# AMERICAN CRIMINAL PROCEDURE: INVESTIGATIVE

## CASES AND COMMENTARY

### [from AMERICAN CRIMINAL PROCEDURE: CASES AND COMMENTARY, TENTH EDITION]

■ ■ ■

by

## Stephen A. Saltzburg

*Wallace and Beverley Woodbury University Professor,*
*George Washington University Law School*

## Daniel J. Capra

*Philip D. Reed Professor of Law*
*Fordham University School of Law*

### AMERICAN CASEBOOK SERIES®

WEST
ACADEMIC
PUBLISHING

Mat #41337543

*American Casebook Series* is a trademark registered in the U.S. Patent and Trademark Office.

© West, a Thomson business, 2007
© 2010 Thomson Reuters
© 2014 LEG, Inc. d/b/a West Academic
   444 Cedar Street, Suite 700
   St. Paul, MN 55101
   1-877-888-1330

West, West Academic Publishing, and West Academic are trademarks of West Publishing Corporation, used under license.

Printed in the United States of America

**ISBN:** 978-0-314-28559-1

*To the women we love,*
*Susan Lee and Anne Capra*

# PREFACE

This book is a complete, unchanged reprint of Chapters 1–6 of Saltzburg & Capra, American Criminal Procedure (10th ed. 2014).

This Tenth Edition plays to what we feel were the strengths of the first nine editions. While the predominant focus is on Supreme Court jurisprudence, we have tried wherever possible to give the reader a sense of what the lower courts are doing with the interesting and exciting issues that abound in criminal procedure. The lower courts are where the day-to-day law is made, and where many of the most interesting fact situations arise. Since our topic is "American" Criminal Procedure, we have made an effort to include cases from all the circuits and state courts throughout the book. As with prior editions, extensive commentary and interesting fact situations are included to assist in doctrinal development. We have also added extensive academic commentary on some of the cutting issues in criminal procedure. Finally, the book covers all problems of criminal investigation and adjudication. It is not limited to constitutional issues. Yet despite the breadth of the book, we have made a special effort to keep it to a manageable and readable length.

The format of the book is the same as the prior editions, although much of the material has been reorganized and updated. Citations to Supreme Court opinions are limited to United States Reports, unless the case is so recent that the U.S. cite is not available. Certiorari denied citations are omitted on the ground that they unnecessarily clutter a book that is primarily for classroom use. Citations included in cases are often omitted without so specifying. Lettered footnotes are from the original materials. Numbered footnotes are ours. Omissions from the text of original material are indicated by asterisks and brackets. We have added more than 1000 headnotes in an effort to make the book as user friendly as possible.

This Edition gives special treatment to some of the more active areas of criminal procedure in the past four years, including important developments after the terrorist attack on 9/11/2001, as well as problems created by developing technology, such as GPS tracking and searches of computer hard-drives. Racially-based stops and encounters are discussed in Chapter 2. The legality of NSA data collection is discussed at the end of Chapter 2. Important questions concerning the right to retained counsel and to counsel's role are also explored in Chapter 10. The fundamental changes wrought in sentencing under the Supreme Court's *Apprendi* line of cases, are explored in Chapters 10 and 11.

Because every criminal procedure teacher likes to cover different material, we have tried to divide the book into numerous subdivisions to enable teachers to pick and choose the subjects they most want to cover. We think that an advanced criminal procedure course is a useful and popular addition to the curriculum. If an advanced course is contemplated, Chapters 9 through 13 could be reserved for that course. An alternative approach is to include Chapter 9 in the basic course and move Chapters 8 and 5 into the advanced course. A third approach is to cover parts of all, or almost all, chapters in the basic course, and to finish them in the advanced course. We believe and hope that the material lends itself to several different divisions that all work well in class and make either a single course or a tandem interesting for all students.

STEPHEN A. SALTZBURG
Washington, D.C.

DANIEL J. CAPRA
New York, N.Y.

April, 2014

# INTRODUCTION

Criminal procedure is one of the courses in law school that generates classroom excitement that continues from the first to the last day of class. Whether it is the opportunity to compare the Warren, Burger and Rehnquist Courts or to predict the likely course of the Roberts Court, criminal procedure as a subject of study is almost always on the cutting edge of the law. It involves the battle between government and individual and the true adversary clash that often results. People like to talk and argue about criminal procedure, and they mind studying it less than they mind studying many other things.

As excited as students of criminal procedure are, too often they leave their courses feeling somewhat frustrated. They have learned a lot of recent law and they know what the latest decisions of the Supreme Court are, but they do not feel comfortable in their understanding of the criminal justice system (to the extent that it is accurate to call the way criminal cases are handled a system) as a whole, or in their knowledge of the doctrinal roots of the numerous concepts that they have examined. This book is an effort to remove some of that frustration, to clarify the way in which the parts of the criminal justice system relate to one another, and to explain how we arrived where we now find ourselves.

To accomplish this task, the book utilizes far more original text and scholarly commentary than is typically found in casebooks on the subject. The text attempts to develop the history of the rules discussed, to point out how judicial treatment of various concepts has changed over time, and to indicate the vices and the virtues of various approaches, past and present. An effort is made to provide students with citations to law journals, books and cases not presented in this book so that those who are interested can examine topics more fully on their own with easy access to the relevant literature.

When a subject is examined, an effort is made to point out inadequacies in judicial opinions or legislative reactions to judicial opinions. Sometimes our own views are stated, either explicitly or implicitly, in an effort to stimulate thinking about new approaches to familiar problems. Where appropriate, students are asked to think about the concepts they have learned in connection with problems that encourage them to develop their own ideas about how best to handle hard cases and close questions.

An effort has been made to reproduce only those Supreme Court cases that are most important. Less important cases are discussed in the textual material. Some of the cases that are offered are not yesterday's

Supreme Court decisions, but those of a more distant Court, because the important opinions may be those that were seminal.

The emphasis on the development of concepts over time indicates a bias that should be confessed here: We believe that the judiciary, especially the Supreme Court, and legislatures, to the extent that they become involved in establishing procedures for criminal cases, attempt to articulate and apply doctrines that will hold their own over time. In other words, we believe that they struggle "to get it right" eventually, if not always at the first crack.

This is not to suggest that right answers are clear or easy to ascertain. In many instances, reasonable minds will differ on the proper solution to questions, and often reasonable minds will find proper solutions to be elusive. We suggest only that approaches that are plainly defective are almost always abandoned or changed, and that it seems that courts and legislatures do attempt to refine the procedures that govern criminal investigations and prosecutions as a result of experience.

Like most criminal procedure books, this one places much emphasis on constitutional rules. This hardly can be avoided, since the Constitution as now interpreted does set minimum standards for many parts of the criminal justice system. But, an attempt is made to indicate when nonconstitutional rules may be more important or more useful than constitutional ones.

To sum up, this book combines elements of traditional casebooks with textual material that might more typically be found in a treatise or hornbook, and it intersperses problems in many chapters. Overall, the idea is to identify clearly the problems of criminal procedure, to offer various ideas about how to handle the problems, and to describe the work that still needs to be done if criminal cases are to be processed fairly.

Some comments on the particular chapters of the book may help to explain how we have approached various topics.

Chapter 1 begins with a development of the criminal justice system. The importance of constitutional rules is discussed, and the incorporation and retroactivity doctrines are examined, since they arise again and again in the cases that are discussed in the following chapters.

Chapter 2 examines all aspects of Fourth Amendment law. It begins with a careful examination of the Amendment's language—including the threshold requirement of "search" or "seizure"—and an exploration of the relationship between the warrant clause and the reasonableness clause. The concepts of probable cause, valid warrants, arrest, stop and frisk, and scrutiny by a detached magistrate are all covered at length. Eavesdropping and wiretapping, and NSA bulk data collection are looked at afterwards. The chapter reserves an examination of the exclusionary rule until the end and attempts thereby to promote an understanding of what the rule is and what its true costs are. This is the longest chapter of the book, covering the many facets of search and seizure law.

Chapter 3 covers self-incrimination and confessions. More than usual attention is paid to traditional Fifth Amendment law and how it relates to the law of confessions. Much space is devoted to laying the historical foundation for present law. Only then are *Miranda, Thompkins, Massiah, Brewer, Henry* and other major cases discussed.

Identification evidence is scrutinized in Chapter 4. The major Supreme Court cases take up most of the chapter, but an attempt is made to point out the shortcomings in the Court's work and to suggest how identification procedures might be improved and how fairer trials might result.

Chapter 5 is about the right to counsel. As the right to counsel may be important in connection with confessions and identifications, as well as later in the process, it might seem strange for this chapter to follow the previous ones. But we believe that the order works and that it is helpful to treat the counsel cases in one place—at the point at which counsel is likely to be involved for the remainder of the process. The doctrines of ineffective assistance and self-representation are not treated here, but are reserved for Chapter 10.

Chapter 6 looks at the decision whether or not to charge a suspect. The roles of the police, the prosecutor and the grand jury are examined, and an effort is made to show how interdependent they are. The current controversy over the utility of the grand jury as a screening device and the dangers of the grand jury serving as an arm of the executive are described and discussed. Preliminary hearings and their relationship to grand juries and charging decisions generally are considered in some detail.

Chapter 7 covers bail and pretrial release. Both constitutional and nonconstitutional rules, especially the 1984 Federal Bail Reform Act, are analyzed. The purposes of bail and the controversy over preventive detention are discussed. Some emphasis is placed on the traditional role of the bondsman and the need for bail reform.

Chapter 8 presents criminal discovery. After a general overview, attention is paid to what the defendant can get from the prosecutor and what the prosecutor can get from the defendant without violating the Constitution. Proposals for liberalizing discovery are considered.

Chapter 9 is devoted to guilty pleas and plea bargaining. An extensive excerpt from a comprehensive study of plea bargaining in the United States begins the chapter. It is followed by a scholarly debate about the merits of plea bargaining, and then by a discussion of the requirements of a valid plea and an analysis of the finality of a plea.

Trial and trial-related rights are treated in Chapter 10. Among the topics covered are speedy trial, joinder of defendants and charges, burdens of persuasion, jury trial, fair-trial—free press conflicts, and effective representation and self-representation. This is the second longest chapter in the book. It addresses in the context of criminal trials many issues that are considered in the context of civil trials in the typical course in Civil Procedure.

Sentencing is the exclusive concern of Chapter 11. Basic options in sentencing are described, as are the roles of judge and jury. The determinate versus indeterminate sentencing controversy is explored, and the Federal Sentencing Guidelines are carefully examined. Also, the procedures that are generally employed in sentencing, and the applicable constitutional rules are set forth.

Chapter 12 covers all aspects of double jeopardy. Most attention is paid to recent decisions of the Supreme Court that clarify (or further confuse, depending on how the decisions are read) a subject that has been puzzling criminal procedure students for years. Collateral estoppel and vindictive prosecutorial conduct also are discussed.

Finally, Chapter 13 focuses on post-trial motions, appeals, and collateral attacks on convictions. An effort is made to examine all important post-sentencing challenges that can be made to a conviction. The section on collateral attack endeavors to explain the development of habeas corpus by the Supreme Court and Congress and the high points of the debate over how much post-conviction attack is desirable in a criminal justice system.

It should be obvious that we have tried to cover all of the significant parts of the criminal justice system and to do so in a reasonable number of pages. To accomplish this, we have worked hard to make the textual portions of the book as informative as possible. This Edition cannot be called a short book, but criminal procedure is not a subject that is easily confined to a few pages. To make the length somewhat more tolerable, we have endeavored to use headnotes as well as several different typesizes, not only for purposes of emphasis, but also to break the monotony of the printed page. To make the book easier to read, we also delete most internal citations in material that we quote from other sources. Thus, most internal cites in the Supreme Court opinions found throughout the book are missing. Footnotes in quoted material generally are deleted also. When we leave internal citations and original footnotes in the quoted material, we do so in the belief that they make a contribution to the overall coverage of the materials. Footnotes that are taken from the original source all have small letters to identify them—i.e., a, b, c, etc.

Our own footnotes are identified by number—i.e., 1, 2, 3, etc. We hope that these choices enhance the "readability" of the book, and that by choosing to delete unnecessary baggage in quoted material, we have been able to pay more attention to the important and interesting questions that make criminal procedure a joy to study.

STEPHEN A. SALTZBURG
Washington, D.C.

DANIEL J. CAPRA
New York, N.Y.

April, 2014

# SUMMARY OF CONTENTS

# TABLE OF CONTENTS

# TABLE OF CASES

The principal cases are in bold type.

---

# TABLE OF AUTHORITIES

# AMERICAN CRIMINAL PROCEDURE: INVESTIGATIVE

## CASES AND COMMENTARY

[from AMERICAN CRIMINAL PROCEDURE:
CASES AND COMMENTARY, TENTH EDITION]

# CHAPTER 1

## BASIC PRINCIPLES

∎ ∎ ∎

### I.   A CRIMINAL CASE

This course covers the procedures that are employed in a criminal case. An important threshold question is whether a sanction that has been chosen is properly classified as "criminal" for purposes of assigning procedural rights. An answer that is frequently given is that criminal cases require proof beyond a reasonable doubt, whereas civil and administrative cases generally do not. But this answer is too circular to be helpful. Proof beyond a reasonable doubt is required once a case is identified as criminal.

Another answer is that the label "criminal" implies jail and prison. But jail and prison are not the usual penalties for many lesser criminal offenses. It is at least generally true that if jail and prison are prescribed penalties for a violation of the law, the law is criminal. But, fines, restitution and other sanctions might be employed as criminal sanctions. If the existence or absence of jail and prison penalties does not determine whether or not a case is criminal, could the determinative factor be whether a penalty is a "punishment" or not? This would appear to be somewhat closer to the mark. Yet, deciding whether a sanction is a punishment itself may present difficulties. Moreover, punitive damages and civil fines are hardly unknown to American law. Thus, the penalty aspect alone cannot identify a criminal case.

### *Legislative Designation*

Something more is needed to identify criminal cases. That something is so obvious that it may appear unsatisfactory at first—it is the label that the legislature chooses to give a sanction. If the legislature calls something criminal, presumably it wants the public to treat an offense as criminal. When this happens, the special procedures of criminal cases will be invoked. See generally Cheh, Constitutional Limits on Using Civil Remedies To Achieve Criminal Law Objectives: Understanding and Transcending the Criminal-Civil Law Distinction, 42 Hastings L.J. 1325 (1991) (proceeding is criminal where labeled as such by the legislature). The question remains, however, whether the legislature's designation of a sanction as other than criminal should always be dispositive.

### Civil Penalty: United States v. L.O. Ward

Usually it is a defendant who argues that his alleged violation is criminal; as such he is seeking to take advantage of certain constitutional rights that are only available in criminal prosecutions. In United States v. L.O. Ward, 448 U.S. 242 (1980), for example, the Supreme Court held that a penalty imposed upon persons discharging hazardous substances into navigable waters was a civil penalty and, therefore, that a reporting requirement for violators did not violate the Fifth Amendment's privilege against compelled self-incrimination. The Court said that the question whether a penalty is criminal or civil is a matter of statutory construction.

> Our inquiry in this regard has traditionally proceeded on two levels. First, we have set out to determine whether Congress, in establishing the penalizing mechanism, indicated either expressly or impliedly a preference for one label or the other. Second, where Congress has indicated an intention to establish a civil penalty, we have inquired further whether the statutory scheme was so punitive either in purpose or effect as to negate that intention. In regard to this latter inquiry, we have noted that "only the clearest proof could suffice to establish the unconstitutionality of a statute on such a ground."

The Court accepted the congressional label of "civil," although Justice Stevens dissented.

### Commitment of Sex Offenders: Allen v. Illinois and Kansas v. Hendricks

In Allen v. Illinois, 478 U.S. 364 (1986), the Court held that commitment proceedings under the Illinois Sexually Dangerous Persons Act were not criminal, and therefore that the Fifth Amendment self-incrimination clause did not prevent the use of the defendant's compelled statements in the case. In Allen, the Court found that the legislature's characterization of the statute as civil and treatment-oriented was crucial, even though persons committed under the Act were kept in a maximum security institution that also housed prisoners in need of psychiatric care.

The Court relied heavily on Allen in Kansas v. Hendricks, 521 U.S. 346 (1997). Hendricks challenged a Kansas statute imposing involuntary civil commitment on sexual predators. Hendricks was committed under the Act just before he was to be released from prison, where he had been incarcerated after a series of sex crime convictions. Hendricks argued that the civil commitment violated his constitutional right against double jeopardy, and also that it operated as an ex post facto law (because the civil commitment statute was passed well after the sexually abusive acts had been committed). Both of these constitutional claims are triggered only when the state imposes criminal "punishment" on the citizen. The case therefore boiled down to whether the involuntary commitment statute was civil or criminal in nature.

Justice Thomas, writing for five members of the Court, held that the statute was civil rather than criminal in nature. He wrote as follows:

> Here, Kansas' objective to create a civil proceeding is evidenced by its placement of the Sexually Violent Predator Act within the Kansas probate code, instead of the criminal code, as well as its description of the Act as creating a "civil commitment procedure." * * *

> Although we recognize that a civil label is not always dispositive, we will reject the legislature's manifest intent only where a party challenging the statute provides the clearest proof that the statutory scheme is so punitive either in purpose or effect as to negate the State's intention to deem it "civil." United States v. Ward. * * * Hendricks, however, has failed to satisfy this heavy burden.

> As a threshold matter, commitment under the Act does not implicate either of the two primary objectives of criminal punishment: retribution or deterrence. The Act's purpose is not retributive because it does not affix culpability for prior criminal conduct. Instead, such conduct is used solely for evidentiary purposes, either to demonstrate that a "mental abnormality" exists or to support a finding of future dangerousness. * * * In addition, the Kansas Act does not make a criminal conviction a prerequisite for commitment—persons absolved of criminal responsibility may nonetheless be subject to confinement under the Act. An absence of the necessary criminal responsibility suggests that the State is not seeking retribution for a past misdeed. * * *

> Nor can it be said that the legislature intended the Act to function as a deterrent. Those persons committed under the Act are, by definition, suffering from a "mental abnormality" or a "personality disorder" that prevents them from exercising adequate control over their behavior. Such persons are therefore unlikely to be deterred by the threat of confinement. And the conditions surrounding that confinement do not suggest a punitive purpose on the State's part. The State has represented that an individual confined under the Act is not subject to the more restrictive conditions placed on state prisoners, but instead experiences essentially the same conditions as any involuntarily committed patient in the state mental institution.

Justice Thomas emphasized that involuntary confinement could be "civil", even if it might be permanent:

Hendricks focuses on his confinement's potentially indefinite duration as evidence of the State's punitive intent. That focus, however, is misplaced. Far from any punitive objective, the confinement's duration is instead linked to the stated purposes of the commitment, namely, to hold the person until his mental abnormality no longer causes him to be a threat to others. If, at any time, the confined person is adjudged "safe to be at large," he is statutorily entitled to immediate release.

Justice Thomas summed up as follows:

Where the State has "disavowed any punitive intent"; limited confinement to a small segment of particularly dangerous individuals; provided strict procedural safeguards; directed that confined persons be segregated from the general prison population and afforded the same status as others who have been civilly committed; recommended treatment if such is possible; and permitted immediate release upon a showing that the individual is no longer dangerous or mentally impaired, we cannot say that it acted with punitive intent. We therefore hold that the Act does not establish criminal proceedings and that involuntary confinement pursuant to the Act is not punitive. Our conclusion that the Act is nonpunitive thus removes an essential prerequisite for both Hendricks' double jeopardy and ex post facto claims.

Justice Breyer, joined by Justices Stevens, Souter and Ginsburg, dissented in *Hendricks*. Justice Breyer contended that the Kansas procedure was punitive because Hendricks received no treatment for his illness.

### Registration of Sex Offenders—Civil Regulation or Criminal Punishment?: Smith v. Doe

In Smith v. Doe, 538 U.S. 84 (2003), the Court upheld Alaska's version of a "Megan's Law" against a challenge that it violated the Ex Post Facto Clause (a clause that applies only to criminal punishment). Megan's Laws, adopted by legislatures throughout the country, require those convicted as sex offenders to register with their state of residence. Information about the offenders is then published over the internet. Alaska's version required sex offenders to register even if they were convicted before the date of the legislation. The Court, in an opinion by Justice Kennedy for five Justices, held that the statutory scheme was civil rather than punitive, and therefore the Ex Post Facto Clause did not apply. Justice Kennedy relied upon *Hendricks* and declared that "an imposition of restrictive measures on sex offenders adjudged to be dangerous is a legitimate nonpunitive governmental objective." The Court also noted that the Alaska law simply requires registration; it "imposes no physical restraint, and so does not resemble the punishment of imprisonment, which is the paradigmatic affirmative disability or restraint."

Justice Kennedy rejected the argument that the registration system was punitive because it was tantamount to probation or supervised release, which clearly are aspects of the criminal justice system. He distinguished registration as a sex offender from probation or supervised release as follows:

> Probation and supervised release entail a series of mandatory conditions and allow the supervising officer to seek the revocation of probation or release in case of infraction. By contrast, offenders subject to the Alaska statute are free to move where they wish and to live and work as other citizens, with no supervision. Although registrants must inform the authorities after they change their facial features (such as growing a beard), borrow a car, or seek psychiatric treatment, they are not required to seek permission to do so. A sex offender who fails to comply with the reporting requirement may be subjected to a criminal prosecution for that failure, but any prosecution is a proceeding separate from the individual's original offense. * * * It suffices to say the registration requirements make a valid regulatory program effective and do not impose punitive restraints in violation of the *Ex Post Facto* Clause.

Justice Thomas wrote a short concurring opinion.

Justice Souter concurred in the judgment. He noted that the Alaska scheme did present some indications of punishment. For example, some of the provisions were located in the criminal code; the touchstone for regulation was the commission of a past crime rather than current dangerousness; and the statute made written notification of the registration requirement a condition of a guilty plea to any sex offense. He also noted that the publication of sex offender status on the internet might be seen to bear "some resemblance to shaming punishments that were used earlier in our history to disable offenders from living normally in the community." Justice Souter, however, concluded as follows:

> To me, the indications of punitive character stated above and the civil indications weighed heavily by the Court are in rough equipoise. * * * What tips the scale for me is the presumption of constitutionality normally accorded a State's law. That presumption gives the State the benefit of the doubt in close cases like this one, and on that basis alone I concur in the Court's judgment.

Justice Stevens dissented in *Smith*. He declared as follows:

> No matter how often the Court may repeat and manipulate multifactor tests that have been applied in wholly dissimilar cases

involving only one or two of these three aspects of these statutory sanctions, it will never persuade me that the registration and reporting obligations that are imposed on convicted sex offenders *and on no one else* as a result of their convictions are not part of their punishment. In my opinion, a sanction that (1) is imposed on everyone who commits a criminal offense, (2) is not imposed on anyone else, and (3) severely impairs a person's liberty, is punishment.

Justice Ginsburg, joined by Justice Breyer, wrote a separate dissent in *Smith*. She argued that the registration and reporting requirements are comparable to conditions of supervised release or parole, and that the public notification regimen called to mind the shaming punishments of the past. She concluded as follows:

> What ultimately tips the balance for me is the Act's excessiveness in relation to its nonpunitive purpose. * * * The Act applies to all convicted sex offenders, without regard to their future dangerousness. And the duration of the reporting requirement is keyed not to any determination of a particular offender's risk of reoffending, but to whether the offense of conviction qualified as aggravated. The reporting requirements themselves are exorbitant: The Act requires aggravated offenders to engage in perpetual quarterly reporting, even if their personal information has not changed. And meriting heaviest weight in my judgment, the Act makes no provision whatever for the possibility of rehabilitation: Offenders cannot shorten their registration or notification period, even on the clearest demonstration of rehabilitation or conclusive proof of physical incapacitation.

### Criminal Procedure Issues in a Civil Context

Occasionally, constitutional guarantees covered in the criminal procedure course will arise in a civil context. The most prevalent situation is an action for damages brought against a police officer under 42 U.S.C. § 1983 for violation of the plaintiff's constitutional rights. For example, if the plaintiff claims that he was wrongly arrested or illegally searched, the court applies Fourth Amendment principles in the same way as if a criminal defendant moves to suppress evidence allegedly obtained in violation of the Fourth Amendment. Many such cases will be discussed throughout this book.

# II.  TWO SPECIAL ASPECTS OF CONSTITUTIONAL LAW: THE INCORPORATION DOCTRINE AND RETROACTIVE APPLICATION OF CONSTITUTIONAL DECISIONS

Most of the cases you will read in this course are decisions of the United States Supreme Court. Before discussing the constitutional law developed by the Supreme Court in these decisions, we believe it is useful to analyze the practical *impact* of a constitutionally-based decision by the Supreme Court. The impact of a Supreme Court decision is governed by two general principles—incorporation and retroactivity. Under the doctrine of incorporation, a constitutionally-based decision ordinarily will bind both the states and the Federal government. Retroactivity principles, on the other hand, determine the extent to which the Court's decision will have an effect on official activity occurring before the date of the decision.

## A.  INCORPORATION

Few individual rights were guaranteed by the original Constitution prior to the adoption of the Bill of Rights. But the ratification of the first ten Amendments in 1791 provided procedural protections that comprise much of what will be examined in this book.

In Barron v. Baltimore, 32 U.S. (7 Pet.) 243 (1833), Chief Justice Marshall, writing for the Court, concluded that the Bill of Rights applied only against the Federal government and not against the states. After the Civil War and the adoption of the Thirteenth, Fourteenth and Fifteenth Amendments, a new question arose: whether these Amendments, particularly the Fourteenth, incorporated the Bill of Rights protections, thus making them applicable against the states. Early cases, like the Slaughter-House Cases, 83 U.S. (16 Wall.) 36 (1872), took a narrow view of the Amendments.

For approximately three quarters of a century the Court struggled to interpret the open-ended language of the Fourteenth Amendment. In 1884, in Hurtado v. California, 110 U.S. 516, the Court held that California could permit criminal proceedings to be instituted by information, rather than by grand jury indictment—that is, the constitutional right to be indicted by a grand jury did not apply to the states. And in 1908, the Court, in Twining v. New Jersey, 211 U.S. 78, held that the privilege against self-incrimination was not binding on the states.

In Palko v. Connecticut, 302 U.S. 319 (1937), Justice Cardozo wrote for the Court to uphold a state procedure that permitted the state to appeal in a criminal case and obtain a new trial. He assumed that the

Double Jeopardy Clause of the Fifth Amendment would have invalidated such an appeal and retrial by the Federal government, but found that the states could take a different approach. Discussing the question whether the Bill of Rights was "absorbed" into the Fourteenth Amendment, Justice Cardozo wrote that the "specific pledges of particular amendments have been found to be implicit in the concept of ordered liberty, and thus, through the Fourteenth Amendment, become valid as against the states." But according to Justice Cardozo, the Double Jeopardy Clause was not one of those guarantees "implicit in the concept of ordered liberty."

A decade after *Palko*, a majority of the Court reaffirmed *Twining* in Adamson v. California, 332 U.S. 46 (1947). Justice Black, joined by Justice Douglas, dissented. Justice Black argued that the language of the first section of the Fourteenth Amendment was intended to assure that no state could deprive its citizens of the privileges and protections of the Bill of Rights. Also, Justice Black rejected what he called the "natural law" formula of *Palko,* which invited the Court to recognize rights "implicit in the concept of ordered liberty" and yet not found in the Bill of Rights.[1] Responding to the opinion by Justice Black and its appendix of constitutional history, Justice Frankfurter took vigorous exception to Black's argument.[2]

Justices Black and Frankfurter continued to disagree for years over the relationship of the Bill of Rights and the Fourteenth Amendment, with Justice Frankfurter generally prevailing on the theory that the Amendment did not make the Bill of Rights applicable to the States, but that it did incorporate such protections as were "implicit in the concept of ordered liberty." See, e.g., Wolf v. Colorado, 338 U.S. 25 (1949); Rochin v. California, 342 U.S. 165 (1952); Irvine v. California, 347 U.S. 128 (1954); Breithaupt v. Abram, 352 U.S. 432 (1957).

In the 1960's a shift took place: the Warren Court—without ever formally abandoning the fundamental fairness standard—began to incorporate more and more Bill of Rights guarantees into the Fourteenth Amendment, under an approach referred to by Justice Black as "selective incorporation." The Court paid little attention to the facts of the case presenting the incorporation issue, and proceeded instead to determine whether the right asserted was fundamental to the American system of

---

[1] Justice Murphy, joined by Justice Rutledge, also dissented. Justice Murphy would have reserved the right to recognize procedural protections not explicitly recognized in the Bill of Rights. Later, Justice Douglas also would move to this position.

[2] Justice Frankfurter relied heavily on the historical analysis in Fairman, Does the Fourteenth Amendment Incorporate the Bill of Rights? The Original Understanding, 2 Stan.L.Rev. 5 (1949). Both Justice Black and Professor Fairman are criticized in Kelly, Clio and the Court: An Illicit Love Affair, 1965 Sup.Ct.Rev. 119. Professor Amar has written an important article that criticizes the Fairman view and concludes that the Fourteenth Amendment was designed to apply the Bill of Rights protections to the States. See Amar, The Bill of Rights and the Fourteenth Amendment, 101 Yale L.J. 1193 (1991).

justice; if so, is was incorporated through the Fourteenth Amendment to apply to the states. Moreover, the Court almost always insisted that, once incorporated, the scope of the Constitutional guarantee would be the same in state as in Federal cases: every detail of the incorporated provision was applicable "jot-for-jot" to the states.

The current approach of the Court, as well as the competing theories, are well illustrated by Duncan v. Louisiana. *Duncan* held that the right to jury trial, guaranteed by the Sixth Amendment, is binding on the states. That particular holding is not the subject of attention here [see Chapter 10 for that part of the case]; rather, the focus is on how the Court reached its result on incorporation. The change in the Court's analysis over time is well-described by the long footnote in the majority opinion.

## DUNCAN V. LOUISIANA
### Supreme Court of the United States, 1968.
### 391 U.S. 145.

### MR. JUSTICE WHITE delivered the opinion of the Court.

\* \* \*

### I

The Fourteenth Amendment denies the States the power to "deprive any person of life, liberty, or property, without due process of law." In resolving conflicting claims concerning the meaning of this spacious language, the Court has looked increasingly to the Bill of Rights for guidance; many of the rights guaranteed by the first eight Amendments to the Constitution have been held to be protected against state action by the Due Process Clause of the Fourteenth Amendment. That clause now protects the right to compensation for property taken by the State;[a] the rights of speech, press, and religion covered by the First Amendment;[b] the Fourth Amendment rights to be free from unreasonable searches and seizures and to have excluded from criminal trials any evidence illegally seized;[c] the right guaranteed by the Fifth Amendment to be free of compelled self-incrimination;[d] and the Sixth Amendment rights to counsel,[e] to a speedy[f] and public[g] trial, to confrontation of opposing witnesses,[h] and to compulsory process for obtaining witnesses.[i]

---

[a]   Chicago, B. & Q. R. Co. v. Chicago, 166 U.S. 226 (1897).

[b]   See, e.g., Fiske v. Kansas, 274 U.S. 380 (1927).

[c]   See Mapp v. Ohio, 367 U.S. 643 (1961).

[d]   Malloy v. Hogan, 378 U.S. 1 (1964).

[e]   Gideon v. Wainwright, 372 U.S. 335 (1963).

[f]   Klopfer v. North Carolina, 386 U.S. 213 (1967).

[g]   In re Oliver, 333 U.S. 257 (1948).

[h]   Pointer v. Texas, 380 U.S. 400 (1965).

[i]   Washington v. Texas, 388 U.S. 14 (1967).

The test for determining whether a right extended by the Fifth and Sixth Amendments with respect to federal criminal proceedings is also protected against state action by the Fourteenth Amendment has been phrased in a variety of ways in the opinions of this Court. The question has been asked whether a right is among those " 'fundamental principles of liberty and justice which lie at the base of all our civil and political institutions,' " Powell v. Alabama, 287 U.S. 45, 67 (1932); whether it is "basic in our system of jurisprudence," In re Oliver, 333 U.S. 257, 273 (1948); and whether it is "a fundamental right, essential to a fair trial," Gideon v. Wainwright, 372 U.S. 335, 343–344 (1963). The claim before us is that the right to trial by jury guaranteed by the Sixth Amendment meets these tests. The position of Louisiana, on the other hand, is that the Constitution imposes upon the States no duty to give a jury trial in any criminal case, regardless of the seriousness of the crime or the size of the punishment which may be imposed. Because we believe that trial by jury in criminal cases is fundamental to the American scheme of justice, we hold that the Fourteenth Amendment guarantees a right of jury trial in all criminal cases which—were they to be tried in a federal court— would come within the Sixth Amendment's guarantee.[j] Since we consider the appeal before us to be such a case, we hold that the Constitution was violated when appellant's demand for jury trial was refused.

* * * A criminal process, which was fair and equitable but used no juries is easy to imagine. It would make use of alternative guarantees and protections which would serve the purposes that the jury serves in the English and American systems. Yet no American State has undertaken to

---

[j]   In one sense recent cases applying provisions of the first eight Amendments to the States represent a new approach to the "incorporation" debate. Earlier the Court can be seen as having asked, when inquiring into whether some particular procedural safeguard was required of a State, if a civilized system could be imagined that would not accord the particular protection. For example, Palko v. Connecticut, 302 U.S. 319, 325 (1937) stated: "The right to trial by jury and the immunity from prosecution except as the result of an indictment may have value and importance. Even so, they are not of the very essence of a scheme of ordered liberty * * *. Few would be so narrow or provincial as to maintain that a fair and enlightened system of justice would be impossible without them." The recent cases, on the other hand, have proceeded upon the valid assumption that state criminal processes are not imaginary and theoretical schemes but actual systems bearing virtually every characteristic of the common-law system that has been developing contemporaneously in England and in this country. The question thus is whether given this kind of system a particular procedure is fundamental—whether, that is, a procedure is necessary to an Anglo-American regime of ordered liberty. It is this sort of inquiry that can justify the conclusions that state courts must exclude evidence seized in violation of the Fourth Amendment, Mapp v. Ohio, 367 U.S. 643 (1961); that state prosecutors may not comment on a defendant's failure to testify, Griffin v. California, 380 U.S. 609 (1965); and that criminal punishment may not be imposed for the status of narcotics addiction, Robinson v. California, 370 U.S. 660 (1962). Of immediate relevance for this case are the Court's holdings that the States must comply with certain provisions of the Sixth Amendment, specifically that the States may not refuse a speedy trial, confrontation of witnesses, and the assistance, at state expense if necessary, of counsel. See cases cited supra. Of each of these determinations that a constitutional provision originally written to bind the Federal Government should bind the States as well it might be said that the limitation in question is not necessarily fundamental to fairness in every criminal system that might be imagined but is fundamental in the context of the criminal processes maintained by the American States.

construct such a system. Instead, every American State, including Louisiana, uses the jury extensively, and imposes very serious punishments only after a trial at which the defendant has a right to a jury's verdict. In every State, including Louisiana, the structure and style of the criminal process—the supporting framework and the subsidiary procedures—are of the sort that naturally complement jury trial, and have developed in connection with and in reliance upon jury trial.

\* \* \*

**MR. JUSTICE BLACK, with whom MR. JUSTICE DOUGLAS joins, concurring.**

\* \* \*

All of these holdings making Bill of Rights' provisions applicable as such to the States mark, of course, a departure from the *Twining* doctrine holding that none of those provisions were enforceable as such against the States. The dissent in this case, however, makes a spirited and forceful defense of that now discredited doctrine. I do not believe that it is necessary for me to repeat the historical and logical reasons for my challenge to the *Twining* holding contained in my *Adamson* dissent and Appendix to it. What I wrote there in 1947 was the product of years of study and research. My appraisal of the legislative history followed 10 years of legislative experience as a Senator of the United States, not a bad way, I suspect, to learn the value of what is said in legislative debates, committee discussions, committee reports, and various other steps taken in the course of passage of bills, resolutions, and proposed constitutional amendments. My Brother Harlan's objections to my *Adamson* dissent history, like that of most of the objectors, relies most heavily on a criticism written by Professor Charles Fairman and published in the Stanford Law Review. 2 Stan.L.Rev. 5 (1949). I have read and studied this article extensively, including the historical references, but am compelled to add that in my view it has completely failed to refute the inferences and arguments that I suggested in my *Adamson* dissent. Professor Fairman's "history" relies very heavily on what was *not* said in the state legislatures that passed on the Fourteenth Amendment. Instead of relying on this kind of negative pregnant, my legislative experience has convinced me that it is far wiser to rely on what *was* said, and most importantly, said by the men who actually sponsored the Amendment in the Congress. \* \* \*

In addition to the adoption of Professor Fairman's "history," the dissent states that "the great words of the four clauses of the first section of the Fourteenth Amendment would have been an exceedingly peculiar way to say that 'The rights heretofore guaranteed against federal intrusion by the first eight Amendments are henceforth guaranteed against state intrusion as well.' " In response to this I can say only that the words "No State shall make or enforce any law which shall abridge the privileges or immunities of citizens of the United States" seem to me an eminently reasonable way of expressing the idea that henceforth the Bill of Rights shall apply to the States. What more precious "privilege" of American citizenship could there be than that privilege to claim the protections of our great Bill of Rights? I suggest that any reading of "privileges or immunities of citizens of the United States" which excludes the Bill of Rights' safeguards renders the words of this section of the Fourteenth Amendment meaningless. * * *

While I do not wish at this time to discuss at length my disagreement with Brother Harlan's forthright and frank restatement of the now discredited *Twining* doctrine, I do want to point out what appears to me to be the basic difference between us. His view, as was indeed the view of *Twining,* is that "due process is an evolving concept" and therefore that it entails a "gradual process of judicial inclusion and exclusion" to ascertain those "immutable principles * * * of free government which no member of the Union may disregard." Thus the Due Process Clause is treated as prescribing no specific and clearly ascertainable constitutional command that judges must obey in interpreting the Constitution, but rather as leaving judges free to decide at any particular time whether a particular rule or judicial formulation embodies an "immutable principl[e] of free government" or is "implicit in the concept of ordered liberty," or whether certain conduct "shocks the judge's conscience" or runs counter to some other similar, undefined and undefinable standard. Thus due process, according to my Brother Harlan, is to be a phrase with no permanent meaning, but one which is found to shift from time to time in accordance with judges' predilections and understandings of what is best for the country. If due process means this, the Fourteenth Amendment, in my opinion, might as well have been written that "no person shall be deprived of life, liberty or property except by laws that the judges of the United States Supreme Court shall find to be consistent with the immutable principles of free government." It is impossible for me to believe that such unconfined power is given to judges in our Constitution that is a written one in order to limit governmental power.

Another tenet of the *Twining* doctrine as restated by my Brother Harlan is that "due process of law requires only fundamental fairness." But the "fundamental fairness" test is one on a par with that of shocking the conscience of the Court. Each of such tests depends entirely on the particular judge's idea of ethics and morals instead of requiring him to depend on the boundaries fixed by the written words of the Constitution. Nothing in the history of the phrase "due process of law" suggests that constitutional controls are to depend on any particular judge's sense of values. * * *

Finally I want to add that I am not bothered by the argument that applying the Bill of Rights to the States, "according to the same standards that protect those personal rights against federal encroachment," interferes with our concept of federalism in that it may prevent States from trying novel social and economic experiments. I have never believed that under the guise of federalism the States should be able to experiment with the protections afforded our citizens through the Bill of Rights. * * *

In closing I want to emphasize that I believe as strongly as ever that the Fourteenth Amendment was intended to make the Bill of Rights applicable to the States. I have been willing to support the selective incorporation doctrine, however, as an alternative, although perhaps less historically supportable than complete incorporation. The selective incorporation process, if used properly, does limit the Supreme Court in the Fourteenth Amendment field to specific Bill of Rights' protections only and keeps judges from roaming at will in their own notions of what policies outside the Bill of Rights are desirable and what are not. And, most importantly for me, the selective incorporation process has the virtue of having already worked to make most of the Bill of Rights' protections applicable to the States.

**MR. JUSTICE HARLAN, whom MR. JUSTICE STEWART joins, dissenting.**

* * *

The Court's approach to this case is an uneasy and illogical compromise among the views of various Justices on how the Due Process Clause should be interpreted. The Court does not say that those who framed the Fourteenth Amendment intended to make the Sixth Amendment applicable to the States. And the Court concedes that it finds nothing unfair about the procedure by which the present appellant was tried. Nevertheless, the Court reverses his conviction: it holds, for some reason not apparent to me that the Due Process Clause incorporates the particular clause of the Sixth Amendment that requires trial by jury in federal criminal cases—including, as I read its opinion, the sometimes trivial accompanying baggage of judicial interpretation in federal contexts. I have raised my voice many times before against the Court's continuing undiscriminating insistence upon fastening on the States federal notions of criminal justice and I must do so again in this instance. With all respect, the Court's approach and its reading of history are altogether topsy-turvy.

* * * I believe I am correct in saying that every member of the Court for at least the last 135 years has agreed that our Founders did not consider the requirements of the Bill of Rights so fundamental that they should operate directly against the States. They were wont to believe

rather that the security of liberty in America rested primarily upon the dispersion of governmental power across a federal system. The Bill of Rights was considered unnecessary by some but insisted upon by others in order to curb the possibility of abuse of power by the strong central government they were creating.

The Civil War Amendments dramatically altered the relation of the Federal Government to the States. The first section of the Fourteenth Amendment imposes highly significant restrictions on state action. But the restrictions are couched in very broad and general terms: citizenship; privileges and immunities; due process of law; equal protection of the laws. * * * Where does the Court properly look to find the specific rules that define and give content to such terms as "life, liberty, or property" and "due process of law"?

A few members of the Court have taken the position that the intention of those who drafted the first section of the Fourteenth Amendment was simply, and exclusively, to make the provisions of the first eight Amendments applicable to state action. This view has never been accepted by this Court. In my view, often expressed elsewhere, the first section of the Fourteenth Amendment was meant neither to incorporate, nor to be limited to, the specific guarantees of the first eight Amendments. The overwhelming historical evidence marshalled by Professor Fairman demonstrates, to me conclusively, that the Congressmen and state legislators who wrote, debated, and ratified the Fourteenth Amendment did not think they were "incorporating" the Bill of Rights[k] and the very breadth and generality of the Amendment's provisions suggest that its authors did not suppose that the Nation would always be limited to mid-19th century conceptions of "liberty" and "due process of law" * * *. In short, neither history, nor sense, supports using the Fourteenth Amendment to put the States in a constitutional straitjacket with respect to their own development in the administration of criminal or civil law.

* * *

Although I therefore fundamentally disagree with the total incorporation view of the Fourteenth Amendment, it seems to me that such a position does at least have the virtue, lacking in the Court's

---

[k]  Fairman, Does the Fourteenth Amendment Incorporate the Bill of Rights? The Original Understanding, 2 Stan.L.Rev. 5 (1949). Professor Fairman was not content to rest upon the overwhelming fact that the great words of the four clauses of the first section of the Fourteenth Amendment would have been an exceedingly peculiar way to say that "The rights heretofore guaranteed against federal intrusion by the first eight Amendments are henceforth guaranteed against state intrusion as well." He therefore sifted the mountain of material comprising the debates and committee reports relating to the Amendment in both Houses of Congress and in the state legislatures that passed upon it. He found that in the immense corpus of comments on the purpose and effects of the proposed amendment, and on its virtues and defects, there is almost no evidence whatever for "incorporation." * * *

selective incorporation approach, of internal consistency: we look to the Bill of Rights, word for word, clause for clause, precedent for precedent because, it is said, the men who wrote the Amendment wanted it that way. * * *.

Apart from the approach taken by the absolute incorporationists, I can see only one method of analysis that has any internal logic. That is to start with the words "liberty" and "due process of law" and attempt to define them in a way that accords with American traditions and our system of government. This approach * * * entails a gradual process of judicial inclusion and exclusion, seeking, with due recognition of constitutional tolerance for state experimentation and disparity, to ascertain those immutable principles of free government which no member of the Union may disregard. * * *

* * *

Today's Court still remains unwilling to accept the total incorporationists' view of the history of the Fourteenth Amendment. This, if accepted, would afford a cogent reason for applying the Sixth Amendment to the States. The Court is also, apparently, unwilling to face the task of determining whether denial of trial by jury in the situation before us, or in other situations, is fundamentally unfair. Consequently, the Court has compromised on the ease of the incorporationist position, without its internal logic. It has simply assumed that the question before us is whether the Jury Trial Clause of the Sixth Amendment should be incorporated into the Fourteenth, jot-for-jot and case-for-case, or ignored. Then the Court merely declares that the clause in question is "in" rather than "out."

The Court has justified neither its starting place nor its conclusion. * * *

### NOTE ON INCORPORATION

The Court has never accepted Justice Black's view that the Fourteenth Amendment incorporates the entirety of the Bill of Rights. So for example, the right to indictment by grand jury is not binding on the states. The Seventh Amendment jury trial right is not binding upon the states in civil cases. And the Bail Clause of the Eighth Amendment has not yet been incorporated into the Fourteenth Amendment by the Supreme Court. But, the "fundamental fairness" approach of *Palko* and *Adamson* has given way to a selective incorporation view that, as Justice Black correctly notes in *Duncan,* has moved the Court a long way toward the total incorporation result that he advocated.

If Justice Black was wrong about the intent of the drafters of the Fourteenth Amendment and they did not intend incorporation, is there any rhyme or reason to the selective incorporation idea? If there is, it has to be that the Court has been willing to assume that the drafters of the Fourteenth Amendment wanted to enforce against the states only those portions of the Bill of Rights whose fundamentality remained evident many years after the first ten Amendments were adopted. Does that kind of prescience seem likely?

Justice Black argued that incorporation of the Bill of Rights is preferable to a case-by-case, fundamental fairness approach, because the latter gives rise to judicial subjectivity in applying the vague term "due process." Are the Bill of Rights protections less susceptible to judicial subjectivity? For instance, does the term "unreasonable searches and seizures" in the Fourth Amendment provide more limitation on judicial subjectivity than the term "due process"?

### Incorporation of the Second Amendment Right to Bear Arms: McDonald v. City of Chicago

The Court had occasion to revisit its history with respect to incorporation in *McDonald v. City of Chicago*, 130 S.Ct. 3020 (2010), in which Justice Alito summarized the holding for a 5–4 Court:

> Two years ago, in District of Columbia v. Heller, 554 U.S. 570 (2008), we held that the Second Amendment protects the right to keep and bear arms for the purpose of self-defense, and we struck down a District of Columbia law that banned the possession of handguns in the home. The City of Chicago (City) and the village of Oak Park, a Chicago suburb, have laws that are similar to the District of Columbia's, but Chicago and Oak Park argue that their laws are constitutional because the Second Amendment has no application to the States. We have previously held that most of the provisions of the Bill of Rights apply with full force to both the Federal Government and the States. Applying the standard that is well established in our case law, we hold that the Second Amendment right is fully applicable to the States.

Four Justices agreed that the Due Process Clause required incorporation while Justice Thomas relied upon the privileges and immunities clause of the Fourteenth Amendment. In a plurality portion of his opinion, Justice Alito noted that Justice Black's "total incorporation" theory was never adopted by the Court, and that "the Court eventually moved in that direction by initiating what has been called a process of 'selective incorporation'." He quoted from *Duncan* and explained that the Court no longer asks whether *any* "civilized system [can] be imagined that would not accord the particular protection" and instead asks "whether a particular Bill of Rights guarantee is fundamental to *our* scheme of ordered liberty and system of justice."

Justice Stevens's dissenting opinion also examined the Court's approach to due process and incorporation and wrote: "In my judgment, this line of cases is best understood as having concluded that, to ensure a criminal trial satisfies essential standards of fairness, some procedures should be the same in state and federal courts: The need for certainty and uniformity is more pressing, and the margin for error slimmer, when criminal justice is at issue."

### NOTE ON STATE CONSTITUTIONAL PROTECTIONS

The Supreme Court has the final say in interpreting federal constitutional protections concerning criminal procedure. But state courts have sometimes provided enhanced protection of constitutional rights through reliance on state constitutions. Of course, state courts cannot construe their own constitutions to provide *less* protections than those granted by the Bill of Rights. But state courts, construing their own constitutions, can provide greater protections than those set by the Supreme Court's construction of the Bill of Rights.

While some states have been more active than others, virtually every state has rejected at least one Supreme Court decision as insufficiently protective of the rights of citizens. Many of these decisions will be discussed in the context of particular Supreme Court rulings, *infra*.

It must be remembered that if the state court explicitly relies on state constitutional law to provide more protection to citizens than the Federal Constitution, the state court's decision on this matter cannot be reviewed by the Supreme Court. This is because there is no Federal question that would control the case. But the state court must be explicit that it is relying on state law. If it appears that the state court may have been relying in whole or part on Federal law, then the Supreme Court can take the case and reject the state court's construction. See generally Michigan v. Long, 463 U.S. 1032 (1983) (state court must place explicit reliance on state law in order to avoid Supreme Court review; otherwise it will be presumed that the state court was construing Federal constitutional law).

For extensive discussions about what has come to be called "state court activism," see Brennan, J., State Constitutions and the Protection of Individual Rights, 90 Harv.L.Rev. 489 (1977); Symposium on Emerging Issues in State Constitutional Law, 65 Temple L.Rev. 1119 (1992); Symposium, Independent State Grounds: Should State Courts Depart From the Fourth Amendment in Construing Their Own Constitutions, and if so, on What Basis Beyond Simple Disagreement With the United States Supreme Court's Result?, 77 Miss. L.Rev. 1 (2007). For a critical view, see Gardner, The Failed Discourse of State Constitutionalism, 90 Mich.L.Rev. 761 (1992).

# B.  RETROACTIVITY

## 1.   The Impact of New Decisions

When the Supreme Court reviews the conduct of government officials in a criminal case, the legal rule it promulgates will obviously apply to all similar government conduct arising after the date of the decision—otherwise the decision would be nothing but an advisory opinion. But an important question is whether the legal rule should also be applied to government conduct occurring *before* the date of the decision. The question of retroactive application is one of competing policies and interests.

For example, when the Supreme Court overrules a prior decision that had permitted certain police behavior, the Court might be concerned that law enforcement officers, who relied on the case law existing at the time of their conduct, in fact acted as competent officers should. The Court might, therefore, be reluctant to see the government disadvantaged as a result of justifiable reliance by government agents. The Court also might be concerned that trial courts that relied on the old rule may be burdened with numerous retrials once the new decision is announced—assuming a retrial is even possible given the passage of time.

On the other hand, if a decision is important enough to be called a "constitutional decision," it is arguable that it ought to benefit all those who suffered the conduct now found to be wrongful.

For many years, the Supreme Court's position on retroactive application was complicated and often inconsistent. But one rule that the Court always has followed, at least to this point,  is to give the benefit of the new rule to the litigant who establishes it—even though that constitutes retroactive application. The Court has done so for two reasons: 1) to provide litigants with incentives to improve past decisions of the Court, because few litigants would ask the Court to establish a new rule that they could not use; and 2) to assure that there is a concrete case or controversy before the Court.

## 2.   Prior Supreme Court Law on Retroactivity, and the Harlan Approach

In Stovall v. Denno, 388 U.S. 293 (1967) and Desist v. United States, 394 U.S. 244 (1969), the Court refused to apply its decisions requiring counsel at certain lineups and its holding in an earlier Fourth Amendment case, Katz v. United States, 389 U.S. 347 (1967), to other cases still pending on direct review. Rather, the Court applied its earlier decisions to reach only the police activity that followed the announcement of the new rules. Essentially, the rulings were given only prospective effect, other than for the litigants in the cases in which the new rule was established.

Justice Harlan dissented in *Desist* and concluded that new constitutional rules must be applied, at a minimum, to all cases pending on direct review when the rules are handed down. (A case is on "direct review" when it is still on appeal from a judgment of conviction. This includes all appellate activity up to and including the Supreme Court's denial of a writ of certiorari). Justice Harlan charged that a decision to apply a ruling on direct review of one case (i.e., the case before the Court), but not to all other similarly situated cases, is an assertion of legislative, not adjudicatory, power. Justice Harlan argued further that, as a general matter, a new rule should *not* be applied in collateral attack (i.e., habeas corpus) proceedings. (Habeas corpus proceedings usually involve federal court review of a state judgment of conviction, and are brought after a defendant's direct appeals through the state appellate courts and the United States Supreme Court have been rejected or foregone; see the discussion in Chapter 13). Justice Harlan identified two situations in which the presumption of nonretroactivity of new rules to habeas corpus cases could be overcome; these were exceptions to the general principle of nonretroactivity in habeas cases. The first exception encompassed habeas corpus petitioners who sought the benefit of a new rule that is so fundamental that it is "implicit in the concept of ordered liberty" (quoting Justice Cardozo's opinion in *Palko*). The second exception covered a petitioner who relied upon a new rule to demonstrate that the conduct for which he was tried was constitutionally protected, so that a trial should never have occurred in the first place. Justice Harlan's view is fully discussed and analyzed by the Court in Teague v. Lane, below.

## 3.   Current Supreme Court Approach to Retroactivity

In a series of cases, the Court finally adopted the Harlan approach to retroactivity, with one slight modification as to the "fundamental fairness" exception to non-retroactivity on habeas. In Griffith v. Kentucky, 479 U.S. 314 (1987), the Court held that its decision the previous term in Batson v. Kentucky, 476 U.S. 79 (1986) (defendant could establish a prima facie case of racial discrimination based on the prosecution's use of peremptory challenges in a single case), would be applied retroactively to all cases still pending on direct review when the decision was announced. Although *Batson* overruled a decision that had withstood attack for more than twenty years, the Court declined to follow *Stovall* and other cases that had barred some or all defendants from benefitting from recently announced decisions even while pursuing direct review. Instead the Court adopted Justice Harlan's analysis of direct review: a new rule is applicable to all cases that are still under court review, up to the time that a petition for certiorari in the United States

Supreme Court has been denied or the time to file such a petition has run out. Justice Blackmun wrote in *Griffith* for six Justices. The Court's analysis in *Griffith* is discussed in Teague v. Lane, immediately below, where the Court adopted the Harlan view that new rules are generally inapplicable to habeas cases. It should be noted, however, that the effect of *Griffith* has been limited in Fourth Amendment cases, as will be discussed in the notes following the next case.

The applicability of *Teague* has been limited somewhat by subsequent Congressional legislation restricting habeas corpus relief. Yet *Teague* is still important because that legislation was promulgated in the spirit of *Teague* (which is generally to limit the retroactive effect of new rules in habeas corpus cases), and there are some situations in which the legislation is inapplicable, thus rendering *Teague* the governing principle. The effect of the legislation is discussed in a Note following *Teague*.

### TEAGUE V. LANE
Supreme Court of the United States, 1989.
489 U.S. 288.

#### JUSTICE O'CONNOR delivered the opinion of the Court.

In Taylor v. Louisiana, 419 U.S. 522 (1975), this Court held that the Sixth Amendment required that the jury venire be drawn from a fair cross section of the community. * * * The principal question presented in this case is whether the Sixth Amendment's fair cross section requirement should now be extended to the petit jury. Because we adopt Justice Harlan's approach to retroactivity for cases on collateral review, we leave the resolution of that question for another day.

* * *

Petitioner, a black man, was convicted by an all-white Illinois jury of three counts of attempted murder, two counts of armed robbery, and one count of aggravated battery. During jury selection for petitioner's trial, the prosecutor used all 10 of his peremptory challenges to exclude blacks. * * *

On appeal, petitioner argued that the prosecutor's use of peremptory challenges denied him the right to be tried by a jury that was representative of the community. The Illinois Appellate Court rejected petitioner's fair cross section claim. The Illinois Supreme Court denied leave to appeal, and we denied certiorari.

Petitioner then filed a petition for a writ of habeas corpus in the United States District Court for the Northern District of Illinois. Petitioner repeated his fair cross section claim * * *. [Both the District Court and the Court of Appeals en banc denied Teague's claim for habeas relief. The Court of Appeals held that the Constitution's fair cross-section requirement was limited to the jury venire—the pool from which the jury that sits in the case (the petit jury) is drawn].

\* \* \*

Petitioner's \* \* \* contention is that the Sixth Amendment's fair cross section requirement applies to the petit jury. \* \* \* Petitioner \* \* \* contends that the *ratio decidendi* of *Taylor* cannot be limited to the jury venire, and he urges adoption of a new rule. Because we hold that the rule urged by petitioner should not be applied retroactively to cases on collateral review, we decline to address petitioner's contention.

\* \* \*

In the past, the Court has, without discussion, often applied a new constitutional rule of criminal procedure to the defendant in the case announcing the new rule, and has confronted the question of retroactivity later when a different defendant sought the benefit of that rule. In several cases, however, the Court has addressed the retroactivity question in the very case announcing the new rule. These two lines of cases do not have a unifying theme, and we think it is time to clarify how the question of retroactivity should be resolved for cases on collateral review.

\* \* \*

In our view, the question "whether a decision [announcing a new rule should] be given prospective or retroactive effect should be faced at the time of [that] decision." Mishkin, Foreword: the High Court, the Great Writ, and the Due Process of Time and Law, 79 Harv. L. Rev. 56, 64 (1965). Retroactivity is properly treated as a threshold question, for, once a new rule is applied to the defendant in the case announcing the rule, evenhanded justice requires that it be applied retroactively to all who are similarly situated. Thus, before deciding whether the fair cross section requirement should be extended to the petit jury, we should ask whether such a rule would be applied retroactively to the case at issue. \* \* \*

It is admittedly often difficult to determine when a case announces a new rule, and we do not attempt to define the spectrum of what may or may not constitute a new rule for retroactivity purposes. In general, however, a case announces a new rule when it breaks new ground or imposes a new obligation on the States or the Federal Government. To put it differently, a case announces a new rule if the result was not dictated by precedent existing at the time the defendant's conviction became final. Given [prior case law stating] that "[f]airness in [jury] selection has never been held to require proportional representation of races upon a jury," application of the fair cross section requirement to the petit jury would be a new rule.

Not all new rules have been uniformly treated for retroactivity purposes. Nearly a quarter of a century ago, in Linkletter v. Walker, 381 U.S. 618 (1965), the Court attempted to set some standards by which to determine the retroactivity of new rules. * * * The *Linkletter* retroactivity standard has not led to consistent results. Instead, it has been used to limit application of certain new rules to cases on direct review, other new rules only to the defendants in the cases announcing such rules, and still other new rules to cases in which trials have not yet commenced. * * *

Application of the *Linkletter* standard led to the disparate treatment of similarly situated defendants on direct review. For example, in * * * Johnson v. New Jersey, 384 U.S. 719, 733–735 (1966), the Court held, under the *Linkletter* standard, that *Miranda* would only be applied to trials commencing after that decision had been announced. Because the defendant in *Johnson*, like the defendants in *Miranda*, was on direct review of his conviction, the Court's refusal to give *Miranda* retroactive effect resulted in unequal treatment of those who were similarly situated. * * *

In Griffith v. Kentucky, 479 U.S. 314 (1987), we rejected as unprincipled and inequitable the *Linkletter* standard for cases pending on direct review at the time a new rule is announced, and adopted the first part of the retroactivity approach advocated by Justice Harlan. We agreed with Justice Harlan that "failure to apply a newly declared constitutional rule to criminal cases pending on direct review violates basic norms of constitutional adjudication." We gave two reasons for our decision. First, because we can only promulgate new rules in specific cases and cannot possibly decide all cases in which review is sought, "the integrity of judicial review" requires the application of the new rule to "all similar cases pending on direct review." * * * Second, because "selective application of new rules violates the principle of treating similarly situated defendants the same," we refused to continue to tolerate the inequity that resulted from not applying new rules retroactively to defendants whose cases had not yet become final. Although new rules that constituted clear breaks with the past generally were not given retroactive effect under the *Linkletter* standard, we held that "a new rule for the conduct of criminal prosecutions is to be applied retroactively to all cases, state or federal, pending on direct review or not yet final, with no exception for cases in which the new rule constitutes a 'clear break' with the past."

* * *

Justice Harlan believed that new rules generally should not be applied retroactively to cases on collateral review. * * * Given the "broad scope of constitutional issues cognizable on habeas," Justice Harlan argued that it is "sounder, in adjudicating habeas petitions, generally to apply the law prevailing at the time a conviction became final than it is to seek to dispose of [habeas] cases on the basis of intervening changes in constitutional interpretation." As he explained * * * "the threat of habeas serves as a necessary additional incentive for trial and appellate courts throughout the land to conduct their proceedings in a manner consistent with established constitutional standards. In order to perform this deterrence function, * * * the habeas court need only apply the constitutional standards that prevailed at the time the original proceedings took place."

Justice Harlan identified only two exceptions to his general rule of nonretroactivity for cases on collateral review. First, a new rule should be applied retroactively if it places "certain kinds of primary, private individual conduct beyond the power of the criminal law-making authority to proscribe." Second, a new rule should be applied retroactively if it requires the observance of "those procedures that . . . are 'implicit in the concept of ordered liberty.' "

* * *

We agree with Justice Harlan's description of the function of habeas corpus. "[T]he Court never has defined the scope of the writ simply by reference to a perceived need to assure that an individual accused of crime is afforded a trial free of constitutional error." Rather, we have recognized that interests of comity and finality must also be considered in determining the proper scope of habeas review. * * *

* * * Application of constitutional rules not in existence at the time a conviction became final seriously undermines the principle of finality which is essential to the operation of our criminal justice system. Without finality, the criminal law is deprived of much of its deterrent effect.

* * *

The "costs imposed upon the State[s] by retroactive application of new rules of constitutional law on habeas corpus * * * generally far outweigh the benefits of this application." In many ways the application of new rules to cases on collateral review may be more intrusive than the enjoining of criminal prosecutions, for it continually forces the States to marshal resources in order to keep in prison defendants whose trials and appeals conformed to then-existing constitutional standards. Furthermore, * * * "[s]tate courts are understandably frustrated when they faithfully apply existing constitutional law only to have a federal court discover, during a [habeas] proceeding, new constitutional commands."

We find these criticisms to be persuasive, and we now adopt Justice Harlan's view of retroactivity for cases on collateral review. Unless they fall within an exception to the general rule, new constitutional rules of criminal procedure will not be applicable to those cases which have become final before the new rules are announced.

* * *

Petitioner's conviction became final in 1983. As a result, the rule petitioner urges would not be applicable to this case, which is on collateral review, unless it would fall within an exception.

The first exception suggested by Justice Harlan—that a new rule should be applied retroactively if it places "certain kinds of primary, private individual conduct beyond the power of the criminal law-making authority to proscribe"—is not relevant here. Application of the fair cross section requirement to the petit jury would not accord constitutional protection to any primary activity whatsoever.

The second exception suggested by Justice Harlan—that a new rule should be applied retroactively if it requires the observance of "those procedures that * * * are 'implicit in the concept of ordered liberty,'" (quoting Palko v. Connecticut)—we apply with a modification. * * *

* * * Were we to employ the *Palko* test without more, we would be doing little more than importing into a very different context the terms of the debate over incorporation. Reviving the *Palko* test now, in this area of law, would be unnecessarily anachronistic. * * * [W]e believe that Justice Harlan's concerns about the difficulty in identifying both the existence and the value of accuracy-enhancing procedural rules can be addressed by limiting the scope of the second exception to those new procedures without which the likelihood of an accurate conviction is seriously diminished.

Because we operate from the premise that such procedures would be so central to an accurate determination of innocence or guilt, we believe it unlikely that many such components of basic due process have yet to emerge. * * *

* * * Because the absence of a fair cross section on the jury venire does not undermine the fundamental fairness that must underlie a conviction or seriously diminish the likelihood of obtaining an accurate conviction, we conclude that a rule requiring that petit juries be composed of a fair cross section of the community would not be a "bedrock procedural element" that would be retroactively applied under the second exception we have articulated.

Were we to recognize the new rule urged by petitioner in this case, we would have to give petitioner the benefit of that new rule even though it would not be applied retroactively to others similarly situated. * * *

If there were no other way to avoid rendering advisory opinions, we might well agree that the inequitable treatment described above is "an insignificant cost for adherence to sound principles of decision-making." But there is a more principled way of dealing with the problem. We can simply refuse to announce a new rule in a given case unless the rule would be applied retroactively to the defendant in the case and to all others similarly situated. We think this approach is a sound one. Not only does it eliminate any problems of rendering advisory opinions, it also avoids the inequity resulting from the uneven application of new rules to similarly situated defendants. We therefore hold that, implicit in the retroactivity approach we adopt today, is the principle that habeas corpus cannot be used as a vehicle to create new constitutional rules of criminal procedure unless those rules would be applied retroactively to all defendants on collateral review through one of the two exceptions we have articulated. * * *

[The opinion of JUSTICE WHITE, concurring in part and concurring in the judgment, is omitted.]

**JUSTICE STEVENS, with whom JUSTICE BLACKMUN joins in relevant part, concurring in part and concurring in the judgment.**

* * *

In general, I share Justice Harlan's views about retroactivity. * * * I am persuaded that the Court should adopt Justice Harlan's analysis of retroactivity for habeas corpus cases as well for cases still on direct review.

I do not agree, however, with the plurality's dicta proposing a "modification" of Justice Harlan's fundamental fairness exception. * * *

* * * I cannot agree that it is "unnecessarily anachronistic" to issue a writ of habeas corpus to a petitioner convicted in a manner that violates fundamental principles of liberty.

* * *

**JUSTICE BRENNAN, with whom JUSTICE MARSHALL joins, dissenting.**

* * * Out of an exaggerated concern for treating similarly situated habeas petitioners the same, the plurality would for the first time preclude the federal courts from considering on collateral review a vast range of important constitutional challenges; where those challenges have merit, it would bar the vindication of personal constitutional rights and deny society a check against further violations until the same claim is presented on direct review. * * *

* * *

[F]rom the plurality's exposition of its new rule, one might infer that its novel fabrication will work no great change in the availability of federal collateral review of state convictions. Nothing could be further from the truth. \* \* \* Few decisions on appeal or collateral review are "dictated" by what came before. Most such cases involve a question of law that is at least debatable, permitting a rational judge to resolve the case in more than one way. Virtually no case that prompts a dissent on the relevant legal point, for example, could be said to be "dictated" by prior decisions. \* \* \* The plurality's approach today can thus be expected to contract substantially the Great Writ's sweep.

\* \* \*

### Commentary on the Teague Rule

In Collins v. Youngblood, 497 U.S. 37 (1990), the Court held that the rule in *Teague,* prohibiting retroactive application or promulgation of new rules to habeas corpus cases, was not jurisdictional and therefore would not be raised by the Court *sua sponte.*

Note that under the Harlan-*Teague* view, defendants are subject to different treatment depending on the efficiency of the appellate courts in the state in which they are convicted. The slower the appellate system, the more likely that the defendant would benefit from new rules, because it is more likely that the case will still be on direct review when the new rule is promulgated.

A different criticism of the Harlan approach, as applied to cases on direct review, is that if new rules are generally applicable to cases not finalized, the cost of a new rule will often be significant. That may deter the Court from promulgating new rules in the first place. See Jenkins v. Delaware, 395 U.S. 213 (1969) (non-retroactivity provides an impetus for the "implementation of long overdue reforms which otherwise could not be practicably effected."); People v. Mitchell, 80 N.Y.2d 519, 591 N.Y.S.2d 990 (1992) (rejecting the Harlan view as a matter of state law and holding that a new rule is not applicable to other cases on direct review: denying retroactive effect to new rules "permits this Court to expand the protection accorded defendants when we might otherwise hesitate to do so because retroactive application threatens to wreak more havoc in society that society's interest in stability will tolerate."). See also Heytens, Managing Transitional Moments in Criminal Cases, 115 Yale L.J. 922 (2006) (noting that the *Griffith* view of retroactivity to cases on direct review has led courts to counter by finding that defendants have forfeited their right to appeal by failing to raise the issue at trial—even though the trial was conducted before the new rule became law).

The academic commentary on *Teague's* limitation on habeas review has been almost uniformly negative. Some examples are: Liebman, More Than "Slightly Retro": The Rehnquist Court's Rout of Habeas Corpus Jurisdiction in Teague v. Lane, 18 N.Y.U. Rev. of Law & Social Change 537 (1991); Dubber, Prudence and Substance: How the Supreme Court's

New Habeas Retroactivity Doctrine Mirrors and Affects Substantive Constitutional Law, 30 Am.Crim.L.Rev. 1 (1992); Meyer, "Nothing We Say Matters": *Teague* and New Rules, 61 Univ.Chi.L.Rev. 423 (1994).

### *What Is a "New Rule"?*

After *Teague,* new rules are generally inapplicable to those whose convictions have been finalized—including the petitioner who initially brings the claim for a new rule on collateral review. However, Justice Harlan, whose views were generally adopted in *Teague,* emphasized that some "new" holdings are not "new" at all, but are merely applications of well-settled principles to different fact situations, and therefore these holdings must apply retroactively to all defendants.

The Court, following Justice Harlan's approach, has mandated that when a decision merely applies settled precedent it is not a "new" rule at all, and is thus completely retroactive. See Yates v. Aiken, 484 U.S. 211 (1988). The rationale is that if a constitutional rule is not "new", the state court should have applied it correctly, and therefore the failure to apply it is proper grounds for habeas relief. The difficulty is in determining if a rule is "new" or merely an old rule applied to a different fact situation. In *Teague,* the Court stated that a case announces a new rule when it was "not dictated by existing precedent."

In Butler v. McKellar, 494 U.S. 407 (1990), the Court expounded further on the *Teague* definition of a "new" rule. The issue was whether Arizona v. Roberson was a new rule or merely an application of Edwards v. Arizona[3] to a somewhat different fact situation. *Edwards* held that once a person in custody has requested counsel, the police may not conduct further interrogation unless counsel is provided or the suspect initiates communications. *Roberson* held that the *Edwards* rule applied even when the officer wants to question the suspect about a crime unrelated to that for which he has been arrested. When Butler was tried in state court, *Edwards* had been decided, but *Roberson* was not decided until Butler's conviction had been finalized. Butler, who confessed to a crime unrelated to that for which he was arrested, argued that the rule in *Roberson* should be retroactively applied to him, on the ground that the *Roberson* Court itself had stated that the rule was not new but merely an application of *Edwards.*

Chief Justice Rehnquist, writing for the majority, stated that a rule is "new" if reasonable minds could have differed about the result of the decision before it was rendered. The majority held that *Roberson* was a new rule, because reasonable-minded lower courts before *Roberson* had differed about whether *Edwards* would apply to questioning about

---

[3]    Both of these cases are discussed in the material on confessions in Chapter 3.

unrelated investigations. The fact that the majority in *Roberson* characterized its decision as indistinguishable from *Edwards* and as a refusal to create an "exception" was not dispositive. According to the Chief Justice, "courts frequently view their decisions as being 'controlled' or 'governed' by prior opinions even when aware of reasonable contrary conclusions reached by lower courts." He stated that "[t]he 'new rule' principle * * * validates reasonable, good-faith interpretations of existing precedents made by state courts even though they are shown to be contrary to later decisions."

Justice Brennan, joined by Justices Marshall, Blackmun and Stevens, dissented in *Butler*.

### Refusal to Promulgate a New Rule as a Decision on the Merits

When the Court refuses to decide a question in a habeas case because to do so would result in the promulgation of a "new rule," has the Court given an opinion on the merits of the proposed rule itself? For example, in *Teague*, did the Court, by refusing to decide the issue of whether the fair cross section requirement applied to the petit jury, effectively signal to the lower courts its view about the merits of such a claim? If you were a lower court judge, would you be inclined to adopt a "new rule" in a direct review case after the Supreme Court had declined to adopt the rule in a habeas case?

The Supreme Court has given some indication that a refusal to render what would be a "new rule" on habeas is similar to a rejection of the proposed rule on the merits. In Johnson v. Texas, 509 U.S. 350 (1993), the Court considered a question of the constitutionality of a capital sentencing statute on direct review. This question was identical to that which the Court had, earlier in the same term, refused to consider on habeas review on the ground that granting relief would require promulgation of a "new rule." Acting on direct review "without the constraints of *Teague*," the Court rejected the constitutional claim on the merits, relying on "much of the reasoning" in the previous habeas case. Justice O'Connor, the author of *Teague*, wrote a dissent in *Johnson* for four Justices. She argued that "cases that reject a claim as requiring a new rule cannot constitute stare decisis on direct review," since a rejection on habeas means only that the issue is "susceptible to debate among reasonable minds."

Is it possible to separate the question of whether a proposed rule is "new" from the question whether a proposed rule is meritorious? See Arkin, The Prisoner's Dilemma: Life in the Lower Federal Courts After Teague v. Lane, 69 No.Car.L.Rev. 371 (1991) (whether a rule is new requires a view into the merits of the rule).

### The Teague Rule and Statutory Limitations on Habeas Corpus Relief

The result mandated by *Teague* and *Butler* essentially has been codified as part of the substantive limitations imposed on habeas corpus relief by the 1996 Antiterrorism and Effective Death Penalty Act (AEDPA). AEDPA severely limits Federal habeas review over state court determinations of constitutional law, but the rule is now phrased as merit-based rather than retroactivity-based. The Act provides, in pertinent part:

> *(d) An application for a writ of habeas corpus on behalf of a person in custody pursuant to the judgment of a State court shall not be granted with respect to any claim that was adjudicated on the merits in State court proceedings unless the adjudication of the claim—*
>
> > *(1) resulted in a decision that was contrary to, or involved an unreasonable application of, clearly established Federal law, as determined by the Supreme Court of the United States; or*
> >
> > *(2) resulted in a decision that was based on an unreasonable determination of the facts in light of the evidence presented in the State court proceeding.*

In Williams v. Taylor, 529 U.S. 362 (2000), the Court, in an opinion by Justice O'Connor, declared that the AEDPA essentially codified a standard of review of state court decisions that is equivalent to the "new rule" jurisprudence of *Teague*. Under AEDPA, a federal court cannot grant relief unless the state court decision is "contrary to, or involved an unreasonable application of, clearly established Federal law, as determined by the Supreme Court of the United States." In *Williams*, Justice O'Connor declared that "whatever would qualify as an old rule under our *Teague* jurisprudence will constitute 'clearly established Federal law, as determined by the Supreme Court of the United States' under § 2254(d)(1). The one caveat, as the statutory language makes clear, is that § 2254(d)(1) restricts the source of clearly established law to this Court's jurisprudence." Consequently, if a habeas petitioner is claiming that a state court misapplied constitutional law that was not clearly established by the United States Supreme Court at the time, the habeas petition must be denied—because the state court decision is not "contrary to" clearly established law as defined by the Supreme Court. It follows that the *Teague* "new rule" jurisprudence has been codified, for all practical purposes, by AEDPA.

Note that in AEDPA there are no exceptions provided comparable to the two limited exceptions permitting retroactive application in *Teague*, i.e., "watershed" rules of constitutional law, or rules that hold certain conduct beyond criminal proscription. The rationale for rejecting these exceptions, according to an official at the Justice Department who was instrumental in drafting the provision, is that the *Teague* exceptions are so narrow that they can never be invoked as a practical matter. The result under AEDPA is that a habeas petitioner cannot seek to invoke a rule of law unless it was already clearly established at the time of the trial—and it makes no difference whether the rule of law proposed by the habeas claimant is a "watershed" rule or a rule that holds certain conduct beyond criminal proscription.

Finally, note that *Teague* itself remains directly applicable in cases where AEDPA does not apply. For example, where a state court never considered a defendant's claim on the merits, the standard of review set forth in AEDPA is by its terms inapplicable. However, for habeas corpus relief to be granted in such a situation, the petitioner's claim must still be based on constitutional law as it existed at the time of his conviction. Any attempt to extend that then-existing law will run into the "new rule" jurisprudence of *Teague* and its progeny. Thus, in Weeks v. Angelone, 176 F.3d 249 (4th Cir. 1999) the habeas petitioner claimed that his due process rights were denied by the state court's failure to provide him an expert in ballistics to assist in his defense. This claim was not covered by AEDPA because the state court had never considered it on the merits, even though asked to do so. But the constitutional claim was still barred by *Teague,* because the law existing at the time of the petitioner's conviction provided only that a defendant was entitled, upon a sufficient showing of need, to a state-appointed *psychiatrist* to assist in the defense. This precedent did not mandate appointment of *non-psychiatric* experts. Extending Supreme Court precedent to provide a guarantee of a non-psychiatric expert would constitute a "new rule", barred by *Teague.*

### *Retroactivity of Fourth Amendment New Rules Does Not Justify Exclusion: Davis v. United States*

In Davis v. United States, 131 S.Ct. 2419 (2011), the defendant sought the application of a new rule that was handed down while his case was still on direct review. The new rule, if applied, would mean that a police search of the defendant's car—which was legal at the time—violated the Fourth Amendment. The Court held that while the new rule of law applied to the search of Davis's car, that did not mean that the evidence should have been excluded. The Court ruled that  the "good faith" exception to the exclusionary rule applied, and because the police thought they were complying at the time, their conduct could not be deterred by the exclusionary rule. Thus, the Court distinguished the law, which was applicable, and the remedy of exclusion, which was not. *Davis* is discussed more fully in the materials on the Fourth Amendment exclusionary rule, and its good faith exception, in Chapter 2.

### Can States Apply a New Supreme Court Rule Retroactively Even if the Supreme Court Does Not? Danforth v. Minnesota

In Danforth v. Minnesota, 552 U.S. 264 (2008), the Court held that *Teague* does not prevent states from giving *more* retroactive effect to new rules than would be given by the Supreme Court. *Danforth* involved a collateral attack under state (rather than federal habeas) law of a finalized conviction. After the conviction was final, the United States Supreme Court decided a case on the confrontation clause that, if applicable, would result in reversal of the state conviction. It was a new rule and so would not be applicable on federal habeas review. But Justice Stevens, writing for the Court, found that *Teague* "was tailored to the unique context of federal habeas and therefore had no bearing on whether States could provide broader relief in their own postconviction proceedings than required by that opinion." He concluded as follows:

> It is important to keep in mind that our jurisprudence concerning the "retroactivity" of "new rules" of constitutional law is primarily concerned, not with the question whether a constitutional violation occurred, but with the availability or nonavailability of remedies. The former is a pure question of federal law, our resolution of which should be applied uniformly throughout the Nation, while the latter is a mixed question of state and federal law.

> A decision by this Court that a new rule does not apply retroactively under *Teague* does not imply that there was no right and thus no violation of that right at the time of trial—only that no remedy will be provided in federal habeas courts. It is fully consistent with a government of laws to recognize that the finality of a judgment may bar relief. It would be quite wrong to assume, however, that the question whether constitutional violations occurred in trials conducted before a certain date depends on how much time was required to complete the appellate process.

Chief Justice Roberts, joined by Justice Kennedy, dissented. He argued that the new rule was, after all, a federal rule, and therefore the decision of retroactivity must be one of federal law. He also noted that if states can vary on whether to hold a new rule retroactive or not, the federal law will vary from state to state.

### Retroactive Application Against the Defendant?: Lockhart v. Fretwell

The cases and statute discussed above deal with whether a defendant can, through retroactive application, receive a benefit from a change in law. But what about changes in law that are *detrimental* to a defendant? In Lockhart v. Fretwell, 506 U.S. 364 (1993), the Supreme Court, in an opinion by Chief Justice Rehnquist, held that detrimental changes in the law must be applied retroactively against petitioners on habeas review. The Chief Justice distinguished *Teague* and reasoned as follows:

> *Teague* stands for the proposition that new constitutional rules of criminal procedure will not be announced or applied on collateral review. * * * [T]his retroactivity rule was motivated by a respect for the States' strong interest in the finality of criminal convictions, and the recognition that a State should not be penalized for relying on the constitutional standards that prevailed at the time the original proceedings took place. The "new rule" principle therefore validates reasonable, good-faith interpretations of existing precedents made by state courts even though they are shown to be contrary to later decisions.

> A federal habeas petitioner has no interest in the finality of the state court judgment under which he is incarcerated: indeed, the very purpose of his habeas petition is to overturn that judgment. Nor does such a petitioner ordinarily have any claim of reliance on past judicial precedent as a basis for his actions * * *. The result of these differences is that the State will benefit from our *Teague* decision in some federal habeas cases, while the habeas petitioner will not.

Justice Stevens, joined by Justice Blackmun, dissented and argued that an "even-handed approach to retroactivity would seem to require that we continue to evaluate defendants' claims under the law as it stood at the time of trial." He reasoned that under *Teague*, a defendant may not take advantage of subsequent changes in the law when they are favorable to him, therefore "there is no self-evident reason why a State should be able to take advantage of subsequent changes in the law when they are adverse to his interests." The dissenters concluded that a "rule that generally precludes defendants from taking advantage of post-conviction changes in the law, but allows the State to do so, cannot be reconciled with this Court's duty to administer justice impartially."

# CHAPTER 2

## SEARCHES AND SEIZURES OF PERSONS AND THINGS

■ ■ ■

## I.  AN INTRODUCTION TO THE FOURTH AMENDMENT

### A.  THE PROBLEM OF GATHERING EVIDENCE

When government focuses its attention on crime detection and crime prevention, frequently it encounters uncooperative individuals. But the police are not compelled to forego investigative and preventive measures for lack of voluntary cooperation. When they seek information without cooperation, they must consider the limitations imposed by the Fourth Amendment, which reads as follows:

> The right of the people to be secure in their persons, houses, papers and effects, against unreasonable searches and seizures shall not be violated, and no Warrants shall issue, but upon probable cause, supported by Oath or affirmation, and particularly describing the place to be searched, and the persons or things to be seized.

### B.  THE BASICS OF THE FOURTH AMENDMENT

A number of points will seem obvious from a reading of the language of the Amendment, even without knowledge of its history and interpretation.

First, the language ascribes the right to *the people*, not to one person as under the Fifth Amendment, or to an accused as under the Sixth Amendment. The wording resembles that found in the Ninth and Tenth Amendments. Professor Amsterdam has suggested that the choice of language might well be important in properly interpreting the Amendment; in his view the courts should focus on how to regulate or control the conduct of the government so that Fourth Amendment violations do not occur, rather than on fashioning remedies for only those individuals who have suffered a personal Fourth Amendment wrong. See Perspectives on the Fourth Amendment, 58 Minn.L.Rev. 335, 367 (1974). But the Supreme Court has instead invoked the term "the people" to narrow the class of those protected by the Fourth Amendment.

### "The People" as a Limiting Term:
### United States v. Verdugo-Urquidez

In United States v. Verdugo-Urquidez, 494 U.S. 259 (1990), a Mexican citizen and resident was apprehended by Mexican police and transported to the United States for trial on drug charges. After his arrest, United States law enforcement officials, working with Mexican officials, conducted warrantless searches of the defendant's residences in Mexico. The lower courts held that the searches violated the Fourth Amendment.

The Supreme Court held that the Fourth Amendment does not apply to a search of property that is owned by a non-resident alien and located in a foreign country. Chief Justice Rehnquist, writing for the Court, reasoned that the Fourth Amendment's reference to "the people," as opposed to a particular person, was a "term of art." He asserted that the term was intended to refer only to a class of persons "who are part of a national community or who have otherwise developed sufficient connection with this country to be considered a part of that community."

The Court held that the defendant, who had been transported against his will to the United States three days before the foreign search was conducted, lacked sufficient connection with the United States to be one of "the people" protected by the Fourth Amendment. The Chief Justice looked to the history of the Amendment and concluded that its purpose was to protect the people of the United States from abuses by their own government and could not fairly be read to limit government action against aliens taken outside the United States.

Justice Brennan, joined by Justice Marshall, dissented. He noted that the defendant was convicted for violating a Federal law, even though his conduct occurred outside the United States. Thus, the defendant had been subject to an extraterritorial application of American criminal law. Justice Brennan argued that it was unfair for the Federal Government to require aliens outside the country to obey Federal laws, and yet refuse to obey its own laws in the course of investigating the very extraterritorial activity that the government has criminalized. According to Justice Brennan, the Fourth Amendment is an "unavoidable correlative" of the government's power to enforce the criminal law. Justice Blackmun wrote a separate dissenting opinion.

### Searches Against Illegal Aliens in the United States?

In *Verdugo-Urquidez,* the Court specifically refused to decide whether an illegal alien who lived in the United States would be one of "the people" protected by the Fourth Amendment. Five Justices, however, (Stevens, Kennedy, Brennan, Marshall and Blackmun), in various opinions in *Verdugo-Urquidez,* indicated that they would hold the Fourth Amendment applicable to searches of illegal aliens conducted within the United States. The reasoning was that an illegal alien living in the United States would have the "connection" with this country required to be one of "the people" protected by the Fourth Amendment.

But *Verdugo-Urquidez* was decided before the terrorist attack of September 11, 2001. Since that time, various government officials have argued that illegal aliens living in the United States do not have the right to invoke Fourth Amendment protections as they do not have a legitimate connection to the United States. What do you think? Should it matter whether the alien has been deported and then illegally re-entered the country?

### *The Reasonableness Clause and the Warrant Clause*

As a second introductory point, the Fourth Amendment is set forth in two parts, the first dealing with unreasonable searches and the second dealing with warrants. Because the term "unreasonable" is used first, it might be thought to predominate so that all searches and seizures must satisfy its command, whereas the warrant clause would come into play only when a warrant is sought to justify government action. But the Supreme Court has purported not to read the language in this way. One observer has suggested that the Court has "stood the amendment on its head" by reading the warrant clause as the controlling clause of the Amendment. T. Taylor, Two Studies in Constitutional Interpretation 23–24 (1969). The Court has stated that searches and seizures are *presumed* to be unreasonable unless carried out pursuant to a warrant. But important exceptions to the presumptive warrant requirement have been created. When an exception to the warrant requirement is applicable, only the reasonableness requirement must be satisfied. It must also be noted that the Court has in some cases explicitly invoked the reasonableness clause as the predominant clause of the Fourth Amendment, most notably when the government's search or seizure serves "special needs" beyond criminal law enforcement.

### *"Probable Cause"*

Third, the term "probable cause" is used to define the minimum showing necessary to support a warrant application; it is not used to demarcate reasonableness generally in search and seizure situations. But despite the placement of the words, the decisions make probable cause a limitation on many searches and seizures even though no warrant is deemed necessary under the circumstances. Also, note that the definition of probable cause is not altogether clear; the Amendment itself contains not a hint as to its meaning. The courts have been left to give meaning to the term, and their efforts will be analyzed later in this Chapter.

### State Action Requirement

Fourth, the Amendment plainly recognizes a right, but does not indicate against whom it applies. Arguably, the people have a right to be free from all searches and seizures that are not reasonable, even if conducted by private persons. But, unlike the Thirteenth Amendment, the Fourth is interpreted as providing protection only against the government and those acting in conjunction with it.

On the other hand, nothing in the language of the Amendment limits the applicability to criminal investigations or to the police. The protection is against all unreasonable searches and seizures conducted by government officials regardless of the purpose of the investigation or the identity of the investigator. Courts have accepted this reading, but do take the nature of the investigation into account in assessing the reasonableness of particular searches and in defining the requirements of a proper warrant.

## C. THE AMENDMENT AND THE EXCLUSIONARY RULE

It is useful to distinguish two questions in thinking about Fourth Amendment problems. First, there is the question whether the Amendment prohibits the kind of governmental conduct described in the cases. If so, the second question is whether evidence obtained by means of a Fourth Amendment violation should be available as proof in criminal trials and other proceedings. The debate over the wisdom of an exclusionary rule is a debate over the second question. Yet, too often analysis of the first question is confused in the process of debating the second. Consider, for example, the following personal editorial by the late Judge Malcolm Wilkey of the United States Court of Appeals for the District of Columbia Circuit:

> Among nations of the civilized world we are unique in two respects: (1) We suffer the most extraordinary crime rate with firearms. (2) In criminal prosecutions, by a rule of evidence which exists in no other country, we exclude the most trustworthy and convincing evidence.

> These two aberrations are not unconnected. In fact, the "exclusionary rule" has made unenforceable the gun control laws we have and will make ineffective any stricter controls which may be devised. Its fetters particularly paralyze police efforts to prevent, detect and punish street crimes involving not only weapons but narcotics.

Why Suppress Valid Evidence, Wall Street Journal, Oct. 7, 1977, at
1, col. 1.

This is an argument by a distinguished jurist who pondered search
and seizure problems for years. Yet, it is fundamentally flawed. "Probable
cause" is a term found in the language chosen by the framers. If the Court
correctly interprets the Fourth Amendment as requiring probable cause
for particular police action such as a search for guns, then it is the
substance of the Fourth Amendment itself (as interpreted by the Court),
not the remedy for a violation, that impairs the ability to enforce firearm
laws. Immediate abolition of the exclusionary rule would not free officers
to search for guns in violation of the substance of the Amendment. They
remain bound by the Constitution.[1] So even with the demise of the
exclusionary rule, some criminal laws still will be hard to enforce. The
cases that comprise the bulk of this Chapter assume that the remedy for
an unconstitutional search and seizure is exclusion.

The costs and benefits of the exclusionary rule are not discussed until
late in the Chapter. Delay should provide an adequate opportunity for an
understanding of the different circumstances in which a Fourth
Amendment violation occurs. But delay in no way is intended to imply
that the exclusionary rule is plainly desirable and that the debate over it
is not important. The debate is important for practical and symbolic
reasons, and delay in reaching it is tantamount to deference to its
significance. But, it is true that even without the exclusionary rule, the
basic problems of deciding what the Amendment means would remain. As
you read the cases, keep in mind that despite the fact that the issues
usually are cast in terms of whether evidence should have been excluded
at trial, the same issues could often arise in some form or other—perhaps
in civil suits rather than criminal cases—even without an exclusionary
rule. So you cannot avoid grappling with the meaning and proper
interpretation of the Fourth Amendment simply by doing away with the
exclusionary rule.

## II.   THRESHOLD REQUIREMENTS FOR FOURTH
##       AMENDMENT PROTECTIONS: WHAT IS A
##       "SEARCH?" WHAT IS A "SEIZURE?"

The Fourth Amendment prohibits unreasonable searches and
seizures. If the government activity is neither a "search" nor a "seizure" it
is not regulated by the Fourth Amendment, and therefore the activity
does not have to be reasonable—at least as far as the federal Constitution
is concerned.

---

[1]   This point is made by another experienced jurist, Justice Stewart, in The Road to *Mapp
v. Ohio* and Beyond: The Origins, Development, and Future of the Exclusionary Rule in Search-
and-Seizure Cases, 83 Colum.L.Rev. 1365 (1989).

It has been argued that in deciding the threshold question of whether a government intrusion is a search or seizure, one should err on the side of the citizen. The consequence of finding a search or seizure is merely that the government is required to act reasonably, whereas the consequence of not finding a search or seizure is that government officials can act unreasonably and arbitrarily. See Amsterdam, Perspectives on the Fourth Amendment, 58 Minn.L.Rev. 349 (1974). In fact, however, the Supreme Court for several decades  has held that a variety of  police investigative activity is neither a search nor a seizure, and is thus free from the strictures of the Fourth Amendment.

## A.  THE REASONABLE EXPECTATION TEST

In the following landmark case, the Court established a general test for determining whether government investigative activity rises to the level of a search—the reasonable expectation of privacy test. As will be seen later in the Chapter, the Court, having  bypassed the "trespass doctrine" in *Katz*, has more recently reinvigorated it and established that the *Katz* test is not the sole ground for finding that a police activity is a search.

### KATZ V. UNITED STATES

Supreme Court of the United States, 1967.
389 U.S. 347.

**MR. JUSTICE STEWART delivered the opinion of the Court.**

The petitioner was convicted in the District Court for the Southern District of California under an eight-count indictment charging him with transmitting wagering information by telephone from Los Angeles to Miami and Boston, in violation of a Federal statute. At trial the Government was permitted, over the petitioner's objection, to introduce evidence of the petitioner's end of telephone conversations, overheard by FBI agents who had attached an electronic listening and recording device to the outside of the public telephone booth from which he had placed his calls. In affirming his conviction, the Court of Appeals rejected the contention that the recordings had been obtained in violation of the Fourth Amendment, because "[t]here was no physical entrance into the area occupied by [the petitioner]." We granted certiorari in order to consider the constitutional questions thus presented.

The petitioner has phrased those questions as follows:

"A. Whether a public telephone booth is a constitutionally protected area so that evidence obtained by attaching an electronic listening recording device to the top of such a booth is obtained in violation of the right to privacy of the user of the booth.

"B. Whether physical penetration of a constitutionally protected area is necessary before a search and seizure can be said to be violative of the Fourth Amendment to the United States Constitution."

We decline to adopt this formulation of the issues. In the first place, the correct solution of Fourth Amendment problems is not necessarily promoted by incantation of the phrase "constitutionally protected area." Secondly, the Fourth Amendment cannot be translated into a general constitutional "right to privacy." That Amendment protects individual privacy against certain kinds of governmental intrusion, but its protections go further, and often have nothing to do with privacy at all. Other provisions of the Constitution protect personal privacy from other forms of governmental invasion. But the protection of a person's *general* right to privacy—his right to be let alone by other people—is like the protection of his property and of his very life, left largely to the law of the individual States.

Because of the misleading way the issues have been formulated, the parties have attached great significance to the characterization of the telephone booth from which the petitioner placed his calls. The petitioner has strenuously argued that the booth was a "constitutionally protected area." The Government has maintained with equal vigor that it was not. But this effort to decide whether or not a given "area," viewed in the abstract, is "constitutionally protected" deflects attention from the problem presented by this case. For the Fourth Amendment protects people, not places. What a person knowingly exposes to the public, even in his own home or office, is not a subject of Fourth Amendment protection. But what he seeks to preserve as private, even in an area accessible to the public, may be constitutionally protected.

The Government stresses the fact that the telephone booth from which the petitioner made his calls was constructed partly of glass, so that he was as visible after he entered it as he would have been if he had remained outside. But what he sought to exclude when he entered the booth was not the intruding eye—it was the uninvited ear. He did not shed his right to do so simply because he made his calls from a place where he might be seen. No less than an individual in a business office, in a friend's apartment, or in a taxicab, a person in a telephone booth may rely upon the protection of the Fourth Amendment. One who occupies it, shuts the door behind him, and pays the toll that permits him to place a call is surely entitled to assume that the words he utters into the mouthpiece will not be broadcast to the world. * * *

The Government contends, however, that the activities of its agents in this case should not be tested by Fourth Amendment requirements, for the surveillance technique they employed involved no physical penetration of the telephone booth from which the petitioner placed his calls. It is true that the absence of such penetration was at one time thought to foreclose further Fourth Amendment inquiry, Olmstead v. United States, 277 U.S. 438, 457, 464, 466; Goldman v. United States, 316 U.S. 129, 134–136, for that Amendment was thought to limit only searches and seizures of tangible property. But "[t]he premise that property interests control the right of the Government to search and seize has been discredited." Warden v. Hayden, 387 U.S. 294, 304. Thus, although a closely divided Court supposed in *Olmstead* that surveillance without any trespass and without the seizure of any material object fell outside the ambit of the Constitution, we have since departed from the narrow view on which that decision rested. Indeed, we have expressly held that the Fourth Amendment governs not only the seizure of tangible items, but extends as well to the recording of oral statements, overheard without any "technical trespass under * * * local property law." Silverman v. United States, 365 U.S. 505, 511. Once this much is acknowledged, and once it is recognized that the Fourth Amendment protects people—and not simply "areas"—against unreasonable searches and seizures, it becomes clear that the reach of that Amendment cannot turn upon the presence or absence of a physical intrusion into any given enclosure.

We conclude that the underpinnings of *Olmstead* and *Goldman* have been so eroded by our subsequent decisions that the "trespass" doctrine there enunciated can no longer be regarded as controlling. The Government's activities in electronically listening to and recording the petitioner's words violated the privacy upon which he justifiably relied while using the telephone booth and thus constituted a "search and seizure" within the meaning of the Fourth Amendment. The fact that the electronic device employed to achieve that end did not happen to penetrate the wall of the booth can have no constitutional significance.

The question remaining for decision, then, is whether the search and seizure conducted in this case complied with constitutional standards. In that regard, the Government's position is that its agents acted in an entirely defensible manner: They did not begin their electronic surveillance until investigation of the petitioner's activities had established a strong probability that he was using the telephone in question to transmit gambling information to persons in other States, in violation of Federal law. Moreover, the surveillance was limited, both in scope and in duration, to the specific purpose of establishing the contents of the petitioner's unlawful telephonic communications. The agents confined their surveillance to the brief periods during which he used the telephone booth, and they took great care to overhear only the conversations of the petitioner himself.

Accepting this account of the Government's actions as accurate, it is clear that this surveillance was so narrowly circumscribed that a duly authorized magistrate, properly notified of the need for such investigation, specifically informed of the basis on which it was to proceed, and clearly apprised of the precise intrusion it would entail, could constitutionally have authorized, with appropriate safeguards, the very limited search and seizure that the Government asserts in fact took place. * * *

* * * Yet the inescapable fact is that this restraint was imposed by the agents themselves, not by a judicial officer. They were not required, before commencing the search, to present their estimate of probable cause for detached scrutiny by a neutral magistrate. They were not compelled, during the conduct of the search itself, to observe precise limits established in advance by a specific court order. Nor were they directed, after the search had been completed, to notify the authorizing magistrate in detail of all that had been seized. In the absence of such safeguards, this Court has never sustained a search upon the sole ground that officers reasonably expected to find evidence of a particular crime and voluntarily confined their activities to the least intrusive means to that end * * *.

* * *

The Government does not question these basic principles. Rather, it urges the creation of a new exception to cover this case. It argues that surveillance of a telephone booth should be exempted from the usual requirement of advance authorization by a magistrate upon a showing of probable cause. We cannot agree. Omission of such authorization

> "bypasses the safeguards provided by an objective predetermination of probable cause, and substitutes instead the far less reliable procedure of an after-the-event justification for the * * * search, too likely to be subtly influenced by the familiar shortcomings of hindsight judgment." Beck v. Ohio, 379 U.S. 89, 96.

And bypassing a neutral predetermination of the *scope* of a search leaves individuals secure from Fourth Amendment violations "only in the discretion of the police."

These considerations do not vanish when the search in question is transferred from the setting of a home, an office, or a hotel room to that of a telephone booth. Wherever a man may be, he is entitled to know that he will remain free from unreasonable searches and seizures. The government agents here ignored "the procedure of antecedent justification * * * that is central to the Fourth Amendment," a procedure that we hold to be a constitutional precondition of the kind of electronic surveillance involved in this case. Because the surveillance here failed to meet that condition, and because it led to the petitioner's conviction, the judgment must be reversed.

\* \* \*

**MR. JUSTICE HARLAN, concurring.**

I join the opinion of the Court, which I read to hold only (a) that an enclosed telephone booth is an area where, like a home, and unlike a field, a person has a constitutionally protected reasonable expectation of privacy; (b) that electronic as well as physical intrusion into a place that is in this sense private may constitute a violation of the Fourth Amendment; and (c) that the invasion of a constitutionally protected area by Federal authorities is, as the Court has long held, presumptively unreasonable in the absence of a search warrant.

As the Court's opinion states, "the Fourth Amendment protects people, not places." The question, however, is what protection it affords to those people. Generally, as here, the answer to that question requires reference to a "place." My understanding of the rule that has emerged from prior decisions is that there is a twofold requirement, first that a person have exhibited an actual (subjective) expectation of privacy and, second, that the expectation be one that society is prepared to recognize as "reasonable." Thus a man's home is, for most purposes, a place where he expects privacy, but objects, activities, or statements that he exposes to the "plain view" of outsiders are not "protected" because no intention to keep them to himself has been exhibited. On the other hand, conversations in the open would not be protected against being overheard, for the expectation of privacy under the circumstances would be unreasonable.

The critical fact in this case is that "[o]ne who occupies it, [a telephone booth] shuts the door behind him, and pays the toll that permits him to place a call is surely entitled to assume" that his conversation is not being intercepted. The point is not that the booth is "accessible to the public" at other times, but that it is a temporarily private place whose momentary occupants' expectations of freedom from intrusion are recognized as reasonable.

\* \* \*

**MR. JUSTICE BLACK, dissenting.**

\* \* \*

My basic objection is twofold: (1) I do not believe that the words of the Amendment will bear the meaning given them by today's decision, and (2) I do not believe that it is the proper role of this Court to rewrite the Amendment in order "to bring it into harmony with the times" and thus reach a result that many people believe to be desirable.

While I realize that an argument based on the meaning of words lacks the scope, and no doubt the appeal, of broad policy discussions and philosophical discourses on such nebulous subjects as privacy, for me the language of the Amendment is the crucial place to look in construing a written document such as our Constitution. * * *

The first clause protects "persons, houses, papers, and effects, against unreasonable searches and seizures * * *." These words connote the idea of tangible things with size, form, and weight, things capable of being searched, seized, or both. The second clause of the Amendment still further establishes its Framers' purpose to limit its protection to tangible things by providing that no warrants shall issue but those "particularly describing the place to be searched, and the persons or things to be seized." A conversation overheard by eavesdropping, whether by plain snooping or wiretapping, is not tangible and, under the normally accepted meanings of the words, can neither be searched nor seized. * * *

Tapping telephone wires, of course, was an unknown possibility at the time the Fourth Amendment was adopted. But eavesdropping (and wiretapping is nothing more than eavesdropping by telephone) was * * * an ancient practice which at common law was condemned as a nuisance. * * * There can be no doubt that the Framers were aware of this practice, and if they had desired to outlaw or restrict the use of evidence obtained by eavesdropping, I believe that they would have used the appropriate language to do so in the Fourth Amendment. They certainly would not have left such a task to the ingenuity of language-stretching judges.

* * *

[JUSTICE MARSHALL took no part in the consideration or decision of this case. Concurring opinions by DOUGLAS, J., joined by BRENNAN, J., and by WHITE, J. are omitted.]

### *Katz as a Two-Pronged Test*

*Katz* has been read to set forth a two-pronged test for determining whether government conduct constitutes a search. First, the government conduct must offend the citizen's subjective manifestation of a privacy interest. Second, the privacy interest invaded must be one that society is prepared to accept as "reasonable" or "legitimate." This two-pronged test comes not from Justice Stewart's majority opinion but rather from Justice Harlan's concurring opinion. It is notable that in the later case of United States v. White, 401 U.S. 745 (1971) (holding that no search occurred where police electronically eavesdropped on a two-party conversation with the consent of one of the parties), Justice Harlan dissented and expressed misgivings about the test that he had promulgated in *Katz:*

While these formulations represent an advance over the unsophisticated trespass analysis of the common law, they too have their limitations and can, ultimately, lead to the substitution of words for analysis. The analysis must, in my view, transcend the search for subjective expectations or legal attribution of assumptions of risk. Our expectations, and the risks we assume, are in large part reflections of laws that translate into rules the customs and values of the past and present.

Justice Harlan's concern was that the reasonableness of an expectation of privacy would be determined by existing laws and practices, and that this could result in the diminution of protected privacy interests; "expectation" of privacy could be based on what government conditions us to expect.

Should the Fourth Amendment threshold be dependent on what we should *expect* from government, or rather on what we can *demand* from government? Consider Professor Clancy's critique of *Katz:*

> The ability to exclude must extend to all invasions, tangible and intangible, and must protect both tangible and intangible aspects of the amendment's protected objects. That was the essential lesson of *Katz*. *Katz* and the privacy theory, however, failed to grasp the essence of the interest protected. Although it may have been Katz's *expectation* that his conversation was not being heard, it was his *right* to exclude others from hearing. It is not privacy which may motivate a person to assert his or her right. It is the right to prevent intrusions—to exclude—which affords personal security.

Clancy, What Does the Fourth Amendment Protect: Property, Privacy, or Security?, 33 Wake Forest L. Rev. 307, 367–8 (1998).

### Privacy and Technological Advances

Has the reasonable expectation of privacy test become outmoded in our technologically advanced society, where very little if any information can be kept private? Professor Henderson, in Nothing New Under the Sun? A Technologically Rational Doctrine of Fourth Amendment Search, 56 Mercer L.Rev. 507 (2005), argues that the reasonable expectation of privacy test should be dropped in favor of a test that evaluates every government intrusion by whether it is reasonable under the circumstances. He explains that if the *Katz* test is retained, "technology will lead to no privacy, and police practice will incorporate that technology to create a reality of no privacy." In contrast, a reasonableness test "is a flexible one that allows courts to continue to protect privacy as we transition into a world in which no intrusion is technologically inconvenient."

## B.  THE RETURN OF THE TRESPASS ANALYSIS

The Court in *Katz* appeared to reject a focus on physical trespass as determining whether a search has occurred. But in the following landmark case, the Court returned to the trespass test to *supplement* the reasonable expectation of privacy test.

## UNITED STATES V. JONES

Supreme Court of the United States, 2012.
132 S.Ct. 945.

### JUSTICE SCALIA delivered the opinion of the Court.

We decide whether the attachment of a Global Positioning-System (GPS) tracking device to an individual's vehicle, and subsequent use of that device to monitor the vehicle's movements on public streets, constitutes a search or seizure within the meaning of the Fourth Amendment.

\* \* \*

In 2004 respondent Antoine Jones, owner and operator of a nightclub in the District of Columbia, came under suspicion of trafficking in narcotics and was made the target of an investigation by a joint FBI and Metropolitan Police Department task force. Officers employed various investigative techniques, including visual surveillance of the nightclub, installation of a camera focused on the front door of the club, and a pen register and wiretap covering Jones's cellular phone. Based in part on information gathered from these sources, in 2005 the Government applied to the United States District Court for the District of Columbia for a warrant authorizing the use of an electronic tracking device on the Jeep Grand Cherokee registered to Jones's wife. A warrant issued, authorizing installation of the device in the District of Columbia and within 10 days.

On the 11th day, and not in the District of Columbia but in Maryland, agents installed a GPS tracking device on the undercarriage of the Jeep while it was parked in a public parking lot. Over the next 28 days, the Government used the device to track the vehicle's movements, and once had to replace the device's battery when the vehicle was parked in a different public lot in Maryland.[a] By means of signals from multiple satellites, the device established the vehicle's location within 50 to 100 feet, and communicated that location by cellular phone to a Government computer. It relayed more than 2,000 pages of data over the 4-week period.

The Government ultimately obtained a multiple-count indictment charging Jones and several alleged coconspirators with, as relevant here, conspiracy to distribute and possess with intent to distribute five kilograms or more of cocaine and 50 grams or more of cocaine base \* \* \*. Before trial, Jones filed a motion to suppress evidence obtained through

---

[a]    In this litigation, the Government has conceded noncompliance with the warrant and has argued only that a warrant was not required.

the GPS device. The District Court granted the motion only in part, suppressing the data obtained while the vehicle was parked in the garage adjoining Jones's residence. It held the remaining data admissible, because " '[a] person traveling in an automobile on public thoroughfares has no reasonable expectation of privacy in his movements from one place to another.' " Jones's trial in October 2006 produced a hung jury on the conspiracy count.

In March 2007, a grand jury returned another indictment, charging Jones and others with the same conspiracy. The Government introduced at trial the same GPS-derived locational data admitted in the first trial, which connected Jones to the alleged conspirators' stash house that contained $850,000 in cash, 97 kilograms of cocaine, and 1 kilogram of cocaine base. The jury returned a guilty verdict, and the District Court sentenced Jones to life imprisonment.

The United States Court of Appeals for the District of Columbia Circuit reversed the conviction because of admission of the evidence obtained by warrantless use of the GPS device which, it said, violated the Fourth Amendment. * * * We granted certiorari.

The Fourth Amendment provides in relevant part that "[t]he right of the people to be secure in their persons, houses, papers, and effects, against unreasonable searches and seizures, shall not be violated." It is beyond dispute that a vehicle is an "effect" as that term is used in the Amendment. We hold that the Government's installation of a GPS device on a target's vehicle, and its use of that device to monitor the vehicle's movements, constitutes a "search."

It is important to be clear about what occurred in this case: The Government physically occupied private property for the purpose of obtaining information. We have no doubt that such a physical intrusion would have been considered a "search" within the meaning of the Fourth Amendment when it was adopted. Entick v. Carrington, 95 Eng. Rep. 807 (C. P. 1765), is a "case we have described as a 'monument of English freedom' 'undoubtedly familiar' to 'every American statesman' at the time the Constitution was adopted, and considered to be 'the true and ultimate expression of constitutional law' " with regard to search and seizure. In that case, Lord Camden expressed in plain terms the significance of property rights in search-and-seizure analysis:

> "[O]ur law holds the property of every man so sacred, that no man can set his foot upon his neighbour's close without his leave; if he does he is a trespasser, though he does no damage at all; if he will tread upon his neighbour's ground, he must justify it by law."

The text of the Fourth Amendment reflects its close connection to property, since otherwise it would have referred simply to "the right of the people to be secure against unreasonable searches and seizures"; the phrase "in their persons, houses, papers, and effects" would have been superfluous.

Consistent with this understanding, our Fourth Amendment jurisprudence was tied to common-law trespass, at least until the latter half of the 20th century. Thus, in Olmstead v. United States, 277 U. S. 438 (1928), we held that wiretaps attached to telephone wires on the public streets did not constitute a Fourth Amendment search because "[t]here was no entry of the houses or offices of the defendants."

Our later cases, of course, have deviated from that exclusively property-based approach. In Katz v. United States, we said that "the Fourth Amendment protects people, not places," and found a violation in attachment of an eavesdropping device to a public telephone booth. Our later cases have applied the analysis of Justice Harlan's concurrence in that case, which said that a violation occurs when government officers violate a person's "reasonable expectation of privacy."

The Government contends that the Harlan standard shows that no search occurred here, since Jones had no "reasonable expectation of privacy" in the area of the Jeep accessed by Government agents (its underbody) and in the locations of the Jeep on the public roads, which were visible to all. But we need not address the Government's contentions, because Jones's Fourth Amendment rights do not rise or fall with the *Katz* formulation. * * * As explained, for most of our history the Fourth Amendment was understood to embody a particular concern for government trespass upon the areas ("persons, houses, papers, and effects") it enumerates.b * * *

* * * *Katz* did not erode the principle that, when the Government does engage in physical intrusion of a constitutionally protected area in order to obtain information, that intrusion may constitute a violation of the Fourth Amendment. We have embodied that preservation of past rights in our very definition of "reasonable expectation of privacy" which we have said to be an expectation "that has a source outside of the Fourth Amendment, either by reference to concepts of real or personal property

---

b    Justice Alito's concurrence * * * doubts the wisdom of our approach because "it is almost impossible to think of late-18th-century situations that are analogous to what took place in this case." But in fact it posits a situation that is not far afield—a constable's concealing himself in the target's coach in order to track its movements. There is no doubt that the information gained by that trespassory activity would be the product of an unlawful search—whether that information consisted of the conversations occurring in the coach, or of the destinations to which the coach traveled.

In any case, it is quite irrelevant whether there was an 18th-century analog. Whatever new methods of investigation may be devised, our task, at a minimum, is to decide whether the action in question would have constituted a "search" within the original meaning of the Fourth Amendment. Where, as here, the Government obtains information by physically intruding on a constitutionally protected area, such a search has undoubtedly occurred.

law or to understandings that are recognized and permitted by society." *Katz* did not narrow the Fourth Amendment's scope.[c]

[The majority distinguishes *Knotts* and *Karo*—two beeper-tracking cases discussed later in this Chapter, in which the Court found that the tracking was not a search—on the ground that *Knotts* did not challenge the placement of the beeper and *Karo* did not involve the government's trespass on private property.][d]

\* \* \*

The concurrence begins by accusing us of applying "18th-century tort law." That is a distortion. What we apply is an 18th-century guarantee against unreasonable searches, which we believe must provide *at a minimum* the degree of protection it afforded when it was adopted. The concurrence does not share that belief. It would apply exclusively *Katz*'s reasonable-expectation-of-privacy test, even when that eliminates rights that previously existed. The concurrence faults our approach for "present[ing] particularly vexing problems" in cases that do not involve physical contact, such as those that involve the transmission of electronic signals. We entirely fail to understand that point. For unlike the concurrence, which would make *Katz* the exclusive test, we do not make trespass the exclusive test. Situations involving merely the transmission of electronic signals without trespass would remain subject to *Katz* analysis.

In fact, it is the concurrence's insistence on the exclusivity of the *Katz* test that needlessly leads us into "particularly vexing problems" in the present case. This Court has to date not deviated from the understanding that mere visual observation does not constitute a search. We accordingly held in *Knotts* that "[a] person traveling in an automobile on public thoroughfares has no reasonable expectation of privacy in his movements from one place to another." Thus, even assuming that the concurrence is correct to say that "[t]raditional surveillance" of Jones for a 4-week period "would have required a large team of agents, multiple vehicles, and perhaps aerial assistance," our cases suggest that such visual observation is constitutionally permissible. It may be that achieving the same result

---

[c] The concurrence notes that post-*Katz* we have explained that "an actual trespass is neither necessary nor sufficient to establish a constitutional violation." That is undoubtedly true, and undoubtedly irrelevant. \* \* \* Trespass alone does not qualify, but there must be conjoined with that what was present here: an attempt to find something or to obtain information. Related to this, and similarly irrelevant, is the concurrence's point that, if analyzed separately, neither the installation of the device nor its use would constitute a Fourth Amendment search. Of course not. A trespass on "houses" or "effects," or a *Katz* invasion of privacy, is not alone a search unless it is done to obtain information; and the obtaining of information is not alone a search unless it is achieved by such a trespass or invasion of privacy.

[d] *Knotts* noted the "limited use which the government made of the signals from this particular beeper," and reserved the question whether "different constitutional principles may be applicable" to "dragnet-type law enforcement practices" of the type that GPS tracking made possible here.

through electronic means, without an accompanying trespass, is an unconstitutional invasion of privacy, but the present case does not require us to answer that question.

And answering it affirmatively leads us needlessly into additional thorny problems. The concurrence posits that "relatively short-term monitoring of a person's movements on public streets" is okay, but that "the use of longer term GPS monitoring in investigations of most offenses" is no good. That introduces yet another novelty into our jurisprudence. There is no precedent for the proposition that whether a search has occurred depends on the nature of the crime being investigated. And even accepting that novelty, it remains unexplained why a 4-week investigation is "surely" too long and why a drug-trafficking conspiracy involving substantial amounts of cash and narcotics is not an "extraordinary offens[e]" which may permit longer observation. What of a 2-day monitoring of a suspected purveyor of stolen electronics? Or of a 6-month monitoring of a suspected terrorist? We may have to grapple with these "vexing problems" in some future case where a classic trespassory search is not involved and resort must be had to *Katz* analysis; but there is no reason for rushing forward to resolve them here.

\* \* \*

## JUSTICE SOTOMAYOR, concurring.

\* \* \*

\* \* \* Justice Alito's approach, which discounts altogether the constitutional relevance of the Government's physical intrusion on Jones' Jeep, erodes that longstanding protection for privacy expectations inherent in items of property that people possess or control. By contrast, the trespassory test applied in the majority's opinion reflects an irreducible constitutional minimum: When the Government physically invades personal property to gather information, a search occurs. The reaffirmation of that principle suffices to decide this case.

Nonetheless, as Justice Alito notes, physical intrusion is now unnecessary to many forms of surveillance. With increasing regularity, the Government will be capable of duplicating the monitoring undertaken in this case by enlisting factory- or owner-installed vehicle tracking devices or GPS-enabled smartphones. In cases of electronic or other novel modes of surveillance that do not depend upon a physical invasion on property, the majority opinion's trespassory test may provide little guidance. But "[s]ituations involving merely the transmission of electronic signals without trespass would remain subject to *Katz* analysis." As Justice Alito incisively observes, the same technological advances that have made possible nontrespassory surveillance techniques will also affect the *Katz* test by shaping the evolution of societal privacy expectations. Under that rubric, I agree with Justice Alito that, at the very least, "longer term GPS monitoring in investigations of most offenses impinges on expectations of privacy."

In cases involving even short-term monitoring, some unique attributes of GPS surveillance relevant to the *Katz* analysis will require particular attention. GPS monitoring generates a precise, comprehensive record of a person's public movements that reflects a wealth of detail about her familial, political, professional, religious, and sexual associations. The Government can store such records and efficiently mine them for information years into the future. And because GPS monitoring is cheap in comparison to conventional surveillance techniques and, by design, proceeds surreptitiously, it evades the ordinary checks that constrain abusive law enforcement practices: limited police resources and community hostility.

Awareness that the Government may be watching chills associational and expressive freedoms. And the Government's unrestrained power to assemble data that reveal private aspects of identity is susceptible to abuse. The net result is that GPS monitoring—by making available at a relatively low cost such a substantial quantum of intimate information about any person whom the Government, in its unfettered discretion, chooses to track—may alter the relationship between citizen and government in a way that is inimical to democratic society. I would take these attributes of GPS monitoring into account when considering the existence of a reasonable societal expectation of privacy in the sum of one's public movements. I would ask whether people reasonably expect that their movements will be recorded and aggregated in a manner that enables the Government to ascertain, more or less at will, their political and religious beliefs, sexual habits, and so on. I do not regard as dispositive the fact that the Government might obtain the fruits of GPS monitoring through lawful conventional surveillance techniques. I would also consider the appropriateness of entrusting to the Executive, in the absence of any oversight from a coordinate branch, a tool so amenable to misuse, especially in light of the Fourth Amendment's goal to curb arbitrary exercises of police power to and prevent a too permeating police surveillance.

More fundamentally, it may be necessary to reconsider the premise that an individual has no reasonable expectation of privacy in information voluntarily disclosed to third parties. This approach is ill suited to the digital age, in which people reveal a great deal of information about themselves to third parties in the course of carrying out mundane tasks. People disclose the phone numbers that they dial or text to their cellular providers; the URLs that they visit and the e-mail addresses with which they correspond to their Internet service providers; and the books, groceries, and medications they purchase to online retailers. Perhaps, as Justice Alito notes, some people may find the "tradeoff" of privacy for convenience "worthwhile," or come to accept this "diminution of privacy" as "inevitable," and perhaps not. I for one doubt that people would accept without complaint the warrantless disclosure to the Government of a list of every Web site they had visited in the last week, or month, or year. But whatever the societal expectations, they can attain constitutionally protected status only if our Fourth Amendment jurisprudence ceases to treat secrecy as a prerequisite for privacy. I would not assume that all information voluntarily disclosed to some member of the public for a limited purpose is, for that reason alone, disentitled to Fourth Amendment protection.

Resolution of these difficult questions in this case is unnecessary, however, because the Government's physical intrusion on Jones' Jeep supplies a narrower basis for decision. I therefore join the majority's opinion.

**JUSTICE ALITO, with whom JUSTICE GINSBURG, JUSTICE BREYER, and JUSTICE KAGAN, join, concurring in the judgment.**

This case requires us to apply the Fourth Amendment's prohibition of unreasonable searches and seizures to a 21st-century surveillance technique, the use of a Global Positioning System (GPS) device to monitor a vehicle's movements for an extended period of time. Ironically, the Court has chosen to decide this case based on 18th-century tort law. By attaching a small GPS device[e] to the underside of the vehicle that respondent drove, the law enforcement officers in this case engaged in conduct that might have provided grounds in 1791 for a suit for trespass to chattels. And for this reason, the Court concludes, the installation and use of the GPS device constituted a search.

This holding, in my judgment, is unwise. It strains the language of the Fourth Amendment; it has little if any support in current Fourth Amendment case law; and it is highly artificial.

I would analyze the question presented in this case by asking whether respondent's reasonable expectations of privacy were violated by the long-term monitoring of the movements of the vehicle he drove.

* * * The Fourth Amendment prohibits "unreasonable searches and seizures," and the Court makes very little effort to explain how the attachment or use of the GPS device fits within these terms. The Court does not contend that there was a seizure. A seizure of property occurs when there is "some meaningful interference with an individual's possessory interests in that property," and here there was none. Indeed, the success of the surveillance technique that the officers employed was dependent on the fact that the GPS did not interfere in any way with the

---

e   Although the record does not reveal the size or weight of the device used in this case, there is now a device in use that weighs two ounces and is the size of a credit card.

operation of the vehicle, for if any such interference had been detected, the device might have been discovered.

The Court does claim that the installation and use of the GPS constituted a search, but this conclusion is dependent on the questionable proposition that these two procedures cannot be separated for purposes of Fourth Amendment analysis. If these two procedures are analyzed separately, it is not at all clear from the Court's opinion why either should be regarded as a search. It is clear that the attachment of the GPS device was not itself a search; if the device had not functioned or if the officers had not used it, no information would have been obtained. And the Court does not contend that the use of the device constituted a search either. On the contrary, the Court accepts the holding in United States v. Knotts, 460 U. S. 276 (1983), that the use of a surreptitiously planted electronic device to monitor a vehicle's movements on public roads did not amount to a search.

The Court argues—and I agree—that we must assure preservation of that degree of privacy against government that existed when the Fourth Amendment was adopted. But it is almost impossible to think of late-18th-century situations that are analogous to what took place in this case. (Is it possible to imagine a case in which a constable secreted himself somewhere in a coach and remained there for a period of time in order to monitor the movements of the coach's owner?[f]) The Court's theory seems to be that the concept of a search, as originally understood, comprehended any technical trespass that led to the gathering of evidence, but we know that this is incorrect. At common law, any unauthorized intrusion on private property was actionable, but a trespass on open fields, as opposed to the "curtilage" of a home, does not fall within the scope of the Fourth Amendment because private property outside the curtilage is not part of a "hous[e]" within the meaning of the Fourth Amendment.

\* \* \*

The Court's reasoning in this case is very similar to that in the Court's early decisions involving wiretapping and electronic eavesdropping, namely, that a technical trespass followed by the gathering of evidence constitutes a search. \* \* \* This trespass-based rule was repeatedly criticized. \* \* \* Katz v. United States finally did away with the old approach, holding that a trespass was not required for a Fourth Amendment violation. \* \* \* Under this approach, as the Court later put it when addressing the relevance of a technical trespass, "an actual trespass is neither necessary nor sufficient to establish a constitutional violation." \* \* \*

---

[f]   The Court suggests that something like this might have occurred in 1791, but this would have required either a gigantic coach, a very tiny constable, or both—not to mention a constable with incredible fortitude and patience.

Disharmony with a substantial body of existing case law is only one of the problems with the Court's approach in this case. I will briefly note four others. First, the Court's reasoning largely disregards what is really important (the use of a GPS for the purpose of long-term tracking) and instead attaches great significance to something that most would view as relatively minor (attaching to the bottom of a car a small, light object that does not interfere in any way with the car's operation). Attaching such an object is generally regarded as so trivial that it does not provide a basis for recovery under modern tort law. But under the Court's reasoning, this conduct may violate the Fourth Amendment. By contrast, if long term monitoring can be accomplished without committing a technical trespass—suppose, for example, that the Federal Government required or persuaded auto manufacturers to include a GPS tracking device in every car—the Court's theory would provide no protection.

Second, the Court's approach leads to incongruous results. If the police attach a GPS device to a car and use the device to follow the car for even a brief time, under the Court's theory, the Fourth Amendment applies. But if the police follow the same car for a much longer period using unmarked cars and aerial assistance, this tracking is not subject to any Fourth Amendment constraints.

\* \* \*

Third, under the Court's theory, the coverage of the Fourth Amendment may vary from State to State. If the events at issue here had occurred in a community property State or a State that has adopted the Uniform Marital Property Act, respondent would likely be an owner of the vehicle, and it would not matter whether the GPS was installed before or after his wife turned over the keys. In non-community-property States, on the other hand, the registration of the vehicle in the name of respondent's wife would generally be regarded as presumptive evidence that she was the sole owner.

Fourth, the Court's reliance on the law of trespass will present particularly vexing problems in cases involving surveillance that is carried out by making electronic, as opposed to physical, contact with the item to be tracked. For example, suppose that the officers in the present case had followed respondent by surreptitiously activating a stolen vehicle detection system that came with the car when it was purchased. Would the sending of a radio signal to activate this system constitute a trespass to chattels? Trespass to chattels has traditionally required a physical touching of the property. In recent years, courts have wrestled with the application of this old tort in cases involving unwanted electronic contact with computer systems, and some have held that even the transmission of electrons that occurs when a communication is sent from one computer to another is enough. But may such decisions be followed in applying the Court's trespass theory? Assuming that what matters under the Court's theory is the law of trespass as it existed at the time of the adoption of the Fourth Amendment, do these recent decisions represent a change in the law or simply the application of the old tort to new situations?

\* \* \*

The *Katz* expectation-of-privacy test avoids the problems and complications noted above, but it is not without its own difficulties. It involves a degree of circularity, and judges are apt to confuse their own expectations of privacy with those of the hypothetical reasonable person to which the *Katz* test looks. In addition, the *Katz* test rests on the assumption that this hypothetical reasonable person has a well-developed and stable set of privacy expectations. But technology can change those expectations. Dramatic technological change may lead to periods in which popular expectations are in flux and may ultimately produce significant changes in popular attitudes. New technology may provide increased convenience or security at the expense of privacy, and many people may find the tradeoff worthwhile. And even if the public does not welcome the diminution of privacy that new technology entails, they may eventually reconcile themselves to this development as inevitable.

On the other hand, concern about new intrusions on privacy may spur the enactment of legislation to protect against these intrusions. This is what ultimately happened with respect to wiretapping. After *Katz*, Congress did not leave it to the courts to develop a body of Fourth Amendment case law governing that complex subject. Instead, Congress promptly enacted a comprehensive statute, and since that time, the regulation of wiretapping has been governed primarily by statute and not by case law. In an ironic sense, although *Katz* overruled *Olmstead*, Chief Justice Taft's suggestion in the latter case that the regulation of wiretapping was a matter better left for Congress has been borne out.

### B

Recent years have seen the emergence of many new devices that permit the monitoring of a person's movements. In some locales, closed-circuit television video monitoring is becoming ubiquitous. On toll roads, automatic toll collection systems create a precise record of the movements of motorists who choose to make use of that convenience. Many motorists purchase cars that are equipped with devices that permit a central station to ascertain the car's location at any time so that roadside assistance may be provided if needed and the car may be found if it is stolen.

Perhaps most significant, cell phones and other wireless devices now permit wireless carriers to track and record the location of users—and as of June 2011, it has been reported, there were more than 322 million wireless devices in use in the United States. * * *

In the pre-computer age, the greatest protections of privacy were neither constitutional nor statutory, but practical. Traditional surveillance for any extended period of time was difficult and costly and therefore rarely undertaken. The surveillance at issue in this case * * * would have required a large team of agents, multiple vehicles, and perhaps aerial assistance. Only an investigation of unusual importance could have justified such an expenditure of law enforcement resources. Devices like the one used in the present case, however, make long-term monitoring relatively easy and cheap. In circumstances involving dramatic technological change, the best solution to privacy concerns may be legislative. A legislative body is well situated to gauge changing public attitudes, to draw detailed lines, and to balance privacy and public safety in a comprehensive way.

To date, however, Congress and most States have not enacted statutes regulating the use of GPS tracking technology for law enforcement purposes. The best that we can do in this case is to apply existing Fourth Amendment doctrine and to ask whether the use of GPS tracking in a particular case involved a degree of intrusion that a reasonable person would not have anticipated.

Under this approach, relatively short-term monitoring of a person's movements on public streets accords with expectations of privacy that our society has recognized as reasonable. But the use of longer term GPS monitoring in investigations of most offenses impinges on expectations of privacy. For such offenses, society's expectation has been that law enforcement agents and others would not—and indeed, in the main, simply could not—secretly monitor and catalogue every single movement of an individual's car for a very long period. In this case, for four weeks, law enforcement agents tracked every movement that respondent made in the vehicle he was driving. We need not identify with precision the point at which the tracking of this vehicle became a search, for the line was surely crossed before the 4-week mark. * * * We also need not consider whether prolonged GPS monitoring in the context of investigations involving extraordinary offenses would similarly intrude on a constitutionally protected sphere of privacy. In such cases, long-term tracking might have been mounted using previously available techniques.

* * *

### GPS Tracking After Jones

After *Jones,* when does GPS tracking in the absence of a trespass constitute a search? For example, GPS tracking through a smartphone does not require a physical trespass. Thus, in United States v. Skinner,

690 F.3d 772 (6th Cir. 2012), the court found that tracking a cellphone's location over three days did not constitute a Fourth Amendment search. The officers used the GPS on the defendant's phone to track him while he drove a motor home transporting narcotics. The court found the tracking not to be a search under *Jones* because here there was no trespass. Nor did the tracking present the concern raised by Justice Alito in *Jones,* as a three-day tracking came "nowhere near" the line of comprehensive tracking that concerned Justice Alito. The court noted that "there is little precedent for what constitutes a level of comprehensive tracking that would violate the Fourth Amendment."

### Pervasive, Prolonged Surveillance After Jones

In Justice Alito's view, police surveillance of a citizen's activity can constitute a search if it is pervasive and "prolonged"—even though the activity is in public. The reason is that prolonged surveillance can tell the government more about the citizen than any member of the public would find out by casual tracking, and more than officers would know by using traditional methods. It is important to note that Justice Alito's interpretation of the *Katz* test, as limiting prolonged surveillance, is joined by five members of the Court—Justice Sotomayor, while joining the majority opinion on trespass, also agrees with Justice Alito's view on the expectation of privacy test. Therefore Justice Alito's opinion about prolonged surveillance provides the standard for judging whether surveillance of public movements constitutes a search.

How does *Jones* apply to surveillance conducted by government security cameras all over town? It is possible these days for police security cameras and other detection devices to track an individual driving through intersections and tollbooths, entering buildings and trains, and on and on. While this kind of tracking is not targeted to an individual, the effect is the same, as the government can put together the information for long-term tracking of an individual's public movements. Could there come a time when this surveillance is too pervasive and prolonged and so would constitute a search under Justice Alito's view?

### Physical Intrusion into the Area Surrounding a Home to Conduct a Canine Sniff: Florida v. Jardines

In the following case, the Court continues what it started in *Jones:* a revival of the focus on physical intrusion for investigative purposes as one way to define a Fourth Amendment search. As will be seen later in this section, the Court has held that a dog sniff of luggage was not a search under the *Katz* test because the sniff can only determine whether contraband is in the luggage, and a person does not have a legitimate expectation of privacy in contraband. But as will be seen in *Jardines,* the majority finds a search without applying the *Katz* reasonable expectation of privacy rationale, and also demonstrates that it is not always easy to apply the trespass doctrine.

## FLORIDA V. JARDINES

Supreme Court of the United States, 2013.
133 S.Ct. 1409.

### JUSTICE SCALIA delivered the opinion of the Court.

We consider whether using a drug-sniffing dog on a homeowner's porch to investigate the contents of the home is a "search" within the meaning of the Fourth Amendment.

\* \* \*

In 2006, Detective William Pedraja of the Miami-Dade Police Department received an unverified tip that marijuana was being grown in the home of respondent Joelis Jardines. One month later, the Department and the Drug Enforcement Administration sent a joint surveillance team to Jardines' home. Detective Pedraja was part of that team. He watched the home for fifteen minutes and saw no vehicles in the driveway or activity around the home, and could not see inside because the blinds were drawn. Detective Pedraja then approached Jardines' home accompanied by Detective Douglas Bartelt, a trained canine handler who had just arrived at the scene with his drug-sniffing dog. The dog was trained to detect the scent of marijuana, cocaine, heroin, and several other drugs, indicating the presence of any of these substances through particular behavioral changes recognizable by his handler.

Detective Bartelt had the dog on a six-foot leash, owing in part to the dog's "wild" nature, and tendency to dart around erratically while searching. As the dog approached Jardines' front porch, he apparently sensed one of the odors he had been trained to detect, and began energetically exploring the area for the strongest point source of that odor. As Detective Bartelt explained, the dog "began tracking that airborne odor by . . . tracking back and forth," engaging in what is called "bracketing," "back and forth, back and forth." Detective Bartelt gave the dog "the full six feet of the leash plus whatever safe distance [he could] give him" to do this—he testified that he needed to give the dog "as much distance as I can." And Detective Pedraja stood back while this was occurring, so that he would not "get knocked over" when the dog was "spinning around trying to find" the source.

After sniffing the base of the front door, the dog sat, which is the trained behavior upon discovering the odor's strongest point. Detective Bartelt then pulled the dog away from the door and returned to his vehicle. He left the scene after informing Detective Pedraja that there had been a positive alert for narcotics.

On the basis of what he had learned at the home, Detective Pedraja applied for and received a warrant to search the residence. When the warrant was executed later that day, Jardines attempted to flee and was arrested; the search revealed marijuana plants, and he was charged with trafficking in cannabis.

[The question for the Court was whether the dog sniff on the porch of the house constituted a search within the meaning of the Fourth Amendment.]

\* \* \*

The Fourth Amendment \* \* \* establishes a simple baseline, one that for much of our history formed the exclusive basis for its protections: When "the Government obtains information by physically intruding" on persons, houses, papers, or effects, "a 'search' within the original meaning of the Fourth Amendment" has "undoubtedly occurred." United States v. Jones, 132 S.Ct. 945 (2012). By reason of our decision in Katz v. United States, property rights are not the sole measure of Fourth Amendment violations—but though *Katz* may add to the baseline, it does not subtract anything from the Amendment's protections when the Government does engage in a physical intrusion of a constitutionally protected area.

That principle renders this case a straightforward one. The officers were gathering information in an area belonging to Jardines and immediately surrounding his house—in the curtilage of the house, which we have held enjoys protection as part of the home itself. And they gathered that information by physically entering and occupying the area to engage in conduct not explicitly or implicitly permitted by the homeowner.

\* \* \* The Fourth Amendment indicates with some precision the places and things encompassed by its protections: persons, houses, papers, and effects. The Fourth Amendment does not, therefore, prevent all investigations conducted on private property; for example, an officer may (subject to *Katz*) gather information in what we have called "open fields"—even if those fields are privately owned—because such fields are not enumerated in the Amendment's text. Hester v. United States, 265 U.S. 57 (1924).

But when it comes to the Fourth Amendment, the home is first among equals. At the Amendment's "very core" stands "the right of a man to retreat into his own home and there be free from unreasonable governmental intrusion." This right would be of little practical value if the State's agents could stand in a home's porch or side garden and trawl for evidence with impunity; the right to retreat would be significantly diminished if the police could enter a man's property to observe his repose from just outside the front window.

We therefore regard the area immediately surrounding and associated with the home—what our cases call the curtilage—as part of the home itself for Fourth Amendment purposes. That principle has ancient and durable roots. * * *

While the boundaries of the curtilage are generally clearly marked, the conception defining the curtilage is at any rate familiar enough that it is easily understood from our daily experience. Here there is no doubt that the officers entered it: The front porch is the classic exemplar of an area adjacent to the home and to which the activity of home life extends.

* * * Since the officers' investigation took place in a constitutionally protected area, we turn to the question of whether it was accomplished through an unlicensed physical intrusion. While law enforcement officers need not shield their eyes when passing by the home on public thoroughfares, an officer's leave to gather information is sharply circumscribed when he steps off those thoroughfares and enters the Fourth Amendment's protected areas. * * * As it is undisputed that the detectives had all four of their feet and all four of their companion's firmly planted on the constitutionally protected extension of Jardines' home, the only question is whether he had given his leave (even implicitly) for them to do so. He had not.

"A license may be implied from the habits of the country," notwithstanding the "strict rule of the English common law as to entry upon a close." McKee v. Gratz, 260 U.S. 127, 136 (1922) (Holmes, J.). We have accordingly recognized that "the knocker on the front door is treated as an invitation or license to attempt an entry, justifying ingress to the home by solicitors, hawkers and peddlers of all kinds." This implicit license typically permits the visitor to approach the home by the front path, knock promptly, wait briefly to be received, and then (absent invitation to linger longer) leave. Complying with the terms of that traditional invitation does not require fine-grained legal knowledge; it is generally managed without incident by the Nation's Girl Scouts and trick-or-treaters. Thus, a police officer not armed with a warrant may approach a home and knock, precisely because that is "no more than any private citizen might do." Kentucky v. King, 131 S.Ct. 1849, 1862 (2011).

But introducing a trained police dog to explore the area around the home in hopes of discovering incriminating evidence is something else. There is no customary invitation to do that. An invitation to engage in canine forensic investigation assuredly does not inhere in the very act of hanging a knocker. To find a visitor knocking on the door is routine (even if sometimes unwelcome); to spot that same visitor exploring the front path with a metal detector, or marching his bloodhound into the garden before saying hello and asking permission, would inspire most of us to—well, call the police. The scope of a license—express or implied—is limited not only to a particular area but also to a specific purpose. * * * Here, the background social norms that invite a visitor to the front door do not invite him there to conduct a search.

The State points to our decisions holding that the subjective intent of the officer is irrelevant. See Whren v. United States, 517 U.S. 806 (1996). But those cases merely hold that a stop or search that is objectively reasonable is not vitiated by the fact that the officer's real reason for making the stop or search has nothing to do with the validating reason. Thus, the defendant will not be heard to complain that although he was speeding the officer's real reason for the stop was racial harassment. Here, however, the question before the court is precisely whether the officer's conduct was an objectively reasonable search. As we have described, that depends upon whether the officers had an implied license to enter the porch, which in turn depends upon the purpose for which they entered. Here, their behavior objectively reveals a purpose to conduct a search, which is not what anyone would think he had license to do.

* * * The State argues that investigation by a forensic narcotics dog by definition cannot implicate any legitimate privacy interest. The State cites for authority our decisions in United States v. Place, 462 U.S. 696 (1983), United States v. Jacobsen, 466 U.S. 109 (1984), and Illinois v. Caballes, 543 U.S. 405 (2005), which held, respectively, that canine inspection of luggage in an airport, chemical testing of a substance that had fallen from a parcel in transit, and canine inspection of an automobile during a lawful traffic stop, do not violate the "reasonable expectation of privacy" described in *Katz*.

Just last Term, we considered an argument much like this. *Jones* held that * * * [t]he *Katz* reasonable-expectations test "has been added to, not substituted for," the traditional property-based understanding of the Fourth Amendment, and so is unnecessary to consider when the government gains evidence by physically intruding on constitutionally protected areas.

Thus, we need not decide whether the officers' investigation of Jardines' home violated his expectation of privacy under *Katz*. One virtue of the Fourth Amendment's property-rights baseline is that it keeps easy cases easy. That the officers learned what they learned only by physically intruding on Jardines' property to gather evidence is enough to establish that a search occurred.

* * *

**JUSTICE KAGAN, with whom JUSTICE GINSBURG and JUSTICE SOTOMAYOR join, concurring.**

\* \* \*

The Court today treats this case under a property rubric; I write separately to note that I could just as happily have decided it by looking to Jardines' privacy interests. A decision along those lines would have looked . . . well, much like this one. It would have talked about "the right of a man to retreat into his own home and there be free from unreasonable governmental intrusion." It would have insisted on maintaining the "practical value" of that right by preventing police officers from standing in an adjacent space and "trawling for evidence with impunity." It would have explained that "privacy expectations are most heightened" in the home and the surrounding area. And it would have determined that police officers invade those shared expectations when they use trained canine assistants to reveal within the confines of a home what they could not otherwise have found there.

**JUSTICE ALITO, with whom THE CHIEF JUSTICE, JUSTICE Kennedy, and JUSTICE BREYER join, dissenting.**

The Court's decision in this important Fourth Amendment case is based on a putative rule of trespass law that is nowhere to be found in the annals of Anglo-American jurisprudence.

The law of trespass generally gives members of the public a license to use a walkway to approach the front door of a house and to remain there for a brief time. This license is not limited to persons who intend to speak to an occupant or who actually do so. (Mail carriers and persons delivering packages and flyers are examples of individuals who may lawfully approach a front door without intending to converse.) Nor is the license restricted to categories of visitors whom an occupant of the dwelling is likely to welcome; as the Court acknowledges, this license applies even to "solicitors, hawkers and peddlers of all kinds." And the license even extends to police officers who wish to gather evidence against an occupant (by asking potentially incriminating questions).

According to the Court, however, the police officer in this case, Detective Bartelt, committed a trespass because he was accompanied during his otherwise lawful visit to the front door of respondent's house by his dog, Franky. Where is the authority evidencing such a rule? Dogs have been domesticated for about 12,000 years; they were ubiquitous in both this country and Britain at the time of the adoption of the Fourth Amendment; and their acute sense of smell has been used in law enforcement for centuries. Yet the Court has been unable to find a single case—from the United States or any other common-law nation—that supports the rule on which its decision is based. Thus, trespass law provides no support for the Court's holding today.

The Court's decision is also inconsistent with the reasonable-expectations-of-privacy test that the Court adopted in Katz v. United States. A reasonable person understands that odors emanating from a house may be detected from locations that are open to the public, and a reasonable person will not count on the strength of those odors remaining within the range that, while detectible by a dog, cannot be smelled by a human.

\* \* \*

As the majority acknowledges, this implied license to approach the front door extends to the police. As we recognized in Kentucky v. King, 131 S.Ct. 1849 (2011), police officers do not engage in a search when they approach the front door of a residence and seek to engage in what is termed a "knock and talk," i.e., knocking on the door and seeking to speak to an occupant for the purpose of gathering evidence. Even when the objective of a "knock and talk" is to obtain evidence that will lead to the homeowner's arrest and prosecution, the license to approach still applies. In other words, gathering evidence—even damning evidence—is a lawful activity that falls within the scope of the license to approach. And when officers walk up to the front door of a house, they are permitted to see, hear, and smell whatever can be detected from a lawful vantage point.

\* \* \*

The Court concludes that Detective Bartelt went too far because he had the "objectiv[e] . . . purpose to conduct a search." What this means, I take it, is that anyone aware of what Detective Bartelt did would infer that his subjective purpose was to gather evidence. But if this is the Court's point, then a standard "knock and talk" and most other police visits would likewise constitute searches. \* \* \* The Court offers no meaningful way of distinguishing the "objective purpose" of a "knock and talk" from the "objective purpose" of Detective Bartelt's conduct here.

The Court contends that a "knock and talk" is different because it involves talking, and "all are invited" to do that. But a police officer who approaches the front door of a house in accordance with the limitations already discussed may gather evidence by means other than talking. The officer may observe items in plain view and smell odors coming from the house. So the Court's "objective purpose" argument cannot stand.

What the Court must fall back on, then, is the particular instrument that Detective Bartelt used to detect the odor of marijuana, namely, his dog. But in the entire body of common-law decisions, the Court has not found a single case holding that a visitor to the front door of a home commits a trespass if the visitor is accompanied by a dog on a leash. On the contrary, the common law allowed even unleashed dogs to wander on private property without committing a trespass.

\* \* \*

For these reasons, the real law of trespass provides no support for the Court's holding today. While the Court claims that its reasoning has "ancient and durable roots," its trespass rule is really a newly struck counterfeit.

### Questions About Jardines

In *Jones,* Justice Scalia determined that the officers had committed a trespass by putting the tracker on Jones's license plate. But if you search his opinion in *Jardines*, the word "trespass" is never used. The term of art is "physical intrusion of a constitutionally protected area." Is that different from a trespass? Note that Justice Alito uses the term "trespass" throughout his dissent, noting that roaming dogs could not commit trespass under the common law; Justice Scalia never engages on this point. So why is Justice Scalia backing away from the term "trespass"? Could it be that the law of trespass varies from state to state, and what might be a trespass in one state is not a trespass in another?

Does *Jardines* prohibit a "knock and talk"—in which an officer simply knocks on a person's door and asks to talk to them? In United States v. Shuck, 713 F.3d 563 (10th Cir. 2013), officers walked up to the defendant's trailer without a warrant, in order to speak to Shuck about reports from his neighbors about the smell of marijuana coming from the trailer. They knocked on the door and received no response. But they did see a PVC pipe coming out of the trailer and one officer kneeled down to smell the end of the pipe, and smelled marijuana. Armed with this and other information, the officers obtained a warrant to search the trailer and found evidence of a growing operation. The court held that the officers' activity in approaching the trailer and smelling the PVC pipe did not constitute a search under *Jardines,* because "the officers used the normal route of access which would be used by anyone visiting this trailer. This is an area that police may approach even without reasonable suspicion if they have a knock and talk purpose, as these officers did." The court concluded that "[a]ny observations that the officers made from the vantage point of the back door, including Detective Grieco's smell of the PVC pipe, are not protected by the Fourth Amendment."

## C. INTERESTS PROTECTED BY THE FOURTH AMENDMENT UNDER *KATZ* AND *JONES*

The Court has held on several occasions after *Katz* that there is no legitimate privacy interest in illegal activity. See United States v. Place, infra (no privacy interest in possession of contraband). If that is the case, it may be wondered why Katz was entitled to protection in the phone booth. Katz was not expressing private, personal thoughts; he was engaging in illegal betting transactions.

One possible answer is that Katz received the protection of the Fourth Amendment because the government was not certain that his activity was illegal *until officials listened to the conversations.* Where guilt is not certain before the intrusion, the police may be invading the legitimate privacy and possessory interests of those who are actually innocent. See Loewy, The Fourth Amendment as a Device for Protecting the Innocent, 81 Mich.L.Rev. 1229 (1983) (Fourth Amendment can be invoked by the guilty "when necessary to protect the innocent"); Colb, Innocence, Privacy, and Targeting in Fourth Amendment Jurisprudence, 96 Colum.L.Rev. 1456 (1996) (discussing the "Innocence Model" of the Fourth Amendment).

But even if Katz is "presumed innocent" before the phone is tapped, couldn't the government in *Katz* have argued that if he were placing an innocent call, he should have no complaint about government surveillance? If the private activity is not criminal, what does the citizen have to hide?

Courts after *Katz* have found that people have three legitimate interests that could be impaired by a government intrusion. First, there is an interest in being free from physical disruption and inconvenience. Thus, an innocent person who is subject to a bodily seizure suffers a Fourth Amendment intrusion; the fact that he or she had nothing to hide is irrelevant. Second, certain information, even though not indicative of criminal activity, may be personal or embarrassing; innocent citizens have a legitimate interest in keeping such information private. Third, the Fourth Amendment prohibits unreasonable seizures of property as well as searches. The citizen has a legitimate interest in control over and use of his or her property, and that interest is obviously implicated when the government exercises dominion and control over such property.

### Seizures and Searches Implicate Different Interests

Note that a seizure may occur without a search, and a search may occur without a seizure. As Justice Stevens explained in his concurring opinion in Texas v. Brown, 460 U.S. 730, 747–48 (1983):

> Although our Fourth Amendment cases sometimes refer indiscriminately to searches and seizures, there are important differences between the two * * *. The Amendment protects two different interests of the citizen—the interest in retaining possession of property and the interest in maintaining personal privacy. A seizure threatens the former, a search the latter. As a matter of timing, a seizure is usually preceded by a search, but when a container is involved the converse is often true. Significantly, the two

protected interests are not always present to the same extent; for example, the seizure of a locked suitcase does not necessarily compromise the secrecy of its contents, and the search of a stopped vehicle does not necessarily deprive its owner of possession.

Justice Stevens's point is that searches and seizures implicate different interests, and that the Fourth Amendment regulates searches and seizures independently. This point was later made by the Court in Soldal v. Cook County, 506 U.S. 56 (1992). The Soldal family resided in a trailer on a rented lot. The owner of the lot removed and towed the trailer prior to an eviction hearing, while deputy sheriffs at the scene declined to intervene. The Soldals brought an action under 42 U.S.C. § 1983, claiming that their Fourth Amendment rights had been violated when their trailer was taken away.

The lower court had dismissed the action, reasoning that the Fourth Amendment was not implicated because the removal and towing did not occur in the course of an investigation for evidence, and did not involve invasion of the privacy interests of those living in the trailer. Justice White, writing for the Court, rejected this position and stated that for Fourth Amendment purposes a "seizure" of property occurs whenever "there is some meaningful interference with an individual's possessory interests in that property." He concluded: "[w]e fail to see how being unceremoniously dispossessed of one's home in the manner alleged to have occurred here can be viewed as anything but a seizure invoking the protection of the Fourth Amendment."

Justice White cited *Katz* for the proposition that privacy rights are not the sole measure of Fourth Amendment violations, and noted that "seizures of property are subject to Fourth Amendment scrutiny even though no search within the meaning of the Amendment has taken place." He rejected the lower court's notion that the Fourth Amendment only applies to efforts to collect evidence.

After *Soldal,* the question of whether a seizure of property has or has not occurred is usually obvious and is rarely contested. More difficult questions have arisen from police efforts to talk to an individual—when does a seizure of a *person* occur? These questions are considered in the discussion of stop and frisk, later in this Chapter.

## D. APPLICATIONS OF THE REASONABLE EXPECTATION OF PRIVACY ANALYSIS (WITH THE TRESPASS SUPPLEMENT)

The cases discussed below illustrate the difficulty that courts have had in applying the Fourth Amendment and the *Katz* test to modern investigative techniques. As you go through this material, keep in mind that if the court finds that the police conduct is a search or seizure, it means only that the Fourth Amendment is applicable, and police activity will still be permissible if it satisfies the requirements of the Fourth Amendment. On the other hand, if the court finds that the police conduct is not a search or seizure, it means that the Fourth Amendment is completely inapplicable; consequently, as far as that Amendment is concerned, the police do not have to explain why they are doing what they are doing. In short, the police can do it to whom they want, when they want, as often as they want, for whatever reason they want—and not violate the Fourth Amendment.

Also keep in mind that after *Jones,* the expectation of privacy analysis is not the exclusive means of determining whether a search has occurred. Under *Jones,* police activity is a search if it involves a trespass (or physical intrusion) onto a person, house, paper or effect, when the officer's purpose is to obtain information. So even if the government does not intrude into an area in which the citizen has a legitimate expectation of privacy, there will still be a search if the government trespasses to obtain information.

## 1. Subjective Manifestation

Individuals must take affirmative steps to protect their privacy interests; otherwise, a police inspection will not constitute a search, due to failure to satisfy the "subjective manifestation" prong of *Katz.* See, e.g., United States v. Bellina, 665 F.2d 1335 (4th Cir.1981) (no search where officer used a step ladder to peer into the interior of a plane; the defendant made no attempt to cover the windows, and therefore did not sufficiently manifest a subjective interest in privacy).

Many cases hold, for example, that abandonment of property is inconsistent with the retention of any subjective privacy or possessory interests, so police detention and investigation of abandoned property does not trigger Fourth Amendment protection. Moreover, abandonment need not be explicit. "Whether abandonment has occurred is a question of intent that may be inferred from acts, words, and other objective facts." United States v. Cofield, 272 F.3d 1303 (11th Cir. 2001). Thus, in United States v. Hoey, 983 F.2d 890 (8th Cir.1993), police entered into an apartment where Hoey had lived, and discovered evidence that was used against her at trial. The court held that the government activity did not constitute a search because the defendant had abandoned the apartment: at the time that the police entered, the defendant was six weeks behind on her rent; she had held a moving sale; and she was seen leaving the apartment two days before the police entry and had not returned. See also United States v. Thomas, 451 F.3d 543 (8th Cir. 2006) (defendant abandoned the mail in his rented post office box; nobody had claimed the mail, or paid the rent on the mailbox, for a year; therefore a police officer's seizure and search of the mail in the box did not implicate the Fourth Amendment).

In contrast, in Smith v. Ohio, 494 U.S. 541 (1990), a defendant carrying a brown paper bag was approached by two plainclothes officers. When the officers identified themselves, the defendant threw the bag on the hood of his car. The officers asked what was in the bag and the defendant tried to grab it. One officer pushed the defendant's hand away and opened the bag. The Court declared that "a citizen who attempts to protect his private property from inspection after throwing it on a car to respond to a police officer's inquiry clearly has not abandoned that property."

Abandonment is often found when a person denies ownership of a container in the face of police inquiries. See, e.g., United States v. McDonald, 100 F.3d 1320 (7th Cir.1996) (police officers discovered contraband in a bag placed in the overhead bin of the passenger compartment of a bus; when the police asked the owner of the bag to claim it, McDonald did not come forward; this constituted an abandonment of McDonald's privacy interest in the bag); United States v. Sanders, 196 F.3d 910 (8th Cir. 1999) ("statements to the officers that he did not own the bag were sufficient to constitute abandonment").

Often the issue of abandonment is considered as a question of whether the defendant has "standing" to assert a Fourth Amendment issue. See, e.g., United States v. Garzon, 119 F.3d 1446 (10th Cir.1997) ("Abandonment is akin to the issue of standing because a defendant lacks standing to complain of an illegal search or seizure of property which has been abandoned.") The concept of "standing" is discussed in the materials on the exclusionary rule, *infra*.

## 2. Open Fields

Prior to *Katz,* the Court had established an "open fields" rule. In Hester v. United States, 265 U.S. 57 (1924), the Court distinguished open fields from constitutionally protected areas like houses, and held that a police entry into open fields was not regulated by the Fourth Amendment. The Court in Oliver v. United States, 466 U.S. 170 (1984) held that the "open fields" doctrine was still valid after *Katz*, because a person does not have a legitimate expectation of privacy in an open field. An important thing to note about *Oliver* is that the term "open fields" was a misnomer as applied to the area searched in that case.[2] Oliver complained that two state police officers trespassed on his farm to investigate reports that he was growing marijuana. They drove past his house to a locked gate with a

---

[2]   See United States v. Van Damme, 48 F.3d 461 (9th Cir.1995) ("The unfortunate use of the term 'open fields' in this body of law causes misunderstanding and confusion, and should be replaced by a term which means what it says, such as 'unprotected area.' ").

"No Trespassing" sign on it. A footpath led around one side of the gate. The officers took it, walked around the gate and along the road for several hundred yards. They found a field of marijuana on the property, about a mile from Oliver's house. The question for the Court was whether this police investigation amounted to a search.

Justice Powell wrote the Court's opinion and was fully supported by four other Justices. Justice White joined the majority on the proposition that the Fourth Amendment "indicates with some precision the places and things encompassed by its protections" and that open fields are not "effects" within the coverage of the Amendment. Justice White did not join the longer parts of the majority opinion concluding that a citizen has no legitimate expectation of privacy in an open field. The lengthy opinion contained the following statements:

1. "An individual may not legitimately demand privacy for activities conducted out of doors in fields, except in the area immediately surrounding the home."

2. "Open fields do not provide the setting for those intimate activities that the Amendment is intended to shelter from government interference or surveillance. There is no societal interest in protecting the privacy of those activities, such as the cultivation of crops, that occur in open fields."

3. "It is not generally true that fences or no trespassing signs effectively bar the public from viewing open fields in rural areas."

4. "[O]nly the curtilage, not the neighboring open fields, warrants the Fourth Amendment protections that attach to the home."

5. "[C]ourts * * * have extended Fourth Amendment protection to the curtilage; and they have defined the curtilage, as did the common law, by reference to the factors that determine whether an individual may expect that an area immediately adjacent to the home will remain private."

6. "An open field need be neither 'open' nor a 'field.'"

The majority in *Oliver* rejected "the suggestion that steps taken to protect privacy establish that expectations of privacy in an open field are legitimate." Although it recognized that Oliver "planted the marijuana upon secluded land and erected fences and no trespassing signs around the property," the Court found that these efforts did not establish that any expectation of privacy was legitimate. In other words, Oliver might have had a *subjective* expectation of privacy in light of his efforts to cordon off his property; but it was not an expectation that society was prepared to accept as legitimate, because there is no legitimate expectation of privacy in an open field.

The *Oliver* majority concluded that even if the officers committed a trespass under state law, the Fourth Amendment was not violated: "in the case of open fields, the general rights of property protected by the common law of trespass have little or no relevancy to the applicability of the Fourth Amendment." Note that the government in *Jones, supra,* cited this passage from *Oliver* to argue against the trespass theory that the *Jones* Court was relying upon. But Justice Scalia's answer was that a trespass for investigation constitutes a search only if the trespass is on a person, house, paper or effect—and under *Oliver* an open field is none of those.

Justice Marshall, joined by Justices Brennan and Stevens, dissented in *Oliver*. He challenged the majority's reasoning that open fields are not protected by the language of the Fourth Amendment, observing that telephone booths and commercial establishments do not fit the language of the Amendment any more than open fields do, yet Supreme Court decisions have found them to be protected by the Fourth Amendment. He also noted that many private activities occur on property outside the curtilage of a home—including romantic activities, nature walks, and secret meetings.

### *QUESTIONS ABOUT OLIVER AND THE OPEN FIELDS DOCTRINE*

Is it now the case that no one—scientist, naturalist, lover, or simply a private person who prefers outdoors to indoors—can rely on the Fourth Amendment to protect against police surveillance of land areas not immediately adjacent to a house? May the police engage in as much surveillance as they care to as often as they want on the theory that there is no violation of any reasonable expectation of privacy? See United States v. Van Damme, 48 F.3d 461 (9th Cir.1995) (no search where police officer trespassed on the defendant's land in the middle of the night, walked through the defendant's forest, and climbed over his wire fence to conduct surveillance). Could it be that such surveillance might be so prolonged and pervasive that it might constitute a search under Justice Alito's concurring opinion in *Jones?*

Suppose police officers jump over a property owner's fence and are traipsing through the owner's field when they come upon a barrel with a lid. If they pry open the lid and look into the barrel, is that a search? May officers in an "open field" lift up a tarpaulin to see what is beneath it? Does it make a difference if the tarpaulin is tied to the ground with stakes? If you would not be willing to let officers open barrels or lift up covers on objects, are you more willing to permit them to roam about and look at uncovered objects? Might the reason that objects are uncovered be that landowners rely on their fence to keep out intruders?[3]

---

[3] The Supreme Court's open field cases are criticized in Saltzburg, Another Victim of Illegal Narcotics: The Fourth Amendment (As Illustrated By the Open Fields Doctrine) 48

## Defining "Curtilage": United States v. Dunn

The Fourth Amendment does not protect open fields, but, as *Oliver* notes, the Amendment does protect "curtilage." Questions arise, of course, on how far "curtilage" extends in any particular case. In United States v. Dunn, 480 U.S. 294 (1987), the Supreme Court held that a barn located approximately fifty yards from the fence surrounding a residence on almost two hundred acres of property was outside the curtilage— therefore police intrusion into that area did not constitute a search. Although Dunn's entire ranch was encircled by a fence and interior fences constructed of posts and barbed wires also were present, Federal and state officers ignored the fences and trespassed without a warrant upon Dunn's land. They crossed over the outer fence and one interior fence before smelling the odor of an acid used in the manufacture of certain drugs. The officers then crossed an interior barbed wire fence surrounding one smaller barn, and another barbed wire interior fence surrounding a larger barn. The larger barn had an open overhang, a wooden fence around it, locked, waist-high gates barring entry into the barn, and netting above the gates. From a distance the officers could not see through the netting. They approached the gates, shined a light through the netting and saw what appeared to a drug laboratory. They left the property without entering the barn, but twice reentered the property without a warrant before obtaining a warrant to search the barn from a Federal magistrate.

Justice White's opinion for the Court declared that curtilage questions should be resolved with particular reference to four factors:

- the proximity of the area claimed to be curtilage to the home;

- whether the area is included within an enclosure surrounding the home;

- the nature of the uses to which the area is put; and

- "the steps taken by the resident to protect the area from observation by people passing by."

Justice White rejected the government's "invitation to adopt a 'bright-line' rule that the curtilage should extend no farther than the nearest fence surrounding a fenced house." Justice White instead applied the four factors and found that the barn was outside the curtilage because it was 60 yards from the house itself, not within the area enclosed by the house fence, there was no objective indication that the barn was used for intimate activities associated with the home, and there was no protection from observation by those standing in open fields. The Court accepted

U.Pitt.L.Rev. 1 (1986). See also Wilkins, Defining the "Reasonable Expectation of Privacy": An Emerging Tripartite Analysis, 40 Vand.L.Rev. 1077 (1987).

arguendo, but did not decide, Dunn's contention that an *entry* into the barn would have been impermissible even though the barn itself was in an open field. Can a barn be an open field?

Justice Scalia concurred in the opinion, except for the portion that focused on whether law enforcement officials possessed objective data indicating that the barn was not being used for intimate activities of the home. In his view, the significant point was that the barn was not being so used, not whether the law enforcement officers knew that. Justice Brennan, joined by Justice Marshall, dissented.[4]

Even if property is within the curtilage, a visual inspection of that property from *outside* the curtilage does not constitute a search. See United States v. Hatfield, 333 F.3d 1189 (10th Cir. 2003) ("[W]e hold that police observation of a defendant's curtilage from a vantage point in the defendant's open field is not a search under the Fourth Amendment. Even though we can conclude that Hatfield had a subjective expectation of privacy in the space immediately behind his house, this is not an expectation of privacy that society regards as reasonable, at least with respect to visual observations made from an adjoining open field.").

## 3. Access by Members of the Public

Even if a person tries to keep information private, it is sometimes the case in society that the person will not get his or her wish. You cannot walk along a public street and reasonably expect that your movement will be free from public viewing. A homeowner cannot demand that planes not fly overhead.

After *Katz,* the Supreme Court held in a series of cases that if an aspect of a person's life is subject to scrutiny by other members of society, then that person has no legitimate expectation in denying equivalent access to police. The Court essentially found that there is no search if the police obtain information that members of the public could obtain.

After *Jones* and *Jardines,* however, it cannot be categorically stated that there is no search where police obtain information that members of the public could obtain. This is for three reasons: 1) the majority in *Jones* holds that trespass-for-investigation constitutes a search even if the citizen exposed the information to members of the public, and the

---

[4] For lower court cases applying the *Dunn* factors, see Daughenbaugh v. City of Tiffin, 150 F.3d 594 (6th Cir.1998) (unattached garage was within curtilage of the house, where it was 50 yards away from the house, within natural boundaries of a river and trees that circled the property, set far back from the road, and the officers had no indication that the defendant was using the garage for any illegal activity); United States v. Traynor, 990 F.2d 1153 (9th Cir.1993) (workshop not within curtilage, where it was 70 feet from the house, and shop and house were not enclosed within a single fenced-in area); United States v. McKeever, 5 F.3d 863 (5th Cir.1993) (area not within curtilage where it was 50 feet from home and not within an immediate fenced-in area); United States v. Swepston, 987 F.2d 1510 (10th Cir.1993) (chicken shed within the curtilage but barn was not).

majority in *Jardines* reaches a similar conclusion; 2) the Alito concurrence in *Jones*—joined by five members of the Court—provides that police surveillance of information known to the public can be a search if it is sufficiently pervasive and prolonged; and 3) Justice Sotomayor, in her concurring opinion, argues that "it may be necessary to reconsider the premise that an individual has no reasonable expectation of privacy in information voluntarily disclosed to third parties" because that approach "is ill-suited to the digital age, in which people reveal a great deal of information about themselves to third parties in the course of carrying out mundane tasks."

So the Supreme Court cases on public access, set forth below, must be read through the prism of the later decision in *Jones*.

### a. *Consensual Electronic Surveillance*

In United States v. White, 401 U.S. 745 (1971), a government informer carrying a radio transmitter engaged the defendant in conversations that were overheard by an agent using a radio receiver. Justice White's opinion for himself, Chief Justice Burger, Justice Stewart and Justice Blackmun concluded that the defendant had no reasonable expectation of privacy in the conversations. The plurality stated that "the law permits the frustration of actual expectations of privacy by permitting authorities to use the testimony of those associates who for one reason or another have determined to turn to the police" and that "one contemplating illegal activities must realize and risk that his companions may be reporting to the police." Justice Black concurred in the judgment for the reasons he stated in *Katz*. Justice Douglas dissented, questioning whether a citizen must "live in fear that every word he speaks may be transmitted or recorded and later repeated to the entire world." Justice Harlan in dissent argued that the assumption of risk approach was not an adequate guide to controlling new threats to privacy. As he put the question, it was not whether the defendant knew there was a risk of third party bugging but whether "we should impose on our citizens the risks of the electronic listener or observer without at least the protection of a warrant requirement." He concluded that "[t]he impact of third-party bugging must * * * be considered to undermine that confidence and sense of security in dealing with another that is characteristic of individual relationships between citizens in a free society." Justice Marshall also dissented.[5] Justice Brennan concurred in the result on a different ground.

The "assumption of risk" analysis applied in *White* is assailed by Professor Maclin in Informants and the Fourth Amendment: a Reconsideration, 74 Wash.Univ.L.Q. 573 (1996) ("A home or private

---

[5]    Some state courts have sided with the dissenters. See, e.g., People v. Beavers, 393 Mich. 554, 227 N.W.2d 511 (1975); State v. Glass, 583 P.2d 872 (Alaska 1978).

conversation should not lose its constitutional protection against promiscuous police intrusion merely because an individual has allowed a third party's presence. When it comes to Fourth Amendment rights, the difference between the police and everyone else matters.").

Courts have applied the *White* analysis to video surveillance as well. In United States v. Gonzalez, 328 F.3d 543 (9th Cir. 2003), Gonzalez and an associate arranged to receive a shipment of drugs in a package addressed to a hospital, where one of them worked in the mailroom. Officers were tipped off to the shipment, and obtained the consent of the hospital to install a hidden video camera in the mailroom. The video showed that when the package arrived, Gonzalez clapped his hands and acted "in a manner usually reserved for post-touchdown endzone celebrations." Gonzalez argued that the suspicious conduct on the video could not be used at trial because the video surveillance was an illegal search. But the court noted that the mailroom was a large, "quasi-public" space at a public hospital, with large windows through which the room was visible, and that it was accessed frequently by hospital employees. The Court concluded as follows:

> Gonzalez would have us adopt a theory of the Fourth Amendment akin to J.K. Rowling's Invisibility Cloak, to create at will a shield impenetrable to law enforcement view even in the most public places. However, the fabric of the Fourth Amendment does not stretch that far. He did not have an expectation of privacy in the public mailroom that society would accept as reasonable.

If Gonzalez did not have a legitimate expectation to be free from video surveillance, why did Katz have a legitimate expectation of privacy in the public telephone booth? If the phone company that owned the booth had consented to the FBI's wiretap, would that have meant that Katz had no reasonable expectation of privacy?

### b. Financial Records

In United States v. Miller, 425 U.S. 435 (1976), Justice Powell's opinion for the Court held that the Fourth Amendment was not implicated by a subpoena issued to a bank to obtain a depositor's records compiled by the bank. Over dissents by Justices Brennan and Marshall, the Court found that because the depositor made the records accessible to the bank, there was no reasonable expectation that they would be free from government surveillance. Justice Sotomayor's concurring opinion in *Jones* suggests that it may be time to reconsider these and other "third party disclosure" cases.

### c.   Pen Registers

In Smith v. Maryland, 442 U.S. 735 (1979), police installed a pen register device in the phone company offices. This device recorded the numbers called by the defendant from his home telephone. Justice Blackmun, writing for six members of the Court, found that the use of the pen register did not constitute a search, and so no warrant or probable cause was required. The majority stated that "a person has no legitimate expectation of privacy in information he voluntarily turns over to third parties" and that "when he used his phone, petitioner voluntarily conveyed numerical information to the telephone company." Justice Stewart, joined by Justice Brennan, dissented, arguing that because private telephone conversations were protected by *Katz,* the numbers dialed from a private telephone were equally protected. Justice Marshall's dissent asserted that "privacy is not a discrete commodity, possessed absolutely or not at all" and that those who disclose information for "a limited business purpose need not assume that this information will be released to other persons for other purposes."

After the Court's decision in *Smith,* Congress imposed statutory limitations on the use of pen registers. The most important statutory enactment is the "pen register" provisions of the Electronic Communications Privacy Act of 1986, 18 U.S.C. § 3121 et seq. The statute prohibits the use of pen registers unless 1) the "provider" gives consent, or 2) a court order is obtained. The court is authorized to issue an order to install a pen register upon a certified statement of a government official that the pen register is likely to uncover information relevant to a criminal investigation. Note that the government does not need to show probable cause, as it would have to do were the use of a pen register a search. Note also that the violation of the statutory requirement does not give rise to the exclusion of any evidence obtained. See United States v. German, 486 F.3d 849 (5th Cir. 2007) (pen register information obtained without court order was properly admitted, as there was no search under *Katz,* and Congress did not provide that a violation of the pen register statute should result in exclusion).

How do pen registers fare under *Jones?* A pen register is installed on the citizen's phone line but it is physically placed in the phone company offices—so it would not appear to be a search under Justice Scalia's trespass test. But query whether a pen register surveillance might be so prolonged in a particular case as to trigger a finding of a search under Justice Alito's concurring opinion in *Jones?* Wouldn't that also be true of the much more pervasive monitoring and collection of phone data by the National Security Administration?

### Carnivore and Computers

The FBI has developed a computer surveillance program called "Carnivore." The program can monitor activity over the Internet. Carnivore is an electronic surveillance system that monitors a targeted user's e-mail, web browsing, and file transfer activity. The system is capable of gathering information associated with Internet activities at two levels. First, in "full collection" mode, Carnivore intercepts the addressing information and content of a targeted user's electronic communication. The FBI readily admits that in "full collection" mode, the use of Carnivore constitutes a search that is regulated by the Fourth Amendment. Second, in "pen collection" mode, Carnivore gathers only the addressing information associated with e-mail, web browsing, and file transfer activity. The FBI argues that this information is equivalent to the numbers dialed on a telephone, and therefore the "pen collection" mode is not a search. The argument is that a computer user has no legitimate expectation of privacy in the web addresses that he visits or the e-mail addresses to which he sends e-mail, as this information is accessible to his Internet service provider. Do you agree? For more discussion of the use of Carnivore, see Schultz, Unrestricted Federal Agent: "Carnivore" and the Need to Revise the Pen Register Statute, 76 Notre Dame L. Rev. 1215 (2001).

Courts have generally found that surveillance of computers for pen-register-like information is not a search. See Guest v. Leis, 255 F.3d 325 (6th Cir. 2001) ("computer users do not have a legitimate expectation of privacy in their subscriber information because they have conveyed it to another person—the system operator"); United States v. Forrester, 512 F.3d 500 (9th Cir. 2008) (use of computer surveillance techniques that revealed "to" and "from" addresses of email messages, addresses of websites visited, and total amount of data transmitted to or from the defendant's internet account did not constitute a "search" because there is no expectation of privacy in such information: "the surveillance techniques the government employed here are constitutionally indistinguishable from the use of a pen register").

Again, these holdings might be altered by *Jones* at least in cases of prolonged surveillance—because, according to Justice Alito, society's expectation "has been that law enforcement agents and others would not—and indeed, in the main, simply could not—secretly monitor and catalogue" every single public activity of a person for a prolonged period.

### d. Trash

In California v. Greenwood, 486 U.S. 35 (1988), police officers asked a neighborhood trash collector to pick up plastic garbage bags that Greenwood left on the curb in front of his house and to turn the bags over to the police. The police rummaged through the bags and found items indicating narcotics use. This information was used to obtain warrants to search Greenwood's house. Greenwood challenged the warrants as the fruit of an illegal search of his trash. Justice White, writing for seven members of the Court, concluded that the officer's inspection of the trash was not a search and therefore was permissible without a warrant or probable cause.

Justice White relied on *Smith* (the pen register case) and asserted that "respondents exposed their garbage to the public sufficiently to defeat their claim to Fourth Amendment protection. It is common knowledge that plastic garbage bags left on or at the side of a public street are readily accessible to animals, children, scavengers, snoops, and other members of the public." Because the public had access to the trash, Justice White reasoned that "the police cannot be reasonably expected to avert their eyes from evidence of criminal activity that could have been observed by any member of the public." Justice White therefore found it irrelevant that Greenwood was prohibited by city ordinance from disposing of his trash in any way other than leaving it for the trash service. The Court's ruling was not based on Greenwood's "abandonment" of property, as that would require some showing of a voluntary relinquishment. Rather, the ruling was based squarely on the premise that Greenwood had no expectation of privacy in property to which members of the public had access.

Justice Brennan, joined by Justice Marshall, dissented. He argued that "scrutiny of another's trash is contrary to commonly accepted notions of civilized behavior" and that "society will be shocked to learn that the Court, the ultimate guarantor of liberty, deems unreasonable our expectation that the aspects of our private lives that are concealed safely in a trash bag will not become public." Justice Brennan concluded as follows:

> The mere *possibility* that unwelcome meddlers *might* open and rummage through the containers does not negate the expectation of privacy in its contents any more than the possibility of a burglary negates an expectation of privacy in the home; or the possibility of a private intrusion negates an expectation of privacy in an unopened package; or the possibility that an operator will listen in on a telephone conversation negates an expectation of privacy in the words spoken on the telephone.

Who more accurately captures societal expectations of the American people, Justice White or Justice Brennan?[6]

---

[6] Professors Slobogin and Schumacher have argued, on the basis of some empirical research, that the Court's conclusions about societal expectations are often at odds with the actual views of most members of society. See Slobogin and Schumacher, Reasonable

## QUESTIONS ABOUT GREENWOOD

What if Greenwood had placed his garbage bags in a trash can just inside his fenced-in backyard? See United States v. Hedrick, 922 F.2d 396 (7th Cir.1991) (not a search even though trash was located near garage, well inside property, because a member of the public could still have reached into the trash can). See also United States v. Redmon, 138 F.3d 1109 (7th Cir.1998) (en banc) (no search where officers walked up the defendant's driveway, took trash out of a trashcan located next to the garage, and rummaged through the trash; the court reasons that members of the public, as well as raccoons, could have obtained access to the trash, so police officers could not be excluded).

Would it make any difference if Greenwood had shredded documents and papers into tiny pieces before depositing them in the trash? The Court in United States v. Scott, 975 F.2d 927 (1st Cir.1992), held that an officer's investigation of shredded trash did not constitute a search:

> What we have here is a failed attempt at secrecy by reason of underestimation of police resourcefulness, not invasion of constitutionally protected privacy. There is no constitutional protection from police scrutiny as to information received from a failed attempt at secrecy. * * * The Fourth Amendment * * * does not protect appellee when a third party expends the effort and expense to solve the jigsaw puzzle created by shredding.

Courts have applied the *Greenwood* holding to find that investigations of other kinds of "waste" are not searches under the Fourth Amendment. See, e.g., Riverdale Mills Corp. v. Pimpare, 392 F.3d 55 (1st Cir. 2004) (manufacturer lacked reasonable expectation of privacy in wastewater discharged from its plant, so the EPA's collection and inspection of wastewater did not constitute a search; any member of the public could have collected and inspected the wastewater).

What if police went through Greenwood's trash every day for four weeks? Would this be a search under Justice Alito's opinion in *Jones*. If so, when would have become a search? After the 30th day? The 31st?

### e.   Public Areas

The "public access" prong of the *Katz* test means that most acts conducted in public are not protected by the Fourth Amendment. But sometimes the question arises as to whether an area is truly "public." For example, can police officers look through the effects of a homeless person (such as a closed cardboard box) without a warrant? Is *Greenwood* good authority for holding that such an inspection is not a search? In Connecticut v. Mooney, 218 Conn. 85, 588 A.2d 145 (1991), the court held that a homeless person had a reasonable expectation of privacy in the

---

Expectations of Privacy and Autonomy in Fourth Amendment Cases: An Empirical Look at "Understandings Recognized and Permitted by Society," 42 Duke L.J. 727 (1993).

contents of a duffel bag and cardboard box kept on public property. The court distinguished *Greenwood* as a case in which defendants placed trash at the curb for the purpose of conveying it to a third party. Is this distinction persuasive? Compare D'Aguanno v. Gallagher, 50 F.3d 877 (11th Cir.1995) (homeless persons did not have reasonable expectation of privacy in belongings stored on private property without landowner's permission).

Is it a search if a police officer peers into a closed public bathroom stall? In United States v. White, 890 F.2d 1012 (8th Cir.1989), an officer surreptitiously observed the defendant in a bathroom stall by looking through the gap between the bathroom stall door and the wall of the stall. In this manner the officer saw the defendant engaged in criminal activity. The court held that the officer's activity did not constitute a search. It stated that while the defendant "could reasonably expect a significant amount of privacy in the bathroom stall," that expectation was not violated "because the design of the stall allowed the officer to make her observations without placing herself in any position that would be unexpected by an occupant of the stall."

### f.	*Aerial Surveillance*

The Court has applied the public-access-therefore-police-access rationale of *Smith* and *Greenwood* to aerial surveillance of private property. In California v. Ciraolo, 476 U.S. 207 (1986), Chief Justice Burger wrote for the Court as it held, 5–4, that the Fourth Amendment was not violated by aerial observation of a fenced-in backyard, from an altitude of 1,000 feet, even though the officers were operating without a warrant or probable cause. Ciraolo had erected two fences, a six foot outer and a ten foot inner fence, to protect his backyard from observation on the ground. But the aerial overflight revealed the fact that Ciraolo was growing marijuana. The majority reasoned that "the mere fact that an individual has taken measures to restrict some views of his activities [does not] preclude an officer's observations from a public vantage point where he has a right to be and which renders the activities clearly visible." Because any member of the public flying in the public airspace could have peered into the yard, the majority concluded that Ciraolo had no reasonable expectation of privacy against aerial surveillance by the police. The defendant argued that a flyover by members of the public would be different in character and purpose from a flyover by law enforcement officers. But the majority rejected any such distinction, and had "difficulty understanding exactly how respondent's expectations of privacy from aerial observation might differ when two airplanes pass overhead at identical altitudes, simply for different purposes."

Justice Powell, joined by Justices Brennan, Marshall and Blackmun, dissented. He relied upon *Katz* and argued that the Court erred in relying solely on the manner of surveillance rather than "focusing on the interests of the individual and of a free society" and suggested that "[a]erial surveillance is nearly as intrusive on family privacy as physical trespass into the curtilage." Does *Jardines* establish that the dissent is correct?

Dow Chemical Co. v. United States, 476 U.S. 227 (1986), was decided the same day by the same vote as *Ciraolo*. The Environmental Protection Agency engaged in aerial photographing of Dow Chemical Co.'s manufacturing plant in Michigan. Dow had maintained elaborate ground security that barred public views of its plant from the ground and had investigated low flights over the plant. It sued for injunctive relief against the EPA, arguing that its Fourth Amendment rights were violated by the aerial overflights. Chief Justice Burger's majority opinion concluded that "the taking of aerial photographs of an industrial plant complex from navigable airspace is not a search prohibited by the Fourth Amendment."

Again Justice Powell wrote for the four dissenters. He relied upon *Katz* to argue that trade secrets laws demonstrate societal recognition of legitimate interests in business privacy, and distinguished *Ciraolo* on the ground that the EPA needed to use a sophisticated camera to discover the details revealed in its photographs.

### Ordinary Overflights: Florida v. Riley

The Court applied *Ciraolo* in Florida v. Riley, 488 U.S. 445 (1989), and held that surveillance of a backyard from a helicopter hovering at 400 feet was not a search. Justice White, writing for a plurality, relied on prior cases for the proposition that if information is made available to the public, then an officer can act as any member of the public could and obtain the information free from Fourth Amendment restrictions.

The crucial question in *Riley* was whether the public could gain access to the information in Riley's backyard by way of aerial surveillance; the information was partially obscured by a greenhouse, precluding observation by airplane. To see what was going on, the officers had to hover over the property in a helicopter at a height of 400 feet. Justice White noted that no law prohibited the public from hovering over Riley's property in a helicopter at that level; therefore the police could do so as well. Justice White relied on FAA regulations that allow helicopters to be operated at virtually any altitude so long as they do not pose a safety hazard. He added that there was no injury to the property or any dust or threat from the visual inspection, and that no intimate activities in the house or curtilage had been observed.

Justice O'Connor concurred in the judgment. She disagreed with the plurality's analysis and contended that the proper test for determining the reasonableness of an expectation of privacy was whether the public *ordinarily* had access to the information sought by the police, not whether it was legally possible for a member of the public to obtain it. Thus, for Justice O'Connor, the question was whether members of the public *ordinarily* hovered over Riley's property at 400 feet in helicopters—if not, the police conduct would be a search. Justice O'Connor nonetheless concurred in the result, asserting that the burden was on Riley, the moving party, to show that members of the public did not regularly hover over his property in helicopters. Because Riley had offered no proof on this point in the lower court, she agreed that a search was not shown on the facts in *Riley*.

Justice Brennan wrote a dissenting opinion joined by Justices Marshall and Stevens. He agreed with Justice O'Connor that the reasonableness of a privacy expectation should be determined by whether the public ordinarily has access to the information, not by whether it is legally possible to obtain access. Justice Brennan urged that judicial notice could be taken of the infrequent nature of lowflying helicopters, and that the burden should be placed upon the government to show that this type of aerial surveillance is so frequent as to render unreasonable a privacy expectation. Justice Blackmun also dissented. He agreed with Justices Brennan and O'Connor that the appropriate test is one of whether public access to the property is potentially frequent as opposed to merely possible. Justice Blackmun agreed with Justice Brennan that the burden should be placed upon the government to show frequency of public access. He argued that a remand would give the government the opportunity to satisfy the burden.

In *Riley* five members of the Court agreed that the mere *possibility* of public access is not enough to render a privacy expectation unreasonable. Isn't that the same point that Justice Brennan made in dissent in *Greenwood*? How can *Riley* and *Greenwood* be reconciled?

How does the Court's opinion in *Jones* affect aerial overflights? They are not trespassory and so they would appear to be unaffected by Justice Scalia's trespass-for-investigation test. But could police conduct overflights on a particular property over such a prolonged period that there would eventually be a search under Justice Alito's opinion in *Jones*?

### g.  *Manipulation of Bags in Public Transit*

In recent years, officers have used many techniques to halt the flow of drug traffic on interstate buses and trains. One method is for officers to enter a bus or train and examine, by touch, the outside of bags that have been placed in the overhead baggage rack. Soft bags are manipulated to determine whether they contain hard objects that could be guns or drugs. In Bond v. United States, 529 U.S. 334 (2000), the Court considered the question whether a law enforcement officer's physical manipulation of a bus passenger's carry-on luggage violated the Fourth Amendment's proscription against unreasonable searches. The Court held that it did. The officer boarded a bus and squeezed a green canvas bag in the baggage area above Bond's seat. He noticed that it contained a "brick-like" object. The question was whether the manipulation of the bag was a search, because the officer did not have probable cause. Bond conceded that other passengers had access to his bag, but contended that the officer manipulated the bag in a way that other passengers would not— specifically he prodded and poked the bag to determine whether there was a brick-like object inside.

Chief Justice Rehnquist, writing for the Court, found that the officer's manipulation of the bag went beyond what would be expected by members of the public, and so constituted a search. He explained that "a bus passenger clearly expects that his bag may be handled," but "[h]e does not expect that other passengers or bus employees will, as a matter of course, feel the bag in an exploratory manner."

Justice Breyer, joined by Justice Scalia, dissented in *Bond,* argued that in modern travel other passengers often squeeze and handle the bags of others in an attempt to cram more bags into baggage compartments, and predicted that "[a]t best, this decision will lead to a constitutional jurisprudence of "squeezes."

### QUESTION ABOUT BOND

*Bond* was decided before September 11, 2001. Do you think it would be decided the same way today? If so, then how is it permissible to conduct the intrusive searches of the luggage and even the persons of air travelers that have become common practice after 9/11? Answers to that last question might be found in the discussion of "special needs" searches and seizures, later in this Chapter.

## 4. Investigation That Can Only Reveal Illegal Activity

Investigation that threatens to uncover innocent, private activity can constitute a search, because it invades a legitimate Fourth Amendment secrecy interest. In contrast, the Supreme Court has held that there is no legitimate expectation of privacy in illegal activity. Therefore—at least under the expectation of privacy test—an investigation is not a search if it can *only* reveal illegal activity.

### a. Canine Sniffs

In United States v. Place, 462 U.S. 696 (1983), the Supreme Court held that a canine sniff of closed luggage for drugs was not a search under the expectation of privacy test.

The Court, in an opinion by Justice O'Connor, said this about "canine sniffs":

A "canine sniff" by a well-trained narcotics detection dog * * * does not require opening the luggage. It does not expose noncontraband items that otherwise would remain hidden from public view, as does, for example, an officer's rummaging through the contents of the luggage. Thus, the manner in which information is obtained through this investigative technique is much less intrusive than a typical search. Moreover, the sniff discloses only the presence or absence of narcotics, a contraband item. Thus, despite the fact that the sniff tells the authorities something about the contents of the luggage, the information obtained is limited. This limited disclosure also ensures that the owner of the property is not subjected to the embarrassment and inconvenience entailed in less discriminate and more intrusive investigative methods.

In these respects, the canine sniff is *sui generis*. We are aware of no other investigative procedure that is so limited both in the manner in which the information is obtained and in the content of the information revealed by the procedure. Therefore, we conclude that the particular course of investigation that the agents intended to pursue here—exposure of respondent's luggage, which was located in a public place, to a trained canine—did not constitute a "search" within the meaning of the Fourth Amendment.

Recall that Justice Scalia distinguished *Place* in *Jardines.* It is obviously true that a suitcase is not a house, but equally obvious is that a suitcase is an "effect" with the meaning of the Fourth Amendment. Given that, does the distinction make sense?

While the dog sniff in *Place* was not a search under *Katz*, the Court nonetheless held that the cocaine found in Place's luggage was illegally obtained. This was because police did not have the dog ready when Place's luggage arrived at the airport; it took 90 minutes to bring the dog to the scene, and Place's luggage was detained for that time. This detention was an exercise of dominion and control over the luggage, which implicated the Fourth Amendment's prohibition against unreasonable *seizures*; and the Court found the 90 minute seizure unreasonable under the circumstances, because the officers were not diligent in their investigation and had no probable cause to detain the luggage.

### Dog Sniffs and Trespass

*Place* was of course decided before the Court in *Jones*, supra, revived the old trespass test as a supplement to the *Katz* reasonable expectation of privacy test. Under the trespass-investigation test of *Jones*, police activity is a search if there is a trespass for investigatory purposes— presumably even if the investigation can only reveal illegal activity. So if a dog, in order to conduct a sniff, physically enters a constitutionally protected space, the dog sniff is a search under *Jones. See Jardines, supra.*

### Dog-Sniff of a Car During a Routine Traffic Stop: *Illinois v. Caballes*

In Illinois v. Caballes, 543 U.S. 405 (2005), the defendant was legally stopped for speeding. While one officer was processing the speeding ticket, another officer came to the scene with a drug-detecting dog, and walked the dog around Caballes's car. The officer had no justification for thinking that Caballes was carrying drugs. The dog alerted at the trunk. Based on that alert, the officers searched the trunk, found marijuana, and arrested Caballes. The entire incident lasted less than 10 minutes. Justice Stevens for the majority stated the question before the Court as follows: "Whether the Fourth Amendment requires reasonable, articulable suspicion to justify using a drug-detection dog to sniff a vehicle during a legitimate traffic stop." Reasonable suspicion would only be required if Caballes was subject to a search or a seizure beyond that permitted by the traffic stop itself (which Caballes did not challenge).

Justice Stevens found no Fourth Amendment violation in the use of the dog. He explained that the dog sniff occurred without extending the time required for the traffic stop, relied on *Place* to say that the dog sniff did not violate any reasonable expectation of privacy, and warned that "[a] seizure that is justified solely by the interest in issuing a warning ticket to the driver can become unlawful if it is prolonged beyond the time reasonably required to complete that mission." The Court concluded as follows:

> Accordingly, the use of a well-trained narcotics-detection dog * * * during a lawful traffic stop, generally does not implicate legitimate privacy interests. In this case, the dog sniff was performed on the exterior of respondent's car while he was lawfully seized for a traffic violation. Any intrusion on respondent's privacy expectations does not rise to the level of a constitutionally cognizable infringement.

Chief Justice Rehnquist did not participate in the decision in *Caballes.* Justice Souter dissented, expressing concern that dog sniffs are fallible—citing examples of one dog with a 70% accuracy rate and another dog that gave false positives 38% of the time. He noted that dog sniffs "are conducted to obtain information about the contents of private spaces beyond anything that human senses could perceive, even when conventionally enhanced."

Justice Ginsburg wrote a separate dissenting opinion. She argued that the use of the dog changed the character of what began as a lawful traffic stop and expressed concern that "[u]nder today's decision, every traffic stop could become an occasion to call in the dogs, to the distress and embarrassment of the law-abiding population."

### b.    Chemical Testing for Drugs

The Court applied the reasoning in *Place* when it upheld the warrantless chemical field-testing of a powder that a Federal agent obtained from a package opened by Federal Express employees in United States v. Jacobsen, 466 U.S. 109 (1984).[7] Justice Stevens' opinion for the Court stated that "[a] chemical test that merely discloses whether or not a particular substance is cocaine does not compromise any legitimate interest in privacy." Even if the results of the test are negative, the results reveal "nothing of special interest." Thus, "[h]ere, as in *Place,* the likelihood that official conduct * * * will actually compromise any legitimate interest in privacy seems much too remote to characterize the testing as a search subject to the Fourth Amendment."

While the field test in *Jacobsen* was not a search, it did constitute a *seizure*, because the powder sample that was tested was destroyed in the process. Thus, the test affected "possessory interests protected by the Amendment, since by destroying a quantity of the powder it converted what had been only a temporary deprivation of possessory interests into a permanent one." However, Justice Stevens found that the seizure involved in the field test was reasonable under the Fourth Amendment— because only a minimal amount of the powder was destroyed, and the officer had a clear indication that the powder was some kind of contraband before he tested it.

Justice Brennan, joined by Justice Marshall, wrote a dissenting opinion in *Jacobsen.* The dissent found it "most startling" that in this case and in *Place* the Court put "its exclusive focus on the nature of the information or item sought and revealed through the use of a surveillance technique, rather than on the context in which the information or item is concealed." Rather than hold that a technique either always or never violates reasonable expectations of privacy, Justice Brennan urged the Court to examine the private nature of the area or item subjected to intrusion.

Does *Jacobsen* mean that an officer can enter a house to do a field test without triggering any Fourth Amendment protection? Would the defendant be able to argue that while the field test itself is not a search, the entry into the house to do the field test is a search? How would that argument play under *Katz?* How would it play under *Jones?*

---

[7]   The portion of the Court's opinion upholding the visual examination and seizure of the plastic bags containing the powder is discussed in the section on mixed public and private searches, *infra.*

### Other Drug Testing

Does *Jacobsen* mean that drug tests on urine samples are not searches? In Skinner v. Railway Labor Executives' Ass'n, 489 U.S. 602 (1989), the Court unanimously held that drug testing of urine was a search. The Court noted that unlike the field testing in *Jacobsen,* drug testing of urine samples could uncover such innocent secret information as epilepsy, pregnancy, or the use of prescription drugs. Moreover, the process of collecting urine samples (including aural observation) was intrusive and embarrassing. The Court concluded that "the collection and testing of urine intrudes upon expectations of privacy that society has long recognized as reasonable."

## 5. Use of Technology to Enhance Inspection

Under *Katz*, visual inspection is not always a "search", as seen in the aerial overflight cases. But what if visual inspection is aided by sophisticated technological devices? And what if it involves a trespass?

### a. Thermal Detection Devices

One technological advance in law enforcement has been the development of an infrared thermal detection device. The use of such a device in detecting a drug-growing operation was reviewed by the Supreme Court in the following case. You may observe that some of Justice Scalia's observations paved the way for his opinions in *Jones* and *Jardines*, considered previously.

## KYLLO V. UNITED STATES

United States Supreme Court, 2001.
533 U.S. 27.

### JUSTICE SCALIA delivered the opinion of the Court.

This case presents the question whether the use of a thermal-imaging device aimed at a private home from a public street to detect relative amounts of heat within the home constitutes a "search" within the meaning of the Fourth Amendment.

* * * In 1991 Agent William Elliott of the United States Department of the Interior came to suspect that marijuana was being grown in the home belonging to petitioner Danny Kyllo, part of a triplex on Rhododendron Drive in Florence, Oregon. Indoor marijuana growth typically requires high-intensity lamps. In order to determine whether an amount of heat was emanating from petitioner's home consistent with the use of such lamps, at 3:20 a.m. on January 16, 1992, Agent Elliott and Dan Haas used an Agema Thermovision 210 thermal imager to scan the triplex. Thermal imagers detect infrared radiation, which virtually all

objects emit but which is not visible to the naked eye. The imager converts radiation into images based on relative warmth—black is cool, white is hot, shades of gray connote relative differences; in that respect, it operates somewhat like a video camera showing heat images. The scan of Kyllo's home took only a few minutes and was performed from the passenger seat of Agent Elliott's vehicle across the street from the front of the house and also from the street in back of the house. The scan showed that the roof over the garage and a side wall of petitioner's home were relatively hot compared to the rest of the home and substantially warmer than neighboring homes in the triplex. Agent Elliott concluded that petitioner was using halide lights to grow marijuana in his house, which indeed he was. Based on tips from informants, utility bills, and the thermal imaging, a Federal Magistrate Judge issued a warrant authorizing a search of petitioner's home, and the agents found an indoor growing operation involving more than 100 plants. Petitioner was indicted on one count of manufacturing marijuana, in violation of 21 U.S.C. § 841(a)(1). He unsuccessfully moved to suppress the evidence seized from his home and then entered a conditional guilty plea.

The Court of Appeals for the Ninth Circuit remanded the case for an evidentiary hearing regarding the intrusiveness of thermal imaging. On remand the District Court found that the Agema 210 "is a non-intrusive device which emits no rays or beams and shows a crude visual image of the heat being radiated from the outside of the house"; it "did not show any people or activity within the walls of the structure"; "[t]he device used cannot penetrate walls or windows to reveal conversations or human activities"; and "[n]o intimate details of the home were observed." Based on these findings, the District Court upheld the validity of the warrant that relied in part upon the thermal imaging, and reaffirmed its denial of the motion to suppress. A divided Court of Appeals * * * held that petitioner had shown no subjective expectation of privacy because he had made no attempt to conceal the heat escaping from his home, and even if he had, there was no objectively reasonable expectation of privacy because the imager "did not expose any intimate details of Kyllo's life," only "amorphous 'hot spots' on the roof and exterior wall." We granted certiorari.

* * * "At the very core" of the Fourth Amendment "stands the right of a man to retreat into his own home and there be free from unreasonable governmental intrusion." Silverman v. United States, 365 U.S. 505, 511 (1961). With few exceptions, the question whether a warrantless search of a home is reasonable and hence constitutional must be answered no.

On the other hand, the antecedent question of whether or not a Fourth Amendment "search" has occurred is not so simple under our precedent. The permissibility of ordinary visual surveillance of a home used to be clear because, well into the 20th century, our Fourth

Amendment jurisprudence was tied to common-law trespass. Visual surveillance was unquestionably lawful because "the eye cannot by the laws of England be guilty of a trespass." Boyd v. United States, 116 U.S. 616, 628 (1886). We have since decoupled violation of a person's Fourth Amendment rights from trespassory violation of his property, but the lawfulness of warrantless visual surveillance of a home has still been preserved. * * *

One might think that the new validating rationale would be that examining the portion of a house that is in plain public view, while it is a "search" despite the absence of trespass, is not an "unreasonable" one under the Fourth Amendment. But in fact we have held that visual observation is no "search" at all—perhaps in order to preserve somewhat more intact our doctrine that warrantless searches are presumptively unconstitutional. In assessing when a search is not a search, we have applied somewhat in reverse the principle first enunciated in Katz v. United States. * * * We have subsequently applied this principle to hold that a Fourth Amendment search does not occur—even when the explicitly protected location of a house is concerned—unless "the individual manifested a subjective expectation of privacy in the object of the challenged search," and "society [is] willing to recognize that expectation as reasonable."

The present case involves officers on a public street engaged in more than naked-eye surveillance of a home. We have previously reserved judgment as to how much technological enhancement of ordinary perception from such a vantage point, if any, is too much. * * *

It would be foolish to contend that the degree of privacy secured to citizens by the Fourth Amendment has been entirely unaffected by the advance of technology. For example, * * * the technology enabling human flight has exposed to public view (and hence, we have said, to official observation) uncovered portions of the house and its curtilage that once were private. The question we confront today is what limits there are upon this power of technology to shrink the realm of guaranteed privacy.

The Katz test—whether the individual has an expectation of privacy that society is prepared to recognize as reasonable—has often been criticized as circular, and hence subjective and unpredictable. While it may be difficult to refine Katz when the search of areas such as telephone booths, automobiles, or even the curtilage and uncovered portions of residences are at issue, in the case of the search of the interior of homes— the prototypical and hence most commonly litigated area of protected privacy—there is a ready criterion, with roots deep in the common law, of the minimal expectation of privacy that exists, and that is acknowledged to be reasonable. To withdraw protection of this minimum expectation would be to permit police technology to erode the privacy guaranteed by the Fourth Amendment. We think that obtaining by sense-enhancing technology any information regarding the interior of the home that could not otherwise have been obtained without physical "intrusion into a constitutionally protected area," constitutes a search—at least where (as here) the technology in question is not in general public use. This assures preservation of that degree of privacy against government that existed when the Fourth Amendment was adopted. On the basis of this criterion, the information obtained by the thermal imager in this case was the product of a search.[a]

* * * The Government maintains, however, that the thermal imaging must be upheld because it detected "only heat radiating from the external surface of the house." The dissent makes this its leading point, contending that there is a fundamental difference between what it calls "off-the-wall" observations and "through-the-wall surveillance." But just as a thermal imager captures only heat emanating from a house, so also a powerful directional microphone picks up only sound emanating from a house—and a satellite capable of scanning from many miles away would pick up only visible light emanating from a house. We rejected such a mechanical interpretation of the Fourth Amendment in *Katz*, where the eavesdropping device picked up only sound waves that reached the exterior of the phone booth. Reversing that approach would leave the homeowner at the mercy of advancing technology—including imaging technology that could discern all human activity in the home. While the technology used in the present case was relatively crude, the rule we adopt must take account of more sophisticated systems that are already in use or in development. * * * As for the dissent's extraordinary assertion that anything learned through "an inference" cannot be a search, that would validate even the "through-the-wall" technologies that the dissent purports to disapprove. Surely the dissent does not believe that the through-the-wall radar or ultrasound technology produces an 8-by-10 Kodak glossy that needs no analysis (i.e., the making of inferences). * * *

The Government also contends that the thermal imaging was constitutional because it did not "detect private activities occurring in private areas." It points out that in Dow Chemical v. United States, 476

---

    [a]  The dissent's repeated assertion that the thermal imaging did not obtain information regarding the interior of the home is simply inaccurate. A thermal imager reveals the relative heat of various rooms in the home. The dissent may not find that information particularly private or important, but there is no basis for saying it is not information regarding the interior of the home. The dissent's comparison of the thermal imaging to various circumstances in which outside observers might be able to perceive, without technology, the heat of the home—for example, by observing snowmelt on the roof—is quite irrelevant. The fact that equivalent information could sometimes be obtained by other means does not make lawful the use of means that violate the Fourth Amendment. The police might, for example, learn how many people are in a particular house by setting up year-round surveillance; but that does not make breaking and entering to find out the same information lawful. In any event, on the night of January 16, 1992, no outside observer could have discerned the relative heat of Kyllo's home without thermal imaging.

U.S. 227 (1986), we observed that the enhanced aerial photography did not reveal any "intimate details." *Dow Chemical*, however, involved enhanced aerial photography of an industrial complex, which does not share the Fourth Amendment sanctity of the home. The Fourth Amendment's protection of the home has never been tied to measurement of the quality or quantity of information obtained. In *Silverman*, for example, we made clear that any physical invasion of the structure of the home, "by even a fraction of an inch," was too much, and there is certainly no exception to the warrant requirement for the officer who barely cracks open the front door and sees nothing but the nonintimate rug on the vestibule floor. In the home, our cases show, all details are intimate details, because the entire area is held safe from prying government eyes. * * *

Limiting the prohibition of thermal imaging to "intimate details" would not only be wrong in principle; it would be impractical in application * * *. To begin with, there is no necessary connection between the sophistication of the surveillance equipment and the "intimacy" of the details that it observes—which means that one cannot say (and the police cannot be assured) that use of the relatively crude equipment at issue here will always be lawful. The Agema Thermovision 210 might disclose, for example, at what hour each night the lady of the house takes her daily sauna and bath—a detail that many would consider "intimate"; and a much more sophisticated system might detect nothing more intimate than the fact that someone left a closet light on. We could not, in other words, develop a rule approving only that through-the-wall surveillance which identifies objects no smaller than 36 by 36 inches, but would have to develop a jurisprudence specifying which home activities are "intimate" and which are not. And even when (if ever) that jurisprudence were fully developed, no police officer would be able to know in advance whether his through-the-wall surveillance picks up "intimate" details—and thus would be unable to know in advance whether it is constitutional.

The dissent's proposed standard—whether the technology offers the "functional equivalent of actual presence in the area being searched"—would seem quite similar to our own at first blush. The dissent concludes that *Katz* was such a case, but then inexplicably asserts that if the same listening device only revealed the volume of the conversation, the surveillance would be permissible. Yet if, without technology, the police could not discern volume without being actually present in the phone booth, JUSTICE STEVENS should conclude a search has occurred. The same should hold for the interior heat of the home if only a person present in the home could discern the heat. Thus the driving force of the dissent, despite its recitation of the above standard, appears to be a distinction among different types of information—whether the "homeowner would even care if anybody noticed." The dissent offers no practical guidance for the application of this standard, and for reasons already discussed, we believe there can be none. The people in their houses, as well as the police, deserve more precision.[b]

* * *

Where, as here, the Government uses a device that is not in general public use, to explore details of the home that would previously have been unknowable without physical intrusion, the surveillance is a "search" and is presumptively unreasonable without a warrant.

* * *

JUSTICE STEVENS, with whom THE CHIEF JUSTICE, JUSTICE O'CONNOR, and JUSTICE KENNEDY join, dissenting.

* * *

All that the infrared camera did in this case was passively measure heat emitted from the exterior surfaces of petitioner's home; all that those measurements showed were relative differences in emission levels, vaguely indicating that some areas of the roof and outside walls were warmer than others. As still images from the infrared scans show, no details regarding the interior of petitioner's home were revealed. * * *

Indeed, the ordinary use of the senses might enable a neighbor or passerby to notice the heat emanating from a building, particularly if it is vented, as was the case here. Additionally, any member of the public might notice that one part of a house is warmer than another part or a nearby building if, for example, rainwater evaporates or snow melts at different rates across its surfaces. Such use of the senses would not convert into an unreasonable search if, instead, an adjoining neighbor allowed an officer onto her property to verify her perceptions with a sensitive thermometer. Nor, in my view, does such observation become an unreasonable search if made from a distance with the aid of a device that merely discloses that the exterior of one house, or one area of the house, is much warmer than another. Nothing more occurred in this case.

* * * Heat waves, like aromas that are generated in a kitchen, or in a laboratory or opium den, enter the public domain if and when they leave a building. A subjective expectation that they would remain private is not only implausible but also surely not "one that society is prepared to recognize as reasonable."

---

[b] The dissent argues that we have injected potential uncertainty into the constitutional analysis by noting that whether or not the technology is in general public use may be a factor. That quarrel, however, is not with us but with this Court's precedent. See *Ciraolo* ("In an age where private and commercial flight in the public airways is routine, it is unreasonable for respondent to expect that his marijuana plants were constitutionally protected from being observed with the naked eye from an altitude of 1,000 feet"). Given that we can quite confidently say that thermal imaging is not "routine," we decline in this case to reexamine that factor.

\* \* \*

Despite the Court's attempt to draw a line that is "not only firm but also bright," the contours of its new rule are uncertain because its protection apparently dissipates as soon as the relevant technology is "in general public use." Yet how much use is general public use is not even hinted at by the Court's opinion, which makes the somewhat doubtful assumption that the thermal imager used in this case does not satisfy that criterion. In any event, putting aside its lack of clarity, this criterion is somewhat perverse because it seems likely that the threat to privacy will grow, rather than recede, as the use of intrusive equipment becomes more readily available.

\* \* \*

## QUESTIONS ABOUT KYLLO

What happens if police use a thermal imaging device on a warehouse rather than a home? Is *Kyllo's* emphasis on the sanctity of the home determinative? Professor Maclin, in *Katz, Kyllo*, and Technology: Virtual Fourth Amendment Protection in the Twenty-First Century, 72 Miss. L.J. 51 (2002), comments that it may be possible in future cases to distinguish the thermal imaging directed at a home from thermal imaging directed at an office or other business facility. Why? Doesn't the citizen have the same right to preserve information as private in her warehouse as she does in her home?

What happens if the use of thermal imaging devices becomes commonplace among members of the public? Doesn't the majority in *Kyllo* admit that the use of the devices by police officers at that point will not be a search? If that is so, then how much has the Court done to protect citizens from technological advances in official investigations?

Note that at least at this point, the Court's holding in *Kyllo* puts an end to the law enforcement use of thermal imaging devices to scan homes. Such a scan would be a search, and searches require probable cause. If an officer has the probable cause necessary to conduct a thermal imaging scan, then he has no need for the thermal imaging scan. He can just get a warrant to search the home. Before *Kyllo*, thermal imagers were used to *obtain* the probable cause necessary to get a warrant. Moreover, thermal imagers rely on a relative comparison of heat emanation. So typically—and as in *Kyllo*—an officer would have to scan other houses in the neighborhood to determine whether the suspect's house emanated heat more than those other houses. Under *Kyllo*, the scan of each of the houses in the neighborhood is an illegal search.

### Kyllo and Trespass

Justice Scalia, at the beginning of his opinion in *Kyllo,* states that notions of trespass were "decoupled" from Fourth Amendment protection in *Katz.* Recall that this passage about "decoupling" Fourth Amendment rights from trespass was written before Justice Scalia's opinion for the Court in *Jones.* After *Jones,* trespass is not "decoupled" but rather provides an alternative protection of Fourth Amendment rights. It is true that the trespass theory would not help Kyllo directly, because the thermal detection device was used off his property. But in fact, Justice Scalia's opinion in *Kyllo* can be seen as a precursor to *Jones,* because it reintroduces trespass concepts to regulate advanced surveillance techniques. At least with regards to a home, the *Kyllo* Court holds that the use of advanced surveillance technology is a search whenever it is used to obtain information that could not be obtained otherwise without a trespass into the home.

### b.   Electronic Tracking Devices

### Tracking Public Movements:
### United States v. Knotts and United States v. Karo

The Court first discussed the use of electronic beepers to track a person's public movements in United States v. Knotts, 460 U.S. 276 (1983). State officers, suspicious that a purchaser of chemicals, Armstrong, might be using them to manufacture drugs, obtained the consent of the company selling the chemicals to install a beeper inside a 5 gallon container of chloroform before Armstrong picked it up. Armstrong placed the container in his car. The officers monitored the beeper signal from the container and followed Armstrong to Petschen's house where the container was transferred to his car. Ultimately the signal became stationary at a location identified as a cabin belonging to Knotts. Because Knotts did not (and could not, for lack of standing) challenge the warrantless installation of the beeper in the container, the Court had no occasion to address the permissibility of that intrusion. Justice Rehnquist's opinion for six Justices quoted from *Katz* and *Smith* (the pen register case) and framed the question presented as whether the officers had invaded any legitimate expectation of privacy held by Knotts when they tracked the container's movement by use of the beeper. The opinion reasoned as follows:

> Visual surveillance from public places along Petschen's route or adjoining Knotts' premises would have sufficed to reveal all of these facts to the police. The fact that the officers in this case relied not only on visual surveillance, but on the use of the beeper to signal the presence of Petschen's automobile to the police receiver, does not alter the situation. Nothing in the Fourth Amendment prohibited the police from augmenting the sensory faculties bestowed upon them at birth with such enhancement as science and technology afforded them in this case.

Knotts argued that if the tracking by beeper was not even a search, it would mean that unlimited surveillance of any citizen would be possible without judicial supervision. But the Court responded that "if such dragnet type law enforcement practices * * * should eventually occur, there will be time enough then to determine whether different constitutional principles may be applicable." It noted too that nothing in the record indicated that the beeper signal was used to monitor any activity in the cabin.

In United States v. Karo, 468 U.S. 705 (1984), officers tracked the movement of a beeper attached to a can of ether. Agents saw Karo pick up the ether from a government informant and followed him to his house. They used the beeper to determine that the ether was still in the house, and they subsequently used it to detect that the ether had been moved to Horton's house. From this house, agents could smell the ether while standing on the sidewalk. A third use of the beeper helped agents discover that the ether had been moved to Horton's father's house, and a fourth use revealed it had been taken to a commercial storage facility. Agents could smell the ether in a row of lockers and used the beeper a fifth time to discover the exact location of the ether. The sixth use led agents to another storage facility where they detected the smell of ether from a locker. They obtained consent to install a closed-circuit camera in the facility and observed a man and woman load the ether into Horton's pick-up truck. While undertaking to follow the truck to another house, the agents used the beeper a seventh time. The eighth use assured the agents that the ether remained in the house when the truck left. Finally, agents obtained a search warrant for the house. They found cocaine and laboratory equipment and made arrests.

Justice White wrote for the Court. He concluded first that no authorization was necessary to place a beeper in the can of ether.

> It is clear that the actual placement of the beeper into the can violated no one's Fourth Amendment rights. The can into which the beeper was placed belonged at the time to the DEA, and by no stretch of the imagination could it be said that respondents then had any legitimate expectation of privacy in it.

Justice White next concluded that the Fourth Amendment was not implicated by the fact that Karo received a can that contained an electronic tracking device.

> The mere transfer to Karo of a can containing an unmonitored beeper infringed no privacy interest. It conveyed no information that Karo wished to keep private, for it conveyed no information at all. To be sure, it created a *potential* for an invasion of privacy, but we have never held that potential, as opposed to actual, invasions of privacy constitute searches for purposes of the Fourth Amendment. A holding

to that effect would mean that a policeman walking down the street carrying a parabolic microphone capable of picking up conversations in nearby homes would be engaging in a search even if the microphone were not turned on. It is the exploitation of technological advances that implicates the Fourth Amendment, not their mere existence.

We likewise do not believe that the transfer of the container constituted a seizure. A "seizure" of property occurs when "there is some meaningful interference with an individual's possessory interests in that property." Although the can may have contained an unknown and unwanted foreign object, it cannot be said that anyone's possessory interest was interfered with in a meaningful way. * * *

### Beepers in the House

Justice White reached a different conclusion in *Karo* as to the monitoring of the beeper "in a private residence, a location not open to visual surveillance".

The monitoring of an electronic device such as a beeper is, of course, less intrusive than a full-scale search, but it does reveal a critical fact about the interior of the premises that the Government is extremely interested in knowing and that it could not have otherwise obtained without a warrant. The case is thus not like *Knotts*, for there the beeper told the authorities nothing about the interior of Knotts' cabin. * * * We cannot accept the Government's contention that it should be completely free from the constraints of the Fourth Amendment to determine by means of an electronic device, without a warrant and without probable cause or reasonable suspicion, whether a particular article—or a person, for that matter—is in an individual's home at a particular time. Indiscriminate monitoring of property that has been withdrawn from public view would present far too serious a threat to privacy interests in the home to escape entirely some sort of Fourth Amendment oversight.

Although the Court condemned warrantless monitoring of a beeper inside a private house, it nonetheless sustained the search warrant that agents obtained at the end of their surveillance. The knowledge that the agents obtained without using the beeper, together with their proper use of the beeper in monitoring travel outside the house, provided sufficient independent information to justify the issuance of a search warrant. Thus, the illegally obtained information (i.e., that the can was inside a house for some period of time) had no effect on the Magistrate's issuance of the warrant.

Justice Stevens, joined by Justices Brennan and Marshall, dissented in part. Justice Stevens observed that "the character of the property is profoundly different when infected with an electronic bug than when it is entirely germ free." He concluded that agents asserted dominion and control over the can of ether when they inserted the beeper and that this amounted to a seizure of the property under the Fourth Amendment. He contended that "the private citizen is entitled to assume, and in fact does assume, that his possessions are not infected with concealed electronic devices." He found "little comfort in the Court's notion that no invasion of privacy occurs until a listener obtains some significant information by use of the device."

But if Justice Stevens felt this way with respect to the use of the beeper in *Karo*, how could he then accept the use of the thermal imaging device in his dissent in *Kyllo*? Is it that the thermal imager operates "on-the-wall" while the beeper operates "through the wall." Or, might it be that the beeper is "planted" by the government into property that most "buyers" would regard as beeper-free, while the heat generated from a home is surely something of which the homeowner is fully aware?

Justice O'Connor, joined by Justice Rehnquist, wrote a separate opinion in *Karo* concurring in most of the Court's opinion and in its judgment. She wrote separately to state her view that a homeowner might not be able to claim that his privacy rights are violated if he permits a third person to enter the home with property that contains a beeper. If, for example, a government undercover agent posing as a drug buyer entered a suspect's home and carried a beeper, the homeowner might not have a valid complaint, because he assumed the risk. Justice White responded in a footnote by saying that he did not necessarily disagree with this analysis. Justice White found it inapplicable to the instant case, where the defendant himself had purchased the beepered can and brought it into the house.

### *Knotts, Karo, and Public Tracking After Jones*

Recall that in United States v. Jones, 132 S.Ct. 945 (2012) set forth after *Katz* in this Chapter, supra, the Court did not read *Knotts* and *Karo* as holding that electronic surveillance of public movements could never be a search. Two limitations on that broad principle were agreed upon by two different five-member coalitions of the Court: 1) if the surveillance device was installed by trespassing on the citizen's person or property, the tracking is a search under pre-*Katz* law; and 2) if the tracking is "prolonged" it is a search under *Katz* because members of the public would not reasonably expect such long-term tracking.

## 6.  Investigative Activity Conducted by Private Citizens

### a.  *Private Activity*

The Fourth Amendment is intended to regulate state actors. Consequently, a search or seizure conducted by a private citizen is not a "search or seizure" within the meaning of the Fourth Amendment. In Burdeau v. McDowell, 256 U.S. 465 (1921), the Supreme Court held that private papers stolen from office safes that were blown open and a desk that was forced open, could be presented to a grand jury by a government prosecutor, because the search was conducted by private parties and so it was not regulated by the Fourth Amendment. Justice Brandeis, joined by Justice Holmes, dissented. See also United States v. Stevenson, 727 F.3d 826 (8th Cir. 2013) (Internet service provider that scanned its users emails for evidence of child pornography, and turned over suspicious information to the government, was a private actor and therefore the search did not violate the Fourth Amendment).

### *Mixed Public and Private Action*

Courts have found the Fourth Amendment to apply if a private individual is acting, under the circumstances, as an agent for the government. Government officials may not avoid Fourth Amendment requirements by enlisting private individuals to do what government officials cannot. See United States v. Walther, 652 F.2d 788 (9th Cir.1981) (airline employee acted as government agent when he expected a DEA reward for his actions and the agency had encouraged him).

In Skinner v. Railway Labor Executives' Ass'n, 489 U.S. 602 (1989), the Court held that drug-testing procedures promulgated by private railroad companies, pursuant to Federal regulations granting authority to the railroads, implicated the Fourth Amendment. The government had mandated that the railroads not bargain away the drug-testing authority granted by the Federal regulations. Also, the Federal regulations made plain a strong preference for testing as well as the government's desire to have access to the results. The Court held that the Fourth Amendment could be applicable even if the government does not actually compel a search by a private party. The Court found "clear indices of the Government's encouragement, endorsement, and participation" sufficient to make the drug testing a government search regulated by the Fourth Amendment. See also United States v. Pierce, 893 F.2d 669 (5th Cir.1990) (for a search by a private person to trigger Fourth Amendment protection, the government must have known about the search in advance, and the private party must be acting for law enforcement purposes).

### b. Government Investigative Activity Subsequent to Private and Other Legal Searches

#### Limits Imposed by the Initial Search: Walter v. United States

Difficult questions can arise when government agents follow up on a private search. Walter v. United States, 447 U.S. 649 (1980), divided the Court on the question whether FBI agents, who received a package of films from a recipient to whom it was misdelivered by a private carrier, could view the films without a warrant. The recipient had opened the package but had not viewed the films. Justice Stevens's opinion, joined by Justice Stewart, concluded that "the unauthorized exhibition of the films constituted an unreasonable invasion of their owner's constitutionally protected interest in privacy," and that "an officer's authority to possess a package is distinct from his authority to examine its contents." So although the agents could receive the films, they could not view them without a warrant, even though a private person not covered by the Fourth Amendment had opened the package. These Justices reasoned that "[a] partial invasion of privacy cannot automatically justify a total invasion." Justice White, joined by Justice Brennan, concurred in part and disagreed with a footnote of Justice Stevens that left open the question "whether the Government projection of the films would have infringed any Fourth Amendment interest if private parties had projected the films before turning them over to the Government." Justice White agreed that a search by private persons could provide probable cause for a warrant, but said it could not excuse the government from the warrant requirement for its own search. Apparently, both opinions agreed that what the FBI observed in plain view was properly observed. Justice Marshall concurred in the judgment without opinion. Justice Blackmun's dissent, joined by Chief Justice Burger and Justices Powell and Rehnquist, argued "that, by the time the FBI received the films, these petitioners had no remaining expectation of privacy in their contents."

#### Reopening Permitted: United States v. Jacobsen

The extent to which government agents may search or seize evidence following searches by private individuals again divided the Court in United States v. Jacobsen, 466 U.S. 109 (1984). A Federal Express supervisor asked an office manager to examine a package that had been torn by a fork lift. Inside a cardboard outer container, the supervisor and manager found, cushioned by five or six pieces of crumpled newspaper, a ten-inch long tube wrapped with the kind of silver tape used on basement ducts. They cut open the tube and found a number of zip-lock bags that contained white powder; they then put the bags back into the tube and closed but did not reseal the tube. They notified the Drug Enforcement

Administration of their finding, and an agent arrived at the office, reopened the tube, opened the zip-lock bags, removed a trace of the powder from each, did a "field test," and discovered that the powder was cocaine.

The Court sustained the agent's actions. Justice Stevens's opinion commanded six votes. He reasoned that the Federal Express employees' actions were not covered by the Fourth Amendment and that *Walter* required an analysis of the extent to which the government exceeded the bounds of the private search.

Justice Stevens observed that there was no Fourth Amendment violation in the employees' describing what they saw and reasoned as follows: when the officer first saw the package he knew that it contained "nothing of significance except a tube containing plastic bags and, ultimately, white powder"; "a manual inspection of the tube and its contents would not tell [the officer] anything more than he already had been told"; the only reason for the inspection was to avoid "the risk of a flaw in the employees' recollection," which did not involve an infringing of privacy rights; the removal of the plastic bags from the tube and the officer's visual inspection "enabled the agent to learn nothing that had not previously been learned during the private search"; the officer's seizure was reasonable because the package already had been opened, it remained unsealed, and the employees invited the agent to inspect its contents; and the warrantless seizure of the bags was reasonable on the ground that they probably contained contraband.

Finally, Justice Stevens reasoned that the field test—to determine only one thing, whether the powder was cocaine—compromised "no legitimate privacy interest." This portion of his opinion, discussed earlier in this Chapter, reasoned that a citizen has no legitimate expectation of privacy in contraband, and therefore an investigation cannot constitute a search if it can only determine whether a substance is contraband or not.

Justice White concurred in part and in the judgment, though he was very critical of the majority's analysis. He argued that the effect of the Court's decision was to permit police to break into a locked car, suitcase, or even a house, if a private person previously did so and reported what he found to the police. Justice White concluded that a warrant should be required in these cases. Justice Brennan, joined by Justice Marshall, dissented and agreed with Justice White's criticism of the majority opinion.

In thinking about the majority's approach in *Jacobsen*, consider whether it really is important that the employees told the agent that the package contained only the bags with the powder. Justice Stevens states that there was nothing of significance in the package other than the bags. On these facts, he probably is correct. What, however, if the newspapers had not been crumpled, or if something else was in the package besides the bags? Does the agent decide what is significant? Or should a magistrate decide?

In considering Justice White's concerns about officers breaking into locked cars and houses simply because a member of the public previously did so, recall that the Court in *Jones* has now restored the trespass-investigation theory as a supplement to *Katz*. How would the trespass-investigation theory be applied to Justice White's examples? How would it be applied to the officer's reopening the tube in *Jacobsen*? Isn't the reopening a physical intrusion into property? If so it is a search under *Jones* even if there is no expectation of privacy under *Katz*.

### *Controlled Deliveries: Illinois v. Andreas*

*Jacobsen* establishes that if an initial intrusion (at least into a container) is not covered by the Fourth Amendment, a later intrusion by police officers to the same extent is also free from Fourth Amendment constraints. While *Jacobsen* dealt with an initial search to which the Fourth Amendment did not apply, its principle has been held equally applicable when initial searches of containers are valid under the Fourth Amendment.

For example, in Illinois v. Andreas, 463 U.S. 765 (1983), government agents conducted a legal customs search of a wooden crate that was being shipped to an address in the United States, and found drugs hidden in a table therein. They then resealed the crate, and followed it to its destination using a surveillance process called a "controlled delivery." Surveilling police ultimately saw Andreas drag the container into his apartment; when he re-emerged with it 30 to 45 minutes later, the agents searched the container without a warrant. Chief Justice Burger, writing for the Court, reasoned that "the simple act of resealing the container to enable the police to make a controlled delivery does not operate to revive or restore the lawfully invaded privacy rights." Thus, the reopening of the container was not a search, because no legitimate expectation of privacy existed in the container at that time.

What if Andreas came out with the crate two days later? If a customs official legally searches a suitcase, can government agents search the same suitcase without a warrant a year later? In *Andreas,* Chief Justice Burger recognized that there may be a gap in surveillance, during which "it is possible that the container will be put to other uses—for example, the contraband may be removed or other items may be placed inside." He concluded, however, that the Fourth Amendment would be applicable to a subsequent reopening only if there is "a substantial likelihood that the contents of the container have been changed during the gap in surveillance." Otherwise, "there is no legitimate expectation of privacy in the contents of a container previously opened under lawful authority." On the facts, the Court found that the re-opening did not implicate a revived privacy interest, due to the unusual size of the container, its specialized purpose, and the relatively short time that Andreas had the container in his apartment.

### 7.   Foreign Officials

Courts have uniformly held that "[e]vidence obtained by foreign police officials from searches conducted in their country is generally admissible * * * regardless of whether the search complied with the Fourth Amendment." United States v. Behety, 32 F.3d 503 (11th Cir.1994). This is because searches by foreign officials do not constitute the kind of "state action" that is circumscribed by the Bill of Rights. There are, however, two very limited exceptions to this general rule. These exceptions are set forth by the court in United States v. Barona, 56 F.3d 1087 (9th Cir.1995):

> One exception * * * occurs if the circumstances of the foreign search and seizure are so extreme that they shock the judicial conscience, so that a federal appellate court in the exercise of its supervisory powers can require exclusion of the evidence. This type of exclusion is not based on our Fourth Amendment jurisprudence, but rather on the recognition that we may employ our supervisory powers when absolutely necessary to preserve the integrity of the criminal justice system. * * *

> The second exception * * * applies when United States agents' participation in the investigation is so substantial that the action is a joint venture between United States and foreign officials.

A suggested approach for identifying foreign searches subject to American constitutional restraints is offered in Saltzburg, The Reach of the Bill of Rights Beyond the Terra Firma of the United States, 20 Va.J.Int'l L. 741 (1980).

Even if the foreign search is conducted by or at the behest of American officials, it will not implicate the Fourth Amendment if the victim of the search is a non-resident alien. In United States v. Verdugo-Urquidez, 494 U.S. 259 (1990), discussed earlier in the Chapter, the Court held that non-resident aliens lack sufficient connection with this Country to be considered as part of "the people" covered by the Fourth Amendment.

### 8.   Jails, Prison Cells, and Convicts

Chief Justice Burger wrote for the Court in Hudson v. Palmer, 468 U.S. 517 (1984), as it held that a prisoner has no constitutionally protected expectation of privacy in his prison cell or in papers or property in his cell. Therefore, the Fourth Amendment was not implicated when prison officials rummaged through Hudson's cell and personal effects and destroyed some of his property in the course of their conduct. The Court concluded that "[t]he uncertainty that attends random searches of cells renders these searches perhaps the most effective weapon of the prison administrator in the constant fight against the proliferation of knives and guns, illicit drugs, and other contraband." It added that prison officials must be free to seize any articles from cells when necessary to serve legitimate institutional interests.

Justice Stevens, joined by Justices Brennan, Marshall and Blackmun, dissented. He did not disagree that prison officials should be able to conduct random searches to protect prison security, but he took exception to the holding that "no matter how malicious, destructive or arbitrary a cell search and seizure may be, it cannot constitute an unreasonable invasion of any privacy or possessory interest that society is prepared to recognize as reasonable." In his opinion, "[t]o hold that a prisoner's possession of a letter from his wife, or a picture of his baby, has no protection against arbitrary or malicious perusal, seizure or destruction would not * * * comport with any civilized standard of decency."

Justice Stevens noted that the majority's holding was limited to a prisoner's papers and effects located in his cell, and that the Court apparently "believes that at least a prisoner's person is secure from unreasonable search and seizure." In Bell v. Wolfish, 441 U.S. 520 (1979), the Court stated that at best prisoners have a reasonable expectation of privacy "of diminished scope" and that strip searches and body cavity searches of pretrial detainees after contact visits were governed by the Fourth Amendment but were reasonable under the circumstances. As to when and whether searches of prisoners are reasonable under the Fourth Amendment, see the section on "special needs" searches later in this Chapter.

## 9. Public Schools and Public Employees

In New Jersey v. T.L.O., 469 U.S. 325 (1985), the Court rejected a state's arguments that students have no legitimate expectation of privacy in their possessions that they take to a public school. Although the Court recognized the need for schools to maintain discipline, it declined to apply its decision in the prisoner case, Hudson v. Palmer, *supra*, to the school context. Justice White wrote for the Court and stated that "[w]e are not yet ready to hold that the schools and the prisons need be equated for purposes of the Fourth Amendment." His opinion also rejected the state's suggestion that a student is free to maintain any privacy interest in personal property simply by leaving the property at home. The opinion concluded that "schoolchildren may find it necessary to carry with them a variety of legitimate, noncontraband items, and there is no reason to conclude that they have necessarily waived all rights to privacy in such items merely by bringing them onto school grounds."

It is important to remember however, that a finding of a legitimate expectation of privacy is simply the first step in the Fourth Amendment inquiry. If the citizen has a legitimate expectation of privacy, then the official intrusion is reviewed for its reasonableness. In *T.L.O.*, the Court held that the school official's inspection of a student's handbag was a search, but concluded that the search was reasonable because the official could reasonably suspect that the student had cigarettes in her bag. This holding on reasonableness is discussed further in the section on "special needs" searches, *infra*.

The Supreme Court in O'Connor v. Ortega, 480 U.S. 709 (1987), unanimously rejected an argument that governmental employees "can never have a reasonable expectation of privacy in their place of work," although the Justices could not agree on an opinion for the Court. State hospital officials, investigating various charges made against a psychiatrist, entered the psychiatrist's office and seized various items from his desk and file cabinets. The psychiatrist brought a civil rights action against the officials, claiming that they had violated his Fourth Amendment rights.

Justice O'Connor's plurality opinion, joined by Chief Justice Rehnquist and Justices White and Powell, declined to decide whether the psychiatrist had a reasonable expectation of privacy in his office, but found that he definitely had one in his desk and file cabinets. The plurality concluded "that public employers' intrusions upon the constitutionally protected privacy interests of government employees for noninvestigatory, work-related purposes, as well as for investigations of work-related misconduct should be judged by the standard of reasonableness under all the circumstances." Applying those reasonableness standards, Justice O'Connor found that the search of the public employee's office was permissible because investigating officials had reasonable suspicion to believe that the employee had stolen government property.

Justice Scalia concurred in the judgment. He objected to the vagueness of the plurality opinion and "would hold * * * that the offices of government employees, and *a fortiori* the drawers and files within those offices, are covered by the Fourth Amendment protections as a general matter. (The qualification is necessary to cover such unusual situations as that in which the office is subject to unrestricted public access * * *.)" But, Justice Scalia also "would hold that government searches to retrieve work-related materials or to investigate violations of workplace rules—searches of the sort that are regarded as reasonable and normal in the private-employer context—do not violate the Fourth Amendment." He agreed with Justice O'Connor that the search in the instant case was reasonable because officials had reasonable suspicion to believe that the employee had stolen property.

Justice Blackmun, joined by Justices Brennan, Marshall, and Stevens, dissented in *Ortega*. The dissenters agreed with Justice Scalia's view that government employees had a reasonable expectation of privacy in their offices. But they argued that the reasonableness of the search should be judged by standards of probable cause rather than the lesser standards of reasonable suspicion. For further discussion on the reasonableness of searches of public employees, see the section on "special needs" searches later in this Chapter.

# III.   THE TENSION BETWEEN THE REASONABLENESS AND THE WARRANT CLAUSES

## A.  THE IMPORTANCE OF THE WARRANT CLAUSE GENERALLY

Searches and seizures conducted without a warrant are presumed to be unreasonable. The language of the Court is that "searches conducted outside the judicial process, without prior approval by judge or magistrate are *per se* unreasonable under the Fourth Amendment—subject only to a few specifically established and well-delineated exceptions." Katz v. United States, 389 U.S. 347, 357 (1967).

But the vision of a tough, sweeping per se warrant rule yielding only to the most demanding claims for exceptions is at odds with reality. Despite the Court's ringing language, the so-called per se rule can be restated as follows:

> A search and seizure in some circumstances is presumed to be unconstitutional if no prior warrant is obtained, but in many other circumstances the prior warrant is unnecessary to justify a search or seizure.

As Justice Scalia stated in his concurring opinion in California v. Acevedo, 500 U.S. 565 (1991), the Court's jurisprudence with respect to the warrant requirement has "lurched back and forth between imposing a categorical warrant requirement and looking to reasonableness alone." According to Justice Scalia, the result is that the warrant requirement has become "so riddled with exceptions that it [is] basically unrecognizable."

## B.  THE REASON FOR THE WARRANT REQUIREMENT

The following case is probably the Supreme Court's most thorough explication and justification of the warrant requirement. It lays the foundation of the current presumption that warrants are required for searches and seizures.

### JOHNSON V. UNITED STATES

Supreme Court of the United States, 1948.
333 U.S. 10.

### MR. JUSTICE JACKSON delivered the opinion of the Court.

Petitioner was convicted of four counts charging violation of federal narcotic laws. The only question which brings the case here is whether it was lawful, without a warrant of any kind, to arrest petitioner and to search her living quarters.

Taking the Government's version of disputed events, decision would rest on these facts:

At about 7:30 p.m. Detective Lieutenant Belland, an officer of the Seattle police force narcotic detail, received information from a confidential informer, who was also a known narcotic user, that unknown persons were smoking opium in the Europe Hotel. The informer was taken back to the hotel to interview the manager, but he returned at once saying he could smell burning opium in the hallway. Belland communicated with federal narcotic agents and between 8:30 and 9 o'clock went back to the hotel with four such agents. All were experienced in narcotic work and recognized at once a strong odor of burning opium which to them was distinctive and unmistakable. The odor led to Room 1. The officers did not know who was occupying that room. They knocked and a voice inside asked who was there. "Lieutenant Belland," was the reply. There was a slight delay, some "shuffling or noise" in the room and then the defendant opened the door. The officer said, "I want to talk to you a little bit." She then, as he describes it, "stepped back acquiescently and admitted us." He said, "I want to talk to you about this opium smell in the room here." She denied that there was such a smell. Then he said, "I want you to consider yourself under arrest because we are going to search the room." The search turned up incriminating opium and smoking apparatus, the latter being warm, apparently from recent use. This evidence the District Court refused to suppress before trial and admitted over defendant's objection at the trial. Conviction resulted and the Circuit Court of Appeals affirmed.

The defendant challenged the search of her home as a violation of the rights secured to her, in common with others, by the Fourth Amendment to the Constitution.

\* \* \*

Entry to defendant's living quarters, which was the beginning of the search, was demanded under color of office. It was granted in submission to authority rather than as an understanding and intentional waiver of a constitutional right.

At the time entry was demanded the officers were possessed of evidence which a magistrate might have found to be probable cause for issuing a search warrant. \* \* \* If the presence of odors is testified to before a magistrate and he finds the affiant qualified to know the odor, and it is one sufficiently distinctive to identify a forbidden substance, \* \* \* it might very well be found to be evidence of most persuasive character.

The point of the Fourth Amendment, which often is not grasped by zealous officers, is not that it denies law enforcement the support of the usual inferences which reasonable men draw from evidence. Its protection consists in requiring that those inferences be drawn by a neutral and detached magistrate instead of being judged by the officer engaged in the often competitive enterprise of ferreting out crime. Any assumption that evidence sufficient to support a magistrate's disinterested determination to issue a search warrant will justify the officers in making a search without a warrant would reduce the Amendment to a nullity and leave the people's homes secure only in the discretion of police officers. Crime, even in the privacy of one's own quarters, is, of course, of grave concern to society, and the law allows such crime to be reached on proper showing. The right of officers to thrust themselves into a home is also a grave concern, not only to the individual but to a society which chooses to dwell in reasonable security and freedom from surveillance. When the right of privacy must reasonably yield to the right of search is, as a rule, to be decided by a judicial officer, not by a policeman or government enforcement agent.

There are exceptional circumstances in which, on balancing the need for effective law enforcement against the right of privacy, it may be contended that a magistrate's warrant for search may be dispensed with. But this is not such a case. No reason is offered for not obtaining a search warrant except the inconvenience to the officers and some slight delay necessary to prepare papers and present the evidence to a magistrate. These are never very convincing reasons and, in these circumstances, certainly are not enough to by-pass the constitutional requirement. No suspect was fleeing or likely to take flight. The search was of permanent premises, not of a movable vehicle. No evidence or contraband was threatened with removal or destruction, except perhaps the fumes which we suppose in time would disappear. But they were not capable at any time of being reduced to possession for presentation to court. The evidence of their existence before the search was adequate and the testimony of the officers to that effect would not perish from the delay of getting a warrant.

If the officers in this case were excused from the constitutional duty of presenting their evidence to a magistrate, it is difficult to think of a case in which it should be required.

[The Court held that the officers had no probable cause to arrest the defendant until they entered the defendant's quarters, and reasoned that the search (entry and visual inspection) preceded the arrest. It was not possible, therefore, to justify the officers' conduct on a search incident to a valid arrest theory. Justices Black, Reed, and Burton, together with Chief Justice Vinson, dissented without opinion.]

### NOTE ON JOHNSON

*Johnson* represents a victory for those who would have the police secure warrants. As the majority intimates, there almost certainly was enough evidence known to the police to justify a magistrate's issuance of a warrant. Yet, because no warrant was sought, the search is deemed constitutionally "unreasonable" or invalid. Why is this the correct result? If you would answer that the Framers assumed that warrants generally would be required, you must recognize that the Warrant Clause is actually designed as a *limitation* on the issuance of warrants ("No warrant shall issue without probable cause . . .") and does not explicitly state a preference for warrants. How does the Court reason from a limitation on warrants to a warrant requirement?

Note that the government did not argue in *Johnson* that a warrant should be excused because of the risk that the evidence would be destroyed by the time they got a warrant. What if they had? See Kentucky v. King, 131 S.Ct. 1849 (2011) (finding exigent circumstances in a similar case and distinguishing *Johnson* as a case in which the government did not argue exigent circumstances). *King* is discussed later in this Chapter in the section on the exigent circumstances exception to the warrant requirement.

## C. THE FUNCTION OF THE WARRANT REQUIREMENT

For searches and seizures that are subject to the warrant requirement, probable cause represents the threshold of proof that must be satisfied before the power to search and seize is legitimated. That proof requirement means that the government must demonstrate a factually-based interest in people, places or things *before* using its power to disturb them. The proof requirement protects against *unjustified* searches and seizures.

Related to the proof requirement are the "Oath or affirmation" and particularity provisions of the Amendment. Probable cause is to be shown by persons willing to swear to or affirm the truth of their statements and thus to be held accountable for their representations. In addition, the applicant for the warrant is committing to a public record the information that is known *before* the search so that, after the search takes place, there is no confusion between the ex-post and ex-ante positions of the applicant. Without an antecedent warrant requirement, an officer questioned about probable cause can work backwards from the search, and fill in the facts as if they were known beforehand.

The specificity requirement implies that the government can only interfere with those persons, places or things that it has shown a valid interest in. Here, too, the written record made in advance of the search may decrease the danger that after a search is completed, the police will claim that whatever is found is exactly what was sought. Also, the specification of objects sought to be seized may inform the magistrate's decision on whether the proposed search is reasonable or excessive. A showing of probable cause, then, does not mean that any search and seizure authorized by a warrant is valid; it means that any search and seizure directed by warrant at the people, places, or things to which the probable cause specifically relates satisfies the warrant clause of the Fourth Amendment. These limitations guard against *arbitrary* searches and seizures.

By placing a magistrate between the citizen and the police, the Amendment, in the words of the *Johnson* majority, establishes that a neutral observer is to decide whether the probable cause and specificity requirements have been satisfied. This is one way in which the Amendment operates to prevent unjustified searches and seizures; the presumption is that a magistrate will make fewer errors than "the officer engaged in the often competitive enterprise of ferreting out crime."

By interposing the magistrate between the "competitors"—the police and the suspect—the Amendment may also serve another function. It gives the neutral magistrate an opportunity to refuse a warrant, even if the application is supported by oath, probable cause and specifics, on the ground that a search and seizure would be unreasonable under the circumstances. For example, if the police have probable cause to believe that A has marijuana cigarettes in his home, and if possession of small quantities of marijuana is punishable by fine only, a magistrate might be inclined to disapprove a warrant to search A's entire house on the ground that the scope of the search would be beyond what reasonable persons would accept in light of the government's minimal interests at stake. The same magistrate might be persuaded to permit a search of A's briefcase. Similarly, if the police obtain a warrant to search A's house on Monday and execute the warrant that same day, but find nothing, a magistrate might hesitate to issue another warrant to search on Tuesday, and perhaps another to look again on Wednesday, even if the police still have probable cause. Or, in an income tax evasion case, if the police asked for authority to search for and seize everything found in a home as evidence of an income greater than that recorded on a tax return, a magistrate might balk at issuing such a warrant. However, the same magistrate might authorize an entry into the house to take photographs. By imposing limitations on searches, a magistrate may prevent *excessive* governmental intrusions.

Another important function of the warrant requirement was identified by the Court in Illinois v. Gates, discussed later in this Chapter. The Court stated that "the possession of a warrant by officers conducting an arrest or search greatly reduces the perception of unlawful or intrusive police conduct, by assuring the individual whose property is searched or seized of the lawful authority of the executing officer, his need to search, and the limits of his power to search."

As you go through the remainder of the Chapter, see if you can identify other goals of the warrant requirement. Might one be to remind police of their obligation to comply with the legal constraints placed upon them? Could it also be argued that without the specific limitation of the warrant requirement, the Fourth Amendment's general command that a search be "reasonable" would be inherently ambiguous and subject to the case-by-case balancing of shifting majorities in the courts? Is it possible for the Supreme Court to give specific and principled guidance under the reasonableness clause, without any reference to a presumption in favor of warrants?

### *The Warrant Requirement in Reality*

The above discussion articulated a number of theoretically sound reasons for the warrant requirement. But does the warrant process, in practice, serve these purposes? For example, the Administrative Office of the United States Courts compiled statistics on warrants issued for electronic surveillance. The New York Times reported on these statistics as follows:

> The figures show that Federal and state judges are largely rubber stamps for law enforcement when it comes to electronic surveillance, despite all the talk of the need for an independent review by the courts of bugs and wiretaps. The last time a court denied a wiretap application was in 1988; all told, only 7 applications out of 8,950 since 1983 have been turned down.

Labaton, Before the Explosion, Officials Saw Little Risk for Building in Oklahoma City, New York Times, May 2, 1995, p. A19. The data is similar for warrants to search for physical evidence.

What is the point of requiring a warrant if the warrant process is simply a formality as a practical matter? Could the almost-certain success of a warrant application be a reason for the Court's expansion of the exceptions to the warrant requirement? Is the Court attempting to focus the warrant requirement on those few areas in which a magistrate's determination might make a difference?

Could it be argued that the success rate for obtaining warrants is attributable not to lax review but to the care that is being put into warrant applications by police officers fearful that their applications will be rejected?

The exceptions to the warrant requirement will be considered shortly. Before reaching them, it is useful to understand what practical protections the warrant application procedure affords.

# IV.   OBTAINING A SEARCH WARRANT: CONSTITUTIONAL PREREQUISITES

## A.  DEMONSTRATING PROBABLE CAUSE

### 1.   Source of Information on Which Probable Cause Is Based

The Fourth Amendment mandates a showing of probable cause as justification for a search warrant. Scant attention was paid to the term *probable cause* until the 1960's, when two major cases were decided, Aguilar v. Texas, 378 U.S. 108 (1964) and Spinelli v. United States, 393 U.S. 410 (1969). *Spinelli* is set forth below; the earlier *Aguilar* decision is discussed in the majority opinion. Both of these cases deal with regulation of the source of information on which probable cause is based. These cases must be read in light of the case that follows, Illinois v. Gates, which tempered the standards for determining probable cause on the basis of informants' tips.

### SPINELLI V. UNITED STATES
Supreme Court of the United States, 1969.
393 U.S. 410.

### MR. JUSTICE HARLAN delivered the opinion of the Court.

William Spinelli was convicted * * * of traveling to St. Louis, Missouri, from a nearby Illinois suburb with the intention of conducting gambling activities proscribed by Missouri law. At every appropriate stage in the proceedings in the lower courts, the petitioner challenged the constitutionality of the warrant which authorized the FBI search that uncovered the evidence necessary for his conviction. * * *

In *Aguilar,* a search warrant had issued upon an affidavit of police officers who swore only that they had "received reliable information from a credible person and do believe" that narcotics were being illegally stored on the described premises. While recognizing that the constitutional requirement of probable cause can be satisfied by hearsay information, this Court held the affidavit inadequate for two reasons. First, the application failed to set forth any of the "underlying circumstances" necessary to enable the magistrate independently to judge of the validity of the informant's conclusion that the narcotics were where he said they were. Second, the affiant-officers did not attempt to support their claim that their informant was " 'credible' or his information 'reliable.' " The Government is, however, quite right in saying that the FBI affidavit in the present case is more ample than that in *Aguilar*. Not only does it contain a report from an anonymous informant, but it also contains a report of an independent FBI investigation which is said to corroborate the informant's tip. We are, then, required to delineate the manner in which *Aguilar's* two-pronged test should be applied in these circumstances.

In essence, the affidavit * * * contained the following allegations:[a]

1.   The FBI had kept track of Spinelli's movements on five days during the month of August 1965. On four of these occasions, Spinelli was seen crossing one of two bridges leading from Illinois into St. Louis, Missouri, between 11 a.m. and 12:15 p.m. On four of the five days, Spinelli was also seen parking his car in a lot used by residents of an apartment house at 1108 Indian Circle Drive in St. Louis, between 3:30 p.m. and 4:45 p.m. On one day, Spinelli was followed further and seen to enter a particular apartment in the building.

2.   An FBI check with the telephone company revealed that this apartment contained two telephones listed under the name of Grace P. Hagen, and carrying the numbers WYdown 4–0029 and WYdown 4–0136.

3.   The application stated that "William Spinelli is known to this affiant and to federal law enforcement agents and local law enforcement agents as a bookmaker, an associate of bookmakers, a gambler, and an associate of gamblers."

4.   Finally, it was stated that the FBI "has been informed by a confidential reliable informant that William Spinelli is operating a handbook and accepting wagers and disseminating wagering information by means of the telephones which have been assigned the numbers WYdown 4–0029 and WYdown 4–0136."

There can be no question that the last item mentioned, detailing the informant's tip, has a fundamental place in this warrant application. Without it, probable cause could not be established. The first two items reflect only innocent-seeming activity and data. Spinelli's travels to and

---

[a]   It is, of course, of no consequence that the agents might have had additional information which could have been given to the Commissioner. "It is elementary that in passing on the validity of a warrant, the reviewing court may consider *only* information brought to the magistrate's attention." Aguilar v. Texas, 378 U.S. 108, 109, n. 1 (emphasis in original). * * *

from the apartment building and his entry into a particular apartment on one occasion could hardly be taken as bespeaking gambling activity; and there is surely nothing unusual about an apartment containing two separate telephones. Many a householder indulges himself in this petty luxury. Finally, the allegation that Spinelli was "known" to the affiant and to other federal and local law enforcement officers as a gambler and an associate of gamblers is but a bald and unilluminating assertion of suspicion that is entitled to no weight in appraising the magistrate's decision.

So much indeed the Government does not deny. Rather, * * * the Government claims that the informant's tip gives a suspicious color to the FBI's reports detailing Spinelli's innocent-seeming conduct and that, conversely, the FBI's surveillance corroborates the informant's tip, thereby entitling it to more weight. It is true, of course that the magistrate is obligated to render a judgment based upon a common-sense reading of the entire affidavit. We believe, however, that the "totality of circumstances" approach taken by the Court of Appeals paints with too broad a brush. Where, as here, the informer's tip is a necessary element in a finding of probable cause, its proper weight must be determined by a more precise analysis.

The informer's report must first be measured against *Aguilar's* standards so that its probative value can be assessed. If the tip is found inadequate under *Aguilar,* the other allegations which corroborate the information contained in the hearsay report should then be considered. At this stage as well, however, the standards enunciated in *Aguilar* must inform the magistrate's decision. He must ask: Can it fairly be said that the tip, even when certain parts of it have been corroborated by independent sources, is as trustworthy as a tip which would pass *Aguilar's* tests without independent corroboration?

* * *

Applying these principles to the present case, we first consider the weight to be given the informer's tip when it is considered apart from the rest of the affidavit. It is clear that a Commissioner could not credit it without abdicating his constitutional function. Though the affiant swore that his confidant was "reliable," he offered the magistrate no reason in support of this conclusion. Perhaps even more important is the fact that *Aguilar's* other test has not been satisfied. The tip does not contain a sufficient statement of the underlying circumstances from which the informer concluded that Spinelli was running a bookmaking operation. We are not told how the FBI's source received his information—it is not alleged that the informant personally observed Spinelli at work or that he had ever placed a bet with him. Moreover, if the informant came by the information indirectly, he did not explain why his sources were reliable.

In the absence of a statement detailing the manner in which the information was gathered, it is especially important that the tip describe the accused's criminal activity in sufficient detail that the magistrate may know that he is relying on something more substantial than a casual rumor circulating in the underworld or an accusation based merely on an individual's general reputation.

The detail provided by the informant in Draper v. United States, 358 U.S. 307 (1959), provides a suitable benchmark. While Hereford, the Government's informer in that case, did not state the way in which he had obtained his information, he reported that Draper had gone to Chicago the day before by train and that he would return to Denver by train with three ounces of heroin on one of two specified mornings. Moreover, Hereford, went on to describe, with minute particularity, the clothes that Draper would be wearing upon his arrival at the Denver station. A magistrate, when confronted with such detail, could reasonably infer that the informant had gained his information in a reliable way.[b] Such an inference cannot be made in the present case. Here, the only facts supplied were that Spinelli was using two specified telephones and that these phones were being used in gambling operations. This meager report could easily have been obtained from an offhand remark heard at a neighborhood bar.

Nor do we believe that the patent doubts *Aguilar* raises as to the report's reliability are adequately resolved by a consideration of the allegations detailing the FBI's independent investigative efforts. At most, these allegations indicated that Spinelli could have used the telephones specified by the informant for some purpose. This cannot by itself be said to support both the inference that the informer was generally trustworthy and that he had made his charge against Spinelli on the basis of information obtained in a reliable way. Once again, *Draper* provides a relevant comparison. Independent police work in that case corroborated much more than one small detail that had been provided by the informant. There, the police, upon meeting the inbound Denver train on the second morning specified by informer Hereford, saw a man whose dress corresponded precisely to Hereford's detailed description. It was then apparent that the informant had not been fabricating his report out of whole cloth; since the report was of the sort which in common experience may be recognized as having been obtained in a reliable way, it was perfectly clear that probable cause had been established.

We conclude, then, that in the present case the informant's tip—even when corroborated to the extent indicated—was not sufficient to provide the basis for a finding of probable cause. This is not to say that the tip

---

[b] While *Draper* involved the question whether the police had probable cause for an arrest without a warrant, the analysis required for an answer to this question is basically similar to that demanded of a magistrate when he considers whether a search warrant should issue.

was so insubstantial that it could not properly have counted in the magistrate's determination. Rather, it needed some further support. When we look to the other parts of the application, however, we find nothing alleged which would permit the suspicions engendered by the informant's report to ripen into a judgment that a crime was probably being committed. As we have already seen, the allegations detailing the FBI's surveillance of Spinelli and its investigation of the telephone company records contain no suggestion of criminal conduct when taken by themselves—and they are not endowed with an aura of suspicion by virtue of the informer's tip. Nor do we find that the FBI's reports take on a sinister color when read in light of common knowledge that bookmaking is often carried on over the telephone and from premises ostensibly used by others for perfectly normal purposes. Such an argument would carry weight in a situation in which the premises contain an unusual number of telephones or abnormal activity is observed, but it does not fit this case where neither of these factors is present.[c] All that remains to be considered is the flat statement that Spinelli was "known" to the FBI and others as a gambler. But just as a simple assertion of police suspicion is not itself a sufficient basis for a magistrate's finding of probable cause, we do not believe it may be used to give additional weight to allegations that would otherwise be insufficient.

\* \* \*

MR. JUSTICE MARSHALL took no part in the consideration or decision of this case.

[Justice White's concurring opinion is omitted.]

**MR. JUSTICE BLACK, dissenting.**

In my view, this Court's decision in Aguilar v. Texas, 378 U.S. 108 (1964), was bad enough. That decision went very far toward elevating the magistrate's hearing for issuance of a search warrant to a full-fledged trial, where witnesses must be brought forward to attest personally to all the facts alleged. But not content with this, the Court today expands *Aguilar* to almost unbelievable proportions. \* \* \* Nothing in our Constitution \* \* \* requires that the facts be established with that degree of certainty and with such elaborate specificity before a policeman can be authorized by a disinterested magistrate to conduct a carefully limited search.

\* \* \*

---

[c]   A box containing three uninstalled telephones was found in the apartment, but only after execution of the search warrant.

**MR. JUSTICE FORTAS, dissenting.**

\* \* \*

A policeman's affidavit should not be judged as an entry in an essay contest. It is not "abracadabra." As the majority recognizes, a policeman's affidavit is entitled to common-sense evaluation. \* \* \*

[Justice Stewart's dissenting opinion is omitted.]

## *Applying Spinelli*

The majority in *Spinelli* appears to accept the following propositions:

- A police officer is presumed to be honest when making an affidavit.

- What may be questioned, however, is the source of the officer's information.

- If the officer avers that she has first-hand knowledge of the facts used to demonstrate probable cause, the only question is whether the sworn facts are sufficient to meet the threshold.

- If the officer is relying on someone else for part or all of the information, then it is necessary to make three additional determinations:

    (i.) Who is the source of the information, and is the source reliable? Reliability is the first prong of the *Spinelli* test.

    (ii.) What are the bases and details of the source's knowledge? Credible information is the second prong of the test.

    (iii.) Assuming reliability of the source, are the facts, either standing alone or taken together with other facts provided by the affiant, sufficient to satisfy the proof threshold, probable cause?

- If the source is not known to the police to be reliable, the police may be able to demonstrate reliability by corroborating the details provided by the informant. The Court in *Spinelli* required a substantial amount of corroboration in such circumstances. Corroborating the fact that Spinelli had two telephone lines in his apartment was not enough to eliminate the concerns about the informant's reliability.

- If the informant's basis of information is unclear, it may be sufficient that the information is so detailed that it could only have come from the informant's personal observation.

- If the information provided by the informant falls short of demonstrating probable cause, the police can gather other information to be included in the application for a warrant.

- When the magistrate looks at all the information provided to assess whether probable cause is shown, she is to take a common sense approach to the application and ask whether the government has shown "the probability" of criminal activity.

*Spinelli* does not impose a limitation where a *crime victim or eyewitness* reports an alleged crime immediately after he or she says it took place. It only addresses warrant applications in which the police rely on 1) tipsters who operate as paid informants or snitches; or 2) anonymous informants. It is these two categories of informants whose reliability is most questionable.

The *Spinelli* majority shows a mistrust of paid and anonymous informants. Is that justified? Consider an anecdote from Dallas, where informants were paid millions of dollars based on tips that certain people were carrying drugs. The informants would pick up migrant laborers, give them a backpack, and tell them to wait to be picked up at a certain corner, where they would be taken to a factory for employment for the day. The bag would contain a powdery substance with trace amounts of cocaine. Then the informants would "tip" the police that a person was standing at a street corner holding a backpack containing narcotics. The "tip" would include a detailed description of the person holding the bag. The scam was not uncovered until years later when the substances were retested and found to be largely ground up masonry, with only trace amounts of cocaine.

Whatever your own opinion is, you should know that *Spinelli* was not well received by law enforcement officials. Generally speaking, law enforcement officers read *Spinelli* as prohibiting warrants based on information from paid or anonymous informants; in the view of law enforcement, the *Spinelli* Court set a standard for corroboration of those tips that was equivalent to independent evidence of criminality approaching probable cause. But if officers had to corroborate with independent evidence approaching or equaling probable cause, it followed that the tip itself was all but irrelevant to the probable cause determination. Also, the decision may have appeared to be more complicated and even more hostile to police than it was intended to be.

## 2. Rejection of a Rigid Two-Pronged Test

In the following case, the Court held that the two-pronged test of *Aguilar* and *Spinelli* would no longer control the determination of probable cause when police obtain information from paid, professional, or anonymous informants. Yet the Court took some pains to emphasize that the *Aguilar-Spinelli* structure still has continuing relevance when police rely in whole or in part on an informant's tip.

## ILLINOIS V. GATES

Supreme Court of the United States, 1983.
462 U.S. 213.

### JUSTICE REHNQUIST delivered the opinion of the Court.

Respondents Lance and Susan Gates were indicted for violation of state drug laws after police officers, executing a search warrant, discovered marijuana and other contraband in their automobile and home. Prior to trial the Gates' moved to suppress evidence seized during this search. The Illinois Supreme Court affirmed the decisions of lower state courts granting the motion. * * *

We granted certiorari to consider the application of the Fourth Amendment to a magistrate's issuance of a search warrant on the basis of a partially corroborated anonymous informant's tip. * * *

* * *

* * * Bloomingdale, Ill., is a suburb of Chicago located in DuPage County. On May 3, 1978, the Bloomingdale Police Department received by mail an anonymous handwritten letter which read as follows:

"This letter is to inform you that you have a couple in your town who strictly make their living on selling drugs. They are Sue and Lance Gates, they live on Greenway, off Bloomingdale Rd. in the condominiums. Most of their buys are done in Florida. Sue his wife drives their car to Florida, where she leaves it to be loaded up with drugs, then Lance flys down and drives it back. Sue flys back after she drops the car off in Florida. May 3 she is driving down there again and Lance will be flying down in a few days to drive it back. At the time Lance drives the car back he has the trunk loaded with over $100,000.00 in drugs. Presently they have over $100,000.00 worth of drugs in their basement.

They brag about the fact they never have to work, and make their entire living on pushers.

I guarantee if you watch them carefully you will make a big catch. They are friends with some big drugs dealers, who visit their house often.

Lance & Susan Gates Greenway in Condominiums"

The letter was referred by the Chief of Police of the Bloomingdale Police Department to Detective Mader, who decided to pursue the tip. Mader learned, from the office of the Illinois Secretary of State, that an Illinois driver's license had been issued to one Lance Gates, residing at a stated address in Bloomingdale. He contacted a confidential informant, whose examination of certain financial records revealed a more recent address for the Gates, and he also learned from a police officer assigned to O'Hare Airport that "L. Gates" had made a reservation on Eastern Airlines flight 245 to West Palm Beach, Fla., scheduled to depart from Chicago on May 5 at 4:15 p.m.

Mader then made arrangements with an agent of the Drug Enforcement Administration for surveillance of the May 5 Eastern Airlines flight. The agent later reported to Mader that Gates had boarded the flight, and that federal agents in Florida had observed him arrive in West Palm Beach and take a taxi to the nearby Holiday Inn. They also reported that Gates went to a room registered to one Susan Gates and that, at 7:00 a.m. the next morning, Gates and an unidentified woman left the motel in a Mercury bearing Illinois license plates and drove northbound on an interstate frequently used by travelers to the Chicago area. In addition, the DEA agent informed Mader that the license plate number on the Mercury registered to a Hornet station wagon owned by Gates. The agent also advised Mader that the driving time between West Palm Beach and Bloomingdale was approximately 22 to 24 hours.

Mader signed an affidavit setting forth the foregoing facts, and submitted it to a judge of the Circuit Court of DuPage County, together with a copy of the anonymous letter. The judge of that court thereupon issued a search warrant for the Gates' residence and for their automobile. The judge, in deciding to issue the warrant, could have determined that the *modus operandi* of the Gates had been substantially corroborated. As the anonymous letter predicted, Lance Gates had flown from Chicago to West Palm Beach late in the afternoon of May 5th, had checked into a hotel room registered in the name of his wife, and, at 7:00 a.m. the following morning, had headed north, accompanied by an unidentified woman, out of West Palm Beach on an interstate highway used by travelers from South Florida to Chicago in an automobile bearing a license plate issued to him.

At 5:15 a.m. on March 7th, only 36 hours after he had flown out of Chicago, Lance Gates, and his wife, returned to their home in Bloomingdale, driving the car in which they had left West Palm Beach some 22 hours earlier. The Bloomingdale police were awaiting them, searched the trunk of the Mercury, and uncovered approximately 350 pounds of marijuana. A search of the Gates' home revealed marijuana, weapons, and other contraband. The Illinois Circuit Court ordered suppression of all these items, on the ground that the affidavit submitted to the Circuit Judge failed to support the necessary determination of probable cause to believe that the Gates' automobile and home contained the contraband in question. This decision was affirmed in turn by the

Illinois Appellate Court and by a divided vote of the Supreme Court of Illinois.

The Illinois Supreme Court concluded—and we are inclined to agree—that, standing alone, the anonymous letter sent to the Bloomingdale Police Department would not provide the basis for a magistrate's determination that there was probable cause to believe contraband would be found in the Gates' car and home. The letter provides virtually nothing from which one might conclude that its author is either honest or his information reliable; likewise, the letter gives absolutely no indication of the basis for the writer's predictions regarding the Gates' criminal activities. Something more was required, then, before a magistrate could conclude that there was probable cause to believe that contraband would be found in the Gates' home and car.

The Illinois Supreme Court also properly recognized that Detective Mader's affidavit might be capable of supplementing the anonymous letter with information sufficient to permit a determination of probable cause. In holding that the affidavit in fact did not contain sufficient additional information to sustain a determination of probable cause, the Illinois court applied a "two-pronged test," derived from our decision in Spinelli v. United States. The Illinois Supreme Court, like some others, apparently understood *Spinelli* as requiring that the anonymous letter satisfy each of two independent requirements before it could be relied on. According to this view, the letter, as supplemented by Mader's affidavit, first had to adequately reveal the "basis of knowledge" of the letter writer—the particular means by which he came by the information given in his report. Second, it had to provide facts sufficiently establishing either the "veracity" of the affiant's informant, or, alternatively, the "reliability" of the informant's report in this particular case.

The Illinois court, alluding to an elaborate set of legal rules that have developed among various lower courts to enforce the "two-pronged test," found that the test had not been satisfied. First, the "veracity" prong was not satisfied because, "there was simply no basis [for] * * * conclud[ing] that the anonymous person [who wrote the letter to the Bloomingdale Police Department] was credible." The court indicated that corroboration by police of details contained in the letter might never satisfy the "veracity" prong, and in any event, could not do so if, as in the present case, only "innocent" details are corroborated. In addition, the letter gave no indication of the basis of its writer's knowledge of the Gates' activities. The Illinois court understood *Spinelli* as permitting the detail contained in a tip to be used to infer that the informant had a reliable basis for his statements, but it thought that the anonymous letter failed to provide sufficient detail to permit such an inference. Thus, it concluded that no showing of probable cause had been made.

We agree with the Illinois Supreme Court that an informant's "veracity," "reliability" and "basis of knowledge" are all highly relevant in determining the value of his report. We do not agree, however, that these elements should be understood as entirely separate and independent requirements to be rigidly exacted in every case, which the opinion of the Supreme Court of Illinois would imply. Rather, as detailed below, they should be understood simply as closely intertwined issues that may usefully illuminate the commonsense, practical question whether there is "probable cause" to believe that contraband or evidence is located in a particular place.

* * * This totality of the circumstances approach is far more consistent with our prior treatment of probable cause than is any rigid demand that specific "tests" be satisfied by every informant's tip. Perhaps the central teaching of our decisions bearing on the probable cause standard is that it is a "practical, nontechnical conception." * * *

[P]robable cause is a fluid concept—turning on the assessment of probabilities in particular factual contexts—not readily, or even usefully, reduced to a neat set of legal rules. Informants' tips doubtless come in many shapes and sizes from many different types of persons. * * *

[T]he "two-pronged test" directs analysis into two largely independent channels—the informant's "veracity" or "reliability" and his "basis of knowledge." There are persuasive arguments against according these two elements such independent status. Instead, they are better understood as relevant considerations in the totality of circumstances analysis that traditionally has guided probable cause determinations: a deficiency in one may be compensated for, in determining the overall reliability of a tip, by a strong showing as to the other, or by some other indicia of reliability.

* * * Unlike a totality of circumstances analysis, which permits a balanced assessment of the relative weights of all the various indicia of reliability (and unreliability) attending an informant's tip, the "two-pronged test" has encouraged an excessively technical dissection of informants' tips,[a] with undue attention being focused on isolated issues

---

[a] Some lower court decisions, brought to our attention by the State, reflect a rigid application of such rules. In Bridger v. State, 503 S.W.2d 801 (Tex.Cr.App.1974), the affiant had received a confession of armed robbery from one of two suspects in the robbery; in addition, the suspect had given the officer $800 in cash stolen during the robbery. The suspect also told the officer that the gun used in the robbery was hidden in the other suspect's apartment. A warrant issued on the basis of this was invalidated on the ground that the affidavit did not satisfactorily describe how the accomplice had obtained his information regarding the gun. Likewise, in People v. Palanza, 371 N.E.2d 687 (Ill.App.1978), the affidavit submitted in support of an application for a search warrant stated that an informant of proven and uncontested reliability had seen, in specifically described premises, "a quantity of a white crystalline substance which was represented to the informant by a white male occupant of the premises to be cocaine. Informant has observed cocaine on numerous occasions in the past and is thoroughly familiar with its appearance. The informant states that the white crystalline powder he observed in the above described premises appeared to him to be cocaine." The warrant issued on the basis of the

that cannot sensibly be divorced from the other facts presented to the magistrate.

* * * Finely-tuned standards such as proof beyond a reasonable doubt or by a preponderance of the evidence, useful in formal trials, have no place in the magistrate's decision. While an effort to fix some general, numerically precise degree of certainty corresponding to "probable cause" may not be helpful, it is clear that "only the probability, and not a prima facie showing, of criminal activity is the standard of probable cause." *Spinelli,* supra.

We have also recognized that affidavits are normally drafted by nonlawyers in the midst and haste of a criminal investigation. * * * The rigorous inquiry into the *Spinelli* prongs and the complex superstructure of evidentiary and analytical rules that some have seen implicit in our *Spinelli* decision, cannot be reconciled with the fact that many warrants are—quite properly—issued on the basis of nontechnical, common-sense judgments of laymen applying a standard less demanding than those used in formal legal proceedings.

* * *

If the affidavits submitted by police officers are subjected to the type of scrutiny some courts have deemed appropriate, police might well resort to warrantless searches, with the hope of relying on consent or some other exception to the warrant clause that might develop at the time of the search. In addition, the possession of a warrant by officers conducting an arrest or search greatly reduces the perception of unlawful or intrusive police conduct, by assuring "the individual whose property is searched or seized of the lawful authority of the executing officer, his need to search, and the limits of his power to search." Reflecting this preference for the warrant process, the traditional standard for review of an issuing magistrate's probable cause determination has been that so long as the magistrate had a "substantial basis for * * * conclud[ing]" that a search would uncover evidence of wrongdoing, the Fourth Amendment requires no more. * * *

Finally, the * * * strictures that inevitably accompany the "two-pronged test" cannot avoid seriously impeding the task of law enforcement. If, as the Illinois Supreme Court apparently thought, that test must be rigorously applied in every case, anonymous tips would be of greatly diminished value in police work. Ordinary citizens * * * generally do not provide extensive recitations of the basis of their everyday observations. Likewise, as the Illinois Supreme Court recognized in this case, the veracity of persons supplying anonymous tips is by hypothesis

---

affidavit was invalidated because "There is no indication as to how the informant or for that matter any other person could tell whether a white substance was cocaine and not some other substance such as sugar or salt."

largely unknown, and unknowable. As a result, anonymous tips seldom could survive a rigorous application of either of the *Spinelli* prongs. Yet, such tips, particularly when supplemented by independent police investigation, frequently contribute to the solution of otherwise "perfect crimes." While a conscientious assessment of the basis for crediting such tips is required by the Fourth Amendment, a standard that leaves virtually no place for anonymous citizen informants is not.

For all these reasons, we conclude that it is wiser to abandon the "two-pronged test" established by our decisions in *Aguilar* and *Spinelli*.[b] In its place we reaffirm the totality of the circumstances analysis that traditionally has informed probable cause determinations. The task of the issuing magistrate is simply to make a practical, common-sense decision whether, given all the circumstances set forth in the affidavit before him, including the "veracity" and "basis of knowledge" of persons supplying hearsay information, there is a fair probability that contraband or evidence of a crime will be found in a particular place. And the duty of a reviewing court is simply to ensure that the magistrate had a "substantial basis for * * * conclud[ing]" that probable cause existed. * * *

Our earlier cases illustrate the limits beyond which a magistrate may not venture in issuing a warrant. A sworn statement of an affiant that "he has cause to suspect and does believe that" liquor illegally brought into the United States is located on certain premises will not do. Nathanson v. United States, 290 U.S. 41 (1933). An affidavit must provide the magistrate with a substantial basis for determining the existence of probable cause, and the wholly conclusory statement at issue in *Nathanson* failed to meet this requirement. An officer's statement that "affiants have received reliable information from a credible person and believe" that heroin is stored in a home, is likewise inadequate. Aguilar v. Texas. As in *Nathanson,* this is a mere conclusory statement that gives the magistrate virtually no basis at all for making a judgment regarding probable cause. Sufficient information must be presented to the magistrate to allow that official to determine probable cause; his action cannot be a mere ratification of the bare conclusions of others. In order to ensure that such an abdication of the magistrate's duty does not occur, courts, must continue to conscientiously review the sufficiency of affidavits on which warrants are issued. But when we move beyond the "bare bones" affidavits present in cases such as *Nathanson* and *Aguilar,* this area simply does not lend itself to a prescribed set of rules, like that

---

b   * * * Whether the allegations submitted to the magistrate in *Spinelli* would, under the view we now take, have supported a finding of probable cause, we think it would not be profitable to decide. There are so many variables in the probable cause equation that one determination will seldom be a useful "precedent" for another. Suffice it to say that while we in no way abandon *Spinelli*'s concern for the trustworthiness of informers and for the principle that it is the magistrate who must ultimately make a finding of probable cause, we reject the rigid categorization suggested by some of its language.

which had developed from *Spinelli.* Instead, the flexible, common-sense standard * * * better serves the purposes of the Fourth Amendment's probable cause requirement.

Justice Brennan's dissent suggests in several places that the approach we take today somehow downgrades the role of the neutral magistrate, because *Aguilar* and *Spinelli* "preserve the role of magistrates as independent arbiters of probable cause. * * *" Quite the contrary, we believe, is the case. * * * Nothing in our opinion in any way lessens the authority of the magistrate to draw such reasonable inferences as he will from the material supplied to him by applicants for a warrant; indeed, he is freer than under the regime of *Aguilar* and *Spinelli* to draw such inferences, or to refuse to draw them if he is so minded.

* * *

* * * Even standing alone, the facts obtained through the independent investigation of Mader and the DEA at least suggested that the Gateses were involved in drug trafficking. In addition to being a popular vacation site, Florida is well-known as a source of narcotics and other illegal drugs. Lance Gates' flight to Palm Beach, his brief, overnight stay in a motel, and apparent immediate return north to Chicago in the family car, conveniently awaiting him in West Palm Beach, is as suggestive of a pre-arranged drug run, as it is of an ordinary vacation trip.

In addition, the magistrate could rely on the anonymous letter which had been corroborated in major part by Mader's efforts—just as had occurred in *Draper.*[c] The Supreme Court of Illinois reasoned that *Draper* involved an informant who had given reliable information on previous occasions, while the honesty and reliability of the anonymous informant in this case were unknown to the Bloomingdale police. While this distinction might be an apt one at the time the police department received the anonymous letter, it became far less significant after Mader's independent investigative work occurred. The corroboration of the letter's predictions that the Gateses' car would be in Florida, that Lance Gates would fly to Florida in the next day or so, and that he would drive the car north toward Bloomingdale all indicated, albeit not with certainty, that the informant's other assertions also were true. "Because an informant is right about some things, he is more probably right about other facts"— including the claim regarding the Gateses' illegal activity. This may well not be the type of "reliability" or "veracity" necessary to satisfy some

---

[c]   The Illinois Supreme Court thought that the verification of details contained in the anonymous letter in this case amounted only to "the corroboration of innocent activity," and that this was insufficient to support a finding of probable cause. We are inclined to agree, however with the observation of Justice Moran in his dissenting opinion that "In this case, just as in *Draper,* seemingly innocent activity became suspicious in the light of the initial tip." And it bears noting that *all* of the corroborating detail established in *Draper, supra,* was of entirely innocent activity * * *.

views of the "veracity prong" of *Spinelli,* but we think it suffices for the practical, common-sense judgment called for in making a probable cause determination. It is enough, for purposes of assessing probable cause, that "corroboration through other sources of information reduced the chances of a reckless or prevaricating tale," thus providing "a substantial basis for crediting the hearsay."

This is perfectly reasonable. As discussed previously, probable cause requires only a probability or substantial chance of criminal activity, not an actual showing of such activity. By hypothesis, therefore, innocent behavior frequently will provide the basis for a showing of probable cause; to require otherwise would be to *sub silentio* impose a drastically more rigorous definition of probable cause than the security of our citizens demands. We think the Illinois court attempted a too rigid classification of the types of conduct that may be relied upon in seeking to demonstrate probable cause. In making a determination of probable cause the relevant inquiry is not whether particular conduct is "innocent" or "guilty," but the degree of suspicion that attaches to particular types of non-criminal acts.

Finally, the anonymous letter contained a range of details relating not just to easily obtained facts and conditions existing at the time of the tip, but to future actions of third parties ordinarily not easily predicted. The letter writer's accurate information as to the travel plans of each of the Gateses' was of a character likely obtained only from the Gateses' themselves, or from someone familiar with their not entirely ordinary travel plans. If the informant had access to accurate information of this type a magistrate could properly conclude that it was not unlikely that he also had access to reliable information of the Gateses' alleged illegal activities.[d] Of course, the Gateses' travel plans might have been learned

---

[d]  Justice Stevens' dissent seizes on one inaccuracy in the anonymous informant's letter—its statement the Sue Gates would fly from Florida to Illinois, when in fact she drove—and argues that the probative value of the entire tip was undermined by this allegedly "material mistake." We have never required that informants used by the police be infallible, and can see no reason to impose such a requirement in this case. Probable cause, particularly when police have obtained a warrant, simply does not require the perfection the dissent finds necessary.

Likewise, there is no force to the dissent's argument that the Gateses' action in leaving their home unguarded undercut the informant's claim that drugs were hidden there. Indeed, the line-by-line scrutiny that the dissent applies to the anonymous letter is akin to that we find inappropriate in reviewing magistrate's decisions. The dissent apparently attributes to the magistrate who issued the warrant in this case the rather implausible notion that persons dealing in drugs always stay at home, apparently out of fear that to leave might risk intrusion by criminals. If accurate, one could not help sympathizing with the self-imposed isolation of people so situated. In reality, however, it is scarcely likely that the magistrate ever thought that the anonymous tip "kept one spouse" at home, much less that he relied on the theory advanced by the dissent. The letter simply says that Sue would fly from Florida to Illinois, without indicating whether the Gateses' made the bitter choice of leaving the drugs in their house, or those in their car, unguarded. The magistrate's determination that there might be drugs or evidence of criminal activity in the Gateses' home was well-supported by the less speculative theory, noted in text, that if the informant could predict with considerable accuracy the somewhat unusual travel plans of the Gateses, he probably also had a reliable basis for his statements that the Gateses kept a large quantity of drugs in their home and frequently were visited by other drug traffickers there.

from a talkative neighbor or travel agent; under the "two-pronged test" developed from *Spinelli*, the character of the details in the anonymous letter might well not permit a sufficiently clear inference regarding the letter writer's "basis of knowledge." But, as discussed previously, probable cause does not demand the certainty we associate with formal trials. It is enough that there was a fair probability that the writer of the anonymous letter had obtained his entire story either from the Gateses or someone they trusted. And corroboration of major portions of the letter's predictions provides just this probability. * * * The judgment of the Supreme Court of Illinois therefore must be

Reversed.

### JUSTICE WHITE, concurring in the judgment.

* * * [I]t is not at all necessary to overrule *Aguilar-Spinelli* in order to reverse the judgment below. Therefore, because I am inclined to believe that, when applied properly, the *Aguilar-Spinelli* rules play an appropriate role in probable cause determinations, and because the Court's holding may foretell an evisceration of the probable cause standard, I do not join the Court's holding.

The Court reasons that the "veracity" and "basis of knowledge" tests are not independent, and that a deficiency as to one can be compensated for by a strong showing as to the other. Thus, a finding of probable cause may be based on a tip from an informant "known for the unusual reliability of his predictions" or from "an unquestionably honest citizen," even if the report fails thoroughly to set forth the basis upon which the information was obtained. If this is so, then it must follow *a fortiori* that "the affidavit of an officer, known by the magistrate to be honest and experienced, stating that [contraband] is located in a certain building" must be acceptable. It would be "quixotic" if a similar statement from an honest informant, but not one from an honest officer, could furnish probable cause. But we have repeatedly held that the unsupported assertion or belief of an officer does not satisfy the probable cause requirement. Thus, this portion of today's holding can be read as implicitly rejecting the teachings of these prior holdings.

The Court may not intend so drastic a result. Indeed, the Court expressly reaffirms the validity of cases such as *Nathanson* that have held that, no matter how reliable the affiant-officer may be, a warrant should not be issued unless the affidavit discloses supporting facts and circumstances. The Court limits these cases to situations involving affidavits containing only "bare conclusions" and holds that, if an affidavit contains anything more, it should be left to the issuing magistrate to decide, based solely on "practical[ity]" and "common-sense," whether there is a fair probability that contraband will be found in a particular place.

Thus, as I read the majority opinion, it appears that the question whether the probable cause standard is to be diluted is left to the common-sense judgments of issuing magistrates. I am reluctant to approve any standard that does not expressly require, as a prerequisite to issuance of a warrant, some showing of facts from which an inference may be drawn that the informant is credible and that his information was obtained in a reliable way. * * *

**JUSTICE BRENNAN, with whom JUSTICE MARSHALL joins, dissenting.**

* * *

[O]ne can concede that probable cause is a "practical, nontechnical" concept without betraying the values that *Aguilar* and *Spinelli* reflect. *Aguilar* and *Spinelli* require the police to provide magistrates with certain crucial information. They also provide structure for magistrates' probable cause inquiries. In so doing, *Aguilar* and *Spinelli* preserve the role of magistrates as independent arbiters of probable cause, insure greater accuracy in probable cause determinations, and advance the substantive value of precluding findings of probable cause, and attendant intrusions, based on anything less than information from an honest or credible person who has acquired his information in a reliable way. Neither the standards nor their effects are inconsistent with a "practical, nontechnical" conception of probable cause. * * *

* * *

**JUSTICE STEVENS, with whom JUSTICE BRENNAN joins, dissenting.**

The fact that Lance and Sue Gates made a 22-hour nonstop drive from West Palm Beach, Florida, to Bloomingdale, Illinois, only a few hours after Lance had flown to Florida provided persuasive evidence that they were engaged in illicit activity. That fact, however, was not known to the magistrate when he issued the warrant to search their home.

What the magistrate did know at that time was that the anonymous informant had not been completely accurate in his or her predictions. The informant had indicated that "Sue drives their car to Florida *where she leaves it to be loaded up with drugs * * *. Sue flies back after she drops the car off in Florida.*" Yet Detective Mader's affidavit reported that she "left the West Palm Beach area driving the Mercury northbound."

The discrepancy between the informant's predictions and the facts known to Detective Mader is significant for three reasons. First, it cast doubt on the informant's hypothesis that the Gateses already had "over $100,000 worth of drugs in their basement." The informant had predicted an itinerary that always kept one spouse in Bloomingdale, suggesting that the Gateses did not want to leave their home unguarded because something valuable was hidden within. That inference obviously could not be drawn when it was known that the pair was actually together over a thousand miles from home.

Second, the discrepancy made the Gateses' conduct seem substantially less unusual than the informant had predicted it would be. It would have been odd if, as predicted, Sue had driven down to Florida on Wednesday, left the car, and flown right back to Illinois. But the mere facts that Sue was in West Palm Beach with the car, that she was joined by her husband at the Holiday Inn on Friday, and that the couple drove north together the next morning are neither unusual nor probative of criminal activity.

Third, the fact that the anonymous letter contained a material mistake undermines the reasonableness of relying on it as a basis for making a forcible entry into a private home.

* * * No one knows who the informant in this case was, or what motivated him or her to write the note. Given that the note's predictions were faulty in one significant respect, and were corroborated by nothing except ordinary innocent activity, I must surmise that the Court's evaluation of the warrant's validity has been colored by subsequent events.

* * *

## NOTE ON GATES

The Court moves to a totality of the circumstances test and abandons, as too rigid, the two-pronged test that it had previously established. Is there any way for a magistrate to independently screen applications for warrants without looking at who provides the underlying information that appears in the applications and how these people obtained their information?

Does the substitution of a totality of the circumstances test for the two-pronged test mean that the two-pronged test is no longer relevant? Or does Illinois v. Gates simply say that the prongs of the *Aguilar* and *Spinelli* are relevant but not necessarily independent or dispositive? See, e.g., United States v. Morales, 171 F.3d 978 (5th Cir.1999) (noting that the *Gates* totality of the circumstances test "includes four factors: (1) the nature of the information; (2) whether there has been an opportunity for the police to see or hear the matter reported; (3) the veracity and the basis of knowledge of the informant; (4) whether there has been any independent verification of the matters reported through police investigation."). See also United States v. Gagnon, 373 F.3d 230 (2d Cir. 2004) (after *Gates* "it is clear that the reliability or veracity of the informant and the basis for the informant's knowledge are but two of several relevant considerations when determining the existence of probable cause based on an informant's tip, and that a deficiency in one may be compensated for, in determining the overall reliability of a tip, by a strong showing as to the other, or by some other indicia of reliability.").

If you were teaching magistrates, which test, the two-pronged *Spinelli* test or the *Gates* totality of the circumstances test, would be more helpful to you in explaining how magistrates are to evaluate warrant applications?

The New York Court of Appeals rejected *Gates* in the context of warrantless police activity in People v. Johnson, 66 N.Y.2d 398, 497 N.Y.S.2d 618, 488 N.E.2d 439 (1985). In so holding, the court followed the lead of the Washington Supreme Court in State v. Jackson, 102 Wash.2d 432, 688 P.2d 136 (1984). See also State v. Jacumin, 778 S.W.2d 430 (Tenn.1989) and State v. Jones, 706 P.2d 317 (Alaska 1985), both rejecting *Gates* in favor of the *Spinelli* two-pronged test. All of these decisions are based on a construction of the respective court's State constitution.

### *Strong Prong/Weak Prong*

Does it make sense that a strong showing on one of the *Spinelli* prongs can make up for a weak showing on the other? For cases in which courts used this reasoning from *Gates* to uphold a finding of probable cause, see Carter v. United States, 729 F.2d 935 (8th Cir.1984) (no specific statement as to informant's basis of knowledge for stating that marijuana was growing on certain property; however, some detail concerning the location of the property was given, and any deficiency in basis of knowledge is compensated for by informant's prior track record of reliable tips); United States v. Phillips, 727 F.2d 392 (5th Cir.1984) (questionable veracity of informant who hated defendant was overcome by wealth of detail in the tip).

### *The Function of Corroboration After Gates*

The biggest effect of *Gates* is its more permissive view of the nature and extent of corroboration necessary to shore up a defective tip. For a post-*Gates* example of the use of corroboration, consider United States v. Warner, 894 F.2d 957 (8th Cir.1990). A "confidential and reliable source" informed the Sheriff's office that he had seen Warner fire a machinegun at Warner's residence. The next day, an anonymous caller reported that Warner had shot a machinegun the previous day at Warner's residence. The officer checked firearms registrations and found that Warner had no registered firearms. On the basis of this information, a warrant was issued to search Warner's house for an unregistered firearm. The court of appeals upheld the magistrate's determination of probable cause, reasoning that the two tips were "mutually corroborative," and that the officer's check of firearms records provided further crucial corroboration. Would this corroboration have been sufficient under *Spinelli*? Did the officer's corroboration mean that Warner had an unlicensed gun, or that he had no gun? How did the court know that the "mutually corroborative" tips came from two different people?

The effect of *Gates* is apparent in cases like United States v. Peyko, 717 F.2d 741 (2d Cir.1983). An officer received an anonymous tip that Peyko was and would be receiving weekly deliveries of drugs by Federal Express. The officer investigated and found that Peyko had been using Federal Express to send and receive packages regularly. The court found that the tip, together with the corroboration, provided probable cause to seize a Federal Express package addressed to Peyko. While the corroboration was of completely innocent activity (regularly sending and receiving packages), it lent color to the tip, which lent color to the corroboration, which led to probable cause under the *Gates* totality of circumstances approach. In light of *Peyko*, is there any risk that an innocent person with enemies will be subject to a search of his house or possessions?

As seen in *Peyko*—and in *Gates* itself—it will be very important to a finding of probable cause if the informant's tip contains some prediction and that prediction bears out. When predictions are corroborated, a magistrate can draw the conclusion that the informant has some inside information about the defendant's activity, and that, because he got one activity correct, he is also correct about his assessment of criminal activity. See, e.g., United States v. Steppello, 664 F.3d 359 (2d Cir. 2011) (probable cause of drug activity existed where informant "predicted just what Steppello would do in response to his cryptic call.").

### *Insufficient Corroboration*

There are a few reported cases finding that police corroboration was insufficient to shore up a defective tip, even under the *Gates* totality of the circumstances approach. One such case is United States v. Leake, 998 F.2d 1359 (6th Cir.1993). An anonymous informant phoned the police narcotics office and stated that he was a tradesman hired to do some work at 4825 Westport Road. While working, he smelled and saw marijuana in the basement. When questioned as to how he knew it was marijuana, he stated that in his "younger days" he had been a marijuana user, but that now he was older, with children, and was very "anti-drug." Surveillance was initiated at 4825 Westport Road. No undue amount of traffic was observed. It was confirmed that the house had a basement. Two vehicles were registered to the address, one owned by Leake. On the basis of the tip and the investigation, the magistrate issued a warrant to search the premises at 4825 Westport Road, and officers recovered over 300 pounds of marijuana in the basement.

The court in *Leake* held that the warrant lacked probable cause. The court first observed that unlike *Gates*, the anonymous caller in *Leake* had not provided much detail. No names of particular individuals were ever mentioned, no dates were provided, and "no planned future activity was described as in *Gates*." Nor was the corroboration sufficient to overcome the defective tip.

The *Leake* court found a moral in this story:

> Ultimately, this case demonstrates the importance of taking sufficient time to verify an anonymous tip before a warrant is requested. Detective Murphy's investigation of the caller's information was inadequate. More police work was needed. The supporting affidavit was too vague and Detective Murphy's limited two-night surveillance was insufficient to verify important elements of the anonymous caller's information.

See also United States v. Wilhelm, 80 F.3d 116 (4th Cir.1996), where the officer received information from a "reliable source" who observed marijuana in the defendant's home and provided directions to that home. The court found, understandably, that this barebones information was not sufficient to establish probable cause, but the government argued that the tip had been corroborated by the facts that: 1) the informant had given accurate directions to the defendant's home and 2) the informant, in describing the defendant's activity, had accurately described what marijuana looks like and how it is packaged and sold. The court found that this corroboration was not enough to cure the defect in the tip under *Gates,* because "[a]lmost anyone can give directions to a particular house without knowing anything of substance about what goes on inside that house, and anyone who occasionally watches the evening news can make generalizations about what marijuana looks like and how it is packaged and sold."

### *The Gates Test Applied: Massachusetts v. Upton*

The Court reiterated its "totality of the circumstances" test in Massachusetts v. Upton, 466 U.S. 727 (1984), a per curiam disposition reversing the state supreme court. The Court described the facts as follows:

> At noon on September 11, 1980, Lt. Beland of the Yarmouth Police Department assisted in the execution of a search warrant for a motel room reserved by one Richard Kelleher at the Snug Harbor Motel in West Yarmouth. The search produced several items of identification, including credit cards, belonging to two persons whose homes had recently been burglarized. Other items taken in the burglaries, such as jewelry, silver and gold, were not found at the motel.

At 3:20 p.m. on the same day, Lt. Beland received a call from an unidentified female who told him that there was "a motor home full of stolen stuff" parked behind #5 Jefferson Ave., the home of respondent George Upton and his mother. She stated that the stolen items included jewelry, silver and gold. As set out in Lt. Beland's affidavit in support of a search warrant:

> She further stated that George Upton was going to move the motor home any time now because of the fact that Ricky Kelleher's motel room was raided and that George Upton had purchased these stolen items from Ricky Kelleher. This unidentified female stated that she had seen the stolen items but refused to identify herself because "he'll kill me," referring to George Upton. I then told this unidentified female that I knew who she was, giving her the name of Lynn Alberico, who I had met on May 16, 1980, at George Upton's repair shop off Summer St., in Yarmouthport. She was identified to me by George Upton as being his girlfriend, Lynn Alberico. The unidentified female admitted that she was the girl that I had named, stating that she was surprised that I knew who she was. She then told me that she'd broken up with George Upton and wanted to burn him. She also told me that she wouldn't give me her address or phone number but that she would contact me in the future, if need be.

Following the phone call, Lt. Beland went to Upton's house to verify that a motor home was parked on the property. Then, while other officers watched the premises, Lt. Beland prepared the application for a search warrant, setting out all the information noted above in an accompanying affidavit. He also attached the police reports on the two prior burglaries, along with lists of the stolen property. A magistrate issued the warrant, and a subsequent search of the motor home produced the items described by the caller and other incriminating evidence. The discovered evidence led to Upton's conviction on multiple counts of burglary, receiving stolen property, and related crimes.

The *Upton* Court explained why the state supreme court's invalidation of the warrant was inconsistent with *Gates*:

[T]he Massachusetts court reasoned, first, that the basis of the informant's knowledge was not "forcefully apparent" in the affidavit. Although the caller stated that she had seen the stolen items and that they were in the motor home, she did not specifically state that she saw them in the motor home. Second, the court concluded that "[n]one of the common bases for determining the credibility of an informant or the reliability of her information is present here." The caller was not a "tried and true" informant, her statement was not against penal interest, and she was not an "ordinary citizen" providing information as a witness to a crime. "She was an anonymous informant, and her unverified assent to the suggestion that she was Lynn Alberico does not take her out of that category."

Finally, the court felt that there was insufficient corroboration of the informant's tip to make up for its failure to satisfy the two-pronged test. The facts that tended to corroborate the informant's story were that the motor home was where it was supposed to be, that the caller knew of the motel raid which took place only three hours earlier, and that the caller knew the name of Upton and his girlfriend. But, much as the Supreme Court of Illinois did in the opinion we reviewed in *Gates*, the Massachusetts court reasoned that each item of corroborative evidence either related to innocent, nonsuspicious conduct or related to an event that took place in public. * * *

The Supreme Court took the Massachusetts Court to task in the following analysis:

We think that the Supreme Judicial Court of Massachusetts misunderstood our decision in *Gates*. We did not merely refine or qualify the "two-pronged test." We rejected it as hypertechnical and divorced from "the factual and practical considerations of everyday life on which reasonable and prudent men, not legal technicians, act." * * *

* * * The court did not consider Lt. Beland's affidavit in its entirety, giving significance to each relevant piece of information and balancing the relative weights of all the various indicia of reliability (and unreliability) attending the tip. Instead, the court insisted on judging bits and pieces of information in isolation against the artificial standards provided by the two-pronged test.

The Supreme Judicial Court also erred in failing to grant any deference to the decision of the magistrate to issue a warrant. Instead of merely deciding whether the evidence viewed as a whole provided a "substantial basis" for the magistrate's finding of probable cause, the court conducted a de novo probable cause determination. We rejected just such after-the-fact, de novo scrutiny in *Gates*. * * *

The *Upton* Court then applied the *Gates* analysis to the facts and found that the warrant was supported by probable cause:

Examined in light of *Gates*, Lt. Beland's affidavit provides a substantial basis for the issuance of the warrant. No single piece of evidence in it is conclusive. But the pieces fit neatly together and, so viewed, support the magistrate's determination that there was "a fair probability that contraband or evidence of crime" would be found in Upton's motor home. The informant claimed to have seen the stolen goods and gave a description of them which tallied with the items taken in recent burglaries. She knew of the raid on the motel room—which produced evidence connected to those burglaries—and that the room had been reserved by Kelleher. She explained the connection between Kelleher's motel room and the stolen goods in Upton's motor home. And she provided a motive both for her attempt at anonymity—fear of Upton's retaliation—and for furnishing the information—her recent breakup with Upton and her desire "to burn him."

The Massachusetts court dismissed Lt. Beland's identification of the caller as a mere "unconfirmed guess." But "probable cause does not demand the certainty we associate with formal trials." Lt. Beland noted that the caller "admitted that she was the girl I had named, stating that she was surprised that I knew who she was." It is of course possible that the caller merely adopted Lt. Beland's suggestion as "a convenient cover for her true identity." But given the caller's admission, her obvious knowledge of who Alberico was and how she was connected with Upton, and her explanation of her motive in calling, Lt. Beland's inference appears stronger than a mere uninformed and unconfirmed guess. It is enough that the inference was a reasonable one and conformed with the other pieces of evidence making up the total showing of probable cause.[8]

On remand in *Upton,* the Massachusetts Supreme Judicial Court declined to follow *Gates* and reaffirmed its commitment to the two-pronged test under the state constitution. Commonwealth v. Upton, 394 Mass. 363, 476 N.E.2d 548 (1985). It reasoned that the two-pronged test "aids lay people, such as the police and certain lay magistrates, in a way that the 'totality of the circumstances' test never could." Did the state supreme court correctly apply the *Spinelli* test to the *Upton* facts?

### 3.   The Citizen Informant

Under both *Spinelli* and *Gates*, the courts have distinguished police informants and anonymous informants from an ordinary citizen who identifies himself and reports a crime. The reason is that paid informants are presumptively unreliable given their dubious character and financial (or other) arrangements, and anonymous informants must be presumed unreliable because they may be using their anonymity for suspect reasons (e.g., to frame or harass an enemy). In contrast, identified citizen informants are considered reliable because they are presumed to be

---

[8]   Justice Stevens concurred in the judgment, expressing the opinion that the state supreme court should have indicated whether the warrant was valid under state law. Justices Brennan and Marshall dissented from the summary reversal of the state court.

motivated by "concern for society or for [their] own safety." State v. Paszek, 50 Wis.2d 619, 184 N.W.2d 836 (1971). See also United States v. Decoteau, 932 F.2d 1205 (7th Cir.1991) (where citizen-informant known to the officer told him that she had seen the defendant with a sawed-off shotgun, the informant's statement itself provided probable cause and corroboration was unnecessary); United States v. Blount, 123 F.3d 831 (5th Cir.1997) (en banc) (information coming from an identified neighbor of the defendant constituted probable cause, because the officers "had no reason to disbelieve Ms. Cooksey, or to question her motives or credibility"). There is also a thought that citizen-informants are not likely to lie directly to police because lying to police is a crime. Are you persuaded that citizen informants should be presumed reliable?

### 4. Accomplices

In United States v. Patterson, 150 F.3d 382 (4th Cir.1998), the police arrested Greene after two masked men robbed a bank. Greene confessed and identified Patterson as his accomplice. On the basis of this statement, the officers searched Patterson's car and found incriminating evidence. Patterson challenged the search as lacking probable cause. But the court held that the confession of a co-participant is itself sufficient to establish probable cause—no corroboration is required. The court noted that a defendant can be *convicted* solely on the basis of the uncorroborated testimony of an accomplice, and reasoned that "it would be contradictory to allow a defendant to be convicted based on the uncorroborated testimony of his co-perpetrator while refusing to find that the same statement would be sufficient to support probable cause." But is the accomplice's testimony under oath at trial really the "same statement" as the accomplice's stationhouse, hearsay confession implicating another in the crime?

### 5. Quantity of Information Required for Probable Cause

*Gates* dealt with the *quality* of information that could be considered in the probable cause determination, i.e., whether the informant's tip is reliable enough to be considered as proof of probable cause. Assuming that all the information is reliable, another question arises: has the information submitted established a "fair probability" of criminal activity? This question arises not only with respect to affidavits submitted to magistrates, but also with warrantless searches and seizures; even if the search or seizure is conducted pursuant to an exception to the warrant requirement, the officer is ordinarily required to have probable cause.

## *Equivocal Activity*

One circumstance in which a "fair probability" question is presented is where it is unknown whether a crime has been or is being committed. For example, what if the officer sees a person at 2:00 a.m. carrying a television and a stereo down the street in a shopping cart? There are many innocent explanations for this activity. Does that mean that there is no fair probability of criminal activity?

Consider United States v. Prandy-Binett, 995 F.2d 1069 (D.C.Cir.1993). Judge Randolph introduced the facts as follows:

> Detective John Centrella saw a small rectangular block wrapped in silver duct tape. To the uninitiated, the object's outward appearance said nothing about its contents. To Detective Centrella, the size, shape and wrapping of the object signified one kilogram of illegal narcotics. * * *
>
> Detective Centrella and another narcotics detective were on duty at Union Station, meeting trains arriving from New York City, a "source city" for drugs. As they watched departing passengers, their attention was drawn to an individual walking through the station faster than the others and trying to get around them. When the individual—Prandy-Binett—made eye contact with the detectives, who were in plain clothes, he moved even more quickly toward the exit. The detectives approached him and identified themselves. After telling the officers he had come from New Jersey, Prandy-Binett produced a one-way train ticket, purchased with cash, showing that his trip originated at Penn Station, New York City. After saying he lived in Washington, D.C., he handed the officers a driver's license showing Hyattsville, Maryland, as his residence. Detective Centrella's suspicions, aroused by these possible inconsistencies, were heightened by the cloth "tote" or "gym" bag Prandy-Binett carried on his shoulder. Prandy-Binett reported having spent a week working in New Jersey. Yet his only luggage was the small bag, which did not appear full. Asked whether the bag contained drugs or guns, Prandy-Binett said no. Detective Centrella then requested permission to search the bag. Prandy-Binett replied that he did not have to consent and that the bag contained only clothing. He took the bag from his shoulder, placed it on the ground, knelt down (as did the detective next to him), unzipped the bag and began pulling out a pair of blue jeans. This action uncovered a miniature shopping bag lying on its side, deep purple in color, a "perfume or a cologne bag" from Elizabeth Taylor Perfume. Unprompted, Prandy-Binett said, in evident reference to the perfume bag, "this is a gift." As Prandy-Binett continued to manipulate the blue jeans, a portion of a rectangular block, wrapped in silver duct tape, slid out of the

perfume bag. Believing the block to contain illegal drugs, Detective Centrella handcuffed Prandy-Binett, examined the wrapped object further, and seized it and the gym bag. A later field test on the contents of the wrapped block revealed cocaine.

Judge Randolph concluded that, based on the totality of circumstances, there was a fair probability that the rectangular block contained drugs, and upheld the narcotics conviction on which the search and seizure were based. He analyzed the fair probability question as follows:

> Somewhere between "less than evidence which would justify conviction" and "more than bare suspicion," probable cause is satisfied. The precise point is indeterminate. * * * This is why the detectives' observations up to the time the block slipped out of the perfume bag cannot be disregarded. * * * Is the probability increased if the passenger moves quickly through the station after leaving the train? Greater if the passenger also gives apparently deceptive answers when the police question him? Greater still if the passenger opens his bag and refers to a package wrapped in duct tape inside a fancy perfume bag as a "gift?" Neither courts nor law enforcement officers, nor anyone else for that matter, can quantify any of this. * * * Still, we are convinced that, up to the sighting of the duct tape package, the conditional probability was low, much too low to have satisfied the Fourth Amendment in light of the interests it protects.

> The case thus comes down to the detectives' inference of narcotics from the appearance of the wrapped block, and on the extent to which that inference enhanced the probability of Prandy-Binett's possessing drugs. We put the question in these terms because "probable cause" is evaluated not only from the perspective of a "prudent man," but also from the particular viewpoint of the officer involved in the search or seizure. * * *

Judge Randolph concluded that the sighting of the rectangular block wrapped in duct tape added enough to the other facts to constitute a fair probability of criminal activity. He noted three factors bearing on this probability assessment:

> There was first the block's bulk. * * * Detective Centrella was quite familiar with the bulk of packages containing one kilogram of cocaine. * * * Detective Centrella * * * thus had good reason for believing that the wrapped block in Prandy-Binett's gym bag was about the size of a package containing one kilogram of cocaine or heroin.

> The second consideration was the rectangular shape of the object. The portion protruding from the perfume bag was consistent with what the detectives knew to be the standard configuration, the

typical "kilo brick." * * * The brick-like shape of the object thus further alerted the detectives, in light of their training and experience, to the possible presence of narcotics.

The third factor was wrapping—silver duct tape (over plastic). Duct tape is attractive to traffickers because fingerprints are difficult to lift from its surface and because some criminals believe— erroneously—that it masks the odor of the drugs from police dogs. * * *

To Detective Centrella the wrapped block thus conveyed the message "one kilo of narcotics" just as surely as if the words were written on the tape. The circumstances leading up to the arrest and the incongruity of the crudely wrapped block inside the fancy perfume bag, together with Prandy-Binett's unsolicited disclaimer "This is a gift," must have confirmed what the detective saw in his mind's eye. * * * We cannot say exactly how probable it was that the block contained drugs, but we are convinced that it amounted, at the least, to a " 'fair probability' " Prandy-Binett was committing an offense.

Judge Edwards wrote a vigorous dissent in *Prandy-Binett*. He complained that the majority, "relying on a bizarre theory of 'conditional probabilities,' holds that probable cause can be based on the appearance of duct tape." He argued that the officers were motivated more by racial profiling than by any assessment of probability:

The circumstances that actually arouse police "suspicion" are obvious to anyone who bothers to look—individuals traveling through Union Station who are evidently poor, or people of color, are the individuals who are approached, questioned, stopped and searched. See Sheri Lynn Johnson, Race and the Decision to Detain a Suspect, 93 Yale L.J. 214, 225–37 (1983) (describing the varied uses of race as a motivation for police detention, and as an element in probable cause and reasonable suspicion analyses); Developments in the Law: Race and the Criminal Process, 101 Harv. L. Rev. 1472, 1496 (1988) (noting studies that reveal that "police use race as an independently significant, if not determinative, factor in deciding whom to follow, detain, search, or arrest").

Judge Edwards dismissed the supposed incongruity of carrying a package wrapped in duct tape as a gift in an expensive bag:

The majority also finds suspicious the "incongruity" of the sight of a "crudely wrapped block inside the fancy perfume bag." Such comment reveals a distinct lack of empathy for some members of our society— those without much disposable income, for example—who readily find use for a discarded shopping bag and who might very well wrap a gift with whatever packaging material is on hand, including duct tape.

Judge Edwards concluded that the placement of a rectangular object wrapped in duct tape inside one's luggage was simply not enough to rise to a fair probability of criminal activity. He argued that the "brick-like shape of a package might provide the observer with a general hint about the size of its contents, but the shape of such a package is too generic to make reasonable the inference that the contents of the package are also brick-shaped."

Who has the better argument in *Prandy-Binett*? Of course it is true that Prandy-Binett might have wrapped some figurines into a rectangular mass of duct tape. But does that mean there wasn't a fair probability that the package contained contraband?

Every circuit has decided cases on probable cause as applied to downloading or distributing child pornography on a computer. Most courts have held that probable cause can be found even without direct evidence that the defendant ever downloaded or distributed illegal images. Is that a proper application of the fair probability standard? See, e.g., United States v. Gourde, 440 F.3d 1065 (9th Cir. 2006) (en banc) (defendant's membership in a website that gave him unlimited access to child pornography on the site provided probable cause to believe that the defendant had actually downloaded illegal images); United States v. Martin, 426 F.3d 68 (2d Cir. 2005) (probable cause to search defendant's home existed on the basis of his membership in a chat group dedicated to child pornography; membership established a fair probability that the defendant did in fact exchange or download child pornography: it is "common-sense that one who voluntarily joins a child-pornography group and remains a member of that group * * * would download such pornography from the website and have it in his possession."). See also United States v. Perez, 484 F.3d 735 (5th Cir. 2007) (association between an IP address used for child pornography and a physical address constitutes a fair probability that criminal activity is occurring at that address: "though it was possible that the transmissions originated outside of the residence to which the IP address was assigned, it remained likely that the source of the transmissions was inside that residence.").

### *Probable Cause to Arrest*

The probable cause requirement applies to arrests as well as to searches. Probable cause to search is determined by whether there is a fair probability that the area or object searched contains evidence of a crime. Probable cause to arrest is determined by whether there is a fair probability to believe that the person arrested has committed a crime. Often these two fair probability assessments are actually one. For example, if there was probable cause to believe that the rectangular object in Prandy-Binett's luggage contained contraband, then there was also probable cause to arrest Prandy-Binett on a narcotics offense. In some situations, however, there may be probable cause to arrest, but not probable cause to search. For example, there may be a fair probability that a person robbed a bank five years ago; but that does not mean there is a fair probability to believe that the defendant's briefcase contains any evidence of the five year-old bank robbery. In other cases, there may be probable cause to search but not probable cause to arrest, such as where a criminal leaves a suitcase full of drugs in the home of an unsuspecting friend.

In the arrest context, the question of fair probability sometimes arises where police know that a crime has been committed, but they are not certain that a suspect is the perpetrator. Consider United States v. Valez, 796 F.2d 24 (2d Cir.1986), where the court set forth the following facts and analysis:

> At 4:30 p.m. on October 16, 1984, New York City Police Sergeant Albert Zarr and Officer James Allen were parked in a surveillance vehicle on West 48th Street between Eighth and Ninth Avenues in Manhattan. Zarr sat near the rear window watching the street with binoculars; Allen remained in the front seat. After observing what appeared to be a narcotics sale on the southeast corner of 48th and Ninth, Zarr sent one of his undercover police officers to make a drug buy.

> Zarr saw the undercover officer hand money to two men at the corner and in return receive two packets that later proved to contain cocaine. Zarr observed that one of the sellers was an Hispanic male in his twenties, wearing a black leather jacket, grey pants with a comb in the back pocket, and a white or off-white V-neck shirt with dark trim on the collar.

> Zarr described the sellers to Allen and radioed the description to the field team. At that point, the seller with the black jacket walked around the corner and disappeared from view. Zarr instructed Allen to follow the subject and make an arrest.

> Allen left the van immediately and proceeded west on 48th Street and then south on Ninth Avenue in search of the seller. Allen walked to the next corner, but did not see his subject. He decided to turn back on the hunch that the seller had ducked into one of the stores. When Allen returned to the corner of 48th and Ninth, he saw a man coming out of a Blimpie's fast food restaurant who matched the description that Zarr had given him. At 4:40 p.m., five to ten minutes after Allen left the surveillance van, he arrested the man. The person whom Allen had arrested was Valez. [Valez was brought

to the station, and a search of his person uncovered packets of cocaine.]

> When Sergeant Zarr and the undercover officer who made the "buy" returned to the stationhouse, they realized that Allen had arrested the wrong man. [Valez moved to suppress the cocaine on the ground that the arrest was illegal for lack of probable cause.] Valez relied primarily on the fact that Zarr's description did not include any mention of facial hair, whereas Valez had a small goatee and a thick moustache. Valez also argued that Zarr's description of the seller was overly general and that the mistaken arrest resulted from the negligent and unorganized conduct of the surveillance team.

The *Valez* Court held that the description of the perpetrator was not overly general, and that the officers had acted properly in arresting Valez, even though he was not in fact involved in the sale to the undercover officer:

> Given Zarr's detailed description of the seller's clothing, his failure to mention that the seller was clean-shaven does not constitute an unreasonable oversight. * * * [T]he police may justifiably place little reliance on the presence or absence of facial hair on a suspect who otherwise matches a description because facial hair may be worn or taken off as a disguise. * * *

Dissenting Judge Oakes argued that Officer Zarr's description was too general to support the conclusion that there was probable cause to arrest:

> By sending an officer into the area with a description only of race, approximate age, and clothing and, oh yes, of a comb in the hip pocket—but not mentioning facial hair or its absence, or the length of the suspect's haircut—Zarr was insufficiently distinguishing the person who made the sale from other Latin males of not uncommon appearance in the immediate area. It was the equivalent of "identifying" a suspect in the Wall Street area by describing him as a white, thirty-ish man with a button-down shirt and dark pinstripe suit, carrying a leather attache case.

Who has the better of the argument on probable cause, the majority or the dissent? Would it have mattered if Zarr had arrested the real seller before Allen had arrested Valez?

Compare the result in *Valez* with that of United States v. Kithcart, 134 F.3d 529 (3d Cir. 1998). Officers received three radio transmissions reporting separate armed robberies. Two robberies were reported in Bensalem Township and one in the adjacent Bristol Township. The time and the exact location of the robbery in Bristol Township was not specified. The perpetrators were described as "two black males in a black sports car." One of the perpetrators might have been wearing white clothes, and the vehicle was described as a "possible Z–28, possible Camaro." Ten minutes after the last radio transmission, concerning the robbery in Bristol Township, Officer Nelson spotted a black Nissan 300ZX, about a mile from Bristol Township. The vehicle was being driven by an African-American male, who appeared to be the only person in the car. Officer Nelson testified that since she had received the last radio transmission, this was the first time she had come upon either a black car or an African-American driver. She signalled the car to pull over, and "saw two sets of arms raised toward the roof of the car, and she realized that there were two people in the car." Eventually the officer searched the car, and found firearms. Kithcart, the driver, was charged with being a felon in possession of a firearm. The trial court denied Kithcart's suppression motion, holding that Officer Nelson had probable cause to arrest Kithcart when she pulled him over, and therefore that the search of the car was a proper search incident to a valid arrest.

The court of appeals, however, held that Officer Nelson did not have probable cause to arrest Kithcart when she pulled him over. The court analyzed the probable cause standard, in light of the facts, as follows:

> The mere fact that Kithcart is black and the perpetrators had been described as two black males is plainly insufficient. * * * Moreover, the match between the description of the perpetrators' car (a black sports car, "possible Z–28, possible Camaro)" and the vehicle in which Kithcart was spotted (a black Nissan 300ZX) was far from precise. Although the Camaro Z–28 and the Nissan 300ZX could be considered "sports cars," there was no evidence offered at the suppression hearing that the shapes of the two cars were sufficiently similar so as to warrant an inference that a 300ZX could be mistaken for a Z–28.

> Nor is probable cause established by either the location or time of the stop. There was no evidence presented as to where in Bristol Township the final robbery occurred; nor was there evidence presented that the Bristol robbery occurred shortly before Officer Nelson stopped the car carrying Kithcart. * * * In other words, armed with information that two black males driving a black sports car were believed to have committed three robberies in the area some relatively short time earlier, Officer Nelson could not justifiably arrest any African-American man who happened to drive by in any type of black sports car.

What accounts for the different results in *Valez* and *Kithcart*? What more could the officer in *Kithcart* have found to make the case for probable cause?

For another interesting case on probable cause, see Valente v. Wallace, 332 F.3d 30 (1st Cir. 2003), where the court found probable cause to arrest an employee for writing notes to the employer containing bomb threats. The arrest was based mostly on the conclusion of a handwriting analyst. The court recognized that handwriting analysis was an "inexact science" but found the expert's conclusion to be a "powerful start" toward probable cause. Added to this was the fact that the letters began shortly after the employee started working for the company; that they were found in the building where she worked; and that she acted nervously when questioned about the notes.

### *Mistaken Arrests*

As indicated by *Valez,* probable cause to arrest (or to search) can exist even though the police are mistaken in believing that the person arrested committed a crime. The question for probable cause is not accuracy but rather fair probability. See Hill v. California, 401 U.S. 797 (1971) (if police have probable cause to arrest Hill and have probable cause to believe that Miller is Hill, they act properly if they arrest Miller); Hirsch v. Burke, 40 F.3d 900 (7th Cir.1994) (police had probable cause to arrest a person for public drunkenness, even though in fact the person was a diabetic in a state of insulin shock).

### *Probabilities with Multiple Suspects*

If a police officer finds drugs in a car, does he have probable cause to arrest everyone in the car? That is the question in the following case.

### MARYLAND V. PRINGLE

Supreme Court of the United States, 2003.
540 U.S. 366.

### CHIEF JUSTICE REHNQUIST delivered the opinion of the Court.

\* \* \*

At 3:16 a.m. on August 7, 1999, a Baltimore County Police officer stopped a Nissan Maxima for speeding. There were three occupants in the car: Donte Partlow, the driver and owner, respondent Pringle, the front-seat passenger, and Otis Smith, the back-seat passenger. The officer asked Partlow for his license and registration. When Partlow opened the glove compartment to retrieve the vehicle registration, the officer observed a large amount of rolled-up money in the glove compartment. The officer returned to his patrol car with Partlow's license and registration to check the computer system for outstanding violations. The computer check did not reveal any violations. The officer returned to the stopped car, had Partlow get out, and issued him an oral warning.

After a second patrol car arrived, the officer asked Partlow if he had any weapons or narcotics in the vehicle. Partlow indicated that he did not. Partlow then consented to a search of the vehicle. The search yielded $763 from the glove compartment and five plastic glassine baggies containing cocaine from behind the back-seat armrest. When the officer began the search the armrest was in the upright position flat against the rear seat. The officer pulled down the armrest and found the drugs, which had been placed between the armrest and the back seat of the car.

The officer questioned all three men about the ownership of the drugs and money, and told them that if no one admitted to ownership of the drugs he was going to arrest them all. The men offered no information regarding the ownership of the drugs or money. All three were placed under arrest and transported to the police station.

Later that morning, Pringle waived his rights under Miranda v. Arizona, and gave an oral and written confession in which he acknowledged that the cocaine belonged to him, that he and his friends were going to a party, and that he intended to sell the cocaine or "use it for sex." Pringle maintained that the other occupants of the car did not know about the drugs, and they were released.

The trial court denied Pringle's motion to suppress his confession as the fruit of an illegal arrest, holding that the officer had probable cause to arrest Pringle. A jury convicted Pringle of possession with intent to distribute cocaine and possession of cocaine. * * * The Court of Appeals of Maryland, by divided vote, reversed, holding that, absent specific facts tending to show Pringle's knowledge and dominion or control over the drugs, "the mere finding of cocaine in the back armrest when [Pringle] was a front seat passenger in a car being driven by its owner is insufficient to establish probable cause for an arrest for possession." We granted certiorari, and now reverse.

\* \* \*

It is uncontested in the present case that the officer, upon recovering the five plastic glassine baggies containing suspected cocaine, had probable cause to believe a felony had been committed. The sole question is whether the officer had probable cause to believe that Pringle committed that crime. Maryland law defines "possession" as "the exercise of actual or constructive dominion or control over a thing by one or more persons."

\* \* \*

In this case, Pringle was one of three men riding in a Nissan Maxima at 3:16 a.m. There was $763 of rolled-up cash in the glove compartment directly in front of Pringle. Five plastic glassine baggies of cocaine were behind the back-seat armrest and accessible to all three men. Upon questioning, the three men failed to offer any information with respect to the ownership of the cocaine or the money.

We think it an entirely reasonable inference from these facts that any or all three of the occupants had knowledge of, and exercised dominion and control over, the cocaine. Thus a reasonable officer could conclude that there was probable cause to believe Pringle committed the crime of possession of cocaine, either solely or jointly.

Pringle's attempt to characterize this case as a guilt-by-association case is unavailing. His reliance on Ybarra v. Illinois [discussed in the section on stop and frisk, infra] * * * is misplaced. In *Ybarra*, police officers obtained a warrant to search a tavern and its bartender for evidence of possession of a controlled substance. Upon entering the tavern, the officers conducted patdown searches of the customers present in the tavern, including Ybarra. Inside a cigarette pack retrieved from Ybarra's pocket, an officer found six tinfoil packets containing heroin. * * * We held that the search warrant did not permit body searches of all of the tavern's patrons and that the police could not pat down the patrons for weapons, absent individualized suspicion.

This case is quite different from *Ybarra*. Pringle and his two companions were in a relatively small automobile, not a public tavern. * * * [A] car passenger—unlike the unwitting tavern patron in *Ybarra*—will often be engaged in a common enterprise with the driver, and have the same interest in concealing the fruits or the evidence of their wrongdoing. Here we think it was reasonable for the officer to infer a common enterprise among the three men. The quantity of drugs and cash in the car indicated the likelihood of drug dealing, an enterprise to which a dealer would be unlikely to admit an innocent person with the potential to furnish evidence against him.

\* \* \*

## QUESTIONS ON PRINGLE

Would the officers have had probable cause to arrest Pringle's 15 year-old son if he were a fourth occupant in the car? What about Pringle's 87 year-old great grandmother? Would the result in *Pringle* have been the same if the officer found no drugs in the car but obtained consent to search the trunk and found the drugs there?

Assume after *Pringle* that officers are in an area known for drug-trafficking and they know that at least one of every three residents is committing drug crimes. They just don't know which ones. Can they arrest every third person that comes walking down the street on the fair probability that they are involved in drug crimes? What about one out of every three residents in the area?

### *Dog Sniffs and Probable Cause: Florida v. Harris*

A dog sniff of luggage is not a search under United States v. Place, *supra*, but what about the *opening* of the luggage after a positive dog sniff? That would be a search because it could uncover legitimate private activity. This is because a dog's positive alert to a piece of luggage does not always mean that drugs are located there. Dogs are fallible.

If a dog positively alerts, the question arises whether that is sufficient to constitute probable cause. The Supreme Court addressed that question in Florida v. Harris, 133 S. Ct. 1050 (2013). Justice Kagan wrote for the Court as it addressed a vehicle stop by an officer with a drug sniffing dog. The dog alerted at the driver's door handle after the suspect appeared nervous and refused consent. A search of the car revealed no drugs the dog was trained to detect but a number of substances used to make methamphetamine. Florida charged Harris with possessing pseudoephedrine for use in manufacturing methamphetamine. While he was released on bail, the same officer stopped him again, the dog alerted at the same place, and nothing was found in a search of the car. A trial judge denied a motion to suppress, and the Florida Supreme Court reversed. Justice Kagan described the issue as follows: * * *

> The Florida Supreme Court * * * [held]  that Wheetley [the officer] lacked probable cause to search Harris's vehicle under the Fourth Amendment. "[W]hen a dog alerts," the court wrote, "the fact that the dog has been trained and certified is simply not enough to establish probable cause." To demonstrate a dog's reliability, the State needed to produce a wider array of evidence:
>
> > "[T]he State must present ... the dog's training and certification records, an explanation of the meaning of the particular training and certification, field performance records (including any unverified alerts), and evidence concerning the experience and training of the officer handling the dog, as well as any other objective evidence known to the officer about the dog's reliability."
>
> * * *

Justice Kagan analyzed the probable cause question, and reliability concerns, as follows:

> Evidence of a dog's satisfactory performance in a certification or training program can itself provide sufficient reason to trust his alert. If a bona fide organization has certified a dog after testing his reliability in a controlled setting, a court can presume (subject to any conflicting evidence offered) that the dog's alert provides probable cause to search. The same is true, even in the absence of formal certification, if the dog has recently and successfully completed a

training program that evaluated his proficiency in locating drugs. After all, law enforcement units have their own strong incentive to use effective training and certification programs, because only accurate drug-detection dogs enable officers to locate contraband without incurring unnecessary risks or wasting limited time and resources.

A defendant, however, must have an opportunity to challenge such evidence of a dog's reliability, whether by cross-examining the testifying officer or by introducing his own fact or expert witnesses. The defendant, for example, may contest the adequacy of a certification or training program, perhaps asserting that its standards are too lax or its methods faulty. So too, the defendant may examine how the dog (or handler) performed in the assessments made in those settings. Indeed, evidence of the dog's (or handler's) history in the field * * * may sometimes be relevant * * *. And even assuming a dog is generally reliable, circumstances surrounding a particular alert may undermine the case for probable cause—if, say, the officer cued the dog (consciously or not), or if the team was working under unfamiliar conditions.

In short, a probable-cause hearing focusing on a dog's alert should proceed much like any other. * * *

Justice Kagan found that the record "amply supported the trial court's determination that Aldo's alert gave Wheetley probable cause to search Harris's truck." The state produced "substantial evidence" of the dog's training and efficiency, as it had completed two recent drug-detection courses and maintained its proficiency through weekly training exercises. Moreover, Harris's cross-examination of the handler failed to rebut the State's showing of reliability. Justice Kagan explained as follows:

Harris principally contended in the trial court that because Wheetley did not find any of the substances Aldo was trained to detect, Aldo's two alerts must have been false. But * * * here we doubt that Harris's logic does justice to Aldo's skills. Harris cooked and used methamphetamine on a regular basis; so as Wheetley later surmised, Aldo likely responded to odors that Harris had transferred to the driver's-side door handle of his truck. A well-trained drug-detection dog *should* alert to such odors; his response to them might appear a mistake, but in fact is not. And still more fundamentally, we do not evaluate probable cause in hindsight, based on what a search does or does not turn up. For the reasons already stated, Wheetley had good cause to view Aldo as a reliable detector of drugs. And no special circumstance here gave Wheetley reason to discount Aldo's usual dependability or distrust his response to Harris's truck.

### Probable Cause for an Arrest Different from the Charge on Which the Defendant Was Arrested: Devenpeck v. Alford

In Devenpeck v. Alford, 543 U.S. 146 (2004), Justice Scalia wrote for a unanimous Court (the Chief Justice not participating) as it addressed "the question whether an arrest is lawful under the Fourth Amendment when the criminal offense for which there is probable cause to arrest is not "closely related" to the offense stated by the arresting officer at the time of arrest." Alford had stopped to assist a disabled automobile before Washington State Patrol Officer Haner came to the scene and Alford left. Haney informed his supervisor, Devenpeck, that Alford appeared to be an impersonator or "wannabe cop". Haney pursued Alford and found that he was listening to a sheriff's office police frequency on a special radio, and that handcuffs and a hand-held police scanner were in the car.

Sergeant Devenpeck arrived at the scene where Haner stopped Alford, was told by Haner that he believed Alford had been impersonating a police officer. Devenpeck discovered that Alford had a tape recorder with the play and record buttons depressed on the passenger seat of his car and asked Alford about his wig-wag headlights. Devenpeck ordered Alford to play the recorded tape, found that Alford was taping his conversations with the officers, and arrested Alford for a violation of the state privacy act.

Haner booked Alford for violating the privacy act and issued a ticket for his flashing headlights. A state court dismissed both charges, and Alford filed suit against the officers for an unlawful arrest, claiming that there was no probable cause warranting arrest. A jury found for the officers despite the fact that it was instructed that at the time of Alford's arrest a state court of appeals had clearly held that the taping of the officers was not a crime.

The court of appeals held 2–1 that there was "no evidence to support the jury's verdict." The majority rejected the argument that probable cause existed to arrest Alford for the offenses of impersonating a law-enforcement officer and obstructing a law-enforcement officer because those offenses were not "closely related" to the offense invoked by Devenpeck as he took Alford into custody.

The Supreme Court reversed. Justice Scalia explained:

> Our cases make clear that an arresting officer's state of mind (except for the facts that he knows) is irrelevant to the existence of probable cause. That is to say, his subjective reason for making the arrest need not be the criminal offense as to which the known facts provide probable cause. * * *

> The rule that the offense establishing probable cause must be "closely related" to, and based on the same conduct as, the offense

identified by the arresting officer at the time of arrest is inconsistent with this precedent. Such a rule makes the lawfulness of an arrest turn upon the motivation of the arresting officer—eliminating, as validating probable cause, facts that played no part in the officer's expressed subjective reason for making the arrest, and offenses that are not "closely related" to that subjective reason. This means that the constitutionality of an arrest under a given set of known facts will vary from place to place and from time to time, depending on whether the arresting officer states the reason for the detention and, if so, whether he correctly identifies a general class of offense for which probable cause exists. An arrest made by a knowledgeable, veteran officer would be valid, whereas an arrest made by a rookie *in precisely the same circumstances* would not. We see no reason to ascribe to the Fourth Amendment such arbitrarily variable protection.

\* \* \* Subjective intent of the arresting officer, *however* it is determined (and of course subjective intent is *always* determined by objective means), is simply no basis for invalidating an arrest. Those are lawfully arrested whom the facts known to the arresting officers give probable cause to arrest.

## 6.  Collective Knowledge

In Whiteley v. Warden, 401 U.S. 560 (1971), the Supreme Court declared that "police officers called upon to aid other officers in executing arrest warrants are entitled to assume that the officers requesting aid offered the magistrate the information requisite to support an independent judicial assessment of probable cause." This approach means that once Officer A demonstrates to a magistrate probable cause to arrest a suspect, any other officer can make the arrest on the assumption that the warrant is valid. The arresting officer need not have independent knowledge of the arrestee's criminal activity. The same rule applies in warrantless arrest cases. If Officer B makes an arrest pursuant to orders from Officer A, and the latter had probable cause for the order, the arrest is valid—Officer B need not be familiar with the facts supporting probable cause. Likewise with searches—the officer who actually conducts the search need not have personal knowledge of the facts supporting probable cause. All that is required is collective knowledge in the police department that rises to the level of probable cause.

## 7.  Staleness of Information

One problem that sometimes arises in assessing probable cause is that the officer's information is dated. For example, an officer may receive information from a reliable informant that the defendant had an ounce of marijuana in his home on January 1. Assuming that the informant's tip satisfies *Gates*, there is still a problem if the search of the defendant's home is conducted on July 1. Certainly, there is no fair probability that the same ounce of marijuana is still in the defendant's house six months later.

An example of a staleness problem arose in United States v. Harris, 20 F.3d 445 (11th Cir.1994). Police had probable cause to believe that Ford was involved in a narcotics conspiracy in 1988. However, the warrant to search Ford's house was not issued until 1990. 1989 had apparently been a bad year for the conspiracy: several drug couriers had been arrested and large amounts of drugs had been seized. Two of Ford's top coconspirators had become embroiled in an altercation, and each had reported the other to the authorities. Ford argued that, under these circumstances, the information that he was involved in a narcotics conspiracy had become stale. The *Harris* Court had this to say about the staleness inquiry:

> When reviewing staleness challenges we do not apply some talismanic rule which establishes arbitrary time limitations * * *. In this case-by-case determination we may consider the maturity of the information, nature of the suspected crime (discrete crimes or ongoing conspiracy), habits of the accused, character of the items sought, and nature and function of the premises to be searched.

Applying these factors, the *Harris* Court found that the information provided to the magistrate established a fair probability that Ford was still involved in a narcotics conspiracy in 1990. The court noted that the conspiracy was "longstanding and protracted" and that the affidavit showed that Ford "had no visible source of income, yet owned a large house" and was still associated with some of his coconspirators. See also United States v. Spikes, 158 F.3d 913 (6th Cir.1998) (four-year-old information concerning drug activity was not stale where it was corroborated by more recent information, to lead to a fair conclusion that the defendant was engaged in continuous large-scale drug activity); United States v. Farmer, 370 F.3d 435 (4th Cir. 2004) (nine month-old information about the defendant's large-scale counterfeiting operation was not stale because it was "unlikely to have been suddenly abandoned" and the information indicated that the operation had been going on for a long time).

## 8.   First Amendment Concerns

In New York v. P.J. Video, 475 U.S. 868 (1986), Justice Rehnquist wrote for the Court as it held that warrants authorizing the seizure of "adult" tapes from a video store were supported by probable cause to believe that the tapes were pornographic. Justice Rehnquist first noted that "an application for a warrant authorizing the seizure of materials presumptively protected by the First Amendment should be evaluated under the same standard of probable cause used to review warrants generally." The Court found that the affidavits in the instant case contained more than enough information to conclude that there was a "fair probability" that the movies satisfied the statutory definition of obscenity (i.e., predominant appeal to prurient interest in sex, specific sexual conduct presented in patently offensive manner, and no serious redeeming social value).

Justice Marshall, joined by Justices Brennan and Stevens, dissented. He argued that the affidavits described only some excerpted scenes, and not the entirety of each film. So in his view the magistrate could not have determined that the sex acts pervaded the films or that the films as a whole lacked artistic value; while the *affidavits* were pervaded with sex acts, it did not necessarily follow that the *films* were obscene. The majority's response to Justice Marshall's argument was that one of the affidavits, for example, described five hardcore sex scenes, taking place in a 93 minute film; therefore the sheer volume of sex acts depicted in the affidavit established at least a fair probability that there was no time left for the film to include any matters of redeeming social value.

When *P.J. Video* returned to the state courts, the New York Court of Appeals held in New York v. P.J. Video, Inc., 68 N.Y.2d 296, 508 N.Y.S.2d 907, 501 N.E.2d 556 (1986), that the state constitution barred reliance on the totality of circumstances approach for warrants directed at allegedly obscene materials. It reasoned that all aspects of the statutory definition of obscenity are significant and that the Supreme Court's approach effectively ignored some of the statutory elements.

## B.  PROBABLE CAUSE, SPECIFICITY AND REASONABLENESS

### 1.  The Things That Can Be Seized

Up until 1967, the Court had consistently held that the Fourth Amendment prohibited the government from searching for or seizing anything other than the "fruits and instrumentalities" of a crime. "Mere evidence" of a crime was considered beyond the scope of a permissible Fourth Amendment search. So for example, if officers had probable cause to believe that the defendant was a narcotics dealer, they could search for and seize narcotics and related paraphernalia, but they would not be permitted to look for phone records or storage locker rental agreements, because these things were "mere evidence" of the crime. Obviously, the mere evidence rule severely constricted the scope of a search that a magistrate could authorize.

In the following case, the Warren Court rejected the "mere evidence" limitation—a decision that dramatically expanded the possibilities for law enforcement, both when searching pursuant to a warrant and when searching pursuant to an exception to the warrant requirement.

## WARDEN V. HAYDEN
Supreme Court of the United States, 1967.
387 U.S. 294.

### JUSTICE BRENNAN delivered the opinion of the Court.

We review in this case the validity of the proposition that there is under the Fourth Amendment a "distinction between merely evidentiary materials, on the one hand, which may not be seized either under the authority of a search warrant or during the course of a search incident to arrest, and on the other hand, those objects which may validly be seized including the instrumentalities and means by which a crime is committed, the fruits of crime such as stolen property, weapons by which escape of the person arrested might be effected, and property the possession of which is a crime."

A Maryland court sitting without a jury convicted respondent of armed robbery. Items of his clothing, a cap, jacket, and trousers, among other things, were seized during a search of his home, and were admitted in evidence without objection. After unsuccessful state court proceedings, he sought and was denied federal habeas corpus relief in the District Court for Maryland. A divided panel of the Court of Appeals for the Fourth Circuit reversed. The Court of Appeals believed that * * * respondent was correct in his contention that the clothing seized was improperly admitted in evidence because the items had "evidential value only" and therefore were not lawfully subject to seizure. * * * We reverse.

* * *

[The Court held that the search of Hayden's house, while without a warrant, was justified by exigent circumstances].

We come, then, to the question whether, even though the search was lawful, the Court of Appeals was correct in holding that the seizure and introduction of the items of clothing violated the Fourth Amendment because they are "mere evidence." The distinction made by some of our cases between seizure of items of evidential value only and seizure of instrumentalities, fruits, or contraband has been criticized by courts and commentators. * * * We today reject the distinction as based on premises no longer accepted as rules governing the application of the Fourth Amendment.

* * *

Nothing in the language of the Fourth Amendment supports the distinction between "mere evidence" and instrumentalities, fruits of crime, or contraband. On its face, the provision assures the "right of the

people to be secure in their persons, houses, papers, and effects . . . ,"
without regard to the use to which any of these things are applied. This
"right of the people" is certainly unrelated to the "mere evidence"
limitation. Privacy is disturbed no more by a search directed to a purely
evidentiary object than it is by a search directed to an instrumentality,
fruit, or contraband. * * * Moreover, nothing in the nature of property
seized as evidence renders it more private than property seized, for
example, as an instrumentality; quite the opposite may be true. Indeed,
the distinction is wholly irrational, since, depending on the
circumstances, the same "papers and effects" may be "mere evidence" in
one case and "instrumentality" in another.

* * *

The requirements of the Fourth Amendment can secure the same
protection of privacy whether the search is for "mere evidence" or for
fruits, instrumentalities or contraband. There must, of course, be a
nexus—automatically provided in the case of fruits, instrumentalities or
contraband—between the item to be seized and criminal behavior. Thus
in the case of "mere evidence," probable cause must be examined in terms
of cause to believe that the evidence sought will aid in a particular
apprehension or conviction. In so doing, consideration of police purposes
will be required. But no such problem is presented in this case. The
clothes found * * * matched the description of those worn by the robber
and the police therefore could reasonably believe that the items would aid
in the identification of the culprit.

* * *

The rationale most frequently suggested for the rule preventing the
seizure of evidence is that "limitations upon the fruit to be gathered tend
to limit the quest itself." But privacy would be just as well served by a
restriction on search to the even-numbered days of the month. * * * And it
would have the extra advantage of avoiding hair-splitting questions * * *.
The "mere evidence" limitation has spawned exceptions so numerous and
confusion so great, in fact, that it is questionable whether it affords
meaningful protection. But if its rejection does enlarge the area of
permissible searches, the intrusions are nevertheless made after fulfilling
the probable cause and particularity requirements of the Fourth
Amendment and after the intervention of "a neutral and detached
magistrate." The Fourth Amendment allows intrusions upon privacy
under these circumstances, and there is no viable reason to distinguish
intrusions to secure "mere evidence" from intrusions to secure fruits,
instrumentalities, or contraband.

The judgment of the Court of Appeals is reversed.

JUSTICE BLACK concurs in the result.

[The concurring opinion by JUSTICE FORTAS, joined by CHIEF JUSTICE WARREN, is omitted].

**JUSTICE DOUGLAS, dissenting.**

\* \* \*

\* \* \* The personal effects and possessions of the individual (all contraband and the like excepted) are sacrosanct from prying eyes, from the long arm of the law, from any rummaging by police. Privacy involves the choice of the individual to disclose or to reveal what he believes, what he thinks, what he possesses. \* \* \* The Framers, who were as knowledgeable as we, knew what police surveillance meant and how the practice of rummaging through one's personal effects could destroy freedom.

\* \* \*

\* \* \* I would \* \* \* leave with the individual the choice of opening his private effects (apart from contraband and the like) to the police or keeping their contents a secret and their integrity inviolate. The existence of that choice is the very essence of the right of privacy. \* \* \*

### NOTE ON THE MERE EVIDENCE RULE

By abrogating the mere evidence limitation, the Warden v. Hayden Court dramatically expanded the search power of police officers. For example, without a mere evidence limitation, an innocent third party's home or office may be the legitimate object of a search; evidence that might be relevant to a crime can be spread far and wide, while the fruits and instrumentalities of a crime are more often kept with the perpetrators. As you proceed through this Chapter, try to determine how the cases discussed would have been resolved under a mere evidence limitation. You will undoubtedly conclude that Warden v. Hayden had a fundamental, pro-prosecution effect on Fourth Amendment law.

Does the result in Warden v. Hayden comport with your impression of the Warren Court's criminal procedure jurisprudence? See Saltzburg, Criminal Procedure in the 1960s: A Reality Check, 42 Drake L.J. 179 (1993) (noting that the Warren Court's pro-defendant reputation is belied by cases like Warden v. Hayden).

### 2.    Probable Cause as to Location of Evidence

Sometimes police have probable cause to believe that a suspect has committed a crime and is in control of certain evidence, but are less sure where the evidence is located. Can they obtain a search warrant for the premises where the suspect lives on the theory that it is the most likely place to search for evidence? The premises where the suspect works? The places that the suspect frequents? In Zurcher v. Stanford Daily, 436 U.S. 547, 556 (1978), the majority stated that "[t]he critical element * * * is reasonable cause to believe that the specific 'things' to be searched for and seized are located on the property to which entry is sought." This will depend on "the type of crime, the nature of the items sought, the suspect's opportunity for concealment and normal inferences about where a criminal might hide" evidence of a crime. See United States v. Jones, 994 F.2d 1051 (3d Cir.1993) (sufficient nexus between robbery and defendants' homes, because items sought, such as cash, were the kinds of things "that criminals like to keep in secure places like their homes").

It follows that probable cause does not automatically exist to search a person's home—or any other particular location—simply because that person has been involved in a crime. For example, in United States v. Lalor, 996 F.2d 1578 (4th Cir.1993), the court held that a warrant to search Lalor's residence was invalid because it lacked probable cause. Investigation showed only that Lalor and others sold drugs on the street. The court reasoned that street sales did not raise a fair probability that Lalor kept evidence of drug activity at his house. The court emphasized that the government offered no information to the magistrate that linked the street sales with any activity at Lalor's house. The court, citing cases, declared that "residential searches have been upheld only where some information links the criminal activity to the defendant's residence." Compare United States v. Pitts, 6 F.3d 1366 (9th Cir.1993) (finding a sufficient nexus between defendant's narcotics activity and his home: "in the case of drug dealers, evidence is likely to be found where the dealers live"). See also United States v. McCoy, 483 F.3d 862 (8th Cir. 2007) (probable cause to believe that the defendant had child pornography in his house did not establish probable cause to search his car).

## 3.   Searches of Non-Suspects' Premises

In some investigations, police may have probable cause to search a person's premises for evidence even though they are not suspected of a crime. That and several other problems arose in Zurcher v. Stanford Daily, 436 U.S. 547 (1978). Officers had probable cause to believe that a Stanford Daily photographer had taken pictures of demonstrators who attacked a group of police officers. A warrant was obtained to search the Daily's offices for negatives, film, and pictures taken at the demonstration. There was no allegation that members of the Daily staff were in any way involved in unlawful acts. The Daily's photographic laboratories, filing cabinets, desks, and wastepaper baskets were searched. Locked drawers and rooms were not opened. No evidence pertinent to the assault on the officers was uncovered. Thereafter, the Daily and some members of its staff brought a civil action seeking declaratory and injunctive relief, alleging that the entry, even though with a warrant, was in violation of the Fourth Amendment.

The lower court in *Zurcher* held that the Fourth Amendment did not permit a warrant to search for materials in possession of one not suspected of a crime, unless it was apparent that a subpoena and a court order would be futile. But the Supreme Court reversed and found the warrant and the search valid, in an opinion by Justice White.

Justice White defined the question presented:

> The issue here is how the Fourth Amendment is to be construed and applied to the "third party" search, the recurring situation where state authorities have probable cause to believe that fruits, instrumentalities, or other evidence of crime is located on identified property but do not then have probable cause to believe that the owner or possessor of the property is himself implicated in the crime that has occurred or is occurring.

Justice White declared that there was nothing special about the search of a third party's premises. The question in any case is whether there is probable cause to believe that evidence of a crime will be found in the place to be searched:

> Under existing law, valid warrants may be issued to search *any* property, whether or not occupied by a third party, at which there is probable cause to believe that fruits, instrumentalities, or evidence of a crime will be found. Nothing on the face of the Amendment suggests that a third-party search warrant should not normally issue. The Warrant Clause speaks of search warrants issued on "probable cause" and "particularly describing the place to be searched, and the persons or things to be seized." * * *.

> \* \* \*

> The critical element in a reasonable search is not that the owner of the property is suspected of crime but that there is reasonable cause to believe that the specific "things" to be searched for and seized are located on the property to which entry is sought. * * *

Justice White emphasized the practical problems that would arise for law enforcement if search warrants could not be issued for third party premises:

> [S]earch warrants are often employed early in an investigation, perhaps before the identity of any likely criminal and certainly before all the perpetrators are or could be known. The seemingly blameless third party in possession of the fruits or evidence may not be innocent at all; and if he is, he may nevertheless be so related to or so sympathetic with the culpable party that he cannot be relied upon to

retain and preserve the articles that may implicate his friends, or at least not to notify those who would be damaged by the evidence that the authorities are aware of its location. In any event, it is likely that the real culprits will have access to the property, and the delay involved in employing the subpoena *duces tecum,* offering as it does the opportunity to litigate its validity, could easily result in the disappearance of the evidence, whatever the good faith of the third party.

Justice White intimated that the reasonableness clause of the Fourth Amendment might impose some limitations on the execution of a search, even if the search was supported by a warrant issued upon probable cause. However, "the courts may not, in the name of Fourth Amendment reasonableness, forbid the States from issuing warrants to search for evidence simply because the owner or possessor of the place to be searched is not then reasonably suspected of criminal involvement."

Finally, Justice White rejected the argument that First Amendment concerns required a limitation on the use of warrants to search the office of a newspaper:

> There is no reason to believe * * * that magistrates cannot guard against searches of the type, scope, and intrusiveness that would actually interfere with the timely publication of a newspaper. Nor, if the requirements of specificity and reasonableness are properly applied, policed, and observed, will there be any occasion or opportunity for officers to rummage at large in newspaper files or to intrude into or to deter normal editorial and publication decisions. * * * Nor are we convinced * * * that confidential sources will disappear and that the press will suppress news because of fears of warranted searches.

Justice Stewart, joined by Justice Marshall, dissented in *Zurcher* and argued that the use of a warrant to search a newspaper constituted an infringement on First Amendment rights.

Justice Stevens wrote a separate dissent, in which he noted that the problem of third party searches had been created by "the profound change in Fourth Amendment law that occurred in 1967, when Warden v. Hayden was decided." He elaborated as follows:

> In the pre-*Hayden* era warrants were used to search for contraband, weapons, and plunder, but not for "mere evidence." The practical effect of the rule prohibiting the issuance of warrants to search for mere evidence was to narrowly limit not only the category of objects, but also the category of persons and the character of the privacy interests that might be affected by an unannounced police search.

Just as the witnesses who participate in an investigation or a trial far outnumber the defendants, the persons who possess evidence that may help to identify an offender, or explain an aspect of a criminal transaction, far outnumber those who have custody of weapons or plunder. Countless law-abiding citizens—doctors, lawyers, merchants, customers, bystanders—may have documents in their possession that relate to an ongoing criminal investigation. The consequences of subjecting this large category of persons to unannounced police searches are extremely serious. The *ex parte* warrant procedure enables the prosecutor to obtain access to privileged documents that could not be examined if advance notice gave the custodian an opportunity to object. The search for the documents described in a warrant may involve the inspection of files containing other private matter. The dramatic character of a sudden search may cause an entirely unjustified injury to the reputation of the persons searched.

Justice Stevens argued that a "showing of probable cause that was adequate to justify the issuance of a warrant to search for stolen goods in the 18th century does not automatically satisfy the new dimensions of the Fourth Amendment in the post-*Hayden* era." He concluded that "[t]he only conceivable justification for an unannounced search of an innocent citizen is the fear that, if notice were given, he would conceal or destroy the object of the search." As there was nothing in the warrant application to indicate that the Daily would destroy evidence, Justice Stevens contended that the search, even though pursuant to a warrant, was unreasonable.

Congress responded to *Zurcher* by enacting the Privacy Protection Act of 1980, 42 U.S.C. § 2000 aa-6(f), which limited searches of the media and the press.

### 4. Describing the Place to Be Searched

The warrant clause requires a particularized description of the place to be searched. The Colonial experience with general warrants was the major reason for including the Fourth Amendment in the Bill of Rights; the particularity requirement is designed to protect against the abuses of a general warrant, i.e., a warrant giving authority to an officer to search wherever the officer wants.

#### *Function of the Particularity Requirement*

The requirement of a particular description of the place to be searched provides at least three protections:

First, if the executing officer has no knowledge of the underlying facts, the particular description of the premises in the warrant operates as a necessary control on his discretion. We would not want an unknowing officer, armed with a single search warrant, to search every "house on Second Avenue," for example. See, e.g., United States v. Nafzger, 965 F.2d 213 (7th Cir.1992) ("By accepting 'the Western District of Wisconsin' as a particular description of the place the truck was to be found we would be giving the government carte blanche to search anywhere in that district that the truck might conceivably be found, condoning the use of the pernicious general warrant, and redacting the particularity requirement from the fourth amendment."). See also United States v. Stefonek, 179 F.3d 1030 (7th Cir.1999) (particularity requirement is necessary to "make sure that the law enforcement officer who executes the warrant stays within the bounds set by the issuer").

Second, even if the executing officer knows the place she wants to search, the particular description in the warrant establishes a specific record of probable cause as to location *prior* to the search. The officer is not permitted, after the fact, to construct the case that would have supported probable cause to search the place she eventually chose.

Finally, the particularity requirement prevents the officer from using the warrant as a blank check to expand a search of a location by relying on an overly general description of the place to be searched. See, e.g., United States v. Cannon, 264 F.3d 875 (9th Cir. 2001) (warrant to search a house did not permit officers to search a building that was unconnected to the house).

### *Reasonable Particularity*

The Fourth Amendment requires that the warrant must set forth the location of the place to be searched with reasonable particularity. Technical precision is not required in all cases. The degree of particularity that is reasonable depends on the nature of the place to be searched and on the information that an officer could reasonably obtain about the location before a warrant is issued.

For example, it is well accepted that "two or more apartments in the same building stand on the same footing as two or more houses. A single warrant cannot describe an entire building when cause is shown for searching only one apartment." Moore v. United States, 461 F.2d 1236, 1238 (D.C.Cir.1972). But in Maryland v. Garrison, 480 U.S. 79 (1987), the Court upheld a warrant authorizing the search of a "third floor apartment" even though there were actually two apartments on the third floor. Baltimore police officers had probable cause to believe that illegal activity was being conducted in an apartment on the third floor of a four-story building, and they conducted an investigation to determine whether there was more than one apartment on the floor. An officer obtained information from the utility company and telephone company that appeared to indicate that the entire third floor consisted of one apartment. The officer checked out the door buzzers outside the apartment building, but they did not indicate how many apartments were on any particular floor—there were seven apartments listed, without specifying the floor, in the four-story building. The officer then obtained a warrant that authorized the search of the "third floor apartment." After entering the apartment building, the officers eventually found that there were two apartments on the third floor, with one door to both apartments, and a shared entryway. McWebb, the suspect, occupied one of the apartments, and Garrison occupied the other. Before the officers realized that they were mistakenly in Garrison's apartment, they discovered contraband leading to Garrison's arrest and used at his trial to obtain his conviction.

The Court in *Garrison*, in an opinion written by Justice Stevens for six Justices, held that the description in the warrant of the place to be searched was sufficiently particular. Justice Stevens reasoned as follows:

> Plainly, if the officers had known, or even if they should have known, that there were two separate dwelling units on the third floor of 2036 Park Avenue, they would have been obligated to exclude [Garrison's] apartment from the scope of the requested warrant. But we must judge the constitutionality of their conduct in light of the information available to them at the time they acted. Those items of evidence that emerge after the warrant is issued have no bearing on whether or not a warrant was validly issued. * * * The validity of the warrant must be assessed on the basis of the information that the officers disclosed, or had a duty to discover and to disclose, to the issuing Magistrate. On the basis of that information, we agree with the conclusion of all three Maryland courts that the warrant, insofar as it authorized a search that turned out to be ambiguous in scope, was valid when it issued.[9]

Compare United States v. Johnson, 26 F.3d 669 (7th Cir.1994), where the warrant authorized the search of an entire duplex occupied by several members of a narcotics conspiracy. Even though the officer was aware that it was a multiple dwelling, the court upheld the warrant as sufficiently particular:

> The defendant argues that in "multiple dwelling" cases we must suppress all the evidence seized pursuant to the overbroad warrant. While that may be true when the warrant authorizes the search of an

---

[9] Of course, a validly issued warrant may be improperly executed. In *Garrison*, however, the Court found that the officers acted reasonably, though mistakenly, by searching Garrison's apartment, because the layout of the two apartments made it appear *as if it actually was a single apartment.* By the time the officers discovered that there were two separate apartments (presumably when they found two kitchens) they had already discovered the evidence that was used against Garrison.

entire structure and the officers do not know which unit contains the evidence of illegal conduct, that analysis does not apply when (1) the officer knows that there are multiple units and believes there is probable cause to search each unit, or (2) the targets of the investigation have access to the entire structure.

Single family dwellings usually present less of a problem of particular description than the multi-family dwellings discussed above. In urban areas, a street address is considered sufficiently particular. In rural areas, less particularized descriptions may be reasonable due to the absence of street addresses. See United States v. Dorrough, 927 F.2d 498 (10th Cir.1991) (warrant sufficiently particular where it describes a well-marked turnoff leading to the house, a quarter mile up a mountain, and the defendant's house is the only one up the mountain). The ultimate question is "whether the place to be searched is described with sufficient particularity to enable the executing officer to locate and identify the premises with reasonable effort, and whether there is any reasonable probability that another premise might be mistakenly searched." United States v. Pelayo-Landero, 285 F.3d 491 (6th Cir. 2002) (trailer home sufficiently described where directions are given to the trailer park and the warrant describes the particular trailer by color, by a certain exterior trim and by a wooden deck).

### The Wrong Address

In some cases, warrants have misdescribed an address. These mistakes arise most often where a building is on a corner or is set back from a street. The fact that the warrant is for the wrong address will not be dispositive if the warrant sufficiently directs the officer to the correct premises. For example, in Lyons v. Robinson, 783 F.2d 737 (8th Cir.1985), the warrant listed the place to be searched as 325 Adkinson Street; Lyons' residence was actually 325 Short Street, on the corner of Short and Adkinson. The *Lyons* Court stated that the description, though inaccurate, was sufficiently particular because it made it unlikely under the circumstances that another premises might be mistakenly searched.

### The Breadth of the Place to Be Searched

The cases discussed above deal with whether the warrant sufficiently describes the location of the premises to be searched. A different particularity question that sometimes arises is whether the warrant sufficiently describes particular places in the general area to be searched. For example, if the warrant authorizes the search of the "premises" at 1825 Elm Street, do the police have the authority to search a freestanding garage behind the house at that address?

In United States v. Earls, 42 F.3d 1321 (10th Cir.1994), the court held that a warrant to search "the premises" at a particular location covered a detached garage, a shed, and an office, each of which was located within the curtilage of the house described in the warrant. See also United States v. Kyles, 40 F.3d 519 (2d Cir.1994) (warrant to search an apartment authorized the agent to search the defendant's locked bedroom, even though the defendant was not named as a suspect; the room was not a separate residence outside the scope of the warrant).

One of the most difficult problems for the courts has been the scope of the search of the property of *persons* who happen to be on the premises that are being searched pursuant to a warrant. Most courts have held that *any* person's property is subject to search so long as the property could physically contain the items described in the warrant. United States v. Gonzalez, 940 F.2d 1413 (11th Cir.1991) (upholding the search of a visitor's briefcase capable of concealing evidence sought in the warrant).

All of these scope rulings are simply an application of the principle that a warrant permitting a search of a house or a building authorizes the police to search anywhere within the building (or curtilage) that is large enough to contain the evidence the police are looking for. The scope of the authority to search a described area is set forth in colorful language by Judge Posner in United States v. Evans, 92 F.3d 540 (7th Cir.1996):

> If they are looking for a canary's corpse, they can search a cupboard, but not a locket. If they are looking for an adolescent hippopotamus, they can search the living room or garage but not the microwave oven. If they are searching for cocaine, they can search a container large enough to hold a gram, or perhaps less.

In *Evans,* the defendant objected to the search of the trunk of his car, which was parked in the detached garage of a house. The warrant authorized a search for drugs in both the house and detached garage. Evans complained, among other things, that he resided at the house (and parked his car there) only intermittently. But Judge Posner found no problem with the search:

> It seems to us that a car parked in a garage is just another interior container, like a closet or a desk. If, as in this case, the trunk or glove compartment is not too small to hold what the search warrant authorizes the police to look for, they can search the trunk and the glove compartment. * * * It does not matter whose [car] it is unless it obviously belonged to someone wholly uninvolved in the criminal activities going on in the house. If an innocent guest leaves a trunk in the host's house and the police obtain a search warrant to search the house for something small enough to fit in the trunk, then, unless it is apparent that the trunk does not belong to anyone

connected with the illegal activity—a condition that will rarely be satisfied—the police can search the trunk and if it happens to contain evidence that the guest is a criminal after all, albeit innocent of any involvement in the criminal activities of his host, he is out of luck.

How could it ever be apparent that a trunk does not belong to someone connected with illegal activity like drugs which can be stored in any type of container?

## 5.  Particularity for Arrest Warrants

An arrest warrant must describe the person to be seized with sufficient particularity. Does the fact that the officers have probable cause to arrest a person mean that the person can be specifically described? Is a warrant authorizing the arrest of "John Doe a/k/a Ed" sufficiently particular? The court in United States v. Doe, 703 F.2d 745 (3d Cir.1983), held that such a warrant was overbroad, and held further that the insufficient description was not cured by the fact that the officer who executed the warrant had independent personal knowledge that the arrestee was the person for whom the warrant was intended. Why doesn't the officer's personal knowledge solve the problem? Would the warrant have been sufficiently particular if it described "John Doe, a/k/a Ed, a white male six feet tall and 200 pounds"?

## 6.  Describing the Things to Be Seized

The warrant clause mandates that a warrant, to be valid, must particularly describe the things that the officers can look for and seize. In essence, this particularity requirement operates to limit the possibility of a general warrant on a particular premises. But how does one determine whether a warrant's description of the things to be seized is sufficiently particular? The following case is the Supreme Court's major pronouncement on the particularity requirement as applied to the things to be seized.

### ANDRESEN V. MARYLAND

Supreme Court of the United States, 1976.
427 U.S. 463.

### MR. JUSTICE BLACKMUN delivered the opinion of the Court.

\* \* \*

In early 1972, a Bi-County Fraud Unit, acting under the joint auspices of the State's Attorneys' Offices of Montgomery and Prince George's Counties, Md., began an investigation of real estate settlement activities in the Washington, D.C., area. At the time, petitioner Andresen was an attorney who \* \* \* specialized in real estate settlements in

Montgomery County. During the Fraud Unit's investigation, his activities
came under scrutiny, particularly in connection with a transaction
involving Lot 13T in the Potomac Woods subdivision of Montgomery
County. The investigation * * * disclosed that petitioner, acting as
settlement attorney, had defrauded Standard-Young Associates, the
purchaser of Lot 13T. Petitioner had represented that the property was
free of liens and that, accordingly, no title insurance was necessary, when
in fact, he knew that there were two outstanding liens on the property. In
addition, investigators learned that the lienholders, by threatening to
foreclose their liens, had forced a halt to the purchaser's construction on
the property. When Standard-Young had confronted petitioner with this
information, he responded by issuing, as an agent of a title insurance
company, a title policy guaranteeing clear title to the property. By this
action, petitioner also defrauded that insurance company by requiring it
to pay the outstanding liens.

The investigators * * * applied for warrants to search petitioner's law
office and the separate office of Mount Vernon Development Corporation,
of which petitioner was incorporator, sole shareholder, resident agent,
and director. The application sought permission to search for specified
documents pertaining to the sale and conveyance of Lot 13T. A judge * * *
concluded that there was probable cause and issued the warrants.

The searches of the two offices were conducted simultaneously during
daylight hours on October 31, 1972. [The searches took a number of
hours; approximately 4% of Andresen's files were seized.]

* * *

[Petitioner contends] that rights guaranteed him by the Fourth
Amendment were violated because the descriptive terms of the search
warrants were so broad as to make them impermissible "general"
warrants * * *.

*The specificity of the search warrants.* Although petitioner concedes
that the warrants for the most part were models of particularity, he
contends that they were rendered fatally "general" by the addition, in
each warrant, to the exhaustive list of particularly described documents,
of the phrase "together with other fruits, instrumentalities and evidence
of crime at this [time] unknown." The quoted language, it is argued, must
be read in isolation and without reference to the rest of the long sentence
at the end of which it appears. When read "properly," petitioner contends,
it permits the search for and seizure of any evidence of any crime.

* * *

* * * [T]he challenged phrase must be read as authorizing only the
search for and seizure of evidence relating to "the crime of false pretenses
with respect to Lot 13T." The challenged phrase is not a separate

sentence. Instead, it appears in each warrant at the end of a sentence containing a lengthy list of specified and particular items to be seized, all pertaining to Lot 13T.[a] We think it clear from the context that the term "crime" in the warrants refers only to the crime of false pretenses with respect to the sale of Lot 13T. The "other fruits" clause is one of a series that follows the colon after the word "Maryland." All clauses in the series are limited by what precedes that colon, namely, "items pertaining to * * * lot 13, block T." The warrants, accordingly, did not authorize the executing officers to conduct a search for evidence of other crimes but only to search for and seize evidence relevant to the crime of false pretenses and Lot 13T.[b]

Petitioner also suggests that the specific list of the documents to be seized constitutes a "general" warrant. We disagree. Under investigation was a complex real estate scheme whose existence could be proved only by piecing together many bits of evidence. Like a jigsaw puzzle, the whole "picture" of petitioner's false-pretense scheme with respect to Lot 13T could be shown only by placing in the proper place the many pieces of evidence that, taken singly, would show comparatively little. The complexity of an illegal scheme may not be used as a shield to avoid detection when the State has demonstrated probable cause to believe that a crime has been committed and probable cause to believe that evidence of this crime is in the suspect's possession.

We recognize that there are grave dangers inherent in executing a warrant authorizing a search and seizure of a person's papers that are not necessarily present in executing a warrant to search for physical objects whose relevance is more easily ascertainable. In searches for papers, it is certain that some innocuous documents will be examined, at least cursorily, in order to determine whether they are, in fact among those papers authorized to be seized. Similar dangers, of course, are

---

[a] "[T]he following items pertaining to sale, purchase, settlement and conveyance of lot 13, block T, Potomac Woods subdivision, Montgomery County, Maryland:

"title notes, title abstracts, title rundowns; contracts of sale and/or assignments from Raffaele Antonelli and Rocco Caniglia to Mount Vernon Development Corporation and/or others; lien payoff correspondence and lien payoff memoranda to and from lienholders and noteholders; correspondence and memoranda to and from trustees of deeds of trust; lenders instructions for a construction loan or construction and permanent loan; disbursement sheets and disbursement memoranda; checks, check stubs and ledger sheets indicating disbursement upon settlement; correspondence and memoranda concerning disbursements upon settlement; settlement statements and settlement memoranda; fully or partially prepared deed of trust releases, whether or not executed and whether or not recorded; books, records, documents, papers, memoranda and correspondence, showing or tending to show a fraudulent intent, and/or knowledge as elements of the crime of false pretenses, in violation of Article 27, Section 140, of the Annotated Code of Maryland, 1957 Edition, as amended and revised, together with other fruits, instrumentalities and evidence of crime at this [time] unknown."

[b] The record discloses that the officials executing the warrants seized numerous papers that were not introduced into evidence. Although we are not informed of their content, we observe that to the extent such papers were not within the scope of the warrants or were otherwise improperly seized, the State was correct in returning them voluntarily and the trial judge was correct in suppressing others.

present in executing a warrant for the "seizure" of telephone conversations. In both kinds of searches, responsible officials, including judicial officials, must take care to assure that they are conducted in a manner that minimizes unwarranted intrusions upon privacy.

\* \* \*

MR. JUSTICE BRENNAN, dissenting.

\* \* \*

\* \* \* After a lengthy and admittedly detailed listing of items to be seized, the warrants in this case further authorized the seizure of "other fruits, instrumentalities and evidence of crime at this [time] unknown." The Court construes this sweeping authorization to be limited to evidence pertaining to the crime of false pretenses with respect to the sale of Lot 13T. \* \* \* The question is not how those warrants are to be viewed in hindsight, but how they were in fact viewed by those executing them. The overwhelming quantity of seized material that was either suppressed or returned to petitioner is irrefutable testimony to the unlawful generality of the warrants. The Court's attempt to cure this defect by *post hoc* judicial construction evades principles settled in this Court's Fourth Amendment decisions. \* \* \*

[JUSTICE MARSHALL also dissented, agreeing with Justice Brennan's Fourth Amendment analysis.]

### *NOTE ON ANDRESEN AND PARTICULARITY*

Justice Blackmun reads the last portion of the *Andresen* warrant as authorizing the police "only to search for and seize evidence relevant to the crime of false pretenses and Lot 13T." Justice Brennan complains that the police reasonably believed the warrant was broader and authorized a search for evidence of other crimes. If a warrant is drafted in such a way that it is subject to two readings, one which would render it valid and another which would invalidate it, should a reviewing court adopt the reading that the police give the warrant, or the reading that the reviewing court believes that the magistrate, presumed to be acting constitutionally, intended? Which approach is more in line with the goals of the Fourth Amendment?

### *Searches of Computers*

The Court in *Andresen* notes that in a search for documents, it is all but inevitable that the police will be required to peruse innocuous private documents. That problem frequently arises when the police search for information stored in a computer. Even a requirement of reasonable particularity will not shield most information stored in a computer from inspection, where police have probable cause to believe that incriminating evidence is somewhere on the hard drive.

Assume, for example, that an officer has a warrant to search for child pornography stored on a computer. In his search, he comes across a folder labeled "grocery lists." Can he open the folder? The answer generally given by the courts is, yes—otherwise a criminal could shield incriminating information from view simply by labeling the folder in a certain way. But this means that the search of the computer will by necessity be extensive and thorough, covering all files, including "cookies", history, deleted files, etc. See Guest v. Leis, 255 F.3d 325 (6th Cir. 2001) (officers with a warrant to search information located on a computer are permitted to seize the computer and conduct a thorough search of all files on the computer, as they are allowed to separate relevant files from unrelated files). As the court put it in United States v. Adjani, 452 F.3d 1140 (9th Cir. 2006), a case in which the defendant complained that the warrant should have restricted the search to a particular email program and specific search terms:

> Computer files are easy to disguise or rename, and were we to limit the warrant to such a specific search protocol, much evidence could escape discovery simply because of Adjani's * * * labeling of the files documenting Adjani's criminal activity. The government should not be required to trust the suspect's self-labeling when executing a warrant.

See also United States v. Giberson, 527 F.3d 882 (9th Cir. 2008) ("While officers ought to exercise caution when executing the search of a computer, just as they ought when sifting through documents that may contain personal information, the potential intermingling of materials does not justify an exception or heightened protection for computers beyond the Fourth Amendment's reasonableness requirement."); United States v. Hill, 459 F.3d 966 (9th Cir. 2006) (no requirement to search only those computer files most likely to contain the documents to be seized: "Computer records are extremely susceptible to tampering, hiding, or destruction, whether deliberate or inadvertent. Images can be hidden in all manner of files, even word processing documents and spreadsheets. Criminals will do all they can to conceal contraband, including the simple expedient of changing the names and extensions of files to disguise their content from the casual observer."); United States v. Triplett, 684 F.3d 500 (5th Cir. 2012) ("Although officers should limit exposure to innocent files, in the end, there may be no practical substitute for actually looking in many (perhaps all) folders, and sometimes at the documents contained within those folders".).

One of the most helpful discussions of the particularity requirement as applied to computers is found in United States v. Richards, 659 F.3d 527 (6th Cir. 2011), a case involving the search of an entire server when there was probable cause to believe that Richards was involved in child pornography:

Courts that have addressed the permissible breadth of computer-related searches have grappled with how to balance two interests that are in tension with each other. On one hand, it is clear that because criminals can—and often do—hide, mislabel, or manipulate files to conceal criminal activity, a broad, expansive search of the hard drive may be required. On the other hand, granting the Government a *carte blanche* to search *every* file on the hard drive impermissibly transforms a limited search into a general one. * * * [G]iven the unique problem encountered in computer searches, and the practical difficulties inherent in implementing universal search methodologies, the majority of federal courts have eschewed the use of a specific search protocol and, instead, have employed the Fourth Amendment's bedrock principle of reasonableness on a case-by-case basis: "While officers must be clear as to what it is they are seeking on the computer and conduct the search in a way that avoids searching files of types not identified in the warrant, . . . a computer search may be as extensive as reasonably required to locate the items described in the warrant based on probable cause." United States v. Burgess, 576 F.3d 1078, 1092 (10th Cir. 2009). We agree with the Tenth Circuit in *Burgess* that it is folly for a search warrant to attempt to structure the mechanics of the search and a warrant imposing such limits would unduly restrict legitimate search objectives. One would not ordinarily expect a warrant to search filing cabinets for evidence of drug activity to prospectively restrict the search to "file cabinets in the basement" or to file folders labeled "Meth Lab" or "Customers." And there is no reason to so limit computer searches. But that is not to say methodology is irrelevant.

A warrant may permit only the search of particularly described places and only particularly described things may be seized. As the description of such places and things becomes more general, the method by which the search is executed becomes more important— the search method must be tailored to meet allowed ends. And those limits must be functional. For instance, unless specifically authorized by the warrant there would be little reason for officers searching for evidence of drug trafficking to look at tax returns (beyond verifying the folder labeled "2002 Tax Return" actually contains tax returns and not drug files or trophy pictures).

Respect for legitimate rights to privacy in papers and effects requires an officer executing a search warrant to first look in the most obvious places and as it becomes necessary to progressively move from the obvious to the obscure. That is the purpose of a search protocol which structures the search by requiring an analysis of the file structure, next looking for suspicious file folders, then looking for files and types of files most likely to contain the objects of the search by doing keyword searches.

But in the end, there may be no practical substitute for actually looking in many (perhaps all) folders and sometimes at the documents contained within those folders, and that is true whether the search is of computer files or physical files. It is particularly true with image files.

Consistent with this rule, the federal courts have not required a second warrant to search a properly seized computer where the evidence obtained in the search did not exceed the probable cause articulated in the original warrant.

Applying a reasonableness analysis on a case-by-case basis, the federal courts have rejected most particularity challenges to warrants authorizing the seizure and search of entire personal or business computers. * * * In other words, in general, so long as the computer search is limited to a search for evidence explicitly authorized in the warrant, it is reasonable for the executing officers to open the various types of files located in the computer's hard drive in order to determine whether they contain such evidence.

In *Richards*, the defendant argued that the warrant to search the entire server was overbroad because he had set it up "in a neatly compartmentalized and segregated fashion, rendering it entirely unnecessary to search beyond the content maintained in the JustinsFriends file directory." But the court responded that "hindsight is 20/20" and also that a forensic evidence procedure could uncover "hidden, erased, compressed, password-protected or encrypted files." Therefore, "searching the entire server was necessary to look for child pornography related to the JustinsFriends websites because individuals often mislabel directory files, the server might contain related websites, and the unallocated server space might contain materials pertaining to those websites."

Compare United States v. Galpin, 720 F.3d 436 (2nd Cir. 2013) ("Once the government has obtained authorization to search the hard drive, the government may claim that the contents of every file it chose to open were in plain view and, therefore, admissible even if they implicate the defendant in a crime not contemplated by the warrant. Thus there is a serious risk that every warrant for electronic information will become, in effect, a general warrant * * *. This threat demands a heightened sensitivity to the particularity requirement in the context of digital searches.").

### *Reasonable Particularity*

Ultimately, the particularity question with respect to items to be seized is one of reasonableness. "While a search warrant must describe items to be seized with reasonable particularity sufficient to prevent a general, exploratory rummaging in a person's belongings, it need only be reasonably specific, rather than elaborately detailed, and the specificity required varies depending on the circumstances of the case and the type of items involved." United States v. Bridges, 344 F.3d 1010 (9th Cir. 2003).

Some property may not be susceptible to anything more than a general description (e.g., "United States currency"). Other property may be reasonably susceptible to a detailed description (e.g., a description of a gun as a murder weapon ordinarily should include the caliber of the gun, whether it is a handgun or shotgun, etc.). The reasonableness inquiry takes into account how much an officer would be expected to know about the property in the course of obtaining probable cause to seize it. See United States v. Fuccillo, 808 F.2d 173 (1st Cir.1987) (warrant to seize "stolen clothing" held insufficiently particular where officers were given a detailed list of the articles stolen before applying for the warrant). Compare United States v. Upham, 168 F.3d 532 (1st Cir.1999) (in a child pornography case, a description of the property to be seized as "any and all visual depictions, in any format or media, or minors engaged in sexually explicit conduct" was sufficiently particular because the officers could not be expected to describe the materials with any more specificity).

In United States v. Strand, 761 F.2d 449 (8th Cir.1985), postal inspectors suspected that Strand, a mail carrier, was stealing items from the mail. They obtained a warrant authorizing the seizure of "stolen mail" from Strand's house. The court held that some items seized from Strand's home were legally obtained, others illegally obtained. The court explained as follows:

> We believe that the term "stolen mail" is sufficiently definite to enable a postal inspector to identify and seize items which clearly fit within such a generic class, such as letters and parcels, neither addressed to nor sent by the person whose property is being searched, bearing postage stamps or marks. A search for "stolen mail" does not, however, permit the seizure of items which do not fit into the generic category. Many of the items seized in the present case under the rubric of stolen mail were not found in parcels of mail, and included items such as socks, a sweatshirt, cosmetics, a sweater, a thermometer, a china plate, and gloves; * * *

Has the court in *Strand* given the searching officers too much or too little discretion to determine whether an item constitutes "stolen mail"? See also United States v. Bridges, 344 F.3d 1010 (9th Cir. 2003) (warrant was overbroad where it did not specify the criminal activity that was being investigated, and yet set forth "a comprehensive laundry list of sundry goods and inventory that one would readily expect to discover in any small or medium-sized business in the United States").

### *Severability*

Even if a clause in the warrant is overbroad, the defect will not ordinarily taint the entire search. Thus, in United States v. Brown, 984 F.2d 1074 (10th Cir.1993), a warrant to search a vehicle dismantling business described with particularity over forty items, including "bumpers, grills, fenders, hoods * * * blank registration forms", etc. But a catch-all clause was included to permit seizure of "[a]ny other item which the Officers determine or have reasonable belief is stolen while executing this search warrant." The Court held that the catch-all provision was overbroad. But this did not taint the evidence seized pursuant to the particular descriptions in the warrant. The Court stated:

> At least eight circuits have held that where a warrant contains both specific as well as unconstitutionally broad language, the broad portion may be redacted and the balance of the warrant considered valid. In such cases only those items confiscated under the overbroad portion of the warrant are suppressed.

### 7.   Reasonableness Limitations on Warranted Searches

A magistrate cannot issue a warrant that violates the reasonableness portion of the Fourth Amendment.

There are a few cases in which searches have been found unreasonable even though conducted with a warrant and probable cause. Most of these cases involve medical procedures. For example, in Winston v. Lee, 470 U.S. 753 (1985), the defendant had been wounded in the course of committing a robbery. The state obtained a court order forcing the defendant to undergo surgery under a general anesthetic to remove a bullet lodged at least 2.5 to 3 centimeters beneath the surface of his skin; the state clearly had probable cause that the search would uncover evidence, and had obtained a court order authorizing the procedure (tantamount to a warrant), but the defendant argued that the procedure was still unreasonable under the Fourth Amendment. Justice Brennan, writing for the Court, agreed with the defendant. He noted that the medical risks of the operation were disputed, and reasoned that the uncertainty militated against a finding that the operation was a reasonable search. Moreover, the Commonwealth failed to show a compelling need for the bullet, as it had substantial other evidence tying the defendant to the robbery and could offer evidence of the location of the bullet in the defendant's body.

It is possible, in light of Supreme Court cases like *Lee,* Griswold v. Connecticut, 381 U.S. 479 (1965) (asking "[w]ould we allow the police to search the sacred precincts of marital bedrooms for telltale signs of the use of contraceptives?"), and Stanley v. Georgia, 394 U.S. 557 (1969) (private possession of obscene material in home constitutionally protected), that some magistrates might decline to issue warrants that would invade areas that traditionally have been regarded as off limits to the government. Similarly, some magistrates might decide that the scope of a warrant is too broad, even though there is probable cause to search and a particularized description of the things to be seized (e.g., a requested authorization to seize all books and records).

### 8.   Details of the Warrant

Federal Rule of Criminal Procedure 41(e)(2)(A) sets forth the basic information that must be included in the warrant:

> [T]he warrant must identify the person or property to be searched, identify any person or property to be seized, and designate the magistrate judge to whom it must be returned. The warrant must command the officer to:
>
>> (i) execute the warrant within a specified time no longer than 14 days;
>>
>> (ii) execute the warrant during the daytime, unless the judge for good cause expressly authorizes execution at another time; and
>>
>> (iii) return the warrant to the magistrate judge designated in the warrant.

Daytime means the hours from 6:00 a.m. to 10:00 p.m. according to local time. Fed.R.Crim.P. 41(a)(2)(B). Searches for narcotics, however, are covered by a specific statute that "requires no special showing for a nighttime search, other than a showing that the contraband is likely to be on the property or person to be searched at the time." Gooding v. United States, 416 U.S. 430 (1974) (citing 21 U.S.C. § 879). See also United States v. Rizzi, 434 F.3d 669 (4th Cir. 2006) (federal statute authorizing nighttime searches for narcotics was not unconstitutionally overbroad; the Fourth Amendment does not prohibit nighttime searches, and intrusion on privacy during daytime activities could be just as burdensome as a nighttime intrusion).

### 9.   Anticipatory Warrants

Can government agents obtain an "anticipatory" search warrant conditioned upon future events that, if fulfilled, would create probable cause? In United States v. Grubbs, 547 U.S. 90 (2006), the Court held that a warrant is not invalid simply because it is contingent on a future occurrence. *Grubbs* involved an investigation into receipt of child pornography. Law enforcement officers obtained a search warrant for Grubbs's house on the basis of an affidavit explaining that the warrant would be executed only after a controlled delivery of child pornography to that location. Specifically, the affidavit stated:

> "Execution of this search warrant will not occur unless and until the parcel has been received by a person(s) and has been physically taken into the residence. . . . At that time, and not before, this search warrant will be executed by me and other United States Postal inspectors, with appropriate assistance from other law enforcement officers in accordance with this warrant's command."

The Magistrate Judge issued the warrant as requested. Two days later, an undercover postal inspector delivered the package. Then a search of the house was conducted pursuant to the warrant.

Justice Scalia, writing for the Court, had this to say about the use and constitutionality of anticipatory warrants:

> An anticipatory warrant is a warrant based upon an affidavit showing probable cause that at some future time (but not presently) certain evidence of crime will be located at a specified place. Most anticipatory warrants subject their execution to some condition precedent other than the mere passage of time—a so-called "triggering condition." * * * If the government were to execute an anticipatory warrant before the triggering condition occurred, there would be no reason to believe the item described in the warrant could be found at the searched location; by definition, the triggering condition which establishes probable cause has not yet been satisfied when the warrant is issued. Grubbs argues that for this reason anticipatory warrants contravene the Fourth Amendment's provision that "no Warrants shall issue, but upon probable cause."

> We reject this view, as has every Court of Appeals to confront the issue. Probable cause exists when there is a fair probability that contraband or evidence of a crime will be found in a particular place. Because the probable-cause requirement looks to whether evidence will be found *when the search is conducted*, all warrants are, in a sense, "anticipatory." In the typical case where the police seek permission to search a house for an item they believe is already located there, the magistrate's determination that there is probable cause for the search amounts to a prediction that the item will still be there when the warrant is executed. * * * Thus, when an anticipatory warrant is issued, the fact that the contraband is not presently located at the place described in the warrant is immaterial, so long as

there is probable cause to believe that it will be there when the search warrant is executed.

Justice Scalia then set forth the requirements for a valid anticipatory warrant.

> Anticipatory warrants are, therefore, no different in principle from ordinary warrants. They require the magistrate to determine (1) that it is *now probable* that (2) contraband, evidence of a crime, or a fugitive *will be* on the described premises (3) when the warrant is executed. It should be noted, however, that where the anticipatory warrant places a condition (other than the mere passage of time) upon its execution, the first of these determinations goes not merely to what will probably be found *if* the condition is met. (If that were the extent of the probability determination, an anticipatory warrant could be issued for every house in the country, authorizing search and seizure *if* contraband should be delivered—though for any single location there is no likelihood that contraband will be delivered.) Rather, the probability determination for a conditioned anticipatory warrant looks also to the likelihood that the condition will occur, and thus that a proper object of seizure will be on the described premises. In other words, for a conditioned anticipatory warrant to comply with the Fourth Amendment's requirement of probable cause, two prerequisites of probability must be satisfied. It must be true not only that *if* the triggering condition occurs there is a fair probability that contraband or evidence of a crime will be found in a particular place, but also that there is probable cause to believe the triggering condition *will occur*. The supporting affidavit must provide the magistrate with sufficient information to evaluate both aspects of the probable-cause determination.

Justice Scalia then applied these requirements to the warrant issued in *Grubbs*.

> In this case, the occurrence of the triggering condition— successful delivery of the videotape to Grubbs' residence—would plainly establish probable cause for the search. In addition, the affidavit established probable cause to believe the triggering condition would be satisfied. Although it is possible that Grubbs could have refused delivery of the videotape he had ordered, that was unlikely. The Magistrate therefore had a substantial basis for concluding that probable cause existed.

Justice Souter, joined by Justices Stevens and Ginsburg, concurred in part and in the judgment. Justice Alito took no part in the decision.

## 10. "Sneak and Peek" Warrants

Fed.R.Crim.P. 41(f)(1)(C) requires that an officer executing a warrant must give a copy to the person whose premises is searched. Thus, secret searches are generally prohibited. But Rule 41(f)(3) provides that a judge may delay any notice "if the delay is authorized by statute." And in reaction to the events of 9/11, there is now statutory authority for secret searches in some circumstances.

Section 213 of Public Law 107–56, 115 Stat. 272, the "Uniting And Strengthening America By Providing Appropriate Tools Required To Intercept And Obstruct Terrorism (USA Patriot Act) Act of 2001," authorizes so-called "sneak and peek" warrants in certain situations. These warrants permit federal agents to enter a person's home or office covertly. The government can delay notice of a search if it can show "reasonable cause to believe that providing immediate notification of the execution of the warrant may have an adverse result." "Adverse result" is defined as (1) endangering the life or physical safety of an individual, (2) flight from prosecution, (3) destruction of or tampering with evidence, (4) intimidation of potential witnesses, or (5) otherwise seriously jeopardizing an investigation or unduly delaying a trial. The government can also seize items without notice if it can show a "reasonable necessity" for the seizure.

Under what circumstances would it be necessary to employ a sneak and peek warrant?

# C. EXECUTING THE WARRANT

## 1. The Knock and Announce Requirement

Statutes throughout the country require that officers executing a warrant knock and announce their presence before attempting to enter a dwelling. Typical of these statutes is 18 U.S.C.A. § 3109.

> The officer may break open any outer or inner door or window of a house, or any part of a house, or anything therein, to execute a search warrant, if, after notice of his authority and purpose, he is refused admittance or when necessary to liberate himself or a person aiding him in the execution of the warrant.

The purposes of the knock and announce requirement are set forth by the court in United States v. Contreras-Ceballos, 999 F.2d 432 (9th Cir.1993):

> The requirement that law enforcement officers give notice of their authority and purpose prior to forcing entry to execute a warrant serves three purposes: it protects citizens and law enforcement

officials from violence; it protects individual privacy rights; and it protects against needless destruction of private property.

### *Constitutional Basis of the Knock and Announce Requirement*

In Wilson v. Arkansas, 514 U.S. 927 (1995), the Court considered whether the Fourth Amendment requires the police to announce their presence before entering a premises. Justice Thomas, writing for a unanimous Court, surveyed the common-law precedents and concluded as follows:

> Given the longstanding common-law endorsement of the practice of announcement, we have little doubt that the Framers of the Fourth Amendment thought that the method of an officer's entry into a dwelling was among the factors to be considered in assessing the reasonableness of a search or seizure. * * * [W]e hold that in some circumstances an officer's unannounced entry into a home might be unreasonable under the Fourth Amendment.

Justice Thomas stressed, however, that the announcement rule was not a rigid constitutional requirement, but rather a component of the Fourth Amendment reasonableness inquiry. He stated that the "Fourth Amendment's flexible requirement of reasonableness should not be read to mandate a rigid rule of announcement that ignores countervailing law enforcement interests." Among the countervailing circumstances that might permit an unannounced entry, the Court mentioned hot pursuit of a suspect, the risk of destruction of evidence, and the safety of officers. Justice Thomas concluded as follows:

> We need not attempt a comprehensive catalog of the relevant countervailing factors here. For now, we leave to the lower courts the task of determining the circumstances under which an unannounced entry is reasonable under the Fourth Amendment. We simply hold that although a search or seizure of a dwelling might be constitutionally defective if police officers enter without prior announcement, law enforcement interests may also establish the reasonableness of an unannounced entry.

The Court remanded to allow the state courts to determine whether circumstances existed sufficient to excuse the fact that officers entered Wilson's home without announcing their presence.

### *"Refused Admittance"*

An officer can break open premises if he has announced his authority and purpose and is refused admittance. Clearly, if the homeowner says "you can't come in", this will justify a forced entry with a warrant. But refused admittance may also be implied from the circumstances. Thus, in

United States v. Knapp, 1 F.3d 1026 (10th Cir.1993), officers smashed down the defendant's door with a battering ram after announcing their presence and waiting in vain for twelve seconds for a response from the defendant, whom they knew was inside. The court found that the failure to respond within twelve seconds constituted a refusal of entry. The court noted that "the phrase 'refused admittance' is not restricted to an affirmative refusal, but encompasses circumstances that constitute constructive or reasonably inferred refusal." On the other hand, in United States v. Moore, 91 F.3d 96 (10th Cir.1996), the officers announced their presence, waited three seconds, and when they got no response, they entered the premises by force. The court found that the forced entry was "virtually instantaneous" with the announcement and that this "precluded any claim that the officers were constructively refused admittance."

Courts have held that citizens should be allowed more time to answer the door when the warrant is executed in the nighttime hours—and accordingly the time can be reduced during the day. See United States v. Jenkins, 175 F.3d 1208 (10th Cir.1999) (where officers waited for 14 seconds after twice announcing their presence, a forced entry was reasonable; the required waiting period "was somewhat reduced because the officers executed the warrant at 10:00 a.m., when most people are awake and engaged in everyday activities."). Another relevant factor is whether the residence is small or large. See United States v. Sargent, 319 F.3d 4 (1st Cir. 2003) (lack of response for five seconds was especially significant, and deemed to be refused admittance, given the small size of the defendant's apartment).

## 2.   Exceptions to the Notice Rule

### *No "Breaking"*

If the door to a residence is already open, police are not required to announce their presence before entering, because the prohibition is against a "breaking" of the door. See United States v. Mendoza, 281 F.3d 712 (8th Cir. 2002) (police officers are not required to knock on the front door of a duplex, as the door opened to a common hallway as to which the defendant had no legitimate expectation of privacy; and they were not required to knock before entering the defendant's own apartment, as that apartment did not have a door on it).

Courts have also held that if the officer can trick the homeowner into opening the door, there is no violation of the knock and announce requirement, because there is no "breaking." See United States v. Alejandro, 368 F.3d 130 (2d Cir. 2004) (officers pretended that they were employees of a utility company checking out a gas leak; when the defendant opened the door and the officers entered, there was no violation of the knock and announce requirement because there was no breaking).

### Emergency Circumstances: Richards v. Wisconsin

As the Supreme Court stated in *Wilson*, supra, officers will be permitted to make an unannounced entry if announcement would create a risk of destruction of evidence or a risk of harm to the officers or others. In Richards v. Wisconsin, 520 U.S. 385 (1997), the Court considered the exigent circumstances exception to the knock and announce requirement in the context of a search of the premises of a suspected drug distribution operation. Justice Stevens, writing for the Court, set forth the facts of the case:

> On December 31, 1991, police officers in Madison, Wisconsin obtained a warrant to search Steiney Richards' hotel room for drugs and related paraphernalia. The search warrant was the culmination of an investigation that had uncovered substantial evidence that Richards was one of several individuals dealing drugs out of hotel rooms in Madison. The police requested a warrant that would have given advance authorization for a "no-knock" entry into the hotel room, but the magistrate explicitly deleted those portions of the warrant.

> The officers arrived at the hotel room at 3:40 a.m. Officer Pharo, dressed as a maintenance man, led the team. With him were several plainclothes officers and at least one man in uniform. Officer Pharo knocked on Richards' door and, responding to the query from inside the room, stated that he was a maintenance man. With the chain still on the door, Richards cracked it open. Although there is some dispute as to what occurred next, Richards acknowledges that when he opened the door he saw the man in uniform standing behind Officer Pharo. He quickly slammed the door closed and, after waiting two or three seconds, the officers began kicking and ramming the door to gain entry to the locked room. At trial, the officers testified that they identified themselves as police while they were kicking the door in. When they finally did break into the room, the officers caught Richards trying to escape through the window. They also found cash and cocaine hidden in plastic bags above the bathroom ceiling tiles.

The Wisconsin Supreme Court had held that the knock and announce requirement was automatically excused in any case in which the police were authorized to search for evidence of a felony drug crime. That court, in establishing a bright-line rule, reasoned that exigent circumstances justifying a no-knock entry are virtually always present in felony drug cases, due to the high risk of destruction of evidence and the likelihood that drug dealers will be armed and dangerous. But the Supreme Court rejected this per se exigent circumstances exception to the knock and announce requirement. Justice Stevens reasoned as follows:

The Wisconsin court explained its blanket exception as necessitated by the special circumstances of today's drug culture, and the State asserted at oral argument that the blanket exception was reasonable in "felony drug cases because of the convergence in a violent and dangerous form of commerce of weapons and the destruction of drugs." But creating exceptions to the knock-and-announce rule based on the "culture" surrounding a general category of criminal behavior presents at least two serious concerns.

First, the exception contains considerable overgeneralization. For example, while drug investigation frequently does pose special risks to officer safety and the preservation of evidence, not every drug investigation will pose these risks to a substantial degree. For example, a search could be conducted at a time when the only individuals present in a residence have no connection with the drug activity and thus will be unlikely to threaten officers or destroy evidence. Or the police could know that the drugs being searched for were of a type or in a location that made them impossible to destroy quickly. In those situations, the asserted governmental interests in preserving evidence and maintaining safety may not outweigh the individual privacy interests intruded upon by a no-knock entry. Wisconsin's blanket rule impermissibly insulates these cases from judicial review.

A second difficulty with permitting a criminal-category exception to the knock-and-announce requirement is that the reasons for creating an exception in one category can, relatively easily, be applied to others. Armed bank robbers, for example, are, by definition, likely to have weapons, and the fruits of their crime may be destroyed without too much difficulty. If a per se exception were allowed for each category of criminal investigation that included a considerable—albeit hypothetical—risk of danger to officers or destruction of evidence, the knock-and-announce element of the Fourth Amendment's reasonableness requirement would be meaningless.

Thus, the fact that felony drug investigations may frequently present circumstances warranting a no-knock entry cannot remove from the neutral scrutiny of a reviewing court the reasonableness of the police decision not to knock and announce in a particular case. Instead, in each case, it is the duty of a court confronted with the question to determine whether the facts and circumstances of the particular entry justified dispensing with the knock-and-announce requirement.

The Court's rejection of a per se exigent circumstances rule did not mean that the no-knock entry in *Richards* was unreasonable. Balancing the interests of the state and the individual, the Court set the standard of exigency that would be sufficient justify a no-knock entry:

> In order to justify a "no-knock" entry, the police must have a reasonable suspicion that knocking and announcing their presence, under the particular circumstances, would be dangerous or futile, or that it would inhibit the effective investigation of the crime by, for example, allowing the destruction of evidence. This standard—as opposed to a probable cause requirement—strikes the appropriate balance between the legitimate law enforcement concerns at issue in the execution of search warrants and the individual privacy interests affected by no-knock entries. Cf. Terry v. Ohio, (requiring a reasonable and articulable suspicion of danger to justify a pat-down search). This showing is not high, but the police should be required to make it whenever the reasonableness of a no-knock entry is challenged.

Thus, officers do not need probable cause to believe that evidence will be destroyed if they announce their presence. The lesser standard of reasonable suspicion is all that is required. Applying this standard to the facts of the case, the Court had little difficulty in determining that the no-knock entry in *Richards* was justified.

For other cases finding reasonable suspicion of exigent circumstances justifying a no-knock entry, see United States v. Sutton, 336 F.3d 550 (7th Cir. 2003) (information that pit bulls had been seen on the property and that individuals with drug or weapons convictions had been seen entering the home, when added to the lack of cover for officers approaching the home, gave officers reasonable suspicion that compliance with the knock and announce requirement might place them in danger); United States v. Weeks, 160 F.3d 1210 (8th Cir.1998) (no-knock entry of drug stash house was justified where officers were informed that the residents answered the door with guns in their hands, one of the residents had been convicted of a firearms offense, and the front door was braced). Compare United States v. Nielson, 415 F.3d 1195 (10th Cir. 2005) (circumstances did not justify a no-knock entry to execute a warrant to search for drugs at the residence of a defendant who 1) had no history of violence, 2) was not involved in trafficking drugs, and 3) had cooperated with police during a previous search).

### *No-Knock Warrants*

The officers in *Richards* asked the magistrate for a no-knock warrant, i.e., a warrant that provided advance authorization excusing the knock and announce requirement. The magistrate refused to issue such a warrant, but that is not to say that such warrants can never be issued. If the officers make an advance showing of conditions at a premises that would excuse the knock and announce requirement, then a no-knock warrant can be valid as issued. As the Supreme Court stated in United States v. Banks, 540 U.S. 31 (2003): "When a warrant applicant gives reasonable grounds to expect futility or to suspect that one or another exigency already exists or will arise instantly upon knocking, a magistrate judge is acting within the Constitution to authorize a 'no-knock' entry."

Indeed it would seem that there should be a preference to have the magistrate determine in advance whether conditions exist that will excuse the knock and announce requirement—rather than leaving the question to the officers in the competitive enterprise of ferreting out crime. According to the courts, though, the preference is a mild one. There is no *requirement* that an officer obtain a no-knock warrant, even if he knows that the conditions at the premises would justify such a warrant at the time it is issued. However, "if police obtain a no-knock warrant prior to the search, the defendant bears the burden to show that the entry method was not justified. If, however, police execute a general search warrant without knocking and announcing, then the government is required to justify use of the no-knock entry." United States v. Esser, 451 F.3d 1109 (10th Cir. 2006).

### No-Knock Entries and Destruction of Property: United States v. Ramirez

In United States v. Ramirez, 523 U.S. 65 (1998), officers had a no-knock warrant to search a house for a dangerous escaped prisoner. Approaching the house in the early morning hours, they announced over a loud speaker system that they had a search warrant. Simultaneously, they broke a single window in the garage and pointed a gun through the opening, hoping to prevent the occupants of the house from rushing to the weapons stash that an informant had told them was in the garage. Awakened by the noise and fearful that his house was being burglarized, the owner of the house, Ramirez, grabbed a pistol and fired it into the garage ceiling. When the officers shouted "police," Ramirez surrendered and was taken into custody. Ramirez was indicted on federal charges of being a felon in possession of a firearm. As it turned out, the escaped prisoner was not on the premises. However, Ramirez did not argue that the police lacked probable cause to search for the escaped prisoner. Rather, he argued that a heightened degree of exigent circumstances is required if the police are going to destroy property during a no-knock warrant entry.

Chief Justice Rehnquist, writing for a unanimous Court, held that officers are not held to a higher standard when a no-knock entry results in the destruction of property. He declared: "Under *Richards*, a no-knock entry is justified if police have a 'reasonable suspicion' that knocking and announcing would be dangerous, futile, or destructive to the purposes of the investigation. Whether such a 'reasonable suspicion' exists depends in no way on whether police must destroy property in order to enter." The Chief Justice recognized that the general Fourth Amendment reasonableness requirement imposes some limitation on the destructiveness of a search. However, in this case, the very limited destruction of property was reasonable, given the fact that the officers were acting to prevent possible violent activity. Compare Mena v. City of Simi Valley, 226 F.3d 1031 (9th Cir. 2000) (Fourth Amendment violated where officers unnecessarily broke down doors that were unlocked and open, with one officer stating "I like to destroy these kind of materials, it's cool").

### 3.   Exigent Circumstances After Knocking

In United States v. Banks, 540 U.S. 31 (2003), the Court discussed how and whether exigent circumstances can allow police to break a door down *after* knocking. Justice Souter, writing for a unanimous Court, described the pertinent facts as follows:

> With information that Banks was selling cocaine at home, [officers] got a warrant to search his two-bedroom apartment. As soon as they arrived there, about 2 o'clock on a Wednesday afternoon, officers posted in front called out "police search warrant" and rapped hard enough on the door to be heard by officers at the back door. There was no indication whether anyone was home, and after waiting for 15 to 20 seconds with no answer, the officers broke open the front door with a battering ram. Banks was in the shower and testified that he heard nothing until the crash of the door, which brought him out dripping to confront the police. The search produced weapons, crack cocaine, and other evidence of drug dealing.

The Court "granted certiorari to consider how to go about applying the standard of reasonableness to the length of time police with a warrant must wait before entering without permission after knocking and announcing their intent in a felony case."

Justice Souter found that exigent circumstances justified the officers' actions in knocking down the door and entering the premises. He explained that while the question was "a close one, we think that after 15 or 20 seconds without a response, police could fairly suspect that cocaine would be gone if they were reticent any longer."

Justice Souter noted that the defendant was confusing two different concepts: the time required to assume that a resident is refusing to answer the door, and the time required for a resident to destroy evidence:

> And the argument that 15 to 20 seconds was too short for Banks to have come to the door ignores the very risk that justified prompt entry. True, if the officers were to justify their timing here by claiming that Banks's failure to admit them fairly suggested a refusal to let them in, Banks could at least argue that no such suspicion can arise until an occupant has had time to get to the door, a time that will vary with the size of the establishment, perhaps five seconds to open a motel room door, or several minutes to move through a townhouse. In this case, however, the police claim exigent need to enter, and the crucial fact in examining their actions is not time to reach the door but the particular exigency claimed. On the record here, what matters is the opportunity to get rid of cocaine, which a prudent dealer will keep near a commode or kitchen sink. * * * And 15 to 20 seconds does not seem an unrealistic guess about the time someone would need to get in a position to rid his quarters of cocaine.

### 4. Does the Violation of the Knock and Announce Requirement Justify Exclusion of Evidence?

In Hudson v. Michigan, 547 U.S. 586 (2006), the Court in a 5–4 decision held that a violation of the knock and announce requirement does not justify exclusion of evidence found in the subsequent search of the premises. Justice Scalia, writing for the majority, explained as follows:

> The interests protected by the knock-and-announce requirement * * * do not include the shielding of potential evidence from the government's eyes.

> One of those interests is the protection of human life and limb, because an unannounced entry may provoke violence in supposed self-defense by the surprised resident. Another interest is the protection of property. * * * The knock-and-announce rule gives individuals the opportunity to comply with the law and to avoid the destruction of property occasioned by a forcible entry. And thirdly, the knock-and-announce rule protects those elements of privacy and dignity that can be destroyed by a sudden entrance. It gives residents the opportunity to prepare themselves for the entry of the police. The brief interlude between announcement and entry with a warrant may be the opportunity that an individual has to pull on clothes or get out of bed. In other words, it assures the opportunity to collect oneself before answering the door.

What the knock-and-announce rule has never protected, however, is one's interest in preventing the government from seeing or taking evidence described in a warrant. Since the interests that *were* violated in this case have nothing to do with the seizure of the evidence, the exclusionary rule is inapplicable.

Justice Scalia found that the exclusionary rule was not necessary to deter violations of the knock and announce requirement, because victims of those violations could bring civil rights actions under 42 U.S.C. § 1983.

Justice Kennedy concurred in part and in the judgment. Justice Breyer, joined by Justices Stevens, Souter and Ginsburg, dissented. He argued that without the threat of exclusion, officers have no reason to comply with the knock and announce rule. *Hudson* receives full-case treatment in the section on the exclusionary rule, at the end of this Chapter.

## 5. Timing and Scope of Execution

In view of the number of search and seizure cases that have been decided, it is surprising that few have discussed the permissible latitude that officers have in *executing* a warrant. Clearly they can only look in places where the objects specified might be found. As the Court stated in United States v. Ross, 456 U.S. 798 (1982): "A lawful search of fixed premises generally extends to the entire area in which the object of the search may be found and is not limited by the possibility that separate acts of entry or entry or opening may be required to complete the search." But beyond probable cause limits as to location, the manner of searching a premises has not received much treatment.

### *Destruction and Excessiveness*

Does the authorization to search wherever evidence may be found mean that officers can break open walls, tear up floors and ceilings, and inflict other permanent damage? The case law, most of it old, offers little guidance. One case with a helpful discussion is Buckley v. Beaulieu, 104 Me. 56, 71 A. 70 (1908), where the court held that officers acted excessively and unreasonably when they searched unsuccessfully for liquor by tearing out the interior walls of a house. The court noted that the officers could have searched for any liquor concealed within the walls by using "some slender probe with comparatively little injury."

In contrast, the court in United States v. Weinbender, 109 F.3d 1327 (8th Cir.1997), found it reasonable for officers to remove a piece of drywall to search for clothes that would have tied the defendant to a crime. The officers found guns in the space behind the drywall. The court observed that the drywall was unfinished; it was a small square apparently covering a storage space; it was removed in a few seconds without tools;

and the officers had been informed that Weinbender used hiding places in his home. The court observed that "the manner in which a warrant is executed is always subject to judicial review to ensure that it does not traverse the general Fourth Amendment proscription against reasonableness." But in this case, the information possessed by the officers and the ease with which the drywall was removed led the court to conclude that the officers' actions were reasonable. And clearly it would be reasonable to do such things as break locks on briefcases and cabinets to search in areas where there is probable cause to believe that evidence exists. Otherwise, a person could stop a warranted search in its tracks simply by locking something up.

### Use of Distraction and Intimidation Devices

Is it ever reasonable for officers to employ distraction and intimidation devices in the course of a warranted search? Is it always reasonable? The use of such a device was considered by the court in United States v. Myers, 106 F.3d 936 (10th Cir.1997). The Kansas Bureau of Investigation (KBI) had probable cause to believe that Myers was growing marijuana inside his home. KBI agents also discovered that Mr. Myers had prior convictions for burglary and theft, and cocaine trafficking. They also found out that, as a juvenile, Myers had been involved in the fire bombing of a jail or police vehicle and had been convicted of possession of an unregistered firearm and possession of a fire bomb.

The KBI obtained a warrant to search Myers's residence; the warrant authorized a night-time search. The agents knocked on Myers' front door and announced that they had a search warrant. They waited ten seconds, then battered down the door and rolled a Deftec Model 25 Distraction Device, also known as a "flash-bang," into the living room. The device exploded, and the agents then stormed the house, finding Mr. Myers, his wife, nineteen-year-old stepson, nine-year-old stepdaughter, and seventeen-month-old daughter. After subduing the family, the KBI conducted a search of the house, which revealed a substantial marijuana growing operation in the attic.

The court noted that the purpose of the flash-bang device is "to distract and disorient any occupants in the vicinity of the entry" and that the device explodes with a "brilliant flash of light and a loud bang." Myers argued that the use of the flash-bang device amounted to a "military-style assault" and was unreasonable. The court was not unsympathetic to the argument, but ultimately rejected it.

> The use of a "flashbang" device in a house where innocent and unsuspecting children sleep gives us great pause. Certainly, we could not countenance the use of such a device as a routine matter.

However, we also recognize that we must review the agents' actions from the perspective of reasonable agents on the scene, who are legitimately concerned with not only doing their job but with their own safety. * * * The district court obviously credited police testimony that Mr. Myers's lengthy pattern of criminal activity—beginning with the fire bombing in 1971 and continuing until the cocaine conviction in 1988—made them apprehensive. The district court also found that the agents knew that there was a fair probability that Mr. Myers's residence contained an illegal marijuana growing operation.

Given the likelihood that a person involved in drugs may also have access to weapons, and may also have committed other crimes, will there ever be a situation during drug searches in which the use of a flash-bang device will be unreasonable? Will flash-bang devices always be reasonable in searches of the premises of suspected terrorists?

If the use of a flash-bang device is unreasonable under the circumstances, should the evidence found in the search be excluded? In United States v. Jones, 214 F.3d 836 (7th Cir. 2000), the court questioned whether the use of a flash-bang device was reasonable where officers invaded the house of a suspected drug dealer, knowing that his girlfriend and her six-year-old child was present. The court noted that "police cannot automatically throw bombs into drug dealers' houses, even if the bomb goes by the euphemism 'flash-bang device.'" But on the question of exclusion, the court reasoned as follows:

> If this were a damages action * * * the claim would be a serious one. But * * * Jones wants us to hold that the fourth amendment precludes the use of the evidence that the officers found in his apartment. That argument must be rejected for a reason unrelated to the strength of the contention that the officers behaved inappropriately: the exclusionary rule depends on causation. * * * A battering ram, flash-bang device, or blow to the neck could affect the seizure [of evidence] only by surprising or stunning the occupants so that they could not destroy evidence. * * * An argument that the occupants could have destroyed the drugs, if only they had more time and full possession of their faculties, is not a good reason to suppress probative evidence of crime.

The analysis in *Jones* receives strong support from the Supreme Court's decision in Hudson v. Michigan, supra, where the Court held that a violation of the knock and announce requirement did not justify exclusion of evidence. Like the court in *Jones,* the *Hudson* Court found no causative connection between the manner of entry and the obtaining of evidence. The defendant could hardly argue, for example, that "if not for the flash-bang device, I wouldn't have been distracted and I would have been able to destroy a lot of the evidence." See also United States v. Ankeny, 502 F.3d 829 (9th Cir. 2007) (relying on *Hudson* to hold that the unreasonable use of a flash-bang device and rubber bullets during a search did not justify exclusion of evidence).

### Unnecessarily Intrusive Searches

An example of an unreasonably intense search arose in Hummel-Jones v. Strope, 25 F.3d 647 (8th Cir.1994), a civil rights action brought by a husband (Jones) and wife (Hummel-Jones) after a 2:00 a.m. raid of the small birthing clinic at which they were staying. The court set forth the facts surrounding the search as follows:

> This dispute arises out of an investigation of the Country Cradle, a well-established and openly-operated alternative birthing clinic located in rural Missouri. A registered nurse operated the clinic. Evidently, the defendants' concern that the nurse might be practicing medicine without a license prompted the search at issue.

> On the afternoon of January 23, 1991, Board of Healing Arts Inspector Kistler became convinced that the nurse was delivering a baby at the clinic, and thereby practicing medicine without a license. Kistler contacted Deputy Sheriff Popplewell about the possibility of an investigation or a search. As a result, a reserve deputy was sent to the clinic that evening at 10 P.M. The couple, their toddler, and their four-hour old newborn were the only occupants at the time the deputy knocked on the door. The deputy told the family that he was a soldier on his way to the Gulf War. He claimed to be having car trouble, so the family admitted him to telephone for help. In reality, he was telephoning waiting officers to inform them that the Country Cradle was occupied by a family with a newborn infant.

> * * * The magistrate issued [a] warrant at approximately 1:00 A.M., and authorized a search for "video tapes, medical records, medical supplies, financial records, video equipment, medications or narcotics, sheets, [and] medical textbooks" being kept at the Country Cradle.

> At 2:00 A.M. four uniformed and armed officers, two prosecuting attorneys, and the inspector raided the Country Cradle. * * * Jones was ordered to sit on the waiting room couch and was questioned. Several others of the search party went into the separate bedroom where the pajama clad Hummel-Jones was attempting to nurse her newborn son, and began to question her. The couple declined to identify themselves. The searchers seized the couple and restricted them to the waiting room couch while the search was conducted. Whenever Hummel-Jones left the couch, an officer accompanied her. Inspector Kistler photographed the family as "evidence." Kistler also

photographed Hummel-Jones's lingerie soaking in the bathroom sink. Popplewell searched Hummel-Jones's overnight bag against her wishes. The searchers seized one of the family's banking slips to establish their identity. The searchers also seized the couple's personal video-tape of Hummel-Jones's afterbirth experience, despite the couple's objections. The search lasted for three and a half hours, or, essentially, throughout the night.

The court held that the search was so excessive—even though conducted pursuant to a warrant and probable cause—as to be unreasonable.

> The primary justification the appellees put forth for performing this search of a well-established and openly-operating birthing clinic at 2:00 A.M. was to ensure that the mother and newborn would be present. Otherwise, we are told, items of evidence, to wit, the mother, newborn, and bloody sheets, might have been lost. Mothers and newborns at a birthing clinic are not "items of evidence." And, neither the warrant nor the warrant application mention either a mother or a newborn when particularly describing the "items" to be searched for and seized. In any case, the mother and newborn were not going to disappear. At worst, they were going to go home. Photographing the mother and her newborn on the clinic premises could not help establish whether or not there was unlicensed practice of medicine occurring at the clinic because it is not illegal to give birth wherever one happens to be when the moment arrives. Nor were the bloody sheets and lingerie attendant to a birth evidence of any illegality.

What should the officers have done in *Hummel-Jones* to make the search reasonable? Is the court simply saying that the crime that the officers suspected was not worth all the havoc they caused? Would the result have been the same if Hummel-Jones had been nursing her newborn in a house full of suspected terrorists or drug dealers?

## When Is the Search Completed?

It is obvious that officers must terminate a search when all of the materials described in the warrant have been found. This standard works pretty well if officers are looking for a discrete object, like a particular stolen television. But sometimes it is difficult to determine whether all the evidence described in the warrant has been found. For example, if officers have a warrant to search for narcotics and paraphernalia, the search need not be terminated as soon as the officers find *some* narcotics. But does it follow that there is really no limitation on the scope and duration of a search for narcotics?

The courts do not seem very interested in imposing temporal or spatial limitations on searches for narcotics and related evidence. For example, in United States v. Stiver, 9 F.3d 298 (3d Cir.1993), officers armed with a search warrant for narcotics, paraphernalia, and proof of residency, entered Stiver's apartment. During the course of the search, which lasted about 80 minutes, the telephone rang many times. An officer answered the phone and pretended to be one of Stiver's associates; he took 12 orders for drugs from the callers. Stiver argued that the officers exceeded their authority by answering the phone and taking orders from his customers. But the court held that this activity was within the scope of the search authorized by the warrant. The court noted that officers are not required to interpret narrowly the terms of the warrant, and reasoned as follows:

> [T]he warrant authorized the officers to search for and seize, among other things, "all drug paraphernalia." In ordinary usage, the term "paraphernalia" is defined to mean "equipment and apparatus used in or necessary for a particular activity." [quoting the Random House Dictionary]. In light of the fact that the officers had ample cause to believe that the defendant had been using the apartment for heroin sales, * * * the officers had an entirely reasonable basis for concluding that the defendant's telephone was a piece of "equipment" or "apparatus" that was used in [drug activity]. The officers therefore acted properly in "searching" the telephone, i.e., answering it.
>
> We also believe that the officers' conduct was authorized by the portion of the warrant permitting them to search for "any items to prove residency." Telephone calls for the defendant at the premises would provide evidence that he resided there.

Does the court's reasoning mean that the officers could occupy Stiver's apartment for a week in order to take more calls from his customers? Could they occupy the apartment for a year?

## 6. Presence of the Warrant

Must the officer who executes a search warrant actually have the warrant in hand at the time of the search? Courts have held that while Fed.R.Crim.P. 41(f) requires the officer to serve upon the person searched a copy of the warrant, it does not require that this be done before the search takes place. See, e.g., United States v. Hepperle, 810 F.2d 836, 839 (8th Cir.1987) ("[w]hile it may be foolhardy to proceed in the absence of the physical presence of the warrant, it is not unconstitutional"). Considering that one reason for the warrant is to provide the executing officer with a lawful show of authority, does this result make sense?

## 7.   Enlisting Private Citizens to Help Search

### *Unwilling Assistance*

In United States v. New York Tel. Co., 434 U.S. 159 (1977), the Court, per Justice White, held that, upon a showing of probable cause, a district judge had power to order an unwilling telephone company to assist the government in installing pen registers. The All Writs Act, 28 U.S.C.A. § 1651(a) states: "The Supreme Court and all courts established by Act of Congress may issue all writs necessary or appropriate in aid of their respective jurisdictions and agreeable to the usages and principles of law." The Act was thought to be sufficient authority for a court to compel a private person to act. Justice Stevens wrote for himself and Justices Brennan and Marshall in dissent. Their position was that Congress did not empower Federal courts to compel private parties to carry out this kind of surveillance. Justice Stewart, also in dissent, agreed with this point. Justice Stevens argued that the majority's decision

> provides a sweeping grant of authority without precedent in our Nation's history. Of course, there is precedent for such authority in the common law—the writ of assistance.

If a warrant is otherwise valid, why shouldn't a person be subject to an order to help the police enforce it? Sometimes such an order might minimize the intrusion the police otherwise would have to make. Would people like Andresen be worse off if secretaries and employees could be compelled to participate in searches in order to minimize intrusions? In the *New York Telephone* case, the majority said that without assistance from the company, the government could not have conducted the surveillance. The same would be true with Internet service providers. Should this make a difference in Fourth Amendment analysis?

### *Willing Assistance*

*New York Telephone* involved civilians who were unwilling to assist the government. Is the Fourth Amendment question different if an individual *agrees* to assist the government in conducting a search of another person's property? In Bellville v. Town of Northboro, 375 F.3d 25 (1st Cir. 2004), the court found no Fourth Amendment violation where an officer asked two corporate employees to assist him in a search of a premises, at which there was probable cause to believe that electronic equipment stolen from the corporation had been stored. The court noted that the civilians were "serving a legitimate investigative function" because they could assist the officer, who did not have the necessary technical expertise to identify the property that belonged to the company. The court noted that the employees did not participate in the search "to further their own personal ends." See also United States v. Bach, 310

F.3d 1063 (8th Cir. 2002) (no error for officers to allow Yahoo technicians to retrieve all of the information from the defendant's Yahoo account in an investigation of child pornography; the court noted that "the technical expertise of Yahoo's technicians far outweighs that of the officers").

In contrast, in Bills v. Aseltine, 958 F.2d 697 (6th Cir.1992), officers had a warrant to search for a stolen generator in the Bills' residence. They also suspected that the Bills had other stolen property on the premises, though the warrant listed only the generator. The officers asked a General Motors official if he wanted to come along on the search for the generator to see if he could identify any property which might have been stolen from General Motors. During the search, the GM official took 231 photographs of various parts and equipment. The court declared:

> [The GM official] was present, not in aid of the officers or their mission, but for his own purposes, involving the recovery of stolen General Motors property not mentioned in any warrant. * * *

> * * * Officers * * * may * * * exceed the scope of the authority implicitly granted them by their warrant when they permit unauthorized invasions of privacy by third parties who have no connection to the search warrant or the officers' purposes for being on the premises.

## 8.  Media Ride Alongs

Are Fourth Amendment problems raised when officers invite the media along when they execute a search? This question was presented in Wilson v. Layne, 526 U.S. 603 (1999). Officers executing an arrest warrant for Dominic Wilson entered the home of his parents late at night. They brought a photographer and a reporter from the Washington Post along with them. Dominic's father became upset, and was subdued on the floor. Dominic's mother came out of the bedroom and witnessed the conflagration in her nightgown. Numerous photographs were taken, but none were ever published.

The Wilsons brought a civil rights action against the officers, contending that the "media ride along" violated their Fourth Amendment rights. The Supreme Court, in an opinion by Chief Justice Rehnquist, unanimously agreed that the media observation of the execution of the arrest warrant in the Wilson's home constituted a Fourth Amendment violation.

The Chief Justice stated that police actions undertaken in execution of a warrant must be "related to the objectives of the authorized intrusion." In this case, "the presence of reporters inside the home was not related to the objectives of the authorized intrusion." The Chief Justice emphasized that this was not a case "in which the presence of the third parties directly aided in the execution of the warrant" and noted that when police enter a home to search for stolen property, "the presence of third parties for the purpose of identifying the stolen property has long been approved by this Court and our common-law tradition."

The officers cited a number of law enforcement objectives that might be met by a media ride along. But the Court rejected these interests as insufficient. The Chief Justice elaborated in the following passage:

> Respondents argue that the presence of the Washington Post reporters in the Wilsons' home nonetheless served a number of legitimate law enforcement purposes. They first assert that officers should be able to exercise reasonable discretion about when it would "further their law enforcement mission to permit members of the news media to accompany them in executing a warrant." But this claim ignores the importance of the right of residential privacy at the core of the Fourth Amendment. It may well be that media ride-alongs further the law enforcement objectives of the police in a general sense, but that is not the same as furthering the purposes of the search. * * *

> Respondents next argue that the presence of third parties could serve the law enforcement purpose of publicizing the government's efforts to combat crime, and facilitate accurate reporting on law enforcement activities. * * * Surely the possibility of good public relations for the police is simply not enough, standing alone, to justify the ride-along intrusion into a private home. And even the need for accurate reporting on police issues in general bears no direct relation to the constitutional justification for the police intrusion into a home in order to execute a felony arrest warrant.

> Finally, respondents argue that the presence of third parties could serve in some situations to minimize police abuses and protect suspects, and also to protect the safety of the officers. While it might be reasonable for police officers to themselves videotape home entries as part of a "quality control" effort to ensure that the rights of homeowners are being respected, or even to preserve evidence, such a situation is significantly different from the media presence in this case. The Washington Post reporters in the Wilsons' home were working on a story for their own purposes. * * *

*Wilson* was a civil action for damages, so the exclusionary rule was not operative. In a footnote, however, the Chief Justice took pains to note that with respect to media ride alongs, "if the police are lawfully present, the violation of the Fourth Amendment is the presence of the media and not the presence of the police in the home." The Court had "no occasion here to decide whether the exclusionary rule would apply to any evidence discovered or developed by the media representatives." For a lower court answer to that question, see United States v. Duenas, 691 F.3d 1070 (9th Cir. 2012):

> Where the media were present, but did not discover or develop any of the evidence later used at trial, the evidence need not be excluded. Here, the media did not expand the scope of the search beyond the warrant's dictates; nor did the media assist the police, or touch, move, handle or taint the admitted evidence in any way. Because the [officers] complied with the terms of the warrant and the media did not disturb any evidence later admitted, the more appropriate remedy here * * * is a *Bivens* or a 42 U.S.C. § 1983 action.

The analysis in *Duenas* receives strong support from the Supreme Court's decision in Hudson v. Michigan, supra, where the Court held that a violation of the knock and announce requirement did not justify exclusion of evidence. Like the court in *Duenas,* the *Hudson* Court found no causative connection between the manner of entry and the obtaining of evidence.

## D.  THE SCREENING MAGISTRATE

### 1.  Neutral and Detached

What is required for a magistrate to be considered neutral and detached, as the Court referred to in *Johnson, supra.* In Coolidge v. New Hampshire, 403 U.S. 443, 449–453 (1971), the Court invalidated a warrant issued by the state's Attorney General, who was authorized by state law to act as a justice of the peace. The Court concluded that an executive officer, the head of law enforcement in the State, could not be the neutral and detached magistrate required by the Constitution. Justice Black, joined by Chief Justice Burger and Justice Blackmun, dissented. That three justices were willing to hold that a law enforcement officer could be the screener in the warrant process suggests something about the teeth they wanted to see that process have. However, in Connally v. Georgia, 429 U.S. 245 (1977), the Court was unanimous in holding that a magistrate who was paid a fee if he issued a warrant, and nothing if he denied an application, was not neutral and detached.

In United States v. McKeever, 906 F.2d 129 (5th Cir.1990), the defendant complained of the magistrate's neutrality on the following grounds: she was formerly involved in law enforcement and retained reserve officer status; her husband was a deputy; and she visited the site of the search while it was being conducted. The court found these factors "troubling" but not enough to show a lack of neutrality. The court stated that a magistrate may retain certain law enforcement duties without losing neutrality; that no showing was made that the magistrate's husband participated in the issuance of the warrant or the search; and that the magistrate went to the site solely out of "curiosity" and did not assist in the search. Compare Lo-Ji Sales, Inc. v. New York, 442 U.S. 319 (1979) (magistrate loses neutral and detached status when he assists in the search).

### *Rubber Stamp*

Of course, if the magistrate issues the warrant without even reading the application, he has become a rubber stamp and cannot be found neutral and detached. See United States v. Decker, 956 F.2d 773 (8th Cir.1992) (magistrate loses neutral and detached status when he fails to read a warrant because he was "intrigued" by the manner in which the officer became suspicious of the defendant). But it is difficult for the defendant to prove that the magistrate actually acted as a rubber stamp. For example, in United States v. Brown, 832 F.2d 991 (7th Cir.1987), the defendant sought to prove that the municipal judge who issued the warrant against him had acted as a rubber stamp. Brown submitted into evidence hundreds of search warrants issued by the municipal judge. Most of the affidavits approved by the judge were form affidavits. The court stated that the volume of warrants issued, especially in comparison to lesser amounts issued by other judges, proved not that the judge was a rubber stamp, but rather that the judge had "extraordinary experience in reviewing warrant applications." The court noted, with considerable understatement, that "it might be difficult for a litigant to establish" that a judge has abandoned her neutral and detached role.

### 2. Legal Training

In Shadwick v. City of Tampa, 407 U.S. 345 (1972), the Court considered whether the Fourth Amendment required a magistrate to have legal training. In Tampa, municipal clerks, who were not lawyers, were authorized to issue arrest warrants for minor offenses. Justice Powell, writing for a unanimous Court, held that the clerks qualified as neutral and detached magistrates despite their lack of legal training. Justice Powell found that the two standards, of neutrality and competence, were met by the Tampa municipal clerks:

> The clerk's neutrality has not been impeached: he is removed from prosecutor or police and works within the judicial branch subject to the supervision of the municipal court judge.
>
> Appellant likewise has failed to demonstrate that these clerks lack capacity to determine probable cause. The clerk's authority extends only to the issuance of arrest warrants for breach of municipal ordinances. We presume from the nature of the clerk's position that he would be able to deduce from the facts on an affidavit before him whether there was probable cause to believe a citizen

guilty of impaired driving, breach of peace, drunkenness, trespass, or the multiple other common offenses covered by a municipal code. There has been no showing that this is too difficult a task for a clerk to accomplish.

Justice Powell emphasized that the Court was not making a categorical rule that the issuance of warrants by non-lawyers would always satisfy the Fourth Amendment requirements of neutrality and detachment. Rather, the Court simply rejected the categorical rule that non-lawyers could never act as neutral and detached magistrates. Justice Powell concluded: "States are entitled to some flexibility and leeway in their designation of magistrates, so long as all are neutral and detached and capable of the probable-cause determination required of them."

### NOTE ON SHADWICK

*Shadwick* dealt with arrest warrants, not search warrants. But, the Court's disclaimers notwithstanding, it is clear that the Court was defining the term "magistrate" for Fourth Amendment purposes. The *Shadwick* Court cited arrest and search cases interchangeably. And in Illinois v. Gates, 462 U.S. 213 (1983), considered supra, the Court assumed that non-lawyers may issue search warrants. Do you believe that the warrant clause is meaningful when the magistrate is not a lawyer? What message, if any, does *Shadwick* send to magistrates about the importance of their screening function?

### 3. Magistrate Decisions

There is no requirement that a magistrate give reasons for finding probable cause or for rejecting a warrant application. Is there an argument that magistrates should have to signify in writing their reasons for finding probable cause before issuing a warrant? Would you be persuaded by a counter-argument that it does not matter whether the magistrate reasoned properly as long as the Fourth Amendment probable cause standard actually is satisfied by the warrant application? Can the Fourth Amendment be satisfied if the magistrate is not reasoning properly?

## V.   TO APPLY OR NOT APPLY THE WARRANT CLAUSE

As stated previously, the Court has held that a search or seizure is presumptively unreasonable in the absence of a warrant based upon probable cause. However, the Court has found that the presumption of unreasonableness can be overcome in a variety of circumstances. Some of the circumstances excuse the officer from obtaining a warrant, but still require the officer to have probable cause. Other circumstances permit a search or seizure even though the officer has neither a warrant nor probable cause. As you read through the "exceptions" to the warrant clause discussed below, be sure to keep straight exactly what requirements the Court retains for each exception. In order to do this, it is helpful to begin with the justification for each exception.

# A.   ARRESTS IN PUBLIC AND IN THE HOME

## 1.   Standards for Warrantless Arrests

Once the point is made that warrants are necessary to search for property and seize it, it might seem that to search for and seize a person would *a fortiori* require a warrant. But this is not the law.

Section 120.1 of the ALI Model Code of Pre-Arraignment Procedure illustrates the powers that police may be given to proceed without a warrant.

### Section 120.1. Arrest Without a Warrant

(1) **Authority to Arrest Without a Warrant.** A law enforcement officer may arrest a person without a warrant if the officer has reasonable cause to believe that such person has committed

(a) a felony;

(b) a misdemeanor, and the officer has reasonable cause to believe that such person

(i) will not be apprehended unless immediately arrested; or

(ii) may cause injury to himself or others or damage to property unless immediately arrested; or

(c) a misdemeanor or petty misdemeanor in the officer's presence.

\* \* \*

Note that even though an arrest is permitted in certain circumstances without a warrant, the officer must always have probable cause to arrest a suspect. See the discussion of probable cause to arrest, earlier in this Chapter.

## 2.   Arrest Versus Summons

Why is it reasonable under the Fourth Amendment to begin the criminal process by arresting a suspect, rather than by simply notifying him to appear in court? In 1791, when the Fourth Amendment was adopted, the prevalence of the death penalty and the incentive it provided offenders to escape might have provided a reason for seizing a person at the time he was charged with any felony. Then, and now, arresting someone who is committing an offense in the officer's presence, especially one who is disturbing the public peace, could be defended on the ground that officers should stop criminal activities before they are completed, if reasonably possible. See, e.g., Diaz v. City of Fitchburg, 176 F.3d 560 (1st Cir.1999) (not unreasonable to effect custodial arrest on persons who violated an ordinance that prohibits the obstruction of public passages: "If the officer always were obligated to allow the criminal obstruction to continue, he or she would be unable to satisfy the Ordinance's apparent purpose of assuring public convenience and safety."). But, why should other cases begin with forcible detention? Is it clear that persons charged with criminal offenses are much more likely to flee than persons named as defendants in civil actions?

In Gustafson v. Florida, 414 U.S. 260, 267 (1973), Justice Stewart suggested that "a persuasive claim might have been made * * * that the custodial arrest of the petitioner for a minor traffic offense violated his rights under the Fourth and Fourteenth Amendments." But that suggestion has never become law.

To the contrary: in Atwater v. City of Lago Vista, 532 U.S. 318 (2001), the Court opted for a bright-line rule that a custodial arrest is *always* reasonable if the officer has probable cause of a criminal violation. Atwater was arrested for a minor traffic offense (a seat belt violation) that was punishable only by a fine. Yet instead of getting a ticket that would operate as a notice to appear, Atwater was detained, brought to the police station and booked. She argued that these custodial actions were unreasonable for such a minor offense. But the Court reasoned, among other things, that it would be too difficult to distinguish among offenses that could justify custodial arrest and those that could not. *Atwater* is set forth in full in the section on arrest powers, *infra*. It is clear after *Atwater* that the decision to proceed by arrest or summons (where custodial arrest is authorized) is totally within the police officer's discretion.

*Atwater* holds that an officer does not need to proceed by summons, even for minor offenses as long as the state authorizes a custodial arrest for the offense. Some states have laws that *require* police officers to arrest anyone suspected of seriously beating a spouse. See "Albany Set to Require Arrest In Domestic Violence Cases," New York Times, June 22, 1994, p.A1, col. 5 (noting the view of the sponsors of such a bill that it "would sharply reduce police discretion in such cases and remedy spotty enforcement of domestic violence laws"). These bills have been criticized by some law enforcement officials on the grounds that they "hamstring police officers" and "force the police to make unwarranted arrests." Id. Is it better to leave the entire question of "arrest versus summons" to the discretion of police officers or to impose some constraints on the decision whether to arrest or issue a citation?

## 3.   The Constitutional Rule: Arrests in Public

The following case sets forth the constitutional basis for permitting a public arrest in the absence of a warrant.

### UNITED STATES V. WATSON

Supreme Court of the United States, 1976.
423 U.S. 411.

### MR. JUSTICE WHITE delivered the opinion of the Court.

This case presents questions under the Fourth Amendment as to the legality of a warrantless arrest * * *.

* * *

The relevant events began on August 17, 1972, when an informant, one Khoury, telephoned a postal inspector informing him that respondent Watson was in possession of a stolen credit card and had asked Khoury to cooperate in using the card to their mutual advantage. On five to 10 previous occasions Khoury had provided the inspector with reliable information on postal inspection matters, some involving Watson. Later that day Khoury delivered the card to the inspector. On learning that Watson had agreed to furnish additional cards, the inspector asked Khoury to arrange to meet with Watson. * * * Khoury met with Watson at a restaurant designated by the latter. Khoury had been instructed that if Watson had additional stolen credit cards, Khoury was to give a designated signal. The signal was given, the officers closed in, and Watson was forthwith arrested. * * * A search having revealed that Watson had no credit cards on his person, the inspector asked if he could look inside Watson's car, which was standing within view. Watson said, "Go ahead," and repeated these words when the inspector cautioned that "[i]f I find anything, it is going to go against you." Using keys furnished by Watson, the inspector entered the car and found under the floor mat an envelope containing two credit cards in the names of other persons. * * *

Prior to trial, Watson moved to suppress the cards, claiming that his arrest was illegal for want of * * * an arrest warrant * * *. The motion was denied, and Watson was convicted of illegally possessing the two cards seized from his car.

[The court of appeals held that Watson's arrest was illegal because the officers had not obtained an arrest warrant, and there were no exigent circumstances to justify the absence of a warrant. The court of appeals further held that the credit cards should have been suppressed as the fruits of the illegal arrest.]

* * *

[T]here is nothing in the Court's prior cases indicating that under the Fourth Amendment a warrant is required to make a valid arrest for a felony. Indeed, the relevant prior decisions are uniformly to the contrary.

The usual rule is that a police officer may arrest without warrant one believed by the officer upon reasonable cause to have been guilty of a felony * * *. * * *

The cases construing the Fourth Amendment thus reflect the ancient common-law rule that a peace officer was permitted to arrest without a warrant for a misdemeanor or felony committed in his presence as well as for a felony not committed in his presence if there was reasonable ground for making the arrest. This has also been the prevailing rule under state constitutions and statutes. * * *

* * *

The balance struck by the common law in generally authorizing felony arrests on probable cause, but without a warrant, has survived substantially intact. It appears in almost all of the States in the form of express statutory authorization. * * *

This is the rule Congress has long directed its principal law enforcement officers to follow. Congress has plainly decided against conditioning warrantless arrest power on proof of exigent circumstances. Law enforcement officers may find it wise to seek arrest warrants where practicable to do so, and their judgments about probable cause may be more readily accepted where backed by a warrant issued by a magistrate. But we decline to transform this judicial preference into a constitutional rule when the judgment of the Nation and Congress has for so long been to authorize warrantless public arrests on probable cause rather than to encumber criminal prosecutions with endless litigation with respect to the existence of exigent circumstances, whether it was practicable to get a warrant, whether the suspect was about to flee, and the like.

Watson's arrest did not violate the Fourth Amendment, and the Court of Appeals erred in holding to the contrary.

* * *

MR. JUSTICE STEVENS took no part in the consideration or decision of this case.

[JUSTICE STEWART's one paragraph opinion concurring in the judgment is omitted.]

**MR. JUSTICE POWELL, concurring.**

\* \* \*

Since the Fourth Amendment speaks equally to both searches and seizures, and since an arrest, the taking hold of one's person, is quintessentially a seizure, it would seem that the constitutional provision should impose the same limitations upon arrests that it does upon searches. Indeed, as an abstract matter an argument can be made that the restrictions upon arrest perhaps should be greater. A search may cause only annoyance and temporary inconvenience to the law-abiding citizen, assuming more serious dimension only when it turns up evidence of criminality. An arrest, however, is a serious personal intrusion regardless of whether the person seized is guilty or innocent. \* \* \*.

But logic sometimes must defer to history and experience. The Court's opinion emphasizes the historical sanction accorded warrantless felony arrests. \* \* \*

[A] constitutional rule permitting felony arrests only with a warrant or in exigent circumstances could severely hamper effective law enforcement. Good police practice often requires postponing an arrest, even after probable cause has been established, in order to place the suspect under surveillance or otherwise develop further evidence necessary to prove guilt to a jury. Under the holding of the Court of Appeals such additional investigative work could imperil the entire prosecution. Should the officers fail to obtain a warrant initially, and later be required by unforeseen circumstances to arrest immediately with no chance to procure a last-minute warrant, they would risk a court decision that the subsequent exigency did not excuse their failure to get a warrant in the interim since they first developed probable cause. If the officers attempted to meet such a contingency by procuring a warrant as soon as they had probable cause and then merely held it during their subsequent investigation, they would risk a court decision that the warrant had grown stale by the time it was used. Law enforcement personnel caught in this squeeze could ensure validity of their arrests only by obtaining a warrant and arresting as soon as probable cause existed, thereby foreclosing the possibility of gathering vital additional evidence from the suspect's continued actions.

\* \* \*

**MR. JUSTICE MARSHALL, with whom MR. JUSTICE BRENNAN joins, dissenting.**

By granting police broad powers to make warrantless arrests, the Court today sharply reverses the course of our modern decisions construing the Warrant Clause of the Fourth Amendment. \* \* \*

\* \* \*

The Government's assertion that a warrant requirement would impose an intolerable burden stems, in large part, from the specious supposition that procurement of an arrest warrant would be necessary as soon as probable cause ripens. There is no requirement that a search warrant be obtained the moment police have probable cause to search. The rule is only that present probable cause be shown and a warrant obtained before a search is undertaken. The same rule should obtain for arrest warrants, where it may even make more sense. Certainly, there is less need for prompt procurement of a warrant in the arrest situation. Unlike probable cause to search, probable cause to arrest, once formed, will continue to exist for the indefinite future, at least if no intervening exculpatory facts come to light.

\* \* \*

It is suggested, however, that even if application of this rule does not require police to secure a warrant as soon as they obtain probable cause, the confused officer would nonetheless be prone to do so. If so, police "would risk a court decision that the warrant had grown stale by the time it was used." This fear is groundless. \* \* \* Just as it is virtually impossible for probable cause for an arrest to grow stale between the time of formation and the time a warrant is procured, it is virtually impossible for probable cause to become stale between procurement and arrest. Delay by law enforcement officers in executing an arrest warrant does not ordinarily affect the legality of the arrest. In short, staleness should be the least of an arresting officer's worries.

\* \* \*

### NOTE ON THE USE OF EXCESSIVE FORCE IN MAKING AN ARREST

The Supreme Court limited the use of deadly force to apprehend a suspect in Tennessee v. Garner, 471 U.S. 1 (1985). The Court held that under the Fourth Amendment, deadly force may not be used to prevent the escape of a felon unless it is necessary to prevent the escape *and* the officer has probable cause to believe that the suspect poses a significant threat of causing death or serious physical injury to the officer or others. The felon who was running from the police in *Garner* had committed a non-violent felony and was not known to be violent. The Court concluded that the felon's Fourth Amendment rights were violated when he was shot and killed by an officer who chased and could not catch him. Justice White wrote for six Justices that "[i]t is not better that all felony suspects die than that they escape."

Justice O'Connor, joined by Chief Justice Burger and Justice Rehnquist, dissented in *Garner*. She argued that "the Court effectively creates a Fourth Amendment right allowing a burglary suspect to flee unimpeded from a police officer who has probable cause to arrest, who has ordered the suspect to halt, and who has no means short of firing his weapon to prevent escape."

After *Garner*, the Supreme Court held in Graham v. Connor, 490 U.S. 386 (1989), that all claims of excessive force in the making of an arrest (whether deadly or not) are to be governed by Fourth Amendment standards of reasonableness. Chief Justice Rehnquist, writing for the Court, indicated that some of the relevant factors in the Fourth Amendment reasonableness inquiry "include the severity of the crime at issue, whether the suspect poses an immediate threat to the safety of the officers or others, and whether he is actively resisting arrest or attempting to evade arrest by flight." Consequently, while an officer may use non-deadly force in apprehending a fleeing or resistant felon, the manner in which the force is asserted might be unreasonable. For example, if the officer uses a police dog that is improperly trained, or fails to give a proper warning or instruction before letting the dog loose, this might be found to be an unreasonable use of force. See, e.g., Vathekan v. Prince George's County, 154 F.3d 173 (4th Cir.1998) (officer who releases an attack dog during a burglary investigation, without giving verbal warning to the suspect, would act unreasonably under the Fourth Amendment).

### *High-Speed Chases: Scott v. Harris*

In Scott v. Harris, 550 U.S. 372 (2007), the Court held a law enforcement official can, consistent with the Fourth Amendment, attempt to stop a fleeing motorist from continuing a public-endangering flight by ramming the motorist's car from behind. Justice Scalia, writing for the Court, declared that officers were not required to avoid a risk to the public by simply stopping their pursuit of a suspect in a car. If that were the rule, drivers could avoid arrest simply by speeding away from the officers. Justice Scalia also noted that in determining reasonableness, it was appropriate to balance the risk to the suspect of ramming his car against the risk to the public of a continued chase. And in doing so, officers could consider the culpability of the suspect against the innocence of members of the public who could be put in danger.

Justice Scalia concluded by stating the rule of law from the case: "A police officer's attempt to terminate a dangerous high-speed car chase that threatens the lives of innocent bystanders does not violate the Fourth Amendment, even when it places the fleeing motorist at risk of serious injury or death."[10]

### 4.  Protections Against Erroneous Warrantless Arrests

*Watson* holds that if an officer has probable cause to believe that a person has committed a felony, he can arrest the suspect in a public place

---

[10]  Justice Ginsburg wrote a short concurring opinion. Justice Stevens dissented.

without a warrant. As discussed earlier in this Chapter, the risk of a warrantless search or seizure is that an officer, in the competitive enterprise of ferreting out crime, may be mistaken in his assessment of probable cause. The Supreme Court has held that while a warrant is not required for a public arrest, certain post-arrest protections are necessary to minimize the intrusion on a person who is arrested without probable cause. In Gerstein v. Pugh, 420 U.S. 103 (1975), the Court declared that if a person is arrested without a warrant, he is entitled to a "prompt" post-arrest assessment of probable cause by a magistrate. The *Gerstein* Court also held, however, that the state need not provide the adversary safeguards associated with a trial. The Court reasoned that the probable cause standard traditionally has been decided by a magistrate in a nonadversary hearing on the basis of hearsay and written testimony.

In County of Riverside v. McLaughlin, 500 U.S. 44 (1991), Justice O'Connor wrote for the Court in a class action by pretrial detainees as it defined what is "prompt" under *Gerstein*. She reasoned as follows:

> Given that *Gerstein* permits jurisdictions to incorporate probable cause determinations into other pretrial procedures, some delays are inevitable. * * * On weekends, when the number of arrests is often higher and available resources tend to be limited, arraignments may get pushed back even further. In our view, the Fourth Amendment permits a reasonable postponement of a probable cause determination while the police cope with the everyday problems of processing suspects through an overly burdened criminal justice system.

> But flexibility has its limits; *Gerstein* is not a blank check. A State has no legitimate interest in detaining for extended periods individuals who have been arrested without probable cause. * * *

* * *

> Our task in this case is to articulate more clearly the boundaries of what is permissible under the Fourth Amendment. Although we hesitate to announce that the Constitution compels a specific time limit, it is important to provide some degree of certainty so that States and counties may establish procedures with confidence that they fall within constitutional bounds. Taking into account the competing interests articulated in *Gerstein,* we believe that a jurisdiction that provides judicial determinations of probable cause within 48 hours of arrest will, as a general matter, comply with the promptness requirement of *Gerstein*. For this reason, such jurisdictions will be immune from systemic challenges.

> This is not to say that the probable cause determination in a particular case passes constitutional muster simply because it is provided within 48 hours. Such a hearing may nonetheless violate

*Gerstein* if the arrested individual can prove that his or her probable cause determination was delayed unreasonably. Examples of unreasonable delay are delays for the purpose of gathering additional evidence to justify the arrest, a delay motivated by ill will against the arrested individual, or delay for delay's sake. In evaluating whether the delay in a particular case is unreasonable, however, courts must allow a substantial degree of flexibility. Courts cannot ignore the often unavoidable delays in transporting arrested persons from one facility to another, handling late-night bookings where no magistrate is readily available, obtaining the presence of an arresting officer who may be busy processing other suspects or securing the premises of an arrest, and other practical realities.

Where an arrested individual does not receive a probable cause determination within 48 hours, the calculus changes. In such a case, the arrested individual does not bear the burden of proving an unreasonable delay. Rather, the burden shifts to the government to demonstrate the existence of a bona fide emergency or other extraordinary circumstance. * * * A jurisdiction that chooses to offer combined proceedings must do so as soon as is reasonably feasible, but in no event later than 48 hours after arrest.

* * *

Justice Scalia dissented and argued that "it is an 'unreasonable seizure' * * * to delay a determination of probable cause for the arrest either (1) for reasons unrelated to arrangement of the probable-cause determination or completion of the steps incident to arrest, or (2) beyond 24 hours after the arrest." He added that "I would treat the time limit as a presumption; when the 24 hours are exceeded the burden shifts to the police to adduce unforeseeable circumstances justifying the additional delay."

Justice Marshall, joined by Justices Blackmun and Stevens also dissented and wrote that "I agree with Justice Scalia that a probable-cause hearing is sufficiently "prompt" under *Gerstein* only when provided immediately upon completion of the 'administrative steps incident to arrest.'"

### Detentions for Less Than 48 Hours

The Court in *McLaughlin* noted that an individual detention might be unreasonable even if it is less than 48 hours. The court in United States v. Davis, 174 F.3d 941 (8th Cir. 1999), found a warrantless detention unreasonable even though it lasted only two hours. Officers arrested Davis for falsely reporting a theft. She was placed in a holding cell for two hours, and was then questioned about her boyfriend, who was suspected of illegally trafficking in firearms. She was released after agreeing to obtain evidence against her boyfriend. Booking procedures on the false report charge were never initiated, and she was never taken before a magistrate to determine whether there was probable cause to arrest her on that charge. Under these circumstances, the court found that Davis had been detained illegally. The court read *McLaughlin* and subsequent lower court cases as having made clear "that a delay may be unreasonable if it is motivated by a desire to uncover additional evidence to support the arrest or to use the suspect's presence solely to investigate the suspect's involvement in other crimes." The court concluded that *McLaughlin* "does not * * * stand for the proposition that authorities may violate the Constitution as long as they do so for only a brief period of time."

Is the court saying that Davis's detention was illegal because the officer had an improper motive in detaining her? Isn't a focus on an officer's motive inconsistent with the Fourth Amendment's standard of objective reasonableness?

### *Remedy for a McLaughlin Violation*

What is the remedy for an unreasonable delay in presentment to a magistrate? Certainly there could be a possible damages recovery, but what about excluding evidence (most likely a confession) that was obtained from the defendant during an unreasonably excessive delay before presentment to the magistrate?

Courts have found that evidence can be excluded only if it was obtained as a result of an unreasonable detention. Thus, exclusion is not required if the magistrate would have found probable cause for the detention even if the hearing had been promptly conducted. See State v. Tucker, 137 N.J. 259, 645 A.2d 111 (1994) (confession made after 48 hour period was admissible, where evidence against the defendant was so strong that he would not have been released had a hearing been held earlier). And exclusion would not be required if the evidence was obtained outside the context of an unreasonably lengthy detention. See United States v. Fullerton, 187 F.3d 587 (6th Cir. 1999) (even though the defendant was detained for 72 hours without a hearing, this did not result in exclusion of evidence obtained from him at the time of the arrest, as there was no causal connection between the *McLaughlin* violation and the seizure of the evidence).

## 5.   Arrests in the Home

### *The Payton Rule*

*Watson* and *Gerstein* left open the question whether a warrant is necessary to enter a home to make an arrest. The Court took up that question in Payton v. New York, 445 U.S. 573 (1980), and held that the exception to the warrant requirement for public arrests did not extend to arrests in the home. The Court described the facts as follows:

> On January 14, 1970, after two days of intensive investigation, New York detectives had assembled evidence sufficient to establish probable cause to believe that Theodore Payton had murdered the manager of a gas station two days earlier. At about 7:30 a.m. on January 15, six officers went to Payton's apartment in the Bronx, intending to arrest him. They had not obtained a warrant. Although light and music emanated from the apartment, there was no response to their knock on the metal door. They summoned emergency assistance and, about 30 minutes later, used crowbars to break open the door and enter the apartment. No one was there. In plain view, however, was a .30-caliber shell casing that was seized and later admitted into evidence at Payton's murder trial.

> In due course Payton surrendered to the police, was indicted for murder, and moved to suppress the evidence taken from his apartment.

Justice Stevens's majority opinion emphasized that the home has always been viewed as an especially private place; set forth a history that indicated there were doubts at common law concerning authority to invade a home to make an arrest; conceded that a majority of state courts addressing the question had permitted warrantless arrests in the home, but observed a trend in the opposite direction in the previous decade; and finally decided that the home deserved special protection. Justice Stevens concluded that "the Fourth Amendment has drawn a firm line at the entrance to the house" and that "absent exigent circumstances, that threshold may not reasonably be crossed without a warrant."[11]

In its penultimate paragraph, the opinion addressed the kind of warrant it required—specifically whether the officers needed a search warrant (with a magistrate's determination that there was probable cause to believe that the arrestee could be found in a particular place) or an arrest warrant (allowing the officers to make an arrest wherever the find the person named in the warrant):

> Finally, we note the State's suggestion that only a search warrant based upon probable cause to believe the suspect is at home at a given time can adequately protect the privacy interests at stake, and since such a warrant requirement is manifestly impractical, there need be no warrant of any kind. We find this ingenious argument

---

[11] If negative consequences could occur in the time it takes to obtain a warrant, the officers are excused from obtaining one under the doctrine of "exigent circumstances." This doctrine applies both to arrest warrants otherwise required by *Payton*, and to search warrants. See the discussion of exigent circumstances later in this Chapter.

unpersuasive. It is true that an arrest warrant requirement may afford less protection than a search warrant requirement [because it is not specific as to location], but it will suffice to interpose the magistrate's determination of probable cause between the zealous officer and the citizen. If there is sufficient evidence of a citizen's participation in a felony to persuade a judicial officer that his arrest is justified, it is constitutionally reasonable to require him to open his doors to the officers of the law. Thus, for Fourth Amendment purposes, an arrest warrant founded on probable cause implicitly carries with it the limited authority to enter a dwelling in which the suspect lives when there is reason to believe the suspect is within.[12]

An in-home arrest is no worse than a public arrest in terms of the seizure that occurs. Both arrestees end up in the same place. So the difference between an in-home arrest and one in public must be that, in conducting the arrest in the home, the officer also ends up *searching* the home.

### Reason to Believe the Suspect Is at Home

*Payton* leaves it to the officer executing the arrest warrant to determine whether there is "reason to believe the suspect is within" the home. Is this consistent with the theory of the warrant clause? Is the officer who executes a search warrant free to determine whether enough information exists to believe that evidence described in the warrant is located in a certain place?

Does the Court in *Payton* mean that an arresting officer must have *probable cause* to believe the suspect is at home? Or does "reason to believe" mean something less than probable cause? In United States v. Magluta, 44 F.3d 1530 (11th Cir.1995), the defendant argued that there was no probable cause to believe that he was at home when the officers entered with an arrest warrant, and the government argued that officers only needed "reason to believe" that he was at home, not probable cause. The court, noting that *Payton* was vague at best on this point, declared as follows:

> We think it sufficient to hold that in order for law enforcement officials to enter a residence to execute an arrest warrant for a resident of the premises, the facts and circumstances within the knowledge of the law enforcement agents, when viewed in the totality, must warrant a reasonable belief that the location to be searched is the suspect's dwelling, and that the suspect is within the residence at the time of entry. * * * In evaluating this on the spot

---

[12] Justice Blackmun wrote a one paragraph concurring opinion. Justice White dissented and was joined by the Chief Justice and Justice Rehnquist. Justice Rehnquist also added a short dissent.

determination * * * courts must be sensitive to common sense factors indicating a resident's presence. For example, officers may take into consideration the possibility that the resident may be aware that police are attempting to ascertain whether or not the resident is at home, and officers may presume that a person is at home at certain times of the day—a presumption which can be rebutted by contrary evidence regarding the suspect's known schedule.

The *Magluta* court found that the officers had "reason to believe" Magluta was at home, because a visitor was on the premises, Magluta's car was in the driveway, and a porch light was on. The fact that the officers had not seen Magluta about the premises that day was not dispositive, because "the officers were entitled to consider that Magluta was a fugitive from justice, wanted on a 24 count drug trafficking indictment, who might have been concealing his presence." Compare United States v. Hill, 649 F.3d 258 (4th Cir. 2011) (mere fact that noise was coming from the premises did not provide reason to believe the defendant was there: "Here, at best, the police had reason to believe that someone was present and that the individual insides was [the defendant's] sister.").

Some courts have held that the "reason to believe" standard must mean less than probable cause, because the Court in *Payton* could have said "probable cause" if it wanted to do so. See United States v. Thomas, 429 F.3d 282 (D.C. Cir. 2005) (it is more likely that "the Supreme Court in *Payton* used a phrase other than 'probable cause' because it meant something other than probable cause"). Other courts have found that the "reason to believe" language in *Payton* was the Court's shorthand for probable cause and so the standards are the same. See United States v. Pruitt, 458 F.3d 477 (6th Cir. 2006) ("Despite some courts' attempt to distinguish between the two monikers, the 'reason to believe' standard directly echoes the underlying definition of probable cause."). See also United States v. Barrera, 464 F.3d 496 (the distinction between probable cause and reasonable belief is "more about semantics than substance").

### *Is the Arrest at Home or in Public?*

In light of *Payton* and *Watson,* it becomes important to determine whether an arrest occurs in the home, where a warrant is generally required, or in public, where it is not. In United States v. Holland, 755 F.2d 253 (2d Cir.1985), the defendant was in his second-floor apartment in a two-family house when he heard someone ring the doorbell to his apartment. To answer the bell, he had to walk down a flight of stairs through a common hallway and open the door in the front of the building. There he was arrested without a warrant. The court found no intent in *Payton* to broaden the definition of "home" so as to include the entranceway to a common hallway. Judge Newman in dissent noted that if Holland had been living in a modern building with a buzzer mechanism, the officer would have had to arrest him at the door to his apartment. He concluded that *Payton* should apply as well to the "humble surroundings" in which the defendant lived.

What if the officers announce their presence and order the citizen to open the door, and the citizen opens the door to his home and is placed under arrest right there? Is that arrest made in the home or in public? Lower courts have split on this question. Some courts have stated that if the defendant is ordered to open the door under a lawful claim of authority, and is arrested upon opening the door, then the arrest occurs in the home and a warrant is required. See United States v. Flowers, 336 F.3d 1222 (10th Cir. 2003). Compare United States v. Vaneaton, 49 F.3d 1423 (9th Cir.1995) (no arrest warrant required where the defendant voluntarily opened the door, and thus "his actions were not taken in response to a claim of lawful authority"). Other courts hold that if the officers remain outside the doorway and inform the defendant that he is under arrest, then the arrest is made in public because the officers never physically entered the home. This latter view leads to difficult fact questions when the officer subsequently enters the home, for example to secure the premises or to follow the defendant while he gets his coat. Under this latter "officer was outside" view, if the arrest was made before the physical entry, then the entry can be justified as incident to the arrest and information discovered during the incident search will be considered legally obtained. However, if the arrest is made after the entry and without a warrant, then there has been a *Payton* violation, and the information discovered during the entry is illegally obtained. See United States v. Berkowitz, 927 F.2d 1376 (7th Cir.1991) (remanding to determine whether the officers informed the defendant that he was under arrest before or after entering his home). Courts holding that a doorway arrest constitutes an arrest in the home do not have to deal with such fine-line distinctions.

If the defendant is in his home, can the officer wait for ten hours for the defendant to come outside and then arrest him without a warrant? See United States v. Bustamante-Saenz, 894 F.2d 114 (5th Cir.1990) (yes). The holding in *Bustamante-Saenz* receives support from the Supreme Court decision in New York v. Harris, 495 U.S. 14 (1990), in which the Court held that a violation of *Payton* constitutes an illegal *search* of the home, but that the warrantless in-home *arrest* is not itself illegal so long as the officer has probable cause to arrest. *Harris* concerned the fruits of an alleged *Payton* violation, and is discussed in the material on the exclusionary rule later in this Chapter.

## Hotels and Motels

The protections against warrantless intrusions into the home announced in *Payton* apply with equal force to a properly rented hotel or motel room during the rental period. See, e.g., United States v. Morales, 737 F.2d 761 (8th Cir.1984). However, this is only the case as long as the arrestee has rightful possession of the room. If the rental period has terminated, or if the person has been ejected from the premises, then the premises can no longer be considered a "home," and an arrest warrant is not required. See, e.g., United States v. Larson, 760 F.2d 852 (8th Cir.1985). See also United States v. Gooch, 6 F.3d 673 (9th Cir.1993) (arrest warrant required for an arrest inside a tent pitched in a public campground: "A guest in Yellowstone Lodge, a hotel on government park land, would have no less an expectation of privacy in his hotel room than a guest in a private hotel, and the same logic would extend to a campsite where the opportunity is extended to spend the night.").

## Arrests in the Home of a Third Party

The Court in *Payton* held that an arrest warrant was sufficient to permit the search of a suspect's house to arrest him there. A search warrant—containing a magistrate's determination of probable cause to believe that the defendant was in his home—was not found necessary. But what if the suspect is arrested in the home of a third person? Does the officer need a search warrant to search that house for the suspect? That was the question in Steagald v. United States, 451 U.S. 204 (1981). Officers obtained an arrest warrant for Ricky Lyons, a federal fugitive wanted on drug charges. They received information that Lyons was staying at a certain house for the next 24 hours. Armed with the arrest warrant, they searched the house. They did not find Lyons, but they did find drugs in the house. These drugs were offered against Steagald, the owner of the house. Steagald moved to suppress the drugs on the ground that the officers failed to secure a search warrant before entering the house to look for Lyons.

Justice Marshall's majority opinion in *Steagald* concluded that a search warrant must be obtained to look for a suspect in the home of a third party, absent exigent circumstances or consent. [Again, the difference between an arrest warrant and a search warrant in this context is that the arrest warrant only requires the magistrate's determination that there is probable cause to arrest a person; it is not specific as to location. A search warrant would require a magistrate to determine that there is probable cause to believe that the suspect is located in the home of the third party.] The majority held that an arrest warrant did not sufficiently protect the privacy interests of *the third party homeowner*. Justice Marshall noted that Steagald's only protection from an illegal search "was the agent's personal determination of probable cause" to believe that Lyons was in Steagald's house. The majority was concerned with the possibility of abuse that could arise if a search warrant were not required in the absence of exigent circumstances: "Armed solely with an arrest warrant for a single person, the police could search all the homes of that individual's friends and acquaintances."

Justice Rehnquist's dissent was joined by Justice White. He focused on the mobility of fugitives—making probable cause determinations as to location quite difficult—and the likelihood of escape. He also observed that when a suspect lives in another's place for a significant period, this may convert the place into the suspect's home and thus justify a search for that suspect under an arrest warrant.

The majority in *Steagald* showed concern that a third party may be the victim of a search where there is no probable cause to believe that the arrestee is on the premises. But what about those third parties who live with the arrestee? See United States v. Litteral, 910 F.2d 547 (9th Cir.1990) ("if the suspect is a co-resident of the third party, then *Steagald* does not apply, and *Payton* allows both arrest of the subject of the arrest warrant and use of evidence found against the third party"). As an arrest warrant is sufficient to arrest a person in his home, aren't those who live with him subject to the same risk that concerned the Court in *Steagald?* Is the real difference between *Payton* and *Steagald* that the officer's error as to probable cause can result in a greater number of mistaken searches in the latter case than in the former? Or does the difference lie in the risk that a person assumes in living with somebody, as opposed to having somebody visit their home temporarily? See United States v. Lovelock, 170 F.3d 339 (2d Cir. 1999) ("A person who occupies premises jointly with another has a reduced expectation of privacy since he assumes the risk that his housemate may engage in conduct that authorized entry into the premises.").

After *Steagald,* it is important for the officer to determine whether the suspect lives in the premises (in which case an arrest warrant is sufficient) or is merely a visitor (in which case a search warrant is required). What considerations should an officer take into account? See United States v. Pallais, 921 F.2d 684 (7th Cir.1990) (suspect who was staying in garage overseeing the renovation of his children's home was a resident, so that arrest warrant was sufficient). What if the officer wants to arrest a person in a third party's home, and knows that the suspect has a residence somewhere else? Does this prohibit the officer from reasonably believing that the suspect might reside in the third party's home as well? See United States v. Risse, 83 F.3d 212 (8th Cir.1996) (officer could enter defendant's home with an arrest warrant to arrest the defendant's girlfriend, even though the officer knew that the girlfriend had her own apartment: "We have found no authority to support Risse's implicit assumption that a person can have only one residence for Fourth Amendment purposes.").

## QUESTIONS OF STANDING

In *Steagald*, the officers entered Steagald's home to arrest the suspect *Lyons*. While trying to find Lyons, the officers discovered evidence that was used against Steagald at trial. The Court held that the evidence should have been suppressed because Steagald's Fourth Amendment rights were violated in the absence of a search warrant. Does that mean that Lyons, the suspect, could have objected to the lack of a search warrant if the officers had found him in the home? The courts have answered in the negative, reasoning that *Steagald* was concerned with the privacy rights of the third-party homeowner, not with the visiting arrestee. See United States v. Underwood, 717 F.2d 482 (9th Cir.1983) (*Steagald* addressed only the right of a third party not named in the arrest warrant to the privacy of his or her home; this right is personal and cannot be asserted vicariously by the person named in the arrest warrant). A contrary rule would be anomalous: the suspect would be entitled to demand a search warrant when arrested in the home of another, while under *Payton* he could demand only an arrest warrant when arrested in his own home. See United States v. Jackson, 576 F.3d 465 (7th Cir. 2009) ("Because it addresses only the Fourth Amendment rights of persons not named in an arrest warrant, *Steagald* did not hold that the subject of an arrest warrant has a higher expectation of privacy in another person's residence than he does in his own.").

## The Rights of an Overnight Guest: Minnesota v. Olson

The Court concluded in Minnesota v. Olson, 495 U.S. 91 (1990), that a warrant was required under *Payton* to arrest a person who was an overnight guest in the home of a third party. [A search warrant would be required to protect the interests of the homeowner under *Steagald*.] Justice White wrote the majority opinion. Chief Justice Rehnquist and Justice Blackmun dissented without opinion. Justice White stressed that a person's "status as an overnight guest is alone enough to show that he had an expectation of privacy in the home that society is prepared to accept as reasonable." The Court specifically rejected the State's argument that a place must be one's own home in order to have a legitimate expectation of privacy there.

## Temporary Visitors

The Court in *Olson* held that an overnight guest had a sufficient expectation of privacy in the premises to be entitled to the protections of the warrant requirement. What if the guest's connection with the premises is less substantial than that of an overnight guest? In Minnesota v. Carter, 525 U.S. 83 (1998), Carter and Johns objected to a warrantless search of an apartment. Their connection with the apartment was that they were there for a couple of hours cutting up cocaine. Chief Justice Rehnquist, writing for the Court, held that the defendants had no expectation of privacy sufficient to trigger their Fourth Amendment rights. The Chief Justice explained as follows:

> If we regard the overnight guest in Minnesota v. Olson as typifying those who may claim the protection of the Fourth Amendment in the home of another, and one merely "legitimately on the premises" as typifying those who may not do so, the present case is obviously somewhere in between. But the purely commercial nature of the transaction engaged in here, the relatively short period of time on the premises, and the lack of any previous connection between respondents and the householder, all lead us to conclude that respondents' situation is closer to that of one simply permitted on the premises. We therefore hold that any search which may have occurred did not violate their Fourth Amendment rights.

## 6. Material Witness

The power to arrest is usually applied to persons suspected of criminal activity. However, the police also have the power to arrest and detain a material witness to a crime under certain circumstances. The Federal material witness statute, 18 U.S.C.A. § 3144, provides as follows:

> If it appears from an affidavit filed by a party that the testimony of a person is material in a criminal proceeding, and if it is shown that it may become impracticable to secure the presence of the person by subpoena, a judicial officer may order the arrest of the person and treat the person [like an arrestee for a crime]. No material witness may be detained because of inability to comply with any condition of release if the testimony of such witness can adequately be secured by deposition, and if further detention is not necessary to prevent a failure of justice. Release of a material witness may be delayed for a reasonable period of time until the deposition of the witness can be taken pursuant to the Federal Rules of Criminal Procedure.

In addition to the Federal statute, every state provides for detention of material witnesses. The Supreme Court has cited the practice with approval in Stein v. New York, 346 U.S. 156, 184 (1953) and Barry v. United States ex rel. Cunningham, 279 U.S. 597, 617 (1929).

There is no constitutional right to monetary compensation for time spent in confinement as a material witness. In Hurtado v. United States, 410 U.S. 578 (1973), the Court held that payment of one dollar per day as compensation did not constitute a "taking" without just compensation or a denial of equal protection.

The expansiveness of the power to arrest a material witness was shown in United States v. Awadallah, 349 F.3d 42 (2d Cir. 2003). A few days after 9/11, Awadallah was detained without probable cause that he was involved in terrorist activity; the detention was based on his purported knowledge of persons so involved. His detention as a material witness lasted for 20 days. Bail was denied. Awadallah eventually testified before a grand jury that he did not know the suspected terrorists named by the government. The government then indicted Awadallah for lying to the grand jury when he denied knowing the suspected terrorists. The court upheld the material witness detention as reasonable, and refused to dismiss the indictment, stating that detention of a witness during a grand jury investigation was permissible, as a grand jury proceeding was a "criminal proceeding" within the meaning of section 3144. [Five years after his initial detention, Awadallah was acquitted of all perjury charges and finally released.]

### *Pretextual Use of Material Witness Detention: Ashcroft v. Al-Kidd*

The dangers of material witness detention, especially after 9/11, are emphasized by Studnicki and Apol in Witness Detention and Intimidation: The History and Future of Material Witness Law, 76 St. John's L.Rev. 483 (2002):

> Material witness law is unique because of the potential *carte blanche* it provides to the government and law enforcement officials who may abuse it. In the aftermath of the September 11, 2001 terrorist attacks, the FBI has been accused of misusing the material witness law to detain people while investigating their backgrounds and activities. Indeed, the United States Attorney General announced that the "aggressive detention" of material witnesses in the wake of September 11th would be the norm. The secrecy surrounding the detention of material witnesses adds to the potential of misuse of this authority as an investigatory tool, rather than a legitimate means of obtaining testimony or protecting a witness. Further, it is easier to arrest an individual as a material witness than as a criminal defendant since there is no required showing of probable cause that the witness has committed a crime.

In Ashcroft v. Al-Kidd, 131 S.Ct. 2074 (2011), the Supreme Court reviewed *Bivens* claims brought against former Attorney General Ashcroft and other officials. The plaintiff alleged that the defendants suspected him of terrorist activity and employed the Material Witness statute to subject him to a long-term detention, even though they had no intent to use him as a witness in any case. Thus, the plaintiff argued that the use of a statute was a pretext to detain him as a terrorism suspect rather than a material witness.

The Court, in an opinion by Justice Scalia, noted first that Al-Kidd "does not assert that Government officials would have acted unreasonably if they had used a material-witness warrant to arrest him for the purpose of securing his testimony for trial. He contests * * * the reasonableness of using the warrant to detain him as a suspected criminal." Justice Scalia rejected Al-Kidd's Fourth Amendment pretext argument because, under cases such as Whren v. United States [discussed in the section in this Chapter on pretextual searches], and *Devenpeck, supra,* the reasonableness of government activity is determined objectively, without regard to an official's state of mind. The Court conceded that the subjective intent of a police officer has been considered in cases where searches were made without suspicion and justified as promoting "special needs" beyond ordinary criminal law enforcement. [See the section on "special needs" searches later in this Chapter.] But the "special needs" cases were not applicable to Al-Kidd's detention, as Justice Scalia explained in the following passage:

> Needless to say, warrantless, suspicionless intrusions pursuant to a general scheme are far removed from the facts of this case. A warrant issued by a neutral Magistrate Judge authorized al-Kidd's arrest. The affidavit accompanying the warrant application (as al-Kidd concedes) gave individualized reasons to believe that he was a material witness and that he would soon disappear. The existence of a judicial warrant based on individualized suspicion takes this case outside the domain of ["special needs" suspicionless searches and seizures].

On the question of pretext, Justice Scalia concluded as follows:

> Because al-Kidd concedes that individualized suspicion supported the issuance of the material-witness arrest warrant; and does not assert that his arrest would have been unconstitutional absent the alleged pretextual use of the warrant; we find no Fourth Amendment violation. Efficient and evenhanded application of the law demands that we look to whether the arrest is objectively justified, rather than to the motive of the arresting officer.

Justice Kennedy, joined by Justices Ginsburg, Breyer, and Sotomayor, wrote a concurring opinion emphasizing that the Court had not decided "whether the Government's use of the Material Witness statute in this case was lawful." That is, Al-Kidd challenged only the pretextual use of the statute, and conceded for argument that detaining a material witness upon satisfying the statutory criteria was a reasonable seizure under the Fourth Amendment. On that broader Fourth Amendment question, Justice Kennedy noted his reservations:

The scope of the statute's lawful authorization is uncertain. For example, a law-abiding citizen might observe a crime during the days or weeks before a scheduled flight abroad. It is unclear whether those facts alone might allow police to obtain a material witness warrant on the ground that it "may become impracticable" to secure the person's presence by subpoena. The question becomes more difficult if one further assumes the traveler would be willing to testify if asked; and more difficult still if one supposes that authorities delay obtaining or executing the warrant until the traveler has arrived at the airport. These possibilities resemble the facts in this case.

In considering these issues, it is important to bear in mind that the Material Witness Statute might not provide for the issuance of warrants within the meaning of the Fourth Amendment's Warrant Clause. The typical arrest warrant is based on probable cause that the arrestee has committed a crime; but that is not the standard for the issuance of warrants under the Material Witness Statute. If material witness warrants do not qualify as "Warrants" under the Fourth Amendment, then material witness arrests might still be governed by the Fourth Amendment's separate reasonableness requirement for seizures of the person. Given the difficulty of these issues, the Court is correct to address only the legal theory put before it, without further exploring when material witness arrests might be consistent with statutory and constitutional requirements.

Justice Ginsburg wrote a separate opinion concurring in the judgment, joined by Justices Breyer and Sotomayor. Justice Sotomayor wrote a separate opinion concurring in the judgment, joined by Justices Ginsburg and Breyer.

## B.  STOP AND FRISK

There are numerous situations in which the police recognize that they do not have probable cause to act, but want to stop a suspicious person for preliminary questioning to determine whether a crime has or is about to occur. From the police perspective, if officers have to wait for probable cause to develop before conducting these preliminary investigations, they would be severely hampered in their efforts to prevent and detect crime. In their view, a standard of proof less demanding than probable cause is needed to nip a crime problem in the bud. Following the adoption in 1964 of a New York statute that became known as the "stop and frisk" law and the conclusion of several important studies of what police do in the real world, the United States Supreme Court placed its first imprimatur on searches and seizures of persons and things on a standard of proof less than probable cause.

## 1.  Stop and Frisk Established

### TERRY V. OHIO

Supreme Court of the United States, 1968.
392 U.S. 1.

#### MR. CHIEF JUSTICE WARREN delivered the opinion of the Court.

This case presents serious questions concerning the role of the Fourth Amendment in the confrontation on the street between the citizen and the policeman investigating suspicious circumstances.

Petitioner Terry was convicted of carrying a concealed weapon and sentenced to the statutorily prescribed term of one to three years in the penitentiary. Following the denial of a pretrial motion to suppress, the prosecution introduced in evidence two revolvers and a number of bullets seized from Terry and a codefendant, Richard Chilton, by Cleveland Police Detective Martin McFadden. At the hearing on the motion to suppress this evidence, Officer McFadden testified that while he was patrolling in plain clothes in downtown Cleveland at approximately 2:30 in the afternoon of October 31, 1963, his attention was attracted by two men, Chilton and Terry, standing on the corner of Huron Road and Euclid Avenue. He had never seen the two men before, and he was unable to say precisely what first drew his eye to them. However, he testified that he had been a policeman for 39 years and a detective for 35 and that he had been assigned to patrol this vicinity of downtown Cleveland for shoplifters and pickpockets for 30 years. He explained that he had developed routine habits of observation over the years and that he would "stand and watch people or walk and watch people at many intervals of the day." He added: "Now, in this case when I looked over they didn't look right to me at the time."

His interest aroused, Officer McFadden took up a post of observation in the entrance to a store 300 to 400 feet away from the two men. * * * He saw one of the men leave the other one and walk southwest on Huron Road, past some stores. The man paused for a moment and looked in a store window, then walked on a short distance, turned around and walked back toward the corner, pausing once again to look in the same store window. He rejoined his companion at the corner, and the two conferred briefly. Then the second man went through the same series of motions, strolling down Huron Road, looking in the same window, walking on a short distance, turning back, peering in the store window again, and returning to confer with the first man at the corner. The two men repeated this ritual alternately between five and six times apiece—in all, roughly a dozen trips. At one point, while the two were standing together on the corner, a third man approached them and engaged them briefly in conversation. This man then left the two others and walked west on Euclid Avenue. Chilton and Terry resumed their measured pacing, peering, and conferring. After this had gone on for 10 to 12 minutes, the two men walked off together, heading west on Euclid Avenue, following the path taken earlier by the third man.

By this time Officer McFadden had become thoroughly suspicious. He testified that after observing their elaborately casual and oft-repeated reconnaissance of the store window on Huron Road, he suspected the two men of "casing a job, a stick-up," and that he considered it his duty as a police officer to investigate further. He added that he feared "they may have a gun." Thus, Officer McFadden followed Chilton and Terry and saw them stop in front of Zucker's store to talk to the same man who had conferred with them earlier on the street corner. Deciding that the situation was ripe for direct action, Officer McFadden approached the three men, identified himself as a police officer and asked for their names. * * * When the men "mumbled something" in response to his inquiries, Officer McFadden grabbed petitioner Terry, spun him around so that they were facing the other two, with Terry between McFadden and the others, and patted down the outside of his clothing. In the left breast pocket of Terry's overcoat Officer McFadden felt a pistol. He reached inside the overcoat pocket, but was unable to remove the gun. At this point, keeping Terry between himself and the others, the officer ordered all three men to enter Zucker's store. As they went in, he removed Terry's overcoat completely, removed a .38-caliber revolver from the pocket and ordered all three men to face the wall with their hands raised. Officer McFadden proceeded to pat down the outer clothing of Chilton and the third man, Katz. He discovered another revolver in the outer pocket of Chilton's overcoat, but no weapons were found on Katz. The officer testified that he only patted the men down to see whether they had weapons, and that he did not put his hands beneath the outer garments of either Terry or Chilton until he felt their guns. So far as appears from the record, he never placed his hands beneath Katz' outer garments. Officer McFadden seized Chilton's gun, asked the proprietor of the store to call a police wagon, and took all three men to the station, where Chilton and Terry were formally charged with carrying concealed weapons.

On the motion to suppress the guns the prosecution took the position that they had been seized following a search incident to a lawful arrest. The trial court rejected this theory, stating that it "would be stretching the facts beyond reasonable comprehension" to find that Officer McFadden had probable cause to arrest the men before he patted them down for weapons. However, the court denied the defendants' motion on the ground that Officer McFadden, on the basis of his experience, "had reasonable cause to believe * * * that the defendants were conducting themselves suspiciously, and some interrogation should be made of their action." Purely for his own protection, the court held, the officer had the right to pat down the outer clothing of these men, who he had reasonable cause to believe might be armed. The court distinguished between an investigatory "stop" and an arrest, and between a "frisk" of the outer clothing for weapons and a full-blown search for evidence of crime. The frisk, it held, was essential to the proper performance of the officer's investigatory duties, for without it "the answer to the police officer may be a bullet, and a loaded pistol discovered during the frisk is admissible."

\* \* \*

The Fourth Amendment provides that "the right of the people to be secure in their persons, houses, papers, and effects, against unreasonable searches and seizures shall not be violated \* \* \*." This inestimable right of personal security belongs as much to the citizen on the streets of our cities as to the homeowner closeted in his study to dispose of his secret affairs. \* \* \*

We would be less than candid if we did not acknowledge that this question thrusts to the fore difficult and troublesome issues regarding a sensitive area of police activity—issues which have never before been squarely presented to this Court. Reflective of the tensions involved are the practical and constitutional arguments pressed with great vigor on both sides of the public debate over the power of the police to "stop and frisk"—as it is sometimes euphemistically termed—suspicious persons.

\* \* \*

In this context we approach the issues in this case mindful of the limitations of the judicial function in controlling the myriad daily situations in which policemen and citizens confront each other on the street. The State has characterized the issue here as "the right of a police officer \* \* \* to make an on-the-street stop, interrogate and pat down for weapons (known in street vernacular as 'stop and frisk')." But this is only partly accurate. For the issue is not the abstract propriety of the police conduct, but the admissibility against petitioner of the evidence uncovered by the search and seizure. [The Court suggests that the exclusionary rule may not deter all Fourth Amendment violations. For example, where an officer is bent on harassment, and doesn't care about whether he finds evidence, the exclusionary rule cannot deter the officer because the exclusionary rule is dependent on litigation-oriented disincentives.]

\* \* \*

Proper adjudication of cases in which the exclusionary rule is invoked demands a constant awareness of these limitations. The wholesale harassment by certain elements of the police community, of which minority groups, particularly Negroes, frequently complain, will not be stopped by the exclusion of any evidence from any criminal trial. Yet a rigid and unthinking application of the exclusionary rule, in futile protest against practices which it can never be used effectively to control, may exact a high toll in human injury and frustration of efforts to prevent crime. * * *

* * *

Our first task is to establish at what point in this encounter the Fourth Amendment becomes relevant. That is, we must decide whether and when Officer McFadden "seized" Terry and whether and when he conducted a "search." There is some suggestion in the use of such terms as "stop" and "frisk" that such police conduct is outside the purview of the Fourth Amendment because neither action rises to the level of a "search" or "seizure" within the meaning of the Constitution. We emphatically reject this notion. It is quite plain that the Fourth Amendment governs "seizures" of the person which do not eventuate in a trip to the station house and prosecution for crime—"arrests" in traditional terminology. It must be recognized that whenever a police officer accosts an individual and restrains his freedom to walk away, he has "seized" that person. And it is nothing less than sheer torture of the English language to suggest that a careful exploration of the outer surfaces of a person's clothing all over his or her body in an attempt to find weapons is not a "search." Moreover, it is simply fantastic to urge that such a procedure performed in public by a policeman while the citizen stands helpless, perhaps facing a wall with his hands raised, is a "petty indignity." It is a serious intrusion upon the sanctity of the person, which may inflict great indignity and arouse strong resentment, and it is not to be undertaken lightly.

* * *

In this case there can be no question, then, that Officer McFadden "seized" petitioner and subjected him to a "search" when he took hold of him and patted down the outer surfaces of his clothing. We must decide whether at that point it was reasonable for Officer McFadden to have interfered with petitioner's personal security as he did. And in determining whether the seizure and search were "unreasonable" our inquiry is a dual one—whether the officer's action was justified at its inception, and whether it was reasonably related in scope to the circumstances which justified the interference in the first place.

* * *

If this case involved police conduct subject to the Warrant Clause of the Fourth Amendment, we would have to ascertain whether "probable cause" existed to justify the search and seizure which took place. However, that is not the case. We do not retreat from our holdings that the police must, whenever practicable, obtain advance judicial approval of searches and seizures through the warrant procedure or that in most instances failure to comply with the warrant requirement can only be excused by exigent circumstances. But we deal here with an entire rubric of police conduct—necessarily swift action predicated upon the on-the-spot observations of the officer on the beat—which historically has not been, and as a practical matter could not be, subjected to the warrant procedure. Instead the conduct involved in this case must be tested by the Fourth Amendment's general proscription against unreasonable searches and seizures.

Nonetheless, the notions which underlie both the warrant procedure and the requirement of probable cause remain fully relevant in this context. In order to assess the reasonableness of Officer McFadden's conduct as a general proposition, it is necessary "first to focus upon the governmental interest which allegedly justifies official intrusion upon the constitutionally protected interests of the private citizen," for there is "no ready test for determining reasonableness other than by balancing the need to search [or seize] against the invasion which the search [or seizure] entails." Camara v. Municipal Court, 387 U.S. 523, 534–535, 536–537 (1967). And in justifying the particular intrusion the police officer must be able to point to specific and articulable facts which, taken together with rational inferences from those facts, reasonably warrant that intrusion. * * * And in making that assessment it is imperative that the facts be judged against an objective standard: would the facts available to the officer at the moment of the seizure or the search "warrant a man of reasonable caution in the belief" that the action taken was appropriate? Anything less would invite intrusions upon constitutionally guaranteed rights based on nothing more substantial than inarticulate hunches, a result this Court has consistently refused to sanction. And simple good faith on the part of the arresting officer is not enough. * * * If subjective good faith alone were the test, the protections of the Fourth Amendment would evaporate, and the people would be secure in their persons, houses, papers, and effects, only in the discretion of the police.

Applying these principles to this case, we consider first the nature and extent of the governmental interests involved. One general interest is of course that of effective crime prevention and detection; it is this interest which underlies the recognition that a police officer may in appropriate circumstances and in an appropriate manner approach a person for purposes of investigating possibly criminal behavior even though there is no probable cause to make an arrest. It was this legitimate investigative function Officer McFadden was discharging when he decided to approach petitioner and his companions. He had observed Terry, Chilton, and Katz go through a series of acts, each of them perhaps innocent in itself, but which taken together warranted further investigation. There is nothing unusual in two men standing together on a street corner, perhaps waiting for someone. Nor is there anything suspicious about people in such circumstances strolling up and down the street, singly or in pairs. Store windows, moreover, are made to be looked in. But the story is quite different where, as here, two men hover about a street corner for an extended period of time, at the end of which it becomes apparent that they are not waiting for anyone or anything; where these men pace alternately along an identical route, pausing to stare in the same store window roughly 24 times; where each completion of this route is followed immediately by a conference between the two men on the corner; where they are joined in one of these conferences by a third man who leaves swiftly; and where the two men finally follow the third and rejoin him a couple of blocks away. It would have been poor police work indeed for an officer of 30 years' experience in the detection of thievery from stores in this same neighborhood to have failed to investigate this behavior further.

The crux of this case, however, is not the propriety of Officer McFadden's taking steps to investigate petitioner's suspicious behavior, but rather, whether there was justification for McFadden's invasion of Terry's personal security by searching him for weapons in the course of that investigation. We are now concerned with more than the governmental interest in investigating crime; in addition, there is the more immediate interest of the police officer in taking steps to assure himself that the person with whom he is dealing is not armed with a weapon that could unexpectedly and fatally be used against him. Certainly it would be unreasonable to require that police officers take unnecessary risks in the performance of their duties. American criminals have a long tradition of armed violence, and every year in this country many law enforcement officers are killed in the line of duty, and thousands more are wounded. Virtually all of these deaths and a substantial portion of the injuries are inflicted with guns and knives.

In view of these facts, we cannot blind ourselves to the need for law enforcement officers to protect themselves and other prospective victims of violence in situations where they may lack probable cause for an arrest. When an officer is justified in believing that the individual whose suspicious behavior he is investigating at close range is armed and presently dangerous to the officer or to others, it would appear to be clearly unreasonable to deny the officer the power to take necessary measures to determine whether the person is in fact carrying a weapon and to neutralize the threat of physical harm.

* * *

Our evaluation of the proper balance that has to be struck in this type of case leads us to conclude that there must be a narrowly drawn authority to permit a reasonable search for weapons for the protection of the police officer, where he has reason to believe that he is dealing with an armed and dangerous individual, regardless of whether he has probable cause to arrest the individual for a crime. The officer need not be absolutely certain that the individual is armed; the issue is whether a reasonably prudent man in the circumstances would be warranted in the belief that his safety or that of others was in danger. And in determining whether the officer acted reasonably in such circumstances, due weight must be given, not to his inchoate and unparticularized suspicion or "hunch," but to the specific reasonable inferences which he is entitled to draw from the facts in light of his experience.

* * *

We need not develop at length in this case * * * the limitations which the Fourth Amendment places upon a protective seizure and search for weapons. These limitations will have to be developed in the concrete factual circumstances of individual cases. Suffice it to note that such a search, unlike a search without a warrant incident to arrest, is not justified by any need to prevent the disappearance or destruction of evidence of crime. The sole justification of the search in the present situation is the protection of the police officer and others nearby, and it must therefore be confined in scope to an intrusion reasonably designed to discover guns, knives, clubs, or other hidden instruments for the assault of the police officer.

The scope of the search in this case presents no serious problem in light of these standards. * * *

V

We conclude that the revolver seized from Terry was properly admitted in evidence against him. At the time he seized petitioner and searched him for weapons, Officer McFadden had reasonable grounds to believe that petitioner was armed and dangerous, and it was necessary for the protection of himself and others to take swift measures to discover the true facts and neutralize the threat of harm if it materialized. The policeman carefully restricted his search to what was appropriate to the discovery of the particular items which he sought. Each case of this sort will, of course, have to be decided on its own facts. We merely hold today that where a police officer observes unusual conduct which leads him reasonably to conclude in light of his experience that criminal activity may be afoot and that the persons with whom he is dealing may be armed and presently dangerous, where in the course of investigating this behavior he identifies himself as a policeman and makes reasonable inquiries, and where nothing in the initial stages of the encounter serves to dispel his reasonable fear for his own or others' safety, he is entitled for the protection of himself and others in the area to conduct a carefully limited search of the outer clothing of such persons in an attempt to discover weapons which might be used to assault him. Such a search is a reasonable search under the Fourth Amendment, and any weapons seized may properly be introduced in evidence against the person from whom they were taken.

MR. JUSTICE BLACK concurs in the judgment and the opinion except where the opinion quotes from and relies upon this Court's opinion in Katz v. United States and the concurring opinion in Warden v. Hayden.

**MR. JUSTICE HARLAN, concurring.**

\* \* \*

A police officer's right to make an on-the-street "stop" and an accompanying "frisk" for weapons is of course bounded by the protections afforded by the Fourth and Fourteenth Amendments. The Court holds, and I agree, that while the right does not depend upon possession by the officer of a valid warrant, nor upon the existence of probable cause, such activities must be reasonable under the circumstances as the officer credibly relates them in court. \* \* \*

\* \* \* The holding has, however, two logical corollaries that I do not think the Court has fully expressed.

In the first place, if the frisk is justified in order to protect the officer during an encounter with a citizen, the officer must first have constitutional grounds to insist on an encounter, to make a *forcible* stop. Any person, including a policeman, is at liberty to avoid a person he considers dangerous. If and when a policeman has a right instead to disarm such a person for his own protection, he must first have a right not to avoid him but to be in his presence. That right must be more than the liberty (again, possessed by every citizen) to address questions to other persons, for ordinarily the person addressed has an equal right to ignore his interrogator and walk away; he certainly need not submit to a frisk for the questioner's protection. I would make it perfectly clear that the right to frisk in this case depends upon the reasonableness of a forcible stop to investigate a suspected crime.

Where such a stop is reasonable, however, the right to frisk must be immediate and automatic if the reason for the stop is, as here, an articulable suspicion of a crime of violence. Just as a full search incident to a lawful arrest requires no additional justification, a limited frisk incident to a lawful stop must often be rapid and routine. There is no reason why an officer, rightfully but forcibly confronting a person suspected of a serious crime, should have to ask one question and take the risk that the answer might be a bullet.

* * *

### MR. JUSTICE WHITE, concurring.

* * * I think an additional word is in order concerning the matter of interrogation during an investigative stop. There is nothing in the Constitution which prevents a policeman from addressing questions to anyone on the street. Absent special circumstances, the person approached may not be detained or frisked but may refuse to cooperate and go on his way. However, given the proper circumstances, such as those in this case, it seems to me the person may be briefly detained against his will while pertinent questions are directed to him. * * *

### MR. JUSTICE DOUGLAS, dissenting.

I agree that petitioner was "seized" within the meaning of the Fourth Amendment. I also agree that frisking petitioner and his companions for guns was a "search." But it is a mystery how that "search" and that "seizure" can be constitutional by Fourth Amendment standards, unless there was "probable cause" to believe that (1) a crime had been committed or (2) a crime was in the process of being committed or (3) a crime was about to be committed.

* * *

The infringement on personal liberty of any "seizure" of a person can only be "reasonable" under the Fourth Amendment if we require the police to possess "probable cause" before they seize him. Only that line draws a meaningful distinction between an officer's mere inkling and the presence of facts within the officer's personal knowledge which would convince a reasonable man that the person seized has committed, is committing, or is about to commit a particular crime. * * *

To give the police greater power than a magistrate is to take a long step down the totalitarian path. Perhaps such a step is desirable to cope with modern forms of lawlessness. But if it is taken, it should be the deliberate choice of the people through a constitutional amendment. * * *

### NOTE ON THE IMPACT OF TERRY

It would be hard to overestimate the effect of *Terry* on Fourth Amendment jurisprudence. The Court not only permitted stops and frisks on less than probable cause; it also explicitly invoked the reasonableness clause over the warrant clause as the governing standard. Perhaps the Court intended to limit use of the reasonableness clause and its balancing approach to the area of stop and frisk; but once that balancing process was launched in one area, it became difficult to prevent its application to other searches and seizures. See Sundby, A Return to Fourth Amendment Basics: Undoing the Mischief of *Camara* and *Terry*, 72 Minn.L.Rev. 383 (1988) (noting that *Terry* has led, in time, to a general diminution of Fourth Amendment protection).

## *Critique of Terry*

Professor Maclin provides a critique on *Terry*, and assesses the impact of that decision on minorities, in Terry v. Ohio's Fourth Amendment Legacy: Black Men and Police Discretion, 72 St.John's L.Rev. 1271, 1278 (1998):

> After *Terry*, police intrusions would be controlled by a malleable "reasonableness" standard that gave enormous discretion to the police. When this reasonableness norm was applied to street encounters between the police and urban residents, the result was predictable—expanded police powers and diminished individual freedom. One of the flaws of *Terry* was that this shift in constitutional doctrine was implemented without a full examination of the consequences for blacks and other disfavored persons most affected by police investigatory methods. Moreover, the result in *Terry* provided a springboard for modern police methods that target black men and others for arbitrary and discretionary intrusions. For some, the *Terry* Court made the right choice. The need for police safety justified the loss of Fourth Amendment freedom. But those that have been the most vocal defenders of *Terry* tend to come from socioeconomic and racial backgrounds that are predominantly free from police harassment. For many blacks and other disfavored groups, however, the *Terry* Court wrongly subordinated their Fourth Amendment rights to police safety. The Court's failure to treat as dispositive the clear correlation between stop and frisk and the violation of their Fourth Amendment rights only served to remind blacks and other minorities of their second-class status in America.

## *An Early Application of Terry—Adams v. Williams*

The *Terry* decision with its companion cases—Sibron v. New York, and Peters v. New York, 392 U.S. 40 (1968)—was only the first step in the articulation of what the Fourth Amendment permits the police to do without probable cause. The Supreme Court's first post-*Terry* effort was Adams v. Williams, 407 U.S. 143 (1972). Williams was convicted of illegal possession of a handgun and possession of heroin, after unsuccessfully challenging a stop and frisk. Justice Rehnquist, writing for the Court, set forth the facts surrounding the stop and frisk as follows:

> Police Sgt. John Connolly was alone early in the morning on car patrol duty in a high-crime area of Bridgeport, Connecticut. At approximately 2:15 a.m. a person known to Sgt. Connolly approached his cruiser and informed him that an individual seated in a nearby vehicle was carrying narcotics and had a gun at his waist.

After calling for assistance on his car radio, Sgt. Connolly approached the vehicle to investigate the informant's report. Connolly tapped on the car window and asked the occupant, Robert Williams, to open the door. When Williams rolled down the window instead, the sergeant reached into the car and removed a fully loaded revolver from Williams' waistband. The gun had not been visible to Connolly from outside the car, but it was in precisely the place indicated by the informant. Williams was then arrested by Connolly for unlawful possession of the pistol. A search incident to that arrest was conducted after other officers arrived. They found substantial quantities of heroin on Williams' person and in the car, and they found a machete and a second revolver hidden in the automobile.

Williams argued that the informant's tip was not a reliable basis on which to conduct the initial stop. But Justice Rehnquist disagreed:

[W]e believe that Sgt. Connolly acted justifiably in responding to his informant's tip. The informant was known to him personally and had provided him with information in the past. This is a stronger case than obtains in the case of an anonymous telephone tip. The informant here came forward personally to give information that was immediately verifiable at the scene. Indeed, under Connecticut law, the informant might have been subject to immediate arrest for making a false complaint had Sgt. Connolly's investigation proved the tip incorrect. Thus, while the Court's decisions indicate that this informant's unverified tip may have been insufficient for a narcotics arrest or search warrant, the information carried enough indicia of reliability to justify the officer's forcible stop of Williams.

In reaching this conclusion, we reject respondent's argument that reasonable cause for a stop and frisk can only be based on the officer's personal observation rather than on information supplied by another person. Informants' tips, like all other clues and evidence coming to a policeman on the scene, may vary greatly in their value and reliability.

Justice Rehnquist also held that the search of Williams' person was permissible in light of the safety risks presented to the officer:

While properly investigating the activity of a person who was reported to be carrying narcotics and a concealed weapon and who was sitting alone in a car in a high-crime area at 2:15 in the morning, Sgt. Connolly had ample reason to fear of his safety. When Williams rolled down his window, rather than complying with the policeman's request to step out of the car so that his movements could more easily be seen, the revolver allegedly at Williams' waist became an even greater threat. Under these circumstances the policeman's action in reaching to the spot where the gun was thought to be hidden constituted a limited intrusion designed to insure his safety, and we conclude that it was reasonable.

Finally, Justice Rehnquist concluded that the search of the passenger compartment of the car, which led to discovery of the heroin, was permissible in light of everything that had gone before—not as a *Terry* search but rather as a search supported by probable cause to arrest Williams.

Justice Douglas, joined by Justice Marshall, dissented in *Williams*. He argued that Williams was illegally arrested, because there was no indication at the time of arrest that it was illegal for Williams to possess a gun.

Justice Brennan wrote a separate dissent in *Williams*, arguing that *Terry* should not be applicable to crimes like narcotics possession, because "[t]here is too much danger that, instead of the stop being the object and the protective frisk an incident thereto, the reverse will be true."

Justice Marshall, joined by Justice Douglas, also wrote a separate dissent in *Williams*. He observed that the informant, on whom the officer relied to stop Williams, had no track record of giving reliable information. He concluded as follows:

> The Court explains what the officer knew about respondent before accosting him. But what is more significant is what he did not know. With respect to the scene generally, the officer had no idea how long respondent had been in the car, how long the car had been parked, or to whom the car belonged. With respect to the gun, the officer did not know if or when the informant had ever seen the gun, or whether the gun was carried legally, as Connecticut law permitted, or illegally. And with respect to the narcotics, the officer did not know what kind of narcotics respondent allegedly had, whether they were legally or illegally possessed, what the basis of the informant's knowledge was, or even whether the informant was capable of distinguishing narcotics from other substances.

> Unable to answer any of these questions, the officer nevertheless determined that it was necessary to intrude on respondent's liberty. I believe that his determination was totally unreasonable. As I read *Terry*, an officer may act on the basis of *reliable* information short of probable cause to make a stop, and ultimately a frisk, if necessary; but the officer may not use unreliable, unsubstantiated, conclusory hearsay to justify an invasion of liberty. *Terry* never meant to approve the kind of knee-jerk police reaction that we have before us in this case.

Do you see anything in the language or tone of *Terry* indicating that the Court never meant to approve the kind of police conduct at issue in

*Williams*? Or is Justice Marshall simply regretful that he didn't join Justice Douglas in dissent in *Terry*?

### Bright Line Rules Under Terry—Pennsylvania v. Mimms

Another case in the Court's early development of the *Terry* doctrine was the per curiam decision in Pennsylvania v. Mimms, 434 U.S. 106 (1977). While on routine patrol, two Philadelphia police officers observed Mimms driving a car with an expired license plate. The officers stopped the car to issue a traffic summons. One of the officers approached and told Mimms to step out of the car and produce his owner's card and operator's license. When Mimms got out of the car, the officer noticed a large bulge under his sports jacket. Thinking that Mimms might be carrying a weapon, the officer frisked Mimms and found that the bulge was a loaded revolver. Mimms unsuccessfully moved to suppress the gun, and was convicted for firearms violations.

The Court held that the officer had acted properly under the *Terry* doctrine, and therefore that the revolver was properly admitted at Mimms' trial. The Court noted that the parties agreed (1) that the officer was justified in stopping Mimms for the traffic violation, and (2) that the officer had sufficient cause to frisk Mimms for a weapon once he observed the bulge. The question in dispute was whether the officer was justified in ordering Mimms to get out of the car. If this seizure was unlawful under *Terry*, then the subsequent frisk would be unlawful as well. But the Court held that officers in the course of a legal stop of an automobile have an *automatic* right under *Terry* to order the driver out of the vehicle. The Court came to its bright line rule in the following analysis:

> We think it too plain for argument that the State's proffered justification—the safety of the officer—is both legitimate and weighty. * * * According to one study, approximately 30% of police shootings occurred when a police officer approached a suspect seated in an automobile. We are aware that not all these assaults occur when issuing traffic summons, but we have before expressly declined to accept the argument that traffic violations necessarily involve less danger to officers than other types of confrontations. * * *

> The hazard of accidental injury from passing traffic to an officer standing on the driver's side of the vehicle may also be appreciable in some situations. Rather than conversing while standing exposed to moving traffic, the officer prudently may prefer to ask the driver of the vehicle to step out of the car and off onto the shoulder of the road where the inquiry may be pursued with greater safety to both.

> Against this important interest we are asked to weigh the intrusion into the driver's personal liberty occasioned not by the initial stop of the vehicle, which was admittedly justified, but by the

order to get out of the car. We think this additional intrusion can only be described as *de minimis*. The driver is being asked to expose to view very little more of his person than is already exposed. * * * What is at most a mere inconvenience cannot prevail when balanced against legitimate concerns for the officer's safety.

Justice Marshall dissented in *Mimms*. He argued that *Terry* requires a nexus between the reason for the stop and the need for self-protection that justifies a further intrusion. He found no nexus between the traffic violation and a subsequent order to get out of the car.

Justice Stevens, joined by Justices Brennan and Marshall, wrote a separate dissent in *Mimms*. He argued that the bright-line rule chosen by the Court could not be supported by safety concerns:

> [Ordering the suspect out of the car] could actually aggravate the officer's danger because the fear of a search might cause a serious offender to take desperate action that would be unnecessary if he remained in the vehicle while being ticketed. Whatever the reason, it is significant that some experts in this area of human behavior strongly recommend that the police officer "never allow the violator to get out of the car * * *."

Justice Stevens strenuously objected to the Court's adoption of a bright line rule to cover all vehicle stops, regardless of the circumstances:

> Until today the law applicable to seizures of a person has required individualized inquiry into the reason for each intrusion, or some comparable guarantee against arbitrary harassment. * * * [T]o eliminate any requirement that an officer be able to explain the reasons for his actions signals an abandonment of effective judicial supervision of this kind of seizure and leaves police discretion utterly without limits. Some citizens will be subjected to this minor indignity while others—perhaps those with more expensive cars, or different bumper stickers, or different-colored skin—may escape it entirely.

### QUESTIONS ABOUT MIMMS

Are the safety concerns cited by the *Mimms* majority likely to arise so often that the Court is justified in adopting a bright line rule? The dissenters consider the safety concerns overstated; but they do not argue that the Court's assessment of the individual right at stake is understated. Given the minimal nature of the intrusion at issue in *Mimms*, why are the dissenters so upset?

What if the driver of the car *wants to get out,* and the officer (perhaps thinking it the safest procedure) *wants the driver to stay in the car*? Is this an additional seizure for Fourth Amendment purposes? Is the dissent's position that the driver can do whatever she wants? What if the officer permits the driver to remain in the car, but says "keep your hands where I can see them"? Does the officer have the automatic right to so order?

### *Mimms and Passengers*

In Maryland v. Wilson, 519 U.S. 408 (1997), the Court considered whether the automatic rule established in *Mimms* applied to passengers as well as drivers. An officer stopped a car traveling on Interstate 95. The car was going 64 miles per hour in a 55 mile per hour zone. The officer ordered the driver and Wilson, a passenger, to get out of the car. The officer did not have reasonable suspicion to believe that Wilson was up to anything special. When Wilson stepped out of the car, a quantity of cocaine allegedly fell to the ground. The state court had held that the *Mimms* rule did not apply to passengers, and therefore that Wilson could not be ordered out of the car in the absence of reasonable suspicion to believe he was involved in a crime. But the Supreme Court, in an opinion by Chief Justice Rehnquist for seven members of the Court, disagreed and held that the bright-line rule of *Mimms* applied to passengers. The Chief Justice balanced the factors discussed in *Mimms*:

> On the public interest side of the balance, the same weighty interest in officer safety is present regardless of whether the occupant of the stopped car is a driver or passenger. Regrettably, traffic stops may be dangerous encounters. In 1994 alone, there were 5,762 officer assaults and 11 officers killed during traffic pursuits and stops. In the case of passengers, the danger of the officer's standing in the path of oncoming traffic would not be present except in the case of a passenger in the left rear seat, but the fact that there is more than one occupant of the vehicle increases the possible sources of harm to the officer.

> On the personal liberty side of the balance, the case for the passengers is in one sense stronger than that for the driver. There is probable cause to believe that the driver has committed a minor vehicular offense, but there is no such reason to stop or detain the passengers. But as a practical matter, the passengers are already stopped by virtue of the stop of the vehicle. The only change in their circumstances which will result from ordering them out of the car is that they will be outside of, rather than inside of, the stopped car.

Justice Stevens, joined by Justice Kennedy, dissented in *Wilson*. He argued that police officers are rarely at risk from passengers during routine automobile stops, and that any "limited additional risk to police officers must be weighed against the unnecessary invasion that will be imposed on innocent citizens under the majority's rule in the tremendous number of routine stops that occur each day." He asserted that "the aggregation of thousands upon thousands of petty indignities has an impact on freedom that I would characterize as substantial, and which in my view clearly outweighs the evanescent safety concerns pressed by the majority."

Justice Kennedy wrote a separate dissent in which he stated that officers should be able to order a passenger out of a car only if necessary under the circumstances to investigate a crime or to protect the officer.

### *Protective Frisk of Passengers: Arizona v. Johnson*

In the later case of Arizona v. Johnson, 555 U.S. 323 (2009), the Court upheld the next step of a process begun by *Mimms*: the protective search of a passenger, when the driver has been lawfully stopped for a traffic violation. The Court stated that "officers who conduct routine traffic stops may perform a patdown of a driver and any passengers upon reasonable suspicion that they may be armed and dangerous." But unlike the seizure involved in making drivers and passenger come out from the car, the power to frisk is not automatic. As the *Johnson* Court notes, the officer must have reasonable suspicion that the passenger or driver is armed and dangerous.

### *Mimms Applied: New York v. Class*

The Court authorized a limited investigative entry into a car during the course of a stop in New York v. Class, 475 U.S. 106 (1986). Class was stopped for a traffic violation. Officers peered through the windshield of Class's car to obtain the vehicle identification, but the number was covered by papers on the dashboard. One officer entered the car to move the papers away, and at that point discovered a gun, which was admitted against Class at his trial for firearms violations. The Court, in a 6–3 opinion by Justice O'Connor, relied on *Mimms* and held that the officer acted reasonably. The Court held that "in order to observe a Vehicle Identification Number (VIN) generally visible from outside an automobile, a police officer may reach into the passenger compartment of a vehicle to move papers obscuring the VIN after its driver has been stopped for a traffic violation and has exited the car." Justice O'Connor reasoned that "[t]he VIN is a significant thread in the web of regulation of the automobile" and that "[a] motorist must surely expect that such regulation will on occasion require the State to determine the VIN of his or her vehicle, and the individual's reasonable expectation of privacy in the VIN is thereby diminished," especially for a driver who has committed a traffic violation.

Justice O'Connor noted that the Court's holding "does not authorize a police officer to enter a vehicle to obtain a dashboard-mounted VIN when the VIN is visible from outside the automobile," because "[i]f the VIN is in the plain view of someone outside the vehicle, there is no justification for governmental intrusion into the passenger compartment to see it."

Justice Powell, joined by Chief Justice Burger, concurred in *Class*, emphasizing the important governmental interest in the VIN, and concluding that "the Fourth Amendment question may be stated simply as whether the officer's efforts to inspect the VIN were reasonable." Justice Brennan, joined by Justices Marshall and Stevens, dissented. He argued that "the mere fact that the state utilizes the VIN in conjunction with regulations designed to promote highway safety does not give the police a reason to *search* for such information every time a motorist violates a traffic law." Justice White, joined by Justice Stevens, also dissented, stating that he was unprepared to accept the Court's reasoning that "the governmental interest in obtaining the VIN by entering a protected area is sufficient to outweigh the owner's privacy interest in the interior of the car."

Car manufacturers now place a second VIN plate somewhere secret in the interior of the car—this is a response to the fact that car thieves often replace the visible VIN plate with a fake. Under *Class,* can an officer conduct a search of the car's interior to look for that second VIN plate?

### *Detention of Occupants of a Residence During Legal Law Enforcement Activity: Note on Michigan v. Summers, Muehler v. Mena, and Bailey v. United States*

In Michigan v. Summers, 452 U.S. 692 (1981), the Court held, 6–3, that police officers with a search warrant for a home can require occupants of the premises, even if leaving when the police arrive, to remain while the search warrant is executed. The Court held that such a seizure would *always* be reasonable, given the state's interest in preventing flight, and the risk that persons leaving the premises would attempt to destroy evidence. The Court noted that the detention in *Summers* was less serious than the street stops sanctioned in *Terry,* because the occupant was being detained inside his home. The Court also observed that the search warrant provided protection against overreaching by the police officers. Does *Mimms* lend support to the result in *Summers*?

The Court applied *Summers* in Muehler v. Mena, 544 U.S. 93 (2005), to uphold a more serious detention—including handcuffing—of a person during the warranted search of the home of a suspected gang member. The Court also found it permissible for the officers to question the detainee about her alienage during the time it took to conduct the search. Officers obtained a search warrant for a premises after a gang-related driveby shooting, based on information that at least one of the gang members lived there. The warrant authorized a broad search for deadly weapons and evidence of gang membership. Because of the violent gang connection, a SWAT team was used to secure the premises during the search. The proceedings started at 7 a.m.. Officers found Mena asleep in her bed and she was handcuffed and placed in a garage that had some furniture. While the search proceeded, officers guarded Mena and three other residents in the garage, all of them remaining in handcuffs for between two and three hours. The officers also notified the Immigration and Naturalization Service (INS) that they would be conducting the search, and an INS officer accompanied the officers executing the warrant. During Mena's detention in the garage, she was asked her name, date and place of birth, and immigration status. The INS officer later asked her for her immigration documentation. Mena's status as a permanent resident was confirmed by her papers. In their lengthy search, the officer found some ammunition, a gun, and some gang paraphernalia, but did not find the gang members they were looking for. Mena was released at the end of the search. She brought a § 1983 suit against the officers, alleging that she was detained "for an unreasonable time and in an unreasonable manner" in violation of the Fourth Amendment.

Chief Justice Rehnquist, writing for the Court, relied on *Summers* to conclude that Mena's Fourth Amendment rights were not violated by her detention and interrogation.

> Mena's detention was, under *Summers*, plainly permissible. An officer's authority to detain incident to a search is categorical; it does not depend on the "quantum of proof justifying detention or the extent of the intrusion to be imposed by the seizure." Thus, Mena's detention for the duration of the search was reasonable under *Summers* because a warrant existed to search 1363 Patricia Avenue and she was an occupant of that address at the time of the search.

> Inherent in *Summers*' authorization to detain an occupant of the place to be searched is the authority to use reasonable force to effectuate the detention. Indeed, *Summers* itself stressed that the risk of harm to officers and occupants is minimized "if the officers routinely exercise unquestioned command of the situation."

The Court noted that while the detention in handcuffs was "more intrusive than that which we upheld in *Summers*" it was nonetheless reasonable given the risk to officer safety presented by a search of the premises.

> [T]his was no ordinary search. The governmental interests in not only detaining, but using handcuffs, are at their maximum when, as here, a warrant authorizes a search for weapons and a wanted gang member resides on the premises. In such inherently dangerous situations, the use of handcuffs minimizes the risk of harm to both

officers and occupants. Though this safety risk inherent in executing a search warrant for weapons was sufficient to justify the use of handcuffs, the need to detain multiple occupants made the use of handcuffs all the more reasonable.

\* \* \* The duration of a detention can, of course, affect the balance of interests \* \* \*. However, the 2- to 3-hour detention in handcuffs in this case does not outweigh the government's continuing safety interests. As we have noted, this case involved the detention of four detainees by two officers during a search of a gang house for dangerous weapons. We conclude that the detention of Mena in handcuffs during the search was reasonable.

Chief Justice Rehnquist found Mena's interrogation during detention to be reasonable as well, explaining that it was not necessary for the officers to have independent reasonable suspicion in order to question Mena concerning her immigration status. He noted that the Court had "held repeatedly that mere police questioning does not constitute a seizure." Because the detention was not prolonged by the questioning, "there was no additional seizure within the meaning of the Fourth Amendment. Hence, the officers did not need reasonable suspicion to ask Mena for her name, date and place of birth, or immigration status."

Justice Kennedy wrote a concurring opinion in *Mena.* Justice Stevens, joined by Justices Souter, Ginsburg and Breyer, wrote an opinion concurring in the judgment.

There are differences between *Summers* and *Mena.* Arguably *Mena* states an overbroad principle. See Saltzburg, The Fourth Amendment: Internal Revenue Code or Body of Principles? 74 Geo.Wash.L.Rev. 956 (2006) ("Suppose that police officers have a search warrant to search a house for a gun belonging to X. They arrive and discover that a Lamaze birthing class is being conducted in a den by X's spouse. According to *Mena,* the officers executing the warrant have a per se right to detain all of the pregnant mothers-to-be and their coaches while the warrant is executed. This is indefensible.").

For a case applying *Summers* and *Mena,* see Los Angeles County v. Rettele, 550 U.S. 609 (2007) (detention at gunpoint of two people found in bed held reasonable even though those detained did not fit the description of those to be arrested: "The deputies needed a moment to secure the room and ensure that other persons were not close by or did not present a danger. Deputies were not required to turn their backs to allow Rettele and Sadler to retrieve clothing or to cover themselves with the sheets.").

In Bailey v. United States, 133 S.Ct. 714 (2013), police officers prepared to conduct a warranted search of an apartment, and saw the defendant leave the apartment and get into a car. They stopped him a mile away from the apartment and brought him back to the apartment while the search was being conducted. That seizure led to evidence and the defendant moved to exclude. The lower court relied on the categorical *Summers* rule—which does not require reasonable suspicion that a resident is involved in a crime—to justify the detention. But the Supreme Court, in an opinion by Justice Kennedy for six Justices, held that the *Summers* rule did not extend to a detention that was made so far away from the premises being searched. Justice Kennedy reasoned that the reasons for the *Summers* rule—to preserve the integrity of the search by detaining the residents—did not apply to a resident who had left the premises and was a mile away when the search began. He also noted that the seizure of Bailey was more intrusive than in *Summers,* where the resident was merely forced to stay on the premises. In contrast, Bailey was stopped in public, placed in a police car, and driven back to the premises. Justice Kennedy summed up as follows:

> Limiting the rule in *Summers* to the area in which an occupant poses a real threat to the safe and efficient execution of a search warrant ensures that the scope of the detention incident to a search is confined to its underlying justification. Once an occupant is beyond the immediate vicinity of the premises to be searched, the search-related law enforcement interests are diminished and the intrusiveness of the detention is more severe.

The *Bailey* Court found it unnecessary to decide how far beyond the premises the *Summers* power to detain residents could extend. Justice Kennedy explained as follows:

> Here, petitioner was detained at a point beyond any reasonable understanding of the immediate vicinity of the premises in question; and so this case presents neither the necessity nor the occasion to further define the meaning of immediate vicinity. In closer cases courts can consider a number of factors to determine whether an occupant was detained within the immediate vicinity of the premises to be searched, including the lawful limits of the premises, whether the occupant was within the line of sight of his dwelling, the ease of reentry from the occupant's location, and other relevant factors.

Justice Scalia, joined by Justices Ginsburg and Kagan, wrote a concurring opinion in *Bailey*. He emphasized the categorical nature of the *Summers* rule. Justice Breyer, joined by Justices Thomas and Alito, dissented. He argued that while the majority purportedly applied a categorical rule, it will be difficult to determine where the line is drawn between residents who are near enough to the premises to be detained, and those who are too far away. He stated that "the majority has substituted a line based on indeterminate geography for a line based on realistic considerations related to basic Fourth Amendment concerns such as privacy, safety, evidence destruction, and flight. In my view, these latter considerations should govern the Fourth Amendment determination at issue here."

## 2. When Does a Seizure Occur? The Line Between "Stop" and "Encounter"

In *Terry,* it was not difficult to determine the precise point at which the stop occurred: the officer physically grabbed Terry and spun him around. However, the Court has had more difficulty determining whether a stop has occurred when the police conduct is not as affirmatively coercive or as physically intrusive as in *Terry.*

### *The Mendenhall "Free to Leave" Test*

In United States v. Mendenhall, 446 U.S. 544 (1980), Mendenhall was observed by Drug Enforcement Administration agents at the Detroit Airport as she arrived on a flight from Los Angeles. They suspected her of being a drug courier. The agents approached her as she was walking through the concourse, identified themselves as DEA agents, and one agent asked to see her identification and airline ticket. The driver's license she produced was in her name, but her ticket was not. She became extremely nervous. The agent gave her back her license and ticket and asked Mendenhall to accompany him to the airport DEA office for further questions. Without saying anything, she did so. In the office the agent asked Mendenhall if she would allow a search of her person and handbag. She said yes. In a strip search of her person drugs were found. Mendenhall was arrested, prosecuted, and convicted.

Justice Stewart, joined only by Justice Rehnquist, addressed an argument that the government had not made in the lower courts and concluded that when Mendenhall was approached in the airport, no "seizure" had occurred, and therefore this initial police-citizen contact was outside the scope of the Fourth Amendment. Just Stewart explained:

> The events took place in the public concourse. The agents wore no uniforms and displayed no weapons. They did not summon the respondent to their presence, but instead approached her and identified themselves as federal agents. They requested, but did not demand to see the respondent's identification and ticket. Such conduct, without more, did not amount to an intrusion upon any constitutionally protected interest. * * *

This conclusion resulted from application of the following rule:

> A person has been "seized" within the meaning of the Fourth Amendment only if, in view of all the circumstances surrounding the incident, a reasonable person would have believed that he was not free to leave. Examples of circumstances that might indicate a

seizure, even where the person did not attempt to leave, would be the threatening presence of several officers, the display of a weapon by an officer, some physical touching of the person of the citizen, or the use of language or tone of voice indicating that compliance with the officer's request might be compelled.

Justice Stewart's "free to leave" test did not command a majority of the Court in *Mendenhall;* seven Justices found that the question of whether a seizure had occurred was not properly raised in the lower court. But subsequent cases have established the "free to leave" test as the initial benchmark for determining whether a person has been stopped within the meaning of *Terry*.[13]

### Applying the "Free to Leave" Test: Florida v. Royer

A plurality of the Court applied the Stewart "free to leave" test in Florida v. Royer, 460 U.S. 491 (1983). Justice White, writing for himself and Justices Marshall, Powell, and Stevens, stated the facts:

> On January 3, 1978, Royer was observed at Miami International Airport by two plain-clothes detectives of the Dade County, Florida, Public Safety Department assigned to the County's Organized Crime Bureau, Narcotics Investigation Section. Detectives Johnson and Magdalena believed that Royer's appearance, mannerisms, luggage, and actions fit the so-called "drug courier profile." Royer, apparently unaware of the attention he had attracted, purchased a one-way ticket to New York City and checked his two suitcases, placing on each suitcase an identification tag bearing the name "Holt" and the destination, "LaGuardia". As Royer made his way to the concourse which led to the airline boarding area, the two detectives approached him, identified themselves as policemen working out of the sheriff's office, and asked if Royer had a "moment" to speak with them; Royer said "Yes."

> Upon request, but without oral consent, Royer produced for the detectives his airline ticket and his driver's license. The airline ticket, like the baggage identification tags, bore the name "Holt," while the driver's license carried respondent's correct name, "Royer." When the detectives asked about the discrepancy, Royer explained that a friend had made the reservation in the name of "Holt." Royer became noticeably more nervous during this conversation, whereupon the detectives informed Royer that they were in fact

---

[13] As will be seen later in this section, the Stewart test has been modified by more recent cases, such as *Bostick* and *Hodari*, to accommodate some specific fact situations arising in police-citizen encounters. But it still remains the basic test for determining whether a person has been stopped under *Terry*.

narcotics investigators and that they had reason to suspect him of transporting narcotics.

The detectives did not return his airline ticket and identification but asked Royer to accompany them to a room, approximately forty feet away, adjacent to the concourse. Royer said nothing in response but went with the officers as he had been asked to do. The room was later described by Detective Johnson as a "large storage closet," located in the stewardesses' lounge and containing a small desk and two chairs. Without Royer's consent or agreement, Detective Johnson, using Royer's baggage check stubs, retrieved the "Holt" luggage from the airline and brought it to the room where respondent and Detective Magdalena were waiting. Royer was asked if he would consent to a search of the suitcases. Without orally responding to this request, Royer produced a key and unlocked one of the suitcases, which the detective then opened without seeking further assent from Royer. Drugs were found in that suitcase. According to Detective Johnson, Royer stated that he did not know the combination to the lock on the second suitcase. When asked if he objected to the detective opening the second suitcase, Royer said "no, go ahead," and did not object when the detective explained that the suitcase might have to be broken open. The suitcase was pried open by the officers and more marihuana was found. Royer was then told that he was under arrest. Approximately fifteen minutes had elapsed from the time the detectives initially approached respondent until his arrest upon the discovery of the contraband.

Justice White observed that Royer had testified that he believed he was not free to leave the officers' presence and that Detective Johnson stated that he did not believe he had probable cause to arrest until after he opened the suitcases. Justice White summarized some of the law regarding "stops."

[L]aw enforcement officers do not violate the Fourth Amendment by merely approaching an individual on the street or in another public place, by asking him if he is willing to answer some questions, by putting questions to him if the person is willing to listen, or by offering in evidence in a criminal prosecution his voluntary answers to such questions. Nor would the fact that the officer identifies himself as a police officer, without more, convert the encounter into a seizure requiring some level of objective justification. The person approached, however, need not answer any question put to him; indeed, he may decline to listen to the questions at all and may go on his way. He may not be detained even momentarily without reasonable, objective grounds for doing so; and his refusal to listen or answer does not, without more, furnish those grounds. If there is no detention—no seizure within the meaning of the Fourth Amendment—then no constitutional rights have been infringed.

The plurality found that a seizure occurred when the officers took Royer's ticket and driver's license and started walking away:

> Here, Royer's ticket and identification remained in the possession of the officers throughout the encounter; the officers also seized and had possession of his luggage. As a practical matter, Royer could not leave the airport without them. In *Mendenhall,* no luggage was involved, the ticket and identification were immediately returned, and the officers were careful to advise that the suspect could decline to be searched. Here, the officers had seized Royer's luggage and made no effort to advise him that he need not consent to the search.

Justice Brennan concurred in the result. Four Justices dissented in *Royer* on the ground that, while Royer may have been seized, the seizure was supported by reasonable suspicion and the police lawfully obtained Royer's consent. Thus, none of the Justices disagreed with the proposition that Royer was seized within the meaning of the Fourth Amendment when the officers retained Royer's ticket and identification.

Does the *Royer* Court give sufficient guidance to the police to determine what type of conduct triggers a Fourth Amendment seizure? Lower courts have tried to impart some guidance. See Johnson v. Campbell, 332 F.3d 199 (3rd Cir. 2003) (motorist was stopped when officer persisted in telling him to roll his window down even after motorist refused: "At that time, Campbell made it clear that Johnson was not free to ignore him and would not be left alone until he complied."); United States v. Madden, 682 F.3d 920 (10th Cir. 2012) ("In this case, what began as a consensual encounter became an investigative detention when Officer Balderrama asked Madden to step out of the vehicle and then * * * directed Madden to sit in the back of his patrol car while he obtained Madden's personal information and ran it through the computer."); United States v. High, 921 F.2d 112 (7th Cir.1990) (suggesting that officers "preface their questions with a statement that the encounter is consensual and that the citizen is free to go"); United States v. Espinoza, 490 F.3d 41 (1st Cir. 2007) (ordering a driver to turn off the engine of his car is a seizure).

### Factory Sweeps: INS v. Delgado

A majority of the Court adopted and applied the *Mendenhall* test in Immigration and Naturalization Service v. Delgado, 466 U.S. 210 (1984), which held that INS officers did not seize workers when they conducted factory surveys in search of illegal aliens. Justice Rehnquist described the surveys as follows:

At the beginning of the surveys several agents positioned themselves near the buildings' exits, while other agents dispersed throughout the factory to question most, but not all, employees at their work stations. The agents displayed badges, carried walkie-talkies, and were armed, although at no point during any of the surveys was a weapon ever drawn. Moving systematically through the factory, the agents approached employees and, after identifying themselves, asked them from one to three questions relating to their citizenship. If the employee gave a credible reply that he was a United States citizen, the questioning ended, and the agent moved on to another employee. If the employee gave an unsatisfactory response or admitted that he was an alien, the employee was asked to produce his immigration papers. During the survey, employees continued with their work and were free to walk around within the factory.

Four employees questioned in one of the surveys filed suit, claiming that the factory sweeps violated the Fourth Amendment and seeking declaratory and injunctive relief. The employees lost in the district court, prevailed in the court of appeals, and lost again in the Supreme Court.

Justice Rehnquist noted that "police questioning, by itself, is unlikely to result in a Fourth Amendment violation. While most citizens will respond to a police request, the fact that people do so, and do so without being told they are free not to respond, hardly eliminates the consensual nature of the response." He rejected the argument that the employees were seized during the entire survey because of the guards being placed at the exits. Because the employees were at work and thus were not going to leave the factory in any event, Justice Rehnquist concluded that the guards at the exit could not have had a coercive or custodial effect. The majority reasoned that "[t]his conduct should have given [the employees] no reason to believe that they would be detained if they gave truthful answers to the questions put to them or if they simply refused to answer." And the majority also rejected an argument that individual employees were seized when they were questioned—because, generally, simple questions from a police officer do not amount to a seizure.

Justice Powell concurred in the result. Justice Brennan, joined by Justice Marshall, dissented from the holding that the individual interrogations were not seizures and argued that the testimony in the case "paints a frightening picture of people subjected to wholesale interrogation under conditions designed not to respect personal security and privacy, but rather to elicit prompt answers from completely intimidated workers."

Put yourself in the workers' place. Would you feel free to leave, or to terminate the questioning? Would you assume the armed guards at the exits were placed there to keep you inside the factory? Would it affect you if, as is likely, all of the other factory members were "cooperating" by answering the officers' questions?

### Can Failure to Cooperate Lead to Reasonable Suspicion to Justify a Stop?

Would you think that the failure to cooperate in an encounter might be treated by the officers as suspicious conduct that would give rise to a more extensive investigation? The Court in *Royer* stated that the failure to cooperate in a consensual encounter cannot be treated as suspicious conduct that would justify a *Terry* stop. Otherwise, the officers would have it both ways: an encounter would be permissible because it is consensual, and yet a stop would be permissible when the individual refuses to consent. But how many people actually *know* that officers cannot treat as suspicious a person's refusal to cooperate in an encounter? And even if not permitted under the law to treat non-cooperation as suspicious, how many officers do *in fact* treat non-cooperation as a reason for detaining an individual?

### Street Encounters

Officers in police cars, marked and unmarked, often seek to question people on the street. When officers pull up to question a person on the street in the absence of any articulable reasonable suspicion, have they violated the person's Fourth Amendment rights? This will depend on whether the officer's conduct amounts to a seizure, or is rather simply an encounter. United States v. Cardoza, 129 F.3d 6 (1st Cir.1997), provides an example. Cardoza arranged a gun purchase for his friend Ragsdale. At the time of the encounter with police officers, Ragsdale was carrying the gun fully loaded, and Cardoza had possession of an extra bullet. The court describes the encounter as follows:

> Sometime after the transaction was completed, Cardoza and Ragsdale began walking along Humboldt Avenue. As they walked, Ragsdale had the handgun in his waistband and Cardoza carried the single round of ammunition in his hand. By this time it was approximately 2:00 a.m. on the morning of July 15. They were spotted walking along Humboldt Avenue by four officers of the Boston Police's Youth Violence Strike Force who were patrolling the area in an unmarked police car. * * * Moving slowly, the police car approached Cardoza and Ragsdale from behind. As the patrol car approached, Cardoza and Ragsdale crossed Humboldt Avenue in order to walk up the sidewalk of Ruthven Street, a one-way thoroughfare that emptied onto Humboldt Avenue. As they crossed in front of the car, Officer Brown, who was sitting in the back seat on the driver's side, recognized Cardoza and directed the driver to make

a left turn off Humboldt, and proceed the wrong way up Ruthven for a short distance. Officer Brown testified that he wanted to ask Cardoza some questions concerning a shooting incident that had occurred some days earlier. The driver took the left turn, and pulled over to the curb just off Humboldt, facing the wrong way on Ruthven Street.

Officer Brown, whose window was rolled down, called out to Cardoza, asking "What's up Freddie? What are you doing out this time of night?" Cardoza stopped, turned, and approached the patrol car. Ragsdale continued walking a short distance. Officer Brown remained in the car conversing with Cardoza through the open car window. As he talked with Officer Brown, Cardoza began to gesture with his hand, exposing the round of ammunition. Seeing the round of ammunition, Brown exited the patrol car, and began to pat-frisk Cardoza. At the same time, two other officers exited the car and approached and pat-frisked Ragsdale, discovering the handgun loaded with eight rounds of ammunition.

Cardoza was convicted of being a felon in possession of a firearm and ammunition. He argued that the evidence should be suppressed because, by the time the officer saw the ammunition, he had been stopped by the officer without reasonable suspicion. But the court disagreed, and found that Cardoza had not been seized within the meaning of the Fourth Amendment. It explained as follows:

To begin with, no sirens or flashing lights were used by the officers to indicate to Cardoza that he should stop in his tracks. Similarly, the police cruiser pulled over and stopped at the curb before Officer Brown called out to Cardoza. And Officer Brown remained in the car when he called out to Cardoza. * * * Officer Brown did not ask Cardoza to stop, or even to approach the car. He simply called out through an open car window with the question "what are you doing out at this time of night?" Those words do not objectively communicate an attempt to restrain Cardoza's liberty. We are therefore unpersuaded that the police officers' actions transformed mere police questioning into a seizure.

If a police car pulled up against traffic on a one-way street to speak to you, would you feel free to leave or to refuse to reply to the officers? Would any person in their right mind (much less reasonable mind) feel free to leave? Obviously not. But the *Cardoza* court had a response to this argument:

We recognize, of course, the import of Cardoza's observation that few people, including himself, would ever feel free to walk away from any police question. Under this reasoning, however, * * * every police-citizen encounter [is transformed] into a seizure. The "free to walk away" test, however, must be read in conjunction with the Court's frequent admonitions that "a seizure does not occur simply because a police officer approaches an individual and asks a few questions." What emerges between the two imperatives, therefore, is the directive that police conduct, viewed from the totality of the circumstances, must objectively communicate that the officer is exercising his or her official authority to restrain the individual's liberty of movement before we can find that a seizure occurred. Because there was no such objective communication in the instant case, we affirm the district court's denial of Cardoza's motion to suppress.

So the court held that the test for a *Terry* stop is not really whether a reasonable person would feel free to leave, but rather whether the police officer was acting coercively. That description of the test seems more realistic, and appears to track the case law: for example, there was a stop in *Royer* because police officers acted coercively when they took Royer's ticket and identification and walked away with the documents. But applying that test to the facts of *Cardoza*: isn't an officer acting coercively when he drives the wrong way down a one-way street at 2 a.m., pulls over, and asks the citizen what he is up to? That's not the kind of conduct you would expect from an ordinary citizen, is it? Compare United States v. Camacho, 661 F.3d 718 (1st Cir. 2011) (seizure found where the officers blocked the defendant's path with their Crown Victoria; both officers were wearing jackets labeled "New Bedford Police" and "Gang Unit"; one officer stepped out of the car and confronted the defendant with "accusatory" questions; and another officer ordered him to place his hands on the hood of the car).

### Problem with the "Freedom to Walk Away" Test

Professor Steinbock takes the Court's "freedom to walk away" test to task in The Wrong Line Between Freedom and Restraint: The Unreality, Obscurity, and Incivility of the Fourth Amendment Consensual Encounter Doctrine, 38 San Diego L.Rev. 507 (2001):

> There are legal fictions and there are legal fictions. One means of differentiating good from bad legal fictions is their relationship to reality * * *. By that measure, in light of the available evidence, the consensual encounter doctrine paints a false picture of reality as applied to encounters involving investigation of the individual being questioned. In so doing, it mislocates the dividing line between freedom and restraint, including on the "freedom" side of this line many people who are effectively restrained or—to put it another way—are restrained in all but the eyes of the law.

* * * The obscurity of the line between freedom and detention bespeaks an uncivil distrust of the persons whose liberty is at stake. It plays on their ignorance and understandable sense of powerlessness in relation to law enforcement officers. Moreover, attempts by citizens to clarify their status, or assert the rights they believe they have, produce additional incivility and friction on both sides. The consensual encounter doctrine virtually invites citizens, as an initial response, to question or rebuff police approaches. * * * Rudeness and confrontation by citizens, which are virtually required in order for citizens to determine whether they are free to go, stimulates rudeness and confrontation in response. This, in turn, poisons the relationship between citizens and their government, creating social friction and disunity.

But what is the alternative? Should it be considered a stop whenever a police officer approaches a citizen to ask questions? See also Saltzburg, The Fourth Amendment: Internal Revenue Code or Body of Principles? 74 Geo.Wash.L.Rev. 956 (2006) ("A better approach is to focus on the conduct of law enforcement officers rather than on the reactions of individuals to law enforcement officers. This approach asks law enforcement officers to pay attention to their own actions, not to predict how reasonable civilians would respond to those actions.").

### Bus Sweeps: Florida v. Bostick and United States v. Drayton

In the following case, the Court considers the permissibility of a "bus sweep" in the absence of reasonable suspicion. The case discusses and applies the Court's first analysis of this subject in Florida v. Bostick.

### UNITED STATES V. DRAYTON

Supreme Court of the United States, 2002.
536 U.S. 194.

### JUSTICE KENNEDY delivered the opinion of the Court.

The Fourth Amendment permits police officers to approach bus passengers at random to ask questions and to request their consent to searches, provided a reasonable person would understand that he or she is free to refuse. Florida v. Bostick, 501 U.S. 429 (1991). This case requires us to determine whether officers must advise bus passengers during these encounters of their right not to cooperate.

* * * On February 4, 1999, respondents Christopher Drayton and Clifton Brown, Jr., were traveling on a Greyhound bus en route from Ft. Lauderdale, Florida, to Detroit, Michigan. The bus made a scheduled stop in Tallahassee, Florida. The passengers were required to disembark so the bus could be refueled and cleaned. As the passengers reboarded, the

driver checked their tickets and then left to complete paperwork inside the terminal. As he left, the driver allowed three members of the Tallahassee Police Department to board the bus as part of a routine drug and weapons interdiction effort. The officers were dressed in plain clothes and carried concealed weapons and visible badges.

Once onboard Officer Hoover knelt on the driver's seat and faced the rear of the bus. He could observe the passengers and ensure the safety of the two other officers without blocking the aisle or otherwise obstructing the bus exit. Officers Lang and Blackburn went to the rear of the bus. Blackburn remained stationed there, facing forward. Lang worked his way toward the front of the bus, speaking with individual passengers as he went. He asked the passengers about their travel plans and sought to match passengers with luggage in the overhead racks. To avoid blocking the aisle, Lang stood next to or just behind each passenger with whom he spoke.

According to Lang's testimony, passengers who declined to cooperate with him or who chose to exit the bus at any time would have been allowed to do so without argument. In Lang's experience, however, most people are willing to cooperate. Some passengers go so far as to commend the police for their efforts to ensure the safety of their travel. Lang could recall five to six instances in the previous year in which passengers had declined to have their luggage searched. It also was common for passengers to leave the bus for a cigarette or a snack while the officers were on board. Lang sometimes informed passengers of their right to refuse to cooperate. On the day in question, however, he did not.

Respondents were seated next to each other on the bus. Drayton was in the aisle seat, Brown in the seat next to the window. Lang approached respondents from the rear and leaned over Drayton's shoulder. He held up his badge long enough for respondents to identify him as a police officer. With his face 12-to-18 inches away from Drayton's, Lang spoke in a voice just loud enough for respondents to hear:

> I'm Investigator Lang with the Tallahassee Police Department. We're conducting bus interdiction [sic], attempting to deter drugs and illegal weapons being transported on the bus. Do you have any bags on the bus?

Both respondents pointed to a single green bag in the overhead luggage rack. Lang asked, "Do you mind if I check it?," and Brown responded, "Go ahead." Lang handed the bag to Officer Blackburn to check. The bag contained no contraband.

Officer Lang noticed that both respondents were wearing heavy jackets and baggy pants despite the warm weather. In Lang's experience drug traffickers often use baggy clothing to conceal weapons or narcotics. The officer thus asked Brown if he had any weapons or drugs in his possession. And he asked Brown: "Do you mind if I check your person?" Brown answered, "Sure," and cooperated by leaning up in his seat, pulling a cell phone out of his pocket, and opening up his jacket. Lang reached across Drayton and patted down Brown's jacket and pockets, including his waist area, sides, and upper thighs. In both thigh areas, Lang detected hard objects similar to drug packages detected on other occasions. Lang arrested and handcuffed Brown. Officer Hoover escorted Brown from the bus.

Lang then asked Drayton, "Mind if I check you?" Drayton responded by lifting his hands about eight inches from his legs. Lang conducted a pat-down of Drayton's thighs and detected hard objects similar to those found on Brown. He arrested Drayton and escorted him from the bus. A further search revealed that respondents had duct-taped plastic bundles of powder cocaine between several pairs of their boxer shorts. Brown possessed three bundles containing 483 grams of cocaine. Drayton possessed two bundles containing 295 grams of cocaine.

[The defendants were charged with drug crimes. The trial court denied motions to suppress the drugs on the ground that the entire procedure was a consensual encounter.]

The Court of Appeals for the Eleventh Circuit reversed and remanded with instructions to grant respondents' motions to suppress. The court held that this disposition was compelled by its previous decisions in United States v. Washington, 151 F. 3d 1354 (1998), and United States v. Guapi, 144 F. 3d 1393 (1998). Those cases had held that bus passengers do not feel free to disregard police officers' requests to search absent "some positive indication that consent could have been refused."

We granted certiorari. The respondents, we conclude, were not seized and their consent to the search was voluntary; and we reverse.

\* \* \*

The Court has addressed on a previous occasion the specific question of drug interdiction efforts on buses. In *Bostick,* two police officers requested a bus passenger's consent to a search of his luggage. The passenger agreed, and the resulting search revealed cocaine in his suitcase. The Florida Supreme Court suppressed the cocaine. In doing so it adopted a *per se* rule that due to the cramped confines onboard a bus the act of questioning would deprive a person of his or her freedom of movement and so constitute a seizure under the Fourth Amendment.

This Court reversed. *Bostick* first made it clear that for the most part *per se* rules are inappropriate in the Fourth Amendment context. The proper inquiry necessitates a consideration of "all the circumstances surrounding the encounter." The Court noted next that the traditional rule, which states that a seizure does not occur so long as a reasonable person would feel free "to disregard the police and go about his business," is not an accurate measure of the coercive effect of a bus encounter. A passenger may not want to get off a bus if there is a risk it will depart before the opportunity to reboard. A bus rider's movements are confined in this sense, but this is the natural result of choosing to take the bus; it says nothing about whether the police conduct is coercive. The proper inquiry "is whether a reasonable person would feel free to decline the officers' requests or otherwise terminate the encounter." Finally, the Court rejected Bostick's argument that he must have been seized because no reasonable person would consent to a search of luggage containing drugs. The reasonable person test, the Court explained, is objective and "presupposes an *innocent* person."

In light of the limited record, *Bostick* refrained from deciding whether a seizure occurred. The Court, however, identified two factors "particularly worth noting" on remand. First, although it was obvious that an officer was armed, he did not remove the gun from its pouch or use it in a threatening way. Second, the officer advised the passenger that he could refuse consent to the search.

Relying upon this latter factor, the Eleventh Circuit has adopted what is in effect a *per se* rule that evidence obtained during suspicionless drug interdiction efforts aboard buses must be suppressed unless the officers have advised passengers of their right not to cooperate and to refuse consent to a search. * * *

The Court of Appeals erred in adopting this approach.

Applying the *Bostick* framework to the facts of this particular case, we conclude that the police did not seize respondents when they boarded the bus and began questioning passengers. The officers gave the passengers no reason to believe that they were required to answer the officers' questions. When Officer Lang approached respondents, he did not brandish a weapon or make any intimidating movements. He left the aisle free so that respondents could exit. He spoke to passengers one by one and in a polite, quiet voice. Nothing he said would suggest to a reasonable person that he or she was barred from leaving the bus or otherwise terminating the encounter.

* * * There was no application of force, no intimidating movement, no overwhelming show of force, no brandishing of weapons, no blocking of exits, no threat, no command, not even an authoritative tone of voice. It is beyond question that had this encounter occurred on the street, it would be constitutional. The fact that an encounter takes place on a bus does not on its own transform standard police questioning of citizens into an illegal seizure. Indeed, because many fellow passengers are present to witness officers' conduct, a reasonable person may feel even more secure

in his or her decision not to cooperate with police on a bus than in other circumstances.

Respondents make much of the fact that Officer Lang displayed his badge. In Florida v. Rodriguez, 469 U.S., at 5–6, however, the Court rejected the claim that the defendant was seized when an officer approached him in an airport, showed him his badge, and asked him to answer some questions. Likewise, in INS v. Delgado, 466 U.S. 210, 212–213 (1984), the Court held that INS agents' wearing badges and questioning workers in a factory did not constitute a seizure. And while neither Lang nor his colleagues were in uniform or visibly armed, those factors should have little weight in the analysis. Officers are often required to wear uniforms and in many circumstances this is cause for assurance, not discomfort. Much the same can be said for wearing sidearms. That most law enforcement officers are armed is a fact well known to the public. The presence of a holstered firearm thus is unlikely to contribute to the coerciveness of the encounter absent active brandishing of the weapon.

Officer Hoover's position at the front of the bus also does not tip the scale in respondents' favor. Hoover did nothing to intimidate passengers, and he said nothing to suggest that people could not exit and indeed he left the aisle clear. * * *

Finally, the fact that in Officer Lang's experience only a few passengers have refused to cooperate does not suggest that a reasonable person would not feel free to terminate the bus encounter. * * * [B]us passengers answer officers' questions and otherwise cooperate not because of coercion but because the passengers know that their participation enhances their own safety and the safety of those around them. * * *

Drayton contends that even if Brown's cooperation with the officers was consensual, Drayton was seized because no reasonable person would feel free to terminate the encounter with the officers after Brown had been arrested. * * * The arrest of one person does not mean that everyone around him has been seized by police. If anything, Brown's arrest should have put Drayton on notice of the consequences of continuing the encounter by answering the officers' questions. * * * And, as the facts above suggest, respondents' consent to the search of their luggage and their persons was voluntary. Nothing Officer Lang said indicated a command to consent to the search. Rather, when respondents informed Lang that they had a bag on the bus, he asked for their permission to check it. And when Lang requested to search Brown and Drayton's persons, he asked first if they objected, thus indicating to a reasonable person that he or she was free to refuse.

\* \* \*

\* \* \* Although Officer Lang did not inform respondents of their right to refuse the search, he did request permission to search, and the totality of the circumstances indicates that their consent was voluntary, so the searches were reasonable.

In a society based on law, the concept of agreement and consent should be given a weight and dignity of its own. Police officers act in full accord with the law when they ask citizens for consent. It reinforces the rule of law for the citizen to advise the police of his or her wishes and for the police to act in reliance on that understanding. When this exchange takes place, it dispels inferences of coercion.

JUSTICE SOUTER, with whom JUSTICE STEVENS and JUSTICE GINSBURG join, dissenting.

\* \* \*

\* \* \* [F]or reasons unexplained, the driver with the tickets entitling the passengers to travel had yielded his custody of the bus and its seated travelers to three police officers, whose authority apparently superseded the driver's own. The officers took control of the entire passenger compartment, one stationed at the door keeping surveillance of all the occupants, the others working forward from the back. With one officer right behind him and the other one forward, a third officer accosted each passenger at quarters extremely close and so cramped that as many as half the passengers could not even have stood to face the speaker. None was asked whether he was willing to converse with the police or to take part in the enquiry. Instead the officer said the police were "conducting bus interdiction," in the course of which they "would like . . . cooperation." The reasonable inference was that the "interdiction" was not a consensual exercise, but one the police would carry out whatever the circumstances; that they would prefer "cooperation" but would not let the lack of it stand in their way. There was no contrary indication that day, since no passenger had refused the cooperation requested, and there was no reason for any passenger to believe that the driver would return and the trip resume until the police were satisfied. The scene was set and an atmosphere of obligatory participation was established by this introduction. Later requests to search prefaced with "Do you mind . . ." would naturally have been understood in the terms with which the encounter began.

It is very hard to imagine that either Brown or Drayton would have believed that he stood to lose nothing if he refused to cooperate with the police, or that he had any free choice to ignore the police altogether. No reasonable passenger could have believed that, only an uncomprehending one. \* \* \*

### NOTE ON BUS SWEEPS

Professor Nadler, in No Need to Shout: Bus Sweeps and the Psychology of Coercion, 2002 Sup.Ct. Rev. 153, argues that the Court's bus sweep cases, while understandable after 9/11, are out of line with social science evidence concerning coercion and consent. She concludes as follows:

> It may be the case that, on balance, it is desirable to permit police to board intercity buses and pose questions to passengers and, in some circumstances, conduct searches of baggage and persons, especially with the current need to be vigilant about potential risks of terrorism. In this way, it is understandable that the *Drayton* Court scrupulously avoided announcing rules in drug cases that would restrict the ability of police to investigate terrorism and other serious threats to public security.

> On the other hand, in its effort to be sensitive to the order-maintenance needs of the government, the Court has promulgated a standard to determining the bounds of consensual police-citizen encounters and voluntary searches that struggles against a wealth of social science evidence, that subjects many innocent people to suspicionless searches and seizures against their will, and that produces disagreement and confusion in the lower courts. It may be that large-scale, suspicionless searches of passengers on common carriers is a price that we ought to be willing to pay to stem the flow of illegal narcotics transported on intercity buses and trains. If this is the determination that underlies the decision in *Drayton*, then the Court should have explicitly stated it and justified it—rather than relying on the implausible assertion that bus passengers, when they are individually confronted by armed police officers who want to search them, feel free to ignore the police or outright refuse their requests.

### *State of Mind Required for a Stop: Brower v. County of Inyo*

Must an officer have a certain state of mind in order to seize a person? Justice Scalia wrote for the Court in Brower v. County of Inyo, 489 U.S. 593 (1989), where officers set up a "blind" roadblock in an attempt to apprehend a fleeing suspect. The suspect, approaching the roadblock from around a curve, was not able to stop before crashing into it. The suspect died in the crash and a wrongful death action was brought alleging that the suspect had been illegally "seized" by the roadblock.

Justice Scalia agreed with the plaintiff that a seizure had occurred. He declared that "a Fourth Amendment seizure does not occur whenever there is a governmentally caused termination of an individual's freedom of movement * * *, nor even whenever there is a governmentally *desired* termination of an individual's freedom of movement * * *, but only when there is a governmental termination of freedom of movement *through means intentionally applied*." In this case, the officers placed the roadblock with the intent to stop the suspect; and in fact the suspect was stopped by means of the roadblock. Therefore, the suspect was seized, even though he was not stopped in precisely the way that the officers intended for him to stop. The means used to stop him were intentionally applied.[14]

Elaborating on this intent-based test, Justice Scalia posed the following hypothetical: suppose police officers park and leave their squad car on a hill, the parking brake accidentally disengages, the car rolls down the hill and just happens to pin a suspected criminal against a wall. Has the criminal been seized? Justice Scalia's answer was "no", because the officers never intentionally applied any means to stop the suspect's freedom of movement. They just got lucky.

Justice Stevens, joined by Justices Brennan, Marshall, and Blackmun, concurred in the judgment. He objected to Justice Scalia's emphasis on an intentional acquisition of physical control as marking the onset of a seizure, and suggested that, since it was clear in the instant case that the roadblock was intended to stop the deceased, "[d]ecision in the case before us is thus not advanced by pursuing a hypothetical inquiry concerning whether an unintentional act might also violate the Fourth Amendment."

How would the *Brower* test apply in the following circumstance? A gunman commandeers a school bus and takes a student as a hostage. A police standoff ensues, and a police officer fires into the bus in an attempt to kill the gunman. The bullet, however, hits the student instead. Has the student been seized under the Fourth Amendment? The court in Medeiros v. O'Connell, 150 F.3d 164 (2d Cir.1998), held that the police conduct did not constitute a seizure of the student, and therefore that summary judgment was properly granted to the officer in a section 1983 case. The court declared that a police officer's deliberate decision to shoot for the purpose of stopping the *gunman* "does not result in the sort of willful detention of the hostage that the Fourth Amendment was designed to govern." The court noted that the officer's intent was not to restrain the hostage's movement—far from it. The court also observed that the instant case was distinguishable "from those in which the police shoot an innocent victim mistakenly believing that he is the suspect whom they are pursuing." In such cases, a seizure occurs because "the victim was indeed the object of an intentional act of seizure, even if the police were mistaken as to the victim's identity." But where a hostage is hit by a bullet intended for the hostage-taker, there is no intentional seizure of the hostage within the meaning of *Brower*.

For an application of the *Brower* test, see Brendlin v. California, 551 U.S. 249 (2007), in which evidence was found on a passenger in a car that

---

[14] The Court in *Brower* remanded for a determination of whether the seizure was unreasonable under the circumstances.

was intentionally stopped by police. The government argued that the passenger was not seized by the mere stop of the car, because the intent of the police was to stop *the driver*. The Court rejected this argument, stating that the intent that counts under the Fourth Amendment "is the intent that has been conveyed to the person confronted, and the criterion of willful restriction on freedom of movement is no invitation to look to subjective intent when determining who is seized." In this case, the officers intended to stop the car, and therefore, under *Brower* a stop occurred with respect to everyone in the car. The Court noted that a reasonable passenger would certainly think that he was not free to walk away when the officers intentionally stop the car in which he is sitting.

### The Suspect Who Does Not Submit: California v. Hodari D.

In California v. Hodari D., 499 U.S. 621 (1991), the Court determined that the *Mendenhall* "freedom to walk away" test needed to be modified when applied to a suspect who refuses to submit to a show of authority. The case arose when officers encountered a group of youths who were huddled around a car and who fled when they saw the officers. Hodari, one of the group who ran, threw away a small rock as a pursuing officer was about to catch him. One officer tackled Hodari, handcuffed him and radioed for assistance. Subsequently, the officer discovered that the discarded rock was crack cocaine. Hodari claimed that the pursuit was a seizure, and because there was no legal cause for the pursuit there was a Fourth Amendment violation, requiring suppression of the fruits including the cocaine.

Justice Scalia, writing for the majority, "consulted the common law" and cited law dictionaries to support the notion that the word "seizure" has meant a "taking possession." Justice Scalia separated seizures into two types: those in which the officer has physically touched the citizen, and those in which the officer has used a non-physical show of authority. As to the former category, Justice Scalia noted that "[t]o constitute an arrest, * * *—the quintessential 'seizure of the person' under our Fourth Amendment jurisprudence—the mere grasping or application of physical force with lawful authority, whether or not it succeeded in subduing the arrestee, was sufficient." However, although "an arrest is effected by the slightest application of physical force," Justice Scalia rejected the idea that "there is a *continuing* arrest during the period of fugitivity."

As to the latter category of *non-physical* displays of authority, at issue under the facts of *Hodari,* Justice Scalia framed the question before the Court as "whether, with respect to a show of authority as with respect to application of physical force, a seizure occurs even though the subject does not yield." The answer was "that it does not."

Justice Scalia observed that *Mendenhall* dealt with non-physical displays of authority, and focused only on whether a reasonable person would feel that he or she was free to leave, rather than on actual submission. Justice Scalia concluded, however, that the "free to leave" test was a necessary, but not sufficient, test for determining whether a seizure occurs. He stated that the *Mendenhall* test when "read carefully" says that a person has been seized "only if", not "whenever" the officer uses a show of authority. Thus, where the officer engages in a non-physical show of authority, it must be such that a reasonable person would not feel free to leave, *and* the citizen must actually submit. This is in contrast to physical touching or grasping, which if intentional is a seizure in any case.

As a matter of policy, Justice Scalia reasoned that the public should be encouraged to comply with police orders; therefore it would not do to reward suspects like Hodari for noncompliance by finding a seizure. Justice Scalia rejected the argument that police officers would abuse a rule that they may automatically chase non-complying suspects. The perceived risk of abuse was that officers, having no reasonable suspicion to support a stop, would routinely use non-physical displays of authority in the hope that suspects would disobey them and evidence would be found. Justice Scalia found this risk overrated. He reasoned that police do not issue orders expecting them to be ignored. Thus, officers would not take the risk that suspects would comply with their orders and render the seizure illegal in the absence of reasonable suspicion.

Justice Stevens, joined by Justice Marshall, dissented. He criticized the majority's "narrow construction" of the term "seizure" as meaning "that a police officer may now fire his weapon at an innocent citizen and not implicate the Fourth Amendment—as long as he misses his target." The dissenters argued that the common law distinction between touching and a show of force was not determinative for Fourth Amendment purposes. Justice Stevens suggested that the common law ought not to govern analyses of current law enforcement practices.

Justice Stevens concluded that the majority erred in focusing on the citizen's reaction to an officer's conduct rather than on the officer's conduct itself. He noted that under the majority's test, police officers could take advantage of citizens by using all their conduct against them in the seconds before they actually submit to authority. For example, an officer could flash his lights to stop a car without adequate cause, and then use any observations made before the car comes to a complete stop. Similarly, a drug enforcement agent could approach a group of passengers in an airport with a drawn gun, announce a baggage search, and then rely on the passengers' reaction to justify a subsequent investigative stop.

Justice Stevens contended that it was "anomalous, at best" to establish different rules for seizures effected by touching and those effected by a show of force. He argued that it was important for an officer to know in advance whether certain conduct would constitute a seizure, and that the majority's test makes this impossible when the officer is using a non-physical show of force.

## QUESTIONS AFTER HODARI

Suppose an officer fires a warning shot in the air and a fleeing suspect stops suddenly and a package falls from his pocket as a result of this sudden stop? Is the package the fruit of a seizure? See Saltzburg, The Fourth Amendment: Internal Revenue Code or Body of Principles? 74 Geo.Wash.L.Rev. 956 (2006) ("Apparently, Justice Scalia would hold that if an officer shot at a suspect to stop him from fleeing, but the bullet missed the suspect because he lunged away to avoid being shot, there would be no seizure. There is little logic to the result that the touch of a finger that fails to restrain a suspect is a seizure, while an unsuccessful attempt to shoot a suspect is not."). See also Mettler v. Whitledge, 165 F.3d 1197 (8th Cir.1999) (sending in an attack dog to subdue the suspect did not constitute an unreasonable seizure, where the citizen shot the dog before the dog got to him).

It should be noted that Hodari was a young, African American, urban male. How suspicious is it for such a person to run when a number of uniformed police come around the corner? See generally Maclin, "Black and Blue Encounters"—Some Preliminary Thoughts About Fourth Amendment Seizures: Should Race Matter?, 26 Val.U.L.Rev. 243 (1991) (arguing that the Court should take account of the race of the citizen in assessing the legality of a police-citizen confrontation under *Terry*).

## *When Does Submission Occur?*

One of the problems left for police officers and the courts after *Hodari* is to determine when, precisely, a suspect has submitted to a non-physical show of authority—i.e., when does the seizure begin. This is important when a citizen tries to dispose of evidence in response to a show of authority. Exemplary is United States v. Lender, 985 F.2d 151 (4th Cir. 1993). The court set forth the pertinent facts as follows:

> At approximately 12:50 a.m., [Officers Hill and Thornell] were patrolling an area in Kinston, North Carolina. The officers knew the area to be one where heavy drug traffic occurred. As they crossed an intersection, the officers observed a group of four or five men, including the defendant, huddled on a corner. The defendant had his hand stuck out with his palm up, and the other men were looking down toward his palm.

Suspecting a drug transaction, the officers stopped their car, got out, and approached the men. Although the officers wore plain clothes and drove an unmarked car, they were readily identifiable as police officers because of their firearms and badges worn at belt-level. As the officers approached, the group began to disperse, and the defendant walked away from the officers with his back to them. Officer Hill called out for the defendant to stop, but the defendant refused. As he walked, the defendant turned and told Hill, "You don't want me; you don't want me."

While Lender continued to walk away, both officers observed him bring his hands to the front of his waist as though reaching for or fumbling with something in that area. Officer Hill again called for the defendant to stop. At this point, the defendant stopped, and a loaded semi-automatic pistol fell from his waist to the ground. [Lender was convicted of possession of a firearm by a felon.]

Lender moved to suppress the gun, arguing that he had been seized without reasonable suspicion by the time he dropped it. But the court disagreed.

Lender argues * * * that he submitted to Officer Hill's second order to stop by coming to a complete halt, and that the gun fell to the ground only after he stopped. Therefore, according to the defendant, the gun fell into plain view after he had been seized.

We do not believe, however, that Lender's momentary halt on the sidewalk with his back to the officers constituted a yielding to their authority. Between Officer Hill's first and second commands for the defendant to stop, both officers heard the defendant say, "You don't want me; you don't want me." They also observed him fumbling with his hands in the area of his waist as if reaching for or adjusting a weapon. Defendant asks us to characterize as capitulation conduct that is fully consistent with preparation to whirl and shoot the officers.

The defendant's actions after he dropped the pistol indicate further that he had not yielded. Lender had stopped for at most an instant when the gun fell. Instead of stopping and standing still, the defendant quickly moved to pick up the weapon. Under the circumstances it cannot be said that the defendant had yielded, and therefore been seized, before the gun fell into the plain view of the officers.

See also United States v. Griffin, 652 F.3d 793 (7th Cir. 2011) (rejecting the defendant's argument that "a seizure does not necessarily occur at a discrete point in time but is better conceived of as a continuing event" that starts at the show of authority and ends when the subject submits; that analysis is directly contrary to *Hodari*; therefore the defendant had not been seized when he refused to pull over when directed to do so by police, and evidence he threw out of the car in a subsequent ""low speed chase" was properly admitted).

## *Summary of Seizure Cases*

Professor Sundby has set forth the following "Accidental Tourist's guidebook" on the state of the law concerning seizures of persons under *Terry*:

> Travel is a considerable problem. One should be aware that law enforcement officers may stop someone and ask permission to look in his luggage even if the traveler has not acted in a fashion that would provoke articulable suspicion of wrongdoing. This is true whether traveling by land, air, or sea. If approached, the innocent traveler should not be alarmed but should state to the officer that he or she has no desire to converse and has other, more important appointments to keep. Although this might strike the traveler at first as rude and abrupt, and perhaps a bit frightening if the questioner is armed, the Supreme Court has made clear that the Fourth Amendment is not for the timid. Consequently, the wise traveler should carry a copy of the Fourth Amendment and display it to the questioner and thus avoid any unnecessary discourse. It is this writer's fervent hope that travel agents soon shall issue copies of the Fourth Amendment as standard procedure when writing airplane, bus, or train tickets.

Sundby, "Everyman's" Fourth Amendment: Privacy or Mutual Trust Between Government and Citizen?, 94 Colum.L.Rev. 1751, 1793 (1994). Is Professor Sundby's assessment overly critical, or just about right?

## 3. Grounds for a Stop: Reasonable Suspicion

The degree of suspicion required to make a stop is referred to as "reasonable suspicion" by the courts. See United States v. Brignoni-Ponce, 422 U.S. 873 (1975). As with the higher standard of probable cause, two separate questions arise in determining whether reasonable suspicion exists. The court must investigate the *source* of information upon which reasonable suspicion is based; and the court must evaluate whether that information is *sufficiently suspicious* to justify a stop.

### a. *Source of Information*

In Adams v. Williams, supra, the Court held that the informant's tip could be credited toward reasonable suspicion. *Adams* did not consider, however, whether reasonable suspicion could be based on a tip from an *anonymous* informant.

### Anonymous Tips: Alabama v. White

The Court relied heavily on *Adams* and Illinois v. Gates (discussed in the material on probable cause) in Alabama v. White, 496 U.S. 325 (1990), and held that an anonymous informant's tip that was "significantly corroborated" by a police officer's investigation provided reasonable suspicion for a stop. Police received an anonymous tip that White would be leaving a particular apartment in a brown Plymouth station wagon with the right taillight broken, and would be driving to Dobey's Motel with a brown attache case containing cocaine. The officers went to the apartment, and saw White enter a brown Plymouth station wagon with a broken right taillight. She was not carrying an attache case. They followed the station wagon as it took the most direct route toward Dobey's Motel. White was stopped just short of Dobey's Motel, and consented to the search of a brown attache case that was in the car. The officers found marijuana in the attache case, and three milligrams of cocaine in White's purse, which was searched during processing at the station. White argued that the stop was illegal because the officers did not have reasonable suspicion, and the evidence should therefore have been excluded as a product of the illegal stop.

Justice White, writing for a six-person majority, held that the stop was supported by reasonable suspicion, derived from the informant's tip and the officers' corroboration of that tip. He noted that under the *Gates* "totality of the circumstances" approach to probable cause, an informant's veracity and basis of knowledge remain "highly relevant" in determining the value of the report of an informant. Justice White stated: "These factors are also relevant in the reasonable suspicion context, although allowance must be made in applying them for the lesser showing required to meet that standard."

Even given the lesser showing required, Justice White acknowledged that the anonymous tip did not itself provide reasonable suspicion, because it failed to show that the informant was reliable (given the fact that the informant was unknown), and it gave no indication of the informant's basis for concluding that White was involved in a drug transaction. But the majority stated: "As there was in *Gates,* however, in this case there is more than the tip itself."

Justice White determined that the corroboration in *White* (i.e., the car was accurately identified and White was going *toward* Dobey's Motel) was not as substantial as that in *Gates.* Yet this was not fatal, because reasonable suspicion is a less stringent standard than probable cause. Justice White explained as follows:

> Reasonable suspicion is a less demanding standard than probable cause not only in the sense that reasonable suspicion can be established with information that is different in quantity or content

than that required to establish probable cause, but also in the sense that reasonable suspicion can arise from information that is less reliable than that required to show probable cause.

The Court found that reasonable suspicion existed even though the corroboration of the tip was not complete, and even though the tip was not correct in some details. Justice White acknowledged that the officer's corroboration of the existence of the car was insignificant, since "anyone could have predicted that fact because it was a condition presumably existing at the time of the call." However, the caller's ability to predict White's future behavior (i.e., getting in the car and driving toward Dobey's Motel) was "important" because:

> [I]t demonstrated inside information—a special familiarity with respondent's affairs. The general public would have had no way of knowing that respondent would shortly leave the building, get in the described car, and drive the most direct route to Dobey's Motel. Because only a small number of people are generally privy to an individual's itinerary, it is reasonable for police to believe that a person with access to such information is likely to also have access to reliable information about that individual's illegal activities. * * * When significant aspects of the caller's predictions were verified, there was reason to believe not only that the caller was honest but also that he was well informed, at least well enough to justify the stop.

Justice Stevens wrote a short dissenting opinion, joined by Justices Brennan and Marshall. The dissenters argued that the activity predicted by the informant and corroborated by the police (leaving an apartment and driving toward a motel) was completely innocent. Justice Stevens concluded as follows:

> Millions of people leave their apartments at about the same time every day carrying an attache case and heading for a destination known to their neighbors. Usually, however, the neighbors do not know what the briefcase contains. An anonymous neighbor's prediction about somebody's time of departure and probable destination is anything but a reliable basis for assuming that the commuter is in possession of an illegal substance—particularly when the person is not even carrying the attache case described by the tipster.

## QUESTIONS AFTER WHITE

Does it make sense that the reasonable suspicion standard is less demanding than probable cause as to both quantity and *quality* of information? Does the Court mean that certain information may be too unreliable to credit toward probable cause, but reliable enough to credit toward reasonable suspicion? How universal is the Court's premise that an informant's accurate prediction of future innocent activity makes it more likely that the informant is correct in his conclusion about the suspect's criminal activity? See generally Rudstein, White on *White:* Anonymous Tips, Reasonable Suspicion, and the Constitution, 79 Ky.L.J. 661 (1991).

### Anonymous Tips Concerning Guns

In the following case, the Court considered whether an anonymous tip concerning possession of a gun constitutes reasonable suspicion when it is not corroborate by any predicted activity.

## FLORIDA v. J.L.
Supreme Court of the United States, 2000.
529 U.S. 266.

### JUSTICE GINSBURG delivered the opinion of the Court.

The question presented in this case is whether an anonymous tip that a person is carrying a gun is, without more, sufficient to justify a police officer's stop and frisk of that person. We hold that it is not.

\* \* \*

On October 13, 1995, an anonymous caller reported to the Miami-Dade Police that a young black male standing at a particular bus stop and wearing a plaid shirt was carrying a gun. So far as the record reveals, there is no audio recording of the tip, and nothing is known about the informant. Sometime after the police received the tip—the record does not say how long—two officers were instructed to respond. They arrived at the bus stop about six minutes later and saw three black males "just hanging out [there]." One of the three, respondent J.L., was wearing a plaid shirt. Apart from the tip, the officers had no reason to suspect any of the three of illegal conduct. The officers did not see a firearm, and J.L. made no threatening or otherwise unusual movements. One of the officers approached J.L., told him to put his hands up on the bus stop, frisked him, and seized a gun from J.L.'s pocket. The second officer frisked the other two individuals, against whom no allegations had been made, and found nothing. J.L., who was at the time of the frisk 10 days shy of his 16th birthday, was charged under state law with carrying a concealed firearm without a license and possessing a firearm while under the age of 18. He moved to suppress the gun as the fruit of an unlawful search, and the trial court granted his motion. The intermediate appellate court reversed, but the Supreme Court of Florida quashed that decision and held the search invalid under the Fourth Amendment.

Anonymous tips, the Florida Supreme Court stated, are generally less reliable than tips from known informants and can form the basis for reasonable suspicion only if accompanied by specific indicia of reliability, for example, the correct forecast of a subject's "not easily predicted" movements. The tip leading to the frisk of J.L., the court observed, provided no such predictions, nor did it contain any other qualifying indicia of reliability. Two justices dissented. The safety of the police and the public, they maintained, justifies a "firearm exception" to the general rule barring investigatory stops and frisks on the basis of bare-boned anonymous tips.

* * * We granted certiorari, and now affirm the judgment of the Florida Supreme Court.

* * *

In the instant case, the officers' suspicion that J.L. was carrying a weapon arose not from any observations of their own but solely from a call made from an unknown location by an unknown caller. Unlike a tip from a known informant whose reputation can be assessed and who can be held responsible if her allegations turn out to be fabricated, see Adams v. Williams, 407 U.S. 143 (1972), "an anonymous tip alone seldom demonstrates the informant's basis of knowledge or veracity," Alabama v. White, 496 U.S., at 329. As we have recognized, however, there are situations in which an anonymous tip, suitably corroborated, exhibits "sufficient indicia of reliability to provide reasonable suspicion to make the investigatory stop." The question we here confront is whether the tip pointing to J.L. had those indicia of reliability.

[Justice Ginsburg points out that in *White*, the Court said it was a "close case."]

The tip in the instant case lacked the moderate indicia of reliability present in *White* and essential to the Court's decision in that case. The anonymous call concerning J.L. provided no predictive information and therefore left the police without means to test the informant's knowledge or credibility. That the allegation about the gun turned out to be correct does not suggest that the officers, prior to the frisks, had a reasonable basis for suspecting J.L. of engaging in unlawful conduct: The reasonableness of official suspicion must be measured by what the officers knew before they conducted their search. All the police had to go on in this case was the bare report of an unknown, unaccountable informant who neither explained how he knew about the gun nor supplied any basis for believing he had inside information about J.L. If *White* was a close case on the reliability of anonymous tips, this one surely falls on the other side of the line.

Florida contends that the tip was reliable because its description of the suspect's visible attributes proved accurate: There really was a young black male wearing a plaid shirt at the bus stop. * * * These contentions misapprehend the reliability needed for a tip to justify a *Terry* stop.

An accurate description of a subject's readily observable location and appearance is of course reliable in this limited sense: It will help the police correctly identify the person whom the tipster means to accuse. Such a tip, however, does not show that the tipster has knowledge of concealed criminal activity. The reasonable suspicion here at issue requires that a tip be reliable in its assertion of illegality, not just in its tendency to identify a determinate person.

A second major argument advanced by Florida and the United States as amicus is, in essence, that the standard *Terry* analysis should be modified to license a "firearm exception." Under such an exception, a tip alleging an illegal gun would justify a stop and frisk even if the accusation would fail standard pre-search reliability testing. We decline to adopt this position.

Firearms are dangerous, and extraordinary dangers sometimes justify unusual precautions. Our decisions recognize the serious threat that armed criminals pose to public safety; *Terry's* rule, which permits protective police searches on the basis of reasonable suspicion rather than demanding that officers meet the higher standard of probable cause, responds to this very concern. But an automatic firearm exception to our established reliability analysis would rove too far. Such an exception would enable any person seeking to harass another to set in motion an intrusive, embarrassing police search of the targeted person simply by placing an anonymous call falsely reporting the target's unlawful carriage of a gun. Nor could one securely confine such an exception to allegations involving firearms. Several Courts of Appeals have held it per se foreseeable for people carrying significant amounts of illegal drugs to be carrying guns as well. If police officers may properly conduct *Terry* frisks on the basis of bare-boned tips about guns, it would be reasonable to maintain under the above-cited decisions that the police should similarly have discretion to frisk based on bare-boned tips about narcotics. As we clarified when we made indicia of reliability critical in *Adams* and *White*, the Fourth Amendment is not so easily satisfied.

The facts of this case do not require us to speculate about the circumstances under which the danger alleged in an anonymous tip might be so great as to justify a search even without a showing of reliability. We do not say, for example, that a report of a person carrying a bomb need bear the indicia of reliability we demand for a report of a person carrying a firearm before the police can constitutionally conduct a frisk. Nor do we hold that public safety officials in quarters where the reasonable expectation of Fourth Amendment privacy is diminished, such as airports, and schools, see New Jersey v. T.L.O., 469 U.S. 325 (1985), cannot conduct protective searches on the basis of information insufficient to justify searches elsewhere.

* * *

JUSTICE KENNEDY, with whom THE CHIEF JUSTICE joins, concurring.

On the record created at the suppression hearing, the Court's decision is correct. The Court says all that is necessary to resolve this case, and I join the opinion in all respects. It might be noted, however, that there are many indicia of reliability respecting anonymous tips that we have yet to explore in our cases.

* * *

It seems appropriate to observe that a tip might be anonymous in some sense yet have certain other features, either supporting reliability or narrowing the likely class of informants, so that the tip does provide the lawful basis for some police action. One such feature, as the Court recognizes, is that the tip predicts future conduct of the alleged criminal. There may be others. For example, if an unnamed caller with a voice which sounds the same each time tells police on two successive nights about criminal activity which in fact occurs each night, a similar call on the third night ought not be treated automatically like the tip in the case now before us. In the instance supposed, there would be a plausible argument that experience cures some of the uncertainty surrounding the anonymity, justifying a proportionate police response. * * *

If an informant places his anonymity at risk, a court can consider this factor in weighing the reliability of the tip. An instance where a tip might be considered anonymous but nevertheless sufficiently reliable to justify a proportionate police response may be when an unnamed person driving a car the police officer later describes stops for a moment and, face to face, informs the police that criminal activity is occurring. * * *

Instant caller identification is widely available to police, and, if anonymous tips are proving unreliable and distracting to police, squad cars can be sent within seconds to the location of the telephone used by the informant. Voice recording of telephone tips might, in appropriate cases, be used by police to locate the caller. It is unlawful to make false reports to the police, and the ability of the police to trace the identity of anonymous telephone informants may be a factor which lends reliability to what, years earlier, might have been considered unreliable anonymous tips.

These matters, of course, must await discussion in other cases, where the issues are presented by the record.

## Tips and Corroboration After J.L.

One court has distilled the following factors for determining whether reasonable suspicion can be found from an informant's tip after *J.L.*:

Although no single factor is dispositive, relevant factors include: (1) whether the informant lacked "true anonymity" (i.e., whether the police knew some details about the informant or had the means to discover them); (2) whether the informant reported contemporaneous, firsthand knowledge; (3) whether the informant provided detailed information about the events observed; (4) the informant's stated motivation for reporting the information; and (5) whether the police were able to corroborate information provided by the informant.

United States v. Chavez, 660 F.3d 1215 (10th Cir. 2011).

## J.L. and a Tip About Reckless Driving

How does the Court's analysis in *J.L.* apply if police receive an anonymous tip that a car is engaged in reckless driving and, when police officers observe the car on the road the driver is not at that point driving recklessly? Can the officers stop the car despite the lack of corroboration of any predictive activity? The court in United States v. Wheat, 278 F.3d 722 (8th Cir. 2001) considered this question and upheld the stop of the identified car. It relied on the language in *J.L.*, implying that the decision would be different if public safety were in imminent risk:

An erratic and possibly drunk driver poses an imminent threat to public safety. Of course, arguably so too does a citizen armed with a gun, yet the Supreme Court firmly declined to adopt an automatic firearm exception to the reliability requirement on that basis. However, there is a critical distinction between gun possession cases and potential drunk driving cases. In the possessory offense cases, law enforcement officers have two less invasive options not available to officers responding to a tip about a drunk driver. First, they may initiate a simple consensual encounter, for which no articulable suspicion is required. Needless to say, that is not possible when the suspect is driving a moving vehicle.

Alternatively, officers responding to a tip about a possessory violation may quietly observe the suspect for a considerable length of time, watching for other indications of incipient criminality that would give them reasonable suspicion to make an investigatory stop—as, for example, in *Terry*, where an experienced officer witnessed several men casing a joint. By contrast, where an anonymous tip alleges erratic and possibly drunk driving, a responding officer faces a stark choice. * * * [H]e can intercept the vehicle immediately and ascertain whether its driver is operating under the influence of drugs or alcohol. Or he can follow and observe, with three possible outcomes: the suspect drives without incident for several miles; the suspect drifts harmlessly onto the shoulder, providing corroboration of the tip and probable cause for an arrest; or the suspect veers into oncoming traffic, or fails to stop at a light, or otherwise causes a sudden and potentially devastating accident. In contradistinction to *J.L.*, where the suspect was merely standing at the bus stop, in this context the suspect is extremely mobile, and potentially highly dangerous. A drunk driver is not at all unlike a "bomb," and a mobile one at that. Thus, we think that there is a substantial government interest in effecting a stop as quickly as possible.

### *J.L. and a Tip About Domestic Violence*

For similar reasons, tips by anonymous informants about domestic violence and related emergencies have been found to be sufficient for a stop even without corroboration through predictive activity. Thus, in United States v. Hicks, 531 F.3d 555 (7th Cir. 2008), a 911 caller reported that "a guy is beating up a woman" and was threatening to shoot her. The caller gave an address, police responded, and they stopped and eventually found a gun on Hicks. Hicks relied on *J.L.*, arguing that the tip was not reliable because it lacked predictive information that would have allowed the officer to test it. But the court distinguished *J.L.* and declared that "police delay while attempting to verify an identity or seek corroboration of a reported emergency may prove costly to public safety and undermine the 911 system's usefulness." The court elaborated as follows:

> A rule requiring a lower level of corroboration before conducting a stop on the basis of an emergency report is not simply an emergency exception to the rule of *J.L.* It is better understood as rooted in the special reliability inherent in reports of ongoing emergencies. * * * Surely, anonymous tips about emergencies cannot always be trusted—although frequency data does not exist, fraudulent 911 calls are agreed to be a dangerous problem. See Rana Simpson, Misuse and Abuse of 911 at 5–7 (U.S. Dept. of Justice, Problem-Oriented Guides for Police Series, No. 19, 2002). But any body of law requiring 911 operators to carefully make credibility determinations would unacceptably delay the necessary responses to *all* emergency calls, including genuine ones.

See also United States v. Wooden, 551 F.3d 647 (7th Cir. 2008) (anonymous tip about domestic violence was sufficient to seize the defendant even though when officers arrived, the couple was chatting amicably; there was a "need for dispatch" that excused any requirement for corroborative evidence, and "domestic violence comes and goes—a man who pulls gun on his wife or girlfriend may do it again at any moment" or may have threatened the woman to "act naturally").

### *J.L. and "Anonymity"*

The Court in *J.L.* distinguishes between known informants (whose tips can be sufficient without corroboration) and anonymous ones. Justice Kennedy points out, however, that under certain circumstances the identity of a tipster may be unknown but the informant is not really "anonymous." For example, in United States v. Heard, 367 F.3d 1275 (11th Cir. 2004), an officer saw Heard and a woman having a loud argument at a train station. The woman accused Heard of owing her money. The officer intervened; Heard admitted owing the woman money, and the officer encouraged Heard to pay her. Heard did so and walked away. The officer walked off in the same direction as the woman. The woman then told the officer that Heard was carrying a weapon. The officer then proceeded back toward Heard, and told the woman to remain at the station to make a statement. But the woman jumped on a waiting train and was never seen again. The officer proceeded to frisk Heard, and found a weapon.

Appealing his conviction for possession of a firearm by a felon, Heard argued that under *J.L.*, there was no reasonable suspicion for the officer to stop and frisk him. The government argued that the woman's tip was more reliable than the purely anonymous tip in *J.L.*, because she spoke face-to-face with the officer.

The court agreed with the government and affirmed the conviction. It explained as follows:

> A face-to-face anonymous tip is presumed to be inherently more reliable than an anonymous telephone tip because the officers receiving the information have an opportunity to observe the demeanor and perceived credibility of the informant.

> In this case, [Officer] Gore had an opportunity to judge the demeanor and credibility of the unknown woman. Gore stated that the woman seemed frightened when she reported Heard's weapon, and Gore reasonably presumed that Heard and the unidentified woman had some sort of relationship—they were arguing over money and Heard paid the woman the amount she demanded. Thus, reasoning that Heard knew the woman, Gore could reasonably conclude that she would have reliable information about whether Heard possessed a weapon.

Heard argued that whatever assurance of reliability was obtained by a face-to-face report, it was lost when the informant jumped on the train and fled the scene. But the court rejected this argument as well:

The reliability of a tip is considered in light of all relevant circumstances, which include—but is not limited to—a consideration of whether the officer can track down the tipster again. In this case, although the unknown woman fled the MARTA station, because she and Heard apparently knew each other, she may have subjected herself to reprisal from Heard based on the tip she gave to Gore— which makes her more reliable. Considering the totality of the circumstances in this case, Gore reasonably concluded that the unknown woman's tip was reliable.

See also United States v. Brown, 496 F.3d 1070 (10th Cir. 2007) (911 caller was not anonymous, and therefore the caller's tip could suffice for reasonable suspicion: "The officers in this case knew the caller was a friend of the alleged victim and was present when the armed man entered her apartment. * * * An unnamed individual who divulges enough distinguishing characteristics to limit his possible identity to only a handful of people may be nameless, but he is capable of being identified and thus is not anonymous."); United States v. Chavez, 660 F.3d 1215 (10th Cir. 2011) (caller was not anonymous even though he refused to provide the police his name: "he stated that he was a Wal-Mart employee at a specific Wal-Mart store and thereby provided the police with information to discover his identity"); United States v. Copening, 506 F.3d 1241 (10th Cir. 2007) (where 911 calls were made from an unblocked number, the caller was not anonymous).

### b. Quantum of Suspicion

The Supreme Court in United States v. Cortez, 449 U.S. 411 (1981), set forth the following oft-cited test for determining whether reasonable suspicion exists in a given set of circumstances:

> [T]he totality of the circumstances—the whole picture—must be taken into account. Based upon that whole picture the detaining officers must have a particularized and objective basis for suspecting the particular person stopped of criminal activity. * * * [P]articularized suspicion contains two elements, each of which must be present before a stop is permissible. First, the assessment must be based upon all the circumstances. The analysis proceeds with various objective observations, information from police reports, if such are available, and considerations of the modes or patterns of operation of certain kinds of lawbreakers. From these data, a trained officer draws inferences and makes deductions—inferences and deductions that might well elude an untrained person.
>
> The process does not deal with hard certainties, but with probabilities. Long before the law of probabilities was articulated as such, practical people formulated certain common sense conclusions about human behavior; * * *.

The second element contained in the idea that an assessment of the whole picture must yield a particularized suspicion is the concept that the process just described must raise a suspicion that the particular individual being stopped is engaged in wrongdoing.

### Comparison to Probable Cause

The Court in *Terry* reasoned that, because a stop was less intrusive than an arrest, it could be justified upon a lesser showing of proof than the probable cause required for an arrest. Courts have struggled with the meaning of reasonable suspicion and with how the reasonable suspicion standard differs from that of probable cause. It is clear, however, that the standards are materially different. There are many cases in which the courts have held that reasonable suspicion existed but probable cause did not. See Florida v. Royer, 460 U.S. 491 (1983) (consent tainted where it was obtained while Royer was under arrest and officers had only reasonable suspicion and not probable cause to believe that Royer was involved in drug activity); United States v. Anderson, 981 F.2d 1560 (10th Cir.1992) (reasonable suspicion but not probable cause existed, where the defendant was twice seen leaving a house in which narcotics were sold, and parked his car a few blocks from the house, near a truck where narcotics were stored; because the defendant was arrested rather than stopped, the evidence obtained as a result of the detention should have been suppressed).

The analytical framework used by the courts in assessing reasonable suspicion is similar to that employed in assessing probable cause. Thus, a court will undertake a common sense analysis of the facts presented; it will give deference to the expertise of law enforcement officers, who may know through experience that certain facts are indicative of criminal activity (e.g., that drug dealers often carry beepers or cellular phones, or speak in code); and it will consider the totality of the circumstances because, while each fact may seem innocent if considered individually, the factors considered in their totality may not be so easily explained away; and it will not expect the officers to be infallible.

The most important difference between reasonable suspicion and probable cause is that reasonable suspicion is a *less demanding standard of proof*—a stop is permissible upon something less than the fair probability standard that defines probable cause. Some courts have defined reasonable suspicion as a fair *possibility* (as opposed to probability) of criminal activity. It is appropriate to think of reasonable suspicion as "possible cause."

A probability-based example of the difference between reasonable suspicion and probable cause is presented by the facts of United States v. Winsor, 846 F.2d 1569 (9th Cir.1988). Officers chased suspected bank robbers fleeing from the bank into a hotel. The hotel had approximately 40 guest rooms, and the officers had no idea where in the hotel the robbers were hiding. The question was whether there was probable cause to search each of the hotel rooms for the suspects. The court found that a one-in-forty probability was too small to support probable cause, but that the low probability did amount to reasonable suspicion: "The odds on discovering the suspect in the first room upon whose door the police knocked were high enough to support a founded suspicion. The odds favoring discovery increase as rooms are searched. At some point, perhaps at the last two or three unsearched rooms, probable cause may be said to exist." Conversely, at some point of improbability, reasonable suspicion would not have existed—for example, if the hotel had 600 rooms, there would not have been reasonable suspicion to believe that the suspects were in any particular room. Because there was only reasonable suspicion and not probable cause in *Winsor*, the court held that the search of the hotel room in which the suspects were actually found was illegal. A search for law enforcement purposes requires probable cause and cannot be justified under *Terry*. What should the police do in a case like Winsor where suspects might be in any of 40 rooms?

### *Assessment of Probabilities*

The Court applied the *Cortez* totality of circumstances test in United States v. Arvizu, 534 U.S. 266 (2002), which involved the stopping of a minivan by a border patrol agent. After stopping the minivan, the agent asked for and obtained permission to search. He found drugs and arrested the driver. The district court denied a motion to suppress evidence, but the Ninth Circuit reversed.

The court of appeals analyzed 10 factors that the district court had considered in denying the motion. Of these, it held that 7 factors—including the driver's slowing down, his failure to acknowledge the agent, the raised position of children's knees in the car, and their odd waving—were entitled to little or no weight in assessing reasonable suspicion. The court of appeals found that other factors—use of the road by smugglers, the temporal proximity between the timing of the trip and the agents' shift change, and the use of minivans by smugglers—were not enough to render the stop permissible.

The Supreme Court reversed in an opinion by Chief Justice Rehnquist, who wrote:

> When discussing how reviewing courts should make reasonable-suspicion determinations, we have said repeatedly that they must look at the "totality of the circumstances" of each case to see whether the detaining officer has a "particularized and objective basis" for suspecting legal wrongdoing. This process allows officers to draw on

their own experience and specialized training to make inferences from and deductions about the cumulative information available to them that "might well elude an untrained person." Although an officer's reliance on a mere "hunch" is insufficient to justify a stop, the likelihood of criminal activity need not rise to the level required for probable cause, and it falls considerably short of satisfying a preponderance of the evidence standard.

Our cases have recognized that the concept of reasonable suspicion is somewhat abstract. But we have deliberately avoided reducing it to a neat set of legal rules. * * *

We think that the approach taken by the Court of Appeals here departs sharply from the teachings of these cases. The court's evaluation and rejection of seven of the listed factors in isolation from each other does not take into account the "totality of the circumstances," as our cases have understood that phrase. The court appeared to believe that each observation by Stoddard [the agent] that was by itself readily susceptible to an innocent explanation was entitled to "no weight." *Terry*, however, precludes this sort of divide-and-conquer analysis. The officer in *Terry* observed the petitioner and his companions repeatedly walk back and forth, look into a store window, and confer with one another. Although each of the series of acts was "perhaps innocent in itself," we held that, taken together, they "warranted further investigation."

The Court of Appeals' view that it was necessary to "clearly delimit" an officer's consideration of certain factors to reduce "troubling . . . uncertainty," also runs counter to our cases and underestimates the usefulness of the reasonable-suspicion standard in guiding officers in the field.

* * * Take, for example, the court's positions that respondent's deceleration could not be considered because "slowing down after spotting a law enforcement vehicle is an entirely normal response that is in no way indicative of criminal activity" and that his failure to acknowledge Stoddard's presence provided no support because there were "no special circumstances rendering innocent avoidance . . . improbable." We think it quite reasonable that a driver's slowing down, stiffening of posture, and failure to acknowledge a sighted law enforcement officer might well be unremarkable in one instance (such as a busy San Francisco highway) while quite unusual in another (such as a remote portion of rural southeastern Arizona). * * * Stoddard was entitled to make an assessment of the situation in light of his specialized training and familiarity with the customs of the area's inhabitants. To the extent that a totality of the circumstances approach may render appellate review less

circumscribed by precedent than otherwise, it is the nature of the totality rule.

Having considered the totality of the circumstances and given due weight to the factual inferences drawn by the law enforcement officer and District Court Judge, we hold that Stoddard had reasonable suspicion to believe that respondent was engaged in illegal activity. It was reasonable for Stoddard to infer from his observations, his registration check, and his experience as a border patrol agent that respondent had set out from Douglas along a little-traveled route used by smugglers to avoid the 191 checkpoint. Stoddard's knowledge further supported a commonsense inference that respondent intended to pass through the area at a time when officers would be leaving their backroads patrols to change shifts. The likelihood that respondent and his family were on a picnic outing was diminished by the fact that the minivan had turned away from the known recreational areas accessible to the east on Rucker Canyon Road. Corroborating this inference was the fact that recreational areas farther to the north would have been easier to reach by taking 191, as opposed to the 40-to-50-mile trip on unpaved and primitive roads. The children's elevated knees suggested the existence of concealed cargo in the passenger compartment. Finally * * * Stoddard's assessment of respondent's reactions upon seeing him and the children's mechanical-like waving, which continued for a full four to five minutes, were entitled to some weight.

### Examples of Reasonable Suspicion

Here are the facts of a case in which reasonable suspicion was found:

At 1:00 p.m. two Boston police detectives in an unmarked car were patrolling that portion of Boston known as the "Combat Zone." The Combat Zone is a high crime area known for prostitution and drug-dealing. As the officers were stopped at a light, they noticed a grey Thunderbird automobile stopped on the curb of Washington Street with a man at the wheel. As the officers watched, a second man approached the Thunderbird from the sidewalk and engaged the driver in a twenty second conversation through the open passenger-side window. The second man got into the car and had an additional five or ten second conversation with the driver. The car then pulled out and proceeded for two blocks until it made a right turn onto Hayward Place, a short street which connects Washington Street and Harrison Avenue. The officers followed in their unmarked car. Hayward Place was deserted. The Thunderbird parked on Hayward Place, and the officers parked well behind it with an unobstructed view. The officers observed the driver and passenger engaged in a thirty second discussion with their heads inclined toward each other. The passenger then got out of the car and walked back toward Washington Street. One officer approached the car, ordered the driver out, noticed a bulge, and pursuant to a pat-down frisk uncovered a spring-activated knife. The officer arrested the driver for carrying an illegal weapon, and in a search incident to arrest eleven grams of cocaine were uncovered.

The court confronted with these facts in United States v. Trullo, 809 F.2d 108 (1st Cir.1987), stated that the officer's seizure of the driver went to the "outermost reaches of a permissible *Terry* stop," and that "today's satisfactory explanation may very well be tomorrow's lame excuse." But the court did uphold the police conduct, relying on the high crime area, the officers' expertise in determining whether drug activity was afoot, the short nature of the conversation between the driver and passenger, and the fact that the passenger walked back toward the place where he had met the car. This latter factor meant that it was "unlikely that the man was seeking transportation." The court concluded that while it would be possible to "hypothesize some innocent explanation" for the conduct, the test for a stop is whether there is reasonable suspicion of criminal activity, and not whether the facts can be construed as innocent. Judge Bownes, in dissent, asked the following question: "If a citizen lets another person into his car on Washington Street, where must he let him off to avoid an armed stop by the police?" Judge Bownes claimed that the majority "seems to allow armed stops of individuals who meet in the Combat Zone on the basis of unlimited deference to police discretion." Who has the better of the argument? Who has more accurately applied the *Cortez* test? See also United States v. Green, 691 F.3d 960 (8th Cir. 2012) (Bank robber described as a black male with a medium build and facial hair wearing white Nike tennis shoes, and Green, who fit the description was found walking two blocks from the bank shortly after the robbery; reasonable suspicion for a stop was found "[g]iven Green's similarities to the description of the suspected robber and his proximity in both time and place to the crime.").

### *Example of Reasonable Suspicion Lacking*

While most of the reported cases assessing reasonable suspicion have found that the officers in question had sufficient proof to justify a stop, there are a few cases in which the facts are so innocent that the reviewing court finds the stop invalid. An example is United States v. Rodriguez, 976 F.2d 592 (9th Cir.1992). Officers sitting in a marked car alongside Interstate 8 in California saw Rodriguez drive toward them in a 1976 Ford Ranchero. They noticed that he looked Hispanic, sat up straight, kept both hands on the wheel, and looked straight ahead. He did not "acknowledge" the agents' presence, which they thought suspicious because all the other traffic passing by had acknowledged the presence of the officers. The agents testified that Interstate 8 is a "notorious route for alien smugglers" and that Ford Rancheros have a space behind the seat where illegal aliens can be concealed. The agents followed Rodriguez. They testified that his car responded sluggishly when it went over a bump, as if heavily loaded, rather than with a "crisp, light movement" that was typical of a Ford Ranchero. They also noted that, while being followed, Rodriguez looked often into his rear view mirror and swerved slightly within his lane. On the basis of this information, the officers stopped Rodriguez's vehicle. A subsequent search pursuant to consent yielded 168 pounds of marijuana. Rodriguez argued that the consent was tainted as a product of an unlawful stop.

The court held that reasonable suspicion did not exist to stop Rodriguez, and therefore the evidence was illegally obtained. It first noted that the testimony of the officers at the suppression hearing was eerily similar to that provided in other cases, so similar that "an inquiring mind may wonder about the recurrence of such fortunate parallelism in the experiences of the arresting agents." The court stated that it could not accept "what has come to appear to be a prefabricated or recycled profile of suspicious behavior very likely to sweep many ordinary citizens into a generality of suspicious appearance merely on hunch." According to the court, the factors cited by the agents "describe too many individuals to create a reasonable suspicion that this particular defendant was engaged in criminal activity." The court concluded as follows:

> In short, the agents in this case saw a Hispanic man cautiously and attentively driving a 16 year-old Ford with a worn suspension, who glanced in his rear view mirror while being followed by agents in a marked Border Patrol car. This profile could certainly fit hundreds or thousands of law abiding daily users of the highways of Southern California.

Is the court's finding of no reasonable suspicion sustainable after *Arvizu*? Are the facts of *Arvizu*, in their totality, more suspicious? See also United States v. Peters, 10 F.3d 1517 (10th Cir.1993) (where two Nigerians in a Ryder truck were pulled over for a traffic violation, and consented to a search that uncovered no evidence, they could not be stopped later down the road on the basis that they appeared nervous when being followed by another marked police car).

In United States v. Manzo-Jurado, 457 F.3d 928 (9th Cir. 2006), the officer saw a group of six Hispanic men and became suspicious that they were illegal aliens. The men were attending a high school football game. The officer testified that he was suspicious because "the group members appeared out of place at the football game." Specifically, "they did not mingle with other attendees, did not appear associated with either high school, and were not familiar to" the officer. The court found that the officer's "unsupported intuition that a group of men keeping to themselves at a football game is indicative of the men's illegal status in this country is not a rational inference that helps establish reasonable suspicion." Is it ever suspicious that a person or group appears "out of place"? What if an obviously destitute person is walking on the street in a wealthy neighborhood?

### Reasonable Suspicion of a Completed Crime: United States v. Hensley

Most of the cases discussed above evaluated whether the officer had reasonable suspicion that the suspect was either committing a crime or about to commit a crime. Can a *Terry* stop be made on the basis of reasonable suspicion to believe that the suspect has *already* committed a crime? The Court in United States v. Hensley, 469 U.S. 221 (1985), confronted these facts:

> Several days after a tavern robbery in St. Bernard, Ohio (a Cincinnati suburb), a St. Bernard police officer interviewed an informant who stated that Hensley drove the getaway car. The officer obtained a written statement from the informant and immediately issued a "wanted flyer" to other police departments in the metropolitan area. The flyer stated that Hensley was wanted for investigation of an aggravated robbery, described Hensley and the date and location of the robbery, warned that Hensley should be considered armed and dangerous, and asked other departments to pick up and hold Hensley for the St. Bernard police.

> In a Kentucky suburb of Cincinnati, an officer who had heard the flyer read aloud several times stopped a car driven by Hensley. Although the officer let Hensley drive away, he inquired whether there was an outstanding warrant for his arrest. Two other officers in separate patrol cars interrupted to say that there might be an Ohio warrant on Hensley. The three officers then looked for Hensley while the dispatcher looked for the flyer and mistakenly telephoned Cincinnati to inquire about the flyer. One of the officers spotted Hensley's car and, after being advised by the dispatcher that Cincinnati was hunting for a warrant, he pulled the car over and approached with a drawn service revolver. A second officer arrived at the scene, saw a gun under the seat of a passenger known to be a convicted felon, arrested the passenger, and searched the car. When another gun was found, Hensley was arrested for illegal handgun possession.

Justice O'Connor, writing for a unanimous Court, held that *Terry* was not confined to prospective crimes; the power granted by *Terry* may also be exercised to investigate completed crimes. Her opinion approved stops where "police have a reasonable suspicion, grounded in specific and articulable facts, that a person they encounter was involved in or is wanted in connection with a completed felony." Relying on the "collective knowledge" doctrine established in Whiteley v. Warden, [discussed in the materials on probable cause], Justice O'Connor concluded that one department or officer could act to make a stop if another officer or department had reasonable suspicion to stop the defendant and asked for assistance. She applied her analysis to the facts and concluded that the St. Bernard police had a reasonable suspicion that Hensley committed a crime, that the Kentucky officers properly relied on the flyer, and that the stop was carried out in compliance with *Terry*.

### *Relevance of the Race of the Suspect*

The court in *Rodriguez, supra,* expressed concern that an overly broad test of reasonable suspicion could result in a dragnet for Hispanics. Can the suspect's race *ever* be taken into account explicitly in determining whether reasonable suspicion exists?

When the question is whether the suspect sufficiently matches the description of a perpetrator of a completed crime, the suspect's race must obviously be considered relevant. For example, if a bank teller describes a robber as an Asian male in his 40's, an officer assessing reasonable suspicion must necessarily consider a person's race in determining whether to stop a person for that crime.

More difficult questions arise, however, when an officer considers a person suspicious simply because he is found in an area ordinarily not frequented by members of the suspect's racial group. Is it appropriate to consider it suspicious that an African-American male is walking down the street of an affluent suburb at 11 p.m., where the same conduct from a white male would not be suspicious in the least? Similarly, difficult questions exist when officers argue that certain crimes are more commonly committed by certain races (such as men of Arab descent and crimes of terrorism). In these cases, police officers essentially argue that activity of a member of a certain race is more suspicious than the same activity by a member of a different race.

The following facts present an example of an officer finding a person's race to be a suspicious factor:

A St. Paul police officer observed Uber's vehicle at about 2:15 a.m. The officer saw the vehicle again about 30 minutes later in the same area. At that time the officer ran a check on the license number and determined that the vehicle was registered to a person in Moundsview, Minnesota, a suburb about 20 miles from St. Paul. Upon learning this information, the officer decided to stop the vehicle, because he thought the driver was seeking to solicit a prostitute. The Summit-University area, in which Uber's car was spotted, is well known as one where prostitution flourishes. The officer did not at that time see prostitutes in the area, nor had Uber slowed down or talked to anyone.

The court in City of St. Paul v. Uber, 450 N.W.2d 623 (Minn.App.1990), held that this information did not create reasonable suspicion to support a stop. The court stated as follows:

> We know of no authority that requires a resident of the State of Minnesota to have any reason to be on the public streets of another town * * *. No one from any suburb needs to justify his or her lawful presence on a public street in Minneapolis or St. Paul. * * * The officer's assumption that [Uber] was seeking prostitution was an inadvertent, but nevertheless invidious, form of discrimination. We would not tolerate the blatant discriminatory proposition that any member of a minority group found on a public street in Edina [an affluent suburb] had better live there, or be required to stop and justify his or her presence to the authorities. * * * Once we clear away the smoke from this case, it is clear that the stop of [Uber] is premised on the belief that after midnight, Caucasian males from the suburbs are only in the Summit-University area for no good, and that after midnight, no good is all the Summit-University area has to offer. Neither the residents of Summit-University nor the residents of Moundsview deserve the implications of this case. * * * Simply being on a public street in an area where one "might" find a prostitute or a drug dealer does not, without more, meet any constitutional standard for a stop by the authorities. See e.g. Brown v. Texas, 443 U.S. 47 (1979) (defendant's mere presence in a neighborhood frequented by drug users held insufficient to justify a stop).

While a person's race, or the existence of a high crime area, may not "without more" constitute reasonable suspicion, how much more is required? What if Uber had been driving ten miles below the speed limit and looking out along the street? Would such conduct be sufficiently suspicious, given the neighborhood, regardless of the suspect's race?[15] For a case consistent with *Uber*, see State v. Barber, 118 Wn.2d 335, 823 P.2d 1068 (1992) ("racial incongruity, i.e., a person of any race being allegedly out of place in a particular geographic area," could not be considered in the reasonable suspicion inquiry).

---

[15] Professor Harris, in Factors for Reasonable Suspicion: When Black and Poor Means Stopped and Frisked, 69 Ind.L.J.659 (1994), argues that *Terry* stops have a disproportionate effect on minorities, even if race is not explicitly taken into account in determining reasonable suspicion. This is because in many courts "an individual's presence in a high crime location plus evasion of the police equals suspicion reasonable enough to allow a stop under *Terry*." Professor Harris argues that minorities, because of where they usually live and how they understandably react toward police, are more likely to trigger these two "suspicious" factors.

Some courts, in contrast to *Uber*, have found it permissible for an officer to consider the race of a person in determining whether the person's conduct is suspicious. These courts hold that while the suspect's race cannot be the *only* factor supporting a stop, it can be considered together with other suspicious factors. In other words, these courts appear to permit a form of racial profiling, so long as race is not the only basis for the stop. As the court put it in United States v. Weaver, 966 F.2d 391 (8th Cir.1992), a case in which the defendant, the only African-American male on a flight from Los Angeles to Kansas City, was stopped on suspicion of drug trafficking:

> Had [Officer] Hicks relied solely on Weaver's race as a basis for his suspicions, we would have a different case before us. As it is, however, facts are not to be ignored simply because they may be unpleasant—and the unpleasant fact in this case is that Hicks had knowledge * * * that young black Los Angeles gangs were flooding the Kansas City area with cocaine. To that extent, then, race, when coupled with the other factors Hicks relied upon, [i.e., that Weaver came from a source city for drugs, had no identification, and appeared unusually nervous when encountered by police officers] was a factor in the decision to approach and ultimately detain Weaver. We wish it were otherwise, but we take the facts as they are presented to us, and not as we would like them to be.

Should the court in *Weaver* have taken the facts as they would have liked them to be, instead of how they were presented? Would it be worth it to hold a person's race to be non-suspicious as a matter of law, regardless of "reality"? Would that encourage the police to be more "race-blind" in their use of the *Terry* power?

What about considering a suspect's Middle Eastern appearance as relevant to terrorism? The court in United States v. Ramos, 629 F.3d 60 (1st Cir. 2010), a case in which the defendants were seized while parked in a van outside a Boston train station, held that officers could take into account that the occupants of the van appeared to be Middle Eastern. The stop was made shortly after bombing attacks on trains in Madrid. The court reasoned as follows:

> While in other situations there may be merit to the argument that a description of ethnic appearance is irrelevant and nothing more than impermissible profiling, the argument fails on the facts here. The MBTA attempted to learn from the lessons of Madrid and had so trained its employees. * * * [E]xplicit warnings * * * of future strikes by the same groups in the United States, meant it was material for the officers to consider, among other facts, the risk of terrorist attacks on train stations in major urban centers and that the persons they were investigating had a Middle Eastern

appearance. This is not a case about stereotyping or selective prosecution.

The *Ramos* court emphasized that its holding on ethnic-based stops could not be taken too far:

> We wish to be very clear. Just as it cannot be said that the appearance, even ethnic appearance, of a suspect is never relevant, it certainly cannot be said that it is always or even generally relevant. If the events in this case took place at a different time or place or under other circumstances, an attribution of "Middle Eastern" appearance may not necessarily be as relevant a fact.

The *Ramos* court also emphasized that the van occupants' Middle Eastern appearance was not the only basis for suspicion. Other factors included the fact that they were in a van, that they were in a commuter parking lot for an extended period of time without dropping anyone off or picking anyone up, that the van had tinted windows, and that it had a temporary, paper license plate from Texas. Would you have found reasonable suspicion on the basis of the facts independent of ethnicity?

Can an officer stop a Hispanic person on suspicion that he is undocumented? In Melendres v. Arpaio, 695 F.3d 990 (9th Cir.2012), the court found that Latino motorists were entitled to a preliminary injunction prohibiting Arizona police officers from detaining individuals based solely on reasonable suspicion that an individual was unlawfully present in the United States. The court noted that "unlike illegal reentry, mere unauthorized presence in the United States is not a crime." Because *Terry* is based on reasonable suspicion of crime, it followed that officers could not conduct a *Terry* stop solely on the basis of suspicion that a Hispanic person is an undocumented alien.

### *Use of Profiles*

In several of the cases above it is apparent that the officers were comparing the activity of the suspect to a profile of a person engaged in certain criminal activity. Officers often use profiles to determine whether the conduct of citizens is sufficiently suspicious to justify a stop. A profile is a list of characteristics compiled by a law enforcement agency, which have been found through experience to be common characteristics of those engaged in a certain type of criminal activity. The most common example is a drug courier profile, but officers also employ other profiles for specific criminal activity, including terrorism. See United States v. Malone, 886 F.2d 1162 (9th Cir.1989) (officer stops the defendant on the basis of a gang member profile).

The use of drug courier profiles was discussed extensively in United States v. Berry, 670 F.2d 583 (5th Cir.1982) (en banc):

\* \* \* We conclude that the profile is nothing more than an administrative tool of the police. The presence or absence of a particular characteristic on any particular profile is of *no* legal significance in the determination of reasonable suspicion.

Two consequences stem from this holding. First, a match between certain characteristics listed on the profile and characteristics exhibited by a defendant does not automatically establish reasonable suspicion. \* \* \* Any checklist of suspicious characteristics cannot be mechanically applied by a court to determine whether a particular search or seizure meets the Supreme Court's standards. A profile does not focus on the particular circumstances at issue. Nor does such a profile indicate in every case that a specific individual who happens to match some of the profile's vague characteristics is involved in actions sufficiently suspicious as to justify a stop.

The second consequence of our holding flows from the first. Although a match between a defendant's characteristics and some of the characteristics on a drug courier profile does not automatically support a finding of reasonable suspicion, the fact that a characteristic of a defendant also happens to appear on the profile does not preclude its use as a justification providing reasonable suspicion for a stop. \* \* \* Our holding is only that we will assign no characteristic greater or lesser weight merely because the characteristic happens to be present on, or absent from, the profile.

The Supreme Court has essentially adopted the *Berry* approach toward profiles. Thus, in United States v. Sokolow, 490 U.S. 1 (1989). DEA agents stopped Sokolow after they learned that he paid $2100 for two airplane tickets from a roll of $20 bills, he traveled under a name that did not match the name under which his telephone was listed, he traveled to Honolulu from Miami and stayed only 48 hours even though a round-trip flight takes 20 hours, he appeared nervous during the trip, and he checked no luggage. Chief Justice Rehnquist wrote for the majority, which found that the above facts, taken together, amounted to reasonable suspicion. The Chief Justice reviewed the facts known to the officers concerning Sokolow, and recognized that "any one of these factors is not by itself proof of any illegal conduct and is quite consistent with innocent travel." But he stated that the relevant inquiry "is not whether particular conduct is innocent or guilty, but the degree of suspicion that attaches to particular types of noncriminal acts."

The Chief Justice rejected Sokolow's argument that the officer's use of a drug courier profile tainted the stop:

A court sitting to determine the existence of reasonable suspicion must require the agent to articulate the factors leading to that conclusion, but the fact that these factors may be set forth in a "profile" does not somehow detract from their evidentiary significance as seen by a trained agent.

The Chief Justice also rejected Sokolow's argument that agents were obligated to use the least intrusive means available to verify or dispel their suspicions—in this case by engaging in an encounter rather than a stop. The majority reasoned that any rule requiring a least intrusive alternative approach would hamper the police in making on-the-spot decisions.

Justice Marshall, joined by Justice Brennan, dissented and complained about the officers' use of the drug courier profile.

> Reflexive reliance on a profile of drug courier characteristics runs a far greater risk than does ordinary, case-by-case police work, of subjecting innocent individuals to unwarranted police harassment and detention. This risk is enhanced by the profile's chameleon-like way of adapting to any particular set of observations.

### Overbroad Profile Factors

It is clear that some profile factors relied on by police are far too broad to support reasonable suspicion in the courts. For example, in United States v. Beck, 140 F.3d 1129 (8th Cir.1998), an officer sought to justify the stop of a motorist in part because he was driving through Arkansas in a car from California, and California was a "source state" for drugs. The criteria for considering the entire state of California to be a profile factor was unexplained. Indeed, the officer testified that he considered not only California to be a drug source state, but also Arizona, Texas, New Mexico, Florida, and Louisiana. The court held that the profile factor was far too broad to be useful in a consideration of reasonable suspicion.

> While we do not suggest that geography is an entirely irrelevant factor, we do not think that the entire state of California, the most populous state in the union, can properly be deemed a source of illegal narcotics such that mere residency in that state constitutes a factor supporting reasonable suspicion. * * * We conclude, in the circumstances of this case, that no specific, articulable basis warranting a reasonable belief that Beck's Buick contained contraband can be gleaned from the mere fact that Beck's Buick was registered and licensed in California.

Note that the *Beck* court does not prevent the officer from using the California profile factor in *deciding* whether to stop a motorist. He simply cannot justify the stop by this factor. If the officer had reasonable suspicion to stop the car on other grounds, the use of the California profile factor would not raise a Fourth Amendment issue.

### Reasonable Suspicion and Flight from the Police

If a person runs upon seeing the police, is this enough to justify a stop of that person? This was a question presented in Illinois v. Wardlow, 528 U.S. 119 (2000). Wardlow fled upon seeing a caravan of police vehicles converge on an area of Chicago known for heavy narcotics trafficking. When Officers Nolan and Harvey caught up with him on the street, Nolan stopped him and conducted a protective pat-down search for weapons because in his experience there were usually weapons in the vicinity of narcotics transactions. Discovering a handgun, the officers arrested Wardlow. The Illinois appellate courts reversed Wardlow's conviction for a firearm violation, reasoning that his flight from the police in a high crime area did not constitute reasonable suspicion. The Supreme Court, in an opinion by Chief Justice Rehnquist for five Justices, found that the officers did have reasonable suspicion under the circumstances, and reinstated Wardlow's conviction.

The Chief Justice analyzed the relevance of Wardlow's flight in a high crime area in the following passage:

> An individual's presence in an area of expected criminal activity, standing alone, is not enough to support a reasonable, particularized suspicion that the person is committing a crime. But officers are not required to ignore the relevant characteristics of a location in determining whether the circumstances are sufficiently suspicious to warrant further investigation. Accordingly, we have previously noted the fact that the stop occurred in a high crime area among the relevant contextual considerations in a Terry analysis. Adams v. Williams.

> In this case, moreover, it was not merely respondent's presence in an area of heavy narcotics trafficking that aroused the officers' suspicion but his unprovoked flight upon noticing the police. * * * Headlong flight—wherever it occurs—is the consummate act of evasion: it is not necessarily indicative of wrongdoing, but it is certainly suggestive of such. In reviewing the propriety of an officer's conduct, courts do not have available empirical studies dealing with inferences drawn from suspicious behavior, and we cannot reasonably demand scientific certainty from judges or law enforcement officers where none exists. Thus, the determination of reasonable suspicion must be based on commonsense judgments and inferences about human behavior. We conclude Officer Nolan was justified in suspecting that Wardlow was involved in criminal activity, and, therefore, in investigating further.

Such a holding is entirely consistent with our decision in Florida v. Royer, where we held that when an officer, without reasonable suspicion or probable cause, approaches an individual, the individual has a right to ignore the police and go about his business. And any refusal to cooperate, without more, does not furnish the minimal level of objective justification needed for a detention or seizure. But unprovoked flight is simply not a mere refusal to cooperate. Flight, by its very nature, is not going about one's business; in fact, it is just the opposite. * * * Respondent and amici also argue that there are innocent reasons for flight from police and that, therefore, flight is not necessarily indicative of ongoing criminal activity. This fact is undoubtedly true, but does not establish a violation of the Fourth Amendment. * * * *Terry* accepts the risk that officers may stop innocent people. Indeed, the Fourth Amendment accepts that risk in connection with more drastic police action; persons arrested and detained on probable cause to believe they have committed a crime may turn out to be innocent. The *Terry* stop is a far more minimal intrusion, simply allowing the officer to briefly investigate further. If the officer does not learn facts rising to the level of probable cause, the individual must be allowed to go on his way. But in this case the officers found respondent in possession of a handgun, and arrested him for violation of an Illinois firearms statute.

Justice Stevens concurred in part and dissented in part in an opinion joined by Justices Souter, Ginsburg and Breyer. Justice Stevens stated that the defendant was pressing for a rule that flight from police officers would *never* equal reasonable suspicion, while the State was pressing for a rule that flight from police officers would *always* equal reasonable suspicion. He agreed with the majority that neither per se rule was appropriate, and that the relevance of flight in the reasonable suspicion inquiry depends on the circumstances. He dissented, however, from the Court's ruling that Wardlow's flight in a high crime area was sufficiently suspicious to justify a *Terry* stop under the circumstances. Justice Stevens emphasized why flight from the police might not be suspicious, particularly in minority communities and high crime neighborhoods:

Among some citizens, particularly minorities and those residing in high crime areas, there is * * * the possibility that the fleeing person is entirely innocent, but, with or without justification, believes that contact with the police can itself be dangerous, apart from any criminal activity associated with the officer's sudden presence. For such a person, unprovoked flight is neither "aberrant" nor "abnormal." * * *

## 4. Limited Searches for Police Protection Under the *Terry* Doctrine

*Terry* and *Adams* indicate that an officer can frisk a suspect, and pull out objects found on the suspect, if there is reasonable suspicion to believe that the search is necessary to protect the officer or others from bodily harm during the course of an otherwise legal stop. See United States v. Preston, 685 F.3d 685 (8th Cir. 2012) ("Officers may conduct a protective pat-down search for weapons during a valid stop when they have objectively reasonable suspicion that a person with whom they are dealing might be armed and presently dangerous."). One obvious concern is that an officer may use the *Terry* frisk doctrine as a pretext to search for evidence of a crime. Thus, the officer may testify that he felt a fear of bodily harm, when in fact he was looking for evidence without having probable cause. Is there an easy way to distinguish *Terry* frisks from impermissible searches for evidence?

### Frisk Cannot Be Used to Search for Evidence: *Minnesota v. Dickerson*

In Minnesota v. Dickerson, 508 U.S. 366 (1993), the Court reaffirmed the principle that *Terry* frisks are justified only for protective purposes and that a search for evidence is not permitted under *Terry*. The officer in *Dickerson*, suspecting drug activity, conducted a lawful stop and patdown, and felt a small, hard object in Dickerson's pocket. The officer determined that it was not a weapon, but nonetheless continued to squeeze and prod the object. This additional investigation led him to the conclusion that the object was crack cocaine. The officer then pulled the object out from Dickerson's pocket, and found that his conclusion was correct. Justice White, writing for the Court, declared that "the police officer in this case overstepped the bounds of the strictly circumscribed search for weapons allowed under *Terry*." He concluded as follows:

> Here, the officer's continued exploration of respondent's pocket after having concluded that it contained no weapon was unrelated to the sole justification of the search under *Terry*: the protection of the police officer and others nearby. It therefore amounted to the sort of evidentiary search that *Terry* expressly refused to authorize, and that we have condemned in subsequent cases.

See also United States v. Miles, 247 F.3d 1009 (9th Cir. 2001) (officer exceeded scope of *Terry* frisk by shaking a small box found in the outer pocket of the suspect's clothing, where the box clearly could not have contained a weapon); United States v. Askew, 529 F.3d 1119 (D.C. Cir. 2008) (en banc) (unzipping a suspect's jacket, in order to facilitate of showup identification, was not justified by *Terry* because it was not a search for self-protection but rather was done to obtain information about a crime; therefore the gun found inside the suspect's jacket was illegally obtained).

### Suspicion Required to Support the Right to Frisk

Evaluate the following facts in light of *Terry* and *Adams*.

> The officer received a radio report of an anonymous 911 call in which the informant stated that he had seen a woman in a blue car with a white top parked in front of 123 West 112th Street, a high crime area in New York City. The woman had passed a handgun to a man seated in the car with her. Finding defendant in a car meeting the description at the specific location indicated by the informant, the officer ordered the defendant out of the car, frisked her, and took a pistol from the area of her waistband.

The New York Court of Appeals held that while the stop was permissible, the frisk was not. The court reasoned as follows:

> A frisk requires reliable knowledge of facts providing reasonable basis for suspecting that the individual to be subjected to that intrusion is armed and may be dangerous. Here, there was no such predicate either in the information received, which indicated that defendant had given a gun to the man but provided no basis for inferring that she had another or that it had been returned to her, or in what occurred during the officer's encounter with defendant. No inquiry was made of defendant so she neither refused to answer nor answered evasively; no suspicious bulge was perceived in her clothing; no furtive movements were made by her; her appearance and movements were not concealed by darkness.

People v. Russ, 61 N.Y.2d 693, 472 N.Y.S.2d 601 (1984). If you were a police officer, would you have found it superfluous to frisk Russ for a gun, after she had already passed a gun in a high crime area?

Most courts have given considerably more deference to police concerns about the risk of harm involved in making a stop. Consider United States v. Rideau, 969 F.2d 1572 (5th Cir.1992) (en banc). Two officers were on patrol in a high crime area of Beaumont, Texas, "where people often carried weapons and transacted drug deals on the street, and where public drunkenness was a recurrent problem." The officers saw a man standing in the road. They flashed a bright light at him. The man turned to step up to the curb, and he stumbled. Officer Ellison, suspecting that the man was drunk, got out of his car and approached. Ellison asked the man his name. The man appeared nervous, did not answer, and began to back away. Ellison "immediately closed the gap and reached out to pat the man's outer clothing." The first place he touched was the man's right front pants pocket, where he felt a gun. The officer put the man up against the patrol car, removed the gun, and arrested him. The man, subsequently identified as Rideau, was convicted for felon firearm possession.

Judge Higginbotham, writing for the majority of the en banc court of appeals, held that the frisk was justified because Officer Ellison had reasonable cause to believe that Rideau posed a threat of harm:

> Rideau's specific moves took place after a detention, at night, in a high crime area where the carrying of weapons is common. * * * Stripped from their context, the backward steps offer no threat, but to a police officer in Ellison's situation, they become very significant in the matrix of the general facts. * * * Of course, that an individual is in a high crime neighborhood at night is not in and of itself enough to support an officer's decision to stop and frisk him. But when someone engages in suspicious activity in a high crime area, where weapons and violence abound, police officers must be particularly cautious in approaching and questioning him.

Judge Smith, together with four other judges of the en banc panel, dissented in *Rideau*. He argued that under the majority's permissive approach, Rideau could have been frisked no matter what he did when Officer Ellison approached: if he had moved forward, this would have been deemed threatening as well; if he had moved to the side, this would have been deemed nervousness or flight; if he had remained motionless, it would have been viewed as "abnormal behavior caused by drugs or alcohol." Judge Smith concluded as follows:

> Perhaps if Rideau had graduated from charm school and had been taught how to look "cool and collected" in the face of approaching uniformed officers, he could have managed to avoid the patdown. Otherwise, he was doomed to the intrusion that in fact occurred. * * *

> * * * Rideau was searched not because of anything he did but because of his *status*—a person in a "bad part of town" where, presumably, people do not belong late at night, on the street, unless they are "up to no good." By that measure, almost any person in the vicinity of Martin Luther King Boulevard and Bonham Street that night could have been stopped and frisked.

Arguably, the New York court in *Russ* gave too little credence to an officer's concern for his safety in making a stop explicitly on a weapons charge. Did the majority in *Rideau* give too much credence to an officer's concern for his safety where the stop had nothing to do with weapons and was at least purportedly an attempt to help Rideau, who appeared drunk?

### Frisking Based on the Type of Crime for Which the Person Is Suspected

Note that reasonable suspicion to conduct a frisk will depend in part on the nature of the crime for which the citizen is suspected. Thus, if there is reasonable suspicion to believe that a person is going to commit a crime of violence with a weapon, there will automatically be reasonable suspicion to frisk that person. On the other hand, if the citizen is suspected of a financial crime, it is less likely that reasonable suspicion to frisk will be found. See Leveto v. Lapina, 258 F.3d 156 (3rd Cir. 2001) (frisk of person suspected of tax offense was illegal, as there was no reason to think that the person was armed and dangerous); United States v. McKoy, 428 F.3d 38 (1st Cir. 2005) (no reasonable suspicion for a pat-down, even though the defendant was in a high crime area, where the basis for the stop was a parking and license plate violation: "this is not a case where the police had reason to suspect the presence of firearms based on the type of crime suspected.").

Courts have expanded the assumption that certain crimes are weapons-related, beyond those crimes that by definition require a weapon (like armed robbery). Thus, in United States v. Snow, 656 F.3d 498 (7th Cir. 2011), officers frisked a person suspected of burglary, even though the person was completely cooperative during the stop and even though the stop occurred during the day in a low-crime area. The court stated that "[b]ecause the facts known to the officers supported a *Terry* stop to investigate whether he in fact had attempted a residential burglary, and because burglary is the type of offense that likely involves a weapon, Andrews' decision to order Snow out of the truck for purposes of a protective frisk was reasonable despite the absence of additional facts suggesting that Snow in particular might be armed." Snow argued that because he was being cooperative, the officers could have simply questioned him about whether he was carrying anything, rather than resorting to a frisk. But the court rejected that suggestion, stating that there was no requirement that officers must take a less onerous alternative in conducting a stop when they have reasonable suspicion that the suspect is armed and dangerous in light of the crime for which he is suspected.

### Protective Searches Beyond the Suspect's Person: Michigan v. Long

The Court held in Michigan v. Long, 463 U.S. 1032 (1983), that the power to search under *Terry* can extend to protective examinations of areas beyond the person of the suspect. Long was stopped by officers who saw him driving erratically before he swerved into a ditch. When the officers stopped him, Long was out of his car and he appeared to be under the influence of drugs or alcohol. Long failed to respond to initial requests that he produce a license and registration and then began to walk toward the passenger compartment of his car. An officer flashed a light into the car and saw a hunting knife. A protective search for weapons was conducted in the passenger compartment and marijuana was found and seized.

Justice O'Connor's opinion for the Court reasoned that *Terry* permits a limited examination of an area from which a person, who police reasonably believe is dangerous, might gain control of a weapon. While Long may not have been able to reach a weapon *during* the stop, Justice O'Connor explained that because a stop is only a temporary intrusion, the suspect "will be permitted to reenter his automobile, and he will then have access to any weapons inside." Thus the officers had a legitimate concern that Long might gain access to a weapon, and use it on the officers, *once he returned to his car after the stop was completed.* Accordingly, it was permissible under the circumstances for the officers to do a cursory inspection of areas in the car from which a weapon could be quickly obtained after the stop was over.[16] Thus while the doctrine is called "stop and frisk", *Long* permits a protective search beyond the suspect's person. After *Long* the more accurate description of *Terry* is "stop and protective search."

The New York Court of Appeals, in People v. Torres, 74 N.Y.2d 224, 544 N.Y.S.2d 796 (1989), rejected the reasoning in *Long* as a matter of state constitutional law. The *Torres* court declared:

> [I]t is unrealistic to assume, as the Supreme Court did in Michigan v. Long, that having been stopped and questioned without incident, a suspect who is about to be released and permitted to proceed on his way would, upon reentry into his vehicle, reach for a concealed weapon and threaten the departing police officer's safety. Certainly, such a far-fetched scenario is an insufficient basis upon which to predicate the substantial intrusion that occurred here.

Is it "far-fetched" to believe that a suspect could present a risk of harm to the officer in a post-stop situation? Would you think it far-fetched if you were a police officer?

### Applying Michigan v. Long

Is it reasonable to assume that those suspected of drug dealing *always* present a risk of harm to the officer when stopped—justifying a protective search of areas that the suspect could reach after a stop? In United States v. Brown, 913 F.2d 570 (8th Cir.1990), the court relied on

---

[16] Justice Blackmun concurred in part and in the judgment. Justice Brennan, joined by Justice Marshall, and Justice Stevens filed dissenting opinions.

*Long* to uphold a search of a locked glove compartment, when the officers had reasonable suspicion of drug activity. The court concluded that "since weapons and violence are frequently associated with drug transactions, the officers reasonably believed that the individuals with whom they were dealing were armed and dangerous." Is there now a per se rule that a search of a passenger compartment for weapons can be conducted upon reasonable suspicion to believe the driver is a drug dealer? See also United States v. Sakyi, 160 F.3d 164 (4th Cir.1998) (finding it permissible to frisk all occupants of a car after a cigar box of marijuana was found in the car; court reasons that "guns often accompany drugs").

For interesting questions about the scope of a search under *Long,* see United States v. McGregor, 650 F.3d 813 (1st Cir. 2011). Officers had reasonable suspicion that gang members in a car were going to commit an act of reprisal after one of their members was shot. They pulled the car over and frisked the suspects and found nothing. Nor was there any weapon laying about in the car. But officer Feeney saw a magnet that he had been trained to suspect as part of a weapons "hide"—which is a series of programmed signals that will open up a secret compartment where a weapon was hidden. The officer, using his expertise, figured out how the "hide" worked, described by the court as follows:

> Put the key in the ignition, fasten a seatbelt, switch on the cruise control, turn on the rear-window defroster, tug on the emergency brake, move the ceiling-light switch to the middle position, move a magnet around a spot on the dashboard (which would trigger a magnetic switch behind the dashboard), and press the sunroof button—doing this activates a series of switches, which starts up a motor under the center console, which opens up the hide so one can reach right through the bottom of the console and into a secret compartment. Feeney did the steps and found [a] round of ammo tucked inside the hide.

The court found that Officer Feeney's inspection of the car, and finding of the "hide" was permissible under *Long* because "McGregor and his buddies could have grabbed the weapon from the console hide in a flash had they gotten back into the car." Feeney had testified that the process took about 20 seconds. Is that within the post-stop parameters of *Long*?

The *Long* rationale is not limited to protective searches of cars. Thus, in United States v. Johnson, 932 F.2d 1068 (5th Cir.1991), the court upheld a cursory inspection of a pair of overalls located a few feet away from a suspect who appeared to be attempting to burglarize a house. The court found that merely separating the suspect from his effects during the stop would not provide sufficient protection to the officers, because if the stop was terminated without an arrest, the officers would have to return the property to the suspect.

## Protective Searches of Persons Other Than the Suspect

In the course of detaining suspects either by a stop or an arrest, officers are often confronted with whether they can frisk persons other than the suspect. In Ybarra v. Illinois, 444 U.S. 85 (1979), the Court refused to uphold the frisk of a patron of a bar who happened to be present when the police arrived to conduct a search of the bar pursuant to a valid search warrant. The Court noted that the patron's mere presence in the bar was not enough to provide a reasonable belief that he posed a risk of harm to the officers, and that no specific facts were shown to indicate that Ybarra was armed and dangerous.

How much information does an officer need, other than mere presence, to support a frisk of a person in the vicinity of an arrest? See United States v. Reid, 997 F.2d 1576 (D.C.Cir.1993) (defendant could be frisked after officers saw him exit from a suspected crack house that they were about to search: "Common sense suggests that there is a much greater likelihood that a person found in a small private residence containing drugs will be involved in the drug activity occurring there than an individual who happens to be in a public tavern where the bartender is suspected of possessing drugs.").

## Inspecting Objects During the Course of a Protective Frisk

Assume that an officer has properly stopped a person and has reasonable suspicion to believe that the person presents a safety risk. The officer then conducts a pat-down and feels an object inside the suspect's coat. Can the officer pull the object out and inspect it? Under *Dickerson*, the answer is that the officer can inspect the object only if it is reasonably likely to be a weapon—*Terry* does not justify a search for evidence. But sometimes there is a dispute about whether an object felt by the officer during a pat-down could reasonably be a weapon.

A case in point is United States v. Swann, 149 F.3d 271 (4th Cir.1998). Officers responded to a report of a theft of a wallet in an office building. Witness reports indicated that the thief had been detained by employees, but broke free and tossed the wallet in the direction of three black males standing near the elevator. One of the men retrieved the wallet and all three men fled the scene. An officer spotted two black males in the basement parking garage. According to the officer, they appeared "really nervous and uneasy and kind of edgy; didn't want to hang around." When the officer told them that he needed to speak with them, one of them tried to circle around him to get behind his back. The officer felt threatened by this action and called for back-up. When another officer arrived, the men were patted down. The officer patting down Swann found a hard object in Swann's left sock. The officer pulled it out and it turned out to be five credit cards belonging to the victim of the theft.

Swann moved to suppress the credit cards on the ground that *Terry* did not permit the officer to inspect the object found in his sock. But the court disagreed, concluding that a reasonable officer "could justifiably have believed that the item was a weapon." The court elaborated:

> [T]he object in Swann's sock was approximately the same size and shape as a box cutter with a sharp blade, which is often used as a weapon.
>
> The location of the object in the sock, as well as its hard character and its shape, made it suspicious. A similarly shaped hard object in Swann's pocket surely would have raised no alarms, as there could be innumerable innocent explanations for it. And a hard rectangular object in one's sock might not be suspicious on a jogger or someone similarly dressed. But these men were both fully dressed, and Swann's pants had pockets that could have contained an item of that size and shape.
>
> Given all the circumstances, it was objectively reasonable for the officer to believe that this particular hard object could likely be a weapon and to seize the item to satisfy himself that it was not something that could be used to inflict harm. Officers making *Terry* stops must make quick decisions as to how to protect themselves and others from possible danger. Were we to disapprove of Officer Martin's actions, we would require an officer to allow a suspicious object to remain within easy reach of demonstrably nervous and potentially aggressive subjects. Our respect for the privacy rights of citizens does not require such an increase in the danger that police officers must face.

Why is it relevant that Swann had pockets and yet decided to use his sock as a storage space? Does that fact indicate that he was trying to hide a weapon? Or rather that he was trying to hide evidence of a crime? Would the result in *Swann* change if the object in Swann's sock was soft to the touch?

### *Protective Sweeps: Maryland v. Buie*

In Maryland v. Buie, 494 U.S. 325 (1990), the Court considered the legality of a "protective sweep," which it defined as a "quick and limited search of a premises, incident to an arrest and conducted to protect the safety of police officers or others." Officers had probable cause to believe that Buie and an associate committed an armed robbery. They arrested

Buie at his home, and conducted a protective sweep of the premises. During the sweep, the officers discovered clothing that tied Buie to the robbery. At the time of the sweep, the officers had reasonable suspicion, but not probable cause, to believe that a dangerous person such as Buie's associate might be hiding in the premises. Buie argued that a protective sweep could not be conducted in the absence of probable cause to believe that there were individuals on the premises who would harm the officers or others. But the Court, by a 7–2 vote, rejected Buie's argument. Justice White, writing for the majority, relied heavily on *Terry* and *Long* to find that a protective sweep could be justified by an officer's reasonable suspicion "that the area swept harbored an individual posing danger to the officer or others." According to Justice White, the reasonable suspicion standard was an appropriate balance between the arrestee's remaining privacy interest in the home and the officer's interest in safety. Justice White emphasized that a protective sweep is a relatively limited intrusion because it "may extend only to a cursory inspection of those spaces where a person may be found," and the sweep can last "no longer than is necessary to dispel the reasonable suspicion of danger." Justice Stevens concurred to emphasize that a protective sweep could only be conducted for safety purposes, not to prevent destruction of evidence.[17] Justice Brennan, joined by Justice Marshall, dissented and noted his continuing criticism "of the emerging tendency on the part of the Court to convert the *Terry* decision from a narrow exception into one that swallows the general rule that searches are 'reasonable' only if based upon probable cause."

Compare *Buie* with United States v. Colbert, 76 F.3d 773 (6th Cir.1996), where the court found that a protective sweep after an arrest was not permitted where there was no indication that anyone other than the arrestee was on the premises: "The facts upon which officers may justify a *Buie* protective sweep are those facts giving rise to a suspicion of danger from attack by a third party during the arrest, not the dangerousness of the arrested individual."

### *Protective Sweep Other Than During an Arrest*

Courts have held that the self-protective principles of *Buie* and *Terry* can permit a protective sweep *even when no arrest is involved*. That is, if the officers are acting in the course of legal activity, and they have reasonable suspicion to believe that a person in the area can obtain access to a weapon and use it on the officers or others, the officers are permitted to conduct a protective sweep for weapons. See, e.g., United States v. Gould, 364 F.3d 578 (5th Cir. 2004) (en banc), in which officers were given

---

[17] See United States v. Hogan, 38 F.3d 1148 (10th Cir.1994) ("[I]t appears that once inside Hogan's property, officers went on a fishing expedition for evidence linking Hogan to the murder. This greatly exceeded the permissible scope of a protective sweep.").

consent to search a particular room in a home. They were concerned, under the circumstances, that they might be walking into a trap, and so conducted a cursory inspection of the entire house. The court found the inspection to be a permissible protective sweep.

> We decline to adopt any across-the-board rule that a protective sweep can never be valid where the initial entry to the home is pursuant to consent, even where the consent does not of itself legally authorize the entry into the area swept. Any such rule either would require officers to forego any and all consent entries or would prevent them, once having so entered, from taking reasonable, minimally intrusive, means for self-protection when reasonable suspicion of danger of ambush arises. * * * [W]e hold that the Fourth Amendment imposes no such Hobson's choice.

### 5.   Brief and Limited Detentions: The Line Between "Stop" and "Arrest"

*Terry* allows a stop upon a standard of proof less than probable cause, in part because a stop is less intrusive than an arrest. But it is often difficult to determine when an intrusion crosses over from a stop to an arrest requiring probable cause. What is it about an arrest that makes it different from a stop? Is it that the officers force the suspect to move to a detention area? Is it that the officers draw their guns or use handcuffs? Is it the length of the detention? This section considers the factors found relevant by the courts.

#### a.   *Forced Movement of the Suspect to a Custodial Area*

In Florida v. Royer, supra, Royer was taken from the public area of an airport into a small room, where the officers sought and obtained Royer's consent to a search of his luggage. The plurality in *Royer* held that the consent was invalid because it was obtained as the result of an arrest without probable cause. Justice White, writing for the plurality, explained as follows:

[A]t the time Royer produced the key to his suitcase, the detention to which he was then subjected was a more serious intrusion on his personal liberty than is allowable on mere suspicion of criminal activity.

> By the time Royer was informed that the officers wished to examine his luggage, he had identified himself when approached by the officers and had attempted to explain the discrepancy between the name shown on his identification and the name under which he had purchased his ticket and identified his luggage. The officers were not satisfied, for they informed him they were narcotics agents and had reason to believe that he was carrying illegal drugs. They

requested him to accompany them to the police room. Royer went with them. He found himself in a small room—a large closet—equipped with a desk and two chairs. He was alone with two police officers who again told him that they thought he was carrying narcotics. He also found that the officers, without his consent, had retrieved his checked luggage from the airlines. What had begun as a consensual inquiry in a public place had escalated into an investigatory procedure in a police interrogation room, where the police, unsatisfied with previous explanations, sought to confirm their suspicions. The officers had Royer's ticket, they had his identification, and they had seized his luggage. Royer was never informed that he was free to board his plane if he so chose, and he reasonably believed that he was being detained. * * * As a practical matter, Royer was under arrest. * * *

Justice White noted that some forced movements of a suspect might be justifiable during a *Terry* stop; he emphasized, however, that probable cause is required if the officer forces the suspect to move in order to further the investigation or to place more pressure on the suspect:

[T]here are undoubtedly reasons of safety and security that would justify moving a suspect from one location to another during an investigatory detention, such as from an airport concourse to a more private area. There is no indication in this case that such reasons prompted the officers to transfer the site of the encounter from the concourse to the interrogation room. It appears, rather, that the primary interest of the officers was not in having an extended conversation with Royer but in the contents of his luggage, a matter which the officers did not pursue orally with Royer until after the encounter was relocated to the police room.

Justice Blackmun dissented in *Royer* and argued that Royer was only detained for 15 minutes, the officers were polite, and the intrusion was minimal. He concluded that Royer was only stopped, not arrested, when he gave consent to the luggage search.

Justice Rehnquist, joined by Chief Justice Burger and Justice O'Connor, also dissented, arguing as follows:

Would it have been more "reasonable" to interrogate Royer about the contents of his suitcases, and to seek his permission to open the suitcases when they were retrieved, in the busy main concourse of the Miami Airport, rather than to find a room off the concourse where the confrontation would surely be less embarrassing to Royer? If the room had been large and spacious, rather than small, if it had possessed three chairs rather than two, would the officers' conduct have been made reasonable by these facts?

See also United States v. Ricardo D., 912 F.2d 337 (9th Cir.1990) (taking person by the arm and placing him in squad car for questioning held impermissible under *Terry*, where there was no showing that the police procedure was "necessary for safety or security reasons").

### b.  Forced Movement for Identification Purposes

In *Royer,* the Court held that an arrest occurred when Royer was forcibly moved to a custodial atmosphere, for purposes of extracting consent to search. The Court noted, however, that an officer can, within the confines of a *Terry* stop, force the suspect to move for purposes of safety and security. Are there any other legitimate reasons to force a suspect to move without probable cause to arrest? Many courts have found that if reasonable suspicion exists, it is permissible to transport the suspect a short distance for purposes of identification by witnesses. In People v. Hicks, 68 N.Y.2d 234, 508 N.Y.S.2d 163 (1986), the New York Court of Appeals found that coercive movement to the crime scene for purposes of identification was within the confines of a permissible *Terry* stop. It explained as follows:

> There were witnesses within a quarter mile of the place of inquiry—approximately one minute away by car—who had just seen the perpetrators and would either identify defendant (in which event he would be arrested) or not identify him (in which event he would be released). A speedy on-the-scene viewing thus was of value both to law enforcement authorities and to defendant, and was appropriate here. The transportation did not unduly prolong the detention. Defendant might, alternatively, have been momentarily detained where he had been stopped and the witnesses brought there, but such a procedure would have entailed first securing defendant and his companion and then arranging transportation for the witnesses, possibly even a more time-consuming process than that chosen. At all events, given the time and distance involved this is a difference without constitutional significance.

See also United States v. Benson, 686 F.3d 498 (8th Cir. 2012) ("The exigencies were such that the officers could not dispel their suspicions that had prompted the *Terry* stop until they transported [the suspect] to the bank for the show-up identification.").

### c.  Investigative Techniques That Are Permissible Within the Confines of a Terry Stop

The purpose of a *Terry* stop is to permit an officer to investigate the facts on which reasonable suspicion is based, in order to determine whether the suspect is involved in criminal activity. It therefore follows that some preliminary investigation, designed to clear up or develop reasonable suspicion, is permissible within the confines of a stop.

However, probable cause will be required if the officers are using the stop for some purpose beyond that which justified the stop.

The most common investigative techniques permitted pursuant to a *Terry* stop are 1) preliminary investigation of the suspect's identity, and 2) questioning concerning the suspicious circumstances giving rise to the stop. See United States v. Guzman, 864 F.2d 1512 (10th Cir.1988) ("An officer conducting a routine traffic stop may request a driver's license and vehicle identification."). The officer may also verify the information obtained from the suspect by communicating with others, or by conducting preliminary investigations such as a vehicle registration check, license check, or a computer search for outstanding warrants. See United States v. Mendez, 118 F.3d 1426 (10th Cir.1997) ("An officer conducting a routine traffic stop may run computer checks on the driver's license, the vehicle registration papers, and on whether the driver has any outstanding warrants or the vehicle has been reported stolen").

Courts have also permitted officers to detain suspects on reasonable suspicion in order to conduct a canine sniff or to conduct a preliminary investigation of other suspicious circumstances. See United States v. Bloomfield, 40 F.3d 910 (8th Cir.1994) (where officers had reasonable suspicion that drugs were in a car, it was proper to detain the suspects while a dog was brought to the scene to sniff the vehicle, because the investigation was "reasonably related in scope to the circumstances that justified the interference in the first place").

### Criminalizing the Refusal to Provide Identification During a Terry Stop: Hiibel v. Sixth Judicial District Court of Nevada

In Hiibel v. Sixth Judicial District Court of Nevada, 542 U.S. 177 (2004), Hiibel was stopped on reasonable suspicion of being involved in a domestic assault. He refused to provide identification. He did not contest the stop, but contended that the state had no power to criminalize his refusal to provide identification during the stop. The Court, in an opinion by Justice Kennedy, upheld the conviction and stressed that an officer has a right to demand identification as part on an investigation during a *Terry* stop. Justice Kennedy explained as follows:

> Our decisions make clear that questions concerning a suspect's identity are a routine and accepted part of many *Terry* stops. Obtaining a suspect's name in the course of a *Terry* stop serves important government interests. Knowledge of identity may inform an officer that a suspect is wanted for another offense, or has a record of violence or mental disorder. On the other hand, knowing identity may help clear a suspect and allow the police to concentrate their efforts elsewhere. * * *

The principles of *Terry* permit a State to require a suspect to disclose his name in the course of a *Terry* stop. The request for identity has an immediate relation to the purpose, rationale, and practical demands of a *Terry* stop. The threat of criminal sanction helps ensure that the request for identity does not become a legal nullity. On the other hand, the Nevada statute does not alter the nature of the stop itself: it does not change its duration, or its location.

Justice Breyer, joined by Justices Souter and Ginsburg, dissented in *Hiibel,* arguing that while the officer can legitimately demand identification during a *Terry* stop, it is unreasonable to criminalize the suspect's refusal.

### d.   Overly Intrusive Investigation Techniques

Some investigative techniques are themselves so intrusive or extensive as to require probable cause. The most obvious example is a search for evidence, which, as stated above, goes beyond the scope of a *Terry* stop. Also, some courts have held that probable cause is required before a suspect can be subjected to a series of demanding physical tests to determine whether he is intoxicated. See People v. Carlson, 677 P.2d 310 (Colo.1984) (holding that the full battery of tests employed was so intrusive as to constitute an arrest). Roadside sobriety tests that are less demanding may be permissible under *Terry*, however. See State v. Wyatt, 67 Haw. 293, 687 P.2d 544 (1984) (limited field sobriety test permissible on reasonable suspicion).

### e.   Investigation of Matters Other Than the Reasonable Suspicion That Supported the Stop: Stop After a Stop

Many courts have held that a *Terry* stop must end when the reason for the stop has come to an end. If the reasonable suspicion supporting the stop has been cleared up (e.g., an identification checks out) or the person has been processed (e.g., the traffic ticket has been issued), then the stop is at an end and the suspect must be released. So for example, an officer who stops someone for a traffic violation cannot continue the stop in order to investigate for drug or gun crimes, in the absence of reasonable suspicion to support such an independent inquiry. A *Terry* stop cannot be used as an excuse for a fishing expedition. United States v. Santiago, 310 F.3d 336 (5th Cir. 2002) (detention after a valid traffic stop was impermissible: "Once a computer check is completed and the officer either issues a citation or determines that no citation should be issued, the detention should end and the driver should be free to leave. In order to continue a detention after such a point, the officer must have a reasonable suspicion supported by articulable facts that a crime has been or is being committed.").

See also United States v. Jenson, 462 F.3d 399 (5th Cir. 2006) (when a traffic stop was completed, an officer was not permitted to ask the defendant where he worked, and then rely on an implausible answer to justify continuing the stop).

### Reasonable Suspicion as to Another Crime

Note that the rulings in the above cases are based on the fact that the officers had no reasonable suspicion to investigate any matter other than the one for which the suspect was stopped. If, however, in the course of a stop to investigate crime "A", the officer obtains reasonable suspicion to investigate crime "B", then the detention can be extended to investigate crime "B" even though the initial justification for the stop no longer exists. There will then be a permissible "stop after a stop." Thus, in United States v. Erwin, 155 F.3d 818 (6th Cir.1998) (en banc), officers pulled Ervin over because they had reasonable suspicion to believe that he was driving while intoxicated. While going through the drill of the traffic stop, it became apparent that Ervin was not intoxicated. But this investigation also uncovered evidence indicating that Ervin was a drug dealer. The court analyzed the situation as follows:

> After the deputies satisfied themselves that Erwin was not drunk or otherwise impaired, they were justified in continuing to detain Erwin if, by then, they had reasonable and articulable suspicion that Erwin was engaged in other criminal activity. We think, as the district court did, that the deputies were reasonably entitled to conclude that Erwin may have been a drug dealer, based on the facts that he (1) was nervous, (2) seemed to try to avoid being questioned by attempting to leave, (3) seemed to have used or was preparing to use a pay telephone to make a call when a cellular telephone was available, (4) seemed to have drug paraphernalia in his vehicle, (5) had a large amount of cash, (6) had no registration or proof of insurance, (7) had a criminal record of drug violations, and (8) had an out-of-place backseat cushion. Although many of these facts are consistent with innocence, all that is required is that the deputies' suspicion be "reasonable" and "articulable," as determined by the totality of the circumstances. We find this standard was met.

See also United States v. Estrada, 459 F.3d 627 (5th Cir. 2006) (continued detention of occupants of a vehicle stopped for a traffic violation was permissible; while waiting for the license check to clear, the officer noticed fresh marks and scratches around the fuel tank, as well as other information raising a reasonable suspicion to believe that the gas tank had a hidden compartment).

### Consensual Encounters After a Stop Has Ended: Ohio v. Robinette

As discussed above, a suspect cannot be detained for investigation of matters different from those which support a stop, in the absence of reasonable suspicion as to those other matters. But what if the suspect is simply *asked* about another crime while the initial stop is ending? Can there be a permissible *encounter* after a stop? The Supreme Court addressed this question in Ohio v. Robinette, 519 U.S. 33 (1996). Robinette was legally stopped for speeding and given a verbal warning. When the officer returned Robinette's license, he said: "One question before you get gone: Are you carrying any illegal contraband in your car? Any weapons of any kind, drugs, anything like that?" Robinette answered "no" to these questions, after which the officer asked if he could search the car. Robinette consented. The officer found drugs and arrested Robinette.

Robinette argued that before valid consent could be obtained, the officer had to tell him that he was free to leave. Otherwise, the detention would still be continuing, and would amount to an illegal arrest as it was a continuing investigation on a matter other than that which gave rise to the initial stop. But Chief Justice Rehnquist, in an opinion for seven members of the Court, disagreed. The Court held that Robinette voluntarily consented to the search, and rejected any bright-line requirement that the suspect be told that the stop is over and he is free to go. The test for whether the continuing discussion was a consensual encounter was based on a totality of the circumstances and not on any one factor—therefore it was not dispositive that Robinette was never specifically told that the stop was over and he was free to go. Justice Ginsburg concurred in the judgment. Justice Stevens dissented.

### f. Interrogations and Fingerprinting

#### Interrogation Beyond the Confines of Terry

In Dunaway v. New York, 442 U.S. 200 (1979), the Court distinguished *Terry* stops from cases in which the police detain a suspect for sustained interrogation. The Court emphasized that *Terry* was a narrow decision and concluded that police cannot detain a suspect and transport him to the stationhouse for questioning without probable cause, even if the detention is not deemed to be an arrest under state law (and there would be no arrest record or formal booking procedure). Justice Brennan, writing for the Court, concluded that "detention for custodial interrogation—regardless of its label—intrudes so severely on interests protected by the Fourth Amendment as necessarily to trigger the traditional safeguards against illegal arrest." He noted that "any 'exception' that could cover a seizure as intrusive as that in this case would threaten to swallow the general rule that Fourth Amendment seizures are reasonable only if based upon probable cause."[18]

### *Fingerprinting*

In Davis v. Mississippi, 394 U.S. 721 (1969), the Court held that a round-up of twenty-five African-American youths for questioning and fingerprinting—in an effort to match prints found around a window entered by a rape suspect—violated the Fourth Amendment. Justice Brennan wrote for the Court that "[i]t is arguable * * * that because of the unique nature of the fingerprinting process, such detentions might, under narrowly defined circumstances, be found to comply with the Fourth Amendment even though there is no probable cause in the traditional sense." He explained that fingerprinting is less serious an intrusion on liberty than other searches, and that it can be done at a convenient time and does not offer opportunities for harassment. In this case, however, the fingerprinting did not comply with the Fourth Amendment because, among other things, "petitioner was unnecessarily required to undergo two fingerprinting sessions; and petitioner was not merely fingerprinted * * * but also subjected to interrogation." And officers did not have probable cause for the fingerprinting dragnet.

Isn't fingerprinting simply a means of identification, and isn't investigation of the suspect's identity permitted in a *Terry* stop? If there is reasonable suspicion but not probable cause, and the officer who makes a stop knows that there were fingerprints found at the scene of a crime, is it permissible for the officer to take fingerprints and delay the suspect long enough to obtain a match?

Justice White addressed some of these questions as he wrote for the Court in Hayes v. Florida, 470 U.S. 811 (1985). Police officers who were investigating a series of rapes had reasonable suspicion but not probable cause to believe that Hayes was the perpetrator. The officers took Hayes to the stationhouse, without his consent, to be fingerprinted. Justice White concluded that this procedure amounted to an arrest. He indicated that the Court adhered to the view that when police forcibly remove a person to the stationhouse, they are making a seizure that must be considered an arrest, requiring probable cause. Justice White added, however, that the Court's reasoning did not imply "that a brief detention in the field for the purpose of fingerprinting, where there is only reasonable suspicion not amounting to probable cause, is necessarily impermissible under the Fourth Amendment." He relied on *Davis* and noted that fingerprinting in itself is a relatively minimal intrusion and a

---

[18] Justice White wrote a short opinion concurring in the judgment. Justice Stevens also wrote a brief concurring opinion. Justice Rehnquist, joined by Chief Justice Burger, dissented.

means of identification not unlike other methods of identification permitted under *Terry*.[19]

Would you permit fingerprinting as part of a *Terry* stop? Would you permit the police to photograph persons who are stopped? What about taking DNA samples of persons who are stopped?

### g.   Time Limits on Terry Stops

The Supreme Court rejected an absolute time limit for *Terry* stops in United States v. Sharpe, 470 U.S. 675 (1985). The facts are described in the next two paragraphs.

> A Drug Enforcement agent was on patrol in an unmarked car on a coastal road in North Carolina at approximately 6:30 a.m. when he saw a blue pickup truck with an attached camper "traveling in tandem with a blue Pontiac Bonneville." The agent saw that the truck was riding low, the camper did not bounce or sway appreciably around turns, and that a quilted material covered the rear and side windows of the camper. The agent followed the vehicles for 20 miles into South Carolina where he decided to make an "investigative stop." He radioed the highway patrol for help and a trooper in a marked patrol car responded to the call. Almost immediately after the trooper caught up with the vehicles, the Pontiac and the pickup turned off the highway onto a campground road. The agent and trooper followed the two vehicles as they sped along the road at double the legal speed until they returned to the main road. The trooper pulled alongside the Pontiac, which was in the lead, turned on his flashing light and motioned for the driver to pull over. As the Pontiac moved to the side, the pickup truck cut between it and the trooper's car, nearly hitting the latter. The trooper pursued the truck while the agent approached the Pontiac and requested identification.

> The agent examined the driver's license. After unsuccessfully attempting to radio the trooper, he radioed the local police for assistance. Two local officers arrived and the agent asked them to "maintain the situation" while he went to find the trooper. The trooper had stopped the pickup, removed the driver from the truck, examined his license and a bill of sale for the truck, and patted him down. When the trooper told the driver that he would be held until a DEA agent arrived, the driver became nervous, stated that he wanted to leave, and asked for the return of the driver's license. Approximately 15 minutes after the truck was stopped, the DEA agent arrived and learned that the name on the registration was the

---

[19] Justice Brennan, joined by Justice Marshall, concurred in the judgment. He objected to "the Court's strained effort to reach the question" of "[t]he validity of on-site fingerprinting." Justice Blackmun concurred in the judgment without opinion. Justice Powell did not participate in the case.

same as the name on the driver's license of the Pontiac's driver. The driver of the pickup denied two requests for permission to search the truck before the agent examined the truck and stated that he could smell marijuana. Without asking again for permission, he removed the keys from the ignition, opened the rear of the camper, and observed a large number of burlap-wrapped bales resembling marijuana. The agent arrested the driver and returned to the Pontiac to arrest its occupants. The total time between his initial stop of the Pontiac and the arrests of its occupants was between 30 and 40 minutes.

The defendants in *Sharpe* argued that the evidence was illegally obtained, because the officers had only reasonable suspicion and not probable cause and by the time of the search of the camper, the defendants had been detained beyond the time limit of a *Terry* stop.

Chief Justice Burger wrote for the Court and held that the detention did not exceed the time limits of a permissible *Terry* stop; therefore the search of the camper was permissible because by that time the officer had smelled the marijuana. The Chief Justice noted the "difficult linedrawing problems in distinguishing an investigative stop from a de facto arrest". He recognized that "if an investigative stop continues indefinitely, at some point it can no longer be justified as an investigative stop." Defendants suggested a bright-line time limit on *Terry* stops of 20 minutes. But the Court rejected a "hard-and-fast time limit" and concluded that it was "appropriate to examine whether the police diligently pursued a means of investigation that was likely to confirm or dispel their suspicions quickly, during which time it was necessary to detain the defendant." The officers satisfied that test, because there was no delay that was "unnecessary to the legitimate investigation of the law enforcement officers"; in part this was because the suspects contributed to the delay through their own actions, by refusing to pull over.

Justice Marshall concurred in the judgment because the evasive actions of the suspects turned a brief encounter with the officers into an extended one. He emphasized, however, that *Terry* stops must be brief "no matter what the needs of law enforcement in the particular case."

Justice Brennan dissented. He objected to treating the brevity limitation upon a stop as an "accordion-like concept that may be expanded outward depending on the law enforcement purposes to be served by the stop." He criticized the officers' handling of the investigation and found that the stop was unduly and unnecessarily lengthy. Justice Stevens dissented without reaching the merits.

## QUESTIONS AFTER SHARPE

After *Sharpe* what kind of conduct, if any, will be considered impermissible delay, as opposed to diligent investigation? See United States v. Davies, 768 F.2d 893 (7th Cir.1985) (reasonable to detain suspects for an additional thirty minutes to await advice from superiors, where detaining officers were inexperienced); United States v. Bloomfield, 40 F.3d 910 (8th Cir.1994) (en banc) ("The one-hour period between the time Roberts pulled Bloomfield over and the time Roberts arrested Bloomfield was not an unreasonable period to wait for a drug dog to verify Roberts' suspicion."); Embody v. Ward, 695 F.3d 577 (6th Cir. 2012) (after Embody was found with a loaded gun in a state park, a two-and-a-half hour detention was not unreasonable under *Terry;* Embody "points to no lack of diligence by [the officer] in trying to confirm (or allay) his suspicions. The officers took the time they needed to determine whether the AK-47 was a handgun, whether Embody had a permit for it, whether he had illegally modified it and whether he posed any other safety threats. A good part of the detention, moreover, came at the beck and call of Embody, who asked to speak to the police supervisor, even after being told it would delay his release.").

### h.  Show of Force During a Terry Stop

A traditional arrest is sometimes accompanied by the officer's use of handcuffs and drawn gun. Can the officer use such coercive tactics within the confines of a *Terry* stop? Courts have routinely relied on *Terry* and *Adams* to uphold the use of handcuffs and guns where there is reasonable suspicion to believe that they are necessary to protect the officer from harm during the course of a stop. See People v. Allen, 73 N.Y.2d 378, 540 N.Y.S.2d 971 (1989) (officers handcuffed suspect who matched the description of an armed bank robber, after chasing him down a dark alley in a high crime area); United States v. Merkley, 988 F.2d 1062 (10th Cir.1993) ("because safety may require the police to freeze temporarily a potentially dangerous situation, both the display of firearms and the use of handcuffs may be part of a reasonable *Terry* stop"; use of such tactics was found permissible in this case where the defendant was suspected of threatening to kill someone).

In United States v. Alexander, 907 F.2d 269 (2d Cir.1990), the court held that officers acted properly when they unholstered their guns to detain two men suspected of purchasing drugs. The two men were in a Jaguar at 6:00 p.m., parked in an area known for drug activity. The court emphasized the "dangerous nature of the drug trade and the genuine need of law enforcement agents to protect themselves from the deadly threat it may pose." Has the court established a per se rule for those who are reasonably suspected of drug activity? Compare United States v. Novak, 870 F.2d 1345 (7th Cir.1989), where nine law enforcement officers working in an airport stopped two suspected drug couriers. One officer drew her gun and pointed it directly at one suspect's head at close range. The court found that an arrest had occurred. The action was clearly excessive given the fact that the suspects had just deplaned and could not have been carrying weapons.

### 6. Detention of Property Under *Terry*

*Terry* concerned seizures of the person, but its principles have been applied to seizures of property as well. The Court in United States v. Van Leeuwen, 397 U.S. 249 (1970), held that some detentions of property could occur upon reasonable suspicion. Officers, acting upon reasonable suspicion, detained a mailed package for more than a day, while an investigation was made for purposes of developing probable cause and obtaining a warrant. A unanimous Court recognized that detention of mail could at some point become an unreasonable seizure, but found that in the instant case the investigation was conducted promptly and diligently. The Court concluded that "[d]etention for this limited time was, indeed, the prudent act rather than letting the packages enter the mails and then, in case the initial suspicions were confirmed, trying to locate them en route." The Court emphasized that the privacy interest in the packages was "not disturbed or invaded until the approval of the magistrate was obtained." See also United States v. Ramirez, 342 F.3d 1210 (10th Cir. 2003) (officers were permitted, on reasonable suspicion, to remove a package from the "mail stream" for 28 hours in order to conduct a canine sniff and investigate other leads). Compare United States v. Dass, 849 F.2d 414 (9th Cir.1988) (reasonable suspicion does not justify detention of mail for 7–23 days, where the delay could have been reduced to 32 hours if officers had acted diligently); United States v. Aldaz, 921 F.2d 227 (9th Cir.1990) (three-day detention of mail permissible upon reasonable suspicion, where drug-sniffing dogs were 700 air miles away, and other delays were caused by remoteness of post office).

The Court in *Van Leeuwen* upheld a one-day detention without probable cause, while an investigation was conducted. Recall the facts of *Sharpe*. Do you think the Court would have allowed the suspects to be detained without probable cause for more than a day, while a diligent investigation was being conducted?[20] If not, what is the difference between the seizure in *Sharpe* and that in *Van Leeuwen?* Could it be argued that the detention in *Van Leeuwen* was no seizure at all, because a person to whom mail is sent has no legitimate expectation of receiving it on a particular day? See United States v. Va Lerie, 424 F.3d 694 (8th Cir.2005) (en banc) (no seizure where officers removed checked luggage from the luggage compartment of a bus and transported it into the bus

---

[20] See United States v. $191,910.00 in Currency, 16 F.3d 1051, 1060 n. 16 (9th Cir.1994) ("[I]f a police officer had sufficient reasonable suspicion to detain a person, he could not hold that person for 24 hours before obtaining probable cause, even if the government was working as quickly as it could to gather evidence establishing probable cause.").

terminal in order to obtain consent to search; officer's removal of the luggage did not delay the passenger's travel or impact his freedom of movement); United States v. Terriques, 319 F.3d 1051 (8th Cir. 2003) (handling and observation of package by mail clerk was not a seizure as it did not delay the time of delivery).

### *Unreasonably Lengthy Detention of Property:*
### *United States v. Place*

The Court in United States v. Place, 462 U.S. 696 (1983), noted that it is often necessary to seize property upon reasonable suspicion, while an investigation of criminal activity continues. The Court recognized, however, that if a person is traveling with his property, then a seizure of that property "intrudes on both the suspect's possessory interest in his luggage as well as his liberty interest in proceeding with his itinerary." It concluded that "the limitations applicable to investigative detentions of the person should define the permissible scope of the person's luggage on less than probable cause."

On the facts, the Court held that the officers detained Place's luggage for such a long period that probable cause was required to support the detention; because the officers had only reasonable suspicion, the detention was illegal. Police officers seized Place's luggage as he arrived at LaGuardia Airport on a flight from Miami. 90 minutes later, they subjected the luggage to a canine sniff. Justice O'Connor, writing for the Court, stated that the 90 minute detention was unreasonable in the absence of probable cause, because the delay was caused by the failure to transport the drug detecting dog from one New York metropolitan airport to another. She reasoned that the dog could have been transported while Place was in the air en route to New York, since the officers had reasonable suspicion during that time. She concluded that the officers had not diligently pursued the investigation, and that "we have never approved a seizure of the person for the prolonged 90-minute period involved here." Finally, the Court noted that the Fourth Amendment violation was "exacerbated by the failure of the agents to inform the respondent of the place to which they were transporting his luggage, of the length of time he might be dispossessed, and of what arrangements would be made for return of the luggage if the investigation dispelled the suspicion." Under these circumstances, the detention of Place's luggage was tantamount to a detention of Place himself.

Justice Brennan, joined by Justice Marshall, concurred in the result. He argued that the *Terry* balancing approach "should not be conducted except in the most limited circumstances." Justice Blackmun also concurred in the result, similarly expressing concern "with what appears to me to be an emerging tendency on the part of the Court to convert the

*Terry* decision into a general statement that the Fourth Amendment requires only that any seizure be reasonable."

### QUESTIONS AFTER PLACE

Does *Place* mean that a 90-minute detention of luggage in transit is *always* unreasonable in the absence of probable cause? The Court in United States v. $191,910.00 in Currency, 16 F.3d 1051 (9th Cir.1994) held that a two-hour detention of a traveler's luggage, pending a dog sniff, violated the Fourth Amendment solely because of its length. Even if "an unforeseeable canine virus" had suddenly afflicted all the available drug-sniffing dogs, that court would have invalidated the two-hour seizure of the person's luggage. Do you agree, or should the officer's diligence in pursuing the investigation be the only factor for determining the reasonableness of the length of the seizure?

Does *Place* mean that officers must have the drug sniffing dog on the premises at the time the luggage is seized? See United States v. Frost, 999 F.2d 737 (3d Cir.1993) (80-minute detention of luggage pending dog sniff was reasonable: "It does not demonstrate a lack of diligence on the part of the detectives that a drug-sniffing unit was not on duty that day, so that he had to be summoned to the airport"; *Place* distinguished because officers in that case had substantial time to bring the dog to the airport before the luggage arrived).

### Seizure of Property with No Deprivation of a Liberty Interest

In United States v. LaFrance, 879 F.2d 1 (1st Cir.1989), police had reasonable suspicion to believe that a Federal Express package, addressed to LaFrance, contained drugs. The package was guaranteed for delivery that day by noon. The officers arranged for a dog sniff, but the dog was several miles away. The sniff began at 1:15 p.m., and was completed by 2:15; the test was positive. Then a warrant was obtained to search the package. LaFrance challenged the reasonableness of the detention of the package. He testified at the suppression hearing that on the basis of prior experience, he expected to receive the package by 11:00 a.m. The court held that "LaFrance's anticipation that he would receive the goods soon after 11 a.m., though based on earlier experiences, is irrelevant. It is hornbook contract law that where a delivery time is agreed upon, a court should not intrude to imply a different reasonable time for delivery." The court recognized that "once noon arrived, the constitutional chemistry was altered" but that the detention from that point was for a limited time, and that the police were diligent in their investigation during that time.

In *LaFrance*, the detention of the package on reasonable suspicion was longer than that held impermissible in *Place*; however, the court reasoned that unlike the traveler in *Place*, LaFrance's liberty interest was not impaired by the detention of the Federal Express package. Place could not really go anywhere without his luggage, whereas LaFrance was at home and free to go wherever he wanted. Because the intrusion was not as severe as that in *Place*, the court reasoned that the somewhat longer detention of the package was permissible so long as the police were acting diligently. Do you agree with the court that LaFrance's liberty interest was not impaired by the detention of the package? Wasn't LaFrance essentially confined to his home by his need to wait for the package?

### 7. Limited Searches for Evidence by Law Enforcement Officers Under *Terry*

*Terry* allows limited investigative seizures of the person or property on the basis of reasonable suspicion. *Terry* also allows limited searches *for self-protection* on the basis of reasonable suspicion. Does *Terry* permit limited, cursory inspections by law enforcement officers searching for *evidence* on the basis of reasonable suspicion rather than probable cause? This was one question encountered by the Court in Arizona v. Hicks, 480 U.S. 321 (1987). Police lawfully entered premises from which a weapon had been fired, and noticed two sets of expensive stereo components in an otherwise squalid apartment. Suspecting that the components were stolen, one officer moved a turntable in order to read the serial number that was on the underside of the unit. The serial number matched that of a turntable that had been reported stolen. The State did not argue that probable cause existed to move the turntable, but rather that the movement and inspection was a "cursory" search that was justified by reasonable suspicion.

Justice Scalia, writing for the Court, rejected the State's argument that a search for evidence could be justified upon reasonable suspicion. He declared that probably cause was required for the search of the turntable, even though it was cursory and minimally intrusive. Justice Scalia stated that "a search is a search, even if it happens to disclose nothing but the bottom of a turntable." He concluded that "we are unwilling to send police and judges into a new thicket of Fourth Amendment law, to seek a creature of uncertain description that is neither a plain-view inspection nor yet a full-blown search. Nothing in the prior opinions of this Court supports such a distinction." Why doesn't the prior opinion of the Court in *Terry* support the distinction that Justice Scalia rejected?

Justice O'Connor, joined by Chief Justice Rehnquist and Justice Powell, dissented. She argued that police officers who have reasonable, articulable suspicion that an object they come across in a lawful search is evidence of crime may make a cursory inspection of the object to verify their suspicion. Justice Powell added a dissenting opinion, joined by the Chief Justice and Justice O'Connor, that suggested that the majority's distinction between observing a serial number while searching (permissible) and moving an object to read a serial number (impermissible) trivialized the Fourth Amendment and would cause uncertainty. See also Minnesota v. Dickerson, 508 U.S. 366 (1993) (*Terry* protective search can be conducted if the officer has reasonable suspicion that the suspect poses a risk of harm to the officer or others; however, a search for contraband by law enforcement officers is outside the *Terry* doctrine and requires probable cause).

## QUESTIONS AFTER HICKS

The State in *Hicks* did not argue that the presence of two new stereos in a squalid apartment constituted probable cause to believe they were stolen. Should this argument have been made?

The holding in *Hicks* has not prevented the government from arguing that cursory inspections can be conducted on reasonable suspicion. In United States v. Winsor, 846 F.2d 1569 (9th Cir.1988) (en banc), officers chased suspected bank robbers fleeing from the crime into a hotel. Given the large number of rooms in the hotel, the court found that there was reasonable suspicion, but not probable cause, to believe that the robbers were in any particular room. At each room, the officers knocked on the door and announced "Police, open the door." After checking a few rooms, they knocked on a door answered by Dennis Winsor. They recognized him as the robber. At this point, the police had probable cause to enter, whereupon they found Peter Winsor, the other robber, as well as incriminating evidence. The Winsors argued that under *Hicks,* the police conducted a search of their room when they knocked on the door, commanded that it be opened, and looked inside. The government argued that the officers had not conducted a full-blown search for evidence, but rather only a cursory inspection that was justified by reasonable suspicion. The court of appeals held that the evidence the officers discovered when the door was opened (and all evidence found in the room thereafter) was illegally obtained:

> We refuse the government's invitation to decide this case by balancing the competing interests at stake. Instead, we adhere to the bright-line rule that *Hicks* appears to have announced: The Fourth Amendment prohibits searches of dwellings without probable cause.

Other courts have taken the contrary view and held—despite *Hicks*—that a minimally intrusive search for evidence is permissible if supported by reasonable suspicion. For example, in United States v. Concepcion, 942 F.2d 1170 (7th Cir.1991), officers took a key found on the defendant, and inserted it into a lock on a door to an apartment in which drugs had been found. The court held that this was a search, because the use of the key in the lock gave the officers information they did not otherwise have, i.e., that the defendant had a key to the apartment. But the search was upheld even though, at the time they used the key, the officers had only reasonable suspicion and not probable cause to connect the defendant with the apartment. The court reasoned that the search was minimally intrusive. It distinguished *Hicks* on the ground that the information uncovered in *Hicks* was more private: the officers in *Concepcion* could have connected the defendant with the apartment in a variety of ways. Is this a meaningful distinction?

## 8. Application of the *Terry* Reasonableness Analysis Outside the Stop and Frisk Context—To Probationers and Parolees

The *Terry* analysis balances the nature of the individual interest at stake in a search and seizure against the interest of the government in investigating and preventing crime. *Terry* applied this reasonableness analysis in the context of the limited intrusion known as stop and frisk. But it is possible that the balancing analysis could be applied in a wide variety of contexts to allow intrusions on less than probable cause, and without a warrant. To do so, however, would raise tension with the Court's position in *Hicks* and *Dickerson* that searches for evidence of a crime, even if not particularly intrusive, require probable cause.

In United States v. Knights, 534 U.S. 112 (2001), Chief Justice Rehnquist wrote for the Court as it held that no more than reasonable suspicion is required to search a probationer's home. He reasoned that "[j]ust as other punishments for criminal convictions curtail an offender's freedoms, a court granting probation may impose reasonable conditions that deprive the offender of some freedoms enjoyed by law-abiding citizens." The Court appeared to apply a reasonableness balancing approach even though the search was for evidence of a crime (as opposed to a *Terry* frisk for the protection of the officer. The Chief Justice declared as follows:

> [W]e conclude that the search of Knights was reasonable under our general Fourth Amendment approach of "examining the totality of the circumstances," with the probation search condition being a salient circumstance.

> The touchstone of the Fourth Amendment is reasonableness, and the reasonableness of a search is determined by assessing, on the one hand, the degree to which it intrudes upon an individual's privacy and, on the other, the degree to which it is needed for the promotion of legitimate governmental interests. Knights's status as a probationer subject to a search condition informs both sides of that balance. * * * Inherent in the very nature of probation is that probationers do not enjoy the absolute liberty to which every citizen is entitled. Just as other punishments for criminal convictions curtail an offender's freedoms, a court granting probation may impose reasonable conditions that deprive the offender of some freedoms enjoyed by law-abiding citizens * * * Although the Fourth Amendment ordinarily requires the degree of probability embodied in the term "probable cause," a lesser degree satisfies the Constitution

when the balance of governmental and private interests makes such a standard reasonable. See, e.g., Terry v. Ohio. Those interests warrant a lesser than probable-cause standard here. When an officer has reasonable suspicion that a probationer subject to a search condition is engaged in criminal activity, there is enough likelihood that criminal conduct is occurring that an intrusion on the probationer's significantly diminished privacy interests is reasonable.

## QUESTIONS ABOUT KNIGHTS

Does the result in *Knights* mean that the reasonableness of *every* search—and accordingly the necessary standard of proof—is based on a balance of the needs of the state and the privacy interests of the individual? If so, what is left of its declaration in *Hicks* that "a search is a search" that requires probable cause even though the particular search is cursory and relatively unintrusive? And what is left of the *Terry* Court's statement that officers during a stop can conduct a search upon reasonable suspicion, but only for self-protection and not to search for evidence?

## Suspicionless Searches of Parolees Found Reasonable: Samson v. California

In Samson v. California, 547 U.S. 843 (2006), the Court answered a question it left open in *Knights*: whether a condition of a parolee's release can so diminish or eliminate his reasonable expectation of privacy that a *suspicionless* search by a law enforcement officer would be permissible under the Fourth Amendment. The case involved a California statute providing that every prisoner eligible for release on state parole "shall agree in writing to be subject to search or seizure by a parole officer or other peace officer at any time of the day or night, with or without a search warrant and with or without cause." Samson so agreed and was paroled. While on parole he was searched without suspicion, and was found in possession of drugs. The Court, in an opinion by Justice Thomas, found that the search was reasonable.

Justice Thomas relied heavily on *Knights,* even though the search in that case was conducted upon reasonable suspicion. Justice Thomas emphasized that the parolee's expectation of privacy is substantially diminished, because his very liberty is conditional. In contrast, the state's interest in conducting a suspicionless search was found "substantial" because "parolees are more likely to commit future criminal offenses." He explained that, "most parolees require intense supervision" and that "a requirement that searches be based on individualized suspicion would undermine the State's ability to effectively supervise parolees and protect the public from criminal acts by reoffenders". In Justice Thomas's view, a reasonable suspicion standard would be deleterious to these state interests, because it "would give parolees greater opportunity to anticipate searches and conceal criminality."

Justice Thomas rejected the argument that the California law permitted "a blanket grant of discretion untethered by any procedural safeguards." He stated that "[t]he concern that California's suspicionless search system gives officers unbridled discretion to conduct searches, thereby inflicting dignitary harms that arouse strong resentment in parolees and undermine their ability to reintegrate into productive society, is belied by California's prohibition on arbitrary, capricious or harassing searches."

Justice Thomas emphasized that the Court did not "address whether California's parole search condition is justified as a special need," [see the discussion of "special needs" searches later in this Chapter] because "our holding under general Fourth Amendment principles renders such an examination unnecessary."

Justice Stevens, joined by Justices Souter and Breyer, dissented in *Samson.* He noted that the search at issue could not possibly have been justified as a "special needs" search, because it was done for criminal law enforcement purposes. Yet the majority, in Justice Stevens's view, unaccountably found a suspicionless search to be reasonable in this case. Justice Stevens elaborated as follows.

> Ignoring just how closely guarded is that category of constitutionally permissible suspicionless searches, the Court for the first time upholds an entirely suspicionless search unsupported by any special need. And it goes further: In special needs cases we have at least insisted upon programmatic safeguards designed to ensure evenhandedness in application; if individualized suspicion is to be jettisoned, it must be replaced with measures to protect against the state actor's unfettered discretion. Here, by contrast, there are no policies in place—no standards, guidelines, or procedures—to rein in officers and furnish a bulwark against the arbitrary exercise of discretion that is the height of unreasonableness.

### Can the Knights/Samson Balancing Test Be Extended Beyond Probationers and Parolees?

*Knights* and *Samson* could be broadly read to allow searches for evidence on less than probable cause whenever the state interest supporting the search outweighs the individual's interest in preventing it—in other words, a free-form balancing test that would allow any number of searches that would, under traditional Fourth Amendment theory (as applied in *Hicks* and *Dickerson, supra*) require probable cause.

The lower courts had generally read *Knights* and *Samson* narrowly, to searches of probationers and parolees, and even then the courts have required something in the probation/parole conditions that authorize a search on less than probable cause. *See, e.g.,* United States v. Freeman, 479 F.3d 743 (10th Cir. 2007) ("We interpret the *Knights-Samson* line of cases as resting on the parolee's diminished expectation of privacy stemming from his own parole agreement and the state regulations applicable to his case."). But the Supreme Court, in Maryland v. King, 133 S.Ct.1958 (2013), seemed to rely on a *Knights/Samson*-like free-form balancing in upholding DNA testing of arrestees. *King* is set forth in full after the treatment of "special needs" searches, infra.

## C. SEARCH INCIDENT TO ARREST: THE ARREST POWER RULE

A warrantless search incident to a valid arrest was an accepted practice at the time the Bill of Rights was adopted. While the principle was and is well-accepted, the application of the arrest power rule to various fact situations, and even the rationale underlying the exception, have been subject to dispute and inconsistent application in the Supreme Court. In the following case, the Court sought to explain the rationale of the search incident to arrest exception, and to limit the scope of an incident search to the rationale supporting the exception.

### 1. Spatial Limitations

### CHIMEL V. CALIFORNIA
Supreme Court of the United States, 1969.
395 U.S. 752.

**MR. JUSTICE STEWART delivered the opinion of the Court.**

This case raises basic questions concerning the permissible scope under the Fourth Amendment of a search incident to a lawful arrest.

The relevant facts are essentially undisputed. Late in the afternoon of September 13, 1965, three police officers arrived at the Santa Ana, California, home of the petitioner with a warrant authorizing his arrest for the burglary of a coin shop. The officers knocked on the door, identified themselves to the petitioner's wife, and asked if they might come inside. She ushered them into the house, where they waited 10 or 15 minutes until the petitioner returned home from work. When the petitioner entered the house, one of the officers handed him the arrest warrant and asked for permission to "look around." The petitioner objected, but was advised that "on the basis of the lawful arrest," the officers would nonetheless conduct a search. No search warrant had been issued.

Accompanied by the petitioner's wife, the officers then looked through the entire three-bedroom house, including the attic, the garage, and a small workshop. * * * After completing the search, they seized numerous items—primarily coins, but also several medals, tokens, and a few other objects. The entire search took between 45 minutes and an hour.

At the petitioner's subsequent state trial on two charges of burglary, the items taken from his house were admitted into evidence against him, over his objection that they had been unconstitutionally seized. * * *

Without deciding the question, we proceed on the hypothesis that the California courts were correct in holding that the arrest of the petitioner was valid under the Constitution. This brings us directly to the question whether the warrantless search of the petitioner's entire house can be constitutionally justified as incident to that arrest. The decisions of this Court bearing upon that question have been far from consistent, as even the most cursory review makes evident.

\* \* \*

[The Court describes its erratic decisions beginning with dictum in Weeks v. United States, 232 U.S. 383 (1914), and continuing through Harris v. United States, 331 U.S. 145 (1947), Trupiano v. United States, 334 U.S. 699 (1948), and United States v. Rabinowitz, 339 U.S. 56 (1950).]

*Rabinowitz* has come to stand for the proposition, *inter alia,* that a warrantless search "incident to a lawful arrest" may generally extend to the area that is considered to be in the "possession" or under the "control" of the person arrested. And it was on the basis of that proposition that the California courts upheld the search of the petitioner's entire house in this case. That doctrine, however, at least in the broad sense in which it was applied by the California courts in this case, can withstand neither historical nor rational analysis.

\* \* \*

* * * When an arrest is made, it is reasonable for the arresting officer to search the person arrested in order to remove any weapons that the latter might seek to use in order to resist arrest or effect his escape. Otherwise, the officer's safety might well be endangered, and the arrest itself frustrated. In addition, it is entirely reasonable for the arresting officer to search for and seize any evidence on the arrestee's person in order to prevent its concealment or destruction. And the area into which an arrestee might reach in order to grab a weapon or evidentiary items must, of course, be governed by a like rule. A gun on a table or in a drawer in front of one who is arrested can be as dangerous to the arresting officer as one concealed in the clothing of the person arrested.

There is ample justification, therefore, for a search of the arrestee's person and the area "within his immediate control"—construing that phrase to mean the area from within which he might gain possession of a weapon or destructible evidence.

There is no comparable justification, however, for routinely searching any room other than that in which an arrest occurs—or, for that matter, for searching through all the desk drawers or other closed or concealed areas in that room itself. Such searches, in the absence of well-recognized exceptions, may be made only under the authority of a search warrant. The "adherence to judicial processes" mandated by the Fourth Amendment requires no less.

\* \* \*

It is argued in the present case that it is "reasonable" to search a man's house when he is arrested in it. But that argument is founded on little more than a subjective view regarding the acceptability of certain sorts of police conduct, and not on considerations relevant to Fourth Amendment interests. Under such an unconfined analysis, Fourth Amendment protection in this area would approach the evaporation point. It is not easy to explain why, for instance, it is less subjectively "reasonable" to search a man's house when he is arrested on his front lawn—or just down the street—than it is when he happens to be in the house at the time of arrest. \* \* \* Thus, although "[t]he recurring questions of the reasonableness of searches" depend upon "the facts and circumstances—the total atmosphere of the case," those facts and circumstances must be viewed in the light of established Fourth Amendment principles.

It would be possible, of course, to draw a line between *Rabinowitz* and *Harris* on the one hand, and this case on the other. For *Rabinowitz* involved a single room, and *Harris* a four-room apartment, while in the case before us an entire house was searched. But such a distinction would be highly artificial. The rationale that allowed the searches and seizures in *Rabinowitz* and *Harris* would allow the searches and seizures in this case. No consideration relevant to the Fourth Amendment suggests any point of rational limitation, once the search is allowed to go beyond the area from which the person arrested might obtain weapons or evidentiary items. The only reasoned distinction is one between a search of the person arrested and the area within his reach on the one hand, and more extensive searches on the other.

The petitioner correctly points out that one result of decisions such as *Rabinowitz* and *Harris* is to give law enforcement officials the opportunity to engage in searches not justified by probable cause, by the simple expedient of arranging to arrest suspects at home rather than elsewhere. We do not suggest that the petitioner is necessarily correct in his assertion that such a strategy was utilized here, but the fact remains that had he been arrested earlier in the day, at his place of employment rather than at home, no search of his house could have been made without a search warrant. * * *

[The concurring opinion of JUSTICE HARLAN is omitted.]

**MR. JUSTICE WHITE, with whom MR. JUSTICE BLACK joins, dissenting.**

* * *

The justifications which make such a search reasonable obviously do not apply to the search of areas to which the accused does not have ready physical access. This is not enough, however, to prove such searches unconstitutional. The Court has always held, and does not today deny, that when there is probable cause to search and it is "impracticable" for one reason or another to get a search warrant, then a warrantless search may be reasonable. This is the case whether an arrest was made at the time of the search or not.

This is not to say that a search can be reasonable without regard to the probable cause to believe that seizable items are on the premises. But when there are exigent circumstances, and probable cause, then the search may be made without a warrant, reasonably. An arrest itself may often create an emergency situation making it impracticable to obtain a warrant before embarking on a related search. Again assuming that there is probable cause to search premises at the spot where a suspect is arrested, it seems to me unreasonable to require the police to leave the scene in order to obtain a search warrant when they are already legally there to make a valid arrest, and when there must almost always be a strong possibility that confederates of the arrested man will in the meanwhile remove the items for which the police have probable cause to search. This must so often be the case that it seems to me as unreasonable to require a warrant for a search of the premises as to require a warrant for search of the person and his very immediate surroundings.

* * *

### Application of Chimel's Case-by-Case Approach to the Permissible Scope of a Search Incident to Arrest

What are the precise spatial limitations on the arrest power rule after *Chimel*? Is the permissible scope of the search determined by where the suspect was arrested, or by where the search occurred? Does it make a difference that the suspect is handcuffed? Infirm? Consider United States v. Lucas, 898 F.2d 606 (8th Cir.1990), where the defendant was convicted of bank robbery based in part upon evidence found in the following search incident to arrest:

> The magistrate found that Lucas was seated at a kitchen table with two other men as the officers stood in the front doorway of the apartment in which he was arrested. As Lucas began to get up from the table, the officers entered the apartment and ran into the kitchen. Two officers attempted to apprehend Lucas, and one officer monitored the other two men seated at the table. By the time the officers reached Lucas, his hand was within inches of the handle on a cabinet door. During the ensuing struggle, which lasted for approximately forty seconds, Lucas and the two officers slid around on the slick floor. At one point, Lucas fell to the floor, and the skirmish continued until Lucas was handcuffed. As an officer pulled Lucas from the floor and moved him toward the living room, another officer immediately stood up, opened the cabinet door that Lucas had been attempting to reach, and found a chrome automatic pistol inside the cabinet. The two men seated at the kitchen table were not handcuffed until after the gun was discovered.

The court upheld the search under *Chimel:*

> Lucas argues that *Chimel* does not justify the search here because he was being escorted, handcuffed, from the kitchen when the search occurred. While relevant under *Chimel,* this is not a determinative factor. * * * [A] warrantless search incident to an arrest may be valid even though a court, operating with the benefit of hindsight in an environment well removed from the scene of the arrest, doubts that the defendant could have reached the items seized during the search. The officers in this case searched a cabinet in a small kitchen immediately after handcuffing Lucas and while removing him from the kitchen. Moreover, two of Lucas' friends who had not been handcuffed were still at the kitchen table when the search took place. On these facts, we conclude that this was a valid warrantless search incident to Lucas' arrest. This conclusion is consistent not only with [this Circuit's opinions] but also with opinions from other circuits. See United States v. Queen, 847 F.2d at 352–54 (holding search valid even though it occurred when arrestee was handcuffed and guarded by two police officers several feet from the searched area).

Does the court in *Lucas* show too much or just enough concern for the safety of the officers? Compare United States v. Blue, 78 F.3d 56 (2d Cir.1996) (search of an area between a mattress and a box spring could not be justified under the arrest power rule; the suspects were on the floor, handcuffed with their hands behind their backs, and many officers were controlling them); United States v. Neely, 345 F.3d 366 (5th Cir.

2003) (officers could not seize the clothing of a suspect who was brought to the hospital and was in surgery: "there are no indications that he could have attempted to destroy the clothing" at the time of the seizure).

In United States v. Currence, 446 F.3d 554 (4th Cir. 2006), the defendant was arrested while on his bicycle. He was suspected of dealing drugs. Officers searched the inside of the handlebars of the bike and found cocaine. The court upheld that search under *Chimel*:

> We believe that because [the officer] was able to remove the handlebar end cap by simply sliding it off * * * there is no basis under *Chimel* to treat the handlebar differently from other items within the immediate control of an arrestee that may be opened in a search incident to an arrest. Just as an arrestee's ability to reach into, for example, a closed container or a locked bag makes those items searchable incident to an arrest, Currence's ability to reach into the easily accessible handlebar likewise makes it searchable.

The court did note, however, that "there are limits to the scope of a search incident to arrest" and that its opinion "should not be construed as a holding that all areas of a bicycle can automatically be searched in every case." So what areas on a bike could not be searched incident to arrest?

### Timing of Grab Area Determination

Should the scope of the grab area be determined by where the arrestee is at the time of the *search*, or rather by where the arrestee *was* at the time of *arrest*? In Davis v. Robbs, 794 F.2d 1129 (6th Cir.1986), the court upheld the seizure of a rifle that had been in close proximity to the arrestee at the time of the arrest. Judge Wellford dissented on this point, noting that the search and seizure occurred after the arrestee was put in the squad car:

> The rationale justifying the search incident to arrest exception is that some exigency exists at the time of the search or seizure, not arrest. Otherwise, no actual exigency, such as danger to the safety of the police or others, would exist. The actual exigency at the time of arrest would become fictional through transplantation to the time of the search and seizure. At the time the police seized the rifle in the present case, [the arrestee] was handcuffed and in the squad car. He no longer had access to the gun nor posed any danger to the police. * * * Thus, the rationale justifying the exception does not support the seizure of the rifle. The danger had passed.

The court in United States v. Abdul-Saboor, 85 F.3d 664 (D.C.Cir.1996) agreed with the majority in *Davis* that the grab area should be determined as of the time of the arrest, not the time of the search. Thus, an officer's search of an area after the arrestee had been taken out of the room was permissible. The court reasoned that "if the courts were to focus exclusively upon the moment of the search, we might create a perverse incentive for an arresting officer to prolong the period during which the arrestee is kept in an area where he could pose a danger to the officer." Do you think this is a realistic possibility?

Since the above cases were decided, the Supreme Court in Arizona v. Gant—discussed infra—held that when a person in a *car* is arrested, the grab area is to be determined as of the time of the *search*—so if at the time of the search the arrestee has been placed in the squad car, the passenger compartment of his vehicle is no longer within the grab area. Some courts have relied on *Gant* to hold that when a person is arrested outside the car context, the grab area must be determined as of the time of the search, not what it was at the time the person was arrested. An example is United States v. Shakir, 616 F.3d 315 (3rd Cir. 2010). Shakir challenged the search of a bag that he was carrying when arrested. He argued that at the time of the search of the bag, he was already handcuffed. The government responded by citing several circuit court decisions that assessed the grab area as of the time of the arrest; the defendant conceded that he had access to the bag at the time he was arrested. The court rejected the government's argument that the *Gant* time of search rule applied only to vehicle searches. It found "no plausible reason" to limit *Gant* to vehicle searches, as opposed to "any situation where the item searched is removed from the suspect's control between the time of the arrest and the time of the search." The court read *Gant* as "refocusing our attention on a suspect's ability (or inability) to access weapons or destroy evidence at the time a search incident to arrest is conducted."

It is notable, though, that the *Shakir* court upheld the search of the defendant's bag under the arrest-power rule. Even as assessed at the time of the search, the search of the bag was reasonably directed to protecting against destruction of evidence and harm to police officers. The court stated that handcuffs are "not fail-safe" and reasoned as follows:

> Although he was handcuffed and guarded by two policemen, Shakir's bag was literally at his feet, so it was accessible if he had dropped to the floor. Although it would have been more difficult for Shakir to open the bag and retrieve a weapon while handcuffed, we do not regard this possibility as remote enough to render unconstitutional the search incident to arrest. This is especially true when we consider that Shakir was subject to an arrest warrant for armed bank robbery, and that he was arrested in a public area near some 20 innocent bystanders, as well as at least one suspected confederate who was guarded only by unarmed hotel security officers.

## Arrest Power Can Be Invoked for Any Custodial Arrest and Can Cover Post-Arrest Movements: Washington v. Chrisman

Does the rationale of *Chimel,* allowing search incident to arrest to protect the officer and preserve the evidence, apply to every arrest? Does it apply even if the arrestee is allowed to move about? In Washington v. Chrisman, 455 U.S. 1 (1982), Chief Justice Burger, writing for the Court, declared that "the absence of an affirmative indication that an arrested person might have a weapon available or might attempt to escape does not diminish the arresting officer's authority to maintain custody over the arrested person" and to conduct an automatic search for evidence and weapons within the grab area. The Court stated that "every arrest must be presumed to present a risk of danger to the arresting officer," because "there is no way for an officer to predict reliably how a particular subject will react to arrest of the degree of potential danger."

The Court in *Chrisman* upheld a search and seizure incident to arrest under the following circumstances: A police officer saw Chrisman, who appeared to be underage, carrying liquor. He asked for identification and Chrisman said it was in his dormitory room. At that point he was placed under arrest and the officer accompanied him to the dorm room to retrieve the identification. As Chrisman entered the room the officer remained in the open doorway, from where he saw Chrisman's roommate become nervous. The officer entered the room and noticed seeds and a small pipe that he concluded were used in marijuana smoking. After warning both roommates of their rights, the officer asked about other drugs and was given additional marijuana. The officer subsequently obtained consent to search the room and found LSD.

Chief Justice Burger reasoned that once the officer placed his suspect under arrest before returning to the suspect's room "[t]he officer had a right to remain literally at the suspect's elbow at all times." This was so even though the officer admitted that he did not think that Chrisman was going up to the room to destroy evidence or get a weapon. The Chief Justice concluded that because the officer had a valid right to enter the room at any time to monitor the movements of the arrested person, he had a right to be where he was when he first saw the seeds and the pipe.

Justice White, joined by Justices Brennan and Marshall, dissented. The thrust of the dissent was that an officer "should not be permitted to invade living quarters any more than is necessary to maintain control and protect himself," which were not the reasons for the invasion in this case.[21]

---

[21] Although the Supreme Court reversed the Washington Supreme Court in *Chrisman,* it was the state supreme court that was to have the last word. On remand, it held that the officer violated the state constitution, which it interpreted to prohibit warrantless entry into a private

## Arrest Leading to Exigent Circumstances

Justice White, dissenting in *Chimel,* argues that when a person is arrested, the fact of the arrest itself will in almost all cases give rise to exigent circumstances to search beyond the grab area of the arrestee. He reasoned that friends, family or business associates of the arrestee will almost always become aware of an arrest and will almost always try to destroy evidence (or police officers) when they learn about the arrest. Justice White does not contend that exigent circumstances will arise after *every* arrest, nor could he: if Chimel was a hermit, there could be no threat that upon his arrest one of his associates would immediately destroy evidence or raise a weapon. Rather, Justice White argues that exigent circumstances will arise *so often* upon an arrest that it makes sense to establish a bright line rule permitting a search, so as to avoid the negative effects of ad hoc judgments by officers on the one hand and the costs of a case-by-case approach by the courts on the other.

Why did Justice White's argument for a bright-line rule not persuade the majority? If, as *Chrisman* states, we presume that the arrestee will destroy evidence or harm the officer even if that is not so in a particular case, why do we not presume that the arrestee's *associates* will learn about the arrest and destroy evidence or harm the officer?

The exigent circumstances exception will be discussed later in this Chapter, but for now it is important to note that the Court requires a showing of exigency on the particular facts of the case; the arrest of a person, while certainly relevant, is not dispositive of whether there is a risk of destruction of evidence or harm to the officers or public that would excuse the warrant requirement. Illustrative is Vale v. Louisiana, 399 U.S. 30 (1970). Officers observing Vale had probable cause to believe that he had engaged in a drug transaction outside his house. When they approached, Vale walked quickly toward the house. He was arrested on his front steps. The officers then searched the house and found narcotics in the back bedroom. Three minutes after the officers entered the house, Vale's mother and brother came home carrying groceries. Justice Stewart wrote for the Court as it held that the officers' warrantless search of the bedroom violated the Fourth Amendment. The Court found that the State had not met its burden of showing that exigent circumstances existed. Justice Stewart stated that "the goods ultimately seized were not in the process of destruction," and rejected the argument that "an arrest on the street can provide its own exigent circumstance so as to justify a warrantless search of the arrestee's house."[22]

---

dwelling by an officer unless he has specific articulable facts justifying the entry. State v. Chrisman, 100 Wash.2d 814, 676 P.2d 419 (1984).

[22] Justice Blackmun did not take part. Justice Black, joined by Chief Justice Burger, dissented. He concluded that the State's burden of showing exigent circumstances was met.

Notwithstanding *Vale,* in many cases an arrest *will* create exigent circumstances due to the risk that the arrestee's friends, family, or criminal associates will destroy evidence or use weapons. In United States v. Socey, 846 F.2d 1439 (D.C.Cir.1988), the court set forth the following standard for determining whether exigent circumstances arise after an arrest:

> Consistent with *Vale,* we believe that a police officer can show an objectively reasonable belief that contraband is being, or will be, destroyed within a home if he can show 1) a reasonable belief that third persons were inside a private dwelling and 2) a reasonable belief that these third persons are aware of an * * * arrest of a confederate outside the premises so that they might see a need to destroy evidence.

The court in *Socey* found that exigent circumstances existed where an arrest was made outside a house in which a large-scale drug operation was being conducted. The court stated that it was not unreasonable for the officers to believe "that such an operation would have some type of look-out system." The court also emphasized the fact that drugs are easily destroyed. Has the court in *Socey* applied a per se rule of exigent circumstances for arrests outside suspected drug operations? Is that consistent with *Chimel* and *Vale?*

### Protective Sweep After an Arrest

Even in the absence of exigent circumstances, police may have the authority, pursuant to the *Terry* doctrine, to search beyond the *Chimel* spatial limitations in order to conduct a "protective sweep" of the place where the arrest is made. In Maryland v. Buie, 494 U.S. 325 (1990), the Court defined a "protective sweep" as a "quick and limited search of a premises, incident to an arrest and conducted to protect the safety of police officers or others." The Court held that a protective sweep could be justified by reasonable suspicion "that the area swept harbored an individual posing a danger to the officer or others." Probable cause was not necessary for such a sweep. Justice White, writing for the Court, concluded that the spatial limitations of *Chimel* were not undermined by allowing a protective sweep on reasonable suspicion. Unlike a search incident to arrest, the protective sweep is limited to areas where persons may be hidden. Nor does the officer have an automatic right to conduct a protective sweep (unlike the automatic right to conduct a search incident to arrest). Justice Stevens concurred to emphasize that a protective sweep could not be conducted to root out those who might destroy evidence but who would not present a safety risk to the officers or others. That is, the protective sweep is a safety-based and not an evidence-based doctrine. Justice Brennan, joined by Justice Marshall dissented.

## 2. Temporal Limitations

### *Sequence of Search and Arrest*

Generally, a search incident to arrest takes place immediately after the arrest itself. But courts will not overly concern themselves with the technicality of which came first—the arrest or the search—when both are nearly simultaneous and probable cause to arrest existed before the search was conducted. As the Court stated in Rawlings v. Kentucky, 448 U.S. 98 (1980): "Where the formal arrest followed quickly on the heels of the challenged search of petitioner's person, we do not believe it particularly important that the search preceded the arrest rather than vice versa." See also United States v. Cutchin, 956 F.2d 1216 (D.C.Cir.1992) ("The sequence makes no difference since police did not need the fruits of the search to establish probable cause.").

While a search can precede the arrest, a search cannot be used to provide the probable cause necessary to make the arrest. As the Court stated in the per curiam opinion in Smith v. Ohio, 494 U.S. 541 (1990): "That reasoning, * * * justifying the arrest by the search and at the same time * * * the search by the arrest, just will not do."

### *Removal from the Arrest Scene*

The term "incident to" implies that if the search is too far removed from the arrest, it will not qualify for the exception. But how removed is too removed? In Chambers v. Maroney, 399 U.S. 42 (1970), officers searched an automobile that had been impounded and brought to the police station after the arrest of its occupants. The Court held that this search could not be justified as incident to the arrests, stating that "once an accused is under arrest and in custody, then a search made at another place, without a warrant, is simply not incident to the arrest." The Court concluded that the reasons for a search incident to arrest "no longer obtain when the accused is safely in custody at the station house." The Court applied the same principle in United States v. Chadwick, 433 U.S. 1 (1977), where a footlocker was searched at the police station, 90 minutes after the arrest of its owner. The Court stated that the search "cannot be viewed as incidental to the arrest or as justified by any other exigency."

In United States v. Edwards, 415 U.S. 800 (1974), the Court held that a suspect, who was arrested and jailed around midnight for attempting to break into a post office, could be searched incident to arrest the next morning. After the arrest, the police discovered that entry into the post office apparently involved prying open a window with an iron bar that caused paint to chip. They seized Edwards's shirt and trousers in the morning and subjected them to analysis that revealed paint chips. Justice

White, writing for the majority, declared that "searches and seizures that could be made on the spot at the time of arrest may legally be conducted later when the accused arrives at the place of detention." He went on to conclude "that the normal processes incident to arrest and custody had not yet been completed when Edwards was placed in his cell." Justice White left open the possibility that a warrant might be required for some post-seizure searches of arrestees, but strongly implied that most searches and seizures of the arrestee's person and things in his possession at the time of the arrest could be examined automatically. Justice Stewart, joined by Justices Douglas, Brennan and Marshall dissented, taking the view that "the considerations that typically justify a warrantless search incident to a lawful arrest were wholly absent here." See also United States v. Johnson, 445 F.3d 793 (5th Cir. 2006) (testing the defendant's hands for gunpowder residue at the police station was a permissible search incident to the arrest: noting that the defendant, or time, could have removed or destroyed the evidence).

*Edwards* was cited by Justice Blackmun in dissent in *Chadwick*. Is there any way to reconcile the two cases? Do they take a different view of what is incident to arrest, or do they merely deal with different types of searches? The next case may have some bearing on this question.

### 3. Searches of the Person—and Containers on the Person— Incident to Arrest

### UNITED STATES V. ROBINSON
Supreme Court of the United States, 1973.
414 U.S. 218.

**MR. JUSTICE REHNQUIST delivered the opinion of the Court.**

Respondent Robinson was convicted in United States District Court for the District of Columbia of the possession and facilitation of concealment of heroin * * *. [T]he Court of Appeals en banc reversed the judgment of conviction, holding that the heroin introduced in evidence against respondent had been obtained as a result of a search which violated the Fourth Amendment to the United States Constitution. * * *

On April 23, 1968, at approximately 11 p.m., Officer Richard Jenks, a 15-year veteran of the District of Columbia Metropolitan Police Department, observed the respondent driving a 1965 Cadillac near the intersection of 8th and C Streets, N.E., in the District of Columbia. Jenks, as a result of previous investigation following a check of respondent's operator's permit four days earlier, determined there was reason to believe that respondent was operating a motor vehicle after the revocation of his operator's permit. This is an offense defined by statute in the District of Columbia which carries a mandatory minimum jail term, a mandatory minimum fine, or both.

Jenks signaled respondent to stop the automobile, which respondent did, and all three of the occupants emerged from the car. At that point Jenks informed respondent that he was under arrest for "operating after revocation and obtaining a permit by misrepresentation." It was assumed by the Court of Appeals, and is conceded by the respondent here, that Jenks had probable cause to arrest respondent, and that he effected a full-custody arrest.

In accordance with procedures prescribed in police department instructions, Jenks then began to search respondent. * * * During this patdown, Jenks felt an object in the left breast pocket of the heavy coat respondent was wearing, but testified that he "couldn't tell what it was" and also that he "couldn't actually tell the size of it." Jenks then reached into the pocket and pulled out the object, which turned out to be a "crumpled up cigarette package." Jenks testified that at this point he still did not know what was in the package. * * *

The officer then opened the cigarette pack and found 14 gelatin capsules of white powder which he thought to be, and which later analysis proved to be, heroin. Jenks then continued his search of respondent to completion, feeling around his waist and trouser legs, and examining the remaining pockets. The heroin seized from the respondent was admitted into evidence at the trial which resulted in his conviction in the District Court.

* * * We conclude that the search conducted by Jenks in this case did not offend the limits imposed by the Fourth Amendment, and we therefore reverse the judgment of the Court of Appeals.

* * *

It is well settled that a search incident to a lawful arrest is a traditional exception to the warrant requirement of the Fourth Amendment. This general exception has historically been formulated into two distinct propositions. The first is that a search may be made of the *person* of the arrestee by virtue of the lawful arrest. The second is that a search may be made of the area within the control of the arrestee.

Examination of this Court's decisions shows that these two propositions have been treated quite differently. The validity of the search of a person incident to a lawful arrest has been regarded as settled from its first enunciation, and has remained virtually unchallenged until the present case. The validity of the second proposition, while likewise conceded in principle, has been subject to differing interpretations as to the extent of the area which may be searched. * * *

\* \* \*

Throughout the series of cases in which the Court has addressed the second proposition relating to a search incident to a lawful arrest—the permissible area beyond the person of the arrestee which such a search may cover—no doubt has been expressed as to the unqualified authority of the arresting authority to search the person of the arrestee.

\* \* \* Since the statements in the cases speak not simply in terms of an exception to the warrant requirement, but in terms of an affirmative authority to search, they clearly imply that such searches also meet the Fourth Amendment's requirement of reasonableness.

\* \* \*

In its decision of this case, the Court of Appeals decided that even after a police officer lawfully places a suspect under arrest for the purpose of taking him into custody, he may not ordinarily proceed to fully search the prisoner. He must, instead, conduct a limited frisk of the outer clothing and remove such weapons that he may, as a result of that limited frisk, reasonably believe and ascertain that the suspect has in his possession. While recognizing that Terry v. Ohio dealt with a permissible "frisk" incident to an investigative stop based on less than probable cause to arrest, the Court of Appeals felt that the principles of that case should be carried over to this probable-cause arrest for driving while one's license is revoked. Since there would be no further evidence of such a crime to be obtained in a search of the arrestee, the court held that only a search for weapons could be justified.

\* \* \*

The justification or reason for the authority to search incident to a lawful arrest rests quite as much on the need to disarm the suspect in order to take him into custody as it does on the need to preserve evidence on his person for later use at trial. The standards traditionally governing a search incident to lawful arrest are not, therefore, commuted to the stricter *Terry* standards by the absence of probable fruits or further evidence of the particular crime for which the arrest is made.

Nor are we inclined, on the basis of what seems to us to be a rather speculative judgment, to qualify the breadth of the general authority to search incident to a lawful custodial arrest on an assumption that persons arrested for the offense of driving while their licenses have been revoked are less likely to possess dangerous weapons than are those arrested for other crimes. It is scarcely open to doubt that the danger to an officer is far greater in the case of the extended exposure which follows the taking of a suspect into custody and transporting him to the police station than in the case of the relatively fleeting contact resulting from the typical *Terry*-type stop. This is an adequate basis for treating all custodial arrests alike for purposes of search justification.

But quite apart from these distinctions, our more fundamental disagreement with the Court of Appeals arises from its suggestion that there must be litigated in each case the issue of whether or not there was present one of the reasons supporting the authority for a search of the person incident to a lawful arrest. * * * A police officer's determination as to how and where to search the person of a suspect whom he has arrested is necessarily a quick *ad hoc* judgment which the Fourth Amendment does not require to be broken down in each instance into an analysis of each step in the search. The authority to search the person incident to a lawful custodial arrest, while based upon the need to disarm and to discover evidence, does not depend on what a court may later decide was the probability in a particular arrest situation that weapons or evidence would in fact be found upon the person of the suspect. A custodial arrest of a suspect based on probable cause is a reasonable intrusion under the Fourth Amendment; that intrusion being lawful, a search incident to the arrest requires no additional justification. It is the fact of the lawful arrest which establishes the authority to search, and we hold that in the case of a lawful custodial arrest a full search of the person is not only an exception to the warrant requirement of the Fourth Amendment, but is also a "reasonable" search under that Amendment.

* * *

MR. JUSTICE POWELL, concurring.

* * *

* * * I believe that an individual lawfully subjected to a custodial arrest retains no significant Fourth Amendment interest in the privacy of his person. Under this view the custodial arrest is the significant intrusion of state power into the privacy of one's person. If the arrest is lawful, the privacy interest guarded by the Fourth Amendment is subordinated to a legitimate and overriding governmental concern. * * *

MR. JUSTICE MARSHALL, with whom MR. JUSTICE DOUGLAS and MR. JUSTICE BRENNAN join, dissenting.

* * *

The majority opinion fails to recognize that the search conducted by Officer Jenks did not merely involve a search of respondent's person. It also included a separate search of effects found on his person. And even were we to assume, *arguendo,* that it was reasonable for Jenks to remove the object he felt in respondent's pocket, clearly there was no justification consistent with the Fourth Amendment which would authorize his opening the package and looking inside.

To begin with, after Jenks had the cigarette package in his hands, there is no indication that he had reason to believe or did in fact believe that the package contained a weapon. More importantly, even if the crumpled-up cigarette package had in fact contained some sort of small weapon, it would have been impossible for respondent to have used it once the package was in the officer's hands. Opening the package, therefore, did not further the protective purpose of the search. * * *

\* \* \*

The Government argues that it is difficult to see what constitutionally protected "expectation of privacy" a prisoner has in the interior of a cigarette pack. One wonders if the result in this case would have been the same were respondent a businessman who was lawfully taken into custody for driving without a license and whose wallet was taken from him by the police. Would it be reasonable for the police officer, because of the possibility that a razor blade was hidden somewhere in the wallet, to open it, remove all the contents, and examine each item carefully? * * * Would it not be more consonant with the purpose of the Fourth Amendment and the legitimate needs of the police to require the officer, if he has any question whatsoever about what the wallet or letter contains, to hold on to it until the arrestee is brought to the precinct station?[a]

### Searches of Smartphones and Other Electronics Found on an Arrestee

*Robinson* held that the officer could thoroughly search the cigarette pack even without any showing on the facts that there was evidence or a weapon in that container. Thus under *Robinson* there would appear to be an automatic right to search any container found on a person subject to a custodial arrest. But maybe some containers are different than others. What if the officer effectuating a custodial arrest for a traffic offense, as in *Robinson,* finds a smartphone in the arrestee's suit pocket? Can the

---

[a]  Nor would it necessarily have been reasonable for the police to have opened the cigarette package at the police station. The Government argued below, as an alternative theory to justify the search in this case, that when a suspect is booked and is about to be placed in station house detention, it is reasonable to search his person to prevent the introduction of weapons or contraband into the jail facility and to inventory the personal effects found on the suspect. Since respondent's cigarette package would have been removed and opened at the station house anyway, the argument goes, the search might just as well take place in the field at the time of the arrest. This argument fails * * *. [A]s the Court of Appeals had indicated in its opinion in United States v. Mills, 472 F.2d 1231 (1972) (en banc), the justification for station-house searches is not the booking process itself, but rather the fact that the suspect will be placed in jail. In the District of Columbia, petty offenses of the sort involved in the present case are bailable, and, as the Government stipulated in *Mills,* the normal procedure is for offenders to be advised of the opportunity to post collateral at the station house and to avoid an inventory search unless they are unable or refuse to do so. One cannot justify a full search in the field on a subsequent event that quite possibly may never take place.

officer open the phone, use the apps, check the arrestee's email, and so forth?

Judge Posner, in United States v. Flores-Lopez, 670 F.3d 803 (7th Cir. 2012), reviewed the constitutionality of a search of a cellphone incident to arrest. Flores-Lopez was arrested for drug violations, and an officer searched a cell phone on his person. The scope of the search was pretty limited. The officer searched the cellphone for its number, then used that information to subpoena the phone company for the call history of the phone. The call history indicated many calls were made between the defendant and other drug dealers.

Judge Posner noted that a cellphone fit the definition of a container, i.e., an object that contains something else. He also noted that under a "fair literal" reading of *Robinson,* any container found on a person who is arrested may be searched incident to that arrest. But Judge Posner thought that there might be some limitations on the *Robinson* rule, because "the Court did not reject the possibility of categorical limits to the rule laid down" in that case. Judge Posner proceeded as follows:

> The potential invasion of privacy in a search of a cell phone is greater than in a search of a "container" in a conventional sense even when the conventional container is a purse that contains an address book (itself a container) and photos. Judges are becoming aware that a computer (and remember that a modern cell phone is a computer) is not just another purse or address book. "[A]nalogizing computers to other physical objects when applying Fourth Amendment law is not an exact fit because computers hold so much personal and sensitive information touching on many private aspects of life. . . . [T]here is a far greater potential for the 'inter-mingling' of documents and a consequent invasion of privacy when police execute a search for evidence on a computer." United States v. Lucas, 640 F.3d 168, 178 (6th Cir.2011). An iPhone application called iCam allows you to access your home computer's webcam so that you can survey the inside of your home while you're a thousand miles away. At the touch of a button a cell phone search becomes a house search, and that is not a search of a "container" in any normal sense of that word, though a house contains data.

Judge Posner noted the limited nature of the search of the cellphone in this case, and analogized it to searches of diaries found on arrestees that have been upheld under *Robinson.*

> [O]pening the diary found on the suspect whom the police have arrested, to verify his name and address and discover whether the diary contains information relevant to the crime for which he has been arrested, clearly is permissible; and what happened in this case was similar but even less intrusive, since a cell phone's phone

number can be found without searching the phone's contents, unless the phone is password-protected—and on some cell phones even if it is. On an iPhone without password protection two steps are required to get the number: touching the "settings" icon and then the "phone" icon. On a Blackberry only one step is required: touching the "phone" icon. Moreover, the phone company knows a phone's number as soon as the call is connected to the telephone network; and obtaining that information from the phone company isn't a search because by subscribing to the telephone service the user of the phone is deemed to surrender any privacy interest he may have had in his phone number. Smith v. Maryland, 442 U.S. 735(1979).

We are quite a distance from the use of the iCam to view what is happening in the bedroom of the owner of the seized cell phone.

It's not even clear that we need a rule of law specific to cell phones or other computers. If police are entitled to open a pocket diary to copy the owner's address, they should be entitled to turn on a cell phone to learn its number. If allowed to leaf through a pocket address book, as they are, United States v. Rodriguez, 995 F.2d 776, 778 (7th Cir.1993), they should be entitled to read the address book in a cell phone. If forbidden to peruse love letters recognized as such found wedged between the pages of the address book, they should be forbidden to read love letters in the files of a cell phone. * * *

Judge Posner also noted that cellphone searches, unlike diaries, might involve the possibility of exigent circumstances, especially in cases involving drug conspiracies:

[A]ssume that justification is required for police who have no warrant to look inside a cell phone even if all they're looking for and all they find is the phone number. The government emphasizes the danger of "remote wiping." Instant wiping, called "local wiping," as by pressing a button on the cell phone that wipes its contents and at the same time sends an emergency alert to a person previously specified, was not a danger in this case once the officers seized the cell phone. But remote-wiping capability is available on all major cell-phone platforms; if the phone's manufacturer doesn't offer it, it can be bought from a mobile-security company. Wiped data may be recoverable in a laboratory, but that involves delay.

According to Apple, a person with a "jailbroken" iPhone (that is, a "self-hacked" iPhone, modified by its owner to enlarge its functionality or run unauthorized applications) could enable anonymous phone calls to be made, a capability that Apple claims "would be desirable to drug dealers." David Kravets, "iPhone Jail-breaking Could Crash Cellphone Towers, Apple Claims," Wired, July 28, 2009, www.wired.com/threatlevel/2009/07/jailbreak/. Apple would like the "jailbreaking" of its phones made illegal, so it is not a disinterested commentator on the use of its phones by those dealers.

Other conspirators were involved in the distribution of methamphetamine besides * * * the defendant, and conceivably could have learned of the arrests (they might even have been monitoring the transaction with the informant in the garage from afar) and wiped the cell phones remotely before the government could obtain and execute a warrant and conduct a search pursuant to it for the cell phone's number; and conceivably the defendant might have had time to warn them before the cell phone was taken from him, giving them time to wipe it. "Conceivably" is not "probably"; but set off against the modest benefit to law enforcement of being able to obtain the cell phone's phone number immediately was only a modest cost in invasion of privacy. Armed with that number the officers could obtain the call history at their leisure, and the defendant does not deny that if the number was lawfully obtained the subpoenaing of the call history from the phone company was also lawful and the history thus obtained could therefore properly be used in evidence against him.

The defendant argues that the officers could have eliminated any possibility of remote wiping just by turning off the cell phone. Without power a cell phone won't be connected to the phone network and so remote wiping will be impossible. But a "roving bug" installed in the phone could record everything that the phone's microphone could pick up even though the phone was turned off (because "turning off" a cell phone often just means a reduction in power—a kind of electronic hibernation). * * * And if the phone is either turned off or powered down to a level at which it appears to be turned off, the police can't obtain information from it, even its phone number, knowledge of which as we said is minimally invasive of privacy. * * *

Judge Posner ultimately concluded that the limited search of the cellphone was reasonable under *Robinson*, and left for another day whether *Robinson* also validates more extensive searches of data on cellphones incident to arrest. He concluded as follows:

We need not consider what level of risk to personal safety or to the preservation of evidence would be necessary to justify a more extensive search of a cell phone without a warrant, especially when we factor in the burden on the police of having to traipse about with * * * mirror-copying technology and having to be instructed in the use of these methods for preventing remote wiping or rendering it ineffectual. We can certainly imagine justifications for a more extensive search. The arrested suspect might have prearranged with coconspirators to call them periodically and if they didn't hear from him on schedule to take that as a warning that he had been seized, and to scatter. Or if conspirators buy prepaid SIM (subscriber identity module) cards, each of which assigns a different phone number to the cell phone in which the card is inserted, and replace the SIM card each day, a police officer who seizes one of the cell phones will have only a short interval within which to discover the phone numbers of the other conspirators. * * * The officer who doesn't make a quick search of the cell phone won't find other conspirators' phone numbers that are still in use.

But these are questions for another day, since the police did not search the contents of the defendant's cell phone, but were content to obtain the cell phone's phone number.

Wouldn't it be easier to treat cellphones the same as any other container of information? Does *Robinson* really invite *any* limitation to its apparent rule that a search of a container found upon an arrestee is automatically reasonable under the arrest power rule? It is true that *Robinson* involved a cigarette pack, and at the time of that case people couldn't be carrying a computer or smartphone on their person. But would that have made a difference to the *Robinson* Court, which appeared to be concerned only with providing bright line rules for police to use? See People v. Diaz, 51 Cal.4th 84, 244 P.3d 501 (2011) (search of cellphone incident to arrest upheld because a cellphone is a container and *Robinson* authorizes all searches of containers found on the person of the arrestee).

For a view different from that of Judge Posner, based on the fact that cellphones and smartphones—unlike the cigarette pack in *Robinson*—can contain so much private information,  see United States v. Wurie, 728 F.3d 1 (1st Cir. 2013) ("the search incident to arrest exception does not authorize the warrantless search of data on a cellphone seized from an arrestee's person, because the government has not convinced us that such a search is ever necessary to protect arresting officers or preserve destructible evidence."). At the time of publication of this casebook, the Court has scheduled *Wurie* for oral argument.

### *Custodial Arrests for Minor Offenses*

The Court in *Robinson* was not called upon to address whether Robinson's custodial arrest was reasonable under the Fourth Amendment. Robinson challenged only the search and not the validity of the arrest for a traffic offense. But why is it reasonable to impose the serious intrusion of a custodial arrest upon a person who has done nothing more than commit a minor traffic offense? Note that one possible limitation on the broad search rights given to police under *Robinson* would be to hold that certain violations are so minimal that they do not justify a custodial arrest. But this option was rejected by the Supreme Court in the following case.

## ATWATER V. CITY OF LAGO VISTA

United States Supreme Court, 2001.
532 U.S. 318.

### JUSTICE SOUTER delivered the opinion of the Court.

The question is whether the Fourth Amendment forbids a warrantless arrest for a minor criminal offense, such as a misdemeanor seatbelt violation punishable only by a fine. We hold that it does not.

* * * In Texas, if a car is equipped with safety belts, a front-seat passenger must wear one, and the driver must secure any small child riding in front. Violation of either provision is a misdemeanor punishable by a fine not less than $25 or more than $50. Texas law expressly authorizes "[a]ny peace officer [to] arrest without warrant a person found committing a violation" of these seatbelt laws, although it permits police to issue citations in lieu of arrest.

In March 1997, Petitioner Gail Atwater was driving her pickup truck in Lago Vista, Texas, with her 3-year-old son and 5-year-old daughter in the front seat. None of them was wearing a seatbelt. Respondent Bart Turek, a Lago Vista police officer at the time, observed the seatbelt violations and pulled Atwater over. According to Atwater's complaint (the allegations of which we assume to be true for present purposes), Turek approached the truck and "yelled" something to the effect of "we've met before" and "you're going to jail." [Turek had previously stopped Atwater for what he had thought was a seatbelt violation, but then had realized that Atwater's son, although seated on the vehicle's armrest, was in fact belted in. Atwater acknowledged that her son's seating position was unsafe, and Turek had issued a verbal warning.] He then called for backup and asked to see Atwater's driver's license and insurance documentation, which state law required her to carry. When Atwater told Turek that she did not have the papers because her purse had been stolen the day before, Turek said that he had "heard that story two-hundred times." Atwater asked to take her "frightened, upset, and crying" children to a friend's house nearby, but Turek told her, "you're not going anywhere." As it turned out, Atwater's friend learned what was going on and soon arrived to take charge of the children. Turek then handcuffed Atwater, placed her in his squad car, and drove her to the local police station, where booking officers had her remove her shoes, jewelry, and eyeglasses, and empty her pockets. Officers took Atwater's "mug shot" and placed her, alone, in a jail cell for about one hour, after which she was taken before a magistrate and released on $310 bond. Atwater was charged with driving without her seatbelt fastened, failing to secure her children in seatbelts, driving without a license, and failing to provide proof of insurance. She ultimately pleaded no contest to the misdemeanor seatbelt offenses and paid a $50 fine; the other charges were dismissed.

* * * Atwater and her husband * * * filed suit * * * under 42 U.S.C. § 1983 against Turek and respondents City of Lago Vista and Chief of Police Frank Miller. So far as concerns us, petitioners (whom we will simply call Atwater) alleged that respondents (for simplicity, the City) had violated Atwater's Fourth Amendment "right to be free from unreasonable seizure," and sought compensatory and punitive damages. * * * Given Atwater's admission that she had "violated the law" * * * the District Court ruled the Fourth Amendment claim "meritless" and granted the City's summary judgment motion. [The Fifth Circuit ultimately agreed with the lower court.]

We granted certiorari to consider whether the Fourth Amendment * * * limits police officers' authority to arrest without warrant for minor criminal offenses. We now affirm.

* * * Atwater's specific contention is that "founding-era common-law rules" forbade peace officers to make warrantless misdemeanor arrests except in cases of "breach of the peace," a category she claims was then understood narrowly as covering only those nonfelony offenses "involving or tending toward violence." Although her historical argument is by no means insubstantial, it ultimately fails.

* * * [Justice Souter engaged in an extensive and detailed analysis of pre-founding English common law and concluded that, "the common-law commentators (as well as the sparsely reported cases) reached divergent conclusions with respect to officers' warrantless misdemeanor arrest power. Moreover, in the years leading up to American independence, Parliament repeatedly extended express warrantless arrest authority to cover misdemeanor-level offenses not amounting to or involving any violent breach of the peace."]

* * * An examination of specifically American evidence is to the same effect. Neither the history of the framing era nor subsequent legal development indicates that the Fourth Amendment was originally understood, or has traditionally been read, to embrace Atwater's position.

[Justice Souter engages in another extensive and detailed analysis of American practice with respect to arrests, both pre-and post-founding. He concludes that there was a basic assumption that a custodial arrest was reasonable for nonviolent misdemeanors.]

* * * Small wonder, then, that today statutes in all 50 States and the District of Columbia permit warrantless misdemeanor arrests by at least some (if not all) peace officers without requiring any breach of the peace, as do a host of congressional enactments. * * * Atwater does not wager all

on history. * * * Atwater * * * argues for a modern arrest rule * * * forbidding custodial arrest, even upon probable cause, when conviction could not ultimately carry any jail time and when the government shows no compelling need for immediate detention.

If we were to derive a rule exclusively to address the uncontested facts of this case, Atwater might well prevail. She was a known and established resident of Lago Vista with no place to hide and no incentive to flee, and common sense says she would almost certainly have buckled up as a condition of driving off with a citation. In her case, the physical incidents of arrest were merely gratuitous humiliations imposed by a police officer who was (at best) exercising extremely poor judgment. Atwater's claim to live free of pointless indignity and confinement clearly outweighs anything the City can raise against it specific to her case.

But we have traditionally recognized that a responsible Fourth Amendment balance is not well served by standards requiring sensitive, case-by-case determinations of government need, lest every discretionary judgment in the field be converted into an occasion for constitutional review. *See, e.g.,* United States v. Robinson. Often enough, the Fourth Amendment has to be applied on the spur (and in the heat) of the moment, and the object in implementing its command of reasonableness is to draw standards sufficiently clear and simple to be applied with a fair prospect of surviving judicial second-guessing months and years after an arrest or search is made. Courts attempting to strike a reasonable Fourth Amendment balance thus credit the government's side with an essential interest in readily administrable rules.

At first glance, Atwater's argument may seem to respect the values of clarity and simplicity, so far as she claims that the Fourth Amendment generally forbids warrantless arrests for minor crimes not accompanied by violence or some demonstrable threat of it (whether "minor crime" be defined as a fine-only traffic offense, a fine-only offense more generally, or a misdemeanor). But the claim is not ultimately so simple, nor could it be, for complications arise the moment we begin to think about the possible applications of the several criteria Atwater proposes for drawing a line between minor crimes with limited arrest authority and others not so restricted.

One line, she suggests, might be between "jailable" and "fine-only" offenses * * *. The trouble with this distinction, of course, is that an officer on the street might not be able to tell. It is not merely that we cannot expect every police officer to know the details of frequently complex penalty schemes, but that penalties for ostensibly identical conduct can vary on account of facts difficult (if not impossible) to know at the scene of an arrest. Is this the first offense or is the suspect a repeat offender? Is the weight of the marijuana a gram above or a gram below

332 SEARCHES AND SEIZURES OF PERSONS AND THINGS CH. 2

the fine-only line? Where conduct could implicate more than one criminal prohibition, which one will the district attorney ultimately decide to charge? And so on. But Atwater's refinements would not end there. She represents that if the line were drawn at nonjailable traffic offenses, her proposed limitation should be qualified by a proviso authorizing warrantless arrests where "necessary for enforcement of the traffic laws or when [an] offense would otherwise continue and pose a danger to others on the road." * * * The proviso only compounds the difficulties. Would, for instance, either exception apply to speeding? At oral argument, Atwater's counsel said that "it would not be reasonable to arrest a driver for speeding unless the speeding rose to the level of reckless driving." But is it not fair to expect that the chronic speeder will speed again despite a citation in his pocket, and should that not qualify as showing that the "offense would * * * continue" under Atwater's rule? And why, as a constitutional matter, should we assume that only reckless driving will "pose a danger to others on the road" while speeding will not?

* * * Atwater's rule therefore would not only place police in an almost impossible spot but would guarantee increased litigation over many of the arrests that would occur. For all these reasons, Atwater's various distinctions between permissible and impermissible arrests for minor crimes strike us as very unsatisfactory lines to require police officers to draw on a moment's notice. * * *.

Just how easily the costs could outweigh the benefits may be shown by asking, as one Member of this Court did at oral argument, "how bad the problem is out there." The very fact that the law has never jelled the way Atwater would have it leads one to wonder whether warrantless misdemeanor arrests need constitutional attention, and there is cause to think the answer is no. So far as such arrests might be thought to pose a threat to the probable-cause requirement, anyone arrested for a crime without formal process, whether for felony or misdemeanor, is entitled to a magistrate's review of probable cause within 48 hours, County of Riverside v. McLaughlin, and there is no reason to think the procedure in this case atypical in giving the suspect a prompt opportunity to request release. Many jurisdictions, moreover, have chosen to impose more restrictive safeguards through statutes limiting warrantless arrests for minor offenses. It is of course easier to devise a minor-offense limitation by statute than to derive one through the Constitution, simply because the statute can let the arrest power turn on any sort of practical consideration without having to subsume it under a broader principle. It is, in fact, only natural that States should resort to this sort of legislative regulation, for * * * it is in the interest of the police to limit petty-offense arrests, which carry costs that are simply too great to incur without good reason. Finally, and significantly, under current doctrine the preference for categorical treatment of Fourth Amendment claims gives way to individualized review when a defendant makes a colorable argument that an arrest, with or without a warrant, was conducted in an extraordinary manner, unusually harmful to his privacy or even physical interests. The upshot of all these influences, combined with the good sense (and, failing that, the political accountability) of most local lawmakers and law-enforcement officials, is a dearth of horribles demanding redress. * * *

Accordingly, we confirm today what our prior cases have intimated: * * * If an officer has probable cause to believe that an individual has committed even a very minor criminal offense in his presence, he may, without violating the Fourth Amendment, arrest the offender.

* * * Atwater's arrest satisfied constitutional requirements. There is no dispute that Officer Turek had probable cause to believe that Atwater had committed a crime in his presence. * * * Turek was accordingly authorized (not required, but authorized) to make a custodial arrest without balancing costs and benefits or determining whether or not Atwater's arrest was in some sense necessary.

Nor was the arrest made in an "extraordinary manner, unusually harmful to [her] privacy or * * * physical interests." * * * Atwater's arrest was surely "humiliating," * * * but it was no more "harmful to privacy or physical interests" than the normal custodial arrest. She was handcuffed, placed in a squad car, and taken to the local police station, where officers asked her to remove her shoes, jewelry, and glasses, and to empty her pockets. They then took her photograph and placed her in a cell, alone, for about an hour, after which she was taken before a magistrate, and released on $310 bond. The arrest and booking were inconvenient and embarrassing to Atwater, but not so extraordinary as to violate the Fourth Amendment.

The Court of Appeals's en banc judgment is affirmed.

**JUSTICE O'CONNOR, with whom JUSTICE STEVENS, JUSTICE GINSBURG, and JUSTICE BREYER join, dissenting**.

* * *

A custodial arrest exacts an obvious toll on an individual's liberty and privacy, even when the period of custody is relatively brief. The arrestee is subject to a full search of her person and confiscation of her possessions. * * * The arrestee may be detained for up to 48 hours without having a magistrate determine whether there in fact was probable cause for the arrest. Because people arrested for all types of violent and nonviolent offenses may be housed together awaiting such review, this detention period is potentially dangerous. And once the period of custody is over, the fact of the arrest is a permanent part of the public record. * * *

\* \* \* The per se rule that the Court creates has potentially serious consequences for the everyday lives of Americans. A broad range of conduct falls into the category of fine-only misdemeanors. In Texas alone, for example, disobeying any sort of traffic warning sign is a misdemeanor punishable only by fine, as is failing to pay a highway toll, and driving with expired license plates. Nor are fine-only crimes limited to the traffic context. In several States, for example, littering is a criminal offense punishable only by fine. \* \* \* Under today's holding, when a police officer has probable cause to believe that a fine-only misdemeanor offense has occurred, that officer may stop the suspect, issue a citation, and let the person continue on her way. Or, if a traffic violation, the officer may stop the car, arrest the driver, search the driver, \* \* \* and impound the car and inventory all of its contents. \* \* \* Such unbounded discretion carries with it grave potential for abuse. \* \* \* Indeed, as the recent debate over racial profiling demonstrates all too clearly, a relatively minor traffic infraction may often serve as an excuse for stopping and harassing an individual. After today, the arsenal available to any officer extends to a full arrest and the searches permissible concomitant to that arrest. An officer's subjective motivations for making a traffic stop are not relevant considerations in determining the reasonableness of the stop. But it is precisely because these motivations are beyond our purview that we must vigilantly ensure that officers' poststop actions—which are properly within our reach—comport with the Fourth Amendment's guarantee of reasonableness.

\* \* \*

### Arrests for Minor Offenses After Atwater

The *Atwater* majority relies in part of a "dearth of horribles"—few if any examples of full custodial arrests for fine-only offenses. After *Atwater* there have indeed been real-life examples of such arrests; one such instance was reviewed by then-Judge Roberts in Hedgepeth v. Washington Metro Area Transit Auth., 386 F.3d 1148 (D.C. Cir. 2004). Judge Roberts described the facts:

> No one is very happy about the events that led to this litigation. A twelve-year-old girl was arrested, searched, and handcuffed. Her shoelaces were removed, and she was transported in the windowless rear compartment of a police vehicle to a juvenile processing center, where she was booked, fingerprinted, and detained until released to her mother some three hours later—all for eating a single french fry in a Metrorail station. The child was frightened, embarrassed, and crying throughout the ordeal.

The arrest was the result of WMATA's "zero-tolerance" policy for violations of the rule prohibiting eating on the subway. The arrest was made by an undercover officer, whose job that day was to pose as a passenger and look for people eating on the subway.

Judge Roberts found that while the arrest was the result of bad policy—a policy subsequently suspended due to public outcry—it was not unreasonable under the Fourth Amendment. The court concluded: "Given the undisputed existence of probable cause, *Atwater* precludes further inquiry into the reasonableness" of the arrest under the Fourth Amendment.

Could the *Atwater* Court take comfort in the fact that after the student's arrest for eating a french fry, the public outcry was so great that the WMATA ended its policy of arresting people for violating the no-eating rule?

### Robinson and Containers in the Arrestee's Grab Area

The Court in *Robinson* established an automatic right to search everything found on a person who has been subjected to a custodial arrest. Does that automatic search power extend to containers found in the arrestee's grab area? In United States v. Chadwick, supra, the Court held that a search of a footlocker at the police station could not be justified as a search incident to arrest because it occurred long after Chadwick was in custody. In a footnote, the Court referred to *Robinson* and distinguished its automatic search rule:

> Unlike searches of the person, searches of possessions within an arrestee's immediate control cannot be justified by any reduced expectations of privacy caused by the arrest. Respondents' privacy interest in the contents of the footlocker was not eliminated simply because they were under arrest.

Does this passage mean that the officer has no automatic right to search containers incident to arrest when they are within the control area but not on the person? This would mean that briefcases, pocketbooks and bookbags could be seized, but they could not be searched without a warrant or exigent circumstances (such as a ticking briefcase); whereas wallets and cigarette packs found on the person could be thoroughly and automatically searched under *Robinson*. Does this distinction based on privacy interests make sense? Wouldn't the things one carries on one's person be more and not less private?

Despite the distinction proffered in *Chadwick*, most lower courts have applied the automatic arrest power rule of *Robinson* to searches of briefcases and the like in the arrestee's grab area. See, e.g., United States v. Morales, 923 F.2d 621 (8th Cir.1991) (distinguishing *Chadwick* as a case involving a search that occurred too long after the arrest was completed and upholding search of a container under the arrest power rule). But see United States v. Gorski, 852 F.2d 692 (2d Cir.1988) (search of bag during arrest must be justified by exigent circumstances, otherwise seizure is all that is permitted).

### 4.   The Arrest Power Rule Applied to Automobiles

Assume that an officer has probable cause to believe that the driver of an automobile has committed a crime for which a custodial arrest is authorized. The officer pulls over the car and places the driver under arrest, handcuffs the driver, and places him in a squad car. Can the officer then search the car incident to the arrest?

### *The Belton Rule*

In New York v. Belton, 453 U.S. 454 (1981), the Court held that the passenger compartment of an automobile constituted the grab area of the car, and therefore officers arresting someone in the car were permitted to search the car incident to the arrest, and also to open any containers that are found in the passenger compartment. (The Court dropped a footnote indicating that the passenger compartment did not include the trunk of the car.) The precise scope of *Belton* was unclear, but most lower courts held that under *Belton* an arresting officer had an *automatic right* to search the passenger compartment and all containers therein, even if the arrestee had absolutely no possible way to reach into the car for evidence or weapons at the time of the search.

The *Belton* Court styled its rule as being nothing more than an application of the *Chimel* grab area rule to the specific situation of cars. But it seemed hard to argue that the *Belton* search had anything to do with preserving evidence or protecting officers—the underlying reasons for permitting a search incident to arrest under *Chimel*.

Thereafter in Thornton v. United States, 541 U.S. 615 (2004), the Court held that the search power granted by *Belton* applied whenever the person arrested was a "recent occupant" of the car to be searched. Officers thought that Thornton was driving a stolen car, but before they could pull him over, Thornton parked the car and got out of the vehicle. Thornton was subjected to a *Terry* frisk that uncovered narcotics. He was arrested a few feet away from the car, and a search of the passenger compartment incident to arrest turned up a gun. The *Thornton* Court held that the search was permissible under *Belton* because Thornton was a recent occupant and any other rule would only encourage drivers to pop out of a car when they saw police coming, in order to avoid a search of the passenger compartment.

Justice Scalia, joined by Justice Ginsburg, concurred in the judgment in *Thornton*, but took the opportunity to question the wisdom and rationale of the *Belton* rule. He argued as follows:

I see three reasons why the search in this case might have been justified to protect officer safety or prevent concealment or destruction of evidence. None ultimately persuades me.

The first is that, despite being handcuffed and secured in the back of a squad car, petitioner might have escaped and retrieved a weapon or evidence from his vehicle—a theory that calls to mind Judge Goldberg's reference to the mythical arrestee "possessed of the skill of Houdini and the strength of Hercules." * * * The risk that a suspect handcuffed in the back of a squad car might escape and recover a weapon from his vehicle is surely no greater than the risk that a suspect handcuffed in his residence might escape and recover a weapon from the next room—a danger we held insufficient to justify a search in *Chimel, supra.*

The second defense of the search in this case is that, since the officer could have conducted the search at the time of arrest (when the suspect was still near the car), he should not be penalized for having taken the sensible precaution of securing the suspect in the squad car first. * * * The weakness of this argument is that it assumes that, one way or another, the search must take place. But conducting a *Chimel* search is not the Government's right; it is an exception—justified by necessity—to a rule that would otherwise render the search unlawful. * * *

The third defense of the search is that, even though the arrestee posed no risk here, *Belton* searches in general are reasonable, and the benefits of a bright-line rule justify upholding that small minority of searches that, on their particular facts, are not reasonable. The validity of this argument rests on the accuracy of *Belton*'s claim that the passenger compartment is "in fact generally, even if not inevitably," within the suspect's immediate control. By the United States' own admission, however, "the practice of restraining an arrestee on the scene before searching a car that he just occupied is so prevalent that holding that *Belton* does not apply in that setting would ... largely render *Belton* a dead letter." Reported cases involving this precise factual scenario—a motorist handcuffed and secured in the back of a squad car when the search takes place—are legion.

So in Justice Scalia's view, an automatic search of the passenger compartment incident to arrest cannot be supported by the reasons cited by *Chimel* for the search power incident to arrest, i.e., the need to protect against the arrestee's destruction of evidence or use of a weapon. Justice Scalia argued, however, that the power to search after an arrest might be justified on another ground. He explained as follows:

If *Belton* searches are justifiable, it is not because the arrestee might grab a weapon or evidentiary item from his car, but simply because the car might contain evidence relevant to the crime for which he was arrested. * * *

Numerous earlier authorities support this approach, referring to the general interest in gathering evidence related to the crime of arrest with no mention of the more specific interest in preventing its concealment or destruction. [Citing cases.] Only in the years leading up to *Chimel* did we start consistently referring to the narrower interest in frustrating concealment or destruction of evidence.

There is nothing irrational about broader police authority to search for evidence when and where the perpetrator of a crime is lawfully arrested. The fact of prior lawful arrest distinguishes the arrestee from society at large, and distinguishes a search for evidence of *his* crime from general rummaging. Moreover, it is not illogical to assume that evidence of a crime is most likely to be found where the suspect was apprehended.

Nevertheless, *Chimel*'s narrower focus on concealment or destruction of evidence also has historical support. [Citing cases.] * * *

*Belton* cannot reasonably be explained as a mere application of *Chimel*. Rather, it is a return to the broader sort of search incident to arrest that we allowed before *Chimel*—limited, of course, to searches of motor vehicles, a category of "effects" which give rise to a reduced expectation of privacy, and heightened law enforcement needs.

### *Limitations on Arrest-Power Rule as Applied to Automobile Searches: Arizona v. Gant*

In the following case, the Court rejected the *Belton* rule, insofar as that rule was read to allow the automatic search of the passenger compartment of a car after a recent occupant of the car was arrested. But it substitutes Justice Scalia's evidence-based view of the arrest power, articulated in his separate opinion in *Thornton*.

### ARIZONA V. GANT

Supreme Court of the United States, 2009.
556 U.S. 332.

### JUSTICE STEVENS delivered the opinion of the Court.

After Rodney Gant was arrested for driving with a suspended license, handcuffed, and locked in the back of a patrol car, police officers searched his car and discovered cocaine in the pocket of a jacket on the backseat.

Because Gant could not have accessed his car to retrieve weapons or evidence at the time of the search, the Arizona Supreme Court held that the search-incident-to-arrest exception to the Fourth Amendment's warrant requirement, as defined in Chimel v. California, and applied to vehicle searches in New York v. Belton, did not justify the search in this case. We agree with that conclusion.

Under *Chimel*, police may search incident to arrest only the space within an arrestee's "immediate control," meaning "the area from within which he might gain possession of a weapon or destructible evidence." The safety and evidentiary justifications underlying *Chimel's* reaching-distance rule determine *Belton's* scope. Accordingly, we hold that *Belton* does not authorize a vehicle search incident to a recent occupant's arrest after the arrestee has been secured and cannot access the interior of the vehicle. Consistent with the holding in Thornton v. United States, and following the suggestion in Justice SCALIA's opinion concurring in the judgment in that case, we also conclude that circumstances unique to the automobile context justify a search incident to arrest when it is reasonable to believe that evidence of the offense of arrest might be found in the vehicle.

[Gant was arrested shortly after getting out of his car. He was handcuffed and locked in the back of a squad car. The officers then searched the passenger compartment and found a gun and some cocaine.]

Gant was charged with two offenses—possession of a narcotic drug for sale and possession of drug paraphernalia (i.e., the plastic bag in which the cocaine was found). He moved to suppress the evidence seized from his car on the ground that * * * *Belton* did not authorize the search of his vehicle because he posed no threat to the officers after he was handcuffed in the patrol car and because he was arrested for a traffic offense for which no evidence could be found in his vehicle. When asked at the suppression hearing why the search was conducted, Officer Griffith responded: "Because the law says we can do it." [The Trial Court refused to suppress the evidence and Gant was convicted. But the Arizona Supreme Court, for reasons discussed *infra,* ruled that the search violated the Fourth Amendment.]

The chorus that has called for us to revisit *Belton* includes courts, scholars, and Members of this Court who have questioned that decision's clarity and its fidelity to Fourth Amendment principles. We therefore granted the State's petition for certiorari.

\* \* \*

In *Belton*, we considered *Chimel's* application to the automobile context. [The Court discusses the facts and arguments of the parties in *Belton*.] There was no suggestion by the parties or amici that *Chimel* authorizes a vehicle search incident to arrest when there is no realistic possibility that an arrestee could access his vehicle.

* * * [W]e held that when an officer lawfully arrests "the occupant of an automobile, he may, as a contemporaneous incident of that arrest, search the passenger compartment of the automobile" and any containers therein. That holding was based in large part on our assumption "that articles inside the relatively narrow compass of the passenger compartment of an automobile are in fact generally, even if not inevitably, within the area into which an arrestee might reach."

The Arizona Supreme Court read our decision in *Belton* as merely delineating "the proper scope of a search of the interior of an automobile" incident to an arrest. That is, when the passenger compartment is within an arrestee's reaching distance, *Belton* supplies the generalization that the entire compartment and any containers therein may be reached. On that view of *Belton*, the state court concluded that the search of Gant's car was unreasonable because Gant clearly could not have accessed his car at the time of the search.

* * *

Despite the textual and evidentiary support for the Arizona Supreme Court's reading of *Belton*, our opinion has been widely understood to allow a vehicle search incident to the arrest of a recent occupant even if there is no possibility the arrestee could gain access to the vehicle at the time of the search. This reading may be attributable to Justice Brennan's dissent in *Belton*, in which he characterized the Court's holding as resting on the "fiction . . . that the interior of a car is always within the immediate control of an arrestee who has recently been in the car." * * *

Under this broad reading of *Belton*, a vehicle search would be authorized incident to every arrest of a recent occupant notwithstanding that in most cases the vehicle's passenger compartment will not be within the arrestee's reach at the time of the search. To read *Belton* as authorizing a vehicle search incident to every recent occupant's arrest would thus untether the rule from the justifications underlying the *Chimel* exception—a result clearly incompatible with our statement in *Belton* that it "in no way alters the fundamental principles established in the *Chimel* case regarding the basic scope of searches incident to lawful custodial arrests." Accordingly, we reject this reading of *Belton* and hold that the *Chimel* rationale authorizes police to search a vehicle incident to a recent occupant's arrest only when the arrestee is unsecured and within reaching distance of the passenger compartment at the time of the search.[a]

---

[a]  Because officers have many means of ensuring the safe arrest of vehicle occupants, it will be the rare case in which an officer is unable to fully effectuate an arrest so that a real possibility

Although it does not follow from *Chimel*, we also conclude that circumstances unique to the vehicle context justify a search incident to a lawful arrest when it is "reasonable to believe evidence relevant to the crime of arrest might be found in the vehicle." *Thornton*, 541 U.S., at 632 (SCALIA, J., concurring in judgment). In many cases, as when a recent occupant is arrested for a traffic violation, there will be no reasonable basis to believe the vehicle contains relevant evidence. But in others, including *Belton* and *Thornton*, the offense of arrest will supply a basis for searching the passenger compartment of an arrestee's vehicle and any containers therein.

Neither the possibility of access nor the likelihood of discovering offense-related evidence authorized the search in this case. Unlike in *Belton*, which involved a single officer confronted with four unsecured arrestees, the five officers in this case outnumbered the three arrestees, all of whom had been handcuffed and secured in separate patrol cars before the officers searched Gant's car. Under those circumstances, Gant clearly was not within reaching distance of his car at the time of the search. An evidentiary basis for the search was also lacking in this case. Whereas Belton and Thornton were arrested for drug offenses, Gant was arrested for driving with a suspended license—an offense for which police could not expect to find evidence in the passenger compartment of Gant's car. * * *

The State does not seriously disagree with the Arizona Supreme Court's conclusion that Gant could not have accessed his vehicle at the time of the search, but it nevertheless asks us to uphold the search of his vehicle under the broad reading of *Belton* discussed above. The State argues that *Belton* searches are reasonable regardless of the possibility of access in a given case because that expansive rule correctly balances law enforcement interests, including the interest in a bright-line rule, with an arrestee's limited privacy interest in his vehicle.

For several reasons, we reject the State's argument. First, the State seriously undervalues the privacy interests at stake. Although we have recognized that a motorist's privacy interest in his vehicle is less substantial than in his home, the former interest is nevertheless important and deserving of constitutional protection. It is particularly significant that *Belton* searches authorize police officers to search not just the passenger compartment but every purse, briefcase, or other container within that space. A rule that gives police the power to conduct such a search whenever an individual is caught committing a traffic offense, when there is no basis for believing evidence of the offense might be found in the vehicle, creates a serious and recurring threat to the privacy of countless individuals.   * * * At the same time as it undervalues these

---

of access to the arrestee's vehicle remains. * * * But in such a case a search incident to arrest is reasonable under the Fourth Amendment.

privacy concerns, the State exaggerates the clarity that its reading of *Belton* provides. Courts that have read *Belton* expansively are at odds regarding how close in time to the arrest and how proximate to the arrestee's vehicle an officer's first contact with the arrestee must be to bring the encounter within *Belton*'s purview and whether a search is reasonable when it commences or continues after the arrestee has been removed from the scene. The rule has thus generated a great deal of uncertainty, particularly for a rule touted as providing a "bright line."

Contrary to the State's suggestion, a broad reading of *Belton* is also unnecessary to protect law enforcement safety and evidentiary interests. Under our view, *Belton* and *Thornton* permit an officer to conduct a vehicle search when an arrestee is within reaching distance of the vehicle or it is reasonable to believe the vehicle contains evidence of the offense of arrest. Other established exceptions to the warrant requirement authorize a vehicle search under additional circumstances when safety or evidentiary concerns demand. For instance, Michigan v. Long, 463 U.S. 1032 (1983), permits an officer to search a vehicle's passenger compartment when he has reasonable suspicion that an individual, whether or not the arrestee, is "dangerous" and might access the vehicle to "gain immediate control of weapons." If there is probable cause to believe a vehicle contains evidence of criminal activity, United States v. Ross, 456 U.S. 798 (1982), authorizes a search of any area of the vehicle in which the evidence might be found. Unlike the searches permitted by Justice SCALIA's opinion concurring in the judgment in *Thornton*, which we conclude today are reasonable for purposes of the Fourth Amendment, *Ross* allows searches for evidence relevant to offenses other than the offense of arrest, and the scope of the search authorized is broader. * * *

These exceptions together ensure that officers may search a vehicle when genuine safety or evidentiary concerns encountered during the arrest of a vehicle's recent occupant justify a search. Construing *Belton* broadly to allow vehicle searches incident to any arrest would serve no purpose except to provide a police entitlement, and it is anathema to the Fourth Amendment to permit a warrantless search on that basis. * * *

Our dissenting colleagues argue that the doctrine of stare decisis requires adherence to a broad reading of *Belton* even though the justifications for searching a vehicle incident to arrest are in most cases absent. The doctrine of stare decisis is of course "essential to the respect accorded to the judgments of the Court and to the stability of the law," but it does not compel us to follow a past decision when its rationale no longer withstands "careful analysis."

* * *

Police may search a vehicle incident to a recent occupant's arrest only if the arrestee is within reaching distance of the passenger compartment at the time of the search or it is reasonable to believe the vehicle contains evidence of the offense of arrest. When these justifications are absent, a search of an arrestee's vehicle will be unreasonable unless police obtain a warrant or show that another exception to the warrant requirement applies. The Arizona Supreme Court correctly held that this case involved an unreasonable search. Accordingly, the judgment of the State Supreme Court is affirmed.

### JUSTICE SCALIA, concurring.

To determine what is an "unreasonable" search within the meaning of the Fourth Amendment, we look first to the historical practices the Framers sought to preserve; if those provide inadequate guidance, we apply traditional standards of reasonableness. Since the historical scope of officers' authority to search vehicles incident to arrest is uncertain, traditional standards of reasonableness govern. It is abundantly clear that those standards do not justify what I take to be the rule set forth in New York v. Belton, and *Thornton*: that arresting officers may always search an arrestee's vehicle in order to protect themselves from hidden weapons. When an arrest is made in connection with a roadside stop, police virtually always have a less intrusive and more effective means of ensuring their safety—and a means that is virtually always employed: ordering the arrestee away from the vehicle, patting him down in the open, handcuffing him, and placing him in the squad car.

\* \* \*

Justice STEVENS acknowledges that an officer-safety rationale cannot justify all vehicle searches incident to arrest, but asserts that that is not the rule *Belton* and Thornton adopted. \* \* \* Justice STEVENS would therefore retain the application of Chimel v. California in the car-search context but would apply in the future what he believes our cases held in the past: that officers making a roadside stop may search the vehicle so long as the "arrestee is within reaching distance of the passenger compartment at the time of the search." I believe that this standard fails to provide the needed guidance to arresting officers and also leaves much room for manipulation, inviting officers to leave the scene unsecured (at least where dangerous suspects are not involved) in order to conduct a vehicle search. In my view we should simply abandon the *Belton-Thornton* charade of officer safety and overrule those cases. I would hold that a vehicle search incident to arrest is ipso facto "reasonable" only when the object of the search is evidence of the crime for which the arrest was made, or of another crime that the officer has probable cause to believe occurred. Because respondent was arrested for driving without a license (a crime for which no evidence could be expected to be found in the vehicle), I would hold in the present case that the search was unlawful.

Justice ALITO insists that the Court must demand a good reason for abandoning prior precedent. That is true enough, but it seems to me ample reason that the precedent was badly reasoned and produces erroneous (in this case unconstitutional) results. We should recognize *Belton's* fanciful reliance upon officer safety for what it was: a return to the broader sort of [evidence-gathering] search incident to arrest that we allowed before *Chimel*.

* * *

No other Justice, however, shares my view that application of *Chimel* in this context should be entirely abandoned. It seems to me unacceptable for the Court to come forth with a 4-to-1-to-4 opinion that leaves the governing rule uncertain. I am therefore confronted with the choice of either leaving the current understanding of *Belton* and *Thornton* in effect, or acceding to what seems to me the artificial narrowing of those cases adopted by Justice STEVENS. The latter, as I have said, does not provide the degree of certainty I think desirable in this field; but the former opens the field to what I think are plainly unconstitutional searches—which is the greater evil. I therefore join the opinion of the Court.

**JUSTICE BREYER, dissenting.**

I agree with Justice ALITO that New York v. Belton is best read as setting forth a bright-line rule that permits a warrantless search of the passenger compartment of an automobile incident to the lawful arrest of an occupant-regardless of the danger the arrested individual in fact poses. I also agree with Justice STEVENS, however, that the rule can produce results divorced from its underlying Fourth Amendment rationale. For that reason I would look for a better rule—were the question before us one of first impression.

The matter, however, is not one of first impression, and that fact makes a substantial difference. The *Belton* rule has been followed not only by this Court in Thornton v. United States, but also by numerous other courts. Principles of stare decisis must apply, and those who wish this Court to change a well-established legal precedent—where, as here, there has been considerable reliance on the legal rule in question—bear a heavy burden. I have not found that burden met. * * *

**JUSTICE ALITO, with whom THE CHIEF JUSTICE and JUSTICE KENNEDY join, and with whom JUSTICE BREYER joins except as to Part II–E, dissenting.**

I

Although the Court refuses to acknowledge that it is overruling *Belton* and *Thornton*, there can be no doubt that it does so.

* * *

The precise holding in *Belton* could not be clearer. The Court stated unequivocally: "[W]e hold that when a policeman has made a lawful custodial arrest of the occupant of an automobile, he may, as a contemporaneous incident of that arrest, search the passenger compartment of that automobile."

Despite this explicit statement, the opinion of the Court in the present case curiously suggests that *Belton* may reasonably be read as adopting a holding that is narrower than the one explicitly set out in the *Belton* opinion, namely, that an officer arresting a vehicle occupant may search the passenger compartment "when the passenger compartment is within an arrestee's reaching distance." * * *

## II

* * *

The opinion of the Court recognizes that *Belton* has been widely taught in police academies and that law enforcement officers have relied on the rule in conducting vehicle searches during the past 28 years. But for the Court, this seemingly counts for nothing.

* * *

* * * Abandonment of the *Belton* rule cannot be justified on the ground that the dangers surrounding the arrest of a vehicle occupant are different today than they were 28 years ago. The Court claims that "[w]e now know that articles inside the passenger compartment are rarely within the area into which an arrestee might reach," but surely it was well known in 1981 that a person who is taken from a vehicle, handcuffed, and placed in the back of a patrol car is unlikely to make it back into his own car to retrieve a weapon or destroy evidence.

* * * The *Belton* rule has not proved to be unworkable. On the contrary, the rule was adopted for the express purpose of providing a test that would be relatively easy for police officers and judges to apply. * * *

The first part of the Court's new rule—which permits the search of a vehicle's passenger compartment if it is within an arrestee's reach at the time of the search—reintroduces the same sort of case-by-case, fact-specific decisionmaking that the *Belton* rule was adopted to avoid. As the situation in *Belton* illustrated, there are cases in which it is unclear whether an arrestee could retrieve a weapon or evidence in the passenger compartment of a car.

Even more serious problems will also result from the second part of the Court's new rule, which requires officers making roadside arrests to determine whether there is reason to believe that the vehicle contains evidence of the crime of arrest. What this rule permits in a variety of situations is entirely unclear.

\* \* \*

## E

\* \* \* The Court is harshly critical of *Belton*'s reasoning, but the problem that the Court perceives cannot be remedied simply by overruling *Belton*. *Belton* represented only a modest—and quite defensible—extension of *Chimel*, as I understand that decision.

\* \* \*

Unfortunately, *Chimel* did not say whether "the area from within which [an arrestee] might gain possession of a weapon or destructible evidence" is to be measured at the time of the arrest or at the time of the search, but unless the *Chimel* rule was meant to be a specialty rule, applicable to only a few unusual cases, the Court must have intended for this area to be measured at the time of arrest.

This is so because the Court can hardly have failed to appreciate the following two facts. First, in the great majority of cases, an officer making an arrest is able to handcuff the arrestee and remove him to a secure place before conducting a search incident to the arrest. Second, because it is safer for an arresting officer to secure an arrestee before searching, it is likely that this is what arresting officers do in the great majority of cases. \* \* \* Thus, if the area within an arrestee's reach were assessed, not at the time of arrest, but at the time of the search, the *Chimel* rule would rarely come into play.

Moreover, if the applicability of the *Chimel* rule turned on whether an arresting officer chooses to secure an arrestee prior to conducting a search, rather than searching first and securing the arrestee later, the rule would "create a perverse incentive for an arresting officer to prolong the period during which the arrestee is kept in an area where he could pose a danger to the officer." United States v. Abdul-Saboor, 85 F.3d 664, 669 (C.A.D.C.1996). If this is the law, the D.C. Circuit observed, "the law would truly be, as Mr. Bumble said, 'a ass.'"

I do not think that this is what the *Chimel* Court intended. Handcuffs were in use in 1969. The ability of arresting officers to secure arrestees before conducting a search—and their incentive to do so—are facts that can hardly have escaped the Court's attention. I therefore believe that the *Chimel* Court intended that its new rule apply in cases in which the arrestee is handcuffed before the search is conducted.

The *Belton* Court, in my view, proceeded on the basis of this interpretation of *Chimel*. Again speaking through Justice Stewart, the *Belton* Court reasoned that articles in the passenger compartment of a car are "generally, even if not inevitably" within an arrestee's reach. This is undoubtedly true at the time of the arrest of a person who is seated in a car but plainly not true when the person has been removed from the car and placed in handcuffs. Accordingly, the *Belton* Court must have proceeded on the assumption that the *Chimel* rule was to be applied at the time of arrest. Viewing *Chimel* as having focused on the time of arrest, *Belton*'s only new step was to eliminate the need to decide on a case-by-case basis whether a particular person seated in a car actually could have reached the part of the passenger compartment where a weapon or evidence was hidden. For this reason, if we are going to reexamine *Belton*, we should also reexamine the reasoning in *Chimel* on which *Belton* rests.

### F

The Court, however, does not reexamine *Chimel* and thus leaves the law relating to searches incident to arrest in a confused and unstable state. The first part of the Court's new two-part rule—which permits an arresting officer to search the area within an arrestee's reach at the time of the search—applies, at least for now, only to vehicle occupants and recent occupants, but there is no logical reason why the same rule should not apply to all arrestees.

The second part of the Court's new rule, which the Court takes uncritically from Justice SCALIA's separate opinion in *Thornton*, raises doctrinal and practical problems that the Court makes no effort to address. Why, for example, is the standard for this type of evidence-gathering search "reason to believe" rather than probable cause? And why is this type of search restricted to evidence of the offense of arrest? It is true that an arrestee's vehicle is probably more likely to contain evidence of the crime of arrest than of some other crime, but if reason-to-believe is the governing standard for an evidence-gathering search incident to arrest, it is not easy to see why an officer should not be able to search when the officer has reason to believe that the vehicle in question possesses evidence of a crime other than the crime of arrest.

Nor is it easy to see why an evidence-gathering search incident to arrest should be restricted to the passenger compartment. The *Belton* rule was limited in this way because the passenger compartment was considered to be the area that vehicle occupants can generally reach, but since the second part of the new rule is not based on officer safety or the preservation of evidence, the ground for this limitation is obscure.

### *QUESTIONS AFTER GANT*

As Justice Alito predicted, the lower courts after *Gant* are now trending toward a time-of-search rule for *all* searches incident to arrest. See the discussion of *Shakir* earlier in this section. Doesn't this mean, as Justice Alito believes, that the arrest-power rule provides little if any utility for officers—because at the time of the search the officer will have put the arrestee in custody so that he no longer presents any risk of destroying evidence or getting a weapon? Is Justice Alito correct that the Court in *Chimel* could not have been going to so much trouble to craft a rule that would seldom if ever be used?

Perhaps, though, a time-of-search rule might still lead to a finding that a passenger car was in the grab area in a particular case. For example, suppose a single officer arrests a driver of a car in which there are five tough-looking occupants, and it is late at night in a high crime area. If the officer searches the passenger compartment before securing all the occupants, do you think a court would find such a search to be valid under *Gant*? See United States v. Salamasina, 615 F.3d 925 (8th Cir. 2010) (search of passenger compartment permissible under *Gant*; while the defendant was secured, his wife was not, and she was repeatedly entering and exiting the vehicle to tend to her children, and was communicating to the defendant in a foreign language despite the officers' direction not to talk to him).

What is the meaning of *Gant's* newly-minted "reason to believe" test? It can't mean that a search of the car is permitted under the arrest-power rule if there is probable cause to believe that there is evidence of the crime for which an arrest has been effectuated. If probable cause were the test, then the doctrine would be completely unnecessary because officers already are permitted to search a car without a warrant if they have probable cause. See the materials on the automobile exception to the warrant requirement later in this Chapter. Accordingly, "reason to believe" must mean that a search of the passenger compartment is permitted upon proof less than probable cause to believe that evidence of the crime that is the subject of arrest will be found. See United States v. Vinton, 594 F.3d 14 (D.C.Cir. 2010) ("Presumably, the 'reason to believe' standard requires less than probable cause, because otherwise *Gant's* evidentiary rationale would merely duplicate the automobile exception, which the Court in *Gant* specifically identified as a distinct exception to the warrant requirement."). Accordingly, the lower courts after *Gant* have interpreted "reason to believe" as equivalent to the reasonable suspicion standard established in *Terry*. Id.

Even as so construed, the "reason to believe" standard appears to be of marginal use to officers as it is specifically limited by the *Gant* Court to evidence of the offense for which the suspect has been arrested. Thus, in a case involving a traffic violation, like *Gant*, the "reason to believe" test will not be useful because there will rarely be evidence of the traffic violation in the passenger compartment. And for arrests on evidence-based crimes, such as drug offenses, the "reason to believe" test will be of little utility because if there is probable cause to arrest the defendant there will, in all but a few cases, be probable cause to believe that there is evidence of that crime in his car—and so the evidence could be found through the automobile exception.

If the "reason to believe" test somehow becomes untethered from the crime for which the person is arrested, *then* it could be useful to the police. For example, if officers have only reasonable suspicion that the defendant is dealing drugs, and arrest him for a traffic offense, the "reason to believe" prong of *Gant*—if it applied—would be very useful to the police. It would come close to the arrest power rules that were granted by *Belton*. Perhaps that is why Justice Alito, in his *Gant* dissent, questions why the "reason to believe" test should be limited to evidence of the crime for which the person is arrested.

Assume a driver is arrested for driving without a license, or driving while texting. Does an officer have "reason to believe" that there is evidence of such offenses when he sees the driver's cellphone in the passenger compartment? Might there be some information on a cellphone about a traffic offense?

## 5. The Arrest Power Rule Where No Custodial Arrest Takes Place

In *Robinson*, the Court established a bright-line rule permitting full-blown searches when a person has been subjected to a custodial arrest; *Gant* allows a search of a passenger compartment upon arrest if the occupant has access at the time of search or if there is "reason to believe" that evidence pertinent to the crime is located there. Each case involved a traffic stop, and in each case a custodial arrest was authorized, but it was not mandatory. What if an officer makes a traffic stop and merely issues a ticket? Does the arrest-power rule apply to permit a search of the person and the grab area? In Knowles v. Iowa, 525 U.S. 113 (1998), the Court held that it was not—the arrest-power rule is limited to situations in which the person is subjected to a custodial arrest. Chief Justice Rehnquist, writing for a unanimous Court, noted that the threat to officer safety from issuing a traffic citation "is a good deal less than in the case of a custodial arrest." Moreover, the threat of destruction of evidence of a traffic stop was nonexistent. In Knowles's case, he was stopped for speeding, and "[n]o further evidence of excessive speed was going to be found either on the person of the offender or in the passenger compartment of the car." The Court also noted that the *Terry* doctrine was in place to protect the interests of officers, should circumstances warrant. Chief Justice Rehnquist concluded as follows:

> In *Robinson*, we held that the authority to conduct a full field search as incident to an arrest was a "bright-line rule," which was based on the concern for officer safety and destruction or loss of evidence, but which did not depend in every case upon the existence of either concern. Here we are asked to extend that "bright-line rule" to a situation where the concern for officer safety is not present to the

same extent and the concern for destruction or loss of evidence is not present at all. We decline to do so.

### QUESTION ON KNOWLES

By denying the right to a search in the absence of a custodial arrest, isn't the Court providing police officers with an incentive to use a custodial arrest rather than a ticket for a minor traffic offense? How does encouraging police officers to act more intrusively further Fourth Amendment values?

## 6. The Arrest Power Rule Where the Arrest Violates State Law

In Virginia v. Moore, 553 U.S. 164 (2008), the Court considered whether a police officer violates the Fourth Amendment by searching a person incident to a custodial arrest based on probable cause, when the custodial arrest was not authorized by state law. Moore was arrested for driving with a suspended license. Officers searched him incident to the arrest and found drugs. State law, however, did not permit a custodial arrest for driving with a suspended license. But the Court, in an opinion by Justice Scalia for eight Justices, held that the search was valid under the Fourth Amendment. Justice Scalia reasoned as follows:

> [L]inking Fourth Amendment protections to state law would cause them to vary from place to place and from time to time. Even at the same place and time, the Fourth Amendment's protections might vary if federal officers were not subject to the same statutory constraints as state officers. In Elkins v. United States, 364 U.S. 206 (1960), we noted the practical difficulties posed by the "silver-platter doctrine," which had imposed more stringent limitations on federal officers than on state police acting independent of them. It would be strange to construe a constitutional provision that did not apply to the States at all when it was adopted to now restrict state officers more than federal officers, solely because the States have passed search-and-seizure laws that are the prerogative of independent sovereigns.

> We conclude that warrantless arrests for crimes committed in the presence of an arresting officer are reasonable under the Constitution, and that while States are free to regulate such arrests however they desire, state restrictions do not alter the Fourth Amendment's protections.

Because the arrest was valid, the Court also found the search of Moore's person to be valid under *Robinson*.[23]

---

[23]  Justice Ginsburg concurred in the judgment.

# D. PRETEXTUAL STOPS AND ARRESTS

The authority we have discussed this far, such as *Terry* and *Robinson,* give police officers the right to conduct certain searches on the basis of a stop or arrest for a minor offense, such as a traffic offense. Is it possible that these investigatory powers as to minor crimes can be used to search for evidence of a more serious crime for which probable cause or reasonable suspicion does not exist? Are you concerned with that possibility? Is it possible that the right to stop/arrest/search pursuant to a minor traffic offense could be used by police as a tool for harassing citizens, particularly minorities? Does the Fourth Amendment protect a citizen from pretextual stops, arrests and searches if the citizen has in fact committed a minor offense? The Supreme Court considered these questions in the following case.

## WHREN V. UNITED STATES

Supreme Court of the United States, 1996.
517 U.S. 806.

### JUSTICE SCALIA delivered the opinion of the Court.

In this case we decide whether the temporary detention of a motorist who the police have probable cause to believe has committed a civil traffic violation is inconsistent with the Fourth Amendment's prohibition against unreasonable seizures unless a reasonable officer would have been motivated to stop the car by a desire to enforce the traffic laws.

* * *

On the evening of June 10, 1993, plainclothes vice-squad officers of the District of Columbia Metropolitan Police Department were patrolling a "high drug area" of the city in an unmarked car. Their suspicions were aroused when they passed a dark Pathfinder truck with temporary license plates and youthful occupants waiting at a stop sign, the driver looking down into the lap of the passenger at his right. The truck remained stopped at the intersection for what seemed an unusually long time—more than 20 seconds. When the police car executed a U-turn in order to head back toward the truck, the Pathfinder turned suddenly to its right, without signaling, and sped off at an "unreasonable" speed. The policemen followed, and in a short while overtook the Pathfinder when it stopped behind other traffic at a red light. They pulled up alongside, and Officer Ephraim Soto stepped out and approached the driver's door, identifying himself as a police officer and directing the driver, petitioner Brown, to put the vehicle in park. When Soto drew up to the driver's window, he immediately observed two large plastic bags of what appeared to be crack cocaine in petitioner Whren's hands. Petitioners were arrested, and quantities of several types of illegal drugs were retrieved from the vehicle.

Petitioners were charged in a four-count indictment with violating various federal drug laws, * * *. At a pretrial suppression hearing, they challenged the legality of the stop and the resulting seizure of the drugs. They argued that the stop had not been justified by probable cause to believe, or even reasonable suspicion, that petitioners were engaged in illegal drug-dealing activity; and that Officer Soto's asserted ground for approaching the vehicle—to give the driver a warning concerning traffic violations—was pretextual. The District Court denied the suppression motion, concluding that "the facts of the stop were not controverted," and "there was nothing to really demonstrate that the actions of the officers were contrary to a normal traffic stop." [The defendants were convicted and the Court of Appeals affirmed.]

* * *

Petitioners accept that Officer Soto had probable cause to believe that various provisions of the District of Columbia traffic code had been violated. See 18 D. C. Mun. Regs. §§ 2213.4 (1995) ("An operator shall . . . give full time and attention to the operation of the vehicle"); 2204.3 ("No person shall turn any vehicle . . . without giving an appropriate signal"); 2200.3 ("No person shall drive a vehicle . . . at a speed greater than is reasonable and prudent under the conditions"). They argue, however, that "in the unique context of civil traffic regulations" probable cause is not enough. Since, they contend, the use of automobiles is so heavily and minutely regulated that total compliance with traffic and safety rules is nearly impossible, a police officer will almost invariably be able to catch any given motorist in a technical violation. This creates the temptation to use traffic stops as a means of investigating other law violations, as to which no probable cause or even articulable suspicion exists. Petitioners, who are both black, further contend that police officers might decide which motorists to stop based on decidedly impermissible factors, such as the race of the car's occupants. To avoid this danger, they say, the Fourth Amendment test for traffic stops should be, not * * * whether probable cause existed to justify the stop; but rather, whether a police officer, acting reasonably, would have made the stop for the reason given.

* * * Petitioners contend that the standard they propose is consistent with our past cases' disapproval of police attempts to use valid bases of action against citizens as pretexts for pursuing other investigatory agendas. We are reminded that in Florida v. Wells, 495 U.S. 1 (1990), we stated that "an inventory search must not be used as a ruse for a general rummaging in order to discover incriminating evidence"; that in Colorado v. Bertine, 479 U.S. 367 (1987), in approving an inventory search, we apparently thought it significant that there had been "no showing that the police, who were following standard procedures, acted in bad faith or for the sole purpose of investigation"; and that in New York v. Burger, 482 U.S. 691 (1987), we observed, in upholding the constitutionality of a

warrantless administrative inspection, that the search did not appear to
be "a 'pretext' for obtaining evidence of . . . violation of . . . penal laws."
But only an undiscerning reader would regard these cases as endorsing
the principle that ulterior motives can invalidate police conduct that is
justifiable on the basis of probable cause to believe that a violation of law
has occurred. In each case we were addressing the validity of a search
conducted in the absence of probable cause. Our quoted statements
simply explain that the exemption from the need for probable cause (and
warrant), which is accorded to searches made for the purpose of inventory
or administrative regulation, is not accorded to searches that are not
made for those purposes.

* * *

* * * Not only have we never held, outside the context of inventory
search or administrative inspection (discussed above), that an officer's
motive invalidates objectively justifiable behavior under the Fourth
Amendment; but we have repeatedly held and asserted the contrary. * * *
In United States v. Robinson, we held that a traffic-violation arrest (of the
sort here) would not be rendered invalid by the fact that it was "a mere
pretext for a narcotics search," and that a lawful postarrest search of the
person would not be rendered invalid by the fact that it was not
motivated by the officer-safety concern that justifies such searches. * * *

We think these cases foreclose any argument that the constitutional
reasonableness of traffic stops depends on the actual motivations of the
individual officers involved. We of course agree with petitioners that the
Constitution prohibits selective enforcement of the law based on
considerations such as race. But the constitutional basis for objecting to
intentionally discriminatory application of laws is the Equal Protection
Clause, not the Fourth Amendment. Subjective intentions play no role in
ordinary, probable-cause Fourth Amendment analysis.

* * * Recognizing that we have been unwilling to entertain Fourth
Amendment challenges based on the actual motivations of individual
officers, petitioners disavow any intention to make the individual officer's
subjective good faith the touchstone of "reasonableness." They insist that
the standard they have put forward—whether the officer's conduct
deviated materially from usual police practices, so that a reasonable
officer in the same circumstances would not have made the stop for the
reasons given—is an "objective" one.

But although framed in empirical terms, this approach is plainly and
indisputably driven by subjective considerations. Its whole purpose is to
prevent the police from doing under the guise of enforcing the traffic code
what they would like to do for different reasons. Petitioners' proposed
standard may not use the word "pretext," but it is designed to combat
nothing other than the perceived "danger" of the pretextual stop, albeit

only indirectly and over the run of cases. Instead of asking whether the individual officer had the proper state of mind, the petitioners would have us ask, in effect, whether (based on general police practices) it is plausible to believe that the officer had the proper state of mind.

Why one would frame a test designed to combat pretext in such fashion that the court cannot take into account actual and admitted pretext is a curiosity that can only be explained by the fact that our cases have foreclosed the more sensible option. If those cases were based only upon the evidentiary difficulty of establishing subjective intent, petitioners' attempt to root out subjective vices through objective means might make sense. But they were not based only upon that, or indeed even principally upon that. Their principal basis—which applies equally to attempts to reach subjective intent through ostensibly objective means—is simply that the Fourth Amendment's concern with "reasonableness" allows certain actions to be taken in certain circumstances, whatever the subjective intent. But even if our concern had been only an evidentiary one, petitioners' proposal would by no means assuage it. Indeed, it seems to us somewhat easier to figure out the intent of an individual officer than to plumb the collective consciousness of law enforcement in order to determine whether a "reasonable officer" would have been moved to act upon the traffic violation. While police manuals and standard procedures may sometimes provide objective assistance, ordinarily one would be reduced to speculating about the hypothetical reaction of a hypothetical constable— an exercise that might be called virtual subjectivity.

Moreover, police enforcement practices, even if they could be practicably assessed by a judge, vary from place to place and from time to time. We cannot accept that the search and seizure protections of the Fourth Amendment are so variable, and can be made to turn upon such trivialities. The difficulty is illustrated by petitioners' arguments in this case. Their claim that a reasonable officer would not have made this stop is based largely on District of Columbia police regulations which permit plainclothes officers in unmarked vehicles to enforce traffic laws "only in the case of a violation that is so grave as to pose an immediate threat to the safety of others." This basis of invalidation would not apply in jurisdictions that had a different practice. And it would not have applied even in the District of Columbia, if Officer Soto had been wearing a uniform or patrolling in a marked police cruiser.

* * *

Petitioners urge as an extraordinary factor in this case that the "multitude of applicable traffic and equipment regulations" is so large and so difficult to obey perfectly that virtually everyone is guilty of violation, permitting the police to single out almost whomever they wish for a stop.

But we are aware of no principle that would allow us to decide at what point a code of law becomes so expansive and so commonly violated that infraction itself can no longer be the ordinary measure of the lawfulness of enforcement. And even if we could identify such exorbitant codes, we do not know by what standard (or what right) we would decide, as petitioners would have us do, which particular provisions are sufficiently important to merit enforcement.

For the run-of-the-mine case, which this surely is, we think there is no realistic alternative to the traditional common-law rule that probable cause justifies a search and seizure.

Here the District Court found that the officers had probable cause to believe that petitioners had violated the traffic code. That rendered the stop reasonable under the Fourth Amendment, the evidence thereby discovered admissible, and the upholding of the convictions by the Court of Appeals for the District of Columbia Circuit correct.

### Questions About Whren

Professor Maclin, in Race and the Fourth Amendment, 51 Vand. L.Rev. 333 (1998), cites statistics that might give some perspective on the impact of *Whren* on Fourth Amendment protections. These statistics were compiled in two separate actions in Maryland and New Jersey, each alleging that State Troopers were engaged in racial profiling of Black motorists. The New Jersey Turnpike data revealed the following:

> A count of the traffic indicated that 13.5% of the automobiles carried a black occupant. A count of the traffic surveyed for speeding indicated that 98.1% of the vehicles on the road exceeded the speed limit. Fifteen percent of the speeding vehicles had a black occupant. Fifteen percent of the automobiles that both violated the speed limit and committed some other moving violation also had a black occupant. * * * [W]hile automobiles with black occupants represented only 15% of the motorists who violated the speeding laws, * * * 35.6% of the race identified stops * * * involved vehicles with black occupants.

In the Maryland case, Wilkins v. Maryland State Police, a state trooper stopped an automobile with four black occupants for speeding in April 1992 in Allegheny County. One of the occupants was Robert Wilkins, a Washington, D.C., criminal defense lawyer, who with his family, was returning to Washington after attending a funeral in Chicago. He was detained for more than 30 minutes, and the officer had a drug-sniffing dog brought to the scene. The canine sniff revealed no narcotics; the officer then permitted Wilson and his family to leave after writing out a speeding ticket.

Wilkins subsequently filed a class action lawsuit alleging Maryland troopers were illegally stopping black motorists because of their race. In addition to the police data, the plaintiffs' expert designed a statistical plan to determine whether Maryland troopers stop and search black motorists at a rate disproportionate to their numbers on the roads. The expert's data indicated that

> 93.3% of the drivers on Interstate 95 "were violating traffic laws and thus were eligible to be stopped by State Police. Of the violators, 17.5% were black, and 74.7% were white." * * * 72.9% of the motorists stopped and searched were black; 80.3% of the motorists searched were black, Hispanic or some other racial minority group; 19.7% of those searched were white. * * * [T]hirteen troopers conducted 85.4% of the searches. With the exception of one trooper, all of these troopers searched black and other minority motorists at much higher rates than these motorists travel on the highway. The trooper (omitting the trooper who searched black motorists at a rate close to their presence on the roads) with the lowest percentage of black motorist searches still searched black motorists at nearly twice the rate they were found to travel on the highway. The trooper with the highest percentage of black motorist searches searched only black motorists. Ten of the thirteen troopers searched minority motorists at least 80% of the time.
>
> * * * Troopers recovered contraband from 28.4% of the black motorists searched and from 28.8% of the white motorists searched. Thus, seventy percent of the searches uncovered no contraband.

The plaintiff's expert in *Wilkins* concluded that "the probability that black Interstate 95 drivers are subjected to searches at so high a rate by chance is less than one in one quintillion. It is wildly significant by statistical measures."

In light of the statistics indicating that traffic stops are used as a pretext to search minorities, did the Court reach the right result in *Whren* when it held that probable cause of a traffic violation ends the Fourth Amendment inquiry? If that is the wrong result, what should the Court have done? Should it have held that officers cannot make stops or arrests for traffic violations? Should it have held that officers can make stops for traffic violations, but that any evidence they find of some other violation cannot be admitted at trial? Would excluding the evidence, even though "legally" found, be justified? Would it deter police officers from stopping for traffic violations simply to harass minority drivers?

Professor Leong, in The Open Road and the Traffic Stop: narratives and Counter-Narratives of the American Dream, 64 Fla L. Rev. 305 (2012), notes that *Whren* provides officers virtually unlimited discretion to stop and search cars, and courts have done little to regulate this discretion:

> Under current doctrine, the legal justification for stopping a car need not be the same as the real reason the police officer wants to stop the car, so long as a reasonable officer would have had probable cause to believe that a traffic infraction in fact took place. [Professor] Paul Butler [now of the Georgetown University Law Center] describes riding in a police cruiser with a police officer friend and playing a game his friend

invented called "Stop that Car!" in which Butler "pick[s] a car—any car—and [the officer] stops it." Butler explains that his friend "is a good cop" because "[h]e waits until he has a legal reason to stop the car. It doesn't take long, never more than three or four blocks of following. There are so many potential traffic infractions that it is impossible to drive without committing one." The reality, then, is that the police are free to pick a car they wish to stop, follow it until the driver inevitably violates one of the vehicle code's myriad obscure provisions, and subsequently pull it over.

For other critiques of *Whren,* see O'Neill, Beyond Privacy, Beyond Probable Cause, Beyond the Fourth Amendment: New Strategies for Fighting Pretext Arrests, 69 Colo.L.Rev. 693 (1998) (arguing that instead of focusing on privacy, the Court in *Whren* should have focused on whether the police officer's conduct in *Whren* was abusive and arbitrary); Fan, The Police Gamesmanship Dilemma in Criminal Procedure, 44 U.C. Davis L.Rev. 1407 (2011) ("*Whren* stands as a controversial landmark of noninquiry and a license to make racial distinctions. *Whren* is a lightning rod for controversy because the Court took a don't ask, don't tell approach allowing police to do whatever it takes—without examining the accuracy of police beliefs about what it takes, basing deference on noninquiry rules rather than data.").

*Atwater* and *Whren* make a powerful combination. See Saltzburg, The Fourth Amendment: Internal Revenue Code or Body of Principles? 74 Geo.Wash.L.Rev. 956 (2006) ("*Atwater* and *Whren* clearly empower police departments to direct officers who see any traffic violation for which an arrest can be made, no matter how minor, to arrest the driver for the specific purpose of searching the car, even though the officer lacks reasonable suspicion that the car contains contraband or evidence of a crime.").

### *Testilying?*

The police officer in *Whren* testified that when he stopped the suspects' vehicle and approached the car, he observed two large plastic bags of crack cocaine in Whren's hands. Was Whren stupid or something? When he saw the officer approach the car, why didn't he try to hide the drugs? Professor Maclin, in Race and the Fourth Amendment, supra, comments on this aspect of *Whren:*

> After reviewing so many cases where police officers testify that they discovered illegal drugs in plain view or after a consent search, judges may begin to wonder why drug dealers are so stupid. * * * Of course, there is an alternative explanation other than drug dealers' desire to cooperate with the police for the type of police testimony seen in *Whren* and other cases where drugs are claimed to be found in plain view or after a consent search: police perjury. As Joseph D. McNamara, the former Police Chief of Kansas City and San Jose, has explained:

(H)undreds of thousands of police officers swear under oath that the drugs were in plain view or that the defendant gave consent to a search. This may happen occasionally but it defies belief that so many drug users are careless enough to leave illegal drugs where the police can see them or so dumb as to give cops consent to search them when they possess drugs.

* * * We can suppose that criminals are not rocket scientists and that Freud's insights apply to criminals no less than to anyone else. But even if a self-destructive error of the sort posited by the police is possible, it is not probable.

### *Equal Protection Issues*

Are there limitations other than those of the Fourth Amendment that might constrain officers who use traffic stops as a pretext to search or harass? In United States v. Scopo, 19 F.3d 777 (2d Cir.1994), the court upheld a firearms conviction based on evidence discovered during a stop for a traffic offense. Judge Newman, concurring, declared as follows:

In upholding Scopo's arrest, we should not be understood to be giving police officers carte blanche to skew their law enforcement activity against any group that displeases them. Though the Fourth Amendment permits a pretext arrest, if otherwise supported by probable cause, the Equal Protection Clause still imposes restraint on impermissibly class-based discriminations.

The Court in *Whren* also cited the Equal Protection Clause as a constraint on police officers in cases where the stop or arrest is reasonable under the Fourth Amendment. But it is extremely difficult to prove an equal protection violation when it comes to police officer conduct in the streets. Professor Maclin, in Race and the Fourth Amendment, supra, elaborates:

Before a black motorist can * * * prevail on the merits of an equal protection claim, he will have to show that he was singled out because of his race or ethnicity, and that similarly situated white motorists were not stopped. In the typical case, this means that a black defendant must show a specific intent or purpose by either the officer or his department to target blacks for traffic stops. * * * Unless an officer were to testify that the motorist was stopped because he was black or Hispanic, the specific intent standard will doom the typical pretextual traffic stop case involving a black motorist. In the atypical case involving a defense able to conduct a systematic study of the enforcement practices of a particular police department, there is a better chance of success if statistics suggest that officers are targeting black motorists. But even where statistics show a strong correlation between race and a particular outcome, the Court has still required the individual criminal defendant to prove that the government officials in his case were motivated by a discriminatory intent.

Finally, even if a black defendant challenging a pretextual traffic stop is able to obtain discovery and prevail on the merits of an equal protection claim, there is the question of remedy. The Court has shown no sign that it interprets the Equal Protection Clause to embody an exclusionary rule remedy, or that the Clause even requires the dismissal of criminal charges in a case involving a race-based prosecution. * * *

For these reasons, successful equal protection challenges to pretextual traffic stops by minority motorists will be rare. Thus, the *Whren* Court's apparent accord with the constitutional challenge in that case, ("We of course agree with petitioners that the Constitution prohibits selective enforcement of the law based on considerations such as race."), seems hollow.

For cases rejecting equal protection challenges to police searches and seizures after *Whren*, see, e.g., Johnson v. Crooks, 326 F.3d 995 (8th Cir. 2003) (even though officer followed a black motorist 11 miles before making a traffic stop, there was no showing of an equal protection violation, as the plaintiff "offered no evidence that Crooks does not stop non-African Americans under similar circumstances."); Bingham v. City of Manhattan Beach, 329 F.3d 723 (9th Cir. 2003) ("Essentially, Bingham argues that because he is African-American, the officer is white, and they disagree about the reasonableness of the traffic stop, these circumstances are sufficient to raise an inference of discrimination. We disagree that this is sufficient to state an equal protection claim."); Bradley v. United States, 299 F.3d 197 (3rd Cir. 2002) (the fact that the plaintiff, an African-American, was thoroughly searched at a Customs checkpoint while several white males were allowed to pass is not enough to show discriminatory intent).

Moreover, as predicted by Professor Maclin, courts have held that even if there is an equal protection violation, the evidence obtained is not excluded. See United States v. Nichols, 512 F.3d 789 (6th Cir. 2008) ("we are aware of no court that has ever applied the exclusionary rule for a violation of the Fourteenth Amendment's Equal Protection Clause, and we decline Nichols's invitation to do so here. Rather, we believe the proper remedy for any alleged violation is a 42 U.S.C. § 1983 action against the offending officers.").

Is it possible that the solution to pretextual stops after *Whren* has been shifted from constitutional regulation to regulation by public outrage and legislation? Public outrage over racial profiling in the use of traffic stops led to personnel changes in New Jersey, as well as new rules requiring Troopers to file reports concerning the race of motorists whom they stop. See "Whitman Admits Police Used Race in Turnpike Stops," New York Times, April 21, 1999, at B1. Legislation exists in a number of states requiring studies of how often racial profiling occurs and requiring police to record the race of each person stopped for a traffic violation. Samborn, "Profiled and Pulled Over," ABA Journal, October, 1999, at 18. Can you think of any other legislation that might be useful in regulating the pretextual use of traffic stops?

### *Probable Cause of a Traffic Violation*

One of the consequences of *Whren* is that courts, in deciding the reasonableness of searches and seizures under the Fourth Amendment, often find themselves immersed in interpreting the intricacies of state and local traffic laws. A traffic stop can only be used as a pretext under *Whren* if the officer has reasonable cause to believe that the motorist has actually violated a traffic law. See United States v. Mariscal, 285 F.3d 1127 (9th Cir. 2002) (*Whren* not applicable because the officer stopped the defendant for something that was not a traffic violation: the defendant turned right without signaling, but the local traffic law prohibited such turns only if "other traffic" would be affected by the turn; in this case, there was no "other traffic" on the road; the fact that the police officer's car was affected by the defendant's turn was irrelevant, because it was affected only "to the extent that the turn energized the officers to swoop down upon their prey"). See also United States v. Sowards, 690 F.3d 583 (4th Cir. 2012) (search made after officer stopped the defendant for speeding was invalid because determination of speeding—that the defendant was driving 75 mph in a 70 mph zone—was based on a visual estimate by an inexperienced officer who testified that he watched the defendant driving for about 100 yards and that "there's 12 feet in a yard" and 12 inches on a yardstick).

### *Reasonable Mistake of Fact, Mistake of Law*

Remember that in assessing probable cause or reasonable suspicion, the officer need not be correct. Reasonable mistakes of fact are excused. So it is with traffic stops and arrests after *Whren*. Thus, in United States v. Flores-Sandoval, 366 F.3d 961 (8th Cir. 2004), the defendant was stopped for not having a front license plate, in violation of the state traffic law. After the stop (and recovery of evidence) it was determined that the car did in fact have a front license plate that was partially obscured from view because it had been mounted below the standard plate bracket. The court held that the evidence was properly admitted. It analyzed the officer's mistake as follows:

> [A] mistake of fact does not automatically negate the validity of the stop. Officer Lippold was justified in making the stop if he had an

objectively reasonable basis for believing that the vehicle was not in conformity with Nebraska's traffic laws. * * *

Officer Lippold testified that he saw an empty front license bracket and assumed that there was no license plate on the front of the car. If credited, Lippold's testimony shows he mistakenly believed that Flores-Sandoval's car did not have a front license plate, in violation of Nebraska law. There is nothing in the record before this court to call into question the credibility determination made by the district court that Officer Lippold believed he had probable cause to stop Flores-Sandoval's vehicle. Officer Lippold's mistake was one of fact, not of law. So, we now turn to the question of whether his mistake of fact was objectively reasonable.

Officer Lippold testified that he relied on a regular practice of observing oncoming traffic-via his rear view mirror-and observing the light that bounced off of the reflective surface on the front license plate of the approaching vehicle. His observation of the Toyota led him to conclude—after seeing no reflection from the front of the vehicle and an empty plate bracket—that the vehicle did not have a front license plate. These perceptions, although flawed, were sufficiently reasonable to provide probable cause to stop the vehicle in which Flores-Sandoval was traveling.

On the other hand, if the officer is mistaken about whether a particular set of facts is in violation of the traffic law, a stop or arrest will be unreasonable. As indicated in *Flores-Sandoval*, the courts distinguish between reasonable mistakes of fact and mistakes of law. See United States v. Chanthasouxat, 342 F.3d 1271 (11th Cir. 2003) (officer's mistaken belief that the city code required vehicles to have an inside rear view mirror did not justify the traffic stop of the defendant's van: "the officer's mistake was one of law" and "an officer's mistake of law cannot provide the objective grounds for reasonable suspicion or probable cause to justify a traffic stop.").

## E. PLAIN VIEW AND PLAIN TOUCH SEIZURES

The concept of plain view underlies much of the law and practice under the *Terry* doctrine and the arrest-power rule, and it applies as well during searches conducted pursuant to a warrant or another exception to the warrant requirement. For example, the officer in *Robinson* seized narcotics in plain view (in the cigarette pack) during the course of a search incident to arrest; the officers in *Long* seized weapons in plain view in Long's car during the course of a search for self-protection under *Terry;* the officer in *Whren* seized evidence that he saw in Whren's hands after making a lawful traffic stop. As the Court put it in Texas v. Brown, 460 U.S. 730, 739 (1983), the plain view doctrine is best understood "not as an independent exception to the warrant clause, but simply as an extension of whatever the prior justification for an officer's access to an object may be."

In Coolidge v. New Hampshire, 403 U.S. 443 (1971), Justice Stewart's plurality opinion stated that if officers have a right to be in a particular place and come upon evidence that they have probable cause to believe is subject to seizure, they may seize it. See also Texas v. Brown, *supra* ("if, while lawfully engaged in an activity in a particular place, police officers perceive a suspicious object, they may seize it immediately"). In the following case, the Court explains the plain view doctrine in detail, and revisits some of the problems of applying that doctrine that divided the Court in *Coolidge*.

## HORTON V. CALIFORNIA
Supreme Court of the United States, 1990.
496 U.S. 128.

### JUSTICE STEVENS delivered the opinion of the Court.

In this case we revisit an issue that was considered, but not conclusively resolved, in Coolidge v. New Hampshire: Whether the warrantless seizure of evidence of crime in plain view is prohibited by the Fourth Amendment if the discovery of the evidence was not inadvertent. We conclude that even though inadvertence is a characteristic of most legitimate "plain view" seizures, it is not a necessary condition.

* * * Petitioner was convicted of the armed robbery of Erwin Wallaker, the treasurer of the San Jose Coin Club. * * *

Sergeant LaRault, an experienced police officer, investigated the crime and determined that there was probable cause to search petitioner's home for the proceeds of the robbery and for the weapons used by the robbers. His affidavit for a search warrant referred to police reports that described the weapons as well as the proceeds, but the warrant issued by the Magistrate only authorized a search for the proceeds, including three specifically described rings.

Pursuant to the warrant, LaRault searched petitioner's residence, but he did not find the stolen property. During the course of the search, however, he discovered the weapons in plain view and seized them. * * * LaRault testified that while he was searching for the rings, he also was interested in finding other evidence connecting petitioner to the robbery. Thus, the seized evidence was not discovered "inadvertently."

* * *

The right to security in person and property protected by the Fourth Amendment may be invaded in quite different ways by searches and seizures. A search compromises the individual interest in privacy; a seizure deprives the individual of dominion over his or her person or property. The "plain view" doctrine is often considered an exception to the general rule that warrantless searches are presumptively unreasonable, but this characterization overlooks the important difference between searches and seizures. If an article is already in plain view, neither its observation nor its seizure would involve any invasion of privacy. A seizure of the article, however, would obviously invade the owner's possessory interest. If "plain view" justifies an exception from an otherwise applicable warrant requirement, therefore, it must be an exception that is addressed to the concerns that are implicated by seizures rather than by searches.

The criteria that generally guide "plain view" seizures were set forth in Coolidge v. New Hampshire. The Court held that the seizure of two automobiles parked in plain view on the defendant's driveway in the course of arresting the defendant violated the Fourth Amendment. Accordingly, particles of gun powder that had been subsequently found in vacuum sweepings from one of the cars could not be introduced in evidence against the defendant. The State endeavored to justify the seizure of the automobiles, and their subsequent search at the police station, on four different grounds, including the "plain view" doctrine. The scope of that doctrine as it had developed in earlier cases was fairly summarized in * * * Justice Stewart's opinion:

* * *

"What the 'plain view' cases have in common is that the police officer in each of them had a prior justification for an intrusion in the course of which he came inadvertently across a piece of evidence incriminating the accused. * * * Of course, the extension of the original justification is legitimate only where it is immediately apparent to the police that they have evidence before them; the 'plain view' doctrine may not be used to extend a general exploratory search from one object to another until something incriminating at last emerges."

* * *

Justice Stewart concluded that the inadvertence requirement was necessary to avoid a violation of the express constitutional requirement that a valid warrant must particularly describe the things to be seized. He explained:

"The rationale of the exception to the warrant requirement, as just stated, is that a plain-view seizure will not turn an initially valid (and therefore limited) search into a 'general' one, while the inconvenience of procuring a warrant to cover an inadvertent discovery is great. But where the discovery is anticipated, where the police know in advance the location of the evidence and intend to seize it, the situation is altogether different. The requirement of a warrant to seize imposes no inconvenience whatever, or at least none which is constitutionally cognizable in a legal system that regards warrantless searches as '*per se* unreasonable' in the absence of 'exigent circumstances.' "

\* \* \*

We find two flaws in this reasoning. First, evenhanded law enforcement is best achieved by the application of objective standards of conduct, rather than standards that depend upon the subjective state of mind of the officer. The fact that an officer is interested in an item of evidence and fully expects to find it in the course of a search should not invalidate its seizure if the search is confined in area and duration by the terms of a warrant or a valid exception to the warrant requirement. If the officer has knowledge approaching certainty that the item will be found, we see no reason why he or she would deliberately omit a particular description of the item to be seized from the application for a search warrant. Specification of the additional item could only permit the officer to expand the scope of the search. On the other hand, if he or she has a valid warrant to search for one item and merely a suspicion concerning the second, whether or not it amounts to probable cause, we fail to see why that suspicion should immunize the second item from seizure if it is found during a lawful search for the first.

\* \* \*

Second, the suggestion that the inadvertence requirement is necessary to prevent the police from conducting general searches, or from converting specific warrants into general warrants, is not persuasive because that interest is already served by the requirements that no warrant issue unless it "particularly describ[es] the place to be searched and the persons or things to be seized," and that a warrantless search be circumscribed by the exigencies which justify its initiation. Scrupulous adherence to these requirements serves the interests in limiting the area and duration of the search that the inadvertence requirement inadequately protects. \* \* \*

\* \* \*

In this case, the scope of the search was not enlarged in the slightest by the omission of any reference to the weapons in the warrant. Indeed, if the three rings and other items named in the warrant had been found at the outset—or if petitioner had them in his possession and had responded to the warrant by producing them immediately—no search for weapons could have taken place. \* \* \*

\* \* \* The prohibition against general searches and general warrants serves primarily as a protection against unjustified intrusions on privacy.

But reliance on privacy concerns that support that prohibition is misplaced when the inquiry concerns the scope of an exception that merely authorizes an officer with a lawful right of access to an item to seize it without a warrant.

\* \* \*

[Based on the above reasoning, the Court rejects the implication in *Coolidge* that a plain view seizure must be inadvertent.]

**JUSTICE BRENNAN, with whom JUSTICE MARSHALL joins, dissenting.**

\* \* \*

[T]here are a number of instances in which a law enforcement officer might deliberately choose to omit certain items from a warrant application even though he has probable cause to seize them, knows they are on the premises, and intends to seize them when they are discovered in plain view. For example, the warrant application process can often be time-consuming, especially when the police attempt to seize a large number of items. An officer interested in conducting a search as soon as possible might decide to save time by listing only one or two hard-to-find items, such as the stolen rings in this case, confident that he will find in plain view all of the other evidence he is looking for before he discovers the listed items. Because rings could be located almost anywhere inside or outside a house, it is unlikely that a warrant to search for and seize the rings would restrict the scope of the search. An officer might rationally find the risk of immediately discovering the items listed in the warrant— thereby forcing him to conclude the search immediately—outweighed by the time saved in the application process.

\* \* \* It is true that the inadvertent discovery requirement furthers no privacy interests. \* \* \* But it does protect possessory interests. \* \* \* The Court today eliminates a rule designed to further possessory interests on the ground that it fails to further privacy interests. I cannot countenance such constitutional legerdemain.

\* \* \*

### *Probable Cause to Seize an Item in Plain View: Arizona v. Hicks*

One of the difficult plain view issues is how closely the police may examine an object to decide whether it is subject to seizure. In the 6–3 decision in Arizona v. Hicks, 480 U.S. 321 (1987), Justice Scalia wrote for the Court as it held that probable cause is necessary to justify a search that precedes a plain view seizure. Arizona police entered Hicks' apartment after a bullet was fired through its floor into the apartment below, injuring a man. The officers looked for the shooter, other victims and weapons. One officer noticed two sets of expensive stereo components that seemed out of place in an "ill-appointed four-room apartment." The officer moved some of the components in order to find serial numbers, telephoned in the numbers, and learned that one turntable he had moved was stolen. He seized the turntable immediately. Later it was learned that other equipment was stolen, and a warrant was obtained.

Justice Scalia rejected the state's argument that the officer's inspection of the underside of the turntable did not amount to a search: "A search is a search, even if it happens to disclose nothing but the bottom of a turntable." He also rejected the argument that the officer had sufficient cause to justify his actions. The state conceded that the officer lacked probable cause for a search, but sought to justify his actions on the basis of reasonable suspicion. Justice Scalia described the plain view doctrine as resting on the "desirability of sparing police, whose viewing of the object in the course of a lawful search is as legitimate as it would have been in a public place, the inconvenience and the risk—to themselves or to preservation of the evidence—of going to get a warrant." He further observed that "[n]o reason is apparent why an object should routinely be seizable on lesser grounds, during an unrelated search and seizure, than would have been needed to obtain a warrant for that same object if it had been known to be on the premises." Justice O'Connor, joined by Chief Justice Rehnquist and Justice Powell, dissented.

After *Hicks*, an officer must have probable cause to seize an item that he views during the course of legal activity. And that probable cause must be *readily apparent*—meaning that probable cause must exist without the necessity of a further search. For cases discussing the probable cause requirement for plain view seizures after *Hicks*, see United States v. Benish, 5 F.3d 20 (3d Cir.1993) (probable cause to seize a marijuana plant was immediately apparent, as the officer had taken classes on identifying marijuana); United States v. Cooper, 19 F.3d 1154 (7th Cir.1994) (probable cause to seize an empty ammunition box was immediately apparent, where it was found together with drugs and weapons: "The ammunition box, unlike a cigar box, is probative of weapons possession and drug dealing."); United States v. Pindell, 336 F.3d 1049 (D.C.Cir. 2003) (probable cause to seize a notebook was immediately apparent, as the victim of a robbery had told the officer that the perpetrator had been disguised as a police officer and had recorded information in a notebook during the robbery; the officer found the notebook lying next to a police uniform in the defendant's car).

## The Plain Touch Doctrine

If an officer, acting in the course of lawful activity, can determine *by touch* that an object is evidence or contraband, can he seize the object? That was the question in Minnesota v. Dickerson, 508 U.S. 366 (1993), where an officer, in the course of a stop and frisk permitted by the *Terry* doctrine, patted-down the suspect and felt a small, hard, pea-shaped object in the suspect's shirt pocket. At the suppression hearing, the officer testified that he examined the object with his fingers "and it slid and it felt to be a lump of crack cocaine in cellophane." Because the suspect had left a house known to be a place for drug activity, the officer concluded that there was probable cause to believe that the pea-shaped object was contraband, and he pulled the object from the suspect's pocket; the object turned out to be a small plastic bag containing crack cocaine.

The state in *Dickerson* argued that the seizure was permissible because the officer obtained probable cause by "plain touch" during a lawful frisk, which was analogized to obtaining probable cause by plain view during a lawful search. The Supreme Court, in an opinion by Justice White, stated that the plain view doctrine "has an obvious application by analogy to cases in which an officer discovers contraband through the sense of touch during an otherwise lawful search."

While the Court found that the Fourth Amendment permits the seizure of evidence discovered through the sense of touch in the course of a lawful search, it also found that the plain touch exception *did not justify the search* under the facts of *Dickerson*. This was because the officer did more than merely touch the object in the course of a lawful *Terry* frisk. Rather, he went beyond the scope of a *Terry* protective frisk, by pushing and prodding the object—after concluding that it was not a weapon—in order to determine whether it was contraband. Thus the officer at that point was conducting a search for evidence, beyond the permissible scope of the *Terry* doctrine.. Justice White evaluated the facts of *Dickerson* as follows:

> Although the officer was lawfully in a position to feel the lump in respondent's pocket, because *Terry* entitled him to place his hands upon respondent's jacket, the court below determined that the incriminating character of the object was not immediately apparent. Rather, the officer determined that the item was contraband only after conducting a further search, one not authorized by *Terry* or any other exception to the warrant requirement. Because the further search of respondent's jacket was constitutionally invalid, the seizure of the cocaine that followed is likewise unconstitutional.

Justice Scalia wrote a short concurring opinion. Chief Justice Rehnquist wrote a short dissenting opinion joined by Justices Blackmun and Thomas. He agreed with the majority's position on the plain touch exception, but argued that a remand was necessary to allow the Minnesota court to apply the exception to the facts of the case.

How much more information would have been required for the officer to find probable cause to believe that a hard, pea-shaped object in Dickerson's pocket was crack cocaine? See United States v. Yamba, 506 F.3d 251 (3rd Cir. 2007) (officer properly frisking for weapons felt a "soft, squishy substance" and what felt like "small buds or seeds" inside the suspect's coat pocket; at that point the officer had probable cause to believe the suspect possessed marijuana); United States v. Williams, 139 F.3d 628 (8th Cir.1998) (officer who conducted *Terry* frisk and felt a package, had probable cause to seize it because the suspect had just been observed taking part in a drug transaction).

## F.  AUTOMOBILES AND OTHER MOVABLE OBJECTS

One of the well-recognized exceptions to the warrant requirement is that which is commonly referred to as the "automobile exception." Under that exception the police may search an automobile without a warrant, so long as they have probable cause to believe it contains evidence of criminal activity. The Court first created the exception in Carroll v. United States, 267 U.S. 132 (1925), and it is sometimes called "the *Carroll* Doctrine." As you study the following material, consider two questions: whether the rationale for the exception can withstand analysis; and whether acceptance of the rationale might logically require its extension to objects other than cars.

### 1.  The *Carroll* Doctrine

Carroll v. United States involved a violation of the National Prohibition Act, as did many early search and seizure cases. In December 1921, Carroll and a cohort were driving westward on a highway between Detroit and Grand Rapids when they were stopped by federal prohibition agents who were patrolling the road. Bootlegging traffic was known to be heavy in the area, due to its proximity to Canada. The officers knew the men had been previously involved in transporting liquor.  Carroll's car was searched without a warrant, and 68 quarts of whiskey and gin were found behind the upholstering of the seats. The defendants were convicted of illegal transportation of intoxicating liquor, a misdemeanor.

The Court, in a 7–2 decision written by Chief Justice Taft, found the search to be constitutional. The major contention was not probable cause, but whether a warrant was required for the search. Justice Taft declared that a warrant could not reasonably have been demanded in light of the mobility of the vehicle:

> [T]he guaranty of freedom from unreasonable searches and seizures by the Fourth Amendment has been construed, practically since the

beginning of the Government, as recognizing a necessary difference between a search of a store, dwelling house or other structure in respect of which a proper official warrant readily may be obtained, and a search of a ship, motor boat, wagon or automobile, for contraband goods, where it is not practicable to secure a warrant because the vehicle can be quickly moved out of the locality or jurisdiction in which the warrant must be sought.

Taft further noted that the right to search and the validity of the seizure were not dependent on the right to arrest, thus clearly distinguishing this search from that of an automobile incident to the arrest of the driver.

## 2. The Progeny of *Carroll*

In the following case, the Court considered whether the *Carroll* doctrine, and its reliance on a car's mobility, could be invoked when a warrantless search of a car occurred after the car had been removed to the police station. A car impounded by the police is hardly mobile within the meaning of *Carroll*. So what can justify a warrantless search of an immobile car?

### CHAMBERS V. MARONEY

Supreme Court of the United States, 1970.
399 U.S. 42.

### MR. JUSTICE WHITE delivered the opinion of the Court.

The principal question in this case concerns the admissibility of evidence seized from an automobile, in which petitioner was riding at the time of his arrest, after the automobile was taken to a police station and was there thoroughly searched without a warrant. The Court of Appeals for the Third Circuit found no violation of petitioner's Fourth Amendment rights. We affirm.

[Officers had probable cause to believe that the petitioner and three other men had robbed a gas station and left in a car. The car was identified and pulled over by officers. The occupants were arrested and the car was driven to the police station. In the course of a thorough search of the car at the station, the police found weapons and other evidence of the crime.]

[The Court holds that the police had probable cause to make an arrest, but that the search of the car at the police station was too removed from the arrest to be justified as a search incident to arrest.]

\* \* \*

\* \* \* *Carroll* holds a search warrant unnecessary where there is probable cause to search an automobile stopped on the highway; the car is movable, the occupants are alerted, and the car's contents may never be found again if a warrant must be obtained. Hence an immediate search is constitutionally permissible.

Arguably, because of the preference for a magistrate's judgment only the immobilization of the car should be permitted until a search warrant is obtained; arguably, only the "lesser" intrusion is permissible until the magistrate authorizes the "greater." But which is the "greater" and which the "lesser" intrusion is itself a debatable question and the answer may depend on a variety of circumstances. For constitutional purposes, we see no difference between on the one hand seizing and holding a car before presenting the probable cause issue to a magistrate and on the other hand carrying out an immediate search without a warrant. Given probable cause to search, either course is reasonable under the Fourth Amendment.

On the facts before us, the blue station wagon could have been searched on the spot when it was stopped since there was probable cause to search and it was a fleeting target for a search. The probable-cause factor still obtained at the station house and so did the mobility of the car unless the Fourth Amendment permits a warrantless seizure of the car and the denial of its use to anyone until a warrant is secured. In that event there is little to choose in terms of practical consequences between an immediate search without a warrant and the car's immobilization until a warrant is obtained.[a] The same consequences may not follow where there is unforeseeable cause to search a house. Compare Vale v. Louisiana [discussed in the section on exigent circumstances]. But as *Carroll,* supra, held, for the purposes of the Fourth Amendment there is a constitutional difference between houses and cars.

\* \* \*

MR. JUSTICE BLACKMUN took no part in the consideration or decision of this case.

**MR. JUSTICE HARLAN, concurring in part and dissenting in part.**

\* \* \*

The Court concedes that the police could prevent removal of the evidence by temporarily seizing the car for the time necessary to obtain a warrant. It does not dispute that such a course would fully protect the interests of effective law enforcement; rather it states that whether temporary seizure is a "lesser" intrusion than warrantless search "is itself a debatable question and the answer may depend on a variety of

---

[a]   It was not unreasonable in this case to take the car to the station house. All occupants in the car were arrested in a dark parking lot in the middle of the night. A careful search at that point was impractical and perhaps not safe for the officers, and it would serve the owner's convenience and the safety of his car to have the vehicle and the keys together at the station house.

circumstances."[b] I believe it clear that a warrantless search involves the greater sacrifice of Fourth Amendment values.

* * * [I]n the circumstances in which this problem is likely to occur, the lesser intrusion will almost always be the simple seizure of the car for the period—perhaps a day—necessary to enable the officers to obtain a search warrant. In the first place, as this case shows, the very facts establishing probable cause to search will often also justify arrest of the occupants of the vehicle. Since the occupants themselves are to be taken into custody, they will suffer minimal further inconvenience from the temporary immobilization of their vehicle. Even where no arrests are made, persons who wish to avoid a search—either to protect their privacy or to conceal incriminating evidence—will almost certainly prefer a brief loss of the use of the vehicle in exchange for the opportunity to have a magistrate pass upon the justification for the search. To be sure, one can conceive of instances in which the occupant, having nothing to hide and lacking concern for the privacy of the automobile, would be more deeply offended by a temporary immobilization of his vehicle than by a prompt search of it. However, such a person always remains free to consent to an immediate search, thus avoiding any delay. Where consent is not forthcoming, the occupants of the car have an interest in privacy that is protected by the Fourth Amendment even where the circumstances justify a temporary seizure. The Court's endorsement of a warrantless invasion of that privacy where another course would suffice is simply inconsistent with our repeated stress on the Fourth Amendment's mandate of adherence to judicial processes.[c]

* * *

### QUESTIONS AFTER CHAMBERS

What implications does *Chambers* have for searches of parked cars, where the police do not make an initial stop? Does it matter where the car is parked, or whether the initial police-vehicle encounter is deliberate or by chance? The Court considered these questions in Coolidge v. New Hampshire, 403 U.S. 443 (1971), in which the police seized the defendant's car from his driveway shortly after the defendant's arrest, and searched it two days later at the police station, and twice more in the following months. A plurality held that the warrantless search was not permissible, because of the absence of

---

[b] The Court, unable to decide whether search or temporary seizure is the "lesser" intrusion, in this case authorizes both. * * * At all times the car and its contents were secure against removal or destruction. Nevertheless, the Court approves the searches without even an inquiry into the officers' ability promptly to take their case before a magistrate.

[c] Circumstances might arise in which it would be impracticable to immobilize the car for the time required to obtain a warrant—for example, where a single police officer must take arrested suspects to the station, and has no way of protecting the suspects' car during his absence. In such situations it might be wholly reasonable to perform an on-the-spot search based on probable cause. However, where nothing in the situation makes impracticable the obtaining of a warrant, I cannot join the Court in shunting aside that vital Fourth Amendment safeguard.

exigency. This is the first and last Supreme Court case in which a warrantless automobile search was held to be unconstitutional for that reason. In *Coolidge*, the government could not argue that it was impracticable to obtain a warrant before seizing the car, because in fact the officers *had* obtained a warrant; the problem was that it was defective because it was not issued by a neutral and detached magistrate. The Court considered whether the potential mobility of the car justified the warrantless seizure (and therefore justified a warrantless search of the car under *Chambers*). Justice Stewart, writing for the plurality, found no exigency based on mobility, because Coolidge had been arrested, his wife had been removed from the premises, and the police had control of the car as it was parked outside Coolidge's house.

Justice Stewart distinguished *Chambers* on the ground that the *initial* intrusion was unjustified without a warrant. That is, the officers did not obtain a proper warrant even though they knew precisely where Coolidge's car was parked at all times, and had been investigating him for weeks. This was unlike the situation in *Chambers*, where the officers were on patrol and happened to *come upon* a car that fit the description of one seen at a gas station robbery; there was no way in which the officers in *Chambers* could have been expected to obtain a warrant *before* they even seized the car. And because they could seize it without a warrant, under the rationale of *Chambers*, they could also search it without a warrant.

Subsequently, the Supreme Court has narrowed *Coolidge* to its facts—it does not stand for the proposition that the car must be actually mobile before officers can search without a warrant. In one post-*Coolidge* case, Cardwell v. Lewis, 417 U.S. 583 (1974), a plurality of the Court explicitly rejected the contention that mobility of the car before it is seized makes a difference: "The fact that the car in *Chambers* was seized after being stopped on a highway, whereas Lewis' car was seized from a public parking lot, has little, if any, legal significance." Similarly, in Texas v. White, 423 U.S. 67 (1975), the Court upheld the warrantless search of an automobile that had been towed to the police department's impound lot. The Court rejected the argument of the dissenters that the police should have been required to provide a justification for removing the car to the stationhouse rather than searching it on the scene. See also Michigan v. Thomas, 458 U.S. 259 (1982) (holding "that the justification to conduct such a warrantless search does not vanish once the car has been immobilized"). An impatient Supreme Court summarily reversed a Florida intermediate appellate court in Florida v. Meyers, 466 U.S. 380 (1984) (per curiam), and, as in Michigan v. Thomas, reiterated the *Chambers* holding that a warrantless search of an automobile may be conducted after it has been immobilized, as long as there is probable cause to believe that the automobile contains evidence of criminal activity.

In light of *White* and *Thomas,* some lower courts have interpreted *Coolidge* to mean that a warrant is required only if the officers had a clear opportunity to obtain a warrant before *seizing* the car. Under this view, *Chambers* is based on the rationale that due to its mobility, a car can be seized pending the obtaining of a warrant; and a search without a warrant is permitted because the search of a car is no more intrusive than would be the seizure of the car pending a warrant. But if the original seizure itself could have been preceded by a warrant, then the premise of *Chambers* is missing and the car exception ought not to apply. This explanation is consistent with the facts of *Chambers,* where the officers clearly could not have obtained a warrant before seizing the car, and with the facts of *Coolidge,* where the officers could have obtained a valid warrant before seizing the car. See, e.g., United States v. Moscatiello, 771 F.2d 589 (1st Cir.1985) (*Coolidge* distinguished where officers seized car after pursuing it in a rapidly developing situation); United States v. Reed, 26 F.3d 523 (5th Cir.1994) (warrantless search of car permitted; *Coolidge* distinguished because the officers "did not know where the car was, nor that it contained the money, until they completed their tracking upon arrival at the house").

### *The Diminished Expectation of Privacy Rationale: California v. Carney*

It is apparent that exigency based on actual mobility is not a sufficient basis for the automobile exception after cases like *Chambers, White* and *Thomas.* The Court has explicitly held that the car exception permits a warrantless search even if the vehicle is immobile. See also See United States v. Howard, 489 F.3d 484 (2nd Cir. 2007) (Sotomayor, J.) ("Even where there is little practical likelihood that the vehicle will be driven away, the exception applies at least when that possibility exists"— requiring actual mobility would "impermissibly graft onto the automobile exception a requirement beyond the inherent mobility of an operational vehicle"); United States v. Navas, 597 F.3d 492 (10th Cir. 2010) (upholding a warrantless search of a trailer unattached to a car: "a vehicle's inherent mobility—not the probability that it might actually be set in motion—is the foundation of the mobility rationale").

In California v. Carney, 471 U.S. 386 (1985), the Court re-evaluated the automobile exception to the warrant requirement and concluded that "the reasons for the vehicle exception are twofold." Chief Justice Burger, writing for the Court, explained as follows:

> The capacity to be quickly moved was clearly the basis of the holding in *Carroll,* and our cases have consistently recognized ready mobility as one of the principal bases of the automobile exception. * * *
>
> However, although ready mobility alone was perhaps the original justification for the vehicle exception, our later cases have made clear that ready mobility is not the only basis for the exception. * * * Besides the element of mobility, less rigorous warrant requirements govern because the expectation of privacy with respect

to one's automobile is significantly less than that relating to one's home or office.

Even in cases where an automobile was not immediately mobile, the lesser expectation of privacy resulting from its use as a readily mobile vehicle justified application of the vehicular exception.

See also United States v. Howard, 489 F.3d 484 (2nd Cir. 2007) (Sotomayor, J.) ("Thus, even if the vehicles searched in the case at hand were not 'readily mobile' within the meaning of the automobile exception, a warrantless search of them would be justified based on the diminished expectation of privacy enjoyed by the drivers and passenger while traveling on the Thruway.").

Why do citizens have a diminished expectation of privacy with respect to their automobiles? The Chief Justice in *Carney* explained that these reduced expectations "derive not from the fact that the area to be searched is in plain view, but from the pervasive regulation of vehicles capable of traveling on the public highways." He stressed that automobiles are "subjected to pervasive and continuing governmental regulation and controls."

In Pennsylvania v. Labron, 518 U.S. 938 (1996), the Court, in a per curiam decision, reaffirmed the principle that exigent circumstances are not required to justify the warrantless search of an automobile. The Court upheld warrantless searches of two cars where the police had probable cause to believe that each contained drugs. It did not matter that there was no risk of destruction of evidence at the time the searches were conducted. Thereafter, in Maryland v. Dyson, 527 U.S. 465 (1999) (per curiam), the Court once again reaffirmed the *Carroll* doctrine, relying on *Labron* to overturn a state court's suppression of evidence. Officers had probable cause to believe that Dyson's car contained drugs, and they conducted a warrantless search. The Maryland court suppressed the evidence because there was no indication of any exigency that would have precluded the police from obtaining a warrant before the search. The Court stated categorically that "the automobile exception has no separate exigency requirement" and that the probable cause finding "alone satisfies the automobile exception to the Fourth Amendment's warrant requirement."

### *Motor Homes*

The Court in *Carney* considered whether the dual justification for the automobile exception (inherent mobility and diminished expectation of privacy) applied to the warrantless search of a motor home. A six-person majority held that police officers validly searched a "Dodge Mini Motor Home" with probable cause but no warrant when the motor home was parked in a lot in a downtown area. Officers had received information that the motor home was used by a person who exchanged marijuana for sex. They watched a youth enter the motor home and remain there for more than an hour. When he left, the officers stopped him and learned that he had received marijuana in exchange for sexual contacts. The officers knocked on the door and Carney stepped out. They identified themselves as officers and entered the motor home where they saw marijuana and related paraphernalia.

Chief Justice Burger rejected the argument that the motor home was different from other vehicles because it was capable of functioning as a home as well as a vehicle. He reasoned that "[t]o distinguish between respondent's motor home and an ordinary sedan for purposes of the vehicle exception would require that we apply the exception depending upon the size of the vehicle and the quality of its appointments" and "to fail to apply the exception to vehicles such as a motor home ignores the fact that a motor home lends itself easily to use as an instrument of illicit drug traffic and other illegal activity." Thus, the Court declined "to distinguish between 'worthy' and 'unworthy' vehicles which are either on the public roads and highways, or situated such that it is reasonable to conclude that the vehicle is not being used as a residence." In a footnote, the Court noted that it did not "pass on the application of the vehicle exception to a motor home that is situated in a way or place that objectively indicates that it is being used as a residence." It suggested, however, some factors that might be relevant in determining whether a warrant would be required: "its location, whether the vehicle is licensed, whether it is connected to utilities, and whether it has convenient access to a public road."[24]

Justice Stevens, joined by Justices Brennan and Marshall, dissented. He argued that the Court "accorded priority to an exception rather than to the general rule." He concluded that because a motor home was a combination of home and car, the general preference for a warrant should govern a close case.

### 3. Movable Containers—In and Out of Cars

If the automobile exception were based totally on exigency due to mobility of the car, then it should also permit warrantless searches of other mobile containers such as briefcases, suitcases, and footlockers—they are potentially mobile as well. However, as seen in *Carney,* the exception is also (and probably primarily) based on the reduced expectation of privacy accorded an automobile. Is there any way to distinguish mobile containers, such as suitcases, from automobiles on privacy grounds? The Supreme Court did just that in United States v.

---

[24] See United States v. Navas, 597 F.3d 492 (2nd Cir. 2010) (warrantless search of a trailer unattached to a vehicle upheld: "the trailer bore no objective indicia of residential use that might give rise to elevated privacy expectations in its contents").

Chadwick, 433 U.S. 1 (1977), where it held that the mobility of a footlocker justified its *seizure* upon probable cause, but that a warrant was required to *search* the footlocker, unless emergency circumstances rendered a seizure insufficient to protect the state interest (e.g., if the footlocker was ticking). Chief Justice Burger, writing for the Court, distinguished mobile containers from cars on the following grounds:

> The factors which diminish the privacy aspects of an automobile do not apply to respondents' footlocker. Luggage contents are not open to public view, except as a condition to a border entry or common carrier travel; nor is luggage subject to regular inspections and official scrutiny on a continuing basis. Unlike an automobile, whose primary function is transportation, luggage is intended as a repository of personal effects. In sum, a person's expectations of privacy in personal luggage are substantially greater than in an automobile.

Because of the higher expectation of privacy in the footlocker, it could not be said, as it could in *Chambers,* that an immediate search would be no more intrusive than a seizure pending a warrant. As the Chief Justice explained in a footnote:

> A search of the interior [of the footlocker] was therefore a far greater intrusion into Fourth Amendment values than the impoundment of the footlocker. Though surely a substantial infringement of respondents' use and possession, the seizure did not diminish respondents' legitimate expectation that the footlocker's contents would remain private.

It was the greatly reduced expectation of privacy in the automobile that made the Court in *Chambers* unwilling to decide whether an immediate search of an automobile constituted a greater intrusion than its seizure pending a warrant. But because there is a higher expectation of privacy in luggage than cars, a search of that luggage was found to be a greater intrusion than seizure pending a warrant.

### QUESTIONS AFTER CHADWICK

The crux of the majority's argument in *Chadwick* is that one has a lesser expectation of privacy in one's car than in movable containers such as luggage. Is the lesser expectation of privacy surrounding autos simply the result of the Supreme Court having said so?

Does the fact that vehicles are used essentially for transportation demand, or even allow, the conclusion that they are seldom used as repositories for personal effects? Would that assertion hold true in the case of a traveling salesman who lives out of his car for several days each week? Do the particular facts of any case make a difference in light of the Court's categorical "diminished expectation" analysis?

## *Mobile Containers in the Car*

With a warrant required for the search of a mobile container, but not required for the search of an automobile, it was only a matter of time before the Court was presented with cases in which the two rules would collide. Which rule applies when an officer finds a mobile container when searching a car without a warrant? In Arkansas v. Sanders, 442 U.S. 753 (1979), the Court held that a warrant was required to search a suitcase that had been placed in the trunk of a taxi. In *Sanders*, officers had probable cause to search the passenger's suitcase, but no probable cause to search anywhere else in the taxi. Thereafter, in United States v. Ross, 456 U.S. 798 (1982), the Court upheld the warrantless search of a paper bag and pouch found during the search of a car. Justice Stevens, writing for a six-person majority, noted that "in neither *Chadwick* nor *Sanders* did the police have probable cause to search the vehicle or anything within it except the footlocker in the former case and the green suitcase in the latter." In contrast, in *Ross* the officers had probable cause to search the entire car for drugs. Justice Stevens noted that the *Carroll* doctrine would largely be nullified if it did not extend to containers such as those in *Ross,* because "contraband goods rarely are strewn across the trunk or floor of a car."

Justice Marshall, joined by Justice Brennan in dissent in *Ross,* emphasized the anomalous results that could occur due to the fine lines drawn between *Ross* and *Sanders.* For example, if officers were informed that a person has drugs in a bag in the trunk, it would appear that probable cause is localized in the bag, and hence *Sanders* would apply. But if they are more generally informed that there are drugs in the trunk, *Ross* would apply. Yet it is notable that the *Ross* dissenters did not challenge the primacy of the *Carroll* doctrine, and accepted the majority's premise that there is a diminished expectation of privacy in an automobile. *Sanders, Ross,* and *Chadwick* are extensively discussed in the next case, in which the Court again tries to resolve the question of whether a warrant is required to search a container placed in a car.

## CALIFORNIA V. ACEVEDO

Supreme Court of the United States, 1991.
500 U.S. 565.

### JUSTICE BLACKMUN delivered the opinion of the Court.

This case requires us once again to consider the so-called "automobile exception" to the warrant requirement of the Fourth Amendment and its application to the search of a closed container in the trunk of a car.

* * * On October 28, 1987, Officer Coleman of the Santa Ana, Cal., Police Department received a telephone call from a federal drug

enforcement agent in Hawaii. The agent informed Coleman that he had seized a package containing marijuana which was to have been delivered to the Federal Express office in Santa Ana and which was addressed to J.R. Daza at 805 West Stevens Avenue in that city. The agent arranged to send the package to Coleman instead. Coleman then was to take the package to the Federal Express office and arrest the person who arrived to claim it.

\* \* \* At about 10:30 a.m. on October 30, a man, who identified himself as Jamie Daza, arrived to claim the package. He accepted it and drove to his apartment on West Stevens. He carried the package into the apartment.

\* \* \*

At 12:30 p.m., respondent Charles Steven Acevedo arrived. He entered Daza's apartment, stayed for about 10 minutes, and reappeared carrying a brown paper bag that looked full. The officers noticed that the bag was the size of one of the wrapped marijuana packages sent from Hawaii. Acevedo walked to a silver Honda in the parking lot. He placed the bag in the trunk of the car and started to drive away. Fearing the loss of evidence, officers in a marked police car stopped him. They opened the trunk and the bag, and found marijuana.

\* \* \*

The California Court \* \* \* concluded that the marijuana found in the paper bag in the car's trunk should have been suppressed. The court concluded that the officers had probable cause to believe that the paper bag contained drugs but lacked probable cause to suspect that Acevedo's car, itself, otherwise contained contraband. Because the officers' probable cause was directed specifically at the bag, the court held that the case was controlled by United States v. Chadwick rather than by United States v. Ross. Although the court agreed that the officers could seize the paper bag, it held that, under *Chadwick,* they could not open the bag without first obtaining a warrant for that purpose. The court then recognized "the anomalous nature" of the dichotomy between the rule in *Chadwick* and the rule in *Ross.* That dichotomy dictates that if there is probable cause to search a car, then the entire car—including any closed container found therein—may be searched without a warrant, but if there is probable cause only as to a container in the car, the container may be held but not searched until a warrant is obtained.

\* \* \*

In United States v. Ross, we held that a warrantless search of an automobile under the *Carroll* doctrine could include a search of a container or package found inside the car when such a search was supported by probable cause. \* \* \* Thus, "[i]f probable cause justifies the search of a lawfully stopped vehicle, it justifies the search of every part of the vehicle and its contents that may conceal the object of the search." In *Ross,* therefore, we clarified the scope of the *Carroll* doctrine as properly including a "probing search" of compartments and containers within the automobile so long as the search is supported by probable cause.

In addition to this clarification, *Ross* distinguished the *Carroll* doctrine from the separate rule that governed the search of closed containers. The Court had announced this separate rule, unique to luggage and other closed packages, bags, and containers, in United States v. Chadwick. In *Chadwick,* federal narcotics agents had probable cause to believe that a 200-pound double-locked footlocker contained marijuana. The agents tracked the locker as the defendants removed it from a train and carried it through the station to a waiting car. As soon as the defendants lifted the locker into the trunk of the car, the agents arrested them, seized the locker, and searched it. In this Court, the United States did not contend that the locker's brief contact with the automobile's trunk sufficed to make the *Carroll* doctrine applicable. Rather, the United States urged that the search of movable luggage could be considered analogous to the search of an automobile.

The Court rejected this argument because, it reasoned, a person expects more privacy in his luggage and personal effects than he does in his automobile. * * *

In Arkansas v. Sanders, the Court extended *Chadwick's* rule to apply to a suitcase actually being transported in the trunk of a car. In *Sanders,* the police had probable cause to believe a suitcase contained marijuana. They watched as the defendant placed the suitcase in the trunk of a taxi and was driven away. The police pursued the taxi for several blocks, stopped it, found the suitcase in the trunk, and searched it. Although the Court had applied the *Carroll* doctrine to searches of integral parts of the automobile itself, (indeed, in *Carroll,* contraband whiskey was in the upholstery of the seats) it did not extend the doctrine to the warrantless search of personal luggage "merely because it was located in an automobile lawfully stopped by the police." * * *

In *Ross,* the Court endeavored to distinguish between *Carroll,* which governed the *Ross* automobile search, and *Chadwick* * * *. It held that the *Carroll* doctrine covered searches of automobiles when the police had probable cause to search an entire vehicle but that the *Chadwick* doctrine governed searches of luggage when the officers had probable cause to search only a container within the vehicle. Thus, in a *Ross* situation, the police could conduct a reasonable search under the Fourth Amendment without obtaining a warrant, whereas in a *Sanders* situation, the police had to obtain a warrant before they searched.

* * *

\* \* \* We now must decide the question deferred in *Ross:* whether the Fourth Amendment requires the police to obtain a warrant to open the sack in a movable vehicle simply because they lack probable cause to search the entire car. We conclude that it does not.

\* \* \* Dissenters in *Ross* asked why the suitcase in *Sanders* was "more private, less difficult for police to seize and store, or in any other relevant respect more properly subject to the warrant requirement, than a container that police discover in a probable-cause search of an entire automobile?" We now agree that a container found after a general search of the automobile and a container found in a car after a limited search for the container are equally easy for the police to store and for the suspect to hide or destroy. In fact, we see no principled distinction in terms of either the privacy expectation or the exigent circumstances between the paper bag found by the police in *Ross* and the paper bag found by the police here. Furthermore, by attempting to distinguish between a container for which the police are specifically searching and a container which they come across in a car, we have provided only minimal protection for privacy and have impeded effective law enforcement.

The line between probable cause to search a vehicle and probable cause to search a package in that vehicle is not always clear, and separate rules that govern the two objects to be searched may enable the police to broaden their power to make warrantless searches and disserve privacy interests. \* \* \* At the moment when officers stop an automobile, it may be less than clear whether they suspect with a high degree of certainty that the vehicle contains drugs in a bag or simply contains drugs. If the police know that they may open a bag only if they are actually searching the entire car, they may search more extensively than they otherwise would in order to establish the general probable cause required by *Ross*.

\* \* \* We cannot see the benefit of a rule that requires law enforcement officers to conduct a more intrusive search in order to justify a less intrusive one.

To the extent that the *Chadwick-Sanders* rule protects privacy, its protection is minimal. Law enforcement officers may seize a container and hold it until they obtain a search warrant. *Chadwick.* Since the police, by hypothesis, have probable cause to seize the property, we can assume that a warrant will be routinely forthcoming in the overwhelming majority of cases. And the police often will be able to search containers without a warrant, despite the *Chadwick-Sanders* rule, as a search incident to a lawful arrest.

* * *

Finally, the search of a paper bag intrudes far less on individual privacy than does the incursion sanctioned long ago in *Carroll*. In that case, prohibition agents slashed the upholstery of the automobile. This Court nonetheless found their search to be reasonable under the Fourth Amendment. If destroying the interior of an automobile is not unreasonable, we cannot conclude that looking inside a closed container is. In light of the minimal protection to privacy afforded by the *Chadwick-Sanders* rule, and our serious doubt whether that rule substantially serves privacy interests, we now hold that the Fourth Amendment does not compel separate treatment for an automobile search that extends only to a container within the vehicle.

* * * The *Chadwick-Sanders* rule not only has failed to protect privacy but it has also confused courts and police officers and impeded effective law enforcement. * * *

The discrepancy between the two rules has led to confusion for law enforcement officers. For example, when an officer, who has developed probable cause to believe that a vehicle contains drugs, begins to search the vehicle and immediately discovers a closed container, which rule applies? The defendant will argue that the fact that the officer first chose to search the container indicates that his probable cause extended only to the container and that *Chadwick* and *Sanders* therefore require a warrant. On the other hand, the fact that the officer first chose to search in the most obvious location should not restrict the propriety of the search. The *Chadwick* rule, as applied in *Sanders,* has devolved into an anomaly such that the more likely the police are to discover drugs in a container, the less authority they have to search it. We have noted the virtue of providing "clear and unequivocal guidelines to the law enforcement profession." The *Chadwick-Sanders* rule is the antithesis of a "clear and unequivocal guideline."

* * *

Although we have recognized firmly that the doctrine of stare decisis serves profoundly important purposes in our legal system, this Court has overruled a prior case on the comparatively rare occasion when it has bred confusion or been a derelict or led to anomalous results. * * * [T]he existence of the dual regimes for automobile searches that uncover containers has proved as confusing as the *Chadwick* and *Sanders* dissenters predicted. We conclude that it is better to adopt one clear-cut rule to govern automobile searches and eliminate the warrant requirement for closed containers set forth in *Sanders*.

\* \* \*

Until today, this Court has drawn a curious line between the search of an automobile that coincidentally turns up a container and the search of a container that coincidentally turns up in an automobile. The protections of the Fourth Amendment must not turn on such coincidences. We therefore interpret *Carroll* as providing one rule to govern all automobile searches. The police may search an automobile and the containers within it where they have probable cause to believe contraband or evidence is contained.

\* \* \*

### JUSTICE SCALIA, concurring in the judgment.

I agree with the dissent that it is anomalous for a briefcase to be protected by the "general requirement" of a prior warrant when it is being carried along the street, but for that same briefcase to become unprotected as soon as it is carried into an automobile. On the other hand, I agree with the Court that it would be anomalous for a locked compartment in an automobile to be unprotected by the "general requirement" of a prior warrant, but for an unlocked briefcase within the automobile to be protected. I join in the judgment of the Court because I think its holding is more faithful to the text and tradition of the Fourth Amendment, and if these anomalies in our jurisprudence are ever to be eliminated that is the direction in which we should travel.

\* \* \*

Although the Fourth Amendment does not explicitly impose the requirement of a warrant, it is of course textually possible to consider that implicit within the requirement of reasonableness. For some years after the (still continuing) explosion in Fourth Amendment litigation that followed our announcement of the exclusionary rule in Weeks v. United States, our jurisprudence lurched back and forth between imposing a categorical warrant requirement and looking to reasonableness alone. (The opinions preferring a warrant involved searches of structures.) See generally Chimel v. California. By the late 1960's, the preference for a warrant had won out, at least rhetorically. See *Chimel;* Coolidge v. New Hampshire.

The victory was illusory. Even before today's decision, the "warrant requirement" had become so riddled with exceptions that it was basically unrecognizable. In 1985, one commentator cataloged nearly 20 such exceptions, including "searches incident to arrest . . . automobile searches . . . border searches . . . administrative searches of regulated businesses . . . exigent circumstances . . . search[es] incident to nonarrest when there is probable cause to arrest . . . boat boarding for document checks . . . welfare searches . . . inventory searches . . . airport searches . . . school search[es]. . . ." Bradley, Two Models of the Fourth Amendment, 83 Mich.L.Rev. 1468, 1473–1474 (1985) (footnotes omitted). * * * Our intricate body of law regarding "reasonable expectation of privacy" has been developed largely as a means of creating these exceptions, enabling a search to be denominated not a Fourth Amendment "search" and therefore not subject to the general warrant requirement.

Unlike the dissent, therefore, I do not regard today's holding as some momentous departure, but rather as merely the continuation of an inconsistent jurisprudence that has been with us for years. * * *

In my view, the path out of this confusion should be sought by returning to the first principle that the "reasonableness" requirement of the Fourth Amendment affords the protection that the common law afforded. I have no difficulty with the proposition that that includes the requirement of a warrant, where the common law required a warrant; and it may even be that changes in the surrounding legal rules * * * may make a warrant indispensable to reasonableness where it once was not. But the supposed "general rule" that a warrant is always required does not appear to have any basis in the common law and confuses rather than facilitates any attempt to develop rules of reasonableness in light of changed legal circumstances, as the anomaly eliminated and the anomaly created by today's holding both demonstrate.

* * *

**JUSTICE WHITE, dissenting.**

Agreeing as I do with most of Justice Stevens' opinion and with the result he reaches, I dissent and would affirm the judgment below.

**JUSTICE STEVENS, with whom JUSTICE MARSHALL joins, dissenting.**

* * *

To the extent there was any "anomaly" in our prior jurisprudence, the Court has "cured" it at the expense of creating a more serious paradox. For, surely it is anomalous to prohibit a search of a briefcase while the owner is carrying it exposed on a public street yet to permit a search once the owner has placed the briefcase in the locked trunk of his car. One's privacy interest in one's luggage can certainly not be diminished by one's removing it from a public thoroughfare and placing it—out of sight—in a privately owned vehicle. * * *

* * *

To support its argument that today's holding works only a minimal intrusion on privacy, the Court suggests that "[i]f the police know that they may open a bag only if they are actually searching the entire car, they may search more extensively than they otherwise would in order to establish the general probable cause required by *Ross*." * * * [T]his fear is unexplained and inexplicable. Neither evidence uncovered in the course of a search nor the scope of the search conducted can be used to provide post hoc justification for a search unsupported by probable cause at its inception.

\* \* \*

* * * No impartial observer could criticize this Court for hindering the progress of the war on drugs. On the contrary, decisions like the one the Court makes today will support the conclusion that this Court has become a loyal foot soldier in the Executive's fight against crime.

\* \* \*

### Probable Cause Issues After Acevedo

Professor Green has pointed out that the rule in *Acevedo* does not eliminate all the uncertainty of the previous law. There will still be difficult questions of whether there is probable cause to search a certain part of the car. See Green, "Power, Not Reason": Justice Marshall's Valedictory and the Fourth Amendment in the Supreme Court's 1990–91 Term, 70 No.Car.L.Rev. 373 (1992). Not surprisingly, the lower courts have reached divergent results on the probable cause/location question after *Acevedo*. Compare United States v. McSween, 53 F.3d 684 (5th Cir.1995) (when officer smelled burnt marijuana, he had probable cause to search under the hood of the defendant's car, even though a search of the passenger compartment had turned up nothing), with United States v. Nielsen, 9 F.3d 1487 (10th Cir.1993) (when officer smelled burnt marijuana and a search of the passenger compartment turned up nothing, his search of the trunk was illegal: "We do not believe under the circumstances that there was a fair probability that the *trunk* contained marijuana, or that a disinterested magistrate would so hold if asked to issue a search warrant.").

### Delayed Search of Containers: United States v. Johns

In United States v. Johns, 469 U.S. 478 (1985), the Court considered whether there are any temporal limitations on the power to search containers in cars without a warrant. Customs agents removed packages from a trunk, placed them in a Drug Enforcement Agency warehouse, and searched the packages three days later. The officers had probable cause, but no warrant. Writing for the Court, Justice O'Connor reasoned that *Ross* would have authorized a warrantless search of the packages when they were removed from the trunk; that previous cases—e.g., Chambers v. Maroney and Texas v. White—authorized a delayed search of the trunk; and that "searches of containers discovered in the course of a vehicle search are [not] subject to temporal restrictions not applicable to the vehicle search itself." The Court indicated that it did not intend to authorize indefinite retention of vehicles or "to foreclose the possibility that the owner of a vehicle or its contents might attempt to prove that delay in the completion of a vehicle search was unreasonable because it adversely affected a privacy or possessory interest." The Court also rejected the defendant's argument that the automobile exception was inapplicable because the agents had taken the packages from the trunk before searching them. Justice O'Connor saw no reason to require officers to keep a container in a car while the search of that container is conducted. Justice Brennan, joined by Justice Marshall, dissented and argued that no exigency precluded reasonable efforts to obtain a warrant.

### Search of Passenger's Property: Wyoming v. Houghton

In *Ross* and *Acevedo*, the Court upheld warrantless searches of containers that were clearly owned by the driver of the car, when there was probable cause to believe that they contained evidence of a crime. Should the situation change if the officer conducts a warrantless search of a passenger's property? The Supreme Court considered that question in Wyoming v. Houghton, 526 U.S. 295 (1999). Justice Scalia, writing for the Court, set forth the facts:

> In the early morning hours of July 23, 1995, a Wyoming Highway Patrol officer stopped an automobile for speeding and driving with a faulty brake light. There were three passengers in the front seat of the car: David Young (the driver), his girlfriend, and respondent. While questioning Young, the officer noticed a hypodermic syringe in Young's shirt pocket. He left the occupants under the supervision of two backup officers as he went to get gloves from his patrol car. Upon his return, he instructed Young to step out of the car and place the syringe on the hood. The officer then asked Young why he had a syringe; with refreshing candor, Young replied that he used it to take drugs.

> At this point, the backup officers ordered the two female passengers out of the car and asked them for identification. Respondent falsely identified herself as "Sandra James" and stated that she did not have any identification. Meanwhile, in light of Young's admission, the officer searched the passenger compartment of the car for contraband. On the back seat, he found a purse, which respondent claimed as hers. He removed from the purse a wallet containing respondent's driver's license, identifying her properly as Sandra K. Houghton. When the officer asked her why she had lied about her name, she replied: "In case things went bad."

Continuing his search of the purse, the officer found a brown pouch and a black wallet-type container. Respondent denied that the former was hers, and claimed ignorance of how it came to be there; it was found to contain drug paraphernalia and a syringe with 60 ccs of methamphetamine. Respondent admitted ownership of the black container, which was also found to contain drug paraphernalia, and a syringe (which respondent acknowledged was hers) with 10 ccs of methamphetamine—an amount insufficient to support the felony conviction at issue in this case. The officer also found fresh needle-track marks on respondent's arms. He placed her under arrest.

The Wyoming Supreme Court found that the search of Houghton's purse violated the Fourth Amendment, because the officer "knew or should have known that the purse did not belong to the driver, but to one of the passengers," and because "there was no probable cause to search the passengers' personal effects and no reason to believe that contraband had been placed within the purse."

Justice Scalia disagreed with the Wyoming Court's assumption that a passenger's property is subject to greater protection than that of the driver. He concluded that the search of the purse was permissible because there was probable cause to believe that drugs were in the car in which the purse was located. Under *Ross*, "[i]f probable cause justifies the search of a lawfully stopped vehicle, it justifies the search of every part of the vehicle and its contents that may conceal the object of the search." While there was no passenger in *Ross*, Justice Scalia reasoned that "if the rule of law that *Ross* announced were limited to contents belonging to the driver, or contents other than those belonging to passengers, one would have expected that substantial limitation to be expressed." * * * Justice Scalia stated that "the critical element in a reasonable search is not that the owner of the property is suspected of crime but that there is reasonable cause to believe that the specific things to be searched for and seized are located on the property to which entry is sought." Justice Scalia concluded as follows:

> When there is probable cause to search for contraband in a car, it is reasonable for police officers—like customs officials in the Founding era—to examine packages and containers without a showing of individualized probable cause for each one. A passenger's personal belongings, just like the driver's belongings or containers attached to the car like a glove compartment, are "in" the car, and the officer has probable cause to search for contraband in the car.
>
> * * * Passengers, no less than drivers, possess a reduced expectation of privacy with regard to the property that they transport in cars, which travel public thoroughfares, seldom serve as the repository of personal effects, are subjected to police stop and

examination to enforce pervasive governmental controls as an everyday occurrence, and, finally, are exposed to traffic accidents that may render all their contents open to public scrutiny.

Houghton relied on the case of United States v. Di Re, 332 U.S. 581 (1948), in which the Court had held that probable cause to search a car did not justify a body search of a passenger. But Justice Scalia distinguished *Di Re* on the basis of "the unique, significantly heightened protection afforded against searches of one's person." Quoting *Terry*, he observed that the search of one's person "must surely be an annoying, frightening, and perhaps humiliating experience" and concluded that "[s]uch traumatic consequences are not to be expected when the police examine an item of personal property found in a car."

In contrast to a passenger's minimal privacy expectations in property placed in a car, Justice Scalia found the government interests at stake in the search to be "substantial." This was because "[e]ffective law enforcement would be appreciably impaired without the ability to search a passenger's personal belongings when there is reason to believe contraband or evidence of criminal wrongdoing is hidden in the car." Justice Scalia explained that a passenger "will often be engaged in a common enterprise with the driver, and have the same interest in concealing the fruits or the evidence of their wrongdoing. A criminal might be able to hide contraband in a passenger's belongings as readily as in other containers in the car—perhaps even surreptitiously, without the passenger's knowledge or permission." Justice Scalia elaborated:

> To be sure, these factors favoring a search will not always be present, but the balancing of interests must be conducted with an eye to the generality of cases. To require that the investigating officer have positive reason to believe that the passenger and driver were engaged in a common enterprise, or positive reason to believe that the driver had time and occasion to conceal the item in the passenger's belongings, surreptitiously or with friendly permission, is to impose requirements so seldom met that a "passenger's property" rule would dramatically reduce the ability to find and seize contraband and evidence of crime. * * * [O]nce a "passenger's property" exception to car searches became widely known, one would expect passenger-confederates to claim everything as their own. And one would anticipate a bog of litigation—in the form of both civil lawsuits and motions to suppress in criminal trials—involving such questions as whether the officer should have believed a passenger's claim of ownership, whether he should have inferred ownership from various objective factors, whether he had probable cause to believe that the passenger was a confederate, or to believe that the driver might have introduced the contraband into the package with or without the passenger's knowledge.

* * *

We hold that police officers with probable cause to search a car may inspect passengers' belongings found in the car that are capable of concealing the object of the search.

Justice Breyer wrote a short concurring opinion in *Houghton,* reasoning that "[i]f the police must establish a container's ownership prior to the search of that container (whenever, for example, a passenger says 'that's mine'), the resulting uncertainty will destroy the workability of the bright-line rule set forth in United States v. Ross. At the same time, police officers with probable cause to search a car for drugs would often have probable cause to search containers regardless. Hence a bright-line rule will authorize only a limited number of searches that the law would not otherwise justify."

Justice Stevens, joined by Justices Souter and Ginsburg, dissented in *Houghton.* He argued that the Court had gone further than it had in *Ross* because it upheld the search of Houghton's purse even though the officer did not actually have probable cause to believe that there was contraband in the purse:

> * * * Ironically, while we concluded in *Ross* that "[p]robable cause to believe that a container placed in the trunk of a taxi contains contraband or evidence does not justify a search of the entire cab," the rule the Court fashions would apparently permit a warrantless search of a passenger's briefcase if there is probable cause to believe the taxidriver had a syringe somewhere in his vehicle.

> [I]n my view, the State's legitimate interest in effective law enforcement does not outweigh the privacy concerns at issue. * * * Certainly the ostensible clarity of the Court's rule is attractive. But that virtue is insufficient justification for its adoption. Moreover, a rule requiring a warrant or individualized probable cause to search passenger belongings is every bit as simple as the Court's rule; it simply protects more privacy.

### QUESTIONS AFTER HOUGHTON

Assume the following facts: the officer properly stops the car driven by Young. Young admits that he is a drug user and that syringes and drugs are in the car. He also says that Houghton, his passenger, is accompanying him to a drug counseling center. Houghton explains that she is a drug counselor fiercely opposed to drug use. Houghton produces identification and a business card that supports her statement. The officer searches under the driver's seat and finds drugs. Can he now search Houghton's purse? The answer appears to be yes under the Court's bright-line rule, because the officer has probable cause to search the car and therefore "may inspect passengers' belongings found in the car that are capable of concealing the object of the search." Does this result make sense under these facts? Are these facts so unlikely that it makes sense to have a bright line rule?

# G. EXIGENT CIRCUMSTANCES

## 1. Exigent Circumstances Generally

It takes time to obtain a warrant. In some cases where police have probable cause to search or arrest, they have to work quickly, because delay 1) could give a suspect the opportunity to escape 2) could give the suspect, or others, an opportunity to take up and use weapons, or hurt others (such as family members during a violent argument), or 3) could give the suspect or others the opportunity to destroy evidence. The exigent circumstance cases concern fact-specific situations in which the state must show that immediate action was reasonably necessary to prevent flight, or to safeguard the police or public, or to protect against the loss of evidence.

The exigent circumstances exception excuses the officer from having to obtain a magistrate's determination that probable cause exists; it does not permit a search in the absence of probable cause. Besides needing probable cause to search, the officer must have probable cause to believe that the persons or items to be searched or seized might be gone, or that some other danger would arise, before a warrant could be obtained.

The exigent circumstances exception applies equally to arrests and to searches. Recall that under Payton v. New York, supra, a warrant is required to arrest a person in his home. However, as the Court there noted, if exigent circumstances are present, a warrant for an in-home arrest is excused. Likewise, officers may search a container, premises, etc. without a warrant if they have probable cause and if exigent circumstances are present. The materials below discuss arrest cases and search cases interchangeably.

## 2. Hot Pursuit

If officers are in "hot pursuit" of a suspect, this will excuse an arrest warrant where one would otherwise be required, and it will also excuse a search warrant where a search of an area is conducted in order to find and apprehend the suspect. The rationale is that it is unrealistic to expect police officers to stop in the middle of a chase and resort to the warrant process. To do so could allow the suspect to get away and thus render the warrant meaningless. The delay of obtaining a warrant could also allow the suspect to destroy evidence or to create a dangerous situation for police officers or members of the public. In these latter respects, the hot pursuit doctrine is really just a variant of the "public safety" and "destruction of evidence" aspects of the exigent circumstances doctrine, to be discussed below.

The leading hot pursuit case in the Supreme Court is Warden v. Hayden, 387 U.S. 294 (1967), the case in which the court rejected the "mere evidence" limitation on searches and seizures. Officers pursued a robbery suspect into what was subsequently determined to be the suspect's house. The suspect's wife answered the door, and the police entered the house to search for the suspect. In the course of looking for him, they also looked for weapons which he might have concealed during the pursuit. The officers found incriminating clothing in a washing machine. The Court held that the warrantless search was justified by the "hot pursuit" exception. The fact that the officers found clothing as opposed to weapons in the washing machine was not problematic, because the officers had the right, in these emergency circumstances, to search the washing machine to look for weapons, and thus the seizure of the clothing was permissible under the plain view doctrine.

The "hot pursuit" doctrine is based on the premise that the suspect, knowing that he is being pursued, may seek to escape, destroy evidence or create a threat to public safety. It follows that the "hot pursuit" doctrine cannot apply where the suspect is unaware that he is being pursued by police officers. Thus, in Welsh v. Wisconsin, 466 U.S. 740 (1984), officers were notified that a car had been driven into a ditch. Eyewitnesses told the officers that the driver had been driving erratically, and had walked away from the scene. The officers quickly went to the address listed on the vehicle registration, and arrested Welsh in his home for driving while intoxicated. The Court held that the "hot pursuit" doctrine could not apply in these circumstances, because Welsh was never aware until he was arrested that he was being pursued by police officers. If the "hot pursuit" doctrine were determined only by how expeditiously the police were pursuing the suspect, then it would exist in virtually every case.

On the other hand, the "hot pursuit" doctrine can cover situations significantly short of high speed car chases. For example, in United States v. Santana, 427 U.S. 38 (1976), officers approached Santana while she was standing in the doorway of her home. They had probable cause to arrest her. When Santana saw the officers, she quickly retreated into her house. The officers told her she was under arrest and then followed her into the house to catch her and place her in custody. The Court, in an opinion by Justice Rehnquist, held that the police officers were permitted to follow Santana into her house under the doctrine of "hot pursuit." Justice Rehnquist noted that the hot pursuit doctrine serves to ensure that "a suspect may not defeat an arrest which has been set in motion in a public place * * * by the expedient of escaping into a private place." He concluded: "the fact that the pursuit here ended almost as soon as it began did not render it any the less a 'hot pursuit' sufficient to justify the warrantless entry."

## 3. Police and Public Safety

A warrant is excused if the delay in obtaining it would result in a significant risk of harm to the police or to members of the public. See, e.g., United States v. Salava, 978 F.2d 320 (7th Cir.1992) (risk to public safety excuses warrant where the defendant was found outside his home with blood on his clothes, and stated that he shot someone inside the home; while it was subsequently discovered that the defendant had wounded himself in a fight with an imaginary opponent, the court must evaluate the risk to public safety from the point of view of the officer at the time of the search). See also United States v. Black, 466 F.3d 1143 (9th Cir.2006) (it was proper for police to enter an apartment without a warrant, after they had received reports of a serious domestic disturbance, even though the house was quiet when they arrived and it turned out that nobody was inside; it was reasonable for the officer to believe that someone inside had been injured or was in danger: "This is a case where the police would be harshly criticized had they not investigated and Walker was in fact in the apartment."). Compare United States v. Williams, 354 F.3d 497 (6th Cir. 2003) (public safety not at stake, and warrant not excused, where officers entered a premises to check out a water leak: "Danger of water damage to a carpet is certainly not urgent within the meaning of the 'risk of danger' exigency.").

### *Public Safety and the Relevance of a Law Enforcement Objective: Brigham City v. Stuart*

The following case applies the "public safety" exception and considers whether it can apply even though the officer is subjectively pursuing law enforcement (rather than public safety) objectives.

### BRIGHAM CITY V. STUART

Supreme Court of the United States, 2006.
547 U.S. 398.

### CHIEF JUSTICE ROBERTS delivered the opinion of the Court.

In this case we consider whether police may enter a home without a warrant when they have an objectively reasonable basis for believing that an occupant is seriously injured or imminently threatened with such injury. We conclude that they may.

\* \* \*

This case arises out of a melee that occurred in a Brigham City, Utah, home in the early morning hours of July 23, 2000. At about 3 a.m., four police officers responded to a call regarding a loud party at a residence. Upon arriving at the house, they heard shouting from inside, and proceeded down the driveway to investigate. There, they observed two juveniles drinking beer in the backyard. They entered the backyard, and saw—through a screen door and windows—an altercation taking place in the kitchen of the home. According to the testimony of one of the officers, four adults were attempting, with some difficulty, to restrain a juvenile. The juvenile eventually "broke free, swung a fist and struck one of the adults in the face." The officer testified that he observed the victim of the blow spitting blood into a nearby sink. The other adults continued to try to restrain the juvenile, pressing him up against a refrigerator with such force that the refrigerator began moving across the floor. At this point, an officer opened the screen door and announced the officers' presence. Amid the tumult, nobody noticed. The officer entered the kitchen and again cried out, and as the occupants slowly became aware that the police were on the scene, the altercation ceased.

The officers subsequently arrested respondents and charged them with contributing to the delinquency of a minor, disorderly conduct, and intoxication. In the trial court, respondents filed a motion to suppress all evidence obtained after the officers entered the home, arguing that the warrantless entry violated the Fourth Amendment. The court granted the motion, and the Utah Court of Appeals affirmed. [The Supreme Court of Utah also affirmed, finding the circumstances not sufficient to justify a warrantless entry, and relying on the fact that the officers were primarily motivated in prosecuting crime rather than in law protecting the public.]

* * *

It is a basic principle of Fourth Amendment law that searches and seizures inside a home without a warrant are presumptively unreasonable. Nevertheless, because the ultimate touchstone of the Fourth Amendment is "reasonableness," the warrant requirement is subject to certain exceptions. We have held, for example, that law enforcement officers may make a warrantless entry onto private property to fight a fire and investigate its cause, Michigan v. Tyler, 436 U.S. 499, 509 (1978), to prevent the imminent destruction of evidence, Ker v. California, 374 U.S. 23, 40 (1963), or to engage in "hot pursuit" of a fleeing suspect, United States v. Santana, 427 U.S. 38, 42–43 (1976). * * *

One exigency obviating the requirement of a warrant is the need to assist persons who are seriously injured or threatened with such injury. * * * Accordingly, law enforcement officers may enter a home without a warrant to render emergency assistance to an injured occupant or to protect an occupant from imminent injury.

Respondents do not take issue with these principles, but instead advance two reasons why the officers' entry here was unreasonable. First, they argue that the officers were more interested in making arrests than quelling violence. They urge us to consider, in assessing the reasonableness of the entry, whether the officers were "indeed motivated primarily by a desire to save lives and property." The Utah Supreme Court also considered the officers' subjective motivations relevant.

Our cases have repeatedly rejected this approach. An action is "reasonable" under the Fourth Amendment, regardless of the individual officer's state of mind, as long as the circumstances, viewed *objectively*, justify the action. The officer's subjective motivation is irrelevant. See Whren v. United States. It therefore does not matter here—even if their subjective motives could be so neatly unraveled—whether the officers entered the kitchen to arrest respondents and gather evidence against them or to assist the injured and prevent further violence.

\* \* \*

Respondents further contend that their conduct was not serious enough to justify the officers' intrusion into the home. They rely on Welsh v. Wisconsin, 466 U.S. 740, 753 (1984), in which we held that "an important factor to be considered when determining whether any exigency exists is the gravity of the underlying offense for which the arrest is being made." This contention, too, is misplaced. *Welsh* involved a warrantless entry by officers to arrest a suspect for driving while intoxicated. There, the "only potential emergency" confronting the officers was the need to preserve evidence (*i.e.*, the suspect's blood-alcohol level)— an exigency that we held insufficient under the circumstances to justify entry into the suspect's home. Here, the officers were confronted with *ongoing* violence occurring *within* the home. *Welsh* did not address such a situation.

We think the officers' entry here was plainly reasonable under the circumstances. The officers were responding, at 3 o'clock in the morning, to complaints about a loud party. As they approached the house, they could hear from within "an altercation occurring, some kind of a fight." \* \* \* The officers heard "thumping and crashing" and people yelling "stop, stop" and "get off me." \* \* \* The noise seemed to be coming from the back of the house; after looking in the front window and seeing nothing, the officers proceeded around back to investigate further. \* \* \* From there, they could see that a fracas was taking place inside the kitchen. A juvenile, fists clenched, was being held back by several adults. As the officers watch, he breaks free and strikes one of the adults in the face, sending the adult to the sink spitting blood.

In these circumstances, the officers had an objectively reasonable basis for believing both that the injured adult might need help and that the violence in the kitchen was just beginning. Nothing in the Fourth Amendment required them to wait until another blow rendered someone "unconscious" or "semi-conscious" or worse before entering. The role of a peace officer includes preventing violence and restoring order, not simply rendering first aid to casualties; an officer is not like a boxing (or hockey) referee, poised to stop a bout only if it becomes too one-sided.

\* \* \*

Accordingly, we reverse the judgment of the Supreme Court of Utah, and remand the case for further proceedings not inconsistent with this opinion.

[The concurring opinion of JUSTICE STEVENS is omitted.]

### Application of Brigham City v. Stuart: Michigan v. Fisher

In Michigan v. Fisher, 558 U.S. 45 (2009), the Court, in a per curiam opinion, applied its analysis in *Brigham City* to uphold a warrantless search of a house by officer responding to a complaint about a domestic disturbance. Upon arriving in response to the complaint, officers found a house "in considerable chaos: a pickup truck in the driveway with its front smashed, damaged fenceposts along the side of the property, and three broken house windows, the glass still on the ground outside. The officers also noticed blood on the hood of the pickup and on clothes inside of it, as well as on one of the doors to the house. \* \* \* Through a window, the officers could see Fisher inside the house screaming and throwing things. The officers knocked, but Fisher refused to answer. They saw that Fisher had a cut on his hand, and they asked him whether he needed medical attention. Fisher ignored these questions and demanded, with accompanying profanity, that the officers go to get a search warrant." The officers entered and saw Fisher pointing a long gun. Fisher was charged with firearms offense and challenged the warrantless entry into his house. The Court found that the public safety interest under the facts was every bit as strong as that found to be sufficient in *Brigham City*. It scolded the state court for dismissing the situation as "a few drops of blood" and not a "life-threatening" emergency. The Court elaborated as follows:

> Officers do not need ironclad proof of "a likely serious, life-threatening" injury to invoke the emergency aid exception. The only injury police could confirm in *Brigham City* was the bloody lip they saw the juvenile inflict upon the adult. Fisher argues that the officers here could not have been motivated by a perceived need to provide medical assistance, since they never summoned emergency medical personnel. This would have no bearing, of course, upon their need to assure that Fisher was not endangering someone else in the house. Moreover, even if the failure to summon medical personnel conclusively established that Goolsby did not subjectively believe, when he entered the house, that Fisher or someone else was seriously

injured (which is doubtful), the test, as we have said, is not what Goolsby believed, but whether there was an objectively reasonable basis for believing that medical assistance was needed, or persons were in danger. * * * It sufficed to invoke the emergency aid exception that it was reasonable to believe that Fisher had hurt himself (albeit nonfatally) and needed treatment that in his rage he was unable to provide, or that Fisher was about to hurt, or had already hurt, someone else. The Michigan Court of Appeals required more than what the Fourth Amendment demands.

Justice Stevens, joined by Justice Sotomayor, dissented in *Fisher*.

### *911 Calls and Public Safety*

If a 911 caller states that, for example, an assault or a murder is occurring in a home, then it goes without saying that officers can enter that home without a warrant unless, upon arriving, it is immediately clear that the call was unjustified. But what if the 911 operator gets a call and there is nothing but static on the other end of the line? If responding officers get to the premises and see nothing one way or the other indicating a risk to public safety, can they enter the home without a warrant? What if, instead, it was a hang-up call? In United States v. Martinez, 643 F.3d 1292 (10th Cir. 2011), the court held that "a static 911 call is insufficient to create an objectively reasonable belief that someone inside the home is in need of aid." The court distinguished static calls from dropped calls, noting that "the two types of calls differ in a fundamental way." The court explained as follows:

> At the very least, 911 hangups inform the police that someone physically dialed 911 and either hung up or was disconnected before he or she could speak to the operator. An unanswered return call [from the operator] gives further information pointing to a probability that after the initial call was placed the caller or the phone has somehow been incapacitated. With a static 911 call, however, there is no such assurance that a person initiated the call. * * * [A]n electrical or weather anomaly can cause such calls * * *.

The court noted that the 911 operator who had received the static call from Martinez's residence returned the call and encountered static on the line, "suggesting there was a line problem." Moreover, "when the officers arrived, they saw no evidence indicating anyone was in the house, much less anyone in need of immediate assistance." The officers contended that the outside of the house was a complete mess, but the court found this irrelevant to any public safety risk under the circumstances, stating that a "person's failure to keep an orderly home should not subject him or her to a warrantless search by police." Accordingly, the court found that the warrantless entry into the home could not be justified under the exigent circumstances exception, and held that the child pornography found in the search of Martinez's home had to be suppressed.

## 4. The Risk of Destruction of Evidence

If evidence will be destroyed in the time it takes to obtain a warrant, then the warrant requirement is excused. The question usually disputed in the cases is whether there was really an imminent risk of destruction of evidence under the facts presented.

Not surprisingly, destruction of evidence issues often arise in drug cases. One such case is the en banc decision of United States v. MacDonald, 916 F.2d 766 (2d Cir.1990). A New York Drug Task Force focused attention on an apartment building. An agent approached an apartment and purchased drugs and witnessed men in the apartment with weapons and counting money.

Ten minutes after the controlled purchase, the agent returned to the apartment with reinforcements. After knocking on the door and identifying themselves, the agents heard the sounds of shuffling feet. They also simultaneously received a radio communication from agents remaining outside the building informing them that the occupants of the first floor apartment were attempting to escape through a bathroom window. The agents at the apartment door then used a battering ram, which they happened to bring with them, to force entry. The agents arrested five men in the apartment and discovered in plain view two loaded weapons, large quantities of cocaine and marijuana, narcotics paraphernalia, packaging materials and several thousand dollars in cash.

The majority of the en banc court found that exigent circumstances existed even before the officers knocked on the door and heard people scurrying around. The court stated as follows:

> The essential question in determining whether exigent circumstances justified a warrantless entry is whether law enforcement agents were confronted by an "urgent need" to render aid or take action. Dorman v. United States, 435 F.2d 385, 391 (D.C.Cir.1970) (in banc). We have adopted the factors set out in *Dorman* as guideposts intended to facilitate the district court's determination. The *Dorman* factors have been summarized as follows:
>
> > (1) the gravity or violent nature of the offense with which the suspect is to be charged; (2) whether the suspect "is reasonably believed to be armed"; (3) "a clear showing of probable cause . . . to believe that the suspect committed the crime"; (4) "strong reason to believe that the suspect is in the premises being entered"; (5) "a likelihood that the suspect will escape if not

swiftly apprehended"; and (6) the peaceful circumstances of the entry.

\* \* \*

Applying the *Dorman* factors to the case at hand, the district court's determination [that exigent circumstances existed] was far from clearly erroneous. First, the ongoing sale and distribution of narcotics constituted a grave offense. Second, the defendant and at least one of his associates were armed with loaded, semi-automatic weapons. Third, the law enforcement agents had not only probable cause to suspect that a crime had been perpetrated but firsthand knowledge that ongoing crimes were transpiring. Fourth, the agents further knew that the defendant and his associates were in the apartment. Fifth, the likelihood that a suspect might escape if not swiftly apprehended was confirmed by the fact that the man who actually made the sale to Agent Agee had apparently escaped during the ten-minute interval that elapsed after the controlled purchase and before the agents entered the apartment. Sixth, the agents acted in accordance with the law, and first attempted to effect a peaceful entry by knocking and announcing themselves.

\* \* \* In addition, the district court's finding that the agents were confronted by an urgent need to prevent the possible loss of evidence cannot be said to be clearly erroneous in light of the information that the suspects were using an unidentified apartment in the building to store narcotics, the ease with which the suspects could have disposed of the cocaine by flushing it down the toilet, and the possibility that the prerecorded five dollar bill used by Agent Agee in the undercover buy would be lost if the ongoing drug transactions were permitted to continue while the agents sought a warrant.

The *MacDonald* majority was unsympathetic to the defendant's claim that the court was creating a per se exigent circumstances exception in large-scale narcotics cases:

The defendant also argues that narcotics-related crimes so frequently involve exigent circumstances that the exception threatens to eviscerate the rule. \* \* \* If it is true that ongoing retail narcotics operations often confront law enforcement agents with exigent circumstances, we fail to see how such a sad reality constitutes a ground for declaring that the exigencies do not, in fact, exist. To disallow the exigent circumstances exception in these cases would be to tie the hands of law enforcement agents who are entrusted with the responsibility of combating grave, ongoing crimes \* \* \*.

Judge Kearse dissented from the majority's decision in *MacDonald*. In her view, the government had not made a factual showing that any risk existed or harm to individuals or destruction of evidence given that there was no evidence that the men in the apartment had been alerted to the presence of the Task Force.

Is the en banc decision in *MacDonald* consistent with the Supreme Court's decision in Vale v. Louisiana, 399 U.S. 30 (1970)? In *Vale,* the Court emphasized the fact-based nature of the exigent circumstances inquiry, and held that exigent circumstances did not exist to search Vale's home, when Vale was arrested outside his home for engaging in a drug transaction and there was no indication that anyone was inside destroying evidence. The Court noted that at the time of the officers' entry into the home, the narcotics were not "in the process of destruction." Does the Court in *Vale* mean that the destruction must have already begun before a warrant is excused? Is the issue whether destruction is "imminent?" Was there an imminent risk of destruction of narcotics in *MacDonald?* Compare United States v. Purcell, 526 F.3d 953 (6th Cir. 2008) (no imminent risk of destruction of evidence despite officers' claim that they thought the defendant was operating a methamphetamine lab in a hotel room; that assumption was based only on the defendant's prior meth lab activities, and not on any real indication that methamphetamine cooking was going on when the officers arrived).

### The Seriousness of the Offense

In assessing whether there is a risk of destruction of evidence sufficient to excuse a warrant, the *Dorman* factors take into account not only the destructibility of the evidence but also the seriousness of the offense—the more serious the offense, the greater the incentive for destroying evidence, and the greater the government interest in protecting against its loss. For example, the serious nature of a narcotics offense was central to the *MacDonald* Court's finding of exigent circumstances.

The "seriousness" factor raises two questions: 1) Could an offense be so serious that exigency should be deemed automatic, without regard to the actual risk of destruction of evidence? and 2) Could an offense be so minor that a warrant should be required regardless of the actual risk of destruction of evidence? The Supreme Court has had something to say about both of these questions.

### Murder Scene

As to the first question, the Court in Mincey v. Arizona, 437 U.S. 385 (1978), considered the government's argument that there should be a "murder scene" exception to the warrant requirement. Mincey shot and killed an officer during a drug bust. Mincey himself was seriously wounded. A protective sweep of the premises resulted in the detention of

Mincey's associates. Ten minutes later, homicide detectives entered the premises without a warrant and began a search for evidence that lasted four days. Every item in the apartment was closely examined and inventoried, and two to three hundred objects were seized.

Justice Stewart wrote for a unanimous Court. He rejected a "scene of the homicide" per se exception to the warrant requirement and stated that the government must make a factual showing of exigent circumstances. Justice Stewart wrote as follows:

> All the persons in Mincey's apartment had been located before the investigating homicide officers arrived there and began their search. And a four-day search that included opening dresser drawers and ripping up carpets can hardly be rationalized in terms of the legitimate concerns that justify an emergency search.

> * * * [T]he State points to the vital public interest in the prompt investigation of the extremely serious crime of murder. No one can doubt the importance of this goal. But the public interest in the investigation of other serious crimes is comparable. If the warrantless search of a homicide scene is reasonable, why not the warrantless search of the scene of a rape, a robbery, or a burglary? No consideration relevant to the Fourth Amendment suggests any point of rational limitation of such a doctrine.

What would be wrong with a rule that allowed automatic searches at the scene of a homicide, rape, or robbery, even the day after the crime has occurred? Won't a search warrant be issued automatically for these kinds of crimes? If the warrant application is perfunctory, what is gained by having the police, who are already at the scene of the crime, seek a warrant?

### Minor Offenses

As to the second question, the Court in Welsh v. Wisconsin, 466 U.S. 740 (1984), considered whether an offense could be so minor as not to justify an exception to the warrant requirement even given an imminent risk of destruction of evidence. Officers arrested Welsh in his home shortly after receiving a report from an observer that Welsh had been driving his car while being intoxicated or very sick. After seeing Welsh driving erratically and ultimately swerving off the road into a ditch, the observer blocked Welsh's car with his own car and saw Welsh walk away from the ditch after being refused a ride. Police came to the scene and discovered a motor vehicle registration in Welsh's abandoned car. The police went to the address listed on the registration and arrested Welsh in his home for driving while under the influence of an intoxicant. Welsh subsequently refused to submit to a breathalyzer test. The state revoked his license due to his refusal, and Welsh challenged this action, arguing that his refusal came about as a result of an illegal warrantless in-home arrest. The state argued that the warrantless arrest was legal because, among other things, the delay in obtaining a warrant would have resulted in the loss of evidence—specifically the loss of proof of Welsh's intoxication.

Justice Brennan's opinion for six members of the Court rejected the destruction of evidence argument and found the warrantless arrest in the home to be illegal. Justice Brennan declared that "it is difficult to conceive of a warrantless home arrest that would not be unreasonable under the Fourth Amendment when the underlying offense is extremely minor." He held that "an important factor to be considered when determining whether any exigency exists is the gravity of the underlying offense for which the arrest is being made" and declared that "application of the exigent-circumstances exception in the context of a home entry should rarely be sanctioned when there is probable cause to believe that only a minor offense, such as the kind at issue in this case, has been committed."

Applying these principles to the facts of the case, Justice Brennan noted that "[t]he State of Wisconsin has chosen to classify the first offense for driving while intoxicated as a noncriminal, civil forfeiture offense for which no imprisonment is possible," and that "[g]iven this expression of the state's interest, a warrantless home arrest cannot be upheld simply because evidence of the petitioner's blood-alcohol level might have dissipated while the police obtained a warrant."

Justice White, joined by Justice Rehnquist, dissented. He reasoned that a warrantless home entry is no more intrusive for a minor offense than a major one and that the majority's approach will force officers who must make quick decisions to assess whether a violation is major or minor for purposes of making an exigency determination.

### *Drawing Blood in a DUI Arrest to Prevent the Loss of Evidence: Missouri v. McNeely*

In Schmerber v. California, 384 U. S. 757 (1966), the Court upheld a warrantless blood test of an individual arrested for driving under the influence of alcohol because the officer "might reasonably have believed that he was confronted with an emergency, in which the delay necessary to obtain a warrant, under the circumstances, threatened the destruction of evidence." But in Missouri v. McNeely, 133 S. Ct. 1552 (2013), the Court held 5–4 that its decision in *Schmerber* did not establish a per se rule that justifies a warrantless seizure of blood in all drunk-driving cases. The court held that exigency must be established case-by-case based on the totality of the circumstances.

An officer stopped McNeely's truck in the early morning hours for speeding and repeatedly crossing the center line.  McNeely did badly on field-sobriety tests and declined to use a portable breath-test device to measure his blood alcohol concentration (BAC).  The officer arrested him and, when McNeely indicated on the way to the station that he would refuse to provide a breath sample, the officer transported him to a hospital.  McNeely refused to consent to a blood test even after being warned that under state law refusal to submit voluntarily to the test would lead to the immediate revocation of his driver's license for one year and could be used against him in a future prosecution. The officer directed a hospital lab technician to take a blood sample, and the sample showed a blood alcohol level almost double the legal limit.

McNeely moved to suppress the results of the test when prosecuted for driving while intoxicated.  The trial judge granted the motion, reasoning that there was no exigency excusing a warrant apart from the fact that "[a]s in all cases involving intoxication, [McNeely's] blood alcohol was being metabolized by his liver."  The Missouri Supreme Court affirmed.  Justice Sotomayor, writing for the Court, agreed with the state courts.

Justice Sotomayor explained that in *Schmerber* the Court "considered all of the facts and circumstances of the particular case and carefully based our holding on those specific facts."  She recognized that "[i]t is true that as a result of the human body's natural metabolic processes, the alcohol level in a person's blood begins to dissipate once the alcohol is fully absorbed and continues to decline until the alcohol is eliminated," but reasoned that this reality did not establish an exigency in every drunk driving case, so that "where police officers can reasonably obtain a warrant before a blood sample can be drawn without significantly undermining the efficacy of the search, the Fourth Amendment mandates that they do so."  Justice Sotomayor observed that times had changed since *Schmerber* was decided and that warrants could be obtained through telephonic and electronic means:

> We by no means claim that telecommunications innovations have, will, or should eliminate all delay from the warrant-application process. Warrants inevitably take some time for police officers or prosecutors to complete and for magistrate judges to review. Telephonic and electronic warrants may still require officers to follow time-consuming formalities designed to create an adequate record, such as preparing a duplicate warrant before calling the magistrate judge. See Fed. Rule Crim. Proc. 41(b)(3). And improvements in communications technology do not guarantee that a magistrate judge will be available when an officer needs a warrant after making a late-night arrest. But technological developments that enable police officers to secure warrants more quickly, and do so without

undermining the neutral magistrate judge's essential role as a check on police discretion, are relevant to an assessment of exigency. That is particularly so in this context, where BAC evidence is lost gradually and relatively predictably.

Justice Sotomayor rejected an alternative test offered by Chief Justice Roberts (and joined in by Justices Breyer and Alito) in an opinion concurring in part and dissenting in part "under which a warrantless blood draw is permissible if the officer could not secure a warrant (or reasonably believed he could not secure a warrant) in the time it takes to transport the suspect to a hospital or similar facility and obtain medical assistance."   One example she offered to explain the problem with that test was a police officer's chance stop of a suspect near an emergency room.   In that example, the test would "enable the officer to conduct a nonconsensual warrantless blood draw even if all agree that a warrant could be obtained with very little delay under the circumstances (perhaps with far less delay than an average ride to the hospital in the jurisdiction)."

Justice Sotomayor rejected a number of arguments for a per se rule, including these: (1) the totality of circumstances test does not provide sufficient guidance to officers; (2) the relatively minor intrusion of a blood test and the motorist's limited expectation of privacy in a car justify a warrantless blood test; and (3) warrantless blood tests are necessary to vindicate the state's strong interest in deterring drunk driving.

Justice Kennedy's short, separate opinion expressed the view that neither the Chief Justice's opinion nor Justice Sotomayor's were required to address the question whether some approach other than a per se rule for all drunk driving cases might satisfy the Fourth Amendment.

Justice Thomas dissented and would have upheld the state's argument for a per se rule that warrantless blood tests are reasonable in drunk driving cases.

## 5.   Impermissibly Created Exigency

In some cases suspects are alerted to the presence of police activity, and at that point there is little dispute about the risk of destruction of evidence or other danger when the officers make an entry. Instead, defendants argue that the police acted impermissibly in revealing their presence—for example, by knocking on a door and yelling "police"—and thus *manufactured* the exigent circumstances.   Does manufacturing exigent circumstances disentitle the officers from relying on the exigent circumstances exception? That question is answered in the following case—in which the Court also addresses whether exigent circumstances can be found even if the officers have an opportunity to obtain a warrant before the exigency arises.

## KENTUCKY V. KING

Supreme Court of the United States, 2011.
131 S.Ct. 1849.

### JUSTICE ALITO delivered the opinion of the Court.

It is well established that exigent circumstances, including the need to prevent the destruction of evidence, permit police officers to conduct an otherwise permissible search without first obtaining a warrant. In this case, we consider whether this rule applies when police, by knocking on the door of a residence and announcing their presence, cause the occupants to attempt to destroy evidence. The Kentucky Supreme Court held that the exigent circumstances rule does not apply in the case at hand because the police should have foreseen that their conduct would prompt the occupants to attempt to destroy evidence. We reject this interpretation of the exigent circumstances rule. The conduct of the police prior to their entry into the apartment was entirely lawful. They did not violate the Fourth Amendment or threaten to do so. In such a situation, the exigent circumstances rule applies.

* * *

This case concerns the search of an apartment in Lexington, Kentucky. Police officers set up a controlled buy of crack cocaine outside an apartment complex. Undercover Officer Gibbons watched the deal take place from an unmarked car in a nearby parking lot. After the deal occurred, Gibbons radioed uniformed officers to move in on the suspect. He told the officers that the suspect was moving quickly toward the breezeway of an apartment building, and he urged them to hurry up and get there before the suspect entered an apartment.

In response to the radio alert, the uniformed officers drove into the nearby parking lot, left their vehicles, and ran to the breezeway. Just as they entered the breezeway, they heard a door shut and detected a very strong odor of burnt marijuana. At the end of the breezeway, the officers saw two apartments, one on the left and one on the right, and they did not know which apartment the suspect had entered. * * * Because they smelled marijuana smoke emanating from the apartment on the left, they approached the door of that apartment.

Officer Steven Cobb * * * testified that the officers banged on the left apartment door as loud as they could and announced, "This is the police" or "Police, police, police." Cobb said that as soon as the officers started banging on the door, they could hear people inside moving, and it sounded as though things were being moved inside the apartment. These noises, Cobb testified, led the officers to believe that drug-related evidence was about to be destroyed.

At that point, the officers announced that they were going to make entry inside the apartment. Cobb then kicked in the door, the officers entered the apartment, and they found three people in the front room: respondent Hollis King, respondent's girlfriend, and a guest who was smoking marijuana. The officers performed a protective sweep of the apartment during which they saw marijuana and powder cocaine in plain view. In a subsequent search, they also discovered crack cocaine, cash, and drug paraphernalia.

Police eventually entered the apartment on the right. Inside, they found the suspected drug dealer who was the initial target of their investigation.

[The lower state courts rejected King's argument that the evidence should be suppressed for lack of exigent circumstances.]

The Supreme Court of Kentucky reversed. [That court] assume[d] for the purpose of argument that exigent circumstances existed. To determine whether police impermissibly created the exigency, the Supreme Court of Kentucky announced a two-part test. First, the court held, police cannot deliberately create the exigent circumstances with the bad faith intent to avoid the warrant requirement. Second, even absent bad faith, the court concluded, police may not rely on exigent circumstances if it was reasonably foreseeable that the investigative tactics employed by the police would create the exigent circumstances. Although the court found no evidence of bad faith, it held that exigent circumstances could not justify the search because it was reasonably foreseeable that the occupants would destroy evidence when the police knocked on the door and announced their presence. We granted certiorari.

\* \* \*

This Court has identified several exigencies that may justify a warrantless search of a home. Under the emergency aid exception, for example, officers may enter a home without a warrant to render emergency assistance to an injured occupant or to protect an occupant from imminent injury. Police officers may enter premises without a warrant when they are in hot pursuit of a fleeing suspect. See United States v. Santana, 427 U.S. 38, 4243 (1976). And what is relevant here the need to prevent the imminent destruction of evidence has long been recognized as a sufficient justification for a warrantless search.

\* \* \*

Over the years, lower courts have developed an exception to the exigent circumstances rule, the so-called police-created exigency doctrine. Under this doctrine, police may not rely on the need to prevent destruction of evidence when that exigency was created or manufactured by the conduct of the police. In applying this exception for the creation or manufacturing of an exigency by the police, courts require something more than mere proof that fear of detection by the police caused the destruction of evidence. An additional showing is obviously needed because * * * in some sense the police always create the exigent circumstances. That is to say, in the vast majority of cases in which evidence is destroyed by persons who are engaged in illegal conduct, the reason for the destruction is fear that the evidence will fall into the hands of law enforcement. Consequently, a rule that precludes the police from making a warrantless entry to prevent the destruction of evidence whenever their conduct causes the exigency would unreasonably shrink the reach of this well-established exception to the warrant requirement.

Presumably for the purpose of avoiding such a result, the lower courts have held that the police-created exigency doctrine requires more than simple causation, but the lower courts have not agreed on the test to be applied. * * *

Despite the welter of tests devised by the lower courts, the answer to the question presented in this case follows directly and clearly from the principle that permits warrantless searches in the first place. As previously noted, warrantless searches are allowed when the circumstances make it reasonable, within the meaning of the Fourth Amendment, to dispense with the warrant requirement. Therefore, the answer to the question before us is that the exigent circumstances rule justifies a warrantless search when the conduct of the police preceding the exigency is reasonable in the same sense. Where, as here, the police did not create the exigency by engaging or threatening to engage in conduct that violates the Fourth Amendment, warrantless entry to prevent the destruction of evidence is reasonable and thus allowed.[a]

We have taken a similar approach in other cases involving warrantless searches. For example, we have held that law enforcement officers may seize evidence in plain view, provided that they have not violated the Fourth Amendment in arriving at the spot from which the observation of the evidence is made. * * *

Similarly, officers may seek consent-based encounters if they are lawfully present in the place where the consensual encounter occurs. If consent is freely given, it makes no difference that an officer may have approached the person with the hope or expectation of obtaining consent.

---

[a] There is a strong argument to be made that, at least in most circumstances, the exigent circumstances rule should not apply where the police, without a warrant or any legally sound basis for a warrantless entry, threaten that they will enter without permission unless admitted. In this case, however, no such actual threat was made, and therefore we have no need to reach that question.

* * *

Some lower courts have adopted a rule that is similar to the one that we recognize today. See United States v. MacDonald, 916 F.2d 766 (C.A.2 1990) (en banc) (law enforcement officers do not impermissibly create exigent circumstances when they act in an entirely lawful manner). But others, including the Kentucky Supreme Court, have imposed additional requirements that are unsound and that we now reject.

*Bad faith.* Some courts, including the Kentucky Supreme Court, ask whether law enforcement officers deliberately created the exigent circumstances with the bad faith intent to avoid the warrant requirement. This approach is fundamentally inconsistent with our Fourth Amendment jurisprudence. Our cases have repeatedly rejected a subjective approach, asking only whether the circumstances, viewed *objectively,* justify the action. * * *

The reasons for looking to objective factors, rather than subjective intent, are clear. Legal tests based on reasonableness are generally objective, and this Court has long taken the view that evenhanded law enforcement is best achieved by the application of objective standards of conduct, rather than standards that depend upon the subjective state of mind of the officer.

*Reasonable foreseeability.* Some courts, again including the Kentucky Supreme Court, hold that police may not rely on an exigency if it was reasonably foreseeable that the investigative tactics employed by the police would create the exigent circumstances. Courts applying this test have invalidated warrantless home searches on the ground that it was reasonably foreseeable that police officers, by knocking on the door and announcing their presence, would lead a drug suspect to destroy evidence.

* * *

Adoption of a reasonable foreseeability test would * * * introduce an unacceptable degree of unpredictability. For example, whenever law enforcement officers knock on the door of premises occupied by a person who may be involved in the drug trade, there is *some* possibility that the occupants may possess drugs and may seek to destroy them. * * *

A simple example illustrates the difficulties that such an approach would produce. Suppose that the officers in the present case did not smell marijuana smoke and thus knew only that there was a 50% chance that the fleeing suspect had entered the apartment on the left rather than the apartment on the right. Under those circumstances, would it have been reasonably foreseeable that the occupants of the apartment on the left would seek to destroy evidence upon learning that the police were at the door? Or suppose that the officers knew only that the suspect had disappeared into one of the apartments on a floor with 3, 5, 10, or even 20 units? If the police chose a door at random and knocked for the purpose of asking the occupants if they knew a person who fit the description of the suspect, would it have been reasonably foreseeable that the occupants would seek to destroy evidence? * * *

*Probable cause and time to secure a warrant.* Some courts, in applying the police-created exigency doctrine, fault law enforcement officers if, after acquiring evidence that is sufficient to establish probable cause to search particular premises, the officers do not seek a warrant but instead knock on the door and seek either to speak with an occupant or to obtain consent to search. This approach unjustifiably interferes with legitimate law enforcement strategies. There are many entirely proper reasons why police may not want to seek a search warrant as soon as the bare minimum of evidence needed to establish probable cause is acquired. Without attempting to provide a comprehensive list of these reasons, we note a few.

First, the police may wish to speak with the occupants of a dwelling before deciding whether it is worthwhile to seek authorization for a search. They may think that a short and simple conversation may obviate the need to apply for and execute a warrant. Second, the police may want to ask an occupant of the premises for consent to search because doing so is simpler, faster, and less burdensome than applying for a warrant. A consensual search also may result in considerably less inconvenience and embarrassment to the occupants than a search conducted pursuant to a warrant. Third, law enforcement officers may wish to obtain more evidence before submitting what might otherwise be considered a marginal warrant application. Fourth, prosecutors may wish to wait until they acquire evidence that can justify a search that is broader in scope than the search that a judicial officer is likely to authorize based on the evidence then available. And finally, in many cases, law enforcement may not want to execute a search that will disclose the existence of an investigation because doing so may interfere with the acquisition of additional evidence against those already under suspicion or evidence about additional but as yet unknown participants in a criminal scheme.

We have said that law enforcement officers are under no constitutional duty to call a halt to criminal investigation the moment they have the minimum evidence to establish probable cause. Faulting the police for failing to apply for a search warrant at the earliest possible time after obtaining probable cause imposes a duty that is nowhere to be found in the Constitution.

*Standard or good investigative tactics.* Finally, some lower court cases suggest that law enforcement officers may be found to have created or manufactured an exigency if the court concludes that the course of their investigation was contrary to standard or good law enforcement practices (or to the policies or practices of their jurisdictions). This approach fails to provide clear guidance for law enforcement officers and authorizes courts to make judgments on matters that are the province of those who are responsible for federal and state law enforcement agencies.

* * * Respondent argues for a rule that differs from those discussed above, but his rule is also flawed. Respondent contends that law enforcement officers impermissibly create an exigency when they engage in conduct that would cause a reasonable person to believe that entry is imminent and inevitable. In respondent's view, relevant factors include the officers' tone of voice in announcing their presence and the forcefulness of their knocks. But the ability of law enforcement officers to respond to an exigency cannot turn on such subtleties.

Police officers may have a very good reason to announce their presence loudly and to knock on the door with some force. A forceful knock may be necessary to alert the occupants that someone is at the door. Furthermore, unless police officers identify themselves loudly enough, occupants may not know who is at their doorstep. Officers are permitted indeed, encouraged to identify themselves to citizens, and in many circumstances this is cause for assurance, not discomfort. Citizens who are startled by an unexpected knock on the door or by the sight of unknown persons in plain clothes on their doorstep may be relieved to learn that these persons are police officers. Others may appreciate the opportunity to make an informed decision about whether to answer the door to the police.

If respondent's test were adopted, it would be extremely difficult for police officers to know how loudly they may announce their presence or how forcefully they may knock on a door without running afoul of the police-created exigency rule. And in most cases, it would be nearly impossible for a court to determine whether that threshold had been passed. The Fourth Amendment does not require the nebulous and impractical test that respondent proposes.[b]

* * *

For these reasons, we conclude that the exigent circumstances rule applies when the police do not gain entry to premises by means of an

---

[b] Contrary to respondent's argument, Johnson v. United States, 333 U.S. 10 (1948), does not require affirmance in this case. In *Johnson,* officers noticed the smell of burning opium emanating from a hotel room. They then knocked on the door and demanded entry. Upon seeing that Johnson was the only occupant of the room, they placed her under arrest, searched the room, and discovered opium and drug paraphernalia. Defending the legality of the search, the Government attempted to justify the warrantless search of the room as a valid search incident to a lawful arrest. The Government did not contend that the officers entered the room in order to prevent the destruction of evidence. Although the officers said that they heard a shuffling noise inside the room after they knocked on the door, the Government did not claim that this particular noise was a noise that would have led a reasonable officer to think that evidence was about to be destroyed. Thus, *Johnson* is simply not a case about exigent circumstances.

actual or threatened violation of the Fourth Amendment. This holding provides ample protection for the privacy rights that the Amendment protects. When law enforcement officers who are not armed with a warrant knock on a door, they do no more than any private citizen might do. And whether the person who knocks on the door and requests the opportunity to speak is a police officer or a private citizen, the occupant has no obligation to open the door or to speak. When the police knock on a door but the occupants choose not to respond or to speak, the investigation will have reached a conspicuously low point, and the occupants will have the kind of warning that even the most elaborate security system cannot provide. And even if an occupant chooses to open the door and speak with the officers, the occupant need not allow the officers to enter the premises and may refuse to answer any questions at any time.

Occupants who choose not to stand on their constitutional rights but instead elect to attempt to destroy evidence have only themselves to blame for the warrantless exigent-circumstances search that may ensue.

[The Court finds no evidence that the officers violated or threatened to violate the Fourth Amendment.]

\* \* \*

### JUSTICE GINSBURG, dissenting.

The Court today arms the police with a way routinely to dishonor the Fourth Amendment's warrant requirement in drug cases. In lieu of presenting their evidence to a neutral magistrate, police officers may now knock, listen, then break the door down, never mind that they had ample time to obtain a warrant. I dissent from the Court's reduction of the Fourth Amendment's force.

\* \* \*

The existence of a genuine emergency depends not only on the state of necessity at the time of the warrantless search; it depends, first and foremost, on actions taken by the police *preceding* the warrantless search. Wasting a clear opportunity to obtain a warrant, therefore, disentitles the officer from relying on subsequent exigent circumstances. S. Saltzburg & D. Capra, American Criminal Procedure 376 (8th ed.2007).

\* \* \*

I \* \* \* would not allow an expedient knock to override the warrant requirement. Instead, I would accord that core requirement of the Fourth Amendment full respect. When possible, a warrant must generally be secured, the Court acknowledges. There is every reason to conclude that securing a warrant was entirely feasible in this case, and no reason to contract the Fourth Amendment's dominion.

### Kentucky v. King and the Relevance of a Prior
### Opportunity to Obtain a Warrant

If the police can foresee that an exigency would arise at a certain time in the future, and have a strong case of probable cause and ample time to obtain a warrant well before that exigency occurs, then that opportunity to obtain the warrant could be argued to prohibit the later invocation of the exigent circumstances exception. For example, assume that an officer knows that a suspect has his house cleaned every Wednesday morning, and that this would destroy relevant forensic evidence. On Wednesday morning, there are exigent circumstances due to the risk of destruction of evidence. But if the officer learned this information on the previous Friday, and had probable cause to search at that time, then he should not be able to invoke the exigent circumstances exception five days later.

The decided cases do not usually present such clean facts, however. In the typical case, the state argues that the officer *did not* have clear probable cause until the exigency arose, and therefore had no prior opportunity to obtain a warrant. The defendant then makes the anomalous argument that the officer *had* probable cause well before that. The state also argues that the officer should not be required to go to the magistrate at the very first moment that probable cause exists—they should have the right to take their time and strengthen their case on probable cause. The state also argues that a rule requiring immediate warrant applications could jeopardize undercover activity and ongoing investigations. See, e.g., United States v. Samboy, 433 F.3d 154 (1st Cir. 2005) (warrantless search upheld, where officers "reasonably delayed not from a desire to avoid seeking a warrant, but because the circumstances of the investigation demanded first caution and then an immediate response.").

In Kentucky v. King, supra, the Court obviously cast substantial doubt on whether a warrantless search based on exigent circumstances could ever be found illegal on the ground that officers had an opportunity to obtain a warrant before the exigency arose. The specific context of *King* was whether police officers' knock on a door impermissibly created exigent circumstances if they had a prior opportunity to obtain a warrant. But the Court's analysis seems to put an end to any argument that officers ever have to exercise a prior opportunity to obtain a warrant if there are in fact exigent circumstances at the time of an entry.

### 6.  Electronic Warrants

As the Court noted in Missouri v. McNeely, supra, warrants can be obtained without having to go to the magistrate in person. Fed.R.Crim.P. 41(d)(3)(A) provides that a magistrate judge "may issue a warrant based on information communicated by telephone or other reliable electronic means." The language "other reliable electronic means" is intended to allow for the use of email or fax warrants. The rule does not mean that warrants can be obtained immediately, however. Under Rule 41, a duplicate original warrant must be prepared by the officer, and must be read or sent in written form verbatim to the magistrate, who must prepare an original warrant for the record. These recording requirements are considered necessary to prevent post hoc reconstructions of probable cause and particularity. It must also be remembered that at certain times (e.g., late at night or on the weekend), it may be difficult to reach a magistrate, telephonically or otherwise.

While not instantaneous, the time involved in obtaining an electronic warrant can be significantly less than it would take to obtain a warrant in person. In *McNeely, supra,* the Court held that exigency must be assessed by the time it takes to obtain an electronic warrant. See also United States v. Patino, 830 F.2d 1413 (7th Cir.1987) (agent who observed fugitive in defendant's yard had adequate opportunity to obtain an electronic warrant during 30-minute wait for back-up assistance). Compare United States v. Berick, 710 F.2d 1035 (5th Cir.1983) (risk of destruction of evidence resulting from arrest of drug seller was so imminent that recourse to even an electronic warrant was unavailable).

## 7.  Seizing Premises in the Absence of Exigent Circumstances

If exigent circumstances do not exist to search a house or other premises, the officers must obtain a search warrant. But can the officers take any protective action to preserve the status quo while a warrant is being obtained? In Segura v. United States, 468 U.S. 796 (1984), officers had probable cause to believe that two individuals, Segura and Luz Colon, were trafficking in cocaine from their New York apartment. They established surveillance, and arrested Segura as he entered the lobby of his apartment building. The agents took Segura to his apartment, and knocked on the door. Luz Colon answered the door. The agents entered without receiving permission, placed Luz Colon under arrest, and conducted a limited security sweep. In the process of the sweep, they saw evidence of drug activity. Luz Colon and Segura were incarcerated, and two officers waited in Segura's apartment while a search warrant was being obtained. Due to "administrative delay" it was 19 hours before the search of the apartment was eventually conducted.

A majority of the Court found it unnecessary to reach the question of whether the officers acted illegally. The majority reasoned that, even if the warrantless entry of the premises was illegal, the later search conducted pursuant to a warrant was based on an independent legal source, i.e., the information the officers already had before they seized the premises. [The "independent source" aspect of the opinion will be discussed later in this Chapter in the materials on the exclusionary rule.] Chief Justice Burger, joined by Justice O'Connor, went further, however, and declared that the seizure of the premises pending a warrant was reasonable, even in the absence of exigent circumstances.

Chief Justice Burger's argument in *Segura* was adopted by a majority of the Court in Murray v. United States, 487 U.S. 533 (1988). Thus it is permissible to seize premises for a reasonable period of time while diligent efforts are being made to obtain a warrant. "Seizing" the premises means that occupants are kept out of the premises, in order to protect against the possible destruction of evidence or risk to public safety while a warrant application is pending. See also United States v. Veillette, 778 F.2d 899 (1st Cir.1985) (48 hour seizure of premises, pending a warrant, held reasonable under *Segura*).

### *Prohibiting Entry While a Warrant Is Being Obtained: Illinois v. McArthur*

In the following case, the Court expanded upon the analysis in *Segura* and firmly established the authority of police officers to maintain the status quo while a warrant is being obtained.

### ILLINOIS V. MCARTHUR

Supreme Court of the United States, 2001.
531 U.S. 326.

### JUSTICE BREYER delivered the opinion of the Court.

Police officers, with probable cause to believe that a man had hidden marijuana in his home, prevented that man from entering the home for about two hours while they obtained a search warrant. We must decide whether those officers violated the Fourth Amendment. We conclude that the officers acted reasonably. They did not violate the Amendment's requirements. And we reverse an Illinois court's holding to the contrary.

\* \* \* On April 2, 1997, Tera McArthur asked two police officers to accompany her to the trailer where she lived with her husband, Charles, so that they could keep the peace while she removed her belongings. The two officers, Assistant Chief John Love and Officer Richard Skidis, arrived with Tera at the trailer at about 3:15 p.m. Tera went inside, where Charles was present. The officers remained outside.

When Tera emerged after collecting her possessions, she spoke to Chief Love, who was then on the porch. She suggested he check the trailer because "Chuck had dope in there." She added (in Love's words) that she had seen Chuck "slid[e] some dope underneath the couch."

Love knocked on the trailer door, told Charles what Tera had said, and asked for permission to search the trailer, which Charles denied. Love then sent Officer Skidis with Tera to get a search warrant.

Love told Charles, who by this time was also on the porch, that he could not reenter the trailer unless a police officer accompanied him. Charles subsequently reentered the trailer two or three times (to get cigarettes and to make phone calls), and each time Love stood just inside the door to observe what Charles did.

Officer Skidis obtained the warrant by about 5 p.m. He returned to the trailer and, along with other officers, searched it. The officers found under the sofa a marijuana pipe, a box for marijuana (called a "one-hitter" box), and a small amount of marijuana. They then arrested Charles.

\* \* \*

Illinois subsequently charged Charles McArthur with unlawfully possessing drug paraphernalia and marijuana (less than 2.5 grams), both misdemeanors. McArthur moved to suppress the pipe, box, and marijuana on the ground that they were the "fruit" of an unlawful police seizure, namely, the refusal to let him reenter the trailer unaccompanied, which would have permitted him, he said, to "have destroyed the marijuana."

The trial court granted McArthur's suppression motion. The Appellate Court of Illinois affirmed, and the Illinois Supreme Court denied the State's petition for leave to appeal. We granted certiorari to determine whether the Fourth Amendment prohibits the kind of temporary seizure at issue here.

\* \* \*

We conclude that the restriction at issue was reasonable, and hence lawful, in light of the following circumstances, which we consider in combination. First, the police had probable cause to believe that McArthur's trailer home contained evidence of a crime and contraband, namely, unlawful drugs. The police had had an opportunity to speak with Tera McArthur and make at least a very rough assessment of her reliability. They knew she had had a firsthand opportunity to observe her husband's behavior, in particular with respect to the drugs at issue. And they thought, with good reason, that her report to them reflected that opportunity.

Second, the police had good reason to fear that, unless restrained, McArthur would destroy the drugs before they could return with a warrant. \* \* \*

Third, the police made reasonable efforts to reconcile their law enforcement needs with the demands of personal privacy. They neither searched the trailer nor arrested McArthur before obtaining a warrant.

Rather, they imposed a significantly less restrictive restraint, preventing McArthur only from entering the trailer unaccompanied. They left his home and his belongings intact—until a neutral Magistrate, finding probable cause, issued a warrant.

Fourth, the police imposed the restraint for a limited period of time, namely, two hours. As far as the record reveals, this time period was no longer than reasonably necessary for the police, acting with diligence, to obtain the warrant. Compare United States v. Place (holding 90-minute detention of luggage unreasonable based on nature of interference with person's travels and lack of diligence of police), with United States v. Van Leeuwen (holding 29-hour detention of mailed package reasonable given unavoidable delay in obtaining warrant and minimal nature of intrusion). Given the nature of the intrusion and the law enforcement interest at stake, this brief seizure of the premises was permissible.

\* \* \*

\* \* \* The Appellate Court of Illinois \* \* \* found negatively significant the fact that Chief Love, with McArthur's consent, stepped inside the trailer's doorway to observe McArthur when McArthur reentered the trailer on two or three occasions. McArthur, however, reentered simply for his own convenience, to make phone calls and to obtain cigarettes. Under these circumstances, the reasonableness of the greater restriction (preventing reentry) implies the reasonableness of the lesser (permitting reentry conditioned on observation).

In sum, the police officers in this case had probable cause to believe that a home contained contraband, which was evidence of a crime. They reasonably believed that the home's resident, if left free of any restraint, would destroy that evidence. And they imposed a restraint that was both limited and tailored reasonably to secure law enforcement needs while protecting privacy interests. In our view, the restraint met the Fourth Amendment's demands.

\* \* \*

[JUSTICE SOUTER, concurring, noted that the law "can hardly raise incentives to obtain a warrant without giving the police a fair chance to take their probable cause to a magistrate and get one."]

[The dissenting opinion of JUSTICE STEVENS is omitted.]

## H.  ADMINISTRATIVE SEARCHES AND OTHER SEARCHES AND SEIZURES BASED ON "SPECIAL NEEDS"

While the warrant clause is still, at least rhetorically, the predominant clause of the Fourth Amendment, the Supreme Court has applied the reasonableness clause to searches conducted for purposes other than traditional criminal law enforcement. The Court has reasoned that the traditional requirement of a warrant based on probable cause is not well-suited to searches for purposes as varied as enforcing school discipline, public safety, and administrative efficiency. If the government search or seizure is designed to effectuate special needs beyond criminal law enforcement, then the Court engages in a balancing of interests under the reasonableness clause to determine what safeguards must apply. Reasonableness analysis balances the need for a particular search or seizure against the degree of invasion upon personal rights that the search or seizure entails. And if the probable cause standard and/or the warrant requirement takes insufficient account of the state interest in light of the degree of the intrusion, then the Court finds it reasonable to dispense with such requirements in favor of lesser standards such as reasonable suspicion, area warrants, or other controls on official discretion.

On the other hand, if the purpose of the search is simply to obtain evidence for purposes of criminal law enforcement, then probable cause and a warrant are presumptively required. See Arizona v. Hicks, 480 U.S. 321 (1987) (holding that, absent "special operational necessities," probable cause is required for a search for evidence); Romo v. Champion, 46 F.3d 1013 (10th Cir.1995) (probable cause not required to search a person driving into a prison parking lot, where the search is conducted for safety purposes; however, if the officers "had executed the search for traditional law enforcement purposes, they presumptively would have needed probable cause.")

It is true that the Court in United States v. Knights and United States v. Samson, supra, in the section on stop and frisk, upheld searches of probationers on less than probable cause (and in *Samson*, without any suspicion at all), and held that it was not necessary in those cases to establish a special need beyond ordinary criminal law enforcement to support the searches; the searches, even though for law enforcement purposes, were found "reasonable" given the state interest on the one hand and the probationer's extremely diminished expectation of privacy on the other. But *Knights* and *Samson* cannot mean that the state is never required to establish special needs to justify searches on less than probable cause: that would be blithely throwing out 30 years of "special needs" case law; and it would also amount to rejecting the *Terry* doctrine's prohibition on using frisks to search for evidence. *Knights* and *Samson* do not contain enough analysis to justify such an extreme result (i.e., that searches for evidence of crime can be done without a warrant and on less than probable cause whenever "reasonable"); and neither case implies that it is doing anything more than deciding whether searches of *probationers and parolees* are reasonable under the circumstances. Yet the Court, in Maryland v. King, set forth later in this section, appears to apply a free-from balancing test of reasonableness to uphold DNA testing of prisoners. So it is fair to state that the integrity of the "special needs" limitation on reasonableness balancing for searches is in some doubt after *King*.

## 1.   Safety Inspections of Homes

In Camara v. Municipal Court, 387 U.S. 523 (1967), a homeowner claimed the right to refuse a warrantless entry by a health inspector who desired to inspect the house as provided for in the San Francisco housing code. The Court held that the Fourth Amendment covered these administrative searches. But Justice White's majority opinion said that government safety inspectors were not required to have probable cause to believe that a particular dwelling was in violation of the code being enforced. Rather, area-wide safety inspections are permissible and "it is obvious that 'probable cause' to issue a warrant to inspect must exist if reasonable legislative or administrative standards for conducting an area inspection are satisfied with respect to a particular dwelling." Thus, while a warrant is required for an administrative safety inspection of a home, the warrant need not be based upon a finding of probable cause that a particular home is in violation of a safety code. Instead, the warrant can be issued upon a finding that a search is in compliance with a reasonable administrative scheme. Finally, the opinion noted that "nothing we say today is intended to foreclose prompt inspections, even without a warrant, that the law had traditionally upheld in emergency situations."

In a companion case, See v. City of Seattle, 387 U.S. 541 (1967), the Court, per Justice White, applied the *Camara* requirements—i.e., a warrant based on either probable cause or demonstrated compliance with some reasonable administrative inspection scheme—to inspections of non-residential commercial structures. But, the Court did "not in any way imply that business premises may not reasonably be inspected in many more situations than private homes."

Justice Clark, joined by Justices Harlan and Stewart, dissented in both *Camara* and *See*. They argued that the area warrant concept and the "boxcar" warrant procedure upheld by the Court would degrade the Fourth Amendment.

### *The Assessment of Cause for a Safety Inspection*

An official who issues a warrant for a home safety inspection under *Camara* necessarily performs a different function than the magistrate assessing a search warrant application in a criminal investigation. This is because the standard of proof required for a home safety inspection is different from the traditional probable cause standard. A home inspection can be conducted on the basis of such generalized facts as passage of time and the nature of the building, or as part of an area-wide inspection. The Court in *Camara* stressed that review of the reasons for a safety inspection should occur "without any reassessment of the basic agency decision to canvass an area." Thus, the officer issuing a safety inspection warrant is not charged with evaluating the legislative and administrative policy decisions as to frequency of inspection, resource expenditures, and the like. The officer need only decide whether an established inspection policy exists and whether the inspection for which a warrant is sought fits within that program.

What danger does an area-wide warrant, which is not based upon probable cause as to any specific home, guard against? What would be wrong with a rule prohibiting safety inspectors from entering a house without probable cause to believe that there was a safety violation? How would a safety inspector obtain enough information to constitute probable cause? Is a safety inspection of a home less intrusive than a search of a home by law enforcement officers investigating a crime?

### *Warrants Without Probable Cause?*

The *Camara* Court imposed a unique requirement—that a warrant would be required, but that the warrant would be issued upon some objective standard other than probable cause. Subsequently, in Griffin v. Wisconsin, 483 U.S. 868 (1987), the Court again addressed the question whether the Fourth Amendment envisions a warrant that is not based upon particularized probable cause. Griffin, a probationer, challenged the search of his home by his probation officer. One argument in the case was that, even if probable cause was not required for the search of a probationer's home (due to a probationer's diminished expectation of privacy and the state's administrative interest in regulating a probationer), the Court should nonetheless require a warrant to be obtained. Justice Scalia, writing for the Court, contended that the Fourth Amendment could not be read to provide for such a warrant. He reasoned that a warrant based on something other than probable cause would violate the specific language in the Fourth Amendment that "no warrant shall issue, but upon probable cause." He distinguished *Camara* as a case where the Court "arguably came to permit an exception to that prescription for administrative search warrants, which may but do not necessarily have to be issued by courts." Justice Scalia emphasized that the general rule for judicial search warrants is that they can only be issued upon particularized probable cause. Thus, the Court refused to accept the solution of a warrant based on less than probable cause as a means of balancing state and individual interests. It held that a probation officer can conduct a warrantless search of a probationer's house, upon reasonable suspicion of a probation violation.

## 2.   Administrative Searches of Businesses

The Court applied the *Camara* protections to businesses in *See,* but it is apparent that administrative searches of businesses involve different issues from searches of residences. For one thing, some entries into business premises may not be searches at all. For example, if a fire inspector walks through a hotel lobby and looks for fire exits, no reasonable expectation of privacy is implicated because it is an area open to the public. See Donovan v. Lone Steer, Inc., 464 U.S. 408 (1984). Also, an administrative search of a business implicates more complex regulatory concerns: the state has an administrative interest not only in whether the business *structure* is safe, but also in whether the business is being safely and properly conducted. Moreover, the businessperson may have a diminished expectation of privacy given the nature of the business conducted. But on the other hand, the risk of an arbitrary use of official power to conduct a regulatory search of a business must be a cause for special concern. It is no secret that businesspersons have occasionally been subject to harassment and extortion by unscrupulous investigators. Moreover, it might be difficult to distinguish between a search done for "administrative" purposes and a search that is done to obtain evidence of a criminal violation. All of these considerations, and the special rules applicable to "closely regulated" businesses, are discussed in the following case.

### NEW YORK V. BURGER

Supreme Court of the United States, 1987.
482 U.S. 691.

### JUSTICE BLACKMUN delivered the opinion of the Court.

This case presents the question whether the warrantless search of an automobile junkyard, conducted pursuant to a statute authorizing such a search, falls within the exception to the warrant requirement for administrative inspections of pervasively regulated industries. The case also presents the question whether an otherwise proper administrative inspection is unconstitutional because the ultimate purpose of the regulatory statute pursuant to which the search is done—the deterrence of criminal behavior—is the same as that of penal laws, with the result that the inspection may disclose violations not only of the regulatory statute but also of the penal statutes.

* * * Respondent Joseph Burger is the owner of a junkyard in Brooklyn, N.Y. His business consists, in part, of the dismantling of automobiles and the selling of their parts. * * * At approximately noon on November 17, 1982, Officer Joseph Vega and four other plainclothes officers, all members of the Auto Crimes Division of the New York City Police Department, entered respondent's junkyard to conduct an

inspection pursuant to N.Y.Veh. & Traf.Law § 415–a5 (McKinney 1986).[a] On any given day, the Division conducts from 5 to 10 inspections of vehicle dismantlers, automobile junkyards, and related businesses.

Upon entering the junkyard, the officers asked to see Burger's license and his "police book"—the record of the automobiles and vehicle parts in his possession. Burger replied that he had neither a license nor a police book. The officers then announced their intention to conduct a § 415–a5 inspection. * * * In accordance with their practice, the officers copied down the Vehicle Identification Numbers (VINs) of several vehicles and parts of vehicles that were in the junkyard. After checking these numbers against a police computer, the officers determined that respondent was in possession of stolen vehicles and parts. Accordingly, Burger was arrested and charged with five counts of possession of stolen property and one count of unregistered operation as a vehicle dismantler, in violation of § 415–a1.

[The trial court denied a motion to suppress, but the New York Court of Appeals reversed, finding that the statute authorizing the warrantless inspection was unconstitutional.]

The Court long has recognized that the Fourth Amendment's prohibition on unreasonable searches and seizures is applicable to commercial premises, as well as to private homes. See v. City of Seattle. An owner or operator of a business thus has an expectation of privacy in commercial property, which society is prepared to consider to be reasonable, see Katz v. United States (Harlan, J., concurring). This expectation exists not only with respect to traditional police searches conducted for the gathering of criminal evidence but also with respect to administrative inspections designed to enforce regulatory statutes. An expectation of privacy in commercial premises, however, is different from, and indeed less than, a similar expectation in an individual's home. This expectation is particularly attenuated in commercial property employed in "closely regulated" industries. * * *

The Court first examined the "unique" problem of inspections of "closely regulated" businesses in two enterprises that had "a long

---

[a] This statute reads in pertinent part:

"Records and identification. (a) * * * Every person required to be registered pursuant to this section shall maintain a record of all motor vehicles, trailers, and major component parts thereof, coming into his possession together with a record of the disposition of any such motor vehicle, trailer or part thereof and shall maintain proof of ownership for any motor vehicle, trailer or major component part thereof while in his possession. * * * Upon request of an agent of the commissioner or of any police officer and during his regular and usual business hours, a vehicle dismantler shall produce such records and permit said agent or police officer to examine them and any vehicles or parts of vehicles which are subject to the record keeping requirements of this section and which are on the premises. . . . The failure to produce such records or to permit such inspection on the part of any person required to be registered pursuant to this section as required by this paragraph shall be a class A misdemeanor."

tradition of close government supervision." In Colonnade Corp. v. United States, 397 U.S. 72 (1970), it considered a warrantless search of a catering business pursuant to several federal revenue statutes authorizing the inspection of the premises of liquor dealers. Although the Court disapproved the search because the statute provided that a sanction be imposed when entry was refused, and because it did not authorize entry without a warrant as an alternative in this situation, it recognized that "the liquor industry [was] long subject to close supervision and inspection." We returned to this issue in United States v. Biswell, 406 U.S. 311 (1972), which [upheld] a warrantless inspection of the premises of a pawnshop operator, who was federally licensed to sell sporting weapons pursuant to the Gun Control Act of 1968. * * * We observed: "When a dealer chooses to engage in this pervasively regulated business and to accept a federal license, he does so with the knowledge that his business records, firearms, and ammunition will be subject to effective inspection."

The *"Colonnade-Biswell"* doctrine, stating the reduced expectation of privacy by an owner of commercial premises in a "closely regulated" industry, has received renewed emphasis in more recent decisions. In Marshall v. Barlow's, Inc., 436 U.S. 307 (1978), we noted its continued vitality but declined to find that warrantless inspections, made pursuant to the Occupational Safety and Health Act of 1970, of *all* businesses engaged in interstate commerce fell within the narrow focus of this doctrine. However, we found warrantless inspections made pursuant to the Federal Mine Safety and Health Act of 1977, proper because they were of a "closely regulated" industry. Donovan v. Dewey, 452 U.S. 594 (1981).

\* \* \*

Because the owner or operator of commercial premises in a "closely regulated" industry has a reduced expectation of privacy, the warrant and probable-cause requirements, which fulfill the traditional Fourth Amendment standard of reasonableness for a government search, have lessened application in this context. Rather, we conclude that, as in other situations of "special need" where the privacy interests of the owner are weakened and the government interests in regulating particular businesses are concomitantly heightened, a warrantless inspection of commercial premises may well be reasonable within the meaning of the Fourth Amendment.

This warrantless inspection, however, even in the context of a pervasively regulated business, will be deemed to be reasonable only so long as three criteria are met. First, there must be a "substantial" government interest that informs the regulatory scheme pursuant to which the inspection is made. See Donovan v. Dewey ("substantial federal interest in improving the health and safety conditions in the Nation's underground and surface mines").

Second, the warrantless inspections must be necessary to further the regulatory scheme. For example, in *Dewey* we recognized that forcing mine inspectors to obtain a warrant before every inspection might alert mine owners or operators to the impending inspection, thereby frustrating the purposes of the Mine Safety and Health Act—to detect and thus to deter safety and health violations.

Finally, the statute's inspection program, in terms of the certainty and regularity of its application, must provide a constitutionally adequate substitute for a warrant." In other words, the regulatory statute must perform the two basic functions of a warrant: it must advise the owner of the commercial premises that the search is being made pursuant to the law and has a properly defined scope, and it must limit the discretion of the inspecting officers. To perform this first function, the statute must be "sufficiently comprehensive and defined that the owner of commercial property cannot help but be aware that his property will be subject to periodic inspections undertaken for specific purposes." Donovan v. Dewey. In addition, in defining how a statute limits the discretion of the inspectors, we have observed that it must be "carefully limited in time, place, and scope." United States v. Biswell.

* * * Searches made pursuant to § 415–a5, in our view, clearly fall within this established exception to the warrant requirement for administrative inspections in "closely regulated" businesses. First, the nature of the regulatory statute reveals that the operation of a junkyard, part of which is devoted to vehicle dismantling, is a "closely regulated" business in the State of New York. The provisions regulating the activity of vehicle dismantling are extensive. An operator cannot engage in this industry without first obtaining a license, which means that he must meet the registration requirements and must pay a fee. Under § 415–a5(a), the operator must maintain a police book recording the acquisition and disposition of motor vehicles and vehicle parts, and make such records and inventory available for inspection by the police or any agent of the Department of Motor Vehicles. The operator also must display his registration number prominently at his place of business, on business documentation, and on vehicles and parts that pass through his business. Moreover, the person engaged in this activity is subject to criminal penalties, as well as to loss of license or civil fines, for failure to comply with these provisions. That other States besides New York have imposed similarly extensive regulations on automobile junkyards further supports the "closely regulated" status of this industry.

In determining whether vehicle dismantlers constitute a "closely regulated" industry, the duration of this particular regulatory scheme has some relevancy. Section 415–a could be said to be of fairly recent vintage, and the inspection provision of § 415–a5 was added only in 1979. But because the automobile is a relatively new phenomenon in our society and because its widespread use is even newer, automobile junkyards and vehicle dismantlers have not been in existence very long and thus do not have an ancient history of government oversight. * * *

The automobile-junkyard business, however, is simply a new branch of an industry that has existed, and has been closely regulated, for many years. The automobile junkyard is closely akin to the secondhand shop or the general junkyard. * * * As such, vehicle dismantlers represent a modern, specialized version of a traditional activity. In New York, general junkyards and secondhand shops long have been subject to regulation. * * *

Accordingly, in light of the regulatory framework governing his business and the history of regulation of related industries, an operator of a junkyard engaging in vehicle dismantling has a reduced expectation of privacy in this "closely regulated" business.

* * * The New York regulatory scheme satisfies the three criteria necessary to make reasonable warrantless inspections pursuant to § 415–a5. First, the State has a substantial interest in regulating the vehicle-dismantling and automobile-junkyard industry because motor vehicle theft has increased in the State and because the problem of theft is associated with this industry. In this day, automobile theft has become a significant social problem, placing enormous economic and personal burdens upon the citizens of different States. * * *

Second, regulation of the vehicle-dismantling industry reasonably serves the State's substantial interest in eradicating automobile theft. It is well established that the theft problem can be addressed effectively by controlling the receiver of, or market in, stolen property. Automobile junkyards and vehicle dismantlers provide the major market for stolen vehicles and vehicle parts. Thus, the State rationally may believe that it will reduce car theft by regulations that prevent automobile junkyards from becoming markets for stolen vehicles and that help trace the origin and destination of vehicle parts.

Moreover, the warrantless administrative inspections pursuant to § 415–a5 "are necessary to further [the] regulatory scheme." Donovan v. Dewey. * * * We explained in *Biswell:*

> "[I]f inspection is to be effective and serve as a credible deterrent, unannounced, even frequent, inspections are essential. In this context, the prerequisite of a warrant could easily frustrate inspection; and if the necessary flexibility as to time, scope, and frequency is to be preserved, the protections afforded by a warrant would be negligible."

\* \* \* Because stolen cars and parts often pass quickly through an automobile junkyard, "frequent" and "unannounced" inspections are necessary in order to detect them. In sum, surprise is crucial if the regulatory scheme aimed at remedying this major social problem is to function at all.

Third, § 415–a5 provides a "constitutionally adequate substitute for a warrant." The statute informs the operator of a vehicle dismantling business that inspections will be made on a regular basis. Thus, the vehicle dismantler knows that the inspections to which he is subject do not constitute discretionary acts by a government official but are conducted pursuant to statute. Section 415–a5 also sets forth the scope of the inspection and, accordingly, places the operator on notice as to how to comply with the statute. In addition, it notifies the operator as to who is authorized to conduct an inspection.

Finally, the "time, place, and scope" of the inspection is limited to place appropriate restraints upon the discretion of the inspecting officers. The officers are allowed to conduct an inspection only "during [the] regular and usual business hours."[b] The inspections can be made only of vehicle-dismantling and related industries. And the permissible scope of these searches is narrowly defined: the inspectors may examine the records, as well as "any vehicles or parts of vehicles which are subject to the record keeping requirements of this section and which are on the premises."

\* \* \* The Court of Appeals, nevertheless, struck down the statute as violative of the Fourth Amendment because, in its view, the statute had no truly administrative purpose but was "designed simply to give the police an expedient means of enforcing penal sanctions for possession of stolen property." The court rested its conclusion that the administrative goal of the statute was pretextual and that § 415–a5 really "authorize[d] searches undertaken solely to uncover evidence of criminality" particularly on the fact that, even if an operator failed to produce his police book, the inspecting officers could continue their inspection for stolen vehicles and parts. The court also suggested that the identity of the inspectors—police officers—was significant in revealing the true nature of the statutory scheme.

In arriving at this conclusion, the Court of Appeals failed to recognize that a State can address a major social problem *both* by way of an administrative scheme *and* through penal sanctions. Administrative statutes and penal laws may have the same *ultimate* purpose of

---

[b] Respondent contends that § 415–a5 is unconstitutional because it fails to limit the number of searches that may be conducted of a particular business during any given period. While such limitations, or the absence thereof, are a factor in an analysis of the adequacy of a particular statute, they are not determinative of the result so long as the statute, as a whole, places adequate limits upon the discretion of the inspecting officers. \* \* \*

remedying the social problem, but they have different subsidiary purposes and prescribe different methods of addressing the problem. An administrative statute establishes how a particular business in a "closely regulated" industry should be operated, setting forth rules to guide an operator's conduct of the business and allowing government officials to ensure that those rules are followed. Such a regulatory approach contrasts with that of the penal laws, a major emphasis of which is the punishment of individuals for specific acts of behavior.

\* \* \* The New York penal laws address automobile theft by punishing it or the possession of stolen property, including possession by individuals in the business of buying and selling property. In accordance with its interest in regulating the automobile-junkyard industry, the State also has devised a regulatory manner of dealing with this problem. Section 415–a, as a whole, serves the regulatory goals of seeking to ensure that vehicle dismantlers are legitimate businesspersons and that stolen vehicles and vehicle parts passing through automobile junkyards can be identified. \* \* \*

If the administrative goals of § 415–a5 are recognized, the difficulty the Court of Appeals perceives in allowing inspecting officers to examine vehicles and vehicle parts even in the absence of records evaporates. The regulatory purposes of § 415–a5 certainly are served by having the inspecting officers compare the records of a particular vehicle dismantler with vehicles and vehicle parts in the junkyard. The purposes of maintaining junkyards in the hands of legitimate businesspersons and of tracing vehicles that pass through these businesses, however, *also* are served by having the officers examine the operator's inventory even when the operator, for whatever reason, fails to produce the police book. Forbidding inspecting officers to examine the inventory in this situation would permit an illegitimate vehicle dismantler to thwart the purposes of the administrative scheme and would have the absurd result of subjecting his counterpart who maintained records to a more extensive search.

Nor do we think that this administrative scheme is unconstitutional simply because, in the course of enforcing it, an inspecting officer may discover evidence of crimes, besides violations of the scheme itself. \* \* \* The discovery of evidence of crimes in the course of an otherwise proper administrative inspection does not render that search illegal or the administrative scheme suspect.[c]

---

[c] The legislative history of § 415–a, in general, and § 415–a5, in particular, reveals that the New York Legislature had proper regulatory purposes for enacting the administrative scheme and was not using it as a "pretext" to enable law enforcement authorities to gather evidence of penal law violations. There is, furthermore, no reason to believe that the instant inspection was actually a "pretext" for obtaining evidence of respondent's violation of the penal laws. It is undisputed that the inspection was made solely pursuant to the administrative scheme. \* \* \*

Finally, we fail to see any constitutional significance in the fact that police officers, rather than "administrative" agents, are permitted to conduct the § 415–a5 inspection. The significance respondent alleges lies in the role of police officers as enforcers of the penal laws and in the officers' power to arrest for offenses other than violations of the administrative scheme. It is, however, important to note that state police officers, like those in New York, have numerous duties in addition to those associated with traditional police work. As a practical matter, many States do not have the resources to assign the enforcement of a particular administrative scheme to a specialized agency. So long as a regulatory scheme is properly administrative, it is not rendered illegal by the fact that the inspecting officer has the power to arrest individuals for violations other than those created by the scheme itself. In sum, we decline to impose upon the States the burden of requiring the enforcement of their regulatory statutes to be carried out by specialized agents.

\* \* \*

**JUSTICE BRENNAN, with whom JUSTICE MARSHALL joins, and with whom JUSTICE O'CONNOR joins in pertinent part, dissenting.**

\* \* \*

The provisions governing vehicle dismantling in New York simply are not extensive. A vehicle dismantler must register and pay a fee, display the registration in various circumstances, maintain a police book, and allow inspections. Of course, the inspections themselves cannot be cited as proof of pervasive regulation justifying elimination of the warrant requirement; that would be obvious bootstrapping. Nor can registration and recordkeeping requirements be characterized as close regulation. New York City, like many States and municipalities, imposes similar, and often more stringent licensing, recordkeeping, and other regulatory requirements on a myriad of trades and businesses. Few substantive qualifications are required of an aspiring vehicle dismantler; no regulation governs the condition of the premises, the method of operation, the hours of operation, the equipment utilized, etc. This scheme stands in marked contrast to, e.g., the mine safety regulations relevant in Donovan v. Dewey.

In sum, if New York City's administrative scheme renders the vehicle-dismantling business closely regulated, few businesses will escape such a finding. \* \* \*

Even if vehicle dismantling were a closely regulated industry, I would nonetheless conclude that this search violated the Fourth Amendment. \* \* \*

\* \* \* There is neither an upper nor a lower limit on the number of searches that may be conducted at any given operator's establishment in any given time period. Neither the statute, nor any regulations, nor any regulatory body, provides limits or guidance on the selection of vehicle dismantlers for inspection. \* \* \*

The Court also maintains that this statute effectively limits the scope of the search. \* \* \* Plainly, a statute authorizing a search which can uncover *no* administrative violations is not sufficiently limited in scope to avoid the warrant requirement. This statute fails to tailor the scope of administrative inspection to the particular concerns posed by the regulated business. \* \* \* The conduct of the police in this case underscores this point. The police removed identification numbers from a walker and a wheelchair, neither of which fell within the statutory scope of a permissible administrative search.

\* \* \* The *sole* limitation I see on a police search of the premises of a vehicle dismantler is that it must occur during business hours; otherwise it is open season. The unguided discretion afforded police in this scheme precludes its substitution for a warrant.

\* \* \*

The fundamental defect in § 415–a5 is that it authorizes searches intended solely to uncover evidence of criminal acts. \* \* \*

Here the State has \* \* \* circumvented the requirements of the Fourth Amendment by altering the label placed on the search. This crucial point is most clearly illustrated by the fact that the police copied the serial numbers from a wheelchair and a handicapped person's walker that were found on the premises, and determined that these items had been stolen. \* \* \* The scope of the search alone reveals that it was undertaken solely to uncover evidence of criminal wrongdoing.

Moreover, it is factually impossible that the search was intended to discover wrongdoing subject to administrative sanction. Burger stated that he was not registered to dismantle vehicles as required by § 415–a1, and that he did not have a police book, as required by § 415–a5(a). At that point he had violated every requirement of the administrative scheme. There is no administrative provision forbidding possession of stolen automobiles or automobile parts. The inspection became a search for evidence of criminal acts when all possible administrative violations had been uncovered.

\* \* \*

The Court thus implicitly holds that if an administrative scheme has certain goals and if the search serves those goals, it may be upheld even if no concrete administrative consequences could follow from a particular search. This is a dangerous suggestion, for the goals of administrative schemes often overlap with the goals of the criminal law. * * * If the Fourth Amendment is to retain meaning in the commercial context, it must be applied to searches for evidence of criminal acts even if those searches would also serve an administrative purpose, unless that administrative purpose takes the concrete form of seeking an administrative violation.

* * *

### Administrative Searches of Businesses After Burger

What precisely are the limitations on administrative inspections of businesses after *Burger?* Has the Court imposed sufficient controls on official discretion? Did Justice Brennan overreact? Analysis in some lower court cases after *Burger* would suggest that he did not. For example, in United States v. Hernandez, 901 F.2d 1217 (5th Cir.1990), an FBI agent who suspected that a commercial truck was carrying drugs followed the truck for twenty-four hours and 600 miles. He then notified the Texas Department of Public Safety that a truck believed to be carrying drugs was traveling on the interstate with no license plates. The DPS officer stopped the truck and demanded a driver's license and a bill of lading describing the cargo. The driver failed to produce evidence of Texas Interstate Commerce Commission Motor Carrier authorization. The officer then walked to the back of the truck and opened an inspection port, a small door used to check the temperature of the cargo. He smelled marijuana, obtained the keys to the cargo door, and a search of the truck uncovered 98 bales of marijuana. The court of appeals found that, while there was probable cause to arrest for the license plate violation, this did not provide probable cause to search the truck; nor was the search permissible as a search incident to arrest, because it went beyond the passenger compartment; nor was it permissible as a protective search under *Terry,* because the officer had no reasonable suspicion of bodily harm that necessitated looking into the cargo area. But the search was permissible as an administrative search under *Burger.* The court concluded that a Texas civil statute regulating motor carriers authorized any Department of Public Safety Officer to inspect any load of commodities being transported for hire over the highways of the state. Could the DPS officer have searched a car to determine whether it was carrying commercial goods without a commercial license? If so, wouldn't that mean that the DPS officer could search any car on the highway without suspicion?

### Substitute for a Warrant

In order to satisfy *Burger's* requirement of a constitutionally adequate substitute for a warrant, a regulatory regime must 1) advise the owner of the regulated business that the inspection is being made pursuant to law; and 2) impose some meaningful limitation on the officer's discretion to search (e.g., time, place and manner restrictions). In *Burger*, discretion was found sufficiently limited by the provision in the statute requiring that the search be made during daytime hours. Is this enough limitation on discretion, given that *Burger* authorizes a suspicionless search? See also United States v. Castelo, 415 F.3d 407 (5th Cir. 2005) (holding that an administrative scheme allowing weighing and inspection of commercial trucks imposed sufficient limits on officer discretion because only commercial vehicles could be inspected, and only when such vehicles were operating on the highways of the state: "These limitations are markedly similar to the limits on officer discretion in *Burger*.").

Although a statute authorizing administrative searches may be constitutional, actual searches purportedly conducted under that authority may not. If a search clearly goes beyond the statutory limitations that substitute for a warrant, it will be found unreasonable under the Fourth Amendment. See Bruce v. Beary, 498 F.3d 1232 (11th Cir. 2007) (search of vehicle dismantling business would be unreasonable if the owner could prove that it lasted 8 hours and involved both a display of automatic weapons by the officers and detention of shop employees: such a search would be "far beyond the statutory authorization" and "hardly seems to be what the Supreme Court in *Burger* had in mind when it held that the Constitution is not offended by * * * the regular, routine inspection of books and records required to be kept by auto salvagers."). See also Turner v. Dammon, 848 F.2d 440 (4th Cir. 1988) (disapproving officers' conduct in performing over 100 administrative inspections of a particular bar, where there was no evidence to support the need for such repeated searches).

### *The Element of Surprise*

The Court justified the warrantless search in *Burger* partly because surprise was necessary. The concern was that the officer would go to Burger's business without a warrant, and would be refused admission; then, when the officer went to get a warrant, Burger would destroy or cover up evidence of an administrative violation. The Court therefore held that Burger had no right to refuse a warrantless inspection; to permit such refusal would deprive the inspector of the element of surprise that is often necessary to further regulatory interests in heavily regulated industries.

But concern about loss of the element of surprise does not really explain why an officer shouldn't have to get a warrant *before* approaching Burger's business the first time around. Then the officer could conduct a surprise inspection *with a warrant*. The court in Lesser v. Espy, 34 F.3d 1301 (7th Cir.1994), confronted the question about the element of surprise discussed in *Burger*, and proffered an explanation. *Lesser* involved the constitutionality of a warrantless inspection of a farm that raised rabbits to be used as laboratory animals. The court discussed the surprise element as follows:

> In rabbit farming many of the potential deficiencies that would violate the [Animal Welfare] Act can be quickly concealed. See, e.g., 9 C.F.R. §§ 3.50(c) (improper storage of food); 3.50(d) (improper waste disposal); 3.50(e) (unclean washrooms); 3.56(a) (unsanitary primary enclosures). Thus the Department correctly observes that preserving the element of surprise and the possibility of frequent inspections is necessary in order to detect violators. In response the Lessers rightly point out that the element of surprise may be easily maintained even with a warrant requirement—a warrant may be issued ex parte and executed without prior notice. Nevertheless, we believe a warrant requirement for the most routine inspection would interfere with the Department's ability to function and unnecessarily increase the cost of the Secretary's operations without a significant increase in privacy, especially since all licensed suppliers of research animals have a reasonable expectation of at least a couple of regular inspections * * * each year.

Thus, the need for surprise is really a false issue—the question is whether officials who undoubtedly need to make surprise inspections should be burdened with a warrant requirement. The *Lesser* court, following *Burger*, determines that the minimal privacy interest protected by a warrant requirement is outweighed by the inconvenience of having to obtain a warrant before every single administrative inspection.

Is the *Lesser* reasoning based on the fact that most businesspersons would find it in their interest to consent to an administrative inspection anyway, which would mean that administrative inspectors would be obtaining warrants that they would by and large never have to use? Is that a legitimate reason for dispensing with the warrant requirement for those business owners who don't consent?

By the way, what would be wrong with having the rabbit farmer "cover up" his violations during the period after his refusal when the administrative inspector would have to go and get a warrant (assuming the inspector did not get one in the first instance)? Doesn't "cover up" mean "fix" in this circumstance? Isn't the goal of the administrative inspection to get the owner to repair the premises?

## Administrative Inspections by Law Enforcement Officers

The Court in *Burger* held that the administrative nature of an inspection was not negated simply because the inspector was a law enforcement officer. Nonetheless, courts after *Burger* have applied a stricter scrutiny to so-called "administrative" searches when they are conducted by law enforcement officers—the concern being that the "administrative" search is simply a pretext to evade the warrant and probable cause requirements that apply to searched for criminal law enforcement. For example, in United States v. Johnson, 994 F.2d 740 (10th Cir.1993), an FBI agent received information (not amounting to probable cause) that Johnson, a taxidermist, was involved in the illegal smuggling of protected animals. He called a state administrative officer, who agreed to accompany the federal agent, ostensibly to conduct an administrative taxidermy inspection. The applicable statute authorized warrantless administrative inspections of taxidermists, but only when performed by state agents. The federal agent drove 300 miles to Johnson's taxidermy shop in order to be present for the inspection; he also participated actively in the search of the business. The investigators discovered several specimens of illegally imported animals. The court held that "the administrative search was employed solely as an instrument of criminal law enforcement." Consequently, all of the evidence was illegally obtained. The court reasoned as follows:

> The presence and active participation of the federal agent during the search of Mr. Johnson's shop, and the federal agent's insistence that the state agent accompany him establish as a matter of law that the federal agent used the state regulatory inspection as a pretext for an investigatory search. Federal agents may not cloak themselves with the authority granted by state inspection statutes in order to seek evidence of criminal activity and avoid the Fourth Amendment's warrant requirement.

Recall the discussion of pretext earlier in this Chapter. Was the inspection in *Johnson* really pretextual, given the fact that the state agent had the right to conduct a warrantless administrative inspection? Or, can it be argued that *Whren* permits otherwise pretextual searches and arrests only when there is probable cause? If that is so, then courts can still regulate for pretext when police officers seek to conduct a suspicionless "administrative" search that is really for purposes of criminal law enforcement. See also United States v. Knight, 306 F.3d 534 (8th Cir. 2002) (police officer's search of a truck, purportedly pursuant to a state safety inspection program, became illegal when it was extended to the trucker's briefcase: "We believe that, as a general matter, rummaging through a person's belongings is more likely to serve the purpose of crime control than the enforcement of a regulatory scheme."). Note that the

Court in *Burger*, in upholding the inspection, specifically noted that there was "no reason to believe that the instant inspection was actually a 'pretext' for obtaining evidence of respondent's violation of the penal laws."

## 3. Searches and Seizures of Individuals Pursuant to "Special Needs"

The Court has used its special needs balancing analysis in a series of cases to uphold civil-based searches of individuals in the absence of a warrant and probable cause. The first cases upheld suspicion-based searches, where the government had reasonable suspicion—but not probable cause—to justify a civil-based search. Then the Court decided a series of cases raising the question whether civil-based searches could be conducted in the absence of any suspicion at all.

### a. Searches and Seizures on the Basis of Reasonable Suspicion Rather Than Probable Cause

In New Jersey v. T.L.O., 469 U.S. 325 (1985), a school official searched the handbag of a student. The official had reasonable suspicion, but not probable cause, to believe that cigarettes were in the student's purse. In the absence of probable cause, the search could not be justified as a criminal-based search for evidence. Nor could the search be justified under the *Terry* doctrine, because *Terry* searches are for safety only, and the school official had no basis for believing that the student posed a risk of bodily harm. Nonetheless, the Court upheld the search. The Court reasoned that the search effectuated "special needs" beyond ordinary criminal law enforcement—specifically the state's need to assure a safe and healthy learning environment. This finding of special needs permitted the Court to balance the state interest at stake in the search against the student's interest in privacy.

The *T.L.O.* Court found that the reasonable suspicion standard was sufficient to protect the student's diminished expectation of privacy in the school environment, while permitting the government the proper degree of leeway in maintaining standards of school discipline. It reasoned that if probable cause were required, school officials would be unable to regulate disciplinary problems at an early stage, before they became serious and intractable problems.  That is, while waiting for probable cause to develop, the state's interest in regulation would already be undermined, as it is important to the state to nip disciplinary problems in the bud. Finally, the Court held that a warrant would not be required for searches conducted by school officials; school officials could not be expected to obtain a judicial warrant before seeking to enforce school disciplinary standards.

The *T.L.O.* analysis was used by the Court to uphold warrantless searches of the office of a government official, and of the house of a probationer. O'Connor v. Ortega, 480 U.S. 709 (1987); Griffin v. Wisconsin, supra. In both *O'Connor* and *Griffin*, as in *T.L.O.*, the Court found that conditioning searches on probable cause would be deleterious to the state interest, and that the reasonable suspicion standard was an appropriate balance between state and (diminished) individual interests in privacy.

### *Limitations on Strip Searches of Students: Safford Unified School District v. Redding*

In *T.L.O.*, the Court required individualized suspicion for a search of a student's handbag. This raises the question whether a "special needs" search could be so intrusive as to require a more substantial showing than mere reasonable suspicion of a school violation. Justice Souter wrote his last opinion for the Court in Safford Unified School District #1 v. Redding, 577 U.S. 364 (2009). He described the issue:

> whether a 13-year-old student's Fourth Amendment right was violated when she was subjected to a search of her bra and underpants by school officials acting on reasonable suspicion that she had brought forbidden prescription and over-the-counter drugs to school.

The Court held that "[b]ecause there were no reasons to suspect the drugs presented a danger or were concealed in her underwear, * * * the search did violate the Constitution, but because there is reason to question the clarity with which the right was established, the official who ordered the unconstitutional search is entitled to qualified immunity from liability."

Justice Souter reasoned that an assistant principal's (Wilson's) suspicion of the student's (Savanah's) distributing drugs to other students was enough to justify a search of her backpack and outer clothing, because "[i]f a student is reasonably suspected of giving out contraband pills, she is reasonably suspected of carrying them on her person and in the carryall that has become an item of student uniform in most places today." But, Justice Souter found that the scope of the search was not justified:

> Here, the content of the suspicion failed to match the degree of intrusion. Wilson knew beforehand that the pills were prescription-strength ibuprofen and over-the-counter naproxen, common pain relievers equivalent to two Advil, or one Aleve. He must have been aware of the nature and limited threat of the specific drugs he was searching for, and while just about anything can be taken in quantities that will do real harm, Wilson had no reason to suspect

that large amounts of the drugs were being passed around, or that individual students were receiving great numbers of pills.

Nor could Wilson have suspected that Savana was hiding common painkillers in her underwear. * * * [N]ondangerous school contraband does not raise the specter of stashes in intimate places, and there is no evidence in the record of any general practice among Safford Middle School students of hiding that sort of thing in underwear. * * *

In sum, what was missing from the suspected facts that pointed to Savana was any indication of danger to the students from the power of the drugs or their quantity, and any reason to suppose that Savana was carrying pills in her underwear. We think that the combination of these deficiencies was fatal to finding the search reasonable.

There were separate opinions of Justices Stevens, Ginsburg and Thomas concurring in part and dissenting in part.

### b. Suspicionless Searches of Persons on the Basis of "Special Needs"

### Drug-Testing of Employees: Skinner v. Railway Labor Executives

*T.L.O.* permitted "special needs" searches on the basis of reasonable suspicion rather than probable cause. The *T.L.O.* Court did not decide whether a "special needs" search could be conducted *without any suspicion* that the person searched has violated any law or regulation. Subsequently the Court, in companion cases, considered the constitutionality of suspicionless drug-testing of public employees. In Skinner v. Railway Labor Executives' Ass'n, 489 U.S. 602 (1989), the Court upheld a program mandating drug tests for all railroad personnel involved in certain train accidents. Thus, the plan called for suspicionless testing of all personnel involved in the accident. Failing the test would result in loss of employment. Justice Kennedy, writing for the Court, made the following points:

1. The program was subject to Fourth Amendment scrutiny, because the drug-testing was essentially required by federal regulation. Therefore, even though it was administered by a private employer, it was not a private party search beyond the purview of the Fourth Amendment.

2. Drug testing of urine is a search within the meaning of the Fourth Amendment, because it can reveal private information (such

as pregnancy or epilepsy), and because the process of monitoring the employee's act of urination implicates privacy interests.

3. The government's interest in regulating the conduct of railroad employees to ensure safety "presents 'special needs' beyond normal law enforcement that may justify departures from the usual warrant and probable-cause requirements."

4. A warrant was not required to subject the railroad employees to drug-testing, because, "in light of the standardized nature of the tests and the minimal discretion vested in those charged with administering the program, there are virtually no facts for a neutral magistrate to evaluate." Moreover, the railroad supervisors responsible for administering the testing program "are not in the business of investigating violations of the criminal laws or enforcing administrative codes, and otherwise have little occasion to become familiar with the intricacies of this Court's Fourth Amendment jurisprudence."

5. The drug-testing program was reasonable even though it provided for testing in the absence of any individualized suspicion of drug use. Justice Kennedy declared: "where the privacy interests implicated by the search are minimal, and where an important governmental interest furthered by the intrusion would be placed in jeopardy by a requirement of individualized suspicion, a search may be reasonable despite the absence of such suspicion." The urine testing was found not very intrusive, because "[t]he regulations do not require that samples be furnished under the direct observation of a monitor, despite the desirability of such a procedure to ensure the integrity of the sample. The sample is also collected in a medical environment, by personnel unrelated to the railroad employer, and is thus not unlike similar procedures encountered often in the context of a regular physical examination." Furthermore, the expectations of privacy of covered employees was "diminished by reason of their participation in an industry that is regulated pervasively to ensure safety, a goal dependent, in substantial part, on the health and fitness of covered employees." On the other side of the balancing equation, the Court found that the state interests at stake were "compelling," and could not be accommodated by a requirement of individualized suspicion. Employees subject to the tests "discharge duties fraught with such risks of injury to others that even a momentary lapse of attention can have disastrous consequences." Drug-testing provides an effective means of deterring drug use, because employees in safety-sensitive positions "know they will be tested upon the occurrence of a triggering event, the timing of which no employee can predict with certainty." Also, drug-testing will "help railroads obtain invaluable information about the causes of major

accidents, and to take appropriate measures to safeguard the general public."

6. The state's interest in a suspicionless testing plan was strengthened by the fact that there was a documented drug problem among railroad employees. Thus, the government was not simply enforcing some hypothetical interest.

7. A requirement of particularized suspicion of drug use would "seriously impede an employer's ability to obtain this information, despite its obvious importance." This is because "[o]btaining evidence that might give rise to the suspicion that a particular employee is impaired, a difficult endeavor in the best of circumstances, is most impracticable in the aftermath of a serious accident."

8. There was no indication that the suspicionless testing was a pretextual means of enforcing the criminal law.

Justice Stevens concurred in part and in the judgment in *Skinner*. He was dubious, however, about the deterrent effect of drug-testing in the railroad context. He noted that the testing was undertaken *after* an accident, not before. He reasoned that workers would "not go to work with the expectation that they may be involved in a major accident," and that "if the risk of serious personal injury does not deter their use of these substances, it seems highly unlikely that the additional threat of loss of employment would have any effect on their behavior."

Justice Marshall, joined by Justice Brennan, dissented in *Skinner*. He criticized the Court for rejecting the probable cause requirement for "a manipulable balancing inquiry under which, upon the mere assertion of a 'special need,' even the deepest dignitary and privacy interests become vulnerable to governmental incursion."

### *Drug-Testing of Employees: National Treasury Employees v. Von Raab*

In National Treasury Employees Union v. Von Raab, 489 U.S. 656 (1989), a case decided the same day as *Skinner,* the Court upheld compelled urinalysis of certain Customs Service employees. Drug tests were made a condition of obtaining employment for three types of positions in the Customs Service: those involving drug interdiction, those requiring the employee to carry a firearm, and those in which the employee would handle "classified documents." The employee was allowed to produce the sample privately, but to protect against adulteration, "a monitor of the same sex as the employee remains close at hand to listen for the normal sounds of urination." Customs employees who tested positive for drugs and who could offer no satisfactory explanation were subject to dismissal from the Service; but the testing results could not be turned over to a criminal prosecutor without the employee's consent.

Justice Kennedy again wrote the opinion for the Court. He found that the drug-testing served special needs beyond criminal law enforcement, specifically the need for safety and to ensure that customs employees responsible for controlling the flow of drugs into the country are not on drugs themselves. Balancing the state and individual interests, Justice Kennedy concluded that a warrant was not required for the testing, because the event that triggered the testing was "the employee's decision to apply for a covered position." There was thus no factual question similar to probable cause for a magistrate to decide.

The *Von Raab* Court found that suspicionless testing was reasonable as applied to two of the three covered types of employees—those involved in drug interdiction and those carrying handguns. Justice Kennedy noted that "the Government has a compelling interest in ensuring that front-line personnel are physically fit, and have unimpeachable integrity and judgment," and that the public interest "likewise demands effective measures to prevent the promotion of drug users to positions that require the incumbent to carry a firearm." The majority asserted that these two classes of employees had a diminished expectation of privacy, because the positions depended uniquely on the employees' "judgment and dexterity." Justice Kennedy also emphasized that the testing procedures were designed to minimize the intrusion involved, to the extent possible without sacrificing the reliability of the test.

The Court in *Von Raab* found itself unable to assess the reasonableness of suspicionless testing as applied to the third category of employees, those handling classified documents. The Court remanded this aspect of the case, and explained as follows:

> It is not clear * * * whether the category defined by the Service's testing directive encompasses only those Customs employees likely to gain access to sensitive information. Employees who are tested under the Service's scheme include those holding such diverse positions as "Accountant," "Accounting Technician," "Animal Caretaker," "Attorney (All)," "Baggage Clerk," "Co-op Student (All)," "Electric Equipment Repairer," "Mail Clerk/Assistant," and "Messenger." * * * [I]t is not evident that those occupying these positions are likely to gain access to sensitive information, and this apparent discrepancy raises in our minds the question whether the Service has defined this category of employees more broadly than is necessary to meet the purposes of the Commissioner's directive.

## *What if There Is No Record of Drug Abuse?*

The most difficult issue for the majority in *Von Raab* was that the Customs Service had implemented the drug-testing program even though there was no documented drug problem among Customs employees. This was unlike the situation in *Skinner,* where the drug problem among railroad employees, and the risk therefrom, was well-documented. Those who challenged the plan in *Von Raab* argued that suspicionless drug-testing was unreasonable unless it could be justified as responsive to and effective against a documented drug problem. Justice Kennedy rejected this argument in the following analysis:

> Detecting drug impairment on the part of employees can be a difficult task, especially where, as here, it is not feasible to subject employees and their work product to the kind of day-to-day scrutiny that is the norm in more traditional office environments. * * * In light of the extraordinary safety and national security hazards that would attend the promotion of drug users to positions that require the carrying of firearms or the interdiction of controlled substances, the Service's policy of deterring drug users from seeking such promotions cannot be deemed unreasonable.

> The mere circumstance that all but a few of the employees tested are entirely innocent of wrongdoing does not impugn the program's validity. * * * The Service's program is designed to prevent the promotion of drug users to sensitive positions as much as it is designed to detect those employees who use drugs. Where, as here, the possible harm against which the Government seeks to guard is substantial, the need to prevent its occurrence furnishes an ample justification for reasonable searches calculated to advance the Government's goal.

In a footnote, Justice Kennedy compared suspicionless drug-testing to suspicionless searches at airports.

> As Judge Friendly explained in a leading case upholding such searches:

> > "When the risk is the jeopardy to hundreds of human lives and millions of dollars of property inherent in the pirating or blowing up of a large airplane, that danger *alone* meets the test of reasonableness, so long as the search is conducted in good faith for the purpose of preventing hijacking or like damage and with reasonable scope and the passenger has been given advance notice of his liability to such a search so that he can avoid it by choosing not to travel by air." United States v. Edwards, 498 F.2d 496, 500 (C.A.2 1974) (emphasis in original).

\* \* \* [W]e would not suppose that, if the validity of these searches be conceded, the Government would be precluded from conducting them absent a demonstration of danger as to any particular airport or airline. It is sufficient that the Government have a compelling interest in preventing an otherwise pervasive societal problem from spreading to the particular context.

Justice Marshall, joined by Justice Brennan, dissented in *Von Raab* for the reasons stated in *Skinner*.

Justice Scalia, joined by Justice Stevens, both of whom found suspicionless drug-testing to be reasonable in *Skinner,* dissented in *Von Raab*. Justice Scalia explained his differing votes in the two cases as follows:

> I joined the Court's opinion [in *Skinner*] because the demonstrated frequency of drug and alcohol use by the targeted class of employees, and the demonstrated connection between such use and grave harm, rendered the search a reasonable means of protecting society. I decline to join the Court's opinion in the present case because neither frequency of use nor connection to harm is demonstrated or even likely. In my view the Customs Service rules are a kind of immolation of privacy and human dignity in symbolic opposition to drug use.

Justice Scalia rejected the majority's generalization that no American workplace is free from the drug problem. He responded that such a generalization could perhaps suffice "if the workplace at issue could produce such catastrophic social harm that no risk whatever is tolerable—the secured areas of a nuclear power plant for example." Justice Scalia noted that suspicionless testing for nuclear power plant employees in sensitive jobs had been upheld even without a showing of a drug problem. See Rushton v. Nebraska Public Power District, 844 F.2d 562 (8th Cir.1988). See also Thomson v. Marsh, 884 F.2d 113 (4th Cir.1989) (suspicionless testing of personnel in chemical weapons plant upheld). He responded, however, that if the majority considered that the threat posed by drug-addicted Customs officials was comparable to that found in *Rushton,* "then the Fourth Amendment has become frail protection indeed." He noted that this reasoning would extend approval of suspicionless drug testing to vast numbers of public employees, including "automobile drivers, operators of other potentially dangerous equipment, construction workers, school crossing guards."

### *Drug-Testing of Schoolchildren*

The Supreme Court has taken up the question of suspicionless testing of schoolchildren in two cases after *Von Raab*: Vernonia School District 47J v. Acton, 515 U.S. 646 (1995), and Board of Education of

Independent School District No. 2 v. Earls, 536 U.S. 822 (2002). In *Vernonia*, the Court upheld (6–3) the suspicionless drug testing of athletes, reasoning that students had a lesser expectation of privacy and that this was especially true of athletes whose privacy was affected by having to dress and shower in close proximity to each other. Justice Scalia wrote for the Court. Justice O'Connor, joined by Justices Stevens and Souter, dissented. In *Earls*, the Court expanded its holding to uphold (5–4) suspicionless drug testing of all students engaged in extracurricular activities. Justice Thomas wrote for the Court in *Earls*. Justice Thomas relied heavily on *Vernonia*. He wrote as follows:

> A student's privacy interest is limited in a public school environment where the State is responsible for maintaining discipline, health, and safety. Schoolchildren are routinely required to submit to physical examinations and vaccinations against disease. Securing order in the school environment sometimes requires that students be subjected to greater controls than those appropriate for adults.

> Respondents argue that because children participating in nonathletic extracurricular activities are not subject to regular physicals and communal undress, they have a stronger expectation of privacy than the athletes tested in *Vernonia*. This distinction, however, was not essential to our decision in *Vernonia,* which depended primarily upon the school's custodial responsibility and authority.

> In any event, students who participate in competitive extracurricular activities voluntarily subject themselves to many of the same intrusions on their privacy as do athletes. Some of these clubs and activities require occasional off-campus travel and communal undress. All of them have their own rules and requirements for participating students that do not apply to the student body as a whole. * * * This regulation of extracurricular activities further diminishes the expectation of privacy among schoolchildren. We therefore conclude that the students affected by this Policy have a limited expectation of privacy.

* * *

> Under the Policy, a faculty monitor waits outside the closed restroom stall for the student to produce a sample and must "listen for the normal sounds of urination in order to guard against tampered specimens and to insure an accurate chain of custody." The monitor then pours the sample into two bottles that are sealed and placed into a mailing pouch along with a consent form signed by the student. This procedure is virtually identical to that reviewed in *Vernonia,* except that it additionally protects privacy by allowing

male students to produce their samples behind a closed stall. Given that we considered the method of collection in *Vernonia* a "negligible" intrusion, the method here is even less problematic.

In addition, the Policy clearly requires that the test results be kept in confidential files separate from a student's other educational records and released to school personnel only on a "need to know" basis. * * * Moreover, the test results are not turned over to any law enforcement authority. Nor do the test results here lead to the imposition of discipline or have any academic consequences. Rather, the only consequence of a failed drug test is to limit the student's privilege of participating in extracurricular activities.

\* \* \*

Given the minimally intrusive nature of the sample collection and the limited uses to which the test results are put, we conclude that the invasion of students' privacy is not significant.

* * * Finally, this Court must consider the nature and immediacy of the government's concerns and the efficacy of the Policy in meeting them. This Court has already articulated in detail the importance of the governmental concern in preventing drug use by schoolchildren. The drug abuse problem among our Nation's youth has hardly abated since *Vernonia* was decided in 1995. * * * The health and safety risks identified in *Vernonia* apply with equal force to Tecumseh's children. Indeed, the nationwide drug epidemic makes the war against drugs a pressing concern in every school.

Additionally, the School District in this case has presented specific evidence of drug use at Tecumseh schools. Teachers testified that they had seen students who appeared to be under the influence of drugs and that they had heard students speaking openly about using drugs. A drug dog found marijuana cigarettes near the school parking lot. Police officers once found drugs or drug paraphernalia in a car driven by a Future Farmers of America member. And the school board president reported that people in the community were calling the board to discuss the "drug situation." We decline to second-guess the finding of the District Court that "[v]iewing the evidence as a whole, it cannot be reasonably disputed that the [School District] was faced with a 'drug problem' when it adopted the Policy."

\* \* \*

Furthermore, this Court has not required a particularized or pervasive drug problem before allowing the government to conduct suspicionless drug testing. For instance, in *Von Raab* the Court upheld the drug testing of customs officials on a purely preventive basis, without any documented history of drug use by such officials.

\* \* \* Likewise, the need to prevent and deter the substantial harm of childhood drug use provides the necessary immediacy for a school testing policy. Indeed, it would make little sense to require a school district to wait for a substantial portion of its students to begin using drugs before it was allowed to institute a drug testing program designed to deter drug use.

\* \* \*

Respondents also argue that the testing of nonathletes does not implicate any safety concerns, and that safety is a "crucial factor" in applying the special needs framework. \* \* \* Respondents are correct that safety factors into the special needs analysis, but the safety interest furthered by drug testing is undoubtedly substantial for all children, athletes and nonathletes alike. We know all too well that drug use carries a variety of health risks for children, including death from overdose.

Justice Thomas challenged the argument that a program requiring reasonable suspicion would be a less intrusive alternative to suspicionless drug testing:

[W]e question whether testing based on individualized suspicion in fact would be less intrusive. \* \* \* A program of individualized suspicion might unfairly target members of unpopular groups. The fear of lawsuits resulting from such targeted searches may chill enforcement of the program, rendering it ineffective in combating drug use. In any case, this Court has repeatedly stated that reasonableness under the Fourth Amendment does not require employing the least intrusive means, because the logic of such elaborate less-restrictive-alternative arguments could raise insuperable barriers to the exercise of virtually all search-and-seizure powers.

Justice Breyer wrote a short concurring opinion that emphasized the fact that "the school board provided an opportunity for the airing of these differences at public meetings designed to give the entire community the opportunity to be able to participate" in developing the drug policy. The board used this "democratic, participatory process to uncover and to resolve differences, giving weight to the fact that the process, in this instance, revealed little, if any, objection to the proposed testing program." He also argued that "a contrary reading of the Constitution, as requiring individualized suspicion in this public school context, could well lead schools to push the boundaries of individualized suspicion to its outer limits, using subjective criteria that may unfairly target members of unpopular groups, or leave those whose behavior is slightly abnormal stigmatized in the minds of others."

Justice Ginsburg, joined by Justices Stevens, O'Connor, and Souter, dissented in *Earls*. She argued that "*Vernonia* cannot be read to endorse invasive and suspicionless drug testing of all students upon any evidence of drug use, solely because drugs jeopardize the life and health of those who use them." She further noted that the Court's reliance on voluntary participation in extracurricular activities was misplaced:

> While extracurricular activities are "voluntary" in the sense that they are not required for graduation, they are part of the school's educational program * * *. Participation in such activities is a key component of school life, essential in reality for students applying to college, and, for all participants, a significant contributor to the breadth and quality of the educational experience. Students "volunteer" for extracurricular pursuits in the same way they might volunteer for honors classes: They subject themselves to additional requirements, but they do so in order to take full advantage of the education offered them.

Justice Ginsburg concluded as follows:

> At the margins, of course, no policy of *random* drug testing is perfectly tailored to the harms it seeks to address. * * * Notwithstanding nightmarish images of out-of-control flatware, livestock run amok, and colliding tubas disturbing the peace and quiet of Tecumseh, the great majority of students the School District seeks to test in truth are engaged in activities that are not safety sensitive to an unusual degree. There is a difference between imperfect tailoring and no tailoring at all.

### QUESTIONS AFTER EARLS

Can a school district now mandate random drug-testing of *all* public school students, whether or not they wish to participate in extracurricular activities? If not, why not?

What about suspicionless searches of student property? Will they be automatically permissible without suspicion, so long as they are done neutrally? See Doe v. Little Rock School Dist., 380 F.3d 349 (8th Cir. 2004) (random suspicionless searches of students belongings were unreasonable; generalized concerns about the presence of weapons and drugs was not sufficient to justify such intrusive searches, even after *Earls*, especially because evidence obtained in the searches was routinely turned over to the police: "Rather than acting *in loco parentis,* with the goal of promoting the students welfare, the government officials conducting the searches are in large part playing a law enforcement role with the goal of ferreting out crime and collecting evidence to be used in prosecuting students.").

How does *Earls* square with *Safford, supra*? *Earls* permits a search of virtually every student in the school without any suspicion at all, while

*Safford* prohibits a search of a particular student even though the official had reasonable suspicion that the student violated the school's rule against possession of medication without permission. How would you advise school officials who want to enforce a drug or medication policy given these two cases?

## *Drug-Testing of Politicians*

In the following case, the Court appeared to draw back somewhat from its previous cases supporting suspicionless drug-testing on the basis of "special needs."

### CHANDLER V. MILLER

Supreme Court of the United States, 1997.
520 U.S. 305.

**JUSTICE GINSBURG delivered the opinion of the Court.**

\* \* \*

Georgia requires candidates for designated state offices to certify that they have taken a drug test and that the test result was negative. We confront in this case the question whether that requirement ranks among the limited circumstances in which suspicionless searches are warranted. Relying on this Court's precedents sustaining drug-testing programs for student athletes, customs employees, and railway employees, \* \* \* the United States Court of Appeals for the Eleventh Circuit judged Georgia's law constitutional. We reverse that judgment. Georgia's requirement that candidates for state office pass a drug test, we hold, does not fit within the closely guarded category of constitutionally permissible suspicionless searches.

\* \* \*

The prescription at issue, approved by the Georgia Legislature in 1990, orders that "each candidate seeking to qualify for nomination or election to a state office shall as a condition of such qualification be required to certify that such candidate has tested negative for illegal drugs." Georgia was the first, and apparently remains the only, State to condition candidacy for state office on a drug test.

Under the Georgia statute, to qualify for a place on the ballot, a candidate must present a certificate from a state-approved laboratory, in a form approved by the Secretary of State, reporting that the candidate submitted to a urinalysis drug test within 30 days prior to qualifying for nomination or election and that the results were negative. The statute lists as "illegal drugs": marijuana, cocaine, opiates, amphetamines, and phencyclidines. The designated state offices are: "the Governor, Lieutenant Governor, Secretary of State, Attorney General, State School

Superintendent, Commissioner of Insurance, Commissioner of Agriculture, Commissioner of Labor, Justices of the Supreme Court, Judges of the Court of Appeals, judges of the superior courts, district attorneys, members of the General Assembly, and members of the Public Service Commission."

* * * A candidate may provide the test specimen at a laboratory approved by the State, or at the office of the candidate's personal physician. Once a urine sample is obtained, an approved laboratory determines whether any of the five specified illegal drugs are present, and prepares a certificate reporting the test results to the candidate.

Petitioners were Libertarian Party nominees in 1994 for state offices subject to the requirements of [the statute]. * * * [P]etitioners requested declaratory and injunctive relief barring enforcement of the statute. * * * In January 1995, the District Court entered final judgment for respondents.

[The Eleventh Circuit upheld the statute, despite the fact that there was no showing of a drug problem among candidates for office. The Court of Appeals relied heavily on *Von Raab*. It stated that "those vested with the highest executive authority to make public policy in general and frequently to supervise Georgia's drug interdiction efforts in particular must be persons appreciative of the perils of drug use." It also found that candidates have a diminished expectation of privacy, because "candidates for high office must expect the voters to demand some disclosures about their physical, emotional, and mental fitness for the position."]

To be reasonable under the Fourth Amendment, a search ordinarily must be based on individualized suspicion of wrongdoing. See *Vernonia*. But particularized exceptions to the main rule are sometimes warranted based on "special needs, beyond the normal need for law enforcement." When such "special needs"—concerns other than crime detection—are alleged in justification of a Fourth Amendment intrusion, courts must undertake a context-specific inquiry, examining closely the competing private and public interests advanced by the parties. * * *

[The Court reviews *Skinner, Von Raab, and Vernonia,* noting as to *Vernonia* that the drug-testing program's "context was critical, for local governments bear large responsibilities, under a public school system, as guardian and tutor of children entrusted to its care."]

* * * Because the State has effectively limited the invasiveness of the testing procedure, we concentrate on the core issue: Is the certification requirement warranted by a special need?

Our precedents establish that the proffered special need for drug testing must be substantial—important enough to override the individual's acknowledged privacy interest, sufficiently vital to suppress the Fourth Amendment's normal requirement of individualized suspicion. Georgia has failed to show * * * a special need of that kind.

Respondents' defense of the statute rests primarily on the incompatibility of unlawful drug use with holding high state office. The statute is justified, respondents contend, because the use of illegal drugs draws into question an official's judgment and integrity; jeopardizes the discharge of public functions, including antidrug law enforcement efforts; and undermines public confidence and trust in elected officials. The statute, according to respondents, serves to deter unlawful drug users from becoming candidates and thus stops them from attaining high state office. Notably lacking in respondents' presentation is any indication of a concrete danger demanding departure from the Fourth Amendment's main rule.

Nothing in the record hints that the hazards respondents broadly describe are real and not simply hypothetical for Georgia's polity. The statute was not enacted, as counsel for respondents readily acknowledged at oral argument, in response to any fear or suspicion of drug use by state officials * * *. A demonstrated problem of drug abuse, while not in all cases necessary to the validity of a testing regime, see *Von Raab*, would shore up an assertion of special need for a suspicionless general search program. Proof of unlawful drug use may help to clarify—and to substantiate—the precise hazards posed by such use. Thus, the evidence of drug and alcohol use by railway employees engaged in safety-sensitive tasks in *Skinner*, and the immediate crisis prompted by a sharp rise in students' use of unlawful drugs in *Vernonia*, bolstered the government's and school officials' arguments that drug-testing programs were warranted and appropriate.

In contrast to the effective testing regimes upheld in *Skinner, Von Raab*, and *Vernonia*, Georgia's certification requirement is not well designed to identify candidates who violate antidrug laws. Nor is the scheme a credible means to deter illicit drug users from seeking election to state office. The test date—to be scheduled by the candidate anytime within 30 days prior to qualifying for a place on the ballot—is no secret. As counsel for respondents acknowledged at oral argument, users of illegal drugs, save for those prohibitively addicted, could abstain for a pretest period sufficient to avoid detection. * * * Moreover, respondents have offered no reason why ordinary law enforcement methods would not suffice to apprehend such addicted individuals, should they appear in the limelight of a public stage. * * *

Respondents and the United States as amicus curiae rely most heavily on our decision in *Von Raab*, which sustained a drug-testing program for Customs Service officers prior to promotion or transfer to certain high-risk positions, despite the absence of any documented drug abuse problem among Service employees. * * *

Hardly a decision opening broad vistas for suspicionless searches, *Von Raab* must be read in its unique context. * * * We stressed that "drug interdiction had become the agency's primary enforcement mission," and that the employees in question would have "access to vast sources of valuable contraband." Furthermore, Customs officers "had been the targets of bribery by drug smugglers on numerous occasions," and several had succumbed to the temptation.

Respondents overlook a telling difference between *Von Raab* and Georgia's candidate drug-testing program. In *Von Raab* it was "not feasible to subject employees [required to carry firearms or concerned with interdiction of controlled substances] and their work product to the kind of day-to-day scrutiny that is the norm in more traditional office environments." Candidates for public office, in contrast, are subject to relentless scrutiny—by their peers, the public, and the press. Their day-to-day conduct attracts attention notably beyond the norm in ordinary work environments.

What is left, after close review of Georgia's scheme, is the image the State seeks to project. By requiring candidates for public office to submit to drug testing, Georgia displays its commitment to the struggle against drug abuse. The suspicionless tests, according to respondents, signify that candidates, if elected, will be fit to serve their constituents free from the influence of illegal drugs. But Georgia asserts no evidence of a drug problem among the State's elected officials, those officials typically do not perform high-risk, safety-sensitive tasks, and the required certification immediately aids no interdiction effort. The need revealed, in short, is symbolic, not "special," as that term draws meaning from our case law.

* * *

* * * However well-meant, the candidate drug test Georgia has devised diminishes personal privacy for a symbol's sake. The Fourth Amendment shields society against that state action.

* * *

We reiterate * * * that where the risk to public safety is substantial and real, blanket suspicionless searches calibrated to the risk may rank as "reasonable"—for example, searches now routine at airports and at entrances to courts and other official buildings. But where, as in this case, public safety is not genuinely in jeopardy, the Fourth Amendment precludes the suspicionless search, no matter how conveniently arranged.

* * *

**CHIEF JUSTICE REHNQUIST, dissenting.**

* * * It would take a bolder person than I to say that * * * widespread drug usage could never extend to candidates for public office such as Governor of Georgia. The Court says that "nothing in the record hints that the hazards respondents broadly describe are real and not simply hypothetical for Georgia's polity." But surely the State need not wait for a drug addict, or one inclined to use drugs illegally, to run for or actually become Governor before it installs a prophylactic mechanism.

* * *

Under normal Fourth Amendment analysis, the individual's expectation of privacy is an important factor in the equation. But here, the Court perversely relies on the fact that a candidate for office gives up so much privacy * * * as a reason for sustaining a Fourth Amendment claim. The Court says, in effect, that the kind of drug test for candidates required by the Georgia law is unnecessary, because the scrutiny to which they are already subjected by reason of their candidacy will enable people to detect any drug use on their part.

* * *

### *Drug-Testing Cases After Chandler*

It should come as no surprise that drug-testing cases are all over the map after *Chandler*. In *Chandler,* the Court second-guessed whether a drug-testing plan would be effective in controlling drug abuse—such second-guessing was missing in the Court's previous cases. In *Chandler*, the Court held that people with minimal privacy interests could not be subject to drug-testing that was relatively non-intrusive. The emphasis in the previous cases was to the contrary.

For a taste of the differing results after *Chandler,* see, e.g., 19 Solid Waste Dept. Mech. v. City of Albuquerque, 156 F.3d 1068 (10th Cir.1998) (invalidating suspicionless searches of trash truck mechanics as not justified by a "special need"; stating that after *Chandler,* "even if the privacy interest is virtually non-existent, the special need requirement prevents suspicionless searches where the government has failed to show either that it has a real interest in testing or that its test will further its proffered interest."); Krieg v. Seybold, 481 F.3d 512 (7th Cir. 2007) (random drug-testing of sanitation workers found reasonable, because they performed a safety-sensitive job and used large and dangerous vehicles); Knox County Educ. Assoc. v. Knox County Board of Education, 158 F.3d 361 (6th Cir.1998) (random testing of all teachers permitted, even though no showing of a drug problem was made; *Chandler* distinguished on the grounds that teachers are more important than politicians, and teachers "are not subject to the same day-to-day scrutiny as are candidates for public office"); United Teachers v. School Bd. Through Holmes, 142 F.3d 853 (5th Cir.1998) (suspicionless testing of all teachers injured in the course of employment violates the Fourth Amendment; the court concluded that "there is an insufficient nexus between suffering an injury at work and drug impairment"); Lanier v. City of Woodburn, 518 F.3d 1147 (9th Cir. 2008) (drug testing of applicants for position of library worker was not reasonable; there was no evidence of a drug problem in the targeted population, and library workers do not perform high-risk or safety-sensitive tasks).

In *19 Solid Waste Dept.*, supra, the court found it necessary after *Chandler* to inquire into the effectiveness of the drug-testing plan. It held the plan ineffective (thus not furthering a "special need") in part because the employees were tested only once every four years. It therefore concluded that "this program is not at all well-designed to detect drug use among its employees and lacks deterrent effect." Would the court have been happier with a plan that required employees to be tested every day? Does the court mean that the more pervasive (and intrusive) the testing plan, the more it is likely to fulfill a special need and thus be reasonable? Can't the same perverse argument be found in *Chandler*, where the Court says that the plan is unreasonable because candidates receive 30 days advance notice? Is the court saying that surprise inspections, though obviously more upsetting to the citizen, are more reasonable?

### NOTE ON VERNONIA, EARLS AND CHANDLER

Does it make sense to you that a 13-year-old who wants to join the school chess team can be forced to take a drug test, while a candidate for Governor of a State cannot be so forced? In light of the privacy interests that each of these people could be thought to have, shouldn't it be the other way around? Can it simply be explained by the fact that the Court considers the school environment, and the state's relationship to schoolchildren, unique? For a critique of the school drug-testing cases and *Chandler*, see Dery, Are Politicians More Deserving of Privacy than Schoolchildren? How Chandler v. Miller Exposed the Absurdities of Fourth Amendment "Special Needs" Balancing, 40 Ariz.L.Rev. 73 (1998).

### Drug-Testing for Special Needs, or for Criminal Law Enforcement? Ferguson v. City of Charleston

In Ferguson v. City of Charleston, 532 U.S, 67 (2001), the Court continued along the difficult path of distinguishing those searches that serve special needs beyond ordinary criminal law enforcement and those that do not. In an opinion by Justice Stevens, the Court struck down a state hospital policy requiring drug testing of pregnant mothers suspected of cocaine use. The Court held that the drug tests were not "special needs" searches because "the central and indispensable feature of the policy" was fulfillment of the State's law enforcement goals. The Medical University of South Carolina (MUSC) was concerned about the effect of drug use by mothers on their babies and instituted a policy that required the drug testing of urine samples from maternity patients suspected of using cocaine. A patient who tested positive was required to undergo subsequent tests and could be arrested and prosecuted if subsequent tests were positive. Police and prosecutors participated in the development and implementation of the program. As the evidence was collected for the specific purpose of incriminating the patients, the Court held that the Fourth Amendment's prohibition against warrantless and suspicionless searches applied in the absence of consent. The Court did not reach the issue of the sufficiency of the evidence with regard to consent and assumed, for purposes of the decision, that the searches were conducted without the patient's consent.

The Court distinguished this case from its previous cases upholding drug tests as fulfilling legitimate "special needs" because the the test results were disseminated to the police and prosecutors, and the program was developed with input of police and prosecutors. The Court found the most critical difference was that in prior cases the "special need" advanced was totally divorced from the State's general interest in law enforcement while the purpose of the MUSC policy was precisely to engage in law enforcement. While the ultimate goal of the policy may have been to help addicted patients (by scaring them straight), the immediate objective was "to generate evidence for law enforcement purposes in order to reach that goal."

Justice Kennedy concurred in the result. Justice Scalia dissented, joined by the Chief Justice and Justice Thomas. Justice Scalia contended that the urine tests were not protected by the Fourth Amendment because they were obtained with the patient's consent.

On remand, the Fourth Circuit held that the mothers did not consent to use of the urine tests in a criminal prosecution. Ferguson v. City of Charleston, 308 F.3d 380 (4th Cir. 2002). The Court remanded for a determination of damages.

### Suspicionless Safety Searches in Airports, Subways, Public Buildings, etc.

In *Von Raab, supra,* the Supreme Court cited favorably some lower court cases from the 1970's that upheld—as reasonable under the "special needs" doctrine—magnetometer searches of persons and carry-on luggage at airports. Those searches were found reasonable because: 1) the searches were safety-based and not primarily intended to enforce the criminal law; 2) the state interest in protecting the safety of air travel was high; 3) the state interest could not be accommodated by limiting the searches to those who were reasonably suspected of presenting a safety risk—suspicionless searches were required because some travelers may pose a safety risk even though they have no intent to violate the law (e.g., a security officer carrying a weapon that might be stolen on board by a highjacker), and because some people might not look suspicious on a cursory view but in fact may be intending to highjack or blow up an airplane; and 4) the searches are minimally intrusive, because a) all travelers are searched (minimizing the humiliation), b) travelers are notified in advance, and c) travelers are free to refuse the search and choose some other form of travel.

After 9/11, it is no secret that suspicionless searches at airports and other public places are now more intrusive and inconvenient than previously. Air passengers are usually required to take their shoes, belts and coats off; at some airports, passengers are required to pass through a machine that blows air at them (and the microscopic particles thus blown off them are tested for traces of explosives); at others, the scan of the person shows everything including genitalia to the officer viewing the monitor; the old x-ray machines have been replaced by more sophisticated 3-D technology so that the viewer can determine, with precision, what property is in handbags, luggage, etc.; some passengers are selected for a more thorough inspection, including the use of an electric wand, a thorough search of personal effects, and what is in effect a *Terry* patdown and frisk. The selection for a more intrusive search is ordinarily done without particularized suspicion; the agents' discretion is purportedly controlled by the use of neutral criteria—the searches are either on a random basis, or because of some factual trigger like purchasing a one-way ticket or setting off the magnetometer.

Are these more intrusive searches reasonable under the special needs line of cases? While the Supreme Court has not yet reviewed the reasonableness of a post 9/11 airport security search, the lower courts have ordinarily upheld these more intrusive searches as within "special needs." For example, in United States v. Marquez, 410 F.3d 612 (9th Cir. 2005), the defendant was randomly selected for an airport wand search and a pat-down, and was found to have two kilograms of cocaine stashed in his pants. The court analyzed the search as follows:

> This case presents a legally novel, yet practically ubiquitous, set of facts. The issue here is whether the random selection of Marquez to go to the selectee lane, where he would automatically be subjected to the wanding of his person with the handheld magnetometer in addition to the walkthrough magnetometer and the x-ray luggage scan, was reasonable. We conclude that it was.

Airport screenings of passengers and their baggage constitute administrative searches and are subject to the limitations of the Fourth Amendment. United States v. Davis, 482 F.2d 893, 908 (9th Cir. 1973) (noting that airport screenings are considered to be administrative searches because they are "conducted as part of a general regulatory scheme" where the essential administrative purpose is "to prevent the carrying of weapons or explosives aboard aircraft"). Thus airport screenings must be reasonable. To judge reasonableness, it is necessary to balance the right to be free of intrusion with society's interest in safe air travel.

In *Davis* and its progeny, we have established a general reasonableness test for airport screenings. An airport screening search is reasonable if: (1) it is no more extensive or intensive than necessary, in light of current technology, to detect weapons or explosives; (2) it is confined in good faith to that purpose; and (3) passengers may avoid the search by electing not to fly.

\* \* \*

It is hard to overestimate the need to search air travelers for weapons and explosives before they are allowed to board the aircraft. As illustrated over the last three decades, the potential damage and destruction from air terrorism is horrifically enormous. The random, additional screening procedure in this case satisfies the *Davis* reasonableness test for airport searches. The procedure is geared towards detection and deterrence of airborne terrorism, and its very randomness furthers these goals. This was a limited search, confined in its intrusiveness (both in duration and scope) and in its attempt to discover weapons and explosives. Given the randomness, the limited nature of the intrusion, the myriad devices that can be used to bring planes down, and the absence of any indicia of improper motive, we hold that the random, more thorough screening involving scanning of Marquez's person with the handheld magnetometer was reasonable. The district court properly denied Marquez's motion to suppress the contraband found during TSA screening

See also United States v. Hartwell, 436 F.3d 174 (3d Cir. 2006) (Alito, J.) (when defendant set off the magnetometer, a wand inspection was reasonable; stating that the search is "less offensive" because air passengers "are on notice that they will be searched" and noting that "the events of September 11, 2001, only emphasize the heightened need to conduct searches" at airports).

Some courts have reasoned that because air travel is "voluntary", the intrusion of an airport search is minimized. Is air travel really voluntary? The Ninth Circuit, in United States v. Aukai, 497 F.3d 955 (9th Cir. 2007), had to confront the relevance of "consent" as diminishing the traveler's expectation of privacy, because Aukai was put in a situation in which he could not just turn around and get to his destination by some other mode of transportation. Aukai checked in at his flight but did not produce an appropriate identification. His ticket was stamped "no ID" and he proceeded to security. He went through the magnetometer without incident, and presented his boarding pass to the TSA officer. Under TSA procedures, a person who has no ID is subjected to a secondary inspection with a wand, etc. During the secondary inspection, Aukai said he no longer wished to board a plane and wanted to leave the airport. But TSA continued the inspection and eventually the agent discovered a glass pipe and a small quantity of drugs. The TSA procedures called for a secondary inspection to continue even if the traveler decides at some point not to fly.

The *Aukai* court began by noting that its case law "has erroneously suggested that the reasonableness of airport screening searches is dependent upon consent, either ongoing consent or irrevocable implied consent." The court explained its "error" and justified the search of Aukai in the following passage:

> The constitutionality of an airport screening search, however, does not depend on consent, and requiring that a potential passenger be allowed to revoke consent to an ongoing airport security search makes little sense in a post-9/11 world. Such a rule would afford terrorists multiple opportunities to attempt to penetrate airport security by "electing not to fly" on the cusp of detection until a vulnerable portal is found. This rule would also allow terrorists a low-cost method of detecting systematic vulnerabilities in airport security, knowledge that could be extremely valuable in planning future attacks. Likewise, given that consent is not required, it makes little sense to predicate the reasonableness of an administrative airport screening search on an irrevocable implied consent theory.

> Rather, where an airport screening search is otherwise reasonable and conducted pursuant to statutory authority, 49 U.S.C. § 44901, all that is required is the passenger's election to attempt entry into the secured area of an airport. Under current TSA regulations and procedures, that election occurs when a prospective passenger walks through the magnetometer or places items on the conveyor belt of the x-ray machine. The record establishes that Aukai elected to attempt entry into the posted secured area of Honolulu International Airport when he walked through the magnetometer, thereby subjecting himself to the airport screening process.

Should we give the *Aukai* court credit for at least being honest, that consent has nothing to do with the reasonableness of a post 9/11 security search?

Another factor used to support security searches is that the public is on notice that the searches are occurring. Does this mean that if the TSA announces a program of random body cavity searches of air travelers, in order to combat terrorism, that those searches are now reasonable because the public has been notified?

Does it make sense that the more intrusive searches are random? Some have suggested that the search plan would be more efficient and reasonable if it was targeted at Muslim men. See Charles Krauthammer, The Case for Profiling, Time Magazine, Mar. 18, 2002, at 104. Professor Maclin rejects the suggestion that racial profiling is necessary or reasonable in "Voluntary" Interviews and Airport Searches of Middle Eastern Men: The Fourth Amendment in a Time of Terror, 73 Miss. L.Rev. 471 (2003). Professor Maclin argues that the proposal for racial profiling of suspect air terrorists relies on the same invalid premise that justified the detention of Japanese citizens during World War II.

In New York City, the police established a search plan for the subway system shortly after the terrorist bombings of commuter trains in Madrid and London. The plan calls for daily inspection checkpoints at selected subway stations. Passengers are randomly selected for a search of their effects before they enter the subway. The targeted stations change from day to day. The court in MacWade v. Kelly, 460 F.3d 260 (2d Cir. 2006), rejected a Fourth Amendment challenge to these searches that was brought by some subway passengers. The court first found that "preventing a terrorist from bombing the subways constitutes a special need that is distinct from ordinary post hoc criminal investigation." Under the special needs doctrine, the program of suspicionless searches of subway passengers was found reasonable, the court determining that:

1) the government interest in searching was "immediate and substantial" given terrorist threats on the system and actual bombings of commuter trains elsewhere;

2) the searches were minimally intrusive, because a) passengers receive notice "and may decline to be searched so long as they leave the subway", b) "police search only those containers capable of concealing explosives" and "inspect eligible containers only to determine whether they contain explosives", c) the searches last only a few seconds, and d) "uniformed personnel conduct the searches out in the open, which reduces the fear and stigma that removal to a hidden area can cause."

The citizens challenging the subway search plan argued that it was ineffective because any terrorist could avoid searches simply by refusing to submit to a search and walking a few blocks to an unmonitored subway station. But in response to that argument, the court stated that it was not its place to conduct "a searching examination of effectiveness" and that officers combating terrorism are entitled to some deference as to the methods chosen and that the  apparent flaw was a strength because "we always have viewed notice and the opportunity to decline as beneficial aspects of a suspicionless search regime because those features minimize intrusiveness" and "if a would-be bomber declines a search, he must leave the subway or be arrested—an outcome that, for the purpose of preventing subway bombings, we consider reasonably effective, especially since the record establishes that terrorists prize predictability."

Is it odd that the citizens are essentially arguing that the plan would be more effective and thus reasonable if all passengers were searched? On the other hand, is it odd that the government is arguing that the plan is reasonable because people can easily avoid searches, and yet the plan is reasonably effective even though people can easily avoid searches?

For other cases upholding post-9/11 security searches, see, e.g., Cassidy v. Chertoff, 471 F.3d 67 (2nd Cir. 2006) (upholding searches of persons, luggage and cars on Lake Ticonderoga ferry; noting that passengers receive ample notice, and that searches promote a special need of preventing terrorist attacks on large vessels engaged in mass transportation: "Although the plaintiffs may be correct that Lake Champlain ferries are a less obvious terrorist target than ferries in, for example, New York City or Los Angeles, the airline cases make it clear that the government, in its attempt to counteract the threat of terrorism, need not show that every airport or every ferry terminal is threatened by terrorism in order to implement a nationwide security policy that includes suspicionless searches."); Johnston v. Tampa Bay Sports Authority, 530 F.3d 1320 (11th Cir. 2008) (upholding pat-down security searches at the Super Bowl on grounds of implied consent).

### *Searching Beyond the Scope of Safety*

A safety-based search must be conducted within the limits of protecting safety. If the officer engages in tactics that are not safety-related, it is possible that the search will be found unreasonable. Illustrative is United States v. McCarty, 648 F.3d 820 (9th Cir. 2011). McCarty was traveling from Hilo Airport to Honolulu. He checked bags that were screened by two TSA screeners (who were, oddly enough, mother and daughter). They were using the "CTX" superscanner machine, and one of the bags set off an alarm for having a dense item requiring further inspection. Under TSA policy, dense items triggering a CTX alarm must be removed and inspected. In this case, the dense item turned out to be an envelope of photos and other papers. Because of the possibility of "sheet explosives"—which may be disguised as a piece of paper or cardboard—the TSA official is required to thumb through papers or photographs that trigger a CTX alarm. The TSA screeners saw in the envelope some photos of children that looked "improper" according to the screeners. The screeners also found letters and newspaper clippings and read through them briefly. These letters and clippings increased the suspicion of a child pornography violation. Eventually the local police were called, and the defendant was arrested and ultimately convicted for transportation and possession of child pornography.

The court noted that "because TSA screeners are limited to the single administrative goal of search for possible safety threats related to explosives, the constitutional bounds of an airport administrative search require that the individual screener's actions be no more intrusive that necessary to determine the existence or absence of explosives that could result in harm to the passengers and aircraft." In this case, the screeners conceded that, at the point when they read the content of the letters and newspaper clippings, they were no longer searching for explosives— rather they were searching to confirm their suspicion that the photos they had thumbed through were evidence of child pornography. The court therefore concluded that the review of the letters and newspaper clippings "clearly fell outside the permissible scope of the lawful administrative search and violated McCarthy's Fourth Amendment rights." In contrast, the screeners' review of the pictures in the envelope was found proper because it was "consistent with the TSA protocol requiring [screeners] to thumb through the photographs in order to clear the bag." The court remanded to determine whether the photographs alone established probable cause of a crime to support McCarty's arrest.

McCarty argued that the screeners, when looking through the photographs, were not motivated by safety but rather were looking for evidence of child pornography. The court found the screeners' motivation to be irrelevant, so long as the search was justified by the safety concerns attendant to sheet explosives. Why would the screeners' motivations be irrelevant?

### *Safety-Based Strip Searches of Detainees Without Reasonable Suspicion: Florence v. Board of Chosen Freeholders*

In Florence v. Board of Chosen Freeholders, 132 S. Ct. 1510 (2012), Justice Kennedy wrote for the Court as it upheld the reasonableness of a policy of strip-searching jail detainees, even when those detainees are arrested on minor offenses.

Florence was arrested for a minor offense and was placed in the Burlington County Detention Center and then in the Essex County Correctional Facility. Justice Kennedy described the procedures in the two facilities:

> Burlington County jail procedures required every arrestee to shower with a delousing agent. Officers would check arrestees for

scars, marks, gang tattoos, and contraband as they disrobed. Petitioner claims he was also instructed to open his mouth, lift his tongue, hold out his arms, turn around, and lift his genitals. (It is not clear whether this last step was part of the normal practice.) Petitioner shared a cell with at least one other person and interacted with other inmates following his admission to the jail.

The Essex County Correctional Facility, where petitioner was taken after six days, is the largest county jail in New Jersey. It admits more than 25,000 inmates each year and houses about 1,000 gang members at any given time. When petitioner was transferred there, all arriving detainees passed through a metal detector and waited in a group holding cell for a more thorough search. When they left the holding cell, they were instructed to remove their clothing while an officer looked for body markings, wounds, and contraband. Apparently without touching the detainees, an officer looked at their ears, nose, mouth, hair, scalp, fingers, hands, arms, armpits, and other body openings. This policy applied regardless of the circumstances of the arrest, the suspected offense, or the detainee's behavior, demeanor, or criminal history. Petitioner alleges he was required to lift his genitals, turn around, and cough in a squatting position as part of the process. After a mandatory shower, during which his clothes were inspected, petitioner was admitted to the facility. He was released the next day, when the charges against him were dismissed.

Florence brought an action under 42 U.S.C. § 1983, contending that persons arrested for a minor offense could not be required to remove their clothing and expose the most private areas of their bodies to close visual inspection as a routine part of the intake process. The lower court granted summary judgment for Florence, reasoning that a policy of strip-searching of minor offenders without reasonable suspicion violates the Fourth Amendment. The court of appeals reversed that order. The Supreme Court affirmed the court of appeals.

After observing that the term "strip search" was imprecise in describing the jail procedures, Justice Kennedy noted that operating a detention center posed major challenges to officials that a court should not underestimate. He cited Bell v. Wolfish, 441 U.S. 520 (1979), which upheld a Federal Bureau of Prisons rule that detainees in any correctional facility were required "to expose their body cavities for visual inspection as a part of a strip search conducted after every contact visit with a person from outside the institution." Justice Kennedy reasoned that correctional officials must be permitted to devise reasonable search policies to detect and deter possession of contraband, to assure that lice and contagious infections were not introduced into the prison population, to discover gang tattoos that might indicate a need for special housing, and to discover weapons that may be especially dangerous in prison settings in which there are feuding gangs.

Florence acknowledged that correctional officials had to conduct effective intake searches and this would include having at least some detainees lift their genitals or cough in a squatting position, but argued that there was little benefit in imposing such procedures on a new detainee who has not been arrested for a serious crime involving weapons or drugs. Justice Kennedy rejected the argument and stated that "[i]t is reasonable * * * for correctional officials to conclude that this standard would be unworkable." One reason is that "[p]eople detained for minor offenses can turn out to be the most devious and dangerous criminals." Another is that "[i]t * * * may be difficult, as a practical matter, to classify inmates by their current and prior offenses before the intake search"; and "[j]ails can be even more dangerous than prisons because officials there know so little about the people they admit at the outset." Justice Kennedy cited *Atwater* for the proposition that it was important that officials in charge of jails, like police officers, can rely on readily administrable rules. In the end, Justice Kennedy stated that "[t]his case does not require the Court to rule on the types of searches that would be reasonable in instances where, for example, a detainee will be held without assignment to the general jail population and without substantial contact with other detainees."

Chief Justice Roberts concurred and emphasized that the majority's opinion does not foreclose the possibility of an exception to the general rule. Justice Alito concurred and emphasized "that the Court does not hold that it is always reasonable to conduct a full strip search of an arrestee whose detention has not been reviewed by a judicial officer and who could be held in available facilities apart from the general population."

Justice Breyer, joined by Justices Ginsburg, Sotomayor and Kagan, dissented and stated that "I have found no convincing reason indicating that, in the absence of reasonable suspicion, involuntary strip searches of those arrested for minor offenses are necessary in order to further the penal interests mentioned above [to detect injuries or diseases, to identify gang tattoos which might reflect a need for special housing, or to detect contraband]."

## *"Special Needs" Search of Text Messages of a Public Employee: City of Ontario v. Quon*

In City of Ontario v. Quon, 560 U.S. 476 (2010), a police officer was given a pager with a monthly text allotment. He exceeded that allotment in a number of consecutive months. This led his supervisors to review his text messages, in order to determine whether they were work-related and whether a greater monthly allotment was required. The review indicated that many of Quon's texts were not work-related, and some were sexually explicit. The supervisors concluded that Quon had violated Police Department rules about use of the department-issued pagers, and Quon was disciplined. Quon challenged the review of his text messages as an unreasonable search. But the Court found no such violation, relying on the "special needs" exception.

Justice Kennedy, writing for eight members of the Court, found that the "there were reasonable grounds for suspecting that the search was necessary for a non-investigatory work-related purpose"—specifically the supervisors were trying to determine whether the character limit under the monthly plan with the provider was sufficient to meet the City's needs. The City and the Police Department "had a legitimate interest in ensuring that employees were not being forced to pay out of their own pockets for work-related expenses, or on the other hand that the City was not paying for extensive personal communications."

Justice Kennedy also found that the review of the text messages was reasonable in scope "because it was an efficient and expedient way to determine whether Quon's overages were the result of work-related messaging or personal use." Moreover, Quon's expectation of privacy, if any, was at least diminished by the fact that the Department had made Quon aware that his text messages were subject to auditing. Justice Kennedy noted that the audit of messages on an employer-provided pager "was not nearly as intrusive as a search of his personal e-mail account or pager, or a wiretap on his phone line, would have been. That the search did reveal intimate details of Quon's life does not make it unreasonable, for under the circumstances a reasonable employer would not expect that such a review would intrude on such matters."

The lower court had found the search of the texts unreasonable because the supervisors could have issued Quon a warning about overages, or they could have had Quon provide the messages to them in redacted form. But Justice Kennedy found that analysis to be inconsistent with the Court's Fourth Amendment jurisprudence. He noted that the Court "has refused to declare that only the 'least intrusive' search practicable can be reasonable under the Fourth Amendment. That rationale could raise insuperable barriers to the exercise of virtually all search-and-seizure powers because judges engaged in post-hoc evaluations of government conduct can always imagine some alternative means by which the objectives of the government might have been accomplished."

It should be noted that the *Quon* Court assumed arguendo that the review of the text messages was a search in the first place. The City contended that Quon had *no* expectation of privacy in his text messages because the Department gave him the pager and he was aware of the possibility of monitoring. Justice Kennedy responded that it was necessary to "proceed with care when considering the whole concept of privacy expectations in communications made on electronic equipment owned by a government employer. The judiciary risks error by elaborating too fully on the Fourth Amendment implications of emerging technology before its role in society has become clear." It was unnecessary to decide whether there was a search, because even if there was, it was reasonable under the special needs exception.

Justice Stevens wrote a concurring opinion in *Quon*. Justice Scalia wrote an opinion concurring in part and concurring in the judgment.

## 4. Roadblocks, Checkpoints and Suspicionless Seizures

### *Individual Stops Without Suspicion*

In Delaware v. Prouse, 440 U.S. 648 (1979), the Court held that an officer could not, in the absence of reasonable suspicion, stop an automobile and detain the driver in order to check his license and registration. The officer in *Prouse* made an ad hoc, suspicionless stop, and the Court expressed its concern with "the unconstrained exercise of discretion." The Court concluded that such an ad hoc stop was not "a sufficiently productive mechanism to justify the intrusion" and that there were other, better ways to effectuate the state interest in vehicle registration and safety, such as yearly inspections. The majority emphasized that it was not foreclosing as one possible alternative the "questioning of all oncoming traffic at roadblock-type stops." In response to the majority's roadblock alternative, Justice Rehnquist argued in dissent that the majority had "elevated the adage 'misery loves company' to a novel role in Fourth Amendment jurisprudence." Why is it better to stop everybody rather than anybody?

### *Permanent Checkpoints*

The dictum in *Prouse* concerning the reasonableness of roadblock-type stops was supported by the Court's earlier decision in United States v. Martinez-Fuerte, 428 U.S. 543 (1976). In *Martinez-Fuerte* the Court, invoking *Terry* principles, approved suspicionless stops at permanent checkpoints removed from the border. The Court emphasized that suspicionless stops were necessary to implement the state interest in regulating the flow of illegal aliens, and noted that the fixed checkpoint was minimally intrusive. Justice Powell, writing for the Court, argued that motorists are not surprised by a fixed checkpoint; that such checkpoints limit the discretion of the officer; and that "the location of a fixed checkpoint is not chosen by officers in the field, but by officials responsible for making overall decisions as to the most effective allocation of limited enforcement resources." Justice Powell stressed that it was permissible to dispense with particularized suspicion because "we deal neither with searches nor with the sanctuary of private dwellings."

### *Temporary Checkpoints to Check for DUI*

The Court upheld suspicionless stops at temporary sobriety checkpoints in Michigan Department of State Police v. Sitz, 496 U.S. 444 (1990). The Michigan program allowed checkpoints to be set up by officers in the field according to a list of considerations including "safety of the location," "minimum inconvenience for the driver," and available space "to pull the vehicle off the traveled portion of the roadway for further inquiry if necessary." Under the program, all motorists passing through the checkpoint were stopped and briefly examined for signs of intoxication. If the driver appeared intoxicated, he or she was directed to another area where license and registration was checked, and further sobriety tests were conducted if warranted. The only checkpoint operated under the program resulted in a stop of 126 vehicles, and one arrest for drunk driving. The challenge in the Supreme Court focused solely on the initial detention and associated preliminary investigation of motorists for signs of intoxication.

Chief Justice Rehnquist's opinion for five members of the Court relied heavily on *Martinez-Fuerte,* and applied the "misery loves company" rationale that then-Justice Rehnquist had criticized in *Prouse.*

Respondents in *Sitz* argued that a reasonableness balancing approach could not be employed to evaluate sobriety checkpoints, because there was no special need beyond criminal law enforcement at stake. They argued that sobriety checkpoints are simply used to enforce criminal laws prohibiting drunk driving.

The majority responded that a special need beyond criminal law enforcement was not required to support reasonableness balancing for stops at fixed checkpoints. The Chief Justice stated that the special needs analysis of *Skinner* et al. "was in no way designed to repudiate our prior cases dealing with police stops." Thus, the Court relied on the *Terry* line of cases rather than on the "special needs" line of cases.

Balancing the interests of the state and the individual, as permitted for law enforcement seizures by *Terry,* the Chief Justice quoted from *Martinez-Fuerte,* and concluded that the intrusiveness of a sobriety checkpoint was extremely limited:

> At traffic checkpoints the motorist can see that other vehicles are being stopped, he can see visible signs of the officers' authority, and he is much less likely to be frightened or annoyed by the

intrusion. * * * Here, checkpoints are selected pursuant to the guidelines, and uniformed police officers stop every approaching vehicle. The intrusion resulting from the brief stop at the sobriety checkpoint is for constitutional purposes indistinguishable from the checkpoint stops we upheld in *Martinez-Fuerte.*

Against this limited intrusion, the Court balanced the State's heavy interest in eradicating drunk driving. Chief Justice Rehnquist rejected the argument that sobriety checkpoints did not effectively advance this undeniable state interest. He stated that references to effectiveness of searches and seizures in previous cases, such as *Prouse,* were not intended "to transfer from politically accountable officials to the courts the decision as to which among reasonable alternative law enforcement techniques should be employed to deal with a serious public danger." The Court concluded that "the choice among such reasonable alternatives remains with the government officials who have a unique understanding of, and a responsibility for, limited public resources." The majority faulted the lower court for its "searching examination" of the effectiveness of sobriety checkpoints.

Justice Stevens wrote a dissenting opinion joined in large part by Justices Brennan and Marshall. He argued that unlike the permanent, fixed checkpoint in *Martinez-Fuerte,* the police operating a sobriety checkpoint "have extremely broad discretion in determining the exact timing and placement of the roadblock." Moreover, a temporary checkpoint is more intrusive because of the element of surprise that it presents:

> A driver who discovers an unexpected checkpoint on a familiar local road will be startled and distressed. She may infer, correctly, that the checkpoint is not simply "business as usual," and may likewise infer, again correctly, that the police have made a discretionary decision to focus their law enforcement efforts upon her and others who pass the chosen point.

### QUESTIONS AFTER SITZ

The Court in *Sitz* chided the lower court for second-guessing the legislature's determination that roadblocks would be an effective means of investigating and deterring drunk driving. Yet in *Chandler,* supra, the Court second-guessed the legislature's determination that its drug-testing plan would be an effective means of detecting and deterring drug use in candidates for public office. How do you square the two cases?

On the problems of figuring out the effectiveness of a sobriety checkpoint—and the consequent need to defer to police on such questions— see Judge Boudin in United States v. William, 603 F.3d 66 (1st Cir. 2010), a case in which the defendant was stopped at a sobriety checkpoint and drugs were eventually found in his car:

> William argues that * * * the data offered to support the use of this checkpoint at this location was inadequate and that the results in arrest numbers were unimpressive. Certainly one can imagine a purported sobriety checkpoint whose location or timing was demonstrably unlikely to be of use. But in *Sitz,* Chief Justice Rehnquist went out of his way to say that whether and where to establish a stop is primarily a judgment for state or local officials. In addition, using the number of drunk driving arrests resulting from a specific checkpoint has at least two problems: one is that the reasonableness of the effort is primarily a forward-looking exercise (in fact, the percentage of arrests in *Sitz* was very low); and the other is that sobriety checkpoints likely have a deterrent value apart from immediate detentions resulting from the stops.

If *Martinez-Fuerte* is the correct analogy, can *Sitz* stand for the proposition that daily stops are permissible at *any* location? Can *Martinez-Fuerte* justify roving or moveable checkpoints? If so, who decides where these checkpoints should be placed? Does it make a difference that the location of the checkpoint in *Martinez-Fuerte* was chosen by high level officials rather than by officers in the field?

## *Drug Checkpoints*

In the following case, the Court essentially revised its analysis in *Sitz* and distinguished sobriety roadblocks from checkpoints designed to check for drugs. The Court invalidates a roadblock program because its primary purpose was to enforce the criminal law. How is a court supposed to determine whether the state has an improper purpose after this case?

### CITY OF INDIANAPOLIS V. EDMOND
Supreme Court of the United States, 2000.
531 U.S. 32.

**JUSTICE O'CONNOR delivered the opinion of the Court.**

In Michigan Dept. of State Police v. Sitz and United States v. Martinez-Fuerte we held that brief, suspicionless seizures at highway checkpoints for the purposes of combating drunk driving and intercepting illegal immigrants were constitutional. We now consider the constitutionality of a highway checkpoint program whose primary purpose is the discovery and interdiction of illegal narcotics.

* * *

In August 1998, the city of Indianapolis began to operate vehicle checkpoints on Indianapolis roads in an effort to interdict unlawful drugs. The city conducted six such roadblocks between August and November that year, stopping 1,161 vehicles and arresting 104 motorists. Fifty-five arrests were for drug-related crimes, while 49 were for offenses unrelated to drugs. The overall "hit rate" of the program was thus approximately nine percent.

The parties stipulated to the facts concerning the operation of the checkpoints by the Indianapolis Police Department (IPD) for purposes of the preliminary injunction proceedings instituted below. At each checkpoint location, the police stop a predetermined number of vehicles. * * * Pursuant to written directives issued by the chief of police, at least one officer approaches the vehicle, advises the driver that he or she is being stopped briefly at a drug checkpoint, and asks the driver to produce a license and registration. The officer also looks for signs of impairment and conducts an open-view examination of the vehicle from the outside. A narcotics-detection dog walks around the outside of each stopped vehicle.

The directives instruct the officers that they may conduct a search only by consent or based on the appropriate quantum of particularized suspicion. The officers must conduct each stop in the same manner until particularized suspicion develops, and the officers have no discretion to stop any vehicle out of sequence. * * * [C]heckpoint locations are selected weeks in advance based on such considerations as area crime statistics and traffic flow. The checkpoints are generally operated during daylight hours and are identified with lighted signs reading, "NARCOTICS CHECKPOINT ___ MILE AHEAD, NARCOTICS K-9 IN USE, BE PREPARED TO STOP." Once a group of cars has been stopped, other traffic proceeds without interruption until all the stopped cars have been processed or diverted for further processing. * * * [T]he average stop for a vehicle not subject to further processing lasts two to three minutes or less.

Respondents James Edmond and Joell Palmer were each stopped at a narcotics checkpoint in late September 1998. Respondents then filed a lawsuit on behalf of themselves and the class of all motorists who had been stopped or were subject to being stopped in the future at the Indianapolis drug checkpoints. Respondents claimed that the roadblocks violated the Fourth Amendment of the United States Constitution. * * * [The court of appeals held that the checkpoints violated the Fourth Amendment.]

* * * A search or seizure is ordinarily unreasonable in the absence of individualized suspicion of wrongdoing. Chandler v. Miller. While such suspicion is not an "irreducible" component of reasonableness, *Martinez-Fuerte*, we have recognized only limited circumstances in which the usual rule does not apply. For example, we have upheld certain regimes of suspicionless searches where the program was designed to serve "special needs, beyond the normal need for law enforcement." [The Court

describes its drug-testing cases.] We have also allowed searches for certain administrative purposes without particularized suspicion of misconduct, provided that those searches are appropriately limited. See, *e.g.,* New York v. Burger (warrantless administrative inspection of premises of "closely regulated" business); Camara v. Municipal Court of City and County of San Francisco (administrative inspection to ensure compliance with city housing code).

\* \* \*

In *Sitz*, we evaluated the constitutionality of a Michigan highway sobriety checkpoint program. The *Sitz* checkpoint involved brief suspicionless stops of motorists so that police officers could detect signs of intoxication and remove impaired drivers from the road. \* \* \* This checkpoint program was clearly aimed at reducing the immediate hazard posed by the presence of drunk drivers on the highways, and there was an obvious connection between the imperative of highway safety and the law enforcement practice at issue. The gravity of the drunk driving problem and the magnitude of the State's interest in getting drunk drivers off the road weighed heavily in our determination that the program was constitutional.

In *Prouse*, we invalidated a discretionary, suspicionless stop for a spot check of a motorist's driver's license and vehicle registration. The officer's conduct in that case was unconstitutional primarily on account of his exercise of "standardless and unconstrained discretion." We nonetheless acknowledged the States' "vital interest in ensuring that only those qualified to do so are permitted to operate motor vehicles, that these vehicles are fit for safe operation, and hence that licensing, registration, and vehicle inspection requirements are being observed." Accordingly, we suggested that "[q]uestioning of all oncoming traffic at roadblock-type stops" would be a lawful means of serving this interest in highway safety.

We further indicated in *Prouse* that we considered the purposes of such a hypothetical roadblock to be distinct from a general purpose of investigating crime. \* \* \*   [T]he common thread of highway safety thus run[s] through *Sitz* and *Prouse* \* \* \*.

It is well established that a vehicle stop at a highway checkpoint effectuates a seizure within the meaning of the Fourth Amendment. The fact that officers walk a narcotics-detection dog around the exterior of each car at the Indianapolis checkpoints does not transform the seizure into a search. See United States v. Place. \* \* \* [W]hat principally distinguishes these checkpoints from those we have previously approved is their primary purpose.

As petitioners concede, the Indianapolis checkpoint program unquestionably has the primary purpose of interdicting illegal narcotics.

In their stipulation of facts, the parties repeatedly refer to the checkpoints as "drug checkpoints" and describe them as "being operated by the City of Indianapolis in an effort to interdict unlawful drugs in Indianapolis." In addition, the first document attached to the parties' stipulation is entitled "DRUG CHECKPOINT CONTACT OFFICER DIRECTIVES BY ORDER OF THE CHIEF OF POLICE.". These directives instruct officers to "[a]dvise the citizen that they are being stopped briefly at a drug checkpoint." * * * Further, * * * the checkpoints are identified with lighted signs reading, "NARCOTICS CHECKPOINT ___ MILE AHEAD, NARCOTICS K-9 IN USE, BE PREPARED TO STOP." * * *

We have never approved a checkpoint program whose primary purpose was to detect evidence of ordinary criminal wrongdoing. * * * [E]ach of the checkpoint programs that we have approved was designed primarily to serve purposes closely related to the problems of policing the border or the necessity of ensuring roadway safety. Because the primary purpose of the Indianapolis narcotics checkpoint program is to uncover evidence of ordinary criminal wrongdoing, the program contravenes the Fourth Amendment.

Petitioners propose several ways in which the narcotics-detection purpose of the instant checkpoint program may instead resemble the primary purposes of the checkpoints in *Sitz* and *Martinez-Fuerte*. Petitioners state that the checkpoints in those cases had the same ultimate purpose of arresting those suspected of committing crimes. Securing the border and apprehending drunk drivers are, of course, law enforcement activities, and law enforcement officers employ arrests and criminal prosecutions in pursuit of these goals. If we were to rest the case at this high level of generality, there would be little check on the ability of the authorities to construct roadblocks for almost any conceivable law enforcement purpose. Without drawing the line at roadblocks designed primarily to serve the general interest in crime control, the Fourth Amendment would do little to prevent such intrusions from becoming a routine part of American life.

Petitioners also emphasize the severe and intractable nature of the drug problem as justification for the checkpoint program. There is no doubt that traffic in illegal narcotics creates social harms of the first magnitude. * * * But the gravity of the threat alone cannot be dispositive of questions concerning what means law enforcement officers may employ to pursue a given purpose. Rather, in determining whether individualized suspicion is required, we must consider the nature of the interests threatened and their connection to the particular law enforcement practices at issue. We are particularly reluctant to recognize exceptions to the general rule of individualized suspicion where governmental authorities primarily pursue their general crime control ends.

Nor can the narcotics-interdiction purpose of the checkpoints be rationalized in terms of a highway safety concern similar to that present in *Sitz*. The detection and punishment of almost any criminal offense serves broadly the safety of the community, and our streets would no doubt be safer but for the scourge of illegal drugs. Only with respect to a smaller class of offenses, however, is society confronted with the type of immediate, vehicle-bound threat to life and limb that the sobriety checkpoint in *Sitz* was designed to eliminate.

Petitioners also liken the anticontraband agenda of the Indianapolis checkpoints to the antismuggling purpose of the checkpoints in *Martinez-Fuerte*. Petitioners cite this Court's conclusion in *Martinez-Fuerte* that the flow of traffic was too heavy to permit "particularized study of a given car that would enable it to be identified as a possible carrier of illegal aliens," and claim that this logic has even more force here. The problem with this argument is that the same logic prevails any time a vehicle is employed to conceal contraband or other evidence of a crime. This type of connection to the roadway is very different from the close connection to roadway safety that was present in *Sitz* and *Prouse*. Further, the Indianapolis checkpoints are far removed from the border context that was crucial in *Martinez-Fuerte*. * * *

* * * We decline to suspend the usual requirement of individualized suspicion where the police seek to employ a checkpoint primarily for the ordinary enterprise of investigating crimes. We cannot sanction stops justified only by the generalized and ever-present possibility that interrogation and inspection may reveal that any given motorist has committed some crime.

Of course, there are circumstances that may justify a law enforcement checkpoint where the primary purpose would otherwise, but for some emergency, relate to ordinary crime control. For example * * * the Fourth Amendment would almost certainly permit an appropriately tailored roadblock set up to thwart an imminent terrorist attack or to catch a dangerous criminal who is likely to flee by way of a particular route. The exigencies created by these scenarios are far removed from the circumstances under which authorities might simply stop cars as a matter of course to see if there just happens to be a felon leaving the jurisdiction. While we do not limit the purposes that may justify a checkpoint program to any rigid set of categories, we decline to approve a program whose primary purpose is ultimately indistinguishable from the general interest in crime control.

Petitioners argue that our prior cases preclude an inquiry into the purposes of the checkpoint program. For example, they cite Whren v. United States, * * * to support the proposition that "where the government articulates and pursues a legitimate interest for a suspicionless stop, courts should not look behind that interest to determine whether the government's 'primary purpose' is valid." These cases, however, do not control the instant situation.

In *Whren*, we held that an individual officer's subjective intentions are irrelevant to the Fourth Amendment validity of a traffic stop that is justified objectively by probable cause to believe that a traffic violation has occurred. * * * In so holding, we expressly distinguished cases where we had addressed the validity of searches conducted in the absence of probable cause. * * *

*Whren* therefore reinforces the principle that, while "[s]ubjective intentions play no role in ordinary, probable-cause Fourth Amendment analysis," programmatic purposes may be relevant to the validity of Fourth Amendment intrusions undertaken pursuant to a general scheme without individualized suspicion. Accordingly, *Whren* does not preclude an inquiry into programmatic purpose in such contexts. It likewise does not preclude an inquiry into programmatic purpose here.

* * *

Petitioners argue that the Indianapolis checkpoint program is justified by its lawful secondary purposes of keeping impaired motorists off the road and verifying licenses and registrations. If this were the case, however, law enforcement authorities would be able to establish checkpoints for virtually any purpose so long as they also included a license or sobriety check. For this reason, we examine the available evidence to determine the primary purpose of the checkpoint program. While we recognize the challenges inherent in a purpose inquiry, courts routinely engage in this enterprise in many areas of constitutional jurisprudence as a means of sifting abusive governmental conduct from that which is lawful. As a result, a program driven by an impermissible purpose may be proscribed while a program impelled by licit purposes is permitted, even though the challenged conduct may be outwardly similar. While reasonableness under the Fourth Amendment is predominantly an objective inquiry, our special needs and administrative search cases demonstrate that purpose is often relevant when suspicionless intrusions pursuant to a general scheme are at issue.[a]

* * *

Our holding also does not affect the validity of border searches or searches at places like airports and government buildings, where the

---

[a]   Because petitioners concede that the primary purpose of the Indianapolis checkpoints is narcotics detection, we need not decide whether the State may establish a checkpoint program with the primary purpose of checking licenses or driver sobriety and a secondary purpose of interdicting narcotics. Specifically, we express no view on the question whether police may expand the scope of a license or sobriety checkpoint seizure in order to detect the presence of drugs in a stopped car.

need for such measures to ensure public safety can be particularly acute. Nor does our opinion speak to other intrusions aimed primarily at purposes beyond the general interest in crime control. Our holding also does not impair the ability of police officers to act appropriately upon information that they properly learn during a checkpoint stop justified by a lawful primary purpose, even where such action may result in the arrest of a motorist for an offense unrelated to that purpose. Finally, we caution that the purpose inquiry in this context is to be conducted only at the programmatic level and is not an invitation to probe the minds of individual officers acting at the scene.

Because the primary purpose of the Indianapolis checkpoint program is ultimately indistinguishable from the general interest in crime control, the checkpoints violate the Fourth Amendment. The judgment of the Court of Appeals is accordingly affirmed.

**CHIEF JUSTICE REHNQUIST, with whom JUSTICE THOMAS joins, and with whom JUSTICE SCALIA joins [in relevant part], dissenting.**

\* \* \*

\* \* \* The only difference between this case and *Sitz* is the presence of the dog. We have already held, however, that a "sniff test" by a trained narcotics dog is not a "search" within the meaning of the Fourth Amendment because it does not require physical intrusion of the object being sniffed and it does not expose anything other than the contraband items. And there is nothing in the record to indicate that the dog sniff lengthens the stop. Finally, the checkpoints' success rate—49 arrests for offenses unrelated to drugs—only confirms the State's legitimate interests in preventing drunken driving and ensuring the proper licensing of drivers and registration of their vehicles. These stops effectively serve the State's legitimate interests; they are executed in a regularized and neutral manner; and they only minimally intrude upon the privacy of the motorists. They should therefore be constitutional.

\* \* \*

[T]he Court's newfound non-law-enforcement primary purpose test is both unnecessary to secure Fourth Amendment rights and bound to produce wide-ranging litigation over the "purpose" of any given seizure. Police designing highway roadblocks can never be sure of their validity, since a jury might later determine that a forbidden purpose exists.

\* \* \* [I]f the Indianapolis police had assigned a different purpose to their activity here, but in no way changed what was done on the ground to individual motorists, it might well be valid. [The Chief Justice cites the majority's footnote concerning the possible permissibility of a checkpoint whose secondary purpose is drug interdiction.] The Court's non-law-enforcement primary purpose test simply does not serve as a proxy for anything that the Fourth Amendment is, or should be, concerned about in the automobile seizure context.

\* \* \*

### JUSTICE THOMAS, dissenting.

Taken together, our decisions in Michigan Dept. of State Police v. Sitz and United States v. Martinez-Fuerte stand for the proposition that suspicionless roadblock seizures are constitutionally permissible if conducted according to a plan that limits the discretion of the officers conducting the stops. I am not convinced that *Sitz* and *Martinez-Fuerte* were correctly decided. Indeed, I rather doubt that the Framers of the Fourth Amendment would have considered "reasonable" a program of indiscriminate stops of individuals not suspected of wrongdoing.

Respondents did not, however, advocate the overruling of *Sitz* and *Martinez-Fuerte,* and I am reluctant to consider such a step without the benefit of briefing and argument. For the reasons given by THE CHIEF JUSTICE, I believe that those cases compel upholding the program at issue here. I, therefore, join his opinion.

### NOTE ON EDMOND AND CHECKPOINTS AFTER 9/11

The *Edmond* majority was concerned that checkpoints would become "a routine part of American life." After 9/11, checkpoints have indeed become routine. Many of the checkpoints are not simply seizures, but intrusive searches as well (e.g., airport checkpoints). But the checkpoints seem to fall within the majority's perhaps prophetic paragraph that permits terrorism-related checkpoints without any showing of suspicion. And if these are "special needs" checkpoints, then the additional step of a search can usually be justified by balancing the government's interest in rooting out terrorism against the individual's diminished interest in privacy.

Terrorism-related checkpoints after 9/11 have routinely been upheld. An example is United States v. Green, 293 F.3d 855 (5th Cir. 2002), upholding a suspicionless roadblock check on an open military installation. The court declared as follows:

> We believe that this case differs substantially from *Edmond* in two respects. First, the protection of the nation's military installations from acts of domestic or international terrorism is a unique endeavour, akin to the policing of our borders, and one in which a greater degree of intrusiveness may be allowed. Second, those cases focusing not on unique, national challenges, but instead on road safety, are concerned with dangers specifically associated with vehicles and therefore justify suspicionless checkpoint seizures. Since we know from painful experience that vehicles are often used to transport and deliver explosives in the form of "car bombs," and that military installations

have historically faced greater risk than civilian communities of such a bombing, vehicles pose a special risk.

The majority in *Edmond* also seemed to approve of emergency roadblocks to catch a dangerous criminal, such as were used during the Washington, D.C. area sniper attacks. Where is the line, then, between crime enforcement and special needs?

### Drug Interdiction as a Secondary Purpose

The majority in *Edmond* dropped a footnote to state that it was not deciding whether checkpoints are invalid if they have drug interdiction as a *secondary* purpose. Throughout the opinion, the Court emphasizes that the *primary* purpose of the Indianapolis checkpoint was drug interdiction, as opposed to a vehicle-related threat to public safety. After *Edmond,* courts have upheld checkpoints where the articulated primary purpose effectuates special needs beyond law enforcement—even though there is also a secondary purpose of drug interdiction. See, e.g., United States v. Davis, 270 F.3d 977 (D.C.Cir. 2001) (checkpoint not invalidated by secondary purpose of drug interdiction, noting that *Edmond* "more than suggests that if the 'primary purpose' had been for a purpose the Court endorsed—such as detecting drunk drivers, or checking licenses—the roadblock would be constitutional."); United States v. Moreno-Vargas, 315 F.3d 489 (5th Cir. 2002) (use of drug-detecting dogs at a permanent fixed immigration checkpoint does not invalidate the checkpoint stops; drug interdiction was a permissible secondary purpose of the checkpoint).

Assuming there is a constitutional distinction between primary and secondary purposes, how hard is it for the government to evade the Court's holding in *Edmond*? What prevents the government from labeling its checkpoint a "sobriety" or "registration" checkpoint, and keeping a drug detecting dog at the checkpoint as part of a specified "secondary" purpose?

### Drug-Detection as a Vehicle-Related Safety Interest

The *Edmond* Court distinguished sobriety checkpoints from the Indianapolis drug interdiction checkpoint on the ground that drunk drivers present an immediate, vehicle-related safety threat while drug dealers do not raise a specific safety issue merely by driving. Does this mean that suspicionless drug checkpoints would be permitted if they are styled as an attempt to detect those who are driving *under the influence* of drugs?

What if the state can make a reasonable argument that drug dealers do indeed create a vehicle-related threat to safety? After all, drug dealers are probably not the safest drivers. They are likely to double park, commit illegal u-turns, and generally act without concern of the traffic laws. In United States v. Davis, 270 F.3d 977 (D.C.Cir. 2001), the court upheld a checkpoint that was in response to community complaints that drug dealers and buyers in cars were speeding, committing illegal u-turns, and causing traffic congestion. The Court noted that the primary purpose of the roadblock was to remedy the traffic problems caused by drug-dealing and "[w]hatever advantage was gained in drug enforcement was coincidental to the principal purpose of the traffic roadblocks." If this is correct, how much is left of the majority opinion in *Edmond*?

## Suspicionless Checkpoints to Obtain Information About a Crime: *Illinois v. Lidster*

In Illinois v. Lidster, 540 U.S. 439 (2004), Justice Breyer wrote for the Court as it upheld a highway checkpoint where motorists were stopped, without suspicion, so that police could ask them about a recent hit-and-run accident. The roadblock was established about a week after the accident on the same highway where the accident occurred and at about the same time of night. Lidster was driving a minivan as he approached the checkpoint, his van swerved and nearly hit one of the officers, and eventually Lidster was arrested for and convicted of driving under the influence.

Justice Breyer reasoned that the checkpoint stop was different from *Edmund* because the officers were not stopping cars to determine whether occupants were committing crimes and the objective of the Illinois roadblock was not to further a "general interest in crime control," He concluded that information-seeking highway stops are less likely to provoke anxiety or to prove intrusive than other stops and "citizens will often react positively when police simply ask for their help as responsible citizens to give whatever information they may have to aid law enforcement." Justice Breyer found that the roadblock was reasonable given that "[t]he relevant public concern was grave" in light of the fact that the accident has resulted in a death, "[t]he stop advanced this grave public concern to a significant degree," and "[t]he police appropriately tailored their checkpoint stops to fit important criminal investigatory needs."

Justice Stevens, joined by Justices Souter and Ginsburg, concurred in part and dissented in part. He agreed that *Edmunds* was not controlling, but found that the reasonableness of the checkpoint was a close question that justified a remand to the state courts so that they could address that question.

## 5.  DNA Testing

When, if ever, is suspicionless DNA testing of individuals reasonable? Can DNA testing—comparing a person's DNA against a database for identification—be justified as promoting "special needs" beyond ordinary criminal law enforcement? The Court considered these questions in the following case.

### MARYLAND V. KING

Supreme Court of the United States, 2013.
133 S.Ct. 1958.

### JUSTICE KENNEDY delivered the opinion of the Court.

In 2003 a man concealing his face and armed with a gun broke into a woman's home in Salisbury, Maryland. He raped her. The police were unable to identify or apprehend the assailant based on any detailed description or other evidence they then had, but they did obtain from the victim a sample of the perpetrator's DNA.

In 2009 Alonzo King was arrested in Wicomico County, Maryland, and charged with first- and second-degree assault for menacing a group of people with a shotgun. As part of a routine booking procedure for serious offenses, his DNA sample was taken by applying a cotton swab or filter paper—known as a buccal swab—to the inside of his cheeks. The DNA was found to match the DNA taken from the Salisbury rape victim. King was tried and convicted for the rape. * * *

The Court of Appeals of Maryland, on review of King's rape conviction, ruled that the DNA taken when King was booked for the 2009 charge was an unlawful seizure because obtaining and using the cheek swab was an unreasonable search of the person. It set the rape conviction aside. This Court granted certiorari and now reverses the judgment of the Maryland court.

### I

When King was arrested on April 10, 2009, for menacing a group of people with a shotgun and charged in state court with both first- and second-degree assault, he was processed for detention in custody at the Wicomico County Central Booking facility. Booking personnel used a cheek swab to take the DNA sample from him pursuant to provisions of the Maryland DNA Collection Act (or Act).

* * *

The advent of DNA technology is one of the most significant scientific advancements of our era. The full potential for use of genetic markers in medicine and science is still being explored, but the utility of DNA identification in the criminal justice system is already undisputed. Since the first use of forensic DNA analysis to catch a rapist and murderer in England in 1986, law enforcement, the defense bar, and the courts have acknowledged DNA testing's unparalleled ability both to exonerate the wrongly convicted and to identify the guilty. * * *

The current standard for forensic DNA testing relies on an analysis of the chromosomes located within the nucleus of all human cells. The DNA material in chromosomes is composed of "coding" and "noncoding" regions. The coding regions are known as genes and contain the information necessary for a cell to make proteins. Non-protein-coding regions are not related directly to making proteins, and have been referred to as "junk" DNA. The adjective "junk" may mislead the layperson, for in fact this is the DNA region used with near certainty to identify a person. The term apparently is intended to indicate that this particular noncoding region, while useful and even dispositive for purposes like identity, does not show more far-reaching and complex characteristics like genetic traits.

* * * The Act authorizes Maryland law enforcement authorities to collect DNA samples from "an individual who is charged with . . . a crime of violence or an attempt to commit a crime of violence; or . . . burglary or an attempt to commit burglary." * * * Once taken, a DNA sample may not be processed or placed in a database before the individual is arraigned (unless the individual consents). It is at this point that a judicial officer ensures that there is probable cause to detain the arrestee on a qualifying serious offense. If all qualifying criminal charges are determined to be unsupported by probable cause the DNA sample [is] immediately destroyed. DNA samples are also destroyed if a criminal action begun against the individual does not result in a conviction, the conviction is finally reversed or vacated and no new trial is permitted, or the individual is granted an unconditional pardon.

The Act also limits the information added to a DNA database and how it may be used. Specifically, only DNA records that directly relate to the identification of individuals [may] be collected and stored. No purpose other than identification is permissible * * *. Tests for familial matches are also prohibited. The officers involved in taking and analyzing respondent's DNA sample complied with the Act in all respects.

Respondent's DNA was collected in this case using a common procedure known as a "buccal swab." Buccal cell collection involves wiping a small piece of filter paper or a cotton swab similar to a Q-tip against the inside cheek of an individual's mouth to collect some skin cells. The procedure is quick and painless. * * *

Respondent's identification as the rapist resulted in part through the operation of a national project to standardize collection and storage of DNA profiles. Authorized by Congress and supervised by the Federal

Bureau of Investigation, the Combined DNA Index System (CODIS) connects DNA laboratories at the local, state, and national level. Since its authorization in 1994, the CODIS system has grown to include all 50 States and a number of federal agencies. CODIS collects DNA profiles provided by local laboratories taken from arrestees, convicted offenders, and forensic evidence found at crime scenes. * * *. [T]he DNA identification is accompanied only by information denoting the laboratory and the analyst responsible for the submission. In short, CODIS sets uniform national standards for DNA matching and then facilitates connections between local law enforcement agencies who can share more specific information about matched * * * profiles.

All 50 States require the collection of DNA from felony convicts, and respondent does not dispute the validity of that practice. Twenty-eight States and the Federal Government have adopted laws similar to the Maryland Act authorizing the collection of DNA from some or all arrestees. * * * At issue is a standard, expanding technology already in widespread use throughout the Nation.

* * * It can be agreed that using a buccal swab on the inner tissues of a person's cheek in order to obtain DNA samples is a search. * * *

A buccal swab is a far more gentle process than a venipuncture to draw blood. It involves but a light touch on the inside of the cheek * * *. The fact than an intrusion is negligible is of central relevance to determining reasonableness, although it is still a search as the law defines that term.

* * *

In some circumstances, such as "[w]hen faced with special law enforcement needs, diminished expectations of privacy, minimal intrusions, or the like, the Court has found that certain general, or individual, circumstances may render a warrantless search or seizure reasonable." Illinois v. McArthur, 531 U.S. 326, 330 (2001). * * * The need for a warrant is perhaps least when the search involves no discretion that could properly be limited by the "interpo[lation of] a neutral magistrate between the citizen and the law enforcement officer." Treasury Employees v. Von Raab.

The instant case can be addressed with this background. The Maryland DNA Collection Act provides that, in order to obtain a DNA sample, all arrestees charged with serious crimes must furnish the sample on a buccal swab applied, as noted, to the inside of the cheeks. The arrestee is already in valid police custody for a serious offense supported by probable cause. The DNA collection is not subject to the judgment of officers whose perspective might be colored by their primary involvement in "the often competitive enterprise of ferreting out crime." Johnson v. United States, 333 U.S. 10, 14 (1948). As noted by this Court in a different but still instructive context involving blood testing, "[b]oth the circumstances justifying toxicological testing and the permissible limits of such intrusions are defined narrowly and specifically in the regulations that authorize them. . . . Indeed, in light of the standardized nature of the tests and the minimal discretion vested in those charged with administering the program, there are virtually no facts for a neutral magistrate to evaluate." *Skinner*, supra, at 622. Here, the search effected by the buccal swab of respondent falls within the category of cases this Court has analyzed by reference to the proposition that the "touchstone of the Fourth Amendment is reasonableness, not individualized suspicion." *Samson.*

Even if a warrant is not required, a search is not beyond Fourth Amendment scrutiny; for it must be reasonable in its scope and manner of execution. To say that no warrant is required is merely to acknowledge that rather than employing a per se rule of unreasonableness, we balance the privacy-related and law enforcement-related concerns to determine if the intrusion was reasonable. This application of traditional standards of reasonableness requires a court to weigh the promotion of legitimate governmental interests against the degree to which the search intrudes upon an individual's privacy. * * *

The legitimate government interest served by the Maryland DNA Collection Act is one that is well established: the need for law enforcement officers in a safe and accurate way to process and identify the persons and possessions they must take into custody. It is beyond dispute that probable cause provides legal justification for arresting a person suspected of crime, and for a brief period of detention to take the administrative steps incident to arrest. Also uncontested is the right on the part of the Government, always recognized under English and American law, to search the person of the accused when legally arrested. * * *

The routine administrative procedure[s] at a police station house incident to booking and jailing the suspect derive from different origins and have different constitutional justifications than, say, the search of a place; for the search of a place not incident to an arrest depends on the fair probability that contraband or evidence of a crime will be found in a particular place. The interests are further different when an individual is formally processed into police custody. Then "the law is in the act of subjecting the body of the accused to its physical dominion." People v. Chiagles, 237 N.Y. 193, 197, 142 N.E. 583, 584 (1923) (Cardozo, J.). When probable cause exists to remove an individual from the normal channels of society and hold him in legal custody, DNA identification plays a critical role in serving those interests.

First, "[i]n every criminal case, it is known and must be known who has been arrested and who is being tried." Hiibel v. Sixth Judicial Dist. Court of Nev., Humboldt Cty., 542 U.S. 177 (2004). An individual's identity is more than just his name or Social Security number, and the government's interest in identification goes beyond ensuring that the proper name is typed on the indictment. * * * It is a well recognized aspect of criminal conduct that the perpetrator will take unusual steps to conceal not only his conduct, but also his identity. * * * An arrestee may be carrying a false ID or lie about his identity, and criminal history records can be inaccurate or incomplete.

A suspect's criminal history is a critical part of his identity that officers should know when processing him for detention. It is a common occurrence that people detained for minor offenses can turn out to be the most devious and dangerous criminals. Police already seek this crucial identifying information. They use routine and accepted means as varied as comparing the suspect's booking photograph to sketch artists' depictions of persons of interest, showing his mugshot to potential witnesses, and of course making a computerized comparison of the arrestee's fingerprints against electronic databases of known criminals and unsolved crimes. In this respect the only difference between DNA analysis and the accepted use of fingerprint databases is the unparalleled accuracy DNA provides.

The task of identification necessarily entails searching public and police records based on the identifying information provided by the arrestee to see what is already known about him. * * * A DNA profile is useful to the police because it gives them a form of identification to search the records already in their valid possession. In this respect the use of DNA for identification is no different than matching an arrestee's face to a wanted poster of a previously unidentified suspect; or matching tattoos to known gang symbols to reveal a criminal affiliation; or matching the arrestee's fingerprints to those recovered from a crime scene. * * * Second, law enforcement officers bear a responsibility for ensuring that the custody of an arrestee does not create inordinate risks for facility staff, for the existing detainee population, and for a new detainee. DNA identification can provide untainted information to those charged with detaining suspects and detaining the property of any felon. For these purposes officers must know the type of person whom they are detaining, and DNA allows them to make critical choices about how to proceed.

* * *

Third, looking forward to future stages of criminal prosecution, the Government has a substantial interest in ensuring that persons accused of crimes are available for trials. A person who is arrested for one offense but knows that he has yet to answer for some past crime may be more inclined to flee the instant charges, lest continued contact with the criminal justice system expose one or more other serious offenses. For example, a defendant who had committed a prior sexual assault might be inclined to flee on a burglary charge, knowing that in every State a DNA sample would be taken from him after his conviction on the burglary charge that would tie him to the more serious charge of rape. * * * Fourth, an arrestee's past conduct is essential to an assessment of the danger he poses to the public, and this will inform a court's determination whether the individual should be released on bail. * * * DNA identification of a suspect in a violent crime provides critical information to the police and judicial officials in making a determination of the arrestee's future dangerousness. * * *

This interest is not speculative. In considering laws to require collecting DNA from arrestees, government agencies around the Nation found evidence of numerous cases in which felony arrestees would have been identified as violent through DNA identification matching them to previous crimes but who later committed additional crimes because such identification was not used to detain them. * * *

Present capabilities make it possible to complete a DNA identification that provides information essential to determining whether a detained suspect can be released pending trial. Regardless of when the initial bail decision is made, release is not appropriate until a further determination is made as to the person's identity in the sense not only of what his birth certificate states but also what other records and data disclose to give that identity more meaning in the whole context of who the person really is. And even when release is permitted, the background identity of the suspect is necessary for determining what conditions must be met before release is allowed. If release is authorized, it may take time for the conditions to be met, and so the time before actual release can be substantial. For example, in the federal system, defendants released conditionally are detained on average for 112 days; those released on unsecured bond for 37 days; on personal recognizance for 36 days; and on other financial conditions for 27 days. During this entire period, additional and supplemental data establishing more about the person's identity and background can provide critical information relevant to the conditions of release and whether to revisit an initial release determination. The facts of this case are illustrative. Though the record is not clear, if some thought were being given to releasing the respondent on bail on the gun charge, a release that would take weeks or months in any event, when the DNA report linked him to the prior rape, it would be relevant to the conditions of his release. * * * Even if an arrestee is released on bail, development of DNA identification revealing the defendant's unknown violent past can and should lead to the revocation of his conditional release. * * *

Finally, in the interests of justice, the identification of an arrestee as the perpetrator of some heinous crime may have the salutary effect of freeing a person wrongfully imprisoned for the same offense. "[P]rompt [DNA] testing . . . would speed up apprehension of criminals before they commit additional crimes, and prevent the grotesque detention of . . . innocent people." J. Dwyer, P. Neufeld, & B. Scheck, Actual Innocence 245 (2000).

\* \* \*

DNA identification represents an important advance in the techniques used by law enforcement to serve legitimate police concerns for as long as there have been arrests, concerns the courts have acknowledged and approved for more than a century. \* \* \* Perhaps the most direct historical analogue to the DNA technology used to identify respondent is the familiar practice of fingerprinting arrestees. From the advent of this technique, courts had no trouble determining that fingerprinting was a natural part of the administrative steps incident to arrest. \* \* \*

DNA identification is an advanced technique superior to fingerprinting in many ways, so much so that to insist on fingerprints as the norm would make little sense to either the forensic expert or a layperson. The additional intrusion upon the arrestee's privacy beyond that associated with fingerprinting is not significant, \* \* \* and DNA is a markedly more accurate form of identifying arrestees. A suspect who has changed his facial features to evade photographic identification or even one who has undertaken the more arduous task of altering his fingerprints cannot escape the revealing power of his DNA.

The respondent's primary objection to this analogy is that DNA identification is not as fast as fingerprinting, and so it should not be considered to be the 21st-century equivalent. But rapid analysis of fingerprints is itself of recent vintage. The FBI's vaunted Integrated Automated Fingerprint Identification System (IAFIS) was only launched on July 28, 1999. Prior to this time, the processing of fingerprint submissions was largely a manual, labor-intensive process, taking weeks or months to process a single submission. \* \* \* The question of how long it takes to process identifying information obtained from a valid search goes only to the efficacy of the search for its purpose of prompt identification, not the constitutionality of the search. Given the importance of DNA in the identification of police records pertaining to arrestees and the need to refine and confirm that identity for its important bearing on the decision to continue release on bail or to impose of new conditions, DNA serves an essential purpose despite the existence of delays such as the one that occurred in this case. Even so, the delay in processing DNA from arrestees is being reduced to a substantial degree by rapid technical advances. See, e.g., Attorney General DeWine Announces Significant Drop in DNA Turnaround Time (Jan. 4, 2013) (DNA processing time reduced from 125 days in 2010 to 20 days in 2012), online at http://ohioattorneygeneral.gov/Media/News-Releases/January-2013/ Attorney-General-DeWine-Announces-Significant-Drop. And the FBI has already begun testing devices that will enable police to process the DNA of arrestees within 90 minutes. An assessment and understanding of the reasonableness of this minimally invasive search of a person detained for a serious crime should take account of these technical advances. * * *

In sum, there can be little reason to question the legitimate interest of the government in knowing for an absolute certainty the identity of the person arrested, in knowing whether he is wanted elsewhere, and in ensuring his identification in the event he flees prosecution. * * * DNA identification of arrestees, of the type approved by the Maryland statute here at issue, is no more than an extension of methods of identification long used in dealing with persons under arrest. In the balance of reasonableness required by the Fourth Amendment, therefore, the Court must give great weight both to the significant government interest at stake in the identification of arrestees and to the unmatched potential of DNA identification to serve that interest.

* * * By comparison to this substantial government interest and the unique effectiveness of DNA identification, the intrusion of a cheek swab to obtain a DNA sample is a minimal one. * * *

The expectations of privacy of an individual taken into police custody necessarily are of a diminished scope. * * *

In this critical respect, the search here at issue differs from the sort of programmatic searches of either the public at large or a particular class of regulated but otherwise law-abiding citizens that the Court has previously labeled as "special needs " searches. Chandler v. Miller, 520 U.S. 305, 314 (1997). * * * Once an individual has been arrested on probable cause for a dangerous offense that may require detention before trial, however, his or her expectations of privacy and freedom from police scrutiny are reduced. DNA identification like that at issue here thus does not require consideration of any unique needs that would be required to justify searching the average citizen. The special needs cases, though in full accord with the result reached here, do not have a direct bearing on the issues presented in this case, because unlike the search of a citizen who has not been suspected of a wrong, a detainee has a reduced expectation of privacy.

The reasonableness inquiry here considers two other circumstances in which the Court has held that particularized suspicion is not categorically required: diminished expectations of privacy and minimal intrusions. * * * This is not to suggest that any search is acceptable solely because a person is in custody. Some searches, such as invasive surgery, or a search of the arrestee's home, involve either greater intrusions or higher expectations of privacy than are present in this case. In those situations, when the Court must balance the privacy-related and law enforcement-related concerns to determine if the intrusion was reasonable, the privacy-related concerns are weighty enough that the search may require a warrant, notwithstanding the diminished expectations of privacy of the arrestee.

Here, by contrast to the approved standard procedures incident to any arrest detailed above, a buccal swab involves an even more brief and still minimal intrusion. A gentle rub along the inside of the cheek does not break the skin, and it involves virtually no risk, trauma, or pain. * * * A brief intrusion of an arrestee's person is subject to the Fourth Amendment, but a swab of this nature does not increase the indignity already attendant to normal incidents of arrest.

* * * In addition the processing of respondent's DNA sample * * * did not intrude on respondent's privacy in a way that would make his DNA identification unconstitutional.

First, as already noted, the CODIS loci come from noncoding parts of the DNA that do not reveal the genetic traits of the arrestee. * * * And even if non-coding alleles could provide some information, they are not in fact tested for that end. It is undisputed that law enforcement officers analyze DNA for the sole purpose of generating a unique identifying number against which future samples may be matched. This parallels a similar safeguard based on actual practice in the school drug-testing context, where the Court deemed it "significant that the tests at issue here look only for drugs, and not for whether the student is, for example, epileptic, pregnant, or diabetic." *Vernonia School Dist. 47J*, 515 U.S., at 658. If in the future police analyze samples to determine, for instance, an arrestee's predisposition for a particular disease or other hereditary factors not relevant to identity, that case would present additional privacy concerns not present here.

Finally, the Act provides statutory protections that guard against further invasion of privacy. As noted above, the Act requires that only DNA records that directly relate to the identification of individuals shall be collected and stored. No purpose other than identification is permissible. * * * The Court need not speculate about the risks posed by a system that [does] not contain comparable security provisions. In light of the scientific and statutory safeguards, once respondent's DNA was lawfully collected the * * * analysis of respondent's DNA pursuant to CODIS procedures did not amount to a significant invasion of privacy that would render the DNA identification impermissible under the Fourth Amendment.

\* \* \* When officers make an arrest supported by probable cause to hold for a serious offense and they bring the suspect to the station to be detained in custody, taking and analyzing a cheek swab of the arrestee's DNA is, like fingerprinting and photographing, a legitimate police booking procedure that is reasonable under the Fourth Amendment. \* \* \*

**JUSTICE SCALIA, with whom JUSTICE GINSBURG, JUSTICE SOTOMAYOR, and JUSTICE KAGAN join, dissenting.**

The Fourth Amendment forbids searching a person for evidence of a crime when there is no basis for believing the person is guilty of the crime or is in possession of incriminating evidence. That prohibition is categorical and without exception; it lies at the very heart of the Fourth Amendment. Whenever this Court has allowed a suspicionless search, it has insisted upon a justifying motive apart from the investigation of crime.

It is obvious that no such noninvestigative motive exists in this case. The Court's assertion that DNA is being taken, not to solve crimes, but to identify those in the State's custody, taxes the credulity of the credulous. And the Court's comparison of Maryland's DNA searches to other techniques, such as fingerprinting, can seem apt only to those who know no more than today's opinion has chosen to tell them about how those DNA searches actually work.

\* \* \*

Although there is a "closely guarded category of constitutionally permissible suspicionless searches," that has never included searches designed to serve "the normal need for law enforcement," Skinner v. Railway Labor Executives' Assn.. Even the common name for suspicionless searches—"special needs" searches—itself reflects that they must be justified, always, by concerns other than crime detection. We have approved random drug tests of railroad employees, yes—but only because the Government's need to "regulat[e] the conduct of railroad employees to ensure safety" is distinct from "normal law enforcement." *Skinner*, supra, at 620. So too we have approved suspicionless searches in public schools—but only because there the government acts in furtherance of its "responsibilities . . . as guardian and tutor of children entrusted to its care." Vernonia School Dist. 47J v. Acton.

So while the Court is correct to note that there are instances in which we have permitted searches without individualized suspicion, "[i]n none of these cases . . . did we indicate approval of a [search] whose primary purpose was to detect evidence of ordinary criminal wrongdoing." Indianapolis v. Edmond. That limitation is crucial. It is only when a governmental purpose aside from crime-solving is at stake that we engage in the free-form "reasonableness" inquiry that the Court indulges at length today. To put it another way, both the legitimacy of the Court's method and the correctness of its outcome hinge entirely on the truth of a single proposition: that the primary purpose of these DNA searches is something other than simply discovering evidence of criminal wrongdoing. As I detail below, that proposition is wrong.

The Court alludes at several points to the fact that King was an arrestee, and arrestees may be validly searched incident to their arrest. But the Court does not really rest on this principle, and for good reason: The objects of a search incident to arrest must be either (1) weapons or evidence that might easily be destroyed, or (2) evidence relevant to the crime of arrest. See Arizona v. Gant. Neither is the object of the search at issue here.

\* \* \*

\* \* \* No matter the degree of invasiveness, suspicionless searches are never allowed if their principal end is ordinary crime-solving. \* \* \*

Sensing (correctly) that it needs more, the Court elaborates at length the ways that the search here served the special purpose of "identifying" King. But that seems to me quite wrong—unless what one means by "identifying" someone is "searching for evidence that he has committed crimes unrelated to the crime of his arrest." \* \* \* If identifying someone means finding out what unsolved crimes he has committed, then identification is indistinguishable from the ordinary law-enforcement aims that have never been thought to justify a suspicionless search. \* \* \* I will therefore assume that the Court means that the DNA search at issue here was useful to "identify" King in the normal sense of that word—in the sense that would identify the author of Introduction to the Principles of Morals and Legislation as Jeremy Bentham.

\* \* \* The portion of the Court's opinion that explains the identification rationale is strangely silent on the actual workings of the DNA search at issue here. To know those facts is to be instantly disabused of the notion that what happened had anything to do with identifying King.

King was arrested on April 10, 2009, on charges unrelated to the case before us. That same day, April 10, the police searched him and seized the DNA evidence at issue here. What happened next? Reading the Court's opinion, particularly its insistence that the search was necessary to know "who [had] been arrested," one might guess that King's DNA was swiftly processed and his identity thereby confirmed—perhaps against some master database of known DNA profiles, as is done for fingerprints. After all, was not the suspicionless search here crucial to avoid "inordinate risks for facility staff" or to "existing detainee population"? Surely, then— surely—the State of Maryland got cracking on those grave risks immediately, by rushing to identify King with his DNA as soon as possible.

Nothing could be further from the truth. Maryland officials did not even begin the process of testing King's DNA that day. Or, actually, the next day. Or the day after that. And that was for a simple reason: Maryland law forbids them to do so. A "DNA sample collected from an individual charged with a crime . . . may not be tested or placed in the statewide DNA data base system prior to the first scheduled arraignment date." Md. Pub. Saf. Code Ann. § 2–504(d)(1). And King's first appearance in court was not until three days after his arrest. (I suspect, though, that they did not wait three days to ask his name or take his fingerprints.)

This places in a rather different light the Court's solemn declaration that the search here was necessary so that King could be identified at "every stage of the criminal process." Does the Court really believe that Maryland did not know whom it was arraigning? The truth, known to Maryland and increasingly to the reader: this search had nothing to do with establishing King's identity.

* * * The FBI's DNA database (known as CODIS) consists of two distinct collections. One of them, the one to which King's DNA was submitted, consists of DNA samples taken from known convicts or arrestees. I will refer to this as the "Convict and Arrestee Collection." The other collection consists of samples taken from crime scenes; I will refer to this as the "Unsolved Crimes Collection." The Convict and Arrestee Collection stores no names or other personal identifiers of the offenders, arrestees, or detainees. Rather, it contains only the DNA profile itself, the name of the agency that submitted it, the laboratory personnel who analyzed it, and an identification number for the specimen. This is because the submitting state laboratories are expected already to know the identities of the convicts and arrestees from whom samples are taken. (And, of course, they do.)

Moreover, the CODIS system works by checking to see whether any of the samples in the Unsolved Crimes Collection match any of the samples in the Convict and Arrestee Collection. That is sensible, if what one wants to do is solve those cold cases, but note what it requires: that the identity of the people whose DNA has been entered in the Convict and Arrestee Collection already be known. If one wanted to identify someone in custody using his DNA, the logical thing to do would be to compare that DNA against the Convict and Arrestee Collection * * *. But that is not what was done. And that is because this search had nothing to do with identification.

* * *

More devastating still for the Court's "identification" theory, the statute does enumerate two instances in which a DNA sample may be tested for the purpose of identification: "to help identify human remains" and "to help identify missing individuals." No mention of identifying arrestees. Inclusio unius est exclusio alterius. And note again that Maryland forbids using DNA records "for any purposes other than those specified"—it is actually a crime to do so.

\* \* \*

The Court also attempts to bolster its identification theory with a series of inapposite analogies.

Is not taking DNA samples the same, asks the Court, as taking a person's photograph? No—because that is not a Fourth Amendment search at all. It does not involve a physical intrusion onto the person, see Florida v. Jardines, and we have never held that merely taking a person's photograph invades any recognized "expectation of privacy." \* \* \*

\* \* \*

It is on the fingerprinting of arrestees, however, that the Court relies most heavily. The Court does not actually say whether it believes that taking a person's fingerprints is a Fourth Amendment search, and our cases provide no ready answer to that question. Even assuming so, however, law enforcement's post-arrest use of fingerprints could not be more different from its post-arrest use of DNA. Fingerprints of arrestees are taken primarily to identify them (though that process sometimes solves crimes); the DNA of arrestees is taken to solve crimes (and nothing else).

\* \* \*

Today, it can fairly be said that fingerprints really are used to identify people—so well, in fact, that there would be no need for the expense of a separate, wholly redundant DNA confirmation of the same information. What DNA adds—what makes it a valuable weapon in the law-enforcement arsenal—is the ability to solve unsolved crimes, by matching old crime-scene evidence against the profiles of people whose identities are already known. That is what was going on when King's DNA was taken, and we should not disguise the fact. Solving unsolved crimes is a noble objective, but it occupies a lower place in the American pantheon of noble objectives than the protection of our people from suspicionless law-enforcement searches. The Fourth Amendment must prevail.

\* \* \* The Court disguises the vast (and scary) scope of its holding by promising a limitation it cannot deliver. The Court repeatedly says that DNA testing, and entry into a national DNA registry, will not befall thee and me, dear reader, but only those arrested for "serious offense[s]." I cannot imagine what principle could possibly justify this limitation, and the Court does not attempt to suggest any. If one believes that DNA will "identify" someone arrested for assault, he must believe that it will "identify" someone arrested for a traffic offense. \* \* \* Make no mistake about it: As an entirely predictable consequence of today's decision, your DNA can be taken and entered into a national DNA database if you are ever arrested, rightly or wrongly, and for whatever reason.

\* \* \*

Today's judgment will, to be sure, have the beneficial effect of solving more crimes; then again, so would the taking of DNA samples from anyone who flies on an airplane (surely the Transportation Security Administration needs to know the "identity" of the flying public), applies for a driver's license, or attends a public school. Perhaps the construction of such a genetic panopticon is wise. But I doubt that the proud men who wrote the charter of our liberties would have been so eager to open their mouths for royal inspection.

I therefore dissent, and hope that today's incursion upon the Fourth Amendment \* \* \* will some day be repudiated.

## 6. Inventory Searches

By now it should be apparent that the line between regulatory searches and law enforcement searches is often blurred. Another example of this overlap occurs with inventory searches. In most jurisdictions it is standard procedure for the police to inventory the contents of automobiles and other containers being held in their custody. An inventory search is not based on probable cause that evidence will be found, and *ostensibly* is unrelated to criminal investigation of any kind. As one court has put it, the police are allowed to conduct inventory searches without a warrant and without suspicion, in order "to protect the owner's property while it is in police custody, to protect the police against claims of lost or stolen property, and to protect the police and the public from potential danger." The traditional requirements of warrant and probable cause are excused because inventory searches serve a "caretaking" function and "are not designed to uncover evidence of criminal activity." United States v. Andrews, 22 F.3d 1328 (5th Cir.1994).

As with other "special needs" searches, the lack of any requirement of probable cause or reasonable suspicion raises the spectre of unregulated police discretion as to what and when to search. To control that discretion, the government must show that the officer was operating pursuant to standard inventory procedures promulgated by the police department. See United States v. Petty, 367 F.3d 1009 (8th Cir. 2004) ("Some degree of standardized criteria or established routine must regulate these police actions \* \* \* to ensure that impoundments and inventory searches are not merely a ruse for general rummaging in order to discover incriminating evidence.").

### Community Caretaking Function

The Supreme Court has analyzed warrantless, suspicionless inventory searches in several instances. In Cady v. Dombrowski, 413 U.S. 433 (1973), the Court approved the search of a car towed to a private garage after an accident that resulted in the hospitalization of the driver. The driver was a Chicago policeman, and the officer who conducted the search testified that he was looking for the driver's service revolver, which he believed Chicago policemen were required to carry at all times. In the course of the search, blood-stained garments were discovered in the trunk, which were later used to convict the defendant of murder. In a 5–4 decision, Justice Rehnquist found that the initial intrusion to search for the gun was reasonable as a "community caretaking function," to protect the public from the possibility that it would fall into the hands of vandals. Therefore, the seizure of evidence found in plain view was also justified.

### Warrantless, Suspicionless Searches: South Dakota v. Opperman

Two years after *Cady,* the Court upheld the warrantless, suspicionless inventory search of a car impounded for a parking violation. Chief Justice Burger, writing for the Court in South Dakota v. Opperman, 428 U.S. 364 (1976), emphasized that the search was conducted pursuant to standard police procedures, which helped to guarantee that the intrusion "would be limited to the scope necessary to carry out the caretaking function." The majority found the search of Opperman's impounded car to be a reasonable means of protecting valuables, which could be seen in plain view on the dashboard. Opperman argued that it was unreasonable for the officers to break open the lock of his car and search the glove compartment, where they found marijuana that was used against him at trial. But the Court held that these actions were reasonable because they were authorized, and indeed mandated, by local police regulations.

As in other special needs cases, the *Opperman* Court balanced the state interest in making the search against the intrusiveness of the search to determine whether inventory searches were reasonable. The Court found that three legitimate state interests supported an inventory search: 1) protection of the police department from false property claims; 2) protection of the property interests of the owner; and 3) protection of the police and public from dangerous items. The Court concluded that these state interests, which could only be effectuated by a suspicionless search, outweighed the owner's privacy interests, especially given the diminished expectation of privacy in automobiles.

Justice Powell, in a concurring opinion, explained why the warrant requirement is inapposite when an inventory search is conducted pursuant to departmental regulations: First, there are no special facts for a neutral magistrate to evaluate so as to determine whether probable cause exists, because inventory searches are non-criminal in nature. Second, there is no danger of discretionary searches or hindsight justifications when searches are conducted in accordance with standard procedures. Third, the danger of arbitrariness is not present where routine searches of all impounded cars are conducted.

Justice Marshall—in a dissent joined by Justices Brennan and Stewart, and in part by Justice White—argued that warrantless, suspicionless inventory searches could not be justified by any "special need." He found the safety rationale—i.e., that inventory searches protected the police and public from dangerous items—to be overbroad. Every automobile and container poses at least some hypothetical threat to safety. Justice Marshall concluded that an "undifferentiated possibility of harm" cannot serve as a basis for an inventory, and that the safety rationale was only implicated where specific circumstances indicate the possibility of a particular danger—such as in *Cady*, where the officers reasonably believed that the defendant had a gun in his car.

Next, Justice Marshall considered the assertion that inventories are necessary to protect the police against lost property claims. In this case, the concern was irrelevant because South Dakota law absolved police of responsibility as "gratuitous depositors" beyond inventorying objects in plain view and locking the car. Furthermore, an inventory does not discourage false claims that an item was stolen prior to the search, or was intentionally omitted from police records. Nor does it ensure that such police misconduct did not in fact occur.

Finally, Justice Marshall derided the assertion that impoundment and search of property is a reasonable means of protecting the owner's property interests. In his view, the property owner's interests are best known by the property owner himself; if the owner feels that impoundment and search are needed to protect his property, then he can simply consent to these intrusions.

### Property Carried by an Arrestee: Illinois v. Lafayette

The Supreme Court relied on South Dakota v. Opperman in Illinois v. Lafayette, 462 U.S. 640 (1983), as it upheld the inventory search at the police station of a shoulder bag belonging to a man arrested for disturbing the peace. The search uncovered drugs. Chief Justice Burger reasoned that the government's interests in an inventory search at the stationhouse "may in some circumstances be even greater that those supporting a search incident to arrest" and that police conduct that might be embarrassingly intrusive on the street could be handled privately at the stationhouse. The Chief Justice asserted that the three interests supporting an inventory search were fully applicable to a stationhouse search of an arrestee's possessions: police need to protect the property of arrested persons, to protect themselves from claims of theft or damage to property, and to remove dangerous instrumentalities from arrestees.

The lower court in *Lafayette* had found the inventory search unreasonable on the ground that preservation of the property could have been achieved in a less intrusive manner—such as by storing the bag rather than investigating its contents. Chief Justice Burger rejected this "less intrusive alternative" reasoning, stating as follows:

> The reasonableness of any particular governmental activity does not necessarily or invariably turn on the existence of alternative less intrusive means. * * * Even if less intrusive means existed of protecting some particular types of property, it would be unreasonable to expect police officers in the everyday course of business to make fine and subtle distinctions in deciding which containers or items may be searched and which must be sealed as a unit.

In a footnote, the Court stated that the inventory search of Lafayette's bag might have been invalid if he was not going to be incarcerated after being booked for disturbing the peace.[25] If the arrestee is going to be released immediately, then the interests supporting an inventory search would not appear to be implicated. Justice Marshall, joined by Justice Brennan, concurred in the judgment.

### *Limits on Police Discretion: Colorado v. Bertine*

*Opperman* and *Lafayette* supported the Supreme Court's decision in Colorado v. Bertine, 479 U.S. 367 (1987), holding that police officers could inventory the contents of a van, including a closed backpack and a nylon bag and other containers within it. Chief Justice Rehnquist's opinion for the Court rejected an argument that the impoundment of the car was unjustified because the driver could have been offered the opportunity to make arrangements for the safekeeping of his property. The Court concluded that "reasonable police regulations relating to inventory procedures administered in good faith satisfy the Fourth Amendment, even though courts might as a matter of hindsight be able to devise equally reasonable rules requiring a different procedure."

The *Bertine* Court also rejected the defendant's claim that the inventory was impermissible because departmental regulations gave police officers discretion to decide whether to impound the van or to park and lock it in a public parking lot. The Chief Justice noted that the

---

[25] A number of courts have held that a preincarceration inventory search is improper if the arrestee, upon posting collateral, has a right to immediate release. See, e.g., United States v. Mills, 472 F.2d 1231 (D.C.Cir.1972); People v. Dixon, 392 Mich. 691, 222 N.W.2d 749 (1974).

regulations established several factors by which the officer was to determine whether to impound the vehicle or instead exercise a park and lock alternative. The regulations permitted impoundment only in two conditions: if leaving the car would present a real risk of damage or vandalism to the car; or if approval to leave the car could not be obtained from the owner. The majority held that these conditions were sufficiently concrete and understandable to reasonably limit the discretion of the officer—providing a satisfactory substitute to the proof requirements of probable cause or reasonable suspicion. The Court concluded that "nothing in *Opperman* or *Lafayette* prohibits the exercise of police discretion so long as that discretion is exercised according to standard criteria and on the basis of something other than suspicion of criminal activity."

Bertine also challenged the opening of the containers found in his car, on the ground that the inventorying officer did not properly weigh the privacy interest in the container against the risk that it might serve as a repository for dangerous or valuable items. The majority again rejected a less intrusive means analysis for opening containers in an inventory search. In a footnote, the Court emphasized that "the police department procedures mandated the opening of closed containers and the listing of their contents." Thus, the officer's discretion as to what to open was limited by the inventory rules that were in place.

Justice Blackmun, joined by Justices Powell and O'Connor, concurred and wrote separately "to underscore the importance of having such inventories conducted only pursuant to standardized police procedures." Justice Marshall, joined by Justice Brennan, dissented. He urged that the officers did not act according to standards that sufficiently controlled their discretion and he repeated the arguments he made in *Opperman* that the government's interests in conducting an inventory did not outweigh the property owner's privacy interests.

## Unlimited Police Discretion Invalidates the Inventory Search: Florida v. Wells

The Court revisited the subject of police discretion in conducting inventory searches in Florida v. Wells, 495 U.S. 1 (1990). The Court unanimously found that the opening of a locked suitcase could not be justified as an inventory search where the Florida Highway Patrol had *no policy whatever* concerning the opening of closed containers. Chief Justice Rehnquist, writing for the Court, found the search to be insufficiently regulated by standardized police procedures. However, the Chief Justice took issue with a statement by the Florida Supreme Court that "the police under *Bertine* must mandate either that all containers will be opened during an inventory search, or that no containers will be opened. There can be no room for discretion." According to the Court in *Wells*, the Fourth Amendment does allow the officer *some* latitude to decide whether a container may be opened in an inventory search. This discretion can be exercised, pursuant to departmental regulations, "in light of the nature of the search and the characteristics of the container itself." The Chief Justice concluded:

> While policies of opening all containers or of opening no containers are unquestionably permissible, it would be equally permissible, for example, to allow the opening of closed containers whose contents officers determine they are unable to ascertain from examining the contents' exteriors. The allowance of the exercise of judgment based on concerns related to the purpose of an inventory search does not violate the Fourth Amendment.

This dictum prompted sharp responses in opinions by Justice Brennan (joined by Justice Marshall), Justice Blackmun, and Justice Stevens, all of whom concurred in the judgment. These Justices generally argued that to allow the individual officer any discretion to determine whether a container should be opened would create an unacceptable risk of abuse. Justice Brennan noted that the *Bertine* Court had allowed the officer some discretion as to whether to impound a car, but no discretion as to whether to open a container therein. He concluded that "attempting to cast doubt on the vitality of the holding in *Bertine* in this otherwise easy case is not justified." In response to Justice Brennan's characterization of the *Bertine* "holding", the Chief Justice stated that while the departmental rules at issue in *Bertine* called for an opening of all containers, the Court did not actually hold that such an all-or-nothing rule was required by the Fourth Amendment.

After *Wells,* would a policy allowing police officers to open containers "if they reasonably appear to contain valuables" be upheld? See United States v. Mundy, 621 F.3d 283 (3rd Cir. 2010): "Though the [police department's inventory policy] does not contain magic words specifically to closed containers, its reference to 'any personal property of value' sufficiently regulated the scope of a permissible inventory search, and therefore authorized the opening of the shoebox in Mundy's trunk to determine if such property was contained therein."   See also United States v. Andrews, 22 F.3d 1328 (5th Cir.1994) (upholding a search of a notebook pursuant to departmental regulations that authorized officers to search property insofar as necessary "to protect the city from claims of lost property").

In the end, there may be no way to completely eliminate the exercise of discretion in an inventory seizure and search. Certainly a rule requiring the "impoundment of all cars" would not be practicable, given the various fact situations in which officers come upon cars that might be subject to impoundment. While an all-or-nothing rule could be applied to opening containers, discretion would still have to be exercised to determine whether a certain item is or is not a container. See generally United States v. Judge, 864 F.2d 1144 (5th Cir.1989). For example, if the inventorying officer finds a fountain pen in a car, can he open up the pen under a policy requiring the opening of all containers? What if he finds a teddy bear? See also United States v. Petty, 367 F.3d 1009 (8th Cir. 2004) (impoundment and inventory regulations "may allow some latitude and exercise of judgment by a police officer when those decisions are based on concerns related to the purposes" of the impoundment or inventory; noting that it is "not feasible for a police department to develop a policy that provides clear-cut guidance" in every potential impoundment or inventory situation).

### *The Problem of Pretext*

The emphasis in *Opperman* and *Bertine* on standardized inventory procedures reflects concern that, absent such guidelines, investigatory searches for evidence of crime may be conducted under the guise of inventories. As we have seen in other areas, however (most notably with roadblocks and searches incident to arrest), the fact that the officer is guided by bright line, all-or-nothing rules does not eliminate the possibility of pretextual searches. And as in other areas, the fact that the officer may have a pretextual motive is usually held irrelevant if the search itself is objectively reasonable. See, e.g., United States v. Hawkins, 279 F.3d 83 (1st Cir. 2002) ("Appellant also challenges the search saying that the inventory was clearly a 'ruse' used to search for drugs. Regardless of what appellant suggests, the law is clear. The subjective intent of the officers is not relevant so long as they conduct a search according to a standardized inventory policy."); United States v. Kanatzar, 370 F.3d 810 (8th Cir.2004) ("The presence of an investigative motive does not invalidate an otherwise valid inventory search.").

On the other hand, if the officer is acting without guidelines, as in *Wells,* or if the officer *disregards guidelines to obtain evidence,* then the search cannot be justified as an inventory search. An example of the latter is where the officer opens only a few containers in an impounded automobile, or fails to file an inventory list where such a filing is required. See United States v. Parr, 716 F.2d 796 (11th Cir.1983) (search cannot be justified as an inventory search where items were selectively investigated). As the court put it in United States v. Rowland, 341 F.3d 774 (8th Cir. 2003), finding an illegal search where officers inventoried the evidence of crime but not other items of value in the car:

> In sum, law enforcement had standardized procedures in place but failed to follow them here. Such failure, coupled with the fact the

officers disregarded items without evidentiary value * * * suggests they did not search the vehicle in order to safeguard the vehicle's contents from loss, or to protect law enforcement personnel from harm, or even to guard the department and county against a possible lawsuit. Rather, it appears law enforcement sifted through the vehicle's contents searching only for and recording only incriminating evidence; something law enforcement may not do.

See also United States v. Proctor, 489 F.3d 1348 (D.C.Cir. 2007) ("Because the officers failed to follow the MPD standard procedure, the impoundment of Proctor's vehicle was unreasonable and thus violated the Fourth Amendment.").

### *Less Onerous Alternatives*

The problem of pretextual inventory searches could be regulated by requiring police officers to use the least onerous alternative in effectuating the state interests involved. For example, impoundment of a car could be prohibited if someone who was not being arrested is on the scene and could simply drive it away—the "drive away" alternative would protect the police from false claims, protect the owner's interest, and protect against safety risks, without necessitating an intrusive seizure. Similarly, a search of the car and containers in the car could be prohibited if the officer could simply seal the car to prevent entry. It would seem that in some circumstances, a container can be sealed or locked, thus protecting the owner's valuables and protecting the police from false claims, without the intrusion of a search. However, these arguments are based on a less intrusive means analysis, which the Supreme Court has rejected in *Lafayette* and *Bertine*. According to those cases, the issue is not whether a less intrusive alternative exists that would equally effectuate state interests. Rather, the issue is whether the alternative chosen is a reasonable means of accommodating the (high) interests of the state and the (low) privacy interests of citizens. So while police departments are free to use these less onerous alternatives, they are not required to do so under the Fourth Amendment. See United States v. Betterton, 417 F.3d 826 (8th Cir. 2005) ("Nothing in the Fourth Amendment requires a police department to allow an arrested person to arrange for another person to pick up his car to avoid impoundment and inventory.").

Why does the Supreme Court reject the less intrusive alternative arguments in the inventory cases? Professor Maclin points out that the Court has required the State to employ less intrusive means when other constitutional rights, such as First Amendment rights, are involved. He proffers the following explanation for this apparent disparity in constitutional standards.

The Court is uninterested in placing the Fourth Amendment in the category of preferred constitutional rights, including the rights of free speech, freedom of religion, and freedom from racial discrimination, despite its specific placement in the Bill of Rights.

\* \* \*

Why is the Fourth Amendment considered a second-class right? My guess is that the Court sees the typical Fourth Amendment claimant as a second-class citizen, and sees the typical police officer as being overwhelmed with the responsibilities and duties of maintaining law and order in our crime-prone society. This dual perception may explain the Court's reluctance to subject police conduct to vigorous judicial oversight.

Maclin, The Central Meaning of the Fourth Amendment, 35 Wm. & Mary L.Rev. 197, 237 (1993). Can you see any reason to distinguish between, for example, First and Fourth Amendment protections? Is the difference that the Fourth Amendment specifically emphasizes reasonableness, while the First Amendment is written in more absolute terms?

### Searches and Seizures That Serve No Inventory Interest

An impoundment or search that effectuates the state interests supporting an inventory search—even though those interests could be met less intrusively—must be distinguished from an impoundment or search that effectuates *none* of those state interests. It is reasonable, under *Bertine,* to impound a vehicle even where alternative arrangements could be made to protect the car. It is also reasonable, under *Bertine* and *Lafayette*, to open a container even though it could otherwise be secured. It is not, however, reasonable to impound a vehicle that is parked in a locked garage attached to the arrestee's home; such a seizure is not necessary to effectuate the interests that support an impoundment in the first place. Likewise, it is not reasonable to vacuum a car's interior to "inventory" carpet fibers: there is no safety risk, no chance of a claim for lost property, and no need to protect the owner from the chance that his carpet fibers will be stolen. See United States v. Showalter, 858 F.2d 149 (3d Cir.1988), where the government sought to justify the search of an entire *residence* under the inventory exception. The court stated that "none of the factors which have been used to justify the warrantless inventory search of an automobile are present \* \* \* when generally applied to the home." See also United States v. Best, 135 F.3d 1223 (8th Cir.1998), where the officer, in the course of an "inventory" search, pried open the door panel of a car and discovered drugs. The court held the search invalid, because it "did not serve the purpose of protecting the car and its contents." The court noted that "Best would not have a legitimate claim for protection of property hidden in the door panel" of his car, and therefore the officer "did not have a legitimate interest in seeking such property."

## 7. Border Searches

Courts are not always persuasive in their inventory search opinions, but they try to state a rationale for not requiring a warrant. This is in sharp contrast with the cases establishing the border search exception to the warrant and probable cause requirements. These cases make little effort to justify the exception on policy grounds. The most persuasive rationale is similar to that used in *Skinner* and *Von Raab*: border searches serve a special need beyond traditional criminal law enforcement. The special need is the interest in protecting American borders, "in order to regulate the collection of duties and to prevent the introduction of contraband into this country." United States v. Johnson, 991 F.2d 1287 (7th Cir.1993). As the Court stated in United States v. Montoya de Hernandez, 473 U.S. 531 (1985):

> At the border, customs officials have more than merely an investigative law enforcement role. They are also charged, along with immigration officials, with protecting this Nation from entrants who may bring anything harmful into this country, whether that be communicable diseases, narcotics, or explosives.

Because the border search serves special needs, it is evaluated under the reasonableness clause of the Fourth Amendment. And given the heavy state interest just stated, as well as the diminished expectation of privacy attendant to a border crossing, border searches are ordinarily reasonable even without a warrant or probable cause, and often without any suspicion at all. See United States v. Robles, 45 F.3d 1 (1st Cir.1995) ("routine border searches, conducted for the purposes of collecting duties and intercepting contraband destined for the interior of the United States, do not require reasonable suspicion, probable cause, or a warrant").

### *Warrantless, Suspicionless Search of International Mail: United States v. Ramsey*

In United States v. Ramsey, 431 U.S. 606 (1977), Customs officials opened eight envelopes sent to the United States from Thailand, as part of an investigation of a heroin-by-mail enterprise in the Washington, D.C. area. Ramsey argued that the envelopes could not be opened without a warrant and probable cause, but the Supreme Court disagreed. Justice Rehnquist found the search to be reasonable under the border search doctrine. He analyzed the constitutionality of border searches as follows:

> That searches made at the border, pursuant to the longstanding right of the sovereign to protect itself by stopping and examining

persons and property crossing into this country, are reasonable simply by virtue of the fact that they occur at the border should, by now, require no extended demonstration. The Congress which proposed the Bill of Rights, including the Fourth Amendment, to the state legislatures on September 25, 1789, 1 Stat. 97, had, some two months prior to that proposal, enacted the first customs statute, Act of July 31, 1789, c. 5, 1 Stat. 29. Section 24 of this statute granted customs officials "full power and authority" to enter and search "any ship or vessel, in which they shall have reason to suspect any goods, wares or merchandise subject to duty shall be concealed * * *." The historical importance of the enactment of this customs statute by the same Congress which proposed the Fourth Amendment is, we think, manifest. * * *

* * *

Border searches, then, from before the adoption of the Fourth Amendment, have been considered to be "reasonable" by the single fact that the person or item in question had entered into our country from outside. There has never been any additional requirement that the reasonableness of a border search depended on the existence of probable cause. This longstanding recognition that searches at our borders without probable cause and without a warrant are nonetheless "reasonable" has a history as old as the Fourth Amendment itself. We reaffirm it now.

The defendant in *Ramsey* argued that the border search doctrine should not apply to international *mail*, because it is not carried across the border by a traveler. But Justice Rehnquist found nothing special about mail when it crosses the border into the United States.

The border-search exception is grounded in the recognized right of the sovereign to control, subject to substantive limitations imposed by the Constitution, who and what may enter the country. It is clear that there is nothing in the rationale behind the border-search exception which suggests that the mode of entry will be critical. It was conceded at oral argument that customs officials could search, without probable cause and without a warrant, envelopes carried by an entering traveler, whether in his luggage or on his person. Surely no different constitutional standard should apply simply because the envelopes were mailed, not carried. The critical fact is that the envelopes cross the border and enter this country, not that they are brought in by one mode of transportation rather than another. It is their entry into this country from without it that makes a resulting search "reasonable."

Justice Stevens, joined by Justices Brennan and Marshall, dissented in *Ramsey*, arguing that Congress did not confer authority to open letters without probable cause. Justice Powell wrote a concurring opinion.

### *"Routine" Border Searches*

The court in United States v. Charleus, 871 F.2d 265 (2d Cir.1989), states that "routine border searches of the personal belongings and effects of entrants may be conducted without regard to probable cause or reasonable suspicion." Such searches are deemed reasonable because of the important state interest involved in regulating the border, the diminished expectation of privacy attendant to crossing the border, and the relatively limited intrusiveness of a "routine" border search. Does the lesser expectation of privacy in luggage carried into the country justify warrantless border searches, or does the existence of such searches reduce one's expectation of privacy?

While suspicionless border searches are generally reasonable, it is possible that "the rule as to nonroutine border searches is, however, different." United States v. Robles, 45 F.3d 1 (1st Cir.1995). Because they are more intrusive, "non-routine" border searches must be supported by some level of individualized suspicion.

In the following case, the Supreme Court criticizes the use of the labels "routine" and "non-routine"—at least as applied to searches of vehicles—and finds a relatively unusual search to be reasonable even in the absence of suspicion.

### UNITED STATES V. FLORES-MONTANO
Supreme Court of the United States, 2004.
541 U.S. 149.

**CHIEF JUSTICE REHNQUIST delivered the opinion of the Court.**

Customs officials seized 37 kilograms—a little more than 81 pounds—of marijuana from respondent Manuel Flores-Montano's gas tank at the international border. The Court of Appeals for the Ninth Circuit * * * held that the Fourth Amendment forbade the fuel tank search absent reasonable suspicion. We hold that the search in question did not require reasonable suspicion.

Respondent, driving a 1987 Ford Taurus station wagon, attempted to enter the United States at the Otay Mesa Port of Entry in southern California. A customs inspector conducted an inspection of the station wagon, and requested respondent to leave the vehicle. The vehicle was then taken to a secondary inspection station.

At the secondary station, a second customs inspector inspected the gas tank by tapping it, and noted that the tank sounded solid.

Subsequently, the inspector requested a mechanic under contract with Customs to come to the border station to remove the tank. Within 20 to 30 minutes, the mechanic arrived. He raised the car on a hydraulic lift, loosened the straps and unscrewed the bolts holding the gas tank to the undercarriage of the vehicle, and then disconnected some hoses and electrical connections. After the gas tank was removed, the inspector hammered off bondo (a putty-like hardening substance that is used to seal openings) from the top of the gas tank. The inspector opened an access plate underneath the bondo and found 37 kilograms of marijuana bricks. The process took 15 to 25 minutes.

\* \* \*

The Government advised the District Court that it was not relying on reasonable suspicion as a basis for denying respondent's suppression motion \* \* \*.

\* \* \* [T]he Court of Appeals \* \* \* asked whether the removal and dismantling of the defendant's fuel tank is a "routine" border search for which no suspicion whatsoever is required. The Court of Appeals stated that "in order to conduct a search that goes beyond the routine, an inspector must have reasonable suspicion," and the "critical factor" in determining whether a search is "routine" is the "degree of intrusiveness."

The Court of Appeals seized on language from our opinion in United States v. Montoya de Hernandez, 473 U.S. 531 (1985), in which we used the word "routine" as a descriptive term in discussing border searches. ("Routine searches of the persons and effects of entrants are not subject to any requirement of reasonable suspicion, probable cause, or warrant"). The Court of Appeals took the term "routine," fashioned a new balancing test, and extended it to searches of vehicles. But the reasons that might support a requirement of some level of suspicion in the case of highly intrusive searches of the person—dignity and privacy interests of the person being searched—simply do not carry over to vehicles. Complex balancing tests to determine what is a "routine" search of a vehicle, as opposed to a more "intrusive" search of a person, have no place in border searches of vehicles.

The Government's interest in preventing the entry of unwanted persons and effects is at its zenith at the international border. Time and again, we have stated that "searches made at the border, pursuant to the longstanding right of the sovereign to protect itself by stopping and examining persons and property crossing into this country, are reasonable simply by virtue of the fact that they occur at the border." United States v. Ramsey. \* \* \* It is axiomatic that the United States, as sovereign, has the inherent authority to protect, and a paramount interest in protecting, its territorial integrity.

That interest in protecting the borders is illustrated in this case by the evidence that smugglers frequently attempt to penetrate our borders with contraband secreted in their automobiles' fuel tank. Over the past 5 1/2 fiscal years, there have been 18,788 vehicle drug seizures at the southern California ports of entry. Of those 18,788, gas tank drug seizures have accounted for 4,619 of the vehicle drug seizures, or approximately 25%. In addition, instances of persons smuggled in and around gas tank compartments are discovered at the ports of entry of San Ysidro and Otay Mesa at a rate averaging 1 approximately every 10 days.

Respondent asserts two main arguments with respect to his Fourth Amendment interests. First, he urges that he has a privacy interest in his fuel tank, and that the suspicionless disassembly of his tank is an invasion of his privacy. But on many occasions, we have noted that the expectation of privacy is less at the border than it is in the interior. We have long recognized that automobiles seeking entry into this country may be searched. It is difficult to imagine how the search of a gas tank, which should be solely a repository for fuel, could be more of an invasion of privacy than the search of the automobile's passenger compartment.

Second, respondent argues that the Fourth Amendment "protects property as well as privacy," and that the disassembly and reassembly of his gas tank is a significant deprivation of his property interest because it may damage the vehicle. He does not, and on the record cannot, truly contend that the procedure of removal, disassembly, and reassembly of the fuel tank in this case or any other has resulted in serious damage to, or destruction of, the property.[a] According to the Government, for example, in fiscal year 2003, 348 gas tank searches conducted along the southern border were negative (*i.e.*, no contraband was found), the gas tanks were reassembled, and the vehicles continued their entry into the United States without incident.

Respondent cites not a single accident involving the vehicle or motorist in the many thousands of gas tank disassemblies that have occurred at the border. A gas tank search involves a brief procedure that can be reversed without damaging the safety or operation of the vehicle. If damage to a vehicle were to occur, the motorist might be entitled to recovery. While the interference with a motorist's possessory interest is not insignificant when the Government removes, disassembles, and

---

[a] Respondent's reliance on cases involving exploratory drilling searches is misplaced. See United States v. Rivas, 157 F.3d 364 (CA5 1998) (drilling into body of trailer required reasonable suspicion); United States v. Robles, 45 F.3d 1 (CA1 1995) (drilling into machine part required reasonable suspicion); United States v. Carreon, 872 F.2d 1436 (CA10 1989) (drilling into camper required reasonable suspicion). We have no reason at this time to pass on the reasonableness of drilling, but simply note the obvious factual difference that this case involves the procedure of removal, disassembly, and reassembly of a fuel tank, rather than potentially destructive drilling. We again leave open the question "whether, and under what circumstances, a border search might be deemed 'unreasonable' because of the particularly offensive manner it is carried out." United States v. Ramsey.

reassembles his gas tank, it nevertheless is justified by the Government's paramount interest in protecting the border.[b]

For the reasons stated, we conclude that the Government's authority to conduct suspicionless inspections at the border includes the authority to remove, disassemble, and reassemble a vehicle's fuel tank. While it may be true that some searches of property are so destructive as to require a different result, this was not one of them. The judgment of the United States Court of Appeals for the Ninth Circuit is therefore reversed, and the case is remanded for further proceedings consistent with this opinion.

It is so ordered.

**JUSTICE BREYER, concurring.**

I join the Court's opinion in full. I also note that Customs keeps track of the border searches its agents conduct, including the reasons for the searches. This administrative process should help minimize concerns that gas tank searches might be undertaken in an abusive manner.

### QUESTIONS AFTER FLORES-MONTANO

The Court dropped a footnote in *Flores-Montano* indicating that it was leaving open whether drilling into a vehicle would be reasonable without suspicion of any crime or violation. Lower courts after *Flores-Montano* have taken that footnote as an invitation to uphold suspicionless drilling and other types of destruction of property at the border. For example, United States v. Chaudhry, 424 F.3d 1051 (9th Cir. 2005), the court upheld a suspicionless border search that included drilling a hole in the bed of a pickup truck. Relying on *Flores-Montano,* the court declared that "a single small diameter hole in a truck bed does not reduce the functionality, operation or safety of the vehicle." The defendant cited cases from other circuits holding that drilling requires reasonable suspicion, but the court noted that all of those cases were decided before *Flores-Montano,* and all of them relied on "the distinction between 'routine' and 'non-routine' searches, a distinction that was specifically limited to searches of the person by the Supreme Court." See also United States v. Cortez-Rocha, 383 F.3d 1093 (9th Cir. 2004) (border search of defendant's vehicle, which included cutting open the defendant's spare tire, did not require reasonable suspicion: "the search of the spare tire,

---

[b] Respondent also argued that he has some sort of Fourth Amendment right not to be subject to delay at the international border and that the need for the use of specialized labor, as well as the hour actual delay here and the potential for even greater delay for reassembly are an invasion of that right. Respondent points to no cases indicating the Fourth Amendment shields entrants from inconvenience or delay at the international border.

The procedure in this case took about an hour (including the wait for the mechanic). At oral argument, the Government advised us that, depending on the type of car, a search involving the disassembly and reassembly of a gas tank may take one to two hours. We think it clear that delays of one to two hours at international borders are to be expected.

which neither damages the vehicle nor decreases the safety of operation of the vehicle, is not so destructive as to be unreasonable").

In *Flores-Montano,* the government "advised the District Court that it was not relying on reasonable suspicion as a basis for denying respondent's suppression motion." This was so even though the defendant avoided eye contact during questioning at the border, his hands were shaking when he produced identification, the agent tapped on the gas tank and noticed that it sounded solid, and a narcotics detection dog alerted on the vehicle. Despite having an excellent case of reasonable suspicion on the facts, the government argued for the broader point that dismantling a gas tank is reasonable at the border, in all cases, even if a car is plucked at random or at the officer's whim. This appears to be a regular tactic that the government has been taking with border searches, i.e., arguing that actions like drilling and dismantling can be done without suspicion, rather than arguing that there is in fact reasonable suspicion in the particular case. This litigation position was criticized by Judge Fletcher in United States v. Chaudhry, 424 F.3d 1051 (9th Cir. 2005), a case in which she concurred in the court's holding that drilling a hole in a flat bed of a pickup truck was permissible without any suspicion. Judge Fletcher expressed her concern about the government's litigation strategy as follows:

> I write separately to express my distaste for the government's game-playing in this case and in two others we heard on the same calendar. In each case there was reasonable and articulable suspicion of drug smuggling. But the government wanted confirmation that no suspicion is required for extensive, intrusive searches at the border. This would have an ancillary benefit for the government—it would not have to prove the reliability of its drug sniffing dogs.

> As a practical matter, border agents are too busy to do extensive searches (removing gas tanks and door panels, boring holes in truck beds) unless they have suspicion. Apparently no suspicionless search case has come along to allow the issue—how destructive and extensive a suspicionless search may be—to be presented in its pure form. So the government seized upon cases where there have been extensive searches based on clearly reasonable, articulable suspicion. In these cases, the government refuses to present evidence to support the suspicion. It prefers to test the limits of its right to search beyond what it can see (by drilling holes, removing gas tanks, etc.) without any suspicion whatsoever.

> \* \* \*

> I see two problems with such an approach to litigation. First, such appeals are essentially a request for an advisory opinion, as the dispute over whether or not a particular search may be conducted in the absence of any suspicion is an entirely fictional construct. \* \* \* The only possible purposes are the government's desire to push the envelope to its limits: to find out just how much destruction it can do without any suspicion,

and to avoid proving it uses reliable dogs. Second, because there is ample suspicion in each case, it is difficult for judges to consider the issue cleanly on an unencumbered record. Evidence of probable criminal activity, especially evidence of narcotics detector dog alerts, cannot help but color judges' views of the facts. We inevitably think "harmless error." I must admit that I take comfort in knowing that the border agents in these cases did not rip apart the defendants' cars on a whim. However, were I to decide a case where there is truly no suspicion, and where five or ten exploratory holes are drilled in the exterior walls of a vehicle, I might reach a different result.

### Border Searches of Ship Cabins

In United States v. Alfaro-Moncada, 607 F.3d 720 (11th Cir. 2010), the defendant was a crew member of a foreign cargo ship that entered the port of Miami. Customs and Border protection officials conducted a search, primarily, for prohibited agricultural materials, including seeds. They inspected the ship from bow to stern—this included a thorough inspection of the cabin of the ship's cook—Alfaro-Moncada. An officer searched the defendant's desk in his cabin and found DVD's, the covers of which showed young girls engaging in sexual acts. The defendant was tried and convicted of child pornography and argued that the search amounted to a search of his *home*, and therefore required reasonable suspicion. But the court disagreed, and noted that the interests supporting a suspicionless border search were fully implicated in this case:

> A home with a fixed location cannot be used as a means to transport into this country contraband or other weapons of mass destruction that threaten national security. A crew member's cabin, like the rest of the ship on which it is located, can and does pose that threat.

* * *

> Stopping agricultural pest and diseases from entering this country is an essential function of homeland security; when they have come across our borders, extensive damage has resulted. [Citing reports of infestation of the Asian longhorned beetle and the emerald ash borer, which led to the destruction of millions of trees.]

Do you think the Customs/Border agent was looking for seeds and bugs in Alfaro-Mancado's desk? Does it make any difference if that answer to that question is no?

### Border Searches and Seizures of Persons

The Court addressed the question of the appropriate standard of proof for highly intrusive border intrusions in United States v. Montoya de Hernandez, 473 U.S. 531 (1985). Justice Rehnquist, writing for a six-person majority, stated that "the detention of a traveler at the border, beyond the scope of a routine customs search and inspection, is justified at its inception if customs agents, considering all the facts surrounding the traveler and her trip, *reasonably suspect* that the traveler is smuggling contraband in her alimentary canal." (emphasis added).

Montoya de Hernandez went through customs in Los Angeles after arriving on a plane from Colombia. Her eight recent trips to either Miami or Los Angeles caused agents to question her about the purpose for her trip. She carried $5,000 cash, mostly $50 bills, with no billfold and stated that she came to purchase goods for her husband's store in Colombia. Although she had no appointments with sellers and no hotel reservation, she stated that she planned to ride around the city visiting retail stores and that she planned to stay at a Holiday Inn. She could not recall how her airline ticket was purchased. In her valise inspectors found four changes of "cold weather" clothing.

These facts, the Court held, were sufficient to warrant seasoned inspectors in arriving at a reasonable suspicion that Montoya de Hernandez was a "balloon swallower" attempting to smuggle drugs into the country. A strip search by a female inspector revealed a fullness in the suspect's abdomen. The inspector noticed that the suspect was wearing two pair of elastic underpants with a paper towel lining the crotch area. Upon receiving this information, the inspector in charge informed the suspect of his suspicion. The inspector gave her the option of returning to Colombia on the next available flight, agreeing to an x-ray or remaining in detention until she produced a monitored bowel movement. She chose the first option, but inspectors were unable to arrange a flight. Sixteen hours later, the suspect had not defecated or urinated and had refused food or drink. It appeared that she was struggling to avoid use of the toilet. Inspectors sought and obtained a warrant authorizing a rectal examination and x-ray, provided that the physician consider the suspect's claim of pregnancy. A pregnancy test was negative, and a rectal examination produced a balloon containing a foreign substance. Investigators arrested the suspect. She later passed 88 cocaine-filled balloons through her system.

The Supreme Court upheld both the initial inspection and the detention, finding that the delay was attributable to the suspect's "heroic" efforts "to resist the call of nature" and that the detention was not unreasonably long even though it "undoubtedly exceed[ed] any other detention we have approved under reasonable suspicion." Justice

Rehnquist emphasized not only the suspect-created delay, but also the heavy state interest and diminished expectation of privacy attendant to a border crossing. He noted that "alimentary canal smuggling cannot be detected in the amount of time in which other illegal activity may be investigated through brief *Terry*-type stops." Justice Stevens concurred in the judgment on the ground that the prolonged detention was attributable to the suspect's choice not to consent to an x-ray. Justice Brennan, joined by Justice Marshall, described the facts as a "disgusting and saddening episode" involving a detention based upon a profile that justified at most reasonable suspicion, and he dissented. He argued that "[i]ndefinite involuntary *incommunicado* detentions 'for investigation' are the hallmark of a police state, not a free society."

### Standard of Proof Between Probable Cause and Reasonable Suspicion?

The lower court in *Montoya* had found that the intrusion was so severe that it had to be justified by a "clear indication" of criminal activity. This was a standard of proof somewhere between reasonable suspicion and probable cause. In *Montoya,* the majority emphatically rejected this approach, and stated that as in *Terry,* there is no relevant standard of proof between reasonable suspicion and probable cause. Justice Rehnquist concluded as follows:

> We do not think that the Fourth Amendment's emphasis upon reasonableness is consistent with the creation of a third verbal standard in addition to reasonable suspicion and probable cause; * * * subtle verbal gradations may obscure rather than elucidate the meaning of the provision in question.

> The reasonable suspicion standard has been applied in a number of contexts and effects a needed balance between private and public interests when law enforcement officials must make a limited intrusion on less than probable cause.

After *Montoya,* there are apparently only two types of intrusions at the border—a "routine" border intrusion that can be done without suspicion, and a "non-routine" border intrusion that requires reasonable suspicion. It could be argued that some intrusions at the border could be so severe as to require probable cause, but given the facts of *Montoya* and the state interest supporting border searches, can you envision such an intrusion? Perhaps compelled surgery? See United States v. Adekunle, 2 F.3d 559 (5th Cir.1993) (reasonable suspicion sufficient for 100 hour incommunicado detention, forced use of laxatives, and monitored bowel movement); United States v. Odofin, 929 F.2d 56 (2d Cir.1991) (24 day detention before bowel movement; reasonable suspicion sufficient).

Depending on their intrusiveness, searches of *persons* at the border can fall on either side of the line the courts have established between "routine" and "non-routine" border searches—the latter requiring reasonable suspicion, the former requiring no suspicion at all. For example, in United States v. Sanders, 663 F.2d 1 (2d Cir.1981), customs officials forced the defendant to take off his artificial leg and inspected it, finding drugs. The court likened the police activity to a body cavity search, well-recognized as more intrusive than the routine border search. See also United States v. Alfaro-Moncada, 607 F.3d 720 (11th Cir. 2010) ("Even at the border, * * * reasonable suspicion is required for highly intrusive searches of a person's body such as a strip search or an x-ray examination."). In contrast, in United States v. Charleus, 871 F.2d 265 (2d Cir.1989), a customs inspector patted down the defendant, felt a hard lump under his clothing, and lifted the back of his shirt, whereupon he found packages of narcotics taped to the defendant's body. The court analyzed the intrusion as follows:

> The [intrusion] arguably straddles the line between the two categories of border searches—searching more than personal belongings or effects such as a purse, wallet, or even outer jacket was involved; but the search was not nearly as intrusive as a body cavity or full strip search. Since the potential indignity resulting from a pat on the back followed by a lifting of one's shirt simply fails to compare with the much greater level of intrusion associated with a body cavity or full strip search, we decline to hold that reasonable suspicion was here required.

See also United States v. Kelly, 302 F.3d 291 (5th Cir. 2002) (canine sniff of a person, including contact with the dog's nose, was a routine border search: "Certainly, a canine sniff, even one involving some bodily contact, is no more intrusive than a frisk or a pat-down, both of which clearly qualify as routine border searches.").

### *Border Searches of Laptops, Video Cameras, Reading Material, etc.*

If you are carrying a laptop across the border into the United States, can an officer—without having any suspicion—turn on the laptop and peruse all the material on the harddrive or SSD? The court in United States v. Ickes, 393 F.3d 501 (4th Cir. 2005), upheld such an inspection as a routine border search. Ickes's van was stopped at a border checkpoint. Officers first turned on Ickes's video camera and saw that he had taken a video of a young ball boy at a tennis match. They then conducted a thorough inspection of his laptop harddrive and computer disks that were in his car. Officers found child pornography and Ickes moved to suppress the evidence. Ickes raised both a Fourth and a First amendment objection

# To Apply or Not Apply the
## WARRANT CLAUSE

to the search. The court quickly disposed of the Fourth Amendment claim, holding that the search was no more intrusive than any other search of a person's effects at the border: such thorough inspections are allowed without suspicion, and there was nothing approaching a strip search or body cavity search that could be labeled "non-routine." As to the First Amendment argument, the court declared as follows:

> [T]he ramifications of accepting Ickes's First Amendment argument would be quite staggering. * * * Particularly in today's world, national security interests may require uncovering terrorist communications, which are inherently "expressive." Following Ickes's logic would create a sanctuary at the border for all expressive material—even for terrorist plans. This would undermine the compelling reasons that lie at the very heart of the border search doctrine. Ickes's argument, at bottom, proves too much.

* * *

> Ickes claims that our ruling is sweeping. He warns that "any person carrying a laptop computer . . . on an international flight would be subject to a search of the files on the computer hard drive." This prediction seems far-fetched. Customs agents have neither the time nor the resources to search the contents of every computer.

For other cases allowing thorough border searches of expressive material without any suspicion, see United States v. Arnold, 533 F.3d 1003 (9th Cir. 2008) (search of laptop without suspicion was reasonable; laptop is nothing more than a container and courts "have long held that searches of closed containers and their contents can be conducted at the border without particularized suspicion"); United States v. Seljan, 547 F.3d 993 (9th Cir. 2008) (suspicionless border search of personal correspondence—revealing sexual misconduct with young children—found reasonable).

In *Seljan, supra,* Judge Kozinski, in dissent, provided a passionate argument against a rule allowing police unfettered discretion to peruse reading and viewing material in a border search. He argued that the majority, in allowing such a practice, failed to give due weight to the language and history of the Fourth Amendment:

> The Fourth Amendment guarantees "[t]he right of the people to be secure in their persons, houses, *papers,* and effects. . . ." The reference to papers is not an accident; it's not a scrivener's error. It reflects the Founders' deep concern with safeguarding the privacy of thoughts and ideas—what we might call freedom of conscience—from invasion by the government. Because my colleagues in the majority don't see this right as very important, they authorize the government to read every scrap of paper that crosses our borders, whether in a pocket or purse, a package, suitcase or envelope. * * *

[T]he Founders were as concerned with invasions of the mind as with those of the body, the home or personal property—which is why they gave papers equal rank in the Fourth Amendment litany. The sum and substance of today's opinion is that we remove papers as an independent sphere of constitutional protection, treating them simply as a species of effects. Because our commission as federal judges does not authorize us to blue-pencil words written by the Founding Fathers, I respectfully dissent.

The majority in *Seljan* relied heavily on *Ramsey, supra,* where the Court upheld the suspicionless search of mail crossing the border. But Judge Kozinski declared that *Ramsey* was readily distinguishable, because *Ramsey* involved mail that included heroin—it "did not involve *reading* anything within the envelopes" and the *Ramsey* Court treated mailed envelopes as effects "because they were simply containers being used for smuggled items."

Judge Kozinski noted that the bedrock cases giving rise to the Fourth Amendment—the libel case involving John Wilkes and the seizure and search of papers in Entick v. Carrington—involved expressive material, and concluded as follows:

The majority's reluctance to step between Mr. Seljan and his well-merited punishment is understandable. Seljan's long career of "sexually educating" children is heinous; it's difficult to regret that he will spend the rest of his life in prison. But this result comes at a high price: allowing serious invasions into the privacy of millions of Americans, innocent as well as guilty. * * *  Every envelope containing birthday cards or trade secrets, every e-mail, every diary, every laptop that crosses the border can be opened and its contents read by government agents, without a warrant or even founded suspicion. Worse yet, by treating these seizures as a trivial annoyance rather than a major intrusion into our freedom of thought, my colleagues open the door for police across the United States to read whatever private papers fall into their hands. This is the power the English government claimed in the Wilkes affair; the power that so outraged the colonists; the power the Fourth Amendment was built to shield us against. We sell this birthright very cheaply today.

Is Judge Kozinski overreacting? How likely is it that Homeland Security will pore over all the reading material of every person crossing the border. They could never hire enough agents to do that, could they? Could they decide to copy all reading material and use Internet cloud storage to be able to access it should they desire to do so?

For more on border seizures and searches of laptops, cellphones, etc., see www.wired.com/threatlevel/2013/02/electronics-border-seizures:

The Department of Homeland Security's civil rights watchdog has concluded that travelers along the nation's borders may have their electronics seized and the contents of those devices examined for any reason whatsoever—all in the name of national security.

The DHS, which secures the nation's border, in 2009 announced that it would conduct a "Civil Liberties Impact Assessment" of its suspicionless search-and-seizure policy pertaining to electronic devices "within 120 days." More than three years later, the DHS office of Civil Rights and Civil Liberties published a two-page executive summary of its findings.

"We also conclude that imposing a requirement that officers have reasonable suspicion in order to conduct a border search of an electronic device would be operationally harmful without concomitant civil rights/civil liberties benefits," the executive summary said.

The President George W. Bush administration first announced the suspicionless, electronics search rules in 2008. The President Barack Obama administration followed up with virtually the same rules a year later. Between 2008 and 2010, 6,500 persons had their electronic devices searched along the U.S. border, according to DHS data.

\* \* \*

Meantime, a lawsuit the ACLU brought on the issue concerns a New York man whose laptop was seized along the Canadian border in 2010 and returned 11 days later after his attorney complained.

At an Amtrak inspection point, Pascal Abidor showed his U.S. passport to a federal agent. He was ordered to move to the cafe car, where they removed his laptop from his luggage and "ordered Mr. Abidor to enter his password," according to the lawsuit.

Agents asked him about pictures they found on his laptop, which included Hamas and Hezbollah rallies. He explained that he was earning a doctoral degree at a Canadian university on the topic of the modern history of Shiites in Lebanon.

He was handcuffed and then jailed for three hours while the authorities looked through his computer while numerous agents questioned him, according to the suit, which is pending in New York federal court.

### Searches Away from the Border

The right to search at the actual border has been extended to its functional equivalent as well. For example, if a plane flies from Mexico City non-stop to Denver, a search by customs officials at the Denver airport is considered a border search. The same standard applies to searches of ships, where the port of call is not at the border itself. United States v. Tilton, 534 F.2d 1363 (9th Cir.1976). In Torres v. Puerto Rico, 442 U.S. 465 (1979), the Court unanimously agreed that a trip from the mainland to Puerto Rico did not result in the crossing of an *international* border and that the border search exception to the warrant requirement did not apply.

A more troubling problem has arisen in connection with searches of vehicles inside the border, pursuant to § 287(a) of the Immigration and Nationality Act [8 U.S.C.A. § 1357(a)], which allows searches for aliens "within a reasonable distance from any external boundary of the United States." A reasonable distance has been defined as 100 air miles from any external border, 8 CFR § 287.1. The Court in United States v. Martinez-Fuerte, 428 U.S. 543, 552–53 (1976), described the kinds of searches that were implemented pursuant to this legislation:

> The Border Patrol conducts three kinds of inland traffic-checking operations in an effort to minimize illegal immigration. Permanent checkpoints, such as those at San Clemente and Sarita, are maintained at or near intersections of important roads leading away from the border. They operate on a coordinated basis designed to avoid circumvention by smugglers and others who transport the illegal aliens. Temporary checkpoints, which operate like permanent ones, occasionally are established in other strategic locations. Finally, roving patrols are maintained to supplement the checkpoint system.

Beginning with Almeida-Sanchez v. United States, 413 U.S. 266 (1973), the Supreme Court decided a series of cases challenging the constitutionality of these law enforcement efforts in border areas. In *Almeida-Sanchez* the defendant was stopped by a roving Border Patrol on an east-west road in California about 25 air miles north of the Mexican border. The officers had no warrant and no suspicion for stopping the car. The officers searched the defendant's vehicle for illegal aliens, discovering instead a large quantity of marijuana. The Court held the stop and search unconstitutional. In a 5–4 decision, Justice Stewart wrote for the majority that a roving patrol away from the border was regulated by the same standards as any other police activity—meaning that suspicionless seizures and searches were not permitted. Justice White's dissent found the search to be a reasonable response to the unique problems of enforcing immigration laws in border areas. See also United States v. Brignoni-Ponce, 422 U.S. 873 (1975), holding that roving border patrols are subject to the same standards as other law enforcement stops under *Terry*.

The use of traffic checkpoints removed from the border also came under scrutiny. In United States v. Ortiz, 422 U.S. 873 (1975), warrantless *searches* at *internal* checkpoints were held unconstitutional unless based on probable cause. The Court found that, at least insofar as searches were concerned, the risk of official abuse of discretion was just as great at a checkpoint as it was at a roving patrol; officers at checkpoints decided which cars to search, and only 3% of the vehicles that were stopped were also searched.

The following year, the Court approved warrantless *stops* of vehicles at *permanent checkpoints* for limited questioning of the occupants. United States v. Martinez-Fuerte, 428 U.S. 543 (1976). No probable cause or reasonable suspicion was required to justify the stops. The Court reasoned that suspicionless checkpoint stops are necessary tools of law enforcement, and that the public interest in making these stops outweighed the constitutionally protected interests of private citizens. In addition, Justice Powell, writing for the Court, stated that motorists could be selectively referred to secondary inspection areas for further questioning, again without any articulable suspicion. He argued that the additional intrusion—although admittedly a seizure—was limited and inoffensive and that use of the questioning techniques tended to minimize the intrusion on the general motoring public, thus protecting other Fourth Amendment interests. However, if the secondary inspection was unduly offensive or intrusive, then individualized suspicion would be required. See also United States v. Machuca-Barrera, 261 F.3d 425 (5th Cir. 2001) (stop at immigration checkpoint can last no longer than necessary to fulfil its immigration-related purpose).

## I.   CONSENT SEARCHES

### 1.   Voluntary Consent

#### *Voluntariness Distinguished from Waiver:*
#### *Schneckloth v. Bustamonte*

A search based upon voluntary consent is reasonable even in the absence of a warrant or any articulable suspicion. The Supreme Court addressed the requirements for valid consent in Schneckloth v. Bustamonte, 412 U.S. 218 (1973). A California police officer at 2:40 a.m. stopped an automobile with a headlight and a license plate light burned out. Six men were in the car. The driver had no license, only one passenger produced his license, and he explained that the car was his brother's. The officer asked the men to step out of the car, they complied, and after two additional officers arrived, the officer asked the person who produced the license if he could search the car. The man replied, "Sure, go ahead," and opened the trunk for the officer. The search produced three stolen checks. The court of appeals held that consent was not valid because the consenting party was never told that he had the right to refuse to give consent. The Supreme Court disagreed.

Justice Stewart's majority opinion cited voluntariness concepts developed in confession cases and concluded that

> the question whether a consent to a search was in fact voluntary or was the product of duress or coercion, express or implied, is a question of fact to be determined from the totality of the circumstances. While knowledge of the right to refuse consent is one factor to be taken into account, the government need not establish such knowledge as the sine qua non of an effective consent.

The defendant argued that warnings of the right to refuse to permit a search—comparable to the *Miranda* warnings, which we shall examine in connection with police interrogation—should be required before consent can be sought. The majority responded that it would be impractical to give such warnings under the "informal and unstructured conditions" in which consent requests are usually made.

Justice Stewart distinguished the traditional concept of waiver of "the safeguards of a fair criminal trial" from consent to search. He concluded that a defendant was to be given "the greatest possible opportunity to utilize every facet of the constitutional model of a fair criminal trial," and that "[a]ny trial conducted in derogation of that model leaves open the possibility that the trial reached an unfair result." But, he found, that "[t]he protections of the Fourth Amendment are of a wholly different order." Justice Stewart concluded that the proper test in consent search cases is not whether there was a waiver of the defendant's Fourth Amendment rights, but whether the consent to search was voluntary under the totality of circumstances. He concluded that the Fourth Amendment does not require that citizens be discouraged from cooperating with the police—which would occur if they were required to be informed of their right to refuse.

The Court concluded that voluntariness of consent must be determined by the totality of the circumstances. The suspect's knowledge of his right to refuse consent is therefore relevant in determining the voluntariness of the consent. But absence of a consent warning is not dispositive.

As applied to the facts of the case, Justice Stewart had no trouble in concluding that the suspect's consent was voluntary—the suspect was not under arrest; the officer used no force and made no threats; and the suspect expressed no unwillingness to consent.

Justice Brennan dissented, arguing that "[i]t wholly escapes me how our citizens can meaningfully be said to have waived something as precious as a constitutional guarantee without ever being aware of its existence." Justice Marshall also dissented. He argued that consent searches are permissible because we permit our citizens to choose not to exercise their constitutional rights, and that "consent cannot be considered a meaningful choice unless he knew that he could in fact exclude the police." His solution was to have the government bear the burden of showing knowledge, which burden could be satisfied by a warning before asking for consent.

### Reaffirming Schneckloth: United States v. Drayton

The Court reaffirmed its totality of the circumstances analysis in United States v. Drayton, 536 U.S. 194 (2002), in which the Court upheld searches of bags and persons made during a bus sweep. The Court found that while the officer did not inform the suspects of their right to refuse consent, "he did request permission to search, and the totality of the circumstances indicates that their consent was voluntary, so the searches were reasonable." The *Drayton* Court concluded as follows:

> In a society based on law, the concept of agreement and consent should be given a weight and dignity of its own. Police officers act in full accord with the law when they ask citizens for consent. It reinforces the rule of law for the citizen to advise the police of his or her wishes and for the police to act in reliance on that understanding. When this exchange takes place, it dispels inferences of coercion.

The Court's opinion in *Drayton* is fully set forth in the section on stops and frisks, supra. See also United States v. Collins, 683 F.3d 697 (6th Cir. 2012) (borrower of car validly consented to search—"when requesting an individual's consent to search, police do not have to inform the individual that others [in this case the owner of the car] could object to the search.").

### The Consequences of Refusing Consent

Is refusal to consent to a search suspicious? Can an officer conclude that a person who refuses to permit a search has something to hide? In United States v. Prescott, 581 F.2d 1343 (9th Cir.1978), the court held that a person cannot be penalized for exercising the right to refuse to permit a search, and that "passive refusal to consent to a warrantless search is privileged conduct which cannot be considered as evidence of criminal wrongdoing." The majority said that its reasoning was necessary "to protect the exercise of a constitutional right." Surprisingly, there was a dissenting opinion that argued that no harm would come if a citizen's decision to invoke Fourth Amendment rights were admissible in evidence against the citizen. See also United States v. Torres, 65 F.3d 1241 (4th Cir.1995) ("Officers cannot use a traveler's refusal to consent to the search of his bags as support for the requisite reasonable, articulable suspicion.").

### The Impact of Custody

In *Schneckloth*, consent was obtained from a person who was not in police custody, a fact emphasized by the Court in its conclusion that its decision was "a narrow one." But in United States v. Watson, 423 U.S. 411 (1976), the Court found that the absence of consent warnings or of proof that Watson knew he could withhold consent was not controlling where the defendant "had been arrested and was in custody, but his consent was given while on a public street, not in the confines of the police station." The majority added that "to hold that illegal coercion is made out from the fact of arrest and the failure to inform the arrestee that he could withhold consent would not be consistent with *Schneckloth*." *Watson* made clear that *Schneckloth* was not as narrow as Justice Stewart had proclaimed. Justice Marshall, joined by Justice Brennan, adhered to his opinion in *Schneckloth*, but added that "even short of this position there are valid reasons for application of such a rule to consents procured from suspects held in custody."

Not surprisingly, *Watson* has been relied upon to uphold consent obtained in all types of custodial situations; while the person's custodial status is relevant to whether the consent was voluntary, it is only one in the totality of circumstances. See, e.g., United States v. Hidalgo, 7 F.3d 1566 (11th Cir.1993) (consent voluntary even though the defendant "was arrested by SWAT team members who broke into his home in the early morning, woke him, and forced him to the ground at gun point"); United States v. Duran, 957 F.2d 499 (7th Cir.1992) (consent voluntary even though the suspect was under arrest and in the police station).

### Totality of the Circumstances

After *Schneckloth* the totality of the circumstances must be examined to determine whether a person has voluntarily consented to a search. In Bumper v. North Carolina, 391 U.S. 543 (1968), the Court placed the burden of proving that consent "was, in fact, freely and voluntarily given" on the government, and declared that "[t]his burden cannot be discharged by showing no more than acquiescence to a claim of lawful authority."

The Supreme Court applied *Schneckloth* and found a valid consent in United States v. Mendenhall, 446 U.S. 544 (1980). Officers encountered Mendenhall in an airport, suspected she was a drug courier, and asked her to accompany them to a private room. She agreed. After a series of polite questions, Mendenhall ultimately agreed to a strip search and a search of her purse. Narcotics were found in the purse and on her person. Although a majority of the Court did not agree on whether to treat

Mendenhall as "seized" when federal agents first approached her, a majority did agree that she voluntarily consented to accompany the agents to their airport office and to have her purse and person searched. In deciding that Mendenhall voluntarily accompanied the agents to their office, the Court observed that she was simply asked to go and was not threatened or physically forced. In deciding that the searches in the office were consensual, the Court emphasized that Mendenhall was twice told that she was free to decline consent. Justice White's dissent for four members of the Court argued that the government failed to meet its burden of proving that Mendenhall consented to accompany the officers to their office. "[T]he Court's conclusion can only be based on the notion that consent can be assumed from the absence of proof that a suspect resisted police authority. This is a notion that we have squarely rejected."

In United States v. Gonzalez-Basulto, 898 F.2d 1011 (5th Cir.1990), the court set forth a non-exclusive list of six factors relevant to whether consent is voluntarily obtained.

> (1) the voluntariness of the defendant's custodial status; (2) the presence of coercive police procedures; (3) the extent and level of the defendant's cooperation with the police; (4) the defendant's awareness of his right to refuse consent; (5) the defendant's education and intelligence; and (6) the defendant's belief that no evidence will be found.

Obviously, none of these factors are dispositive. For example, *Watson* found a consent voluntary even though the defendant was under arrest, and *Schneckloth* found voluntary consent even though the defendant was unaware of his right to refuse. However, a weak showing by the government on several of the factors substantially increases the likelihood that consent will be found involuntary.

The facts and resolution of *Gonzalez-Basulto,* supra, are typical of consent cases after *Schneckloth.* Border patrol agents at a permanent checkpoint suspected that Gonzalez-Basulto was carrying drugs in a refrigerated tractor-trailer rig. He was referred to a secondary inspection area to verify his claim that he was an American citizen. Gonzalez produced immigration documentation, and looked nervously about at the drug sniffing dogs present at the checkpoint. The agent asked whether Gonzalez would mind opening the trailer for an inspection. Gonzalez replied "no problem" and unlocked and opened the trailer, which contained boxes of oranges and lemons. A drug-sniffing dog was hoisted into the trailer, and gave a positive alert. The agents opened many boxes, and finally found cocaine in boxes near the front of the trailer. The court found that Gonzalez voluntarily consented to the search.

> The agents did not brandish weapons or threaten Gonzalez in any way. Gonzalez was not placed under arrest until the search

uncovered the cocaine. Gonzalez cooperated with the agent who requested permission to search by responding "no problem" to the request and by unlocking and opening the trailer doors. While the agent admitted that he did not inform Gonzalez of his right to refuse to consent, the agent emphasized that he did not put any kind of pressure on Gonzalez to get his consent. He merely asked for permission. Gonzalez was not well-educated but he exhibited a sufficient degree of understanding to indicate his "no problem" response was intelligent. Gonzalez may well have believed that no drugs would be found because the cocaine was hidden in boxes toward the front of the trailer and there was little crawl space in the trailer.

Compare United States v. Isiofia, 370 F.3d 226 (2d Cir. 2004) (consent not voluntary where the defendant was never informed of his right to refuse consent, the agents demanded consent, yelled at the defendant and used abusive language, and told him that he would be jailed and deported and never see his family again unless he consented to the search).

Consider the sixth factor discussed in *Gonzalez-Basulto,* i.e. the defendant's belief that no evidence would be found. In United States v. Mendenhall, *supra,* the Court categorically rejected the argument that Mendenhall could not have voluntarily consented to a strip search because it would disclose the drugs that she carried. The Court stated that, while the suspect may later regret having given consent, "the question is not whether she acted in her ultimate self-interest, but whether she acted voluntarily." Wouldn't the contrary view—that a person could not give voluntary consent if the search would be likely to uncover incriminating evidence—all but do away with consent searches?

### *Threats of Action if Consent Is Refused*

Suppose an officer says, "I would like you to consent, but if you don't, I'll just come back a little later with a warrant." Does this threat render a subsequent consent involuntary? The court considered this question in United States v. Duran, 957 F.2d 499 (7th Cir.1992), in which Karen Duran consented to the search of an outbuilding after officers told her that they would obtain a warrant if she didn't consent. The court stated:

> This may have induced Karen to grant her consent, but it was not coercive under the fourth amendment. Although empty threats to obtain a warrant may at times render a subsequent consent involuntary, see United States v. Talkington, 843 F.2d 1041 (7th Cir.1988) (consent invalid when police lied in telling suspect that they were in the process of getting a search warrant); Dotson v. Somers, 175 Conn. 614, 402 A.2d 790 (1978) (consent invalid where police had insufficient grounds upon which to base a warrant

application), the threat in this case was firmly grounded. Karen's admission that [her husband, the defendant] dealt marijuana would have provided the police probable cause had they sought a search warrant, so their threat to do so in the event she refused consent was entirely proper.

On the relevance of police threats of action, and the rationality of giving consent, consider United States v. Welch, 683 F.3d 1304 (9th Cir. 2012). Officers were conducting a lawful protective sweep and came upon Welch in his bedroom. The officers had guns drawn. They asked for consent to search the room and Welch said "no." One officer then said, "Fine, but we're going to have to get a search warrant." Welch said nothing. The officer then said, "it could take awhile." Welch then said "okay you can search." The search uncovered a gun and ammunition and Welch was charged with felon-firearm-possession. He argued that he had not voluntarily consented, but the court disagreed.

> The explicit threat here is that Welch might have to stand around with nothing to do for some substantial period of time, much as we all do whenever we are stuck in a line. It would be a delicate will indeed that might be overborne by the threat of a period of idleness and wasted time. Yet that threat, "it would take a while," is what changed Welch's "no" to a "yes."

> The district judge provided a persuasive explanation of why Welch changed his mind. Welch, the court found, "reasonably believed that the officers would eventually be able to obtain a search warrant" and that, because he would have to wait on the balcony while they did, he would not be able to go into the apartment, retrieve the pistol and ammunition, and somehow dispose of them before the police came back with a warrant. So "it made sense for [Welch] to agree to the search rather than wait for the warrant to be obtained and, because of where the items were hidden, hope for the best." That was a rational gamble, but one that Welch lost. Welch's consent was not coerced, just constrained, by having to place his bet on one of two poor alternatives. Maybe if he let them in, the police would want to get the search done quickly and fail to find his contraband. Or maybe if he put them to the trouble of getting a search warrant, they would search more thoroughly because he had inconvenienced them.

### Must a Person Who Is Stopped Be Told That He Is Free to Leave?: Ohio v. Robinette

In Ohio v. Robinette, 519 U.S. 33 (1996), Robinette was lawfully stopped for speeding and given a warning. After the officer returned his license, he asked Robinette: "One question before you get gone: Are you carrying any illegal contraband in your car? Any weapons of any kind, drugs, anything like that?" Robinette answered in the negative, and when the officer asked to search the car, Robinette consented. The officer found drugs in the car.

The state court held that Robinette's consent could not be voluntary because the officer never informed him that the stop had ended and he was free to go. The Court, in an opinion by Chief Justice Rehnquist for seven Justices, found no such bright-line requirement in the Fourth Amendment. The Chief Justice reasoned as follows:

> We have previously rejected a per se rule very similar to that adopted by the Supreme Court of Ohio in determining the validity of a consent to search. In Schneckloth v. Bustamonte, it was argued that such a consent could not be valid unless the defendant knew that he had a right to refuse the request. We rejected this argument: "While knowledge of the right to refuse consent is one factor to be taken into account, the government need not establish such knowledge as the sine qua non of an effective consent." And just as it "would be thoroughly impractical to impose on the normal consent search the detailed requirements of an effective warning," so too would it be unrealistic to require police officers to always inform detainees that they are free to go before a consent to search may be deemed voluntary.

Justice Ginsburg concurred in the judgment in *Robinette,* emphasizing that while a "tell-then-ask" rule made good sense, imposing it as a constitutional requirement was inconsistent with the totality of circumstances approach mandated by *Schneckloth.*

Justice Stevens dissented. He argued that, by asking whether Robinette had contraband, the officer was continuing the detention, even though the initial reason for the detention had ended. Justice Stevens concluded from this that the continued interrogation, in the absence of reasonable suspicion, constituted an illegal seizure, which tainted Robinette's consent.

### *Did the Person Consent?*

In some cases, the question is not whether the defendant consented voluntarily, but whether he consented at all. For example, in United States v. Price, 54 F.3d 342 (7th Cir.1995), Officer Brown stopped Pierce's car, became suspicious, and asked whether there were any drugs in the car. Pierce replied in the negative. Officer Brown then asked Pierce, "Do you mind if I take a look?" and Pierce quickly replied "Sure." Brown searched the car, and Pierce looked on without objection. Narcotics were discovered. At the suppression hearing, Pierce testified that when he said

"Sure" what he meant was "Sure, I *mind*." The court of appeals responded to this argument as follows:

> Perhaps in the abstract one could say that given the phrasing of Brown's question, Pierce's response to it is ambiguous and thus capable of being interpreted as either "Go ahead" or "No way." But * * * [t]he only conclusion to be drawn from the totality of the evidence is that Pierce's immediate response "Sure" meant, "Sure, go ahead." The crucial fact is Pierce's failure to protest upon learning that Brown understood his response as a consent to the search. Had Pierce not agreed to the search, now was the time to make that clear. Yet when confronted with Brown's understanding of his response, Pierce offered no objection at all; instead, he submitted to a pat-down search and took a seat in Brown's patrol car in order to get out of the rain. Given these circumstances it was not clear error for the district court to find that Pierce's response "Sure" meant that he agreed to the search.

Assume that you are in Pierce's situation and that you really mean "Sure, I mind," not "Sure, go ahead." What would your reaction be if Officer Brown ignores you and goes ahead with the search anyway? Would telling him to stop have a positive effect, do you think? See also United States v. Bautista, 362 F.3d 584 (9th Cir. 2004) (no consent where the occupant of a motel room opened the door after the police demanded entrance, and stepped back as officers proceeded into the room); United States v. Williams, 521 F.3d 902 (8th Cir. 2008) ("The precise question is not whether [the defendant] consented subjectively, but whether his conduct would have caused a reasonable person to believe that he consented.").

## 2.  Third Party Consent

Can a third party consent to the search of an area in which a suspect has an expectation of privacy? Frazier v. Cupp, 394 U.S. 731 (1969), upheld the search of a defendant's duffle bag when his cousin, a joint user of the bag, voluntarily consented. The Court rejected the argument that because the cousin had authority to use only one compartment of the bag, he could not consent to a search of the remainder, stating that it would not "engage in such metaphysical subtleties," and that the defendant, who allowed his cousin to use the bag, must "have assumed the risk" he would consent to let others see inside.

### *Actual Authority: United States v. Matlock*

The leading third-party consent case is United States v. Matlock, 415 U.S. 164 (1974). Matlock was arrested in the front yard of a house. Mrs. Graff admitted the police to the house and told them she shared the house with Matlock. She consented to a search. The Court found the search to be reasonable because Mrs. Graff had actual authority to consent to the search. The Court stated the rationale for permitting third-party consent searches in the following analysis:

> The authority which justifies the third-party consent does not rest upon the law of property, with its attendant historical and legal refinements, but rests rather on mutual use of the property by persons generally having joint access or control for most purposes, so that it is reasonable to recognize that any of the co-inhabitants has the right to permit the inspection in his own right and that the others have assumed the risk that one of their number might permit the common area to be searched.

See also United States v. Kimoana, 383 F.3d 1215 (10th Cir. 2004) (individual who had stayed overnight in a motel room, who left his possessions there, and who had a room key, had actual authority to consent to a search of the room, even though he was not the registered guest who paid for the room).

### Apparent Authority: Illinois v. Rodriguez

The Court in Illinois v. Rodriguez, 497 U.S. 177 (1990), considered whether a search is valid when based on the consent of a third party who has *apparent* but not *actual* authority. The third party in *Rodriguez* was Rodriguez's woman friend, who had, unknown to the officers, moved out of his apartment a month before the search and retained a key without permission. When speaking to the officers who were seeking consent, she referred to the premises as "our apartment" and opened the door with a key and let them in.

Justice Scalia, writing for a six-person majority, agreed with the lower courts that the friend did not have actual authority to consent to a search of the apartment, in that she had no joint access or control of the premises after moving out. According to the majority, however, the entry was valid if the officers had reasonable belief that the friend had authority to consent. The Court rejected the defendant's argument that permitting a search on the basis of apparent but not actual authority would amount to an unauthorized waiver of the defendant's Fourth Amendment rights. Justice Scalia relied on *Schneckloth* and distinguished between a waiver of constitutional rights and the voluntary consent to search. He explained that while a waiver of a constitutional right must be personal, the validity of a consent search is determined by whether the search is reasonable:

> We would assuredly not permit * * * evidence seized in violation of the Fourth Amendment to be introduced on the basis of a trial court's mere reasonable belief—derived from statements by unauthorized persons—that the defendant has waived his objection.

But one must make a distinction between, on the one hand, trial rights that derive from the violation of constitutional guarantees and, on the other hand, the nature of those constitutional guarantees themselves. * * *

What Rodriguez is assured by the trial right of the exclusionary rule, where it applies, is that no evidence seized in violation of the Fourth Amendment will be introduced at his trial unless he consents. What he is assured by the Fourth Amendment itself, however, is not that no government search of his house will occur unless he consents; but that no search will occur that is "unreasonable." * * *

Justice Scalia concluded that the question of authority to consent should be governed by the same standard of reasonableness—and allowance for reasonable mistakes—as had been applied in other areas of Fourth Amendment jurisprudence, such as probable cause, the execution of a warrant, and the existence of exigent circumstances. The Court remanded for a determination of whether the officers could have reasonably believed that Rodriguez's friend had actual authority to consent to a search of his apartment. Justice Marshall, joined by Justices Brennan and Stevens, dissented.

### Mistakes of Law

In Stoner v. California, 376 U.S. 483 (1964), the government argued that the officers relied on the apparent authority of the hotel desk clerk to consent to a search of Stoner's room. The Court rejected that argument, stating that "the rights protected by the Fourth Amendment are not to be eroded by unrealistic doctrines of apparent authority." Is the result and language in *Stoner* inconsistent with *Rodriguez?* Or can it be explained by the reasonableness standards that are applicable to third party consent searches? Is *Stoner* really an apparent authority case? See, e.g., United States v. Brown, 961 F.2d 1039 (2d Cir.1992) (stating that *Rodriguez* does not validate "a search premised upon an erroneous view of the law" and that "an investigator's erroneous belief that landladies are generally authorized to consent to a search of a tenant's premises could not provide the authorization necessary for a warrantless search").

### The Duty to Investigate Third Party Authority to Consent

Does *Rodriguez* mean that the police can presume third party consent upon the simple assertion of the third party that she has common authority? If a babysitter answers the door, and asserts that she has actually been granted authority over the entire premises, can police search the entire house upon the babysitter's consent? In United States v. Dearing, 9 F.3d 1428 (9th Cir.1993), the court held that a live-in babysitter lacked apparent authority to consent to a search of his employer's bedroom. The court declared that "the police are not allowed to proceed on the theory that ignorance is bliss," and concluded that the officer should have inquired into the extent of the babysitter's authorized access into his employer's bedroom. See also United States v. Kimoana, 383 F.3d 1215 (10th Cir. 2004) (government's burden of proving valid third party consent "cannot be met if agents, faced with an ambiguous situation, nevertheless proceed without making further inquiry").

### Third Party Consent Where the Defendant Is Present and Objecting: Georgia v. Randolph

In Georgia v. Randolph, 547 U.S. 103 (2006), Justice Souter wrote for the Court as it held that even though one occupant consents, a physically present co-occupant's stated refusal to permit entry prevails, rendering the warrantless search unreasonable and invalid as to him.

Randolph and his wife had separated, she moved away with their son, and returned to the home to get some belongings; thereafter she complained to the police that after a domestic dispute her husband took their son away, and when officers reached the house she told them that her husband was a cocaine user whose habit had caused financial troubles. She stated there was evidence of drugs in the house. Eventually officers went to the house and both Mr. and Mrs. Randolph answered the door. An officer asked for consent to search. Mr. Randolph unequivocally refused, but Mrs. Randolph readily gave consent. The police entered and found drugs.

Justice Souter wrote that "[t]he constant element in assessing Fourth Amendment reasonableness in the consent cases, * * * is the great significance given to widely shared social expectations, which are naturally enough influenced by the law of property, but not controlled by its rules." Looking to widely shared social expectations he reasoned as follows:

> [I]t is fair to say that a caller standing at the door of shared premises would have no confidence that one occupant's invitation was a sufficiently good reason to enter when a fellow tenant stood there saying, "stay out." Without some very good reason, no sensible person would go inside under those conditions. Fear for the safety of the occupant issuing the invitation, or of someone else inside, would be thought to justify entry, but the justification then would be the personal risk, the threats to life or limb, not the disputed invitation.

> The visitor's reticence without some such good reason would show not timidity but a realization that when people living together disagree over the use of their common quarters, a resolution must come through voluntary accommodation, not by appeals to authority. Unless the people living together fall within some recognized

hierarchy, like a household of parent and child or barracks housing military personnel of different grades, there is no societal understanding of superior and inferior. \* \* \* In sum, there is no common understanding that one co-tenant generally has a right or authority to prevail over the express wishes of another, whether the issue is the color of the curtains or invitations to outsiders.

Justice Souter explicitly stated that "this case has no bearing on the capacity of police to protect domestic victims" and "[t]he undoubted right of the police to enter in order to protect a victim, however, has nothing to do with the question in this case \* \* \*." At the end of his opinion, he noted the State did not argue exigent circumstances or that Janet Randolph gave any indication of a need for protection inside the house.

Justice Souter then considered the limits of a rule prohibiting entry on third party consent when the defendant is present and objecting:

> Although the *Matlock* defendant was not present with the opportunity to object, he was in a squad car not far away; the *Rodriguez* defendant was actually asleep in the apartment, and the police might have roused him with a knock on the door before they entered with only the consent of an apparent co-tenant. If those cases are not to be undercut by today's holding, we have to admit that we are drawing a fine line; if a potential defendant with self-interest in objecting is in fact at the door and objects, the co-tenant's permission does not suffice for a reasonable search, whereas the potential objector, nearby but not invited to take part in the threshold colloquy, loses out.

> This is the line we draw, and we think the formalism is justified. So long as there is no evidence that the police have removed the potentially objecting tenant from the entrance for the sake of avoiding a possible objection, there is practical value in the simple clarity of complementary rules, one recognizing the co-tenant's permission when there is no fellow occupant on hand, the other according dispositive weight to the fellow occupant's contrary indication when he expresses it. \* \* \* Better to accept the formalism of distinguishing *Matlock* from this case than to impose a requirement, time-consuming in the field and in the courtroom, with no apparent systemic justification.

Chief Justice Roberts, joined by Justice Scalia, dissented. He argued as follows:

> A wide variety of often subtle social conventions may shape expectations about how we act when another shares with us what is otherwise private, and those conventions go by a variety of labels— courtesy, good manners, custom, protocol, even honor among thieves. The Constitution, however, protects not these but privacy, and once

privacy has been shared, the shared information, documents, or places remain private only at the discretion of the confidant.

\* \* \*

Just as the source of the majority's rule is not privacy, so too the interest it protects cannot reasonably be described as such. That interest is not protected if a co-owner happens to be absent when the police arrive, in the backyard gardening, asleep in the next room, or listening to music through earphones so that only his co-occupant hears the knock on the door. That the rule is so random in its application confirms that it bears no real relation to the privacy protected by the Fourth Amendment. What the majority's rule protects is not so much privacy as the good luck of a co-owner who just happens to be present at the door when the police arrive. Usually when the development of Fourth Amendment jurisprudence leads to such arbitrary lines, we take it as a signal that the rules need to be rethought. We should not embrace a rule at the outset that its *sponsors* appreciate will result in drawing fine, formalistic lines.

The Chief Justice expressed the view that the decision would have serious consequences in domestic abuse situations because "[t]he majority's rule apparently forbids police from entering to assist with a domestic dispute if the abuser whose behavior prompted the request for police assistance objects." He opined that the majority's reliance on exigent circumstances "is a strange way to justify a rule, and the fact that alternative justifications for entry might arise does not show that entry pursuant to consent is unreasonable."

Justice Scalia and Justice Thomas also dissented. Justice Stevens and Breyer wrote concurring opinions. Justice Alito did not participate.

### NOTE ON RANDOLPH

After *Randolph,* what does it mean to be "present" and "objecting" at the time the third party consents to a search? On the question of "presence" the Supreme Court held, in Fernandez v. California, 134 S.Ct. 1126 (2014), that the defendant's wife's consent to search the premises was valid even though the defendant had objected to the search when the officers initially approached his apartment. At the time of that approach, officers saw that Fernandez's wife appeared to be battered and bleeding. They arrested Fernandez, then returned to the apartment and obtained consent from his wife. Justice Alito, writing for six members of the Court, declared that the Court in *Randolph* "went to great lengths to make clear that its holding was limited to situations in which the objecting occupant is present" at the time the consent search is conducted. The Court held that the officers were justified in removing Fernandez and that the *Randolph* rule could not apply where officers are "objectively reasonable" in removing the objector from the premises. The Court also rejected the defendant's argument that the objection he made while he *was* present was enough to bar third party consent at a later point when he was not. Justice Alito reasoned that the objection could not last forever, and to limit its duration to a "reasonable" time would create a host of practical problems and would be inconsistent with the bright line rule established in *Randolph*. Justice Ginsburg, joined by Justices Sotomayor and Kagan, dissented in *Fernandez*.

As to whether a defendant is *objecting* at the time third-party consent is given, see, e.g., United States v. Uscanga-Ramirez, 475 F.3d 1024 (8th Cir. 2007) (defendant denied that there was a gun in his house and said his girlfriend was lying about it, but he never explicitly objected when the girlfriend granted consent to search, therefore the gun that was found was properly admitted); United States v. Hicks, 539 F.3d 566 (7th Cir. 2008) (defendant who objected to his arrest and removal from the premises did not explicitly object to a search of the premises, so third-party consent was valid).

As to whether a defendant is *present* at the time third-party consent is granted, see, e.g., United States v. Alama, 486 F.3d 1062 (8th Cir. 2007) (where defendant refused to come to the door in order to avoid arrest, he was not present and objecting when third-party search was granted); United States v. Lopez, 547 F.3d 397 (2nd Cir. 2008) (officers arrested the defendant on the first floor of his house, then escorted his girlfriend to the second floor bedroom to get the defendant's clothes, and at that point sought consent from her to search the bedroom; third-party consent was valid because the defendant was not present and there was no indication that the marshals removed Lopez for the purpose of avoiding his potential objection: "the ease with which law enforcement officers might seek the defendant's permission to search when a co-occupant has already consented is irrelevant").

## 3.   Scope of Consent

Even if a person voluntarily gives consent, there may be a question about whether the consent extended to the areas actually searched by the officer. A search beyond the scope of the consent granted cannot be justified as a consent search. See United States v. Neely, 564 F.3d 346 (4th Cir. 2009) (defendant's consent to search his trunk did not extend to a search of the passenger compartment of the car). The question, of course, is whether a given search is beyond the scope of a given consent.

### *Scope Defined by the Object of the Search: Florida v. Jimeno*

In Florida v. Jimeno, 500 U.S. 248 (1991), Chief Justice Rehnquist, writing for a majority of seven justices, relied on *Rodriguez* and *Schneckloth* to conclude that the scope of a consent is determined by a standard of objective reasonableness. The Court held that an officer could reasonably conclude that when a suspect gave general consent to a search of his car, he also consented to a search of a paper bag lying on the floor of the car. The officer had informed Jimeno that he was looking for narcotics in the car and obtained consent to search. Jimeno did not place any explicit limitation on the scope of the search. The Chief Justice reasoned that the general consent to search the car included consent to search containers in the car that might contain drugs. He stated that "the scope of a search is generally defined by its expressed object" and that "a reasonable person might be expected to know that narcotics are carried in some form of container." The Chief Justice distinguished the instant case from one in which an officer, given consent to search the trunk of a car, pried open a locked briefcase found inside the trunk. He explained that "it is very likely unreasonable to think that a suspect, by consenting to the search of his trunk, has agreed to the breaking open of a locked briefcase within the trunk, but it is otherwise with a paper bag."

The *Jimeno* majority rejected the defendant's argument that police officers should be required to request separate permission to search each container found in a car. The Chief Justice saw "no basis for adding this sort of superstructure to the Fourth Amendment's basic tenet of reasonableness." He noted that a container-by-container requirement would result in fewer consents being given—which would be contrary to the community's interest in encouraging citizens to cooperate with the authorities.

Justice Marshall, joined by Justice Stevens, dissented. Justice Marshall noted that, at best, general consent is ambiguous, and police can avoid ambiguity by asking specifically at the outset for permission to search the contents of a car, or by asking for additional permission to search a container when it is found within a car. Justice Marshall concluded by attacking the majority's expressed interest in encouraging consent searches:

> The majority's real concern is that if the police were required to ask for additional consent to search a closed container * * * an individual who did not mean to authorize such additional searching would have an opportunity to say no. In essence, then, the majority is claiming that the community has a real interest not in encouraging citizens to *consent* to investigatory efforts of their law enforcement agents, but rather in encouraging individuals to be *duped* by them. That is not the community that the Fourth Amendment contemplates.

### Ambiguity Construed Against the Citizen

After *Jimeno,* it is up to the citizen rather than the officer to clarify any ambiguity concerning the scope of consent. See United States v. Berke, 930 F.2d 1219 (7th Cir.1991) (consent to officer's "looking" into bag allows a thorough search of the bag; defendant did not ask for clarification of what the officers meant when they said they wanted to "look"); United States v. Luken, 560 F.3d 741 (8th Cir. 2009) (forensic analysis of hard drive on defendant's computer did not exceed the scope of consent; before defendant gave consent, the officer explained that they would be able to recover deleted files and images, and defendant did not place any explicit limitations on the search).

Imagine that you are in Jimeno's position and the officer asks if he can search your car. Assume further that you want to limit the scope of this search. Because it is up to you to clarify any ambiguity, how would you go about doing so? Would you be concerned that by limiting the scope of the search, you will direct the officer's attention to the very area that you want to exclude from the search? Does it make sense for Jimeno to say, "yes, you can search the car, but not that bag in the back seat"?

While ambiguity is construed against the citizen, there are certainly situations in which the officers' search will be beyond what could be reasonably contemplated by the consent. For example, in United States v. Turner, 169 F.3d 84 (1st Cir.1999), Turner's next door neighbor was attacked with a knife, and blood was found around Turner's window. Officers thought the assailant might be hiding in Turner's house and asked for consent to search. They also had thoughts that Turner might be the assailant. They asked to search for any signs that the suspect might have been inside Turner's apartment, or might have left evidence of his presence there. Turner consented. An officer saw a picture on Turner's computer screen that resembled the victim. This got him curious, and so he sat down and started searching through the computer's hard drive. He discovered files containing child pornography, and Turner was prosecuted for that offense. But the court held that the search exceeded the scope of consent, and therefore that the files were illegally obtained:

> We think that an objectively reasonable person assessing in context the exchange between Turner and these detectives would have understood that the police intended to search only in places where an intruder hastily might have disposed of any physical evidence of the Thomas assault immediately after it occurred; for example, in places where a fleeing suspect might have tossed a knife or bloody clothing. Whereas, in sharp contrast, it obviously would have been impossible to abandon physical evidence of this sort in a personal computer hard drive, and bizarre to suppose—nor has the government suggested—that the suspected intruder stopped to enter incriminating evidence into the Turner computer.

It is also likely that a search will be beyond the scope of the consent if it involves *destructive activity*—as in an example given by the Court in *Jimeno*, involving breaking open a locked briefcase. See United States v. Strickland, 902 F.2d 937 (11th Cir.1990) (consent to search a car does not extend to officer's slashing open a spare tire); United States v. Osage, 235

F.3d 518 (10th Cir. 2000) (consent to search a bag does not permit the opening of a sealed can labeled "Tamales in Gravy" found in the bag: "before an officer may actually destroy or render completely useless a container which would otherwise be within the scope of a permissive search, the officer must obtain explicit authorization, or have some other, lawful, basis upon which to proceed."). Compare United States v. Jackson, 381 F.3d 984 (10th Cir. 2004) (consent to search for narcotics allowed the officer to pry open the top of a baby powder container: "removing the lid of the baby powder container did not exceed the scope of Jackson's consent because it did not destroy or render the container useless").

## 4. Withdrawing Consent

Because there is a right to refuse consent initially, and a right to control the scope of consent, it follows that there is also a right to revoke a consent once given. Of course, consent cannot be revoked retroactively after the officer has found incriminating information. United States v. Dyer, 784 F.2d 812 (7th Cir.1986) (revocation must be made before the search is completed). Also, the revocation of consent must be *clear and explicit*. See United States v. Gray, 369 F.3d 1024 (8th Cir. 2004) (expression of impatience with how long the consent search is taking is not sufficient to terminate consent: "Withdrawal of consent need not be effectuated through particular magic words, but an intent to withdraw consent must be made by unequivocal act or statement.").

Suppose that an officer obtains voluntary consent to search a home and then, when he is about to enter a closet, the defendant revokes consent and forbids entry to the closet. Can the officer consider the defendant's actions as proof that there is something incriminating in the closet? As one court put it: "The constitutional right to withdraw one's consent would be of little value if the very fact of choosing to exercise that right could serve as any part of the basis for finding the reasonable suspicion that makes consent unnecessary." United States v. Carter, 985 F.2d 1095 (D.C.Cir.1993).

This principle is fact-sensitive, however. For example, in *Carter,* where the court set forth the principle that revocation of consent cannot be considered suspicious, the court actually upheld a search that was made after consent was revoked. The court found the principle it stated "immaterial" where the following sequence of events occurred: 1) Officers suspected Carter of drug trafficking based on various profile factors and suspicious answers to questions during the encounter; 2) Carter permitted the officer to look through his tote bag; 3) the officer pulled out a paper bag from the tote bag; 4) Carter snatched the paper bag from the officer and volunteered to show the officer the food that he claimed was in the paper bag; 5) Carter put his hand inside the paper bag, felt around, and finally withdrew his hand—which was empty; and 6) Carter then rolled up the paper bag and stood looking at the officer.

The *Carter* court held that the officer could reasonably take Carter's conduct with respect to the paper bag into account, "as part of the totality of the circumstances, regardless whether it occurred before or, as here, after Carter had given and then withdrawn his consent to a search." This was because Carter's "peculiar" way of retracting consent could legitimately be considered suspicious, independent of the withdrawal of consent itself.

Judge Wald, in dissent, complained that under the majority's approach, Carter "was entitled to just say no to any further search of the bag, [but] he had to do so in a way that would not raise the detective's suspicion that he had something to hide; not an easy feat under the circumstances." She concluded as follows:

> Permitting the police to rely on the atmospherics of the refusal or withdrawal of consent to supply the reasonable suspicion necessary to objectively justify an otherwise unlawful search strips the legal right of withdrawal of all practical value. * * * If the right to withdraw consent for a "consensual" encounter is to have any meaning on the streets, as well as in the jurisprudence, it must encompass the manner as well as the fact of its exercise.

For a different perspective on "suspicious" withdrawal of consent, see United States v. Wilson, 953 F.2d 116 (4th Cir.1991) (angry refusal to allow search of coat, after consenting to search of luggage and person, should not have counted as a factor in the analysis of reasonable suspicion; except in extraordinary circumstances, officers must have evidence independent of the withdrawal of consent and the manner in which it is executed).

## 5. Credibility Determinations

Consent cases often come down to a credibility determination between the officer's and the defendant's accounts of what happened. Typically, the officers testify that they acted politely, asked the defendant to consent, informed him of his right to refuse, and the defendant readily consented. In contrast, defendants testify that the officers either never even sought consent, or the defendant never consented, or that the officers did obtain consent but only after using threatening and coercive tactics. In the typical consent case, there is little evidence other than the testimony of the opposing sides that is or can be produced on the consent question. It is fair to state, at least by viewing the reported opinions, that courts routinely find officers to be more credible than defendants. See United States v. Dean, 550 F.3d 626 (7th Cir. 2008) ("Altogether, it was perfectly rational for the district court to have believed that Dean's desire to avoid another conviction provided a greater motive for him to fabricate a story than any motive that could be attributed to the officers.").

In New York City, the Mollen Commission reviewed the activities of the New York City Police Department and concluded that police officers often commit perjury on the witness stand. The Commission found that perjury is "prevalent enough in the department that it has its own nickname: 'testilying.'" Sexton, New York Police Often Lie Under Oath, Report Says, New York Times, April 22, 1994, p.1, col. 1. See also Slobogin, Testilying and What To Do About It, 67 Colo. L.Rev. 1037 (1996) (citing surveys of defense attorneys, prosecutors and judges, who estimated that police perjury at Fourth Amendment suppression hearings occurs in as much as fifty percent of the cases).

Professor Lassiter, in Eliminating Consent from the Lexicon of Traffic Stop Interrogations, 27 Cap. L.Rev. 79 (1998), argues that "testilying" goes hand in hand with racial profiling. That is, officers single out minorities for traffic and other stops, and then lie at the suppression hearing about things like consent. He considers whether a rule should be promulgated that a suspect cannot consent to a search without a lawyer present, but dismisses that solution as "impractical" when applied to consents obtained on the street. He states that in light of the twin problems of racial profiling and testilying, the possibility that citizens truly and voluntarily consent to a search that uncovers evidence is so remote that the *entire concept of voluntary consent should be rejected.*

Can you think of any other solutions to the problem of testilying? What about subjecting officers to polygraph tests before they testify that the defendant voluntarily consented to a search that uncovered incriminating evidence? See also McClurg, Good Cop, Bad Cop: Using Cognitive Dissonance Theory to Reduce Police Lying, 32 U.C. Davis L.Rev. 389 (1999) (suggesting changes in police training and mentoring to reduce testilying).

# VI.   ELECTRONIC SURVEILLANCE, UNDERCOVER ACTIVITY, AND THE OUTER REACHES OF THE FOURTH AMENDMENT

The Supreme Court has struggled in its attempts to consider the Fourth Amendment's applicability to various types of surreptitious investigative activity.

## A. CONSTITUTIONAL LIMITATIONS ON ELECTRONIC SURVEILLANCE

### Physical Trespass Required: Olmstead v. United States

In 1928, Chief Justice Taft's majority opinion in Olmstead v. United States, 277 U.S. 438, declared that the interception of voice communications over telephone lines without entry into Olmstead's premises was not within the coverage of the Amendment. "The evidence was secured by the use of the sense of hearing and that only. There was no entry of the house or offices of the defendants." Justices Brandeis and Holmes wrote separate dissenting opinions. Justice Brandeis observed that "[t]he makers of our Constitution * * * conferred, as against the government, the right to be let alone—the most comprehensive of rights and the right most valued by civilized men." He argued that "every unjustifiable intrusion upon the privacy of the individual, by whatever means employed, must be deemed a violation of the Fourth Amendment." And he warned, in now familiar words, that "[o]ur government is the potent, the omnipresent teacher. For good or ill, it teaches the whole people by its example. Crime is contagious. If the government becomes a lawbreaker, it breeds contempt for law; it invites every man to become a law unto himself; it invites anarchy."

### Continuing the Trespass Analysis: Goldman v. United States and on Lee v. United States

In Goldman v. United States, 316 U.S. 129 (1942), the Court found that the use of a detectaphone placed against an office wall to hear conversations next door did not violate the Fourth Amendment because there was no trespass. A decade later the Court held by a 5–4 majority in On Lee v. United States, 343 U.S. 747 (1952), that the Fourth Amendment was not implicated when the government wired an undercover agent for sound by means of a microphone that transmitted sounds to another officer outside the laundry in which the undercover agent was conversing with On Lee. There was no trespass. In a separate opinion, Justice Frankfurter said that the dissenting view in *Goldman* was correct: *Olmstead* and its trespass analysis should be overruled. Justice Douglas's dissent expressed dissatisfaction that he had voted with the majority in *Goldman*.

### Trespass Not Required: Silverman v. United States and Katz v. United States

Nine years later came the first Supreme Court condemnation of eavesdropping under the Fourth Amendment. Justice Stewart's unanimous opinion in Silverman v. United States, 365 U.S. 505 (1961), found a constitutional violation in the placement of a spike, a foot long with a microphone attached, under a baseboard into a party wall, so that it made contact with the heating duct that ran through the entire house and served as a sounding board. The Court said that its decision did "not turn upon the technicality of a trespass upon a party wall as a matter of local law. It is based upon the reality of an intrusion into a constitutionally protected area." Finally, in Katz v. United States, 389 U.S. 347 (1967), the Court stated that the Fourth Amendment would apply to electronic surveillance whenever it violated a person's justifiable expectation of privacy. *Katz* is set forth, and discussed in detail, in the section on the threshold requirements for Fourth Amendment protection, *supra*.

It is important to note that *Katz* found that a trespass was not *necessary* for Fourth Amendment protection. It might have appeared, upon a reading of *Katz* and the cases that followed it for more than 40 years, that the whole concept of connecting physical trespass to Fourth Amendment protection had been scrapped. But in the landmark case of United States v. Jones, 132 S.Ct. 945 (2012), the Court held that the *Katz* "reasonable expectation of privacy" test did not *reject* the old cases finding that the Fourth Amendment protected against trespassory investigations. Rather, *Katz* held that the Fourth Amendment does not protect *only* against trespassory investigations. In other words, the reasonable expectation of privacy test is a *supplement* to and not a substitute for the common-law premise that trespassory investigations constitute searches regulated by the Fourth Amendment. *Jones* is set forth earlier in this Chapter in the section on searches.

# B.  UNDERCOVER AGENTS

### *Surreptitious Recording: Lopez v. United States*

Lopez v. United States, 373 U.S. 427 (1963), involved an IRS agent who, having received an unsolicited bribe and having reported it to his superiors, concealed a wire recorder on his person, as directed by his superiors, when he met Lopez. Justice Harlan's majority opinion found no Fourth Amendment violation. "[T]he device was used only to obtain the most reliable evidence possible of a conversation in which the Government's own agent was a participant and which that agent was fully entitled to disclose." The opinion concluded that "the risk that petitioner took in offering a bribe * * * fairly included the risk that the offer would be accurately reproduced in court, whether by faultless memory or mechanical recording."

### Undercover Agents in the Home: Lewis v. United States

Chief Justice Warren wrote for the Court in Lewis v. United States, 385 U.S. 206 (1966), and shed additional light on the Fourth Amendment's application to undercover government investigative activities. An undercover narcotics agent had telephoned Lewis's home asking about the possibility of purchasing marijuana. Arrangements were made and a sale was consummated. Subsequently, another sale took place in Lewis's home. Only Justice Douglas dissented from the Warren view that, because Lewis invited the agent into his home "for the specific purpose of executing a felonious sale of narcotics," the fact that Lewis believed he was dealing with a fellow lawbreaker did not require constitutional protection for the belief. The Chief Justice rejected the defendant's argument that the privacy interests in a home required heightened protection:

> [W]hen, as here, the home is converted into a commercial center to which outsiders are invited for purposes of transacting unlawful business, that business is entitled to no greater sanctity than if it were carried on in a store, a garage, a car, or on the street. A government agent, in the same manner as a private person, may accept an invitation to do business and may enter upon the premises for the very purposes contemplated by the occupant.

### Limits on the Scope of Undercover Activity: Gouled v. United States

In upholding the undercover activity in *Lewis*, the Court took pains to distinguish Gouled v. United States, 255 U.S. 298 (1921). In *Gouled,* a business associate of the defendant, acting under orders from federal officers, obtained entry into the defendant's office by pretending that he was paying a social visit, when in fact he rummaged through papers in the office while Gouled was temporarily absent. The Court in *Gouled* invalidated the search. The *Lewis* Court explained that the search in *Gouled* was invalidated because the undercover informant's search went well beyond the scope of Gouled's invitation into the home.

### Misplaced Confidence: Hoffa v. United States

A similar result to that in *Lewis* was reached in Hoffa v. United States, 385 U.S. 293 (1966). Union leader James Hoffa was convicted for attempting to bribe jurors in a previous trial. Much of the government's case depended on the testimony of a local union official who, after being released from jail with federal and state charges pending against him, spent a great deal of time in the Hoffa camp at the time of the bribe attempts. Justice Stewart's majority opinion assumed that the witness had been an undercover agent from the first visit to Hoffa, but found that "no interest legitimately protected by the Fourth Amendment" was involved in the case. Justice Stewart wrote that "[w]hat the Fourth Amendment protects is the security a man relies upon when he places himself or his property within a constitutionally protected area * * *." He concluded that the undercover agent invaded no protected area because he was invited into Hoffa's hotel room. Under these circumstances, Hoffa was not relying on the security of the hotel room, but upon his "misplaced confidence" that the union official would not reveal his statements. Such a risk, according to Justice Stewart, is "the kind of risk we necessarily assume whenever we speak."

### *Analysis of Eavesdropping and Undercover Informant Cases*

The Court struggled in the early wiretapping and eavesdropping cases just to identify the right issues. Faced with new techniques of evidence gathering, the Court first found no Fourth Amendment violation unless a trespass occurred. Then, it found that any trespassory investigation was enough to require a finding that the Fourth Amendment was violated. *Katz* ultimately supplemented the trespass test with a reasonable expectation of privacy test. But the *Katz* test does not change the results in *Lewis, Gouled* or *Hoffa,* because the Court in those cases held that a person has no reasonable expectation of privacy from undercover activity *when he assumes the risk that his friends or associates would disclose his guilty secrets.* See also United States v. Davis, 326 F.3d 361 (2d Cir. 2003) (no Fourth Amendment violation where defendant invited an undercover informant into his home for a drug transaction, and the informant secretly videotaped the proceedings; the court noted that it was not deciding "the constitutionality of video surveillance conducted by an invited visitor equipped with a hidden camera with the power to depict items and details unobservable by the human eye").

Why does a person assume the risk that a friend will record an incriminating conversation, but not the risk that the government will use a wiretap and record an incriminating conversation?

## C.  STATUTORY REGULATION OF DOMESTIC ELECTRONIC SURVEILLANCE

### *Procedural Protections Required: Berger v. New York*

Berger v. New York, 388 U.S. 41 (1967), seemed to evince a different judicial attitude toward electronic eavesdropping. The case arose out of a state investigation of alleged bribery of officials responsible for liquor licenses. An eavesdropping order was obtained pursuant to a New York statute, under which a justice could enter an order upon a finding of a "reasonable ground to believe that evidence of crime" might be obtained. The statute required that the order particularly describe "the person or persons whose communications, conversations or discussions are to be overheard or recorded." The orders at issue in *Berger* permitted the installation of recording devices in an attorney's office and another person's office for 60 days. After two weeks, a conspiracy was uncovered and Berger was indicted as part of it. Relevant portions of the recordings were admitted into evidence.

Justice Clark's majority opinion found serious fault with the New York statute. Justice Clark viewed the statute as a "blanket grant" of permission to eavesdrop, "without adequate supervision or protective procedures." Among the procedural flaws, Justice Clark noted that: 1) there was a conspicuous absence of any requirement that a particular crime be named; 2) there was no requirement of a particular description of the conversations sought; 3) the length of time eavesdropping was permitted was too extensive; 4) extensions of the time period were granted on an insufficient showing that such extensions were "in the public interest"; 5) there was no provision for terminating the conversation once the evidence sought was found; and 6) the statute lacked notice and return procedures. The opinion concluded as follows: "Our concern with the statute here is whether its language permits a trespassory invasion of the home, by general warrant, contrary to the command of the Fourth Amendment. As it is written, we believe that it does."

### *The Federal Statutory Response: Title III and Its Amendments*

One year after *Berger*, Congress enacted a new scheme of regulating wiretapping and electronic eavesdropping as part of the Omnibus Crime Control and Safe Streets Act of 1968. This legislation—which does not regulate eavesdropping conducted with the consent of one of the parties— is commonly known as "Title III." Title III was modified by Title I of the 1986 Electronic Communications Privacy Act, to account for technological advances and to correct perceived gaps in the statute. Other amendments were made by the Stored Communications Act. Title III was further amended by the USA PATRIOT ACT, passed almost immediately after the 9/11 terrorist attacks, and then again by the Homeland Security Act of 2002 (which makes it easier for agencies to share information obtained through interceptions permitted by Title III); and subsequent minor changes have been added from time to time.

The basic provisions of Title III as amended (18 U.S.C. §§ 2510–2522) are as follows:

**1.** *Coverage:* The statute covers any "wire, oral or electronic communication" It regulates any "intercept" which is defined as "the aural or other acquisition of the contents of any wire, electronic, or oral communication through the use of any electronic, mechanical, or other device."

**2.  *Prohibition and Exclusion:*** Section 2511 prohibits the unauthorized willful interception, use, or disclosure of wire, oral, or electronic communications covered by the Act; but it does not apply to interception conducted with the consent of one of the parties.[26] Section 2515 states that no information obtained in violation of Title III, and no evidence derived therefrom, may be admitted in any proceeding.

**3.  *Authorization:*** Title III provides that a court order may be obtained authorizing or approving the interception of wire or oral communications when such interception may provide or has provided evidence of—a long list of specified crimes. Title III was amended by the USA PATRIOT ACT to add to the list of crimes those related to computer fraud and abuse, use of chemical weapons, and terrorism.

**4.  *Procedural Requirements for Application:*** To obtain an order authorizing interception of a wire, oral, or electronic communication, an officer must make a written filing under oath or affirmation to a judge of competent jurisdiction and must include, among other things:

> "a full and complete statement of the facts and circumstances relied upon by the applicant, to justify his belief that an order should be issued, including details as to the particular offense that has been, is being, or is about to be committed";

> unless the application is for a "roving" wiretap, "a particular description of the nature and location of the facilities from which or the place where the communication is to be intercepted";

> "a particular description of the type of communications sought to be intercepted";

> "the identity of the person, if known, committing the offense and whose communications are to be intercepted";

> "a full and complete statement as to whether or not other investigative procedures have been tried and failed or why they reasonably appear to be unlikely to succeed if tried or to be too dangerous";

---

[26] Inadvertent interceptions do not violate the Act. See Adams v. Sumner, 39 F.3d 933 (9th Cir.1994) (switchboard operator at hotel inadvertently hears an incriminating conversation; no error to admit at trial). See also United States v. Wuliger, 981 F.2d 1497 (6th Cir.1992) (attorney who uses intercepted conversations to cross-examine a witness cannot be convicted under the Act unless he knows or has reason to know that the communications were intercepted in violation of the Act).

"a statement of the period of time for which the interception is required to be maintained"; and

a full and complete statement of any prior applications made with judges to intercept communications with any of the targets.

**5.  *Order Issued by the Court:*** Upon a proper submission, the court "may enter an ex parte order * * * authorizing or approving interception of wire, oral or electronic communications" if the court finds that:

there is probable cause to believe that an individual is committing, has committed, or is about to commit an enumerated offense;

there is probable cause to believe that particular communications concerning that offense will be obtained through the interception;

"normal investigative procedures have been tried and have failed or reasonably appear to be unlikely to succeed if tried or to be too dangerous";[27] and

there is probable cause to believe that the place where the communications are coming from are being used, or are about to be used, in connection with the commission of the specified offense.

**6.  *Particularity Requirements*:** A court order authorizing interception of communications must provide the following particularized information:

"the identity of the person, if known, whose communications are to be intercepted";[28]

"the nature and location of the communications facilities as to which, or the place where, authority to intercept is granted";

"a particular description of the type of communication sought to be intercepted, and a statement of the particular offense to which it relates";

"the identity of the agency authorized to intercept the communications, and of the person authorizing the application"; and

---

[27] The statute's reference to other available investigative methods is known as the "necessity" requirement. But it is not an "exhaustion" requirement. As the Court stated in United States v. Giordano, 416 U.S. 505 (1974), the statute was intended to ensure not that wiretaps are used only as a last resort, "but that they were not to be routinely employed as the initial step in a criminal investigation." Thus, the statute does not require that alternative investigative procedures have been tried and failed, "but only that the success of other methods of investigation appear unlikely." United States v. Rivera, 527 F.3d 891 (9th Cir.2008) (necessity requirement met where it was clear that officers did not use the wiretap as the initial step in the investigation but instead used numerous techniques, and considered using several others, over the course of a 19-month investigation, before applying for the wiretap).

[28] In United States v. Kahn, 415 U.S. 143 (1974), the Court held that where the government knew of the existence of a person but did not know she was using the phone for illegal purposes, she was not a person whose identity must be disclosed under this section.

"the period of time during which such interception is authorized, including a statement as to whether or not the interception shall automatically terminate when the described communication has been first obtained."

**7. *Time Limits*:** An order permitting interception of communications under Title III must be limited in duration. It cannot authorize interception "for any period longer than is necessary to achieve the objective of the authorization, nor in any event longer than thirty days." Extensions of an order may be granted, but only upon application for an extension establishing necessity. The period of extension can be no longer than the judge deems necessary to achieve the purposes for which it was granted and in no event for longer than thirty days.

**8. *Minimization:*** Every order under Title III must contain a provision that the interception "shall be conducted in such a way as to minimize the interception of communications not otherwise subject to interception." This "minimization" requirement means that officers must stop monitoring a conversation as soon as it becomes apparent that it is not about the criminal activity that justified the court's order.[29]

**9. *Exigent Circumstances:*** Officers with probable cause can intercept communications without a court order, for a period no more than 48 hours, if an emergency situation exists that involves "immediate danger of death or serious physical injury to any person, conspiratorial activities threatening the national security interest, or conspiratorial activities characteristic of organized crime."

**10. *Inventory:*** Within a reasonable time and in no case more than 90 days of the issuance of a court order, the party whose communications were intercepted must receive an inventory which must include among other things notice of the fact and date of the entry of the order, and the fact that communications were intercepted. The court may in its discretion make available for inspection "such portions of the intercepted communications, applications and orders as the judge determines to be in the interest of justice." On an ex parte showing of good cause the court may order that the delivery of the inventory be postponed.[30]

---

[29] In Scott v. United States, 436 U.S. 128 (1978), the Court held it irrelevant that officers had no subjective intent to comply with the minimization requirement. What is controlling, said the Court, is whether the agents actually intercepted conversations that were not otherwise subject to interception under the Act.

[30] In United States v. Donovan, 429 U.S. 413 (1977), the Court held that when the government inadvertently excluded persons from its list of those intercepted and thus deprived them of the inventory notice, suppression of evidence was not warranted because the requirements did not play a "substantive role" in the statutory scheme. The Court in United States v. Ojeda Rios, 495 U.S. 257 (1990), held that a failure to comply with the Title III requirement that tapes be immediately sealed would not result in suppression if the government's error was the result of a good faith, objectively reasonable misinterpretation of the statute.

**11.** *Remedies:* Any "aggrieved person" may move to suppress the contents of any intercepted "wire or oral communication, or evidence derived therefrom," on the grounds that—

the communication was unlawfully intercepted;

the order of authorization or approval under which it was intercepted is insufficient on its face; or

the interception was not made in conformity with the order of authorization or approval.

**12.** *Roving Wiretaps:* Title III now allows for "roving" wiretaps, i.e., interception of communications that are not tied to a particular location. An order for a roving wiretap can be issued upon a detailed showing that a stationary wiretap will not be a sufficient means for intercepting the targeted communications. See United States v. Oliva, 686 F.3d 1106 (9th Cir. 2012) (orders allowing surveillance of cellphones authorized the government to transform the cellphones into roving electronic bugs through the use of sophisticated technology; government needed to specifically request that authority in order to have it provided).

For an attack on Title III as being insufficiently protective, see Schwartz, The Legitimization of Electronic Eavesdropping: The Politics of "Law and Order," 67 Mich.L.Rev. 455 (1969). The Supreme Court's handling of important questions under the statute is criticized in Goldsmith, The Supreme Court and Title III; Rewriting the Law of Electronic Surveillance, 74 J.Crim.L. & Crim. 1 (1983).

For an article analyzing the changes wrought to Title III by the PATRIOT ACT, including the authorization of "roving wiretaps", see Orin Kerr, Internet Surveillance After the USA PATRIOT ACT: The Big Brother That Isn't, 97 Nw.U. L.Rev. 607 (2003).

## D. THE FOREIGN INTELLIGENCE SURVEILLANCE ACT

Title III exempts interceptions of communications involving foreign intelligence, as Congress determined that matters of national security could not be accommodated by the strictures of Title III: it provides that "nothing contained [herein], shall be deemed to affect the acquisition by the United States Government of foreign intelligence information from international or foreign communications, or foreign intelligence activities conducted in accordance with otherwise applicable Federal law involving a foreign electronic communications system."

Interception of communications pertinent to foreign intelligence are governed by the Foreign Intelligence Surveillance Act of 1978, 50

U.S.C.A. § 1801 et seq. FISA differs from Title III in several important respects:

1) The government does not need to show traditional probable cause that a crime has been or will be committed. All that must be shown is that "the target of the electronic surveillance is a foreign power or agent of a foreign power." This includes a so-called "Lone Wolf" who is not directly affiliated but who engages in "international terrorism." See, e.g., United States v. Wen, 471 F.3d 777 (7th Cir. 2006) (probable cause to believe that a foreign agent was communicating with his controllers outside the United States was sufficient to support a FISA warrant; if, while conducting this surveillance, agents discover evidence of a domestic crime, they may use it to prosecute for that offense).

2) Requests for an order are made to one of eleven federal district judges specially selected by the Chief Justice of the Supreme Court. In order to secure an order, the application must set forth the identity or description of the target, and a statement of facts or circumstances relied upon to justify the officer's belief that the target is a foreign power or agent of a foreign power and that each facility or location to be subjected to surveillance is being used or is about to be used by the target.

3) Notice and inventory requirements are much less stringent; in fact, a target need *never* be notified of FISA surveillance if the Attorney General determines that there is a national security interest in continuing to maintain the secrecy of the search.

4) If there is a motion to suppress, the government may withhold the application it submitted to the FISA court, as well as the court order, on grounds of national security.

5) The "exigent circumstances" exception allows interceptions without a court order for up to 72 hours for an individual and for up to a year for foreign governmental entities.

6) Court review of a FISA application is extremely limited: "[I]n the absence of a prima facie showing of a fraudulent statement by the certifying officer, procedural regularity is the only determination to be made if a non-United States person is the target." United States v. Campa, 529 F.3d 980 (11th Cir. 2008). If a United States person is a target, the review is only over whether "some of the certifications are clearly erroneous." Defendants have argued that FISA is invalid because it does not assure adequate judicial review. But these arguments have been rejected. See United States v. Stewart, 590 F.3d 93 (2nd Cir. 2009) (upholding FISA surveillance of a lawyer representing a defendant charged with conspiracy to bomb the World Trade Center).

Up until 9/11/2001, FISA was used exclusively to conduct foreign counterintelligence investigations. But Section 218 of the PATRIOT ACT amended FISA to authorize electronic surveillance even in investigations whose primary purpose is criminal prosecution. See United States v. Ning Wen, 477 F.3d 896 (7th Cir. 2007) (FISA now applies to interceptions that have international intelligence as a "significant purpose"); United States v. Stewart, 590 F.3d 93 (2nd Cir. 2009) (reviewing and rejecting defendant's argument that the primary purpose for wiretapping her under FISA was to pursue a criminal investigation). "Since the passage of the PATRIOT ACT, the government has instituted a significant number of criminal prosecutions involving evidence gathered through FISA surveillance. In 2004, the federal government requested and obtained 1,754 FISA orders to conduct searches and surveillance, more than seven times the number of FISA orders issued in the year 2000." Siegler, The PATRIOT ACT's Erosion of Constitutional Rights, 32 Litigation 18 (2006). For a case finding that the FISA "significant purpose" test is reasonable under the Fourth Amendment, see United States v. Duka, 671 F.3d 329 (3rd Cir. 2011).

Despite the very mild limitations on surveillance imposed by FISA, the Bush Administration argued that it needed more flexibility in monitoring suspected terrorist activity. Congress responded by enacting the FISA Amendments Act of 2008. The Amendment left much of FISA intact, but it established a new and independent source of intelligence collection authority, beyond that granted in traditional FISA. Section 702 of FISA, 50 U.S.C. § 1881a, which was enacted as part of the FISA Amendments Act, supplements pre-existing FISA authority by creating a new framework under which the Government may seek the FISA court's authorization of certain foreign intelligence surveillance targeting the communications of non-U.S. persons located abroad. Unlike traditional FISA surveillance, § 1881a does not require the Government to demonstrate probable cause that the target of the electronic surveillance is a foreign power or agent of a foreign power. And, unlike traditional FISA, § 1881a does not require the Government to specify the nature and location of each of the particular facilities or places at which the electronic surveillance will occur. All that is required in a showing to the court is that the surveillance is of "persons reasonably believed to be located outside the United States" and that the targeting concerns "foreign intelligence information." Surveillance under § 1881a may not be intentionally targeted at any person known to be in the United States or any U.S. person reasonably believed to be located abroad Additionally, acquisitions under § 1881a must comport with the Fourth Amendment. § 1881a(b)(5). Moreover, surveillance under § 1881a is subject to congressional oversight and several types of Executive Branch review.

Section 1881a mandates that the Government obtain the Foreign Intelligence Surveillance Court's approval of "targeting" procedures, "minimization" procedures, and a governmental certification regarding proposed surveillance. Among other things, the Government's certification must attest that (1) procedures are in place "that have been approved, have been submitted for approval, or will be submitted with the certification for approval by the [FISC] that are reasonably designed" to ensure that an acquisition is "limited to targeting persons reasonably believed to be located outside" the United States; (2) minimization procedures adequately restrict the acquisition, retention, and dissemination of nonpublic information about unconsenting U.S. persons, as appropriate; (3) guidelines have been adopted to ensure compliance with targeting limits and the Fourth Amendment; and (4) the procedures and guidelines referred to above comport with the Fourth Amendment.

### Data Mining Under—and Around—FISA

In 2013, information was leaked that the National Security Agency obtained FISA orders to engage in data mining of phone calls, emails, and internet activity of millions of Americans. The orders purportedly did not allow interception of content, but did allow collection of metadata—i.e., the length of a call, the number called, the recipient of an email, the fact of access to an internet page, etc. The following is a report by the **Huffington Post** on the FISA-authorized data mining:

> A massive email surveillance program run by the National Security Agency is not directed at Americans and is legally permissible and highly useful for anti-terror operation, a senior administration official said in a statement Thursday night.

> The statement, provided on condition of anonymity, came hours after news outlets revealed the existence of the PRISM program, which provides the NSA with access to records of America's largest Internet companies. The statement is an implicit confirmation of the program's existence. It also is the first defense of the massive surveillance effort that, until Thursday evening, the public did not know existed.

> The Guardian and Washington Post articles refer to collection of communications pursuant to Section 702 of the Foreign Intelligence Surveillance Act. This law does not allow the targeting of any U.S. citizen or of any person located within the United States.

> The program is subject to oversight by the Foreign Intelligence Surveillance Court, the Executive Branch, and Congress. It involves extensive procedures, specifically approved by the court, to ensure that only non-U.S. persons outside the U.S. are targeted, and that

minimize the acquisition, retention and dissemination of incidentally acquired information about U.S. persons.

This program was recently reauthorized by Congress after extensive hearings and debate.

Information collected under this program is among the most important and valuable intelligence information we collect, and is used to protect our nation from a wide variety of threats.

The Government may only use Section 702 to acquire foreign intelligence information, which is specifically, and narrowly, defined in the Foreign Intelligence Surveillance Act. This requirement applies across the board, regardless of the nationality of the target.

Coming on the heels of revelations that the NSA had obtained phone call data from several of the biggest providers (as well as, reportedly, credit card information) it remains to be seen if the White House explanation will suffice. Top senators were quick to defend the NSA's phone surveillance program on Thursday. But others expressed concern, if not dismay, that it violated privacy rights.

This was before news of PRISM. It seems likely that lawmakers who reauthorized the Foreign Intelligence Surveillance Act will say that they anticipated that it would never be used to collect search histories, email contents or live chat transcripts.

### From the Washington Post, June 18, 2013

### Google challenges U.S. gag order, citing First Amendment

Google asked the secretive Foreign Intelligence Surveillance Court on Tuesday to ease long-standing gag orders over data requests the court makes, arguing that the company has a constitutional right to speak about information it is forced to give the government.

The legal filing, which invokes the First Amendment's guarantee of free speech, is the latest move by the California-based tech giant to protect its reputation in the aftermath of news reports about broad National Security Agency surveillance of Internet traffic.

Revelations about the program, called PRISM, have opened fissures between U.S. officials and the involved companies, which have scrambled to reassure their users without violating strict rules against disclosing information that the government has classified as top secret.

A high-profile legal showdown might help Google's efforts to portray itself as aggressively resisting government surveillance, and a victory could bolster the company's campaign to portray government surveillance requests as targeted narrowly and affecting only a small number of users.

\* \* \*

In its petition, Google sought permission to publish information about how many government data requests the surveillance court approves and how many user accounts are affected. Google long has made regular reports with regard to other data demands from the U.S. government and other governments worldwide, but it has been forced to exclude requests from the surveillance court, which oversees an array of official monitoring efforts that target foreigners.

\* \* \*

Surveillance court requests typically are known only to small numbers of a company's employees. Discussing the requests openly, either within or beyond the walls of the company, can violate federal law.

Yet even if Google is permitted to say how many requests the surveillance court has made, the information may not shed much light on PRISM. The program does not require individual warrants from the surveillance court each time a search is made.

Even overall numbers of surveillance court requests would offer insight "only at a very high level of abstraction," said Stephen Vladeck, an American University law professor. "I don't think we'll learn anything other than how pervasive this practice has been. . . . It will only be a piece of a much larger puzzle."

The court, based in downtown Washington and composed of 11 federal judges appointed by Chief Justice John G. Roberts Jr., rarely rejects government requests for information. Of 1,789 requests it received in 2012, it approved all but one, which was withdrawn.

In 2008, the court rejected a challenge from a technology company that argued that a government request for information on foreign users was too broad to be constitutional. The court redacted the name of the company and other details when it published the ruling. Few of its decisions are ever made public. Appeals are handled by a secretive review court and can reach the Supreme Court.

The sharply limited public window into the legal infrastructure of surveillance review has made it difficult for outsiders to evaluate its decisions or the value of the secrecy it maintains.

\* \* \*

All of the technology companies involved in PRISM, including Facebook, Apple, Microsoft, Google and Yahoo, have struggled to respond to the revelations about NSA surveillance.

Most of the companies have issued carefully crafted denials, saying that they do not permit wholesale data collection while acknowledging that they comply with legal government information requests. In Tuesday's legal filing, Google called the Post and Guardian reports about PRISM "misleading."

Those articles cited an NSA Power-Point presentation that said the agency connected directly to the servers of Facebook, Google, Microsoft and other tech industry giants—an assertion immediately denied by the companies. * * *

### *From Reuters, August 21, 2013:*

The National Security Agency's surveillance network has the capacity to reach around 75 percent of all U.S. Internet communications in the hunt for foreign intelligence, the Wall Street Journal reported on Tuesday.

Citing current and former NSA officials, the newspaper said the 75 percent coverage is more of Americans' Internet communications than officials have publicly disclosed.

The Journal said the agency keeps the content of some emails sent between U.S. citizens and also filters domestic phone calls made over the Internet.

The NSA's filtering, carried out with telecom companies, looks for communications that either originate or end abroad, or are entirely foreign but happen to be passing through the United States, the paper said.

But officials told the Journal the system's broad reach makes it more likely that purely domestic communications will be incidentally intercepted and collected in the hunt for foreign ones.

In response to a request for comment, NSA said its intelligence mission "is centered on defeating foreign adversaries who aim to harm the country. We defend the United States from such threats while fiercely working to protect the privacy rights of U.S. persons."

The Journal said that these surveillance programs show the NSA can track almost anything that happens online, so long as it is covered by a broad court order, the Journal said.

Edward Snowden, a former NSA contractor, first disclosed details of secret U.S. programs to monitor Americans' telephone and Internet traffic earlier this summer.

In 2013, the FISA court renewed its authorization of the NSA plan to search the metadata of every American's phone calls. The court declared that the plan was constitutional under Smith v. Maryland, supra, the pen register case, which held that because the phone company had access to the numbers called by a person, the government could have such access in equal measure. The court acknowledged that under United States v. Jones, supra, the long-term surveillance of a person's location could be a search, but the court declared that the Supreme Court's *Jones* decision was grounded in trespass, and the NSA committed no trespass by monitoring calls. Moreover, NSA was not involved in location-tracking, as were the police in *Jones*. The Court declared that "[t]he Supreme Court may someday revisit the third-party disclosure principle in the context of 21st century technology, but that day has not arrived."

Is there a difference between aggregated location tracking and aggregated call tracking? Don't both types of aggregation risk disclosure of intimate details of a person's life? Is it relevant that FISA courts render rulings after hearing only the government's side?

It should be noted that the FISA court found that the NSA had violated the limits on the order allowing collection of phone call metadata—i.e., the NSA had looked at the contents of some calls. The FISA judge who discovered the violations reprimanded the NSA for violating the order prohibiting inspection of the content of calls in the absence of reasonable suspicion to believe that the calls were linked to terrorism. In fact only 10% of the calls monitored for content satisfied the reasonable suspicion standard. See NSA Violated Rules on Use of Phone Logs, Intelligence Court Found in 2009, New York Times, Sept. 11, 2013, p. A14.

Since the FISA court's decision on the data collection program, two district courts have reviewed the program, as of the date of this publication. One court upheld the program, relying on Smith v. Maryland, thus equating metadata collection to pen registers. The other court held that *Smith* dealt with quaint technology and was too thin a reed on which to rest the massive data collection that the NSA had undertaken.

Public outcry over the NSA data collection program led President Obama to make some changes by executive order and to suggest others through legislation. The most important change is that prior FISA court approval is now necessary before an analyst can gain access to calling records (except in emergencies). Also, a board of advocates has been appointed to argue the civil liberties side when FISA courts are ruling on cases that present novel and important policy issues. But the changes do not question the constitutionality of the data collection program and do not impose any limitation on NSA's collection of telephone call and internet data. See Obama Outlines Calibrated Curbs on Phone Spying, New York Times, Jan. 18, 2014, p.1.

———

For more on the use of FISA procedures after 9/11, see Maclin, The Bush Administration's Terrorist Surveillance Program and the Fourth Amendment's Warrant Requirement: Lessons from Justice Powell and the *Keith* case. 41 U.C. Davis L. Rev. 1259 (2008).

# VII.   REMEDIES FOR FOURTH AMENDMENT VIOLATIONS

## A.  THE BACKGROUND OF THE EXCLUSIONARY RULE

The exclusionary rule, in its broadest conception, provides that evidence obtained in violation of the Fourth Amendment must be excluded from trial. But the exclusionary rule was not born contemporaneously with the Fourth Amendment. The Bill of Rights is not explicit as to remedies. For over a century after the adoption of the Fourth Amendment, virtually the only remedies available to victims of illegal searches were suits in trespass for damages, or in replevin for return of the goods seized. The trespass alternative was usually impractical, and replevin had no chance of success if the goods seized were contraband, or the fruits or instrumentalities of crime, because these items were considered forfeited to the state regardless of the legality of the seizure.

### *Exclusionary Rule for the Federal Courts:*
### *Weeks v. United States*

The Court in Weeks v. United States, 232 U.S. 383 (1914), held that evidence obtained in violation of the Fourth Amendment must be excluded from evidence in federal courts. Justice Day wrote for a unanimous Court that if evidence obtained in violation of the Fourth Amendment could be used against a criminal defendant, then "the protection of the Fourth Amendment declaring his right to be secure against such searches and seizures is of no value." The Court noted that the officers who obtained the evidence illegally were "doubtless prompted by the desire to bring further proof to the aid of the Government." It concluded that "[t]o sanction such proceedings would be to affirm by judicial decision a manifest neglect if not an open defiance of the prohibitions of the Constitution intended for the protection of the people against such unauthorized action."

*Weeks* was limited to cases where the illegal search was conducted by federal officers and the evidence was sought to be admitted in a federal criminal proceeding. It was essentially an exercise of the Court's supervisory power over the federal courts.

Two themes articulated in *Weeks,* and finding recurrent expression in later cases dealing with the rationale for excluding evidence, were that the exclusionary rule is the only effective means of protecting Fourth Amendment rights, and that the interest in judicial integrity requires that the courts not sanction illegal searches by admitting the fruits of illegality into evidence. In Silverthorne Lumber Co. v. United States, 251 U.S. 385 (1920), these considerations were held to prohibit the copying of illegally seized documents, and their use as the basis for a subpoena of the originals, which had been returned pursuant to a motion by the defendant. The Court stressed that "[t]he essence of a provision forbidding the acquisition of evidence in a certain way is [not merely that] evidence so acquired shall not be used before the Court but that it shall not be used at all."

## B. THE EXCLUSIONARY RULE AND THE STATES

*Weeks,* which was grounded in the Court's supervisory power over federal courts, explicitly rejected the notion that the exclusionary rule should apply to violations by state or local police. Because the exclusionary rule after *Weeks* did not affect the conduct of state officials, federal officials would often allow state officers to obtain evidence illegally and then serve it to the federal officers on a "silver platter." The silver platter method of avoiding Fourth Amendment protections was used until 1960 when Elkins v. United States, 364 U.S. 206, abolished it. Then the Court took the next step and applied the exclusionary rule to the states. Mapp v. Ohio, 367 U.S. 643 (1961).

The rationale underlying these developments in Fourth Amendment remedies can best be understood by contrasting two major opinions of that period: Wolf v. Colorado and Mapp v. Ohio. As you study the two opinions, consider not only the debate over the efficacy of the exclusionary rule, but also the sensitive issues of federal-state relations.

### WOLF V. COLORADO
Supreme Court of the United States, 1949.
338 U.S. 25.

#### MR. JUSTICE FRANKFURTER delivered the opinion of the Court.

\* \* \*

The security of one's privacy against arbitrary intrusion by the police—which is at the core of the Fourth Amendment—is basic to a free society. It is therefore implicit in "the concept of ordered liberty" and as such enforceable against the States through the Due Process Clause. The knock at the door, whether by day or by night, as a prelude to a search, without authority of law but solely on the authority of the police, did not need the commentary of recent history to be condemned as inconsistent with the conception of human rights enshrined in the history and the basic constitutional documents of English-speaking peoples.

Accordingly, we have no hesitation in saying that were a State affirmatively to sanction such police incursion into privacy it would run counter to the guaranty of the Fourteenth Amendment. But the ways of enforcing such a basic right raise questions of a different order. How such arbitrary conduct should be checked, what remedies against it should be afforded, the means by which the right should be made effective, are all questions that are not to be so dogmatically answered as to preclude the varying solutions which spring from an allowable range of judgment on issues not susceptible of quantitative solution.

In Weeks v. United States, this Court held that in a federal prosecution the Fourth Amendment barred the use of evidence secured through an illegal search and seizure. This ruling * * * was not derived from the explicit requirements of the Fourth Amendment; it was not based on legislation expressing Congressional policy in the enforcement of the Constitution. The decision was a matter of judicial implication. Since then it has been frequently applied and we stoutly adhere to it. But the immediate question is whether the basic right to protection against arbitrary intrusion by the police demands the exclusion of logically relevant evidence obtained by an unreasonable search and seizure because, in a federal prosecution for a federal crime, it would be excluded. As a matter of inherent reason, one would suppose this to be an issue as to which men with complete devotion to the protection of the right of privacy might give different answers. When we find that in fact most of the English-speaking world does not regard as vital to such protection the exclusion of evidence thus obtained, we must hesitate to treat this remedy as an essential ingredient of the right. The contrariety of views of the States is particularly impressive in view of the careful reconsideration which they have given the problem in the light of the *Weeks* decision.

[Justice Frankfurter summarized state case law on the issue of admissibility of evidence, contrasting pre-and post-*Weeks* decisions. In 1949, 31 states had rejected the *Weeks* doctrine and 16 states were in agreement with it.]

The jurisdictions which have rejected the *Weeks* doctrine have not left the right to privacy without other means of protection. Indeed, the exclusion of evidence is a remedy which directly serves only to protect those upon whose person or premises something incriminating has been found. We cannot, therefore, regard it as a departure from basic standards to remand such persons, together with those who emerge scatheless from a search, to the remedies of private action and such protection as the internal discipline of the police, under the eyes of an alert public opinion, may afford. Granting that in practice the exclusion of evidence may be an effective way of deterring unreasonable searches, it is not for this Court to condemn as falling below the minimal standards assured by the Due Process Clause a State's reliance upon other methods which, if consistently enforced, would be equally effective. We cannot brush aside the experience of States which deem the incidence of such conduct by the police too slight to call for a deterrent remedy not by way of disciplinary measures but by overriding the relevant rules of evidence. * * *

We hold, therefore, that in a prosecution in a State court for a State crime the Fourteenth Amendment does not forbid the admission of evidence obtained by an unreasonable search and seizure. * * *

**MR. JUSTICE MURPHY, with whom MR. JUSTICE RUTLEDGE joins, dissenting.**

* * *

The conclusion is inescapable that but one remedy exists to deter violations of the search and seizure clause. That is the rule which excludes illegally obtained evidence. Only by exclusion can we impress upon the zealous prosecutor that violation of the Constitution will do him no good. And only when that point is driven home can the prosecutor be expected to emphasize the importance of observing constitutional demands in his instructions to the police.

* * *

[JUSTICE RUTLEDGE's separate dissent is omitted, as is JUSTICE DOUGLAS' dissent. JUSTICE BLACK's concurring opinion, stating that the exclusionary rule "is not a command of the Fourth Amendment" also is omitted.]

### NOTE ON WOLF AND THE ROAD TO MAPP

Although the Court was divided 6–3 in *Wolf,* the division was over the applicability of the exclusionary rule to the States. The Justices unanimously agreed that the prohibition against unreasonable searches and seizures was a fundamental right applied to the States through the Due Process Clause of the Fourteenth Amendment. They disagreed on whether the exclusionary rule was a constitutionally required remedy.

In the next decade, the issue received the Court's attention twice more. In Rochin v. California, 342 U.S. 165 (1952), the shocking method used by the State to obtain incriminating evidence—pumping the defendant's stomach—was held to so offend "a sense of justice" as to require exclusion at a state trial. Two years later, in Irvine v. California, 347 U.S. 128 (1954), *Wolf* was reaffirmed, 5–4, and evidence was admitted where the search of a home, although illegal, did not involve a physical assault on the suspect's person.

In 1961, the Supreme Court once again considered the question in Mapp v. Ohio. *Mapp* appeared to be exclusively a First Amendment case (whether Miss Mapp had the right to possess obscene material in her home); the exclusionary rule issue was neither briefed nor argued. Yet, *Wolf* was overruled 5–3. The change is partly explained by the fact that six members of the *Wolf* Court were no longer on the Bench.

## MAPP V. OHIO

Supreme Court of the United States, 1961.
367 U.S. 643.

### MR. JUSTICE CLARK delivered the opinion of the Court.

\* \* \*

Some five years after *Wolf,* in answer to a plea made here Term after Term that we overturn its doctrine on applicability of the *Weeks* exclusionary rule, this Court indicated that such should not be done until the States had "adequate opportunity to adopt or reject the [*Weeks*] rule." Irvine v. California. \* \* \*

\* \* \* Today we once again examine *Wolf's* constitutional documentation of the right to privacy free from unreasonable state intrusion, and, after its dozen years on our books, are led by it to close the only courtroom door remaining open to evidence secured by official lawlessness in flagrant abuse of that basic right, reserved to all persons as a specific guarantee against that very same unlawful conduct. We hold that all evidence obtained by searches and seizures in violation of the Constitution is, by that same authority, inadmissible in a state court.

\* \* \* Since the Fourth Amendment's right of privacy has been declared enforceable against the States through the Due Process Clause of the Fourteenth, it is enforceable against them by the same sanction of exclusion as is used against the Federal Government. \* \* \* [T]he admission of the new constitutional right by *Wolf* could not consistently tolerate denial of its most important constitutional privilege, namely, the exclusion of the evidence which an accused had been forced to give by reason of the unlawful seizure. To hold otherwise is to grant the right but in reality to withhold its privilege and enjoyment. \* \* \*

Indeed, we are aware of no restraint, similar to that rejected today, conditioning the enforcement of any other basic constitutional right. The right to privacy, no less important than any other right carefully and particularly reserved to the people, would stand in marked contrast to all other rights declared as basic to a free society. This Court has not hesitated to enforce as strictly against the States as it does against the

Federal Government the rights of free speech and of a free press, the rights to notice and to a fair, public trial, including, as it does, the right not to be convicted by use of a coerced confession, however logically relevant it be, and without regard to its reliability. * * * Why should not the same rule apply to what is tantamount to coerced testimony by way of unconstitutional seizure of goods, papers, effects, documents, etc.? * * *

\* \* \*

There are those who say, as did Justice (then Judge) Cardozo, that under our constitutional exclusionary doctrine "[t]he criminal is to go free because the constable has blundered." People v. Defore, 242 N.Y. at 21. In some cases this will undoubtedly be the result. But * * * there is another consideration—the imperative of judicial integrity. The criminal goes free, if he must, but it is the law that sets him free. Nothing can destroy a government more quickly than its failure to observe its own laws, or worse, its disregard of the charter of its own existence. * * *

The ignoble shortcut to conviction left open to the States tends to destroy the entire system of constitutional restraints on which the liberties of the people rest. Having once recognized that the right to privacy embodied in the Fourth Amendment is enforceable against the States, and that the right to be secure against rude invasions of privacy by state officers is, therefore, constitutional in origin, we can no longer permit that right to remain an empty promise. Because it is enforceable in the same manner and to like effect as other basic rights secured by the Due Process Clause, we can no longer permit it to be revocable at the whim of any police officer who, in the name of law enforcement itself, chooses to suspend its enjoyment. Our decision, founded on reason and truth, gives to the individual no more than that which the Constitution guarantees him, to the police officer no less than that to which honest law enforcement is entitled, and, to the courts, that judicial integrity so necessary in the true administration of justice. * * *

\* \* \*

[JUSTICE BLACK concurred in a separate opinion, arguing that the Constitutional basis for the majority rule was the Fourth Amendment in conjunction with the Fifth Amendment's ban against compelled self-incrimination. The concurrences of Justices Douglas and Stewart have been omitted. Justice Stewart did not reach the Fourth Amendment question, preferring to decide the case on First Amendment grounds.]

**MR. JUSTICE HARLAN, whom MR. JUSTICE FRANKFURTER and JUSTICE WHITTAKER join, dissenting.**

\* \* \*

I would not impose upon the States this federal exclusionary remedy. The reasons given by the majority for now suddenly turning its back on *Wolf* seem to me notably unconvincing.

\* \* \*

[T]he majority now finds an incongruity in *Wolf's* discriminating perception between the demands of "ordered liberty" as respects the basic right of "privacy" and the means of securing it among the States. That perception, resting both on a sensitive regard for our federal system and a sound recognition of this Court's remoteness from particular state problems, is for me the strength of that decision.

\* \* \*

### *NOTE ON MAPP*

What is the basis for the majority's conclusion that the exclusionary rule is required by the Constitution? Obviously, the texts of the Fourth and Fourteenth Amendments lend no support to the proposition. The origins of the rule likewise throw no historical weight behind its acceptance. In the final analysis, isn't the majority implicitly deciding that the exclusion of evidence is the only effective sanction, and that the right to be free from unreasonable searches is "a dead letter" without a sanction? If other alternatives had proved effective in deterring violations, would the Court have found exclusion to be a constitutional requirement?

Would a showing that exclusion of evidence has no deterrent effect whatsoever have required a different result? Professor Dripps, in Living with *Leon*, 95 Yale L.J. 906 (1986), argues that if no sanction attaches to a Fourth Amendment violation, the Amendment does not qualify as a *law*, thus betraying "the fundamental principle of constitutionalism, which is after all that the Constitution states the law." He argues that "even if the sanction does not deter, the refusal to apply it or anything else expresses the judgment that the underlying norm is of little importance."

As we will see in *Leon, infra,* the Court has held that despite its decision in *Mapp,* the exclusionary rule *is not constitutionally required for all Fourth Amendment violations*, in part because the violation of a Fourth Amendment right occurs at the time of the original police intrusion. The argument is that later exclusion from the trial has nothing to do with the already completed violation, and that introduction of the evidence at trial is not a separate violation of privacy. For an argument that the Fourth Amendment violation is not complete at the time of the intrusion, and that the exclusionary rule is constitutionally required, see Heffernan, On Justifying Fourth Amendment Exclusion, 1989 Wis.L.Rev. 1193.

## C. ARGUMENTS FOR AND AGAINST THE EXCLUSIONARY RULE

Many judges are not enamoured of the exclusionary rule. For example, Judge Bowman had this to say about the exclusionary rule in United States v. Jefferson, 906 F.2d 346 (8th Cir.1990), a case in which the entire court agreed that evidence obtained during a stop without reasonable suspicion had to be excluded due to the exclusionary rule:

> This case vividly illustrates the perversity of the exclusionary rule. Here, an officer's educated hunch led to the discovery of evidence (nine kilograms of cocaine) of substantial criminal activity. This discovery occurred as a result of information the officer developed by asking questions and examining documents in the course of his routine check of a parked car and its occupants at a highway rest stop. The ordinary law-abiding citizen, I believe, would think the officer should be commended for his fine work, and the cocaine dealers punished. Instead, because we hold (as I agree, under the existing case law, we must) that a "seizure" within the meaning of the Fourth Amendment occurred before the officer had formed an objectively reasonable basis for suspecting the defendants of criminal activity, the exclusionary rule requires that the evidence be suppressed. The defendants thus exit unpunished, free to continue dealing illegal drugs to the pathetic addicts and contemptible scofflaws who comprise the national market for these substances. As for the officer, far from his being commended, it is judicially recorded that he blundered, and the point once again is driven home that legalistic observance of even the most technical of the judge-created rules of search and seizure—rules which, like the Fourth Amendment itself, seek to protect law-abiding citizens from intrusive conduct by officers of the state—is more important than intelligent, courageous, and vigorous initiative to expose criminal activity and bring those responsible for it to the bar of justice.

> It has been reported that since 1961, when [*Mapp* was decided], "the murder rate has doubled, rape has quadrupled and robbery has quintupled." *Wall St.J.,* May 7, 1990, at A14, Col. 1. While it would be foolish to blame the exclusionary rule for all of this alarming increase in violent crime, I believe it is equally foolish to pretend that the exclusionary rule, and the *zeitgeist* it has created, is to blame for none of it.

Judge Bowman's comments prompted Chief Judge Lay to respond as follows:

> If police are not deterred from illegal intrusions of privacy by excluding whatever evidence is seized, the Fourth Amendment will have no meaning or force. Surely an appreciation for the history and

purpose of our basic freedoms will never allow emotional fear to justify an environment where there is no check on the abuse of police power.

The Fourth Amendment protects the good guy as well as the bad. It would mean very little to anyone if it did not. The argument that since 1961 murders have doubled, rapes quadrupled, and robbery quintupled in part because of the exclusionary rule is a statement more fitting for headlines of the National Enquirer. It is irrational hyperbole totally unsupported in fact or in law.

Supporters of the exclusionary rule generally make four points in its favor: 1. The rule preserves judicial integrity, by insulating the courts from tainted evidence; 2. The rule prevents the government from profiting from its own wrong; 3. The rule is not costly, because it only excludes what should never have been obtained in the first place; and 4. The rule is necessary to deter police misconduct. See, e.g., Barnett, Resolving the Dilemma of the Exclusionary Rule: An Application of Restitutive Principles of Justice, 32 Emory L.J. 937 (1983).

Professor Amar, in Fourth Amendment First Principles, 107 Harv.L.Rev. 757 (1994), attacks each of the justifications listed by Judge Lay. As to the judicial integrity rationale, Amar responds: "we must remember that integrity and fairness are also threatened by excluding evidence that will help the justice system to reach a true verdict. Thus, the courts best affirm their integrity not by closing their eyes to truthful evidence, but by opening their doors to any civil suit brought against wayward government officials, even one brought by a convict."

Professor Amar continues his critique of the exclusionary rule as follows:

Consider next the nice-sounding idea that government should not profit from its own wrongdoing. Our society, however, also cherishes the notion that cheaters—or murderers or rapists, for that matter—should not prosper. When the murderer's bloody knife is introduced, it is not only the government that profits; the people also profit when those who truly do commit crimes against person and property are duly convicted on the basis of reliable evidence. * * *

The classic response is that setting criminals free is a cost of the Fourth Amendment itself, and not of the much-maligned exclusionary rule. If the government had simply obeyed the Fourth Amendment it would never have found the bloody knife. Thus, excluding the knife simply restores the status quo ante and confers no benefit on the murderer. The classic response is too quick.

In many situations, it is far from clear that the illegality of a search is indeed a but-for cause of the later introduction of an item found in the search. Suppose the police could easily get a warrant, but fail to do so because they think the case at hand falls into a judicially recognized exception to the warrant requirement. A court later disagrees—and so, under current doctrine, the search was unconstitutional. But if the court goes on to exclude the bloody knife, it does indeed confer a huge benefit on the murderer. The police could easily have obtained a warrant before the search, so the illegality is not a but-for cause of the introduction of the knife into evidence.

\* \* \*

But even if a defendant could conclusively establish but-for causation, the bloody knife should still come in as evidence. Not all but-for consequences of an illegal search are legally cognizable. \* \* \* [I]f an illegal search turns up a ton of marijuana, the government need not return the contraband even if the government's possession of the marijuana is clearly a but-for consequence of its illegal search. Indeed, the government may sell the marijuana (say, for legitimate medical uses) and use the proceeds to finance the continued war on drugs. In a very real way, the government *has* profited from its own wrong.

Finally, Professor Amar critiques the deterrence rationale of the exclusionary rule, and decries the fact that deterrence comes by way of benefit to criminal defendants.

Deterrence is concerned with the government, it is concerned with systematic impact. It treats the criminal defendant merely as a surrogate for the larger public interest in restraining the government. The criminal defendant is a kind of private attorney general.

But the worst kind. He is self-selected and self-serving. He is often unrepresentative of the larger class of law-abiding citizens. Indeed, he is often despised by the public, the class he implicitly is supposed to represent. He will litigate on the worst set of facts, heedless that the result will be a bad precedent for the Fourth Amendment generally. He cares only about the case at hand—his case—and has no long view. He is not a sophisticated repeat player. He rarely hires the best lawyer. He cares only about exclusion—and can get only exclusion—even if other remedies (damages or injunctions) would better prevent future violations. \* \* \* He is, in short, an awkward champion of the Fourth Amendment.

He is also overcompensated. \* \* \* In a criminal case, if we insist on using criminal defendants as private attorneys general, why not give a defendant who successfully establishes a Fourth Amendment violation only a ten percent sentence discount—surely a tangible incentive—and substitute for the remaining ninety percent some other structural remedy, injunctive or damages, that will flow to the direct benefit of law-abiding citizens? * * *

Put differently, if deterrence is the key, the idea is to make the government pay, in some way, for its past misdeeds, in order to discourage future ones. But why should that payment flow to the guilty? Under the exclusionary rule, the more guilty you are, the more you benefit. * * * In sum, when it comes to private attorneys general, the exclusionary rule's deterrence rationale looks in the wrong place—to paradigmatically guilty criminal defendants rather than to prototypically law-abiding civil plaintiffs.

Professor Slobogin, in Why Liberals Should Chuck the Exclusionary Rule, 1999 Univ. Ill. L.Rev. 363, argues that the exclusionary rule should be replaced by an effective remedy of monetary damages.

[I]f optimal deterrence of illegal searches and seizures is the goal, the exclusionary rule is a poor solution. Changing or suppressing behavior is a complex and difficult task. It is especially difficult when, as is true with many types of illegal searches and seizures, the behavior is implicitly or explicitly endorsed by peers, superiors, and a large segment of the general public. Without a strong disincentive to engage in such conduct, it will continue. Thus, a regime that directly sanctions officers and their departments is preferable to the [exclusionary] rule. Although there are many versions of such a regime, it should have several core components: (1) a liquidated damages/penalty for all unconstitutional actions, preferably based on the average officer's salary; (2) personal liability, at the liquidated damages sum, of officers who knowingly or recklessly violate the Fourth Amendment; (3) entity liability, at the liquidated damages sum, for all other violations; (4) state-paid legal assistance for those with Fourth Amendment claims; and (5) a judicial decisionmaker.

That such a regime is a better deterrent than the exclusionary rule does not establish that it should be adopted, of course. The exclusionary rule clearly does have some deterrent effect. If it proves to be considerably less costly than a damages regime, perhaps it should remain the sanction of choice. It is unlikely that the rule is significantly "cheaper," however, whether one looks at financial or other types of costs. * * * A conservative estimate is that approximately 10,000 felons and 55,000 misdemeanants evade punishment each year because of successful Fourth Amendment suppression motions. Other costs of the rule are more subtle. These include the threat to the Fourth Amendment posed by judges and prosecutors concerned with freeing criminals, the psychic and systemic costs of routine perjury by police officers, the distracting impact of suppression hearings on the quality of defense representation on other issues, and the damage to courts and government generally because of public outrage at the huge benefit criminals receive when the cases against them are dismissed or damaged by exclusion.

* * *

[A] favorite liberal argument on behalf of the rule has been * * * that any alternative that truly works will result in at least as many lost convictions as the rule. A first response to this argument is that if we can avoid flaunting the costs of the Fourth Amendment and still achieve its goals, so much the better. More importantly, the assumption that an effective alternative prevents us from catching any criminal the exclusionary rule prevents us from convicting is wrong. The point of an effective deterrent is not only to discourage unconstitutional actions but to encourage constitutional ones. With an effective deterrent in place, police who lack probable cause will not necessarily give up; the more reasonable assumption is that they will simply get more cause. That is precisely the behavior a damages regime would systematically induce and what the exclusionary rule fails to encourage in any concerted way.

For more arguments about the value of the exclusionary rule and alternative remedies, see Stuntz The Virtues and Vices of the Exclusionary Rule, 20 Harv.J.L and Pub.Pol. 443 (1997); Perrin et al., If It's Broken, Fix It: Moving Beyond the Exclusionary Rule—A New and Extensive Empirical Study of the Exclusionary Rule and a Call for a Civil Administrative Remedy to Partially Replace the Rule, 83 Iowa L.Rev. 669 (1998).

For a debate over the exclusionary rule by two titans of the law, see Calabresi and Kamisar, Debate on the Search and Seizure Exclusionary Rule, 26 Harv. J. L. & Pub. Pol. 4 (2003). Judge Calabresi proposes an alternative to the exclusionary rule: that defendants could object to illegally obtained evidence, but only at *sentencing*, and if the motion is successful the defendant would receive a sentence reduction. In addition, Judge Calabresi would impose direct administrative sanctions on police officers for illegal searches and seizures. Professor Kamisar expresses doubt that administrative sanctions on wrongdoing police officers will be imposed in practice.

## D.  ALTERNATIVES TO EXCLUSION

The most common argument in support of the exclusionary rule is the alleged absence of alternative means of enforcing Fourth Amendment protections. The efficacy of the alternatives are, however, as hotly debated as the rule itself. In this section, other possible remedies will be evaluated, both in terms of deterrent value and workability.

It should be noted at the outset that most of these remedies could be used as *supplements* to, rather than replacements for, suppression of evidence.

## 1. Civil Damages Recovery

At present several forms of damage actions are available to the victim of an illegal search or seizure. Common law tort actions include false arrest, false imprisonment and trespass. More importantly, a federal civil rights action under 42 U.S.C.A. § 1983 is available when state officers, acting under color of law, violate a constitutional right. In Bivens v. Six Unknown Named Agents of Federal Bureau of Narcotics, 403 U.S. 388 (1971), the Supreme Court created a federal common law counterpart to § 1983 for violations by *federal* officials.

The two major problems involved in civil actions against police for violation of constitutional rights are first, winning, and second, collecting on the judgment. Obstacles such as governmental immunity exist in many states. Magistrates who issue invalid warrants are immune from suit. Pierson v. Ray, 386 U.S. 547, 553–55 (1967). Police officers exercising discretion are entitled to qualified immunity, so that even if they violate the Fourth Amendment, the citizen does not recover unless the law was clearly established at the time of the conduct.[31] How much Fourth Amendment law can be considered clearly established? (See *Safford, supra,* in the section on *Terry,* in which a strip search of a student was found illegal under the Fourth Amendment, but the official was found not liable because the law against such an action was not clearly established at the time of the search).

Besides the daunting prospect of overcoming qualified immunity, the "moral aspects of the case" make recovery in a jury trial difficult. Many victims of illegal police practices are not very sympathetic plaintiffs. In a false arrest action, for example, proof of the plaintiff's prior convictions often can be used to impeach his credibility or to show that probable cause existed for the arrest. "Respectable" persons have the greatest chance of recovering, because they will not be tainted by their past, but the "respectable" person is probably least likely to be subject to arbitrary arrest and harassment, and thus least likely to require a tort remedy.

If a plaintiff succeeds in proving liability, the next obstacle is proving—and collecting—damages adequate to make the suit worth the effort. In a trespass action, where damages are limited to actual property

---

[31] In Malley v. Briggs, 475 U.S. 335 (1986), the Court states that the question to be asked on qualified immunity with respect to an illegal search is "whether a reasonably well-trained officer * * * would have known that his affidavit failed to establish probable cause and that he should not have applied for the warrant." The opinion observes that "[i]t is true that in an ideal system an unreasonable request for a warrant would be harmless, because no judge would approve it," but that "ours is not an ideal system, and it is possible that a magistrate, working under docket pressures, will fail to perform as a magistrate should."

loss, the award is usually small except in the most extreme search cases. Nominal damages provide no incentive for an aggrieved citizen to sue, and thus prevent private persons from effectively enforcing the public policy against police illegality. A § 1983 action, which provides for attorney fees for the prevailing party, avoids some of the drawbacks of common law tort remedies. However, proof of the requisite intent and measuring the value of constitutional rights impose additional problems.

If the plaintiff receives a substantial damage award, the final problem is collecting on the judgment. Where sovereign immunity prevents actions against the government, a plaintiff is left to attempt recovery from the offending officers, who are often unable to pay. In § 1983 actions, the governmental unit employing the officer is not liable simply because one of its officers has violated the plaintiff's Fourth Amendment rights. In order to hold the government entity liable, the plaintiff must show that his injury resulted from the entity's custom or policy; otherwise the plaintiff is left to recover against the individual officer. Monell v. Department of Social Services, 436 U.S. 658 (1978) (applying the custom or policy requirement for municipal liability in § 1983 actions).

### Supreme Court View on Civil Damage Recovery as an Alternative to the Exclusionary Rule: Hudson v. Michigan

Despite all these limitations on civil damages recovery for a Fourth Amendment violation, the Supreme Court in Hudson v. Michigan, 547 U.S. 586 (2006), seemed to find § 1983 actions to be a viable alternative to the exclusionary rule. The Court in *Hudson* held that a violation of the knock-and-announce requirement does not justify exclusion of evidence found in the home.[32] The defendant argued that without the exclusionary rule, such violations would not be deterred. Justice Scalia, writing for the majority, responded to that argument, and more broadly to the argument that the exclusionary rule was necessary to deter other Fourth Amendment violations, in the following passage:

> We cannot assume that exclusion in this context is necessary deterrence simply because we found that it was necessary deterrence in different contexts and long ago. That would be forcing the public today to pay for the sins and inadequacies of a legal regime that existed almost half a century ago. Dollree Mapp could not turn to 42 U.S.C. § 1983 for meaningful relief; Monroe v. Pape, 365 U.S. 167 (1961), which began the slow but steady expansion of that remedy, was decided the same Term as *Mapp*. It would be another 17 years before the § 1983 remedy was extended to reach the deep pocket of

---

[32] *Hudson* is set forth in detail in the section on the fruit of causation and attenuation, *infra*.

municipalities, Monell v. New York City Dept. of Social Servs., 436 U.S. 658 (1978). Citizens whose Fourth Amendment rights were violated by federal officers could not bring suit until 10 years after *Mapp,* with this Court's decision in Bivens v. Six Unknown Fed. Narcotics Agents, 403 U.S. 388 (1971).

Hudson complains that "it would be very hard to find a lawyer to take a case such as this", but 42 U.S.C. § 1988(b) answers this objection. Since some civil-rights violations would yield damages too small to justify the expense of litigation, Congress has authorized attorney's fees for civil-rights plaintiffs. This remedy was unavailable in the heydays of our exclusionary-rule jurisprudence, because it is tied to the availability of a cause of action. For years after *Mapp,* "very few lawyers would even consider representation of persons who had civil rights claims against the police," but now "much has changed. Citizens and lawyers are much more willing to seek relief in the courts for police misconduct." M. Avery, D. Rudovsky, & K. Blum, Police Misconduct: Law and Litigation, p. v (3d ed. 2005). The number of public-interest law firms and lawyers who specialize in civil-rights grievances has greatly expanded.

Is the Court saying that the exclusionary rule is no longer necessary to deter *any* Fourth Amendment violation, because of the modern strength and viability of § 1983 actions? What about the limitations on §1983 liability that Justice Scalia did not discuss in *Hudson*—such as defenses of qualified immunity, and the absence of respondeat superior liability? What about the fact that many victims of Fourth Amendment violations are people with whom a jury will have little sympathy?

### *Fortified Civil Damages Remedy*

It should be noted that after *Hudson,* any talk of a fortified damages remedy may be hypothetical, because the Court seems to think that existing damages remedies provide a sufficiently effective alternative to exclusion. Nonetheless, Professor Amar, in Fourth Amendment First Principles, 107 Harv.L.Rev.757 (1994), recommends five steps that would strengthen the deterrent effects of the existing civil damages remedy for Fourth Amendment violations. He contends that if these steps are employed, the damages remedy will provide effective deterrence against illegal police activity; the exclusionary rule can then be abolished.

Professor Amar's suggestions are as follows: First, the government should be made liable for illegal police behavior—that is, the current bar on respondeat superior liability should be abrogated. Not only would this provide a financially responsible defendant, but it would apply the deterrent at the level where policy is made. Second, damage multipliers and punitive damages should be made available—with some of the excess recovery going to a "Fourth Amendment Fund to educate Americans about the Amendment and comfort victims of crime and police brutality." Third, claims for small damage amounts should be entitled to reasonable attorney's fees and the possibility of class action consolidation. Fourth, the procedural limitations on injunctive relief for Fourth Amendment violations should be liberalized. Fifth, administrative channels should be established so that claims can be processed quickly and efficiently without the need for a court action.

Would this fortified damages remedy be more effective than the exclusionary rule? Does it make more sense than the exclusionary rule because it potentially provides compensation to innocent people, whereas the exclusionary rule can by definition be invoked only by guilty people?

Some have argued that one of the costs of the exclusionary rule is that it results in judicial cutbacks on the Fourth Amendment's substantive protections—the argument is that courts, when they see the consequences of exclusion of evidence (letting the guilty go free), tend to hold that there is no Fourth Amendment violation in the first place. Would the courts be more prone to find Fourth Amendment violations if the only consequence was a monetary remedy, as opposed to allowing a guilty person to go free?

### Proposals in Congress for Alternatives to the Exclusionary Rule

Members of Congress have from time to time proposed legislation that would abrogate the exclusionary rule and replace it with a fortified tort remedy. As of yet, no such proposal has been enacted. A typical example is a proposal providing that the United States would be liable for damages resulting from an illegal search or seizure of an investigative or law enforcement officer. Punitive damages are capped at $10,000; awards to anyone convicted of an offense in which the illegally obtained evidence was used would be limited to damages for actual physical injury and property damage; and attorney's fees and costs would be awarded to claimants who prevail.

The Committee on Federal Legislation of the Association of the Bar of the City of New York had this to say about tort recovery alternatives to the exclusionary rule:

> [E]ven if a tort remedy could be fashioned that would result in meaningful monetary recovery for the victims of Fourth Amendment violations, we would object to it as a replacement for (rather than a supplement to) the exclusionary rule. The tort remedy is based upon the premise that Fourth Amendment rights can and should be left to the marketplace—that the government can make an economic decision to violate a person's Fourth Amendment rights, so long as it

is willing to pay its way out of it. We do not believe that Fourth Amendment rights are susceptible to such a market analysis. * * *

* * * We find it troubling that the government could establish a budget line for Fourth Amendment violations as part of its war on crime. It cannot be the case that a Fourth Amendment violation is truly remedied simply because the government cuts a check.

Proposed Changes to the Exclusionary Rule, 50 The Record of the Association of the Bar of the City of New York 385 (1995).

Does Congress even have the power under the Constitution to abrogate the exclusionary rule and replace it with another remedy?

## 2. Criminal Prosecutions of Offending Officers

Criminal prosecution of offending officers is sometimes suggested as the only real deterrent to police misconduct. A federal statute has been in existence since 1921 that makes federal officers who participate in illegal searches guilty of a misdemeanor and subject to substantial fines. 18 U.S.C.A. § 2236. To our knowledge, however, no officer has ever been convicted under the statute. Many states have similar statutes that also remain dormant. A fair number of criminal actions have been brought under state and federal law for actions of police officers that have resulted in death or serious injury of persons who are arrested. The cases involving the beatings of Rodney King (an African-American construction worker who was beaten by Los Angeles police officers following a high-speed car chase in 1991) and Abner Louima (arrested in a nightclub in 1997 and sexually assaulted by police officers in a stationhouse bathroom) are two notorious examples. But again, few criminal prosecutions are brought against police officers who simply make illegal searches.

Why has there been such a dearth of prosecutions? The most likely answer is that prosecutors are reluctant to press charges against the police, except in the most extreme cases involving physical injury, because they rely heavily on cooperation with the department. In addition, juries are reluctant to convict policemen of crime, unless the circumstances are egregious.

More fundamentally, it can be argued that the threat of a direct criminal sanction on the officer who conducts an illegal search is an *over-deterrent*. It may lead to an officer "second-guessing" himself in fast-developing situations, and deciding, for example, not to enter a premises, when to enter might be needed to protect a member of the public. Isn't the systemic deterrence provided by the exclusionary rule more appropriate in these circumstances?

### 3.  Police Rulemaking and Other Administrative Solutions

A third alternative remedy for Fourth Amendment violations is police regulation, education, training and discipline. In Hudson v. Michigan, supra, the Court extolled the virtues of internal police regulations and training programs to comply with the Fourth Amendment—which programs generally did not exist at the time of *Mapp*—as an alternative to the exclusionary rule for deterring police misconduct.

> Another development over the past half-century that deters civil-rights violations is the increasing professionalism of police forces, including a new emphasis on internal police discipline. * * * [W]e now have increasing evidence that police forces across the United States take the constitutional rights of citizens seriously. There have been "wide-ranging reforms in the education, training, and supervision of police officers." S. Walker, Taming the System: The Control of Discretion in Criminal Justice 1950–1990, p. 51 (1993). Numerous sources are now available to teach officers and their supervisors what is required of them under this Court's cases, how to respect constitutional guarantees in various situations, and how to craft an effective regime for internal discipline. [Citing treatises and manuals used by police.] Failure to teach and enforce constitutional requirements exposes municipalities to financial liability. See Canton v. Harris, 489 U.S. 378, 388 (1989). Moreover, modern police forces are staffed with professionals; it is not credible to assert that internal discipline, which can limit successful careers, will not have a deterrent effect. There is also evidence that the increasing use of various forms of citizen review can enhance police accountability.

While police education, training and discipline on Fourth Amendment issues has surely increased dramatically since *Mapp,* couldn't it be argued that all of these innovations occurred *because* the exclusionary rule finally made the Fourth Amendment relevant, as a practical matter, to police departments? Why was there no significant training on Fourth Amendment standards in the state before *Mapp*? If the exclusionary rule were abolished, would there be the same incentive to train officers in Fourth Amendment law and discipline them when they violate it?

### 4.  Sentence Reductions

Some of the commentary discussed above suggest that instead of excluding illegally obtained evidence from the trial, a more fair and balanced result would allow or require the sentencing court to reduce a defendants sentence if illegally obtained evidence was used against him at trial. It is argued that the sentencing alternative would limit the costs to society and avoid a windfall for the defendant.

Would the threat of a reduction of sentence deter illegal searches and seizures? Would officers and police departments take account of a sentencing discount in determining whether to conduct a search or seizure? Or would these actors be focused on convicting the guilty?

# E.  LIMITATIONS ON EXCLUSION

There are a number of important situations in which evidence has been illegally obtained, and yet it will not be excluded. This section considers those limitations on the exclusionary rule.

## 1.  "Good Faith"—Reasonable Reliance on the Decisions of Magistrates and Others

In the following case, the Court adopted a "good faith" exception for searches conducted pursuant to a warrant that is later found to be invalid. As you read the case, keep in mind that the Court is not promulgating an "absolute" exception. Rather, there are "exceptions to the exception," where a good faith argument will be rejected and the evidence excluded. Also note that the Court clearly holds that the Constitution does not require exclusion of evidence as a remedy for a Fourth Amendment violation. Does this mean that *Mapp* is overruled? If so, are the States permitted to abolish the exclusionary rule entirely and admit *all* illegally obtained evidence, as they were before *Mapp*?

### UNITED STATES V. LEON

Supreme Court of the United States, 1984.
468 U.S. 897.

### JUSTICE WHITE delivered the opinion of the Court.

This case presents the question whether the Fourth Amendment exclusionary rule should be modified so as not to bar the use in the prosecution's case-in-chief of evidence obtained by officers acting in reasonable reliance on a search warrant issued by a detached and neutral magistrate but ultimately found to be unsupported by probable cause. * * *

[On the basis of information from an informant and other investigation, Officer Rombach obtained a facially valid search warrant. The ensuing searches produced large quantities of drugs and related evidence that the government proffered against several alleged coconspirators. The district court found that the warrant was issued without probable cause. The court of appeals affirmed the order of suppression, finding that the affidavit was insufficient to establish probable cause under the then-applicable *Spinelli* test. One court of appeals judge dissented from this ruling.]

The Government's petition for certiorari expressly declined to seek review of the lower courts' determinations that the search warrant was unsupported by probable cause and presented only the question "[w]hether the Fourth Amendment exclusionary rule should be modified so as not to bar the admission of evidence seized in reasonable, good-faith reliance on a search warrant that is subsequently held to be defective." * * *

We have concluded that, in the Fourth Amendment context, the exclusionary rule can be modified somewhat without jeopardizing its ability to perform its intended functions. Accordingly, we reverse the judgment of the Court of Appeals.

* * *

Language in opinions of this Court and of individual Justices has sometimes implied that the exclusionary rule is a necessary corollary of the Fourth Amendment, or that the rule is required by the conjunction of the Fourth and Fifth Amendments. These implications need not detain us long. The Fifth Amendment theory has not withstood critical analysis or the test of time, and the Fourth Amendment has never been interpreted to proscribe the introduction of illegally seized evidence in all proceedings or against all persons.

* * * The Fourth Amendment contains no provision expressly precluding the use of evidence obtained in violation of its commands, and an examination of its origin and purposes makes clear that the use of fruits of a past unlawful search or seizure "works no new Fourth Amendment wrong." The wrong condemned by the Amendment is "fully accomplished" by the unlawful search or seizure itself, and the exclusionary rule is neither intended nor able to "cure the invasion of the defendant's rights which he has already suffered." The rule thus operates as "a judicially created remedy designed to safeguard Fourth Amendment rights generally through its deterrent effect, rather than a personal constitutional right of the party aggrieved."

Whether the exclusionary sanction is appropriately imposed in a particular case, our decisions make clear, is "an issue separate from the question whether the Fourth Amendment rights of the party seeking to invoke the rule were violated by police conduct." Only the former question is currently before us, and it must be resolved by weighing the costs and benefits of preventing the use in the prosecution's case-in-chief of inherently trustworthy tangible evidence obtained in reliance on a search warrant issued by a detached and neutral magistrate that ultimately is found to be defective.

The substantial social costs exacted by the exclusionary rule for the vindication of Fourth Amendment rights have long been a source of concern. * * * An objectionable collateral consequence of this interference with the criminal justice system's truth-finding function is that some guilty defendants may go free or receive reduced sentences as a result of favorable plea bargains. Particularly when law enforcement officers have acted in objective good faith or their transgressions have been minor, the magnitude of the benefit conferred on such guilty defendants offends basic concepts of the criminal justice system. * * *

Close attention to those remedial objectives has characterized our recent decisions concerning the scope of the Fourth Amendment exclusionary rule.

[Justice White notes that the Court had by this time: confined the rule to criminal trials; required "standing" on the part of defendants who seek suppression; permitted use of illegally seized evidence to impeach the defendant; and allowed evidence to be admitted where its link to a violation is attenuated.]

As yet, we have not recognized any form of good-faith exception to the Fourth Amendment exclusionary rule. But the balancing approach that has evolved during the years of experience with the rule provides strong support for the modification currently urged upon us. * * *

Because a search warrant provides the detached scrutiny of a neutral magistrate, which is a more reliable safeguard against improper searches than the hurried judgment of a law enforcement officer "engaged in the often competitive enterprise of ferreting out crime," we have expressed a strong preference for warrants and declared that "in a doubtful or marginal case a search under a warrant may be sustainable where without one it would fail." Reasonable minds frequently may differ on the question whether a particular affidavit establishes probable cause, and we have thus concluded that the preference for warrants is most appropriately effectuated by according "great deference" to a magistrate's determination.

\* \* \*

* * * To the extent that proponents of exclusion rely on its behavioral effects on judges and magistrates in these areas, their reliance is misplaced. First, the exclusionary rule is designed to deter police misconduct rather than to punish the errors of judges and magistrates. Second, there exists no evidence suggesting that judges and magistrates are inclined to ignore or subvert the Fourth Amendment or that lawlessness among these actors requires application of the extreme sanction of exclusion.

Third, and most important, we discern no basis, and are offered none, for believing that exclusion of evidence seized pursuant to a warrant will have a significant deterrent effect on the issuing judge or magistrate. * * * Judges and magistrates are not adjuncts to the law enforcement team; as neutral judicial officers, they have no stake in the outcome of particular criminal prosecutions. * * * Imposition of the exclusionary sanction is not necessary to inform judicial officers of their errors, and we cannot conclude that admitting evidence obtained pursuant to a warrant while at the same time declaring that the warrant was somehow defective will in any way reduce judicial officers' professional incentives to comply with the Fourth Amendment, encourage them to repeat their mistakes, or lead to the granting of all colorable warrant requests.

If exclusion of evidence obtained pursuant to a subsequently invalidated warrant is to have any deterrent effect, therefore, it must alter the behavior of individual law enforcement officers or the policies of their departments. One could argue that applying the exclusionary rule in cases where the police failed to demonstrate probable cause in the warrant application deters future inadequate presentations or "magistrate shopping" and thus promotes the ends of the Fourth Amendment. Suppressing evidence obtained pursuant to a technically defective warrant supported by probable cause also might encourage officers to scrutinize more closely the form of the warrant and to point out suspected judicial errors. We find such arguments speculative and conclude that suppression of evidence obtained pursuant to a warrant should be ordered only on a case-by-case basis and only in those unusual cases in which exclusion will further the purposes of the exclusionary rule.[a]

We have frequently questioned whether the exclusionary rule can have any deterrent effect when the offending officers acted in the objectively reasonable belief that their conduct did not violate the Fourth Amendment. * * * But even assuming that the rule effectively deters some police misconduct and provides incentives for the law enforcement profession as a whole to conduct itself in accord with the Fourth Amendment, it cannot be expected, and should not be applied, to deter objectively reasonable law enforcement activity. * * *[b]

This is particularly true, we believe, when an officer acting with objective good faith has obtained a search warrant from a judge or magistrate and acted within its scope. In most such cases, there is no police illegality and thus nothing to deter. It is the magistrate's responsibility to determine whether the officer's allegations establish

---

[a] Our discussion of the deterrent effect of excluding evidence obtained in reasonable reliance on a subsequently invalidated warrant assumes, of course, that the officers properly executed the warrant and searched only those places and for those objects that it was reasonable to believe were covered by the warrant. * * *

[b] We emphasize that the standard of reasonableness we adopt is an objective one. Many objections to a good-faith exception assume that the exception will turn on the subjective good faith of individual officers. Grounding the modification in objective reasonableness, however, retains the value of the exclusionary rule as an incentive for the law enforcement profession as a whole to conduct themselves in accord with the Fourth Amendment. The objective standard we adopt, moreover, requires officers to have a reasonable knowledge of what the law prohibits.

probable cause and, if so, to issue a warrant comporting in form with the requirements of the Fourth Amendment. In the ordinary case, an officer cannot be expected to question the magistrate's probable cause determination or his judgment that the form of the warrant is technically sufficient. * * * Penalizing the officer for the magistrate's error, rather than his own, cannot logically contribute to the deterrence of Fourth Amendment violations.

* * * We conclude that the marginal or nonexistent benefits produced by suppressing evidence obtained in objectively reasonable reliance on a subsequently invalidated search warrant cannot justify the substantial costs of exclusion. We do not suggest, however, that exclusion is always inappropriate in cases where an officer has obtained a warrant and abided by its terms. * * * [T]he officer's reliance on the magistrate's probable-cause determination and on the technical sufficiency of the warrant he issues must be objectively reasonable, and it is clear that in some circumstances the officer[c] will have no reasonable grounds for believing that the warrant was properly issued.

Suppression therefore remains an appropriate remedy if the magistrate or judge in issuing a warrant was misled by information in an affidavit that the affiant knew was false or would have known was false except for his reckless disregard of the truth. The exception we recognize today will also not apply in cases where the issuing magistrate wholly abandoned his judicial role in the manner condemned in Lo-Ji Sales, Inc. v. New York [where the magistrate issued the warrant and then participated in the search]; in such circumstances, no reasonably well-trained officer should rely on the warrant. Nor would an officer manifest objective good faith in relying on a warrant based on an affidavit so lacking in indicia of probable cause as to render official belief in its existence entirely unreasonable. Finally, depending on the circumstances of the particular case, a warrant may be so facially deficient—i.e., in failing to particularize the place to be searched or the things to be seized—that the executing officers cannot reasonably presume it to be valid.

In so limiting the suppression remedy, we leave untouched the probable-cause standard and the various requirements for a valid warrant. * * *

Nor are we persuaded that application of a good-faith exception to searches conducted pursuant to warrants will preclude review of the

---

c  References to "officer" throughout this opinion should not be read too narrowly. It is necessary to consider the objective reasonableness, not only of the officers who eventually executed a warrant, but also of the officers who originally obtained it or who provided information material to the probable-cause determination. Nothing in our opinion suggests, for example, that an officer could obtain a warrant on the basis of a "bare bones" affidavit and then rely on colleagues who are ignorant of the circumstances under which the warrant was obtained to conduct the search.

constitutionality of the search or seizure, deny needed guidance from the courts, or freeze Fourth Amendment law in its present state. * * *

If the resolution of a particular Fourth Amendment question is necessary to guide future action by law enforcement officers and magistrates, nothing will prevent reviewing courts from deciding that question before turning to the good-faith issue. Indeed, it frequently will be difficult to determine whether the officers acted reasonably without resolving the Fourth Amendment issue. Even if the Fourth Amendment question is not one of broad import, reviewing courts could decide in particular cases that magistrates under their supervision need to be informed of their errors and so evaluate the officers' good faith only after finding a violation. In other circumstances, those courts could reject suppression motions posing no important Fourth Amendment questions by turning immediately to a consideration of the officers' good faith. * * *

When the principles we have enunciated today are applied to the facts of this case, it is apparent that the judgment of the Court of Appeals cannot stand. * * *

\* \* \*

Officer Rombach's application for a warrant clearly was supported by much more than a "bare bones" affidavit. The affidavit related the results of an extensive investigation and, as the opinions of the divided panel of the Court of Appeals make clear, provided evidence sufficient to create disagreement among thoughtful and competent judges as to the existence of probable cause. Under these circumstances, the officers' reliance on the magistrate's determination of probable cause was objectively reasonable, and application of the extreme sanction of exclusion is inappropriate.

**JUSTICE BLACKMUN, concurring.**

* * * I believe that the rule announced today advances the legitimate interests of the criminal justice system without sacrificing the individual rights protected by the Fourth Amendment. I write separately, however, to underscore what I regard as the unavoidably provisional nature of today's decisions.

\* \* \*

* * * By their very nature, the assumptions on which we proceed today cannot be cast in stone. To the contrary, they now will be tested in the real world of state and federal law enforcement, and this Court will attend to the results. If it should emerge from experience that, contrary to our expectations, the good faith exception to the exclusionary rule results in a material change in police compliance with the Fourth Amendment, we shall have to reconsider what we have undertaken here.

* * *

**JUSTICE BRENNAN, with whom JUSTICE MARSHALL joins, dissenting.**[d]

* * *

[A]s critics of the exclusionary rule never tire of repeating, the Fourth Amendment makes no express provision for the exclusion of evidence secured in violation of its commands. A short answer to this claim, of course, is that many of the Constitution's most vital imperatives are stated in general terms and the task of giving meaning to these precepts is therefore left to subsequent judicial decisionmaking. * * *

A more direct answer may be supplied by recognizing that the Amendment, like other provisions of the Bill of Rights, restrains the power of the government as a whole; * * *. The judiciary is responsible, no less than the executive, for ensuring that constitutional rights are respected.

* * * Because seizures are executed principally to secure evidence, and because such evidence generally has utility in our legal system only in the context of a trial supervised by a judge, it is apparent that the admission of illegally obtained evidence implicates the same constitutional concerns as the initial seizure of that evidence. Indeed, by admitting unlawfully seized evidence, the judiciary becomes a part of what is in fact a single governmental action prohibited by the terms of the Amendment. * * *

[I]f the Amendment is to have any meaning, police and the courts cannot be regarded as constitutional strangers to each other; because the evidence-gathering role of the police is directly linked to the evidence-admitting function of the courts, an individual's Fourth Amendment rights may be undermined as completely by one as by the other.

* * *

[T]he Court has frequently bewailed the "cost" of excluding reliable evidence. In large part, this criticism rests upon a refusal to acknowledge the function of the Fourth Amendment itself. If nothing else, the Amendment plainly operates to disable the government from gathering information and securing evidence in certain ways. * * * Thus, some criminals will go free *not,* in Justice (then Judge) Cardozo's misleading epigram, "because the constable has blundered," but rather because official compliance with Fourth Amendment requirements makes it more difficult to catch criminals.

---

[d]  The dissent addresses both *Leon* and the companion case, *Sheppard* discussed infra.

\* \* \*

\* \* \* The key to the Court's conclusion \* \* \* is its belief that the prospective deterrent effect of the exclusionary rule operates only in those situations in which police officers, when deciding whether to go forward with some particular search, have reason to know that their planned conduct will violate the requirements of the Fourth Amendment. \* \* \*

\* \* \* But what the Court overlooks is that the deterrence rationale for the rule is not designed to be, nor should it be thought of as, a form of "punishment" of individual police officers for their failures to obey the restraints imposed by the Fourth Amendment. Instead, the chief deterrent function of the rule is its tendency to promote institutional compliance with Fourth Amendment requirements on the part of law enforcement agencies generally. \* \* \*

If the overall educational effect of the exclusionary rule is considered, application of the rule to even those situations in which individual police officers have acted on the basis of a reasonable but mistaken belief that their conduct was authorized can still be expected to have a considerable long-term deterrent effect. If evidence is consistently excluded in these circumstances, police departments will surely be prompted to instruct their officers to devote greater care and attention to providing sufficient information to establish probable cause when applying for a warrant, and to review with some attention the form of the warrant that they have been issued, rather than automatically assuming that whatever document the magistrate has signed will necessarily comport with Fourth Amendment requirements.

\* \* \*

Although the Court brushes these concerns aside, a host of grave consequences can be expected to result from its decision to carve this new exception out of the exclusionary rule. A chief consequence of today's decision will be to convey a clear and unambiguous message to magistrates that their decisions to issue warrants are now insulated from subsequent judicial review. \* \* \*

Moreover, the good faith exception will encourage police to provide only the bare minimum of information in future warrant applications. The police will now know that if they can secure a warrant, so long as the circumstances of its issuance are not "entirely unreasonable," all police conduct pursuant to that warrant will be protected from further judicial review. \* \* \*

[E]ven if one were to believe, as the Court apparently does, that police are hobbled by inflexible and hypertechnical warrant procedures, today's decision cannot be justified. This is because, given the relaxed standard for assessing probable cause established just last Term in

Illinois v. Gates, the Court's newly fashioned good faith exception, when applied in the warrant context, will rarely, if ever, offer any greater flexibility for police than the *Gates* standard already supplies. * * * Given such a relaxed standard, it is virtually inconceivable that a reviewing court, when faced with a defendant's motion to suppress, could first find that a warrant was invalid under the new *Gates* standard, but then, at the same time, find that a police officer's reliance on such an invalid warrant was nevertheless "objectively reasonable" under the test announced today. Because the two standards overlap so completely, it is unlikely that a warrant could be found invalid under *Gates* and yet the police reliance upon it could be seen as objectively reasonable; otherwise, we would have to entertain the mindboggling concept of objectively reasonable reliance upon an objectively unreasonable warrant.

* * * [T]he full impact of the Court's regrettable decision will not be felt until the Court attempts to extend this rule to situations in which the police have conducted a warrantless search solely on the basis of their own judgment about the existence of probable cause and exigent circumstances. When that question is finally posed, I for one will not be surprised if my colleagues decide once again that we simply cannot afford to protect Fourth Amendment rights.

* * *

**JUSTICE STEVENS, concurring in the judgment in [*Sheppard*], and dissenting in [*Leon*].**[e]

* * *

The Court assumes that the searches in these cases violated the Fourth Amendment, yet refuses to apply the exclusionary rule because the Court concludes that it was "reasonable" for the police to conduct them. In my opinion an official search and seizure cannot be both "unreasonable" and "reasonable" at the same time.

* * *

Today's decisions do grave damage to [the exclusionary rule's] deterrent function. Under the majority's new rule, even when the police know their warrant application is probably insufficient, they retain an incentive to submit it to a magistrate, on the chance that he may take the bait. No longer must they hesitate and seek additional evidence in doubtful cases. * * *

* * * Today, for the first time, this Court holds that although the Constitution has been violated, no court should do anything about it at any time and in any proceeding. In my judgment, the Constitution requires more. * * * Nor should we so easily concede the existence of a

---

[e] Justice Stevens expressed the view that there was no constitutional violation in *Sheppard*.

constitutional violation for which there is no remedy. To do so is to convert a Bill of *Rights* into an unenforced honor code that the police may follow in their discretion. The Constitution requires more; it requires a *remedy*. If the Court's new rule is to be followed, the Bill of Rights should be renamed.

### NOTE ON MASSACHUSETTS V. SHEPPARD

Massachusetts v. Sheppard, 468 U.S. 981 (1984), is the companion case to *Leon*. In the course of a murder investigation in Roxbury, Officer O'Malley obtained probable cause to arrest Sheppard and to search his residence. Officer O'Malley's affidavit described in detail the property to be seized in the search of Sheppard's house, e.g., the victim's clothing. Detective O'Malley showed the affidavit to the district attorney, the district attorney's first assistant, and a sergeant, who all concluded that it set forth probable cause for the search and the arrest, and that a warrant based on the affidavit would particularly describe the things to be seized. The *Sheppard* Court described what happened next:

> Because it was Sunday, the local court was closed, and the police had a difficult time finding a warrant application form. Detective O'Malley finally found a warrant form previously in use in the Dorchester District. The form was entitled "Search Warrant—Controlled Substance G.L. c. 276 §§ 1 through 3A." Realizing that some changes had to be made before the form could be used to authorize the search requested in the affidavit, Detective O'Malley deleted the subtitle "controlled substance" with a typewriter. He also substituted "Roxbury" for the printed "Dorchester" and typed Sheppard's name and address into blank spaces provided for that information. However, the reference to "controlled substance" was not deleted in the portion of the form that constituted the warrant application and that, when signed, would constitute the warrant itself.

> Detective O'Malley then took the affidavit and the warrant form to the residence of a judge who had consented to consider the warrant application. The judge examined the affidavit and stated that he would authorize the search as requested. Detective O'Malley offered the warrant form and stated that he knew the form as presented dealt with controlled substances. He showed the judge where he had crossed out the subtitles. After unsuccessfully searching for a more suitable form, the judge informed O'Malley that he would make the necessary changes so as to provide a proper search warrant. The judge then took the form, made some changes on it, and dated and signed the warrant. However, he did not change the substantive portion of the warrant, which continued to authorize a search for controlled substances; nor did he alter the form so as to incorporate the affidavit. The judge returned the affidavit and the warrant to O'Malley, informing him that the warrant was sufficient authority in form and content to carry out the search as

requested. * * * The scope of the ensuing search was limited to the items listed in the affidavit, and several incriminating pieces of evidence were discovered. Sheppard was then charged with first degree murder.

The *Sheppard* Court stated that "[t]here is no dispute that the officers believed that the warrant authorized the search that they conducted." The Court found that there was an objectively reasonable basis for the officers' mistaken belief. If an error of constitutional dimension was made, the Court found that it was the judge who made it, and the Court therefore declined to suppress the evidence. The Court concluded that the officers "took every step that could reasonably be expected of them," and that O'Malley was not required "to disbelieve a judge who has just advised him, by word and by action, that the warrant he possesses authorizes him to conduct the search he has requested." The Court refused to decide whether the warrant was in fact invalid for lack of particularity. It stated that this was "a fact-bound issue of little importance since similar situations are unlikely to arise with any regularity." Justice Stevens argued in his opinion concurring in the judgment that there was no error of constitutional dimension and therefore no need to suppress evidence.

For cases following *Sheppard*, see United States v. Kelley, 140 F.3d 596 (5th Cir.1998) (officers could reasonably rely on the warrant even though it was defective because the magistrate hadn't signed it: "The rare occasion when a magistrate accidentally fails to sign a warrant cannot be eliminated by suppressing the evidence" and "it is unlikely that police will wilfully and recklessly attempt to evade getting a warrant signed"); United States v. Russell, 960 F.2d 421 (5th Cir.1992) (warrant fails to include an attachment of the items to be seized, but the officer specifically described the items in an affidavit; judge committed the "clerical error" of failing to incorporate the affidavit in the warrant).

### Reasonable Reliance on Unreasonable Warrants

The *Leon* Court rejects a good faith test that would depend on the subjective state of mind of the officer. Instead, the Court establishes a concept of "reasonable" reliance on an invalid warrant. Justices Stevens and Brennan contend that it is impossible to rely reasonably on an unreasonable warrant. But reasonable minds can and often do differ as to what is reasonable. For example, in a typical negligence trial both sides can make reasonable arguments about whether the defendant acted unreasonably—if there was no such thing as a reasonable argument about whether the defendant acted reasonably, then no negligence case would ever get to a jury. And in terms of warrants, one person might think that a warrant is valid while two others might think it defective; certainly there could be a reasonable disagreement when it comes to Fourth Amendment standards that are often ambiguous and fact-dependent.

What the *Leon* Court appears to mean is that in cases where some or most people would think that a warrant is invalid—for lack of probable cause, or particularity, or other procedural details—the good faith exception will apply so long as reasonable minds can differ on the point. Where no reasonable argument can be made that the warrant is valid, then the good faith exception will not apply because no reasonable officer could rely on the magistrate's determination. It is at that point an error by the *officer* to rely on the warrant—and officers can be deterred by the exclusionary rule.

Thus, the good faith exception is similar to the standard used for reviewing jury verdicts in civil cases—the standard is not whether the jury was correct or whether the reviewing court would have decided the case another way, but rather whether no reasonable person could have decided the way the jury did. So long as there is room for argument, then, the good faith exception will apply.

Another useful analogy comes from the qualified immunity cases decided under the civil rights statute, 42 U.S.C. § 1983. Even if the plaintiff's constitutional rights are violated, an official is not liable unless he violated clearly established law; if the law was not clearly established at the time of the officer's action, then there is room for argument as to whether the officer's conduct was lawful. The Supreme Court has equated the standards of qualified immunity with the objective reasonableness standard of the good faith exception to the exclusionary rule. See Anderson v. Creighton, 483 U.S. 635 (1987) (rejecting the argument that an officer may not reasonably act unreasonably).

Because an officer can reasonably act unreasonably, there are three types of errors after *Leon:*

(1) reasonable mistakes that are not a violation of the Fourth Amendment at all, such as a mistake of fact;

(2) unreasonable mistakes that in fact violate the Fourth Amendment, but at the time of the conduct reasonable minds could have differed about whether the officer was acting lawfully; and

(3) unreasonable mistakes where the officer violated clearly established law, so that no reasonable argument could be made that the action was lawful.

Illinois v. Rodriguez, (discussed in the materials on third party consent)—where the officers made a reasonable mistake about the authority of a third party to consent to a search—falls into the first category; *Leon* falls into the second; and reliance on a warrant issued on the basis of a barebones affidavit falls into the third.

### *Leon, Gates and Warrants Clearly Lacking in Probable Cause*

In Justice Brennan's view, the good faith standard and the *Gates* standard for probable cause overlap completely, so that if a warrant is lacking in probable cause under the permissible test of *Gates* it must be so deficient, so clearly lacking in probable cause, that it could not possibly be reasonably relied upon. This view has not been adopted by the courts after *Leon*, however. There are a number of cases in which courts have found the good faith exception applicable because reasonable minds could differ about whether the *Gates* standards were satisfied. These cases indicate that there is some grey area between the *Gates* standard and a warrant that clearly lacks probable cause. See, e.g., United States v. Gibson, 928 F.2d 250 (8th Cir.1991) (*Gates* standard not satisfied because police only corroborated a few "innocent details," but good faith exception applies because reasonable minds could differ on whether *Gates* standard is satisfied on such minimal corroboration); United States v. Brunette, 256 F.3d 14 (1st Cir. 2001) (it was error for the magistrate to issue a warrant to search for internet child pornography where the magistrate relied solely on the officer's conclusion that the pictures posted by the defendant were pornographic; however, "although we hold that the omission of images or a description of them was a serious defect in the warrant application, the uncertain state of the law at the time made reliance on the warrant objectively reasonable."); United States v. Paull, 551 F.3d 516 (6th Cir. 2009) (while information about the defendant's possession of child pornography was very dated, the warrant did not "clearly lack" probable cause because of this stale information; the officer had experience in child pornography investigations that caused her to believe the evidence was still on the premises: "even where an officer's experience provides too little evidence to establish probable cause, it suffices to make the affidavit not bare bones by providing a reasonable connection between the defendant and the alleged crime.").

There are also a fair number of cases in which probable cause is found lacking under *Gates*, and the court further finds that the officer was *not* objectively reasonable in relying on the warrant. See, e.g., United States v. Doyle, 650 F.3d 460 (4th Cir. 2011) (warrant to search for child pornography clearly lacked probable cause where "[t]he bulk of the information supplied in the affidavit concerned allegations of sexual assault"; the court found that "evidence of child molestation alone does not support probable cause to search for child pornography"); United States v. John, 654 F.3d 412 (3rd Cir. 2011) (warrant to search the defendant's home for child pornography clearly lacked probable cause where it was based solely on the fact that the defendant had molested his students on school property and kept evidence of those crimes at his home); United States v. Baxter, 889 F.2d 731 (6th Cir.1989) (affidavit describing tip from anonymous informant, with corroboration only of defendant's address and prior conviction on drug charges, is a barebones affidavit, and officer was not objectively reasonable in relying on the warrant); United States v. Helton, 314 F.3d 812 (6th Cir. 2003) ("A reasonable officer knows that evidence of three calls a month to known drug dealers from a house, a description of that house, and an allegation that a drug dealer stores drug proceeds with his brother and his brother's girlfriend (neither of whom live at or are known to visit that house) falls well short of establishing probable cause that the house contains evidence of a crime.").

The case of United States v. Carpenter, 360 F.3d 591 (6th Cir. 2004), is instructive on the difference between facts that are reasonably close to probable cause and facts where probable cause is clearly lacking. Officers obtained a warrant to search the defendant's residence based on an affidavit stating that marijuana was growing in a field "near" the residence and "there is a road connecting the above described residence to the marijuana plants." The court held that the warrant issued on the basis of this affidavit lacked probable cause, "because it did not provide the required nexus between the residence and the illegal activity." However, the evidence found in the residence was not excluded because the affidavit did not clearly lack a showing of probable cause as to location. The court stated that "the affidavit was not completely devoid of any nexus between the residence and the marijuana that the police observed." Rather, it noted both that the marijuana was growing near the residence and that there was a road connecting the residence and the marijuana plants. The court found a "useful contrast" in the facts of United States v. Hove, 848 F.2d 137 (9th Cir. 1988), where a warrant was found clearly lacking in probable cause because the officer "obtained a warrant to search a particular residence after submitting to the issuing magistrate an affidavit that failed to provide *any* nexus between the residence and illegal activity".

### Good Faith and Qualified Immunity: Messerschmidt v. Miller

In Messerschmidt v. Millender, 132 S.Ct. 1235 (2012), the Supreme Court reversed the Ninth Circuit's denial of qualified immunity to two officers who executed a search warrant for firearms and gang-related material based solely on a violent altercation between the defendant and his girlfriend. The Court, in an opinion by Chief Justice Roberts, noted (as it had in previous cases) that the standard for qualified immunity in cases alleging Fourth Amendment violations was the same as provided in the good-faith exception under *Leon*:

> Where the alleged Fourth Amendment violation involves a search or seizure pursuant to a warrant, the fact that a neutral magistrate has issued a warrant is the clearest indication that the

officers acted in an objectively reasonable manner or, as we have sometimes put it, in "objective good faith." Nonetheless * * * the fact that a neutral magistrate has issued a warrant authorizing the allegedly unconstitutional search or seizure does not end the inquiry into objective reasonableness. Rather, we have recognized an exception allowing suit when "it is obvious that no reasonably competent officer would have concluded that a warrant should issue." The "shield of immunity" otherwise conferred by the warrant will be lost, for example, where the warrant was "based on an affidavit so lacking in indicia of probable cause as to render official belief in its existence entirely unreasonable." *Leon*.

Because the officers in this case had obtained a warrant, the major question in the case was whether that warrant was so lacking in probable cause as to a gang-related offense that it could not have been reasonably relied upon. Chief Justice Roberts found a number of plausible reasons for allowing a search for gang-related material, among them that gang-related evidence would tie the defendant to the premises and show his control over the property. He also noted that reasonable officers could have concluded that what was going on in the house was more than a domestic dispute: "A reasonable officer could certainly view Bowen's attack as motivated not by the souring of his romantic relationship with Kelly but instead by a desire to prevent her from disclosing details of his gang activity to the police." The Chief Justice concluded as follows:

> The question in this case is not whether the magistrate erred in believing there was sufficient probable cause to support the scope of the warrant he issued. It is instead whether the magistrate so obviously erred that any reasonable officer would have recognized the error. * * * Even if the warrant in this case were invalid, it was not so obviously lacking in probable cause that the officers can be considered "plainly incompetent" for concluding otherwise.

Justice Breyer wrote a short concurring opinion. Justice Kagan wrote an opinion concurring in part and dissenting in part. Justice Sotomayor, joined by Justice Ginsburg, dissented, accusing the Court of sanctioning a "general warrant" based on the faulty premise that "four wrongs apparently make a right."

### *Leon and Warrants Lacking Particularity*

Applying the *Leon* framework to particularity questions, it would appear that the good faith exception would apply to a search pursuant to an overbroad or unparticularized warrant, so long as reasonable minds could differ about whether the warrant is in fact overbroad. On the other hand, if all reasonable people would agree that the warrant is deficient, then the officer cannot reasonably rely upon it.

United States v. Dahlman, 13 F.3d 1391 (10th Cir.1993), is an example of *Leon*-applicability. Officers searching for narcotics obtained a warrant to search two "lots" in a subdivision. As conducted, the search encompassed a camping trailer and a cabin on one of the lots, as well as the lots themselves. The court found that the warrant was defective as applied to the cabin: "a warrant authorizing the search of a lot of land without a more precise definition of the scope of the search is inconsistent with the particularity requirement of the Fourth Amendment, and does not suffice to authorize a search of a residence located on the land." Still, the court held that the evidence obtained in the cabin was admissible under the good faith exception. It noted that two other circuits had held similar warrants to be sufficiently particular, and therefore that reasonable minds could differ about whether the warrant was in fact overbroad. See also United States v. Otero, 563 F.3d 1127 (10th Cir. 2009) (warrant to search computer was overbroad because it authorized the seizure of "any and all information" stored on the computer, and the subject matter limitations were placed in a different part of the affidavit; but the good faith exception applied because "one could see how a reasonable officer might have thought that the limitations in the first portion of Attachment B would be read to also apply to the second portion").

In contrast, some cases have found a warrant to be so overbroad that it could not reasonably be relied upon. In United States v. Fuccillo, 808 F.2d 173 (1st Cir.1987), officers searched a clothing warehouse and retail clothing store, with search warrants authorizing the seizure of "women's clothing" believed to be stolen. They seized virtually all the clothing found at each of the premises (including men's clothing). The court ruled that the warrants were insufficiently particular, because the officers "could have obtained specific information for presentment to the magistrate and placement in the warrant which would have enabled the agents [executing the warrants] to differentiate contraband cartons of women's clothing from legitimate ones." In fact the officers had a detailed list of the stolen clothing, but they failed to include it in the warrant application. The court further held that the good faith exception could not justify the searches and seizures. It reasoned that the officers were "reckless in not including in the affidavit information which was known or easily accessible to them," and that the warrant was so overbroad that the executing officers could not reasonably presume it to be valid. See also United States v. Stubbs, 873 F.2d 210 (9th Cir.1989) (good faith exception unavailable where warrant authorizes seizure of virtually all business documents, and probable cause existed as to only one transaction).

## *Leon and Untrue or Omitted Statements in the Warrant Application*

An exception to the good faith exception arises if the officer includes material information in the application that he "knew was false or would have known was false except for his reckless disregard of the truth." *Leon.* Exclusion also occurs if the officer knowingly omits material information that would have resulted in the magistrate's refusing to issue the warrant. The good faith exception cannot apply in these instances because the error is the officer's, not the magistrate's. Determining whether the officer has made such an error is sometimes difficult, however.

Consider United States v. Johnson, 78 F.3d 1258 (8th Cir.1996). A police officer received a call from an anonymous informant who stated that he had been present when marijuana had been delivered to Johnson's residence. The officer verified Johnson's address and discovered that Johnson had been arrested previously for marijuana possession. The officer then prepared an affidavit to obtain a search warrant of Johnson's address. The affidavit for search warrant had a printed form attached, Attachment B. This form had a section relating to whether the informant was anonymous or confidential, and a section with four printed reasons why the informant is reliable. The officer checked two reasons why the anonymous caller was reliable: "C. Information he has supplied has been corroborated by law enforcement personnel." and "D. He has not given false information in the past." The warrant was issued and a search turned up drugs. The government conceded that the tip was too conclusory and the corroboration too thin to support probable cause under *Gates*; but the government argued that the information provided was close enough that reasonable minds could differ about whether the *Gates* standards were satisfied.

Because the officer had corroborated at least some part of the informant's tip as asserted in the warrant application, the question was whether the officer had knowingly or recklessly disregarded the truth in checking the line stating that the informant had not given false information in the past. The Court held that the officer's assertion did not trigger the "officer misrepresentation" exception to *Leon.* The court reasoned as follows:

> The officer took the literal view of the phrase that the caller had not given false information in the past even though this was the informant's first call. We do not believe that checking this statement rises to the level of making a false statement knowingly or intentionally or with a reckless disregard for the truth. * * * [W]e do not subject law enforcement officers to absolute syllogistic precision.

Judge Arnold, in dissent, disagreed and argued that the affidavit was deceptive and outside the realm of *Leon* good faith:

> This is hardly a matter of requiring law enforcement officers to observe "syllogistic precision". It is, rather, a matter of common ordinary speech. A statement that an informant had not previously given false information is clearly calculated to influence the magistrate to whom the application for warrant was to be submitted. The statement could hardly have been other than deliberate. To read the statement absolutely literally seems disingenuous to me, and certainly not the way one would understand the statement under the circumstances. * * * For this reason, it seems to me that the affidavit falls clearly within one of the exceptions to the *Leon* "good faith" rule, and that the motion to suppress should have been granted.

Why did the form affidavit have a "fill in the blank" for whether the informant had ever given *false* information in the past? Why wasn't the issue phrased as whether the informant had ever given *truthful* information in the past? Isn't that the important question under *Gates*? If it is the form itself that is deceptive, should *Leon* apply?

For a case in which *Leon* was found inapplicable due to officer misrepresentations in the warrant application, see United States v. Vigeant, 176 F.3d 565 (1st Cir.1999). Officers filed a detailed affidavit, based in large part on a tip from a confidential informant (CI) alleging that Vigeant was engaged in money-laundering resulting from sales of drugs. Among the allegations was that Vigeant was unemployed, and yet had purchased a "pleasure boat"—the inference being that he must have done so with laundered funds. One problem with the case, however, was that Vigeant filed a proper Currency Transaction Report (CTR) for each of his financial transactions, and made no attempt to disguise the electronic or paper trail of any transaction. The court reviewed the affidavit and found it insufficient to establish probable cause; it also found the good faith exception inapplicable due to the various misrepresentations and omissions in the affidavit. It elaborated as follows:

> We believe this is a case in which excluding the evidence will have a substantial deterrent effect on the police. Our conclusion rests on the fact that a finding of good faith is inconsistent with the numerous material omissions excluded from—and false and misleading statements included in—the underlying affidavit. * * * Officer Botelho's numerous omissions of material facts were at least reckless. An enumeration of Botelho's omissions follows.

> First, and most important, Botelho neglected to mention the CI's long criminal history, his numerous aliases, his recent plea agreement, and other indicia of his unreliability. Second, Botelho failed to note that Vigeant had filed the necessary CTR, yet Botelho

included in the affidavit such minute details about the transaction as that it involved "small bills"—a fact he presumably obtained from the CTR. Filing a CTR, like failing to "structure" the transaction to avoid the reporting requirement, is evidence manifestly inconsistent with money laundering. Third, Botelho mentioned an additional deposit by cashier's check, but neglected to say that Vigeant's grandmother, who was above suspicion in this case, was the purchaser of the check. Fourth, Botelho could have (but did not) obtain Vigeant's employment status from the probation office, apparently deciding instead to infer (without informing the magistrate that he had done so) Vigeant's present unemployment from a blank space marked "current employment" on a two-year-old bank application. Fifth, Botelho stated that "the evidence indicates that Robert Vigeant has created front companies," which implies the existence of underlying evidence not disclosed. Such evidence did not, in fact, exist. Sixth, the government failed to note that the supposed "pleasure boat" mentioned in the affidavit was, in fact, a stripped-down craft in poor condition in need of considerable repair and refurbishing before it could be sold at a profit. Seventh, the affidavit implies that the CI personally witnessed a marijuana transaction and personally received $10,000; neither is true. * * *

The government offers no rational explanation for these omissions and foundationless conclusions. Instead, the government argues in its brief—with information obtained after the search in question—that Vigeant is a bad person. Be that as it may, even unsavory persons have constitutional rights. We conclude that a reasonable officer in Botelho's position—that is, in possession of the omitted information—would have known that he should not have applied for the warrant, at least not without further investigation.

### Leon and the Abdicating Magistrate

United States v. Decker, 956 F.2d 773 (8th Cir.1992), is a rare case in which the court held that *Leon* could not apply because the magistrate abdicated his neutral and detached role. Agents subjected a suspicious-looking UPS package to a canine sniff, and the dog positively alerted to drugs. The agents then made a controlled delivery, and followed the package to Decker's house. Decker was arrested when he received the package. A search of his person revealed a small amount of narcotics. An agent prepared an affidavit setting forth these facts and applying for permission to seize narcotics at Decker's house. The magistrate issued a warrant to search Decker's house, but the warrant failed to list any items to be seized other than the UPS package, which was already in the possession of the agents. The search warrant was a standard form relating to stolen property, not to drugs, and referred to the UPS package as "unlawfully stolen." The magistrate later admitted that the flaws in the warrant were his fault and attributed these errors "to the fact that he was intrigued by the manner in which Agent Hicks became suspicious of the package and the ensuing investigation and therefore did not focus on the language of the warrant." Pursuant to the warrant, the officers seized more than 300 items from Decker's house, including a clock radio, two lamps, a microwave oven, and a weed eater. The court found that the magistrate signed the warrant without reading it, that he acted as "a rubber stamp," and that the agents could not reasonably rely on the warrant. So the evidence had to be suppressed. Compare United States v. Breckenridge, 782 F.2d 1317 (5th Cir.1986), where the court held that the good faith exception applied even though the judge who issued the warrant never read the officer's affidavit. The court reasoned that the officer could reasonably rely on the warrant because, while the judge did not read the affidavit, he "appeared to Agent Alexander to be doing so."

The good faith exception will not apply if the person who issues the warrant is affiliated with law enforcement. See, e.g., United States v. Lucas, 451 F.3d 492 (8th Cir. 2006) (officers could not reasonably rely on a warrant issued by the Director of Corrections, a member of the executive branch: "the good faith exception does not apply when the individual who issued the warrant is not neutral and detached.").

### *The Teaching Function*

The *Leon* dissenters were concerned that appellate courts will routinely refuse to decide Fourth Amendment questions about the validity of a warrant, preferring instead to reach the easier holding that the officer was not totally unreasonable in relying on a magistrate's determination that the warrant was valid. Lower court decisions suggest that the dissenters' concerns were justified—many courts are avoiding decisions about substantive Fourth Amendment law and ruling instead on the easier question of good faith. For example, in United States v. Henderson, 746 F.2d 619 (9th Cir.1984), defendants convicted of drug offenses challenged an order authorizing beeper surveillance. Rather than rule on whether the order was valid, the court sustained the search by citing *Leon* and relying upon the good faith of the agents. Thus, in future cases, the agents have no guidance as to the validity of similar orders. Presumably, officers continue to act in good faith until a similar order actually is invalidated. Likewise, in United States v. Tedford, 875 F.2d 446 (5th Cir.1989), the court bypassed a probable cause question and proceeded directly to the issue of good faith. The court stated that the probable cause issue was fact-bound, and resolution would not provide important guidance on Fourth Amendment limitations. See also United States v. Perez, 393 F.3d 457 (4th Cir. 2004) ("Assuming without deciding that the * * * search warrant was invalid for lack of probable cause, we exercise our discretion to proceed directly to the question of good faith."; assuming arguendo that the warrant lacked probable cause, it was close enough for reasonable minds to differ, and therefore evidence could not be excluded).

Despite the general trend to avoid Fourth Amendment questions after *Leon*, there are some courts that have taken their teaching function seriously. Illustrative is United States v. Dahlman, 13 F.3d 1391 (10th Cir.1993), discussed above. In *Dahlman*, the court held that a warrant authorizing the search of a certain "lot", without mentioning a residence, was insufficiently particular to justify a search of the residence. Then the court found that the good faith exception applied to the search of the residence, because the law on particularity, as applied to the search of a "lot", was unsettled at the time of the search. The court had this to say about the teaching function after *Leon*:

> This court could have simply affirmed the trial court on the good faith issue without first discussing the underlying Fourth Amendment issue, i.e., the validity of the warrant. * * * However, a close reading of *Leon* reveals that, while the Supreme Court intended to vest lower courts with discretion, the preferred sequence is to address the Fourth Amendment issues before turning to the good faith issue unless there is no danger of "freezing" Fourth Amendment jurisprudence or unless the case poses "no important Fourth Amendment questions."

> * * * If we were to have avoided addressing the underlying Fourth Amendment question today, a magistrate could legitimately issue an identical warrant tomorrow and the officers could engage in the same conduct without consequence—since there would be no adverse ruling to guide the magistrate or the officers, the warrant would be issued and the search would once again be valid under principles of good faith. In effect, Fourth Amendment jurisprudence would be frozen on this issue because of this never-ending cycle. Thus, the policy of avoiding "freezing" Fourth Amendment jurisprudence, discussed by the Court in *Leon*, compels us in this case to resolve the constitutional issue so that magistrates and law enforcement officers do not continue to make the same mistake indefinitely.

Once a court, such as in *Dahlman*, declares a particular practice illegal—though without an attendant exclusion of evidence in that case—an officer who thereafter engages in the conduct is acting unreasonably, and the good faith exception will not apply. See United States v. Buck, 813 F.2d 588 (2d Cir.1987), where the court held that a warrant with a catch-all clause was insufficiently particular, but nonetheless applied the good faith exception because "what the officers failed to do was to anticipate our holding today that the particularity clause of the Fourth

Amendment prohibits the use of a catch-all description in a search warrant, unaccompanied by any list of particular items or any other limiting language." However, the court stated in a footnote that "with respect to searches conducted hereafter, police officers may no longer invoke the reasonable-reliance exception to the exclusionary rule when they attempt to introduce as evidence the fruits of searches undertaken on the basis of warrants containing only a catch-all description of the property to be seized." And the court was true to its word. In United States v. George, 975 F.2d 72 (2d Cir.1992), the court invalidated a warrant similar to that in *Buck,* and refused to apply the good faith exception "in light of the settled nature of the law."

## 2.   The Good Faith Exception and Warrantless Searches

The Court in *Leon* applied the good faith exception because an officer reasonably relied on the magistrate's decision. The Court reasoned that the magistrate, rather than the officer, made the error, and that magistrates cannot be deterred by the exclusionary rule. An important question is whether this reasoning can be applied to excuse illegal but "good faith," objectively reasonable—but illegal—searches *without a warrant.*

### *Reasonable Reliance on Legislative Acts: Illinois v. Krull*

In Illinois v. Krull, 480 U.S. 340 (1987), Illinois had enacted a statute authorizing warrantless searches by state officials to inspect the records of dealers in motor vehicles, automobile parts, or automobile scrap metal. Officers searched Krull's premises without a warrant, under the authority of the statute. The statute was found unconstitutional after the search. The government argued that while the search was illegal, the error was that of the legislature, not the officer, and so exclusion was unwarranted.

Justice Blackmun's majority opinion reasoned that, as in *Leon,* the presence of an intermediary upon whom the officer could reasonably rely meant that the officer could not be deterred by the exclusionary rule. Justice Blackmun recognized that the legislature made a mistake by passing an unconstitutional statute, but reasoned that the legislature could not be deterred from passing unconstitutional laws by application of the exclusionary rule. According to the Court, legislators enact statutes for "broad programmatic purposes, not for the purpose of procuring evidence in particular criminal investigations."

The *Krull* Court decided, as in *Leon,* that a good faith claim must have an objective basis, so that "[a] statute cannot support objectively reasonable reliance if, in passing the statute, the legislature wholly abandoned its responsibility to enact constitutional laws," and "a law enforcement officer [cannot] be said to have acted in good-faith reliance upon a statute if its provisions are such that a reasonable officer should have known that the statute was unconstitutional." But neither of these exceptions were applicable to the facts of the case.

Justice O'Connor, joined by Justices Brennan, Marshall and Stevens, dissented. She distinguished legislators from magistrates, finding that "[t]he judicial role is particularized, fact-specific and nonpolitical," and argued that "[p]roviding legislatures a grace period during which the police may freely perform unreasonable searches in order to convict those who might have otherwise escaped creates a positive incentive to promulgate unconstitutional laws." See also United States v. Duka, 671 F.3d 329 (3rd Cir. 2011) (finding that FISA amendment allowing domestic wiretapping was reasonable and even if it were not, officer's reliance on it was objectively reasonable and so exclusion was unwarranted).

### Clerical Errors and Reliance on Court Clerical Personnel: *Arizona v. Evans*

The Court continued to adhere to the *Leon* framework in Arizona v. Evans, 514 U.S. 1 (1995), a case that arose from a clerical error attributed to the judicial branch. Evans was stopped for a traffic violation. The officer entered Evans's name in a computer data terminal, and the computer inquiry indicated that there was an outstanding misdemeanor warrant for Evans' arrest. On the basis of that information, the officer arrested Evans, and in a search incident to the arrest, the officer found marijuana. Subsequently, it was discovered that the arrest warrant had been quashed well before Evans had been stopped by the officer, but that an entry to that effect had never been made in the computer records of outstanding warrants. The Supreme Court assumed that the error was caused by court clerical personnel who, contrary to standard procedure, never called the Sheriff's office with notification that Evans' arrest warrant had been quashed.

Chief Justice Rehnquist, writing for a seven-person majority, held that the critical analysis under "the *Leon* framework" was whether the government official who makes a mistake that leads to an illegal search or seizure can be deterred by operation of the exclusionary rule. Applying this reasoning to errors of court clerical personnel, the Chief Justice stated as follows:

> [T]here is no basis for believing that application of the exclusionary rule in these circumstances will have a significant effect on court employees responsible for informing the police that a warrant has been quashed. Because court clerks are not adjuncts to the law enforcement team engaged in the often competitive enterprise of ferreting out crime, they have no stake in the outcome of particular criminal prosecutions. The threat of exclusion of

evidence could not be expected to deter such individuals from failing to inform police officials that a warrant had been quashed.

The next question under the *Leon* framework is whether application of the exclusionary rule would deter misconduct of *police officers* where the initial mistake was made by a different government official. The Chief Justice concluded that officers could not be deterred when they reasonably rely on erroneous computer records prepared and maintained by court clerical personnel.

Justice O'Connor, joined by Justices Souter and Breyer, wrote a concurring opinion emphasizing that the Court had not decided whether the good faith exception should apply if the computer error was caused by police personnel rather than court personnel. She also stated that the exclusionary rule should be applicable if police officers rely on a court recordkeeping system that is known to be rife with error. She elaborated as follows:

> Surely it would not be reasonable for the police to rely, say, on a recordkeeping system, their own or some other agency's, that has no mechanism to ensure its accuracy over time and that routinely leads to false arrests, even years after the probable cause for any such arrest has ceased to exist (if it ever existed).
>
> In recent years, we have witnessed the advent of powerful, computer-based recordkeeping systems that facilitate arrests in ways that have never before been possible. The police, of course, are entitled to enjoy the substantial advantages this technology confers. They may not, however, rely on it blindly.

Justice Souter, joined by Justice Breyer, wrote a separate, short concurring opinion in which he left open the possibility that the exclusionary rule might be necessary as a last resort to combat erroneous computerized recordkeeping by non-police personnel.

Justice Stevens dissented from the Court's opinion in *Evans*. He contended that court clerical personnel often "work in the same building with police officers and may have more regular and direct contact with police than with judges or magistrates." Justice Stevens found it "outrageous" for a citizen to be "arrested, handcuffed, and searched on a public street simply because some bureaucrat has failed to maintain an accurate computer data base."

Justice Ginsburg wrote a separate dissent that was joined by Justice Stevens. She noted her concern with the risk to privacy that could result from errors in computer entries. She explained the scope of the problem in the following passage:

> Widespread reliance on computers to store and convey information generates, along with manifold benefits, new possibilities

of error, due to both computer malfunctions and operator mistakes. Most germane to this case, computerization greatly amplifies an error's effect, and correspondingly intensifies the need for prompt correction; for inaccurate data can infect not only one agency, but the many agencies that share access to the database. * * *

Evans' case is not idiosyncratic. Rogan v. Los Angeles, 668 F.Supp. 1384 (C.D.Cal.1987), similarly indicates the problem. There, the Los Angeles Police Department, in 1982, had entered into the NCIC computer an arrest warrant for a man suspected of robbery and murder. Because the suspect had been impersonating Terry Dean Rogan, the arrest warrant erroneously named Rogan. Compounding the error, the Los Angeles Police Department had failed to include a description of the suspect's physical characteristics. During the next two years, this incorrect and incomplete information caused Rogan to be arrested four times, three times at gunpoint, after stops for minor traffic infractions in Michigan and Oklahoma.

Justice Ginsburg concluded that, in light of the enormity and relative recency of the problem arising from illegal searches based on computer error, the Court should have dismissed the grant of certiorari and allowed the issue to be developed and argued throughout the lower courts.

### *Good-Faith Exception Applied Where Error Was the Result of Negligence Attenuated from the Arrest or Search: Herring v. United States*

### HERRING V. UNITED STATES

Supreme Court of the United States, 2009.
555 U.S. 135.

#### CHIEF JUSTICE ROBERTS delivered the opinion of the Court.

What if an officer reasonably believes there is an outstanding arrest warrant, but that belief turns out to be wrong because of a negligent bookkeeping error by another police employee? The parties here agree that the ensuing arrest is still a violation of the Fourth Amendment, but dispute whether contraband found during a search incident to that arrest must be excluded in a later prosecution.

Our cases establish that such suppression is not an automatic consequence of a Fourth Amendment violation. Instead, the question turns on the culpability of the police and the potential of exclusion to deter wrongful police conduct. Here the error was the result of isolated negligence attenuated from the arrest. We hold that in these circumstances the jury should not be barred from considering all the evidence.

Herring was arrested by Coffee County Officer Anderson after Anderson sought and received information that there was an outstanding warrant for his arrest in nearby Dale County. There had, however, been a mistake about the warrant. It had been quashed, but the database had not been changed to reflect that fact. Unlike in *Evans,* though, the clerical error was made by a law enforcement officer. By the time Anderson found out about the error, Herring had already been arrested, and evidence had been found in a search incident to arrest. The court of appeals found that the good faith exception applied and so the evidence was properly admitted.]

In analyzing the applicability of the [exclusionary] rule, *Leon* admonished that we must consider the actions of all the police officers involved. * * * The Coffee County officers did nothing improper. Indeed, the error was noticed so quickly because Coffee County requested a faxed confirmation of the warrant.

* * *

1.   * * * [E]xclusion has always been our last resort, not our first impulse, and our precedents establish important principles that constrain application of the exclusionary rule. * * *

2.   The extent to which the exclusionary rule is justified by these deterrence principles varies with the culpability of the law enforcement conduct. As we said in *Leon,* "an assessment of the flagrancy of the police misconduct constitutes an important step in the calculus" of applying the exclusionary rule. * * *

Anticipating the good-faith exception to the exclusionary rule, Judge Friendly wrote that "[t]he beneficent aim of the exclusionary rule to deter police misconduct can be sufficiently accomplished by a practice ... outlawing evidence obtained by flagrant or deliberate violation of rights." The Bill of Rights as a Code of Criminal Procedure, 53 Calif. L.Rev. 929, 953 (1965).

Indeed, the abuses that gave rise to the exclusionary rule featured intentional conduct that was patently unconstitutional. In *Weeks,* a foundational exclusionary rule case, the officers had broken into the defendant's home (using a key shown to them by a neighbor), confiscated incriminating papers, then returned again with a U.S. Marshal to confiscate even more. Not only did they have no search warrant, which the Court held was required, but they could not have gotten one had they tried. * * * Equally flagrant conduct was at issue in Mapp v. Ohio, which * * * extended the exclusionary rule to the States. Officers forced open a door to Ms. Mapp's house, kept her lawyer from entering, brandished what the court concluded was a false warrant, then forced her into handcuffs and canvassed the house for obscenity. An error that arises from nonrecurring and attenuated negligence is thus far removed from the core concerns that led us to adopt the rule in the first place. And in fact since *Leon*, we have never applied the rule to exclude evidence obtained in violation of the Fourth Amendment, where the police conduct was no more intentional or culpable than this.

3. To trigger the exclusionary rule, police conduct must be sufficiently deliberate that exclusion can meaningfully deter it, and sufficiently culpable that such deterrence is worth the price paid by the justice system. As laid out in our cases, the exclusionary rule serves to deter deliberate, reckless, or grossly negligent conduct, or in some circumstances recurring or systemic negligence. The error in this case does not rise to that level.[a]

We do not suggest that all recordkeeping errors by the police are immune from the exclusionary rule. In this case, however, the conduct at issue was not so objectively culpable as to require exclusion. * * * If the police have been shown to be reckless in maintaining a warrant system, or to have knowingly made false entries to lay the groundwork for future false arrests, exclusion would certainly be justified under our cases should such misconduct cause a Fourth Amendment violation. We said as much in *Leon*, explaining that an officer could not "obtain a warrant on the basis of a 'bare bones' affidavit and then rely on colleagues who are ignorant of the circumstances under which the warrant was obtained to conduct the search." Petitioner's fears that our decision will cause police departments to deliberately keep their officers ignorant, are thus unfounded.

* * * In a case where systemic errors were demonstrated, it might be reckless for officers to rely on an unreliable warrant system. But there is no evidence that errors in Dale County's system are routine or widespread. * * *

––––––––––

Petitioner's claim that police negligence automatically triggers suppression cannot be squared with the principles underlying the exclusionary rule, as they have been explained in our cases. In light of our repeated holdings that the deterrent effect of suppression must be substantial and outweigh any harm to the justice system, we conclude that when police mistakes are the result of negligence such as that described here, rather than systemic error or reckless disregard of constitutional requirements, any marginal deterrence does not pay its

---

[a] We do not quarrel with Justice GINSBURG's claim that "liability for negligence . . . creates an incentive to act with greater care," and we do not suggest that the exclusion of this evidence could have no deterrent effect. But our cases require any deterrence to be weighed against the substantial social costs exacted by the exclusionary rule, and here exclusion is not worth the cost.

way. In such a case, the criminal should not "go free because the constable has blundered." People v. Defore, 242 N.Y. 13, 21, 150 N.E. 585, 587 (1926) (opinion of the Court by Cardozo, J.).

**JUSTICE GINSBURG, with whom JUSTICE STEVENS, JUSTICE SOUTER, and JUSTICE BREYER join, dissenting.**

* * *

Electronic databases form the nervous system of contemporary criminal justice operations. In recent years, their breadth and influence have dramatically expanded. Police today can access databases that include not only the updated National Crime Information Center (NCIC), but also terrorist watchlists, the Federal Government's employee eligibility system, and various commercial databases. Moreover, States are actively expanding information sharing between jurisdictions. As a result, law enforcement has an increasing supply of information within its easy electronic reach.

The risk of error stemming from these databases is not slim. Herring's amici warn that law enforcement databases are insufficiently monitored and often out of date. Government reports describe, for example, flaws in NCIC databases, terrorist watchlist databases, and databases associated with the Federal Government's employment eligibility verification system.

* * * The Court assures that "exclusion would certainly be justified" if "the police have been shown to be reckless in maintaining a warrant system, or to have knowingly made false entries to lay the groundwork for future false arrests." This concession provides little comfort.

First, by restricting suppression to bookkeeping errors that are deliberate or reckless, the majority leaves Herring, and others like him, with no remedy for violations of their constitutional rights. There can be no serious assertion that relief is available under 42 U.S.C. § 1983. The arresting officer would be sheltered by qualified immunity, and the police department itself is not liable for the negligent acts of its employees. Moreover, identifying the department employee who committed the error may be impossible.

Second, I doubt that police forces already possess sufficient incentives to maintain up-to-date records. The Government argues that police have no desire to send officers out on arrests unnecessarily, because arrests consume resources and place officers in danger. The facts of this case do not fit that description of police motivation. Here the officer wanted to arrest Herring and consulted the Department's records to legitimate his predisposition.

Third, even when deliberate or reckless conduct is afoot, the Court's assurance will often be an empty promise: How is an impecunious defendant to make the required showing? If the answer is that a defendant is entitled to discovery (and if necessary, an audit of police databases), then the Court has imposed a considerable administrative burden on courts and law enforcement.

**JUSTICE BREYER, with whom JUSTICE SOUTER joins, dissenting.**

I agree with Justice GINSBURG and join her dissent. I write separately to note one additional supporting factor that I believe important. In Arizona v. Evans, we held that recordkeeping errors made by a court clerk do not trigger the exclusionary rule, so long as the police reasonably relied upon the court clerk's recordkeeping. The rationale for our decision was premised on a distinction between judicial errors and police errors * * *.

Distinguishing between police recordkeeping errors and judicial ones not only is consistent with our precedent, but also is far easier for courts to administer than THE CHIEF JUSTICE's case-by-case, multifactored inquiry into the degree of police culpability. I therefore would apply the exclusionary rule when police personnel are responsible for a recordkeeping error that results in a Fourth Amendment violation.

\* \* \*

## *New Rules and Retroactivity: Davis v. United States*

Justice Alito wrote for the Court in Davis v. United States, 131 S. Ct. 2419 (2011), as it held that the exclusionary rule did not require suppression of evidence when police officers executed a search in compliance with binding Supreme Court authority that was later overruled. In *Davis*, officers stopped a car, arrested the driver for driving under the influence and a passenger for giving a false name to the police, and searched the passenger compartment of the car in reliance on New York v. Belton, supra. They found a revolver in Davis's jacket pocket. Davis was prosecuted and convicted for being a felon in possession of the firearm. While his conviction was on appeal, the Court decided Arizona v. Gant, supra, and limited searches of automobiles following an arrest.

Justice Alito agreed that *Gant* applied on direct review, given the Court's approach to direct and collateral review spelled out in Griffith v. Kentucky (discussed in Chapter 1). But, Justice Alito concluded that the question was not whether *Gant* applied, but whether suppression was required where "the police conduct in this case was in no way culpable." He reasoned that "this acknowledged absence of police culpability dooms Davis's claim." In other words, *Gant* applied retroactively but the question of whether evidence should be excluded had to run through the Court's exclusionary rule cost-benefit analysis. Justice Alito concluded that exclusion was unwarranted because officers were reasonably applying the law as it existed at the time of their conduct. Thus, there would be no deterrent effect in exclusion of evidence based on a case decided after that conduct.

Justice Sotomayor concurred in the judgment and stated that "[i]n my view, whether an officer's conduct can be characterized as 'culpable' is not itself dispositive," but "an officer's culpability is relevant because it may inform the overarching inquiry whether exclusion would result in appreciable deterrence."

Justice Breyer, joined by Justice Ginsburg, dissented. He argued that under the majority's position, no defendant would have an incentive to seek a change in Fourth Amendment law, because they would not get the benefit of its application.

### *Davis and the Applicability of the Supreme Court's Jones Ruling on GPS Tracking*

In United States v. Pineda-Moreno, 688 F.3d 1087 (9th Cir. 2012), officers tracked the defendant's movements by attaching an electronic tracking device to the undercarriage of his car. This tracking occurred before the Supreme Court's decision in Jones v. United States, supra, where the Court held that physically installing a tracking device constituted a search. By the time of appeal to the Ninth Circuit, *Jones* had been decided. The court concluded that while *Jones* was retroactive and therefore the tracking was illegal, the evidence should not be excluded, because at the time of the tracking, "circuit precedent held that placing an electronic tracking device on the undercarriage of a car was neither a search nor a seizure under the Fourth Amendment." But didn't the Court in *Jones* hold that its trespass theory—upon which both Jones and Pineda-Moreno relied—had *never* been rejected and had *always* been applicable to protect citizens by supplementing the *Katz* expectation of privacy test? And if that is so, isn't it the case that Pineda-Morena was not seeking to rely on a new rule of law? Also, why did Jones get the benefit of the ruling in *his* case? Weren't the officers in *Jones* reasonably relying on pre-*Jones* case law permitting public tracking of cars?

### *Good Faith Where the Arresting/Searching Officer Is at Fault?*

The Supreme Court has not addressed the question whether the good faith exception applies to illegal searches and seizures where the fault is that of the searching or seizing officer, i.e., where that officer is relying only his or her own mistaken judgment. Can the officer argue that he was wrong in thinking that there was, e.g., voluntary consent, exigent circumstances, etc., but reasonable minds could differ about whether he was wrong and therefore the evidence should not be excluded?

The rationale of *Leon*, *Krull*, and *Evans* does not easily extend to "good faith" mistakes by police officers who rely on their own mistaken judgment. In each of those cases, the Court held that mistakes of intermediary officials (such as magistrates and legislators) cannot be deterred by the exclusionary rule, but presumed that an officer in the competitive enterprise of ferreting out crime *can* be deterred by strict operation of the exclusionary rule. How could the Court then turn around and say that officers cannot be deterred by the exclusionary rule when they wrongly, but reasonably, interpret Fourth Amendment law?

That turnaround becomes a bit easier after *Herring*, however. *Herring* is the first case in which the good faith exception was applied to excuse an error by a police department official. (In *Davis* it is the court that has made the error, which it recognizes by overruling a prior case). The wrinkle in *Herring* is that the error, though by a police official, was not by the officer who actually made the arrest and conducted the search. As the Court put it, the error was "attenuated" from the arrest and search. There is much in *Herring*, however, that could lead to the conclusion that the good faith exception is to apply to *all* police errors, even those of the officer directly involved. The majority spends a good deal of time arguing that the exclusionary rule can only deter reckless or intentional misconduct. That analysis could be used by the government to argue that while the searching officer made a mistake and violated the Fourth Amendment, reasonable minds could differ about the illegality and therefore the evidence should not be excluded.

How exactly could an officer be deterred from violating the law if reasonable minds can differ about whether it is a violation? Doesn't the majority in *Herring* have it right? One possible response is that police departments, with the exclusionary rule in mind, will train officers to follow a *strict application* of Fourth Amendment law, and will instruct them not to "push the envelope" for fear that action on the frontier of Fourth Amendment reasonableness will result in exclusion. In contrast, if officers are entitled to good faith protection for their own mistakes, police departments will have an incentive to conduct searches that are of dubious legality, so long as reasonable minds can differ on whether the search is legal.

For a post-*Herring* case adopting the good-faith exception for officer error—and applying what Justice Breyer in dissent in *Herring* referred to as the majority's "case-by-case, multifactored inquiry" into the degree of police culpability required for exclusion, see United States v. Julius, 610 F.3d 60 (2nd Cir. 2010). Julius had violated parole, and officers arrested him in his girlfriend's apartment where he was residing. The girlfriend consented to entry into the apartment, and the officers found Julius on the bed in a bedroom, with his son. Julius offered no resistance to the arrest. After he was taken out of the room, an officer noticed that the mattress of the bed hung over the box spring by about a foot. The officer lifted the mattress and found a gun. Julius was charged with felon-firearm possession. The lower court found that the search was illegal, because: 1) the officers had taken Julius out of the room so the search was not within his grab area for purposes of search incident to arrest; and 2) the officers did not have the reasonable suspicion required to support a search of a parolee's premises under cases like Samson v. California, discussed earlier in this Chapter. In a decision rendered *before Herring,* the lower court excluded the evidence because it was illegally obtained. But on appeal, the Second Circuit remanded in light of the intervening decision in *Herring.* The Second Circuit did *not* read *Herring* as applying the good faith exception only when the error is attenuated from the illegal search—if it had, there would have been no need to remand, because the error in *Julius* was by the officer who *did* the search. The Second Circuit held that *Herring* mandates "a case-by-case, multifactored inquiry into the degree of police culpability." It provided the following analysis of how *Herring* might apply to the search that found the gun.

> Unlike in *Herring,* in which the alleged error was attenuated from the search, the error here was made by the searching officer. Also unlike *Herring*, this case involves a warrantless search, which entails different concerns about deterrence of police misconduct. * * * Wood, the officer who conducted the search, however, testified that he thought he had a right to search the area within the arrestee's reach at the time of the arrest regardless of the arrestee's status at the time of the search as long as it was within a reasonable amount of time after the arrest. The district court may consider whether the other circumstances of the search support a finding that the law enforcement officers had knowledge, or may properly be charged with knowledge, that the search was unconstitutional under the Fourth Amendment, requiring suppression [under] *Herring*. The district court may consider whether any of the * * * grounds relied upon by the government as justifying Deputy Wood's initial search * * * suggested the requisite level of culpability on the part of the officers.

> On the other hand, there is no question that the arrest of Julius was justified because it is undisputed that he was in violation of the terms of his special parole. The search itself was not prolonged; Officer Barry testified that "less than two minutes" had elapsed between the arrest of Julius and Deputy Wood's announcement that he had found a gun. Further, the court may also consider the issue of officer safety when deciding whether the conduct of the officers was "the result of . . . systemic error or reckless disregard of constitutional requirements." *Herring.* Deputy Wood articulated a concern for the safety of the officers and others. He explained there

was minimal possibility that Julius could have obtained the gun "because he was restrained," but that there was a risk that the minor child "could have accessed the weapon accidently" or that [the girlfriend] could have obtained the weapon if allowed to get clothes for Julius. Additionally, immediately upon finding the firearm, Deputy Wood and his colleagues: (1) ceased searching; (2) obtained [the girlfriend's] permission to search the entire residence, permission that the district court found was properly obtained; and (3) contacted New Haven police officers for assistance. We do not conclude that any of these circumstances are necessarily dispositive.

We emphasize that *Herring* should not serve as an enticement for law enforcement personnel to depart from search procedures which comply with the Fourth Amendment. Rather, *Herring* requires careful consideration by district courts of whether the goal of deterring violations of the Fourth Amendment outweighs the costs to truth-seeking and law enforcement objectives in each case.

But how can an exclusionary rule deter officer misconduct where it is subject to a multifactor, case-by-case application that must be applied by officers before the search? Are we expecting officers, before searching, to try to figure out how a court will apply an indefinite case-by-case application to the search? Or is all this just code for telling the officer that everything will be okay so long as the violation of the Fourth Amendment is not egregious? And if that is the message, how much deterrent effect does the exclusionary rule have after *Herring*?

## 3. Establishing a Violation of a Personal Fourth Amendment Right

Fourth Amendment rights are personal rights. It therefore follows that for a defendant to be entitled to exclusion of evidence, he must establish that his own personal rights were affected by the government's search or seizure. This has been characterized by many courts as a question of "standing"—though as will be seen below, the Supreme Court has chafed at this label. The question of "standing" is determined by whether the person seeking to suppress the evidence has had his own Fourth Amendment rights violated.

In the 1960's, the Court developed a generous view of a defendant's ability to invoke the exclusionary rule. Jones v. United States, 362 U.S. 257 (1960), held that a defendant had "automatic standing" to challenge the legality of the search that produced the very drugs that he was charged with possessing at the time of the search. The Court in *Jones* also stated that a search could be challenged by anyone "legitimately on the premises where a search occurs." In the following case the Court substantially cuts back on *Jones* and, more importantly, recharacterizes "standing" questions so that they are now resolved by substantive standards of Fourth Amendment law.

## RAKAS V. ILLINOIS
Supreme Court of the United States, 1978.
439 U.S. 128.

### JUSTICE REHNQUIST delivered the opinion of the Court.

[Officers received a radio call concerning a robbery and describing the getaway car. They stopped a vehicle which matched the description. Petitioners and two female companions were ordered out of the car. The officers searched the passenger compartment and found a box of rifle shells in the glove compartment and a sawed-off rifle under the front passenger seat. Petitioners had been passengers in the car; the owner of the car was driving when the car was stopped. The lower court denied the motion to suppress, reasoning that petitioners lacked standing, and the Illinois appellate courts affirmed. The Supreme Court found that petitioners had the burden of proof as to standing, and that they failed to meet their burden of showing ownership of the rifle or shells. The Court proceeded to consider whether standing could be established in the absence of ownership of the property seized].

\* \* \*

Petitioners first urge us to relax or broaden the rule of standing enunciated in Jones v. United States, so that any criminal defendant at whom a search was "directed" would have standing to contest the legality of that search and object to the admission at trial of evidence obtained as a result of the search. Alternatively, petitioners argue that they have standing to object to the search under *Jones* because they were "legitimately on [the] premises" at the time of the search.

\* \* \* Adoption of the so-called "target" theory advanced by petitioners would in effect permit a defendant to assert that a violation of the Fourth Amendment rights of a third party entitled him to have evidence suppressed at his trial. If we reject petitioners' request for a broadened rule of standing such as this, and reaffirm the holding of *Jones* and other cases that Fourth Amendment rights are personal rights that may not be asserted vicariously, we will have occasion to re-examine the "standing" terminology emphasized in *Jones*. For we are not at all sure that the determination of a motion to suppress is materially aided by labeling the inquiry identified in *Jones* as one of standing, rather than simply recognizing it as one involving the substantive question of whether or not the proponent of the motion to suppress has had his own Fourth Amendment rights infringed by the search and seizure which he seeks to challenge. \* \* \*

We decline to extend the rule of standing in Fourth Amendment cases in the manner suggested by petitioners. * * * A person who is aggrieved by an illegal search and seizure only through the introduction of damaging evidence secured by a search of a third person's premises or property has not had any of his Fourth Amendment rights infringed. And since the exclusionary rule is an attempt to effectuate the guarantees of the Fourth Amendment, it is proper to permit only defendants whose Fourth Amendment rights have been violated to benefit from the rule's protections. There is no reason to think that a party whose rights have been infringed will not, if evidence is used against him, have ample motivation to move to suppress it. Even if such a person is not a defendant in the action, he may be able to recover damages for the violation of his Fourth Amendment rights, or seek redress under state law for invasion of privacy or trespass.

\* \* \*

In Alderman v. United States, 394 U.S. 165 (1969) * * * Mr. Justice Harlan [dissenting] * * * identified administrative problems posed by the target theory:

> "[T]he [target] rule would entail very substantial administrative difficulties. In the majority of cases, I would imagine that the police plant a bug with the expectation that it may well produce leads to a large number of crimes. A lengthy hearing would, then, appear to be necessary in order to determine whether the police knew of an accused's criminal activity at the time the bug was planted and whether the police decision to plant a bug was motivated by an effort to obtain information against the accused or some other individual * * *"

When we are urged to grant standing to a criminal defendant to assert a violation, not of his own constitutional rights but of someone else's, we cannot but give weight to practical difficulties such as those foreseen by Mr. Justice Harlan in the quoted language.

Conferring standing to raise vicarious Fourth Amendment claims would necessarily mean a more widespread invocation of the exclusionary rule during criminal trials. * * * Each time the exclusionary rule is applied it exacts a substantial social cost for the vindication of Fourth Amendment rights. Relevant and reliable evidence is kept from the trier of fact and the search for truth at trial is deflected. * * *

* * * [H]aving rejected petitioners' target theory * * * the question necessarily arises whether it serves any useful analytical purpose to consider this principle a matter of standing, distinct from the merits of a defendant's Fourth Amendment claim. We can think of no decided cases of this Court that would have come out differently had we concluded, as we do now, that the type of standing requirement discussed in *Jones* and

reaffirmed today is more properly subsumed under substantive Fourth Amendment doctrine. * * * The inquiry under either approach is the same. But we think the better analysis forthrightly focuses on the extent of a particular defendant's rights under the Fourth Amendment, rather than on any theoretically separate, but invariably intertwined concept of standing.

* * *

Analyzed in these terms, the question is whether the challenged search and seizure violated the Fourth Amendment rights of a criminal defendant who seeks to exclude the evidence obtained during it. That inquiry in turn requires a determination of whether the disputed search and seizure has infringed an interest of the defendant which the Fourth Amendment was designed to protect. We are under no illusion that by dispensing with the rubric of standing used in *Jones* we have rendered any simpler the determination of whether the proponent of a motion to suppress is entitled to contest the legality of a search and seizure. But by frankly recognizing that this aspect of the analysis belongs more properly under the heading of substantive Fourth Amendment doctrine than under the heading of standing, we think the decision of this issue will rest on sounder logical footing.

* * *

Here petitioners, who were passengers occupying a car which they neither owned nor leased, seek to analogize their position to that of the defendant in Jones v. United States. In *Jones,* petitioner was present at the time of the search of an apartment which was owned by a friend. The friend had given Jones permission to use the apartment and a key to it, with which Jones had admitted himself on the day of the search. He had a suit and shirt at the apartment and had slept there "maybe a night," but his home was elsewhere. At the time of the search, Jones was the only occupant of the apartment because the lessee was away for a period of several days. Under these circumstances, this Court stated that while one wrongfully on the premises could not move to suppress evidence obtained as a result of searching them, "anyone legitimately on premises where a search occurs may challenge its legality." Petitioners argue that their occupancy of the automobile in question was comparable to that of Jones in the apartment and that they therefore have standing to contest the legality of the search—or as we have rephrased the inquiry, that they, like Jones, had their Fourth Amendment rights violated by the search.

We do not question the conclusion in *Jones* that the defendant in that case suffered a violation of his personal Fourth Amendment rights if the search in question was unlawful. Nonetheless, we believe that the phrase "legitimately on premises" coined in *Jones* creates too broad a gauge for measurement of Fourth Amendment rights. For example, applied literally, this statement would permit a casual visitor who has never seen, or been permitted to visit, the basement of another's house to object to a search of the basement if the visitor happened to be in the kitchen of the house at the time of the search. Likewise, a casual visitor who walks into a house one minute before a search of the house commences and leaves one minute after the search ends would be able to contest the legality of the search. * * *

We think that *Jones* on its facts merely stands for the unremarkable proposition that a person can have a legally sufficient interest in a place other than his own home so that the Fourth Amendment protects him from unreasonable governmental intrusion into that place. * * *

Katz v. United States, provides guidance in defining the scope of the interest protected by the Fourth Amendment. * * * [T]he Court in *Katz* held that capacity to claim the protection of the Fourth Amendment depends not upon a property right in the invaded place but upon whether the person who claims the protection of the Amendment has a legitimate expectation of privacy in the invaded place. Viewed in this manner, the holding in *Jones* can best be explained by the fact that Jones had a legitimate expectation of privacy in the premises he was using and therefore could claim the protection of the Fourth Amendment with respect to a governmental invasion of those premises, even though his "interest" in those premises might not have been a recognized property interest at common law.

* * * In abandoning "legitimately on premises" for the doctrine that we announce today, we are not forsaking a time-tested and workable rule, which has produced consistent results when applied, solely for the sake of fidelity to the values underlying the Fourth Amendment. Rather, we are rejecting blind adherence to a phrase which at most has superficial clarity and which conceals underneath that thin veneer all of the problems of line drawing which must be faced in any conscientious effort to apply the Fourth Amendment. * * * We would not wish to be understood as saying that legitimate presence on the premises is irrelevant to one's expectation of privacy, but it cannot be deemed controlling.

* * *

Judged by the foregoing analysis, petitioners' claims must fail. They asserted neither a property nor a possessory interest in the automobile, nor an interest in the property seized. And as we have previously indicated, the fact that they were "legitimately on [the] premises" in the sense that they were in the car with the permission of its owner is not determinative of whether they had a legitimate expectation of privacy in the particular areas of the automobile searched. * * *

JUSTICE POWELL, with whom CHIEF JUSTICE BURGER joins, concurring.

\* \* \*

This is not an area of the law in which any "bright line" rule would safeguard both Fourth Amendment rights and the public interest in a fair and effective criminal justice system. The range of variables in the fact situations of search and seizure is almost infinite. Rather than seek facile solutions, it is best to apply principles broadly faithful to Fourth Amendment purposes.

JUSTICE WHITE, with whom JUSTICE BRENNAN, JUSTICE MARSHALL, and JUSTICE STEVENS join, dissenting.

\* \* \* Insofar as passengers are concerned, the Court's opinion today declares an "open season" on automobiles. However unlawful stopping and searching a car may be, absent a possessory or ownership interest, no "mere" passenger may object, regardless of his relationship to the owner. \* \* \*

More importantly, the ruling today undercuts the force of the exclusionary rule in the one area in which its use is most certainly justified—the deterrence of bad-faith violations of the Fourth Amendment. This decision invites police to engage in patently unreasonable searches every time an automobile contains more than one occupant. Should something be found, only the owner of the vehicle, or of the item, will have standing to seek suppression, and the evidence will presumably be usable against the other occupants. The danger of such bad faith is especially high in cases such as this one where the officers are only after the passengers and can usually infer accurately that the driver is the owner. \* \* \*

## NOTE ON RAKAS

The Rakas Court ties standing to the *Katz* reasonable expectation of privacy test. But after Jones v. United States—the landmark case on electronic tracking discussed earlier in this Chapter—the reasonable expectation of privacy test is not the only test for determining whether the Fourth Amendment applies. The Court in *Jones* held that a trespass for investigatory purposes constituted a search even if the investigation does not intrude on a reasonable expectation of privacy. Because *Rakas* evaluates standing by whether a person has a Fourth Amendment right at all, it follows that if a person's Fourth Amendment right is triggered under *either Katz* or *Jones,* then that person will have standing to raise the Fourth Amendment claim. This is why Jones himself was allowed to raise the argument that his Fourth Amendment rights were violated even if he had no expectation of privacy in his public movements.

## Abolition of Automatic Standing: United States v. Salvucci

*Rakas* was relied upon by the Supreme Court in United States v. Salvucci, 448 U.S. 83 (1980) (stolen checks found in apartment of one defendant's mother; only defendants whose Fourth Amendment rights were violated can challenge warrant), which finally overruled *Jones* and abolished the automatic standing doctrine. The notion of automatic standing was that possession of property gave a person an automatic right to complain about the search or seizure of that property. Justice Rehnquist's majority opinion concluded that possession of a seized good should not be used as a substitute for a factual finding that the owner of the good had a legitimate expectation of privacy in the area searched. The automatic standing rule had been based on fairness concerns—that it would be unfair for the government to argue at the suppression hearing that the defendant did not possess the property sought to be suppressed, and then to turn around and argue at trial that the defendant did possess the same property. According to the *Salvucci* majority, however, *Rakas* and other cases "clearly establish that a prosecutor may simultaneously maintain that a defendant criminally possessed the seized good, but was not subject to a Fourth Amendment deprivation, without legal contradiction." This was because, after *Rakas,* a "person in legal possession of a good seized during an illegal search has not necessarily been subject to a Fourth Amendment deprivation." Thus, there was no unfairness or inconsistency in arguing, for example, that the defendant constructively possessed a gun, but had no Fourth Amendment protection in the area that was searched to find the gun.

## Ownership of Seized Property Does Not Necessarily Confer Standing: Rawlings v. Kentucky

Rawlings v. Kentucky, 448 U.S. 98 (1980), demonstrated the significance of *Salvucci*. Rawlings was convicted of trafficking in and possession of various controlled substances. These substances were seized from the purse of a woman who, along with Rawlings, was visiting the premises when police arrived. The Supreme Court found that Rawlings had no right to object to the search of the purse because he had no legitimate expectation of privacy in the purse. The Court added that even assuming that the woman consented to have the drugs stored in the purse, "the precipitous nature of the transaction hardly supports a reasonable inference that petitioner took normal precautions to maintain his privacy." Ownership of the drugs was not enough to confer a right to object to the search, because the question was whether Rawlings had a legitimate expectation of privacy in the area that was searched, i.e., the purse. Justice Marshall, joined by Justice Brennan, dissented.

While ownership of the property seized does not necessarily provide the right to object to a search, it does provides right to object to a *seizure* of that property—because a seizure is by definition an intrusion on an ownership interest. Of course, this did not help Rawlings, because the seizure of his property was completely reasonable—the officers searched the purse and found contraband. Rawlings did not have a legitimate possessory interest in contraband.

### Targets Without Standing: United States v. Payner

United States v. Payner, 447 U.S. 727 (1980), shows the consequences of the Court's rejection of the "target" theory of standing in *Rakas.* An IRS investigation of American citizens doing business in the Bahamas focused on a certain Bahamian bank. When an official of that bank visited the United States, IRS agents stole his briefcase and removed and photographed hundreds of documents. They did this to obtain evidence against Payner. Under *Rakas,* Payner had no right to object to the search of the briefcase, even though he was the target of the illegal search. Payner argued that the federal district court should exercise its supervisory power to exclude the evidence and thus to deter such purposefully illegal tactics. The district court agreed with Payner and excluded the evidence given the officers' bad intent, but the Supreme Court held "that the supervisory power does not authorize a federal court to suppress otherwise admissible evidence on the ground that it was seized unlawfully from a third party not before the court." Justice Marshall, joined by Justices Brennan and Blackmun, dissented and argued that the government agents acted in bad faith by manipulating the standing rules in order to conduct an unconstitutional search; therefore, suppression of the illegally seized evidence was essential to protect the integrity of the judiciary whose rules were being manipulated.

### Presence in the Home of Another: Minnesota v. Carter

Assume that you are at a party and police officers enter and conduct a thorough search of the premises, and they find evidence that is being used against you in a criminal trial. If the search of the premises is illegal, do you, as a partygoer, have the right to complain that the search was a violation of your Fourth Amendment rights? In Minnesota v. Carter, 525 U.S. 83 (1998), the defendants complained about a search of a premises in which they were visitors—bagging cocaine with the owner. Chief Justice Rehnquist, writing for the Court, held that persons who are temporarily on the premises for a commercial transaction have no Fourth Amendment rights at stake in a search of the premises. He accepted the fact that a person might have a reasonable expectation of privacy in the home of another as did the overnight guest in Minnesota v. Olson, discussed earlier in this Chapter, but he concluded that "the purely commercial nature of the transaction engaged in here, the relatively short period of time on the premises, and the lack of any previous connection between respondents and the householder, all lead us to conclude that respondents' situation is closer to that of one simply permitted on the premises."

Justice Scalia, joined by Justice Thomas, wrote a concurring opinion. Justice Kennedy wrote a concurring opinion emphasizing that social guests might have expectations that business visitors do not. Justice Breyer wrote an opinion concurring in the judgment. Justice Ginsburg, joined by Justices Stevens and Souter, dissented.

### Cars, Drivers, Passengers

Standing questions arise quite frequently when vehicles are stopped and searched. It is clear that the owner of a car has standing to object to a search. But there are several problematic questions, such as: 1. What if the owner is not present? 2. What if the owner is in the car but somebody else is driving? 3. Can a passenger ever have a protectible Fourth Amendment interest in the car? and 4. Who can object to the seizure of the car, as distinct from the search?

Some of these questions are discussed in United States v. Carter, 14 F.3d 1150 (6th Cir.1994). Carter was a passenger in a van owned and operated by Locklear. The police stopped the car for a traffic violation, then illegally searched suitcases in the back of the van and found drugs. Locklear was able to suppress the evidence and was never tried. Carter sought in turn to suppress the evidence. Carter argued that he had standing he had agreed to accompany Locklear on a lengthy trip; that he had taken toilet articles and a change of clothing with him in the van; that he had entertained an expectation of privacy in the vehicle throughout the duration of the trip; and that he had been detained in violation of his Fourth Amendment rights during the time the vehicle was illegally searched. Carter had no ownership interest in the van and no control over it; he had no possessions in the van other than a change of clothes (a pair of jeans and a shirt) and a shaving kit found in the front of the vehicle; and he claimed no possessory or other interest in the suitcases filled with marijuana.

The court held that Carter had the right to challenge the *seizure* of his person that occurred when the van was searched, but the evidence could not be excluded as the fruit of Carter's seizure. It was the search of the car that uncovered the evidence, and that search was not connected to Carter's seizure. The court explained with a hypothetical:

> Suppose that at the time of the driver's arrest the police had summoned a taxi cab for Mr. Carter and told him he was free to

leave. The marijuana would still have been discovered, because it was located in a van owned and controlled by Mr. Locklear (who was not going anywhere until his vehicle had been searched) and not in a vehicle controlled by Mr. Carter.

As to the search of the back of the van, the court held that the presence of the shaving kit and change of clothing in the front of the van did not give Carter a legitimate expectation that the police would not open the van's back door. Thus, Carter did not meet his burden of showing that his expectation of privacy was violated by the search. [Nor would he have been any more successful under the trespassory investigation theory of *Jones,* because he had no ownership or control of the van.]

Would the result in *Carter* have been different if his shaving kit and change of clothing had been in the back of the van? What if he could show that he had been traveling in the van across country for a week before it was stopped by the police?

United States v. Lopez, 474 F.Supp. 943 (C.D.Cal.1979), holds that defendants who had been given keys to a truck, who had permission to use it and who did use it, had the right to challenge a search of the truck. Compare United States v. Tropiano, 50 F.3d 157 (2d Cir.1995) ("a defendant who knowingly possesses a stolen car has no legitimate expectation of privacy in the car"). In United States v. Powell, 929 F.2d 1190 (7th Cir.1991), the court held that where the owner of a car was absent at the time the car was stopped and searched, he had the right to object to the search but not to the stop. Does this make sense?

### *Disassociation from Property*

If a person disassociates himself from certain property, then he loses standing to object to a search of that property, at least under the resonable expectation of privacy theory of *Rakas.* United States v. Boruff, 909 F.2d 111 (5th Cir.1990), provides an example. A pick-up truck driven by Taylor and a rented car driven by Boruff were involved in a drug-smuggling scheme. The truck had been purchased by Boruff, but title, registration and insurance were put in Taylor's name. Boruff added improvements to the truck, and it was understood that if the truck were sold, the money would go to Boruff. The car was rented by Boruff's girlfriend in her own name. The standard rental agreement signed by the girlfriend stated that only she could drive the car and that the car would not be used for any illegal purpose. Boruff and Taylor drove to Mexico, loaded marijuana into the pick-up truck, and started back. They travelled 100 yards apart on the highway. When a suspicious Border Patrol agent began to pursue the pick-up truck, Boruff did two u-turns in an effort to divert the agent's attention. A second agent pursued Boruff, while the first agent stopped the truck, searched it, found drugs, and placed Taylor under arrest. The second agent stopped Boruff, searched the rented car and found incriminating evidence. Boruff argued that both searches were illegal and moved to suppress all the evidence. As to the truck, the court held that Boruff had failed to establish an expectation of privacy, even though he paid for it.

> Despite his asserted ownership interest, Boruff did everything he could to disassociate himself from the truck in the event it was stopped by law enforcement officials. [Besides placing all documentation in Taylor's name], during the smuggling operation, Taylor, not Boruff, drove the truck. Boruff travelled in a separate vehicle, * * * and left his position in front of the truck after spotting the Border Patrol vehicle. * * * In addition, Boruff was not present when the truck was stopped or searched. See Rakas v. Illinois (legitimate presence at time of search an important factor). * * * Boruff also disavowed any knowledge of the truck and its contents after his own vehicle was stopped.

As to the rental car, the court found that Boruff had no standing to contest the search because his girlfriend was the only legal operator of the vehicle under the terms of the agreement and thus "had no authority to give control of the car to Boruff. The rental agreement also expressly forbade any use of the vehicle for illegal purposes." Do you agree with the court? Shouldn't Boruff have had some expectation of privacy somewhere?

For another case in which disavowal of ownership resulted in a loss of "standing", see United States v. Mangum, 100 F.3d 164 (D.C.Cir.1996). Mangum was a passenger in a car that was stopped by police. Mangum conceded that there was reasonable suspicion for the stop. A knapsack was removed from the trunk and Mangum, when asked, denied that it was his and said it belonged to the driver. The officer searched the bag and found that it contained a loaded handgun and Mangum's driver's license. The court held that because Mangum denied ownership, "he abandoned his property and waived any legitimate privacy interest in it. Courts have long held that, when a person voluntarily denies ownership of property in response to a police officer's question, he forfeits any privacy interest in the property; consequently, police may search it without a warrant."

Query whether these "disassociation" cases rejecting standing have been altered by the holding in United States v. Jones that the Fourth Amendment protects against trespassory investigation regardless of whether a reasonable expectation of privacy has been invaded. Couldn't Boruff claim that the search of the truck was a trespass because, despite his efforts to disassociate himself from the property, he was still the owner? Would the answer depend on the niceties of the state tort law on trespass?

### Coconspirator "Standing" Rejected: United States v. Padilla

A unanimous Supreme Court held in United States v. Padilla, 508 U.S. 77 (1993) (per curiam), that a person does not have an automatic right to challenge a search or seizure simply because he is a member of the conspiracy that owned the property that was searched or seized. In *Padilla,* the lower court held that the defendants could contest the legality of the stop and search of a car that was being operated by a coconspirator, even though the defendants were not present during the stop and did not own the car. But the Supreme Court reversed, explaining that a "coconspirator standing" rule "squarely contradicts" *Rakas,* under which each person must establish an individual expectation of privacy, or a legitimate possessory interest, that has been affected by the search or seizure.

The Court concluded: "Expectations of privacy and property interests govern the analysis of Fourth Amendment search and seizure claims. Participants in a criminal conspiracy may have such expectations or interests, but the conspiracy itself neither adds nor detracts from them." The Court remanded the case so that the lower court could consider "whether each respondent had either a property interest protected by the Fourth Amendment that was interfered with by the stop of the automobile" or "a reasonable expectation of privacy that was invaded by the search thereof." On remand, the court of appeals held that the conspirators had no right to object to the seizure of the car: they did not own the car, and they were not driving it. United States v. Padilla, 111 F.3d 685 (9th Cir.1997).

### 4. The Requirement of Causation and the Exception for Attenuation

The exclusionary rule does not apply unless there is a substantial causal connection between the illegal activity and the evidence offered at trial. Deterrence is unjustified in the absence of that causal link. Determining whether a causal link exists is often a difficult inquiry.

### Searches and Seizures That Produce No Evidence: The Ker-Frisbie Doctrine

The exclusionary rule cannot apply unless evidence is seized as a result of a search or arrest. See United States v. Occhipinti, 998 F.2d 791 (10th Cir. 1993) (legality of protective sweep need not be decided because no evidence was obtained, so there was nothing to exclude). In Ker v. Illinois, 119 U.S. 436 (1886), and Frisbie v. Collins, 342 U.S. 519 (1952), the Supreme Court held that an illegal arrest of a person did not deprive the court of jurisdiction to try that person. That is, the body of the person, as distinct from evidence, was not subject to exclusion. The *Ker-Frisbie* doctrine has been used to uphold the abduction of suspects from foreign countries in order for them to be tried in the United States. See United States v. Alvarez-Machain, 504 U.S. 655 (1992) (holding that because the U.S.-Mexican Extradition Treaty did not explicitly prohibit abduction, "the rule in *Ker* applies, and the court need not inquire as to how respondent came before it.").

## Causal Connection: Evidence Found After a Fourth Amendment Violation

Wong Sun v. United States, 371 U.S. 471 (1963) and the following case, Brown v. Illinois, are the Court's leading cases on whether there is a sufficient causal connection between proffered evidence and an illegal search or seizure to justify exclusion. In these cases, the defendant asserts that there is a direct link between the illegality and the proffered evidence. The government, while admitting at least for argument's sake that there was an illegal search or seizure, nonetheless contends that the relationship between the illegality and the proffered evidence is too attenuated to justify exclusion. *Wong Sun* is discussed in detail in *Brown*.

## BROWN V. ILLINOIS

Supreme Court of the United States, 1975.
422 U.S. 590.

### MR. JUSTICE BLACKMUN delivered the opinion of the Court.

\* \* \*

As petitioner Richard Brown was climbing the last of the stairs leading to the rear entrance of his Chicago apartment in the early evening of May 13, 1968, he happened to glance at the window near the door. He saw, pointed at him through the window, a revolver held by a stranger who was inside the apartment. The man said: "Don't move, you are under arrest." Another man, also with a gun, came up behind Brown and repeated the statement that he was under arrest. It was about 7:45 p.m. The two men turned out to be Detectives William Nolan and William Lenz of the Chicago police force. \* \* \* As both officers held him at gunpoint, the three entered the apartment. Brown was ordered to stand against the wall and was searched. No weapon was found. \* \* \* Detective Lenz informed him that he was under arrest for the murder of Roger Corpus, handcuffed him, and escorted him to the squad car.

The two detectives took petitioner to the Maxwell Street police station. [While at the station, Brown was twice given *Miranda* warnings and twice confessed. The first confession occurred 90 minutes after the arrest, the second occurred seven hours after the arrest. Brown moved to suppress the confessions as having been caused by an arrest without probable cause. The trial court denied the motion, and Brown was convicted. The Illinois Supreme Court found that Brown had been arrested without probable cause, but nonetheless held that the motion to suppress was properly denied because the confessions were too attenuated from the illegal arrest to justify exclusion].

\* \* \* The [Illinois] court appears to have held that the *Miranda* warnings in and of themselves broke the causal chain so that any subsequent statement, even one induced by the continuing effects of unconstitutional custody, was admissible so long as, in the traditional sense, it was voluntary and not coerced in violation of the Fifth and Fourteenth Amendments.

\* \* \*

In *Wong Sun,* the Court pronounced the principles to be applied where the issue is whether statements and other evidence obtained after an illegal arrest or search should be excluded. In that case, federal agents elicited an oral statement from defendant Toy after forcing entry at 6 a.m. into his laundry, at the back of which he had his living quarters. The agents had followed Toy down the hall to the bedroom and there had placed him under arrest. The Court of Appeals found that there was no probable cause for the arrest. This Court concluded that that finding was "amply justified by the facts clearly shown on this record." Toy's statement, which bore upon his participation in the sale of narcotics, led the agents to question another person, Johnny Yee, who actually possessed narcotics. Yee stated that heroin had been brought to him earlier by Toy and another Chinese known to him only as "Sea Dog." Under questioning, Toy said that "Sea Dog" was Wong Sun. Toy led agents to a multifamily dwelling where, he said, Wong Sun lived. Gaining admittance to the building through a bell and buzzer, the agents climbed the stairs and entered the apartment. One went into the back room and brought Wong Sun out in handcuffs. After arraignment, Wong Sun was released on his own recognizance. Several days later, he returned voluntarily to give an unsigned confession.

This Court ruled that Toy's declarations and the contraband taken from Yee were the fruits of the agents' illegal action and should not have been admitted as evidence against Toy. It held that the statement did not result from "an intervening independent act of a free will," and that it was not "sufficiently an act of free will to purge the primary taint of the unlawful invasion." With respect to Wong Sun's confession, however, the Court held that in the light of his lawful arraignment and release on his own recognizance, and of his return voluntarily several days later to make the statement, the connection between his unlawful arrest and the statement "had become so attenuated as to dissipate the taint." The Court said:

> "We need not hold that all evidence is 'fruit of the poisonous tree' simply because it would not have come to light but for the illegal actions of the police. Rather, the more apt question in such a case is whether, granting establishment of the primary illegality, the evidence to which instant objection is made has been come at by exploitation of that illegality or instead by means sufficiently distinguishable to be purged of the primary taint."

\* \* \*

The Illinois courts refrained from resolving the question, as apt here as it was in *Wong Sun,* whether Brown's statements were obtained by exploitation of the illegality of his arrest. They assumed that the *Miranda* warnings, by themselves, assured that the statements (verbal acts, as contrasted with physical evidence) were of sufficient free will as to purge the primary taint of the unlawful arrest. *Wong Sun,* of course, preceded *Miranda.*

\* \* \*

\* \* \* In order for the causal chain, between the illegal arrest and the statements made subsequent thereto, to be broken, *Wong Sun* requires not merely that the statement meet the Fifth Amendment standard of voluntariness but that it be "sufficiently an act of free will to purge the primary taint." \* \* \*

If *Miranda* warnings, by themselves, were held to attenuate the taint of an unconstitutional arrest, regardless of how wanton and purposeful the Fourth Amendment violation, the effect of the exclusionary rule would be substantially diluted. \* \* \* Any incentive to avoid Fourth Amendment violations would be eviscerated by making the warnings, in effect, a "cure-all," and the constitutional guarantee against unlawful searches and seizures could be said to be reduced to "a form of words."

\* \* \*

While we therefore reject the *per se* rule which the Illinois courts appear to have accepted, we also decline to adopt any alternative *per se* or "but for" rule. \* \* \* The question whether a confession is the product of a free will under *Wong Sun* must be answered on the facts of each case. No single fact is dispositive. \* \* \* The *Miranda* warnings are an important factor, to be sure, in determining whether the confession is obtained by exploitation of an illegal arrest. But they are not the only factor to be considered. The temporal proximity of the arrest and the confession, the presence of intervening circumstances, and, particularly, the purpose and flagrancy of the official misconduct are all relevant. * * * And the burden of showing admissibility rests, of course, on the prosecution.

* * * We conclude that the State failed to sustain the burden of showing that the evidence in question was admissible under *Wong Sun*.

Brown's first statement was separated from his illegal arrest by less than two hours, and there was no intervening event of significance whatsoever. In its essentials, his situation is remarkably like that of James Wah Toy in *Wong Sun*.[a] We could hold Brown's first statement admissible only if we overrule *Wong Sun*. We decline to do so. And the second statement was clearly the result and the fruit of the first.

The illegality here, moreover, had a quality of purposefulness. The impropriety of the arrest was obvious; awareness of that fact was virtually conceded by the two detectives when they repeatedly acknowledged, in their testimony, that the purpose of their action was "for investigation" or for "questioning." The arrest, both in design and in execution, was investigatory. The detectives embarked upon this expedition for evidence in the hope that something might turn up. The manner in which Brown's arrest was effected gives the appearance of having been calculated to cause surprise, fright, and confusion.

* * *

[The concurring opinion of JUSTICE WHITE is omitted.]

**MR. JUSTICE POWELL, with whom MR. JUSTICE REHNQUIST joins, concurring in part.**

I join the Court insofar as it holds that the *per se* rule adopted by the Illinois Supreme Court for determining the admissibility of petitioner's two statements inadequately accommodates the diverse interests underlying the Fourth Amendment exclusionary rule. I would, however, remand the case for reconsideration under the general standards articulated in the Court's opinion and elaborated herein.

* * *

* * * If an illegal arrest merely provides the occasion of initial contact between the police and the accused, and because of time or other intervening factors the accused's eventual statement is the product of his own reflection and free will, application of the exclusionary rule can serve little purpose: the police normally will not make an illegal arrest in the hope of eventually obtaining such a truly volunteered statement. * * * Bearing these considerations in mind, and recognizing that the deterrent

---

[a]  The situation here is thus in dramatic contrast to that of Wong Sun himself. Wong Sun's confession, which the Court held admissible, came several days after the illegality, and was preceded by a lawful arraignment and a release from custody on his own recognizance.

value of the Fourth Amendment exclusionary rule is limited to certain kinds of police conduct, the following general categories can be identified.

Those most readily identifiable are on the extremes: the flagrantly abusive violation of Fourth Amendment rights, on the one hand, and "technical" Fourth Amendment violations, on the other. In my view, these extremes call for significantly different judicial responses.

I would require the clearest indication of attenuation in cases in which official conduct was flagrantly abusive of Fourth Amendment rights. * * * In such cases the deterrent value of the exclusionary rule is most likely to be effective * * *. I thus would require some demonstrably effective break in the chain of events leading from the illegal arrest to the statement, such as actual consultation with counsel or the accused's presentation before a magistrate for a determination of probable cause, before the taint can be deemed removed.

At the opposite end of the spectrum lie "technical" violations of Fourth Amendment rights * * *.

* * * [In "technical" violation cases], with the exception of statements given in the immediate circumstances of the illegal arrest * * * I would not require more than proof that effective *Miranda* warnings were given and that the ensuing statement was voluntary in the Fifth Amendment sense. * * *

Between these extremes lies a wide range of situations that defy ready categorization, and I will not attempt to embellish on the factors set forth in the Court's opinion other than to emphasize that the *Wong Sun* inquiry always should be conducted with the deterrent purpose of the Fourth Amendment exclusionary rule sharply in focus. * * *

### Statements Tainted by an Illegal Arrest: Dunaway v. New York, Taylor v. Alabama, and Kaupp v. Texas

*Brown* is followed in Dunaway v. New York, 442 U.S. 200 (1979), where the defendant was arrested without probable cause, taken down to the station, and confessed after receiving *Miranda* warnings. The Court found that Dunaway's situation was "virtually a replica of the situation in *Brown*." As in *Brown,* the Court was concerned that officers would "violate the Fourth Amendment with impunity, safe in the knowledge that they could wash their hands in the procedural safeguards of the Fifth."

*Brown* and *Dunaway* were deemed to be dispositive in Taylor v. Alabama, 455 U.S. 1014 (1982). Police arrested Taylor for a grocery store robbery without probable cause, searched him, took him to the station for questioning and gave him *Miranda* warnings. At the station, he was fingerprinted, re-advised of his rights, questioned and placed in a lineup.

Police told Taylor that his fingerprints matched those on some grocery items that had been handled by a participant in the robbery, and after a short visit with his girlfriend and a male companion, Taylor signed a *Miranda* waiver and confessed. Although the length of time between the illegal arrests and the confessions in *Brown* and *Dunaway* was two hours and in this case it was six hours, the Court said that "a difference of a few hours is not significant where, as here, petitioner was in police custody, unrepresented by counsel, and he was questioned on several occasions, fingerprinted and subjected to a line-up." Although Taylor was given *Miranda* warnings three times, the Court found that this was insufficient to break the connection with the illegal arrest and detention. Four dissenters agreed on the applicable law but disagreed on its application to the facts of the case.

The Court applied *Brown, Dunaway* and *Taylor* in Kaupp v. Texas, 538 U.S. 626 (2003) (per curiam) as it held that a suspect's confession was, on the record before it, the fruit of an arrest without probable cause. Police officers suspected Kaupp, an adolescent, of involvement in a murder, but did not have probable cause to arrest him. The officers entered Kaupp's house at 3 a.m., went to his bedroom, woke him up, placed him in handcuffs, and took him in his underwear to a patrol car. They drove and stopped for 5 to 10 minutes at the site where the victim's body had been found, and then went on to the sheriff's headquarters, where they removed his handcuffs, gave him *Miranda* warnings, and told him that the victim's brother had confessed to the crime and implicated him as an accomplice. Kaupp then admitted to some part in the crime. The Court analyzed the situation as follows:

> Since Kaupp was arrested before he was questioned, and because the state does not even claim that the sheriff's department had probable cause to detain him at that point, well-established precedent requires suppression of the confession unless that confession was an act of free will sufficient to purge the primary taint of the unlawful invasion. Demonstrating such purgation is, of course, a function of circumstantial evidence, with the burden of persuasion on the state. Relevant considerations include observance of *Miranda*, the temporal proximity of the arrest and the confession, the presence of intervening circumstances, and, particularly, the purpose and flagrancy of the official misconduct.

> The record before us shows that only one of these considerations, the giving of *Miranda* warnings, supports the state, and we held in *Brown* that "*Miranda* warnings, *alone* and *per se*, cannot always . . . break, for Fourth Amendment purposes, the causal connection between the illegality and the confession." All other factors point the opposite way. There is no indication from the record that any substantial time passed between Kaupp's removal from his home in

handcuffs and his confession after only 10 or 15 minutes of interrogation. In the interim, he remained in his partially clothed state in the physical custody of a number of officers, some of whom, at least, were conscious that they lacked probable cause to arrest. In fact, the state has not even alleged any meaningful intervening event between the illegal arrest and Kaupp's confession.

### Statements Not Tainted by an Illegal Arrest: Rawlings v. Kentucky

*Brown* was distinguished in Rawlings v. Kentucky, 448 U.S. 98 (1980). The Court assumed that Rawlings and others were improperly detained in a house while police went to get a search warrant, but found that the improper detention did not require suppression of statements made by Rawlings after evidence was discovered. Justice Rehnquist's majority opinion observed that *Miranda* warnings were given (also true in *Brown*); that the 45 minute detention was in a congenial atmosphere; that the statements were apparently spontaneous reactions to the discovery of evidence rather than the product of the illegal detention; that the police action did not involve flagrant misconduct; and that no argument was made that the statements were involuntary. Justices White and Stewart would have remanded for consideration of the "fruit" question. Justices Marshall and Brennan thought that the statements "were obviously the fruit of the illegal detention."

### Warrantless In-Home Arrest Is Not Causally Connected to a Subsequent Confession: New York v. Harris

*Brown, Dunaway* and *Taylor* each excluded confessions as the fruit of an arrest made without probable cause. In New York v. Harris, 495 U.S. 14 (1990), the defendant confessed at the station after police made a warrantless in-home arrest, with probable cause but without a warrant— and so the in-home arrest was in violation of Payton v. New York, *supra* (holding that an arrest warrant is necessary for an in-home arrest in the absence of exigent circumstances). The challenged confession was made at the station an hour after the arrest. Justice White concluded for the Court that there was no substantial causative connection between the *Payton* violation and the confession, because unlike the prior cases, the defendant was not unlawfully in custody when he made the confession. Justice White reasoned that "the rule in *Payton* was designed to protect the physical integrity of the home; it was not intended to grant criminal suspects * * * protection for statements made outside their premises where the police have probable cause to arrest the suspect." Thus, a violation of *Payton* constitutes an illegal *search* of the home, but it does not result in an illegal arrest, so long as there is probable cause; and while evidence obtained in the warrantless search of the home is subject to exclusion, there is no automatic connection between that search and a subsequent confession outside the home.

Justice Marshall dissented in an opinion joined by Justices Brennan, Blackmun and Stevens. Justice Marshall contended that the rule adopted by the majority would give the police an incentive to violate *Payton*. He reasoned that the officer might find it beneficial to enter the arrestee's home illegally in order to save time, and perhaps to rattle the suspect and increase the likelihood of a confession. Excluding evidence found in the house would be no deterrent, because such suppression would make the officer no worse off than if he had waited outside to make the arrest.

In *Harris* the *Payton* violation turned up no evidence; nothing incriminating was seen in Harris's home. Would exclusion be required if the officers found incriminating evidence in Harris's house in the course of making a warrantless arrest, and subsequently used that evidence to obtain a stationhouse confession from Harris? In United States v. Beltran, 917 F.2d 641, 645 (1st Cir.1990), police arrested Beltran in her home without a warrant. During the arrest the police saw cocaine in plain view. They took the defendant to the stationhouse where she made incriminating statements. The court stated that "whether or the extent to which *Harris* applies may turn on questions of fact such as when the police seized the items in question or what motivated Ms. Beltran's statements" and remanded the case to the district court for a factual determination. Does this mean that if Beltran was rattled into a confession by the fact that the police saw the cocaine—rather than by the arrest—then *Harris* would not apply and the confession would be excluded?

### *Insufficient Causal Connection Between a Knock-and-Announce Violation and Evidence Found in the Home: Hudson v. Michigan*

In Hudson v. Michigan, 547 U.S. 586 (2006), Justice Scalia wrote for the Court as it decided a violation of the knock-and-announce requirement does not justify the exclusion of evidence found in the warranted search. The Court uses an analysis like that found in Harris v. New York, supra. But the case has broader importance as it seems to signal that the Court is questioning whether the exclusionary rule is necessary *at all* given developments since *Mapp*.

Police had a warrant to search Hudson's house for drugs and firearms. They executed the warrant and found both. The only question before the Supreme Court was whether the fact that the officers only waited several seconds after announcing themselves before turning the doorknob and entering the house required exclusion of the evidence because the knock-and-announce rule was violated.

Justice Scalia found that exclusion was not required:

[E]xclusion may not be premised on the mere fact that a constitutional violation was a "but-for" cause of obtaining evidence. Our cases show that but-for causality is only a necessary, not a sufficient, condition for suppression. In this case, of course, the constitutional violation of an illegal *manner* of entry was *not* a but-for cause of obtaining the evidence. Whether that preliminary misstep had occurred *or not*, the police would have executed the warrant they had obtained, and would have discovered the gun and drugs inside the house. But even if the illegal entry here could be characterized as a but-for cause of discovering what was inside, we have never held that evidence is fruit of the poisonous tree simply because it would not have come to light but for the illegal actions of the police. Rather, but-for cause * * * can be too attenuated to justify exclusion. * * *

Attenuation can occur, of course, when the causal connection is remote. Attenuation also occurs when, even given a direct causal connection, the interest protected by the constitutional guarantee that has been violated would not be served by suppression of the evidence obtained. * * * Thus, in New York v. Harris, where an illegal warrantless arrest was made in Harris' house, we held that suppressing Harris's statement taken outside the house would not serve the purpose of the [*Payton*] rule that made Harris' in-house arrest illegal. * * *

For this reason, cases excluding the fruits of unlawful warrantless searches say nothing about the appropriateness of exclusion to vindicate the interests protected by the knock-and-announce requirement. * * * Exclusion of the evidence obtained by a warrantless search vindicates that entitlement. The interests protected by the knock-and-announce requirement are quite different—and do not include the shielding of potential evidence from the government's eyes.

Justice Scalia had this to say about the exclusionary rule:

Quite apart from the requirement of unattenuated causation, the exclusionary rule has never been applied except where its deterrence benefits outweigh its substantial social costs. The costs here are considerable. In addition to the grave adverse consequence that exclusion of relevant incriminating evidence always entails (viz., the risk of releasing dangerous criminals into society), imposing that massive remedy for a knock-and-announce violation would generate a constant flood of alleged failures to observe the rule, and claims that any asserted * * * justification for a no-knock entry had inadequate support. The cost of entering this lottery would be small, but the jackpot enormous: suppression of all evidence, amounting in many cases to a get-out-of-jail-free card. Courts would experience as never before the reality that the exclusionary rule frequently requires extensive litigation to determine whether particular evidence must be excluded. * * *

\* \* \*

Next to these "substantial social costs" we must consider the deterrence benefits, existence of which is a necessary condition for exclusion. * * * To begin with, the value of deterrence depends upon the strength of the incentive to commit the forbidden act. Viewed from this perspective, deterrence of knock-and-announce violations is not worth a lot. Violation of the warrant requirement sometimes produces incriminating evidence that could not otherwise be obtained. But ignoring knock-and-announce can realistically be expected to achieve absolutely nothing except the prevention of destruction of evidence and the avoidance of life-threatening resistance by occupants of the premises—dangers which, if there is even "reasonable suspicion" of their existence, *suspend the knock-and-announce requirement anyway*. Massive deterrence is hardly required.

It seems to us not even true, as Hudson contends, that without suppression there will be no deterrence of knock-and-announce violations at all. Of course even if this assertion were accurate, it would not necessarily justify suppression. Assuming (as the assertion must) that civil suit is not an effective deterrent, one can think of many forms of police misconduct that are similarly "undeterred." When, for example, a confessed suspect in the killing of a police officer, arrested (along with incriminating evidence) in a lawful warranted search, is subjected to physical abuse at the station house, would it seriously be suggested that the evidence must be excluded, since that is the only "effective deterrent"? And what, other than civil suit, is the "effective deterrent" of police violation of an already-confessed suspect's Sixth Amendment rights by denying him prompt access to counsel? Many would regard these violated rights as more significant than the right not to be intruded upon in one's nightclothes—and yet nothing but "ineffective" civil suit is available as a deterrent. And the police incentive for those violations is arguably greater than the incentive for disregarding the knock-and-announce rule.

\* \* \*

In sum, the social costs of applying the exclusionary rule to knock-and-announce violations are considerable; the incentive to such violations is minimal to begin with, and the extant deterrences against them are substantial—incomparably greater than the factors deterring warrantless entries when *Mapp* was decided. Resort to the massive remedy of suppressing evidence of guilt is unjustified.

Justice Kennedy concurred in part and in the judgment and wrote as follows:

> Today's decision does not address any demonstrated pattern of knock-and-announce violations. If a widespread pattern of violations were shown, and particularly if those violations were committed against persons who lacked the means or voice to mount an effective protest, there would be reason for grave concern. Even then, however, the Court would have to acknowledge that extending the remedy of exclusion to all the evidence seized following a knock-and-announce violation would mean revising the requirement of causation that limits our discretion in applying the exclusionary rule. That type of extension also would have significant practical implications, adding to the list of issues requiring resolution at the criminal trial questions such as whether police officers entered a home after waiting 10 seconds or 20.

Justice Breyer, joined by Justices Stevens, Souter and Ginsburg, dissented and wrote that "the Court destroys the strongest legal incentive to comply with the Constitution's knock-and-announce requirement"; "the Court does so without significant support in precedent"; "[t]oday's opinion is thus doubly troubling"; "[i]t represents a significant departure from the Court's precedents"; and "it weakens, perhaps destroys, much of the practical value of the Constitution's knock-and-announce protection."

### *Consent as Breaking the Chain of Causation*

Police often argue that an illegal search or seizure should not result in exclusion of evidence because the suspect voluntarily consented to the search that ultimately uncovered that evidence. For example, assume that the defendant is illegally pulled over while driving. After a short period, the officer asks nicely whether the defendant would permit a search of the trunk; the defendant is told of his right to refuse; the defendant consents and weapons are found in the trunk. The defendant argues that there is a direct causal link between the illegal stop and the discovery of the evidence. The government argues that the voluntary consent broke the chain of causation.

The question in such cases is whether the voluntary consent is enough to break the chain of causation running from the illegal police activity to the evidence ultimately uncovered. The answer is dependent on the circumstances, and the analysis is no different from that employed in *Brown* to determine whether an admittedly voluntary confession should be excluded as the fruit of an illegal arrest. As one court put it:

> To determine whether the defendant's consent was an independent act of free will, breaking the causal chain * * * we must consider three factors: 1) the temporal proximity of the illegal conduct and the consent; 2) the presence of intervening circumstances; and 3) the purpose and flagrancy of the initial misconduct.

United States v. Hernandez, 279 F.3d 302 (5th Cir. 2002). In *Hernandez*, the court found that the defendant voluntarily consented to a search of luggage, but that this voluntary act was not sufficient to break the chain of causation from the officer's initial illegal search. Hernandez was traveling on a bus when police seized her bag and manipulated it in such a way as to determine that a hard package was inside it. This manipulation constituted an illegal search under United States v. Bond, discussed earlier in this Chapter. The officer then immediately sought and obtained consent from Hernandez to open the suitcase. The Court found that there were no intervening circumstances, and therefore the opening of the suitcase was a fruit of the *Bond* violation. The Court stated that while the police misconduct was not flagrant, the officer exploited the illegality as the officer's suspicions were aroused only after manipulating Hernandez's suitcase. As a result, "even though Hernandez voluntarily consented to Officer Ordaz's opening her suitcase and searching it, her consent did not cure the Fourth Amendment violation caused by Officer Ordaz's prior manipulation of the suitcase." For a contrary result, see United States v. Becker, 333 F.3d 858 (8th Cir. 2003) (voluntary consent severed the chain of causation from an illegal detention to the evidence obtained: consent was removed in time from the detention, and the officers were not engaged in flagrant misconduct).

### Other Ways of Breaking the Chain

Suppose a police officer makes a *Terry* stop of a car without reasonable suspicion, discovers that someone in the car has an outstanding warrant, arrests the person, does a search incident and finds drugs or an illegal firearm. Must the evidence be suppressed or does the warrant break the chain that began with the illegal stop? United States v. Gross, 662 F.3d 393 (6th Cir. 2011), is just such a case. The court in *Gross* held that discovery of a warrant during an illegal stop constituted an intervening circumstance and held, 2–1, that "where there is a stop with no legal purpose, the discovery of a warrant during that stop may be a relevant factor in the intervening circumstance analysis, but it is not itself dispositive." The court explained that "[t]o hold otherwise would create a rule that potentially allows for a new form of police investigation" and "would create perverse incentives."

### Witness Testimony After Illegal Arrests and Searches: *United States v. Ceccolini*

Courts are reluctant to suppress the testimony from a live witness that is alleged to be the product of an illegal search or arrest. The witness's decision to testify is ordinarily enough to break any causal connection between the illegality and the testimony. The leading case is United States v. Ceccolini, 435 U.S. 268 (1978), where an officer stopped to talk with a friend who was in Ceccolini's flower shop. While there, the officer illegally picked up and opened an envelope, and found money and gambling slips. He then learned from his friend, who did not know about this discovery, that the envelope belonged to Ceccolini. The officer relayed his information to detectives who in turn transmitted it to the FBI. Four months later, an FBI agent questioned the officer's friend who had been in the flower shop, without mentioning the illegally discovered gambling slips. The friend expressed a willingness to testify against Ceccolini, and did so before the grand jury and at Ceccolini's trial.

Justice Rehnquist, writing for the Court, declined to adopt a rule that the testimony of a live witness could never be excluded. But he stated that "the exclusionary rule should be invoked with much greater reluctance where the claim is based on a causal relationship between a constitutional violation and the discovery of a live witness than when a similar claim is advanced to support suppression of an inanimate object." The Court noted that the willingness of the witness to testify is very likely, if not certain, to break the chain of causation under *Wong Sun*. Justice Rehnquist also noted that exclusion of a live witness would have a serious cost, as it would "perpetually disable a witness from testifying about relevant and material facts, regardless of how unrelated such testimony might be to the purpose of the originally illegal search or the evidence discovered thereby." Because of this cost, the Court concluded that the exclusionary rule could only apply if there is a very close and direct link between the illegality and the witness's testimony. The Court found no such close link under the facts in *Ceccolini,* where the witness was willing to testify, four months passed between the illegality and the agent's contact with the witness, and the witness was unaware of the illegality. Justice Marshall, in a dissent joined by Justice Brennan, found no meaningful distinction between live witnesses and inanimate evidence. He argued that "the same tree" cannot bear "two different kinds of fruit, with one kind less susceptible than the other to exclusion."

After *Ceccolini,* can you think of facts that would result in the exclusion of a live witness? See United States v. Akridge, 346 F.3d 618

(6th Cir. 2003) (stating that after *Ceccolini*, the question of causal connection between an illegality and witness testimony is determined by the following factors: "(a) the degree of free will exercised by the witnesses; (b) the role of the illegality in obtaining the testimony; (c) the time elapsed between the illegal behavior, the decision to cooperate, and the actual testimony at trial; and (d) the purpose and flagrancy of the officials' misconduct.").

## 5.  Independent Source

Evidence will not be excluded if it is obtained independently from and without reliance on any illegal police activity. The "independent source" doctrine allows "the introduction of evidence discovered initially during an unlawful search if the evidence is discovered later through a source that is untainted by the initial illegality." United States v. Markling, 7 F.3d 1309 (7th Cir.1993).

In Segura v. United States, 468 U.S. 796 (1984), and in the following case, Murray v. United States, the Court considered whether an illegal search of premises could be cured when the officers later obtained a warrant, and where the probable cause supporting the warrant was not derived from information obtained in the illegal search. *Segura* is discussed in detail in *Murray*.

### MURRAY V. UNITED STATES
Supreme Court of the United States, 1988.
487 U.S. 533.

### JUSTICE SCALIA delivered the opinion of the Court.

In Segura v. United States, we held that police officers' illegal entry upon private premises did not require suppression of evidence subsequently discovered at those premises when executing a search warrant obtained on the basis of information wholly unconnected with the initial entry. In these consolidated cases we are faced with the question whether, again assuming evidence obtained pursuant to an independently obtained search warrant, the portion of such evidence that had been observed in plain view at the time of a prior illegal entry must be suppressed.

\* \* \* Based on information received from informants, federal law enforcement agents had been surveilling petitioner Murray and several of his co-conspirators. At about 1:45 p.m. on April 6, 1983, they observed Murray drive a truck and Carter drive a green camper, into a warehouse in South Boston. When the petitioners drove the vehicles out about 20 minutes later, the surveilling agents saw within the warehouse two individuals and a tractor-trailer rig bearing a long, dark container. Murray and Carter later turned over the truck and camper to other drivers, who were in turn followed and ultimately arrested, and the vehicles lawfully seized. Both vehicles were found to contain marijuana.

After receiving this information, several of the agents converged on the South Boston warehouse and forced entry. They found the warehouse unoccupied, but observed in plain view numerous burlap-wrapped bales that were later found to contain marijuana. They left without disturbing the bales, kept the warehouse under surveillance, and did not reenter it until they had a search warrant. In applying for the warrant, the agents did not mention the prior entry, and did not rely on any observations made during that entry. When the warrant was issued—at 10:40 p.m., approximately eight hours after the initial entry—the agents immediately reentered the warehouse and seized 270 bales of marijuana and notebooks listing customers for whom the bales were destined.

[The motion to suppress was denied and the Court of Appeals affirmed.]

* * *

Almost simultaneously with our development of the exclusionary rule, * * * we also announced what has come to be known as the "independent source" doctrine. That doctrine, which has been applied to evidence acquired not only through Fourth Amendment violations but also through Fifth and Sixth Amendment violations, has recently been described as follows:

> "[T]he interest of society in deterring unlawful police conduct and the public interest in having juries receive all probative evidence of a crime are properly balanced by putting the police in the same, not a *worse,* position than they would have been in if no police error or misconduct had occurred. . . . When the challenged evidence has an independent source, exclusion of such evidence would put the police in a worse position than they would have been in absent any error or violation." Nix v. Williams, 467 U.S. 431, 443 (1984).

The dispute here is over the scope of this doctrine. Petitioners contend that it applies only to evidence obtained for the first time during an independent lawful search. The Government argues that it applies also to evidence initially discovered during, or as a consequence of, an unlawful search, but later obtained independently from activities untainted by the initial illegality. We think the Government's view has better support in both precedent and policy.

Our cases have used the concept of "independent source" in a more general and a more specific sense. The more general sense identifies *all* evidence acquired in a fashion untainted by the illegal evidence-gathering activity. Thus, where an unlawful entry has given investigators knowledge of facts $x$ and $y$, but fact $z$ has been learned by other means, fact *z* can be said to be admissible because derived from an "independent source." This is how we used the term in Segura v. United States. In that case, agents unlawfully entered the defendant's apartment and remained there until a search warrant was obtained. The admissibility of what they discovered while waiting in the apartment was not before us, but we held that the evidence found for the first time during the execution of the valid and untainted search warrant was admissible because it was discovered pursuant to an "independent source."

The original use of the term, however, and its more important use for purposes of this case, was more specific. It was originally applied in the exclusionary rule context * * * with reference to that particular category of evidence acquired by an untainted search *which is identical to the evidence unlawfully acquired*—that is, in the example just given, to knowledge of facts *x* and *y* derived from an independent source.

* * *

Petitioners' asserted policy basis for excluding evidence which is initially discovered during an illegal search, but is subsequently acquired through an independent and lawful source, is that a contrary rule will remove all deterrence to, and indeed positively encourage, unlawful police searches. As petitioners see the incentives, law enforcement officers will routinely enter without a warrant to make sure that what they expect to be on the premises is in fact there. If it is not, they will have spared themselves the time and trouble of getting a warrant; if it is, they can get the warrant and use the evidence despite the unlawful entry. We see the incentives differently. An officer with probable cause sufficient to obtain a search warrant would be foolish to enter the premises first in an unlawful manner. By doing so, he would risk suppression of all evidence on the premises, both seen and unseen, since his action would add to the normal burden of convincing a magistrate that there is probable cause the much more onerous burden of convincing a trial court that no information gained from the illegal entry affected either the law enforcement officers' decision to seek a warrant or the magistrate's decision to grant it. Nor would the officer *without* sufficient probable cause to obtain a search warrant have any added incentive to conduct an unlawful entry, since whatever he finds cannot be used to establish probable cause before a magistrate.[a]

---

[a]   * * * To say that a district court must be satisfied that a warrant would have been sought without the illegal entry is not to give dispositive effect to police officers' assurances on the point. Where the facts render those assurances implausible, the independent source doctrine will not apply.

We might note that there is no basis for pointing to the present cases as an example of a "search first, warrant later" mentality. The District Court found that the agents entered the warehouse "in an effort to apprehend any participants who might have remained inside and to guard against the destruction of possibly critical evidence." While they may have misjudged the existence of sufficient exigent circumstances to justify the warrantless entry * * * there is

It is possible to read petitioners' briefs as asserting the more narrow position that the "independent source" doctrine does apply to independent acquisition of evidence previously derived *indirectly* from the unlawful search, but does not apply to what they call "primary evidence," that is, evidence acquired during the course of the search itself. In addition to finding no support in our precedent, this strange distinction would produce results bearing no relation to the policies of the exclusionary rule. It would mean, for example, that the government's knowledge of the existence and condition of a dead body, knowledge lawfully acquired through independent sources, would have to be excluded if government agents had previously observed the body during an unlawful search of the defendant's apartment; but not if they had observed a notation that the body was buried in a certain location, producing consequential discovery of the corpse.

\* \* \*

To apply what we have said to the present cases: Knowledge that the marijuana was in the warehouse was assuredly acquired at the time of the unlawful entry. But it was also acquired at the time of entry pursuant to the warrant, and if that later acquisition was not the result of the earlier entry there is no reason why the independent source doctrine should not apply. Invoking the exclusionary rule would put the police (and society) not in the *same* position they would have occupied if no violation occurred, but in a *worse* one.

We think this is also true with respect to the tangible evidence, the bales of marijuana. It would make no more sense to exclude that than it would to exclude tangible evidence found upon the corpse in *Nix,* if the search in that case had not been abandoned and had in fact come upon the body. \* \* \* The independent source doctrine does not rest upon such metaphysical analysis, but upon the policy that, while the government should not profit from its illegal activity, neither should it be placed in a worse position than it would otherwise have occupied.

The ultimate question, therefore, is whether the search pursuant to warrant was in fact a genuinely independent source of the information and tangible evidence at issue here. This would not have been the case if the agents' decision to seek the warrant was prompted by what they had seen during the initial entry, or if information obtained during that entry was presented to the Magistrate and affected his decision to issue the warrant. \* \* \* The District Court found that the agents did not reveal their warrantless entry to the Magistrate and that they did not include in their application for a warrant any recitation of their observations in the warehouse. It did not, however, explicitly find that the agents would have

---

nothing to suggest that they went in merely to see if there was anything worth getting a warrant for.

sought a warrant if they had not earlier entered the warehouse. * * * To be sure, the District Court did determine that the purpose of the warrantless entry was in part "to guard against the destruction of possibly critical evidence," and one could perhaps infer from this that the agents who made the entry already planned to obtain that "critical evidence" through a warrant-authorized search. That inference is not, however, clear enough to justify the conclusion that the District Court's findings amounted to a determination of independent source.

Accordingly, we vacate the judgment and remand these cases to the Court of Appeals with instructions that it remand to the District Court for determination whether the warrant-authorized search of the warehouse was an independent source of the challenged evidence in the sense we have described.

JUSTICE BRENNAN and JUSTICE KENNEDY took no part in the consideration or decision of this litigation.

**JUSTICE MARSHALL, with whom JUSTICE STEVENS and JUSTICE O'CONNOR join, dissenting.**

* * * In holding that the independent source exception may apply to the facts of these cases, I believe the Court loses sight of the practical moorings of the independent source exception and creates an affirmative incentive for unconstitutional searches. * * *

* * * Obtaining a warrant is inconvenient and time consuming. Even when officers have probable cause to support a warrant application, therefore, they have an incentive first to determine whether it is worthwhile to obtain a warrant. Probable cause is much less than certainty, and many "confirmatory" searches will result in the discovery that no evidence is present, thus saving the police the time and trouble of getting a warrant. If contraband is discovered, however, the officers may later seek a warrant to shield the evidence from the taint of the illegal search. The police thus know in advance that they have little to lose and much to gain by forgoing the bother of obtaining a warrant and undertaking an illegal search.

Under the Court's view, today's decision does not provide an incentive for unlawful searches, because the officer undertaking the search would know that "his action would add to the normal burden of convincing a magistrate that there is probable cause the much more onerous burden of convincing a trial court that no information gained from the illegal entry affected either the law enforcement officers' decision to seek a warrant or the magistrate's decision to grant it." The Court, however, provides no hint of why this risk would actually seem significant to the officers. Under the circumstances of these cases, the officers committing the illegal search have both knowledge and control of the factors central to the trial court's determination. First, it is a simple matter, as was done in these cases, to exclude from the warrant application any information gained from the initial entry so that the magistrate's determination of probable cause is not influenced by the prior illegal search. Second, today's decision makes the application of the independent source exception turn entirely on an evaluation of the officers' intent. It normally will be difficult for the trial court to verify, or the defendant to rebut, an assertion by officers that they always intended to obtain a warrant, regardless of the results of the illegal search. The testimony of the officers conducting the illegal search is the only direct evidence of intent, and the defendant will be relegated simply to arguing that the officers should not be believed. Under these circumstances, the litigation risk described by the Court seems hardly a risk at all; it does not significantly dampen the incentive to conduct the initial illegal search.

\* \* \*

[The dissenting opinion of JUSTICE STEVENS is omitted.]

### QUESTIONS ABOUT MURRAY

The majority in *Murray* expresses concern about a "confirmatory" search, and states that the subsequent search will be invalidated if the officer's testimony denying a confirmatory motivation is "implausible." The officer denying a confirmatory motivation must explain why he or she made the original search without a warrant, and after *Murray* this explanation must rise only to the level of plausibility. In *Murray,* the explanation found plausible was that the officers thought they had exigent circumstances, even though in fact they did not. (If they did have exigent circumstances, *Murray* would not be an exclusionary rule case, because the original search would have been legal). Recall the discussion of exigent circumstances earlier in the Chapter. Under what facts could the officers be *so wrong* about exigent circumstances that their explanation on that point would not even be plausible? Could that *ever* happen in a narcotics case?

Has the Court in *Murray* established a good faith exception for warrantless searches that are later sanitized by a warrant? As in *Leon,* discussed *infra,* the search, though illegal, does not result in exclusion so long as the officers are not totally unreasonable in believing that they were acting legally. For criticism of *Murray* on these points, see Bradley, Murray v. United States: The Bell Tolls for the Search Warrant Requirement, 64 Ind.L.J. 907 (1989). See also United States v. Johnson, 994 F.2d 980 (2d Cir.1993) (independent source doctrine applies where officers made an initial search under the mistaken impression that it was incident to an arrest; while mistaken, the officers were not totally unreasonable).

Is the primary purpose of the exclusionary rule to deter police misconduct, or to restore the situation to what it was before the illegal search? If the primary purpose is deterrence, can it be argued that it is sometimes necessary to place the government in a worse position than if the illegal search had not occurred?

## 6.  Inevitable Discovery

The inevitable discovery exception has been termed the "hypothetical independent source" exception. See Forbes, The Inevitable Discovery Exception, Primary Evidence, and the Emasculation of the Fourth Amendment, 55 Fordham L.Rev. 1221 (1987). For the exception to apply, the government must show that the illegally obtained evidence *would have been* discovered through legitimate means independent of the official misconduct. Note that if the evidence is *actually* discovered through legitimate independent means, the independent source exception would apply. So the inevitable discovery exception is one step removed from the independent source exception.

### *Establishing the Exception: Nix v. Williams*

The Supreme Court approved the inevitable discovery limitation upon the exclusionary rule for the first time in Nix v. Williams, 467 U.S. 431 (1984), which is discussed in *Murray*. Seven years earlier, the Court had held that Williams's conviction for murdering a 10-year-old girl was tainted when a police officer managed to obtain statements from Williams in violation of Williams's Sixth Amendment right to counsel. In the course of making statements, Williams led police to the girl's body. Although the Court held that the statements must be suppressed, it left open the question whether evidence as to the location and condition of the body might be admissible in a new trial.

At Williams's second trial, a state court judge found that the government proved by a preponderance of the evidence that a search party, which had suspended its activities once Williams agreed to lead the police to the body, would have found the body shortly afterwards anyway and that the body would have been found in essentially the same condition as when Williams led the police to it. Thus, the judge admitted evidence concerning the body's location and condition on the ground that it would have been inevitably discovered through legal means. But a federal court on habeas review found that the inevitable discovery rule could not be invoked where a police officer acted in bad faith, as it found the officer had in dealing with Williams.

Chief Justice Burger wrote for a majority as it reversed the federal court. He treated the independent source and inevitable discovery doctrines as related, reasoning that both doctrines limit the exclusionary rule so that the government is not denied evidence it would have had even without the officers' illegal activity. The Court indicated that the exclusionary rule works to assure that police do not benefit from constitutional violations, and that the inevitable discovery exception simply recognizes that the government actually obtains no advantage from illegal conduct *if* the government can prove that it would have obtained the evidence legally anyway.

The Court declined to restrict the inevitable discovery limitation to situations in which an officer acts in good faith. It found that a "good faith" requirement is not needed to deter officers from violating constitutional rules, because officers seeking to gather evidence cannot know in advance whether the government will be able to prove that their evidence would have been discovered inevitably through legal means. Thus, sufficient deterrence flows from the uncertainty that any evidence would have been inevitably obtained legally. The Chief Justice found that excluding evidence that would have been inevitably discovered legally, on the ground that officers acted in bad faith, "would put the police in a *worse* position than they would have been if no unlawful conduct had transpired" and that the exclusionary rule could not be used to punish the state in that way.

The Court in *Nix* held that to invoke the inevitable discovery exception, the government must prove by a *preponderance* that the challenged evidence would have been discovered through independent legal means. Chief Justice Burger rejected the more stringent clear and convincing evidence standard, stating that "we are unwilling to impose added burdens on the already difficult task of proving guilt in criminal cases by enlarging the barrier to placing evidence of unquestioned truth before juries." Applying the preponderance of the evidence standard to the facts, the Chief Justice found that the government had established its burden that the body would have been found by the search team only a short time after Williams directed the officers there.

Justice Stevens concurred in the judgment. He expressed concern, however, that the majority emphasized the "societal costs" of the exclusionary rule without also emphasizing the "societal costs" of unconstitutional police conduct.

Justice Brennan, joined by Justice Marshall, dissented in *Nix*. Justice Brennan accepted the inevitable discovery doctrine but emphasized that inevitable discovery was a more hypothetical concept than independent source, and so concluded that the government should have to prove inevitability by clear and convincing evidence.

Although *Williams* was a case involving a Sixth Amendment violation, the Court discussed the exclusionary rules it has adopted to enforce Fourth, Fifth and Sixth Amendment standards. The Court's opinion strongly suggests that the inevitable discovery doctrine limits the exclusionary rule under all three amendments. Both before and after *Nix,* lower courts have applied the inevitable discovery exception to Fourth

Amendment violations. See, e.g., United States v. Jackson, 901 F.2d 83 (7th Cir.1990) (even if defendant did not give voluntary consent to a search of his person, officers would have inevitably conducted a *Terry* frisk and uncovered crack cocaine in defendant's pockets); United States v. Kennedy, 61 F.3d 494 (6th Cir.1995) (evidence discovered by airport police in an illegal search of lost luggage was properly admitted, because if the police had not searched the suitcase, they would have returned it to the airline, and the airline's policy was to open lost luggage to determine the identity of the owner).

### Inevitable Discovery Through a Hypothetical Inventory Search

An oft-repeated example of inevitable discovery in the Fourth Amendment context is presented in United States v. Andrade, 784 F.2d 1431 (9th Cir.1986), where officers searched Andrade's bag and found cocaine after he was arrested for a drug violation. The search did not occur until an hour after the arrest. The court held that even if the search could not be justified as incident to arrest and was thus unlawful, "the cocaine was admissible because it would have been inevitably discovered through a routine inventory search." The court noted that it was normal DEA procedure to inventory the contents of bags held by arrestees, and that such a procedure was valid under Illinois v. Lafayette, *supra*. Judge Reinhardt, concurring, agreed that the "confluence" of *Nix* and *Lafayette* required this result, but concluded that "the result we are required to reach will serve only to encourage illegal and unconstitutional searches." See also United States v. Seals, 987 F.2d 1102 (5th Cir.1993) (evidence found in car held admissible where it "would have been discovered pursuant to an authorized inventory search").

If *Andrade* is correct that the existence of routine inventory procedures allows admission of the evidence obtained from the illegal search of a car or container, then why would an officer ever have to comply with the rules that still limit searches of cars or containers? For example, probable cause is required to search the trunk of a car of an arrestee. But does the probable cause requirement mean anything if the inevitable discovery exception applies by way of the (hypothetical) inventory search of anything found in the trunk? Is there any reason for an officer even to follow the standardized inventory procedures themselves, given the fact that standards are in place to permit an argument that such an inventory would have been conducted? See United States v. Martin, 982 F.2d 1236 (8th Cir.1993) (improper inventory excused because a proper one would have been conducted under police guidelines).

In United States v. $639,558.00 in United States Currency, 955 F.2d 712 (D.C.Cir.1992), the court refused to apply the inevitable discovery rule to situations in which the hypothetical independent source is an inventory search. The court reasoned as follows:

> If the evidence stemming from the violation is nevertheless admissible on the basis that the bags inevitably would have been opened when they were inventoried, the practical consequence is apparent. In the vast run of cases, there would be no incentive whatever for police to go to the trouble of seeking a warrant (or, we should add, of waiting for a lawful inventory to occur during normal processing). The police could readily make this assessment on their own. Contrary to what *Nix* supposed, they would almost invariably be in a position to calculate whether the evidence would inevitably have been discovered, because they would know that inventory procedures were in place.

Note that even if a court follows the "inevitable discovery through a hypothetical inventory" analysis, the government will have to prove that the search conducted would have been permissible under the inventory standards. Thus, if the officer searches the door panels of a car, the inevitable discovery exception will not work because a search of door panels cannot be justified under the inventory rules. See the discussion in United States v. Martinez, 512 F.3d 1268 (10th Cir. 2008) (noting cases excluding evidence found in door panels because "searching behind the door panel of a vehicle does not qualify as standard police inventory procedure").

### *"We Would Have Obtained a Warrant"*

Under the inevitable discovery exception, what is to stop the government from making the following argument:

> "We realize that we conducted an illegal warrantless search. Sorry. However, we had probable cause, and we would have obtained a warrant on that basis. Because we had probable cause, the warrant inevitably would have issued, and we would have searched pursuant to the warrant (if we had bothered to obtain it). So all the evidence we obtained is admissible under the inevitable discovery exception."

Do *Nix* and *Murray* require that such an argument must be accepted? If so, is there anything left of the warrant requirement?

Most courts have rejected government arguments that the inevitable discovery exception is met on the simple assertion that the officers had probable cause and would have obtained a warrant. Judge Easterbrook rejected that argument in United States v. Brown, 64 F.3d 1083 (7th Cir.1995):

> What makes a discovery "inevitable" is not probable cause alone, * * * but probable cause plus a chain of events that would have led to a

warrant (or another justification) independent of the search. Otherwise the requirement of a warrant for a residential entry will never be enforced by the exclusionary rule. A warrant requirement matters only when the police have probable cause, because otherwise they can't get one. (Under the second clause of the fourth amendment, "no Warrants shall issue, but upon probable cause".) To say that a warrant is required for a search is to say that the police must get judicial approval before acting. Yet if probable cause means that discovery is inevitable, then the prior-approval requirement has been nullified.

See also United States v. Johnson, 22 F.3d 674 (6th Cir.1994) ("to hold that simply because the police could have obtained a warrant, it was therefore inevitable that they would have done so would mean that there is inevitable discovery and no warrant requirement whenever there is probable cause"); United States v. Echegoyen, 799 F.2d 1271 (9th Cir.1986) ("to excuse the failure to obtain a warrant merely because the officers had probable cause and could have inevitably obtained a warrant would completely obviate the warrant requirement of the fourth amendment").

Some decisions can be found, however that rely on *Nix* to hold that evidence found in an illegal warrantless search was admissible because a warrant could and would have been obtained. See, e.g., United States v. Goins, 437 F.3d 644 (7th Cir.2006) (excusing an illegal search because police inevitably would have sought a search warrant and a magistrate would have issued one).

### *Establishing Inevitability*

*Nix* holds that the government must prove by a preponderance that the illegally obtained evidence inevitably would have been discovered by legal means. In United States v. Feldhacker, 849 F.2d 293 (8th Cir.1988), the court cautioned that in deciding whether the inevitable discovery exception applies, courts must focus on what the officers actually *would have done*, not on what they *could possibly have done*.

> There are reasonable limits to the scope that courts will impute to the hypothetical untainted investigation. An investigation conducted over an infinite time with infinite thoroughness will, of course, ultimately or inevitably turn up any and all pieces of evidence in the world. Prosecutors may not justify unlawful extractions of information post hoc where lawful methods present only a theoretical possibility of discovery. While the hypothetical discovery by lawful means need not be reached as rapidly as that actually reached by unlawful means, the lawful discovery must be inevitable through means that would actually have been employed.

Similar concerns arose in United States v. Allen, 159 F.3d 832 (4th Cir.1998). The government sought to avoid exclusion after Officer Tackett illegally searched a bag in a bus sweep. The government argued, and Officer Tackett testified, that if she hadn't opened the bag and discovered drugs, she would have called the K-9 unit and had a dog sniff the bag. The government presented testimony that a dog unit was at the bus terminal that day, and that the dog would have had no problem alerting to the drugs in Allen's bag. Officer Tackett testified that if the dog alerted, she would have sought a search warrant to search the bag. But the court found this scenario speculative.

> Our initial problem * * * lies in the lack of evidentiary support for the conclusion that Tackett would have used the dog. We have no doubt that Tackett *could* have used the dog, but whether she *would* have presents an entirely different question. Tackett testified specifically that if she had not conducted the illegal search and if she had thought the bag "could have been Allen's," she would have used the drug dog to sniff the bag. However, when Detective Kennedy (the dog's handler) testified, he did not so much as suggest that his dog had ever been used to sniff bags located inside the passenger compartment of a bus. Instead, he stated that his usual duty involved sending his dog into the undercarriage of the bus, as he had done that day. Furthermore, nothing in the record indicates that Tackett had ever previously called for a police dog to sniff baggage inside a bus, and Tackett conceded as much. * * *

> A finding of inevitable discovery necessarily rests on facts that did not occur. However, by definition the occurrence of these facts must have been likely, indeed "inevitable," absent the government's misconduct. On the record here, * * * we cannot possibly conclude that the government inevitably would have discovered the cocaine by employing a drug dog to establish probable cause.

## 7. Use of Illegally Seized Evidence Outside the Criminal Trial Context

Where it applies, the exclusionary rule operates to exclude evidence at a criminal trial. But in a series of cases, the Court has held that the exclusionary rule generally does not apply outside the context of a criminal trial on the merits. This is because, according to the Court, exclusion from the criminal prosecution's case-in-chief is all that is necessary to deter Fourth Amendment violations. The cost of exclusion in other "collateral" contexts generally has been held to outweigh the benefits in deterrence that the rule provides.

## *Grand Jury Proceedings*

In United States v. Calandra, 414 U.S. 338 (1974), agents illegally seized certain documents located at Calandra's place of business. The documents related to loansharking activities. A grand jury was convened to investigate these activities, and Calandra was subpoenaed to appear so that he might be questioned on the basis of the information obtained from the illegally seized documents. Calandra moved to suppress the documents and refused to answer the grand jury's questions. The Supreme Court held that Calandra had no right to refuse to answer the questions, because the exclusionary rule does not apply to grand jury proceedings. The Court concluded that the marginal deterrent effect of allowing a witness to raise a Fourth Amendment claim before the grand jury was outweighed by the disruption of investigations that exclusion of evidence would produce. The Court declared that sufficient deterrence flowed from exclusion of the illegally obtained evidence at trial. Justice Brennan, whose dissent was joined by Justices Douglas and Marshall, de-emphasized the deterrent rationale of the rule and focused instead on the benefits of keeping courts from lending their assistance to unconstitutional practices.

The fact that indictments can be based on illegally seized evidence is another arrow in the government's quiver. It means that the government will get some benefits from an illegal search. On the other hand, there is something to the *Calandra* Court's assertion that it will ordinarily be impractical to use tainted evidence to obtain an indictment; because that evidence would not be admissible at trial, it seems that the chances of obtaining a conviction would be remote. See United States v. Puglia, 8 F.3d 478 (7th Cir.1993) ("Prosecutors will not waste their time seeking indictments of individuals against whom they do not have enough evidence to convict.").

Yet prosecutors have sometimes been quoted as saying that it is important to indict someone even if they are not convicted—that is, the indictment can be used as punishment in the public eye, and as a means of imposing inconvenience and distress on a suspected criminal. For example, the special prosecutor in the case against former Secretary of Agriculture Mike Espy was quoted as being content with Espy's acquittal, because law enforcement and deterrence interests were substantially furthered by the indictment itself. If prosecutors can use an indictment as an end in itself, did the Court get it right in *Calandra* when it reasoned that sufficient deterrence flows from excluding illegally obtained evidence at trial?

## *Civil Tax Proceedings*

The Court has held that evidence illegally seized by state police can be used by federal tax officials in civil tax litigation. United States v. Janis, 428 U.S. 433 (1976). The Court in *Janis* found the deterrent effect of the exclusionary rule "attenuated when the punishment imposed upon the offending criminal enforcement officer is the removal of that evidence from a civil suit by or against a different sovereign." This attenuation, coupled with the "existing deterrence" effected by exclusion of the evidence from both state and federal criminal trials, tilted the cost-benefit analysis in favor of admitting the evidence.

## *Civil Deportation Proceedings*

In Immigration and Naturalization Service v. Lopez-Mendoza, 468 U.S. 1032 (1984), the question was whether illegally obtained statements could be used in deportation proceedings. INS officials had illegally obtained confessions from aliens concerning their immigration status. Justice O'Connor's opinion for the Court found that the consequence of exclusion would be especially severe, because exclusion could mean that a person who is committing a criminal offense *at the time of the proceeding* would be allowed to go free. Finding that the cost of exclusion outweighed the benefits in deterrence of misconduct, the Court held that illegally seized evidence may be used in a deportation proceeding.

Justice O'Connor reasoned specifically as follows:

- no matter how an arrest is made, deportation will still be possible when evidence derived independently of the arrest is available, and evidence of alienage alone might be sufficient to warrant deportation—thus, the use of illegally obtained evidence will ordinarily be harmless;

- as a practical matter, it is highly unlikely that deportees will raise exclusionary rule claims and therefore it is equally unlikely that the rule would deter INS agents;

- the INS has its own scheme for deterring Fourth Amendment violations by its agents;

- declaratory relief is available to restrain institutional practices by the INS that violate the Fourth Amendment;

- deportation currently requires only a simple hearing, and it would be inappropriate to add complex issues of exclusion to these hearings;

- INS agents handle so many cases that they might have difficulty accounting for exactly how they handled each suspected alien; and

- "[a]pplying the exclusionary rule in proceedings that are intended not to punish past transgressions but to prevent their continuance or renewal would require the courts to close their eyes to ongoing violations of the law."

Justice White dissented. He reasoned that INS agents seek to gather evidence specifically for use in deportation proceedings, and that their activities are closely analogous to those of police officers who seek to obtain evidence for criminal trials. So in his view the deterrent effect of the exclusionary rule is the same as it would be for criminal prosecutions. Justices Brennan, Marshall and Stevens each filed a short dissenting opinion.

Note that some courts have found that the exclusionary rule can apply to deportation proceedings under dicta in Justice O'Connor's opinion indicating that exclusion "might" be justified for "egregious violations of Fourth Amendment or other liberties that might transgress notions of fundamental fairness and undermine the probative value of the evidence obtained." For a case involving egregious circumstances, see Cotzojay v. Holder, 725 F.3d 172 (2nd Cir. 2013)(forced entry into a home, made in pre-dawn hours in order to coerce consent by startling sleeping residents).

### Habeas Corpus Proceedings

In Stone v. Powell, 428 U.S. 465 (1976), the Court, using its familiar cost-benefit analysis, held that the exclusionary rule could not be invoked in habeas corpus proceedings to challenge Fourth Amendment violations that resulted in evidence being admitted at a state trial. The Court stated that in the context of habeas proceedings, "the contribution of the exclusionary rule, if any, to the effectuation of the Fourth Amendment is minimal and the substantial societal costs of application of the rule persist with special force." The deterrent effect of exclusion was considered low because the habeas proceeding is collateral to the criminal trial and therefore not something officers would think about in deciding whether to conduct an illegal search. And the costs of exclusion are especially high because reversing a state conviction on habeas review implicates serious federalism and finality interests. The practical consequence of *Stone* is that unless the Supreme Court grants certiorari, no federal court will ever review a state court ruling on a Fourth Amendment issue.

### Parole Revocation Proceedings

In Pennsylvania Board of Probation and Parole v. Scott, 524 U.S. 357 (1998), Scott's parole was revoked and he was returned to prison to serve the remainder of his sentence, on the basis of evidence uncovered in an illegal search. The Court upheld the revocation, concluding that the exclusionary rule was not applicable in parole revocation proceedings.

Justice Thomas wrote the majority opinion for five members of the Court. Justice Thomas found that the cost of applying the exclusionary rule in parole revocation proceedings outweighed the benefits in deterrence of official misconduct. His "cost" argument proceeded as follows:

> The costs of excluding reliable, probative evidence are particularly high in the context of parole revocation proceedings. * * * In most cases, the State is willing to extend parole only because it is able to condition it upon compliance with certain requirements. The State thus has an overwhelming interest in ensuring that a parolee complies with those requirements and is returned to prison if he fails to do so. The exclusion of evidence establishing a parole violation, however, hampers the State's ability to ensure compliance with these conditions by permitting the parolee to avoid the consequences of his noncompliance. * * *

> The exclusionary rule, moreover, is incompatible with the traditionally flexible, administrative procedures of parole revocation. * * * Most States * * * have adopted informal, administrative parole revocation procedures in order to accommodate the large number of parole proceedings. These proceedings generally are not conducted by judges, but instead by parole boards, members of which need not be judicial officers or lawyers. * * * Nor are these proceedings entirely adversarial, as they are designed to be predictive and discretionary as well as factfinding.

> Application of the exclusionary rule would significantly alter this process. The exclusionary rule frequently requires extensive litigation to determine whether particular evidence must be excluded. Such litigation is inconsistent with the nonadversarial, administrative processes established by the States. Although States could adapt their parole revocation proceedings to accommodate such litigation, such a change would transform those proceedings from a predictive and discretionary effort to promote the best interests of both parolees and society into trial-like proceedings less attuned to the interests of the parolee. We are simply unwilling so to intrude into the States' correctional schemes. Such a transformation ultimately might disadvantage parolees because in an adversarial proceeding, the hearing body may be less tolerant of marginal deviant behavior and feel more pressure to reincarcerate than to continue nonpunitive rehabilitation. And the financial costs of such a system could reduce the State's incentive to extend parole in the first place, as one of the purposes of parole is to reduce the costs of

criminal punishment while maintaining a degree of supervision over the parolee.

The majority's "benefit" argument found little deterrence value to the exclusionary rule in the context of parole revocation proceedings:

> [A]pplication of the exclusionary rule to parole revocation proceedings would have little deterrent effect upon an officer who is unaware that the subject of his search is a parolee. In that situation, the officer will likely be searching for evidence of criminal conduct with an eye toward the introduction of the evidence at a criminal trial. The likelihood that illegally obtained evidence will be excluded from trial provides deterrence against Fourth Amendment violations, and the remote possibility that the subject is a parolee and that the evidence may be admitted at a parole revocation proceeding surely has little, if any, effect on the officer's incentives.

Justice Thomas further rejected the lower court's position that the exclusionary rule should at least be applicable when the government official conducts an illegal search *for the specific purpose* of using illegally obtained evidence in the parole revocation proceeding, as opposed to a criminal trial. Despite the apparent deterrent effect of excluding the evidence in these circumstances, Justice Thomas was unpersuaded:

> We have never suggested that the exclusionary rule must apply in every circumstance in which it might provide marginal deterrence. Furthermore, such a piecemeal approach to the exclusionary rule would add an additional layer of collateral litigation regarding the officer's knowledge of the parolee's status.

Justice Stevens wrote a short dissenting opinion in *Scott*, emphasizing his continuing position that the Constitution requires exclusion of illegally obtained evidence. Justice Souter, in a dissenting opinion joined by Justices Ginsburg and Breyer, took issue with the majority's assessment of the costs and benefits of the exclusionary rule in the parole revocation context. He argued that the costs of applying the exclusionary rule in parole revocation proceedings are certainly no greater than the costs of applying the rule in a criminal trial. As to the benefits of applying the rule, Justice Souter noted that the parole revocation proceeding often takes the place of a criminal trial, rendering it the only venue in which illegally obtained evidence would be used against a parolee, and consequently raising the deterrent value of exclusion. He reasoned as follows:

> [P]arole revocation will frequently be pursued instead of prosecution as the course of choice, * * * because of the procedural ease of recommitting the individual on the basis of a lesser showing by the State.

The reasons for this tendency to skip any new prosecution are obvious. If the conduct in question is a crime in its own right, the odds of revocation are very high. Since time on the street before revocation is not subtracted from the balance of the sentence to be served on revocation, the balance may well be long enough to render recommitment the practical equivalent of a new sentence for a separate crime. And all of this may be accomplished without shouldering the burden of proof beyond a reasonable doubt; hence the obvious popularity of revocation in place of new prosecution.

The upshot is that without a suppression remedy in revocation proceedings, there will often be no influence capable of deterring Fourth Amendment violations when parole revocation is a possible response to new crime.

### *Sentencing Proceedings*

The Supreme Court has not considered whether illegally obtained evidence can be used in sentencing proceedings. But the lower courts have found the exclusionary rule inapplicable to sentencing hearings. United States v. Tejada, 956 F.2d 1256 (2d Cir.1992), is an example of the predominant approach. The *Tejada* court analyzed the costs and benefits of exclusion of illegally obtained evidence at sentencing as follows:

> [The defendants] posit that police and prosecutors with enough lawfully obtained evidence for a conviction of a relatively minor offense that has a broad sentencing range could guarantee a heavier sentence by seizing other evidence illegally and introducing it at sentencing. * * *
>
> Defendants * * * do not explain why this supposed incentive to violate the Fourth Amendment will prove incrementally stronger than the rewards that already exist. Illegally seized evidence long has played a role in our legal system, and many of its uses might motivate a police officer to violate the Fourth Amendment. [Citing *Lopez-Mendoza*, *Janis*, and *Calandra*]. The Supreme Court has held that these uses for illegally seized evidence do not diminish deterrence sufficiently to justify the exclusion of probative evidence. We see no reason why this additional use of illegally seized evidence justifies different treatment.

The *Tejada* court asserted that "[g]reat rewards still exist for following accepted police procedures." If evidence cannot be used at trial, the government may never get to the sentencing proceeding due to the weakness of its case. Against the perceived minimal deterrent effect of exclusion at the sentencing hearing, the court weighed the need for sentencing courts to have "as much information as possible at sentencing." The result:

We conclude that the benefits of providing sentencing judges with reliable information about the defendant outweigh the likelihood that allowing consideration of illegally seized evidence will encourage unlawful police conduct. Absent a showing that officers obtained evidence expressly to enhance a sentence, a district judge may not refuse to consider relevant evidence at sentencing, even if that evidence has been seized in violation of the Fourth Amendment.

Note that the *Tejada* court provided a possible exception for cases in which officials obtain evidence expressly to enhance a sentence. Presumably those are cases in which application of the exclusionary rule would have some deterrent effect. But *Tejada* was written before the Supreme Court's decision in *Scott, supra*, in which the Court held that the exclusionary rule does not apply to parole revocation proceedings, even if it is clear that the officer conducted an illegal search for the specific purpose of using the evidence at the parole revocation proceeding. The Court reasoned that excluding the evidence depending on the mindset of the particular officer would be micromanaging the exclusionary rule. Presumably the rationale of *Scott* applies to the sentencing context as well, meaning that illegally obtained evidence can be considered even if it was obtained solely for purposes of using it at the sentencing proceeding.

### 8.   Use of Illegally Obtained Evidence for Impeachment Purposes

#### *Opening the Door on Direct Examination:*
#### *Walder v. United States*

In Walder v. United States, 347 U.S. 62 (1954), Walder testified on direct examination in a trial on narcotics charges that he had never possessed or sold narcotics in his life. The Supreme Court held that he was properly impeached with evidence of heroin that had been illegally seized from his home in an earlier, unrelated case. The Court reasoned that Walder had "opened the door" to this evidence and that the exclusionary rule could not be used as a license for perjury.

#### *Opening the Door on Cross-Examination:*
#### *United States v. Havens*

United States v. Havens, 446 U.S. 620 (1980), extended the impeachment exception to the exclusionary rule that had been applied in *Walder*. Officers stopped McLeroth and Havens coming off a flight. They illegally searched Havens's suitcase and found a shirt from which the pocket had been torn out. McLeroth was also searched, and officers found a pocket, matching the shirt found in Havens's bag, sewn into McLeroth's clothing. The officers found cocaine in the pocket. At his trial, Havens took the stand and denied being involved with McLeroth in the transportation of cocaine; he did not mention anything about the shirt or the pocket. On cross-examination, Havens was asked specifically whether he had been involved in sewing a pocket into McLeroth's clothing, and whether he had a shirt in his own suitcase from which that pocket had been torn out. Havens answered in the negative, and this testimony was impeached by introduction of the illegally seized shirt. The court of appeals held that the evidence was improperly admitted. It reasoned that *Walder* permitted impeachment only if the defendant opened the door to it—and Havens had not done so in this case because he hadn't mentioned the shirt on direct.

But in a 5–4 decision written by Justice White, the Supreme Court held that illegally obtained evidence can be used to impeach the defendant's testimony no matter when that testimony is elicited. Justice White argued that there was no difference of constitutional magnitude between impeachment of direct testimony and impeachment of testimony elicited on cross-examination, so long as the questions put to the defendant on cross-examination "are plainly within the scope" of the direct. He stated that a contrary rule would severely impede the normal function of cross-examination. Justice White concluded as follows:

> [T]he policies of the exclusionary rule no more bar impeachment here than they did in *Walder* * * *. [The incremental deterrence which occurs] by forbidding impeachment of the defendant who testifies was deemed [in *Walder*] insufficient to permit or require that false testimony go unchallenged, with the resulting impairment of the integrity of the fact-finding goals of the criminal trial. We reaffirm this assessment of the competing interests * * *.

Justice Brennan, joined by Justices Stewart, Marshall and Stevens, dissented. He complained that the majority had passed control of the impeachment exception to the government, "since the prosecutor can lay the predicate for admitting otherwise suppressible evidence with his own questioning." He argued that after *Havens,* a defendant who has been the victim of an illegal search will have to forego testifying on his own behalf, because it is impossible for the defendant to testify to anything on direct that would not open him up to impeachment through illegally obtained evidence on cross-examination.

### Impeachment of Defense Witnesses: James v. Illinois

In James v. Illinois, 493 U.S. 307 (1990), the Court refused to extend the impeachment exception to allow impeachment of defense *witnesses* (as opposed to the defendant) with illegally obtained evidence. James made a statement to police officers that he had changed his hair color and style the day after taking part in a shooting. The trial court suppressed this statement because it was the fruit of an arrest made without probable cause. Prosecution witnesses at trial identified James, though they admitted that his hair color at trial was different from that of the perpetrator at the time of the shooting. To rebut the identification testimony, James called a family friend, who testified that just before the shooting, James's hair color and style was the same as it was at trial. The trial court, relying on the impeachment exception to the exclusionary rule, allowed the prosecution to introduce James's suppressed statement to impeach the credibility of the defense witness—a mode of impeachment known as "contradiction."

The Supreme Court reversed in an opinion by Justice Brennan for five members of the Court. Justice Brennan found a compelling distinction between impeachment of a defendant's own testimony and that of defense witnesses. Despite his prior dissents on the impeachment exception, Justice Brennan argued that as applied to the defendant, the impeachment exception serves salutary purposes: it "penalizes defendants for committing perjury," and yet "leaves defendants free to testify truthfully on their own behalf." According to the Court, the impeachment exception keeps perjury out and allows truthful testimony in, thus furthering the search for truth.

In contrast, the Court found that expanding the impeachment exception to encompass the testimony of all defense witnesses would result in the loss of truthful testimony. Justice Brennan argued that the fear of impeachment of one's witnesses likely would discourage defendants from even presenting the testimony of others. He posited that the defendant could carefully limit his own truthful testimony to avoid reference to matters that could be impeached by illegally obtained evidence. But the defendant's witnesses could not be so easily controlled.

Justice Brennan also argued that impeachment was not needed to deter defense witnesses from offering perjurious testimony. Unlike the defendant, defense witnesses are sufficiently deterred by the threat of a perjury prosecution.

Justice Brennan concluded that the exclusionary rule would be robbed of significant deterrent effect if illegally obtained evidence could be used to impeach not only the defendant but the defendant's witnesses. He argued that illegally obtained evidence would have greater value to the government because it could be used to prevent defendants from calling witnesses to give truthful testimony. Justice Brennan asserted that a rule allowing impeachment of defense witnesses "would leave officers with little to lose and much to gain by overstepping constitutional limits on evidence gathering."

Justice Kennedy, joined by Chief Justice Rehnquist and Justices O'Connor and Scalia, dissented. The dissenters complained that the majority had granted the defendant "broad immunity to introduce whatever false testimony it can produce from the mouth of a friendly witness." Justice Kennedy argued that impeachment is even more vital for attacking untruthful testimony of a defense witness than it is for attacking the defendant's testimony:

> It is natural for jurors to be skeptical of self-serving testimony by the defendant. Testimony by a witness said to be independent has the greater potential to deceive. And if a defense witness can present false testimony with impunity, the jurors may find the rest of the prosecution's case suspect, for ineffective and artificial cross-examination will be viewed as a real weakness in the State's case. * * * The State must * * * suffer the introduction of false testimony and appear to bolster the falsehood by its own silence.

The majority in *James* bases its decision on the assumption that the defendant can restrict his testimony to avoid impeachment, while the defendant's witnesses cannot be so controlled. After *Havens*—which allowed impeachment on cross-examination even though the direct testimony was carefully tailored to avoid any reference to the shirt—is it ever possible for the defendant to avoid impeachment with illegally obtained evidence? If not, isn't the majority's decision in *James* based on a faulty premise? Is Justice Brennan simply making the best of what he thinks is bad law? *James* is criticized in Note, The Pinocchio Defense Witness Impeachment Exception to the Exclusionary Rule: Combatting a Defendant's Right to Use with Impunity the Perjurious Testimony of Defense Witnesses, 1990 U.Ill.L.Rev. 375.

## F.  PROCEDURAL ASPECTS OF THE EXCLUSIONARY RULE

### 1.  Attacking the Warrant

If the search was pursuant to a warrant, the judge ruling on a motion to suppress will consider the sworn evidence presented to the magistrate who issued the warrant. The Fourth Amendment determination will be made on the basis of only this evidence. No after-acquired evidence can be considered because the issue is whether the magistrate properly issued the warrant on the basis of the information available to her. See generally Kaiser v. Lief, 874 F.2d 732 (10th Cir.1989) (magistrate may rely on affidavit, complaint, and other affidavits contemporaneously presented for other warrants).

### *Challenging the Truthfulness of the Warrant Application:*
### *Franks v. Delaware*

In Franks v. Delaware, 438 U.S. 154 (1978), the Court held that a defendant has a limited right to attack the truthfulness of statements made in warrant applications. But the Court emphasized that it is difficult for a defendant to mount a successful challenge, because in order to obtain a hearing the defendant must make a case that the officers preparing the application engaged in deliberate falsification or reckless disregard for the truth that materially affected the showing of probable cause.

> \* \* \* There is, of course, a presumption of validity with respect to the affidavit supporting the search warrant. To mandate an evidentiary hearing, the challenger's attack must be more than conclusory and must be supported by more than a mere desire to cross-examine. There must be allegations of deliberate falsehood or of reckless disregard for the truth, and those allegations must be accompanied by an offer of proof. They should point out specifically the portion of the warrant affidavit that is claimed to be false; and they should be accompanied by a statement of supporting reasons. Affidavits or sworn or otherwise reliable statements of witnesses should be furnished, or their absence satisfactorily explained. Allegations of negligence or innocent mistake are insufficient. The deliberate falsity or reckless disregard whose impeachment is permitted today is only that of the affiant, not of any nongovernmental informant. Finally, if these requirements are met, and if, when material that is the subject of the alleged falsity or reckless disregard is set to one side, there remains sufficient content in the warrant affidavit to support a finding of probable cause, no hearing is required. On the other hand, if the remaining content is insufficient, the defendant is entitled, under the Fourth Amendment, to his hearing. Whether he will prevail at that hearing is, of course, another issue.

The Court found that where defendants could make the required preliminary showing, the need to assure that the police act in good faith outweighed the drain on resources that the limited hearing requirement would necessitate. Justice Rehnquist, joined by Chief Justice Burger, dissented, arguing that, even if "some inaccurate or falsified information may have gone into the making of the determination" to issue a warrant, "I simply do not think the game is worth the candle in this situation." When you recall that the warrant application is made ex parte and the magistrate makes nothing like a credibility determination, what would become of the warrant requirement if Justice Rehnquist's view had prevailed?

United States v. Johns, 851 F.2d 1131 (9th Cir.1988), provides an example of a showing sufficient to warrant a *Franks* hearing. In *Johns*, probable cause was based in material part on the officer's averment that he had detected the odor of methamphetamine emanating from the defendant's premises. The defendant submitted affidavits from two experts stating that in light of the way the methamphetamine was stored, it would have been impossible for the officer outside the premises to smell it. *Johns* was distinguished in United States v. Mueller, 902 F.2d 336 (5th Cir.1990), where the officer averred that he could smell methamphetamine emanating from the defendant's house while standing across the street. The defendant submitted an expert affidavit to the effect that it would have been unlikely to pick up such a smell given the officer's distance from the house and the prevailing winds. The court denied a *Franks* hearing, noting that Mueller's expert merely concluded that the officer's story was "unlikely," while the experts in *Johns* concluded that the officer's story was "impossible."

### *Materiality Requirement*

To obtain relief under *Franks*, the defendant must show that the deliberate falsehood or reckless disregard for the truth had a material effect on the issuance of the warrant. An officer's misstatement is not material under *Franks* if probable cause would exist even without the misstatement. See United States v. Campbell, 878 F.2d 170 (6th Cir.1989), citing cases in every circuit applying this test. In *Campbell,* the court found the search warrant valid even though the affidavit included a statement attributed to an informant known by the affiant to be fictitious. The court held that untainted information in the affidavit from three reliable informants was sufficient to establish probable cause under Illinois v. Gates, supra. Essentially, the officer's fabrication constituted harmless error.

## 2. Challenging a Warrantless Search

If no warrant was obtained, the government must justify the search. Generally, the state must prove by a preponderance of the evidence that an exception to the warrant requirement was satisfied. See United States v. Matlock, 415 U.S. 164 (1974) (government must prove voluntariness of consent by a preponderance of the evidence). This allocation of the burden of proof reflects the Court's mild preference for warrants. See generally Saltzburg, Standards of Proof and Preliminary Questions of Fact, 27 Stan.L.Rev. 271 (1975).

## 3. The Suppression Hearing and Judicial Review

At the hearing on the motion to suppress evidence, the government will have a privilege to protect the identity of informants. See McCray v.

Illinois, 386 U.S. 300 (1967) (holding that it is constitutional to withhold informant's identity on issue of probable cause). But the judge may in her discretion require the prosecution, *in camera,* to disclose to her the identity of the informant, or produce the informant for questioning. "If the judge does so require, the information or testimony so obtained shall be kept securely under seal and, in the event of an appeal from the judge's disposition of the motion, transmitted to the appellate court." § 290.4, ALI Model Code of Pre-Arraignment Procedure.

In a suppression hearing, the ordinary rules of evidence are not applicable, with the exception of rules of privilege. A judge can, for example, rely on hearsay to determine the legality of a search or seizure. In United States v. Matlock, 415 U.S. 164 (1974), the Court reasoned that "in proceedings where the judge himself is considering the admissibility of evidence, the exclusionary rules, aside from rules of privilege, should not be applicable; and the judge should receive the evidence and give it such weight as his judgment and experience counsel." The *Matlock* Court concluded that at a suppression hearing "the judge should be empowered to hear any relevant evidence, such as affidavits or other reliable hearsay."

### *Limitations on Use of Suppression Hearing Testimony at Trial: Simmons v. United States*

At the suppression hearing, the defendant may testify in support of his claim of a Fourth Amendment violation. Simmons v. United States, 390 U.S. 377 (1968), holds that when a defendant testifies on the question of "standing" (a subject discussed infra) at a suppression hearing, the government may not use his testimony against him on the question of guilt or innocence. So for example, the defendant to establish standing might testify at the suppression hearing that the briefcase searched by police that was full of narcotics was his. That statement cannot be used against him as an admission of guilt at trial. Justice Harlan's opinion for the 6–2 majority in *Simmons* reasoned that defendants would be unduly inhibited from making Fourth Amendment claims absent protection against automatic use of suppression hearing testimony at trial. In light of the way the opinion is written, it is likely that it extends to all Fourth Amendment questions (e.g., consent) considered at the hearing, not just to "standing" questions.

Can the testimony at the suppression hearing be used at trial to impeach a defendant who takes the stand and changes his testimony? *Simmons* left the impeachment question open. But lower courts have held that *Simmons* does not prevent the use of suppression hearing testimony for impeachment purposes. See, e.g., United States v. Beltran-Gutierrez, 19 F.3d 1287 (9th Cir.1994) (defendant's statements at a suppression hearing can be used to impeach him if his trial testimony is inconsistent with them). Thus, a defendant who testifies at the suppression hearing that he owned the briefcase full of drugs will run into difficulty if the evidence is not suppressed and he takes the stand at trial to testify that the briefcase was not his. His suppression hearing testimony can be offered as a prior inconsistent statement to impeach him. He will be entitled to have the jury instructed that the prior statement is not to be used as substantive evidence that the briefcase was actually his, but only for its bearing on the defendant's credibility. But that limiting instruction is likely to have little practical effect.

If the defendant calls a witness to testify at the suppression hearing (e.g., a friend who testifies that the briefcase was the defendant's), the government is not precluded by *Simmons* from using that testimony against the defendant. This is because *Simmons* was designed to protect defendants from sacrificing one constitutional right (the Fifth Amendment right against self-incrimination) for another (the Fourth Amendment right). When the defendant calls a witness at the suppression hearing, the defendant's Fifth Amendment rights are not implicated. As the court stated in United States v. Boruff, 870 F.2d 316 (5th Cir.1989):

> While a defendant's decision to call third-parties to corroborate his testimony at a suppression hearing might be affected by his knowledge that the government may subsequently utilize that testimony at trial, this dilemma does not rise to the level of a constitutional problem.

### *Appellate Review*

If a motion to suppress is granted, federal law permits immediate appellate review of the ruling subject to certain conditions. 18 U.S.C. § 3731. Most states are in accord. The federal statute provides that three conditions must be satisfied before the government can appeal from a suppression order: 1. The government cannot appeal if the defendant has been put in jeopardy, within the meaning of the Double Jeopardy Clause; 2. An appeal must not be taken for the purpose of delay; and 3. The suppressed evidence must be substantial proof of a fact material to the proceedings. See United States v. Gantt, 179 F.3d 782 (9th Cir.1999), for an application of these factors.

Most jurisdictions deny the defendant the right to an immediate appeal. This includes the federal courts, where an appeal from the denial of a suppression motion must await a judgment of conviction. It must be kept in mind that prosecutors cannot appeal the merits of an adverse judgment; only defendants can. Thus, prosecutors have to get an immediate appeal or none at all. If the defendant is convicted, the denial of a suppression motion may be a subject of the appeal.

Where the case stands or falls on admitting the challenged evidence, and the court has denied the motion to suppress, a defendant may wish to plead guilty on condition that he reserves the right to appeal the court's Fourth Amendment ruling. Fed.R.Crim.P. 11(a)(2) permits a defendant, with the approval of the court and the consent of the government, to enter a conditional plea of guilty, reserving the right to appeal the court's denial of a motion to suppress. A defendant who prevails on appeal "may then withdraw the plea."

# CHAPTER 3

## SELF-INCRIMINATION AND CONFESSIONS

■ ■ ■

### I.  THE PRIVILEGE AGAINST COMPELLED SELF-INCRIMINATION

#### A.  THE POLICIES OF THE PRIVILEGE AGAINST COMPELLED SELF-INCRIMINATION

**1.  The Need to Examine Policies**

The Fifth Amendment provides that no person "shall be compelled in any criminal case to be a witness against himself * * *." Judge Friendly pointed out the need for careful examination of the policies supporting this privilege in his oft-cited article, The Fifth Amendment Tomorrow: The Case For Constitutional Change, 37 U.Cin.L.Rev. 679–81, 698 (1968):

> It is still true, as Bentham wrote 140 years ago, that the main obstacle to rational discussion of the privilege is the *assumption of the propriety of the rule,* as a proposition too plainly true to admit of dispute * * *.

> A good way to start dissipating the lyricism now generally accompanying any reference to the privilege is to note how exceptional it is in the general setting of jurisprudence and morality. While it carries the burden of impeding ascertainment of the truth that is common to all testimonial privileges, it has uncommon burdens as well. Most other privileges, for example, communications between husband and wife, attorney and client, doctor and patient, priest and penitent, promote and preserve relationships possessing social value. * * * In contrast, the fifth amendment privilege extends, by hypothesis, only to persons who have been breakers of the criminal law or believe they may be charged as such.

> Again, while the other privileges accord with notions of decent conduct generally accepted in life outside the court room, the privilege against self-incrimination defies them. No parent would teach such a doctrine to his children; the lesson parents preach is that while a misdeed, even a serious one, will generally be forgiven, a failure to make a clean breast of it will not be. Every hour of the day people are being asked to explain their conduct to parents, employers

and teachers. Those who are questioned consider themselves to be morally bound to respond, and the questioners believe it proper to take action if they do not.

* * * The privilege not only stands in the way of convictions but often prevents restitution to the victim—of goods, of money, even of a kidnapped child. In contrast to the rare case where it may protect an innocent person, it often may do the contrary. A man in suspicious circumstances but not in fact guilty is deprived of official interrogation of another whom he knows to be the true culprit * * *.

One would suppose that such a collection of detriments would have led the Supreme Court to expound the basis for the privilege thoughtfully and carefully before asking the country to accept extensions in no way called for by the fifth amendment's words or history. It thus is strange how rarely one encounters in the Court's opinions on the privilege the careful weighing of *pros* and *cons,* the objective investigation of how rules of law actually work, and, above all, the consideration whether a less extreme position might not adequately meet the needs of the accused without jeopardizing other important interests, which ought to characterize constitutional adjudication before the Court goes beyond the ordinary meaning of the language.

See also Tague, The Fifth Amendment: If an Aid to the Guilty Defendant, an Impediment to the Innocent One, 78 Geo.L.J. 1 (1989) (Fifth Amendment "can shackle the innocent defendant from attempting to prove that another person committed the crime").

## 2.   A Chart to Assist Analysis

The chart below lists the most commonly offered justifications for the privilege against self-incrimination, critical responses to those justifications, and sources in which these arguments are discussed.[1] As you study the chart, consider which of the asserted policies are valid rationales for the privilege. Which responses adequately dispose of the

---

[1]    Sources that are referred to several times are cited in shorthand form. The full citations follow:

Murphy v. Waterfront Comm., 378 U.S. 52 (1964).

Fortas, The Fifth Amendment: Nemo Tenetur Prodere Seipsum, 25 Clev.Bar Assn.J. 91 (1954).

Friendly, The Fifth Amendment Tomorrow: The Case for Constitutional Change, 37 U.Cin.L.Rev. 671 (1968).

McKay, Self-Incrimination and the New Privacy, 1967 Sup.Ct.Rev. 193.

L. Mayers, Shall We Amend the Fifth Amendment (1959).

8 J. Wigmore, Evidence in Trials at Common Law (McNaughten rev. 1961).

The usual rationales for the privilege against self-incrimination are found wanting in Dolinko, Is There a Rationale for the Privilege Against Self-Incrimination, 33 U.C.L.A.L.Rev. 1063 (1986).

policy arguments? Are there convincing responses to any of the criticisms? To all of them?

1.   *Protection of the Innocent:* The privilege protects the innocent defendant from convicting himself by a bad performance on the witness stand. *Murphy,* 378 U.S. at 55; Mayers, at 61.

1.   There is no proof that it protects the innocent. In fact, juries are unlikely to give a defendant the benefit of an innocent explanation of his silence in the face of evidence against him. Mayers, at 26, 61–67. It is admittedly possible that an innocent defendant will invoke the privilege to avoid impeachment with prior convictions. However, the problem of threatened impeachment does not require a constitutionally-based solution protecting all defendants. A better solution is to impose appropriate limitations on the use of prior convictions. See Montana Rule of Evidence 609 (prior convictions not admissible to attack credibility). Finally, the privilege historically—and by hypothesis—protects the guilty, i.e., those whose testimony would implicate them of a crime. Fortas, at 98–100.

2.   *The Cruel Trilemma:* We are unwilling to subject those suspected of crime to the cruel trilemma of self-accusation, perjury, or contempt. Brown v. Walker, 161 U.S. 591, 637 (1896)(Field, J., dissenting).

2.   This problem is not peculiar to self-incrimination: it exists whenever a witness is reluctant to testify for whatever reason. Any such witness is subject to the trilemma of testifying despite an interest in not doing so, perjury, or contempt. We do subject friends, lovers, parents, teachers, and most people to the discomfort of having to testify against individuals about whom they might care the most. Why is the incrimination interest protected and other interests not? Wigmore, § 2251, at 316. Also, the Supreme Court has ridiculed the "cruel trilemma" analysis. See Brogan v. United States, 522 U.S. 398 (1998) (dismissing the "cruel trilemma" as a "bon mot" and noting that "an innocent person will not find himself in a similar quandary" because the

innocent person "lacks even a lemma").

3. *Deter Perjury:* If there were no privilege, people compelled to testify would commit perjury rather than incriminate themselves. Rampant perjury would burden the courts. Wigmore, § 2251, at 311.

3. Perjury is prevalent despite the existence of the privilege. Silence is also a burden on the truth-finding function of the criminal process. Friendly, at 680. There is no reason to believe that a defendant who concludes that perjury will succeed will not attempt it. Nor is there reason to believe that a defendant who concludes that perjury will fail will attempt it or succeed if an attempt is made.

4. *Unreliability of Coerced Statements:* We do not trust self-deprecatory statements, particularly when they are the product of coercion. *Murphy,* 378 U.S. at 55.

4. If reliability is the primary concern, there is no need to exclude compelled testimony that can be independently corroborated. Moreover, testimony at trial is likely to be cast by the defense in its most favorable light. It will not always be self-deprecatory. Also, it is more likely to be reliable than statements obtained by police interrogation, which are admitted as evidence.

5. *Preference for Accusatorial System:* We prefer an accusatorial rather than inquisitorial system of criminal justice. *Murphy,* 378 U.S. at 55.

5. "Language like this, no matter how often repeated, no matter how eloquently intoned, is merely restatement of the privilege itself." McKay, at 209.

6. *Deter Improper Police Practices:* Self-incriminating statements are likely to be elicited by inhumane treatment and abuses. The privilege has historically protected against such forms of torture. *Murphy,* 378 U.S. at 55.

6. Torture is unacceptable on its own merits, regardless of the existence of a privilege. Wigmore, § 2251, at 315. The privilege is unnecessary to guard against objectionable police practices—adequate protection is afforded by the Due Process clauses of the Fifth and Fourteenth Amendments. Testimony in court is subject to the safeguards of the judicial process.

7. *Fair State-Individual Balance:* "The privilege contributes towards a fair state-individual balance by

7. First, the probable cause requirements for search and arrest provide adequate protection against

requiring the government to leave the individual alone until good cause is shown for disturbing him and by requiring the government in its contest with the individual to shoulder the entire load." Wigmore, § 2251, at 317.

unwarranted governmental disturbance. Second, the argument relies on a notion of the criminal trial as "a jousting contest where the rules bear equally on both participants and neither is expected to be of the slightest help to the other"—a concept that bears no relation to reality. Third, even assuming that the ideal balance between state and defendant could be determined, manipulating the scope of the privilege is not necessarily the best way to achieve that balance. Friendly, at 693–94. Finally, the fact is that the government is not required to "shoulder the entire load" in a criminal prosecution. For example, the government can compel the defendant to produce DNA samples, voice prints, and physical evidence. Compelled production of this evidence is not covered by the Fifth Amendment. So what is it about testimony that makes it free from compulsion?

8. *Preservation of Official Morality:* "Any system * * * which permits the prosecution to trust habitually to compulsory self-disclosure as a source of proof must itself suffer morally thereby. 8 J. Wigmore, § 2251 (3d ed. 1940).

8. Wigmore's statement was based on two debatable assumptions: First, he believed the privilege applied only in the courtroom. When extended to the stationhouse, this rationale would disallow most police questioning—an untenable proposition. Second, he assumed that the privilege developed historically because the balance struck by the English judicial system had become morally unacceptable. Friendly, at 691.

9. *Privacy Rationale:* "Our respect for the inviolability of the human personality and of the right of each individual 'to a private enclave where he may lead a private life' " justifies the privilege. *Murphy,* 378 U.S. at 55.

9. If the basis for the privilege is a general freedom of silence to protect one's privacy, it is inconsistent first with immunity statutes—which require testimony no matter how private the matter; second, with rules requiring information of a far more private nature in civil suits (e.g., annulment suits); and

third, with the Fourth Amendment, which clearly does protect privacy, but only to the extent that intrusions are unreasonable. This privacy rationale enjoys historical support only when crimes of belief or association are involved. It is immoral to suggest that a murderer in a typical criminal case is justified in withholding his aid because he "prefers to remain in a 'private enclave.'" Friendly, at 689–90.

10. *First Amendment Rationale:* The privilege affords "a shelter against governmental snooping and oppression concerning political and religious beliefs." Friendly, at 696.

10. The First Amendment is the appropriate vehicle for dealing with this problem, as the Court implicitly recognized in cases such as NAACP v. Alabama, 357 U.S. 449 (1958). Furthermore, this justification, even if valid, would apply only in free speech, religion, or association situations, not in the typical criminal investigation and prosecution. Wigmore, § 2251, at 314.

Consider how one's choice of rationale necessarily affects one's view of the legitimate scope of the Amendment. For example, if the privilege is primarily intended to prevent "the cruel trilemma" and to deter perjury, then it should be applicable only when testimony under oath is involved. If one is concerned that the government bear its burden of proof without assistance, then voice or handwriting exemplars and other physical evidence extracted from a defendant would be protected. In the cases that follow, try to determine which policies underlie the Supreme Court's analysis of the privilege.

Judge Friendly criticizes the Fifth Amendment as protecting only the guilty. Professors Seidmann and Stein argue to the contrary in The Right to Silence Helps the Innocent: A Game-Theoretic Analysis of the Fifth Amendment Privilege, 114 Harv. L.Rev. 430 (2000). The professors assume that under the current law, guilty defendants will rely on the Fifth Amendment and choose not to testify. Therefore, an innocent person who actually *does* have an alibi will testify and be believed by the jury. If there were no Fifth Amendment, juries would have difficulty distinguishing between all of the false and true defendant-testimony. Query, though, whether juries are aware of the game theory going on and savvy enough to draw the assumption that the defendant has thought through the game and therefore must be innocent because he is testifying.

Professor Bibas, in The Right to Remain Silent Helps Only the Guilty, 88 Iowa L.Rev.421 (2003), disagrees with Seidmann and Stein. He states that their "elegant game-theoretic construct avails them little" because their premises do not mirror reality. Bibas points out that most guilty defendants *do* confess in an attempt to cooperate with the government, and very few go to trial. He also notes that juries are instructed to consider a witness's stake in the outcome in deciding their credibility, and so there is no working assumption that only innocent defendants testify.

## B. SCOPE OF THE PRIVILEGE

### 1. Proceedings in Which the Privilege Applies

Read literally, the language of the Fifth Amendment would seem to indicate that the privilege against self-incrimination applies only to testimony sought to be compelled in a *criminal case*. However, the Supreme Court has consistently given the privilege a broader interpretation, holding that it

> not only protects the individual against being involuntarily called as a witness against himself in a criminal prosecution but also privileges him not to answer official questions put to him in any other proceeding, civil or criminal, formal or informal, where his answers might incriminate him in future criminal proceedings.

Lefkowitz v. Turley, 414 U.S. 70, 77 (1973).

### *Applicability to Non-Criminal Cases: Counselman v. Hitchcock*

This policy of allowing invocation of the Fifth Amendment privilege outside a criminal case was developed in Counselman v. Hitchcock, 142 U.S. 547, 562 (1892). The issue in *Counselman* was whether a grand jury witness could claim the privilege. The Court held that a grand jury investigation of a criminal matter was a "criminal case," but the Court went further and declared that the privilege was available in *any* proceeding, if the testimony sought from a party or witness might later be *used* in a criminal prosecution against that person.

> It is impossible that the meaning of the constitutional provision can only be, that a person shall not be compelled to be a witness against himself in a criminal prosecution against himself. * * * The object was to insure that a person should not be compelled, when acting as a witness in any investigation, to give testimony which might tend to show that he himself had committed a crime. The privilege is limited to criminal matters, but it is as broad as the mischief against which it seeks to guard.

Thus, *Counselman* established that a person called as a witness in any federal proceeding could invoke the privilege against self-incrimination to avoid testifying to matters that could possibly tend to be damaging in a *subsequent* criminal prosecution. That rule now binds the states as well as the federal government. See Malloy v. Hogan, 378 U.S. 1 (1964) (right to be free from compelled self-incrimination is incorporated by the Fourteenth Amendment to apply against the states).

## 2.  Criminal Cases

While witnesses in civil cases can invoke the Fifth Amendment protection, the actual *use* of compelled testimony in a civil case does not itself violate the Fifth Amendment. Thus, in Minnesota v. Murphy, 465 U.S. 420 (1984), the Court held that a person has no right to refuse to answer questions on the ground that they might be used against him in subsequent probation revocation proceedings, because those proceedings are civil and not criminal. See also Piemonte v. United States, 367 U.S. 556 (1961) (privilege does not prevent use of compelled testimony for purposes of private retribution).

What makes a proceeding in which compelled testimony is used a "criminal case" that triggers Fifth Amendment protection? The discussion here was foreshadowed in Chapter 1.

### *Civil Penalties: United States v. L.O. Ward*

When incarceration is not available as a penalty, a legislative determination that a proceeding is "civil" is likely to be upheld. United States v. L.O. Ward, 448 U.S. 242 (1980), held, for example, that a statute imposing a "civil penalty" upon persons discharging hazardous material into navigable waters was not "quasi-criminal" so as to invalidate a reporting requirement imposed upon polluters. The Court distinguished Boyd v. United States, 116 U.S. 616 (1886)—which held that a forfeiture proceeding was a "criminal case" in which compelled testimony could not be used—suggesting that *Boyd* involved penalties that had no correlation with the damages sustained by society or the costs of enforcing the law. It also noted that in *Boyd* the forfeiture provision was listed along with fine and imprisonment as possible punishments for customs fraud. Justice Stevens dissented.

### *Detention for "Treatment"*

In Allen v. Illinois, 478 U.S. 364 (1986), the Court held 5–4 that proceedings under the Illinois Sexually Dangerous Persons Act were not criminal for self-incrimination purposes. Thus, the state court properly relied upon statements made by Allen to psychiatrists who subjected him to compulsory examination to determine whether he should be committed for treatment under the Act. (Though of course the compelled statements could not have been used against Allen in a criminal trial for sexual assault). The argument for applying the privilege focused on the fact that the state could not file a petition under the Act unless it had already filed criminal charges; the Act provided some of the same safeguards found in criminal proceedings; and a person committed for treatment was kept in a maximum security institution that also housed prisoners in need of psychiatric care.

Justice Rehnquist's majority opinion dismissed these factors and stated that the question of whether a proceeding is criminal for Fifth Amendment purposes was "first of all a question of statutory construction." The majority relied heavily on the fact that the Illinois Legislature had expressly provided that proceedings under the Act would "be civil in nature." Justice Rehnquist concluded that the state's decision to limit proceedings under the Act to persons charged with criminal acts did not turn a civil proceeding into a criminal one. Nor did the presence of some safeguards also found in criminal cases do so. The majority found that the conditions of the institution were not incompatible with the state's interest in treatment. Finally, it held that due process did not require recognition of the privilege, because the privilege would decrease, not increase, the reliability of the fact finding.

Justice Stevens, joined by Justices Brennan, Marshall, and Blackmun, dissented. He argued that a treatment goal was insufficient to render the privilege inapplicable and that the Court was "permitting a State to create a shadow criminal law without the fundamental protection of the Fifth Amendment."

For a case applying *Allen*, see United States v. Phelps, 955 F.2d 1258 (9th Cir.1992) (insanity acquittee who seeks release from involuntary commitment has no Fifth Amendment right to refuse to speak to state psychiatrist; release proceeding is civil because the emphasis is on treatment rather than punishment, the acquittee bears the burden of proof, and there is no right to a jury determination).

### Invoking the Privilege in a Civil Case to Prevent Use of Statements in a Criminal Case

As noted earlier, the privilege can be invoked in almost any proceeding, whether judicial, administrative, or legislative, in order to protect against the use of incriminating statements in a subsequent criminal proceeding. So for example, Fifth Amendment claims have been upheld when asserted by a party in a bankruptcy case. McCarthy v. Arndstein, 266 U.S. 34 (1924). Fifth Amendment claims also can be asserted by the subject of an investigation into possible wrongdoing by public contractors, Lefkowitz v. Turley, 414 U.S. 70 (1973) (architect); by public employees, Garrity v. New Jersey, 385 U.S. 493 (1967) (policemen); by prisoners, Baxter v. Palmigiano, 425 U.S. 308 (1976); or by lawyers (in disbarment proceedings), Spevack v. Klein, 385 U.S. 511 (1967). In none of these cases, however, did the Court hold that the proceeding itself was a "criminal case," although substantial penalties—loss of professional status or even more severe incarceration in the case of prisoners—were often at stake.

### 3.   Foreign Prosecution

As will be discussed below, a grant of use immunity allows the state to compel a witness's testimony. The immunity grant means that neither the statement nor its fruits can be used against the person in either a state or a federal prosecution. But what if there is a risk of *foreign* prosecution? A grant of use immunity by an American prosecutor has no binding effect on a foreign government. Can the witness refuse to testify, regardless of a grant of domestic immunity, on the ground that the compelled testimony could incriminate him in a foreign prosecution? Put another way—is a foreign prosecution a "criminal" case, so that the threat of use of a compelled statement in that case is prohibited by the Fifth Amendment?

In United States v. Balsys, 524 U.S. 666 (1998), the Court held that "concern with foreign prosecution is beyond the scope of the Self-Incrimination Clause." Justice Souter wrote the majority opinion that was joined in full by four other Justices, and joined in substantial part by Justices Scalia and Thomas. Balsys had refused to answer questions in a deportation proceeding in which the government alleged that he had committed atrocities during World War II. Balsys asserted the Fifth Amendment privilege on the ground that his testimony could be used against him in a criminal prosecution in either Israel or Lithuania.

Justice Souter analyzed the policies of the Fifth Amendment, as asserted by the Court in Murphy v. Waterfront Commission, 378 U.S. 52 (1964), to determine whether these policies demanded application of Fifth Amendment protection against the risk of foreign prosecution. In particular, *Murphy* had stated that the Fifth Amendment reflects

> "our unwillingness to subject those suspected of crime to the cruel trilemma of self-accusation, perjury or contempt; our preference for an accusatorial rather than an inquisitorial system of criminal justice; our fear that self-incriminating statements will be elicited by inhumane treatment and abuses; our sense of fair play which dictates a fair state-individual balance by requiring the government to leave the individual alone until good cause is shown for disturbing him and by requiring the government in its contest with the individual to shoulder the entire load; our respect for the inviolability of the human personality and of the right of each individual to a

private enclave where he may lead a private life, our distrust of self-deprecatory statements; and our realization that the privilege, while sometimes a shelter to the guilty, is often a protection to the innocent."

Applying this grounding of the privilege by the *Murphy* Court to the risk of foreign prosecution, Justice Souter found that the Fifth Amendment did not protect against that risk. He reasoned as follows:

> Some of the policies listed would seem to point no further than domestic arrangements and so raise no basis for any privilege looking beyond fear of domestic prosecution. Others, however, might suggest a concern broad enough to encompass foreign prosecutions and accordingly to support a more expansive theory of the privilege * * *.

> \* \* \*

> The most general of *Murphy's* policy items ostensibly suggesting protection as comprehensive as that sought by Balsys is listed in the opinion as "the inviolability of the human personality and . . . the right of each individual to a private enclave where he may lead a private life." * * * If in fact these values were reliable guides to the actual scope of protection under the Clause, they would be seen to demand a very high degree of protection indeed * * *.

> The Fifth Amendment tradition, however, offers no such degree of protection. If the Government is ready to provide the requisite use and derivative use immunity, see Kastigar v. United States [discussed infra in the section on immunity], the protection goes no further: no violation of personality is recognized and no claim of privilege will avail. * * * [Moreover,] when a witness's response will raise no fear of criminal penalty, there is no protection for testimonial privacy at all.

> Thus, what we find in practice is not the protection of personal testimonial inviolability, but a conditional protection of testimonial privacy subject to basic limits recognized before the framing and refined through immunity doctrine in the intervening years. Since the Judiciary could not recognize fear of foreign prosecution and at the same time preserve the Government's existing rights to seek testimony in exchange for immunity (because domestic courts could not enforce the immunity abroad), it follows that extending protection as Balsys requests would change the balance of private and governmental interests that has seemingly been accepted for as long as there has been Fifth Amendment doctrine. * * *

Justice Stevens wrote a short concurring opinion in *Balsys*, emphasizing that the costs of extending the privilege to protect against the risk of foreign prosecutions were too great to bear. If a person could refuse to testify due to a risk of foreign prosecution, "we would confer power on foreign governments to impair the administration of justice in this country." Like the majority, Justice Stevens appears to be concerned that sophisticated lawbreakers could manufacture foreign contacts to bring domestic prosecutions to a halt. In the modern era of international transactions, it might be possible to make a credible argument that there is a risk of foreign prosecution for many individuals involved in organized crime. Justice Stevens wrote that "[a] law enacted by a foreign power making it a crime for one of its citizens to testify in an American proceeding against another citizen of that country would immunize those citizens from being compelled to testify in our courts."

Justice Ginsburg wrote a short dissenting opinion in *Balsys* and joined Justice Breyer's far more extensive opinion. Justice Breyer disagreed with the majority's assessment that applying the privilege to claims of foreign incrimination would substantially impair law enforcement:

> [T]hat fear is overstated. After all, "foreign application" of the privilege would matter only in a case where an individual could not be prosecuted domestically but the threat of foreign prosecution is substantial. * * * [R]elatively few witnesses face deportation or extradition, and a witness who will not be forced to enter a country disposed to prosecute him, cannot make the showing of "real and substantial" fear that the Fifth Amendment would require.

### 4. Compulsion of Statements Never Admitted at a Criminal Trial

In Chavez v. Martinez, 538 U.S. 760 (2003), the Court considered whether the Fifth Amendment is violated when police compel a statement from a suspect during interrogation but the statement *is never admitted* against the suspect in a criminal trial. Martinez brought a civil rights action under 42 U.S.C. § 1983 for violation of his Fifth Amendment rights. Chavez was a police officer who interrogated Martinez after Martinez was shot in a fight with police officers. The interrogation session occurred while Martinez was in the hospital being treated for bullet wounds. Martinez made some inculpatory statements. For purposes of the appeal, the Court assumed that the statements made by Martinez would have been excluded under the Fifth Amendment as compelled self-incrimination, had the statements been offered at a criminal trial. However, Martinez was never charged with a crime, and the statements were never used against him in a criminal prosecution.

A majority found that the Fifth Amendment provides no relief when statements are compelled but are never admitted in a criminal case. However, there was no opinion for the Court on this question. Justice

Thomas, joined by Chief Justice Rehnquist and Justices O'Connor and Scalia, provided the broadest opinion, declaring that the Fifth Amendment simply did not apply because Martinez's confession was ever admitted against him in a criminal case. Justice Thomas reasoned as follows:

> Although Martinez contends that the meaning of "criminal case" should encompass the entire criminal investigatory process, including police interrogations, we disagree. In our view, a "criminal case" at the very least requires the initiation of legal proceedings. * * * Here, Martinez was never made to be a "witness" against himself in violation of the Fifth Amendment's Self-Incrimination Clause because his statements were never admitted as testimony against him in a criminal case. Nor was he ever placed under oath and exposed to the cruel trilemma of self-accusation, perjury or contempt.

Justice Souter, joined by Justice Breyer, concurred in the judgment, agreeing with the general proposition that the Fifth Amendment does not protect against compulsion of statements that are never used in a criminal case. Justice Souter expressed concern over the stopping point for a rule of law providing that compelled confessions are actionable in themselves.

> If obtaining Martinez's statement is to be treated as a stand-alone violation of the privilege subject to compensation, why should the same not be true whenever the police obtain any involuntary self-incriminating statement, or whenever the government so much as threatens a penalty in derogation of the right to immunity, or whenever the police fail to honor *Miranda?* Martinez offers no limiting principle or reason to foresee a stopping place short of liability in all such cases.

Justice Kennedy, joined by Justices Stevens and Ginsburg, dissented. He argued as follows:

> The conclusion that the Self-Incrimination Clause is not violated until the government seeks to use a statement in some later criminal proceeding strips the Clause of an essential part of its force and meaning. * * * To tell our whole legal system that when conducting a criminal investigation police officials can use severe compulsion or even torture with no present violation of the right against compelled self-incrimination can only diminish a celebrated provision in the Bill of Rights. * * *

Justice Ginsburg added a separate dissenting opinion.

In Aleman v. Village of Hanover Park, 662 F.3d 897 (7th Cir. 2011), the court held when police continued to interrogate a suspect who asked for counsel after receiving *Miranda* warnings and his statement became an indispensable ground of his indictment for murder, the *Miranda* violation was actionable in a civil suit even though the statement was never actually used in a criminal trial. Similarly, in Stoot v. City of Everett, 582 F.3d 910 (9th Cir. 2009), the court found that a statement coerced from a suspect was "used" in a criminal case against him in the affidavit filed in support of the information charging him with child molestation and in a pretrial arraignment and bail hearing. And in Higazy v. Templeton, 505 F.3d 161 (2d Cir. 2007), the court held that use of a compelled statement at a bail or pretrial release hearing constituted use in a criminal case. Other courts, in contrast, hold that a statement is not "used" against a person unless it is admitted at trial. Some examples are Burrell v. Virginia, 395 F.3d 508 (4th Cir. 2005); and Murray v. Earle, 405 F.3d 278 (5th Cir. 2005).

## C. WHAT IS COMPULSION?

The Fifth Amendment protects against self-incrimination only if it is *compelled* by the government. It is sometimes difficult to determine whether a particular pressure imposed by the government on a citizen rises to the level of compulsion.

### 1. Use of the Contempt Power

Use of the contempt power is the classic form of compulsion, because it imposes a substantial punishment on the witness who is exercising the right to remain silent, and it presents the witness with a cruel trilemma: remain silent and face imprisonment; tell the truth and face imprisonment; or tell a lie and face imprisonment for perjury. Thus, a witness cannot be subjected to contempt for refusing to testify, if the testimony could create a risk of self-incrimination in a criminal case.

### 2. Other State-Imposed Sanctions

The Supreme Court has extended the concept of compulsion well beyond its original grounding in the contempt power. For example, the Court in Miranda v. Arizona, discussed *infra,* found compulsion in the setting of custodial interrogation. The Court has also found other state-imposed sanctions for silence, of less severity than contempt, to constitute compulsion. The following case provides an example of the Court's approach.

**LEFKOWITZ V. TURLEY**

Supreme Court of the United States, 1973.
414 U.S. 70.

**MR. JUSTICE WHITE delivered the opinion of the Court:**

[New York statutes required public contracts to provide that if a contractor refused to waive immunity or to testify concerning state contracts, existing contracts could be canceled and future contracts could be denied for five years. Contractors in this case refused to answer questions that could incriminate them, and were denied the right to future contracts under the statute.]

\* \* \*

It is true that the State has a strong, legitimate interest in maintaining the integrity of its civil service and of its transactions with independent contractors furnishing a wide range of goods and services; and New York would have it that this interest is sufficiently strong to override the privilege. The suggestion is that the State should be able to interrogate employees and contractors about their job performance without regard to the Fifth Amendment, to discharge those who refuse to answer or to waive the privilege by waiving the immunity to which they would otherwise be entitled, and to use any incriminating answers obtained in subsequent criminal prosecutions. But claims of overriding interests are not unusual in Fifth Amendment litigation and they have not fared well.

\* \* \*

[I]n almost the very context here involved, this court has only recently held that employees of the State do not forfeit their constitutional privilege and that they may be compelled to respond to questions about the performance of their duties but only if their answers cannot be used against them in subsequent criminal prosecutions. Garrity v. New Jersey, 385 U.S. 493 (1967); Gardner v. Broderick, 392 U.S. 273 (1968); Sanitation Men v. Sanitation Comm'r, 392 U.S. 280 (1968).

\* \* \*

In Garrity v. New Jersey, certain police officers were summoned to an inquiry being conducted by the Attorney General concerning the fixing of traffic tickets. They were asked questions following warnings that if they did not answer they would be removed from office and that anything they said might be used against them in any criminal proceeding. No immunity of any kind was offered or available under state law. The questions were answered and the answers later used over their objections, in their prosecutions for conspiracy. The Court held that "protection of the individual under the Fourteenth Amendment against coerced statements prohibits use in subsequent criminal proceedings of statements obtained under threat of removal from office, and that it extends to all, whether they are policemen or other members of our body politic." \* \* \*

The issue in Gardner v. Broderick, supra, was whether the State might discharge a police officer who, after he was summoned before a grand jury to testify about the performance of his official duties and was advised of his right against compulsory self-incrimination, then refused to waive that right as requested by the State. Conceding that appellant could be discharged for refusing to answer questions about the performance of his official duties, if not required to waive immunity, the Court held that the officer could not be terminated, as he was, for refusing to waive his constitutional privilege. * * *

The companion case, Sanitation Men v. Sanitation Com'r, supra, was to the same effect. * * *

These cases, and their predecessors, ultimately rest on a reconciliation of the well-recognized policies behind the privilege of self-incrimination, and the need of the State, as well as the Federal Government, to obtain information "to assure the effective functioning of government." Immunity is required if there is to be "rational accommodation between the imperatives of the privilege and the legitimate demands of government to compel citizens to testify." It is in this sense that immunity statutes have "become part of our constitutional fabric."

* * * *Garrity, Gardner,* and *Sanitation Men* control the issue now before us. The State sought to interrogate appellees about their transactions with the State and to require them to furnish possibly incriminating testimony by demanding that they waive their immunity and by disqualifying them as public contractors when they refused. It seems to us that the State intended to accomplish what *Garrity* specifically prohibited—to compel testimony that had not been immunized. The waiver sought by the State, under threat of loss of contracts, would have been no less compelled than a direct request for the testimony without resort to the waiver device. A waiver secured under threat of substantial economic sanction cannot be termed voluntary.

* * *

## *The Function of Immunity*

If the contractor in *Lefkowitz* had been given immunity from criminal prosecution, could he then be denied public contracts for refusing to testify? If he spoke pursuant to a grant of immunity, could he then be denied public contracts on the basis of incriminating statements made in his testimony? The court explained the relevant principles in National Federation of Federal Employees v. Greenberg, 983 F.2d 286 (D.C.Cir.1993), a case in which government employees were subject to firing for refusing to answer questions, and relevant statutes prevented use of the compelled statements in a criminal prosecution:

The government * * * may fire employees who refuse, on the basis of their Fifth Amendment privilege, to answer questions concerning the performance of their duties, so long as the employees' answers could not be used against them in a criminal prosecution. For purposes of the Fifth Amendment, the threat of firing or other economic sanctions may constitute compulsion. But the protection of the privilege extends only to criminal prosecutions. A government employee would not be incriminating himself within the meaning of the Fifth Amendment if his answers could not be used against him in a criminal case.

This means that a contractor could be denied public contracts on the basis of compelled testimony, so long as the statements could not be *used against him in a criminal case.* Denial of public contracts would not itself constitute a criminal case.

### *Threat of Disbarment as Compulsion*

Spevack v. Klein, 385 U.S. 511 (1967), forbids disbarment of a lawyer for invoking the privilege during a bar investigation, where any statements could be used against the lawyer in a subsequent criminal prosecution. But, can an applicant for the bar exam refuse to answer questions on an application and still insist on admission to the bar? This requires a look at the Court's approach to benefits and penalties.

### *The Benefit-Penalty Distinction*

What if the government does not impose a penalty for silence, as in *Turley,* but instead conditions a benefit on the waiver of the privilege? Is this "compulsion" within the meaning of the Fifth Amendment? The basic answer is that denial of a benefit is not a penalty, and therefore is not compulsion.

The benefit/penalty distinction has often been applied when a defendant is required to provide incriminating information in order to receive a reduction in sentence. For example, in United States v. Cruz, 156 F.3d 366 (2d Cir.1998), the defendant was subject to a mandatory minimum sentence of ten years for a drug crime. However, a federal statute provides for "safety valve" relief from mandatory minimums in some narcotics cases if, among other things, the defendant "has truthfully provided to the Government all information and evidence the defendant has concerning the offense or offenses that were part of the same course of conduct or of a common scheme or plan." The defendant in *Cruz* argued that this disclosure provision compelled him to incriminate himself, because in order to receive the waiver of the mandatory minimum, he would have to implicate himself in other drug transactions for which he was not yet charged. But the court found no compulsion, noting that the penalty cases "have all involved some kind of loss or reduction from the status quo" such as the loss of public employment or disbarment. "A defendant facing a particular sentence, however, with the option of obtaining a lower sentence if he or she waives the Fifth Amendment privilege is not presented with the same 'negative' sanction as presented in the penalty cases." The court declared that "the choice confronting the defendant gives rise to no more compulsion than that present in a typical plea bargain." If the defendant had actually suffered an *enhanced* sentence for remaining silent, this would have amounted to compulsion. But conditioning a *reduction* of sentence on cooperation is permitted.

### Self-Incrimination and Clemency Proceedings: Ohio Adult Parole Authority v. Woodard

The Supreme Court considered the benefit-penalty distinction in Ohio Adult Parole Authority v. Woodard, 523 U.S. 272 (1998). The Parole Authority commenced a clemency proceeding in accordance with state law, after Woodard's appeal from his capital murder conviction had been denied. Under Ohio law, the Parole Authority must conduct a clemency hearing within 45 days of the scheduled date of execution. Prior to the hearing, the inmate may request an interview with one or more parole board members. The Authority must hold the hearing, complete its clemency review, and make a recommendation to the Governor. Woodard did not request an interview. Instead, he brought a section 1983 action in federal court, arguing, among other things, that the clemency proceeding left him with a "Hobson's choice": to have any chance of clemency, he would have to subject himself to an interview, thereby opening himself up to incrimination both on the current charge (given the possibility of successful post-conviction proceedings) as well as on other charges.

The Supreme Court, in a unanimous opinion on this point, rejected Woodard's Fifth Amendment argument and held that the clemency procedure did not *compel* him to incriminate himself. Chief Justice Rehnquist, writing for the Court, reasoned as follows:

> It is difficult to see how a voluntary interview could "compel" respondent to speak. He merely faces a choice quite similar to the sorts of choices that a criminal defendant must make in the course of criminal proceedings, none of which has ever been held to violate the Fifth Amendment.

> Long ago we held that a defendant who took the stand in his own defense could not claim the privilege against self-incrimination when the prosecution sought to cross-examine him. Brown v. Walker, 161 U.S. 591 (1896). A defendant who takes the stand in his own behalf may be impeached by proof of prior convictions without violation of the Fifth Amendment privilege. Spencer v. Texas, 385 U.S. 554, 561

(1967). A defendant whose motion for acquittal at the close of the Government's case is denied must then elect whether to stand on his motion or to put on a defense, with the accompanying risk that in doing so he will augment the Government's case against him. McGautha v. California, 402 U.S. 183 (1971). In each of these situations, there are undoubted pressures—generated by the strength of the Government's case against him—pushing the criminal defendant to testify. But it has never been suggested that such pressures constitute "compulsion" for Fifth Amendment purposes.

\* \* \*

Here, respondent has the same choice of providing information to the Authority—at the risk of damaging his case for clemency or for postconviction relief—or of remaining silent. But this pressure to speak in the hope of improving his chance of being granted clemency does not make the interview compelled.

### The Benefit-Penalty Distinction and Penalties Imposed on Incarcerated Sex Offenders: McKune v. Lile

In McKune v. Lile, 536 U.S. 24 (2002), a divided Court considered whether the benefit-penalty distinction works when applied to a program for rehabilitating incarcerated sex offenders. The Court also considered whether certain inconveniences can be imposed on a prisoner for remaining silent without rising to the level of compulsion.

Lile was convicted in state court of rape, aggravated sodomy and aggravated kidnaping in 1982. In 1994, prison officials in Kansas ordered him to participate in a Sexual Abuse Treatment Program. Participating inmates are required to complete and sign an "Admission of Responsibility" form, in which they discuss and accept responsibility for the crimes of conviction. They are also required to complete a sexual history form in which they detail all prior sexual activities, regardless of whether such activities constitute uncharged criminal offenses. The veracity of their answers is checked by polygraph examination. The information that the participants disclose is not privileged and can be used in future criminal prosecutions.

Lile refused to participate on the ground that the required disclosures would violate his privilege against self-incrimination. Department officials responded that if he refused to participate in the SATP, his privilege status would be reduced from Level III to Level I and, as a result, his visitation rights, earnings, work opportunities, ability to send money to family, canteen expenditures, access to a personal television, and other privileges automatically would be curtailed. One other detriment for non-participation was a transfer to a maximum-security unit, where his movement would be more limited, he would be moved from a two-person to a four-person cell, and he would be in a potentially more dangerous environment. Believing that the threatened response was a penalty for his invocation of his privilege, Lile sued in federal court to enjoin the prison officials from withdrawing his privileges.

Justice Kennedy, writing for himself, Chief Justice Rehnquist, Justice Scalia, and Justice Thomas, declared that the program did not constitute compulsion within the meaning of the Fifth Amendment. With respect to the losses suffered by Lile for not participating, Justice Kennedy declared as follows:

> The consequences in question here—a transfer to another prison where television sets are not placed in each inmate's cell, where exercise facilities are not readily available, and where work and wage opportunities are more limited—are not ones that compel a prisoner to speak about his past crimes despite a desire to remain silent. The fact that these consequences are imposed on prisoners, rather than ordinary citizens, moreover, is important in weighing respondent's constitutional claim.

Justice Kennedy rejected Lile's attempt to claim that he was faced with penalties:

> Respondent is mistaken as well to concentrate on the so-called reward/penalty distinction and the illusory baseline against which a change in prison conditions must be measured. The answer to the question whether the government is extending a benefit or taking away a privilege rests entirely in the eye of the beholder. For this reason, emphasis of any baseline, while superficially appealing, would be an inartful addition to an already confused area of jurisprudence. * * *

> * * * Respondent's reasoning would provide States with perverse incentives to assign all inmates convicted of sex offenses to maximum security prisons until near the time of release, when the rehabilitation program starts. The rule would work to the detriment of the entire class of sex offenders who might not otherwise be placed in maximum-security facilities. And prison administrators would be forced, before making routine prison housing decisions, to identify each inmate's so-called baseline and determine whether an adverse effect, however marginal, will result from the administrative decision. * * *

> Respondent's analysis also would call into question the constitutionality of an accepted feature of federal criminal law: the downward adjustment for acceptance of criminal responsibility provided in § 3E1.1 of the United States Sentencing Guidelines. If

the Constitution does not permit the government to condition the use of a personal television on the acceptance of responsibility for past crimes, it is unclear how it could permit the government to reduce the length of a prisoner's term of incarceration based upon the same factor. By rejecting respondent's theory, we do not, in this case, call these policies into question.

Justice O'Connor concurred in the judgment and reasoned as follows:

I do not believe the consequences facing respondent in this case are serious enough to compel him to be a witness against himself. * * * These changes in living conditions seem to me minor. Because the prison is responsible for caring for respondent's basic needs, his ability to support himself is not implicated by the reduction in wages he would suffer as a result. While his visitation is reduced as a result of his failure to incriminate himself, he still retains the ability to see his attorney, his family, and members of the clergy. The limitation on the possession of personal items, as well as the amount that respondent is allowed to spend at the canteen, may make his prison experience more unpleasant, but seems very unlikely to actually compel him to incriminate himself.

\* \* \*

Justice Stevens dissented and was joined by Justices Souter, Ginsburg and Breyer. He stated that "[u]ntil today the Court has never characterized a threatened harm as 'a minimal incentive.' Nor have we ever held that a person who has made a valid assertion of the privilege may nevertheless be ordered to incriminate himself and sanctioned for disobeying such an order. This is truly a watershed case."

Justice Stevens relied upon the distinction between benefits and penalties:

We have recognized that the government can extend a benefit in exchange for incriminating statements, but cannot threaten to take away privileges as the cost of invoking Fifth Amendment rights. Based on this distinction, nothing that I say in this dissent calls into question the constitutionality of *downward* adjustments for acceptance of responsibility under the United States Sentencing Guidelines. Although such a reduction in sentence creates a powerful incentive for defendants to confess, it completely avoids the constitutional issue that would be presented if the Guidelines operated like the scheme here and authorized an *upward* adjustment whenever a defendant refused to accept responsibility. * * * By obscuring the distinction between penalties and incentives, it is the plurality that calls into question both the Guidelines and plea bargaining.

## 3.   Comment on the Invocation of the Privilege

### *The Griffin Rule*

In Griffin v. California, 380 U.S. 609 (1965), the Court held that adverse comment to the jury, by either the judge or the prosecutor, on the defendant's election not to testify constitutes punishment for the invocation of silence, which is tantamount to compulsion and therefore violates the Fifth Amendment. Thus, the fact that the defendant did not take the stand cannot be used as information against him.[2]

The Court extended *Griffin* in Carter v. Kentucky, 450 U.S. 288 (1981). Carter asked the trial judge to instruct the jurors that they were not to draw an adverse inference from the fact that Carter did not testify. The trial judge denied the request, reasoning that such an instruction would only draw attention to the fact that the defendant had not testified. The Supreme Court held that the trial judge was required to give the instruction upon request, "to minimize the danger that the jury will give evidentiary weight to a defendant's failure to testify."

Lakeside v. Oregon, 435 U.S. 333 (1978), presented the opposite situation from *Carter*. The trial judge instructed the jury not to draw an adverse inference from Lakeside's failure to testify, and Lakeside *objected* to the instruction presumably because he was concerned that an instruction would only highlight the failure to take the stand. He argued that he was being penalized for not testifying when the trial judge gave the instruction against his wishes. But the Court rejected Lakeside's argument. It reasoned that *Griffin* was concerned with "adverse comment", and the instruction in this case was anything but an adverse comment. The instruction was designed to *dispel* the compulsion that might otherwise exist due to the negative inferences that could be drawn from the defendant's failure to testify.

The Court distinguished *Griffin* in United States v. Robinson, 485 U.S. 25 (1988), and held that a prosecutor properly pointed out in closing argument that the defendant had an opportunity to testify. The prosecutor was responding to defense counsel's closing argument that the defendant had not been permitted to explain his side of the story. How does an adverse inference "punish" a defendant who refuses to testify? Consider the assessment of Judge Posner, writing in United States v. Castillo, 965 F.2d 238 (7th Cir.1992). He argued that the "punishment" found impermissible in *Griffin* was "slight, because juries are perfectly

---

[2]   For a criticism of *Griffin,* see Ayer, The Fifth Amendment and the Inference of Guilt from Silence: Griffin v. California After Fifteen Years, 78 Mich.L.Rev. 841 (1980) (arguing that *Griffin* is an ill-advised exception to the rule that attorneys may draw any reasonable inference from the facts legitimately within the jury's knowledge). For a defense of *Griffin,* see Saltzburg, Foreword: The Flow and Ebb of Constitutional Criminal Procedure in the Warren and Burger Courts, 69 Geo.L.J. 151, 204 (1980).

capable of drawing an adverse inference from a defendant's refusal to testify on their own, without having to be told to do so." Do you agree?

### Adverse Inferences at Sentencing: Mitchell v. United States

The defendant in Mitchell v. United States, 526 U.S. 314 (1999), pleaded guilty to federal charges of conspiring to distribute five or more kilograms of cocaine and of distributing cocaine. But she reserved the right to contest at sentencing the drug quantity attributable to her under the conspiracy count. Before accepting her plea, the District Court made the inquiries required by Fed.R.Crim.P. 11 (see Chapter 9); told petitioner that she faced a mandatory minimum of one year in prison for distributing cocaine, but a 10-year minimum for conspiracy if the Government could show that she was involved in a quantity more than 5 kilograms; and explained that by pleading guilty she would be waiving her right "at trial to remain silent." Indicating that she had done "some of" the proffered conduct, Mitchell confirmed her guilty plea. At her sentencing hearing, three codefendants testified that she had sold 1 1/2 to 2 ounces of cocaine twice a week for 1 1/2 years, and another person testified that Mitchell had sold her two ounces of cocaine. This was enough to take the quantity over the 5 kilogram threshold for an enhancement of Mitchell's sentence. Mitchell put on no evidence at the sentencing hearing, choosing instead to attack the credibility of the codefendant-witnesses. The sentencing court found that the codefendants' testimony put her over the 5-kilogram threshold, thus mandating the 10-year minimum, and noted specifically that Mitchell's failure to testify at sentencing was a factor in persuading the court to rely on the codefendants' testimony.

Thus, one question in *Mitchell* was whether the sentencing court was permitted to draw an adverse inference from Mitchell's silence. In a 5–4 opinion written by Justice Kennedy, the Court relied on *Griffin* and held that a defendant could not be subject to an adverse inference upon invoking the right to remain silent at a sentencing proceeding. Justice Kennedy's analysis of *Griffin*, and its applicability to sentencing, proceeded as follows:

> [A] sentencing hearing is part of the criminal case—the explicit concern of the self-incrimination privilege. In accordance with the text of the Fifth Amendment, we must accord the privilege the same protection in the sentencing phase of "any criminal case" as that which is due in the trial phase of the same case.
>
> The concerns which mandate the rule against negative inferences at a criminal trial apply with equal force at sentencing. Without question, the stakes are high: Here, the inference drawn by

the District Court from petitioner's silence may have resulted in decades of added imprisonment.

Justice Scalia, joined by Chief Justice Rehnquist and Justices O'Connor and Thomas in dissent, argued that an adverse inference "does not 'compel' anyone to testify." He launched into an extensive historical analysis, concluding, on the basis of common-law cases and the understanding of the Framers, that *Griffin's* "pedigree" is "dubious." He asserted that "the text and history of the Fifth Amendment give no indication that there is a federal constitutional prohibition on the use of the defendant's silence as demeanor evidence." He explained as follows:

> Our hardy forebears, who thought of compulsion in terms of the rack and oaths forced by the power of law, would not have viewed the drawing of a commonsensical inference as equivalent pressure. And it is implausible that the Americans of 1791, who were subject to adverse inferences for failing to give unsworn testimony, would have viewed an adverse inference for failing to give sworn testimony as a violation of the Fifth Amendment.

Justice Scalia also noted that the *Griffin* rule "runs exactly counter to normal evidentiary inferences: If I ask my son whether he saw a movie I had forbidden him to watch, and he remains silent, the import of the silence is clear."

Justice Scalia next contested the application of *Griffin* to sentencing proceedings:

> Our case law has long recognized a natural dichotomy between the guilt and penalty phases. The jury-trial right contained in the Sixth Amendment—whose guarantees apply "[i]n all criminal prosecutions," a term indistinguishable for present purposes from the Fifth Amendment's "in any criminal case"—does not apply at sentencing. Nor does the Sixth Amendment's guarantee of the defendant's right "to be confronted with the witnesses against him." (The sentencing judge may consider, for example, reports of probation officers and psychiatrists without affording any cross-examination.)

Justice Thomas wrote a separate dissenting opinion in *Mitchell*, in which he stated that he was prepared to revisit the *Griffin* rule *in toto*. He attacked the analysis in *Griffin* in the following passage:

> Prosecutorial comments on a defendant's decision to remain silent at trial surely impose no greater "penalty" on a defendant than threats to indict him on more serious charges if he chooses not to enter into a plea bargain—a practice that this Court previously has validated. * * * [A]t bottom, *Griffin* constitutionalizes a policy choice that a majority of the Court found desirable at the time. * * * This sort of

undertaking is not an exercise in constitutional interpretation but an act of judicial willfulness that has no logical stopping point.

## *Adverse Inferences Drawn in Civil Cases*

In Baxter v. Palmigiano, 425 U.S. 308 (1976), the Court declared that "the Fifth Amendment does not forbid inferences against parties to civil actions when they refuse to testify in response to probative evidence offered against them: the Amendment does not preclude the inference where the privilege is claimed by a party to a civil cause." The *Baxter* Court explained that in ordinary civil cases, the party confronted with the invocation of the privilege by the opposing side has no capacity to avoid it, say, by offering immunity from prosecution. Thus the rule allowing invocation of the privilege—though at the risk of suffering an adverse inference and possibly an adverse civil judgment—accommodates the right not to be a witness against oneself while still permitting civil litigation to proceed. For a discussion of what courts should do when the privilege against self-incrimination is raised in civil cases, see Heidt, The Conjurer's Circle, The Fifth Amendment Privilege in Civil Cases, 91 Yale L.J. 1062 (1982).

## 4.   Compulsion and the "Exculpatory No" Doctrine

The Court in Brogan v. United States, 522 U.S. 398 (1998), considered whether the Fifth Amendment prohibited the criminal punishment of a person who lies to government investigators during the course of a criminal investigation. Justice Scalia, writing for the Court, summarized the facts.

> While acting as a union officer * * * petitioner James Brogan accepted cash payments from JRD Management Corporation, a real estate company whose employees were represented by the union. On October 4, 1993, federal agents from the Department of Labor and the Internal Revenue Service visited petitioner at his home. The agents identified themselves and explained that they were seeking petitioner's cooperation in an investigation of JRD and various individuals. * * *

> The agents then asked petitioner if he would answer some questions, and he agreed. One question was whether he had received any cash or gifts from JRD when he was a union officer. Petitioner's response was "no." At that point, the agents disclosed that a search of JRD headquarters had produced company records showing the contrary. They also told petitioner that lying to federal agents in the course of an investigation was a crime. Petitioner did not modify his answers, and the interview ended shortly thereafter.

Petitioner was indicted for accepting unlawful cash payments from an employer * * *, and making a false statement within the jurisdiction of a federal agency in violation of 18 U.S.C. § 1001.

Section 1001, in essential part, imposes a criminal penalty on anyone who wilfully makes a false statement to the government. Brogan admitted that his denial of involvement was covered by the statute, but argued that he could not be convicted because of lower court case law that had developed the "exculpatory no doctrine." The rationale of the doctrine is that section 1001 should not criminalize simple denials of guilt to government investigators, because to do so would violate the "spirit" of the Fifth Amendment.

Justice Scalia categorically rejected the "exculpatory no" doctrine, and the Court upheld the false statement conviction. Justice Scalia dismissed the Fifth Amendment argument by noting that Brogan was not *compelled*, in any sense, to deny criminal responsibility when he said "no" to the agents. He could simply have remained silent without penalty.

Justices Ginsburg, joined by Justice Souter, concurred only in the judgment in *Brogan*, inviting Congress to consider the possibility that section 1001 might be used for overreaching, i.e., to prosecute people who are not aware that denying criminal responsibility in a situation like Brogan's is in fact a criminal act. Justice Stevens, joined by Justice Breyer, dissented.

## D. TO WHOM DOES THE PRIVILEGE BELONG?

The privilege against self-incrimination is a personal right, belonging only to the person who is himself incriminated by his own testimony. For example, an employer may not claim the privilege on the ground that his testimony might incriminate his employee; nor may the employee complain about the employer's compelled testimony. Which of the rationales for the privilege, discussed above, justify this limitation? Consider the Court's policy analysis in the following case.

### FISHER v. UNITED STATES
Supreme Court of the United States, 1976.
425 U.S. 391.

### MR. JUSTICE WHITE delivered the opinion of the Court.

[Taxpayers, who were under investigation for possible civil or criminal tax violations, obtained documents relating to the preparation of their tax returns from their accountants. Shortly thereafter, they transferred these documents to the lawyers handling their cases. The IRS served summonses on the attorneys directing them to produce the records, but the attorneys refused to comply on Fifth Amendment grounds.]

## II

All of the parties in these cases and the Court of Appeals for the Fifth Circuit have concurred in the proposition that if the Fifth Amendment would have excused a *taxpayer* from turning over the accountant's papers had he possessed them, the *attorney* to whom they are delivered for the purpose of obtaining legal advice should also be immune from subpoena. Although we agree with this proposition * * * we are convinced that, under our decision in Couch v. United States, 409 U.S. 322 (1973), it is not the taxpayer's Fifth Amendment privilege that would excuse the *attorney* from production.

The relevant part of that Amendment provides:

> "No person * * * shall be *compelled* in any criminal case to be a *witness against himself.*" (Emphasis added.)

The taxpayer's privilege under this Amendment is not violated by enforcement of the summonses involved in these cases because enforcement against a taxpayer's lawyer would not "compel" the taxpayer to do anything—and certainly would not compel him to be a "witness" against himself. * * * In Couch v. United States, supra, we recently ruled that the Fifth Amendment rights of a taxpayer were not violated by the enforcement of a documentary summons directed to her accountant and requiring production of the taxpayer's own records in the possession of the accountant. We did so on the ground that in such a case "the ingredient of personal compulsion against an accused is lacking."

Here, the taxpayers are compelled to do no more than was the taxpayer in *Couch.* The taxpayers' Fifth Amendment privilege is therefore not violated by enforcement of the summonses directed toward their attorneys. This is true whether or not the Amendment would have barred a subpoena directing the taxpayer to produce the documents while they were in his hands.

* * * In Hale v. Henkel, 201 U.S. 43, 69–70 (1906), the Court said that the privilege "was never intended to permit [a person] to plead the fact that some third person might be incriminated by his testimony, even though he were the agent of such person * * *. [T]he Amendment is limited to a person who shall be compelled in any criminal case to be a witness against *himself.*" (Emphasis in original.) "It is extortion of information from the accused himself that offends our sense of justice."

* * *

The Court of Appeals for the Fifth Circuit suggested that because legally and ethically the attorney was required to respect the confidences of his client, the latter had a reasonable expectation of privacy for the records in the hands of the attorney and therefore did not forfeit his Fifth Amendment privilege with respect to the records by transferring them in order to obtain legal advice. * * *

\* \* \*

We cannot cut the Fifth Amendment completely loose from the moorings of its language, and make it serve as a general protector of privacy—a word not mentioned in its text and a concept directly addressed in the Fourth Amendment. We adhere to the view that the Fifth Amendment protects against "compelled self-incrimination, not [the disclosure of] private information."

\* \* \*

[In Part III, the Court held that the attorney-client privilege protects against disclosure of documents that would have been protected by the Fifth Amendment had they been in the taxpayer's possession. However, in Part IV it concluded that the documents in question would not be privileged even in the hands of the taxpayer. See infra for the Court's discussion of the latter issue.]

### NOTE ON THE COLLECTIVE ENTITY RULE

The Fifth Amendment prevents the state from compelling a "person" to be a "witness against himself." The Court in Bellis v. United States, 417 U.S. 85 (1974), held that the textual limitation to a "person" meant that partnerships have no Fifth Amendment protection. The partnership in *Bellis* was a law firm with three partners and a handful of employees. Justice Marshall, writing for the Court, stated broadly that the privilege against compelled self-incrimination is a "purely personal" one, which applies "only to natural individuals." Therefore, "no artificial organization may utilize the personal privilege against compulsory self-incrimination." Justice Marshall concluded that the partnership in *Bellis* had "an established institutional identity independent of its individual partners." Therefore, the partnership could be placed in contempt for failing to comply with an order to produce information, even though that information could be used in a criminal case to impose a penalty on the partnership.

In United States v. Doe, 465 U.S. 605 (1984), the Court distinguished *Bellis* and held that a *sole proprietorship* was entitled to Fifth Amendment protection. A sole proprietorship was not considered an entity distinct from the individual. However, in Braswell v. United States, 487 U.S. 99 (1988), the Court held that a corporation—even one wholly owned and operated by a single individual—was not itself entitled to Fifth Amendment protection. Chief Justice Rehnquist, writing for the Court, distinguished *Doe* as follows:

Had petitioner conducted his business as a sole proprietorship, *Doe* would require that he be provided the opportunity to show that his act of production would entail testimonial self-incrimination. But petitioner has operated his business through the corporate form, and we have long recognized that for purposes of the Fifth Amendment, corporations and other collective entities are treated differently from individuals.

See also In re Grand Jury Subpoena, 973 F.2d 45 (1st Cir.1992) (trust established by two brothers for purposes of conducting real estate transactions held an entity not entitled to Fifth Amendment protection).

Corporations have Fourth Amendment rights (see Marshall v. Barlow's in Chapter 2); they have First Amendment rights (First National Bank v. Bellotti, 435 U.S. 765 (1978)); they have due process rights (International Shoe Co. v. Washington, 326 U.S. 310 (1945)); why don't they have Fifth Amendment rights? Why is it of constitutional importance that Braswell operated a business as a wholly owned corporation rather than as a sole proprietorship?

# E.  WHAT IS PROTECTED

The privilege only protects a person when that person is being compelled to be a "witness" against himself. Thus, it does not protect against *all* forms of compelled self-incrimination. If a person is forced to give information other than what a "witness" would provide, the privilege is inapplicable. In the cases that follow, the Court attempts to define the scope of information protected by the privilege.

## 1.  Non-Testimonial Evidence

### SCHMERBER V. CALIFORNIA
Supreme Court of the United States, 1966.
384 U.S. 757.

**MR. JUSTICE BRENNAN delivered the opinion of the Court.**

Petitioner was convicted in Los Angeles Municipal Court of the criminal offense of driving an automobile while under the influence of intoxicating liquor. He had been arrested at a hospital while receiving treatment for injuries suffered in an accident involving the automobile that he had apparently been driving. At the direction of a police officer, a blood sample was then withdrawn from petitioner's body by a physician at the hospital. The chemical analysis of this sample revealed a percent by weight of alcohol in his blood at the time of the offense which indicated intoxication, and the report of this analysis was admitted in evidence at the trial. Petitioner objected to receipt of this evidence of the analysis on the ground that the blood had been withdrawn despite his refusal, on the advice of his counsel, to consent to the test. He contended that in that circumstance the withdrawal of the blood and the admission of the analysis in evidence denied him * * * his privilege against self-incrimination under the Fifth Amendment * * *.

* * * We hold that the privilege protects an accused only from being compelled to testify against himself, or otherwise provide the State with evidence of a testimonial or communicative nature,[a] and that the withdrawal of blood and use of the analysis in question in this case did not involve compulsion to these ends.

It could not be denied that in requiring petitioner to submit to the withdrawal and chemical analysis of his blood the State compelled him to submit to an attempt to discover evidence that might be used to prosecute him for a criminal offense. * * * The critical question, then, is whether petitioner was thus compelled "to be a witness against himself."

If the scope of the privilege coincided with the complex of values it helps to protect, we might be obliged to conclude that the privilege was violated. * * *

* * * [H]owever, the privilege has never been given the full scope which the values it helps to protect suggest. History and a long line of authorities in lower courts have consistently limited its protection to situations in which the State seeks to submerge those values by obtaining the evidence against an accused through "the cruel, simple expedient of compelling it from his own mouth. * * * In sum, the privilege is fulfilled only when the person is guaranteed the right 'to remain silent unless he chooses to speak in the unfettered exercise of his own will." * * *

It is clear that the protection of the privilege reaches an accused's communications, whatever form they might take * * *. On the other hand, both federal and state courts have usually held that it offers no protection against compulsion to submit to fingerprinting, photographing, or measurements, to write or speak for identification, to appear in court, to stand, to assume a stance, to walk, or to make a particular gesture. The distinction which has emerged, often expressed in different ways, is that the privilege is a bar against compelling "communications" or "testimony," but that compulsion which makes a suspect or accused the source of "real or physical evidence" does not violate it.

---

[a]   A dissent suggests that the report of the blood test was "testimonial" or "communicative," because the test was performed in order to obtain the testimony of others, communicating to the jury facts about petitioner's condition. Of course, all evidence received in court is "testimonial" or "communicative" if these words are thus used. But the Fifth Amendment relates only to acts on the part of the person to whom the privilege applies, and we use these words subject to the same limitations. A nod or head-shake is as much a "testimonial" or "communicative" act in this sense as are spoken words. But the terms as we use them do not apply to evidence of acts noncommunicative in nature as to the person asserting the privilege, even though, as here, such acts are compelled to obtain the testimony of others.

* * *

* * * Not even a shadow of testimonial compulsion upon or enforced communication by the accused was involved either in the extraction or in the chemical analysis. Petitioner's testimonial capacities were in no way implicated; indeed, his participation, except as a donor, was irrelevant to the results of the test, which depend on chemical analysis and on that alone. Since the blood test evidence, although an incriminating product of compulsion, was neither petitioner's testimony nor evidence relating to some communicative act or writing by the petitioner, it was not inadmissible on privilege grounds.

* * *

**MR. JUSTICE BLACK with whom MR. JUSTICE DOUGLAS joins, dissenting.**

* * * [I]t seems to me that the compulsory extraction of petitioner's blood for analysis so that the person who analyzed it could give evidence to convict him had both a "testimonial" and a "communicative nature." The sole purpose of this project which proved to be successful was to obtain "testimony" from some person to prove that petitioner had alcohol in his blood at the time he was arrested. And the purpose of the project was certainly "communicative" in that the analysis of the blood was to supply information to enable a witness to communicate to the court and jury that petitioner was more or less drunk.

* * *

[The concurring opinion of JUSTICES HARLAN and STEWART and the dissenting opinions of CHIEF JUSTICE WARREN and JUSTICE FORTAS are omitted.]

### NOTE ON TESTIMONIAL VS. NON-TESTIMONIAL EVIDENCE

The holding of *Schmerber* has been reaffirmed and applied several times. One year after that decision, the Court held that requiring a suspect to participate in a police line-up did not violate the Fifth Amendment. In United States v. Wade, 388 U.S. 218 (1967), the defendant was arrested for robbing a bank. He was forced to stand in a line-up with several other prisoners, each of whom wore strips of tape on their faces, as had the actual robber. In addition, the defendant, for identification purposes, was required to utter the words allegedly spoken by the robber. The Court held:

> We have no doubt that compelling the accused merely to exhibit his person for observation by a prosecution witness prior to trial involves no compulsion of the accused to give evidence having testimonial significance. It is compulsion of the accused to exhibit his physical characteristics, not compulsion to disclose any knowledge he might have. It is no different from compelling Schmerber to provide a blood sample

* * *. [C]ompelling Wade to speak within hearing distance of the witnesses, even to utter words purportedly uttered by the robber, was not compulsion to utter statements of a "testimonial" nature; he was required to use his voice as an identifying physical characteristic, not to speak his guilt.

Justice Black again dissented on the Fifth Amendment issue, because requiring a suspect to stand in a line-up and speak certain words is "forcing [that] person to supply proof of his own crime."

Justice Fortas filed a separate opinion challenging the constitutionality of forcing a suspect to speak in the line-up.

> *Schmerber,* which authorized the forced extraction of blood from the veins of an unwilling human being, did not compel the person actively to cooperate—to accuse himself by a volitional act which differs only in degree from compelling him to act out the crime, which, I assume, would be rebuffed by the Court. It is the latter feature which places the compelled utterance by the accused squarely within the history and noble purpose of the Fifth Amendment's commandment.

What other physical characteristics are exempt from Fifth Amendment protection? In Gilbert v. California, 388 U.S. 263 (1967), a companion case to *Wade,* the Court held that handwriting exemplars may be compelled from an unwilling defendant. In United States v. Dionisio, 410 U.S. 1 (1973), the same rule was applied to voice-prints. While one's voice and handwriting are means of communication, the Court's view is that the sample itself, in contrast to the content of the communication, is merely an identifying physical characteristic—outside the protection of the Fifth Amendment because it is not the kind of evidence that a witness would provide.

Of course, another view of voice and handwriting exemplars is that the suspect is saying "this is my real voice and handwriting." If, in fact, the suspect attempts to distort the exemplar, this may be considered as evidence of guilt. Viewed in this light, do the cases make sense? Note that your answer may depend upon the policy arguments that you accept as a valid basis for the privilege.

Is evidence about a tattoo testimonial? In United States v. Greer, 631 F.3d 608 (2nd Cir. 2011), a police officer testified about Greer's physical appearance when he was arrested for being a felon in possession of a firearm. The officer testified that Greer had a tattoo that said "Tangela." That evidence was used to tie him to the car owned by a Tangela Hudson, in which the gun was found. The defendant argued that the testimony regarding his tattoo violated his right against compelled self-incrimination. The government argued that the tattoo was not testimonial, but the court disagreed. It stated that in the context of the case, the tattoo was more than just a physical feature: the government relied on the tattoo not simply as an identifying physical characteristic, but rather for its expressive content, i.e., "I know Tangela." However, the court found no Fifth Amendment violation because while the tattoo, in context, was testimonial, that testimony was not compelled by the government. The detective merely viewed the tattoo on Greer's arm after his arrest. The court concluded that the "voluntary tattooing of an incriminating word to Greer's arm was * * * not the product of government compulsion. In the absence of compulsion, Greer's Fifth Amendment claim fails."

### Testimonial Evidence and the Cruel Trilemma: Pennsylvania v. Muniz

The Court in Pennsylvania v. Muniz, 496 U.S. 582 (1990), finally articulated a rationale for understanding the *Schmerber* line of cases. It held that the line between testimonial and non-testimonial evidence must be determined by whether the witness faces the "cruel trilemma" in disclosing the evidence. Muniz was pulled over on suspicion of drunk driving. After he failed sobriety tests, police officers placed Muniz under arrest and transported him to a booking center. There they asked Muniz, among other things, the date of his sixth birthday. The officers did not give Muniz *Miranda* warnings. Muniz responded with slurred speech, stumbled over his answers, and said that he did not know the date of his sixth birthday. Both the manner of speech and the content of Muniz's answers were used at trial as evidence that he was under the influence of alcohol. In the Supreme Court, the Court assumed that the defendant had been custodially interrogated, without warnings; the issue in dispute was whether the evidence compelled from Muniz was *testimonial* and therefore protected by the Fifth Amendment.

Writing for eight members of the Court, Justice Brennan concluded that evidence of the slurred nature of Muniz's speech was not testimonial under *Schmerber* and its progeny. The slurred speech in *Muniz* was held to be physical evidence, because its relevance was divorced from the content of the words themselves. The Court stated that "[r]equiring a suspect to reveal the physical manner in which he articulates words, like requiring him to reveal the physical properties of the sound produced by his voice * * * does not, without more, compel him to provide a 'testimonial' response for purposes of the privilege." Only Justice Marshall dissented on this point.

The Court did not decide whether a person's performance on a sobriety test (e.g., standing on one leg for thirty seconds and counting) was testimonial, because Muniz did not challenge the lower court's decision that such evidence was non-testimonial under *Schmerber*. The Court noted, however, that many lower courts have held that such tests merely measure physical capacity such as reflex, dexterity, and balance, and consequently do not compel testimony under *Schmerber*. See People v. Hager, 69 N.Y.2d 141, 512 N.Y.S.2d 794, 505 N.E.2d 237 (1987) ("physical performance tests do not reveal a person's subjective knowledge or thought processes but, rather, exhibit a person's degree of physical coordination.").

With respect to the answer to the sixth birthday question, Justice Brennan, writing on this point for five members of the Court, held that Muniz's response *was* testimonial, and therefore that the use of it as evidence at trial was error. The State argued that an answer to the sixth birthday question did not trigger Fifth Amendment protection because the only evidence derived would concern the physiological functioning of Muniz's brain. Justice Brennan rejected this argument, reasoning "that the 'fact' to be inferred might be said to concern the physical status of Muniz's brain merely describes the way in which the inference is incriminating. The correct question * * * is whether the incriminating inference of mental confusion is drawn from a testimonial act or from physical evidence." Thus, when facts about a person's physical condition are obtained through testimonial evidence, the Fifth Amendment applies. For example, if police had compelled Schmerber to answer questions about the alcohol in his blood, his oral responses (e.g., "I am drunk") would be testimonial even though the fact proven would concern Schmerber's physical condition.

Justice Brennan found that Muniz's answer to the sixth birthday question was protected by the "core meaning" of the self-incrimination clause. He explained as follows:

> Because the privilege was designed primarily to prevent a recurrence of the Inquisition and the Star Chamber * * * it is evident that a suspect is compelled to be a witness against himself at least whenever he must face the modern day analog of the historic trilemma. * * * Whenever a suspect is asked for a response requiring him to communicate an express or implied assertion of fact or belief, the suspect confronts the trilemma of truth, falsity or silence and hence the response (whether based on truth or falsity) contains a testimonial component.

The State argued that Muniz did not face the cruel trilemma in answering the sixth birthday question, because the State was not interested in the actual date of Muniz's sixth birthday. Justice Brennan concluded, however, that Muniz was indeed "confronted with the trilemma." He reasoned as follows:

> By hypothesis, the inherently coercive environment created by the custodial interrogation precluded the option of remaining silent. * * * Muniz was left with the choice of incriminating himself by admitting that he did not then know the date of his sixth birthday, or answering untruthfully by reporting a date that he did not then believe to be accurate (an incorrect guess would be incriminating as well as untruthful). The content of his truthful answer supported an

inference that his mental faculties were impaired, because his assertion (he did not know the date of his sixth birthday) was different from the assertion (he knew the date was [correct date]) that the trier of fact might reasonably have expected a lucid person to provide. Hence, the incriminating inference of impaired mental faculties stemmed, not just from the fact that Muniz slurred his response, but also from a testimonial aspect of that response.

Chief Justice Rehnquist, joined by Justices White, Blackmun, and Stevens, dissented from the Court's holding that the content of Muniz's answer to the sixth birthday question was testimonial. The Chief Justice argued that the question was designed to elicit the physical fact of Muniz's mental coordination. The dissenters reasoned that because the police could extract Schmerber's blood "to determine how much that part of his system had been affected by alcohol," the police could likewise "examine the functioning of Muniz's mental processes for the same purpose."

### Express or Implied Assertions of Fact: Doe v. United States

*Muniz* does not stand for the proposition that *all* compelled oral statements are testimonial. To be testimonial, the communication must be an express or implied assertion of fact that can be true or false: otherwise there is no risk of perjury, and no cruel trilemma (of punishment for truth, falsity, or silence) is presented. For example, in Doe v. United States, 487 U.S. 201 (1988), the Court held that a person's compelled signature on a bank consent form, directing the release of bank records—*assuming* such records existed—was not testimonial because there was no assertion of fact that the records did or did not exist. A simple authorization is not an implied assertion of fact—it cannot be false, and therefore cannot expose the citizen to the truth-falsity-silence trilemma. See In re Grand Jury Subpoena, 826 F.2d 1166 (2d Cir.1987) ("the directives here * * * do not contain any assertions by appellants regarding the existence of, or control over, foreign bank accounts. They authorize disclosure of records and information only if such accounts exist."). Compare United States v. Davis, 767 F.2d 1025 (2d Cir.1985) (consent form may be testimonial if there is an implied assertion that bank records actually exist).

### Psychological Evaluations

Estelle v. Smith, 451 U.S. 454 (1981), holds that a defendant who is to be interviewed by a government psychiatrist who will testify at sentencing (in this case the death penalty was involved) has a right to be warned that what he says may be used against him in the sentencing proceeding. Writing for the Court, Chief Justice Burger rejected the state's argument that the psychiatrist's assessment was not made on the basis of testimonial communications, but rather upon physical manifestations and demeanor. The Court found instead that the doctor based his testimony, at least in part, on the defendant's statements about the crime and omissions from his statements. Three Justices concurred in the judgment on right to counsel grounds.

### Drawing an Adverse Inference for Refusing to Produce Non-Testimonial Evidence

When a suspect refuses to supply physical evidence or to participate in a line-up, what sanctions are available to the state? One possibility is an action for contempt. Contempt, while compulsion, is permissible because the suspect has no constitutional right to refuse production of non-testimonial evidence.

Another possibility is that an adverse inference could be drawn against the person who refuses to supply non-testimonial evidence. Justice O'Connor wrote for seven members of the Court in South Dakota v. Neville, 459 U.S. 553 (1983), and explained why an adverse inference permissibly could be drawn. Neville was stopped for drunken driving and was asked to submit to a blood-alcohol test. He refused, saying he was too drunk to pass the test. The state courts suppressed evidence of the refusal on self-incrimination grounds, but the Supreme Court reversed. It reasoned as follows: *Schmerber* authorized a state to force a person to take such a test; South Dakota, therefore, had the power to administer a test to Neville *without* his consent; the state could therefore impose a qualification on Neville's refusal—use of his refusal to take the test as evidence against him at trial. Nor was the officer required to inform Neville that his refusal might be used as evidence against him. The Court found no "implicit promise to forego use of evidence that would unfairly 'trick' " a person.

### 2. Documents and Other Information Existing Before Compulsion

In Boyd v. United States, 116 U.S. 616 (1886), the Court held that a subpoena of one's private books and papers violates the Fifth Amendment, when the *content* of those papers are incriminating. In *Fisher*, supra, the Court found that the privilege cannot be asserted to prevent the government from obtaining evidence from third parties. The rationale is that the incriminated person has not been *compelled* to do anything when the evidence is gathered from third parties. The same rationale served as a basis for the holding in Andresen v. Maryland, 427 U.S. 463 (1976) (discussed in the previous chapter), that the use at trial of the defendant's business records, seized pursuant to a valid warrant, did not violate the Fifth Amendment. The Court explained:

> [I]n this case, petitioner was not asked to say or to do anything. The records seized contained statements that petitioner had voluntarily committed to writing. The search for and seizure of these records were conducted by law enforcement personnel. Finally, when these records were introduced at trial, they were authenticated by a handwriting expert, not by petitioner. Any compulsion of petitioner to speak, other than the inherent psychological pressure to respond at trial to unfavorable evidence, was not present.

The rationale of *Fisher* and *Andresen* is inconsistent with the *Boyd* holding that a person may rely on the privilege to resist a formal governmental demand for private papers in existence when the demand is made. If the document was prepared before the demand, then the government did not compel the content of the document. However, as seen in the excerpt from *Fisher* immediately below, in some circumstances a person may properly refuse to respond to a subpoena: if the *production itself* is communicative (testimonial) and that communication could tend to incriminate the party producing the documents.

## FISHER v. UNITED STATES

Supreme Court of the United States, 1976.
425 U.S. 391.

\* \* \*

It is also clear that the Fifth Amendment does not independently proscribe the compelled production of every sort of incriminating evidence but applies only when the accused is compelled to make a *testimonial* communication that is incriminating. \* \* \*

A subpoena served on a taxpayer requiring him to produce an accountant's workpapers in his possession without doubt involves substantial compulsion. But it does not compel oral testimony; nor would it ordinarily compel the taxpayer to restate, repeat, or affirm the truth of the contents of the documents sought. Therefore, the Fifth Amendment would not be violated by the fact alone that the papers on their face might incriminate the taxpayer, for the privilege protects a person only against being incriminated by his own compelled testimonial communications.

\* \* \* [T]he preparation of all of the papers sought in these cases was wholly voluntary, and they cannot be said to contain compelled testimonial evidence, either of the taxpayers or of anyone else.[a] The

---

[a]    The fact that the documents may have been written by the person asserting the privilege is insufficient to trigger the privilege, and, unless the Government has compelled the subpoenaed

taxpayer cannot avoid compliance with the subpoena merely by asserting that the item of evidence which he is required to produce contains incriminating writing, whether his own or that of someone else.

The act of producing evidence in response to a subpoena nevertheless has communicative aspects of its own, wholly aside from the contents of the papers produced. Compliance with the subpoena tacitly concedes the existence of the papers demanded and their possession or control by the taxpayer. It also would indicate the taxpayer's belief that the papers are those described in the subpoena. The elements of compulsion are clearly present, but the more difficult issues are whether the tacit averments of the taxpayer are both "testimonial" and "incriminating" for purposes of applying the Fifth Amendment. These questions perhaps do not lend themselves to categorical answers; their resolution may instead depend on the facts and circumstances of particular cases or classes thereof. In light of the records now before us, we are confident that however incriminating the contents of the accountant's workpapers might be, the act of producing them—the only thing which the taxpayer is compelled to do—would not itself involve testimonial self-incrimination.

It is doubtful that implicitly admitting the existence and possession of the papers rises to the level of testimony within the protection of the Fifth Amendment. The papers belong to the accountant, were prepared by him, and are the kind usually prepared by an accountant working on the tax returns of his client. Surely the Government is in no way relying on the "truthtelling" of the taxpayer to prove the existence of or his access to the documents. The existence and location of the papers are a foregone conclusion and the taxpayer adds little or nothing to the sum total of the Government's information by conceding that he in fact has the papers. Under these circumstances by enforcement of the summons no constitutional rights are touched. The question is not of testimony but of surrender.

\* \* \*

As for the possibility that responding to the subpoena would authenticate the workpapers, production would express nothing more than the taxpayer's belief that the papers are those described in the subpoena. The taxpayer would be no more competent to authenticate the accountant's workpapers or reports by producing them than he would be to authenticate them if testifying orally. The taxpayer did not prepare the papers and could not vouch for their accuracy. The documents would not be admissible in evidence against the taxpayer without authenticating

---

person to write the document, the fact that it was written by him is not controlling with respect to the Fifth Amendment issue. Conversations may be seized and introduced in evidence under proper safeguards, if not compelled. In the case of a documentary subpoena the only thing compelled is the act of producing the document and the compelled act is the same as the one performed when a chattel or document not authored by the producer is demanded.

testimony. Without more, responding to the subpoena in the circumstances before us would not appear to represent a substantial threat of self-incrimination.

Whether the Fifth Amendment would shield the taxpayer from producing his own tax records in his possession is a question not involved here; for the papers demanded here are not his "private papers." We do hold that compliance with a summons directing the taxpayer to produce the accountant's documents involved in these cases would involve no incriminating testimony within the protection of the Fifth Amendment.

\* \* \*

### Application of the Fisher Analysis: United States v. Doe and the Act of Production

The Court applied *Fisher* in United States v. Doe, 465 U.S. 605 (1984), holding that the owner of several sole proprietorships properly invoked his privilege against self-incrimination in response to grand jury subpoenas for business documents and records. A district judge had found that the act of producing the documents would have required the owner to "admit that the records exist, that they are in his possession, and that they are authentic." Justice Powell's opinion for the Court stated that the privilege did not protect the content of records prepared voluntarily by Doe, because the government did not compel the owner to make incriminating records. Justice Powell recognized, however, that the privilege may be invoked when the *act of producing* documents involves "testimonial self-incrimination." All Justices agreed with him on this point. Justice O'Connor added a one paragraph concurring opinion stating "that the Fifth Amendment provides absolutely no protection for the contents of private papers of any kind." Justice Marshall, joined by Justice Brennan, offered a short opinion, arguing that the Court had not decided whether the content of some private papers might be protected by the privilege.

### Private Papers

Both *Fisher* and *Doe* held that the Fifth Amendment does not protect the content of documents that were voluntarily prepared; even if production of these documents is compelled and the content would be incriminating, the Fifth Amendment is inapplicable because the government did not compel the preparation (as opposed to the production) of the documents. *Fisher* and *Doe* dealt with business papers. Does the rationale of those cases apply to private papers as well? For example, can the government compel a criminal defendant to turn over a diary in which the defendant has written an account of how he committed the crime? In such a case, the act of production itself is not incriminating, because by production the defendant is simply admitting that the diary exists, that he has it, and that it's the document the government demanded. The existence of a diary is not an incriminating fact; having custody of your own diary is not incriminating; and so long as the government can prove that the authenticity of the diary in some way other than the act of production (e.g., by testimony of someone familiar with the defendant's handwriting), the defendant's act of production itself is not incriminating. The only thing incriminating is the—voluntarily prepared—content of the diary.

Most courts have agreed with Justice O'Connor's concurring opinion in *Doe,* that the contents of voluntarily prepared documents are *never* protected by the Fifth Amendment. See In re Grand Jury Proceedings on February 4, 1982, 759 F.2d 1418 (9th Cir.1985) (no distinction between business and personal records); In re Grand Jury Subpoena Duces Tecum, 1 F.3d 87 (2d Cir.1993) ("Self-incrimination analysis now focuses on whether the creation of the thing demanded was compelled and, if not, whether the act of producing it would constitute compelled testimonial communication."). Other courts still draw a business/personal distinction, and hold that the contents of personal records are protected; this position obviously creates problems in determining which records are business and which are personal. United States v. Stone, 976 F.2d 909 (4th Cir.1992) (affirming a lower court finding, after a hearing, that beach house utility records were business-related and not personal). Given the rationale of *Fisher* and *Doe,* how can one validly distinguish between voluntarily prepared business records and voluntarily prepared personal records?

## When Is the Act of Production Incriminating?

In *Fisher,* the Court found that the *act of producing* documents is, testimonial. By producing documents in response to a subpoena, the individual admits that the documents exist; that he has custody of the documents; and that the documents are those that are described in the subpoena. This last admission is pertinent to *authenticating* the documents. If the documents are to be admitted at a trial, the government would have to establish that they are authentic, meaning that the documents are what the government says they are, e.g., the defendant's diary and not a forgery. See Federal Rule of Evidence 901. One possible way of proving authenticity is through the defendant's own admission, by way of production in response to a subpoena, that the documents are those demanded by the subpoena—at least this is so if the documents were prepared by him or ones he knows personally.

While every production of documents in response to a subpoena admits existence, control, and authenticity, it does not follow that the

Fifth Amendment prohibits *every* compelled act of document production. The Fifth Amendment applies only if the compelled testimonial act of production could *incriminate* the person responding to the subpoena. In *Fisher*, the testimonial aspects of the act of production were not incriminating, because existence and control of the documents was a "foregone conclusion", and because the defendant was not competent to authenticate the accountant's workpapers. (The *contents* of the documents were incriminating, but the Fifth Amendment provided no protection as to content, because the documents were voluntarily prepared.) In *Doe,* the Court accepted the finding of the District Court that the act of production would have incriminated the taxpayer. So just when is the act of production, independent of the contents of the documents, incriminating?

A simple admission of the mere existence of documents is rarely incriminating. For example, it is not incriminating for a business to have inventory records, so when someone turns them over to the government, a compelled admission of their existence is not protected by the Fifth Amendment. See United States v. Stone, 976 F.2d 909 (4th Cir.1992) (act of producing utility records for a beach house was not privileged, because there was nothing incriminating about the existence of such records). However, in certain unusual cases the fact that records exist can itself tend to incriminate. Thus, if a corporation has a *second set* of books and records, that fact is incriminating independent of the content of the records. See also United States v. Argomaniz, 925 F.2d 1349 (11th Cir.1991) (existence of documents would show that taxpayer had income for a year when he claimed not to have any). Similarly admission of existence of a document would be incriminating if a person had previously testified, under oath, that a document did not exist. The act of production of that document would be an admission of perjury.

The producer of documents in response to a subpoena admits not only existence but also that he has custody of the documents. Again, however, it is ordinarily not incriminating to control documents, independent of their content. See United States v. Stone, 976 F.2d 909 (4th Cir.1992)(act of producing utility records for a beach house was not privileged, because as the owner of the house, it was not incriminating for the defendant to have the utility bills for the house). For example, the fact that a records custodian has control of corporate records is not inherently incriminating. However, in some limited cases the admission of control creates an inference of affiliation with another person or business that itself tends to incriminate. Thus, in In re Sealed Case, 832 F.2d 1268 (D.C.Cir.1987), a person allegedly involved in the Iran-Contra scandal was served with a subpoena to produce the records of eight foreign companies involved in covert and illegal activity. The court found that by producing the records, thus admitting custody of them, the person would be admitting that he was intimately involved with these corporations—you couldn't possess their records unless you were intimately involved with them. See also Smith v. Richert, 35 F.3d 300 (7th Cir.1994) (defendant charged with not reporting income could be incriminated by act of production of W-2 forms: "by producing them Smith would have acknowledged having received them, foreclosing any defense of nonwilfulness").

Finally, while admission of authenticity is potentially incriminating, it is sometimes the case that the act of production is insufficient to authenticate the records. In *Fisher,* for example, the Court found that the taxpayer's admission could not be used to authenticate the documents, because they were prepared by the accountant. In such cases, there is no risk of an incriminating admission of authentication.

Even in the limited cases where the act of production would be incriminating, the Fifth Amendment will not apply if existence, control, and authentication are in *Fisher's* words, a "foregone conclusion." This will be the case when the government has substantial independent evidence that the records exist, that the witness controls them, and that the records produced are authentic. For example, existence and control can be shown through other witnesses, when the records have either been prepared by or shown to them. See United States v. Clark, 847 F.2d 1467 (10th Cir.1988) (existence and control of records that the defendant had once given to his accountant to prepare his tax return is proven by subpoenaing the accountant to testify; existence and control of bank records can be proven through testimony of bank officials). Persons in similar situations can testify that in their jobs, records such as those subpoenaed exist and they have custody over them. See S.E.C. v. First Jersey Securities, Inc., 843 F.2d 74 (2d Cir.1988) (possession of parallel documents by other branch managers). Existence and control is often admitted, though perhaps unwittingly, by the witness at some time before the subpoena is served. See United States v. Rue, 819 F.2d 1488 (8th Cir.1987) (dentist demurs to voluntary inspection on grounds that his records are too voluminous to produce); In re Grand Jury Subpoena Duces Tecum, 1 F.3d 87 (2d Cir.1993) ("Since Doe produced a copy of the calendar to the SEC and testified about his possession and use of it, its existence and location are foregone conclusions, and his production of the original adds little or nothing to the sum total of the government's information."). Finally, authenticity can be shown in a variety of ways other than through the act of production, such as by handwriting exemplars, testimony by those who prepared the documents, and comparison to similar documents. See In re Grand Jury Subpoena Duces Tecum, 1 F.3d 87 (2d Cir.1993) (noting that the defendant's "authentication is a foregone conclusion if someone else can verify that the records are in fact what they purport to be"); United States v. Stone, 976 F.2d 909 (4th Cir.1992) (defendant's authentication of utility records for a beach house was unnecessary to the government's case, because authentication "could easily be obtained from the utilities involved").

### Act of Production as a Roadmap for the Government: United States v. Hubbell

Even if an act of production of documents would be incriminating, the government can *still* obtain the documents—by giving immunity to the party holding them. That immunity, as discussed later in the Chapter, will mean that the government cannot use the incriminating admissions in the act of production, and also cannot use any "fruits" of those incriminating admissions. In United States v. Hubbell, 530 U.S. 27 (2000), the Court found that the compelled act of production of personal documents was incriminating, because it provided the government information about a trail of documentation of which it had not been aware—thus it provided incriminating evidence of the producing defendant's thought process on how the documents were organized and related. This incrimination was not solved by a grant of use immunity. See also In re Grand Jury Subpoena Duces Tecum, 670 F.3d 1335 (11th Cir. 2012) (compelling a person to decrypt the contents of a harddrive violated the Fifth Amendment because decryption "would require the use of the contents of Doe's mind").

### Production of Corporate Documents: Braswell v. United States

Recall that in *Bellis* the Court held that business entities are not entitled to Fifth Amendment protection. But a business entity *itself* cannot be compelled to produce incriminating evidence—except through individual agents of the entity. If the act of production of an entity's documents would be personally incriminating to an agent of the entity, can the agent invoke his personal Fifth Amendment privilege? This was the question in Braswell v. United States, 487 U.S. 99 (1988). Braswell formed two corporations in which he was the sole shareholder. A grand jury issued a subpoena to him—in his capacity as agent—to produce the books and records of the two companies. Braswell invoked his personal privilege against self-incrimination on the ground that the act of production might incriminate him. Chief Justice Rehnquist, writing for the Court, relied on the "collective entity" rule to deny the Fifth Amendment claim. The Chief Justice described that rule as follows:

> The official records and documents of the organization that are held [by the agent] in a representative rather than in a personal capacity cannot be the subject of the personal privilege against self-incrimination, even though production of the papers might tend to incriminate [the agent] personally.

The Chief Justice explained the obligations of a corporate agent:

The custodian of corporate or entity records holds those documents in a representative rather than a personal capacity * * * and a custodian's assumption of his representative capacity leads to certain obligations, including the duty to produce corporate records on proper demand by the Government. Under those circumstances, the custodian's act of production is not deemed a personal act, but rather an act of the corporation.

Braswell sought support from Curcio v. United States, 354 U.S. 118 (1957), where Curcio was served with a subpoena to testify in his capacity as a secretary-treasurer of a local union. Curcio refused to answer any questions as to the whereabouts of the books and records of the union. The Court in *Curcio* held that the collective entity rule did not require "the giving of oral testimony by the custodian" where that testimony could incriminate him personally. The Chief Justice distinguished *Curcio* in *Braswell,* stating that a corporate agent assumes the risk of producing *documents* as part of the job, but not the risk of being compelled to give incriminating *oral testimony*.

The Chief Justice reasoned that recognizing a privilege on the part of records custodians would essentially render meaningless the prior cases holding that corporations do not have a Fifth Amendment privilege— corporations engaged in wrongdoing would effectively have a back-door privilege through the personal invocation by the corporate agent.

Although a custodian like Braswell is not permitted to claim the privilege in response to a subpoena for corporate records, the Court recognized that "certain consequences flow from the fact that the custodian's act of production is one in his representative rather than personal capacity." The Court noted that the government had conceded that "it may make no use of the 'individual act' against the individual," which means, "[f]or example, in a criminal prosecution the Government may not introduce into evidence before the jury the fact that the subpoena was served upon and the corporation's documents were delivered by one particular individual, the custodian."

This is not to say, however, that the government may not use the act of production as evidence; the *corporation's* act of production may be used as evidence against the custodian. The jury cannot be told that the individual defendant produced the records as a corporate agent, but it can be told that the corporation produced the records. The *Braswell* Court concluded that "the jury may draw from the corporation's act of production the conclusion that the records in question are authentic corporate records, which the corporation possessed, and which it produced in response to the subpoena, and if the defendant held a prominent position within the corporation that produced the records, the jury may, just as it would had someone else produced the documents, reasonably infer that he had possession of the documents or knowledge of their contents."

As a result of the limits on the use of the corporate agent's act of production, the Court concluded that Braswell was not incriminated by the fact of personal production, only by the fact of corporate production. The Court left open "the question whether the agency rationale supports compelling a custodian to produce corporate records when the custodian is able to establish, by showing for example that he is the sole employee and officer of the corporation, that the jury would inevitably conclude that he produced the records."

Justice Kennedy, joined by Justices Brennan, Marshall, and Scalia, dissented and argued that "[t]he Court today denies an individual his Fifth Amendment privilege against self-incrimination in order to vindicate the rule that a collective entity which employs him has no privilege itself." He concluded that the majority's approach to the privilege—i.e., holding that it did not apply to a corporate custodian but that the custodian's act of production could not be used as evidence— "avoided and manipulated" basic Fifth Amendment principles. He asserted that the only way to obtain corporate documents from an agent whose act of production would be personally incriminating was to grant use immunity to the agent.

### The Difference Between a Corporate Agent's Compelled Oral Testimony and Compelled Document Production

In *Curcio,* the Court held that the corporate agent had a privilege to refuse to testify on the whereabouts of corporate documents. But in *Braswell,* the Court held that the agent had no privilege to refuse their production. What is the difference between a corporate agent's compelled oral testimony and compelled document production? Judge Kravitch proffered this explanation in In re Grand Jury Subpoena Dated April 9, 1996 v. Smith, 87 F.3d 1198 (11th Cir.1996):

> In drawing a line between acts of production and oral testimony, the Court appears to have relied on one fact that distinguishes these two types of testimony: the corporation owns the documents. In contrast, to the extent that one's thoughts and statements can be said to "belong" to anyone, they belong to the witness herself. A custodian has no personal right to retain corporate books. Because the documents belong to the corporation, the state may exercise its right to review the records. For Fifth Amendment analysis, oral statements are different. The government has no right to compel a person to speak the contents of her mind when doing so would incriminate that person.

The corporate agent in *Grand Jury Subpoena* did not refuse to produce corporate documents. Rather, she claimed not to possess them, and refused to testify as to their location. The court stated that this case was controlled by *Curcio*, because the government was demanding oral testimony, and the answer could have personally incriminated the defendant (the answer probably being, "I destroyed them, that's where they are"). Accordingly, the subpoena demanding oral testimony was quashed.

### Production of a Person in Response to a Court Order: Baltimore City Dept. of Social Services v. Bouknight

In Baltimore City Dept. of Social Services v. Bouknight, 493 U.S. 549 (1990), the Court relied in part upon the collective entity rule to find the Fifth Amendment inapplicable to an act of production of a *child*. Suspecting child abuse, the Department of Social Services obtained a court order removing Maurice Bouknight from his mother's control. The Department obtained a further order declaring Maurice to be a "child in need of assistance" under Maryland law. That court order gave the Department jurisdiction over Maurice. Maurice was returned to his mother, but only under conditions imposed by a protective order. Ms. Bouknight did not comply with those conditions, and the Juvenile Court granted the Department's petition again to remove Maurice from his mother's control. Ms. Bouknight failed to produce Maurice, and Department officials feared that he might be dead. The case was referred to the police homicide division. The Juvenile Court directed that Ms. Bouknight be held in contempt for failing to produce Maurice. That court rejected her argument that the Fifth Amendment protected her from any incrimination that might result from the act of producing Maurice.

Justice O'Connor wrote the majority opinion for the Supreme Court. She assumed, without deciding, that Bouknight's act of producing Maurice could be potentially incriminating, as an "implicit communication of control over Maurice at the moment of production." However, Justice O'Connor concluded that Bouknight could not invoke the privilege "because she has assumed custodial duties related to production and because production is required as part of a noncriminal regulatory regime." Justice O'Connor found an analogy to *Braswell*. She argued that by "accepting care of Maurice subject to the custodial order's conditions," Bouknight accepted the consequent obligations of production.

Justice Marshall, joined by Justice Brennan, dissented. He rejected the analogy to the collective entity rule and *Braswell*. He reasoned that Bouknight "is not the agent for an artificial entity that possesses no Fifth Amendment privilege. Her role as Maurice's parent is very different from the role of a corporate custodian who is merely the instrumentality through whom the corporation acts."

## 3. Required Records

Even if documents are prepared under compulsion, their contents as well as the act of production will be unprotected by the Fifth Amendment if the *government requires the documents to be kept for a legitimate administrative purpose* that is not focused solely on those inherently suspected of criminal activity. This principle is embodied in the "required records" exception to the Fifth Amendment. Under the exception, the government can require records to be kept; it can punish those who do not keep the records; it can punish those who keep false records; and it can punish those who truthfully admit criminal activity in the compelled records. The justification is that the state has legitimate administrative functions that would be impaired by a strict application of the Fifth Amendment, because any citizen could simply refuse to comply with the recordkeeping requirement by claiming that keeping the records would tend to incriminate them.

In Shapiro v. United States, 335 U.S. 1 (1948), a 5–4 decision, Chief Justice Vinson wrote for the Court as it held that the compelled production of defendant's customary business records, which were required to be kept under the Emergency Price Control Act, did not implicate the Fifth Amendment:

> It may be assumed at the outset that there are limits which the Government cannot constitutionally exceed in requiring the keeping of records which may be inspected by an administrative agency and may be used in prosecuting statutory violations committed by the record-keeper himself. But no serious misgiving that those bounds have been overstepped would appear to be evoked when there is a sufficient relation between the activity sought to be regulated and the public concern so that the Government can constitutionally regulate or forbid the basic activity concerned, and can constitutionally require the keeping of particular records, subject to inspection by the Administrator. It is not questioned here that Congress has constitutional authority to prescribe commodity prices as a war emergency measure, and that the licensing and record-keeping requirements of the Price Control Act represent a legitimate exercise of that power. * * *

In a dissenting opinion, Justice Frankfurter expressed concern about the scope of the required records exception. He suggested that the government might use the exception to set up a recordkeeping scheme as a device to force criminal targets to incriminate themselves.

## *Limitations on the Required Records Exception*

The majority opinion in *Shapiro* refers to "limits which the Government cannot constitutionally exceed" in requiring that records be kept or produced for inspection. What are those limits? In 1968, the Court decided several cases in which the scope of the required records doctrine was an issue. Marchetti v. United States, 390 U.S. 39 (1968), involved a defendant who had been convicted for willfully failing to register and to pay an occupational tax for engaging in the business of accepting unlawful gambling wagers. Marchetti claimed that he failed to register and pay because to do so would provide an incriminating admission that he was involved in illegal gambling. While acknowledging Congress's authority to tax unlawful activities, the Court reversed the convictions, stating that "those who properly assert the constitutional privilege as to these provisions may not be criminally punished for failure to comply with their requirements."

Justice Harlan, writing for the Court in *Marchetti*, distinguished *Shapiro* and explained why the required records doctrine did not apply:

> Each of the three principal elements of the [required records] doctrine, as it is described in *Shapiro,* is absent from this situation. First, petitioner Marchetti was not, by the provisions now at issue, obliged to keep and preserve records "of the same kind as he has customarily kept"; he was required simply to provide information, unrelated to any records which he may have maintained, about his wagering activities. This requirement is not significantly different from a demand that he provide oral testimony. Second, whatever "public aspects" there were to the records at issue in *Shapiro,* there are none to the information demanded from Marchetti. The Government's anxiety to obtain information known to a private individual does not without more render that information public; if it did, no room would remain for the application of the constitutional privilege. * * * Third, the requirements at issue in *Shapiro* were imposed in "an essentially non-criminal and regulatory area of inquiry" while those here are directed to a "selective group inherently suspect of criminal activities."

In Haynes v. United States, 390 U.S. 85 (1968), decided the same day as *Marchetti*, the Court reversed a conviction for failing to register a sawed-off shotgun as required by the National Firearms Act. Other sections of the Act provided that possession of a sawed-off shotgun was itself a criminal offense. The reversal was grounded on a finding that the registration statute created real and appreciable hazards of incrimination, because it was "directed principally at those persons who * * * are immediately threatened by criminal prosecution" under other sections of the Act.

Justice Harlan again found the required records doctrine to be inapplicable because the registration did not involve records of the kind "customarily kept," the statutory provisions were directed at "a highly selective group inherently suspect of criminal activities," they were not concerned essentially with non-criminal and regulatory inquiries, and the records involved were in no sense "public."

How does one distinguish between legislation that has a noncriminal or regulatory purpose, such as the production of tax revenue, and one that is essentially targeted at criminals? If both require self-reporting that may be incriminating, what is the basis for differential application of the Fifth Amendment? See, e.g., In re Grand Jury Proceedings, 707 F.3d 1262 (11th Cir. 2013) (provisions of Bank Secrecy Act requiring person to keep and produce records concerning foreign bank accounts were within the required records exception: "That a statute relates both to criminal law and to civil regulatory matters does not strip the statute of its status as essentially regulatory * * * There is nothing inherently illegal about having or being a beneficiary of an offshore foreign banking account.").

### Compelled Reporting of an Accident: California v. Byers

In California v. Byers, 402 U.S. 424 (1971), the constitutionality of California's "hit and run" statute was in issue. Byers was convicted of a misdemeanor for failing to stop at the scene of an accident and to leave his name and address. The Court found that the statute was valid under the required records exception—so the defendant could be convicted for failing to report, and his incriminatory statements could be used against him if he did report. In a plurality opinion, Chief Justice Burger stressed that the statutory scheme was essentially regulatory and noncriminal; it was directed to the motoring public at large, rather than to "a highly selective group inherently suspect of criminal activities;" and self-reporting was indispensable to fulfillment of its purposes. Even if incrimination was a danger, Chief Justice Burger argued, the Fifth Amendment was not implicated. The act of stopping at the scene of an accident was no more "testimonial" than standing in a line-up, and disclosure of identity "is an essentially neutral act." It would be an extravagant extension of the Fifth Amendment, the Chief Justice concluded, to hold that there is a constitutional right "to flee the scene of an accident in order to avoid the possibility of legal involvement."

Justice Harlan, in his opinion concurring in the result in *Byers*, disagreed with the Chief Justice's analysis. Justice Harlan was willing to call the information sought by the statute testimonial and he recognized that it was potentially incriminatory. Thus, he agreed with the four dissenting Justices that the plurality was wrong to say that the information was neither testimonial nor incriminating. But he argued that the state had legitimate regulatory interests in controlling dangerous driving.

### Is the Target Group Inherently Suspect?

In Baltimore City Dept. of Social Services v. Bouknight, discussed supra, the Court relied in part upon the required records exception to find the Fifth Amendment inapplicable to an act of production of a child who was feared dead. The mother, upon whom the order to produce the child was served, claimed that the Fifth Amendment protected her from the incriminating aspects of the act of production. The Court held that the collective entity rule and the required records exception each applied, so that the mother was not protected from incrimination.

With regard to the required records exception, Justice O'Connor, writing for the majority, relied heavily on *Shapiro* and *Byers*. As in those cases, the State's demand for information was imposed in an "essentially non-criminal and regulatory area of inquiry" and was not "directed to a selective group inherently suspect of criminal activities." Justice O'Connor reasoned that the State's efforts to gain access to "children in need of assistance" did not focus solely on criminal conduct, and were motivated by the proper regulatory purpose of concern for the child's safety and welfare.

Justice Marshall, joined by Justice Brennan, dissented. He rejected the analogy to the required records exception. He noted that as a matter of fact, the State's scheme was "narrowly targeted at parents who through abuse or neglect deny their children the minimal reasonable level of care and attention," and argued that the State's goal of protecting children from abuse "inevitably intersects" with criminal provisions that serve the same goal.

In Bionic Auto Parts and Sales, Inc. v. Fahner, 721 F.2d 1072 (7th Cir.1983), the court held that the privilege against self-incrimination barred a state from enforcing a regulation requiring a record of any serial number or identifying mark that was removed from an auto or an auto part. It said that "[a]lthough there is a fine line between a regulatory purpose and the specific effort to root out criminal activity, we are hard pressed to articulate a regulatory rationale for the record-keeping requirement in question." The recordkeeping scheme was directly solely at autos and parts that are likely to be stolen. Compare that same court's decision in United States v. Lehman, 887 F.2d 1328 (7th Cir.1989), which held that a statute requiring buyers and sellers of livestock to keep records was within the required records exception. The court stated that "there is nothing ordinarily criminally suspect in buying and selling livestock." See also United States v. Garcia-Cordero, 610 F.3d 613 (11th Cir. 2010) (statute requiring that anyone transporting aliens must present them to immigration officials upon arrival was valid under the required records exception: "The 'bring and present' requirement is part of the federal regulatory scheme through which the government controls our national borders. * * * The statute imposes the bring and present requirement on all who transport aliens to this country—not just those who do so illegally.").

18 U.S.C. § 922(e) makes it a crime to knowingly fail to provide written notice to an airline before transporting firearms. Does a defendant who fails to comply have a Fifth Amendment defense? Courts have held that the statute is within the required records exception, as a legitimate exercise of regulatory activity. Therefore there is no privilege to refuse to comply, even if the report would be incriminating. See, e.g., United States v. Alkhafaji, 754 F.2d 641 (6th Cir.1985). The courts rely on the fact that transporting firearms on an airline is not always illegal, and therefore the statute does not focus on a group inherently suspected of criminal activity. Moreover there is a legitimate regulatory interest in knowing that firearms are being transported.

For a general approach to required records, see Saltzburg, The Required Records Doctrine: Its Lessons for the Privilege Against Self-Incrimination, 53 U.Chi.L.Rev. 6 (1986). See also Rajah v. Mukasey, 544 F.3d 427 (2nd Cir. 2008) (Fifth Amendment did not protect aliens from having to file information concerning their immigration status as part of a special call-in registration program: "Just as a taxpayer's W-2 forms are required records not subject to the Fifth Amendment because they are a mandatory part of a civil regulatory regime, so too are the passports and [disclosure forms] in the current case.").

## F. PROCEDURAL ASPECTS OF SELF-INCRIMINATION CLAIMS

### 1. Determining the Risk of Incrimination

If a criminal defendant decides not to take the stand, there is no need for the court to decide whether this exercise of the privilege is valid, for it clearly is. But when the privilege is invoked by someone who is *testifying* at a proceeding, it must be decided whether the witness, by answering a particular question, would subject herself to the risk of incrimination within the meaning of the Fifth Amendment. The risk of incrimination must of course be assessed without compelling the witness to divulge the information that the witness claims is protected by the privilege. Thus, the task of determining the risk of incrimination is both delicate and murky—and in most cases the claim is sustained. The Supreme Court has stated that the risk of incrimination is determined by whether it is *perfectly clear,* from a careful consideration of all the circumstances in the case, that the witness is mistaken, and that the answers *cannot possibly* have such tendency to incriminate.

Hoffman v. United States, 341 U.S. 479, 488 (1951). The Court in *Hoffman* detailed the standards for determining whether testimony could tend to incriminate a witness within the meaning of the Fifth Amendment:

> If a person cannot possibly be prosecuted in the future—e.g., a complete pardon has been issued, double jeopardy clearly bars future prosecution, or immunity [as discussed infra] has been granted—then the privilege cannot be relied upon. [The privilege] extends to answers that would in themselves support a conviction * * * but likewise embraces those which would furnish a link in the chain of evidence needed to prosecute * * *. [I]f the witness, upon interposing his claim, were required to prove the hazard * * * he would be compelled to surrender the very protection which the privilege is designed to guarantee. To sustain the privilege, it need only be evident from the implications of the question, in the setting in which it is asked, that a responsive answer to the question or an explanation of why it cannot be answered might be dangerous because injurious disclosure could result.

See also Malloy v. Hogan, 378 U.S. 1 (1964) (even after Malloy was convicted and served a prison sentence for gambling activities, he could not be compelled to identify his associates in those activities, because disclosure of these names "might furnish a link in a chain of evidence sufficient to connect the petitioner with a more recent crime for which he might still be prosecuted"); Kastigar v. United States, 406 U.S. 441 (1972) (Fifth Amendment protects against compelled disclosures "that the witness reasonably believes could be used in a criminal prosecution or could lead to other evidence that might be so used.").

In sum, the threshold for "tendency" to incriminate is not high, and as a practical matter in most cases, it is self-executing. If a person says that testifying will tend to incriminate him, or might lead to evidence that would do so, it is an unusual case in which a court will disagree and compel that person to testify. But as the following case illustrates, there are indeed some unusual situations in which a statement's tendency to incriminate is extremely doubtful.

*Compelled Self-Identification and the Tendency to Incriminate*

## HIIBEL V. SIXTH JUDICIAL DISTRICT COURT OF NEVADA, HUMBOLDT COUNTY

Supreme Court of the United States, 2004.
542 U.S. 177.

### JUSTICE KENNEDY delivered the opinion of the Court.

[The defendant was convicted for refusing to give his name to a police officer during a lawful *Terry* stop. The Court first holds that Hiibel's Fourth Amendment rights were not violated because officers are permitted to determine the suspect's identity during the course of a lawful *Terry* stop.]

Petitioner further contends that his conviction violates the Fifth Amendment's prohibition on compelled self-incrimination. * * *

In this case petitioner's refusal to disclose his name was not based on any articulated real and appreciable fear that his name would be used to incriminate him, or that it "would furnish a link in the chain of evidence needed to prosecute" him. Hoffman v. United States, 341 U.S. 479, 486 (1951). As best we can tell, petitioner refused to identify himself only because he thought his name was none of the officer's business. Even today, petitioner does not explain how the disclosure of his name could have been used against him in a criminal case. While we recognize petitioner's strong belief that he should not have to disclose his identity, the Fifth Amendment does not override the Nevada Legislature's judgment to the contrary absent a reasonable belief that the disclosure would tend to incriminate him.

The narrow scope of the disclosure requirement is also important. One's identity is, by definition, unique; yet it is, in another sense, a universal characteristic. Answering a request to disclose a name is likely to be so insignificant in the scheme of things as to be incriminating only in unusual circumstances. In every criminal case, it is known and must be known who has been arrested and who is being tried. Even witnesses who plan to invoke the Fifth Amendment privilege answer when their names are called to take the stand. Still, a case may arise where there is a substantial allegation that furnishing identity at the time of a stop would have given the police a link in the chain of evidence needed to convict the individual of a separate offense. In that case, the court can then consider whether the privilege applies, and, if the Fifth Amendment has been violated, what remedy must follow. We need not resolve those questions here.

The judgment of the Nevada Supreme Court is

Affirmed.

JUSTICE STEVENS, dissenting.

\* \* \*

\* \* \* A name can provide the key to a broad array of information about the person, particularly in the hands of a police officer with access to a range of law enforcement databases. And that information, in turn, can be tremendously useful in a criminal prosecution. \* \* \*

[The dissenting opinion of JUSTICE BREYER, joined by JUSTICES SOUTER and GINSBURG, is omitted.]

## The Risk of Incrimination and Denial of Guilt: Ohio v. Reiner

Can a witness invoke the Fifth Amendment privilege if she denies guilt of any crime? This question was faced by the Court in Ohio v. Reiner, 532 U.S. 17 (2001) (per curiam). Reiner was charged with involuntary manslaughter in connection with the death of his infant son. He blamed it on the babysitter. The babysitter refused to testify, claiming a Fifth Amendment privilege. She was granted immunity, then testified as a prosecution witness that she had nothing to do with the infant's death or with other injuries to the infant's brother. Reiner was convicted but the state court reversed on the ground that the babysitter should not have been granted immunity. In the state court's view, the babysitter's testimony "did not incriminate her, because she denied any involvement in the abuse. Thus, she did not have a valid Fifth Amendment privilege."

The Supreme Court reinstated the conviction; it found that the babysitter faced a risk of self-incrimination even though she denied wrongdoing, and therefore the grant of immunity was not unlawful. The Court reasoned as follows:

> We have held that the privilege's protection extends only to witnesses who have "reasonable cause to apprehend danger from a direct answer." Hoffman v. United States. That inquiry is for the court; the witness' assertion does not by itself establish the risk of incrimination. A danger of "imaginary and unsubstantial character" will not suffice. But we have never held, as the Supreme Court of Ohio did, that the privilege is unavailable to those who claim innocence. To the contrary, we have emphasized that one of the Fifth Amendment's "basic functions \* \* \* is to protect innocent men \* \* \* who otherwise might be ensnared by ambiguous circumstances." Grunewald v. United States, 353 U.S. 391, 421 (1957). In *Grunewald*, we recognized that truthful responses of an innocent witness, as well as those of a wrongdoer, may provide the government with incriminating evidence from the speaker's own mouth.

> The Supreme Court of Ohio's determination that Batt [the babysitter] did not have a valid Fifth Amendment privilege because

she denied any involvement in the abuse of the children clearly conflicts with *Hoffman* and *Grunewald*. Batt had "reasonable cause" to apprehend danger from her answers if questioned at respondent's trial. Batt spent extended periods of time alone with Alex [the infant]. She was with Alex within the potential timeframe of the fatal trauma. The defense's theory of the case was that Batt, not respondent, was responsible for Alex's death and his brother's uncharged injuries. In this setting, it was reasonable for Batt to fear that answers to possible questions might tend to incriminate her. Batt therefore had a valid Fifth Amendment privilege against self-incrimination.

## 2. Immunity

If a witness is guaranteed that no criminal prosecution having anything to do with statements given to the government will take place, then there is no possibility of incrimination. Thus, a person who receives immunity has no right to refuse to testify and may be punished by imprisonment for contempt for so refusing. A person who receives immunity is not subject to the cruel trilemma of punishment for truth, silence and falsity—because there is no punishment for telling the truth when immunized.

A broad guarantee against future prosecution is called *transactional immunity*, to signify that no transaction about which a witness testifies can be the subject of a future prosecution against the witness. The Federal immunity statute, 18 U.S.C. § 6002, provides for a more limited kind of immunity known as *use and derivative use* (or use-fruits) immunity. That statute provides:

> Whenever a witness refuses, on the basis of his privilege against self-incrimination, to testify or provide other information in a proceeding before or ancillary to [a Federal court, grand jury, agency proceeding, or Congressional proceeding], and the person presiding over the proceeding communicates to the witness an order issued under this part, the witness may not refuse to comply with the order on the basis of his privilege against self-incrimination; but no testimony or other information compelled under the order (or any information directly or indirectly derived from such testimony or other information) may be used against the witness in any criminal case, except a prosecution for perjury, giving a false statement, or otherwise failing to comply with the order.

### The Constitutionality of Use Immunity:
### Kastigar v. United States

At one time, it appeared that the Supreme Court might require transactional immunity (i.e., immunity from prosecution for the acts that are the subject of the compelled testimony) as the cost to the government of forcing a witness to testify. In Counselman v. Hitchcock, 142 U.S. 547 (1892), the Court held that a statute, providing that no "evidence obtained from a party or witness by means of a judicial proceeding * * * shall be given in evidence; or in any matter used against him * * * in any court of the United States," was insufficient to supplant the privilege against self-incrimination.

But, in the landmark case of Kastigar v. United States, 406 U.S. 441 (1972),[3] the Court explained that *Counselman* did not require transactional immunity; what it required was use and "derivative use" or "use-fruits" immunity. The defect in the statute rejected in *Counselman* was that it did not "prevent the use of his testimony to search out other testimony to be used in evidence against him [the immunized witness]." In *Kastigar,* the Court upheld 18 U.S.C.A. § 6002 and stated that use-fruits immunity was "a rational accommodation between the imperatives of the privilege and the legitimate demands of government to compel citizens to testify." The Court concluded that use-fruits immunity "leaves the witness and the prosecutorial authorities in substantially the same position as if the witness had claimed the Fifth Amendment privilege. The immunity therefore is coextensive with the privilege and suffices to supplant it."

The *Kastigar* Court declared that after immunity is granted and a witness is compelled to testify, the burden is on the government "to prove that the evidence it proposes to use is derived from a legitimate source wholly independent of the compelled testimony."

Justice Marshall dissented in *Kastigar*, arguing that the burden placed on the government was not adequate protection for the witness, "[f]or the paths of information through the investigative bureaucracy may well be long and winding, and even a prosecutor acting in the best of faith cannot be certain that somewhere in the depths of his investigative apparatus, often including hundreds of employees, there was not some prohibited use of the compelled testimony."[4]

---

[3]   Prior to *Kastigar,* the Court had held in Murphy v. Waterfront Comm., 378 U.S. 52 (1964), that a state grant of immunity prevented the federal government from using the compelled testimony or its fruits, and that this protection was sufficient to supplant the Fifth Amendment privilege against self-incrimination. Until *Kastigar,* no one was sure whether the *Murphy* rule applied when the same sovereign granted the immunity and subsequently sought to bring a criminal charge against an immunized witness.

[4]   Justice Douglas also dissented. Justices Brennan and Rehnquist did not participate. States may still require transactional immunity as a matter of state constitutional or statutory

## Proving That Immunized Testimony Was Not Used

When a witness gives immunized testimony and is later prosecuted, the question of whether the government has used the fruits of the immunized testimony inevitably arises. One way for the government to satisfy its burden of showing that its evidence is not the fruit of immunized testimony is to establish a "Wall of Silence" between the prosecutors exposed to the testimony and the prosecutors who bring the case against the witness. See United States v. Schwimmer, 882 F.2d 22 (2d Cir.1989) (recommending the "Wall of Silence" approach); U.S. Dep't of Justice, U.S. Attorneys' Manual, § 1–11.–400 (to demonstrate that no use has been made of the compelled testimony, prosecution should be handled by an attorney unfamiliar with its substance). See also United States v. Harris, 973 F.2d 333 (4th Cir.1992) (while there is no per se rule requiring withdrawal of a prosecutor who was exposed to immunized testimony, "a prosecutor's failure to withdraw certainly makes it more difficult for the government to prove that the compelled testimony did not contribute to the prosecution"). How likely is it that a "Wall of Silence" will be effective? See also United States v. Slough, 641 F.3d 544 (D.C. Cir. 2011) (noting difficulties in determining whether the government evidence is tainted when it only partially overlaps immunized information).

## Impeachment, Perjury

The Supreme Court has made clear that once use immunity is granted, the testimony that is extracted from the immunized witness is coerced and cannot be used as evidence against the witness in a subsequent case against the witness, *even for impeachment purposes.* New Jersey v. Portash, 440 U.S. 450 (1979). However, the Court held in United States v. Apfelbaum, 445 U.S. 115 (1980), that an immunized witness has no right to lie, and that evidence of lying under a grant of immunity could be used in a subsequent prosecution for perjury, false statements, or obstruction of justice. Justice Rehnquist, writing for the Court, noted that if a person could not be punished for lying while immunized, an option would be created that would make a mockery of conferring immunity on a witness because the very purpose of granting immunity would be defeated. Justice Brennan and Justice Blackmun, joined by Justice Marshall, concurred in the result. The court in United States v. Veal, 153 F.3d 1233 (11th Cir.1998), put it this way:

---

law. See, e.g., Attorney General v. Colleton, 387 Mass. 790, 444 N.E.2d 915 (1982); N.Y.C.P.L. 190.40. Even though a state gives transactional immunity, the witness can still be prosecuted in a federal court or a court in another state, so long as the testimony and its fruits are not used. United States v. Gallo, 863 F.2d 185 (2d Cir.1988).

When an accused has been accorded immunity to preserve his right against self-incrimination, he must choose either to relinquish his Fifth Amendment right and testify truthfully, knowing that his statements cannot be used against him in a subsequent criminal prosecution regarding the matter being investigated, or continue to assert the privilege and suffer the consequences. There is no third option for testifying falsely without incurring potential prosecution for perjury or false statements.

For a discussion of *Apfelbaum* and *Portash,* see Hoffman, The Privilege Against Self-Incrimination and Immunity Statutes: Permissible Uses of Immunized Testimony, 16 Crim.L.Bull. 421 (1980).

### *Subsequent Statements: Pennsylvania v. Conboy*

What happens if a witness testifies pursuant to a grant of immunity, then later makes a statement that is identical to the immunized statement? Can the later statement be used against the witness? Put another way, does a witness who testifies under a grant of immunity have a Fifth Amendment right to refuse to give an identical statement at a later point? In Pillsbury Co. v. Conboy, 459 U.S. 248 (1983), the Court upheld the right of a witness at a deposition in a civil case to claim the privilege against self-incrimination, even though he had previously been granted use immunity in related criminal proceedings. Conboy was a former executive of a company involved in an antitrust case. He testified before a grand jury after receiving use immunity. Subsequently, his grand jury testimony was provided to lawyers in related civil litigation. The lawyers decided to depose Conboy, and at the deposition, they read from the grand jury transcript in the course of asking questions. Conboy invoked his privilege against self-incrimination, but the district court found that the former immunity grant required him to answer and held him in contempt. A majority of the Court concluded that the prior grant of immunity was not sufficient protection to assure Conboy that nothing that he said at the deposition could be used against him in later criminal proceedings. The Court held that a new immunity grant would be required before the witness could be forced to answer. Justice Marshall wrote a concurring opinion, and Justices Brennan and Blackmun concurred in the judgment. Justice Stevens, joined by Justice O'Connor, dissented.

## 3. Invoking the Privilege

### *The Requirement of Expressly Invoking the Privilege: Garner v. United States, Minnesota v. Murphy and Salinas v. Texas*

When a person is compelled by the government to answer questions that might tend to incriminate that person in a subsequent criminal case, the person can refuse to answer and rely on the Fifth Amendment privilege against self-incrimination. However, if the person *does* answer, the privilege will be deemed waived and the answer can be used as evidence. For example, in Garner v. United States, 424 U.S. 648 (1976), the Court held that a taxpayer lost whatever privilege he might have had when he answered questions on a tax return, rather than invoking the privilege.

In Minnesota v. Murphy, 465 U.S. 420 (1984), the Court reiterated its view that generally a person who is asked to answer questions must invoke his privilege against self-incrimination or lose its protection. It held that a probationer lost the protection of the privilege when he answered questions of his probation officer concerning crimes for which he had not yet been charged.

In Salinas v. Texas, 133 S.Ct. 2174 (2013), Salinas was being questioned by police officers about a murder. He was not in custody and he did not receive *Miranda* warnings—as seen later in this Chapter, *Miranda* warnings are required only if the police are engaged in custodial interrogation. Salinas answered a number of questions voluntarily but balked and did not answer when the officer asked whether a ballistics test of shell casings found at the crime scene would match his shotgun. He answered a few other questions when the officer moved on from the ballistics test. At trial, prosecutors argued that Salinas's silence regarding the outcome of a ballistics test constituted an admission of guilt, and the defendant claimed that the use of his silence violated his Fifth Amendment right.

The Supreme Court held that Salinas's Fifth Amendment right was not violated by the use of his silence, but there was no opinion for the Court. Justice Alito wrote an opinion for the plurality, joined by Chief Justice Roberts and Justice Kennedy. Justice Alito relied on Minnesota v. Murphy and other cases to conclude that Salinas could not rely on his Fifth Amendment right at trial because he had not invoked it at the time he was questioned. Justice Alito elaborated as follows:

> Petitioner's Fifth Amendment claim fails because he did not expressly invoke the privilege against self-incrimination in response to the officer's question. It has long been settled that the privilege "generally is not self-executing" and that a witness who desires its protection "must claim it." Minnesota v. Murphy. Although no

ritualistic formula is necessary in order to invoke the privilege, a witness does not do so by simply standing mute.

\* \* \*

The privilege against self-incrimination is an exception to the general principle that the Government has the right to everyone's testimony. To prevent the privilege from shielding information not properly within its scope, we have long held that a witness who "desires the protection of the privilege . . . must claim it" at the time he relies on it. *Murphy.*

That requirement ensures that the Government is put on notice when a witness intends to rely on the privilege so that it may either argue that the testimony sought could not be self-incriminating, or cure any potential self-incrimination through a grant of immunity. The express invocation requirement also gives courts tasked with evaluating a Fifth Amendment claim a contemporaneous record establishing the witness' reasons for refusing to answer. In these ways, insisting that witnesses expressly invoke the privilege assures that the Government obtains all the information to which it is entitled.

Justice Alito noted two recognized exceptions to the invocation requirement: 1) Griffin v. California, supra, holding that a criminal defendant need not take the stand and assert the privilege at his own trial; and 2) "we have held that a witness' failure to invoke the privilege must be excused where governmental coercion makes his forfeiture of the privilege involuntary." For this latter exception, Justice Alito cited *Miranda* and the cases holding that threats to withdraw a government benefit for being silent constitute compulsion, e.g., Lefkowitz v. Turley, supra. Justice Alito concluded that Salinas could not come within the exceptions because

it is undisputed that his interview with police was voluntary. \* \* \* That places petitioner's situation outside the scope of *Miranda* and other cases in which we have held that various forms of governmental coercion prevented defendants from voluntarily invoking the privilege. \* \* \* The critical question is whether, under the circumstance of this case, petitioner was deprived of the ability to voluntarily invoke the Fifth Amendment. He was not. We have before us no allegation that petitioner's failure to assert the privilege was involuntary, and it would have been a simple matter for him to say that he was not answering the officer's question on Fifth Amendment grounds. Because he failed to do so, the prosecution's use of his noncustodial silence did not violate the Fifth Amendment.

Justice Alito declined Salinas's invitation to establish a new exception to the Fifth Amendment invocation requirement—for cases "in which a witness stands mute and thereby declines to give an answer that officials suspect would be incriminating." Justice Alito declared that such an exception "would needlessly burden the Government's interests in obtaining testimony and prosecuting criminal activity" and would be inconsistent with *Murphy,* where the Court held "that the express invocation requirement applies even when an official has reason to suspect that the answer to his question would incriminate the witness." He further analyzed the possibility of an "under suspicion" exception to the invocation requirement in the following passage:

> In support of their proposed exception to the invocation requirement, petitioner and the dissent argue that reliance on the Fifth Amendment privilege is the most likely explanation for silence in a case such as this one. But whatever the most probable explanation, such silence is insolubly ambiguous. To be sure, someone might decline to answer a police officer's question in reliance on his constitutional privilege. But he also might do so because he is trying to think of a good lie, because he is embarrassed, or because he is protecting someone else. Not every such possible explanation for silence is probative of guilt, but neither is every possible explanation protected by the Fifth Amendment. Petitioner alone knew why he did not answer the officer's question, and it was therefore his burden to make a timely assertion of the privilege.

Justice Alito rejected Salinas's argument that an invocation requirement was unfair to suspects who are not schooled in the law—and who might think that being silent is the best way to invoke the Fifth Amendment right to silence:

> [P]opular misconceptions notwithstanding, the Fifth Amendment * * * does not establish an unqualified "right to remain silent." A witness' constitutional right to refuse to answer questions depends on his reasons for doing so, and courts need to know those reasons to evaluate the merits of a Fifth Amendment claim.
>
> In any event, it is settled that forfeiture of the privilege against self-incrimination need not be knowing. Statements against interest are regularly admitted into evidence at criminal trials, see Fed. Rule of Evid. 804(b)(3), and there is no good reason to approach a defendant's silence any differently.

Finally, Justice Alito rejected the argument that an invocation requirement in the context of noncustodial police questioning would be too difficult to apply:

> Petitioner and the dissent suggest that our approach will "unleash complicated and persistent litigation" over what a suspect must say to invoke the privilege, but our cases have long required that a witness assert the privilege to subsequently benefit from it.

That rule has not proved difficult to apply. * * * Notably, petitioner's approach would produce its own line-drawing problems, as this case vividly illustrates. When the interviewing officer asked petitioner if his shotgun would match the shell casings found at the crime scene, petitioner did not merely remain silent; he made movements that suggested surprise and anxiety. At precisely what point such reactions transform "silence" into expressive conduct would be a difficult and recurring question that our decision allows us to avoid.

* * * Petitioner worries that officers could unduly pressure suspects into talking by telling them that their silence could be used in a future prosecution. But as petitioner himself concedes, police officers have done nothing wrong when they accurately state the law. * * * So long as police do not deprive a witness of the ability to voluntarily invoke the privilege, there is no Fifth Amendment violation.

Justice Thomas, joined by Justice Scalia, concurred in the judgment in *Salinas*, but used a completely different theory to get to the result. Justice Thomas declared that it didn't matter whether Salinas invoked his Fifth Amendment right because even if he had done so, "the prosecutor's comments regarding his precustodial silence did not compel him to give self-incriminating testimony." Justice Thomas repeated the position that he and Justice Scalia had previously taken regarding Griffin v. California, supra, in which the Court held that the Fifth Amendment prohibits a prosecutor or judge from commenting on a defendant's failure to testify. Justice Thomas wrote as follows:

> Salinas argues that we should extend *Griffin's* no-adverse-inference rule to a defendant's silence during a precustodial interview. I have previously explained that the Court's decision in *Griffin* "lacks foundation in the Constitution's text, history, or logic" and should not be extended. I adhere to that view today.

Justice Breyer, joined by Justices Ginsburg, Sotomayor and Kagan, dissented in *Salinas*. He argued that allowing the prosecutor to comment on pre-custodial silence puts the citizen "in an impossible predicament. He must either answer the question or remain silent. If he answers the question, he may well reveal, for example, prejudicial facts, disreputable associates, or suspicious circumstances—even if he is innocent. If he remains silent, the prosecutor may well use that silence to suggest a consciousness of guilt. And if the defendant then takes the witness stand in order to explain either his speech or his silence, the prosecution may introduce, say for impeachment purposes, a prior conviction that the law would otherwise make inadmissible." Justice Breyer concluded that under the circumstances of the police interview, there was "a reasonable inference that Salinas' silence derived from an exercise of his Fifth

Amendment rights. * * * The nature of the surroundings, the switch of topic, the particular question—all suggested that the right we have and generally know we have was at issue at the critical moment here. Salinas, not being represented by counsel, would not likely have used the precise words 'Fifth Amendment' to invoke his rights because he would not likely have been aware of technical legal requirements, such as a need to identify the Fifth Amendment by name."

## 4. Waiver of the Privilege

Voluntary testimony waives the privilege for the simple reason that the person is by definition not being compelled to testify. But there are sometimes difficult questions about the scope of a waiver of the privilege.

### *Determining the Scope of a Waiver*

If a witness elects to testify, has the witness waived the privilege completely? On direct examination, the witness ordinarily can control what she says, but not on cross-examination. The usual rule is that a witness who takes the stand waives the privilege as to any subject matter within the scope of the direct examination. The witness is subject to cross-examination only to the extent necessary to fairly test the statements made upon direct examination and inferences that might be drawn from such statements.

United States v. Hearst, 563 F.2d 1331 (9th Cir.1977), involved the scope of a waiver in a famous criminal trial. The defendant was charged with bank robbery. She admitted participation, but testified that at the time of the robbery, she was under duress from members of the Symbionese Liberation Army. The court held that by so testifying she waived the privilege with respect to questions on cross-examination concerning a later period in which she allegedly lived with SLA members voluntarily. The court found that the government's questions were "reasonably related" to the subjects covered by the direct testimony. Consequently, it was not error to allow the jury to hear Hearst invoke a privilege against self-incrimination in response to the questions: *Griffin* was not violated because Hearst's invocation of the privilege was invalid.

Hearst unsuccessfully relied on Calloway v. Wainwright, 409 F.2d 59 (5th Cir.1968), a case in which the defendant testified at trial that his confession was involuntarily obtained. The *Calloway* court held that by challenging his confession, the defendant had not waived the privilege concerning the substance of the charges against him, and therefore that the prosecutor's reference to Calloway's failure to testify on these matters violated *Griffin*. Why was *Calloway* not helpful to Hearst?

### *Waiver of the Privilege at a Guilty Plea Hearing?*
### *Mitchell v. United States*

The defendant in Mitchell v. United States, 526 U.S. 314 (1999), pleaded guilty to federal charges of conspiring to distribute five or more kilograms of cocaine and of distributing cocaine. But she reserved the right to contest at sentencing the drug quantity attributable to her under the conspiracy count. One of the questions in *Mitchell* was whether the defendant had waived her Fifth Amendment privilege, insofar as sentencing was concerned, by pleading guilty and admitting to "some of" the conduct at her plea colloquy. If so, there would be no constitutional problem in penalizing her silence at sentencing. The Supreme Court, in an opinion by Justice Kennedy, held that Mitchell had not waived her privilege. Justice Kennedy's analysis of the waiver question proceeded as follows:

> It is well established that a witness, in a single proceeding, may not testify voluntarily about a subject and then invoke the privilege against self-incrimination when questioned about the details. The privilege is waived for the matters to which the witness testifies, and the scope of the "waiver is determined by the scope of relevant cross-examination." * * *

> The justifications for the rule of waiver in the testimonial context are evident: A witness may not pick and choose what aspects of a particular subject to discuss without casting doubt on the trustworthiness of the statements and diminishing the integrity of the factual inquiry. * * * [A] contrary rule would open the way to distortion of facts by permitting a witness to select any stopping place in the testimony. It would * * * "make of the Fifth Amendment not only a humane safeguard against judicially coerced self-disclosure but a positive invitation to mutilate the truth a party offers to tell." * * *

> We may assume for purposes of this opinion, then, that if petitioner had pleaded not guilty and, having taken the stand at a trial, testified she did "some of it," she could have been cross-examined on the frequency of her drug deliveries and the quantity of cocaine involved. The concerns which justify the cross-examination when the defendant testifies are absent at a plea colloquy, however. The purpose of a plea colloquy is to protect the defendant from an unintelligent or involuntary plea. The Government would turn this constitutional shield into a prosecutorial sword by having the defendant relinquish all rights against compelled self-incrimination upon entry of a guilty plea, including the right to remain silent at sentencing.

\* \* \* Unlike the defendant taking the stand, \* \* \* the defendant who pleads guilty puts nothing in dispute regarding the essentials of the offense. Rather, the defendant takes those matters out of dispute, often by making a joint statement with the prosecution or confirming the prosecution's version of the facts. Under these circumstances, there is little danger that the court will be misled by selective disclosure. \* \* \* Here, petitioner's statement that she had done "some of" the proffered conduct did not pose a threat to the integrity of factfinding proceedings, for the purpose of the District Court's inquiry was simply to ensure that petitioner understood the charges and that there was a factual basis for the Government's case.[5]

## *Psychiatric Defenses*

In Buchanan v. Kentucky, 483 U.S. 402 (1987), the Court found no Fifth Amendment violation in the use of a psychiatric evaluation of the defendant to rebut a psychiatric defense. Justice Blackmun wrote for the Court and stated that if the defendant presents psychiatric evidence in defense, "then, at the very least, the prosecution may rebut this presentation with evidence from the reports of the examination that the defendant requested." Thus, the Court found a waiver of Fifth Amendment rights in this circumstance. Justice Marshall, joined by Justice Brennan, dissented.

Justice Sotomayor wrote for a unanimous Court in Kansas v. Cheever, 134 S. Ct. 596 (2013), as it held that the state did not violate the defendant's privilege against self-incrimination when it used evidence from a court-ordered examination to rebut the defendant's presentation of expert testimony to support a voluntary intoxication defense. The defendant was charged with capital murder for shooting a sheriff who had come to a residence to arrest him and others for methamphetamine offenses. The defendant had cooked and smoked methamphetamine prior to the shooting and presented a pharmaceutical expert to testify that his use of the drug had rendered him incapable of premeditation. The prosecution presented testimony in rebuttal from the expert who had examined the defendant at the order of a federal judge when he was facing federal charges arising from the murder. Justice Sotomayor relied on *Buchanan* and reasoned that "[w]hen a defendant presents evidence through a psychological expert who has examined him, the government likewise is permitted to use the only effective means of challenging that evidence: testimony from an expert who has examined him." She

---

[5]   Justice Scalia, joined by the Chief Justice and Justices O'Connor and Thomas, dissented in *Mitchell*. He agreed, however, with the majority's position that Mitchell could invoke her Fifth Amendment right to silence at the sentencing proceeding. In Justice Scalia's view, while Mitchell could invoke her privilege, there was nothing in the Fifth Amendment to prohibit the sentencing judge from drawing an adverse inference from her silence. This aspect of the decision in *Mitchell* is discussed *supra* in this Chapter.

concluded that the Kansas Supreme Court had erred in limiting *Buchanan* to cases in which the defendant relies on a mental disease or defect defense and observed that *Buchanan* addressed "mental status" and covered cases like this one regardless of whether the defense is based on a temporary state of mind.

## II.   CONFESSIONS AND DUE PROCESS

### A.  INTRODUCTION

The United States Supreme Court has relied on three constitutional provisions in regulating the admissibility of confessions:

>(1) From 1936 to the present, the due process clauses of the Fifth and Fourteenth Amendments have been used to exclude *involuntary* confessions.

>(2) From 1964 to the present, the Sixth Amendment *right to counsel* has been applied in determining the admissibility of a confession obtained from a defendant who has been charged with a crime.

>(3) From 1966 to the present, the Fifth Amendment's privilege against self-incrimination has been applied to statements made during *custodial interrogation*, unless the suspect, after receiving warnings, makes a knowing and voluntary waiver of the right.

These developments have not been as smooth as this brief description might suggest. The changing nature of claims to exclude confessions and of the Court's approach to them is an important part of the development of constitutionally-based criminal procedure. Thus, it warrants careful attention.

In 1884, the Court reviewed a federal criminal conviction in Hopt v. People of Territory of Utah, 110 U.S. 574.[6] It recognized that there was a common-law rule prohibiting the use of confessions obtained by inducements, promises and threats. The common-law rule was based on the premise that confessions resulting from promises or threats are unreliable—therefore they could not be admitted into evidence. The same desire to prevent erroneous convictions led the Court to cite treatises on evidence and to follow the common-law rule. (There is no indication that the Court was relying on any constitutional language.)

Thirteen years later, in Bram v. United States, 168 U.S. 532 (1897) (suspect in custody of police was stripped, searched, and questioned), the Court abruptly departed from an emphasis on the reliability of confessions, and relied on the self-incrimination clause of the Fifth

---

[6]   This section on the background of confessions law draws heavily from O. Stephens, The Supreme Court and Confessions of Guilt 19–26 (1973).

Amendment to find that statements of an accused, which were introduced to establish his guilt, were made involuntarily and therefore admitting them at trial violated the constitutional prohibition against compelled incrimination. *Bram* was sharply criticized by a number of legal scholars as an erroneous union of the right against self-incrimination and the common-law confessions rule.[7]

The proposition that the Fifth Amendment is the proper basis on which to assess the admissibility of confessions "was not itself developed in subsequent decisions," Miranda v. Arizona, 384 U.S. 436, 506 (1966) (Harlan, J., dissenting). Although it did not overrule *Bram*, for two-thirds of a century the Court never explicitly and exclusively relied on the privilege against self-incrimination to suppress the use of a confession in another federal case. See generally, Developments in the Law: Confessions, 79 Harv.L.Rev. 935, 959–61 (1966).[8] After *Bram* and until 1964, the Court turned to the Due Process Clause to decide coerced confession cases.

For an argument that the Fifth Amendment, rather than the Due Process Clause, is the better source for regulating police-induced confessions, see Godsey, Rethinking the Involuntary Confessions Rule: Toward a Workable Test for Identifying Compelled Self-Incrimination, 93 Calif. L. Rev. 465 (2005).

## B. THE DUE PROCESS CASES

### *The Involuntariness Test: Brown v. Mississippi*

The Court made its first important decision on confessions under the Due Process Clause of the Fourteenth Amendment in Brown v. Mississippi, 297 U.S. 278 (1936). The facts surrounding the Brown case indicate why the Supreme Court found it necessary to invoke due process to regulate confessions. The facts below are quoted from the dissenting opinion of Judge Griffith in the Mississippi state court; Judge Griffin dissented from the majority's decision that a confession obtained through torture was admissible because the Fifth Amendment protection against compelled self-incrimination was not applicable to the States:

> The crime with which these defendants, all ignorant negroes, are charged, was discovered about one o'clock p.m. on Friday, March 30, 1934. On that night one Dial, a deputy sheriff, accompanied by others, came to the home of Ellington, one of the defendants, and requested him to accompany them to the house of the deceased, and

---

[7]  See, e.g., 3 J. Wigmore, Evidence § 823 (Chadbourn Rev. 1981).

[8]  The Court could not rely on *Bram* in reviewing state confession cases until 1964 when the Fifth Amendment's self-incrimination clause was incorporated into the Fourteenth Amendment and thereby made applicable to the states.

there a number of white men were gathered, who began to accuse the defendant of the crime. Upon his denial they seized him, and with the participation of the deputy they hanged him by a rope to the limb of a tree, and having let him down, they hung him again, and when he was let down the second time, and he still protested his innocence, he was tied to a tree and whipped, and still declining to accede to the demands that he confess, he was finally released and he returned with some difficulty to his home, suffering intense pain and agony. The record of the testimony shows that the signs of the rope on his neck were plainly visible during the so-called trial. A day or two thereafter the said deputy, accompanied by another, returned to the home of the said defendant and arrested him, and departed with the prisoner towards the jail in an adjoining county, but went by a route which led into the State of Alabama; and while on the way, in that State, the deputy stopped and again severely whipped the defendant, declaring that he would continue the whipping until he confessed, and the defendant then agreed to confess to such a statement as the deputy would dictate, and he did so, after which he was delivered to jail.

The other two defendants, Ed Brown and Henry Shields, were also arrested and taken to the same jail. On Sunday night, April 1, 1934, the same deputy, accompanied by a number of white men, one of whom was also an officer, and by the jailer, came to the jail, and the two last named defendants were made to strip and they were laid over chairs and their backs were cut to pieces with a leather strap with buckles on it, and they were likewise made by the said deputy definitely to understand that the whipping would be continued unless and until they confessed, and not only confessed, but confessed in every matter of detail as demanded by those present; and in this manner the defendants confessed the crime, and as the whippings progressed and were repeated, they changed or adjusted their confession in all particulars of detail so as to conform to the demands of their torturers. When the confessions had been obtained in the exact form and contents as desired by the mob, they left with the parting admonition and warning that, if the defendants changed their story at any time in any respect from that last stated, the perpetrators of the outrage would administer the same or equally effective treatment.

* * *

The defendants were brought to the courthouse of the county on * * * April 5th, and the so-called trial was opened, and was concluded on the next day, April 6, 1934, and resulted in a pretended conviction with death sentences. The evidence upon which the conviction was obtained was the so-called confessions. * * *. The defendants were put on the stand, and by their testimony the facts and the details thereof as to the manner by which the confessions were extorted from them were fully developed, and it is further disclosed by the record that the same deputy, Dial, under whose guiding hand and active participation the tortures to coerce the confessions were administered, was actively in the performance of the supposed duties of a court deputy in the courthouse and in the presence of the prisoners during what is denominated, in complimentary terms, the trial of these defendants. This deputy was put on the stand by the state in rebuttal, and admitted the whippings. It is interesting to note that in his testimony with reference to the whipping of the defendant Ellington, and in response to the inquiry as to how severely he was whipped, the deputy stated, "Not too much for a negro; not as much as I would have done if it were left to me." Two others who had participated in these whippings were introduced and admitted it—not a single witness was introduced who denied it.

So the defendants in *Brown* were sentenced to death, within a week of the crime, on the basis of confessions obtained by torture. One would think that if due process is to mean anything, it must mean that it was violated under the facts of *Brown*. And that is how the Supreme Court saw it. The Court declared as follows:

> The rack and torture chamber may not be substituted for the witness stand. The State may not permit an accused to be hurried to conviction under mob domination—where the whole proceeding is but a mask—without supplying corrective process. * * * [The trial] is a mere pretense where the state authorities have contrived a conviction resting solely upon confessions obtained by violence. The due process clause requires that state action, whether through one agency or another, shall be consistent with the fundamental principles of liberty and justice which lie at the base of all our civil and political institutions. It would be difficult to conceive of methods more revolting to the sense of justice than those taken to procure the confessions of these petitioners, and the use of the confessions thus obtained as the basis for conviction and sentence was a clear denial of due process.

The Court decided thirty-five confession cases between *Brown* in 1936 and Massiah v. United States, 377 U.S. 201, in 1964. It struggled in the ensuing cases—which involved more subtle and less physical methods of obtaining confessions—to define appropriate constitutional limitations on the interrogation methods used by police. Case-by-difficult-case, the Court attempted to describe the reach of the Due Process Clause, and its role in controlling the methods by which government agents seek confessions.

### Pre-Miranda Cases: Circumstances Relevant to Involuntariness

A summary, by no means exhaustive, might convey the breadth of circumstances—with none being dispositive—that the Court considered when it tried to determine the validity of confessions under the Due Process Clause:

- *The personal characteristics of the accused.* The Court was concerned not only with the youthfulness of the suspect, but also with the educational background of the accused in cases such as Payne v. Arkansas, 356 U.S. 560 (1958)(fifth grade education), and Fikes v. Alabama, 352 U.S. 191 (1957)(illiterate). In addition, the Court was sensitive to any mental deficiency of the defendant as illustrated by Culombe v. Connecticut, 367 U.S. 568, 620 (1961)(illiterate mental defective), and Blackburn v. Alabama, 361 U.S. 199, 207 (1960)(strong probability that the accused was insane at the time he allegedly confessed). Conversely, the Court was less likely to find undue coercion if the defendant was well-educated as in Crooker v. California, 357 U.S. 433 (1958)(accused had completed one year of law school), or was a hardened veteran of criminal proceedings as in Stein v. New York, 346 U.S. 156, 185 (1953)(defendants were not "young, soft, ignorant or timid").

- *Physical deprivation or mistreatment.* The Court not only disapproved of severe brutality like that found in *Brown,* supra, but also of the denial of food, *Payne,* supra (accused was given no food for twenty-four hours), or sleep, Ashcraft v. Tennessee, 322 U.S. 143 (1944) (defendant was not permitted to sleep for thirty-six hours). If the accused was permitted certain amenities, the Court responded favorably. In *Crooker,* supra, for instance, the confession was found admissible and the Court pointed out that the defendant was provided with food and was permitted to smoke during interrogations.

- *Psychological pressure.* Use of threats, humiliation, isolation, etc., was accorded great weight by the Court. Although the Court stated that a voluntary statement need not be volunteered, it refused to hold that only physical brutality was impermissible. In Watts v. Indiana, 338 U.S. 49, 53 (1949), the Court said that:

> if [the confession] is the product of sustained pressure by the police it does not issue from a free choice. When a suspect speaks because he is overborne, it is immaterial whether he has been subjected to a physical or mental ordeal. Eventual yielding to questioning under such circumstances is plainly the product of the suction process of interrogation and therefore the reverse of voluntary.

In *Watts,* as in Haley v. Ohio, 332 U.S. 596 (1948), the Court paid special attention to whether the accused was denied the aid of family, friends, or counsel. Incommunicado confinement consistently was viewed as an element of coercion. Another form of psychological influence was trickery, though this was only one factor in the due process calculus. See generally White, Police Trickery in Inducing Confessions, 127 U.Pa.L.Rev. 581 (1979).

The Court recognized the pressure inherent in such psychological techniques as sustained interrogation, *Ashcraft,* supra, and the threat of mob violence, *Payne,* supra (defendant was told thirty to forty people would be waiting to get him unless he confessed). The Court also was concerned about rewards and inducements to confess, which had been condemned in *Hopt,* supra. New techniques as well as old were carefully scrutinized. For example, in Leyra v. Denno, 347 U.S. 556 (1954), the Court took exception to the use of a trained psychiatrist to extract a confession through skillful and suggestive questioning.

• *Warnings.* Finally, the Court considered—as one factor in the totality—whether the accused was aware or had been apprised of his right to remain silent and the possibility of obtaining legal counsel.

It should be apparent from this overview that the voluntariness standard required a case-by-case scrutiny of the circumstances surrounding a particular confession to determine if the methods by which it was obtained comported with due process. The Court considered both the police conduct in procuring the confession and the defendant's ability to withstand coercion; therefore, the "totality of the circumstances" was determinative of the voluntariness of the confession.

### Criticism of the Involuntariness Test

Although the Court refined its analysis of the voluntariness test in the course of deciding over 30 full-length opinions under the due process standard, some members of the Court recognized the shortcomings of the totality-of-circumstances voluntariness approach. Justice Frankfurter, a supporter of the due process standard, noted in *Culombe* that "[n]o single litmus-paper test for constitutionally impermissible interrogations has been evolved." The word "voluntary" hardly offered clear guidance to law enforcement officers and to lower court judges. It had to be applied anew in every case. Because the Court could not possibly pass on all of the confession cases in which review was sought, usually certiorari was limited to death penalty cases or others of special concern. That the Justices themselves often disagreed on the proper application of the test compounded the problem.

The totality of circumstances test gave little guidance to the police. For example, the instruction "don't overbear the will of the suspect" has little defined content outside the realm of physical force. Professor Schulhofer has criticized the indeterminacy of the involuntariness test in the following passage:

> In theory, brutality is ruled out by the due process test * * * but in operation the due process test sends police a fatally mixed message. The job of the interrogator, of course, is to get the reticent suspect to "come clean." When a tired, confused, or shaky prisoner shows signs of starting to "crack," is the interrogator supposed to keep up the pressure, or back off to avoid breaking the suspect's will? In effect, under the due process test, the officer is expected to do both. Instances of overbearing coercion are bound to occur under such a system, not because some officers will deliberately flout the law but because even the best of professionals will inevitably misjudge the elusive psychological line.

Schulhofer, *Miranda's* Practical Effect: Substantial Benefits and Vanishingly Small Costs, 90 Nw. Univ.L.Rev. 500 (1996).

### Increasing Emphasis on Assistance of Counsel: Spano v. New York

The growing dissatisfaction of certain members of the Court with the voluntariness standard became very apparent in Spano v. New York, 360 U.S. 315 (1959). Four concurring justices expressed more concern about the fact that the defendant Spano had been indicted and was refused permission to see his attorney than about the "voluntariness" of the confession under the totality of the circumstances. Spano, a 25-year old immigrant with a junior high school education, shot a person after a bar fight. He left the scene and disappeared for a week or so, and was indicted for murder during this period. The facts surrounding Spano's confession were set forth by Chief Justice Warren as follows:

> On February 3, 1957, petitioner called one Gaspar Bruno, a close friend of [Spano] who had attended school with him. Bruno was a fledgling police officer, having at that time not yet finished attending police academy. According to Bruno's testimony, petitioner told him "that he took a terrific beating, that the deceased hurt him real bad and he dropped him a couple of times and he was dazed; he didn't know what he was doing and that he went and shot at him." Petitioner told Bruno that he intended to get a lawyer and give himself up. Bruno relayed this information to his superiors.

> The following day, February 4, at 7:10 p.m., petitioner, accompanied by counsel, surrendered himself to the authorities * * *. His attorney had cautioned him to answer no questions, and left him

in the custody of the officers. He was promptly taken to the office of the Assistant District Attorney and at 7:15 p.m. the questioning began, being conducted by Assistant District Attorney Goldsmith, Lt. Gannon, Detectives Farrell, Lehrer and Motta, and Sgt. Clarke. The record reveals that the questioning was both persistent and continuous. Petitioner, in accordance with his attorney's instructions, steadfastly refused to answer. * * * He asked one officer, Detective Ciccone, if he could speak to his attorney, but that request was denied. Detective Ciccone testified that he could not find the attorney's name in the telephone book. He was given two sandwiches, coffee and cake at 11 p.m.

At 12:15 a.m. on the morning of February 5, after five hours of questioning in which it became evident that petitioner was following his attorney's instructions, on the Assistant District Attorney's orders petitioner was transferred to the 46th Squad, Ryer Avenue Police Station. The Assistant District Attorney also went to the police station and to some extent continued to participate in the interrogation. Petitioner arrived at 12:30 and questioning was resumed at 12:40. * * * But petitioner persisted in his refusal to answer, and again requested permission to see his attorney, this time from Detective Lehrer. His request was again denied.

It was then that those in charge of the investigation decided that petitioner's close friend, Bruno, could be of use. * * * Although, in fact, his job was in no way threatened, Bruno was told to tell petitioner that petitioner's telephone call had gotten him "in a lot of trouble," and that he should seek to extract sympathy from petitioner for Bruno's pregnant wife and three children. Bruno developed this theme with petitioner without success, and petitioner, also without success, again sought to see his attorney, a request which Bruno relayed unavailingly to his superiors. After this first session with petitioner, Bruno was again directed by Lt. Gannon to play on petitioner's sympathies, but again no confession was forthcoming. But the Lieutenant a third time ordered Bruno falsely to importune his friend to confess, but again petitioner clung to his attorney's advice. Inevitably, in the fourth such session directed by the Lieutenant, lasting a full hour, petitioner succumbed to his friend's prevarications and agreed to make a statement. Accordingly, at 3:25 a.m. the Assistant District Attorney, a stenographer, and several other law enforcement officials entered the room where petitioner was being questioned, and took his statement in question and answer form with the Assistant District Attorney asking the questions. The statement was completed at 4:05 a.m.

But this was not the end. At 4:30 a.m. three detectives took petitioner to Police Headquarters in Manhattan. On the way they attempted to find the bridge from which petitioner said he had thrown the murder weapon. They crossed the Triborough Bridge into Manhattan, arriving at Police Headquarters at 5 a.m., and left Manhattan for the Bronx at 5:40 a.m. via the Willis Avenue Bridge. When petitioner recognized neither bridge as the one from which he had thrown the weapon, they reentered Manhattan via the Third Avenue Bridge, which petitioner stated was the right one, and then returned to the Bronx well after 6 a.m. During that trip the officers also elicited a statement from petitioner that the deceased was always "on [his] back," "always pushing" him and that he was "not sorry" he had shot the deceased. All three detectives testified to that statement at the trial.

Spano argued that his *Sixth Amendment* right to counsel was violated when he was interrogated, despite his repeated request for counsel, after he had been formally charged with the crime. Chief Justice Warren found it unnecessary to decide the Sixth Amendment's applicability, because the use of Spano's confessions was "inconsistent with the Fourteenth Amendment under traditional principles." The Chief Justice surveyed the law governing involuntary confessions:

> The abhorrence of society to the use of involuntary confessions does not turn alone on their inherent untrustworthiness. It also turns on the deep-rooted feeling that the police must obey the law while enforcing the law; that in the end life and liberty can be as much endangered from illegal methods used to convict those thought to be criminals as from the actual criminals themselves. * * * The facts of no case recently in this Court have quite approached the brutal beatings in Brown v. Mississippi, or the 36 consecutive hours of questioning present in Ashcraft v. Tennessee, 322 U.S. 143 (1944). But as law enforcement officers become more responsible, and the methods used to extract confessions more sophisticated, our duty to enforce federal constitutional protections does not cease. It only becomes more difficult because of the more delicate judgments to be made.

The Court found that the following factors in their totality constituted substantial police misconduct that caused an involuntary confession: 1) Spano was young, foreign-born, relatively uneducated, emotionally unstable, and inexperienced in the criminal justice system; 2) Spano "did not make a narrative statement, but was subject to the leading questions of a skillful prosecutor in a question and answer confession"; 3) he was questioned virtually incessantly by a number of officers, throughout the night; 4) the questioning "persisted in the face of his repeated refusals to answer on the advice of his attorney"; 5) the officers "ignored his reasonable requests to contact the local attorney whom he had already retained and who had personally delivered him into the custody of these officers"; and 6) the officers used Bruno, Spano's friend to extract the confession by using false statements.

Justice Douglas, joined by Justice Black and Justice Brennan, wrote a concurring opinion that emphasized the officers' denial of Spano's request for counsel:

> We have often divided on whether state authorities may question a suspect for hours on end when he has no lawyer present and when he has demanded that he have the benefit of legal advice. But here we deal not with a suspect but with a man who has been formally charged with a crime. The question is whether after the indictment and before the trial the Government can interrogate the accused *in secret* when he asked for his lawyer and when his request was denied. * * * Depriving a person, formally charged with a crime, of counsel during the period prior to trial may be more damaging than denial of counsel during the trial itself.

Justice Stewart, joined by Justice Douglas and Justice Brennan wrote a separate concurring opinion that also emphasized the right to counsel:

> Our Constitution guarantees the assistance of counsel to a man on trial for his life in an orderly courtroom, presided over by a judge, open to the public, and protected by all the procedural safeguards of the law. Surely a Constitution which promises that much can vouchsafe no less to the same man under midnight inquisition in the squad room of a police station.

### The Importance of Spano

The concurring Justices in *Spano* believed that once a person is formally charged by an indictment or information, his constitutional right to counsel begins, at least when counsel previously has been retained. Although the majority of the Court analyzed the confession under the traditional voluntariness standard, the majority did not reject the views expressed in the concurring opinions. It left the counsel question for another day, which was not long in coming, as we shall soon see. Thus, while *Spano* is a due process case, it provided a doctrinal bridge for the Court to consider the applicability of other constitutional limitations on police efforts to obtain confessions.

### The Continuing Relevance of Due Process Protection

Despite the Court's eventual regulation of confessions through the Sixth Amendment in *Massiah* and through the Fifth Amendment in *Miranda* (both discussed later in this Chapter), the totality of the circumstances voluntariness test is in some cases a suspect's only protection from police coercion. The Sixth Amendment does not apply until the suspect has been formally charged (Moran v. Burbine, infra). *Miranda* applies only during police "custodial interrogation," and that term does not cover all potentially coercive police practices. See United States v. Murphy, 763 F.2d 202 (6th Cir.1985) (sending an attack dog to apprehend the suspect is not custodial interrogation, but confession made while dog was attacking held involuntary); United States v. Lall, 607 F.3d 1277 (11th Cir. 2010) ("Even if Lall was not in custody (and thus *Miranda* warnings were not required), we would still be required to address the voluntariness of his confession."). Moreover, *Miranda* and Sixth Amendment rights can be waived, while the right to be free from coercion cannot (nobody argues, for example, that the defendants in Brown v. Mississippi could have waived the right to be free from physical beating). Thus, if the defendant has made a valid waiver of *Miranda* (and, if applicable, Sixth Amendment) rights, his only protection from subsequent police pressure is the due process involuntariness test. See, e.g., United States v. Astello, 241 F.3d 965 (8th Cir. 2001) (court considers whether confession was involuntary after the defendant made a valid waiver of *Miranda* rights). Finally, the Court has found several exceptions to *Miranda*, so that a *Miranda*-defective confession can be used for impeachment (Harris v. New York, infra), the fruits of such a confession are generally admissible (Oregon v. Elstad, infra), and the confession itself can be admitted if obtained under emergency circumstances (New York v. Quarles, infra). However, even where *Miranda* and *Massiah* are inapplicable, the confession is still excluded under the Due Process Clause if obtained through police coercion. Thus, the due process involuntariness test retains vitality today, and cases are still being decided under that doctrine.

### *Modern Due Process Cases*

It is the rare and extreme case, however, in which a court will find that a suspect confessed involuntarily. See White, Interrogation Without Questions, 78 Mich.L.Rev. 1209 (1980). Examples of cases denying involuntariness claims are Sumpter v. Nix, 863 F.2d 563 (8th Cir.1988) (suspect with I.Q. of 89 and psychological problems, promised treatment, and interrogated for more than seven hours); McCall v. Dutton, 863 F.2d 454 (6th Cir.1988) (defendant was wounded, and officers interrogated with guns drawn); Moore v. Dugger, 856 F.2d 129 (11th Cir.1988) (suspect with an I.Q. of 62, who functioned at the level of an 11-year old, had been without food or sleep for 25 hours at the time he confessed); and United States v. Kelley, 953 F.2d 562 (9th Cir.1992) (suspect confessed while handcuffed and suffering from heroin withdrawal).

Grano, Voluntariness, Free Will, and the Law of Confessions, 65 Va.L.Rev. 859 (1979), argues that an involuntary confession is "any confession produced by interrogation pressures that a person of reasonable firmness, with some of the defendant's characteristics, would not resist." How would *Spano* be resolved under this standard?

Others have argued that a confession is involuntary only where police tactics are such as would force an innocent person to confess. This is a reflection of the premise of some scholars that "the Constitution seeks to protect the innocent." Amar, The Constitution and Criminal Procedure: First Principles 154 (1997). This would mean that threats of harm, and physical violence, would be prohibited, but tactics that could be used to trick a person to confess (e.g., false expressions of sympathy, or understating the significance of the crime) would be permitted.

### *Deception and False Promises by the Police*

What effect does the use of police deception and similar psychological ploys have on the voluntariness inquiry? The Court in *Bram* had stated that a confession induced by "any direct or implied promises, however slight" must be suppressed. But courts have not followed that language from *Bram*.

For example, in Green v. Scully, 850 F.2d 894 (2d Cir.1988), Green was taken to the station by two New York detectives to be interrogated as a murder suspect. He waived his *Miranda* rights. Thereafter, Detective Byrnes threatened him with the electric chair, even though there was at that time no capital punishment in New York. Then Byrnes left the room. During a lengthy interrogation, Detective Hazel consistently asserted that the police had all the evidence they needed to convict Green, stating that he had personally checked it out. This was false. When Green stated that he would never confess because he would not be able to face his and the victim's families, Hazel said he could help Green with that and suggested that Green must have been mentally ill when he committed the murder. Hazel referred to Green as "brother" and said that he would try to get psychiatric help for Green. Then Hazel took a different tack, appeared frustrated, and threatened to leave the interrogation over to the "bad cop," Byrnes. Byrnes then came in and stated that he had found Green's palm prints at the scene, with blood stains on them. This was not true. Byrnes told Green that he was lucky that Hazel was there, because Hazel cared about him while Byrnes did not. Green then began to consider cooperating, after again receiving assurance from Hazel that he would obtain psychiatric help and would avoid capital punishment. In the course of his confession, Green stated that he suffered from blackouts, that he was confessing out of fear that if he were not convicted of this crime he might kill someone else, and that confessing would be the only way to obtain psychiatric help.

The court held that the confession was voluntary. It concluded that despite *Bram,* "the presence of a direct or implied promise of help or leniency alone has not barred the admission of a confession" and that "promises do not require an analysis separate from or different than the totality of circumstances rule." The court found that Green was of above average intelligence and streetwise, that the interrogation session was only two hours long, and that Green was not handcuffed or in pain during that time. As to the psychological tactics, the court found the police conduct "troubling." But the use of these tactics was not enough to taint the confession, in part because Green had his own motivation for confessing.

> [T]he scare tactics, false representation as to the evidence, good cop/bad cop routine, and whatever hopes were instilled from the promises or fears from the reference to the "chair" considered together did not overbear Green's will and bring about his confession. He confessed—as he candidly admitted—because he was afraid that what he had done to the victims in a blackout would be something he was going to do to his own family—maybe even his mother.

Did the court overlook the fact that Green confessed not precisely to take himself "off the street," but because in doing so he would obtain psychiatric help? See generally White, Confessions Induced by Broken Government Promises, 43 Duke L.J. 947 (1994).

A leading interrogation manual, authored by Inbau, Reid and Buckley, argues the merits of deceptive interrogation techniques in leading to confessions. The techniques they recommend include:

- showing fake sympathy for the suspect by acting like his friend (e.g., by falsely telling a rape suspect that the officer himself had once "roughed it up" with a girl in an attempt to have intercourse with her);

- reducing the suspect's feelings of guilt through lies (e.g., by telling a person suspected of killing his wife that he was not as "lucky" as the officer, who at one time was just about to "pound" his wife when the doorbell rang);

- exaggerating the crime in an effort to get the suspect to negotiate, or in hopes of obtaining a denial which will indirectly inculpate the suspect (e.g., accusing the suspect of stealing $40,000 when only $20,000 is involved, or accusing the suspect of murder where the victim, while shot, survived the incident);

- lying that implies that "the game is up" because the evidence is so strong (e.g., stating that the suspect was identified at the scene when in fact he was not); and

- playing one codefendant against another (e.g., leading one to believe the other has confessed when no confession has occurred).

Inbau, Reid & Buckley, Criminal Interrogation and Confessions 98–132 (3rd ed. 1986).

Tactics such as these are routinely permitted by the courts in applying the voluntariness test. See, e.g., Frazier v. Cupp, 394 U.S. 731 (1969) (use of "false friend" and "game is up" techniques, although relevant to the due process inquiry, were not sufficient to render the confession involuntary); United States v. Whitfield, 695 F.3d 288 (4th Cir. 2012) (officers' misrepresentation about the offenses they were investigating—allowing the defendant to believe that he was only being investigated for a minor crime—did not render the defendant's confession involuntary: "we are satisfied that Whitfield's capacity for self-determination was not critically impaired by Sergeant Reynolds's misrepresentations."); Miller v. Fenton, 796 F.2d 598 (3d Cir. 1986) (use of "false friend" technique, together with a ruse that the victim had not died when in fact she had, does not render confession involuntary). See also Young, Unnecessary Evil: Police Lying in Interrogations, 28 Conn. L.Rev. 425 (1996) (providing citations to lower court cases refusing to exclude confessions obtained after the suspect was exposed to lies about matters such as the strength of the case, fabricated evidence, suggestions that the suspect was not at fault, and lies about the identity of the interrogator).

Are deception techniques permitted because the courts tacitly assume that suspects are not naive enough to believe that police will tell them the absolute truth during an interrogation? After all, it is an interrogation, not a picnic, right? But if suspects anticipate police mendacity, what good are these deceptive practices? See Paris, Trust, Lies and Interrogation, 3 Va.J.Soc.Pol. & L. 3 (1995) (arguing for a rule prohibiting police from lying, on the ground that such a rule would lead to more reliable confessions, not less: "suspects would be able to relax their guard if assured that lying interrogators would be punished" and will be more prone "to trust their interrogators and confess in situations in which confessions will serve their interests").

For a case where police deception was found to cause an involuntary confession, see Aleman v. Village of Hanover Park, 662 F.3d 897 (7th cir. 2011), in which Aleman, who ran a day care home, sued police officers who extracted a confession from him about the death of a child. (Aleman was charged and incarcerated but eventually released—because the evidence actually showed that the child's mother had beaten the child severely before dropping him off at Aleman's day care home). Aleman had shaken the child in an attempt to revive him.   During Aleman's interrogation, an officer falsely reported that a medical report indicated the child's death was caused by shaking—when in fact the medical doctors had not excluded other possibilities. Aleman responded that "if the only way to cause [the injuries] is to shake that baby, then, when I shook that baby, I hurt that baby." Judge Posner explained why this statement was involuntary:

> Courts have been reluctant to deem trickery by police a basis for excluding a confession on the ground that the tricks made the confession coerced and thus involuntary. * * * The confession must be excluded only if the government feeds the defendant false information that seriously distorts his choice * * * in other words, only if the false statement destroyed the information that he required for a rational choice.

> In this case a false statement did destroy the information required for a rational choice. Not being a medical expert, Aleman could not contradict what was represented to him as settled medical opinion. He had shaken Joshua, albeit gently; but if medical opinion excluded any other possible cause of the child's death, then, gentle as the shaking was, and innocently intended, it *must* have been the cause of death. Aleman had no rational basis, given his ignorance of medical science, to deny that he had to have been the cause.

What is the difference between falsely reporting medical evidence— found coercive in *Aleman*—and falsely reporting that eyewitnesses saw the defendant at the scene of the crime, which is a trick that is routinely permitted?

### *False Documentary Evidence*

In Florida v. Cayward, 552 So.2d 971 (Fla.App.1989), police fabricated a scientific report for use as a ploy in interrogating the defendant. The report was prepared on stationery of Lifecodes, Inc., a DNA testing service, and it indicated that DNA testing showed that bodily fluids on the victim came from the defendant. The defendant confessed when shown the false report. The court found the resulting confession involuntary, reasoning as follows:

> The reporters are filled with examples of police making false verbal assertions to a suspect, but * * * we perceive an intrinsic distinction between verbal assertions and manufactured documentation. * * * It may well be that a suspect is more impressed and thereby more easily induced to confess when presented with tangible, official-looking reports as opposed to merely being told that some tests have implicated him. In addition to our spontaneous distaste for the conduct we have reviewed in this matter, we have practical concerns regarding the use of the false reports beyond the inducement of a confession. Unlike oral misrepresentations,

manufactured documents have the potential of indefinite life and the facial appearance of authenticity. * * * Such reports have the potential of finding their way into the courtroom.

Do you agree that there is a per se distinction between false verbal statements and false documentary evidence? Is the distinction that an innocent person may shrug off an officer's verbal statement that the suspect's DNA was found at the scene, whereas even an innocent person might have to think about confessing where the forensic test apparently incriminates him?

### Honest Promises vs. False Promises

The fact that an interrogating officer makes a promise does not mean that it is necessarily a false promise. Judge Posner, in United States v. Baldwin, 60 F.3d 363 (7th Cir.1995), had this to say about a confession obtained after a police officer's promise to the defendant that any cooperation by him would be brought to the prosecutor's attention:

> A false promise of lenience would be an example of forbidden tactics, for it would impede the suspect in making an informed choice as to whether he was better off confessing or clamming up. But government is not forbidden to buy information with honest promises of consideration. And as it is well known that the suspect's cooperation, by lightening the government's burdens of investigation and prosecution, is looked upon favorably by prosecutors and judges, what the agent told the defendant was very close to a truism; * * * and the defendant was not a tyro or ignoramus, but a 39-year-old with a long history of involvement in the criminal justice system.

See also United States v. Fraction, 795 F.2d 12 (3d Cir. 1986) (officer promises to relate the fact of the suspect's cooperation to the prosecutor, but does not represent that he has authority to affect the outcome of the case; confession voluntary). But as Judge Posner recognizes, there will be a due process concern when the officer makes a *specific* promise that the defendant's statement will not be used against him or that he will get a specific benefit for confessing, and then such a promise is not kept. See, e.g., United States v. Walton, 10 F.3d 1024 (3d Cir. 1993) (confession involuntary where the officer, a long-time friend of the defendant, promises to keep a conversation "off the record" and then does not do so); United States v. Lall, 607 F.3d 1277 (11th Cir. 2010) (officer stated that anything the defendant said would not be used to prosecute him; admission of defendant's confession in response violated the defendant's due process rights).

## Threats of Physical Violence: Arizona v. Fulminante

Justice White wrote for a majority in Arizona v. Fulminante, 499 U.S. 279 (1991), as it found that a confession made by a prisoner to an informant—when made to ward off a threat of physical violence—was coerced and thus involuntary under the Fifth and Fourteenth Amendments. Fulminante was suspected of murdering his stepdaughter in Arizona, but had not been arrested or charged before he was incarcerated in New Jersey on an unrelated firearms conviction. He became friends with another inmate who was a paid informant for the FBI and who masqueraded as an organized crime figure. When the informant learned that Fulminante was suspected of killing a child, he suggested to Fulminante that he could protect him from other inmates, who did not look kindly upon suspected child killers. But this protection would be provided only if Fulminante told him the truth about what had occurred. This offer resulted in the confession, which the informant related at Fulminante's trial.

Justice White observed that the *Bram* standard, which condemned any confession obtained by any direct or implied promises, however slight, or by the exertion of any improper influence, had been replaced by a *totality of the circumstances* test. In applying that test, he concluded that a credible threat of physical violence had existed, and that Fulminante confessed due to his misplaced hope for protection from that violence. Therefore the confession was involuntary. Justice White stressed that "a finding of coercion need not depend upon actual violence by a government agent; a credible threat is sufficient." The majority analogized Fulminante's plight to that of the defendant in Payne v. Arkansas, supra, where the Court found a confession to be coerced when an interrogating officer threatened that unless Payne confessed, the officer would leave him to an angry mob just outside the jailhouse door.

Chief Justice Rehnquist, joined by Justices O'Connor, Kennedy, and Souter, dissented. He emphasized that Fulminante offered no evidence that he believed his life was in danger or that he confessed to obtain protection.

After *Fulminante,* is a credible threat of physical violence a per se factor? If so, why is it different from a threat of the electric chair, as in *Green,* or an assertion that the suspect's fingerprints were found at the scene? Is the distinction that even an innocent person might confess to avoid a beating?

### *Focus on Police Misconduct Causing the Confession to be Made: Colorado v. Connelly*

The Supreme Court held in Colorado v. Connelly, 479 U.S. 157 (1986), that the due process focus is primarily on *police misconduct* rather than the suspect's state of mind. Connelly approached a uniformed officer on the street and stated that he had murdered someone and wanted to talk about it. The officer warned Connelly that he had the right to remain silent, that anything he said could be used against him in court, and that he had a right to an attorney before any questioning. Connelly stated that he understood his rights and wanted to talk about the murder. A homicide detective arrived and repeated the warnings. Connelly then stated that he needed to confess to the murder of a young girl whom he had killed months earlier. The officers took him to the police station, examined their records, discovered that an unidentified female body had been found, talked with Connelly concerning the murder, and took Connelly in a police car to point out the location of the crime. The next morning Connelly began to appear disoriented, and he stated that "voices" had told him to confess. He was initially found incompetent to assist in his own defense, but later was declared fit to proceed to trial.

An expert witness testified in support of Connelly's motion to suppress that at the time he confessed Connelly was experiencing "command hallucinations," which interfered with his ability to make free and rational choices. The state courts suppressed the confessions on the ground that Connelly only confessed because the voices told him to, and therefore his confession was involuntary. But the Supreme Court reversed. Writing for the Court, Chief Justice Rehnquist reasoned that the *police* applied absolutely no pressure on Connelly to confess. The state courts failed "to recognize the essential link between coercive activity of the State, on the one hand, and a resulting confession by a defendant, on the other." The Court held that "coercive police activity is a necessary predicate to the finding that a confession is not 'voluntary' within the meaning of the Due Process Clause."

The Chief Justice asserted that suppressing a statement in the absence of police coercion "would serve absolutely no purpose in enforcing constitutional guarantees" because it would not deter future police conduct.

The Court concluded as follows:

> Only if we were to establish a brand new constitutional right— the right of a criminal defendant to confess to his crime only when totally rational and properly motivated—could respondent's present claim be sustained. * * * Respondent would now have us require sweeping inquiries into the state of mind of a criminal defendant who has confessed, inquiries quite divorced from any coercion brought to

bear on the defendant by the State. We think the Constitution rightly leaves this sort of inquiry to be resolved by state laws governing the admission of evidence * * *. A statement rendered by one in the condition of respondent might be proved to be quite unreliable, but this is a matter to be governed by the evidentiary laws of the forum.

Justice Brennan, joined by Justice Marshall, dissented from this holding. He argued that the absence of police wrongdoing was not conclusive and "[t]he requirement that a confession be voluntary reflects a recognition of the importance of free will and of reliability in determining the admissibility of a confession, and thus demands an inquiry into the totality of the circumstances surrounding the confession."

The effect of *Connelly* can be seen in such cases as United States v. Erving L., 147 F.3d 1240 (10th Cir.1998), where the suspect's mother coerced him into confessing to the authorities. The court relied on *Connelly* to find no due process violation. Courts have also held after *Connelly* that it is irrelevant that the suspect was drunk, on drugs, mentally impaired, emotionally vulnerable, etc., when he confessed. As one court put it, "*Connelly* makes it clear that personal characteristics of the defendant are constitutionally irrelevant absent proof of police coercion." United States v. Rohrbach, 813 F.2d 142 (8th Cir.1987). See also United States v. Williamson, 706 F.3d 405 (4th Cir. 2013) (secretly recording the suspect's statement to an associate did not render statement involuntary because the statements were not the product of coercion).

### *Problems with a Test Based on Free Will*

Is "free will" a workable standard for confession cases? Judge Posner in United States v. Rutledge, 900 F.2d 1127 (7th Cir.1990), had this to say about the "overbearing of free will" test:

> Taken seriously it would require the exclusion of virtually all fruits of custodial interrogation, since few choices to confess can be thought truly "free" when made by a person who is incarcerated and is being questioned by * * * officers without the presence of counsel or anyone else to give him moral support. The formula is not taken seriously. *Connelly* may have driven the stake through its heart by holding that a confession which is not a product of the defendant's free choice * * * is admissible so long as whatever it was that destroyed the defendant's power of choice was not police conduct. In any event, very few incriminating statements, custodial or otherwise, are held to be involuntary, though few are the product of a choice that the interrogators left completely free.

> An alternative approach, which is implied by *Connelly* and may well describe the courts' actual as distinct from articulated standard,

is to ask whether the government has made it impossible for the defendant to make a *rational* choice as to whether to confess—has made it in other words impossible for him to weigh the pros and cons of confessing and go with the balance as it appears at the time. This approach * * * implies, for example, that if the government feeds the defendant false information that seriously distorts his choice, by promising him that if he confesses he will be set free, or if the government drugs him so that he cannot make a conscious choice at all, then the confession must go out. * * * The police are allowed to play on a suspect's ignorance, his anxieties, his fears, and his uncertainties; they just are not allowed to magnify those fears, uncertainties and so forth to the point where rational decision becomes impossible.

Is Judge Posner saying that confessions are involuntary only when police tactics are such as would cause an innocent person to confess (e.g., a statement "if you confess you go free")? Is his analysis consistent with *Fulminante*?

### Coercive Interrogation of Suspected Terrorists

After 9/11, suspected terrorists detained abroad or at Guantanamo have been subject to interrogation techniques that would be found coercive under the due process test. Examples include "waterboarding" (simulated drowning); forcing Muslim men to wear women's clothing and to disrobe in front of women; simulated dog attacks; jarring music and lighting; extended isolation; prolonged sleep deprivation; exposure to excessive cold; and food deprivation. Details on the techniques that have actually been used remain classified. Supporters of "enhanced interrogation" techniques take the position that they do not allow "torture," but that coercive techniques are necessary to crack terrorists and save lives.

Note, however, that if a person is charged with a terrorism-related crime in a civilian court, the Due Process Clause is fully applicable. See United States v. Abu Ali, 528 F.3d 210 (4th Cir. 2008) (will of defendant was not overborne during interrogation in Saudi Arabia, where defendant had responded to his interrogators' questions in Arabic, officials provided defendant with a prayer rug and the Koran among other accommodations, defendant was confined under reasonable conditions, including three meals per day, a bed, blanket and pillow, and the defendant began to confess just two days after interrogation started); In re Terrorist Bombings of U.S. Embassies, 548 F.3d 237 (2nd Cir. 2008) (confession was voluntary even though the defendant was detained incommunicado for 14 days; defendant was not abused, and he was motivated to confess by a desire to air his grievances in a United States court).

# III.   FIFTH AMENDMENT LIMITATIONS ON CONFESSIONS

As discussed above, the Court became dissatisfied with the due process-totality of the circumstances test as an exclusive means of regulating confessions. After *Spano*, the Court applied the Sixth Amendment right to counsel to exclude two confessions. Massiah v. United States, 377 U.S. 201 (1964); Escobedo v. Illinois, 378 U.S. 478 (1964). But Sixth Amendment protection does not begin until there is a "criminal prosecution"—the Court came to doubt whether that Amendment's protections could apply to the *investigatory* stage, before the defendant has been formally accused of a crime. And it is during the investigatory stage that most police interrogation occurs and most confessions are obtained. The Court therefore began to shift to a different constitutional amendment—the Fifth Amendment, which is not temporally limited to criminal prosecutions.[9]

## A.   MIRANDA v. ARIZONA

In 1964, the Court in Malloy v. Hogan, 378 U.S. 1, paved the way for its decision in *Miranda* by ruling that the Fifth Amendment privilege against self-incrimination is applicable to the states through the Fourteenth Amendment. Two years later, in *Miranda,* the Court declared that the Fifth Amendment is the touchstone for determining the admissibility of any statements obtained through custodial interrogation by government officials. The advantage seen in Fifth Amendment application was that the threshold for the official pressure on a suspect that is required to trigger Fifth Amendment protections is substantially less than the pressure required to trigger due process protections.

### MIRANDA V. ARIZONA
Supreme Court of the United States, 1966.
384 U.S. 436.

### MR. CHIEF JUSTICE WARREN delivered the opinion of the Court.

The cases before us raise questions which go to the roots of our concepts of American criminal jurisprudence: the restraints society must observe consistent with the Federal Constitution in prosecuting individuals for crime. More specifically, we deal with the admissibility of statements obtained from an individual who is subjected to custodial

---

[9]   Eventually the Court was to return to the Sixth Amendment as an additional control over police interrogations. *Massiah* and its progeny are discussed after the materials on the *Miranda* doctrine.

police interrogation and the necessity for procedures which assure that the individual is accorded his privilege under the Fifth Amendment to the Constitution not to be compelled to incriminate himself.

\* \* \*

Our holding will be spelled out with some specificity in the pages which follow but briefly stated it is this: the prosecution may not use statements, whether exculpatory or inculpatory, stemming from custodial interrogation of the defendant unless it demonstrates the use of procedural safeguards effective to secure the privilege against self-incrimination. By custodial interrogation, we mean questioning initiated by law enforcement officers after a person has been taken into custody or otherwise deprived of his freedom of action in any significant way. As for the procedural safeguards to be employed, unless other fully effective means are devised to inform accused persons of their right of silence and to assure a continuous opportunity to exercise it, the following measures are required. Prior to any questioning, the person must be warned that he has a right to remain silent, that any statement he does make may be used as evidence against him, and that he has a right to the presence of an attorney, either retained or appointed. The defendant may waive effectuation of these rights, provided the waiver is made voluntarily, knowingly and intelligently. If, however, he indicates in any manner and at any stage of the process that he wishes to consult with an attorney before speaking there can be no questioning. Likewise, if the individual is alone and indicates in any manner that he does not wish to be interrogated, the police may not question him. The mere fact that he may have answered some questions or volunteered some statements on his own does not deprive him of the right to refrain from answering any further inquiries until he has consulted with an attorney and thereafter consents to be questioned.

\* \* \* The constitutional issue we decide in each of these cases is the admissibility of statements obtained from a defendant questioned while in custody or otherwise deprived of his freedom of action in any significant way. In each, the defendant was questioned by police officers, detectives, or a prosecuting attorney in a room in which he was cut off from the outside world. In none of these cases was the defendant given a full and effective warning of his rights at the outset of the interrogation process. In all the cases, the questioning elicited oral admissions, and in three of them, signed statements as well which were admitted at their trials. They all thus share salient features—incommunicado interrogation of individuals in a police-dominated atmosphere, resulting in self-incriminating statements without full warnings of constitutional rights.

An understanding of the nature and setting of this in-custody interrogation is essential to our decisions today. The difficulty in depicting what transpires at such interrogations stems from the fact that in this country they have largely taken place incommunicado. From extensive factual studies undertaken in the early 1930's, including the famous Wickersham Report to Congress by a Presidential Commission, it is clear that police violence and the "third degree" flourished at that time. * * *

* * *

[T]he modern practice of in-custody interrogation is psychologically rather than physically oriented. * * * Interrogation still takes place in privacy. Privacy results in secrecy and this in turn results in a gap in our knowledge as to what in fact goes on in the interrogation rooms. A valuable source of information about present police practices, however, may be found in various police manuals and texts which document procedures employed with success in the past, and which recommend various other effective tactics. These texts are used by law enforcement agencies themselves as guides. It should be noted that these texts professedly present the most enlightened and effective means presently used to obtain statements through custodial interrogation. By considering these texts and other data, it is possible to describe procedures observed and noted around the country.

The officers are told by the manuals that the "principal psychological factor contributing to a successful interrogation is *privacy*—being alone with the person under interrogation." * * *

To highlight the isolation and unfamiliar surroundings, the manuals instruct the police to display an air of confidence in the suspect's guilt and from outward appearance to maintain only an interest in confirming certain details. The guilt of the subject is to be posited as a fact. The interrogator should direct his comments toward the reasons why the subject committed the act, rather than court failure by asking the subject whether he did it. Like other men, perhaps the subject has had a bad family life, had an unhappy childhood, had too much to drink, had an unrequited desire for women. The officers are instructed to minimize the moral seriousness of the offense, to cast blame on the victim or on society. These tactics are designed to put the subject in a psychological state where his story is but an elaboration of what the police purport to know already—that he is guilty. Explanations to the contrary are dismissed and discouraged.

The texts thus stress that the major qualities an interrogator should possess are patience and perseverance. * * *

The manuals suggest that the suspect be offered legal excuses for his actions in order to obtain an initial admission of guilt. * * *

When the techniques described above prove unavailing, the texts recommend they be alternated with a show of some hostility. * * *

The interrogators sometimes are instructed to induce a confession out of trickery. The technique here is quite effective in crimes which require identification or which run in series. In the identification situation, the interrogator may take a break in his questioning to place the subject among a group of men in a line-up. "The witness or complainant (previously coached, if necessary) studies the line-up and confidently points out the subject as the guilty party." Then the questioning resumes "as though there were now no doubt about the guilt of the subject." A variation on this technique is called the "reverse line-up":

> "The accused is placed in a line-up but this time he is identified by several fictitious witnesses or victims who associated him with different offenses. It is expected that the subject will become desperate and confess to the offense under investigation in order to escape from the false accusations."

* * *

Even without employing brutality, the "third degree" or the specific stratagems described above, the very fact of custodial interrogation exacts a heavy toll on individual liberty and trades on the weakness of individuals. * * *

In the cases before us today, given this background, we concern ourselves primarily with this interrogation atmosphere and the evils it can bring. In No. 759, Miranda v. Arizona, the police arrested the defendant and took him to a special interrogation room where they secured a confession. In No. 760, Vignera v. New York, the defendant made oral admissions to the police after interrogation in the afternoon, and then signed an inculpatory statement upon being questioned by an assistant district attorney later the same evening. In No. 761, Westover v. United States, the defendant was handed over to the Federal Bureau of Investigation by local authorities after they had detained and interrogated him for a lengthy period, both at night and the following morning. After some two hours of questioning, the federal officers had obtained signed statements from the defendant. Lastly, in No. 584, California v. Stewart, the local police held the defendant five days in the station and interrogated him on nine separate occasions before they secured his inculpatory statement.

In these cases, we might not find the defendants' statements to have been involuntary in traditional terms. Our concern for adequate safeguards to protect precious Fifth Amendment rights is, of course, not lessened in the slightest. In each of the cases, the defendant was thrust into an unfamiliar atmosphere and run through menacing police interrogation procedures. The potentiality for compulsion is forcefully apparent, for example, in *Miranda,* where the indigent Mexican defendant was a seriously disturbed individual with pronounced sexual fantasies, and in *Stewart,* in which the defendant was an indigent Los Angeles Negro who had dropped out of school in the sixth grade. To be sure, the records do not evince overt physical coercion or patent psychological ploys. The fact remains that in none of these cases did the officers undertake to afford appropriate safeguards at the outset of the interrogation to insure that the statements were truly the product of free choice.

It is obvious that such an interrogation environment is created for no purpose other than to subjugate the individual to the will of his examiner. This atmosphere carries its own badge of intimidation. To be sure, this is not physical intimidation, but it is equally destructive of human dignity. The current practice of incommunicado interrogation is at odds with one of our Nation's most cherished principles—that the individual may not be compelled to incriminate himself. Unless adequate protective devices are employed to dispel the compulsion inherent in custodial surroundings, no statement obtained from the defendant can truly be the product of his free choice.

From the foregoing, we can readily perceive an intimate connection between the privilege against self-incrimination and police custodial questioning. It is fitting to turn to history and precedent underlying the Self-Incrimination Clause to determine its applicability in this situation.

[The Court briefly traces the roots of the Fifth Amendment and how the privilege against self-incrimination obtained constitutional status in the United States.]

The question in these cases is whether the privilege is fully applicable during a period of custodial interrogation. * * * We are satisfied that all the principles embodied in the privilege apply to informal compulsion exerted by law-enforcement officers during in-custody questioning. An individual swept from familiar surroundings into police custody, surrounded by antagonistic forces, and subjected to the techniques of persuasion described above cannot be otherwise than under compulsion to speak. As a practical matter, the compulsion to speak in the isolated setting of the police station may well be greater than in courts or other official investigations, where there are often impartial observers to guard against intimidation or trickery.

This question, in fact could have been taken as settled in federal courts almost 70 years ago, when, in Bram v. United States, 168 U.S. 532, 542 (1897), this Court held:

"In criminal trials, in the courts of the United States, wherever a question arises whether a confession is incompetent because not voluntary, the issue is controlled by that portion of the Fifth Amendment * * * commanding that no person 'shall be compelled in any criminal case to be a witness against himself.' "

* * *

Today, then, there can be no doubt that the Fifth Amendment privilege is available outside of criminal court proceedings and serves to protect persons in all settings in which their freedom of action is curtailed in any significant way from being compelled to incriminate themselves. We have concluded that without proper safeguards the process of in-custody interrogation of persons suspected or accused of crime contains inherently compelling pressures which work to undermine the individual's will to resist and to compel him to speak where he would not otherwise do so freely. In order to combat these pressures and to permit a full opportunity to exercise the privilege against self-incrimination, the accused must be adequately and effectively apprised of his rights and the exercise of those rights must be fully honored.

It is impossible for us to foresee the potential alternatives for protecting the privilege which might be devised by Congress or the States in the exercise of their creative rule-making capacities. Therefore we cannot say that the Constitution necessarily requires adherence to any particular solution for the inherent compulsions of the interrogation process as it is presently conducted. Our decision in no way creates a constitutional straitjacket which will handicap sound efforts at reform, nor is it intended to have this effect. We encourage Congress and the States to continue their laudable search for increasingly effective ways of protecting the rights of the individual while promoting efficient enforcement of our criminal laws. However, unless we are shown other procedures which are at least as effective in apprising accused persons of their right of silence and in assuring a continuous opportunity to exercise it, the following safeguards must be observed.

At the outset, if a person in custody is to be subjected to interrogation, he must first be informed in clear and unequivocal terms that he has the right to remain silent. For those unaware of the privilege, the warning is needed simply to make them aware of it—the threshold requirement for an intelligent decision as to its exercise. More important, such a warning is an absolute prerequisite in overcoming the inherent pressures of the interrogation atmosphere. It is not just the subnormal or woefully ignorant who succumb to an interrogator's imprecations, whether implied or expressly stated, that the interrogation will continue until a confession is obtained or that silence in the face of accusation is itself damning and will bode ill when presented to a jury.[a] Further, the

---

[a]  In accord with our decision today it is impermissible to penalize an individual for exercising his Fifth Amendment privilege when he is under police custodial interrogation. The

warning will show the individual that his interrogators are prepared to recognize his privilege should he choose to exercise it.

The Fifth Amendment privilege is so fundamental to our system of constitutional rule and the expedient of giving an adequate warning as to the availability of the privilege so simple, we will not pause to inquire in individual cases whether the defendant was aware of his rights without a warning being given. Assessments of the knowledge the defendant possessed, based on information as to his age, education, intelligence, or prior contact with authorities, can never be more than speculation; a warning is a clearcut fact. More important, whatever the background of the person interrogated, a warning at the time of the interrogation is indispensable to overcome its pressures and to insure that the individual knows he is free to exercise the privilege at that point in time.

The warning of the right to remain silent must be accompanied by the explanation that anything said can and will be used against the individual in court. This warning is needed in order to make him aware not only of the privilege, but also of the consequences of forgoing it. It is only through an awareness of these consequences that there can be any assurance of real understanding and intelligent exercise of the privilege. Moreover, this warning may serve to make the individual more acutely aware that he is faced with a phase of the adversary system—that he is not in the presence of persons acting solely in his interest.

The circumstances surrounding in-custody interrogation can operate very quickly to overbear the will of one merely made aware of his privilege by his interrogators. Therefore, the right to have counsel present at the interrogation is indispensable to the protection of the Fifth Amendment privilege under the system we delineate today. Our aim is to assure that the individual's right to choose between silence and speech remains unfettered throughout the interrogation process. A once-stated warning, delivered by those who will conduct the interrogation, cannot itself suffice to that end among those who most require knowledge of their rights. A mere warning given by the interrogators is not alone sufficient to accomplish that end. Prosecutors themselves claim that the admonishment of the right to remain silent without more "will benefit only the recidivist and the professional." Even preliminary advice given to the accused by his own attorney can be swiftly overcome by the secret interrogation process. Thus, the need for counsel to protect the Fifth Amendment privilege comprehends not merely a right to consult with counsel prior to questioning, but also to have counsel present during any questioning if the defendant so desires.

---

prosecution may not, therefore, use at trial the fact that he stood mute or claimed his privilege in the face of accusation.

That presence of counsel at the interrogation may serve several significant subsidiary functions as well. If the accused decides to talk to his interrogators, the assistance of counsel can mitigate the dangers of untrustworthiness. With a lawyer present the likelihood that the police will practice coercion is reduced, and if coercion is nevertheless exercised the lawyer can testify to it in court. The presence of a lawyer can also help to guarantee that the accused gives a fully accurate statement to the police and that the statement is rightly reported by the prosecution at trial.

An individual need not make a pre-interrogation request for a lawyer. While such request affirmatively secures his right to have one, his failure to ask for a lawyer does not constitute a waiver. No effective waiver of the right to counsel during interrogation can be recognized unless specifically made after the warnings we here delineate have been given. The accused who does not know his rights and therefore does not make a request may be the person who most needs counsel. * * *

* * *

Accordingly we hold that an individual held for interrogation must be clearly informed that he has the right to consult with a lawyer and to have the lawyer with him during interrogation under the system for protecting the privilege we delineate today. As with the warnings of the right to remain silent and that anything stated can be used in evidence against him, this warning is an absolute prerequisite to interrogation. No amount of circumstantial evidence that the person may have been aware of this right will suffice to stand in its stead. Only through such a warning is there ascertainable assurance that the accused was aware of this right.

If an individual indicates that he wishes the assistance of counsel before any interrogation occurs, the authorities cannot rationally ignore or deny his request on the basis that the individual does not have or cannot afford a retained attorney. The financial ability of the individual has no relationship to the scope of the rights involved here. The privilege against self-incrimination secured by the Constitution applies to all individuals. The need for counsel in order to protect the privilege exists for the indigent as well as the affluent. In fact, were we to limit these constitutional rights to those who can retain an attorney, our decisions today would be of little significance. The cases before us as well as the vast majority of confession cases with which we have dealt in the past involve those unable to retain counsel. While authorities are not required to relieve the accused of his poverty, they have the obligation not to take advantage of indigence in the administration of justice. Denial of counsel to the indigent at the time of interrogation while allowing an attorney to those who can afford one would be no more supportable by reason or logic than the similar situation at trial and on appeal. * * *

In order fully to apprise a person interrogated of the extent of his rights under this system then, it is necessary to warn him not only that he has the right to consult with an attorney, but also that if he is indigent a lawyer will be appointed to represent him. Without this additional warning, the admonition of the right to consult with counsel would often be understood as meaning only that he can consult with a lawyer if he has one or has the funds to obtain one. The warning of a right to counsel would be hollow if not couched in terms that would convey to the indigent—the person most often subjected to interrogation—the knowledge that he too has a right to have counsel present. As with the warnings of the right to remain silent and of the general right to counsel, only by effective and express explanation to the indigent of this right can there be assurance that he was truly in a position to exercise it.[b]

Once warnings have been given, the subsequent procedure is clear. If the individual indicates in any manner, at any time prior to or during questioning, that he wishes to remain silent, the interrogation must cease.[c] At this point he has shown that he intends to exercise his Fifth Amendment privilege; any statements taken after the person invokes his privilege cannot be other than the product of compulsion, subtle or otherwise. Without the right to cut off questioning, the setting of in-custody interrogation operates on the individual to overcome free choice in producing a statement after the privilege has been once invoked. If the individual states that he wants an attorney, the interrogation must cease until an attorney is present. At that time, the individual must have an opportunity to confer with the attorney and to have him present during any subsequent questioning. If the individual cannot obtain an attorney and he indicates that he wants one before speaking to police, they must respect his decision to remain silent.

This does not mean, as some have suggested, that each police station must have a "station house lawyer" present at all times to advise prisoners. It does mean, however, that if police propose to interrogate a person they must make known to him that he is entitled to a lawyer and that if he cannot afford one, a lawyer will be provided for him prior to any interrogation. If authorities conclude that they will not provide counsel

---

[b]    While a warning that the indigent may have counsel appointed need not be given to the person who is known to have an attorney or is known to have ample funds to secure one, the expedient of giving a warning is too simple and the rights involved too important to engage in *ex post facto* inquiries into financial ability when there is any doubt at all on that score.

[c]    If an individual indicates his desire to remain silent, but has an attorney present, there may be some circumstances in which further questioning would be permissible. In the absence of evidence of overbearing, statements then made in the presence of counsel might be free of the compelling influence of the interrogation process and might fairly be construed as a waiver of the privilege for purposes of these statements.

during a reasonable period of time in which investigation in the field is carried out, they may refrain from doing so without violating the person's Fifth Amendment privilege so long as they do not question him during that time.

If the interrogation continues without the presence of an attorney and a statement is taken, a heavy burden rests on the government to demonstrate that the defendant knowingly and intelligently waived his privilege against self-incrimination and his right to retained or appointed counsel. This Court has always set high standards of proof for the waiver of constitutional rights, and we reassert these standards as applied to in-custody interrogation. Since the State is responsible for establishing the isolated circumstances under which the interrogation takes place and has the only means of making available corroborated evidence of warnings given during incommunicado interrogation, the burden is rightly on its shoulders.

An express statement that the individual is willing to make a statement and does not want an attorney followed closely by a statement could constitute a waiver. But a valid waiver will not be presumed simply from the silence of the accused after warnings are given or simply from the fact that a confession was in fact eventually obtained. * * *

* * * Moreover, where in-custody interrogation is involved, there is no room for the contention that the privilege is waived if the individual answers some questions or gives some information on his own prior to invoking his right to remain silent when interrogated.

Whatever the testimony of the authorities as to waiver of rights by an accused, the fact of lengthy interrogation or incommunicado incarceration before a statement is made is strong evidence that the accused did not validly waive his rights. In these circumstances the fact that the individual eventually made a statement is consistent with the conclusion that the compelling influence of the interrogation finally forced him to do so. It is inconsistent with any notion of a voluntary relinquishment of the privilege. Moreover, any evidence that the accused was threatened, tricked, or cajoled into a waiver will, of course, show that the defendant did not voluntarily waive his privilege. The requirement of warnings and waiver of rights is a fundamental with respect to the Fifth Amendment privilege and not simply a preliminary ritual to existing methods of interrogation.

The warnings required and the waiver necessary in accordance with our opinion today are, in the absence of a fully effective equivalent, prerequisites to the admissibility of any statement made by a defendant. No distinction can be drawn between statements which are direct confessions and statements which amount to "admissions" of part or all of an offense. The privilege against self-incrimination protects the individual from being compelled to incriminate himself in any manner; it does not distinguish degrees of incrimination. Similarly, for precisely the same reason, no distinction may be drawn between inculpatory statements and statements alleged to be merely "exculpatory." If a statement made were in fact truly exculpatory it would, of course, never be used by the prosecution. In fact, statements merely intended to be exculpatory by the defendant are often used to impeach his testimony at trial or to demonstrate untruths in the statement given under interrogation and thus to prove guilt by implication. These statements are incriminating in any meaningful sense of the word and may not be used without the full warnings and effective waiver required for any other statement. * * *

The principles announced today deal with the protection which must be given to the privilege against self-incrimination when the individual is first subjected to police interrogation while in custody at the station or otherwise deprived of his freedom of action in any significant way. * * * Under the system of warnings we delineate today or under any other system which may be devised and found effective, the safeguards to be erected about the privilege must come into play at this point.

Our decision is not intended to hamper the traditional function of police officers in investigating crime. When an individual is in custody on probable cause, the police may, of course, seek out evidence in the field to be used at trial against him. Such investigation may include inquiry of persons not under restraint. General on-the-scene questioning as to facts surrounding a crime or other general questioning of citizens in the fact-finding process is not affected by our holding. It is an act of responsible citizenship for individuals to give whatever information they may have to aid in law enforcement. In such situations the compelling atmosphere inherent in the process of in-custody interrogation is not necessarily present.

In dealing with statements obtained through interrogation, we do not purport to find all confessions inadmissible. Confessions remain a proper element in law enforcement. Any statement given freely and voluntarily without any compelling influences is, of course, admissible in evidence.

* * *

Because of the nature of the problem and because of its recurrent significance in numerous cases, we have to this point discussed the relationship of the Fifth Amendment privilege to police interrogation without specific concentration on the facts of the cases before us. We turn now to these facts to consider the application to these cases of the constitutional principles discussed above. In each instance, we have concluded that statements were obtained from the defendant under circumstances that did not meet constitutional standards for protection of the privilege.

\* \* \*

**MR. JUSTICE CLARK, dissenting in Nos. 759, 760, and 761, and concurring in the result in No. 584.**

It is with regret that I find it necessary to write in these cases. However, I am unable to join the majority because its opinion goes too far on too little, while my dissenting brethren do not go quite far enough. Nor can I join in the Court's criticism of the present practices of police and investigatory agencies as to custodial interrogation. The materials it refers to as "police manuals" are, as I read them, merely writings in this field by professors and some police officers. \* \* \*

\* \* \* Such a strict constitutional specific inserted at the nerve center of crime detection may well kill the patient. Since there is at this time a paucity of information and an almost total lack of empirical knowledge on the practical operation of requirements truly comparable to those announced by the majority, I would be more restrained lest we go too far too fast.

**MR. JUSTICE HARLAN, whom MR. JUSTICE STEWART and MR. JUSTICE WHITE join, dissenting.**

I believe the decision for the Court represents poor constitutional law and entails harmful consequences for the country at large. How serious these consequences may prove to be only time can tell. But the basic flaws in the Court's justification seem to me readily apparent now once all sides of the problem are considered.

\* \* \*

\* \* \* The new rules are not designed to guard against police brutality or other unmistakably banned forms of coercion. Those who use third-degree tactics and deny them in court are equally able and destined to lie as skillfully about warnings and waivers. Rather, the thrust of the new rules is to negate all pressures, to reinforce the nervous or ignorant suspect, and ultimately to discourage any confession at all. The aim in short is toward "voluntariness" in a utopian sense, or to view it from a different angle, voluntariness with a vengeance.

\* \* \*

[Justice Harlan surveys the limits on confessions the Court evolved under the Due Process Clause of the Fourteenth Amendment.]

I turn now to the Court's asserted reliance on the Fifth Amendment, an approach which I frankly regard as a *trompe l'oeil*. The Court's opinion in my view reveals no adequate basis for extending the Fifth Amendment's privilege against self-incrimination to the police station.

Far more important, it fails to show that the Court's new rules are well supported, let alone compelled, by Fifth Amendment precedents. Instead, the new rules actually derive from quotation and analogy drawn from precedents under the Sixth Amendment, which should properly have no bearing on police interrogation.

The Court's opening contention, that the Fifth Amendment governs police station confessions, is perhaps not an impermissible extension of the law but it has little to commend itself in the present circumstances. Historically, the privilege against self-incrimination did not bear at all on the use of extra-legal confessions, for which distinct standards evolved. * * * Even those who would readily enlarge the privilege must concede some linguistic difficulties since the Fifth Amendment in terms proscribes only compelling any person "in any criminal case to be a witness against himself."

* * *

Having decided that the Fifth Amendment privilege does apply in the police station, the Court reveals that the privilege imposes more exacting restrictions than does the Fourteenth Amendment's voluntariness test. * * *

The more important premise is that pressure on the suspect must be eliminated though it be only the subtle influence of the atmosphere and surroundings. The Fifth Amendment, however, has never been thought to forbid *all* pressure to incriminate one's self in the situations covered by it. * * * This is not to say that short of jail or torture any sanction is permissible in any case; policy and history alike may impose sharp limits. However, the Court's unspoken assumption that *any* pressure violates the privilege is not supported by the precedents and it has failed to show why the Fifth Amendment prohibits that relatively mild pressure the Due Process Clause permits.

The Court appears similarly wrong in thinking that precise knowledge of one's rights is a settled prerequisite under the Fifth Amendment to the loss of its protections. * * * No Fifth Amendment precedent is cited for the Court's contrary view. There might of course be reasons apart from Fifth Amendment precedent for requiring warning or any other safeguard on questioning but that is a different matter entirely.

A closing word must be said about the Assistance of Counsel Clause of the Sixth Amendment, which is never expressly relied on by the Court but whose judicial precedents turn out to be linchpins of the confession rules announced today. * * *

* * * The sound reason why [the Sixth Amendment] right is so freely extended for a criminal trial is the severe injustice risked by confronting an untrained defendant with a range of technical points of law, evidence,

and tactics familiar to the prosecutor but not to himself. This danger shrinks markedly in the police station where indeed the lawyer in fulfilling his professional responsibilities of necessity may become an obstacle to truthfinding. * * *

**MR. JUSTICE WHITE, with whom MR. JUSTICE HARLAN and MR. JUSTICE STEWART join, dissenting.**

The proposition that the privilege against self-incrimination forbids in-custody interrogation without the warnings specified in the majority opinion and without a clear waiver of counsel has no significant support in the history of the privilege or in the language of the Fifth Amendment. As for the English authorities and the common-law history, the privilege, firmly established in the second half of the seventeenth century, was never applied except to prohibit compelled judicial interrogations. * * * Morgan, The Privilege Against Self-Incrimination, 34 Minn.L.Rev. 1, 18 (1949).

[Justice White surveyed the history of the Fifth Amendment and the Court's prior treatment of confession cases in support of this proposition.]

* * *

[E]ven if one assumed that there was an adequate factual basis for the conclusion that all confessions obtained during in-custody interrogation are the product of compulsion, the rule propounded by the Court would still be irrational, for, apparently, it is only if the accused is also warned of his right to counsel and waives both that right and the right against self-incrimination that the inherent compulsiveness of interrogation disappears. But if the defendant may not answer without a warning a question such as "Where were you last night?" without having his answer be a compelled one, how can the Court ever accept his negative answer to the question of whether he wants to consult his retained counsel or counsel whom the court will appoint? * * * The Court apparently realizes its dilemma of foreclosing questioning without the necessary warnings but at the same time permitting the accused, sitting in the same chair in front of the same policemen, to waive his right to consult an attorney. It expects, however, that the accused will not often waive the right; and if it is claimed that he has, the State faces a severe, if not impossible burden of proof.

All of this makes very little sense in terms of the compulsion which the Fifth Amendment proscribes. That amendment deals with compelling the accused himself. It is his free will that is involved. Confessions and incriminating admissions, as such, are not forbidden evidence; only those which are compelled are banned. I doubt that the Court observes these distinctions today. * * *

\* \* \*

The obvious underpinning of the Court's decision is a deep-seated distrust of all confessions. As the Court declares that the accused may not be interrogated without counsel present, absent a waiver of the right to counsel, and as the Court all but admonishes the lawyer to advise the accused to remain silent, the result adds up to a judicial judgment that evidence from the accused should not be used against him in any way, whether compelled or not. This is the not so subtle overtone of the opinion—that it is inherently wrong for the police to gather evidence from the accused himself. And this is precisely the nub of this dissent. I see nothing wrong or immoral, and certainly nothing unconstitutional, in the police's asking a suspect whom they have reasonable cause to arrest whether or not he killed his wife or in confronting him with the evidence on which the arrest was based, at least where he has been plainly advised that he may remain completely silent \* \* \*. Particularly when corroborated, as where the police have confirmed the accused's disclosure of the hiding place of implements or fruits of the crime, such confessions have the highest reliability and significantly contribute to the certitude with which we may believe the accused is guilty. \* \* \*

### *Analysis of Miranda*

*Miranda* brought the Fifth Amendment into the stationhouse. *Miranda* was viewed by many as a radical change in the law, as the scope of the Fifth Amendment had been thought limited to protecting against formal modes of state compulsion—such as contempt of court. But the history of the privilege against self-incrimination is ambiguous enough that reasonable people easily may reach different conclusions as to whether it should reach into the modern day stationhouse. For a defense of the majority's approach, see Kamisar, A Dissent From the Miranda Dissents: Some Comments on the "New" Fifth Amendment and the Old "Voluntariness" Test, 65 Mich.L.Rev. 59 (1966).

*Miranda's* importation of the Fifth Amendment into the stationhouse, and the Court's rationale for doing so, is explained by Professor Schulhofer in *Miranda's* Practical Effect: Substantial Benefits and Vanishingly Small Social Costs, 90 Nw.U.L.Rev. 500 (1996):

> Police do not have to violate KGB standards in order to violate the Fifth Amendment. \* \* \* [W]hatever one may think of *Miranda*, it is clear—and uncontroversial—that pressure need not rise to the level of overbearing physical or psychological coercion, in the due process sense, before it is sufficiently compelling to violate the Fifth Amendment. Outside the context of police interrogation, the law has long been settled, before *Miranda* and since, that the Fifth Amendment is violated by any pressure or penalty deliberately

imposed for the purpose of getting a criminal suspect to speak. [citing cases such as *Lefkowitz* and *Griffin*, discussed earlier in this Chapter]. \* \* \* The opposing view, pressed so hard by *Miranda's* critics—that Fifth Amendment compulsion and due-process coercion are identical concepts—would, if taken seriously and applied to contexts other than police interrogation, make shreds of the entire fabric of Fifth Amendment doctrine and tradition.

*Miranda's* innovation was to hold that police interrogation could no longer be treated as a world apart. Prior to *Miranda*, the courts had uniformly held that police interrogation, because it imposed no formal penalty for silence, was immune from the Fifth Amendment limitations that apply in every other context. Because there was no formal legal obligation to speak, and thus no duty against which a formal privilege of silence could be applied, there simply was no privilege for the arrested suspect to waive \* \* \*. *Miranda*, in a radical break with prior precedent, rejected that view. The Court's central holding was not the now-famous warnings, but the principle that Fifth Amendment standards would henceforth apply. And the two premises cited to support that conclusion, though hotly contested then, are surely uncontroversial now: that a formalistic showing of compulsion by legal process or official punishment cannot be essential, and that from every practical vantage point, once a suspect is isolated in police custody and deprived of his freedom to leave, interrogation involves pressures that can dwarf those that were decisive in cases like *Griffin* and *Lefkowitz*. The pressures are normally compelling in this practical sense, as even *Miranda's* most committed critics now acknowledge. \* \* \* As a result, the typical custodial police interrogation, even if not brutally coercive in the due process sense, will readily (perhaps almost invariably) violate the Fifth Amendment bar on the use of compelling pressure, at least in the absence of safeguards sufficient to dispel that pressure.

In thinking about *Miranda*, it might be useful to ask whether a suspect who is compelled to undergo interrogation in the police station might believe that the police have the power to keep him in custody and to ask questions until he confesses. If so, the warnings simply clarify that the suspect may be confined against his will but not compelled to speak. See Saltzburg, Miranda v. Arizona Revisited: Constitutional Law or Judicial Fiat, 26 Washburn L.Rev. 1 (1986).

### *Judicial Review and Education of the Public*

The Court in *Miranda* appears to have two distinct goals, and it is useful to consider them separately. First, the Court was clearly concerned that under the due process test it was impossible to have meaningful judicial review over police interrogation practices. It is difficult after an interrogation to determine how coercive it really was, especially when the usual witnesses are police officers and the suspect—none of whom are neutral observers. One purpose of *Miranda* is therefore to create a prophylactic rule to aid in judicial review: If the warnings are not given, then a confession in response to custodial interrogation is irrebuttably presumed to be tainted. If warnings are given, then the confession still may not be voluntary, but at least courts have some greater confidence in any confession that is obtained. But, to the extent that *Miranda* was intended to ease the task of judicial review of confessions, it is subject to attack on the ground that tape recording of interrogations and the placement of a heavy burden on the government to demonstrate voluntariness would have been a sufficient, and perhaps a better, way to promote effective review. The wisdom of the Court's approach also can be challenged on the ground that the courts remain dependent on testimony (and perhaps "testilying") to determine whether and how the warnings were ever given and what happened afterwards.

Second, *Miranda* signifies that no person should be deemed to confess voluntarily and intelligently unless she knows of the right to remain silent and that statements made can be used as evidence against her. If our educational process taught law like reading, writing, and arithmetic, *Miranda* might not have been necessary. But, prior to *Miranda* it was the rare person who could articulate her constitutional rights to refuse cooperation to the police. Although the Court could not compel that law be taught to all, it had a way of making the government the teacher in custody situations. Thus, part of *Miranda* involves educating suspects about the real choice they have to make in the interrogation process. See generally Thomas, Separated at Birth but Siblings Nonetheless: *Miranda* and the Due Process Notice Cases, 99 U. Mich. L.Rev. 1081 (2001).

The educational aspect of *Miranda* has its own problems, however. The Court was depending on the very police officers about whom it was concerned to give the warnings. How effective could the Court have expected police officers to be as teachers of constitutional rights to their adversaries? We do not rely on an officer "in the competitive enterprise of ferreting out crime" to protect our Fourth Amendment rights, but instead we impose a judicial officer as an intermediary. Why do we rely on a police officer to protect our Fifth Amendment rights? On the other hand, what is the alternative? That no custodial interrogation can occur until the suspect is brought before a magistrate and given warnings? How would that rule affect the state's ability to obtain confessions? See Kamisar, Kauper's "Judicial Examination of the Accused" Forty Years Later—Some Comments on a Remarkable Article, 73 Mich.L.Rev. 15 (1974) (suggesting that no custodial interrogation should be permitted until the suspect is presented to a judicial officer and told he has the right to remain silent).

Even as a set of warnings, *Miranda* is not wholly adequate. Despite the fact that Chief Justice Warren repeats the Court's holding in several places, it is arguable that there are subtle differences in different parts of the opinion. Test yourself on this by stating what you think the Court's required warning is. Then ask someone else to do the same. Compare your warnings. You may find some significant differences. Also, ask yourself what you have *not* told the suspect. For example, have you communicated *what happens* if the suspect remains silent? Have you invited the person to ask questions to assure an understanding of the warnings? Have you informed the suspect that if he wants to talk, he can change his mind at any time? Have you told the suspect how long it will take to provide counsel if the suspect wants counsel?

### *The Impact of Miranda*

What effect has *Miranda* had? Some empirical evidence appears to indicate that the costs imposed by *Miranda* are limited. See generally Stephens, The Supreme Court and Confessions of Guilt 179–200 (1973), and authorities cited therein. See also Medalie, Leitz and Alexander, Custodial Police Interrogation in Our Nation's Capital: The Attempt to Implement *Miranda*, 66 Mich.L.Rev. 1347 (1968). Although in some places the absolute number of confessions may have fallen after *Miranda,* it does not appear that the conviction rates of law enforcement agencies has ever suffered. See Seeburger & Wettick, *Miranda* in Pittsburgh—A Statistical Study, 29 U.Pitt.L.Rev. 1 (1967). Certainly the published cases in which confessions are excluded and convictions reversed under *Miranda*—when the confessions would not have been excluded anyway under the involuntariness test—are few. See Guy and Huckabee, Going Free on a Technicality: Another Look at the Effect of the *Miranda* Decision on the Criminal Justice Process, 4 Crim.J.Res.Bull. 1 (1988) (*Miranda* issue raised in 9% of appeals, but only 5.6% of those claims were successful, resulting in a reversal rate of .51% of all criminal appeals).

Among the writings asserting that *Miranda* has hurt law enforcement are Office of Legal Policy, Report on the Law of Pretrial Interrogation (Feb. 12, 1986), defended in Markman, The Fifth Amendment and Custodial Questioning: A Response to "Reconsidering *Miranda*," 54 U.Chi.L.Rev. 938 (1987), and Caplan, Questioning *Miranda*, 38 Vand.L.Rev. 1417 (1985). An attempt to reevaluate the empirical data to consider all relevant costs, including lost cases and more lenient plea bargains, can be found in Cassell, *Miranda's* Social Costs: An Empirical Reassessment, 90 Nw.U.L.Rev. 387 (1996). Professor Cassell finds the costs of *Miranda* significant, especially in light of less onerous alternatives that he asserts are available to deal with the concerns of the *Miranda* majority. In a later article, Cassell argues that *Miranda* has imposed substantial harms on the innocent, including victims of criminals not caught due to the *Miranda* safeguards, and innocent people who are accused of crime because police are not permitted to obtain a confession from another suspect. See Cassell, Protecting the Innocent From False Confessions and Lost Confessions—and From *Miranda*, 88 J.Crim.L. & Crim. 497 (1998).

Contrary views are found in Schulhofer, The Fifth Amendment at Justice: A Reply, 54 U.Chi.L.Rev. 950 (1987); Schulhofer, Reconsidering *Miranda*, 54 U.Chi.L.Rev. 435 (1987); and White, Defending *Miranda*: A Reply to Professor Caplan, 39 Vand.L.Rev. 1 (1986). Professor White concludes that "the great weight of empirical evidence supports the conclusion that *Miranda's* impact on the police's ability to obtain confessions has not been significant." And a special committee of the ABA Criminal Justice Section reported that a "very strong majority of those surveyed—prosecutors, judges and police officers—agree that compliance with *Miranda* does not present serious problems for law enforcement." Special Committee on Criminal Justice in a Free Society, Criminal Justice Section, ABA, Criminal Justice In Crisis 28–29 (1988).

Professors Inbau and Manak assess another cost of *Miranda* in Miranda v. Arizona: Is It Worth the Cost? (A Sample Survey, with Commentary, of the Expenditure of Court Time and Effort), 24 Cal.Western L.Rev. 185 (1988). They conclude that *Miranda* questions take up a disproportionate amount of time in trial and appellate courts. They do not factor in, however, the amount of court time that would be expended if *Miranda* were overruled and the courts returned to the old case-by-case voluntariness test to regulate confessions.

If you agree with the supporters of *Miranda* that it has had no real effect on police officers' ability to obtain confessions, then you have to ask yourself, "what good is *Miranda* anyway?" Wasn't the point of *Miranda* to limit confessions? Professor Schulhofer addresses this question in *Miranda's* Practical Effect: Substantial Benefits and Vanishingly Small Social Costs, 90 Nw.U.L.Rev. 500 (1996):

> If *Miranda* really has so little impact on confession and conviction rates, why bother defending it? Isn't *Miranda* simply a hollow promise for civil libertarians and an inconvenient nuisance for law enforcement? If the *Miranda* Court's goal was to reduce or eliminate confessions, the decision was an abject failure. Plainly, however, the Warren Court had no such thought in mind; it explicitly structured *Miranda's* warning and waiver requirements to ensure that confessions could continue to be elicited and used. *Miranda's*

stated objective was not to eliminate confessions, but to eliminate compelling pressure in the interrogation process.

\* \* \*

For those concerned with the "bottom line," *Miranda* may appear to be a mere symbol. But the symbolic effects of criminal procedure safeguards are important. Those guarantees help shape the self-conception and define the role of conscientious police professionals; they underscore our constitutional commitment to restraint in an area in which emotions easily run uncontrolled.

*Miranda* is, in any event, more than a mere symbol. In a constitutional system, procedure matters; the means to the end are never irrelevant. *Miranda* does not protect suspects from conviction but only from a particular method of conviction. The rate of confessions has not changed, but those confessions are now mostly the result of persuasion and the suspect's overconfidence, not of pressure and fear. That difference in method is crucial.

As you read further, you will see that evaluating the "costs" of *Miranda* is an ongoing process, as the Court has trimmed away much of the protection that the Court in 1966 clearly assumed would be present going forward.

### *Miranda's Costs on Habeas Review: Withrow v. Williams*

In Withrow v. Williams, 507 U.S. 680 (1993), the Court downplayed the costs of deciding *Miranda* issues, as it held that *Miranda* claims can be pursued on collateral review of a state court conviction. Justice Souter, writing for five Justices, concluded if *Miranda* claims were barred on habeas it "would not significantly benefit the federal courts." Justice Souter explained this assertion as follows:

> [E]liminating habeas review of *Miranda* issues would not prevent a state prisoner from simply converting his barred *Miranda* claim into a due process claim that his conviction rested on an involuntary confession. \* \* \*

> If that is so, the federal courts would certainly not have heard the last of *Miranda* on collateral review. Under the due process approach, \* \* \* courts look to the totality of circumstances to determine whether a confession was voluntary. Those potential circumstances \* \* \* include the failure of police to advise the defendant of his rights to remain silent and to have counsel present during custodial interrogation. We could lock the front door against *Miranda,* but not the back.

We thus fail to see how abdicating *Miranda's* bright line (or, at least, brighter line) rules in favor of an exhaustive totality-of-circumstances approach on habeas would do much of anything to lighten the burdens placed on busy federal courts.[10]

## *Miranda's Impact on Review of Confessions for Voluntariness*

If a defendant is interrogated while in custody, *Miranda* requires that he receive warnings before a confession is admissible. But it also provides that the suspect can waive his *Miranda* rights. But of course, if there is a waiver, this does not mean that officers can then beat or threaten the suspect. Any confession made after *Miranda* warnings must still be voluntary.

Yet some have argued that *Miranda* has had a negative effect on the voluntariness inquiry. The argument is that once courts know that *Miranda* warnings have been given and the rights have been voluntarily waived, they tend to think that everything worked out fine. There is an indication in the case law that *Miranda* distracts judges from the propriety of the interrogation that follows the waiver of *Miranda* rights. For more on this point, see Stuntz, The Collapse of American Criminal Justice 235 (2011).

## *The Miranda Compromise*

Part of the reason *Miranda* may not have much of an adverse effect on law enforcement is that the *Miranda* opinion is not as drastic as its opponents initially feared. *Miranda* does not put an end to confessions without counsel, nor does it prohibit stationhouse interrogation. *Miranda* does impose a warning requirement, but these warnings are given by a police officer, not a judicial officer. *Miranda* provides a right to silence and to counsel, but the decision whether to *invoke* these rights (and conversely whether to waive them) is made by the suspect, *in the same coercive atmosphere* that the Court was so concerned about. *Miranda* does not impose a videotaping requirement, and so what goes on in the stationhouse can be as difficult to determine as under the old voluntariness test.

The Court in *Miranda* specifically rejected the suggestion—which would seem to flow from the premise that stationhouse interrogation is inherently coercive—that a suspect must have a nonwaivable right to an attorney before being interrogated. Thus, *Miranda* struck a compromise. See Benner, Requiem for *Miranda:* The Rehnquist Court's Voluntariness Doctrine in Historical Perspective, 67 Wash.U.L.Q. 59 (1989) ("confronted

---

[10] Justice O'Connor wrote a dissenting opinion joined by the Chief Justice, while Justice Scalia wrote a dissenting opinion joined by Justice Thomas.

with the storm of controversy that *Escobedo* [implying an absolute right to counsel] created, the Court retreated in *Miranda,* and struck a compromise" that "transformed the debate about self-incrimination into a debate about waiver"); Saltzburg, Miranda v. Arizona Revisited: Constitutional Law or Judicial Fiat, 26 Washburn L.J. 1 (1986) ("*Miranda* is more of a compromise than most critics would care to admit").

For an argument that the *Miranda* Court did not go far enough and that "all suspects should have a nonwaivable right to consult with a lawyer before being interrogated by police," see Ogletree, Are Confessions Really Good for the Soul? A Proposal to Mirandize *Miranda,* 100 Harv.L.Rev. 1826 (1987). If *Miranda* had gone that far, would it have been overruled by now? Would a rule imposing an absolute right to counsel have garnered a majority of the *Miranda* Court?

## *Alternatives to Miranda*

The *Miranda* Court emphasized that its system of warnings and waivers was not the only means possible for regulating the problem of custodial interrogation. According to Professor Cassell, however, the Court's invitation to alternatives "was in reality empty because it did not specify what alternatives would be deemed acceptable." Consequently, since *Miranda*, "reform efforts have been virtually nonexistent." In Cassell's view, the lack of experimentation results from the reluctance of the states to spend resources on alternatives that the Court might simply strike down. Cassell, *Miranda's* Social Costs: An Empirical Reassessment, 90 Nw.U.L.Rev. 387 (1996). Undaunted, Professor Cassell proposes the following alternative to *Miranda*:

> Videotaping interrogations would be at least as effective as *Miranda* in preventing police coercion. The *Miranda* regime appears to have had little effect on what police misconduct exists. In contrast, videotaping, when it has been used, has often reduced claims of police coercion and probably real coercion as well. To be sure, police could conceivably alter tapes or deploy force off-camera. But if you were facing a police officer with a rubber hose, would you prefer a world in which he was required to mumble the *Miranda* warnings and have you waive your rights, all as reported by him in later testimony? Or a world in which the interrogation is videorecorded and the burden is on law enforcement to explain if it is not; where date and time are recorded on the videotape; where your physical appearance and demeanor during the interrogation are permanently recorded?

Do you agree that videotaping will be a better solution than *Miranda* to the problem of police coercion?[11] Professor Schulhofer, in *Miranda's Practical Effect: Substantial Benefits and Vanishingly Small Social Costs*, 90 Nw.U.L.Rev. 500 (1996), argues that a videotaping requirement would be a valuable *supplement* to, but a problematic replacement for, the *Miranda* safeguards.

> In effect, the proposal to substitute videotaping for *Miranda* amounts to a police offer in the form, "We'll stop lying about what we do, if you allow us to do it." No doubt a videotaped record would often prevent police abuse and manipulation of the "swearing contest." But without clear substantive requirements against which to test the police behavior that the videotape will reveal, the objective record will lack any specific legal implications. * * * Thus, videotaping, though an excellent idea, does not meet the constitutional concerns about compulsion to which the *Miranda* safeguards are addressed. Videotaping could provide a useful complement to the *Miranda* protections, but it cannot replace them.

Can you think of any other means by which police coercion can be controlled, without the loss of reliable evidence? Amar and Lettow, in Fifth Amendment First Principles: The Self-Incrimination Clause, 93 Mich.L.Rev. 857 (1995), suggest "a prophylactic rule that no police-station confession by a defendant is ever allowed in, unless volunteered by a suspect in the presence of an on-duty defense lawyer or ombudsman in the police station." In place of custodial interrogation, Amar and Lettow propose that at a pretrial hearing before a judge, the government would be permitted to compel a suspect to provide evidence against himself. The suspect would be given only "testimonial" immunity as opposed to use-fruits immunity, meaning that his statement could not be used as evidence against him, but the government could use the statement as a means of finding other information such as physical evidence and adverse witnesses. If the suspect refuses to make a statement at this pretrial hearing, Amar and Lettow propose that the suspect could be jailed for contempt, and that an adverse inference could be drawn at trial. Is this a better system than *Miranda*? Is this system possible given the Court's interpretation of the privilege against self-incrimination?

---

[11] Some state courts have relied on their own constitutions to mandate videotaping of all custodial interrogations. See, e.g., Kane, No More Secrets: Minnesota State Due Process Requirement that Law Enforcement Officers Electronically Record Custodial Interrogation and Confessions, 77 Minn.L.Rev.983 (1993). These requirements are, however, in addition to and not in replacement of the *Miranda* safeguards. See also Leonard Post, Illinois to Tape Police Questioning, Nat'l L.J., 8/4/2003 p.1 (noting some police officers are critical of taping because "it absolutely hasn't shortened evidentiary hearings or the swearing contests" and that "When suspects have to go to the bathroom, we chase them with tape recorders.").

## B.  DID CONGRESS OVERRULE *MIRANDA*?

In 1968, Congress passed 18 U.S.C. § 3501, which provides, among other things, that a confession "shall be admissible in evidence if it is voluntarily given," and that voluntariness is to be determined on the basis of "all the circumstances surrounding the giving of the confession," including whether the defendant received warnings and counsel. Thus, warnings and counsel are simply factors in the voluntariness analysis— the absence of warnings or the failure to provide counsel do not themselves render a confession inadmissible under the statute. The expressed intent of Congress was to "overrule" *Miranda* in favor of a return to the due process "voluntariness" standard. The Supreme Court considered whether Congress had the power to overrule *Miranda* in the following case.

### DICKERSON V. UNITED STATES

Supreme Court of the United States, 2000.
530 U.S. 428.

**CHIEF JUSTICE REHNQUIST delivered the opinion of the Court.**

In Miranda v. Arizona, we held that certain warnings must be given before a suspect's statement made during custodial interrogation could be admitted in evidence. In the wake of that decision, Congress enacted 18 U.S.C. § 3501, which in essence laid down a rule that the admissibility of such statements should turn only on whether or not they were voluntarily made. We hold that *Miranda*, being a constitutional decision of this Court, may not be in effect overruled by an Act of Congress, and we decline to overrule *Miranda* ourselves. We therefore hold that *Miranda* and its progeny in this Court govern the admissibility of statements made during custodial interrogation in both state and federal courts.

[Dickerson was charged with bank robbery and related offenses. He moved to suppress a confession on the ground that he didn't receive *Miranda* warnings. The Court of Appeals held that § 3501 was satisfied because Dickerson was not coerced. It then concluded that our decision in *Miranda* was not a constitutional holding, and that therefore Congress could reject the *Miranda* safeguards.].

\* \* \*

Two years after *Miranda* was decided, Congress enacted § 3501. \* \* \* Given § 3501's express designation of voluntariness as the touchstone of admissibility, its omission of any warning requirement, and the instruction for trial courts to consider a nonexclusive list of factors relevant to the circumstances of a confession, we agree with the Court of Appeals that Congress intended by its enactment to overrule *Miranda*. Because of the obvious conflict between our decision in *Miranda* and

§ 3501, we must address whether Congress has constitutional authority to thus supersede *Miranda*. If Congress has such authority, § 3501's totality-of-the-circumstances approach must prevail over *Miranda's* requirement of warnings; if not, that section must yield to *Miranda's* more specific requirements.

\* \* \* Congress retains the ultimate authority to modify or set aside any judicially created rules of evidence and procedure that are not required by the Constitution. But Congress may not legislatively supersede our decisions interpreting and applying the Constitution. This case therefore turns on whether the *Miranda* Court announced a constitutional rule or merely exercised its supervisory authority to regulate evidence in the absence of congressional direction.

Recognizing this point, the Court of Appeals surveyed *Miranda* and its progeny to determine the constitutional status of the *Miranda* decision. Relying on the fact that we have created several exceptions to *Miranda's* warnings requirement and that we have repeatedly referred to the *Miranda* warnings as "prophylactic," New York v. Quarles, and "not themselves rights protected by the Constitution," Michigan v. Tucker, [These cases are discussed immediately infra in the section on exceptions to *Miranda*.] the Court of Appeals concluded that the protections announced in *Miranda* are not constitutionally required.

We disagree with the Court of Appeals' conclusion, although we concede that there is language in some of our opinions that supports the view taken by that court. But first and foremost of the factors on the other side—that *Miranda* is a constitutional decision—is that both *Miranda* and two of its companion cases applied the rule to proceedings in state courts—to wit, Arizona, California, and New York. Since that time, we have consistently applied *Miranda's* rule to prosecutions arising in state courts. It is beyond dispute that we do not hold a supervisory power over the courts of the several States.

The *Miranda* opinion itself begins by stating that the Court granted certiorari "to explore some facets of the problems . . . of applying the privilege against self-incrimination to in-custody interrogation, and to give concrete constitutional guidelines for law enforcement agencies and courts to follow." In fact, the majority opinion is replete with statements indicating that the majority thought it was announcing a constitutional rule. \* \* \*

The Court of Appeals also relied on the fact that we have, after our *Miranda* decision, made exceptions from its rule in cases such as New York v. Quarles, and Harris v. New York, also discussed immediately infra]. \* \* \* These decisions illustrate the principle—not that *Miranda* is not a constitutional rule—but that no constitutional rule is immutable. No court laying down a general rule can possibly foresee the various circumstances in which counsel will seek to apply it, and the sort of modifications represented by these cases are as much a normal part of constitutional law as the original decision.

The Court of Appeals also noted that in Oregon v. Elstad, 470 U.S. 298 (1985), we stated that "[t]he Miranda exclusionary rule . . . serves the Fifth Amendment and sweeps more broadly than the Fifth Amendment itself." Our decision in that case—refusing to apply the traditional "fruits" doctrine developed in Fourth Amendment cases—does not prove that *Miranda* is a nonconstitutional decision, but simply recognizes the fact that unreasonable searches under the Fourth Amendment are different from unwarned interrogation under the Fifth Amendment.

As an alternative argument for sustaining the Court of Appeals' decision, the court-invited amicus curiae contends that the section complies with the requirement that a legislative alternative to *Miranda* be equally as effective in preventing coerced confessions. See Brief for Paul G. Cassell as Amicus Curiae 28–39. \* \* \* *Miranda* requires procedures that will warn a suspect in custody of his right to remain silent and which will assure the suspect that the exercise of that right will be honored. As discussed above, § 3501 explicitly eschews a requirement of pre-interrogation warnings in favor of an approach that looks to the administration of such warnings as only one factor in determining the voluntariness of a suspect's confession. The additional remedies cited by amicus do not, in our view, render them, together with § 3501 an adequate substitute for the warnings required by *Miranda*.

The dissent argues that it is judicial overreaching for this Court to hold § 3501 unconstitutional unless we hold that the *Miranda* warnings are required by the Constitution, in the sense that nothing else will suffice to satisfy constitutional requirements. But we need not go farther than *Miranda* to decide this case. In *Miranda*, the Court noted that reliance on the traditional totality-of-the-circumstances test raised a risk of overlooking an involuntary custodial confession, a risk that the Court found unacceptably great when the confession is offered in the case in chief to prove guilt. The Court therefore concluded that something more than the totality test was necessary. As discussed above, § 3501 reinstates the totality test as sufficient. Section 3501 therefore cannot be sustained if *Miranda* is to remain the law.

Whether or not we would agree with *Miranda's* reasoning and its resulting rule, were we addressing the issue in the first instance, the principles of stare decisis weigh heavily against overruling it now. \* \* \*

We do not think there is such justification for overruling *Miranda*. *Miranda* has become embedded in routine police practice to the point where the warnings have become part of our national culture. While we have overruled our precedents when subsequent cases have undermined their doctrinal underpinnings, we do not believe that this has happened to the *Miranda* decision. If anything, our subsequent cases have reduced the impact of the *Miranda* rule on legitimate law enforcement while reaffirming the decision's core ruling that unwarned statements may not be used as evidence in the prosecution's case in chief.

The disadvantage of the *Miranda* rule is that statements which may be by no means involuntary, made by a defendant who is aware of his "rights," may nonetheless be excluded and a guilty defendant go free as a result. But experience suggests that the totality-of-the-circumstances test which § 3501 seeks to revive is more difficult than *Miranda* for law enforcement officers to conform to, and for courts to apply in a consistent manner. The requirement that *Miranda* warnings be given does not, of course, dispense with the voluntariness inquiry. But as we said in Berkemer v. McCarty, 468 U.S. 420 (1984), "[c]ases in which a defendant can make a colorable argument that a self-incriminating statement was 'compelled' despite the fact that the law enforcement authorities adhered to the dictates of *Miranda* are rare."

In sum, we conclude that *Miranda* announced a constitutional rule that Congress may not supersede legislatively. Following the rule of stare decisis, we decline to overrule *Miranda* ourselves. The judgment of the Court of Appeals is therefore

Reversed.

**JUSTICE SCALIA, with whom JUSTICE THOMAS joins, dissenting.**

\* \* \*

It was once possible to characterize the so-called *Miranda* rule as resting (however implausibly) upon the proposition that what the statute here before us permits—the admission at trial of un-*Mirandized* confessions—violates the Constitution. That is the fairest reading of the *Miranda* case itself. \* \* \*

So understood, *Miranda* was objectionable for innumerable reasons, not least the fact that cases spanning more than 70 years had rejected its core premise that, absent the warnings and an effective waiver of the right to remain silent and of the (hitherto unknown) right to have an attorney present, a statement obtained pursuant to custodial interrogation was necessarily the product of compulsion. Moreover, history and precedent aside, the decision in *Miranda*, if read as an explication of what the Constitution requires, is preposterous. There is, for example, simply no basis in reason for concluding that a response to the very first question asked, by a suspect who already knows all of the rights described in the *Miranda* warning, is anything other than a volitional act. And even if one assumes that the elimination of compulsion absolutely requires informing even the most knowledgeable suspect of his right to remain silent, it cannot conceivably require the right to have counsel present. * * * Thus, what is most remarkable about the *Miranda* decision—and what made it unacceptable as a matter of straightforward constitutional interpretation in the *Marbury* tradition—is its palpable hostility toward the act of confession per se, rather than toward what the Constitution abhors, compelled confession.

* * *

As the Court today acknowledges, since *Miranda* we have explicitly, and repeatedly, interpreted that decision as having announced, not the circumstances in which custodial interrogation runs afoul of the Fifth or Fourteenth Amendment, but rather only "prophylactic" rules that go beyond the right against compelled self-incrimination. * * * The Court has squarely concluded that it is possible—indeed not uncommon—for the police to violate *Miranda* without also "violating the Constitution."

[Justice Scalia discusses cases in which the Court stated that the *Miranda* warnings are prophylactic safeguards rather than constitutional rights, including New York v. Quarles and Oregon v. Elstad, discussed infra in this Chapter.]

In light of these cases, * * * it is simply no longer possible for the Court to conclude, even if it wanted to, that a violation of *Miranda's* rules is a violation of the Constitution. * * * By disregarding congressional action that concededly does not violate the Constitution, the Court flagrantly offends fundamental principles of separation of powers, and arrogates to itself prerogatives reserved to the representatives of the people.

The Court seeks to avoid this conclusion in two ways: First, by misdescribing these post-*Miranda* cases as mere dicta. The Court concedes only "that there is language in some of our opinions that supports the view" that *Miranda's* protections are not "constitutionally required." It is not a matter of language; it is a matter of holdings. The proposition that failure to comply with *Miranda's* rules does not establish a constitutional violation was central to the holdings of *Tucker, Hass, Quarles, and Elstad.*

The second way the Court seeks to avoid the impact of these cases is simply to disclaim responsibility for reasoned decisionmaking. * * * [I]f confessions procured in violation of *Miranda* are confessions "compelled" in violation of the Constitution, the post-*Miranda* decisions I have discussed do not make sense. The only reasoned basis for their outcome was that a violation of *Miranda* is not a violation of the Constitution. * * *

* * *

Neither am I persuaded by the argument for retaining *Miranda* that touts its supposed workability as compared with the totality-of-the-circumstances test it purported to replace. *Miranda's* proponents cite ad nauseam the fact that the Court was called upon to make difficult and subtle distinctions in applying the "voluntariness" test in some 30-odd due process "coerced confessions" cases in the 30 years between Brown v. Mississippi and *Miranda*. It is not immediately apparent, however, that the judicial burden has been eased by the "bright-line" rules adopted in *Miranda*. In fact, in the 34 years since *Miranda* was decided, this Court has been called upon to decide nearly 60 cases involving a host of *Miranda* issues, most of them predicted with remarkable prescience by Justice White in his *Miranda* dissent. * * * But even were I to agree that the old totality-of-the-circumstances test was more cumbersome, it is simply not true that *Miranda* has banished it from the law and replaced it with a new test. Under the current regime, which the Court today retains in its entirety, courts are frequently called upon to undertake both inquiries.

* * *

I dissent from today's decision, and, until § 3501 is repealed, will continue to apply it in all cases where there has been a sustainable finding that the defendant's confession was voluntary.

### NOTE ON DICKERSON

The Court in *Dickerson* seemed to be between a rock and a hard place: it had rendered decisions binding state courts, which it could only do if *Miranda* were a constitutional decision, and yet repeatedly referred to *Miranda* as a non-constitutional, prophylactic rule that did not compel exclusion of evidence that appeared to be taken in violation of the rule. Thus, the Court had held the decision both constitutional and non-constitutional. Court-watchers may have thought that the Court was finally going to have to choose between these polar opposite approaches. As it turned out the Court, much to the dismay of Justice Scalia, appeared to have its cake and eat it too: the *Miranda* safeguards are constitutionally required, and yet all of the exceptions are retained, though now as exceptions to a constitutional rule.

For more on *Dickerson* and its effect on the *Miranda* exceptions, see Klein, *Miranda's* Exceptions in a Post-*Dickerson* World, 91 J.Crim.L. & Criminology 567 (2001).

### *§ 3501, McNabb-Mallory, and Fed. R. Crim. P. 5*

Before *Miranda*, the Supreme Court—exercising its supervisory power over federal courts—sought to protect suspects in custody by requiring their *prompt presentment before a magistrate*. The idea was that the magistrate would inform the suspect of their rights to silence and counsel. If police did not comply with the prompt presentment requirement, statements made after the time at which the suspect should have been brought before a magistrate were held inadmissible. The "prompt presentment" requirement—and exclusion of confessions made in violation of it—became known as the *McNabb-Mallory* rule. That rule was, and still is, embodied in Fed. R. Crim.P. 5. That rule provides that a person making an arrest within the United States "must take the defendant without unnecessary delay before a magistrate judge."

Congress passed 18 U.S.C. § 3501 shortly after *Miranda* was decided. That statute was designed to legislatively overrule *Miranda* (an attempt found unsuccessful in Dickerson v. United States, *supra*)—and it was *also* designed to limit the *McNabb-Mallory* rule. Subsection (a) of § 3501 provides that "[i]n any criminal prosecution brought by the United States . . . , a confession . . . shall be admissible in evidence if it is voluntarily given"; subsection (b) lists several considerations for courts to address in assessing voluntariness. Subsection (c), which focused specifically on *McNabb-Mallory*, provides that in any federal prosecution, a confession made while under arrest "shall not be inadmissible solely because of delay in bringing such person before a magistrate judge * * * if such confession is found by the trial judge to have been made voluntarily * * * and if such confession was made * * * within six hours" of the arrest. The six-hour time limit is extended when further delay is "reasonable considering the means of transportation and the distance to be traveled to the nearest available" magistrate.

In Corley v. United States, 556 U.S. 303 (2009), Justice Souter wrote for the Court as it examined the effect of § 3501 on the *McNabb-Mallory* rule: "The question here is whether Congress intended 18 U.S.C. § 3501 to discard, or merely to narrow, the rule in McNabb v. United States, 318 U.S. 332 (1943), and Mallory v. United States, 354 U.S. 449 (1957), under which an arrested person's confession is inadmissible if given after an unreasonable delay in bringing him before a judge. We hold that Congress meant to limit, not eliminate, *McNabb-Mallory*."

Corley was arrested for bank robbery. He was detained and confessed about 9 hours after arrest. He was presented to a magistrate about 20 hours after that. Corley moved unsuccessfully to suppress his confessions under Rule 5(a) and *McNabb-Mallory*. The lower court that held that § 3501 entirely abrogated the *McNabb-Mallory* rule and replaced it with a pure voluntariness test. To that court, unreasonable delay is irrelevant as long as the confession was voluntary.

The Government's argument in the Supreme Court relied on § 3501(a), which provides that any confession "shall be admissible in evidence" in federal court "if it is voluntarily given." The government maintained that subsection (a) means that once a district court looks to the considerations in § 3501(b) and finds a confession voluntary it is admissible so subsection (a) entirely eliminates *McNabb-Mallory*. Corley argued to the Court that § 3501(a) was meant to overrule *Miranda* and nothing more, and had no effect on *McNabb-Mallory*, which § 3501 touches only in subsection (c)—by giving police a 6-hour grace period.

Justice Souter concluded that "Corley has the better argument," and the Court held as follows:

> We hold that § 3501 modified *McNabb-Mallory* without supplanting it. Under the rule as revised by § 3501(c), a district court with a suppression claim must find whether the defendant confessed within six hours of arrest (unless a longer delay was reasonable considering the means of transportation and the distance to be traveled to the nearest available magistrate). If the confession came within that period, it is admissible, subject to the other Rules of Evidence, so long as it was "made voluntarily and . . . the weight to be given [it] is left to the jury." If the confession occurred before presentment and beyond six hours, however, the court must decide whether delaying that long was unreasonable or unnecessary under the *McNabb-Mallory* cases, and if it was, the confession is to be suppressed.

The Court remanded the case to the Third Circuit for application of the Court's interpretation of § 3501.

Justice Alito, joined by Chief Justice Roberts, and Justices Scalia and Thomas, dissented and argued that "[u]nless the unambiguous language of § 3501(a) is ignored, petitioner's confession may not be suppressed." Justice Alito also questioned whether the *McNabb-Mallory* rule retained its significance:

> [T]he need for the *McNabb-Mallory* exclusionary rule is no longer clear. That rule, which was adopted long before *Miranda*, originally served a purpose that is now addressed by the giving of *Miranda* warnings upon arrest. * * * In the pre-*Miranda* era, the requirement of prompt presentment ensured that persons taken into custody would, within a relatively short period, receive advice about their rights. Now, however, *Miranda* ensures that arrestees receive such advice at an even earlier point, within moments of being taken into custody. * * * [I]t is certainly not clear that the *McNabb-Mallory* rule adds much protection beyond that provided by *Miranda*.

## C.  EXCEPTIONS TO THE *MIRANDA* RULE OF EXCLUSION

In a number of cases after *Miranda*, the Court found exceptions to the *Miranda* rule—meaning that confessions made during custodial interrogation are admissible, in certain circumstances, even though *Miranda* warnings have not been given or the suspect's invocation of *Miranda* has not been respected. These cases originally relied on the premise that the *Miranda* safeguards were merely prophylactic rules and not constitutionally required. After *Dickerson,* however, that analysis can no longer stand. Rather, these exceptions to the *Miranda* rule of exclusion are now, just that: exceptions to a constitutional rule.

## 1. Impeaching the Defendant-Witness

One of the most significant cases limiting the Court's decision in *Miranda* is Harris v. New York, 401 U.S. 222 (1971). Harris was charged with selling heroin to undercover police officers, and he took the stand in his own defense. On cross-examination, he was asked if he had made statements to the police immediately after his arrest that partially contradicted his direct testimony. The statements were not admissible as substantive evidence under *Miranda,* because Harris was not warned of his right to counsel prior to his in-custody interrogation. However, Chief Justice Burger, writing for the Court, declared that the *Miranda* safeguards are not required by the Constitution, and therefore that Harris's *Miranda*-defective statements could be admitted for purposes of impeaching his credibility.[12]

While this "*Miranda* is non-constitutional" analysis is no longer viable after *Dickerson*, the impeachment exception *remains intact.* Perhaps the reason for this retention stems from the Court's cost-benefit analysis in *Harris*. It found that the cost of excluding *Miranda*-defective confessions when offered for impeachment outweighed the benefit in deterring *Miranda* violations. The *Harris* Court explained its cost-benefit balance as follows:

> * * * The impeachment process here undoubtedly provided valuable aid to the jury in assessing petitioner's credibility, and the benefits of this process should not be lost, in our view, because of the speculative possibility that impermissible police conduct will be encouraged thereby. Assuming that the exclusionary rule has a deterrent effect on proscribed police conduct, sufficient deterrence flows when the evidence in question is made unavailable to the prosecution in its case in chief.

> The shield provided by *Miranda* cannot be perverted into a license to use perjury by way of a defense, free from the risk of confrontation with prior inconsistent utterances. We hold, therefore, that petitioner's credibility was appropriately impeached by use of his earlier conflicting statements.

---

[12] Justices Black, Brennan, Douglas, and Marshall dissented. Arguably, the Court strained, to the point of distorting the record, to use this case to cabin *Miranda*. See Ely & Dershowitz, Harris v. New York: Some Anxious Observations on the Candor and Logic of the Emerging Nixon Majority, 80 Yale L.J. 1198 (1971).

Can the decision in *Harris* be reconciled with the language in *Miranda*? Does it diminish the effectiveness of *Miranda*? If so, how?

The Court reaffirmed *Harris* in Oregon v. Hass, 420 U.S. 714 (1975). In *Hass,* the defendant had received the full *Miranda* warnings and had said that he would like to call a lawyer. He was told that he could not telephone an attorney until he and the police officer reached the police station. Thereafter, the defendant made inculpatory statements before he was given an opportunity to call a lawyer. Thus the violation of *Miranda* was not in the failure to warn, but in the refusal of the police to respect the defendant's invocation of his *Miranda* rights. Finding that *Hass* was controlled by *Harris,* the Court held that the statements were admissible to impeach the defendant, who had taken the stand and offered direct testimony in conflict with the incriminating information with knowledge that the inculpatory statements had been ruled inadmissible as substantive evidence.[13]

The Court's decisions in *Harris* and *Hass* leave a defendant who has made a *Miranda*-defective confession with a practical problem. The defendant may not want to take the stand, because if he does the jury may learn about the confession. Even though the jury will be told that the confession can be used for impeachment purposes only, such an instruction is very difficult for a lay jury to follow. It's entirely possible that the jury will disregard the instruction and use the confession as evidence of guilt. On the other hand, if the defendant does not take the stand in order to avoid impeachment, the chance of conviction increases appreciably. See H. Kalven & H. Zeisel, The American Jury 160 (1960).

A police training tape entitled "Questioning Outside *Miranda*" provides a lecture from an Assistant District Attorney suggesting options that an officer might consider if the suspect, when given *Miranda* warnings, decides not to talk. The ADA suggests that the questioning continue "outside *Miranda*" because such questioning can help the police officer even if the confession is inadmissible at trial. The ADA notes, for example, that obtaining a confession "outside *Miranda*"

> forces the defendant to commit to a statement that will prevent him from pulling out some defense and using it at trial—that he's cooked up with some defense lawyer—that wasn't true. So if you get a statement "outside *Miranda*" and he tells you that he did it and how he did it or if he gives you a denial of some sort, he's tied to that, he's married to that, because * * * we can use statements outside *Miranda* to impeach or rebut. We can't use them for our case-in-chief. The D.A. can't trot them out to the jury before he says "I rest," but * * * we can use his "outside *Miranda*" statements to impeach him. * * * I mean we can't use them for any purpose if you beat them out

---

[13] Justices Brennan and Marshall dissented. Justice Douglas took no part in the decision.

of him, but if they're voluntary statements, the fact that they weren't Mirandized will mean that we cannot use them in the case-in-chief but it does not mean we can't use them to impeach or rebut. So you see you got all those legitimate purposes that could be served by statements taken "outside *Miranda*."

Given the value to the prosecution of a *Miranda*-defective confession after *Harris* and *Hass,* as emphasized in the police training video, do you think the Chief Justice was correct in asserting that sufficient deterrence flows from exclusion of the confession in the case-in-chief? For a critique of *Harris*, see Weisselberg, Saving *Miranda*, 84 Cornell L.Rev. 109 (1998).

### *Involuntary Confessions and Impeachment*

In Mincey v. Arizona, 437 U.S. 385 (1978), the Court distinguished *Harris* and *Hass* and held that if a confession is *involuntary*, as opposed to merely *Miranda*-defective, it cannot be admitted even for impeachment purposes. The Court reasoned that the Due Process Clause operates to prohibit the use of coerced confessions *for any purpose*.

### *Impeachment with Prior Silence*

Under standard evidentiary principles, a defendant can be impeached with prior silence if a reasonable person would have spoken at the time about the matter to which the defendant later testifies. For example, if Joe is sitting in his yard and his neighbor comes up to Joe and accuses him of stealing money from the neighbor's home, and Joe says nothing, Joe can be impeached at trial with this silence if he later testifies that he did not steal the money. The silence is considered *inconsistent* with the later testimony—much as if Joe had said, "yes, I did steal the money."

Is it different if *Miranda* warnings are given? In Doyle v. Ohio, 426 U.S. 610 (1976), the defendant had been given *Miranda* warnings at the time of his arrest and chose to remain silent. At his trial, he took the stand and related an exculpatory story that he had not told to the police when Mirandized. On cross-examination, he was asked why he had not given the exculpatory explanation before; the jury was instructed that it could consider Doyle's silence as bearing on his credibility as a witness. Doyle appealed his conviction, arguing that the reference to post-*Mirandized* silence violated his constitutional rights.

The *Doyle* Court held that after *Miranda* warnings are given, the Due Process Clause prohibits the government from using the defendant's silence against him, even for impeachment purposes.[14] In reaching this conclusion, the Court said that "while it is true that the *Miranda* warnings contain no express assurance that silence will carry no penalty, such assurance is implicit to any person who receives the warnings. In such circumstances, it would be fundamentally unfair and a deprivation of due process to allow the arrested person's silence to be used to impeach an explanation subsequently offered at trial."[15]

The Court later held that a person who *waived* his rights after receiving *Miranda* warnings and who spoke to the police could be asked at trial why his pretrial statement differed from his trial testimony, even if the question focused on a relevant omission in the pretrial statement. Anderson v. Charles, 447 U.S. 404 (1980). This is because the *Miranda* promise—that silence will not carry a penalty—is inoperative where the defendant chose to speak.

### *Pre-Arrest Silence*

In Jenkins v. Anderson, 447 U.S. 231 (1980), the Court considered whether the use of *pre*-arrest silence for impeachment purposes was prohibited by *Doyle*. Jenkins stabbed and killed Redding, and at his trial for murder he contended that the killing was in self-defense. Jenkins waited until two weeks after the killing to turn himself in. On cross-examination and in closing argument, the prosecutor emphasized that Jenkins' two-week waiting period was inconsistent with his later claim of self-defense, i.e., if he had really acted in self-defense, he would have come forward right away rather than remaining at large. Justice Powell, writing for the Court, found *Doyle* inapplicable, reasoning as follows:

> In this case, no governmental action induced petitioner to remain silent before arrest. The failure to speak occurred before the petitioner was taken into custody and given *Miranda* warnings. Consequently, the fundamental unfairness present in *Doyle* is not present in this case. We hold that impeachment by use of pre-arrest silence does not violate the Fourteenth Amendment.

---

[14] Justices Stevens, Blackmun, and Rehnquist dissented. Prior to *Doyle,* the Court had limited the use of silence upon arrest for impeachment, but as an evidentiary, not a constitutional, ruling. See United States v. Hale, 422 U.S. 171 (1975).

[15] The Supreme Court found no violation of *Doyle* in Greer v. Miller, 483 U.S. 756 (1987). When Miller took the stand in his trial for kidnaping, robbery, and murder, he testified that he had taken no part in the criminal activity, and that two other defendants had come to his trailer and confessed to the crimes shortly after they occurred. The prosecutor asked Miller why he didn't tell his story to anyone after he was arrested. Miller's lawyer objected and moved for a mistrial. The trial judge denied the motion and instructed the jury to "ignore the question, for the time being." Justice Powell's opinion for the Court concluded that the trial judge in Miller's case, unlike the judge in *Doyle*, did not permit the inquiry into silence after receipt of warnings. Once objection was made, no further question or argument concerning silence was heard. Justice Stevens filed an opinion concurring in the judgment. Justice Brennan filed a dissenting opinion, in which Justices Marshall and Blackmun joined.

Justice Stevens, joined by Justice Stewart, concurred in the judgment, stating that "the admissibility of petitioner's failure to come forward with the excuse of self-defense shortly after the stabbing raised a routine evidentiary question that turns on the probative significance of that evidence and presented no issue under the Federal Constitution." Justices Marshall and Brennan dissented.

Assume you are a criminal lawyer and a client comes to you and tells you facts that might indicate possible criminal activity. What do you advise? If you tell your client to tell the police everything she knows, you are a more effective agent for the government than the police can be under *Miranda*. If you tell your client to do nothing, *Jenkins* suggests that the client may suffer as a result. Could you tell your client to send an anonymous letter to the police stating that she is not guilty of criminal activity and that her failure to come forward represents a decision not to risk misinterpretation of the facts and concomitant incrimination? Would this bar use of silence as evidence under *Jenkins*?

For a criticism of *Jenkins*, see Saltzburg, Foreword: The Flow and Ebb of Constitutional Criminal Procedure in the Warren and Burger Courts, 69 Geo.L.J. 151, 203–05 (1980).

### *Post-Arrest, Pre-Miranda Silence*

In Fletcher v. Weir, 455 U.S. 603 (1982), the Court considered whether *Doyle* prohibited the use of a suspect's *post-arrest* silence for impeachment purposes, when that silence *preceded* the giving of *Miranda* warnings. Weir testified at trial that he acted in self-defense, and the prosecutor asked why he did not offer this explanation when he was arrested. The Court, per curiam, held that "in the absence of the sort of affirmative assurances embodied in the *Miranda* warnings," impeachment with post-arrest silence was constitutionally permissible. The Court stated that the arrest by itself does not implicitly induce a suspect to remain silent.[16] See also United States v. Frazier, 394 F.3d 612 (8th Cir. 2005) (allowing the use of post-arrest, pre-*Miranda* silence in the government's *case-in-chief* because the defendant was under no compulsion to speak and therefore silence can be deemed an admission).

### 2. Admitting the Fruits of a *Miranda* Violation

By its terms (and even after *Harris*), *Miranda* requires that if the police engage in custodial interrogation and give no warnings or incomplete warnings, the resulting confession must be excluded from the case-in-chief. But what about the *fruits* of that confession? Some possible fruits of a *Miranda*-defective confession are: investigative leads pursued

---

[16] Some state courts have rejected *Fletcher* as a matter of state law. See Nelson v. State, 691 P.2d 1056 (Alaska App.1984); State v. Davis, 38 Wash.App. 600, 686 P.2d 1143 (1984).

as a result of the confession; physical evidence; and a second confession by the suspect. In Michigan v. Tucker, 417 U.S. 433 (1974), and Oregon v. Elstad, 470 U.S. 298 (1985), the Court severely limited the exclusionary impact of *Miranda* on the fruits of confessions, relying on two propositions: 1) that exclusion of the fruit of a poisonous tree is only justified if a constitutional right is violated (i.e., the "poison" must be a constitutional violation); and 2) that a violation of *Miranda* is not by itself a violation of the Fifth Amendment. This second argument is no longer valid after *Dickerson*. However, the Court in *Dickerson* specifically held that the "fruits" exception to *Miranda* retained validity even though the *Miranda* safeguards are constitutionally based.

### Leads to Witnesses: Michigan v. Tucker

In *Tucker,* the defendant was arrested for rape. Before he was interrogated, he was advised of his right to remain silent and his right to counsel, but was not told that he had the right to appointed counsel if he was indigent. The defendant told the police that he was with his friend Henderson at the time the crime was committed. The police then went to talk to Henderson. But Henderson gave information tending to incriminate the defendant. Before trial, the defendant moved to exclude Henderson's expected testimony because the defendant's *Miranda*-defective statement had led them to Henderson. In Tucker's view, Henderson's statement was the fruit of the poisonous tree. The motion was denied and the defendant was convicted.

The Court found that the failure to give the full *Miranda* warnings required exclusion of Tucker's confession, but not Henderson's testimony. The Court found "no reason to believe that Henderson's testimony is untrustworthy simply because [Tucker] was not advised of *his* right to appointed counsel." Justice Rehnquist, writing for the majority, declared that exclusion of this reliable evidence was not required simply because it proceeded from Tucker's *Miranda*-defective confession. He concluded that the *Miranda* warnings were "procedural safeguards" that "were not themselves rights protected by the Constitution but were instead measures to insure that the right against compulsory self-incrimination was protected." While this rationale is, again, no longer applicable after *Dickerson*, the *Tucker* rule has been retained by *Dickerson*, perhaps because the Court still agrees with the cost-benefit analysis that the Court conducted in *Tucker.*

Justice Rehnquist in *Tucker* considered whether the benefits of exclusion (deterring future *Miranda* violations) outweighed the costs of exclusion (the loss of reliable evidence). He reasoned that the deterrent effect of excluding Henderson's testimony would be minimal, because sufficient deterrence already existed by excluding Tucker's confession from the case-in-chief. The Court weighed the minimal incremental deterrence resulting from exclusion of derivative evidence, against the cost of excluding Henderson's reliable testimony, and found that the *Miranda* exclusionary rule should not apply.

Justice Rehnquist noted, however, that if Tucker's confession had been *involuntary*, the Due Process Clause would require exclusion of the confession as well as its fruits. Justices Brennan and Marshall concurred in the judgment.

### *Subsequent Confessions: Oregon v. Elstad and Missouri v. Seibert*

Justice O'Connor, writing for the Court in *Elstad,* extended the *Tucker* analysis to a case where a second confession resulted from a *Miranda*-defective confession. Justice O'Connor rejected the argument that the second confession had to be excluded as tainted by the first. Again, the Court relied on its now-discredited premise that the *Miranda* safeguards are not constitutionally-grounded. The Court held that "since there was no actual infringement of the suspect's *constitutional* rights" the case was not controlled "by the doctrine expressed in *Wong Sun* that fruits of a *constitutional* violation must be suppressed." Justice O'Connor recognized that if Elstad's first confession was *involuntary* within the meaning of the Due Process Clause, then the second confession would have to be excluded if it were derived from the first: the fruits doctrine applies to due process violations.

While the "non-constitutional" rationale of *Elstad* is no longer viable, the *Dickerson* Court reaffirmed the result in *Elstad*, i.e., statements that are the "fruit" of a *Miranda*-defective confession are not excluded. Again, the Court's retention of the *Elstad* rule may be based on the cost-benefit analysis conducted in that case: even if *Miranda* is a constitutional rule, the costs of compliance by excluding fruits were thought to outweigh the benefits of deterrence.

Justice Brennan, in *Elstad,* argued that the majority had dealt a "crippling blow to *Miranda*," by allowing police officers to obtain an unwarned confession virtually secure in the knowledge that by giving warnings they could then obtain a second (admissible) confession "because the suspect knows that the authorities know of his earlier statements and most frequently will believe that those statements have already sealed his fate."

The status of *Elstad* after *Dickerson*, and concerns that police may use the *Elstad* rule to end-run *Miranda*, are discussed in the following case, which involves "the Missouri two-step" approach to *Miranda*.

## MISSOURI V. SEIBERT

Supreme Court of the United States, 2004.
542 U.S. 600.

JUSTICE SOUTER announced the judgment of the Court and delivered an opinion, in which JUSTICE STEVENS, JUSTICE GINSBURG, and JUSTICE BREYER join.

This case tests a police protocol for custodial interrogation that calls for giving no warnings of the rights to silence and counsel until interrogation has produced a confession. Although such a statement is generally inadmissible, since taken in violation of Miranda v. Arizona, the interrogating officer follows it with *Miranda* warnings and then leads the suspect to cover the same ground a second time. The question here is the admissibility of the repeated statement. Because this midstream recitation of warnings after interrogation and unwarned confession could not effectively comply with *Miranda*'s constitutional requirement, we hold that a statement repeated after a warning in such circumstances is inadmissible.

\* \* \*

Respondent Patrice Seibert's 12-year-old son Jonathan had cerebral palsy, and when he died in his sleep she feared charges of neglect because of bedsores on his body. In her presence, two of her teenage sons and two of their friends devised a plan to conceal the facts surrounding Jonathan's death by incinerating his body in the course of burning the family's mobile home, in which they planned to leave Donald Rector, a mentally ill teenager living with the family, to avoid any appearance that Jonathan had been unattended. Seibert's son Darian and a friend set the fire, and Donald died.

Five days later, the police awakened Seibert at 3 a.m. at a hospital where Darian was being treated for burns. In arresting her, Officer Kevin Clinton followed instructions from Rolla, Missouri, officer Richard Hanrahan that he refrain from giving *Miranda* warnings. After Seibert had been taken to the police station and left alone in an interview room for 15 to 20 minutes, Hanrahan questioned her without *Miranda* warnings for 30 to 40 minutes, squeezing her arm and repeating "Donald was also to die in his sleep." After Seibert finally admitted she knew Donald was meant to die in the fire, she was given a 20-minute coffee and cigarette break. Officer Hanrahan then turned on a tape recorder, gave Seibert the *Miranda* warnings, and obtained a signed waiver of rights from her. He resumed the questioning with "Ok, 'trice, we've been talking for a little while about what happened on Wednesday the twelfth, haven't we?," and confronted her with her prewarning statements:

Hanrahan: "Now, in discussion you told us, you told us that there was an understanding about Donald."

Seibert: "Yes."

Hanrahan: "Did that take place earlier that morning?"

Seibert: "Yes."

Hanrahan: "And what was the understanding about Donald?"

Seibert: "If they could get him out of the trailer, to take him out of the trailer."

Hanrahan: "And if they couldn't?"

Seibert: "I, I never even thought about it. I just figured they would."

Hanrahan: " 'Trice, didn't you tell me that he was supposed to die in his sleep?"

Seibert: "If that would happen, 'cause he was on that new medicine, you know. . . ."

Hanrahan: "The Prozac? And it makes him sleepy. So he was supposed to die in his sleep?"

Seibert: "Yes."

After being charged with first-degree murder for her role in Donald's death, Seibert sought to exclude both her prewarning and postwarning statements. At the suppression hearing, Officer Hanrahan testified that he made a "conscious decision" to withhold *Miranda* warnings, thus resorting to an interrogation technique he had been taught: question first, then give the warnings, and then repeat the question "until I get the answer that she's already provided once." He acknowledged that Seibert's ultimate statement was "largely a repeat of information . . . obtained" prior to the warning.

The trial court suppressed the prewarning statement but admitted the responses given after the *Miranda* recitation. A jury convicted Seibert of second-degree murder. On appeal, the Missouri Court of Appeals affirmed, treating this case as indistinguishable from Oregon v. Elstad.

The Supreme Court of Missouri reversed, holding that "in the circumstances here, where the interrogation was nearly continuous, . . . the second statement, clearly the product of the invalid first statement, should have been suppressed." The court distinguished *Elstad* on the ground that warnings had not intentionally been withheld there * * *.

* * *

The technique of interrogating in successive, unwarned and warned phases raises a new challenge to *Miranda*. Although we have no statistics on the frequency of this practice, it is not confined to Rolla, Missouri. An officer of that police department testified that the strategy of withholding *Miranda* warnings until after interrogating and drawing out a confession

SELF-INCRIMINATION AND CONFESSIONS

was promoted not only by his own department, but by a national police training organization and other departments in which he had worked. Consistently with the officer's testimony, the Police Law Institute, for example, instructs that "officers may conduct a two-stage interrogation. . . . At any point during the pre-*Miranda* interrogation, usually after arrestees have confessed, officers may then read the *Miranda* warnings and ask for a waiver. If the arrestees waive their *Miranda* rights, officers will be able to repeat any *subsequent* incriminating statements later in court." Police Law Institute, Illinois Police Law Manual 83 (Jan.2001/Dec.2003). The upshot of all this advice is a question-first practice of some popularity, as one can see from the reported cases describing its use, sometimes in obedience to departmental policy.

* * * The object of question-first is to render *Miranda* warnings ineffective by waiting for a particularly opportune time to give them, after the suspect has already confessed.

* * * The threshold issue when interrogators question first and warn later is thus whether it would be reasonable to find that in these circumstances the warnings could function "effectively" as *Miranda* requires. Could the warnings effectively advise the suspect that he had a real choice about giving an admissible statement at that juncture? Could they reasonably convey that he could choose to stop talking even if he had talked earlier? For unless the warnings could place a suspect who has just been interrogated in a position to make such an informed choice, there is no practical justification for accepting the formal warnings as compliance with *Miranda*, or for treating the second stage of interrogation as distinct from the first, unwarned and inadmissible segment.[a]

* * * By any objective measure, applied to circumstances exemplified here, it is likely that if the interrogators employ the technique of withholding warnings until after interrogation succeeds in eliciting a confession, the warnings will be ineffective in preparing the suspect for successive interrogation, close in time and similar in content. * * * Upon

---

[a] Respondent Seibert argues that her second confession should be excluded from evidence under the doctrine known by the metaphor of the "fruit of the poisonous tree," developed in the Fourth Amendment context in Wong Sun v. United States, 371 U.S. 471 (1963): evidence otherwise admissible but discovered as a result of an earlier violation is excluded as tainted, lest the law encourage future violations. But the Court in *Elstad* rejected the *Wong Sun* fruits doctrine for analyzing the admissibility of a subsequent warned confession following "an initial failure . . . to administer the warnings required by *Miranda*." * * *. *Elstad* held that "a suspect who has once responded to unwarned yet uncoercive questioning is not thereby disabled from waiving his rights and confessing after he has been given the requisite *Miranda* warnings." In a sequential confession case, clarity is served if the later confession is approached by asking whether in the circumstances the *Miranda* warnings given could reasonably be found effective. If yes, a court can take up the standard issues of voluntary waiver and voluntary statement; if no, the subsequent statement is inadmissible for want of adequate *Miranda* warnings, because the earlier and later statements are realistically seen as parts of a single, unwarned sequence of questioning.

hearing warnings only in the aftermath of interrogation and just after making a confession, a suspect would hardly think he had a genuine right to remain silent, let alone persist in so believing once the police began to lead him over the same ground again. * * * What is worse, telling a suspect that "anything you say can and will be used against you," without expressly excepting the statement just given, could lead to an entirely reasonable inference that what he has just said will be used, with subsequent silence being of no avail. Thus, when *Miranda* warnings are inserted in the midst of coordinated and continuing interrogation, they are likely to mislead and deprive a defendant of knowledge essential to his ability to understand the nature of his rights and the consequences of abandoning them. By the same token, it would ordinarily be unrealistic to treat two spates of integrated and proximately conducted questioning as independent interrogations subject to independent evaluation simply because *Miranda* warnings formally punctuate them in the middle.

* * *

Missouri argues that a confession repeated at the end of an interrogation sequence envisioned in a question-first strategy is admissible on the authority of Oregon v. Elstad, 470 U.S. 298 (1985), but the argument disfigures that case. In *Elstad*, the police went to the young suspect's house to take him into custody on a charge of burglary. Before the arrest, one officer spoke with the suspect's mother, while the other one joined the suspect in a "brief stop in the living room," where the officer said he "felt" the young man was involved in a burglary. The suspect acknowledged he had been at the scene. This Court noted that the pause in the living room "was not to interrogate the suspect but to notify his mother of the reason for his arrest," and described the incident as having "none of the earmarks of coercion." The Court, indeed, took care to mention that the officer's initial failure to warn was an "oversight" that "may have been the result of confusion as to whether the brief exchange qualified as 'custodial interrogation' or . . . may simply have reflected . . . reluctance to initiate an alarming police procedure before [an officer] had spoken with respondent's mother." At the outset of a later and systematic station house interrogation going well beyond the scope of the laconic prior admission, the suspect was given *Miranda* warnings and made a full confession. * * *. Although the *Elstad* Court expressed no explicit conclusion about either officer's state of mind, it is fair to read *Elstad* as treating the living room conversation as a good-faith *Miranda* mistake, not only open to correction by careful warnings before systematic questioning in that particular case, but posing no threat to warn-first practice generally.

The contrast between *Elstad* and this case reveals a series of relevant facts that bear on whether *Miranda* warnings delivered midstream could be effective enough to accomplish their object: the completeness and detail of the questions and answers in the first round of interrogation, the overlapping content of the two statements, the timing and setting of the first and the second, the continuity of police personnel, and the degree to which the interrogator's questions treated the second round as continuous with the first. In *Elstad*, it was not unreasonable to see the occasion for questioning at the station house as presenting a markedly different experience from the short conversation at home; since a reasonable person in the suspect's shoes could have seen the station house questioning as a new and distinct experience, the *Miranda* warnings could have made sense as presenting a genuine choice whether to follow up on the earlier admission.

At the opposite extreme are the facts here, which by any objective measure reveal a police strategy adapted to undermine the *Miranda* warnings.[b] The unwarned interrogation was conducted in the station house, and the questioning was systematic, exhaustive, and managed with psychological skill. When the police were finished there was little, if anything, of incriminating potential left unsaid. The warned phase of questioning proceeded after a pause of only 15 to 20 minutes, in the same place as the unwarned segment. When the same officer who had conducted the first phase recited the *Miranda* warnings, he said nothing to counter the probable misimpression that the advice that anything Seibert said could be used against her also applied to the details of the inculpatory statement previously elicited. In particular, the police did not advise that her prior statement could not be used.[c] Nothing was said or done to dispel the oddity of warning about legal rights to silence and counsel right after the police had led her through a systematic interrogation, and any uncertainty on her part about a right to stop talking about matters previously discussed would only have been aggravated by the way Officer Hanrahan set the scene by saying "we've been talking for a little while about what happened on Wednesday the twelfth, haven't we?" The impression that the further questioning was a mere continuation of the earlier questions and responses was fostered by references back to the confession already given. It would have been reasonable to regard the two sessions as parts of a continuum, in which it would have been unnatural to refuse to repeat at the second stage what had been said before. These circumstances must be seen as challenging the comprehensibility and efficacy of the *Miranda* warnings to the point that a reasonable person in the suspect's shoes would not have

---

[b] Because the intent of the officer will rarely be as candidly admitted as it was here (even as it is likely to determine the conduct of the interrogation), the focus is on facts apart from intent that show the question-first tactic at work.

[c] We do not hold that a formal addendum warning that a previous statement could not be used would be sufficient to change the character of the question-first procedure to the point of rendering an ensuing statement admissible, but its absence is clearly a factor that blunts the efficacy of the warnings and points to a continuing, not a new, interrogation.

understood them to convey a message that she retained a choice about continuing to talk.

\* \* \*

Because the question-first tactic effectively threatens to thwart *Miranda*'s purpose of reducing the risk that a coerced confession would be admitted, and because the facts here do not reasonably support a conclusion that the warnings given could have served their purpose, Seibert's postwarning statements are inadmissible. The judgment of the Supreme Court of Missouri is affirmed.

### JUSTICE BREYER, concurring.

In my view, the following simple rule should apply to the two-stage interrogation technique: Courts should exclude the "fruits" of the initial unwarned questioning unless the failure to warn was in good faith. I believe this is a sound and workable approach to the problem this case presents. Prosecutors and judges have long understood how to apply the "fruits" approach, which they use in other areas of law. And in the workaday world of criminal law enforcement the administrative simplicity of the familiar has significant advantages over a more complex exclusionary rule.

I believe the plurality's approach in practice will function as a "fruits" test. The truly "effective" *Miranda* warnings on which the plurality insists will occur only when certain circumstances—a lapse in time, a change in location or interrogating officer, or a shift in the focus of the questioning—intervene between the unwarned questioning and any postwarning statement.

I consequently join the plurality's opinion in full. I also agree with Justice Kennedy's opinion insofar as it is consistent with this approach and makes clear that a good-faith exception applies.

### JUSTICE KENNEDY, concurring in the judgment.

The interrogation technique used in this case is designed to circumvent Miranda v. Arizona. It undermines the *Miranda* warning and obscures its meaning. The plurality opinion is correct to conclude that statements obtained through the use of this technique are inadmissible. Although I agree with much in the careful and convincing opinion for the plurality, my approach does differ in some respects, requiring this separate statement.

\* \* \* In my view, *Elstad* was correct in its reasoning and its result. *Elstad* reflects a balanced and pragmatic approach to enforcement of the *Miranda* warning. An officer may not realize that a suspect is in custody and warnings are required. The officer may not plan to question the suspect or may be waiting for a more appropriate time. Skilled investigators often interview suspects multiple times, and good police work may involve referring to prior statements to test their veracity or to refresh recollection. In light of these realities it would be extravagant to treat the presence of one statement that cannot be admitted under *Miranda* as sufficient reason to prohibit subsequent statements preceded by a proper warning. * * *

This case presents different considerations. The police used a two-step questioning technique based on a deliberate violation of *Miranda*. The *Miranda* warning was withheld to obscure both the practical and legal significance of the admonition when finally given. * * *

The technique used in this case distorts the meaning of *Miranda* and furthers no legitimate countervailing interest. The *Miranda* rule would be frustrated were we to allow police to undermine its meaning and effect. * * * When an interrogator uses this deliberate, two-step strategy, predicated upon violating *Miranda* during an extended interview, postwarning statements that are related to the substance of prewarning statements must be excluded absent specific, curative steps.

The plurality concludes that whenever a two-stage interview occurs, admissibility of the postwarning statement should depend on "whether the *Miranda* warnings delivered midstream could have been effective enough to accomplish their object" given the specific facts of the case. This test envisions an objective inquiry from the perspective of the suspect, and applies in the case of both intentional and unintentional two-stage interrogations. In my view, this test cuts too broadly. *Miranda*'s clarity is one of its strengths, and a multifactor test that applies to every two-stage interrogation may serve to undermine that clarity. I would apply a narrower test applicable only in the infrequent case, such as we have here, in which the two-step interrogation technique was used in a calculated way to undermine the *Miranda* warning.

The admissibility of postwarning statements should continue to be governed by the principles of *Elstad* unless the deliberate two-step strategy was employed. If the deliberate two-step strategy has been used, postwarning statements that are related to the substance of prewarning statements must be excluded unless curative measures are taken before the postwarning statement is made. Curative measures should be designed to ensure that a reasonable person in the suspect's situation would understand the import and effect of the *Miranda* warning and of the *Miranda* waiver. For example, a substantial break in time and circumstances between the prewarning statement and the *Miranda* warning may suffice in most circumstances, as it allows the accused to distinguish the two contexts and appreciate that the interrogation has taken a new turn. Alternatively, an additional warning that explains the likely inadmissibility of the prewarning custodial statement may be sufficient. No curative steps were taken in this case, however, so the postwarning statements are inadmissible and the conviction cannot stand.

For these reasons, I concur in the judgment of the Court.

**JUSTICE O'CONNOR, with whom THE CHIEF JUSTICE, JUSTICE SCALIA, and JUSTICE THOMAS join, dissenting.**

\* \* \*

I would analyze the two-step interrogation procedure under the voluntariness standards central to the Fifth Amendment and reiterated in *Elstad*. *Elstad* commands that if Seibert's first statement is shown to have been involuntary, the court must examine whether the taint dissipated through the passing of time or a change in circumstances \* \* \*. In addition, Seibert's second statement should be suppressed if she showed that it was involuntary despite the *Miranda* warnings. Although I would leave this analysis for the Missouri courts to conduct on remand, I note that, unlike the officers in *Elstad*, Officer Hanrahan referred to Seibert's unwarned statement during the second part of the interrogation when she made a statement at odds with her unwarned confession. Such a tactic may bear on the voluntariness inquiry.

\* \* \*

### QUESTIONS AFTER SEIBERT

*Seibert* was a 4–1–4 decision. With no majority opinion, how is it to be interpreted? The lower courts have held that Justice Kennedy's opinion is controlling because it is the narrowest view on which five members of the Court could agree. This means that a confession made after a *Miranda*-defective confession will be admissible unless, 1) the officers were in *bad faith* in not giving the warnings before the first confession; and 2) the second confession proceeded directly from the first. The court in United States v. Stewart, 388 F.3d 1079 (7th Cir. 2004), explained the state of the law after *Seibert* and the importance of Justice Kennedy's position:

> What emerges from the split opinions in *Seibert* is this: at least as to deliberate two-step interrogations in which *Miranda* warnings are intentionally withheld until after the suspect confesses, the central voluntariness inquiry of *Elstad* has been replaced by a presumptive rule of exclusion, subject to a multifactor test for change in time, place, and circumstances from the first statement to the second. According to the plurality, the multifactor test—timing and location of interrogations, continuity of police personnel, overlapping content of statements, etc.— measures the "effectiveness" of midstream *Miranda* warnings and applies in all cases involving sequential unwarned and warned admissions. In Justice Kennedy's view, however, an inquiry into change in time and circumstances between the prewarning and postwarning

statements—what he called "curative steps"—is necessary only in cases involving the deliberate use of a two-step interrogation strategy calculated to evade the requirements of *Miranda*. Justice Kennedy thus provided a fifth vote to depart from *Elstad*, but only where the police set out deliberately to withhold *Miranda* warnings until after a confession has been secured. Where the initial violation of *Miranda* was not part of a deliberate strategy to undermine the warnings, *Elstad* appears to have survived *Seibert*.

See also United States v. Kiam, 432 F.3d 524 (3d Cir. 2006) ("Once we determine that the *Miranda* violation was not deliberate, we must fall back on *Elstad* as instructed by Justice Kennedy.").

So under Justice Kennedy's controlling view, the bad faith of the interrogating officer is the controlling factor. How can you tell if the officer's failure to give *Miranda* warnings was a bad faith attempt to engage in a two-step interrogation process with midstream warnings? In *Seibert* the officers *admitted* that they intended to evade *Miranda* by using a two-step interrogation process. How many officers are going to admit that?

For an application of the Justice Kennedy "bad faith" test see United States v. Terry, 400 F.3d 575 (8th Cir. 2005), where the defendant was convicted of violating a federal law prohibiting a person from possessing a firearm if that person has been previously convicted of a crime of domestic violence. Officers responded to a call about a domestic dispute and arrested Terry, who appeared drunk. At the station, an officer asked a single question without giving *Miranda* warnings—whether Terry had been previously convicted of domestic violence. Terry answered "yes" and seemed eager to talk further, but the officer stopped the conversation. Later he was given warnings and admitted that he had brandished a gun during the current domestic dispute. The court held that the confession made after warnings was admissible under *Seibert*. The court found "no evidence that the police engaged in a deliberate strategy to undermine the *Miranda* warnings. Accordingly, the concerns of Justice Kennedy * * * in *Seibert* are not present here." See also United States v. Williams, 681 F.3d 35 (2nd Cir. 2012) ("public safety considerations plausibly account for [the officer's] limited questioning of Williams at the apartment in a way that militates against finding that the first interview was a premeditated attempt to evade *Miranda*"; officer asked only three questions about ownership and location of guns); United States v. Stewart, 536 F.3d 714 (7th Cir. 2008) (failure to give warnings was not in bad faith—officer was distracted because he was in a rush to release information on the defendant's accomplice, who was at large after a bank robbery). Compare United States v. Barnes, 713 F.3d 1200 (9th Cir. 2013) (court finds that warnings were deliberately delayed for fear that the suspect would be less willing to talk about another suspect that the agents were targeting; mid-stream warnings were ineffective where the subject of the interrogations was the same, there was no break in the interrogation, and the officers "treated the second round of interrogation as continuous with the first").

### Is There a Seibert Violation if the Mirandized Statement Is Not Repetitive of the Unwarned Statement?: Bobby v. Dixon

In Bobby v. Dixon, 132 S.Ct. 26 (2011), the Court in a unanimous per curiam opinion reversed the Sixth Circuit, which had granted habeas relief because of a *Seibert* violation. The Court found that *Seibert* could not apply where the unwarned statement and the Mirandized statement are about different (even if related) crimes. Police had three encounters with the defendant. The first was when he came to the stationhouse to retrieve his car. When a detective issued *Miranda* warnings and asked him about the murder victim's disappearance, the defendant refused to answer questions without a lawyer. Later, as the investigation continued, the police determined that the defendant had forged the victim's name on a check the defendant received as a result of selling the victim's car. The police arrested the defendant and deliberately interrogated him without *Miranda* warnings. The defendant admitted obtaining an identification card in the victim's name and signing the victim's name on the check but claimed he had permission to sell the car and that he did not know where the victim was. The interrogation occurred intermittently for a total of 45 minutes over about four hours, and the police brought the defendant to a correctional facility where he was booked on a forgery charge. The same afternoon another suspect led police to the victim's body and said that the defendant had told him where the victim was buried. The police released the other suspect and had the defendant brought back to the stationhouse.

Upon arriving at the station, several hours after he had left it, the defendant said that he had heard the police had found a body and asked whether the other suspect was in custody. The police said "no," whereupon the defendant said that "I talked to my attorney, and I want to tell you what happened." The police provided *Miranda* warnings, the defendant talked, the police then used a tape recorder and, after again advising of *Miranda* warnings, taped the defendant's detailed confession of murder. At the defendant's trial, the confession of forgery was excluded from the trial but the confession to murder was admitted.

The Court found this case to be very different from *Seibert*. The Court described the result in *Seibert* and distinguished it in the following passage:

> In this case, no two-step interrogation technique of the type that concerned the Court in *Seibert* undermined the *Miranda* warnings Dixon received. In *Seibert*, the suspect's first, unwarned interrogation left "little, if anything, of incriminating potential left unsaid," making it "unnatural" not to "repeat at the second stage what had been said before." But in this case Dixon steadfastly maintained during his first, unwarned interrogation that he had "[n]othing whatsoever" to

do with Hammer's disappearance. Thus, unlike in *Seibert*, there is no concern here that police gave Dixon *Miranda* warnings and then led him to repeat an earlier murder confession, because there was no earlier confession to repeat. * * * Nor is there any evidence that police used Dixon's earlier admission to forgery to induce him to waive his right to silence later: Dixon declared his desire to tell police what happened to Hammer before the second interrogation session even began. * * *

The Court concluded as follows:

> The admission of Dixon's murder confession was consistent with this Court's precedents: Dixon received *Miranda* warnings before confessing to Hammer's murder; the effectiveness of those warnings was not impaired by the sort of "two-step interrogation technique" condemned in *Seibert*; and there is no evidence that any of Dixon's statements was the product of actual coercion. That does not excuse the detectives' decision not to give Dixon *Miranda* warnings before his first interrogation. But the Ohio courts recognized that failure and imposed the appropriate remedy: exclusion of Dixon's forgery confession and the attendant statements given without the benefit of *Miranda* warnings. Because no precedent of this Court required Ohio to do more, the Sixth Circuit was without authority to overturn the reasoned judgment of the State's highest court.

### Physical Evidence Derived from Miranda-Defective Confessions

In the following case, the Court holds that, even after *Dickerson*, the exclusionary rule does not bar the physical fruits of a *Miranda*-defective confession.

### UNITED STATES V. PATANE

Supreme Court of the United States, 2004.
542 U.S. 630.

**JUSTICE THOMAS announced the judgment of the Court and delivered an opinion, in which THE CHIEF JUSTICE and JUSTICE SCALIA join.**

In this case we must decide whether a failure to give a suspect the warnings prescribed by Miranda v. Arizona requires suppression of the physical fruits of the suspect's unwarned but voluntary statements. * * * Because the *Miranda* rule protects against violations of the Self-Incrimination Clause, which, in turn, is not implicated by the introduction at trial of physical evidence resulting from voluntary statements, we answer the question presented in the negative.

* * * In June 2001, respondent, Samuel Francis Patane, was arrested for harassing his ex-girlfriend, Linda O'Donnell. He was released on bond, subject to a temporary restraining order that prohibited him from contacting O'Donnell. Respondent apparently violated the restraining order by attempting to telephone O'Donnell. On June 6, 2001, Officer Tracy Fox of the Colorado Springs Police Department began to investigate the matter. On the same day, a county probation officer informed an agent of the Bureau of Alcohol, Tobacco, and Firearms (ATF), that respondent, a convicted felon, illegally possessed a .40 Glock pistol. The ATF relayed this information to Detective Josh Benner, who worked closely with the ATF. Together, Detective Benner and Officer Fox proceeded to respondent's residence.

After reaching the residence and inquiring into respondent's attempts to contact O'Donnell, Officer Fox arrested respondent for violating the restraining order. Detective Benner attempted to advise respondent of his *Miranda* rights but got no further than the right to remain silent. At that point, respondent interrupted, asserting that he knew his rights, and neither officer attempted to complete the warning.

Detective Benner then asked respondent about the Glock. Respondent was initially reluctant to discuss the matter, stating: "I am not sure I should tell you anything about the Glock because I don't want you to take it away from me." Detective Benner persisted, and respondent told him that the pistol was in his bedroom. Respondent then gave Detective Benner permission to retrieve the pistol. Detective Benner found the pistol and seized it.

A grand jury indicted respondent for possession of a firearm by a convicted felon * * *. [The court of appeals held that the gun should have been suppressed as the fruit of a *Miranda*-defective confession.] The court rejected the Government's argument that this Court's decisions in *Elstad* and *Tucker* foreclosed application of the fruit of the poisonous tree doctrine of Wong Sun v. United States, 371 U.S. 471 (1963), to the present context. These holdings were, the Court of Appeals reasoned, based on the view that *Miranda* announced a prophylactic rule, a position that it found to be incompatible with this Court's decision in *Dickerson, supra* ("*Miranda* announced a constitutional rule that Congress may not supersede legislatively"). The Court of Appeals thus equated *Dickerson's* announcement that *Miranda* is a constitutional rule with the proposition that a failure to warn pursuant to *Miranda* is itself a violation of the Constitution (and, more particularly, of the suspect's Fifth Amendment rights). * * *

As we explain below, the *Miranda* rule is a prophylactic employed to protect against violations of the Self-Incrimination Clause. The Self-Incrimination Clause, however, is not implicated by the admission into evidence of the physical fruit of a voluntary statement. Accordingly, there is no justification for extending the *Miranda* rule to this context. And just as the Self-Incrimination Clause primarily focuses on the criminal trial, so too does the *Miranda* rule. The *Miranda* rule is not a code of police conduct, and police do not violate the Constitution (or even the *Miranda* rule, for that matter) by mere failures to warn. For this reason, the exclusionary rule articulated in cases such as *Wong Sun* does not apply. * * *

* * * For present purposes, it suffices to note that the core protection afforded by the Self-Incrimination Clause is a prohibition on compelling a criminal defendant to testify against himself at trial. The Clause cannot be violated by the introduction of nontestimonial evidence obtained as a result of voluntary statements.

To be sure, the Court has recognized and applied several prophylactic rules designed to protect the core privilege against self-incrimination. For example, although the text of the Self-Incrimination Clause at least suggests that its coverage is limited to compelled testimony that is used against the defendant in the trial itself, potential suspects may, at times, assert the privilege in proceedings in which answers might be used to incriminate them in a subsequent criminal case.

Similarly, in *Miranda*, the Court concluded that the possibility of coercion inherent in custodial interrogations unacceptably raises the risk that a suspect's privilege against self-incrimination might be violated. To protect against this danger, the *Miranda* rule creates a presumption of coercion, in the absence of specific warnings, that is generally irrebuttable for purposes of the prosecution's case in chief.

But because these prophylactic rules (including the *Miranda* rule) necessarily sweep beyond the actual protections of the Self-Incrimination Clause, any further extension of these rules must be justified by its necessity for the protection of the actual right against compelled self-incrimination. * * *

* * *

Finally, nothing in *Dickerson*, including its characterization of *Miranda* as announcing a constitutional rule, changes any of these observations.

* * *

Our cases also make clear the related point that a mere failure to give *Miranda* warnings does not, by itself, violate a suspect's constitutional rights or even the *Miranda* rule. * * * This, of course, follows from the nature of the right protected by the Self-Incrimination Clause, which the *Miranda* rule, in turn, protects. It is a fundamental *trial* right.

It follows that police do not violate a suspect's constitutional rights (or the *Miranda* rule) by negligent or even deliberate failures to provide the suspect with the full panoply of warnings prescribed by *Miranda*. Potential violations occur, if at all, only upon the admission of unwarned statements into evidence at trial. And, at that point, the exclusion of unwarned statements is a complete and sufficient remedy for any perceived *Miranda* violation.

Thus, unlike unreasonable searches under the Fourth Amendment or actual violations of the Due Process Clause or the Self-Incrimination Clause, there is, with respect to mere failures to warn, nothing to deter. There is therefore no reason to apply the "fruit of the poisonous tree" doctrine of *Wong Sun*. The admission of such fruit presents no risk that a defendant's coerced statements (however defined) will be used against him at a criminal trial. In any case, the exclusion of unwarned statements is a complete and sufficient remedy for any perceived *Miranda* violation. * * * Our decision not to apply *Wong Sun* to mere failures to give *Miranda* warnings was sound at the time *Tucker* and *Elstad* were decided, and we decline to apply *Wong Sun* to such failures now.

* * * [A]lthough it is true that the Court requires the exclusion of the physical fruit of actually coerced statements, it must be remembered that statements taken without sufficient *Miranda* warnings are presumed to have been coerced only for certain purposes and then only when necessary to protect the privilege against self-incrimination. For the reasons discussed above, we decline to extend that presumption further.

* * *

Accordingly, we reverse the judgment of the Court of Appeals and remand the case for further proceedings consistent with this opinion.

**JUSTICE KENNEDY, with whom JUSTICE O'CONNOR joins, concurring in the judgment.**

In Oregon v. Elstad, New York v. Quarles, and Harris v. New York, evidence obtained following an unwarned interrogation was held admissible. This result was based in large part on our recognition that the concerns underlying the Miranda v. Arizona rule must be accommodated to other objectives of the criminal justice system. I agree with the plurality that Dickerson v. United States did not undermine these precedents and, in fact, cited them in support. Here, it is sufficient to note that the Government presents an even stronger case for admitting the evidence obtained as the result of Patane's unwarned statement. Admission of nontestimonial physical fruits (the Glock in this case), even more so than the postwarning statements to the police in *Elstad* * * * does not run the risk of admitting into trial an accused's coerced incriminating statements against himself. In light of the important probative value of reliable physical evidence, it is doubtful that exclusion can be justified by a deterrence rationale sensitive to both law enforcement interests and a suspect's rights during an in-custody interrogation. Unlike the plurality, however, I find it unnecessary to decide whether the detective's failure to give Patane the full *Miranda* warnings should be characterized as a violation of the *Miranda* rule itself, or whether there is "anything to deter" so long as the unwarned statements are not later introduced at trial.

With these observations, I concur in the judgment of the Court.

**JUSTICE SOUTER, with whom JUSTICE STEVENS and JUSTICE GINSBURG join, dissenting.**

The issue actually presented today is whether courts should apply the fruit of the poisonous tree doctrine lest we create an incentive for the police to omit *Miranda* warnings before custodial interrogation. In closing their eyes to the consequences of giving an evidentiary advantage to those who ignore *Miranda*, the majority adds an important inducement for interrogators to ignore the rule in that case.

\* \* \*

There is no way to read this case except as an unjustifiable invitation to law enforcement officers to flout *Miranda* when there may be physical evidence to be gained. The incentive is an odd one, coming from the Court on the same day it decides Missouri v. Seibert. I respectfully dissent.

**JUSTICE BREYER, dissenting.**

For reasons similar to those set forth in Justice Souter's dissent and in my concurring opinion in Missouri v. Seibert, I would extend to this context the "fruit of the poisonous tree" approach, which I believe the Court has come close to adopting in *Seibert*. Under that approach, courts would exclude physical evidence derived from unwarned questioning unless the failure to provide *Miranda* warnings was in good faith. Because the courts below made no explicit finding as to good or bad faith, I would remand for such a determination.

### QUESTIONS AFTER PATANE

*Patane* and *Seibert* were decided the same day. One holds that the physical fruits of a *Miranda* violation are never excluded; the other holds that testimonial fruits of a *Miranda* violation must be excluded under certain circumstances. Is there a difference between physical and testimonial fruits that would justify such a difference in treatment?

Note that Justice Thomas's opinion—which essentially questions the constitutional status of the *Miranda* safeguards—does not command a majority of the Court. The controlling opinion is that of Justice Kennedy, as the narrowest opinion on which five members of the Court can agree. That opinion is basically, "Even if *Miranda* is constitutionally-based, the physical fruits of a *Miranda* violation are not excluded." See United States v. Jackson, 506 F.3d 1358 (11th Cir. 2007): noting that Justice Kennedy's opinion controls, and concluding that "the *Patane* plurality and concurrence agreed, at least, that *Miranda* does not require the exclusion of physical evidence that is discovered on the basis of a voluntary, although unwarned, statement. As several of our sister circuits have recognized, this narrow agreement is the holding of *Patane*."

Justice Thomas's opinion reads as if *Dickerson* was never written. How can the *Miranda* safeguards be simply "prophylactic" and not guaranteed by the Constitution, after *Dickerson* said that *Miranda* was a constitutional decision that could not be legislatively overruled? And how could Chief Justice Rehnquist, who wrote *Dickerson*, sign on to such an opinion? Is *Miranda* "constitutional enough" that it must be complied with by the states and respected by Congress, but not "constitutional enough" to require exclusion of evidence where the Court decides that the evidence should be admitted?

## 3. An Emergency Exception

### *New York v. Quarles*

In New York v. Quarles, 467 U.S. 649 (1984), the Court concluded that "overriding considerations of public safety" can justify an officer's failure to provide *Miranda* warnings, and that an unwarned confession obtained under such circumstances is admissible *in the government's case-in-chief* despite *Miranda*. The Court relied on the now-discredited rationale that a violation of *Miranda* was not a violation of the Constitution. After *Dickerson*, the *Quarles* public safety exception to *Miranda* is apparently justified as a necessity exception to the constitutionally-based *Miranda* rule—much like the exigent circumstances exception to the Fourth Amendment warrant requirement. See United States v. Talley, 275 F.3d 560 (6th Cir. 2001) ("the *Dickerson* majority expressly incorporated existing decisions, like *Quarles*, into the 'constitutional' right to a *Miranda* warning").

Justice Rehnquist wrote for the majority in *Quarles* and stated the facts as follows:

> On September 11, 1980, at approximately 12:30 a.m., Officer Frank Kraft and Officer Sal Scarring were on road patrol in Queens, New York, when a young woman approached their car. She told them that she had just been raped by a black male, approximately six feet tall, who was wearing a black jacket with the name "Big Ben" printed in yellow letters on the back. She told the officers that the man had just entered an A & P supermarket located nearby and that the man was carrying a gun.

The officers drove the woman to the supermarket, and Officer Kraft entered the store while Officer Scarring radioed for assistance. Officer Kraft quickly spotted respondent, who matched the description given by the woman, approaching a check-out counter. Apparently upon seeing the officer, respondent turned and ran toward the rear of the store, and Officer Kraft pursued him with a drawn gun. When respondent turned the corner at the end of an aisle, Officer Kraft lost sight of him for several seconds, and upon regaining sight of respondent, ordered him to stop and put his hands over his head.

Although more than three other officers had arrived on the scene by that time, Officer Kraft was the first to reach respondent. He frisked him and discovered that he was wearing a shoulder holster which was then empty. After handcuffing him, Officer Kraft asked him where the gun was. Respondent nodded in the direction of some empty cartons and responded, "the gun is over there." Officer Kraft thereafter retrieved a loaded .38 caliber revolver from one of the cartons.

The Court agreed with the state courts that the facts demonstrated custodial interrogation and thus the confession would appear to fall within the exclusionary rule of *Miranda,* because Quarles never received the warnings. But it explained the need for an exception for emergency circumstances as follows:

The police in this case, in the very act of apprehending a suspect, were confronted with the immediate necessity of ascertaining the whereabouts of a gun which they had every reason to believe the suspect had just removed from his empty holster and discarded in the supermarket. So long as the gun was concealed somewhere in the supermarket, with its actual whereabouts unknown, it obviously posed more than one danger to the public safety: an accomplice might make use of it, a customer or employee might later come upon it.

In such a situation, if the police are required to recite the familiar *Miranda* warnings before asking the whereabouts of the gun, suspects in Quarles' position might well be deterred from responding. Procedural safeguards which deter a suspect from responding were deemed acceptable in *Miranda* in order to protect the Fifth Amendment privilege; when the primary social cost of those added protections is the possibility of fewer convictions, the *Miranda* majority was willing to bear that cost. Here, had *Miranda* warnings deterred Quarles from responding to Officer Kraft's question about the whereabouts of the gun, the cost would have been something more than merely the failure to obtain evidence useful in convicting Quarles. Officer Kraft needed an answer to his question not simply to make his case against Quarles but to insure that further danger to the public did not result from the concealment of the gun in a public area.

\* \* \* We decline to place officers such as Officer Kraft in the untenable position of having to consider, often in a matter of seconds, whether it best serves society for them to ask the necessary questions without the *Miranda* warnings and render whatever probative evidence they uncover inadmissible, or for them to give the warnings in order to preserve the admissibility of evidence they might uncover but possibly damage or destroy their ability to obtain that evidence and neutralize the volatile situation confronting them.

Although the Court recognized that it had "to some degree \* \* \* lessen[ed] the desirable clarity of" the *Miranda* rule, it stated that "we recognize here the importance of a workable rule to guide police officers, who have only limited time and expertise to reflect on and balance the social and individual interests involved in the specific circumstances they confront." It expressed the belief that "the exception we recognize today lessens the necessity of that on-the-scene balancing process." The Court held that the both the gun and the statement revealing its location were therefore admissible despite the *Miranda* violation.

Justice O'Connor concurred in part and dissented in part. She dissented from the public safety exception created by the Court on the ground that it would be confusing and contrary to *Miranda's* bright line approach. While disagreeing with the majority's implementation of a public safety exception, and thus dissenting from the Court's ruling that Quarles' statement was admissible, Justice O'Connor concurred in the result as to the admission of the gun. In her view, the gun was admissible because *Miranda* does not require exclusion of the fruits of *Miranda*-defective confessions—a view eventually adopted by the Court in *Patane, supra.*

Justice Marshall dissented and was joined by Justices Brennan and Stevens. He found no emergency on the facts of the case:

[C]ontrary to the majority's intimations, no customers or employees were wandering about the store in danger of coming across Quarles' discarded weapon. Although the supermarket was open to the public, Quarles' arrest took place during the middle of the night when the store was apparently deserted except for the clerks at the checkout counter. The police could easily have cordoned off the store and searched for the missing gun. Had they done so, they would have found the gun forthwith. The police were well aware that Quarles had discarded his weapon somewhere near the scene of the arrest.

### The Scope of the Public Safety Exception

How "exigent" must the circumstances be before the public safety exception applies? See United States v. Mobley, 40 F.3d 688 (4th Cir.1994), where the court found that an officer's question concerning the location of a gun in a house was *not* within the public safety exception. The officers went to the defendant's house to arrest him for a narcotics violation, the defendant was naked when he answered the door, and before asking the question about the gun, the officers had already conducted a protective sweep and found that no other persons were present. The court found no "immediate need" to ask about a gun and declared that "[t]here is nothing that separates these facts from those of an ordinary arrest scenario." Therefore the defendant's statement about the location of the gun could not be admitted under *Miranda*. See also United States v. Jackson, 544 F.3d 351 (1st Cir. 2008) (public safety exception does not apply to unwarned statements the defendant made concerning the presence of a gun in the cereal box of his refrigerator; at the time of questioning, the defendant was outside the residence and surrounded by police officers, and the residence was unoccupied). Compare United States v. Liddell, 517 F.3d 1007 (8th Cir. 2008): where officers had already obtained a gun from the defendant's car, their question—"Is there anything else we need to know about?"—was within the public safety exception because officers "had good reason to believe that additional weapons might pose a threat to their safety when they searched Liddell's car incident to a late night arrest."

What kind of questions can be asked within the rubric of public safety? The Court in *Quarles* held that questions without warnings, to be permissible, must be addressed to the public safety risk. So for, example, it was permissible to ask Quarles about the location of the gun, but it would not have been within the public safety exception to ask whether he had committed the crime that he was arrested for. See United States v. Newton, 369 F.3d 659 (2d Cir. 2004) (asking the defendant about the location of a gun was within the public safety exception, but asking why he needed the gun was not).

### Categorical Application of the Public Safety Exception

Can the public safety exception be applied categorically to certain arrest situations? Consider United States v. Carrillo, 16 F.3d 1046 (9th Cir.1994). Carrillo was arrested after a narcotics transaction, and transported to a detention facility. At that point, Officer Weeks decided to search Carrillo. Before beginning the search, however, the officer asked Carrillo if he had any drugs or needles on his person. Carrillo responded, "No, I don't use drugs, I sell them." This statement was used against Carrillo as an admission at trial. Carrillo argued that the statement should have been suppressed because it was made before he had been given a *Miranda* warning. But the court held that the statement was properly admitted under the "public safety" exception to *Miranda*. The court noted that at the suppression hearing, Officer Weeks testified that during past searches he had been poked by needles and suffered headaches and skin irritation from contact with illegal drugs.

Does the *Carrillo* holding mean that "public safety" permits an officer to dispense with *Miranda* warnings and ask *any* arrestee (e.g., those arrested for theft or white collar crime) whether they are carrying drugs or syringes? See also United States v. Lackey, 334 F.3d 1224 (10th Cir. 2003) (it was proper, under the public safety exception, to ask an arrestee whether he was carrying any guns or sharp objects, before conducting a search incident to the arrest; the defendant's response, "no I am not, but there is a gun in the car" was properly admitted under *Quarles*).

## D. OPEN QUESTIONS AFTER *MIRANDA*

What does it mean for the suspect to be "in custody"? When is a suspect being "interrogated"? Must the warnings be given pursuant to a standard and precise script? These and other important questions are discussed in this section.

### 1. What Is Custody?

If the defendant who confesses is not in custody, *Miranda* does not apply, and the admissibility of the confession depends on whether it was given voluntarily under the totality of the circumstances. As one court put it: "Because the presence of *both* a custodial setting and official interrogation is required to trigger the *Miranda* right * * * absent one or the other, *Miranda* is not implicated." Alston v. Redman, 34 F.3d 1237 (3d Cir.1994). It follows that if the defendant is not in custody, it wouldn't matter if the suspect invokes his right to remain silent or his right to counsel—those invocations need not be respected because they are only triggered by custodial interrogation. See United States v. Infante, 701 F.3d 386 (1st Cir. 2012) (defendant was not in custody at the time of an interrogation, "obviating the need for *Miranda* warnings and for heeding Infante's invocation of his rights.").

#### *Arrest Is Custody*

According to *Miranda,* the test for custody is whether a person is deprived of his freedom of action in any significant way. In several cases subsequent to *Miranda,* the Court specifically addressed the custody question. In Orozco v. Texas, 394 U.S. 324 (1969), it held that the defendant was in custody when four armed policemen entered his bedroom at 4:00 a. m. and tried to elicit incriminating information from him. In so deciding, the Court noted that one of the four officers had testified that the defendant was under arrest and not free to leave his bedroom. If a person is arrested, he is in custody.

Conversely, in Beckwith v. United States, 425 U.S. 341 (1976), the Court found that the defendant was not in custody for purposes of receiving *Miranda* warnings where two I.R.S. agents arrived at his house at 8:00 p.m., were invited in, and sat with the defendant at his dining room table to discuss their investigation of his federal income tax returns. The agents were looking into the possibility of criminal tax fraud. The Court maintained that although Beckwith was the focus of a tax investigation, he was not in a custodial situation when he talked with the agents in his home. The Court stated that if the defendant is not in custody the inherently coercive atmosphere that triggers the need for *Miranda* warnings is not present. See also United States v. Courtney, 463 F.3d 333 (5th Cir. 2006) (confession was not custodial where the agents met with the defendant in public, at a restaurant of her choice, agents were not in uniform and did not display weapons, she was not told that she had to meet with the agents, and she was allowed to leave after the interview).

### *Objective Test: Stansbury v. California*

In Stansbury v. California, 511 U.S. 318 (1994) (per curiam), the Court held, "not for the first time, that an officer's subjective and undisclosed view concerning whether the person being interrogated is a suspect is irrelevant to the assessment whether the person is in custody." An officer questioned Stansbury about a murder, thinking that Stansbury was a potential witness. When the questioning began, the officer believed that another man was the prime suspect. But after Stansbury gave incriminating information in response to a few questions, it became clear to the officer that Stansbury was the perpetrator. At that point, the officer gave Stansbury *Miranda* warnings. There was no indication that the officer's initial lack of suspicion had been imparted to Stansbury.

The question for the Court was whether Stansbury's initial statements had been obtained in violation of *Miranda*. Stansbury argued that he was in custody during the period of initial questioning because he was questioned in the jail part of the police station, by officers whose guns were visible. But the lower courts found that Stansbury was not in custody until the *officer's suspicions* shifted to him as a result of the initial questioning.

The Supreme Court unanimously held that the lower courts were incorrect in focusing on the officer's undisclosed state of mind. It reasoned as follows:

It is well settled * * * that a police officer's subjective view that the individual under questioning is a suspect, if undisclosed, does not bear upon the question whether the individual is in custody for purposes of *Miranda*. The same principle obtains if an officer's undisclosed assessment is that the person being questioned is not a suspect. In either instance, one cannot expect the person under interrogation to probe the officer's innermost thoughts. * * *

* * * [A]n officer's views concerning the nature of an interrogation, or beliefs concerning the potential culpability of the individual being questioned, may be one among many factors that bear upon the assessment whether that individual was in custody, but only if the officer's views or beliefs were somehow manifested to the individual under interrogation and would have affected how a reasonable person in that position would perceive his or her freedom to leave.

The Court remanded to the lower court to determine the question of custody without relying on the officer's subjective and undisclosed opinions. See also United States v. Panak, 552 F.3d 462 (6th Cir. 2009) (officer's knowledge about evidence incriminating the suspect "is relevant only if (1) it was somehow manifested to the individual under interrogation and (2) it would have affected how a reasonable person in that position would perceive his or her freedom to leave.").

### *The Relevance of the Suspect's Youth: J.D.B. v. North Carolina*

In J.D.B. v. North Carolina, 131 S. Ct. 2394 (2011), Justice Sotomayor wrote for the Court as it reasoned that

[i]t is beyond dispute that children will often feel bound to submit to police questioning when an adult in the same circumstances would feel free to leave," and "[s]eeing no reason for police officers or courts to blind themselves to that commonsense reality, we hold that a child's age properly informs the *Miranda* custody analysis."

J.D.B. was a 13-year-old, seventh-grade student attending class at Smith Middle School in Chapel Hill, North Carolina when he was removed from his classroom by a uniformed police officer, escorted to a closed-door conference room, and questioned by police for at least half an hour regarding two home break-ins. After learning of the prospect of juvenile detention, J.D.B. confessed that he and a friend were responsible for the break-ins. The officer only then informed J.D.B. that he could refuse to answer the investigator's questions and that he was free to leave.

Justice Sotomayor concluded that "so long as the child's age was known to the officer at the time of police questioning, or would have been objectively apparent to a reasonable officer, its inclusion in the custody analysis is consistent with the objective nature of that test." Justice Alito, with whom The Chief Justice, Justice Scalia, and Justice Thomas joined, dissented. Justice Alito argued that the decision was "fundamentally inconsistent with one of the main justifications for the *Miranda* rule: the perceived need for a clear rule that can be easily applied in all cases."

### Prisoners in Custody: Mathis v. United States and Howes v. Fields

In Mathis v. United States, 391 U.S. 1 (1968), the defendant was interrogated, while in jail, by I.R.S. agents about his alleged tax evasion. The Court found that although the defendant was in jail for reasons unrelated to the tax investigation, he was under the circumstances in custody, and the failure to give him his *Miranda* warnings violated his constitutional rights.

Subsequent cases have refused to read *Mathis* as establishing a per se rule that prisoners are always in custody for *Miranda* purposes. Rather, the question is whether prison officials' conduct would cause "a reasonable person to believe his freedom of movement had been *further* diminished." Garcia v. Singletary, 13 F.3d 1487 (11th Cir.1994).

In Howes v. Fields, 132 S. Ct. 1181 (2012), the Supreme Court rejected the Sixth Circuit's categorical rule—purportedly based on *Mathis*—that interrogation is per se custodial when a prisoner is questioned in private about conduct occurring outside the prison. Justice Alito wrote the majority opinion for six Justices. While Fields was incarcerated, he was escorted to a conference room in the prison and interrogated, without *Miranda* warnings, about committing a crime unrelated to his incarceration. He confessed after an interrogation session that took between five and seven hours.

Justice Alito first stated that "our decisions do not clearly establish that a prisoner is always in custody for purposes of *Miranda* whenever a prisoner is isolated from the general prison population and questioned about conduct outside the prison." He went on to observe that a determination of custody must focus on all features of the interrogation, and incarceration is only one such feature. Justice Alito found that two factors pointed in favor of a finding of custody under the facts presented: the interrogation was lengthy (well past the time when the prisoners generally went to bed), and Fields was not informed of his right to refuse to speak to the deputies. However, Justice Alito found those factors were offset by others. Most importantly, Fields was told twice that he was free to leave and return to his cell. Further, Fields was not physically restrained and the door to the conference room was sometimes left open.

The Court also suggested that the interests protected by *Miranda* may apply with less force to prisoners. It identified three reasons that might be so: Questioning a person already in custody does not involve the "shock" that generally accompanies arrest; a prisoner is unlikely to be lured into speaking based on the hope of prompt release; and a prisoner knows that the law enforcement officers conducting the interrogation probably lack the authority to affect the duration of his sentence.

Justice Ginsburg, joined by Justices Breyer and Sotomayor, concurred in part and dissented in part. Justice Ginsburg recognized that the case law did not support an automatic rule that prison interrogation was always custodial. But she concluded that Fields was in custody at the time of his interrogation. She stated: "I would not train, as the Court does, on the question whether there can be custody within custody. Instead, I would ask, as *Miranda* put it, whether Fields was subjected to "incommunicado interrogation . . . in a police-dominated atmosphere," whether he was placed, against his will, in an inherently stressful situation, and whether his freedom of action was curtailed in any significant way. Those should be the key questions, and to each I would answer "Yes.""

### Interrogation at the Police Station: Oregon v. Mathiason

In Oregon v. Mathiason, 429 U.S. 492 (1977), a per curiam opinion, the Court ruled that an individual questioned at a police station is not necessarily in custody. Mathiason was out on parole when an officer telephoned him to say that he wanted to discuss something with him and asked if they could meet somewhere. Mathiason had no preference, so the policeman asked if he could come down to the station house. Mathiason agreed, and arriving a short time later, was told that he was not under arrest. Mathiason was ushered into an office, the door was closed and the two sat across a desk. No *Miranda* warnings were given. The officer told Mathiason about the burglary he was investigating, that he believed Mathiason was involved, and that his fingerprints were found at the scene (which was not true). Mathiason confessed, and was then allowed to leave the police station.

The Court concluded that Mathiason's freedom was not restrained so as to render him in custody under *Miranda*. The Court stressed that Mathiason went down to the station voluntarily, was informed that he was not under arrest, and left the station without hindrance after he confessed. The dissenters, Justices Brennan, Marshall, and Stevens, stressed that Mathiason was a parolee and so it could not be truly said that he went down to the station of his own accord. Does *Mathiason* encourage suspects to be cooperative with the police? If it is important that a suspect is allowed to leave, can't that factor be manipulated by officers after *Mathiason*?

In California v. Beheler, 463 U.S. 1121 (1983), the Court extended *Mathiason* to find that the suspect was not in custody when he agreed to accompany police officers down to the station for questioning. He was told he was not under arrest and was released after confessing. Should there be a difference between going to the station unaccompanied and going to the station with police officers? See also Yarborough v. Alvarado, 541 U.S. 652 (2004), where the Court found that a teenager who was brought to the station by his parents, at the request of police, was not in custody when he was interrogated in the stationhouse for two hours.

### *Meetings with a Probation Officer: Minnesota v. Murphy*

Justice White wrote for six Justices in Minnesota v. Murphy, 465 U.S. 420 (1984), as the Court held that the privilege against self-incrimination was not violated when a probation officer called Murphy, a probationer, to her office and questioned him about the rape and murder of a teenage girl. Murphy had admitted the offenses to a counselor as part of the treatment prescribed as a condition of probation. The Court held that *Miranda* did not require the officer to warn Murphy of his rights prior to asking questions about crimes he might have committed, because Murphy was not arrested or otherwise in custody even though he was required to meet with the officer. Although the Court recognized that the officer sought incriminating information, it declared that warnings are not required simply because an investigation has focused upon a suspect.

Justice Marshall, joined by Justice Stevens and in part by Justice Brennan, dissented. He argued that a reasonable man in Murphy's position would have believed that his duty to answer questions honestly as a condition of probation required him to respond to the questions put by the officer.

### *Terry Stops: Berkemer v. McCarty*

If a police officer interrogates a suspect during a *Terry* stop, must the officer give *Miranda* warnings? In Berkemer v. McCarty, 468 U.S. 420 (1984), the Court in an opinion by Justice Marshall held that *Terry* stops are not custodial for *Miranda* purposes. Justice Marshall noted that *Terry* stops are typically of brief duration; questioning is limited, because the officer can ask only a "moderate number of questions to determine identity and to try to obtain information confirming or dispelling the officer's suspicions;" the detainee is not obliged to respond (though he must provide identification); and unless probable cause arises in a short time, the detainee must be released. Justice Marshall concluded that

*Terry* stops were "comparatively nonthreatening" and hence unlike the custodial situations required to trigger *Miranda.* If the stop escalates to an arrest, however, *Miranda* will apply.

Thus, the law distinguishing *Terry* stops from arrests discussed in Chapter 2 (see, e.g., Dunaway v. New York, supra) also determines whether custody exists under *Miranda.* See Saltzburg, Foreword: The Flow and Ebb of Constitutional Criminal Procedure in the Warren and Burger Courts, 69 Geo.L.J. 151, 200–03 (1980). See also United States v. Ozuna, 170 F.3d 654 (6th Cir.1999) (limited interrogation at customs checkpoint is not custodial within the meaning of *Miranda:* "All persons attempting to enter the United States must anticipate detention while answering a few basic questions and this cuts against the potentially coercive aspect of the Customs inquiry.").

### *Summary on Custody: Relevant Factors*

One court has set forth six indicia for determining whether a suspect is in custody for *Miranda* purposes:

(1) whether the suspect was informed at the time of questioning that the questioning was voluntary, that the suspect was free to leave or request the officers to do so, or that the suspect was not considered under arrest; (2) whether the suspect possessed unrestrained freedom of movement during questioning; (3) whether the suspect initiated contact with authorities or voluntarily acquiesced to official request to respond to questions; (4) whether strong arm tactics or deceptive stratagems were employed during questioning; (5) whether the atmosphere of the questioning was police dominated; and (6) whether the suspect was placed under arrest at the termination of the questioning.

United States v. Brown, 990 F.2d 397 (8th Cir.1993). The *Brown* court stated that "[t]he presence of the first three indicia tends to mitigate the existence of custody at the time of questioning" while "the presence of the last three indicia aggravate the existence of custody."

How would the above six-factor test apply to the following facts?

On February 25, 1989, the Twin Cities Federal Savings and Loan Association (TCF) was robbed by two men armed with a shotgun and possibly a handgun. [Eyewitness descriptions and other information led the officers to focus on Griffin as a suspect. The officers telephoned Griffin's house].

* * * Griffin's stepfather answered the phone and informed the agents that Griffin would be home early that evening. Agents Waldie and Tremper proceeded to Griffin's home, arriving at 7 p.m., and were invited into the living room by Griffin's stepfather. The purpose

of the interview was to determine what Griffin knew of the bank robbery. The officers did not intend to arrest him at that time. The agents waited in the living room until 8:15 p.m. when Griffin was heard approaching the house outside. The agents moved to the hall near the front door to meet Griffin as he entered the house. Waldie and Tremper identified themselves as F.B.I. agents investigating a bank robbery and informed Griffin that they needed to speak with him. At that point, before any other words were spoken, Griffin stated, "The gun wasn't loaded."

The agents explained to Griffin's parents that it was necessary for them to speak to Griffin in private and, accordingly, the three went into the dining room and sat down. The agents did not draw their guns, handcuff Griffin, or place him under formal arrest. Griffin's parents retired to the upstairs of the house where they remained throughout the course of the questioning.

Neither of the agents informed Griffin that he was not under arrest, that he was free to request the agents to leave without speaking to them, nor did they inform him of his *Miranda* rights. Twice during the two-hour interview Griffin asked to obtain cigarettes from other places in the house and each time Agent Waldie required that Agent Tremper escort him. Griffin was told he was to stay in their view at all times. The agents used this procedure to ensure their personal safety because a weapon had been used in the course of the robbery, although this was not explained to Griffin at the time.

During the interview, Griffin appeared nervous, "sort of choked up for words" and "fearful" of the agents. In the course of the questioning Griffin implicated himself and Chapman in the robbery. The agents questioned Griffin for approximately two hours. At the conclusion of the interview the agents placed Griffin under arrest. Griffin was then transported to the F.B.I. office where, three hours after his initial confrontation with the agents, he was advised of his *Miranda* rights for the first time.

In United States v. Griffin, 922 F.2d 1343 (8th Cir.1990), the Court analyzed the above facts and held that Griffin was in custody when he confessed. Do you agree? Which of the factors cut most strongly in Griffin's favor? Which cut most strongly in the government's favor?

Another court has espoused a list of (nondispositive) circumstances relevant to whether a defendant is in custody that is different from the *Griffin* court.

We have identified five factors relevant to the custody determination: 1) the language used to summon the individual; 2) the extent to which the defendant is confronted with evidence of guilt;

3) the physical surroundings of the interrogation; 4) the duration of the detention; and 5) the degree of pressure applied to detain the individual.

United States v. Bassignani, 560 F.3d 989 (9th Cir. 2009). Applying the above factors to circumstances very similar to those presented in *Griffin*—a lengthy interrogation at the defendant's workplace—the court found that the defendant was *not* in custody. Does that tell you anything about which list of factors is superior? Or does it tell you about the indeterminacy of any test based on a totality of the circumstances?

## 2. What Is Interrogation?

In addition to the custody requirement, the police must also be interrogating the individual before the need for *Miranda* warnings arises. Thus, volunteered statements or "threshold" confessions (where the defendant walks into the police station and immediately confesses) are not barred by the fact that they were made without *Miranda* warnings.

The following case sets forth the Supreme Court's guidelines for determining when interrogation can be found.

### RHODE ISLAND V. INNIS
Supreme Court of the United States, 1980.
446 U.S. 291.

#### MR. JUSTICE STEWART delivered the opinion of the Court.

In Miranda v. Arizona, the Court held that, once a defendant in custody asks to speak with a lawyer, all interrogation must cease until a lawyer is present. The issue in this case is whether the respondent was "interrogated" in violation of the standards promulgated in the *Miranda* opinion.

[Innis was identified as the perpetrator in the shooting death of a cab driver. Some time later, Innis was seen on the street and arrested by Patrolman Lovell. He was unarmed. Lovell gave Innis *Miranda* warnings.]

Within minutes, Sergeant Sears arrived at the scene of the arrest, and he also gave the respondent the *Miranda* warnings. Immediately thereafter, Captain Leyden and other police officers arrived. Captain Leyden advised the respondent of his *Miranda* rights. The respondent stated that he understood those rights and wanted to speak with a lawyer. Captain Leyden then directed that the respondent be placed in a "caged wagon," a four-door police car with a wire screen mesh between the front and rear seats, and be driven to the central police station. Three officers, Patrolmen Gleckman, Williams, and McKenna, were assigned to accompany the respondent to the central station. They placed the respondent in the vehicle and shut the doors. Captain Leyden then instructed the officers not to question the respondent or intimidate or coerce him in any way. The three officers then entered the vehicle, and it departed.

While enroute to the central station, Patrolman Gleckman initiated a conversation with Patrolman McKenna concerning the missing shotgun. As Patrolman Gleckman later testified:

> "At this point, I was talking back and forth with Patrolman McKenna stating that I frequent this area while on patrol and [that because a school for handicapped children is located nearby,] there's a lot of handicapped children running around in this area, and God forbid one of them might find a weapon with shells and they might hurt themselves."

Patrolman McKenna apparently shared his fellow officer's concern:

> "I more or less concurred with him [Gleckman] that it was a safety factor and that we should, you know, continue to search for the weapon and try to find it."

While Patrolman Williams said nothing, he overheard the conversation between the two officers:

> "He [Gleckman] said it would be too bad if the little—I believe he said girl—would pick up the gun, maybe kill herself."

The respondent then interrupted the conversation, stating that the officers should turn the car around so he could show them where the gun was located. * * * At the time the respondent indicated that the officers should turn back, they had traveled no more than a mile, a trip encompassing only a few minutes.

The police vehicle then returned to the scene of the arrest where a search for the shotgun was in progress. There, Captain Leyden again advised the respondent of his *Miranda* rights. The respondent replied that he understood those rights but that he "wanted to get the gun out of the way because of the kids in the area in the school." The respondent then led the police to a nearby field, where he pointed out the shotgun under some rocks by the side of the road.

[A motion to suppress was denied by the trial court and Innis was convicted. But the state appellate court found that Innis had been subject to interrogation about the gun and so his statements should have been suppressed.]

* * *

In the present case, the parties are in agreement that the respondent was fully informed of his *Miranda* rights and that he invoked his *Miranda* right to counsel when he told Captain Leyden that he wished to consult with a lawyer. It is also uncontested that the respondent was "in custody" while being transported to the police station.

The issue, therefore, is whether the respondent was "interrogated" by the police officers in violation of the respondent's undisputed right under *Miranda* to remain silent until he had consulted with a lawyer.[a] In resolving this issue, we first define the term "interrogation" under *Miranda* before turning to a consideration of the facts of this case.

\* \* \*

The starting point for defining "interrogation" in this context is, of course, the Court's *Miranda* opinion. There the Court observed that "[b]y custodial interrogation, we mean *questioning* initiated by law enforcement officers after a person has been taken into custody or otherwise deprived of his freedom of action in any significant way." This passage and other references throughout the opinion to "questioning" might suggest that the *Miranda* rules were to apply only to those police interrogation practices that involve express questioning of a defendant while in custody.

We do not, however, construe the *Miranda* opinion so narrowly. The concern of the Court in *Miranda* was that the "interrogation environment" created by the interplay of interrogation and custody would "subjugate the individual to the will of his examiner" and thereby undermine the privilege against compulsory self-incrimination. The police practices that evoked this concern included several that did not involve express questioning. \* \* \*

This is not to say, however, that all statements obtained by the police after a person has been taken into custody are to be considered the product of interrogation. \* \* \* It is clear therefore that the special procedural safeguards outlined in *Miranda* are required not where a suspect is simply taken into custody, but rather where a suspect in custody is subjected to interrogation. "Interrogation," as conceptualized in the *Miranda* opinion, must reflect a measure of compulsion above and beyond that inherent in custody itself.[b] \* \* \*

---

[a] Since we conclude that the respondent was not "interrogated" for *Miranda* purposes, we do not reach the question whether the respondent waived his right under *Miranda* to be free from interrogation until counsel was present.

[b] There is language in the opinion of the Rhode Island Supreme Court in this case suggesting that the definition of "interrogation" under *Miranda* is informed by this Court's decision in Brewer v. Williams [discussed infra in the section on the Sixth Amendment]. This suggestion is erroneous. Our decision in *Brewer* rested solely on the Sixth and Fourteenth Amendment right to counsel. That right, as we held in *Massiah*, prohibits law enforcement officers from "deliberately eliciting" incriminating information from a defendant in the absence of counsel after a formal charge against the defendant has been filed. Custody in such a case is not controlling; \* \* \*. By contrast, the right to counsel at issue in the present case is based not on the Sixth and Fourteenth Amendments, but rather on the Fifth and Fourteenth Amendments as interpreted in the *Miranda* opinion. The definitions of "interrogation" under the Fifth and Sixth Amendments, if indeed the term "interrogation" is even apt in the Sixth Amendment context, are

We conclude that the *Miranda* safeguards come into play whenever a person in custody is subjected to either express questioning or its functional equivalent. That is to say, the term "interrogation" under *Miranda* refers not only to express questioning, but also to any words or actions on the part of the police (other than those normally attendant to arrest and custody) that the police should know are reasonably likely to elicit an incriminating response[c] from the suspect. The latter portion of this definition focuses primarily upon the perceptions of the suspect, rather than the intent of the police. This focus reflects the fact that the *Miranda* safeguards were designed to vest a suspect in custody with an added measure of protection against coercive police practices, without regard to objective proof of the underlying intent of the police. A practice that the police should know is reasonably likely to evoke an incriminating response from a suspect thus amounts to interrogation.[d] But, since the police surely cannot be held accountable for the unforeseeable results of their words or actions, the definition of interrogation can extend only to words or actions on the part of police officers that they *should have known* were reasonably likely to elicit an incriminating response.[e]

* * * Turning to the facts of the present case, we conclude that the respondent was not "interrogated" within the meaning of *Miranda*. It is undisputed that the first prong of the definition of "interrogation" was not satisfied, for the conversation between Patrolmen Gleckman and McKenna included no express questioning of the respondent. Rather, that conversation was, at least in form nothing more than a dialogue between the two officers to which no response from the respondent was invited.

* * *

Moreover, it cannot be fairly concluded that the respondent was subjected to the "functional equivalent" of questioning. * * * There is nothing in the record to suggest that the officers were aware that the respondent was peculiarly susceptible to an appeal to his conscience concerning the safety of handicapped children, or that the police knew that the respondent was unusually disoriented or upset at the time of his arrest.

---

not necessarily interchangeable, since the policies underlying the two constitutional protections are quite distinct.

[c] By "incriminating response" we refer to any response—whether inculpatory or exculpatory—that the *prosecution* may seek to introduce at trial. * * *

[d] This is not to say that the intent of the police is irrelevant, for it may well have a bearing on whether the police should have known that their words or actions were reasonably likely to evoke an incriminating response. In particular, where a police practice is designed to elicit an incriminating response from the accused, it is unlikely that the practice will not also be one which the police should have known was reasonably likely to have that effect.

[e] Any knowledge the police may have had concerning the unusual susceptibility of a defendant to a particular form of persuasion might be an important factor in determining whether the police should have known that their words or actions were reasonably likely to elicit an incriminating response from the suspect.

The case thus boils down to whether, in the context of a brief conversation, the officers should have known that the respondent would suddenly be moved to make a self-incriminating response. Given the fact that the entire conversation appears to have consisted of no more than a few off-hand remarks, we cannot say that the officers should have known that it was reasonably likely that Innis would so respond. This is not a case where the police carried on a lengthy harangue in the presence of the suspect. Nor does the record support the respondent's contention that, under the circumstances, the officers' comments were particularly "evocative."

* * *

[JUSTICE WHITE's concurring opinion, and CHIEF JUSTICE BURGER's opinion concurring in the judgment, are omitted].

**MR. JUSTICE MARSHALL, with whom MR. JUSTICE BRENNAN joins, dissenting.**

I am substantially in agreement with the Court's definition of "interrogation" within the meaning of Miranda v. Arizona. In my view, the *Miranda* safeguards apply whenever police conduct is intended or likely to produce a response from a suspect in custody. * * *

I am utterly at a loss, however, to understand how this objective standard as applied to the facts before us can rationally lead to the conclusion that there was no interrogation. * * *

One can scarcely imagine a stronger appeal to the conscience of a suspect—*any* suspect—than the assertion that if the weapon is not found an innocent person will be hurt or killed. And not just any innocent person, but an innocent child—a little girl—a helpless, handicapped little girl on her way to school. The notion that such an appeal could not be expected to have any effect unless the suspect were known to have some special interest in handicapped children verges on the ludicrous.

* * *

I firmly believe that this case is simply an aberration, and that in future cases the Court will apply the standard adopted today in accordance with its plain meaning.

**JUSTICE STEVENS, dissenting.**

* * *

* * * In my view any statement that would normally be understood by the average listener as calling for a response is the functional equivalent of a direct question, whether or not it is punctuated by a question mark. The Court, however, takes a much narrower view. It holds that police conduct is not the "functional equivalent" of direct questioning unless the police should have known that what they were saying or doing

was likely to elicit an incriminating response from the suspect. This holding represents a plain departure from the principles set forth in *Miranda.*

\* \* \*

[T]he Court's test creates an incentive for police to ignore a suspect's invocation of his rights in order to make continued attempts to extract information from him. If a suspect does not appear susceptible to a particular type of psychological pressure, the police are apparently free to exert that pressure on him despite his request for counsel, so long as they are careful not to punctuate their statements with question marks. And if, contrary to all reasonable expectations, the suspect makes an incriminating statement, that statement can be used against him at trial. \* \* \*

### Application of Innis: Arizona v. Mauro

Applying the *Innis* test, the Court found no interrogation when a suspect confessed to his wife in the presence of a police officer who recorded the statements. Arizona v. Mauro, 481 U.S. 520 (1987). Police received a telephone call stating that a man had entered a store claiming to have killed his son. When officers reached the store, Mauro freely admitted that he had killed his son and directed officers to the body. The police arrested Mauro and gave him two sets of *Miranda* warnings. After the second set, given at the police station, Mauro indicated that he wished to say nothing more without a lawyer. Mrs. Mauro, who was being questioned separately, asked to speak with her husband. The police were reluctant to permit her to do so, but ultimately agreed to her request. An officer told the Mauros, however, that they could speak together only if an officer were present to observe and hear what was said. The officer placed a tape recorder in plain view. During the conversation between husband and wife, Mrs. Mauro expressed despair, and Mr. Mauro consoled her by saying that "You tried to stop me as best you can." Mauro's defense at trial was insanity, and the prosecutor played the tape at trial in rebuttal, arguing that it demonstrated that Mauro was sane.

Justice Powell wrote for the majority, as it concluded that there was no evidence that the officers sent Mrs. Mauro in to see her husband for the purpose of eliciting statements. Even though the officers conceded that they recognized a *possibility* that Mauro would incriminate himself while talking with his wife, Justice Powell concluded that "officers do not interrogate a suspect simply by hoping that he will incriminate himself." Justice Powell determined that "Mauro was not subjected to compelling influences, psychological ploys, or direct questioning," and "his volunteered statements cannot properly be considered the result of police interrogation." He added that "[p]olice departments need not adopt inflexible rules barring suspects from speaking with their spouses, nor must they ignore legitimate security concerns by allowing spouses to meet in private."

Justice Stevens, joined by Justices Brennan, Marshall, and Blackmun, dissented. He concluded that "it was not only likely, but highly probable, that one of the suspects would make a statement that the prosecutor might seek to introduce at trial," and that "[i]t follows that the police conduct in this case was the functional equivalent of deliberate, direct interrogation."

Suppose the police officers refused to permit Mrs. Mauro to speak with her husband, and he had made a statement to the police. Wouldn't Mauro have argued that the refusal to permit contact was itself interrogation? If the dissenters are correct in *Mauro,* what advice would they give to police confronted with the *Mauro* facts? See also United States v. Swift, 623 F.3d 618 (8th Cir. 2010) (police officers' act of leaving two defendants alone in a monitored interrogation room was not the functional equivalent of interrogation; even though officers hoped that they would make incriminating statements when left alone, the conduct did not put pressure on the defendants).

### *Appeals to the Welfare of Others as Interrogation?*

In *Innis*, the Court held that an average suspect would not likely be moved by an appeal based on a risk of harm to innocent children; the fact that Innis himself *was* so moved was not dispositive, because the test is whether an incriminating response would have been likely from an *average suspect*—and apparently an average suspect doesn't care about whether children could be harmed by a gun. Would an average suspect be affected by an appeal based on possible harm to a loved one? Consider United States v. Calisto, 838 F.2d 711 (3rd Cir.1988), where officers searched Calisto's home and found large quantities of drugs in a bedroom. Calisto was placed under arrest by Officer McKeefry and invoked his right to silence. The officers knew that Calisto lived with his adult daughter. One of the searching officers came up to McKeefry and said that he had found both men's and women's clothing in the bedroom where the drugs had been located. Officer McKeefry responded, "Well, then we'll have to get an arrest warrant for the daughter." Calisto, who was a few feet away from McKeefry, said "Don't lock my daughter up. She has nothing to do with that stuff. That's mine. I'm the one you want." The court found that McKeefry's statement concerning the daughter was not interrogation, reasoning that his remark "was not directed at Calisto, was the kind of remark that an officer would normally make in carrying out his duties under the circumstances that confronted him, and was not made in a provocative manner." The court concluded that "even if it could be said that reasonable officers might have expected a protest of some kind from Calisto upon his hearing of his daughter's possible arrest, we do not think it was reasonable to expect an *inculpatory* response from Calisto." (emphasis added).

Why do the courts in *Innis* and *Calisto* take such a dim view of the character of an average suspect?

### Confronting the Suspect with Incriminating Evidence

In Edwards v. Arizona, 451 U.S. 477 (1981), the Court found that Edwards had been interrogated when officers played for him a recorded statement of Edwards' associate that implicated Edwards in the crime. See also People v. Ferro, 63 N.Y.2d 316, 482 N.Y.S.2d 237 (1984) (interrogation found where officers placed the fruits of Ferro's crime in front of his jail cell); United States v. Green, 541 F.3d 176 (3rd Cir. 2008) ("we can hardly imagine a more prototypical example of the functional equivalent of interrogation than when a suspect is shown a video in which he is depicted as engaging in a criminal act").

Why does confronting the suspect with incriminating evidence constitute interrogation, while confronting the same suspect with a risk of harm to innocent children, as in *Innis*, does not?

It should be noted that despite the holding in *Edwards,* courts have not been uniform in finding interrogation whenever a suspect in custody is confronted with incriminating evidence. See Shedelbower v. Estelle, 885 F.2d 570 (9th Cir.1989) (lying to the defendant that he had just been identified by an eyewitness was not reasonably likely to elicit an incriminating response). The court in United States v. Payne, 954 F.2d 199 (4th Cir.1992), argued that it would be inappropriate to apply *Miranda* to every instance in which a person in custody is told about incriminating evidence against them:

> That no comment on the evidence in a case will ever issue in the presence of a criminal suspect seems to us neither realistic nor desirable as an absolute rule derived from the Fifth Amendment. Indeed, it may even be in the interest of a defendant to be kept informed about matters relating to the charges against him. * * * Information about the evidence against a suspect may also contribute to the intelligent exercise of his judgment regarding what course of conduct to follow.

> * * * It simply cannot be said that all such statements are objectively likely to result in incriminating responses by those in custody. The inquiry mandated by *Innis* into the perceptions of the suspect is necessarily contextual, and whether descriptions of incriminating evidence constitute the functional equivalent of

interrogation will depend on circumstances that are too numerous to catalogue.

Of course it is true, as the *Payne* court states, that a suspect may have an interest in being apprised of the evidence against him. But does that mean that *Miranda* is inapplicable? *Miranda* does not prevent an officer from speaking to a suspect, it just requires that a confession in response to the officer must be preceded by warnings and waiver in order for that confession to be admissible. Hasn't the *Payne* court overlooked the fact that an officer who is trying to "help" the defendant by keeping him informed, can also help him by providing the warnings? If there is no per se rule, how does one tell whether confronting a suspect with incriminating evidence will constitute interrogation? See also Easley v. Frey, 433 F.3d 969 (7th Cir. 2006) ("statements by law enforcement officers to a suspect regarding the nature of the evidence against him do not constitute interrogation as a matter of law").

### Direct vs. Indirect Statements

One factor mentioned in *Innis* as cutting against a finding of interrogation was that the officers were ostensibly talking among themselves; they did not direct their comments at Innis. Likewise, the officer's statement in *Calisto*, supra—about arresting the defendant's daughter—was found not to be interrogation in part because it was not made in a "provocative" manner. The reasoning is that a comment not even directed at a suspect is less likely to produce an incriminating response.

Conversely, if an officer is addressing the suspect directly, an incriminating response is presumably more likely. Illustrative is United States v. Soto, 953 F.2d 263 (6th Cir.1992). Soto was stopped for a traffic violation, gave suspicious answers to preliminary questions, and ultimately consented to a search of his car. The officer discovered narcotics in an opaque bag in the trunk, and Soto was placed under arrest. The officer continued to search the car, and came upon a photograph of Soto's wife and child. The officer pointed to the narcotics and said "What are you doing with crap like that when you have these two waiting for you at home?" Soto gave an incriminating answer. The court held that the officer's comment constituted impermissible interrogation. It reasoned that while the remark "was not couched in formal question and answer form, in substance it was a direct inquiry into Soto's reasons for committing the offense he appeared to have committed, and it elicited an incriminating response." Do you think the officer in *Soto* was trying to obtain an incriminating statement? Does that make any difference under *Innis*? See also United States v. Rambo, 365 F.3d 906 (10th Cir. 2004) (directly addressing the defendant to tell him that "most of the blame will fall on your shoulders" constitutes interrogation).

## QUESTIONS ATTENDANT TO CUSTODY:
## PENNSYLVANIA V. MUNIZ

In *Innis*, the Court's definition of interrogation excludes questions "attendant to custody." Thus, officers can ask custody-related questions without *Miranda* warnings, and if the suspect's answer is incriminating, it is admissible at trial. This *"booking exception"* was further developed in Pennsylvania v. Muniz, 496 U.S. 582 (1990). Muniz was stopped on suspicion of drunk driving. He failed sobriety tests and was brought to a booking center, where he was asked, among other things, his name, address, height, weight, eye color, date of birth, and current age. Muniz stumbled over the answers and gave incorrect information on some points. His responses were admitted at his trial as evidence of drunkenness. Justice Brennan, writing for a plurality of four members of the Court, held that Muniz's answers to the questions were admissible, even though in response to custodial interrogation, because they fell within a "routine booking question exception which exempts from *Miranda's* coverage questions to secure the biographical data necessary to complete booking or pretrial services." The plurality noted that the booking exception would not apply if such questions were "designed to elicit incriminatory admissions."

Chief Justice Rehnquist, joined by Justices White, Blackmun, and Stevens, concurred in the result. The Chief Justice did not find it necessary to consider whether the questions to Muniz fell within a booking exception to *Miranda*. He found Muniz's answers to these questions to be non-testimonial, and hence not protected by the Fifth Amendment in the first place, because they were used at trial only to show that Muniz's mental processes were not operating properly. (This aspect of the case is discussed earlier in this Chapter in the section on the Fifth Amendment). However, Chief Justice Rehnquist assumed that a booking exception to *Miranda* does exist.

Justice Marshall dissented. He argued that a booking exception would lead to difficult, time-consuming litigation concerning its scope and application, contrary to the *Miranda* bright-line approach.

### Determining the Scope of the Booking Questions Exception

How is a court able to tell whether an officer's question about biographical information is, as *Muniz* puts it, "designed to elicit incriminatory admissions?" Is it a subjective test? Lower courts have looked to objective factors such as whether there could be a proper administrative purpose for the question, whether the question is asked by an officer who routinely books suspects, and whether the officer would need to know the information for booking purposes. See, e.g., United States v. Pacheco-Lopez, 531 F.3d 420 (6th Cir. 2008): In a drug case, questions concerning when the suspect arrived at the house where drugs were sent and how he got there were not within the booking questions exception—questions did not serve an administrative purpose, questioning was done on the scene and not at the station, and no effort was made to document the suspect's answers in any arrest-related paperwork. Compare United States v. Washington, 462 F.3d 1124 (9th Cir. 2006) (questions about defendant's gang affiliation and gang moniker were proper booking questions: "agents routinely obtain gang moniker and gang affiliation information for the United States Marshals and Metropolitan Detention Center in order to ensure prisoner safety").

In United States v. Carmona, 873 F.2d 569 (2d Cir.1989), officers arresting Carmona asked his name, even though they knew who he was. He answered with a false name, and this answer was used as evidence of consciousness of guilt at his trial. The court held that the question "what's your name?" is *always* within the booking exception, even if the officer knows the information in advance. The court noted that it is prudent practice for officers to make sure that the person arrested is the correct person. Was the question in *Carmona* "designed to elicit incriminating information?" What kind of answer were they expecting?

### 3.  Does *Miranda* Apply to Undercover Activity?

What if a suspect in custody does not know that he is speaking to a police officer or agent? In Illinois v. Perkins, 496 U.S. 292 (1990), authorities suspected that Perkins was involved in a murder. Perkins was in prison on charges unrelated to the murder. An undercover officer was placed as Perkins' cellmate, with the hope that he could obtain incriminating statements from Perkins about the murder. In the course of conversation concerning a planned escape, the undercover officer asked Perkins whether he had ever killed anybody. Perkins said yes and described the murder that was being investigated. For obvious reasons, Perkins had received no *Miranda* warnings. The Court held that Perkins's unwarned statement was admissible because "*Miranda* was not meant to protect suspects from boasting about their criminal activities in front of persons who they believe to be their cellmates." Justice Kennedy wrote the opinion for seven members of the Court. He reasoned that *Miranda* was concerned with the pressures upon a suspect in a police-dominated atmosphere. If the suspect does not even know that he is talking to a police officer, the problems with which the Court was concerned in *Miranda* do not exist. Justice Kennedy explained as follows:

> It is the premise of *Miranda* that the danger of coercion results from the interaction of custody and official interrogation. * * * Questioning by captors, who appear to control the suspect's fate, may create mutually reinforcing pressures that the Court has assumed will weaken the suspect's will, but where a suspect does not know

that he is conversing with a government agent, these pressures do not exist.

One of the virtues of *Miranda,* often recognized by the Court, is its bright-line character. Perkins argued that the creation of an "undercover investigations exception" to *Miranda* would destroy the clarity of the rule. But the majority rejected this argument, reasoning that the *Perkins* rule *itself* is a bright-line rule: if there is an undercover investigation (and it is easy to determine whether there is one) then *Miranda* is completely inapplicable. Justice Kennedy stated that "law enforcement officers will have little difficulty putting into practice our holding that undercover agents need not give *Miranda* warnings to incarcerated suspects."

Justice Brennan concurred in the judgment. He agreed that when a suspect does not know he is talking to a police agent, *Miranda* warnings are not required. Justice Brennan argued, however, that undercover activity constituted trickery, which could raise a "substantial claim that the confession was obtained in violation of the Due Process Clause."

Justice Marshall dissented. He argued that undercover questioning of an incarcerated suspect constituted both "custody" and "interrogation," and that the majority's opinion was thus an unjustified "exception" to *Miranda.* Justice Marshall also expressed concern that police would use the majority's decision to circumvent *Miranda* requirements by using undercover agents.

See also Cook v. Warden, 677 F.3d 1133 (11th Cir. 2012): admission of the defendant's custodial confession did not violate *Miranda,* where he was questioned by an FBI agent—who was his father. The father testified that he was not thinking of his job at the time and wanted to protect his son and convince him to cooperate for leniency. Under the circumstances, the defendant was not talking to a law enforcement officer within the meaning of *Miranda.*

### 4. Does *Miranda* Protection Depend on the Seriousness of the Offense?

The Court in Berkemer v. McCarty, 468 U.S. 420 (1984), established that there is no distinction between felonies and misdemeanors insofar as *Miranda* is concerned.

Writing for the Court, Justice Marshall rejected the felony-misdemeanor distinction on the ground that it would remove one of *Miranda's* principal advantages—the clarity of the rule.

> The exception to *Miranda* proposed * * * would substantially undermine this crucial advantage of the doctrine. The police often are unaware when they arrest a person whether he may have committed a misdemeanor or a felony. * * * Indeed, the nature of his offense

may depend upon circumstances unknowable to the police, such as whether the suspect has previously committed a similar offense or has a criminal record of some other kind. It may even turn upon events yet to happen, such as whether a victim of the accident dies. It would be unreasonable to expect the police to make guesses as to the nature of the criminal conduct at issue before deciding how they may interrogate the suspect.

Equally importantly, the doctrinal complexities that would confront the courts if we accepted [the misdemeanor-felony distinction] would be byzantine. Difficult questions quickly spring to mind: For instance, investigations into seemingly minor offenses sometimes escalate gradually into investigations into more serious matters; at what point in the evolution of an affair of this sort would the police be obliged to give *Miranda* warnings to a suspect in custody? * * * The litigation necessary to resolve such matters would be time-consuming and disruptive of law enforcement. And the end result would be an elaborate set of rules, interlaced with exceptions and subtle distinctions, discriminating between different kinds of custodial interrogations. Neither the police nor criminal defendants would benefit from such a development.

If the bright-line aspect of *Miranda* is so important, why did the Court in *Quarles* establish a public safety exception? Is a public safety exception to *Miranda* any easier to apply than a misdemeanor exception?

## 5. How Complete and Accurate Must the Warnings Be?

The Court in *Miranda* promulgated a set of detailed warnings. Yet it left unclear whether something less than a verbatim transcription of the Court's warnings would suffice. In California v. Prysock, 451 U.S. 1301 (1981), the Court concluded that police should be given some flexibility— so long as they provide the suspect with the gist of the warnings. Prysock was informed that he had "the right to talk to a lawyer before you are questioned, have him present while you are being questioned, and all during the questioning" and also that he had "the right to have a lawyer appointed to represent you at no cost to yourself." Prysock argued that he was never informed of his right to have an attorney appointed *before being questioned*. Thus, he was left with the impression that he could only have an attorney if he agreed to answer questions. The Court declared, however, that it had "never indicated that the rigidity of *Miranda* extends to the precise formulation of the warnings," and that "*Miranda* itself indicates that no talismanic incantation" is required. Under the circumstances, the warnings gave sufficient information, and were not misrepresentative. They didn't specifically say, for example, that Prysock had no right to an attorney unless he agreed to talk.

Chief Justice Rehnquist wrote for the Court in Duckworth v. Eagan, 492 U.S. 195 (1989), as it found no *Miranda* violation in a police officer's reading a printed waiver form to a suspect, which provided:

> "Before we ask you any questions, you must understand your rights. You have the right to remain silent. Anything you say can be used against you in court. *You have the right to talk to a lawyer for advice before we ask you any questions, and to have him with you during questioning.* You have this right to the advice and presence of a lawyer even if you cannot afford to hire one. We *have no way of giving you a lawyer, but one will be appointed for you, if you wish, if and when you go to court.* If you wish to answer questions now without a lawyer present, you have the right to stop answering questions at any time. You also have the right to stop answering at any time until you've talked to a lawyer." (emphasis added)

The Chief Justice noted that the Court has never insisted that *Miranda* warnings be given in the exact form described in Chief Justice Warren's opinion, and concluded that the inclusion of the "if and when you go to court" language accurately described state procedure and did not fail to apprise the defendant of his rights.

Justice Marshall, joined by Justices Brennan, Blackmun, and Stevens, dissented. He argued that the "if and when" language led the defendant to believe that a lawyer would not be appointed until some future time after questioning took place.

### *Ambiguity About the Right to Have an Attorney Present Throughout the Questioning: Florida v. Powell*

### FLORIDA V. POWELL
Supreme Court of the United States, 2010.
559 U.S. 50.

#### JUSTICE GINSBURG delivered the opinion of the Court.

In Miranda v. Arizona, the Court held that an individual must be 'clearly informed,' prior to custodial questioning, that he has, among other rights, 'the right to consult with a lawyer and to have the lawyer with him during interrogation.' The question presented in this case is whether advice that a suspect has 'the right to talk to a lawyer before answering any of [the law enforcement officers'] questions,' and that he can invoke this right 'at any time . . . during th[e] interview,' satisfies *Miranda*. We hold that it does."

[Powell was arrested on suspicion of robbery, and officers found a weapon in his residence. Powell was taken to the police station.] Once there, and before asking Powell any questions, the officers read Powell the standard Tampa Police Department Consent and Release Form 310. The form states:

> "You have the right to remain silent. If you give up the right to remain silent, anything you say can be used against you in court. You have the right to talk to a lawyer before answering any of our questions. If you cannot afford to hire a lawyer, one will be appointed for you without cost and before any questioning. You have the right to use any of these rights at any time you want during this interview."

Acknowledging that he had been informed of his rights, that he "underst[oo]d them," and that he was "willing to talk" to the officers, Powell signed the form. He then admitted that he owned the handgun found in the apartment. Powell knew he was prohibited from possessing a gun because he had previously been convicted of a felony, but said he had nevertheless purchased and carried the firearm for his protection.

Powell was charged in state court with possession of a weapon by a prohibited possessor * * *. Contending that the *Miranda* warnings were deficient because they did not adequately convey his right to the presence of an attorney during questioning, he moved to suppress his inculpatory statements. The trial court denied the motion, concluding that the officers had properly notified Powell of his right to counsel. A jury convicted Powell of the gun-possession charge.

* * *

The [lower] court found that the advice Powell received was misleading because it suggested that Powell could "only consult with an attorney before questioning" and did not convey Powell's entitlement to counsel's presence throughout the interrogation. Nor, in the court's view, did the final catchall warning—"[y]ou have the right to use any of these rights at any time you want during this interview"—cure the defect the court perceived in the right-to-counsel advice: "The catch-all phrase did not supply the missing warning of the right to have counsel present during police questioning," the court stated, for "a right that has never been expressed cannot be reiterated."

* * *

We granted certiorari, and now reverse the judgment of the Florida Supreme Court.

* * *

The four warnings *Miranda* requires are invariable, but this Court has not dictated the words in which the essential information must be conveyed. See California v. Prysock. The inquiry is simply whether the warnings reasonably convey to a suspect his rights as required by *Miranda*.

[JUSTICE GINSBURG discusses the facts and results in California v. Prysock and Duckworth v. Eagan].

The Tampa officers * * * informed Powell that he had "the right to talk to a lawyer before answering any of [their] questions" and "the right to use any of [his] rights at any time [he] want[ed] during th[e] interview." The first statement communicated that Powell could consult with a lawyer before answering any particular question, and the second statement confirmed that he could exercise that right while the interrogation was underway. In combination, the two warnings reasonably conveyed Powell's right to have an attorney present, not only at the outset of interrogation, but at all times.

To reach the opposite conclusion, i.e., that the attorney would not be present throughout the interrogation, the suspect would have to imagine an unlikely scenario: To consult counsel, he would be obliged to exit and reenter the interrogation room between each query. A reasonable suspect in a custodial setting who has just been read his rights, we believe, would not come to the counterintuitive conclusion that he is obligated, or allowed, to hop in and out of the holding area to seek his attorney's advice. Instead, the suspect would likely assume that he must stay put in the interrogation room and that his lawyer would be there with him the entire time.

The Florida Supreme Court found the warning misleading because it believed the temporal language—that Powell could "talk to a lawyer before answering any of [the officers'] questions"—suggested Powell could consult with an attorney only before the interrogation started. In context, however, the term "before" merely conveyed when Powell's right to an attorney became effective—namely, before he answered any questions at all. Nothing in the words used indicated that counsel's presence would be restricted after the questioning commenced. Instead, the warning communicated that the right to counsel carried forward to and through the interrogation: Powell could seek his attorney's advice before responding to "any of [the officers'] questions" and "at any time . . . during th[e] interview." Although the warnings were not the clearest possible formulation of *Miranda's* right-to-counsel advisement, they were sufficiently comprehensive and comprehensible when given a commonsense reading.

Pursuing a different line of argument, Powell points out that most jurisdictions in Florida and across the Nation expressly advise suspects of the right to have counsel present both before and during interrogation. If we find the advice he received adequate, Powell suggests, law enforcement agencies, hoping to obtain uninformed waivers, will be tempted to end-run *Miranda* by amending their warnings to introduce ambiguity. But  * * *  law enforcement agencies have little reason to assume the litigation risk of experimenting with novel *Miranda* formulations; instead, it is desirable police practice and in law enforcement's own interest to state warnings with maximum clarity.

For these reasons, all federal law enforcement agencies explicitly advise suspects of the full contours of each *Miranda* right, including the right to the presence of counsel during questioning. The standard warnings used by the Federal Bureau of Investigation are exemplary. They provide, in relevant part: "You have the right to talk to a lawyer for advice before we ask you any questions. You have the right to have a lawyer with you during questioning." This advice is admirably informative, but we decline to declare its precise formulation necessary to meet *Miranda*'s requirements. Different words were used in the advice Powell received, but they communicated the same essential message.

---

For the reasons stated, the judgment of the Supreme Court of Florida is reversed, and the case is remanded for further proceedings not inconsistent with this opinion.

[The dissenting opinion of Justice Stevens, joined in part by Justice Breyer, is omitted.]

## 6. Do the *Miranda* Safeguards Apply to Custodial Interrogations of Foreigners Conducted Abroad?

Courts have struggled with whether and to what extent United States officials are bound by the *Miranda* requirements when interrogating suspects on foreign soil. See United States v. Mohammed, 693 F.3d 192 (D.C.Cir. 2012) ("We need not resolve the novel question whether *Miranda* applies to the overseas custodial interrogation of a person who is not a U.S. citizen" because any error in admitting the confession was harmless).

The question of *Miranda's* applicability to interrogations of foreigners on foreign soil arises most often in cases involving charges of terrorism.[17] For example, the court in In re Terrorist Bombings, U.S. Embassies, East Africa, 552 F.3d 177 (2d Cir. 2008), considered whether and how the *Miranda* safeguards applied to custodial interrogation of a suspected terrorist in Kenya. United States investigators[18] gave the suspect an

---

[17] Note that if a terrorism-related case is brought in a military commission proceeding, as opposed to a civilian judicial tribunal, the questions of the admissibility of any confession may be different. See the discussion in the section on voluntariness, supra.

[18] Note that foreign investigators questioning a suspect in a foreign jurisdiction are not bound by the *Miranda* requirements. In re Terrorist Bombings, 552 F.3d 177 (2nd Cir. 2008) ("Recognizing that the threat of suppression in U.S. courts for failure to comply with *Miranda*

Advice of Rights form, which stated that the suspect did not have to speak or answer any questions and that anything he said could be used against him "in a court in the United States or elsewhere." The Advice of Rights form then informed the suspect of his right to counsel *if he were being questioned in the United States*. It then proceeded as follows:

> Because we are not in the United States, we cannot ensure that you will have a lawyer appointed for you before any questioning.

The suspect was given a further oral warning, and eventually waived his rights and confessed. He complained at trial and on appeal that he did not receive the full panoply of *Miranda* protections. The court found no error in admitting the confession. It first addressed whether *Miranda* was applicable *at all* to a foreign interrogation in which United States officials participate. It proceeded on the assumption that *Miranda* was applicable, reasoning that United States officials could be deterred by the risk of exclusion, and so "the twin goals of ensuring trustworthiness and deterring misconduct might compel the application of *Miranda*." But it noted that even assuming *Miranda* was applicable, its "warning/waiver framework" has been applied by many courts "in a flexible fashion to accommodate the exigencies of local conditions."

Applying that flexible approach to the facts of the case, the court found that the Advice of Rights form and the subsequent oral warning presented the suspect with a "factually accurate" statement of the right to counsel, given the fact that there was no such right under Kenyan law— the controlling law under the circumstances. The court concluded as follows:

> In cases where a suspect has no entitlement to counsel under the law of the foreign land, it would be misleading to inform him falsely that the was guaranteed the presence or appointment of an attorney—and *Miranda* does not require the provision of false assurances.

The court also held that the United States officials had no affirmative obligation to urge local officials to provide counsel to the suspect. It declared that *"Miranda* requires government agents to be the conduits of *information* to detained suspects" but it does not "compel the police to serve as *advocates* for detainees before local authorities, endeavoring to expand the rights and privileges available under local law."

The court therefore concluded that the suspect was properly informed of his rights; it also found the waiver to be knowing and voluntary and therefore the confession was properly admitted under *Miranda*. The court did note, however, that the Advice of Rights form "created a needless risk of misunderstanding by stating, albeit accurately, what the right to

---

holds little sway over foreign authorities, we have declined to suppress un-warned statements obtained overseas by foreign officials.")

counsel would have been had the interrogation occurred in the United States." According to the court, an advice of rights form "should state only what rights are available, not what rights would be available if circumstances were different."

# E. WAIVER OF *MIRANDA* RIGHTS

## 1. Waiver and the Role of Counsel

The *Miranda* Court stated that the accused may waive the rights to silence and counsel, but only if, under all the circumstances, the rights are waived "voluntarily, knowingly, and intelligently." Thus, the validity of a waiver is a question of fact in any particular case. According to *Miranda,* a valid waiver will not be assumed from the silence of the accused after the warnings are given, nor merely from the fact that a confession is eventually obtained. However, the Court later held in North Carolina v. Butler, 441 U.S. 369 (1979), that neither an express statement of waiver nor a written waiver is required, so long as there is sufficient evidence to show that the suspect understood his rights and voluntarily waived them. The *Butler* Court stated that "the question is not one of form, but rather whether the defendant in fact knowingly and voluntarily waived the rights delineated in the *Miranda* case." Of course, while a written waiver is not required, it certainly supports the government's claim that a knowing and voluntary waiver was obtained.

For more on implied waivers, see the watershed case of Berghuis v. Thompkins, set forth in full in the section on invoking the right to silence, infra. There the Court found that a suspect who understood the warnings impliedly waived his rights when he confessed, even though he was silent for more than two hours while being interrogated.

### *Knowing and Voluntary*

The Court in Moran v. Burbine, 475 U.S. 412 (1986), held that two requirements must be met before a suspect can be found to have waived his *Miranda* rights:

> First, the relinquishment of the right must have been voluntary in the sense that it was the product of a free and deliberate choice rather than intimidation, coercion, or deception. Second, the waiver must have been made with a full awareness both of the nature of the right being abandoned and the consequences of the decision to abandon it.

In Tague v. Louisiana, 444 U.S. 469 (1980) (per curiam), the Court held that a waiver of *Miranda* rights was not proven by an officer's testimony that he read a suspect his rights from a card and the suspect then confessed. The officer could not remember whether he asked the suspect if he understood them or whether he made an effort to determine if the suspect "was literate or otherwise capable of understanding his rights." Thus, a valid waiver could not be found simply by the fact that the warnings are given and the suspect confesses.

On the other hand, a waiver can be found if it seems apparent from the giving of the warnings and the suspect's reaction that the suspect understood his *Miranda* rights and freely waived them. For example, in United States v. Frankson, 83 F.3d 79 (4th Cir.1996), the officer read Frankson his rights, asked him if he understood those rights, and Frankson said "yes." Immediately after that, Frankson answered a number of questions posed by the officer, providing extensive details on how he evaded detection for drug activity: he would find a house where no one was ordinarily home during the day, instruct his drug supplier to send a package of drugs via UPS to that house, and then pick up the package when it was left on the home's doorstep. The court held that the circumstances indicated a knowing and voluntary waiver:

> A defendant's subsequent willingness to answer questions after acknowledging his *Miranda* rights is sufficient to constitute an implied waiver. * * * Even though Frankson never "formally" waived his *Miranda* rights, such cooperation, when coupled with his acknowledgment of his *Miranda* rights, constituted a valid waiver.

See also United States v. Banks, 78 F.3d 1190 (7th Cir.1996) (waiver found, even though waiver form not signed, where defendant was familiar with the criminal justice system, and answered some questions and refused to answer others); United States v. Smith, 218 F.3d 777 (7th Cir. 2000) (waiver found where the defendant refused to sign a waiver form, but then immediately began to talk to police officers and continued to do so for an hour).

For more on applying the standards for knowing and voluntary waiver, see the Supreme Court's decision in Berghuis v. Thompkins, set forth in the section on invoking the right to silence, *infra*. There the Court held that after warnings are given, the police can continue to interrogate, and obtain a knowing and voluntary waiver, until the suspect explicitly invokes his right to remain silent. That is, a waiver need not be obtained *before* interrogation is conducted; rather, interrogation can be conducted until the suspect invokes his *Miranda* rights or confesses.

### *Relationship of Waiver Standards to the Test for Voluntary Confessions*

Even after *Miranda* warnings are given, a confession can still be coerced under traditional due process standards. For example, the suspect may make a valid waiver of his rights, but the subsequent confession may be involuntary due to overbearing police pressure after the waiver of rights. See United States v. Syslo, 303 F.3d 860 (8th Cir. 2002) (statements were properly suppressed even though the defendant had voluntarily waived her *Miranda* rights, where after waiver the suspect had her young children at the police station and was informed that they could not be picked up by a relative until she confessed). Or it may be that warnings are given but the police pressure is so great that it cannot be said that the suspect voluntarily waived his *Miranda* rights. See, e.g., Commonwealth v. Perry, 475 Pa. 1, 379 A.2d 545 (1977) (a confession was involuntary even when warnings were given, because the statement was taken while the defendant was in the hospital and in a great deal of pain).

The Supreme Court held in Colorado v. Connelly, 479 U.S. 157 (1986)—the decision holding that coercive police activity is a prerequisite to a finding that a confession is involuntary—that "[t]here is obviously no reason to require more in the way of a 'voluntariness' inquiry in the *Miranda* waiver context than in the Fourteenth Amendment confession context." Thus, "[t]he voluntariness of a waiver of this privilege [against self-incrimination] has always depended on the absence of police overreaching, not on 'free choice' in any broader sense of the word." The Court found that a defendant voluntarily waived his *Miranda* rights because he decided to confess after receiving warnings, without the police engaging in any coercive behavior: "Respondent's perception of coercion flowing from the 'voice of God,' however important or significant such a perception may be in other disciplines, is a matter to which the United States Constitution does not speak." Chief Justice Rehnquist's majority opinion did not address the question whether Connelly actually understood the warnings and thus made a *knowing* waiver. That question was left for the state courts on remand.

### *Understanding the Miranda Warnings*

Subsequent to *Connelly* and its remand on the issue of whether Connelly *understood* his rights as well as voluntarily waived them, several courts have held that persons who are deranged or mentally defective cannot knowingly and intelligently waive their *Miranda* rights. In Smith v. Zant, 887 F.2d 1407 (11th Cir.1989) (en banc), the court concluded that "the *Connelly* Court addressed only voluntariness," and noted the "continued vitality of the knowing and intelligent requirement." The court found that the state did not satisfy its burden of showing that the defendant in that case was capable of understanding his *Miranda* rights; the defendant had an I.Q. of 65, he was under extreme stress, and the warnings were read to him only once, very quickly.

Similarly, courts have held that a waiver might not be "knowing and understanding" if the suspect could not understand the *Miranda* warnings due to some language barrier. Thus, in United States v. Garibay, 143 F.3d 534 (9th Cir.1998), the suspect was given *Miranda* warnings in English and said he understood them. Nonetheless, the Court held that the government failed to satisfy its burden that Garibay *actually* understood the warnings. The court noted that Garibay's primary language was Spanish; that he received D+ grades in English in high school, and only passed because those classes were taught in Spanish; that he was "borderline retarded with extremely low verbal-English comprehension skills"; and that he had no previous experience with the criminal justice system, so that his "personal life experiences do not indicate that he was familiar with his *Miranda* rights and with his option to waive those rights." The court concluded that its result would have changed if Garibay either had been given the warnings in Spanish, or if he had signed a waiver form in English.

### *Conditional Waivers: Connecticut v. Barrett*

Is it possible for the suspect to give a limited or conditional waiver of *Miranda* rights? In Connecticut v. Barrett, 479 U.S. 523 (1987), Barrett received *Miranda* warnings and then signed a form indicating that he would talk to the police about a sexual assault investigation. He stated he had "no problem" in talking about the assault, but that he would not give a written statement. He was given *Miranda* warnings several times, and eventually gave an oral confession which was admitted at trial. In an opinion by Chief Justice Rehnquist, the Court held that Barrett had knowingly and voluntarily waived his *Miranda* rights. The Chief Justice reasoned that the police had complied with Barrett's conditions, because they never sought to obtain a written statement. He emphasized that Barrett gave affirmative indications that he was willing to make an oral statement. The fact that Barrett's decision may have been "illogical" was held irrelevant, "for we have never embraced the theory that a defendant's ignorance of the full consequences of his decisions vitiates their voluntariness."

Justice Brennan concurred in the judgment. He argued that if Barrett was laboring under the misimpression that oral statements could not be admitted against him at trial, his waiver would have been invalid. However, Barrett's testimony at trial that he understood the warnings (to the effect that *any* statement could be used against him) demonstrated a valid waiver. Justice Stevens, joined by Justice Marshall, dissented.

Another question of limited waiver arises when a suspect says he will talk about "x" but not about "y". If the police then question him on "y", they have violated *Miranda* because the suspect never waived his rights with respect to "y". For example, in United States v. Soliz, 129 F.3d 499 (9th Cir.1997), the defendant was arrested on suspicion of an immigration violation as well as smuggling activity. He agreed to talk to police officers about his citizenship. The police then began asking him about the smuggling and Soliz said "I thought this was just about my citizenship." The questioning continued about the smuggling and Soliz made admissions concerning the smuggling. The court held that those statements had to be excluded. It found that Soliz had made an unequivocal invocation of his right to remain silent on all issues other than citizenship. Accordingly, the officers were required to respect the conditions Soliz placed on his waiver.

### Information Needed for an Intelligent Waiver: The Scope of the Interrogation—Colorado v. Spring

How much information must a suspect have to make a "knowing and intelligent" waiver of *Miranda* rights? This question arose in three Supreme Court cases, in each of which defendants argued that the *Miranda* warnings did not give them enough information. The Court rejected this argument in each case.

In Colorado v. Spring, 479 U.S. 564 (1987), Spring was arrested in Missouri when he tried to sell stolen firearms to an undercover agent. Agents also had information that Spring had been involved in a killing in Colorado. Spring was given warnings and signed a waiver form. He was first questioned about the firearms. Then the agents asked him whether he had ever shot anyone. He said that he had "shot another guy once." Eventually Spring gave a complete confession to the killing. Spring argued that he had not knowingly and intelligently waived his *Miranda* rights concerning the Colorado shooting, because the agents had not warned him that he would be questioned about that matter. Justice Powell, writing for seven members of the Court, rejected Spring's argument that the warnings must be tied to the planned subject matter of the interrogation. Justice Powell reasoned as follows:

> Spring understood that he had the right to remain silent and that anything he said could be used as evidence against him. The Constitution does not require that a criminal suspect know and understand every possible consequence of a waiver of the Fifth Amendment privilege. * * * The *Miranda* warnings protect this privilege by ensuring that a suspect knows that he may choose not to talk to law enforcement officers, to talk only with counsel present, or to discontinue talking at any time. * * * [A] suspect's awareness of all the possible subjects of questioning in advance of interrogation is not relevant to determining whether the suspect voluntarily, knowingly, and intelligently waived his Fifth Amendment privilege.

Spring also argued that his waiver was invalid because the agents "tricked" him into believing that they were only concerned with the firearms charge. Justice Powell rejected this argument as well, stating that while trickery could vitiate the voluntariness of a waiver, trickery could not be found through "mere silence" on the part of the police. Here, the agents had not affirmatively misrepresented the intended scope of their questioning; they simply said nothing about it.

Justice Marshall, joined by Justice Brennan, dissented. He argued that a suspect's decision to waive the privilege will "necessarily be influenced by his awareness of the scope and seriousness of the matters under investigation." He claimed that the majority's rule would allow officers to take "unfair advantage of the suspect's psychological state."

### Information Needed for an Intelligent Waiver: The Inadmissibility of a Previous Confession—Oregon v. Elstad

In Oregon v. Elstad, 470 U.S. 298 (1985), Elstad gave a *Miranda*-defective confession, then he received warnings, signed a waiver, and made a formal confession. Only this second confession was admitted at his trial. Elstad argued that the waiver he made before giving his second confession was not knowing and intelligent. Justice O'Connor described the argument, and rejected it, in the following passage:

> Respondent * * * has argued that he was unable to give a fully *informed* waiver of his rights because he was unaware that his prior statement could not be used against him. Respondent suggests that Deputy McAllister, to cure this deficiency, should have added an additional warning to those given him at the Sheriff's office. Such a requirement is neither practicable nor constitutionally necessary. In many cases, a breach of *Miranda* procedures may not be identified as such until long after full *Miranda* warnings are administered and a valid confession obtained. The standard *Miranda* warnings explicitly inform the suspect of his right to consult a lawyer before speaking. Police officers are ill equipped to pinch-hit for counsel, construing the murky and difficult questions of when "custody" begins or whether a given unwarned statement will ultimately be held admissible.

> This Court has never embraced the theory that a defendant's ignorance of the full consequences of his decisions vitiates their voluntariness. * * *

### Information Needed for an Intelligent Waiver: Efforts of a Lawyer to Contact the Suspect—Moran v. Burbine

The Court in Moran v. Burbine, 475 U.S. 412 (1986), again considered whether the basic *Miranda* warnings were sufficient to establish the knowledge required for a knowing and intelligent waiver of

*Miranda* rights. Justice O'Connor's majority opinion begins with a useful summary of the case:

> After being informed of his rights pursuant to Miranda v. Arizona, and after executing a series of written waivers, respondent confessed to the murder of a young woman. At no point during the course of the interrogation, which occurred prior to arraignment, did he request an attorney. While he was in police custody, his sister attempted to retain a lawyer to represent him. The attorney telephoned the police station and received assurances that respondent would not be questioned until the next day. In fact, the interrogation session that yielded the inculpatory statements began later that evening. The question presented is whether either the conduct of the police or respondent's ignorance of the attorney's efforts to reach him taints the validity of the waivers and therefore requires exclusion of the confessions.

Justice O'Connor concluded first that Burbine's waiver was valid despite the fact that he was not informed that an attorney sought to contact him. She reasoned as follows:

> The voluntariness of the waiver is not at issue. As the Court of Appeals correctly acknowledged, the record is devoid of any suggestion that police resorted to physical or psychological pressure to elicit the statements. * * * Nor is there any question about respondent's comprehension of the full panoply of rights set out in the *Miranda* warnings and of the potential consequences of a decision to relinquish them. * * *

> Events occurring outside of the presence of the suspect and entirely unknown to him surely can have no bearing on the capacity to comprehend and knowingly relinquish a constitutional right. [Accepting Burbine's argument would mean that] the same defendant, armed with the same information and confronted with precisely the same police conduct, would have knowingly waived his *Miranda* rights had a lawyer not telephoned the police station to inquire about his status. Nothing in any of our waiver decisions or in our understanding of the essential components of a valid waiver requires so incongruous a result. No doubt the additional information would have been useful to respondent; perhaps even it might have affected his decision to confess. But we have never read the Constitution to require that the police supply a suspect with a flow of information to help him calibrate his self interest in deciding whether to speak or stand by his rights. Once it is determined that a suspect's decision not to rely on his rights was uncoerced, that he at all times knew he could stand mute and request a lawyer, and that he was aware of the state's intention to use his statements to secure

a conviction, the analysis is complete and the waiver is valid as a matter of law.

### State of Mind of Police Irrelevant

In the *Burbine* majority's view, the fact that the police acted *deliberately* to deprive the suspect of information concerning counsel's attempt to reach him did not affect the validity of the waiver. Justice O'Connor reasoned as follows:

> [W]hether intentional or inadvertent, the state of mind of the police is irrelevant to the question of the intelligence and voluntariness of respondent's election to abandon his rights. Although highly inappropriate, even deliberate deception of an attorney could not possibly affect a suspect's decision to waive his *Miranda* rights unless he were at least aware of the incident. Nor was the failure to inform respondent of the telephone call the kind of "trickery" that can vitiate the validity of a waiver. * * * Because respondent's voluntary decision to speak was made with full awareness and comprehension of all the information *Miranda* requires the police to convey, the waivers were valid.

### The Role of Counsel Under Miranda

The defendant in *Burbine* argued that apart from the waiver issue, *Miranda* should be read to prohibit the police from deliberately deceiving counsel, or from denying counsel's request to see the suspect. According to the defendant, *Miranda* should be read to provide some protection of the right to counsel *independent of the suspect's decision whether to invoke that right*. The majority, however, declined "to further extend *Miranda's* reach." Justice O'Connor explained the Court's position as follows:

> [W]hile we share respondent's distaste for the deliberate misleading of an officer of the court, reading *Miranda* to forbid police deception of an *attorney* would cut [the decision] completely loose from its own explicitly stated rationale. * * * Clearly, a rule that focuses on how the police treat an attorney—conduct that has no relevance at all to the degree of compulsion experienced by the defendant during interrogation—would ignore both *Miranda's* mission and its only source of legitimacy.

In other words, it is the suspect who has the right to counsel under *Miranda*; and counsel has a role only after the suspect has invoked the right. Because the defendant never asked for counsel in *Burbine*, counsel had *no independent rights* to assert. His presence at the police station was irrelevant.

### No Requirement to Inform the Suspect of Counsel's Efforts

Finally, the *Burbine* Court declined to "extend" *Miranda* to require the police to inform the suspect of an attorney's efforts to reach him. Such a requirement would be inconsistent with *Miranda's* bright-line approach. Justice O'Connor explained as follows:

> As we have stressed on numerous occasions, "[o]ne of the principal advantages" of *Miranda* is the ease and clarity of its application. We have little doubt that the approach urged by respondent * * * would have the inevitable consequence of muddying *Miranda's* otherwise relatively clear waters. The legal questions it would spawn are legion: To what extent should the police be held accountable for knowing that the accused has counsel? Is it enough that someone in the station house knows, or must the interrogating officer himself know of counsel's efforts to contact the suspect? Do counsel's efforts to talk to the suspect concerning one criminal investigation trigger the obligation to inform the defendant before interrogation may proceed on a wholly separate matter?

Justice O'Connor also argued that an extra warning requirement would be too costly to law enforcement interests, and thus was inconsistent with the *Miranda* compromise:

> * * * [R]eading *Miranda* to require the police in each instance to inform a suspect of an attorney's efforts to reach him would work a substantial and, we think, inappropriate shift in the subtle balance struck in that decision. Custodial interrogations implicate two competing concerns. On the one hand, the need for police questioning as a tool for effective enforcement of criminal laws cannot be doubted. Admissions of guilt are more than merely desirable, they are essential to society's compelling interest in finding, convicting and punishing those who violate the law. On the other hand, the Court has recognized that the interrogation process is "inherently coercive" and that, as a consequence, there exists a substantial risk that the police will inadvertently traverse the fine line between legitimate efforts to elicit admissions and constitutionally impermissible compulsion.

> *Miranda* attempted to reconcile these opposing concerns by giving the *defendant* the power to exert some control over the course of the interrogation. Declining to adopt the more extreme position that the actual presence of a lawyer was necessary to dispel the coercion inherent in custodial interrogation, the Court found that the suspect's Fifth Amendment rights could be adequately protected by less intrusive means. Police questioning, often an essential part of the investigatory process, could continue in its traditional form, the Court held, but only if the suspect clearly understood that, at any

time, he could bring the proceeding to a halt or, short of that, call in an attorney to give advice and monitor the conduct of his interrogators.

The position urged by respondent would upset this carefully drawn approach in a manner that is both unnecessary for the protection of the Fifth Amendment privilege and injurious to legitimate law enforcement. * * * Because neither the letter nor purposes of *Miranda* require this additional handicap on otherwise permissible investigatory efforts, we are unwilling to expand the *Miranda* rules to require the police to keep the suspect abreast of the status of his legal representation.

### Dissent in Burbine

Justice Stevens, joined by Justices Brennan and Marshall, dissented in *Burbine*. He argued that the Court's holding "exalts incommunicado interrogation, sanctions police deception, and demeans the right to consult with an attorney." In his view, "[p]olice interference with communications between an attorney and his client is a recurrent problem." Justice Stevens responded to the majority's reliance on *Miranda's* careful balance with the observation that a rule requiring the police to inform a suspect of an attorney's call would serve *Miranda's* goal of dispelling the compulsion inherent in custodial interrogation. He responded to the majority's concern for clarity with the suggestion that no state that required the police to tell a suspect of an attorney's call had experienced problems. Justice Stevens argued that the police deliberately deceived the suspect's agent, his attorney, and that "as a matter of law, the police deception of Munson [the attorney] was tantamount to deception of Burbine himself."

### Abstract Right to Counsel vs. Concrete Offer of Assistance

In Connecticut v. Stoddard, 206 Conn. 157, 537 A.2d 446 (1988), the court rejected *Burbine* as a matter of state constitutional law, and held that a waiver could not be knowing if the suspect is unaware of a lawyer's attempt to contact him. The court reasoned as follows:

> *Miranda* warnings refer only to an abstract right to counsel. That a suspect validly waives the presence of counsel only means that for the moment the suspect is forgoing the exercise of that conceptual privilege. Faced with a concrete offer of assistance, however, a suspect may well decide to reclaim his or her continuing right to legal assistance. We cannot therefore conclude that a decision to forgo the abstract offer contained in *Miranda* embodies an implied rejection of a specific opportunity to confer with a known lawyer.

Has the *Stoddard* court effectively addressed the concerns of the majority in *Burbine?*

## 2. Waiver After Invocation of *Miranda* Rights—And Questions of Whether Those Rights *Have* Been Invoked

In all the above cases, the suspect had never invoked his *Miranda* rights, and the government argued that the suspect waived his rights and confessed. What if the suspect first invokes his *Miranda* rights and later confesses? It's obviously more difficult to argue waiver in such circumstances. If rights aren't invoked the suspect may have at all times wanted to speak with the police. But where the suspect has initially invoked his rights, *something* must have changed his mind. The government must show that this change of mind came from the suspect, and not from police harassment. Where the suspect has invoked his rights, the Supreme Court has shown far greater sensitivity to the waiver issue than in cases where there was no invocation.

A suspect can invoke two rights in response to the *Miranda* warnings—the right to silence, and the right to counsel. The Court has held that the rules on waiver differ depending on which right is invoked. And the Court has also made a number of rulings on *whether* the rights have been properly invoked under a variety of circumstances.

### a. Invocation of the Right to Silence

#### Scrupulous Honor: Michigan v. Mosley

In Michigan v. Mosley, 423 U.S. 96 (1975), the defendant was arrested in connection with certain robberies, given *Miranda* warnings, and told that he could remain silent. Mosley said that he did not want to discuss the robberies, and the detective refrained from questioning him further. Approximately two hours later *Miranda* warnings were given again, and a different detective questioned Mosley about a murder that was not related to the robberies. Mosley signed a waiver form, and made an incriminating statement, which was admitted at his murder trial, in which he was convicted.

Justice Stewart, writing for the Court, found that the admission of the incriminating statements did not violate *Miranda*. In reaching this decision, the Court found it necessary to interpret the following language from *Miranda:*

> If the individual indicates in any manner, at any time prior to or during questioning, that he wishes to remain silent, the interrogation must cease. At this point he has shown that he intends to exercise his Fifth Amendment privilege; any statement taken after the person

invokes his privilege cannot be other than the product of compulsion, subtle or otherwise.

The *Mosley* Court concluded that the *Miranda* Court could not have meant that interrogation is *forever barred* simply because the defendant invoked his right to silence at some point. Justice Stewart concluded that the only sensible reading of the above language was that the suspect's right to cut off questioning must be "*scrupulously honored.*" If the right to silence was scrupulously honored, then police interrogation could be permitted and a knowing and voluntary waiver could be found. Reviewing the circumstances of Mosley's second interrogation, the Court found:

> This is not a case * * * where the police failed to honor a decision of a person in custody to cut off questioning, either by refusing to discontinue the interrogation upon request or by persisting in repeated efforts to wear down his resistance and make him change his mind. In contrast to such practices, the police here immediately ceased the interrogation, resumed questioning only after the passage of a significant period of time and the provision of a fresh set of warnings, and restricted the second interrogation to a crime that had not been a subject of the earlier interrogation.

Justice Stewart indicated that the Court would not tolerate repetitive and continuous attempts to interrogate a defendant who wanted to remain silent. But he concluded *Miranda* should not be a per se bar to resumption of questioning.

### Scrupulously Honoring an Invocation of Silence

It may be wondered how an officer can "scrupulously honor" a suspect's right to remain silent and yet resume interrogation. Generally speaking, courts have found the most important factor to be whether the officers gave the suspect a "cooling off" period after he invoked the right to silence. See United States v. Rambo, 365 F.3d 906 (10th Cir. 2004) ("Whatever else *Mosley* might require, it is clear that some break in the interrogation must occur."); Charles v. Smith, 894 F.2d 718 (5th Cir.1990) (waiver invalid where suspect was asked whether he owned a certain hat and coat, two minutes after invoking the right to silence); United States v. Ramsey, 992 F.2d 301 (11th Cir.1993) (waiver invalid where defendant was given a last "opportunity to help himself", twenty minutes after invoking the right to silence); Grooms v. Keeney, 826 F.2d 883 (9th Cir.1987) (waiver valid after four hour break in questioning).

Multiple attempts to get the suspect to speak are considered problematic. See Vujosevic v. Rafferty, 844 F.2d 1023 (3d Cir.1988) (waiver invalid where suspect was approached four times to determine whether he had changed his mind about not talking, and where officers had no reason to believe that he had changed his mind). If the officers give fresh *Miranda* warnings when they approach the suspect, this is evidence (though not dispositive) that they are scrupulously honoring the suspect's right to silence, as well as evidence that defendant knowingly and voluntarily waived his rights if a confession is obtained. See Otey v. Grammer, 859 F.2d 575 (8th Cir.1988) (waiver found where warnings were given frequently and defendant was allowed to control the subject matter of the questioning).

What if the officers use a tactic designed to impress upon the defendant the seriousness of the situation? Is this permissible when the defendant has invoked his right to silence? In United States v. Tyler, 164 F.3d 150 (3d Cir. 1998), the defendant was arrested for murdering a witness who was scheduled to testify at his brother's criminal trial. He invoked his right to silence, and was placed in a room at the police station. The walls of the room contained a time line of the murder investigation and crime scene photographs, including two photos of the body of the victim. Tyler remained in the room, alone, for hours. When the officers came to question him again, Tyler immediately confessed. The Court found that this confession had to be excluded under *Mosley*. Do you agree? See also United States v. Lafferty, 503 F.3d 293 (3rd Cir. 2007) (officers did not scrupulously honor the right to remain silent when they put the suspect in an interrogation room with her alleged accomplice after he had agreed to give a confession).

### *Right to Silence Must Be Clearly Invoked; Waiver Can Be Implied from the Confession Itself; and Interrogation After Warnings Is Permissible So Long as Waiver Is Ultimately Found: Berghuis v. Thompkins*

The *Mosley* standards presume that the suspect has invoked the right to silence after receiving *Miranda* warnings. If the suspect, in response to the warnings, says "I don't want to talk about anything," then he has clearly triggered the protections provided by *Mosley*. Not all invocations are so clear, however. What if the suspect says "If I knew what was good for me, I wouldn't be talking to you," or "I'd like to cooperate, but my brother would kill me if I did"? If it is unclear whether the suspect is invoking his right to silence, must the police stop the interrogation?

The following case takes up a number of important questions concerning waiver of *Miranda* rights. The case concerns specifically whether the *Miranda* right to silence is invoked by remaining silent. But the Court also provides important rules on when a waiver of *Miranda* rights can be found in the absence of an invocation.

## BERGHUIS V. THOMPKINS

Supreme Court of the United States, 2010.
560 U.S. 370.

### JUSTICE KENNEDY delivered the opinion of the Court

The United States Court of Appeals for the Sixth Circuit, in a habeas corpus proceeding challenging a Michigan conviction for first-degree murder and certain other offenses, ruled that * * * a statement by the accused, relied on at trial by the prosecution, had been elicited in violation of Miranda v. Arizona. [That contention] had been rejected in Michigan courts and in the habeas corpus proceedings before the United States District Court. Certiorari was granted to review the decision by the Court of Appeals on both points. * * *

On January 10, 2000, a shooting occurred outside a mall in Southfield, Michigan. Among the victims was Samuel Morris, who died from multiple gunshot wounds. The other victim, Frederick France, recovered from his injuries and later testified. Thompkins, who was a suspect, fled. About one year later he was found in Ohio and arrested there.

Two Southfield police officers traveled to Ohio to interrogate Thompkins, then awaiting transfer to Michigan. The interrogation began around 1:30 p.m. and lasted about three hours. The interrogation was conducted in a room that was 8 by 10 feet, and Thompkins sat in a chair that resembled a school desk * * *. At the beginning of the interrogation, one of the officers, Detective Helgert, presented Thompkins with a form derived from the *Miranda* rule. It stated:

"NOTIFICATION OF CONSTITUTIONAL RIGHTS AND STATEMENT

"1. You have the right to remain silent.

"2. Anything you say can and will be used against you in a court of law.

"3. You have a right to talk to a lawyer before answering any questions and you have the right to have a lawyer present with you while you are answering any questions.

"4. If you cannot afford to hire a lawyer, one will be appointed to represent you before any questioning, if you wish one.

"5. You have the right to decide at any time before or during questioning to use your right to remain silent and your right to talk with a lawyer while you are being questioned."

Helgert asked Thompkins to read the fifth warning out loud. Thompkins complied. Helgert later said this was to ensure that Thompkins could read, and Helgert concluded that Thompkins understood English. Helgert then read the other four *Miranda* warnings out loud and asked Thompkins to sign the form to demonstrate that he understood his rights. Thompkins declined to sign the form. The record contains conflicting evidence about whether Thompkins then verbally confirmed that he understood the rights listed on the form.

Officers began an interrogation. At no point during the interrogation did Thompkins say that he wanted to remain silent, that he did not want to talk with the police, or that he wanted an attorney. Thompkins was "[l]argely" silent during the interrogation, which lasted about three hours. He did give a few limited verbal responses, however, such as "yeah," "no," or "I don't know." And on occasion he communicated by nodding his head. Thompkins also said that he "didn't want a peppermint" that was offered to him by the police and that the chair he was "sitting in was hard."

About 2 hours and 45 minutes into the interrogation, Helgert asked Thompkins, "Do you believe in God?" Thompkins made eye contact with Helgert and said "Yes," as his eyes "well[ed] up with tears." Helgert asked, "Do you pray to God?" Thompkins said "Yes." Helgert asked, "Do you pray to God to forgive you for shooting that boy down?" Thompkins answered "Yes" and looked away. Thompkins refused to make a written confession, and the interrogation ended about 15 minutes later.

Thompkins was charged with first-degree murder * * *. He moved to suppress the statements made during the interrogation. He argued that he had invoked his Fifth Amendment right to remain silent, requiring police to end the interrogation at once, see Michigan v. Mosley, that he had not waived his right to remain silent, and that his inculpatory statements were involuntary. The trial court denied the motion. [Thompkins was convicted. His state appeals were rejected. The district court denied a writ of habeas corpus but the Sixth Circuit reversed.]

* * *

All concede that the warning given in this case was in full compliance with these requirements. The dispute centers on the response—or nonresponse—from the suspect.

Thompkins makes various arguments that his answers to questions from the detectives were inadmissible. He first contends that he invoked his privilege to remain silent by not saying anything for a sufficient period of time, so the interrogation should have ceased before he made his inculpatory statements.

This argument is unpersuasive. In the context of invoking the *Miranda* right to counsel, the Court in Davis v. United States [discussed *infra* in the section on invoking the right to counsel], held that a suspect must do so "unambiguously." If an accused makes a statement concerning the right to counsel "that is ambiguous or equivocal" or makes no statement, the police are not required to end the interrogation, or ask questions to clarify whether the accused wants to invoke his or her *Miranda* rights.

The Court has not yet stated whether an invocation of the right to remain silent can be ambiguous or equivocal, but there is no principled reason to adopt different standards for determining when an accused has invoked the *Miranda* right to remain silent and the *Miranda* right to counsel at issue in *Davis*. Both protect the privilege against compulsory self-incrimination, by requiring an interrogation to cease when either right is invoked.

There is good reason to require an accused who wants to invoke his or her right to remain silent to do so unambiguously. A requirement of an unambiguous invocation of *Miranda* rights results in an objective inquiry that avoids difficulties of proof and provides guidance to officers on how to proceed in the face of ambiguity. If an ambiguous act, omission, or statement could require police to end the interrogation, police would be required to make difficult decisions about an accused's unclear intent and face the consequence of suppression if they guess wrong. Suppression of a voluntary confession in these circumstances would place a significant burden on society's interest in prosecuting criminal activity. Treating an ambiguous or equivocal act, omission, or statement as an invocation of *Miranda* rights might add marginally to *Miranda's* goal of dispelling the compulsion inherent in custodial interrogation. But as *Miranda* holds, full comprehension of the rights to remain silent and request an attorney are sufficient to dispel whatever coercion is inherent in the interrogation process.

Thompkins did not say that he wanted to remain silent or that he did not want to talk with the police. Had he made either of these simple, unambiguous statements, he would have invoked his right to cut off questioning. Michigan v. Mosley. Here he did neither, so he did not invoke his right to remain silent.

\* \* \*

We next consider whether Thompkins waived his right to remain silent. Even absent the accused's invocation of the right to remain silent, the accused's statement during a custodial interrogation is inadmissible at trial unless the prosecution can establish that the accused in fact knowingly and voluntarily waived *Miranda* rights when making the statement. The waiver inquiry has two distinct dimensions: waiver must be voluntary in the sense that it was the product of a free and deliberate choice rather than intimidation, coercion, or deception, and "made with a full awareness of both the nature of the right being abandoned and the consequences of the decision to abandon it." Moran v. Burbine.

Some language in *Miranda* could be read to indicate that waivers are difficult to establish absent an explicit written waiver or a formal, express oral statement. * * *

The course of decisions since *Miranda*, informed by the application of *Miranda* warnings in the whole course of law enforcement, demonstrates that waivers can be established even absent formal or express statements of waiver that would be expected in, say, a judicial hearing to determine if a guilty plea has been properly entered. * * *

One of the first cases to decide the meaning and import of *Miranda* with respect to the question of waiver was North Carolina v. Butler. The *Butler* Court, after discussing some of the problems created by the language in *Miranda*, established certain important propositions. *Butler* interpreted the *Miranda* language concerning the "heavy burden" to show waiver, in accord with usual principles of determining waiver, which can include waiver implied from all the circumstances. And in a later case, the Court stated that this "heavy burden" is not more than the burden to establish waiver by a preponderance of the evidence. Colorado v. Connelly

The prosecution therefore does not need to show that a waiver of *Miranda* rights was express. * * * *Butler* made clear that a waiver of *Miranda* rights may be implied through "the defendant's silence, coupled with an understanding of his rights and a course of conduct indicating waiver." The Court in *Butler* therefore retreated from the language and tenor of the *Miranda* opinion, which suggested that the Court would require that a waiver be specifically made.

If the State establishes that a *Miranda* warning was given and the accused made an uncoerced statement, this showing, standing alone, is insufficient to demonstrate a valid waiver of *Miranda* rights. The prosecution must make the additional showing that the accused understood these rights. Where the prosecution shows that a *Miranda* warning was given and that it was understood by the accused, an accused's uncoerced statement establishes an implied waiver of the right to remain silent.

Although *Miranda* imposes on the police a rule that is both formalistic and practical when it prevents them from interrogating suspects without first providing them with a *Miranda* warning, it does not impose a formalistic waiver procedure that a suspect must follow to relinquish those rights. As a general proposition, the law can presume that an individual who, with a full understanding of his or her rights, acts in a manner inconsistent with their exercise has made a deliberate choice to relinquish the protection those rights afford. * * *

The record in this case shows that Thompkins waived his right to remain silent. * * * First, there is no contention that Thompkins did not understand his rights; and from this it follows that he knew what he gave up when he spoke. There was more than enough evidence in the record to conclude that Thompkins understood his *Miranda* rights. Thompkins received a written copy of the *Miranda* warnings; Detective Helgert determined that Thompkins could read and understand English; and Thompkins was given time to read the warnings. * * * Helgert, moreover, read the warnings aloud.

Second, Thompkins's answer to Detective Helgert's question about whether Thompkins prayed to God for forgiveness for shooting the victim is a "course of conduct indicating waiver" of the right to remain silent. *Butler*. If Thompkins wanted to remain silent, he could have said nothing in response to Helgert's questions, or he could have unambiguously invoked his *Miranda* rights and ended the interrogation. The fact that Thompkins made a statement about three hours after receiving a *Miranda* warning does not overcome the fact that he engaged in a course of conduct indicating waiver. Police are not required to rewarn suspects from time to time. Thompkins's answer to Helgert's question about praying to God for forgiveness for shooting the victim was sufficient to show a course of conduct indicating waiver. This is confirmed by the fact that before then Thompkins had given sporadic answers to questions throughout the interrogation.

Third, there is no evidence that Thompkins's statement was coerced. * * * Thompkins does not claim that police threatened or injured him during the interrogation or that he was in any way fearful. The interrogation was conducted in a standard-sized room in the middle of the afternoon. It is true that apparently he was in a straight-backed chair for three hours, but there is no authority for the proposition that an interrogation of this length is inherently coercive. Indeed, even where interrogations of greater duration were held to be improper, they were accompanied, as this one was not, by other facts indicating coercion, such as an incapacitated and sedated suspect, sleep and food deprivation, and threats. The fact that Helgert's question referred to Thompkins's religious beliefs also did not render Thompkins's statement involuntary. The Fifth Amendment privilege is not concerned with moral and psychological pressures to confess emanating from sources other than official coercion. In these circumstances, Thompkins knowingly and voluntarily made a statement to police, so he waived his right to remain silent.

* * *

Thompkins next argues that, even if his answer to Detective Helgert could constitute a waiver of his right to remain silent, the police were not allowed to question him until they obtained a waiver first. *Butler* forecloses this argument. The *Butler* Court held that courts can infer a waiver of *Miranda* rights "from the actions and words of the person interrogated." This principle would be inconsistent with a rule that requires a waiver at the outset. The *Butler* Court thus rejected the rule proposed by the *Butler* dissent, which would have "requir[ed] the police to obtain an express waiver of [*Miranda* rights] before proceeding with interrogation." This holding also makes sense given that the primary protection afforded suspects subjected to custodial interrogation is the *Miranda* warnings themselves. * * *

Interrogation provides the suspect with additional information that can put his or her decision to waive, or not to invoke, into perspective. As questioning commences and then continues, the suspect has the opportunity to consider the choices he or she faces and to make a more informed decision, either to insist on silence or to cooperate. When the suspect knows that *Miranda* rights can be invoked at any time, he or she has the opportunity to reassess his or her immediate and long-term interests. * * *

In order for an accused's statement to be admissible at trial, police must have given the accused a *Miranda* warning. If that condition is established, the court can proceed to consider whether there has been an express or implied waiver of *Miranda* rights. In making its ruling on the admissibility of a statement made during custodial questioning, the trial court, of course, considers whether there is evidence to support the conclusion that, from the whole course of questioning, an express or implied waiver has been established. Thus, after giving a *Miranda* warning, police may interrogate a suspect who has neither invoked nor waived his or her *Miranda* rights. On these premises, it follows the police were not required to obtain a waiver of Thompkins's *Miranda* rights before commencing the interrogation.

* * *

In sum, a suspect who has received and understood the *Miranda* warnings, and has not invoked his *Miranda* rights, waives the right to remain silent by making an uncoerced statement to the police. Thompkins did not invoke his right to remain silent and stop the questioning. Understanding his rights in full, he waived his right to remain silent by making a voluntary statement to the police. The police, moreover, were not required to obtain a waiver of Thompkins's right to remain silent before interrogating him. The state court's decision rejecting Thompkins's *Miranda* claim was thus correct under de novo review and therefore necessarily reasonable under the more deferential AEDPA standard of review.

* * *

**JUSTICE SOTOMAYOR, with whom JUSTICE STEVENS, JUSTICE GINSBURG, and JUSTICE BREYER join, dissenting.**

The Court concludes today that a criminal suspect waives his right to remain silent if, after sitting tacit and uncommunicative through nearly three hours of police interrogation, he utters a few one-word responses. The Court also concludes that a suspect who wishes to guard his right to remain silent against such a finding of "waiver" must, counterintuitively, speak—and must do so with sufficient precision to satisfy a clear-statement rule that construes ambiguity in favor of the police. Both propositions mark a substantial retreat from the protection against compelled self-incrimination that *Miranda* has long provided during custodial interrogation. * * *.

\* \* \*

That Thompkins did not make the inculpatory statements at issue until after approximately 2 hours and 45 minutes of interrogation serves as strong evidence against waiver. *Miranda* and *Butler* expressly preclude the possibility that the inculpatory statements themselves are sufficient to establish waiver. * * *

Today's dilution of the prosecution's burden of proof to the bare fact that a suspect made inculpatory statements after *Miranda* warnings were given and understood takes an unprecedented step away from the high standards of proof for the waiver of constitutional rights this Court has long demanded. * * *

\* \* \*

I cannot agree with the Court's * * * ruling that a suspect must clearly invoke his right to silence by speaking. Taken together with the Court's reformulation of the prosecution's burden of proof as to waiver, today's novel clear-statement rule for invocation invites police to question a suspect at length—notwithstanding his persistent refusal to answer questions—in the hope of eventually obtaining a single inculpatory response which will suffice to prove waiver of rights. * * *

I disagree with [the Court's] novel application of *Davis*. Neither the rationale nor holding of that case compels today's result. *Davis* involved the right to counsel, not the right to silence. * * *

\* \* \*

In my mind, a more appropriate standard for addressing a suspect's ambiguous invocation of the right to remain silent is the constraint *Mosley* places on questioning a suspect who has invoked that right: The suspect's "right to cut off questioning" must be "scrupulously honored." Such a standard is necessarily precautionary and fact specific. * * *

To be sure, such a standard does not provide police with a bright-line rule. But * * * *Mosley* itself does not offer clear guidance to police about when and how interrogation may continue after a suspect invokes his rights. Given that police have for nearly 35 years applied *Mosley's* fact-specific standard in questioning suspects who have invoked their right to remain silent * * * I see little reason to believe today's clear-statement rule is necessary to ensure effective law enforcement.

*Davis'* clear-statement rule is also a poor fit for the right to silence. Advising a suspect that he has a "right to remain silent" is unlikely to convey that he must speak (and must do so in some particular fashion) to ensure the right will be protected. By contrast, telling a suspect he has the right to the presence of an attorney, and that if he cannot afford an attorney one will be appointed for him prior to any questioning if he so desires implies the need for speech to exercise that right. * * *

Conversely, the Court's concern that police will face "difficult decisions about an accused's unclear intent" and suffer the consequences of "guessing wrong," is misplaced. If a suspect makes an ambiguous statement or engages in conduct that creates uncertainty about his intent to invoke his right, police can simply ask for clarification. It is hardly an unreasonable burden for police to ask a suspect, for instance, "Do you want to talk to us?" * * *

--------

Today's decision turns *Miranda* upside down. Criminal suspects must now unambiguously invoke their right to remain silent—which, counterintuitively, requires them to speak. At the same time, suspects will be legally presumed to have waived their rights even if they have given no clear expression of their intent to do so. Those results, in my view, find no basis in *Miranda* or our subsequent cases and are inconsistent with the fair-trial principles on which those precedents are grounded. * * *

### Custodial Interrogation Requirement

*Mosley's* requirement of "scrupulous honor" applies only if the defendant's explicit invocation of the right to silence occurs in the context of custodial interrogation. For example, in United States v. Kelly, 329 F.3d 624 (8th Cir. 2003), the defendant argued that his confession had to be excluded under *Mosley* because he had previously invoked his right to silence when he spoke to police officers in an initial interview, and then confessed when the officers interrogated him later. The court, however, noted that the defendant was not in custody during the initial interview; accordingly, he had no *Miranda* rights to invoke. The court concluded that "Kelly's termination of the voluntary encounter posed no independent barrier to later questioning."

### b.  Invocation of the Right to Counsel

### Bright Line Rule: Edwards v. Arizona

In Edwards v. Arizona, 451 U.S. 477 (1981), the Court determined whether and under what circumstances a waiver can be found after the suspect invokes his right to *counsel*. The Court adopted a per se approach:

> [A]dditional safeguards are necessary when the accused asks for counsel; and we now hold that when an accused has invoked his right to have counsel present during custodial interrogation, a valid waiver of that right cannot be established by showing only that he responded to further police-initiated custodial interrogation even if he has been advised of his rights. We further hold that an accused, such as Edwards, having expressed his desire to deal with the police only through counsel, *is not subject to further interrogation by the authorities until counsel has been made available to him, unless the accused himself initiates further communication, exchanges or conversations with the police.*[19]

### Relationship Between Edwards and Innis

*Edwards* holds that police must terminate and cannot re-initiate an interrogation of a suspect who has invoked his right to counsel. But if police-renewed contact does not rise to the level of custodial interrogation, *Miranda* itself is inapplicable to a resulting confession, and therefore so is *Edwards*. This is shown by the facts of *Innis*. Innis invoked his right to counsel, but the Court found it unnecessary to reach the question of waiver, because the officers never interrogated him after he invoked. They had *contact* with him—the officer's statement in the cruiser about the gun possibly being picked up by a handicapped child—but they did not interrogate him.

So if the suspect invokes his right to counsel, what *Edwards* holds is that police may not *interrogate* him while in custody unless the suspect initiates the conversation and then knowingly and voluntarily waives his *Miranda* rights. See, e.g., Van Hook v. Anderson, 444 F.3d 830 (6th Cir. 2006) (after defendant invoked his right to counsel, the officer spoke with the defendant's mother, then approached the defendant and said "I just spoke to your mother, we need to talk"; this was interrogation, so the subsequent confession was obtained in violation of *Edwards*).

---

[19] Chief Justice Burger and Justices Powell and Rehnquist agreed with the result, but expressed concern about the seemingly per se aspects of the majority rule which they found to be an unnecessary embellishment on the standard knowing and intelligent waiver rule.

### *Defining Initiation: Oregon v. Bradshaw*

*Edwards* requires that a suspect "initiate" further communication before a waiver can be found. Whether a suspect has initiated reinterrogation is often a difficult question. In Oregon v. Bradshaw, 462 U.S. 1039 (1983), Oregon police were investigating the death of Lowell Reynolds, a minor who apparently died in the wreck of his pickup truck. Bradshaw was asked and consented to come to the police station for questioning. Once there, he was advised of his rights and admitted providing liquor to Reynolds. He was arrested for furnishing liquor to a minor. When an officer suggested that Bradshaw might have been driving Reynolds' truck, Bradshaw invoked his right to an attorney. Questioning stopped. Thereafter, during or just before a 10 or 15 mile trip from the police station to the jail, Bradshaw asked, "Well, what is going to happen to me now?" An officer answered that Bradshaw had requested an attorney and that Bradshaw should not be talking with the officer unless he desired to do so. The two had a conversation concerning where Bradshaw was being taken and what the charges against him would be. The officer suggested that Bradshaw might help himself by taking a lie detector test, and Bradshaw agreed to take one. The next day, following new warnings, he took the test. The examiner expressed doubts that Bradshaw had told the truth and Bradshaw then admitted he was driving the vehicle in which Reynolds was killed. The trial court admitted Bradshaw's confession.

A plurality of the Supreme Court found that *Edwards* was satisfied, because Bradshaw initiated the contact with the police officer after invoking his right to counsel, and then made a knowing and voluntary waiver of his *Miranda* rights. Justice Rehnquist's plurality opinion, joined by Chief Justice Burger and Justices White and O'Connor, found initiation by reasoning as follows:

> There can be no doubt in this case that in asking, "Well, what is going to happen to me now?" respondent "initiated" further conversation in the ordinary dictionary sense of that word. While we doubt that it would be desirable to build a superstructure of legal refinements around the word "initiate" in this context, there are undoubtedly situations where a bare inquiry by either a defendant or by a police officer should not be held to "initiate" any conversation or dialogue. There are some inquiries, such as a request for a drink of water or a request to use a telephone that are so routine that they cannot be fairly said to represent a desire on the part of an accused to open up a more generalized discussion relating directly or indirectly to the investigation. Such inquiries or statements, by either an accused or a police officer, relating to routine incidents of the

custodial relationship, will not generally "initiate" a conversation in the sense in which that word was used in *Edwards*.

Although ambiguous, the respondent's question in this case as to what was going to happen to him evinced a willingness and a desire for a generalized discussion about the investigation; it was not merely a necessary inquiry arising out of the incidents of the custodial relationship. It could reasonably have been interpreted by the officer as relating generally to the investigation. That the police officer so understood it is apparent from the fact that he immediately reminded the accused that "you do not have to talk to me," and only after the accused told him that he "understood" did they have a generalized conversation. On these facts we believe that there was not a violation of the *Edwards* rule.

The plurality clarified that a finding of initiation by the suspect was not enough to constitute a waiver under *Edwards*. Justice Rehnquist stated that even if the suspect initiates communication, "where reinterrogation follows, the burden remains upon the prosecution to show that subsequent events indicated a waiver of the Fifth Amendment right to have counsel present during the interrogation."

Thus, the Court uses a two-step analysis to determine whether a suspect waives his rights after invoking the right to counsel:

- The first step is the bright-line prophylactic safeguard of the suspect-initiation requirement.

- The second step is the familiar totality of circumstances test of a knowing and voluntary waiver.

The plurality in *Bradshaw* found that after initiating communication, Bradshaw knowingly and voluntarily waived his *Miranda* rights, because he was given fresh warnings and it was clear he understood them and voluntarily waived them.

Justice Marshall, joined by Justices Brennan, Blackmun, and Stevens, dissented. The dissenters applied the same two-step approach as had the majority, but they differed as to the application of the threshold requirement of "initiation" to the facts. Justice Marshall argued that the plurality's definition of "initiation" was overbroad, and "drastically undermined" the protection erected in *Edwards*. In Justice Marshall's view, initiation could not be found unless the suspect expresses a willingness to discuss the *specific subject matter of the investigation*. He argued that Bradshaw's question was merely a response to his custodial surroundings, rather than an expression of willingness to discuss his crime.

The deciding vote in *Bradshaw* was cast by Justice Powell, who concurred in the result. He expressed concern about the bright line initiation requirement. Justice Powell preferred to rely on the totality of the circumstances, which in this case indicated that Bradshaw had knowingly and voluntarily waived his *Miranda* rights.

## Applications of Bradshaw

While the Court split 4–4 in *Bradshaw* as to the proper test for initiation, the lower courts have consistently followed Justice Rehnquist's view that any ambiguity in whether the suspect expressed an intent to reopen the dialogue should be construed in favor of finding an initiation. The court in United States v. Velasquez, 885 F.2d 1076 (3d Cir.1989), relied on the *Bradshaw* plurality to hold that the suspect's statement "what is going to happen?" was an initiation under *Edwards*. The court stated that the plurality's test was a reasonable compromise between individual and state interests, and that Justice Marshall's test "might convert the prophylactic value of the initiation requirement * * * into an overly stringent substantive hurdle." The Court felt it was unnecessary to apply the initiation requirement aggressively, because the government continues to have the burden of showing that the suspect knowingly and voluntarily waived his *Miranda* rights.

Even under the plurality's view of initiation in *Bradshaw*, however, it does not follow that every statement from a suspect's mouth evinces a desire to "talk generally about his case." See, e.g., United States v. Soto, 953 F.2d 263 (6th Cir.1992) (indicating desire to keep belongings separate from those of co-defendant is not initiation); Jacobs v. Singletary, 952 F.2d 1282 (11th Cir.1992) (asking officer "Where are my children?" is not initiation).

## Ambiguous Invocation of the Right to Counsel: Davis v. United States

As with invocation of the right to silence, questions sometimes arise as to whether the suspect has *in fact* invoked a right to counsel. If there is no invocation, then there is no initiation requirement, and the analysis reverts to whether the defendant knowingly and voluntarily waived his *Miranda* rights.

In Davis v. United States, 512 U.S. 452 (1994), the Court held that a suspect must *clearly and unequivocally* invoke the right to counsel in order to trigger the protections of *Edwards*. If the invocation is ambiguous or equivocal, police questioning can continue; and such questioning need not be limited to that necessary to clarify the suspect's desire with respect to counsel. [As discussed above, the Court thereafter in Berghuis v. Thompkins applied the *Davis* explicit invocation requirement to the right to silence.]

After waiving his *Miranda* rights, Davis answered questions about a killing; about 90 minutes into the interview, he said, "Maybe I should talk to a lawyer." The officers then asked clarifying questions to determine whether Davis wanted a lawyer. He said that he did not. A short break was taken, Davis was reminded of his rights, and the interview continued for another hour, until Davis said, "I think I want a lawyer before I say anything else." At that point, questioning ceased. In the Supreme Court, Davis argued that the statements he made after his first reference to counsel were improperly admitted at his trial.

The Supreme Court, in an opinion by Justice O'Connor for five Justices, rejected Davis's argument and held that the statements Davis made after referring to counsel were properly admitted at his trial. Justice O'Connor set forth the standards applicable to the invocation of the *Miranda* right to counsel, and the protections of *Edwards,* in the following analysis:

> [T]he suspect must unambiguously request counsel. Although a suspect need not "speak with the discrimination of an Oxford don," he must articulate his desire to have counsel present sufficiently clearly that a reasonable police officer in the circumstances would understand the statement to be a request for an attorney. If the statement fails to meet the requisite level of clarity, *Edwards* does not require that the officers stop questioning the suspect.

> We decline petitioner's invitation to extend *Edwards* and require law enforcement officers to cease questioning immediately upon the making of an ambiguous or equivocal reference to an attorney. The rationale underlying *Edwards* is that the police must respect a suspect's wishes regarding his right to have an attorney present during custodial interrogation. But when the officers conducting the questioning reasonably do not know whether or not the suspect wants a lawyer, a rule requiring the immediate cessation of questioning would * * * needlessly prevent the police from questioning a suspect in the absence of counsel even if the suspect did not wish to have a lawyer present. Nothing in *Edwards* requires the provision of counsel to a suspect who consents to answer questions without the assistance of a lawyer.

Davis argued that if police were permitted to continue interrogation in the face of an ambiguous invocation of counsel, they could take unfair advantage of inarticulate and overmatched suspects. But Justice O'Connor held that these concerns were not of sufficient weight to prevent the continuation of police questioning:

> We recognize that requiring a clear assertion of the right to counsel might disadvantage some suspects who—because of fear, intimidation, lack of linguistic skills, or a variety of other reasons—

will not clearly articulate their right to counsel although they actually want to have a lawyer present. But the primary protection afforded suspects subject to custodial interrogation is the *Miranda* warnings themselves. * * * A suspect who knowingly and voluntarily waives his right to counsel after having that right explained to him has indicated his willingness to deal with the police unassisted. Although *Edwards* provides an additional protection—if a suspect subsequently requests an attorney, questioning must cease—it is one that must be affirmatively invoked by the suspect.

Justice O'Connor further declared that the continued questioning after a suspect's ambiguous reference to counsel need not be limited to questions clarifying whether the suspect really wants a lawyer:

> Of course, when a suspect makes an ambiguous or equivocal statement it will often be good police practice for the interviewing officers to clarify whether or not he actually wants an attorney. That was the procedure followed by the [officers] in this case. Clarifying questions help protect the rights of the suspect by ensuring that he gets an attorney if he wants one, and will minimize the chance of a confession being suppressed due to subsequent judicial second-guessing as to the meaning of the suspect's statement regarding counsel. But we decline to adopt a rule requiring officers to ask clarifying questions. If the suspect's statement is not an unambiguous or unequivocal request for counsel, the officers have no obligation to stop questioning him.

Finally, Justice O'Connor found no reason to disturb the rulings of the lower courts that Davis' statement—"Maybe I should talk to a lawyer"—was not a sufficiently explicit request for counsel.

Justice Souter, joined by Justices Blackmun, Stevens, and Ginsburg, concurred only in the judgment in *Davis*. He agreed with the Court that Davis's position—i.e., questioning must cease completely whenever the suspect invokes counsel, even if the invocation is ambiguous—was overprotective of suspects and too costly to law enforcement. He disagreed, however, with the Court's position that an ambiguous invocation was essentially irrelevant and placed no limits on subsequent questioning.

Justice Souter preferred the view taken by the majority of courts prior to *Davis*—that questioning could continue, but that the questions must be limited to clarifying whether or not the suspect wanted to invoke the right to counsel. Justice Souter expressed concern that the majority's explicit invocation test, without a safety valve requirement that officers ask only clarifying questions, would fall hard on many criminal suspects:

> [C]riminal suspects who may (in *Miranda's* words) be "thrust into an unfamiliar atmosphere and run through menacing police

interrogation procedures," would seem an odd group to single out for the Court's demand of heightened linguistic care. A substantial percentage of them lack anything like a confident command of the English language; many are "woefully ignorant;" and many more will be sufficiently intimidated by the interrogation process or overwhelmed by the uncertainty of their predicament that the ability to speak assertively will abandon them.

## QUESTIONS AFTER DAVIS

What is the difference between Davis's first statement—"Maybe I should talk to a lawyer"—and his second statement—"I think I want a lawyer before I say anything else"? Are you as convinced as the Court that the first one was an ambiguous statement that did not constitute a request for counsel, while the second one was a clear invocation of the right to counsel? The majority in *Davis* opted for the "clarity" of a bright-line rule. Are you convinced that the rule is as bright a line as the *Davis* Court suggests?

Here are three examples of statements that have been found insufficiently specific to constitute an invocation of the right to counsel after *Davis*:

- "My daddy wants me to get a lawyer"—held insufficiently specific in Hyatt v. Branker, 569 F.3d 162 (4th Cir. 2009).

- "My lawyer told me to keep my mouth shut"—held insufficiently specific in Sechrest v. Ignacio, 549 F.3d 789 (9th Cir. 2008).

- "I guess you better get me a lawyer, then"—held insufficiently specific (because "I guess" is defined as equivocal in the Oxford Dictionary) in United States v. Havlik, 710 F.3d 818 (8th Cir. 2013).

Compare Moore v. Berghuis, 700 F.3d 882 (6th Cir. 2012) ("Moore invoked his constitutional right to counsel by requesting that the police officer call his attorney's phone number."); United States v. Wysinger, 683 F.3d 784 (7th Cir. 2012) ("Do you think I should have a lawyer at this point?" is not an explicit invocation, but later question "Can I call one now?" was an explicit invocation).

## Consequences of Explicit Invocation: Smith v. Illinois

In Smith v. Illinois, 469 U.S. 91 (1984), a suspect who was asked whether he understood his right to have a lawyer present stated, "Uh, yeah, I'd like that." The Court rejected the state's argument that this statement was too vague to be considered an invocation of counsel that triggered the protections of *Edwards*. It found that "with the possible exception of the word 'uh' the defendant's statement in this case was neither indecisive nor ambiguous." The Court concluded that "where nothing about the request for counsel or the circumstances leading up to the request would render it ambiguous, all questioning must cease."

When the officer questioned Smith after his "uh" response to the warnings, ostensibly to clarify the request, Smith did make ambiguous statements concerning his desire for counsel. But the Court dismissed this *later* ambiguity as irrelevant. It declared that "using an accused's subsequent responses to cast doubt on the adequacy of the initial request *itself* is * * * intolerable" and that a contrary rule would lead to abusive use of "clarifying" questions.[20]

### Unrelated Crimes: Arizona v. Roberson

Does *Edwards* permit officers to initiate interrogation on crimes other than the one for which the suspect invoked his right to counsel? In Arizona v. Roberson, 486 U.S. 675 (1988), the Court answered this question in the negative and held that an invocation of the right to counsel under *Edwards* was not offense-specific. Such an invocation prevents police-initiated interrogation *on any crime*.

Roberson was arrested at the scene of a just-completed burglary. After he was given *Miranda* warnings, he stated that he wanted a lawyer before answering any questions. Three days later while the defendant remained in custody, a different officer, who was unaware of the previous request for a lawyer, gave new *Miranda* warnings and obtained a statement concerning another burglary. Justice Stevens wrote for the Court as it declared that "*Edwards* serves the purpose of providing clear and unequivocal guidelines to the law enforcement profession," and that "there is nothing ambiguous about the requirement that after a person in custody has expressed his desire to deal with the police only through counsel, he is not subject to further interrogation by the authorities until counsel has been made available to him, unless the accused himself initiates further communication, exchanges, or conversations with the police."

The Court concluded that "to a suspect who has indicated his inability to cope with the pressures of custodial interrogation by requesting counsel, any further interrogation without counsel having been provided will surely exacerbate whatever compulsion to speak the suspect may be feeling." The government argued that a suspect might have good reason to want to speak to police about a new investigation. But Justice Stevens responded that "[t]he simple answer is that the suspect, having requested counsel, can determine how to deal with the separate investigations with counsel's advice." He added that "even if the

---

[20] Justice Rehnquist, joined by Chief Justice Burger and Justice Powell, dissented. He argued that Smith's statement was ambiguous under the circumstances, and that the majority's rule preventing consideration of post-request statements was overbroad.

police have decided temporarily not to provide counsel, they are free to inform the suspect of the facts of the second investigation as long as such communication does not constitute interrogation."

Justice Kennedy, joined by Chief Justice Rehnquist, dissented, complaining that the Court's ruling was unnecessary to protect a suspect's rights and unduly restricted legitimate investigations of crimes other than those for which a suspect has been arrested. He described the breadth of the Court's rule as follows:

> The rule announced today will bar law enforcement officials, even those from some other city or other jurisdiction, from questioning a suspect about an unrelated matter if he is in custody and has requested counsel to assist in answering questions put to him about the crime for which he was arrested.

Justice Kennedy attacked the Court's presumption "that a suspect has made the decision that he does not wish to talk about that [separate investigation] without counsel present, although that decision was made when the suspect was unaware of even the existence of a second investigation," and argued that "[a]llowing authorities who conduct a separate investigation to read the suspect his *Miranda* rights and ask him whether he wishes to invoke them strikes an appropriate balance."

### Waiver After the Suspect Has Consulted with Counsel: Minnick v. Mississippi

Suppose the suspect invokes his *Miranda* right to counsel and then the police let him confer with counsel. After counsel leaves, can the police approach the suspect and ask him if he would *now* like to talk to them? This was the question in Minnick v. Mississippi, 498 U.S. 146 (1990). The Court in *Minnick* held that the protection of *Edwards* continues *even after the suspect has consulted with an attorney*. Justice Kennedy, who dissented in *Roberson,* wrote the majority opinion for six justices. Minnick committed murders in Mississippi, and was apprehended in California. After making inculpatory statements at an FBI interview (which were excluded from Minnick's trial as violative of *Edwards*) an appointed attorney met with Minnick on two or three occasions. The attorney told Minnick not to say anything, and not to sign any waiver forms. After these consultations, a Mississippi Deputy Sheriff initiated an interrogation of Minnick. Minnick was given *Miranda* warnings, refused to sign a waiver of rights form, and confessed. The trial court held that the confession to the Deputy Sheriff was not excluded by *Edwards,* reasoning that *Edwards* was inapplicable once counsel had been made available to Minnick.

Justice Kennedy declared that under *Edwards*, police-initiated interrogation after an invocation of counsel may occur only if counsel is *actually present* during the interrogation. The Court relied upon language in *Miranda* and *Edwards,* which stated that "the interrogation must cease until an attorney is present" and that the suspect has the right "to have counsel present during custodial interrogation." Justice Kennedy reasoned that two policies underlying *Edwards* rendered its application in this case "appropriate and necessary":

- the bright line *Edwards* rule provides clarity and certainty; and

- the rule guarantees that suspects will not be badgered by police officers and provides prophylactic protection against police coercion.

On the issue of clarity, the Court found that a rule allowing police-initiated interrogation after consultation with counsel "would undermine the advantages flowing from *Edwards'* clear and unequivocal character." Justice Kennedy observed that a rule denying *Edwards* protection after consultation with a lawyer would be vague because "consultation is not a precise concept, for it may encompass variations from a telephone call to say that the attorney is in route, to a hurried exchange, * * * to a lengthy in-person conference."

As to the *Edwards* policy of preventing badgering and coercion, the Court found that mere consultation with an attorney would be insufficient to protect against the risk of harassment and exploitation of the suspect by the police. Justice Kennedy stated that "a single consultation with an attorney does not remove the suspect from persistent attempts by officials to persuade him to waive his rights, or from the coercive pressures that accompany custody and that may increase as custody is prolonged."

In a vigorous dissent, Justice Scalia, joined by Chief Justice Rehnquist, attacked the Court's "irrebuttable presumption" that a suspect who has invoked his right to counsel "can never validly waive that right during any police-initiated encounter, even after the suspect has been provided multiple *Miranda* warnings and has actually consulted with his attorney." Justice Scalia contended that a suspect who has consulted with counsel knows "that he has an advocate on his side, and that the police will permit him to consult with that advocate. He almost certainly also has a heightened awareness (above what the *Miranda* warning itself will provide) of his right to remain silent."

Justice Scalia concluded with a broad attack on the prophylactic rules of *Edwards* and *Miranda* itself:

> Both holdings are explicable * * * only as an effort to protect suspects against what is regarded as their own folly. The procedural protections of the Constitution protect the guilty as well as the innocent, but it is not their objective to set the guilty free. That some

clever criminals may employ those protections to their advantage is poor reason to allow criminals who have not done so to escape justice.

Thus, even if I were to concede that an honest confession is a foolish mistake, I would welcome rather than reject it * * *. While every person is entitled to stand silent, it is more virtuous for the wrongdoer to admit his offense and accept the punishment he deserves. * * * We should, then, rejoice at an honest confession, rather than pity the "poor fool" who has made it.

### The Requirement of Continuous Custody for Edwards Protection: Maryland v. Shatzer

In Maryland v. Shatzer, 559 U.S. 98 (2010), the Court held that the prophylactic safeguards of *Edwards* do not apply if the suspect, after invoking his right to counsel, is released from custody on the crime for which he is suspected, for an extended period. In that circumstance, the officers are free to take the suspect back into custody and initiate interrogation, and a resulting confession is admissible so long as the suspect knowingly and voluntarily waives his *Miranda* rights.

Shatzer was serving time on a child sex abuse offense, when officers sought to interrogate him about another crime—the abuse of his son. Shatzer invoked his right to counsel and was returned to the prison population. Two years and six months later, officers initiated a new interrogation on the abuse of his son. Shatzer, who was still incarcerated, waived his rights and confessed. All agreed that if *Edwards* applied, the confession would be inadmissible, because Shatzer did not initiate the new interrogation.

Justice Scalia, writing for seven members of the Court, held that *Edwards* did not apply, because he was not in custody for the offense of abusing his son for an extended period of time. Justice Scalia explained as follows:

> It is easy to believe that a suspect may be coerced or badgered into abandoning his earlier refusal to be questioned without counsel in * * * a case in which the suspect has been arrested for a particular crime and is held in uninterrupted pretrial custody while that crime is being actively investigated. After the initial interrogation, and up to and including the second one, he remains cut off from his normal life and companions, "thrust into" and isolated in an "unfamiliar," "police-dominated atmosphere," *Miranda,* where his captors "appear to control [his] fate," Illinois v. Perkins. * * *

> When * * * a suspect has been released from his pretrial custody and has returned to his normal life for some time before the later attempted interrogation, there is little reason to think that his

change of heart regarding interrogation without counsel has been coerced. He has no longer been isolated. He has likely been able to seek advice from an attorney, family members, and friends. And he knows from his earlier experience that he need only demand counsel to bring the interrogation to a halt; and that investigative custody does not last indefinitely. In these circumstances, it is far fetched to think that a police officer's asking the suspect whether he would like to waive his *Miranda* rights will any more wear down the accused than did the first such request at the original attempted interrogation—which is of course not deemed coercive. His change of heart is less likely attributable to "badgering" than it is to the fact that further deliberation in familiar surroundings has caused him to believe (rightly or wrongly) that cooperating with the investigation is in his interest. Uncritical extension of *Edwards* to this situation would not significantly increase the number of genuinely coerced confessions excluded. The justification for a conclusive presumption disappears when application of the presumption will not reach the correct result most of the time.

At the same time that extending the *Edwards* rule yields diminished benefits, extending the rule also increases its costs: the in-fact voluntary confessions it excludes from trial, and the voluntary confessions it deters law enforcement officers from even trying to obtain. * * *

The only logical endpoint of *Edwards* disability is termination of *Miranda* custody and any of its lingering effects. Without that limitation—and barring some purely arbitrary time-limit—every *Edwards* prohibition of custodial interrogation of a particular suspect would be eternal. * * *

We conclude that such an extension of *Edwards* is not justified; we have opened its protective umbrella far enough. The protections offered by *Miranda*, which we have deemed sufficient to ensure that the police respect the suspect's desire to have an attorney present the first time police interrogate him, adequately ensure that result when a suspect who initially requested counsel is reinterrogated after a break in custody that is of sufficient duration to dissipate its coercive effects.

Justice Scalia addressed the possibility that police officers might seek to evade the *Edwards* protections by releasing suspects for only a short period of time, then putting them into custody and reinterrogating them:

We think it appropriate to specify a period of time to avoid the consequence that continuation of the *Edwards* presumption will not reach the correct result most of the time. It seems to us that period is 14 days. That provides plenty of time for the suspect to get reacclimated to his normal life, to consult with friends and counsel, and to shake off any residual coercive effects of his prior custody.

The 14-day limitation meets Shatzer's concern that a break-in-custody rule lends itself to police abuse. He envisions that once a suspect invokes his *Miranda* right to counsel, the police will release the suspect briefly (to end the *Edwards* presumption) and then promptly bring him back into custody for reinterrogation. But once the suspect has been out of custody long enough (14 days) to eliminate its coercive effect, there will be nothing to gain by such gamesmanship—nothing, that is, except the entirely appropriate gain of being able to interrogate a suspect who has made a valid waiver of his *Miranda* rights.

Finally, Justice Scalia addressed Shatzer's argument that he *was* in continuous custody—he was imprisoned the entire time between his invocation of the right to counsel and the reinterrogation (albeit on a different charge):

> Without minimizing the harsh realities of incarceration, we think lawful imprisonment imposed upon conviction of a crime does not create the coercive pressures identified in *Miranda*.

> Interrogated suspects who have previously been convicted of crime live in prison. When they are released back into the general prison population, they return to their accustomed surroundings and daily routine-they regain the degree of control they had over their lives prior to the interrogation. Sentenced prisoners, in contrast to the *Miranda* paradigm, are not isolated with their accusers. They live among other inmates, guards, and workers, and often can receive visitors and communicate with people on the outside by mail or telephone.

Justice Thomas concurred in part and concurred in the result in *Shatzer*. He objected to the Court's 14-day rule as arbitrary. Justice Stevens dissented. He contended that the majority had ignored "the compulsion caused by a second (or third, or fourth) interrogation of an indigent suspect who was told that if he requests a lawyer, one would be provided for him" and that if a suspect is reinterrogated without a lawyer "the suspect is likely to feel that the police lied to him and that he really does not have any right to a lawyer."

### Which Constitutional Right to Counsel Is Invoked?
### McNeil v. Wisconsin

Besides the *Miranda* right to counsel, a defendant who has been formally charged with a crime (e.g., indicted) also has a Sixth Amendment right to counsel, as discussed later in this Chapter. When a formally charged defendant appears at an arraignment and invokes the right to counsel, is that an invocation of the *Miranda* right to counsel or the Sixth Amendment right to counsel? And why would it make any difference?

The Court in McNeil v. Wisconsin, 501 U.S. 171 (1991), held that an accused who is arraigned and asks for counsel is invoking the Sixth Amendment, rather than the *Miranda*, right to counsel, and that there *is* a difference in the protections provided. As we will see, the *Edwards* initiation requirement is a protection available only if *Miranda* rights are invoked. It's not available for invocations of the Sixth Amendment right to counsel.

McNeil was formally charged with armed robbery, and at his initial appearance before a judicial officer, he invoked his right to counsel. Police thereafter initiated questioning of McNeil. McNeil then waived his *Miranda* rights and confessed. McNeil argued that he was denied his protection under *Edwards* and *Roberson,* because the police had initiated interrogation after he had invoked his right to counsel. Justice Scalia, writing for a six-person majority, stated that McNeil had invoked his Sixth Amendment right, not his *Miranda* right. He explained as follows:

> To invoke the Sixth Amendment interest is, as a matter of fact, not to invoke the *Miranda-Edwards* interest. One might be quite willing to speak to the police without counsel present concerning many matters, but not the matter under prosecution. It can be said, perhaps, that it is likely that one who has asked for counsel's assistance in defending against a prosecution would want counsel present for all custodial interrogation, even interrogation unrelated to the charge. * * * But even if that were true, the likelihood that a suspect would wish counsel to be present is not the test for applicability of *Edwards*. The rule of that case * * * requires, at a minimum, some statement that can reasonably be construed to be expression of a desire for the assistance of an attorney in dealing with custodial interrogation by the police. Requesting the assistance of an attorney at a bail hearing does not bear that construction.

### Can Edwards Protections Be Triggered in Advance of Interrogation?

*McNeil* holds that when a suspect is arraigned before a judicial officer and asks for counsel, he is invoking his Sixth Amendment right, not his *Miranda* right, and therefore gets no protection from *Edwards*, which is a prophylactic rule designed to safeguard *Miranda* rights. So if it is a Sixth Amendment invocation, officers are free to approach the person who has invoked and ask him if he has changed his mind. Then, if the person makes a knowing and voluntary waiver, the confession will be admissible.

This raises the question of whether someone in McNeil's position could find a way to invoke his *Miranda* right to counsel instead of, or in addition to, his Sixth Amendment right. Would it make a difference, for example, if at the arraignment, McNeil tells the judge that "I want a lawyer under *Miranda*" or in some other way specifically indicates that he wants a *Miranda* right to counsel?

Justice Stevens, dissenting in *McNeil*, argued that the case amounted to little because suspects being arraigned could simply specify that they want their *Miranda* right to counsel, and thereby get the protection of *Edwards* that the majority had denied to McNeil. Thus, Justice Stevens assumed that the *Miranda* right to counsel can be invoked *in advance of police interrogation*. But this assumption was challenged by Justice Scalia in a footnote in the *McNeil* majority opinion. Justice Scalia asserted that "we have never held that a person can invoke his *Miranda* rights anticipatorily, in a context other than custodial interrogation—which a preliminary hearing will not always, or even usually, involve." He stated that such reasoning would lead to the unacceptable conclusion that *Miranda* rights could be invoked "in a letter prior to arrest, or indeed even prior to identification as a suspect."

Subsequently the Court in Montejo v. Louisiana (infra in the section on Sixth Amendment waiver) expressly stated that the protections of *Edwards* can only be obtained by invoking the right to counsel "in the context of custodial interrogation."

See also United States v. Wyatt, 179 F.3d 532 (7th Cir.1999) (suspect could not invoke his *Miranda* right to counsel when he was not yet in custody; therefore there was no violation of *Edwards* when officers later initiated interrogation, gave warnings, and the defendant voluntarily confessed).

# IV.    CONFESSIONS AND THE SIXTH AMENDMENT RIGHT TO COUNSEL

## A.   THE *MASSIAH* RULE

In addition to the Fifth Amendment and the Due Process Clause, the Court has also extended the protections of the Sixth Amendment to some police-induced confessions. Recall that in *Spano*, the concurring Justices heavily emphasized the fact that Spano had been formally charged with a crime, and yet was interrogated without his counsel being present. In the following case, the Supreme Court explicitly relied on the Sixth Amendment to exclude a confession.

## MASSIAH V. UNITED STATES

Supreme Court of the United States, 1964.
377 U.S. 201.

### MR. JUSTICE STEWART delivered the opinion of the Court.

\* \* \*

[Massiah was a merchant seaman. Drugs were found on a ship and connected to Massiah. He was arrested, arraigned, and subsequently indicted for possession of narcotics aboard a United States vessel. Thereafter, a superseding indictment was returned, charging Massiah, Colson with narcotics offenses and conspiracy. Massiah, who had retained a lawyer, pleaded not guilty and was released on bail, along with Colson.]

A few days later, and quite without the petitioner's knowledge, Colson decided to cooperate with the government agents in their continuing investigation of the narcotics activities in which the petitioner, Colson, and others had allegedly been engaged. Colson permitted an agent named Murphy to install a Schmidt radio transmitter under the front seat of Colson's automobile, by means of which Murphy, equipped with an appropriate receiving device, could overhear from some distance away conversations carried on in Colson's car.

On the evening of November 19, 1959, Colson and the petitioner held a lengthy conversation while sitting in Colson's automobile, parked on a New York street. By prearrangement with Colson, and totally unbeknown to the petitioner, the agent Murphy sat in a car parked out of sight down the street and listened over the radio to the entire conversation. The petitioner made several incriminating statements during the course of this conversation. At the petitioner's trial these incriminating statements were brought before the jury through Murphy's testimony, despite the insistent objection of defense counsel. The jury convicted the petitioner of several related narcotics offenses, and the convictions were affirmed by the Court of Appeals.

\* \* \* [I]t is said that the petitioner's Fifth and Sixth Amendment rights were violated by the use in evidence against him of incriminating statements which government agents had deliberately elicited from him after he had been indicted and in the absence of his retained counsel.

[The Court discusses *Spano,* paying more attention to the concurring opinions than to the majority opinion. It also discusses right to counsel precedents, which are discussed in Chapter 5, infra. The Court ultimately finds the Sixth Amendment right to counsel to be determinative.]

\* \* \* We hold that the petitioner was denied the basic protections of that [Sixth Amendment] guarantee when there was used against him at his trial evidence of his own incriminating words, which federal agents had deliberately elicited from him after he had been indicted and in the absence of his counsel. It is true that in the *Spano* case the defendant was interrogated in a police station, while here the damaging testimony was elicited from the defendant without his knowledge while he was free on bail. But, as Judge Hays pointed out in his dissent in the Court of Appeals, "if such a rule is to have any efficacy it must apply to indirect and surreptitious interrogations as well as those conducted in the jailhouse. In this case, Massiah was more seriously imposed upon * * * because he did not even know that he was under interrogation by a government agent."

The Solicitor General * * * has strenuously contended that the federal law enforcement agents had the right, if not indeed the duty, to continue their investigation of the petitioner and his alleged criminal associates even though the petitioner had been indicted. He points out that the Government was continuing its investigation in order to uncover not only the source of narcotics found on the S. S. *Santa Maria,* but also their intended buyer. He says that the quantity of narcotics involved was such as to suggest that the petitioner was part of a large and well-organized ring, and indeed that the continuing investigation confirmed this suspicion, since it resulted in criminal charges against many defendants. Under these circumstances the Solicitor General concludes that the government agents were completely "justified in making use of Colson's cooperation by having Colson continue his normal associations and by surveilling them."

* * * We do not question that in this case, as in many cases, it was entirely proper to continue an investigation of the suspected criminal activities of the defendant and his alleged confederates, even though the defendant had already been indicted. All that we hold is that the defendant's own incriminating statements, obtained by federal agents under the circumstances here disclosed, could not constitutionally be used by the prosecution as evidence against *him* at his trial.

**MR. JUSTICE WHITE, with whom MR. JUSTICE CLARK and MR. JUSTICE HARLAN join, dissenting.**

* * *

Massiah was not prevented from consulting with counsel as often as he wished. No meetings with counsel were disturbed or spied upon. Preparation for trial was in no way obstructed. It is only a sterile syllogism—an unsound one, besides—to say that because Massiah had a right to counsel's aid before and during the trial, his out-of-court conversations and admissions must be excluded if obtained without counsel's consent or presence. The right to counsel has never meant as much before, and its extension in this case requires some further explanation, so far unarticulated by the Court.

* * *

[T]he Court's newly fashioned exclusionary principle goes far beyond the constitutional privilege against self-incrimination, which neither requires nor suggests the barring of voluntary pre-trial admissions. * * *

At the time of the conversation in question, petitioner was not in custody but free on bail. He was not questioned in what anyone would call an atmosphere of official coercion.

* * *

## *The Rationale of Massiah*

Massiah was certainly not pressured to confess in the same way that Spano was. Indeed, he suffered less pressure than Miranda, because he didn't even know that he was speaking with a government agent. So the Sixth Amendment protection established in *Massiah* must be directed toward something *other* than police-created pressure to confess. What is the rationale for Sixth Amendment regulation of confessions? Judge Higginbotham, in United States v. Johnson, 954 F.2d 1015 (5th Cir.1992), explained it this way:

> [The Sixth Amendment] recognizes that once the government has brought formal charges against an individual the adversary relationship between the parties is cemented. Once an accused has chosen to retain an attorney to act as his representative in the adversary process, the government may not try to circumvent the protection afforded by the presence of counsel during questioning. The vice is not deprivation of privacy, but interference with the parity required by the Sixth Amendment.

Thus, the *Massiah* right is basically a constitutionalized version of a rule of professional (and litigation) ethics: that an adverse party, in advance of litigation, may be contacted only through her lawyer. This rule protects the attorney-client relationship and guards against overreaching by the adversary. See Model Rules of Professional Conduct 4.2. This is not to say that the ethics rules *define* the constitutional right. But it is to say that the principles behind the ethics rule of proceeding through counsel, once litigation has begun, are the same principles that animate the Sixth Amendment right to counsel.[21]

## NOTE ON ESCOBEDO V. ILLINOIS

In Escobedo v. Illinois, 378 U.S. 478 (1964), the Court undertook a short-lived experiment to extend the Sixth Amendment right to counsel to suspects

---

[21] For an eloquent defense of the *Massiah* doctrine, in response to an attack on that doctrine by the Justice Department, see Tomkovicz, The Truth About *Massiah*, 23 U.Mich.J.L.Ref. 641 (1990).

who have *not yet been formally charged*. Escobedo was taken into custody on suspicion of murder. He asked for a lawyer several times, but his request was denied. His mother retained a lawyer for him, and the lawyer went to the police station, but the police would not let the lawyer speak to Escobedo. Escobedo was confronted with incriminating evidence, while handcuffed in a standing position, and was given false promises that if he confessed, he would be allowed to go home. While these facts established a strong case for holding Escobedo's confession involuntary, the Court, in this pre-*Miranda* case, relied explicitly on the Sixth Amendment to invalidate the confession. Justice Goldberg, writing for the Court, recognized that unlike Spano and Massiah, Escobedo had not been indicted at the time he confessed; but he argued that "in the context of this case, that fact should make no difference." This was because the police had *focused* on Escobedo as a *prospective* criminal defendant. Justice Goldberg stated that when Escobedo was denied his request for counsel, "the investigation had ceased to be a general investigation of an unsolved crime" and that Escobedo had become the "accused."

Justices Harlan, Stewart, White, and Clark dissented in *Escobedo*. The dissenters were concerned that the majority's "focus" test would result in an extravagant extension of the Sixth Amendment right to counsel, which by its terms applies to criminal "prosecutions," not criminal "investigations." As Justice Stewart put it:

> [T]he institution of formal, meaningful judicial proceedings, by way of indictment, information, or arraignment, marks the point at which a criminal investigation has ended and adversary litigative proceedings have commenced. * * * [T]he Court today converts a routine police investigation of an unsolved murder into a distorted analogue of a judicial trial. It imports into this investigation constitutional concepts historically applicable only after the onset of formal prosecutorial proceedings.

As a Sixth Amendment case, *Escobedo* has no continuing relevance. In Moran v. Burbine, 475 U.S. 412 (1986), discussed in the section on *Miranda*, Burbine was being interrogated as a suspect in a murder. His family retained counsel for him, but police officers denied counsel's request to see Burbine. Burbine had not been formally charged at the time he confessed, but he was certainly the focus of the police investigation. Burbine relied on *Escobedo* to argue that his Sixth Amendment rights were violated, but Justice O'Connor, writing for the majority, rejected that argument. She stated that "subsequent decisions foreclose any reliance on *Escobedo* * * * for the proposition that the Sixth Amendment right, in any of its manifestations, applies prior to the initiation of adversary criminal proceedings." She concluded that *Escobedo* is in retrospect best understood as a *Fifth* Amendment case, because the prime purpose of the Court in *Escobedo* was not to vindicate the right to counsel as such but rather to guarantee "the full effectuation of the privilege against self-incrimination."

While *Escobedo* is therefore mainly of historical note on the Court's road to *Miranda,* the Sixth Amendment right to counsel has significant contemporary relevance where information is sought from a person who *has* been formally charged. After the Court decided *Miranda,* it returned to *Massiah* and gave it a broad reading. These cases are discussed immediately below.

## B. OBTAINING INFORMATION FROM FORMALLY CHARGED DEFENDANTS

After *Massiah*, the Supreme Court for several years virtually ignored the Sixth Amendment as a means of regulating confessions. As you know, the Court turned to the Fifth Amendment in *Miranda.* However, in 1977, the Court unexpectedly returned to the Sixth Amendment as an additional source for excluding confessions.

### BREWER V. WILLIAMS
Supreme Court of the United States, 1977.
430 U.S. 387.

**MR. JUSTICE STEWART delivered the opinion of the Court.**

\* \* \*

On the afternoon of December 24, 1968, a 10-year-old girl named Pamela Powers went with her family to the YMCA in Des Moines, Iowa, to watch a wrestling tournament in which her brother was participating. When she failed to return from a trip to the washroom, a search for her began. The search was unsuccessful.

Robert Williams, who had recently escaped from a mental hospital, was a resident of the YMCA. Soon after the girl's disappearance Williams was seen in the YMCA lobby carrying some clothing and a large bundle wrapped in a blanket. He obtained help from a 14-year-old boy in opening the street door of the YMCA and the door to his automobile parked outside. When Williams placed the bundle in the front seat of his car the boy "saw two legs in it and they were skinny and white." Before anyone could see what was in the bundle Williams drove away. His abandoned car was found the following day in Davenport, Iowa, roughly 160 miles east of Des Moines. A warrant was then issued in Des Moines for his arrest on a charge of abduction.

On the morning of December 26, a Des Moines lawyer named Henry McKnight went to the Des Moines police station and informed the officers present that he had just received a long distance call from Williams, and that he had advised Williams to turn himself in to the Davenport police. Williams did surrender that morning to the police in Davenport, and they booked him on the charge specified in the arrest warrant and gave him the warnings required by Miranda v. Arizona. The Davenport police then telephoned their counterparts in Des Moines to inform them that Williams had surrendered. McKnight, the lawyer, was still at the Des Moines police headquarters, and Williams conversed with McKnight on the telephone. In the presence of the Des Moines chief of police and a police detective named Leaming, McKnight advised Williams that Des Moines police officers would be driving to Davenport to pick him up, that the officers would not interrogate him or mistreat him, and that Williams was not to talk to the officers about Pamela Powers until after consulting with McKnight upon his return to Des Moines. As a result of these conversations, it was agreed between McKnight and the Des Moines police officials that Detective Leaming and a fellow officer would drive to Davenport to pick up Williams, that they would bring him directly back to Des Moines, and that they would not question him during the trip.

In the meantime Williams was arraigned before a judge in Davenport on the outstanding arrest warrant. The judge advised him of his *Miranda* rights and committed him to jail. Before leaving the courtroom, Williams conferred with a lawyer named Kelly, who advised him not to make any statements until consulting with McKnight back in Des Moines.

Detective Leaming and his fellow officer arrived in Davenport about noon to pick up Williams and return him to Des Moines. Soon after their arrival they met with Williams and Kelly, who, they understood, was acting as Williams' lawyer. Detective Leaming repeated the *Miranda* warnings, and told Williams:

> "[W]e both know that you're being represented here by Mr. Kelly and you're being represented by Mr. McKnight in Des Moines, and * * * I want you to remember this because we'll be visiting between here and Des Moines."

Williams then conferred again with Kelly alone, and after this conference Kelly reiterated to Detective Leaming that Williams was not to be questioned about the disappearance of Pamela Powers until after he had consulted with McKnight back in Des Moines. When Leaming expressed some reservations, Kelly firmly stated that the agreement with McKnight was to be carried out—that there was to be no interrogation of Williams during the automobile journey to Des Moines. Kelly was denied permission to ride in the police car back to Des Moines with Williams and the two officers.

The two detectives, with Williams in their charge, then set out on the 160-mile drive. At no time during the trip did Williams express a willingness to be interrogated in the absence of an attorney. Instead, he stated several times that "[w]hen I get to Des Moines and see Mr. McKnight, I am going to tell you the whole story." Detective Leaming knew that Williams was a former mental patient, and knew also that he was deeply religious.

The detective and his prisoner soon embarked on a wide-ranging conversation covering a variety of topics, including the subject of religion. Then, not long after leaving Davenport and reaching the interstate highway, Detective Leaming delivered what has been referred to in the briefs and oral arguments as the "Christian burial speech." Addressing Williams as "Reverend," the detective said:

> "I want to give you something to think about while we're traveling down the road. * * * Number one, I want you to observe the weather conditions, it's raining, it's sleeting, it's freezing, driving is very treacherous, visibility is poor, it's going to be dark early this evening. They are predicting several inches of snow for tonight, and I feel that you yourself are the only person that knows where this little girl's body is, that you yourself have only been there once, and if you get a snow on top of it you yourself may be unable to find it. And, since we will be going right past the area on the way into Des Moines, I feel that we could stop and locate the body, that the parents of this little girl should be entitled to a Christian burial for the little girl who was snatched away from them on Christmas [E]ve and murdered. And I feel we should stop and locate it on the way in rather than waiting until morning and trying to come back out after a snow storm and possibly not being able to find it at all."

Williams asked Detective Leaming why he thought their route to Des Moines would be taking them past the girl's body, and Leaming responded that he knew the body was in the area of Mitchellville—a town they would be passing on the way to Des Moines.[a] Leaming then stated: "I do not want you to answer me. I don't want to discuss it any further. Just think about it as we're riding down the road."

As the car approached Grinnell, a town approximately 100 miles west of Davenport, Williams asked whether the police had found the victim's shoes. When Detective Leaming replied that he was unsure, Williams directed the officers to a service station where he said he had left the shoes; a search for them proved unsuccessful. As they continued towards Des Moines, Williams asked whether the police had found the blanket, and directed the officers to a rest area where he said he had disposed of the blanket. Nothing was found. The car continued towards Des Moines, and as it approached Mitchellville, Williams said that he would show the officers where the body was. He then directed the police to the body of Pamela Powers.

---

[a] The fact of the matter, of course, was that Detective Leaming possessed no such knowledge.

Williams was indicted for first-degree murder. Before trial, his counsel moved to suppress all evidence relating to or resulting from any statements Williams had made during the automobile ride from Davenport to Des Moines. After an evidentiary hearing the trial judge denied the motion. * * * The jury found Williams guilty of murder. [The Iowa Supreme Court affirmed 4–3. But Williams was successful below in his federal habeas corpus action.]

\* \* \*

[T]he District Court based its judgment in this case on three independent grounds. The Court of Appeals appears to have affirmed the judgment on two of those grounds. We have concluded that only one of them need be considered here.

Specifically, there is no need to review in this case the doctrine of Miranda v. Arizona, a doctrine designed to secure the constitutional privilege against compulsory self-incrimination. It is equally unnecessary to evaluate the ruling of the District Court that Williams' self-incriminating statements were, indeed, involuntarily made. For it is clear that the judgment before us must in any event be affirmed upon the ground that Williams was deprived of a different constitutional right—the right to the assistance of counsel.

\* \* \*

There can be no doubt in the present case that judicial proceedings had been initiated against Williams before the start of the automobile ride from Davenport to Des Moines. A warrant had been issued for his arrest, he had been arraigned on that warrant before a judge in a Davenport courtroom, and he had been committed by the court to confinement in jail. The State does not contend otherwise.

There can be no serious doubt, either, that Detective Leaming deliberately and designedly set out to elicit information from Williams just as surely as—and perhaps more effectively than—if he had formally interrogated him. Detective Leaming was fully aware before departing for Des Moines that Williams was being represented in Davenport by Kelly and in Des Moines by McKnight. Yet he purposely sought during Williams' isolation from his lawyers to obtain as much incriminating information as possible. Indeed, Detective Leaming conceded as much when he testified at Williams' trial:

"Q. In fact, Captain, whether he was a mental patient or not, you were trying to get all the information you could before he got to his lawyer, weren't you?

"A. I was sure hoping to find out where that little girl was, yes, sir.

\* \* \*

"Q. Well, I'll put it this way: You was [*sic*] hoping to get all the information you could before Williams got back to McKnight, weren't you?

"A. Yes, sir."

\* \* \*

The circumstances of this case are thus constitutionally indistinguishable from those presented in Massiah v. United States. \* \* \*

That the incriminating statements were elicited surreptitiously in the *Massiah* case, and otherwise here, is constitutionally irrelevant. Rather, the clear rule of *Massiah* is that once adversary proceedings have commenced against an individual, he has a right to legal representation when the government interrogates him.[b] It thus requires no wooden or technical application of the *Massiah* doctrine to conclude that Williams was entitled to the assistance of counsel guaranteed to him by the Sixth and Fourteenth Amendments.

\* \* \*

The Iowa courts recognized that Williams had been denied the constitutional right to the assistance of counsel. They held, however, that he had waived that right during the course of the automobile trip from Davenport to Des Moines. \* \* \*

[I]t was incumbent upon the State to prove "an intentional relinquishment or abandonment of a known right or privilege." That standard has been reiterated in many cases. We have said that the right to counsel does not depend upon a request by the defendant, and that courts indulge in every reasonable presumption against waiver. This strict standard applies equally to an alleged waiver of the right to counsel whether at trial or at a critical stage of pretrial proceedings.

\* \* \* [J]udged by these standards, the record in this case falls far short of sustaining petitioner's burden. It is true that Williams had been informed of and appeared to understand his right to counsel. But waiver requires not merely comprehension but relinquishment, and Williams' consistent reliance upon the advice of counsel in dealing with the authorities refutes any suggestion that he waived that right. He consulted McKnight by long distance telephone before turning himself in. He spoke with McKnight by telephone again shortly after being booked. After he was arraigned, Williams sought out and obtained legal advice from Kelly. Williams again consulted with Kelly after Detective Leaming

---

[b] The only other significant factual difference between the present case and *Massiah* is that here the police had *agreed* that they would not interrogate Williams in the absence of his counsel. This circumstance plainly provides petitioner with no argument for distinguishing away the protection afforded by *Massiah*.

and his fellow officer arrived in Davenport. Throughout, Williams was advised not to make any statements before seeing McKnight in Des Moines, and was assured that the police had agreed not to question him. His statements while in the car that he would tell the whole story *after* seeing McKnight in Des Moines were the clearest expressions by Williams himself that he desired the presence of an attorney before any interrogation took place. But even before making these statements, Williams had effectively asserted his right to counsel by having secured attorneys at both ends of the automobile trip, both of whom, acting as his agents, had made clear to the police that no interrogation was to occur during the journey. Williams knew of that agreement and, particularly in view of his consistent reliance on counsel, there is no basis for concluding that he disavowed it.

Despite Williams' express and implicit assertions of his right to counsel, Detective Leaming proceeded to elicit incriminating statements from Williams. Leaming did not preface this effort by telling Williams that he had a right to the presence of a lawyer, and made no effort at all to ascertain whether Williams wished to relinquish that right. The circumstances of record in this case thus provide no reasonable basis for finding that Williams waived his right to the assistance of counsel.

The Court of Appeals did not hold, nor do we, that under the circumstances of this case Williams *could not,* without notice to counsel, have waived his rights under the Sixth and Fourteenth Amendments. It only held, as do we, that he did not.

\* \* \*

The judgment of the Court of Appeals is affirmed.

[Evidence of the body, its condition, and location were admitted on retrial. See Nix v. Williams, in the materials on inevitable discovery, in Chapter 2.]

### MR. JUSTICE MARSHALL, concurring.

\* \* \*

Leaming knowingly isolated Williams from the protection of his lawyers and during that period he intentionally "persuaded" him to give incriminating evidence. It is this intentional police misconduct—not good police practice—that the Court rightly condemns. \* \* \*

\* \* \*

### MR. JUSTICE POWELL, concurring.

\* \* \*

I join the opinion of the Court which also finds that the efforts of Detective Leaming "to elicit information from Williams," as conceded by counsel for petitioner at oral argument, were a skillful and effective form of interrogation. Moreover, the entire setting was conducive to the psychological coercion that was successfully exploited. Williams was known by the police to be a young man with quixotic religious convictions and a history of mental disorders. The date was the day after Christmas, the weather was ominous, and the setting appropriate for Detective Leaming's talk of snow concealing the body and preventing a "Christian burial." * * *

### MR. JUSTICE STEVENS, concurring.

* * *

Underlying the surface issues in this case is the question, whether a fugitive from justice can rely on his lawyer's advice given in connection with a decision to surrender voluntarily. The defendant placed his trust in an experienced Iowa trial lawyer who in turn trusted the Iowa law enforcement authorities to honor a commitment made during negotiations which led to the apprehension of a potentially dangerous person. Under any analysis, this was a critical stage of the proceeding in which the participation of an independent professional was of vital importance to the accused and to society. * * * If, in the long run, we are seriously concerned about the individual's effective representation by counsel, the State cannot be permitted to dishonor its promise to this lawyer.

### MR. CHIEF JUSTICE BURGER, dissenting.

* * *

Williams is guilty of the savage murder of a small child; no member of the Court contends he is not. While in custody, and after no fewer than *five* warnings of his rights to silence and to counsel, he led police to the concealed body of his victim. The Court concedes Williams was not threatened or coerced and that he spoke and acted voluntarily and with full awareness of his constitutional rights. In the face of all this, the Court now holds that because Williams was prompted by the detective's statement—not interrogation but a statement—the jury must not be told how the police found the body.

* * *

The evidence is uncontradicted that Williams had abundant knowledge of his right to have counsel present and of his right to silence. Since the Court does not question his mental competence, it boggles the mind to suggest that Williams could not understand that leading police to the child's body would have other than the most serious consequences. All of the elements necessary to make out a valid waiver are shown by the record and acknowledged by the Court; we thus are left to guess how the Court reached its holding.

* * *

**MR. JUSTICE WHITE, with whom MR. JUSTICE BLACKMUN and MR. JUSTICE REHNQUIST join, dissenting.**

* * *

Respondent relinquished his right not to talk to the police about his crime when the car approached the place where he had hidden the victim's clothes. Men usually intend to do what they do and there is nothing in the record to support the proposition that respondent's decision to talk was anything but an exercise of his own free will. * * * The statement by Leaming was not coercive; it was accompanied by a request that respondent not respond to it; and it was delivered hours before respondent decided to make any statement. Respondent's waiver was thus knowing and intentional.

* * *

**MR. JUSTICE BLACKMUN, with whom MR. JUSTICE WHITE and MR. JUSTICE REHNQUIST join, dissenting.**

* * *

First, the police did not deliberately seek to isolate Williams from his lawyers so as to deprive him of the assistance of counsel. The isolation in this case was a necessary incident of transporting Williams to the county where the crime was committed.

Second, Leaming's purpose was not solely to obtain incriminating evidence. The victim had been missing for only two days, and the police could not be certain that she was dead. Leaming, of course, and in accord with his duty, was "hoping to find out where that little girl was," but such motivation does not equate with an intention to evade the Sixth Amendment.

* * *

In summary, it seems to me that the Court is holding that *Massiah* is violated whenever police engage in any conduct, in the absence of counsel, with the subjective desire to obtain information from a suspect after arraignment. Such a rule is far too broad.

* * *

### Would Williams Be Decidedly Differently Under the Later Case of Berghuis v. Thompkins?

In Berghuis v. Thompkins, supra, the Court held that Thompkins had voluntarily waived *Miranda* rights even though he was silent for more than two hours, then confessed when asked about his religious beliefs. The waiver was found voluntary because his answer about God was a "course of conduct indicating waiver" and he could have said nothing or invoked his rights in response to the question; he waived his right to remain silent "by making a voluntary statement to police." If the facts of *Williams* are evaluated under the implied waiver standards in *Thompkins,* wouldn't the court have to find that Williams waived his rights? Put another way, is the waiver discussion in *Williams* still good law after *Berghuis*?

## Sixth Amendment Attaches at Formal Charge: United States v. Gouveia

Reaffirming that the Sixth Amendment right to counsel attaches only after adversarial proceedings have begun, the Supreme Court held in United States v. Gouveia, 467 U.S. 180 (1984), that prison officials did not violate the right to counsel of inmates suspected of two murders when the officials placed them in administrative detention for periods of 19 and 8 months prior to their being indicted. Justice Rehnquist's opinion for the Court stated that "both inside and outside the prison, it may well be true that in some cases pre-indictment investigation could help a defendant prepare a better defense. But, * * * our cases have never suggested that the purpose of the right to counsel is to provide a defendant with a pre-indictment private investigator, and we see no reason to adopt that novel interpretation of the right to counsel in this case." Justice Marshall dissented and argued that administrative detention was part of an accusatorial process.

The Supreme Court held in Moran v. Burbine, supra, that there was no violation of a suspect's Sixth Amendment right to counsel when police failed to disclose to him that a lawyer had called and had been falsely told that the suspect would not be interrogated until the next day. Justice O'Connor's majority opinion observed that the suspect had not been formally charged, cited *Gouveia* as well as *Massiah, Brewer,* and other cases drawing a line between pre-and post-charge situations, and declined to adopt a rule that would make the right to counsel depend "on the fortuity of whether the suspect or his family happens to have retained counsel prior to interrogation."

## On the Meaning of "Deliberate" Elicitation

The Sixth Amendment prohibits a government agent from "deliberately eliciting" incriminating information from an "accused" in the absence of counsel or a waiver. This means, does it not, that the officer must be *trying* to obtain incriminating information from the accused? For example, the Court found deliberate elicitation in Brewer v. Williams because Leaming actually admitted that he was trying to pump Williams for information about the location of the body. But what if the officer can plausibly argue that he was not trying to obtain incriminating information? Can there still be a violation of the Sixth Amendment?

The court in Bey v. Morton, 124 F.3d 524 (3d Cir. 1997), considered this question. Bey was on death row. The only people he was permitted to talk to were corrections officers. Bey struck up a relationship with Officer Pearson, and they engaged in a number of conversations, covering many different topics, including sports, women and the news. In the course of their extensive discourse, Bey confessed to the murder of two women—the murders for which he was sitting on death row. Then his convictions were reversed and he had to be retried. At the retrials, the Officer testified and related Bey's confessions. Bey argued that these confessions had to be excluded because Officer Pearson had deliberately elicited these confessions from him in violation of his right to counsel. But the court disagreed. It analyzed the deliberate elicitation question as follows:

> The critical distinction between this case and the *Massiah* [line of cases] is that Pearson, while a state actor, was not a state actor deliberately engaged in trying to secure information from the defendant for use in connection with the prosecution that was the subject matter of counsel's representation. * * *

> * * * First, Pearson had no responsibility for eliciting or reporting information for use in the prosecution of Bey's case and was not working with anyone who had such responsibility. Second, and most importantly, Pearson did not behave like someone who intended to secure incriminating statements from Bey. The record lacks evidence of any questions designed to elicit the statement that Bey had raped and beaten a woman to death on the beach, and merely reveals Pearson's asking "why" Bey had committed the act and seeking clarification "if it was something [he] didn't understand." Pearson did not take any notes or compile any reports of his conversations with Bey. In fact, Pearson disclosed the confession to no one for five years. It was only through the systematic efforts of the investigator that the prosecutor's office uncovered Bey's statements. Even Pearson's testimony in Bey's case was "reluctantly given." Thus, the state's receipt of Bey's confession was not the result of any deliberate elicitation by Pearson for use in connection with Bey's prosecution, and the state's use of Bey's confession at trial did not violate the Sixth Amendment.

If the focus of the Sixth Amendment is on whether the officer is *trying* to get information from a person charged with a crime, won't it be difficult for a court to assess the intent of the officer?

### Application of the Deliberate Elicitation Standard: Fellers v. United States

In Fellers v. United States, 540 U.S. 519 (2004), the Supreme Court, in an opinion by Justice O'Connor, found that the lower court had improperly applied *Miranda* rules to a *Massiah* case. A grand jury indicted Fellers on drug charges. Police went to his home to arrest him, knocked on the door, asked for entry and were admitted, and advised Fellers they had come to discuss his involvement in methamphetamine distribution. They informed Fellers that they had a federal warrant for his arrest and that a grand jury had indicted him for conspiracy to distribute methamphetamine that involved certain individuals, four of whom they named. Fellers then told the officers that he knew the four people and had used methamphetamine during his association with them. Fellers later made statements at the jailhouse after being warned of his rights. He moved to suppress both his statements at home and at the jail.

The Court of Appeals held that Fellers' Sixth Amendment rights were not violated by the post-charge discussion because "the officers did not interrogate [petitioner] at his home." It further held that later statements by Fellers, made at the jailhouse, could not be excluded as the fruits of an illegally obtained statement—even assuming, arguendo, that Fellers' first statement was illegally obtained. It relied on the *Miranda*-based decision of Oregon v. Elstad, which held that the testimonial fruits of a *Miranda*-defective confession are not subject to *Miranda's* exclusionary rule. In essence, the lower court looked at the case as one involving *Miranda* rather than the Sixth Amendment.

Justice O'Connor noted that the Sixth Amendment "deliberately elicited" standard was distinct from "interrogation" and found that "there is no question that the officers in this case deliberately elicited information" from Fellers. Accordingly, she concluded that the lower court erred in finding that Fellers' Sixth Amendment right to counsel was not violated in his house. But, she also concluded that the Court had not decided whether *Elstad* applied to a Sixth Amendment violation and therefore remanded for further proceedings.

## C.  USE OF UNDERCOVER OFFICERS AND STATE AGENTS

In one respect, the Sixth Amendment is less protective in regulating confessions than is the Fifth: it applies only to those who have been formally charged, whereas *Miranda* applies to all suspects facing custodial interrogation. In another respect, however, the Sixth Amendment is more protective than the Fifth: it limits the use of undercover tactics, whereas (according to Illinois v. Perkins, supra)

*Miranda* only applies when the suspect knows that he is speaking to a police officer.

### Jailhouse Plant: United States v. Henry

The Court in United States v. Henry, 447 U.S. 264 (1980), considered the application of the Sixth Amendment right to counsel when charged and incarcerated defendants are questioned by informants. Henry's cellmate, Nichols, testified at Henry's bank robbery trial to incriminating statements that Henry had made. At the time of those statements, Henry had already been indicted and was incarcerated awaiting trial. Nichols was a prisoner who operated as a paid government informant. An FBI agent told Nichols, who was kept in the same jail as Henry, of the government's interest in several individuals who were housed in the jail, including Henry. The agent told Nichols not to initiate conversations with Henry, but to pay attention to anything Henry said about the robbery.

Citing both *Massiah* and *Brewer*, the Chief Justice wrote that "[t]he question here is whether * * * a government agent deliberately elicited incriminating statements from Henry within the meaning of *Massiah*." The Chief Justice found "deliberate" elicitation even though the state denied that the officers had the intent to elicit a confession from Henry. On the question of "deliberateness", the court reasoned as follows:

> Three factors are important. First, Nichols was acting under instructions as a paid informant for the Government; second, Nichols was ostensibly no more than a fellow inmate of Henry; and third, Henry was in custody and under indictment at the time he was engaged in conversation by Nichols.

> * * * Even if the agent's statement that he did not intend that Nichols would take affirmative steps to secure incriminating information is accepted, he must have known that such propinquity would lead to that result.

> The Government argues that the federal agents instructed Nichols not to question Henry about the robbery. Yet according to his own testimony, Nichols was not a passive listener; rather, he had "some conversations with Mr. Henry" while he was in jail and Henry's incriminatory statements were "the product of this conversation." While affirmative interrogation, absent waiver, would certainly satisfy *Massiah*, we are not persuaded, as the Government contends, that Brewer v. Williams modified *Massiah's* "deliberately elicited" test. * * *

> The Government argues that this Court should apply a less rigorous standard under the Sixth Amendment [to undercover activity] than where the accused is speaking in the hearing of

persons he knows to be Government officers. That line of argument, however, seeks to infuse Fifth Amendment concerns * * * into the Sixth Amendment protection * * *.

Moreover, the concept of a knowing and voluntary waiver of Sixth Amendment rights does not apply in the context of communications with an undisclosed undercover informant acting for the Government. In that setting, Henry, being unaware that Nichols was a Government agent expressly commissioned to secure evidence, cannot be held to have waived his right to the assistance of counsel.

Finally, Henry's incarceration at the time he was engaged in conversation by Nichols is also a relevant factor. * * * [T]he mere fact of custody imposes pressures on the accused; confinement may bring into play subtle influences that will make him particularly susceptible to the ploys of undercover Government agents.

The Court concluded that "[b]y intentionally creating a situation likely to induce Henry to make incriminating statements without the assistance of counsel, the government violated Henry's Sixth Amendment's right to counsel."

Justice Blackmun, joined by Justice White, dissented. He argued that the Court purported to retain the "deliberately elicited" test, but that in reality it was extending *Massiah* to "cover even a 'negligent' triggering of events resulting in reception of disclosures." He concluded that a deliberateness standard "imposes the exclusionary sanction on that conduct that is most culpable, most likely to frustrate the purpose of having counsel, and most susceptible to being checked by a deterrent." He went on to criticize the Court's application of its own test to the facts, which in his view did not reveal that anything the government agent did was " 'likely to induce' Nichols' successful prompting of Henry."

Justice Rehnquist filed a separate dissent. He urged another look at the doctrinal underpinnings of the *Massiah* doctrine. After observing that in cases like this one the government has done nothing to impair the defendant's ability to consult with an attorney, Justice Rehnquist observed:

The role of counsel in an adversary system is to offer advice and assistance in the preparation of a defense and to serve as a spokesman for the accused in technical legal proceedings. And the Sixth Amendment, of course, protects the confidentiality of communications between the accused and his attorney. But there is no constitutional or historical support for concluding that an accused has a right to have his attorney serve as a sort of guru who must be present whenever an accused has an inclination to reveal incriminating information to anyone who acts to elicit such information at the behest of the prosecution. To the extent the accused is protected from revealing evidence that may be incriminatory, the focus must be on the Fifth Amendment privilege against compulsory self-incrimination.

### *The Listening Post: Kuhlmann v. Wilson*

The Court distinguished *Henry* in Kuhlmann v. Wilson, 477 U.S. 436 (1986), as it held that the Sixth Amendment was not violated when police put a jailhouse informant in close proximity to a defendant and the defendant made statements to the informant without any serious effort on the informant's part to elicit the statements. The Court stated that, to prove a Sixth Amendment violation, a defendant must show that the police took some action, beyond merely listening, that was deliberately designed to elicit incriminating remarks. *No elicitation* was found on the facts of the case.

The basic facts were the following: Prior to the defendant's arrival at a jail following an arraignment for robbery and murder, an officer entered into an agreement with inmate Lee under which Lee would listen to the defendant's conversations and report them, but Lee would ask no questions and would simply "keep his ears open." The defendant, without prompting, told Lee that he had been present during the robbery but denied knowing the robbers. Lee responded that the explanation "didn't sound too good." The defendant changed details over the next few days. Finally, after a visit from his brother, the defendant, again without prompting, admitted to Lee that he and two other men had committed the robbery and murder.

Justice Powell, writing for the Court, distinguished *Henry* on the ground that the informant in *Henry* had "stimulated" the conversations with Henry and that Lee had not done so in the instant case. The Court stated that a defendant does not show a Sixth Amendment violation "simply by showing that an informant, either through prior arrangement or voluntarily, reported his incriminating statements to the police." Justice Powell found it insignificant that Lee had said that the defendant's version of the crimes didn't sound too good. Just that one remark did not bring the case out of the realm of the "passive recording device"; that single remark did not constitute "elicitation".

Chief Justice Burger filed a short concurring opinion stating that "[t]here is a vast difference between placing an 'ear' in the suspect's cell and placing a voice in the cell to encourage conversation for the 'ear' to record." Justice Brennan, joined by Justice Marshall, dissented in *Wilson* and found the case to be virtually indistinguishable on its facts from *Henry*. Justice Stevens also dissented briefly and agreed with Justice Brennan.

See also United States v. York, 933 F.2d 1343 (7th Cir.1991): The court found no deliberate elicitation where the informant responded with neutral comments when incriminating topics were brought up by the defendant. The court observed that informants are not required to risk revealing their status by refusing to participate in the natural flow of conversation.

### Is the Informant a State Agent?

Sixth Amendment protection under *Henry* requires that the informant must have been working for the government at the time the information was obtained from the accused—otherwise there is no state action implicated in the deliberate elicitation.

Whether the informant is a state agent, or is simply working on his own account, is often a difficult question. For example, in United States v. Watson, 894 F.2d 1345 (D.C.Cir.1990), Watson argued that the jailhouse informant was working as a government agent at the time he elicited incriminating statements from Watson. The informant had worked for the DEA for two years and was in regular contact with the DEA while he was in jail. But the court found "no evidence that the DEA in any way encouraged" the informant to talk to Watson; that the informant was in contact with the DEA on unrelated cases, and did not mention Watson until after Watson made incriminating statements; and that the informant "was acting as an entrepreneur." The court stated that the informant "may have hoped to make a sale to the government when he spoke with Watson, but that does not make the government responsible for his actions, any more than a person who has bought an article from a salesman in the past is responsible if the salesman then steals something similar in the hope of making a second sale."

The court in Ayers v. Hudson, 623 F.3d 301 (10th Cir. 2010), has noted the dispute among the courts on what is necessary for an informant to be a government agent for Sixth Amendment purposes:

> Some of [the] circuits employ a bright-line rule, deciding that an informant becomes a government agent only when the informant has been instructed by the police to get information about the particular defendant. Other circuits, however, flatly reject this approach, [and consider] the facts and circumstances of each case. Embracing this broader approach, at least two of these circuits require only some evidence that an agreement, express or implied, between the individual and a government official existed at the time the elicitation took place. [citations omitted]

The *Ayers* court agreed with the broader, totality of circumstances approach, noting that under *Henry*, a Sixth Amendment violation can occur even if the State specifically instructs its informant *not* to initiate any conversation. Thus the court found the bright-line rule requiring a specific instruction to the informant to be inconsistent with *Henry*. The court also noted that if the State could avoid a finding of agency simply by not explicitly instructing the informant to get information from the defendant, this "would allow the State to accomplish with a wink and a nod what it cannot do overtly."

## D. CONTINUING INVESTIGATIONS

A defendant who is formally charged has a right to be free from deliberate attempts by state agents to elicit incriminating information in the absence of defendant's counsel. But defendants who have been formally charged are often suspected of committing crimes in addition to those charged. Does the Sixth Amendment prohibit an officer from obtaining information from the defendant concerning *uncharged* crimes?

### *Maine v. Moulton*

That was the question in Maine v. Moulton, 474 U.S. 159 (1985). Moulton and a codefendant, Colson, were charged with theft of automobiles and parts. Colson, along with his lawyer, informed the Chief of Police of threatening telephone calls to his house and of the fact that Moulton had spoken of killing a key witness. Colson cooperated with the police. The police wired Colson with a transmitter when he agreed to meet with Moulton. The codefendants, at their meeting, spoke of eliminating witnesses. Moulton rejected the idea, and Colson led Moulton into talking about their theft activities, as well as burglaries that were related to the thefts. Both the recorded telephone statements and the recorded meeting were used as evidence at trial. Moulton was convicted.

Justice Brennan wrote for the Court as it reversed Moulton's conviction. He found it irrelevant that the meeting with the informant was initiated by Moulton, concluding that "knowing exploitation by the State of an opportunity to confront the accused without counsel being present is as much a breach of the State's obligation not to circumvent the right to the assistance of counsel as is the intentional creation of such an opportunity."

Justice Brennan also rejected the argument that Moulton's statements should be admissible because the police were investigating new crimes, including threats to the safety of witnesses. Justice Brennan emphasized that police may investigate crimes separate from the crimes charged and may use statements made by a suspect in a *later trial* for those crimes. But he concluded that "incriminating statements pertaining to pending charges are inadmissible at the trial of those charges, notwithstanding the fact that the police were also investigating other crimes, if, in obtaining the evidence, the State violated the Sixth

Amendment by knowingly circumventing the accused's right to the assistance of counsel." He stated that the Sixth Amendment guarantees the accused "the right to rely on counsel as a 'medium' between him and the State."

The government argued that the elicitation of information about the charged crime was not "deliberate" because the officers instructed the informant to limit the scope of discussion to the subject matter of killing witnesses. But the majority was unpersuaded. Justice Brennan stated that the agents should have known that despite their instructions, the conversation between the informant and Moulton would be likely to turn to the crime for which both were charged. Justice Brennan noted that "direct proof of the State's knowledge will seldom be available," but that "proof that the State must have known that its agent was likely to obtain incriminating statements" suffices to establish the "deliberate" elicitation prohibited by the Sixth Amendment.

Thus, the officer's actions in *Moulton* constituted "deliberate" elicitation even though there was no showing of specific intent on the part of the officers to obtain information about the charged crime. "Deliberate" elicitation is found whenever the officers should have known that their investigative tactic would lead to incriminating information from a charged defendant in the absence of counsel.

Chief Justice Burger dissented in *Moulton*, joined by Justices White and Rehnquist and in part by Justice O'Connor. The Chief Justice argued that the Sixth Amendment term "deliberate elicitation" focuses upon a bad purpose—to use statements in connection with pending charges—and that suppression should not be required unless police institute the investigation of separate charges in bad faith to avoid the dictates of *Massiah*.

## E. WAIVER OF SIXTH AMENDMENT PROTECTIONS

Under what circumstances can an accused be held to have *waived* his Sixth Amendment rights to be free from deliberate elicitation in the absence of counsel? Is the test for waiver similar or identical to that applied for waiver of *Miranda* rights? In the *Miranda* section, we noted two distinct waiver situations: 1) where the defendant receives warnings and waives his rights; and 2) where the defendant receives his warnings, invokes his rights, and then subsequently is argued to have waived his rights. Similar situations arise in the Sixth Amendment context.

### Waiving Sixth Amendment Rights After Receiving Miranda Warnings: Brewer v. Williams, Berghuis v. Thompkins, and Patterson v. Illinois

Where the defendant receives warnings and waives his rights, the question is simply whether the waiver was knowing and voluntary. The Court in Brewer v. Williams, supra, held that the government, to prove a waiver of Sixth Amendment rights, *must show more than simply that the defendant received warnings and elected to speak.* The majority in *Williams* found nothing to indicate that Williams had actually relinquished his rights. Analogizing from *Miranda*, evidence of relinquishment could be found in myriad ways, for example by the defendant's signing a waiver form; answering some questions but not others; showing a high level of cooperation; or providing an extremely detailed and lengthy confession. But none of this was shown to the majority's satisfaction in Brewer v. Williams. [Though as noted in the commentary after Brewer v. Williams, supra, the standards for finding an implied voluntary waiver of *Miranda* have been substantially relaxed by the Court in Berghuis v. Thompkins; and there is no reason to think that those relaxed standards would be inapplicable to an inquiry on voluntary waiver of Sixth Amendment rights.]

Assuming that the government can show that the defendant voluntarily relinquished his Sixth Amendment rights, another question arises: whether the defendant was sufficiently informed of his rights to make a *knowing* waiver. In the *Miranda* context, the Court held that the *Miranda* warnings provide a suspect with all the information he needs to make a knowing waiver. Does the same hold true for a waiver of the Sixth Amendment right to counsel?

The Court's answer to this question came in Patterson v. Illinois, 487 U.S. 285 (1988). Patterson was indicted, received *Miranda* warnings, and signed the waiver form and confessed. He had never invoked his Sixth Amendment right to counsel. He argued that his waiver, while voluntary, was not knowing and intelligent, because he received only the *Miranda* warnings, and these warnings did not adequately inform him of his Sixth Amendment right to counsel. Justice White, writing for the Court, rejected this argument in the following analysis:

> By telling petitioner that he had a right to consult with an attorney, to have a lawyer present while he was questioned, and even to have a lawyer appointed for him if he could not afford to retain one on his own, [the officers] conveyed to petitioner the sum and substance of the rights that the Sixth Amendment provided him. * * * [The *Miranda*] warning also sufficed * * * to let petitioner know what a lawyer could do for him during the postindictment

questioning; namely, advise petitioner to refrain from making any [incriminating] statements * * *

Our conclusion is supported by petitioner's inability, in the proceedings before this Court, to articulate with precision what additional information should have been provided to him before he would have been competent to waive his right to counsel. * * * The State's decision to take an additional step and commence formal adversarial proceedings against the accused does not substantially increase the value of counsel to the accused at questioning, or expand the limited purpose that an attorney serves when the accused is questioned by authorities. With respect to this inquiry, we do not discern a substantial difference between the usefulness of a lawyer to a suspect during custodial interrogation, and his value to an accused at postindictment questioning. * * * Because the role of counsel at questioning is relatively simple and limited, we see no problem in having a waiver procedure at that stage which is likewise simple and limited.

Justice White distinguished Faretta v. California, 422 U.S. 806 (1975), where the Court required copious warnings to be conveyed to an accused before an informed waiver of the right to counsel *at trial* could be found.[22] Justice White explained that the "full dangers and disadvantages of self-representation during questioning are less substantial and more obvious to an accused than they are at trial." That is, counsel can do a lot for you at trial, and so extensive warnings are necessary so that you understand what you are giving up; in contrast, counsel's role during police questioning is less complex—if counsel is there, she will tell you to shut up. And the *Miranda* warnings give the necessary information of counsel's role in that context.

Justice Stevens, joined by Justices Brennan, Marshall, and Blackmun dissented in *Patterson*. Justice Stevens argued that the majority had underplayed the significance of the initiation of formal proceedings and the multifaceted role of counsel after an indictment. He noted that the lawyer might examine the indictment for legal sufficiency, or might be able to negotiate a plea bargain, and that the *Miranda* warnings did not apprise the accused of these possibilities. Therefore, he concluded the person indicted is not fully aware of the value of an attorney if he simply receives the *Miranda* warnings.

---

[22] The breadth and detail of the required *Faretta* warnings are discussed in Chapter 10.

### Two Situations in Which Sixth Amendment Waiver Standards Might Be Different

In a footnote in *Patterson*, Justice White stressed that there are some limited situations in which a valid waiver might be found under *Miranda* but not under the Sixth Amendment. He gave two examples where Sixth Amendment waiver standards would be different from the standards applicable to *Miranda*. First,

> we have permitted a waiver to stand where a suspect was not told that his lawyer was trying to reach him during questioning [Moran v. Burbine]; in the Sixth Amendment context, this waiver would not be valid.

Second,

> a surreptitious conversation between an undercover police officer and an unindicted suspect would not give rise to any *Miranda* violation [Illinois v. Perkins]; however, once the accused is indicted, such questioning would be prohibited [and a waiver could not be found].

Why should these two circumstances preclude a finding of a knowing and voluntary waiver of Sixth Amendment rights?

### Indictment Warnings

The Court in *Patterson* left open whether an indicted suspect is entitled to a warning that he has been indicted before a waiver of the Sixth Amendment right to counsel can be found; Patterson had been so informed. But the sweeping language in *Patterson*, to the effect that *Miranda* warnings impart the necessary information for a Sixth Amendment waiver, has led courts to hold that an "indictment warning" is not required. See United States v. Chadwick, 999 F.2d 1282 (8th Cir.1993) ("law enforcement officers need not inform an accused that he has been indicted before seeking a waiver of his right to counsel").

### Waiving the Sixth Amendment Right to Counsel After Invoking It: Michigan v. Jackson and Montejo v. Louisiana

In Michigan v. Jackson, 475 U.S. 625 (1986), the accused formally requested counsel at an arraignment. Later he was interrogated by police officers about the crime for which he had been charged. Jackson did not initiate the contact, but he signed a waiver form, and confessed. Justice Stevens wrote for the Court as it held that Jackson had not knowingly and voluntarily waived his Sixth Amendment rights. He stated that when an accused invokes his Sixth Amendment right to counsel, the standards of Edwards v. Arizona, supra, govern the waiver of Sixth Amendment rights. Accordingly, Jackson could only have waived his Sixth

Amendment rights if he had initiated a later conversation and also knowingly and voluntarily waived his rights; this he had not done. Justice Stevens contended that "the reasons for prohibiting the interrogation of an uncounseled prisoner are even stronger after he has been formally charged with an offense than before."

In the following case, the Court reconsidered—and rejected—the extension of *Edwards* to the Sixth Amendment waiver context. This means that there is a major difference between Fifth and Sixth Amendment waiver after the right to counsel has been invoked. If a charged defendant invokes his Sixth Amendment right—typically, at an arraignment or other hearing—police officers remain free to approach him and seek a knowing and voluntary waiver as to the crime for which he has been charged. In contrast, if the suspect invokes his *Miranda* right to counsel—which could only be done when getting *Miranda* warnings from police officers in the context of custodial interrogation—then there can be no waiver unless the defendant initiates a new conversation with the officers.

## MONTEJO v. LOUISIANA

Supreme Court of the United States, 2009.
556 U.S. 778.

### JUSTICE SCALIA delivered the opinion of the Court.

We consider in this case the scope and continued viability of the rule announced by this Court in Michigan v. Jackson, 475 U.S. 625 (1986), forbidding police to initiate interrogation of a criminal defendant once he has requested counsel at an arraignment or similar proceeding.

\* \* \*

Petitioner Jesse Montejo was arrested on September 6, 2002, in connection with the robbery and murder of Lewis Ferrari, who had been found dead in his own home one day earlier. Suspicion quickly focused on Jerry Moore, a disgruntled former employee of Ferrari's dry cleaning business. Police sought to question Montejo, who was a known associate of Moore.

Montejo waived his rights under Miranda v. Arizona, and was interrogated at the sheriff's office by police detectives through the late afternoon and evening of September 6 and the early morning of September 7. During the interrogation, Montejo repeatedly changed his account of the crime, at first claiming that he had only driven Moore to the victim's home, and ultimately admitting that he had shot and killed Ferrari in the course of a botched burglary. These police interrogations were videotaped.

On September 10, Montejo was brought before a judge for what is known in Louisiana as a "72-hour hearing"—a preliminary hearing required under state law. [Montejo did not expressly state that he wanted a lawyer, but the court ordered that counsel be appointed for Montejo.]

Later that same day, two police detectives visited Montejo back at the prison and requested that he accompany them on an excursion to locate the murder weapon (which Montejo had earlier indicated he had thrown into a lake). * * * Montejo was again read his *Miranda* rights and agreed to go along; during the excursion, he wrote an inculpatory letter of apology to the victim's widow. Only upon their return did Montejo finally meet his court-appointed attorney, who was quite upset that the detectives had interrogated his client in his absence.

At trial, the letter of apology was admitted over defense objection. The jury convicted Montejo of first-degree murder, and he was sentenced to death.

[The lower court found that Montejo's waiver was knowing and voluntary and that *Jackson/Edwards* was not applicable because Montejo had never explicitly requested counsel. Justice Scalia rejected the Louisiana rule that the *Jackson/Edwards* protection was contingent on an explicit invocation of the Sixth Amendment right to counsel at an arraignment. He noted among other things that in almost half the states the appointment of counsel is automatic upon a finding of indigency and in others the court appoints counsel sua sponte. In these states, the affirmative invocation requirement would be unworkable.]

But if the Louisiana Supreme Court's application of *Jackson* is unsound as a practical matter, then Montejo's solution is untenable as a theoretical and doctrinal matter. Under his approach, once a defendant is represented by counsel, police may not initiate any further interrogation. Such a rule would be entirely untethered from the original rationale of *Jackson*.

* * *

Our precedents * * * place beyond doubt that the Sixth Amendment right to counsel may be waived by a defendant, so long as relinquishment of the right is voluntary, knowing, and intelligent. Patterson v. Illinois; Brewer v. Williams. The defendant may waive the right whether or not he is already represented by counsel; the decision to waive need not itself be counseled. And when a defendant is read his *Miranda* rights (which include the right to have counsel present during interrogation) and agrees to waive those rights, that typically does the trick, even though the *Miranda* rights purportedly have their source in the Fifth Amendment * * *.

The only question raised by this case, and the only one addressed by the *Jackson* rule, is whether courts must presume that such a waiver is invalid under certain circumstances. We created such a presumption in *Jackson* by analogy to a similar prophylactic rule established to protect the Fifth Amendment based *Miranda* right to have counsel present at any custodial interrogation. * * *

*Jackson* represented a wholesale importation of the *Edwards* rule into the Sixth Amendment. The *Jackson* Court decided that a request for counsel at an arraignment should be treated as an invocation of the Sixth Amendment right to counsel "at every critical stage of the prosecution," despite doubt that defendants "actually inten[d] their request for counsel to encompass representation during any further questioning," because doubts must be "resolved in favor of protecting the constitutional claim." Citing *Edwards*, the Court held that any subsequent waiver would thus be "insufficient to justify police-initiated interrogation." In other words, we presume such waivers involuntary "based on the supposition that suspects who assert their right to counsel are unlikely to waive that right voluntarily" in subsequent interactions with police.

With this understanding of what *Jackson* stands for and whence it came, it should be clear that Montejo's interpretation of that decision—that no represented defendant can ever be approached by the State and asked to consent to interrogation—is off the mark. * * * No reason exists to assume that a defendant like Montejo, who has done nothing at all to express his intentions with respect to his Sixth Amendment rights, would not be perfectly amenable to speaking with the police without having counsel present. And no reason exists to prohibit the police from inquiring. *Edwards* and *Jackson* are meant to prevent police from badgering defendants into changing their minds about their rights, but a defendant who never asked for counsel has not yet made up his mind in the first instance.

* * *

The upshot is that even on *Jackson's* own terms, it would be completely unjustified to presume that a defendant's consent to police-initiated interrogation was involuntary or coerced simply because he had previously been appointed a lawyer.

* * *

So on the one hand, requiring an initial "invocation" of the right to counsel in order to trigger the *Jackson* presumption is consistent with the theory of that decision, but * * * would be unworkable in more than half the States of the Union. On the other hand, eliminating the invocation requirement would render the rule easy to apply but depart fundamentally from the *Jackson* rationale.

We do not think that *stare decisis* requires us to expand significantly the holding of a prior decision—fundamentally revising its theoretical basis in the process—in order to cure its practical deficiencies. To the contrary, the fact that a decision has proved "unworkable" is a traditional ground for overruling it. * * *

Beyond workability, the relevant factors in deciding whether to adhere to the principle of stare decisis include the antiquity of the precedent, the reliance interests at stake, and of course whether the decision was well reasoned. The first two cut in favor of abandoning *Jackson*: the opinion is only two decades old, and eliminating it would not upset expectations. Any criminal defendant learned enough to order his affairs based on the rule announced in *Jackson* would also be perfectly capable of interacting with the police on his own. Of course it is likely true that police and prosecutors have been trained to comply with *Jackson*, but that is hardly a basis for retaining it as a constitutional requirement. If a State wishes to abstain from requesting interviews with represented defendants when counsel is not present, it obviously may continue to do so.

Which brings us to the strength of *Jackson's* reasoning. When this Court creates a prophylactic rule in order to protect a constitutional right, the relevant "reasoning" is the weighing of the rule's benefits against its costs. * * * We think that the marginal benefits of *Jackson* (viz., the number of confessions obtained coercively that are suppressed by its bright-line rule and would otherwise have been admitted) are dwarfed by its substantial costs (viz., hindering society's compelling interest in finding, convicting, and punishing those who violate the law).

What does the *Jackson* rule actually achieve by way of preventing unconstitutional conduct? Recall that the purpose of the rule is to preclude the State from badgering defendants into waiving their previously asserted rights. The effect of this badgering might be to coerce a waiver, which would render the subsequent interrogation a violation of the Sixth Amendment. Even though involuntary waivers are invalid even apart from *Jackson*, mistakes are of course possible when courts conduct case-by-case voluntariness review. A bright-line rule like that adopted in *Jackson* ensures that no fruits of interrogations made possible by badgering-induced involuntary waivers are ever erroneously admitted at trial.

But without *Jackson*, how many would be? The answer is few if any. The principal reason is that the Court has already taken substantial other, overlapping measures toward the same end. * * * Under *Miranda's* prophylactic protection of the right against compelled self-incrimination, any suspect subject to custodial interrogation has the right to have a lawyer present if he so requests, and to be advised of that right. Under

*Edwards'* prophylactic protection of the *Miranda* right, once such a defendant "has invoked his right to have counsel present," interrogation must stop. And under *Minnick's* prophylactic protection of the *Edwards* right, no subsequent interrogation may take place until counsel is present, "whether or not the accused has consulted with his attorney."

These three layers of prophylaxis are sufficient. * * *

* * *

Under the *Miranda-Edwards-Minnick* line of cases (which is not in doubt), a defendant who does not want to speak to the police without counsel present need only say as much when he is first approached and given the *Miranda* warnings. At that point, not only must the immediate contact end, but "badgering" by later requests is prohibited. If that regime suffices to protect the integrity of a suspect's voluntary choice not to speak outside his lawyer's presence before his arraignment, it is hard to see why it would not also suffice to protect that same choice after arraignment, when Sixth Amendment rights have attached. And if so, then *Jackson* is simply superfluous.

* * *

On the other side of the equation are the costs of adding the bright-line *Jackson* rule on top of *Edwards* and other extant protections. The principal cost of applying any exclusionary rule is, of course, letting guilty and possibly dangerous criminals go free. *Jackson* not only operates to invalidate a confession given by the free choice of suspects who have received proper advice of their *Miranda* rights but waived them nonetheless, but also deters law enforcement officers from even trying to obtain voluntary confessions. The ready ability to obtain uncoerced confessions is not an evil but an unmitigated good. Without these confessions, crimes go unsolved and criminals unpunished. These are not negligible costs, and in our view the *Jackson* Court gave them too short shrift.

* * * Montejo expresses concern that courts will have to determine whether statements made at preliminary hearings constitute *Edwards* invocations—thus implicating all the practical problems of the Louisiana rule we discussed above. That concern is misguided. We have * * * never held that a person can invoke his *Miranda* rights anticipatorily, in a context other than custodial interrogation. What matters for *Miranda* and *Edwards* is what happens when the defendant is approached for interrogation, and (if he consents) what happens during the interrogation—not what happened at any preliminary hearing.

In sum, when the marginal benefits of the *Jackson* rule are weighed against its substantial costs to the truth-seeking process and the criminal justice system, we readily conclude that the rule does not "pay its way." Michigan v. Jackson should be and now is overruled.

\* \* \*

Although our holding means that the Louisiana Supreme Court correctly rejected Montejo's claim under *Jackson*, we think that Montejo should be given an opportunity to contend that his letter of apology should still have been suppressed under the rule of *Edwards*. If Montejo made a clear assertion of the right to counsel when the officers approached him about accompanying them on the excursion for the murder weapon, then no interrogation should have taken place unless Montejo initiated it. Even if Montejo subsequently agreed to waive his rights, that waiver would have been invalid had it followed an unequivocal election of the right.

Montejo understandably did not pursue an *Edwards* objection, because *Jackson* served as the Sixth Amendment analogy to *Edwards* and offered broader protections. Our decision today, overruling *Jackson*, changes the legal landscape and does so in part based on the protections already provided by *Edwards*. Thus we think that a remand is appropriate so that Montejo can pursue this alternative avenue for relief. \* \* \*

[The concurring opinion by JUSTICE ALITO, joined by JUSTICE KENNEDY, is omitted.]

**JUSTICE STEVENS, with whom JUSTICE SOUTER and JUSTICE GINSBURG join, and with whom JUSTICE BREYER joins [in pertinent part] dissenting.**

\* \* \*

The majority's analysis flagrantly misrepresents *Jackson's* underlying rationale and the constitutional interests the decision sought to protect. While it is true that the rule adopted in *Jackson* was patterned after the rule in *Edwards*, the *Jackson* opinion does not even mention the anti-badgering considerations that provide the basis for the Court's decision today. Instead, *Jackson* relied primarily on cases discussing the broad protections guaranteed by the Sixth Amendment right to counsel— not its Fifth Amendment counterpart. *Jackson* emphasized that the purpose of the Sixth Amendment is to "protec[t] the unaided layman at critical confrontations with his adversary" by giving him "the right to rely on counsel as a 'medium' between him[self] and the State." \* \* \*

Once *Jackson* is placed in its proper Sixth Amendment context, the majority's justifications for overruling the decision crumble. \* \* \*

[The dissenting opinion of JUSTICE BREYER is omitted.]

## F.  THE SIXTH AMENDMENT EXCLUSIONARY RULE

In *Moulton,* Chief Justice Burger argued in dissent that even if there were a Sixth Amendment violation, the exclusionary rule should not be used to exclude the evidence of Moulton's reliable incriminatory statements. Citing the good faith exception to the Fourth Amendment exclusionary rule (discussed in Chapter 2), the Chief Justice argued that "the Sixth Amendment claims at issue here closely parallel claims under the Fourth Amendment where we have found the exclusionary rule to be inapplicable by weighing the costs and benefits of its applications."

In *Dickerson,* the Court held that exclusion of *Miranda*-defective confessions was required by the Fifth Amendment, but that there are certain exceptions to the exclusionary rule, such as for fruits, impeachment, and public safety. On the other hand, a violation of the Due Process Clause carries with it an automatic rule of exclusion, as the Court has consistently stated in cases such as Mincey v. Arizona. Does the Constitution require exclusion of a confession obtained in violation of the Sixth Amendment, or is Chief Justice Burger correct in *Moulton*?

Several commentators have argued that the Constitution requires exclusion of evidence obtained as a result of a Sixth Amendment violation. They reason that a violation of the *Massiah* right to counsel is not complete until the confession is admitted at trial. It is only at that point that the effectiveness of trial counsel envisioned by *Massiah* is impaired. As such, a *Massiah* violation is, according to these commentators, unlike a Fourth Amendment violation, which occurs at the time of the intrusion. See Loewy, Police Obtained Evidence and the Constitution: Distinguishing Unconstitutionally Obtained Evidence from Unconstitutionally Used Evidence, 87 Mich.L.Rev. 907 (1989).

But the Supreme Court rejected the "violation at time of admission at trial" argument in Kansas v. Ventris, 556 U.S. 586 (2009)—and in doing so the Court adopted an "impeachment" exception to the Sixth Amendment exclusionary rule that is analogous to the impeachment exceptions to the Fourth Amendment and to *Miranda.*

The police deliberately elicited information from Ventris after he had been charged. In the Supreme Court the government conceded a *Massiah* violation. But the confession was only admitted to impeach Ventris's trial testimony. The Court, in an opinion by Justice Scalia for seven Justices, found that Ventris was properly impeached with the *Massiah*-defective confession. Justice Scalia addressed the "violation at the time of admission at trial" argument in the following passage:

> Whether otherwise excluded evidence can be admitted for purposes of impeachment depends upon the nature of the constitutional guarantee that is violated. Sometimes that explicitly

mandates exclusion from trial, and sometimes it does not. The Fifth Amendment guarantees that no person shall be compelled to give evidence against himself, and so is violated whenever a truly coerced confession is introduced at trial, whether by way of impeachment or otherwise. The Fourth Amendment, on the other hand, guarantees that no person shall be subjected to unreasonable searches or seizures, and says nothing about excluding their fruits from evidence; exclusion comes by way of deterrent sanction rather than to avoid violation of the substantive guarantee. Inadmissibility has not been automatic, therefore, but we have instead applied an exclusionary-rule balancing test. * * * Respondent argues that the Sixth Amendment's right to counsel is a "right an accused is to enjoy a[t] trial." * * * It is illogical to say that the right is not violated until trial counsel's task of opposing conviction has been undermined by the statement's admission into evidence. A defendant is not denied counsel merely because the prosecution has been permitted to introduce evidence of guilt—even evidence so overwhelming that the attorney's job of gaining an acquittal is rendered impossible. In such circumstances the accused continues to enjoy the assistance of counsel; the assistance is simply not worth much. The assistance of counsel has been denied, however, at the prior critical stage which produced the inculpatory evidence. * * * It is that deprivation which demands a remedy.

Accordingly, the Court found that the remedy for the violation should be the same as for the violation of the Fourth Amendment or *Miranda*: exclusion from the case-in-chief, but permitting impeachment of the defendant's inconsistent testimony.

# CHAPTER 4

## IDENTIFYING SUSPECTS

■ ■ ■

## I.   INTRODUCTION

Even in the days of DNA matching, eyewitness identification is an important part of many criminal prosecutions. Many types of crimes cannot usually be solved by DNA evidence, e.g., bank robbery, fraud, drugs, etc. Indeed most cases in which identity is disputed will turn on whether witnesses are believed. Yet, it is well known that eyewitness evidence is often not very reliable and that police procedures may render identifications even less reliable than they otherwise would be.

The late Circuit Judge McGowan explained more than 40 years ago that many experts believe that erroneous identifications are "conceivably the greatest single threat to the achievement of our ideal that no innocent man shall be punished." Constitutional Interpretation and Criminal Identification, 12 Wm. & Mary L.Rev. 235, 238 (1970). There is growing evidence that suggestive law enforcement conduct may exacerbate the problems of securing accurate identifications from victims and witnesses who often experience crime in circumstances of stress and poor observation conditions. The Innocence Project offers a compelling statistic about the impact of eyewitness identification on wrongful convictions and some examples of mistaken identifications:

> Eyewitness misidentification is the single greatest cause of wrongful convictions nationwide, playing a role in more than 75% of convictions overturned through DNA testing. While eyewitness testimony can be persuasive evidence before a judge or jury * * * research shows that the human mind is not like a tape recorder; we neither record events exactly as we see them, nor recall them like a tape that has been rewound. Instead, witness memory is like any other evidence at a crime scene; it must be preserved carefully and retrieved methodically, or it can be contaminated.

In case after case, DNA has proven what scientists already know—that eyewitness identification is frequently inaccurate. In the wrongful convictions caused by eyewitness misidentification, the circumstances varied, but judges and juries all relied on testimony that could have been more accurate if reforms proven by science had been implemented. The Innocence Project has worked on cases in which:

- A witness made an identification in a "show-up" procedure from the back of a police car hundreds of feet away from the suspect in a poorly lit parking lot in the middle of the night.

- A witness in a rape case was shown a photo array where only one photo—of the person police suspected was the perpetrator—was marked with an "R."

- Witnesses substantially changed their description of a perpetrator (including key information such as height, weight and presence of facial hair) after they learned more about a particular suspect.

- Witnesses only made an identification after multiple photo arrays or lineups—and then made hesitant identifications (saying they "thought" the person "might be" the perpetrator, for example), but at trial the jury was told the witnesses did not waver in identifying the suspect.

[www.innocenceproject.org]

Another documented problem is that an identification may be more in accord with the witness's expectation than with reality. This may be particularly so where a witness of one race identifies a person of another race as the perpetrator. See Johnson, Cross-Racial Identification Errors in Criminal Cases, 69 Cornell L.Rev. 934 (1984). An American Bar Association Report prepared in 2008 explained the problem with cross-racial identification.

Research results vary but they show a generally consistent pattern. Persons of one racial group may have greater difficulty distinguishing among individual faces of persons in another group than among faces of persons in own group. Persons who primarily interact within their own racial group, especially if they are in the majority group, will better perceive and process the subtlety of facial features of persons within their own racial group than persons of other racial groups. In terms of personal experience, who has never heard the phrase, "they all look alike to me"?

[Report Accompanying Resolution 104 D, 2008 Annual Meeting, http://www.abanet.org/leadership/2008/annual/recommendations/OneHundredFourD.doc]

Indeed there is a substantial body of social science data indicating reliability problems with virtually every possible type of identification process. Problems include:

- Where the lineup administrator is involved in the investigation, "the overall probability that administrator expectations do not influence the subject is near zero." New Jersey v. Henderson, 208 N.J. 208, 27 A.3d 872 (2011) (citing analysis of 345 studies).

- Where a weapon is used in the crime, the identifying witness is likely to be impaired by "weapons focus" and thus less likely to reliably identify the perpetrator. Thus, "an analysis of 19 weapon-focus studies involving 2082 identifications found that, on average, identification accuracy decreased approximately 10 percent when a weapon was present." Young v. Conway, 698 F.3d 69 (2nd Cir. 2012).

- High levels of stress have been shown to "induce a defensive mental state that can result in a diminished ability accurately to process and recall events, leading to inaccurate identifications. For example, a review of 16 studies involving 1727 participants found that accurate identifications decreased 22.2% under high stress conditions." *Young,* supra.

- Use of disguises—even subtle ones like hats—can substantially impair accurate identifications. Cutler et. al., The Reliability of Eyewitness Identification: The Role of System and Estimator Variables, 11 Law & Hum. Behavior, 233 (1987) (reporting results of an experiment showing that when the "perpetrator" wore a hat, only 27% of participants' identifications were accurate, as opposed to 45% accuracy when no hat was worn).

- Once a witness has made an identification—even an inaccurate one—they can suffer "unconscious transference" or a "mugshot exposure effect" that affects any subsequent identification. This occurs because "the witness is unable to partition his or her memory in such a way as to know that the suspect's increased familiarity is due to the [prior identification procedure] rather than the suspect's presence at the time of the crime." *Young,* supra.

As you will see, the Supreme Court took an interest in eyewitness identification beginning in 1967 but over subsequent years has become more tolerant of suggestive police procedures. Indeed, although eyewitness identification mistakes continue to pose a major problem for American criminal justice, the Supreme Court has largely left the playing field since 1977. There is irony here, given the fact that the search and seizure rules discussed in Chapter 2 and the privilege against self-incrimination and confession cases discussed in Chapter 3 largely deal with attempts to suppress evidence by suspects who often are guilty of serious crime, while eyewitness identification rules deal with attempts to prevent innocent individuals from being convicted. Fortunately, conscientious prosecutors  and courts have in some jurisdictions adopted non-constitutional measures—discussed later in this Chapter—to reduce the likelihood of erroneous identifications and the possibility that police suggestiveness will contribute to wrongful convictions. Some federal and state courts have also filled part of the void by giving jury instructions on identification testimony that cautions jurors to view such testimony with care.

## II.    THE JUDICIAL RESPONSE

## A.  IDENTIFICATIONS AND THE RIGHT TO COUNSEL

### 1.  The *Wade-Gilbert* Rule

With so much evidence casting doubt on the identification techniques commonly used by the police, sooner or later the judiciary was going to have to examine them. One morning in June of 1967, the Court handed down three major opinions designed to protect those suspected and accused of crime from unfair identification tactics.

The first case was the following one:

### UNITED STATES V. WADE

Supreme Court of the United States, 1967.
388 U.S. 218.

**MR. JUSTICE BRENNAN delivered the opinion of the Court.**

The question here is whether courtroom identifications of an accused at trial are to be excluded from evidence because the accused was exhibited to the witnesses before trial at a post-indictment lineup conducted for identification purposes without notice to and in the absence of the accused's appointed counsel.

The federally insured bank in Eustace, Texas, was robbed on September 21, 1964. A man with a small strip of tape on each side on his face entered the bank, pointed a pistol at the female cashier and the vice president, the only persons in the bank at the time, and forced them to fill a pillowcase with the bank's money. The man then drove away with an accomplice who had been waiting in a stolen car outside the bank. On March 23, 1965, an indictment was returned against respondent, Wade, and two others for conspiring to rob the bank, and against Wade and the accomplice for the robbery itself. Wade was arrested on April 2, and counsel was appointed to represent him on April 26. Fifteen days later an FBI agent, without notice to Wade's lawyer, arranged to have the two bank employees observe a lineup made up of Wade and five or six other prisoners and conducted in a courtroom of the local county courthouse. Each person in the line wore strips of tape such as allegedly worn by the robber and upon direction each said something like "put the money in the bag," the words allegedly uttered by the robber. Both bank employees identified Wade in the lineup as the bank robber.

At trial, the two employees, when asked on direct examination if the robber was in the courtroom, pointed to Wade. The prior lineup identification was then elicited from both employees on cross-examination. * * *

[T]he confrontation compelled by the State between the accused and the victim or witnesses to a crime to elicit identification evidence is peculiarly riddled with innumerable dangers and variable factors which might seriously, even crucially, derogate from a fair trial. The vagaries of eyewitness identification are well-known; the annals of criminal law are rife with instances of mistaken identification. * * * A major factor contributing to the high incidence of miscarriage of justice from mistaken identification has been the degree of suggestion inherent in the manner in which the prosecution presents the suspect to witnesses for pretrial identification. * * * Suggestion can be created intentionally or unintentionally in many subtle ways. And the dangers for the suspect are particularly grave when the witness' opportunity for observation was insubstantial, and thus his susceptibility to suggestion the greatest.

Moreover, it is a matter of common experience that, once a witness has picked out the accused at the lineup, he is not likely to go back on his word later on, so that in practice the issue of identity may (in the absence of other relevant evidence) for all practical purposes be determined there and then, before the trial.

The pretrial confrontation for purpose of identification may take the form of a lineup, also known as an "identification parade" or "showup," as in the present case, or presentation of the suspect alone to the witness. * * * It is obvious that risks of suggestion attend either form of confrontation and increase the dangers inhering in eyewitness identification. But as in the case with secret interrogations, there is serious difficulty in depicting what transpires at lineups and other forms of identification confrontations. * * * [T]he defense can seldom reconstruct the manner and mode of lineup identification for judge or jury at trial. Those participating in a lineup with the accused may often be police officers; in any event, the participants' names are rarely recorded or divulged at trial. The impediments to an objective observation are increased when the victim is the witness. Lineups are prevalent in rape and robbery prosecutions and present a particular hazard that a victim's understandable outrage may excite vengeful or spiteful motives. In any event, neither witnesses nor lineup participants are apt to be alert for conditions prejudicial to the suspect. And if they were, it would likely be of scant benefit to the suspect since neither witnesses nor lineup participants are likely to be schooled in the detection of suggestive influences.[a] Improper influences may go undetected by a suspect, guilty or not, who experiences the emotional tension which we might expect in one being confronted with potential accusers. Even when he does observe abuse, if he has a criminal record he may be reluctant to take the stand and open up the admission of prior convictions. Moreover, any protestations by the suspect of the fairness of the lineup made at trial are likely to be in vain; the jury's choice is between the accused's unsupported version and that of the police officers present. In short, the accused's inability effectively to reconstruct at trial any unfairness that occurred at the lineup may deprive him of his only opportunity meaningfully to attack the credibility of the witness' courtroom identification.

\* \* \*

Insofar as the accused's conviction may rest on a courtroom identification in fact the fruit of a suspect pretrial identification which the accused is helpless to subject to effective scrutiny at trial, the accused is deprived of that right of cross-examination which is an essential safeguard to his right to confront the witnesses against him. And even though cross-examination is a precious safeguard to a fair trial, it cannot be viewed as an absolute assurance of accuracy and reliability. Thus in the present context, where so many variables and pitfalls exist, the first line of defense must be the prevention of unfairness and the lessening of the hazards of eyewitness identification at the lineup itself. The trial which might determine the accused's fate may well not be that in the courtroom but that at the pretrial confrontation, with the State aligned against the accused, the witness the sole jury, and the accused unprotected against the overreaching, intentional or unintentional, and with little or no effective appeal from the judgment there rendered by the witness—"that's the man."

Since it appears that there is grave potential for prejudice, intentional or not, in the pretrial lineup, which may not be capable of reconstruction at trial, and since presence of counsel itself can often avert prejudice and assure a meaningful confrontation at trial, there can be little doubt that for Wade the post-indictment lineup was a critical stage of the prosecution at which he was as much entitled to such aid of counsel as at the trial itself. Thus both Wade and his counsel should have been notified of the impending lineup, and counsel's presence should have been a requisite to conduct of the lineup, absent an "intelligent waiver." No substantial countervailing policy considerations have been advanced against the requirement of the presence of counsel. Concern is expressed

---

[a]  An additional impediment to the detection of such influences by participants, including the suspect, is the physical conditions often surrounding the conduct of the lineup. In many, lights shine on the stage in such a way that the suspect cannot see the witness. In some a one-way mirror is used and what is said on the witness' side cannot be heard.

that the requirement will forestall prompt identifications and result in obstruction of the confrontations. As for the first, we note that in the two cases in which the right to counsel is today held to apply, counsel had already been appointed and no argument is made in either case that notice to counsel would have prejudicially delayed the confrontations. Moreover, we leave open the question whether the presence of substitute counsel might not suffice where notification and presence of the suspect's own counsel would result in prejudicial delay. And to refuse to recognize the right to counsel for fear that counsel will obstruct the course of justice is contrary to the basic assumptions upon which this Court has operated in Sixth Amendment cases. * * * In our view counsel can hardly impede legitimate law enforcement; on the contrary, for the reasons expressed, law enforcement may be assisted by preventing the infiltration of taint in the prosecution's identification evidence.

* * *

We come now to the question whether the denial of Wade's motion to strike the courtroom identification by the bank witnesses at trial because of the absence of his counsel at the lineup required * * * the grant of a new trial at which such evidence is to be excluded. * * * Where, as here, the admissibility of evidence of the lineup identification itself is not involved, a *per se* rule of exclusion of courtroom identification would be unjustified. A rule limited solely to the exclusion of testimony concerning identification at the lineup itself, without regard to admissibility of the courtroom identification, would render the right to counsel an empty one. The lineup is most often used, as in the present case, to crystallize the witnesses' identification of the defendant for future reference. We have already noted that the lineup identification will have that effect. * * * Counsel is then in the predicament in which Wade's counsel found himself—realizing that possible unfairness at the lineup may be the sole means of attack upon the unequivocal courtroom identification, and having to probe in the dark in an attempt to discover and reveal unfairness, while bolstering the government witness' courtroom identification by bringing out and dwelling upon his prior identification. Since counsel's presence at the lineup would equip him to attack not only the lineup identification but the courtroom identification as well, limiting the impact of violation of the right to counsel to exclusion of evidence only of identification at the lineup itself disregards a critical element of that right.

We think it follows that the proper test to be applied in these situations is that quoted in Wong Sun v. United States, 371 U.S. 471, 488, "[W]hether, granting establishment of the primary illegality, the evidence to which instant objection is made has been come at by exploitation of that illegality or instead by means sufficiently distinguishable to be purged of the primary taint." Application of this test in the present context requires consideration of various factors; for example, the prior opportunity to observe the alleged criminal act, the existence of any discrepancy between any pre-lineup description and the defendant's actual description, any identification prior to lineup of another person, the identification by picture of the defendant prior to the lineup, failure to identify the defendant on a prior occasion, and the lapse of time between the alleged act and the lineup identification. It is also relevant to consider those facts which, despite the absence of counsel, are disclosed concerning the conduct of the lineup.

\* \* \*

On the record now before us we cannot make the determination whether the in-court identifications had an independent origin. \* \* \* We therefore think the appropriate procedure to be followed is to vacate the conviction pending a hearing to determine whether the in-court identifications had an independent source, or whether, in any event, the introduction of the evidence was harmless error \* \* \*.

\* \* \*

[Separate opinions by JUSTICE FORTAS (joined by CHIEF JUSTICE WARREN), JUSTICE BLACK, JUSTICE CLARK, and JUSTICE DOUGLAS are omitted.]

MR. JUSTICE WHITE, whom MR. JUSTICE HARLAN and MR. JUSTICE STEWART join, dissenting in part and concurring in part.

The Court has again propounded a broad constitutional rule barring use of a wide spectrum of relevant and probative evidence, solely because a step in its ascertainment or discovery occurs outside the presence of defense counsel. This was the approach of the Court in Miranda v. Arizona. I objected then to what I thought was an uncritical and doctrinaire approach without satisfactory factual foundation. \* \* \*

The Court's opinion is far-reaching. It proceeds first by creating a new *per se* rule of constitutional law: a criminal suspect cannot be subjected to a pretrial identification process in the absence of his counsel without violating the Sixth Amendment. \* \* \*

\* \* \* The Court apparently believes that improper police procedures are so widespread that a broad prophylactic rule must be laid down, requiring the presence of counsel at all pretrial identifications, in order to detect recurring instances of police misconduct. I do not share this pervasive distrust of all official investigations. None of the materials the Court relies upon supports it.

\* \* \*

## NOTE ON THE MEANING OF WADE

In *Wade* the lineup was held improper because of the absence of counsel, substitute counsel, or waiver of counsel. But, when Wade was tried, the lineup was not mentioned by the prosecution; its results were not a part of the evidence until brought up by the defense in cross-examination. Thus, the controlling question was whether the *in-court identification* was tainted by the unconstitutional lineup—i.e., whether the in-court identification, which the prosecutor used, would have been made had there been no counsel-free lineup.

Evidence of an out-of-court identification, offered for its truth, was hearsay not subject to any exception at the time of the federal trial in *Wade.* The prosecution could make no direct use of the prior identification unless the defense "opened the door" by attacking the identifying witness at trial. But a federal prosecutor would no longer be so constrained, because Rule 801(d)(1)(C) of the Federal Rules of Evidence provides for admissibility of prior identifications as "not hearsay" when the person who made the identification is "subject to cross-examination."

### Evidence of the Prior Identification Itself: Gilbert v. California

In Gilbert v. California, 388 U.S. 263 (1967), one of the companion cases to *Wade,* the out-of-court identification made in the absence of counsel was actually admitted in the prosecution's case-in-chief, under a state hearsay exception. Gilbert was convicted of armed bank robbery and the murder of a police officer who entered the bank during the course of the robbery. At the time of the challenged identification procedure, Gilbert had been indicted for robbery. Justice Brennan, writing for the Court, noted that the lineup was on a stage behind bright lights, which prevented those in the line from seeing the audience. Upwards of 100 persons were in the audience, each an eyewitness to one of the several robberies charged to Gilbert. Doubtful witnesses were allowed to call Gilbert out of the lineup to make him repeat a phrase in a particular way or to walk in a particular way. The witnesses talked to each other and made their identifications in each other's presence.

As in *Wade,* the Court held that the in-court identifications would be excluded unless they proceeded from a source independent of the tainted identification, such as a substantial opportunity to view the perpetrator at the time of the crime. As in *Wade,* the Court remanded for an independent source determination. And as to the use of the out-of-court identifications as evidence, the Court adopted a per se rule of exclusion. Justice Brennan explained:

Only a *per se* exclusionary rule as to such testimony can be an effective sanction to assure that law enforcement authorities will respect the accused's constitutional right to the presence of his counsel at the critical lineup. In the absence of legislative regulations adequate to avoid the hazards to a fair trial which inhere in lineups as presently conducted, the desirability of deterring the constitutionally objectionable practice must prevail over the undesirability of excluding relevant evidence. That conclusion is buttressed by the consideration that the witness' testimony of his lineup identification will enhance the impact of his in-court identification on the jury and seriously aggravate whatever derogation exists of the accused's right to a fair trial.

### The Role of a Lawyer at a Lineup

The Court in *Wade* and *Gilbert* was concerned about inadequate identification procedures and the lasting effect they may have in some cases. But did the Court, in imposing a counsel requirement, fashion a remedy that suited the problems it identified? The Court's counsel remedy is criticized in Read, Lawyers at Lineups: Constitutional Necessity or Avoidable Extravagance?, 17 U.C.L.A.L.Rev. 339, 362–67 (1969). Read makes the following arguments:

- *Wade* viewed counsel as essentially an observer, i.e., a passive participant.

- A passive observer is unlikely to be able to improve the quality of lineups.

- If the defendant is not a very good witness in a hearing on a lineup because of obvious bias, his lawyer is likely to be almost as biased and thus no better a witness.

- Recording devices would depict the lineup more effectively than testimony by participants.

- Counsel is no more schooled than other participants in psychology and may be insensitive to lineup conditions that might be prejudicial to a defendant.

The presence of a lawyer at a lineup might do *some* good, however. A lawyer who is used to bargaining with law enforcement officials—even though only an observer—may be able to persuade them as to the unfairness of some procedures at lineups. Moreover, knowledge that a lawyer is present may tend to make officials more careful—just like having lawyers present at elections is thought to make them more fair. Lawyers may not be trained psychologists, but they should know the kinds of suggestive factors that make lineups vulnerable and can urge case law on police and prosecutors. Even without formal interdisciplinary training, lawyers may be careful listeners and should be able to identify certain forms of suggestiveness—e.g., leading questions to witnesses. Finally, cross-examination of identification witnesses is likely to be more effective when the lawyer has actually seen the identification process.

If the lawyer is only a passive observer at the lineup, could police permissibly dispense with a lawyer's presence by simply videotaping the identification and giving the tape to counsel? In United States v. LaPierre, 998 F.2d 1460 (9th Cir.1993), the court refused to decide whether videotaping could ever be a substitute for the presence of counsel. It found, however, that videotaping was inadequate under the facts because the videotape showed only the people in the lineup, and did not record anything that occurred in the witness room.

## 2. Limits on the Right to Counsel at Identification Procedures

The Sixth Amendment right to counsel invoked in *Wade* applies to all "criminal prosecutions." As seen in the discussion of *Massiah* and *Escobedo* in Chapter 3, the Court has held that a criminal prosecution within the meaning of the Sixth Amendment does not begin until the suspect has been *formally charged* with a crime. Both Wade and Gilbert had been formally charged, although the Court did not emphasize that in its discussion of the need for counsel when the identification might be the real "trial." In Kirby v. Illinois, 406 U.S.682, the Court held, 5–4, that it would not "extend" its Sixth Amendment reasoning to identifications made before an individual was indicted or otherwise formally charged. Justice Stewart wrote a plurality opinion. Justice Powell concurred in the result.

The plurality opinion in *Kirby* states that "[t]he Due Process Clause of the Fifth and Fourteenth Amendments forbids a lineup that is unnecessarily suggestive and conducive to irreparable mistaken identification." The cases reviewing claims of "unnecessary suggestiveness" under the Due Process Clause are examined in the next section. The bottom line, though, is that the vast majority of identification procedures are conducted *before* a formal charge has been filed. Indeed lineups and other identifications are ordinarily conducted to obtain evidence with which to bring a formal charge. Thus, *Kirby* strips the *Wade* counsel requirement of significant practical effect.

As a practical matter, the Court in *Kirby* must have been concerned with the implications of extending the *Wade* right to counsel rule to all or virtually all identifications. Many identifications are made *on the street* only minutes after the event. Application of the *Wade* rule in these circumstances obviously presents problems; the delay resulting from waiting for counsel to arrive may perversely decrease the reliability of the identification due to the fading memory of witnesses. In light of these problems, the result in *Kirby* is understandable, so long as the Due Process Clause provides meaningful protection against mistaken identifications in cases where the *Wade* rule does not apply. As we will see, though, this has not always been the case.

Does *Kirby* create an incentive for the government to delay an indictment in order to conduct an identification procedure in the absence of counsel? Does a suspect have a constitutional right to be indicted at a certain point? Courts have stated that if adversary proceedings are "deliberately delayed" in order to evade the *Wade* rule, the resulting identification will be invalidated. See, e.g., United States ex rel. Burbank v. Warden, 535 F.2d 361 (7th Cir.1976). However, proving that an indictment was deliberately delayed is difficult, to say the least. See United States ex rel. Hall v. Lane, 804 F.2d 79 (7th Cir.1986) (no evidence that delay in obtaining indictment was caused by bad faith, therefore there was no right to counsel at the pre-indictment identification).

### Post-Charge Photographic Identifications: United States v. Ash

In United States v. Ash, 413 U.S. 300 (1973), the Court again restricted the *Wade* rule, holding that a defendant has no right to counsel at a *photographic* identification, whether conducted before or after indictment or formal charge. Justice Blackmun's majority opinion described the right to counsel as a defendant's right to have a spokesperson or advisor while being subject to an identification procedure. The Court stated that "the accused himself is not present at the time of the photographic display and asserts no right to be present" and therefore "no possibility arises that the accused might be misled by his lack of familiarity with the law or overpowered by his professional adversary."

The *Ash* Court noted that photo arrays are unlike lineups, because an "accurate reconstruction" of a photographic array is possible at trial. It concluded that "the opportunity to cure defects at trial causes the pretrial confrontation to cease to be critical." The Court also saw photo displays as a mere preparatory step in the gathering of evidence where the defense counsel had an "equal ability * * * to seek and interview witnesses himself."

Professor Grano, in *Kirby, Biggers*, and *Ash*: Do Any Constitutional Safeguards Remain Against the Danger of Protecting the Innocent?, 72 Mich.L.Rev. 717 (1974), suggests that there are myriad possibilities of suggestiveness in photographic identifications. While it might be true that the photograph array itself can be reproduced at trial, what about the conditions surrounding the identification of the photo?—such as police suggestion as to whom to pick, whether the witness was completely certain in his choice, etc. Doesn't counsel need to know about all of these factors in order to effectively cross-examine the identifying witness? How can counsel know these factors if she wasn't there?

What if a charged defendant is identified in a *photograph of a lineup*? Does the lineup rule of *Wade* control, so that counsel is required? In United States v. Barker, 988 F.2d 77 (9th Cir.1993), the court held that *Ash* rather than *Wade* applied to such an identification. It explained as follows:

> This case is a hybrid: it involves a photograph of a lineup. The fact that the lineup is depicted in the photograph, though, does not call into question the reasoning behind the decision in *Ash*. Counsel must be present where there is a potential "that the accused might be misled by his lack of familiarity with the law or overpowered by his professional adversary," or where counsel would "produce equality in a trial-like adversary confrontation." Here, as in *Ash*, the defendant is not present when the photograph of the lineup is shown and thus cannot be "misled" or "overpowered," and the "adversary mechanism remains as effective for a photographic display as for other parts of a pretrial interview" whether the photos concerned are of a lineup or an array of suspects.

While it is probably true that the rationale of *Ash* is applicable to all photographic identifications, did the Court in *Ash* adequately state the rationale of *Wade*? Was counsel required in *Wade* in order to keep the *defendant* from being misled or overpowered? Or did the Court think that counsel was required in order to guarantee adequate cross-examination of the identification witnesses? If adequate cross-examination was the goal, why would counsel's presence not be required at a photographic identification?

## B. DUE PROCESS LIMITATIONS ON IDENTIFICATION EVIDENCE

### 1.   The Foundations of a Due Process Test

#### *Stovall v. Denno*

On the same day that it decided *Wade* and *Gilbert,* the Court ruled that those decisions applied prospectively only (which meant that only Wade and Gilbert would get the benefit of the decisions and that the counsel requirement would only apply to future lineups or showups). Stovall v. Denno, 388 U.S. 293 (1967) (applying retroactivity analysis that has since been rejected by the Court; see Chapter 1). The important point from *Stovall* today is not about retroactivity but rather about what protections exist for identification procedures where the right to counsel does not apply. The Court in *Stovall* held that a *due process-fundamental fairness* approach would be used in assessing identification procedures that are not governed by *Wade* and *Gilbert*. As stated above, after *Kirby* and *Ash,* the application of *Wade* and *Gilbert* is limited to post-indictment corporeal identifications. The due process test set forth in *Stovall,* and developed in later cases discussed below, therefore governs the admissibility of most identification evidence. Justice Brennan, again writing for the Court, described the relevant facts in *Stovall*:

> Dr. Paul Behrendt was stabbed to death in the kitchen of his home in Garden City, Long Island, about midnight August 23, 1961. Dr. Behrendt's wife, also a physician, had followed her husband to the kitchen and jumped at the assailant. He knocked her to the floor and stabbed her 11 times. The police found a shirt on the kitchen floor and keys in a pocket which they traced to petitioner. They arrested him on the afternoon of August 24. An arraignment was promptly held but was postponed until petitioner could retain counsel.

> Mrs. Behrendt was hospitalized for major surgery to save her life. The police, without affording petitioner time to retain counsel, arranged with her surgeon to permit them to bring petitioner to her hospital room about noon of August 25, the day after the surgery. Petitioner was handcuffed to one of five police officers who, with two members of the staff of the District Attorney, brought him to the hospital room. Petitioner was the only Negro in the room. Mrs. Behrendt identified him from her hospital bed after being asked by an officer whether he "was the man" and after petitioner repeated at the direction of an officer a "few words for voice identification." None of the witnesses could recall the words that were used. Mrs. Behrendt and the officers testified at the trial to her identification of the petitioner in the hospital room, and she also made an in-court identification of petitioner in the courtroom.

> Petitioner was convicted and sentenced to death. * * *

After holding that *Wade* and *Gilbert* would not be applied retroactively, the Court considered Stovall's contention that "in any event the confrontation conducted in this case was so unnecessarily suggestive and conducive to irreparable mistaken identification that he was denied due process of law." Justice Brennan analyzed this question by focusing on whether it was necessary for the police to act as they did.

> The practice of showing suspects singly to persons for the purpose of identification, and not as part of a lineup, has been widely condemned. However, a claimed violation of due process of law in the conduct of a confrontation depends on the totality of the circumstances surrounding it, and the record in the present case

reveals that the showing of Stovall to Mrs. Behrendt in an immediate hospital confrontation was imperative.

Justice Brennan then quoted approvingly from the Court of Appeals' decision finding no due process violation:

"Here was the only person in the world who could possibly exonerate Stovall. Her words, and only her words, 'He is not the man' could have resulted in freedom for Stovall. The hospital was not far distant from the courthouse and jail. No one knew how long Mrs. Behrendt might live. Faced with the responsibility of identifying the attacker, with the need for immediate action and with the knowledge that Mrs. Behrendt could not visit the jail, the police followed the only feasible procedure and took Stovall to the hospital room. Under these circumstances, the usual police station lineup, which Stovall now argues he should have had, was out of the question."

Note that the Court in *Stovall* did not mention the possible unreliability of the identification, even though Stovall was handcuffed and was the only African-American man in the room. Does the Court mean that even *unreliable* identifications are constitutionally permissible so long as the police have a legitimate excuse for conducting a suggestive identification? Conversely, if the police had no good reason for acting as they did, would the Court then be concerned about whether the identification was reliable? These questions were taken up by the Court in such cases as Manson v. Brathwaite and Perry v. New Hampshire, discussed below.

Note also that Mrs. Behrendt, the witness who made the identification in *Stovall,* survived her attack and testified at trial. Of course, her survival was a happy event; but could this lead you to question whether there was really such an emergency as to excuse the suggestive activity in *Stovall?* Part of the reason the hospital show-up was held permissible was that this was the only procedure that could have resulted in exoneration for Stovall. But if that is the case, why not let Stovall decide whether he wants to be subject to a show-up identification in handcuffs? If Stovall had been given the option to "exonerate" himself in this way, what do you think he would have done?

### *Permissible Suggestiveness?*

Cases arise from time to time in which the government argues, as in *Stovall*, that there was a legitimate excuse for conducting a suggestive identification procedure. Sometimes these claims are rebuffed. For example, in Neil v. Biggers, 409 U.S. 188 (1972), Biggers was identified in a one-on-one showup by the victim of a rape. The government offered an excuse for conducting the one-on-one showup: the officers tried to conduct a lineup, but when they checked the city jail and the juvenile home for people who looked similar to Biggers, they found no one at either place fitting the suspect's "unusual physical description." The Court stated that it was "inclined to agree with the courts below that the police did not exhaust all possibilities in seeking persons physically comparable to respondent." Yet in *Biggers*, the unnecessarily suggestive identification was nonetheless held admissible. Cases such as Manson v. Brathwaite, infra, discuss how this could be so.

On the other hand, street identifications held immediately after the crime have often been excused as "necessarily" suggestive. Whenever a court finds necessary suggestiveness, it does not conduct examine the reliability of the identification. A typical analysis is found in United States v. Bautista, 23 F.3d 726 (2nd Cir.1994), a case in which the suspects were presented, in handcuffs, for an identification by a confidential informant (CI) immediately after a drug raid:

> We find that the presentation of the suspects to the CI immediately following the raid was not *unnecessarily* suggestive. * * * [A] prompt showing of a detained suspect at the scene of arrest has a very valid function: to prevent the mistaken arrest of innocent persons. Indeed, this court has instructed law enforcement officials that where an officer has or should have doubts whether a detained suspect is in fact the person sought, the officer must make immediate reasonable efforts to confirm the suspect's identity.
>
> * * *
>
> The fact that the suspects were handcuffed, in the custody of law enforcement officers, and illuminated by flashlights * * * did not render the pre-trial identification procedure unnecessarily suggestive. In this case, handcuffs, custody, and flashlights were all necessary incidents of an on-the-scene identification immediately following a night-time narcotics raid. Because the on-the-scene identification was necessary to allow the officers to release the innocent, the incidents of that identification were also necessary.

See also United States v. Martinez, 462 F.3d 903 (8th Cir.2006) ("Police officers need not limit themselves to station house lineups when an opportunity for a quick, on-the-scene identification arises. Such identifications are essential to free innocent suspects and to inform the police if further investigation is necessary."); Brisco v. Ercole, 565 F.3d 80 (2nd Cir. 2009) (show-up immediately after the crime was not unnecessarily suggestive: "If no identification was made at the showup, the officers could resume their search for the offender"); United States v. Sanders, 708 F.3d 976 (7th Cir. 2013) (identification of the perpetrator from photos found in a car at the scene was not unnecessary: "It would have taken significantly more time for the police to leave the scene, go to the station house, locate photos similar to those found in the car, and return. A dangerous suspect could have used that extra time to facilitate his escape.").

## 2.  Applying the Due Process Test

### *Simmons v. United States*

In Simmons v. United States, 390 U.S. 377 (1968), a bank was robbed by two men. Andrews and Simmons were suspected. The FBI had shown the bank employees at least six pictures, mostly group photos of Andrews, Simmons, and others, and some individual snapshots of Simmons and Andrews. Simmons and Andrews were identified; the witnesses identified Simmons at his trial, but the prosecution made no mention of the pre-trial identification. Simmons challenged the identification procedures under the Due Process Clause. The Court stated that the due process test protects against identifications that are "so impermissibly suggestive as to give rise to a very substantial likelihood of irreparable misidentification." Applying that test to the facts, the Court emphasized the following factors: the officers had a pressing need for fast action; Simmons was readily identified by the witnesses, while Andrews was not, even though Andrews was in many of the same pictures as Simmons; the witnesses had an excellent opportunity to observe the robbery and the perpetrators; and the identification was made shortly after the robbery.

The *Simmons* Court found no due process violation "even though the identification procedure employed may have in some respects fallen short of the ideal." The Court concluded that the witnesses' bases for making the identification was so strong that it was unaffected by any police suggestiveness.

### *Violation of Due Process: Foster v. California*

In Foster v. California, 394 U.S. 440 (1969), the Court found for the first time—and so far the only time—that a police procedure was so impermissibly suggestive as to create a substantial risk of mistaken identification under the Due Process Clause. The eyewitness was called to the station to view a three-person lineup. Foster, who was six feet tall, was placed between two men who were both six inches shorter. Only Foster wore a jacket similar to that of the perpetrator. The witness could not positively identify Foster. Foster was then brought into an office for a one-on-one showup. The witness could still not make a positive identification. A week later, the witness viewed a second lineup. Only Foster remained from the first lineup. At this point, the witness positively identified Foster. This identification was admitted at trial pursuant to the California hearsay exception discussed in *Gilbert*, and the witness also identified Foster at trial.

The Supreme Court stated that the "suggestive elements in this identification procedure made it all but inevitable that [the witness] would identify petitioner whether or not he was in fact the man," and that the procedure "so undermined the reliability of the eyewitness identification as to violate due process." The Court held that both the in-court and out-of-court identifications were improperly admitted, because both were tainted by the police suggestiveness.

### The Independent Source: Neil v. Biggers

In Neil v. Biggers, 409 U.S. 188 (1972), the defendant was convicted of rape, after the victim identified him at trial and described her pretrial identification of Biggers. For seven months after the rape, the victim viewed lineups, one person showups, and photographs, but was unable to identify her assailant. One day the police arrested Biggers on an unrelated charge. They brought the victim to the police station, walked Biggers past her, and directed him to utter certain words. The victim identified Biggers. Justice Powell's opinion for the Court stated that "the primary evil to be avoided is a very substantial likelihood of irreparable misidentification." Thus, the question was whether the identification was reliable "even though the confrontation procedure was suggestive." On the facts, the Court found that the police suggestiveness did not cause the identification to be made, and therefore "the identification was reliable even though the confrontation procedure was suggestive." Essentially, the Court found that the witness had an independent source for the identification—her experience with the perpetrator at the time of the crime.

Thus, the Court's approach to admissibility under the Due Process Clause is whether the witness had an accurate picture of the perpetrator in his or her mind *before* the unnecessary police suggestiveness occurred, and whether that suggestiveness altered that picture in any way. To determine whether suggestiveness *caused* the identification, a court must investigate how clear the witness's pre-identification picture was; this is determined by such factors as how good a look the witness got during or before the crime, how attentive the witness was, and whether memory loss has faded the picture in the witness's mind by the time of the identification. Inferences are drawn about the clarity of the picture in the witness's mind by descriptions given by the witness, by whether the witness has mistakenly identified another person as the criminal, by whether the witness's description fits the person that is identified, and by the certainty of the witness at the time the defendant is identified. After *Biggers,* police suggestiveness is not the predominant inquiry that it may have appeared to be in *Stovall.* Rather, it is only one factor among the totality of circumstances to be considered. The following case makes this clear.

## 3.  Unnecessary Police Suggestiveness Is Not Enough

### MANSON V. BRATHWAITE
Supreme Court of the United States, 1977.
432 U.S. 98.

**MR. JUSTICE BLACKMUN delivered the opinion of the Court.**

This case presents the issue as to whether the Due Process Clause of the Fourteenth Amendment compels the exclusion, in a state criminal trial, apart from any consideration of reliability, of pretrial identification evidence obtained by a police procedure that was both suggestive and unnecessary. This Court's decisions in Stovall v. Denno and Neil v. Biggers are particularly implicated.

\* \* \*

Jimmy D. Glover, a full-time trooper of the Connecticut State Police, in 1970 was assigned to the Narcotics Division in an undercover capacity. On May 5 of that year, about 7:45 p.m., e.d.t., and while there was still daylight, Glover and Henry Alton Brown, an informant, went to an apartment building at 201 Westland, in Hartford, for the purpose of purchasing narcotics from "Dickie Boy" Cicero, a known narcotics dealer. Cicero, it was thought, lived on the third floor of that apartment building. Glover and Brown entered the building, observed by backup Officers D'Onofrio and Gaffey, and proceeded by stairs to the third floor. Glover knocked at the door of one of the two apartments served by the stairway. The area was illuminated by natural light from a window in the third floor hallway. The door was opened 12 to 18 inches in response to the knock. Glover observed a man standing at the door and, behind him, a woman. Brown identified himself. Glover then asked for "two things" of narcotics. The man at the door held out his hand, and Glover gave him two $10 bills. The door closed. Soon the man returned and handed Glover two glassine bags. While the door was open, Glover stood within two feet of the person from whom he made the purchase and observed his face. Five to seven minutes elapsed from the time the door first opened until it closed the second time.

Glover and Brown then left the building. This was about eight minutes after their arrival. Glover drove to headquarters where he described the seller to D'Onofrio and Gaffey. \* \* \* He described him as being "a colored man, approximately five feet eleven inches tall, dark complexion, black hair, short Afro style, and having high cheekbones, and of heavy build. He was wearing at the time blue pants and a plaid shirt." D'Onofrio, suspecting from this description that respondent might be the seller, obtained a photograph of respondent from the Records Division of the Hartford Police Department. He left it at Glover's office. D'Onofrio was not acquainted with respondent personally, but did know him by sight and had seen him "[s]everal times" prior to May 5. Glover, when alone, viewed the photograph for the first time upon his return to headquarters on May 7; he identified the person shown as the one from whom he had purchased the narcotics. * * * No explanation was offered by the prosecution for the failure to utilize a photographic array or to conduct a lineup.

[The photo identification was admitted at trial, and Glover also identified the defendant at trial. The defendant was convicted, but the Second Circuit reversed the conviction on the ground that the officers engaged in impermissible suggestiveness during the identification procedure. It did not matter to the Second Circuit that the identification might have been made despite, rather than because of, the suggestive procedure.]

[The Court discusses its precedents, all of which have been discussed, supra.]

* * *

Petitioner at the outset acknowledges that "the procedure in the instant case was suggestive [because only one photograph was used] and unnecessary" [because there was no emergency or exigent circumstance]. The respondent, in agreement with the Court of Appeals, proposes a *per se* rule of exclusion that he claims is dictated by the demands of the Fourteenth Amendment's guarantee of due process. * * *

Since the decision in *Biggers,* the Courts of Appeals appear to have developed at least two approaches to [identification] evidence. The first, or *per se* approach, employed by the Second Circuit in the present case, focuses on the procedures employed and requires exclusion of the out-of-court identification evidence, without regard to reliability, whenever it has been obtained through unnecessarily suggestive confrontation procedures. The justifications advanced are the elimination of evidence of uncertain reliability, deterrence of the police and prosecutors, and the stated "fair assurance against the awful risks of misidentification."

The second, or more lenient, approach is one that continues to rely on the totality of the circumstances. It permits the admission of the confrontation evidence if, despite the suggestive aspect, the out-of-court identification possesses certain features of reliability. Its adherents feel that the *per se* approach is not mandated by the Due Process Clause of the Fourteenth Amendment. This second approach, in contrast to the other, is *ad hoc* and serves to limit the societal costs imposed by a sanction that excludes relevant evidence from consideration and evaluation by the trier of fact.

The respondent here stresses * * * the need for deterrence of improper identification practice, a factor he regards as pre-eminent.

Photographic identification, it is said, continues to be needlessly employed. * * * He argues that a totality rule cannot be expected to have a significant deterrent impact; only a strict rule of exclusion will have direct and immediate impact on law enforcement agents. Identification evidence is so convincing to the jury that sweeping exclusionary rules are required. * * *

There are, of course, several interests to be considered and taken into account. The driving force behind United States v. Wade and Gilbert v. California (right to counsel at a post-indictment lineup), and *Stovall,* all decided on the same day, was the Court's concern with the problems of eyewitness identification. Usually the witness must testify about an encounter with a total stranger under circumstances of emergency or emotional stress. The witness' recollection of the stranger can be distorted easily by the circumstances or by later actions of the police. Thus, *Wade* and its companion cases reflect the concern that the jury not hear eyewitness testimony unless that evidence has aspects of reliability. It must be observed that both approaches before us are responsive to this concern. The *per se* rule, however, goes too far since its application automatically and peremptorily, and without consideration of alleviating factors, keeps evidence from the jury that is reliable and relevant.

The second factor is deterrence. Although the *per se* approach has the more significant deterrent effect, the totality approach also has an influence on police behavior. The police will guard against unnecessarily suggestive procedures under the totality rule, as well as the *per se* one, for fear that their actions will lead to the exclusion of identifications as unreliable.

The third factor is the effect on the administration of justice. Here the *per se* approach suffers serious drawbacks. Since it denies the trier reliable evidence, it may result, on occasion, in the guilty going free. Also, because of its rigidity, the *per se* approach may make error by the trial judge more likely than the totality approach. And in those cases in which the admission of identification evidence is error under the *per se* approach but not under the totality approach—cases in which the identification is reliable despite an unnecessarily suggestive identification procedure— reversal is a Draconian sanction. Certainly, inflexible rules of exclusion, that may frustrate rather than promote justice, have not been viewed recently by this Court with unlimited enthusiasm.

* * *

We therefore conclude that reliability is the linchpin in determining the admissibility of identification testimony for both pre-and post-*Stovall* confrontations. The factors to be considered are set out in *Biggers.* These include the opportunity of the witness to view the criminal at the time of the crime, the witness' degree of attention, the accuracy of his prior description of the criminal, the level of certainty demonstrated at the confrontation, and the time between the crime and the confrontation. Against these factors is to be weighed the corrupting effect of the suggestive identification itself.

V

We turn, then, to the facts of this case and apply the analysis:

1. *The opportunity to view.* Glover testified that for two to three minutes he stood at the apartment door, within two feet of the respondent. The door opened twice, and each time the man stood at the door. The moments passed, the conversation took place, and payment was made. Glover looked directly at his vendor. It was near sunset, to be sure, but the sun had not yet set, so it was not dark or even dusk or twilight. Natural light from outside entered the hallway through a window. There was natural light, as well, from inside the apartment.

2. *The degree of attention.* Glover was not a casual or passing observer, as is so often the case with eyewitness identification. Trooper Glover was a trained police officer on duty—and specialized and dangerous duty—when he called at the third floor of 201 Westland in Hartford on May 5, 1970. Glover himself was a Negro and unlikely to perceive only general features of "hundreds of Hartford black males," as the Court of Appeals stated. It is true that Glover's duty was that of ferreting out narcotics offenders and that he would be expected in his work to produce results. But it is also true that, as a specially trained, assigned, and experienced officer, he could be expected to pay scrupulous attention to detail, for he knew that subsequently he would have to find and arrest his vendor. In addition, he knew that his claimed observations would be subject later to close scrutiny and examination at any trial.

3. *The accuracy of the description.* Glover's description was given to D'Onofrio within minutes after the transaction. It included the vendor's race, his height, his build, the color and style of his hair, and the high cheekbone facial feature. It also included clothing the vendor wore. No claim has been made that respondent did not possess the physical characteristics so described. D'Onofrio reacted positively at once. Two days later, when Glover was alone, he viewed the photograph D'Onofrio produced and identified its subject as the narcotics seller.

4. *The witness' level of certainty.* There is no dispute that the photograph in question was that of respondent. Glover, in response to a question whether the photograph was that of the person from whom he made the purchase, testified: "There is no question whatsoever." This positive assurance was repeated.

5. *The time between the crime and the confrontation.* Glover's description of his vendor was given to D'Onofrio within minutes of the

crime. The photographic identification took place only two days later. We do not have here the passage of weeks or months between the crime and the viewing of the photograph.

These indicators of Glover's ability to make an accurate identification are hardly outweighed by the corrupting effect of the challenged identification itself. Although identifications arising from single-photograph displays may be viewed in general with suspicion, we find in the instant case little pressure on the witness to acquiesce in the suggestion that such a display entails. D'Onofrio had left the photograph at Glover's office and was not present when Glover first viewed it two days after the event. There thus was little urgency and Glover could view the photograph at his leisure. And since Glover examined the photograph alone, there was no coercive pressure to make an identification arising from the presence of another. The identification was made in circumstances allowing care and reflection. * * *

Surely, we cannot say that under all the circumstances of this case there is "a very substantial likelihood of irreparable misidentification." Short of that point, such evidence is for the jury to weigh. We are content to rely upon the good sense and judgment of American juries, for evidence with some element of untrustworthiness is customary grist for the jury mill. Juries are not so susceptible that they cannot measure intelligently the weight of identification testimony that has some questionable feature.

* * *

**MR. JUSTICE STEVENS, concurring.**

* * * [I]n evaluating the admissibility of particular identification testimony it is sometimes difficult to put other evidence of guilt entirely to one side. Mr. Justice Blackmun's opinion for the Court carefully avoids this pitfall and correctly relies only on appropriate indicia of the reliability of the identification itself. Although I consider the factual question in this case extremely close, I am persuaded that the Court has resolved it properly.

**MR. JUSTICE MARSHALL, with whom MR. JUSTICE BRENNAN joins, dissenting.**

Today's decision can come as no surprise to those who have been watching the Court dismantle the protections against mistaken eyewitness testimony erected a decade ago * * *. But it is still distressing to see the Court virtually ignore the teaching of experience embodied in those decisions and blindly uphold the conviction of a defendant who may well be innocent.

\* \* \*

[T]he Court gives passing consideration to the dangers of eyewitness identification recognized in the *Wade* trilogy. It concludes, however, that the grave risk of error does not justify adoption of the *per se* approach because that would too often result in exclusion of relevant evidence. In my view, this conclusion totally ignores the lessons of *Wade.* \* \* \*

Finally, the Court errs in its assessment of the relative impact of the two approaches on the administration of justice. \* \* \* [O]ther exclusionary rules have been criticized for preventing jury consideration of relevant and usually reliable evidence in order to serve interests unrelated to guilt or innocence, such as discouraging illegal searches or denial of counsel. Suggestively obtained eyewitness testimony is excluded, in contrast, precisely because of its unreliability and concomitant irrelevance.

\* \* \*

[Justice Marshall applies the majority's "totality of circumstances" test to the facts of the case. He points out that the transaction occurred quickly and the opportunity for observation was brief, argues that the witness's degree of certainty is worthless as a guarantee of reliability, notes that the greatest memory loss occurs within hours after an event, and concluded that Glover's description "was actually no more than a general summary of the seller's appearance."]

### QUESTIONS AFTER MANSON

In evaluating who has the better of the argument in *Manson* on whether exclusion should occur *solely* because of police suggestiveness, consider the following hypothetical. A victim of a kidnaping, who lived in close quarters with the perpetrator for six months, finally escapes. He contacts the police and describes the kidnapper in perfect detail, including a distinctive scar on the kidnapper's forehead. The defendant is apprehended, and the victim views him in a one-on-one show-up, while the defendant is in handcuffs and prison clothing. The defendant has the distinctive scar described by the victim. The victim immediately identifies the defendant with absolute certainty. The police had no reason for failing to conduct a lineup.

Under the per se rule rejected in *Manson,* this identification would be inadmissible; but the in-court identification would be admissible because it proceeded from an independent source. Does this make sense? One could argue that it does because otherwise police will not be deterred from conducting suggestive identifications. Moreover, the cost of exclusion to the state is not significant because the in-court identification will still be admissible, and the police could always conduct a lineup *after* this suggestive procedure. The identification from that subsequent lineup, like the in-court identification, would proceed from an independent source and would therefore be admissible. But if the rule of exclusion can be so easily evaded, is it worth having? Ultimately, the question is whether the *per se* rule would be a more effective deterrent than the totality of circumstances test chosen by the Court. There is certainly strong evidence that the *Manson* test, at least as applied by the courts, does little to deter the police from using suggestive identification procedures. For example, the Court has denounced the use of unnecessary show-ups in most of the cases arising between *Wade* and *Braithwaite*. Yet, in 1990, the court in Rodriguez v. Young, 906 F.2d 1153 (7th Cir.), noted with distress "that we continue to review cases both of showups and other suggestive procedures," and that "in few of these cases do we ever find an explanation, by the prosecution, for the failure to conduct a lineup." Of course, the court in *Rodriguez* held that the identification was admissible despite the police suggestiveness (because the witness had a good view of the suspect at the time of the crime), so it will continue to hear more such cases.

Some state courts have called the reasoning of *Manson* into question and have required trial judges to take special care in assessing the reliability of eyewitness testimony. Two such cases are State v. Lawson, 352 Ore. 724, 291 P.3d 673 (2012); and State v. Henderson, 208 N.J. 208, 27 A.3d 872 (2011). Efforts by these and other courts to improve the reliability of the identification process are discussed later in this Chapter.

## 4. Unnecessary Police Suggestiveness Required for a Due Process Violation.

In the following case, the court clarifies whether due process regulation of identifications is concerned only with regulating unreliability, or whether police misconduct is a threshold requirement.

### PERRY V. NEW HAMPSHIRE

Supreme Court of the United States, 2012.
132 S.Ct. 716.

### JUSTICE GINSBURG delivered the opinion of the Court.

\* \* \*

An identification infected by improper police influence, our case law holds, is not automatically excluded. Instead, the trial judge must screen the evidence for reliability pretrial. If there is a very substantial likelihood of irreparable misidentification, the judge must disallow presentation of the evidence at trial. But if the indicia of reliability are strong enough to outweigh the corrupting effect of the police-arranged suggestive circumstances, the identification evidence ordinarily will be admitted, and the jury will ultimately determine its worth.

We have not extended pretrial screening for reliability to cases in which the suggestive circumstances were not arranged by law enforcement officers. Petitioner requests that we do so because of the grave risk that mistaken identification will yield a miscarriage of justice. Our decisions, however, turn on the presence of state action and aim to deter police from rigging identification procedures, for example, at a lineup, showup, or photograph array. When no improper law enforcement activity is involved, we hold, it suffices to test reliability through the rights and opportunities generally designed for that purpose, notably, the presence of counsel at postindictment lineups, vigorous cross-examination, protective rules of evidence, and jury instructions on both the fallibility of eyewitness identification and the requirement that guilt be proved beyond a reasonable doubt.

\* \* \*

Around 3 a.m. on August 15, 2008, Joffre Ullon called the Nashua, New Hampshire, Police Department and reported that an African-American male was trying to break into cars parked in the lot of Ullon's apartment building. Officer Nicole Clay responded to the call. Upon arriving at the parking lot, Clay heard what "sounded like a metal bat hitting the ground." She then saw petitioner Barion Perry standing between two cars. Perry walked toward Clay, holding two car-stereo amplifiers in his hands. A metal bat lay on the ground behind him. Clay asked Perry where the amplifiers came from. "[I] found them on the ground," Perry responded.

Meanwhile, Ullon's wife, Nubia Blandon, woke her neighbor, Alex Clavijo, and told him she had just seen someone break into his car. Clavijo immediately went downstairs to the parking lot to inspect the car. He first observed that one of the rear windows had been shattered. On further inspection, he discovered that the speakers and amplifiers from his car stereo were missing, as were his bat and wrench. Clavijo then approached Clay and told her about Blandon's alert and his own subsequent observations.

By this time, another officer had arrived at the scene. Clay asked Perry to stay in the parking lot with that officer, while she and Clavijo went to talk to Blandon. Clay and Clavijo then entered the apartment building and took the stairs to the fourth floor, where Blandon's and Clavijo's apartments were located. They met Blandon in the hallway just outside the open door to her apartment.

Asked to describe what she had seen, Blandon stated that, around 2:30 a.m., she saw from her kitchen window a tall, African-American man roaming the parking lot and looking into cars. Eventually, the man circled Clavijo's car, opened the trunk, and removed a large box.[b]

---

[b] The box, which Clay found on the ground near where she first encountered Perry, contained car-stereo speakers.

Clay asked Blandon for a more specific description of the man. Blandon pointed to her kitchen window and said the person she saw breaking into Clavijo's car was standing in the parking lot, next to the police officer. Perry's arrest followed this identification. About a month later, the police showed Blandon a photographic array that included a picture of Perry and asked her to point out the man who had broken into Clavijo's car. Blandon was unable to identify Perry.

\* \* \*

[The State courts rejected Perry's challenge to Blandon's identification. They found that the police had not engaged in any unnecessarily suggestive tactics, and therefore found it unnecessary to decide whether the identification was reliable.]

We granted certiorari to resolve a division of opinion on the question whether the Due Process Clause requires a trial judge to conduct a preliminary assessment of the reliability of an eyewitness identification made under suggestive circumstances not arranged by the police.

\* \* \*

The Constitution, our decisions indicate, protects a defendant against a conviction based on evidence of questionable reliability, not by prohibiting introduction of the evidence, but by affording the defendant means to persuade the jury that the evidence should be discounted as unworthy of credit. Constitutional safeguards available to defendants to counter the State's evidence include the Sixth Amendment rights to counsel, compulsory process, and confrontation plus cross-examination of witnesses. Apart from these guarantees, we have recognized, state and federal statutes and rules ordinarily govern the admissibility of evidence, and juries are assigned the task of determining the reliability of the evidence presented at trial. \* \* \* Only when evidence is so extremely unfair that its admission violates fundamental conceptions of justice, have we imposed a constraint tied to the Due Process Clause. See, e.g., Napue v. Illinois, 360 U.S. 264, 269 (1959) (Due process prohibits the State's "knowin[g] use [of] false evidence," because such use violates "any concept of ordered liberty.").

Contending that the Due Process Clause is implicated here, Perry relies on a series of decisions involving police-arranged identification procedures. [The Court discusses Stovall v. Denno, Simmons v. United States, Foster v. California, Neil v. Biggers, and Manson v. Brathwaite.]

A rule requiring automatic exclusion, the [*Manson*] Court reasoned, would go too far, for it would keep evidence from the jury that is reliable and relevant, and may result, on occasion, in the guilty going free. \* \* \*

Instead of mandating a *per se* exclusionary rule, the [*Manson*] Court held that the Due Process Clause requires courts to assess, on a case-by-case basis, whether improper police conduct created a "substantial likelihood of misidentification." "[R]eliability [of the eyewitness identification] is the linchpin" of that evaluation * * *. Where the "indicators of [a witness's] ability to make an accurate identification" are "outweighed by the corrupting effect" of law enforcement suggestion, the identification should be suppressed. Otherwise, the evidence (if admissible in all other respects) should be submitted to the jury.

* * *

Perry concedes that, in contrast to every case in the *Stovall* line, law enforcement officials did not arrange the suggestive circumstances surrounding Blandon's identification. * * * He contends, however, that it was mere happenstance that each of the *Stovall* cases involved improper police action. The rationale underlying our decisions, Perry asserts, supports a rule requiring trial judges to prescreen eyewitness evidence for reliability any time an identification is made under suggestive circumstances. We disagree.

Perry's argument depends, in large part, on the Court's statement in *Brathwaite* that "reliability is the linchpin in determining the admissibility of identification testimony." If reliability is the linchpin of admissibility under the Due Process Clause, Perry maintains, it should make no difference whether law enforcement was responsible for creating the suggestive circumstances that marred the identification.

Perry has removed our statement in *Brathwaite* from its mooring, and thereby attributes to the statement a meaning a fair reading of our opinion does not bear. [T]he *Brathwaite* Court's reference to reliability appears in a portion of the opinion concerning the appropriate remedy *when the police use an unnecessarily suggestive identification procedure.* The Court adopted a judicial screen for reliability as a course preferable to a *per se* rule requiring exclusion of identification evidence whenever law enforcement officers employ an improper procedure. The due process check for reliability, *Brathwaite* made plain, comes into play only after the defendant establishes improper police conduct. The very purpose of the check, the Court noted, was to avoid depriving the jury of identification evidence that is reliable, *notwithstanding* improper police conduct.

Perry's contention that improper police action was not essential to the reliability check *Brathwaite* required is echoed by the dissent. Both ignore a key premise of the *Brathwaite* decision: A primary aim of excluding identification evidence obtained under unnecessarily suggestive circumstances, the Court said, is to deter law enforcement use of improper lineups, showups, and photo arrays in the first place. Alerted to the prospect that identification evidence improperly obtained may be excluded, the Court reasoned, police officers will "guard against unnecessarily suggestive procedures." This deterrence rationale is inapposite in cases, like Perry's, in which the police engaged in no improper conduct.

* * *

Perry's argument, reiterated by the dissent, thus lacks support in the case law he cites. Moreover, his position would open the door to judicial preview, under the banner of due process, of most, if not all, eyewitness identifications. External suggestion is hardly the only factor that casts doubt on the trustworthiness of an eyewitness's testimony. As one of Perry's *amici* points out, many other factors bear on "the likelihood of misidentification,"—for example, the passage of time between exposure to and identification of the defendant, whether the witness was under stress when he first encountered the suspect, how much time the witness had to observe the suspect, how far the witness was from the suspect, whether the suspect carried a weapon, and the race of the suspect and the witness. There is no reason why an identification made by an eyewitness with poor vision, for example, or one who harbors a grudge against the defendant, should be regarded as inherently more reliable, less of a "threat to the fairness of trial," than the identification Blandon made in this case. To embrace Perry's view would thus entail a vast enlargement of the reach of due process as a constraint on the admission of evidence.

Perry maintains that the Court can limit the due process check he proposes to identifications made under "suggestive circumstances." Even if we could rationally distinguish suggestiveness from other factors bearing on the reliability of eyewitness evidence, Perry's limitation would still involve trial courts, routinely, in preliminary examinations. Most eyewitness identifications involve some element of suggestion. Indeed, all in-court identifications do. Out-of-court identifications volunteered by witnesses are also likely to involve suggestive circumstances. * * *

* * * In urging a broadly applicable due process check on eyewitness identifications, Perry maintains that eyewitness identifications are a uniquely unreliable form of evidence. We do not doubt either the importance or the fallibility of eyewitness identifications. * * * We have concluded in other contexts, however, that the potential unreliability of a type of evidence does not alone render its introduction at the defendant's trial fundamentally unfair. * * * We reach a similar conclusion here: The fallibility of eyewitness evidence does not, without the taint of improper state conduct, warrant a due process rule requiring a trial court to screen such evidence for reliability before allowing the jury to assess its creditworthiness.

Our unwillingness to enlarge the domain of due process as Perry and the dissent urge rests, in large part, on our recognition that the jury, not the judge, traditionally determines the reliability of evidence. We also take account of other safeguards built into our adversary system that caution juries against placing undue weight on eyewitness testimony of questionable reliability. These protections include the defendant's Sixth Amendment right to confront the eyewitness. Another is the defendant's right to the effective assistance of an attorney, who can expose the flaws in the eyewitness's testimony during cross-examination and focus the jury's attention on the fallibility of such testimony during opening and closing arguments. Eyewitness-specific jury instructions, which many federal and state courts have adopted, likewise warn the jury to take care in appraising identification evidence. See, e.g., United States v. Telfaire, 469 F.2d 552, 558–559 (CADC 1972) (per curiam) (D. C. Circuit Model Jury Instructions) ("If the identification by the witness may have been influenced by the circumstances under which the defendant was presented to him for identification, you should scrutinize the identification with great care."). * * * The constitutional requirement that the government prove the defendant's guilt beyond a reasonable doubt also impedes convictions based on dubious identification evidence.

State and federal rules of evidence, moreover, permit trial judges to exclude relevant evidence if its probative value is substantially outweighed by its prejudicial impact or potential for misleading the jury. See, e.g., Fed. Rule Evid. 403; N. H. Rule Evid. 403 (2011) . . .   In appropriate cases, some States also permit defendants to present expert testimony on the hazards of eyewitness identification evidence. See, e.g., State v. Clopten, 2009 UT 84, P33, 223 P. 3d 1103, 1113 ("We expect . . . that in cases involving eyewitness identification of strangers or near-strangers, trial courts will routinely admit expert testimony [on the dangers of such evidence].").

Many of the safeguards just noted were at work at Perry's trial. During her opening statement, Perry's court-appointed attorney cautioned the jury about the vulnerability of Blandon's identification. (Blandon, "the eyewitness that the State needs you to believe[,] can't pick [Perry] out of a photo array. How carefully did she really see what was going on? . . . How well could she really see him?"). While cross-examining Blandon and Officer Clay, Perry's attorney constantly brought up the weaknesses of Blandon's identification. She highlighted: (1) the significant distance between Blandon's window and the parking lot, (2) the lateness of the hour, (3) the van that partly obstructed Blandon's view, (4) Blandon's concession that she was "so scared [she] really didn't pay attention" to what Perry was wearing, (5) Blandon's inability to describe Perry's facial features or other identifying marks, (6) Blandon's failure to pick Perry out of a photo array, and (7) Perry's position next to a uniformed, gun-bearing police officer at the moment Blandon made her identification. Perry's counsel reminded the jury of these frailties during her summation. (Blandon "wasn't able to tell you much about who she saw. . . . She couldn't pick [Perry] out of a lineup, out of a photo array. . . . [Blandon said] [t]hat guy that was with the police officer, that's who was circling. Again, think about the context with the guns, the uniforms. Powerful, powerful context clues.").

After closing arguments, the trial court read the jury a lengthy instruction on identification testimony and the factors the jury should consider when evaluating it. The court also instructed the jury that the defendant's guilt must be proved beyond a reasonable doubt, and specifically cautioned that "one of the things the State must prove [beyond a reasonable doubt] is the identification of the defendant as the person who committed the offense."

Given the safeguards generally applicable in criminal trials, protections availed of by the defense in Perry's case, we hold that the introduction of Blandon's eyewitness testimony, without a preliminary judicial assessment of its reliability, did not render Perry's trial fundamentally unfair.

* * *

For the foregoing reasons, we agree with the New Hampshire courts' appraisal of our decisions. Finding no convincing reason to alter our precedent, we hold that the Due Process Clause does not require a preliminary judicial inquiry into the reliability of an eyewitness identification when the identification was not procured under unnecessarily suggestive circumstances arranged by law enforcement. Accordingly, the judgment of the New Hampshire Supreme Court is

*Affirmed.*

### JUSTICE THOMAS, concurring.

The Court correctly concludes that its precedents establish a due process right to the pretrial exclusion of an unreliable eyewitness identification only if the identification results from police suggestion. I therefore join its opinion. I write separately because I would not extend Stovall v. Denno and its progeny even if the reasoning of those opinions applied to this case. The *Stovall* line of cases is premised on a "substantive due process" right to "fundamental fairness." * * * In my view, those cases are wrongly decided because the Fourteenth Amendment's Due Process Clause is not a "secret repository of substantive guarantees against 'unfairness.'" * * * Accordingly, I would limit the Court's suggestive eyewitness identification cases to the precise circumstances that they involved.

### JUSTICE SOTOMAYOR, dissenting.

Our due process concern * * * arises not from the act of suggestion, but rather from the corrosive effects of suggestion on the reliability of the resulting identification. By rendering protection contingent on improper police arrangement of the suggestive circumstances, the Court effectively grafts a *mens rea* inquiry onto our rule. The Court's holding enshrines a murky distinction—between suggestive confrontations intentionally orchestrated by the police and, as here, those inadvertently caused by police actions—that will sow confusion. It ignores our precedents' acute sensitivity to the hazards of intentional and unintentional suggestion alike and unmoors our rule from the very interest it protects, inviting arbitrary results. And it recasts the driving force of our decisions as an interest in police deterrence, rather than reliability. Because I see no warrant for declining to assess the circumstances of this case under our ordinary approach, I respectfully dissent.

\* \* \*

As this case illustrates, police intent is now paramount. As the Court acknowledges, Perry alleges an "accidental showup." He was the only African-American at the scene of the crime standing next to a police officer. For the majority, the fact that the police did not intend that showup, even if they inadvertently caused it in the course of a police procedure, ends the inquiry. The police were questioning the eyewitness, Blandon, about the perpetrator's identity, and were intentionally detaining Perry in the parking lot—but had not intended for Blandon to identify the perpetrator from her window. Presumably, in the majority's view, had the police asked Blandon to move to the window to identify the perpetrator, that could have made all the difference.

\* \* \*

Today's opinion renders the applicability of our ordinary inquiry contingent on a murky line-drawing exercise. Whereas our two-step inquiry focuses on overall reliability—and could account for the spontaneity of the witness' identification and degree of police manipulation under the totality of the circumstances—today's opinion forecloses that assessment by establishing a new and inflexible step zero.

\* \* \*

\* \* \* We once described the "primary evil to be avoided" as the likelihood of misidentification. Today's decision, however, means that even if that primary evil is at its apex, we need not avoid it at all so long as the suggestive circumstances do not stem from improper police arrangement.

\* \* \*

[T]he majority emphasizes that we should rely on the jury to determine the reliability of evidence. But our cases are rooted in the assumption that eyewitness identifications upend the ordinary expectation that it is "the province of the jury to weigh the credibility of competing witnesses." As noted, jurors find eyewitness evidence unusually powerful and their ability to assess credibility is hindered by a witness' false confidence in the accuracy of his or her identification. That disability in no way depends on the intent behind the suggestive circumstances.

\* \* \*

It would be one thing if the passage of time had cast doubt on the empirical premises of our precedents. But just the opposite has happened. A vast body of scientific literature has reinforced every concern our precedents articulated nearly a half-century ago, though it merits barely a parenthetical mention in the majority opinion. Over the past three decades, more than two thousand studies related to eyewitness identification have been published. \* \* \*

\* \* \* Study after study demonstrates that eyewitness recollections are highly susceptible to distortion by post-event information or social cues; that jurors routinely overestimate the accuracy of eyewitness identifications; that jurors place the greatest weight on eyewitness confidence in assessing identifications even though confidence is a poor gauge of accuracy; and that suggestiveness can stem from sources beyond police orchestrated procedures. The majority today nevertheless adopts an artificially narrow conception of the dangers of suggestive identifications at a time when our concerns should have deepened.

\* \* \*

### Independent Source for In-Court Identification?

If an out-of-court identification is excluded under the Due Process Clause, can the witness identify the defendant in court? Recall that under *Wade,* the witness could make an in-court identification if it was free from the taint of the lineup conducted in the absence of counsel. But if the prior identification was caused by *police suggestiveness*, as required for exclusion after *Perry*—and as distinguished from a counsel-free lineup which may not have changed the picture of the perpetrator in the witness's mind—there can by definition be no independent source for the in-court identification. If there were an independent source, then the out-of-court identification *itself* would be admissible. It follows that if the pretrial identification is excluded under the Due Process Clause, the in-court identification must be as well. See Marsden v. Moore, 847 F.2d 1536 (11th Cir.1988) (single photograph procedure creates substantial risk of mistaken identification where witness had only a fleeting glimpse of the perpetrator two years before the identification; in-court identification must be excluded as well); Dispensa v. Lynaugh, 847 F.2d 211 (5th Cir.1988) (identification caused by police suggestiveness requires exclusion of both in-court and out-of-court identification).

## 5. Determining Whether Unnecessary Suggestiveness Caused an Unreliable Identification

There are a lot of reported cases evaluating whether unnecessary police suggestiveness caused an unreliable identification to be made. It is fair to state that in most cases, the courts have refused to find causation, relying on the *Manson* factors: opportunity to view, degree of attention, accuracy of the description, certainty of the witness, and the time between the crime and the identification. See, e.g., Archuleta v. Kirby, 864 F.2d 709 (10th Cir. 1989) (one-on-one showup, with the defendant in cuffs, did not cause an unreliable identification because the witnesses got a lock at the perpetrator's face after the crime, the identification was made 30 minutes after the crime, and the witnesses were certain about their identifications; while the witnesses gave descriptions inconsistent with each other, and both overestimated his height, these discrepancies were "minor errors."

It should be noted that the *Manson* factors have been challenged by the substantial social science that has developed since that case. The American Psychological Association, in a brief filed in *Perry*, urged the Court to revisit its assumptions in *Manson*:

> [M]ost of [the *Manson*] factors are indeed relevant to probable accuracy—with the notable exception of witness certainty. But given that notable exception, and given the plethora of other accuracy-related factors that researchers have identified since *Biggers* and *Manson*, APA urges the Court, in an appropriate case, to revisit the *Manson* framework so as to bring it in line with current scientific knowledge.

It turns out that *Perry* was not an appropriate case, because the Court held that in the absence of police misconduct, there is no call to review the identification for possible unreliability. As one court said, the Court "bypassed this topic in *Perry*, leaving to the future any inquiry into the *Biggers* framework." Phillips v. Allen, 668 F.2d 912 (7th Cir. 2012). See also State v. Henderson, 208 N.J. 208, 27 A.3d 872 (2011): relying on comprehensive review of social science data by a Special Master, the court concluded that the *Manson* factors "do[ ] not offer an adequate measure for reliability."

### *Certainty of the Witness*

How important is it that the witness is *certain* about an identification? The court in Rodriguez v. Young, 906 F.2d 1153 (7th Cir.1990), had this to say about the certainty factor relied upon in *Manson*:

We are skeptical about equating certainty with reliability. Determinations of the reliability suggested by a witness's certainty after the use of suggestive procedures are complicated by the possibility that the certainty may reflect the corrupting effect of the suggestive procedures themselves. Also, the most certain witnesses are not invariably the most reliable ones. We consider certainty a relevant factor but consider it warily.

Empirical data indicates the lack of a significant correlation between certainty and accuracy. See American Psychology Association Brief in *Perry,* supra:

Jurors' evident belief that eyewitness confidence correlates with accurate identifications was once shared by many in the judiciary. Indeed, in *Biggers* this Court stated, albeit without citing any scientific authorities, that confidence is an indication of accuracy. Subsequent research, however, has called this notion into very serious question. As one report concluded, "[t]he outcomes of empirical studies, reviews, and meta-analyses have converged on the conclusion that the confidence-accuracy relationship for eyewitness identification is weak, with average confidence-accuracy correlations generally estimated between little more than 0 and .29." Brewer et al., *The Confidence-Accuracy Relationship in Eyewitness Identification,* 8 J. Experimental Psychol. Applied 44, 44–45 (2002). Even these various correlation figures are likely overestimates, moreover, because the confidence of eyewitnesses in actual cases, unlike in controlled experiments, may be infected by positive feedback received in the investigative process (for example, an officer stating during a photo array or line-up, "good, you identified the suspect").

## 6.   The Effect of Identification Procedures on Trials

Some of the defects in pre-trial lineups may even have an impact on trials aside from possibly tainting identification evidence. If the government uses "mug shots" in a photo identification, the suggestion to the witness will be that the mug shot reflects a prior criminal record of the person photographed. Although the courts will balance the need for the evidence against its possible prejudicial effect, in many cases the photos will be admitted because the circumstances of the identification procedure will be critical to the evidentiary weight to which it is entitled. See, e.g., United States v. Stevens, 935 F.2d 1380 (3d Cir.1991) (submitting "wanted board," with which defendant was identified, to the jury, was permissible under Federal Rule of Evidence 403, even though others on the board were violent felons and defendant had no record of violent activity: "Allowing the jury to inspect the board in its unaltered condition would permit the jurors to determine what, if anything, drew the victims' attention to Stevens"). Thus, the defendant identified by mug shot may have to choose between challenging the identification and protecting against disclosure of a prior record. United States v. McCoy, 848 F.2d 743 (6th Cir.1988) (introducing mug shots prohibited by Rule 403 where the defendant never challenged the suggestiveness of the identification, and therefore did not "open the door").

Can the defendant call *expert witnesses* to testify to the unreliability of identification evidence? How will that testimony help the jury? What kind of people have expertise on this subject? See United States v. Rincon, 28 F.3d 921 (9th Cir.1994) (upholding trial court's exclusion of such evidence on the ground that the expert's testimony was not sufficiently scientific, but emphasizing that there is no per se rule of exclusion); United States v. Brien, 59 F.3d 274 (1st Cir.1995) (finding no abuse of discretion in the trial court's exclusion of the defense expert on the unreliability of identification evidence; the expert's proffered testimony was very general, and did not fit with many of the circumstances underlying the identifications in this case; nor did the expert explicate the methodology by which he concluded that the identifications were unreliable). Compare United States v. Smith, 122 F.3d 1355 (11th Cir. 1997) (expert testimony concerning the unreliability of identification procedures is inadmissible because it does not assist the jury; it is not needed, "because the jury [can] determine the reliability of identification with the tools of cross-examination."). See also United States v. Jones, 689 F.3d 12 (1st Cir. 2012) (trial court did not abuse discretion in excluding expert testimony on identifications and choosing instead to instruct the jury on potential areas of unreliability).

## 7.   The Unreliability of In-Court Identifications

Speaking of unreliable identifications, what can be more suggestive than an identification that occurs *at the trial*? Unfortunately for defendants, any challenge to an in-court identification does not rise to a constitutional argument. This is because, after *Perry,* the Due Process Clause regulates the reliability of identifications only if they have been caused by police misconduct. And there is no police misconduct in an in-court identification. See United States v. Whatley, 719 F.3d 1206 (11th Cir. 2013) (holding that the circuit's previous cases reviewing in-court identifications under the Due Process Clause had been overruled by *Perry*: "under *Perry,* the admission of the in-court identifications of Whatley cannot violate his right to due process because he cannot establish that the suggestive circumstances of the identifications were the result of improper police conduct.")

Can anything be done about the suggestiveness inherent in an identification at trial? Defense counsel in United States v. Brien, 59 F.3d 274 (1st Cir.1995), moved for permission to have the defendant seated in the spectator section of the courtroom and asked leave to "salt the audience with three or four individuals of the same general description as the bank robber." The trial judge responded that he would agree to a "fairly staged courtroom lineup" but that he was concerned about the risk of unfairness to the prosecution in defense counsel's open-ended proposal. Defense counsel did not take the judge up on his offer, and the defendant appealed the conviction as based on an unfair in-court identification. The court of appeals responded as follows:

> If Brien had presented the court with a detailed plan for a fair in-court lineup, and the court had rejected the plan without a plausible justification, then on the present facts we think that a significant issue would be presented. But Brien's motion is not within a country mile of such a proposal. As the trial court sensibly explained, Brien's plan left room for a scenario fully capable of misleading the jury. To alter the standard practice, it was up to Brien's counsel to propose a plan that would guard against unfairness to either side.

Why do you suppose Brien's counsel did not accept the trial judge's offer of a fairly staged courtroom lineup? Why was it Brien's obligation to propose a plan that would guard against unfairness to both sides? Isn't that the prosecution's obligation? See also United States v. Burdeau, 168 F.3d 352 (9th Cir.1999) (trial court has discretion to order an in-court lineup, but no obligation to do so).

## 8.  Voice Identification

Do *voice* identifications raise problems that are different from those encountered in photograph identifications, lineups, show-ups, etc.? Courts use the *Manson* standards for voice identification. But as discussed above, the *Manson* test gives only minimal protection against police suggestiveness for any identification procedure, whether by sight or voice. For example, in United States v. Patton, 721 F.2d 159 (6th Cir.1983), the defendant was charged with making threatening phone calls. The witness identified the defendant's voice at a pretrial "show-up." The court held that the *Manson* test "applies with full force to aural identification." But then the court found that the show-up had not caused a mistaken identification. Applying the *Manson* factors, the court concluded that the witness had an opportunity to hear the defendant's voice during four phone calls; that the witness was attentive to these calls, as evidenced by her description of their content; that the time between the crime and the voice "show-up" was only three weeks; and that, upon hearing the defendant's voice at the "show-up" the witness "immediately recoiled, instantly recognizing the voice." Is the likelihood of mistaken identification any greater with voice identifications than with visual identifications?

## C. NON-CONSTITUTIONAL PROTECTIONS AGAINST UNRELIABLE IDENTIFICATIONS

The effect of police suggestiveness, and the unreliability of many pretrial identifications, are well-documented, as indicated in the excerpt from the Innocence Project set forth at the beginning of this Chapter. It's also fair to state that the Supreme Court has not provided much in the way of constitutional protections that would guarantee the reliability of identification evidence. The lack of constitutional protection has led a number of actors in the criminal justice system in various parts of the country—lawyers, law enforcement officials, and courts included—to propose and to adopt a number of procedures designed to increase the reliability of pretrial identifications.

In 1999, the Justice Department published guidelines developed by the Office of Justice Programs for refining investigative practices dealing with eyewitness identifications. Eyewitness Evidence: A Guide For Law Enforcement (Nat'l Inst. of Justice, Office of Justice Programs, U.S. Dep't of Justice, Oct. 1999); see also Eyewitness Evidence: A Trainer's Manual For Law Enforcement (Nat'l Inst. of Justice, Office of Justice Programs, U.S. Dep't of Justice, Sept. 2003) (together "guidelines"). The guidelines emphasize: (1) the importance of selecting other subjects in arrays and lineups who resemble the suspect in respect to significant features described by the witnesses; (2) the dangers of simultaneous identification procedures—a number of people or photographs brought before the witness at one time—that encourage inaccurate relative judgments; and (3) the inherent suggestiveness of identifications in which only one individual is shown to a witness. The guidelines suggest, among other things, the following:

- Cautionary instructions to the witness that "the person who committed the crime may or may not be present" and that "it is just as important to clear innocent persons from suspicion as to identify guilty parties."

- Instructions to the witness that the procedure requires the investigator to state, in the witness's own words, how certain the witness is of any identification (designed to guard against post-identification inflation of certainty from the confirming feedback of police officers).

- Sequential presentation (designed to discourage a witness's tendency to engage in a relative judgment by identifying the person who looks more like the perpetrator than any of the other alternatives). (See Steblay et al., Eyewitness Accuracy Rates in Sequential and Simultaneous Lineup Presentations, 25 L. & Human Behavior 459 (2001)).

- Blind administration—meaning that the officer who conducts the procedure does not know who the suspect is—thus avoiding the threat of conscious or unconscious influence by the officer.

A number of courts throughout the country have adopted some or all of these standards as conditions for admitting identification evidence. See Fisher, Eyewitness Identification Reform in Massachusetts, 91 Mass. L. Rev. 52 (2008).

One interesting experiment was undertaken by Ramsey County, Minnesota District Attorney, Susan Gaertner, and St. Paul Minnesota Police Chief John Harrington along with other cooperating law enforcement agencies. They describe the experiment, and similar practice in other states, in the April 2009 issue of The Police Chief:

> Ramsey County decided to move ahead in 2005 with a year-long pilot project to test whether implementation of blind sequential lineups was feasible and practical for law enforcement practitioners. The pilot was successful and, in April 2006, the new lineup protocol was adopted as countywide policy by all law enforcement agencies in the jurisdiction. * * * After almost four years of experience with this protocol, the county has concluded that it is feasible, practical, and superior to past eyewitness identification procedures.

> * * *

> The traditional photo identification procedure in Ramsey County, as it has been across the United States, was the simultaneous photo array. The typical photo array contained six photos. It was the usual practice for an investigator with knowledge of the case to show the photo lineup to witnesses.

> The first meta-analysis assessing all laboratory studies comparing the simultaneous and sequential lineup formats came in 2001. It showed that identification errors are significantly more likely (up to three times higher) in a simultaneous format; conversely, the sequential procedure produces fewer misidentifications. The sequential format also produces fewer correct identifications overall. However, the reduction in correct identifications using this method is offset by the much larger reduction of incorrect identifications.

> * * *

> On reflection, the startling scientific evidence that the traditional law enforcement method of offering photo displays might have inadvertently increased the likelihood of misidentification makes sense objectively for two reasons:

- The risk of administrator influence on lineup results can be essentially eliminated by having someone other than the investigator, who knows the identity of the suspect, conduct the photo lineup, whether the lineup is simultaneous or sequential. (Ramsey County has the utmost confidence in the integrity and professionalism of its investigators but recognizes that even the most well-intentioned investigator who knows which person in the lineup is the suspect cannot eliminate all possibility of unintentionally cueing the witness or responding to the witness's identification or nonidentification of that person.)

- Simultaneous photo display tends to encourage relative judgment; that is, a witness comparing photos side by side can more easily pick the person who looks most like the perpetrator—regardless of whether that person is, in fact, the perpetrator.

The scientific evidence made clear that both components were necessary and that each accomplished a different objective. If a nonblind administrator is used, switching from simultaneous to sequential photo displays alone may even increase misidentification, since there is a danger of inadvertently highlighting an individual suspect photo. On the other hand, while recognizing the necessity of blind administration, the county understood the practical realities of conducting photo lineups under the time pressures and the personnel constraints in a criminal investigation and that, especially in a small department, the investigator with knowledge of the case (a nonblind administrator) might be the only one available. The county therefore set up a practical alternative that still maintained the blind component: If no independent administrator is available, the investigator must use a method that is the functional equivalent (FE)—that is, a method that assures that the investigator does not know and cannot see the order in which the photos are presented and that the witness knows this (and therefore will not be looking to the administrator for cues). This is sometimes called a "blinded" method.

* * *

After one year [of the pilot project], the results were clear: investigators who used this method found it not only workable but no more difficult to apply than the traditional method. There were no associated administrative difficulties or additional overtime costs. However, there was an unexpected benefit: most investigators involved in the pilot came to prefer the new method and felt more confident in the eyewitness identifications that resulted. * * *

* * *

Ramsey County is not alone in the adoption of this new eyewitness identification protocol. * * * In addition to the statewide adoption of this procedure in New Jersey and North Carolina, the Wisconsin Attorney General's Office has formally recommended that this change be adopted statewide, and more than 200 Wisconsin law enforcement agencies, including those in Milwaukee and Madison, have done so to date. * * * These examples indicate that the protocol can be adapted for large and small agencies in a variety of settings, urban, suburban, small-town, and rural.

* * *

### *Jury Instructions*

Federal and State courts throughout the country instruct juries to consider the potential unreliability of identification procedures. These instructions are of course tailored to the case, but they cover factors like the difference between a sequential identification and an identification in which all options are present at one time; the questionable validity of a witness being certain of an identification; problems of cross-racial identification; the effect of stress on the reliability of an identification; the threat to reliability if the administrator of the identification procedure is involved in the investigation; the phenomenon of weapons focus; and the impact of disguises and clothing on identifications. For a discussion of jury instructions provided by courts, see American Bar Association Policy 104D: Cross-Racial Identification, 37 Sw. U. L.Rev. 917 (2008).

### *Should These Protections Be Constitutionalized?*

As stated above, the Supreme Court has adhered to its *Manson* test for assessing reliability of eyewitness identifications, even though at least one of the factors—witness certainty—has been discredited by social science, and even though other valid factors such as stress and weapons focus are not on the list. Should the *Manson* analysis be retooled in light of the convincing social science data indicating that it is partially inadequate and clearly incomplete? See Thompson, Eyewitness Identifications and State Courts as Guardians Against Wrongful Conviction, 7 Ohio State Journal of Criminal Law, 603 (2010) (noting state courts that have revised the *Manson* factors to accord with social science data, relying on their own state constitutions.)

# CHAPTER 5

# THE RIGHT TO COUNSEL

∎ ∎ ∎

## I.   THE BACKGROUND

The Sixth Amendment provides that "[i]n all criminal prosecutions, the accused shall enjoy the right * * * to have the Assistance of Counsel for his defence."[1] The right to counsel embodied in the Amendment deviated from the English common-law practice at the time of the American Revolution. Under English law, an accused had a right to have counsel in misdemeanor, but not felony, cases. Although Parliament granted special treatment to those accused under the Treason Act of 1695, and required the court to appoint counsel upon the request of the accused, in ordinary felony cases in England the defendant was not permitted to have counsel until 1836.[2]

When the Constitution was adopted, twelve of the thirteen original states had rejected the English common-law rule and had fully recognized the right to counsel in criminal prosecutions. Powell v. Alabama, 287 U.S. 45, 64–65 (1932). Adoption of the Sixth Amendment formalized this practice. As such, it conveyed the idea that the right to counsel was a grant of privilege—i.e., eliminating the prohibition on counsel—rather than a requirement that counsel be appointed. This can be contrasted with the Federal Crimes Act of 1790, which imposed a statutory *duty* on federal courts in capital cases to assign counsel. 1 Stat. 118 (1790). Although no statute required appointment of counsel in noncapital cases

---

[1] The right to counsel is important in many stages of the criminal process. This is already apparent from the previous chapters. The *Massiah* rule, for example, governed attempts to elicit statements from an accused following an indictment or other formal charge. And the *Wade* and *Gilbert* rules governing lineups following a formal charge also involved a right to counsel. The chapters that follow this one involve the decision to bring formal charges against a suspect, the treatment of the suspect while charges are pending, trials and guilty pleas, sentencing and post-trial procedures. Counsel is important in most of the stages of the criminal process that will be examined. At some point it is useful to look at the *development* of the right to counsel. That look is provided in this Chapter. The discussion of counsel here is limited to establishing how the right to counsel developed and to examining the stages of the process to which the right extends. In Chapter 10, which covers trial rights, the right to counsel at trial is more extensively examined. The doctrine of effective assistance will be discussed there, along with the right of self-representation.

[2] See Faretta v. California, 422 U.S. 806, 821–826 (1975); W. Beaney, The Right to Counsel in American Courts 8–15 (1955); F. Heller, The Sixth Amendment (1951); Holtzoff, The Right of Counsel Under the Sixth Amendment, 20 N.Y.U.L.Rev. 1–22 (1944). Despite the absence of a right to counsel, in practice English courts frequently allowed counsel to argue points of law and to assume other defense functions. W. Beaney at 9–11.

and no one originally read the Sixth Amendment as so requiring, the practice developed of appointing counsel for indigents in serious federal cases.[3]

## II.   THE EARLY DEVELOPMENT OF THE RIGHT

In Johnson v. Zerbst, 304 U.S. 458 (1938), the Court held that the Sixth Amendment requires counsel in federal court in all criminal proceedings, unless the defendant waives the assistance of counsel. (At that point, the Sixth Amendment was not applicable to the States). The Court viewed counsel as a jurisdictional prerequisite to a federal court's authority to deprive an accused of life or liberty.

The right to counsel in state prosecutions for many years was determined exclusively by state law. In 1932, even before Johnson v. Zerbst, the famous "Scottsboro Case" raised the question of whether a failure of the state to make an effective appointment of counsel to indigent defendants in a capital case could deprive the defendants of their rights to due process.

### The Right to Appointed Counsel in Felony Cases

### POWELL V. ALABAMA
Supreme Court of the United States, 1932.
287 U.S. 45.

### MR. JUSTICE SUTHERLAND delivered the opinion of the Court.

\* \* \*

The petitioners, hereinafter referred to as defendants, are negroes charged with the crime of rape, committed upon the persons of two white girls. The crime is said to have been committed on March 25, 1931. The indictment was returned in a state court of first instance on March 31, and the record recites that on the same day the defendants were arraigned and entered pleas of not guilty. \* \* \*

There was a severance upon the request of the state, and the defendants were tried in three \* \* \* groups \* \* \*. Each of the three trials was completed within a single day. Under the Alabama statute the punishment for rape is to be fixed by the jury, and in its discretion may be from ten years imprisonment to death. The juries found defendants guilty and imposed the death penalty upon all.

---

[3] Before 1938, some courts would appoint counsel for indigents, but the practice was not uniform. See W. Beaney, supra note 2, at 29–33; Holtzoff, supra note 2, at 8.

* * *

The record shows that on the day when the offense is said to have been committed, these defendants, together with a number of other negroes, were upon a freight train on its way through Alabama. On the same train were seven white boys and the two white girls. A fight took place between the negroes and the white boys, in the course of which the white boys, with the exception of one named Gilley, were thrown off the train. A message was sent ahead, reporting the fight and asking that every negro be gotten off the train. The participants in the fight, and the two girls, were in an open gondola car. The two girls testified that each of them was assaulted by six different negroes in turn, and they identified the seven defendants as having been among the number. None of the white boys was called to testify, with the exception of Gilley, who was called in rebuttal.

Before the train reached Scottsboro, Alabama, a sheriff's posse seized the defendants and two other negroes. Both girls and the negroes then were taken to Scottsboro, the county seat. Word of their coming and of the alleged assault had preceded them, and they were met at Scottsboro by a large crowd. It does not sufficiently appear that the defendants were seriously threatened with, or that they were actually in danger of, mob violence; but it does appear that the attitude of the community was one of great hostility. The sheriff thought it necessary to call for the militia to assist in safeguarding the prisoners. * * * It is perfectly apparent that the proceedings, from beginning to end, took place in an atmosphere of tense, hostile and excited public sentiment. During the entire time, the defendants were closely confined or were under military guard. The record does not disclose their ages, except that one of them was nineteen; but the record clearly indicates that most, if not all, of them were youthful, and they are constantly referred to as "the boys." They were ignorant and illiterate. All of them were residents of other states, where all members of their families or friends resided.

* * *

[U]ntil the very morning of the trial no lawyer had been named or definitely designated to represent the defendants. Prior to that time, the trial judge had "appointed all the members of the bar" for the limited "purpose of arraigning the defendants." Whether they would represent the defendants thereafter if no counsel appeared in their behalf, was a matter of speculation only, or, as the judge indicated, of mere anticipation on the part of the court. Such a designation, even if made for all purposes, would, in our opinion, have fallen far short of meeting, in any proper sense, a requirement for the appointment of counsel. How many lawyers were members of the bar does not appear; but, in the very nature of things, whether many or few, they would not, thus collectively named, have been given that clear appreciation of responsibility or impressed with that individual sense of duty which should and naturally would accompany the appointment of a selected member of the bar, specifically named and assigned.

\* \* \*

The defendants, young, ignorant, illiterate, surrounded by hostile sentiment, haled back and forth under guard of soldiers, charged with an atrocious crime regarded with especial horror in the community where they were to be tried, were thus put in peril of their lives within a few moments after counsel for the first time charged with any degree of responsibility began to represent them.

It is not enough to assume that counsel thus precipitated into the case thought there was no defense, and exercised their best judgment in proceeding to trial without preparation. Neither they nor the court could say what a prompt and thoroughgoing investigation might disclose as to the facts. No attempt was made to investigate. No opportunity to do so was given. Defendants were immediately hurried to trial. \* \* \* Under the circumstances disclosed, we hold that defendants were not accorded the right of counsel in any substantial sense.

\* \* \*

The Constitution of Alabama provides that in all criminal prosecutions the accused shall enjoy the right to have the assistance of counsel; and a state statute requires the court in a capital case, where the defendant is unable to employ counsel, to appoint counsel for him. The state supreme court held that these provisions had not been infringed, and with that holding we are powerless to interfere. The question, however, which it is our duty and within our power, to decide, is whether the denial of the assistance of counsel contravenes the due process clause of the Fourteenth Amendment to the federal Constitution.

[The Court discussed the historical development of the right to counsel in England and the colonies. One test for determining whether due process has been accorded is to examine whether the settled "usages and modes of proceeding" were followed. The Court concluded that the procedures employed in this case deviated from traditionally accepted practices.]

\* \* \*

The right to be heard would be, in many cases, of little avail if it did not comprehend the right to be heard by counsel. Even the intelligent and educated layman has small and sometimes no skill in the science of law. If charged with crime, he is incapable, generally, of determining for himself whether the indictment is good or bad. He is unfamiliar with the rules of evidence. Left without the aid of counsel he may be put on trial without a proper charge, and convicted upon incompetent evidence, or evidence irrelevant to the issue or otherwise inadmissible. He lacks both the skill and knowledge adequately to prepare his defense, even though he have a perfect one. He requires the guiding hand of counsel at every step in the proceedings against him. Without it, though he be not guilty, he faces the danger of conviction because he does not know how to establish his innocence. If that be true of men of intelligence, how much more true is it of the ignorant and illiterate, or those of feeble intellect.

\* \* \*

In the light of the facts outlined in the forepart of this opinion—the ignorance and illiteracy of the defendants, their youth, the circumstances of public hostility, the imprisonment and the close surveillance of the defendants by the military forces, the fact that their friends and families were all in other states and communication with them necessarily difficult, and above all that they stood in deadly peril of their lives—we think the failure of the trial court to give them reasonable time and opportunity to secure counsel was a clear denial of due process.

\* \* \* [W]e are of opinion that, under the circumstances just stated, the necessity of counsel was so vital and imperative that the failure of the trial court to make an effective appointment of counsel was likewise a denial of due process within the meaning of the Fourteenth Amendment. Whether this would be so in other criminal prosecutions, or under other circumstances, we need not determine. All that it is necessary now to decide, as we do decide, is that in a capital case, where the defendant is unable to employ counsel, and is incapable adequately of making his own defense because of ignorance, feeble mindedness, illiteracy, or the like, it is the duty of the court, whether requested or not, to assign counsel for him as a necessary requisite of due process of law; and that duty is not discharged by an assignment at such a time or under such circumstances as to preclude the giving of effective aid in the preparation and trial of the case. \* \* \*

\* \* \*

[JUSTICE BUTLER dissented.]

## NOTE ON BETTS V. BRADY

Although the Court found that the defendants' due process rights were violated in *Powell,* the Court did not require counsel in *all* state prosecutions. Ten years later, in fact, the Court held explicitly that the Due Process Clause of the Fourteenth Amendment did not incorporate the specific guarantees of the Sixth Amendment, i.e., an automatic right to counsel. Betts v. Brady, 316 U.S. 455 (1942). The Court endorsed a case-by-case inquiry into the fundamental fairness of the proceeding, in light of the totality of the facts in a given case. The Court considered the circumstances of the case in *Betts*, a prosecution for robbery, and concluded as follows:

> [T]he accused was not helpless, but was a man forty-three years old, of ordinary intelligence, and ability to take care of his own interests on the trial of this narrow issue [alibi defense]. He had once before been in a criminal court, pleaded guilty to larceny and served a sentence and was not wholly unfamiliar with criminal procedure. It is quite clear that in Maryland, if the situation had been otherwise and it had appeared that the petitioner was, for any reason, at a serious disadvantage by reason of the lack of counsel, a refusal to appoint would have resulted in the reversal of judgment of conviction. * * *

The Court in *Betts* held that the Due Process Clause required appointment of counsel only where "special circumstances" indicated that the defendant could not perform adequately on his own.

### *Between Betts and Gideon*

The case-by-case, "special circumstances" approach to appointment of counsel in *Betts* was undermined by a number of cases decided before *Betts* was overruled in Gideon v. Wainwright, 372 U.S. 335 (1963), set forth infra. The Court faced difficult problems in deciding in what circumstances due process required appointment of counsel. Two cases in particular, in which counsel was not appointed, effectively undercut *Betts*. In Hudson v. North Carolina, 363 U.S. 697 (1960), the Court held that the defendant needed a lawyer to protect against the prejudicial effect of his co-defendant's plea of guilty to a lesser charge in the presence of the jury. In Chewning v. Cunningham, 368 U.S. 443 (1962), the Court reversed the defendant's conviction under a recidivist statute. The defendant was denied due process because the difficult legal questions in the case presented too great a potential for prejudice to the defendant.

Furthermore, the Court held in Hamilton v. Alabama, 368 U.S. 52 (1961), that there was an unqualified right to counsel in state capital cases. The distinction between a case involving capital punishment, where counsel was mandated, and one involving a maximum punishment of life imprisonment, where counsel was not absolutely required, proved to be tenuous, at best. By the time of *Gideon,* the *Betts* rule had been eroded to such an extent that it was ripe for a fall.

## III.   A NEW AND SWEEPING RIGHT AND ITS LIMITS

### A.  APPOINTED COUNSEL FOR INDIGENTS IN FELONY PROSECUTIONS

#### GIDEON V. WAINWRIGHT

Supreme Court of the United States, 1963.
372 U.S. 335.

**MR. JUSTICE BLACK delivered the opinion of the Court.**

Petitioner was charged in a Florida state court with having broken and entered a poolroom with intent to commit a misdemeanor. This offense is a felony under Florida law. Appearing in court without funds and without a lawyer, petitioner asked the court to appoint counsel for him, whereupon the following colloquy took place:

"The Court: Mr. Gideon, I am sorry, but I cannot appoint Counsel to represent you in this case. Under the laws of the State of Florida, the only time the Court can appoint Counsel to represent a Defendant is when that person is charged with a capital offense. I am sorry, but I will have to deny your request to appoint Counsel to defend you in this case.

"The Defendant: The United States Supreme Court says I am entitled to be represented by Counsel."

Put to trial before a jury, Gideon conducted his defense about as well as could be expected from a layman. He made an opening statement to the jury, cross-examined the State's witnesses, presented witnesses in his own defense, declined to testify himself, and made a short argument "emphasizing his innocence to the charge contained in the Information filed in this case." The jury returned a verdict of guilty, and petitioner was sentenced to serve five years in the state prison. * * * Since 1942, when Betts v. Brady was decided by a divided Court, the problem of a defendant's federal constitutional right to counsel in a state court has been a continuing source of controversy and litigation in both state and federal courts. To give this problem another review here, we granted certiorari. Since Gideon was proceeding *in forma pauperis,* we appointed counsel to represent him and requested both sides to discuss in their briefs and oral arguments the following: "Should this Court's holding in Betts v. Brady be reconsidered?"

[The Court discussed the facts of Betts v. Brady, which were virtually indistinguishable from those in *Gideon.* The Court noted that *Betts* addressed the circumstance of an indigent charged with a felony.]

\* \* \* Upon full reconsideration we conclude that Betts v. Brady should be overruled.

\* \* \*

We accept Betts v. Brady's assumption, based as it was on our prior cases, that a provision of the Bill of Rights which is "fundamental and essential to a fair trial" is made obligatory upon the States by the Fourteenth Amendment. We think the Court in *Betts* was wrong, however, in concluding that the Sixth Amendment's guarantee of counsel is not one of these fundamental rights. Ten years before Betts v. Brady, this Court, after full consideration of all the historical data examined in *Betts,* had unequivocally declared that "the right to the aid of counsel is of this fundamental character." Powell v. Alabama. While the Court at the close of its *Powell* opinion did by its language, as this Court frequently does, limit its holding to the particular facts and circumstances of that case, its conclusions about the fundamental nature of the right to counsel are unmistakable.

\* \* \*

\* \* \* The fact is that in deciding as it did—that "appointment of counsel is not a fundamental right, essential to a fair trial"—the Court in Betts v. Brady made an abrupt break with its own well-considered precedents. In returning to these old precedents, sounder we believe than the new, we but restore constitutional principles established to achieve a fair system of justice. Not only these precedents but also reason and reflection require us to recognize that in our adversary system of criminal justice, any person haled into court, who is too poor to hire a lawyer, cannot be assured a fair trial unless counsel is provided for him. This seems to us to be an obvious truth. Governments, both state and federal, quite properly spend vast sums of money to establish machinery to try defendants accused of crime. Lawyers to prosecute are everywhere deemed essential to protect the public's interest in an orderly society. Similarly, there are few defendants charged with crime, few indeed, who fail to hire the best lawyers they can get to prepare and present their defenses. That government hires lawyers to prosecute and defendants who have the money hire lawyers to defend are the strongest indications of the widespread belief that lawyers in criminal courts are necessities, not luxuries. The right of one charged with crime to counsel may not be deemed fundamental and essential to fair trials in some countries, but it is in ours. From the very beginning, our state and national constitutions and laws have laid great emphasis on procedural and substantive safeguards designed to assure fair trials before impartial tribunals in which every defendant stands equal before the law. This noble ideal cannot be realized if the poor man charged with crime has to face his accusers without a lawyer to assist him. \* \* \*

The Court in Betts v. Brady departed from the sound wisdom upon which the Court's holding in Powell v. Alabama rested. Florida, supported by two other States, has asked that Betts v. Brady be left intact. Twenty-two States, as friends of the Court, argue that *Betts* was "an anachronism when handed down" and that it should now be overruled. We agree.

The judgment is reversed and the cause is remanded to the Supreme Court of Florida for further action not inconsistent with this opinion.

[JUSTICES DOUGLAS, CLARK, and HARLAN wrote separate concurring opinions. JUSTICE HARLAN questioned whether *Betts* was an abrupt break with history. He viewed the *Betts* rule as one that did not work, but argued that it was "entitled to a more respectful burial than has been accorded."]

## *Establishing Indigency*

*Gideon* requires the state to appoint counsel for indigents in felony cases, but what does it mean to be "indigent?" Consider Barry v. Brower, 864 F.2d 294 (3d Cir.1988), where the defendant was denied a request for the appointment of counsel on the ground that he and his wife had an $80,000 equity in their home and $7,500 in a money market fund. Barry claimed that his debts exceeded his assets, his wife opposed selling their property to pay for his legal expenses, and that he had consulted six attorneys recommended by the public defender, all of whom had refused to represent him without a substantial "up-front" payment. The court held that Barry was entitled to appointed counsel. It stated that "indigence is not equivalent to destitution," and that "if by their nature an accused's assets cannot be timely reduced to cash and cash is required, the present financial inability to obtain counsel which defines indigence for Sixth Amendment purposes appears." The court noted that the state may require reasonable reimbursement if the defendant's indigency is temporary.

The federal standard for appointment of counsel "for any person financially unable to obtain adequate representation" is codified in the Criminal Justice Act, 18 U.S.C. § 3006A. For an application of the federal statute, see United States v. Bauer, 956 F.2d 693 (7th Cir.1992) ("It is not enough to claim inability to hire a lawyer and back up the claim with an affidavit. The statute provides for 'appropriate inquiry' into the veracity of that claim."). The court in *Bauer* held that it is the defendant's burden to establish indigency, and that the defendant has no right to appointed counsel at a hearing to establish indigency.

## B. THE RIGHT TO APPOINTED COUNSEL IN MISDEMEANOR CASES

After *Gideon,* the Court was asked to determine whether a defendant charged with a misdemeanor was inherently more capable of self-representation than a felony defendant. The right to counsel grew with the answer.

### ARGERSINGER V. HAMLIN

Supreme Court of the United States, 1972.
407 U.S. 25.

**MR. JUSTICE DOUGLAS delivered the opinion of the Court.**

Petitioner, an indigent, was charged in Florida with carrying a concealed weapon, an offense punishable by imprisonment up to six months, a $1,000 fine, or both. The trial was to a judge, and petitioner was unrepresented by counsel. He was sentenced to serve 90 days in jail, and brought this habeas corpus action in the Florida Supreme Court, alleging that, being deprived of his right to counsel, he was unable as an indigent layman properly to raise and present to the trial court good and sufficient defenses to the charge for which he stands convicted. The Florida Supreme Court * * * in ruling on the right to counsel, followed the line we marked out in Duncan v. Louisiana, 391 U.S. 145, 159, as respects the right to trial by jury and held that the right to court-appointed counsel extends only to trials "for non-petty offenses punishable by more than six months imprisonment."

[The Court noted that the Sixth Amendment was binding on the states through the Fourteenth Amendment and proceeded to examine the Amendment's requirements of a public trial, the right to be informed of the nature and cause of the accusation, the right of confrontation, and the right of compulsory process. These rights have never been limited to felonies or to serious offenses. Although Duncan v. Louisiana limited the right to trial by jury to trials where the potential punishment was imprisonment for six months or more (as discussed in Chapter 10, infra), the Court concluded that "there is no support for a similar limitation on the right to assistance of counsel." The Court relied heavily on the rationale in *Powell* and *Gideon* and utilized lengthy quotations from both opinions.]

\* \* \*

The requirement of counsel may well be necessary for a fair trial even in a petty-offense prosecution. We are by no means convinced that legal and constitutional questions involved in a case that actually leads to imprisonment even for a brief period are any less complex than when a person can be sent off for six months or more.

\* \* \*

Beyond the problem of trials and appeals is that of the guilty plea, a problem which looms large in misdemeanor as well as in felony cases. Counsel is needed so that the accused may know precisely what he is doing, so that he is fully aware of the prospect of going to jail or prison, and so that he is treated fairly by the prosecution.

\* \* \*

We must conclude, therefore, that the problems associated with misdemeanor and petty offenses often require the presence of counsel to insure the accused a fair trial. Mr. Justice Powell suggests that these problems are raised even in situations where there is no prospect of imprisonment. We need not consider the requirements of the Sixth Amendment as regards the right to counsel where loss of liberty is not involved, however, for here petitioner was in fact sentenced to jail. [T]he prospect of imprisonment for however short a time will seldom be viewed by the accused as a trivial or petty matter and may well result in quite serious repercussions affecting his career and his reputation. \* \* \*

We hold, therefore, that absent a knowing and intelligent waiver, no person may be imprisoned for any offense, whether classified as petty, misdemeanor, or felony, unless he was represented by counsel at his trial.

\* \* \*

[JUSTICE BRENNAN filed a concurring opinion. CHIEF JUSTICE BURGER concurred in the result, and JUSTICE POWELL filed an opinion concurring in the result, in which JUSTICE REHNQUIST joined. JUSTICE BRENNAN emphasized the availability of law students to assist indigents. THE CHIEF JUSTICE expressed concern that trial judges would have difficulty deciding whether to appoint counsel before hearing evidence in a case. He pointed out that the judge probably will rely on representations of the prosecutor. JUSTICE POWELL preferred an approach that, like Betts v. Brady, would have afforded counsel only when necessary to a fair trial. He was bothered by the fact that indigents would receive counsel in cases in which relatively poor non-indigents would be forced by circumstances to forego counsel. Also of concern to him was the lack of attorney resources available to courts in some areas and the increased burden that appointing counsel represented for overworked judges.]

### *The Actual Imprisonment Rule for Misdemeanor Cases: Scott v. Illinois*

Argersinger was imprisoned after a trial in which he was forced to proceed without counsel. The Court did not decide whether the right to counsel extends to a misdemeanor defendant who is punished only with a fine. In Scott v. Illinois, 440 U.S. 367 (1979), the Court considered whether the Sixth Amendment requires appointed counsel when a defendant actually is fined, but the offense is *punishable* by fine or imprisonment. Scott was convicted of shoplifting and fined, after a trial in which he was denied the right to counsel. Shoplifting carried a sentence of either a fine or imprisonment of less than a year.

In *Scott,* the Court stated that there was a line drawn in *Argersinger* between actual imprisonment and other forms of punishment. Even though the statute under which Scott was convicted authorized a year of incarceration, he was not entitled to counsel because he was not sentenced to prison. The majority reasoned as follows:

> Although the intentions of the *Argersinger* Court are not unmistakably clear from its opinion, we conclude today that *Argersinger* did indeed delimit the constitutional right to appointed counsel in state criminal proceedings. Even were the matter *res nova,* we believe that the central premise of *Argersinger*—that actual imprisonment is a penalty different in kind from fines or the mere threat of imprisonment—is eminently sound and warrants adoption of actual imprisonment as the line defining the constitutional right to appointment of counsel. *Argersinger* has proved reasonably workable, whereas any extension would create confusion and impose unpredictable, but necessarily substantial, costs on 50 quite diverse States. We therefore hold that the Sixth and Fourteenth Amendments to the United States Constitution require only that no indigent criminal defendant be sentenced to a term of imprisonment unless the State has afforded him the right to assistance of appointed counsel in his defense.

Justice Powell concurred, although he expressed reservations about the rule enunciated in *Argersinger* and reaffirmed in *Scott.* He argued that the Constitution does not mandate the rule in *Argersinger,* and preferred a more flexible due process approach to the appointment of counsel. Nevertheless, in *Scott* he recognized a need to provide clear guidance to lower courts.

Justice Brennan, joined by Justices Marshall and Stevens, dissented. The dissenters focused on the need for counsel to defend against a charge, and concluded that counsel should be furnished whenever imprisonment is *authorized* for an offense. They noted that public defender systems are economically feasible, and that many states actually require counsel where any imprisonment is authorized.

Justice Brennan argued in *Scott* that the actual imprisonment approach was unworkable because it forces the judge to consider sentencing factors before the case has even begun. He explained as follows:

[T]he judge will be forced to decide in advance of trial—and without hearing the evidence—whether he will forego entirely his judicial discretion to impose some sentence of imprisonment and abandon his responsibility to consider the full range of punishments established by the legislature. His alternatives, assuming the availability of counsel, will be to appoint counsel and retain the discretion vested in him by law, or to abandon this discretion in advance and proceed without counsel.

Justice Brennan argued that another salutary effect of the authorized imprisonment approach would be to encourage state legislatures to update criminal statutes. As Justice Brennan put it, "a state legislature or local government might determine that it no longer desired to authorize incarceration for certain minor offenses in light of the expense of meeting the requirements of the Constitution. In my view, this re-examination is long overdue."

Justice Blackmun also dissented in *Scott*. He agreed that *Argersinger* did not decide this question, but would have held that an indigent defendant must be given counsel in any prosecution for an offense punishable by more than six months imprisonment (or, under *Argersinger,* when the defendant is actually subjected to a term of imprisonment). This approach would make the right to counsel co-extensive with the right to a jury trial, also guaranteed by the Sixth Amendment and discussed in Chapter 10, infra.

For a critical analysis of *Scott,* see Herman & Thompson, Scott v. Illinois and the Right to Counsel: A Decision in Search of a Doctrine? 17 Am.Crim.L.Rev. 71 (1979).

One lower court had this to say about *Scott:*

In essence, the *Scott* holding set up a trade-off whereby states could choose between providing indigent defendants with appointed counsel and foregoing jail time for convictions obtained without appointed counsel. *Scott* holds that, if the state wants to incarcerate an indigent defendant, the state must provide appointed counsel.

Moore v. Jarvis, 885 F.2d 1565 (11th Cir.1989). Does the "trade-off" approach described have anything to do with the Sixth Amendment right to counsel in "all criminal prosecutions?" Does it have anything to do with the right to due process, which extends to deprivations of both liberty and property?

### Applying the Actual Imprisonment Approach

Recall that in Berkemer v. McCarty (Chapter 3) the Court held that the protections of Miranda v. Arizona applied to arrests for misdemeanors. Thus, an indigent person subject to custodial questioning for a misdemeanor has a right to appointed counsel during that questioning. But then at trial, he has no right to appointed counsel unless he receives a prison sentence. Is the *Miranda* right more important than the right to counsel at trial in misdemeanor cases?

If a defendant is not provided counsel at trial, can the court impose a suspended sentence and probation under *Scott*? The Court in Alabama v. Shelton, 535 U.S. 654 (2002), held in the negative. Justice Ginsburg, writing for the Court, declared that a suspended sentence is "a prison term imposed for the offense of conviction" upon the defendant's violation of probation and that once the prison term is triggered, "the defendant is incarcerated not for the probation violation, but for the underlying offense." Justice Scalia, joined by Chief Justice Rehnquist, Justice Kennedy, and Justice Thomas, dissented in *Shelton*. He argued that the threat of a suspended sentence could deter many probation violations.

### Use of Uncounseled Convictions to Enhance a Sentence: Baldasar v. Illinois and Nichols v. United States

Suppose an indigent defendant is denied counsel and convicted of a misdemeanor. Under *Scott*, he can only be fined. Suppose further that the same defendant is later charged with another crime, given counsel, and convicted. Can the first uncounseled conviction be used to enhance his sentence for the second crime? In Baldasar v. Illinois, 446 U.S. 222 (1980), a divided Supreme Court held that a defendant was denied his right to counsel under *Argersinger* and *Scott* when his misdemeanor theft conviction was transformed into a felony because of a previous conviction for the same offense, where the defendant had not had counsel when previously convicted and fined. The Court reasoned that *Scott* was violated because Baldasar "was sentenced to an increased term of imprisonment *only* because he had been convicted in a previous prosecution in which he had *not* had the assistance of appointed counsel."

But the Court overruled *Baldasar* in Nichols v. United States, 511 U.S. 738 (1994). Nichols was sentenced under the Federal Sentencing Guidelines after pleading guilty to a federal drug felony. He had previously been convicted on a DUI offense, which was a misdemeanor for which he received no jail time; he was not provided counsel at that previous trial. The DUI conviction was used to place Nichols in a higher criminal history category for sentencing on the drug offense. As a consequence, Nichols received a sentence longer than he would otherwise have received. Chief Justice Rehnquist, in an opinion for five members of the Court, declared that "an uncounseled misdemeanor conviction, valid under *Scott* because no prison term was imposed, is also valid when used to enhance punishment at a subsequent conviction."

The Chief Justice reasoned that "[e]nhancement statutes, whether in the nature of criminal history provisions such as those contained in the Sentencing Guidelines, or recidivist statutes which are commonplace in state criminal laws, do not change the penalty imposed for the earlier conviction." To the contrary, enhancement statutes penalize "only the last offense committed by the defendant." The Chief Justice also argued that the unrestricted use of valid uncounseled convictions was consistent with the "less exacting" standards applicable to the sentencing process. Under the Sentencing Guidelines, a defendant's prior bad acts can be taken into account as part of his criminal history, whenever the government can prove by a preponderance of the evidence that the defendant committed the acts. Thus, Nichols's DUI offense could have been used against him to enhance the sentence *even if he had never been convicted*. The Chief Justice concluded that "it must be constitutionally permissible to consider a prior uncounseled misdemeanor conviction based on the same conduct where that conduct must be proven beyond a reasonable doubt." Justice Souter concurred in the judgment.

Justice Blackmun, joined by Justices Stevens and Ginsburg, dissented. He contended that "a rule that an uncounseled conviction *never* can form the basis for a term of imprisonment is faithful to the principle born of *Gideon* and announced in *Argersinger* that an uncounseled misdemeanor, like an uncounseled felony, is not reliable enough to form the basis for the severe sanction of incarceration."[4]

## IV.   THE SCOPE OF THE RIGHT

### A.  CRITICAL STAGES

*Gideon, Argersinger*, and *Scott* analyze the right of an indigent to appointed trial counsel. But as we have already seen in connection with confessions and identification procedures, counsel may be needed *before* a trial starts. And counsel may be needed after it ends. Other "critical stages"—stages where the presence of counsel is critical—are so labeled when it is said that counsel is essential in order to protect against substantial prejudice to a defendant's rights.

### *Definition of a Critical Stage: United States v. Wade*

The justification for and development of the "critical stage" analysis is expressed in United States v. Wade, 388 U.S. 218 (1967), a case

---

[4]  It must be remembered that Nichols' prior conviction, while uncounseled, was a *valid* conviction because Nichols received no jail time for it. In contrast, if the prior uncounseled conviction is invalid under *Gideon* and its progeny, the conviction cannot be used to enhance a later sentence. Thus, in Custis v. United States, 511 U.S. 485 (1994), the Court stated that, where a prior conviction is being used to enhance a sentence, the defendant can collaterally attack the prior conviction at the sentencing hearing if it was rendered in violation of *Gideon*.

examined in the preceding chapter on identification. The *Wade* Court wrote as follows:

> * * * When the Bill of Rights was adopted, there were no organized police forces as we know them today. The accused confronted the prosecutor and the witnesses against him, and the evidence was marshalled, largely at the trial itself. In contrast, today's law enforcement machinery involves critical confrontations of the accused by the prosecution at pretrial proceedings where the results might well settle the accused's fate and reduce the trial itself to a mere formality. In recognition of these realities of modern criminal prosecution, our cases have construed the Sixth Amendment guarantee to apply to "critical" stages of the proceedings. * * *

[The Court discusses *Powell, Escobedo, Massiah, Miranda,* and other cases.]

> In sum, the principle of Powell v. Alabama and succeeding cases requires that we scrutinize *any* pretrial confrontation of the accused to determine whether the presence of his counsel is necessary to preserve the defendant's basic right to a fair trial as affected by his right meaningfully to cross-examine the witnesses against him and to have effective assistance of counsel at the trial itself. It calls upon us to analyze whether potential substantial prejudice to defendant's rights inheres in the particular confrontation and the ability of counsel to help avoid that prejudice.

The Court concluded, as Chapter 4 revealed, that there was great potential for suggestiveness in a lineup, and "the accused's inability effectively to reconstruct at trial any unfairness that occurred at the lineup may deprive him of his only opportunity meaningfully to attack the credibility of the witness' courtroom identification."

### *Preliminary Hearings: Coleman v. Alabama*

Using this "critical stage" method of analysis, the Court found in Coleman v. Alabama, 399 U.S. 1 (1970), that Alabama's preliminary hearing was a critical stage requiring the appointment of counsel for the indigent defendant. Although preliminary hearings have not yet been examined, it is sufficient for present purposes to note that the major purpose of the preliminary hearing is to determine whether there is sufficient evidence against the accused to bind the defendant over for trial. The Court in *Coleman* declared as follows:

> Plainly the guiding hand of counsel at the preliminary hearing is essential to protect the indigent accused against an erroneous or improper prosecution. First, the lawyer's skilled examination and cross-examination of witnesses may expose fatal weaknesses in the

State's case that may lead the magistrate to refuse to bind the accused over. Second, in any event, the skilled interrogation of witnesses by an experienced lawyer can fashion a vital impeachment tool for use in cross-examination of the State's witnesses at the trial, or preserve testimony favorable to the accused of a witness who does not appear at the trial. Third, trained counsel can more effectively discover the case the State has against his client and make possible the preparation of a proper defense to meet that case at the trial. Fourth, counsel can also be influential at the preliminary hearing in making effective arguments for the accused on such matters as the necessity for an early psychiatric examination or bail.

### *Other Pre-Trial Critical Stages*

The right to counsel has not been extended to all pretrial phases of a criminal investigation. Kirby v. Illinois, 406 U.S. 682 (1972), for instance, provided a substantial temporal limitation on the Sixth Amendment right to counsel. Unless counsel is provided to safeguard an independent constitutional right, as in *Miranda,* generally one can say that adversary proceedings must be formally initiated before a particular phase of a prosecution can be considered a critical stage requiring counsel. (Recall Massiah v. United States, and Moran v. Burbine). Adversary criminal proceedings plainly can be initiated by formal charge, preliminary hearing, indictment, information, or arraignment. It is not clear what the Supreme Court means by "formal charge," but presumably the Court is focusing on the filing of some statement with the court that expresses the government's belief that the criminal process leading to conviction should begin against a suspect. Before this formal filing, an investigation generally does not trigger counsel rights. Thus, counsel is not constitutionally required at the grand jury stage, because no charges have yet been filed. See, e.g., In re Grand Jury Subpoenas, 906 F.2d 1485 (10th Cir.1990) (subpoenaing attorney to testify before the grand jury to give information against his client does not violate defendant's right to counsel, even though it may result in defense attorney's disqualification from representation; no Sixth Amendment rights attach prior to indictment).

Even where the criminal process has begun, there are limitations on the extension of the right to counsel to pre-trial proceedings. United States v. Ash, 413 U.S. 300 (1973), holding that a photographic identification at which the accused was not present was not a critical stage, illustrates this point. After reviewing the history and expansion of the Sixth Amendment counsel guarantee, the *Ash* Court redefined the approach used in extending the right to counsel: "[T]he test utilized by the Court has called for examination of the event in order to determine whether the accused required aid in coping with legal problems or assistance in meeting his adversary." The Court distinguished the lineup in *Wade* because in *Ash* there was no confrontation between the accused and the prosecution. After stating that there is no right to counsel because the accused has no right to be present at a photographic array, the Court went on to make the following argument:

> A substantial departure from the historical test would be necessary if the Sixth Amendment were interpreted to give Ash a right to counsel at the photographic identification in this case. Since the accused himself is not present at the time of the photographic display, and asserts no right to be present, no possibility arises that the accused might be misled by his lack of familiarity with the law or overpowered by his professional adversary. Similarly, the counsel guarantee would not be used to produce equality in a trial-like adversary confrontation. * * *

After *Ash*, what kind of post-charge, pre-trial situations will be deemed critical stages? See, e.g., Commonwealth v. Holzer, 480 Pa. 93, 389 A.2d 101 (1978) (indigent has right to appointed counsel at search and seizure suppression hearing).

## B.  POST-TRIAL STAGES

The right to counsel has been extended to certain stages of a criminal prosecution following trial. Generally speaking, extension appears to be based on whether counsel's presence is necessary to provide the defendant with a minimum level of fairness.

### MEMPA V. RHAY

Supreme Court of the United States, 1967.
389 U.S. 128.

#### MR. JUSTICE MARSHALL delivered the opinion of the Court.

These consolidated cases raise the question of the extent of the right to counsel at the time of sentencing where the sentencing has been deferred subject to probation.

Petitioner Jerry Douglas Mempa was convicted in the Spokane County Superior Court on June 17, 1959, of the offense of "joyriding." This conviction was based on his plea of guilty entered with the advice of court-appointed counsel. He was then placed on probation for two years on the condition, *inter alia,* that he first spend 30 days in the county jail, and the imposition of sentence was deferred * * *.

About four months later the Spokane County prosecuting attorney moved to have petitioner's probation revoked on the ground that he had been involved in a burglary on September 15, 1959. A hearing was held in the Spokane County Superior Court on October 23, 1959. Petitioner

Mempa, who was 17 years old at the time, was accompanied to the hearing by his stepfather. He was not represented by counsel and was not asked whether he wished to have counsel appointed for him. Nor was any inquiry made concerning the appointed counsel who had previously represented him.

At the hearing Mempa was asked if it was true that he had been involved in the alleged burglary and he answered in the affirmative. A probation officer testified without cross-examination that according to his information petitioner had been involved in the burglary and had previously denied participation in it. * * * [T]he court immediately entered an order revoking petitioner's probation and then sentenced him to 10 years in the penitentiary, * * *.

* * *

In 1948 this Court held in Townsend v. Burke, 334 U.S. 736, that the absence of counsel during sentencing after a plea of guilty coupled with "assumptions concerning his criminal record which were materially untrue" deprived the defendant in that case of due process. Mr. Justice Jackson there stated in conclusion, "in this case, counsel might not have changed the sentence, but he could have taken steps to see that the conviction and sentence were not predicated on misinformation or misreading of court records, a requirement of fair play which absence of counsel withheld from this prisoner." [The Court discusses other pre-Gideon cases.]

There was no occasion in Gideon to enumerate the various stages in a criminal proceeding at which counsel was required, but [these earlier cases] clearly stand for the proposition that appointment of counsel for an indigent is required at every stage of a criminal proceeding where substantial rights of a criminal accused may be affected. * * *

The State, however, argues that the petitioners were sentenced at the time they were originally placed on probation and that the imposition of sentence following probation revocation is, in effect, a mere formality constituting part of the probation revocation proceeding. It is true that sentencing in Washington offers fewer opportunities for the exercise of judicial discretion than in many other jurisdictions. The applicable statute requires the trial judge in all cases to sentence the convicted person to the maximum term provided by law for the offense of which he was convicted. The actual determination of the length of time to be served is to be made by the Board of Prison Terms and Paroles within six months after the convicted person is admitted to prison.

On the other hand, the sentencing judge is required by statute, together with the prosecutor, to furnish the Board with a recommendation as to the length of time that the person should serve, in addition to supplying it with various information about the circumstances of the crime and the character of the individual. We were informed during oral argument that the Board places considerable weight on these recommendations, although it is in no way bound by them. Obviously to the extent such recommendations are influential in determining the resulting sentence, the necessity for the aid of counsel in marshaling the facts, introducing evidence of mitigating circumstances and in general aiding and assisting the defendant to present his case as to sentence is apparent.

Even more important in a case such as this is the fact that certain legal rights may be lost if not exercised at this stage. For one, Washington law provides that an appeal in a case involving a plea of guilty followed by probation can only be taken after sentence is imposed following revocation of probation. Therefore in a case where an accused agreed to plead guilty, although he had a valid defense, because he was offered probation, absence of counsel at the imposition of the deferred sentence might well result in loss of the right to appeal. * * *

Likewise the Washington statutes provide that a plea of guilty can be withdrawn at any time prior to the imposition of sentence, if the trial judge in his discretion finds that the ends of justice will be served. Without undertaking to catalog the various situations in which a lawyer could be of substantial assistance to a defendant in such a case, it can be reiterated that a plea of guilty might well be improperly obtained by the promise to have a defendant placed on the very probation the revocation of which furnishes the occasion for desiring to withdraw the plea. An uncounseled defendant might very likely be unaware of this opportunity.

The two foregoing factors assume increased significance when it is considered that * * * the eventual imposition of sentence on the prior plea of guilty is based on the alleged commission of offenses for which the accused is never tried.

In sum, we do not question the authority of the State of Washington to provide for a deferred sentencing procedure coupled with its probation provisions. Indeed, it appears to be an enlightened step forward. All we decide here is that a lawyer must be afforded at this proceeding whether it be labeled a revocation of probation or a deferred sentencing. We assume that counsel appointed for the purpose of the trial or guilty plea would not be unduly burdened by being requested to follow through at the deferred sentencing stage of the proceeding.

* * *

## *Limitations on Mempa*

Today, it is likely to come as no surprise that sentencing is treated as part of the trial process and as requiring the assistance of counsel.

However, courts have held that *Mempa* does not mean that every step in the sentencing process is "critical" within the meaning of the Sixth Amendment. In United States v. Johnson, 935 F.2d 47 (4th Cir.1991), the defendant was sentenced in part on the basis of *ex parte* communications between his probation officer and the sentencing judge. The court rejected the argument that the right to counsel attached to those meetings. It found the communications to be "nonadversarial," reasoning that under the Federal Sentencing Guidelines, the probation officer is an agent of the court and assists the court in arriving at a just sentence. Do you agree that a conference between the probation officer and the judge is not a critical stage?

### *Right to Counsel on Appeal: Douglas v. California and Ross v. Moffitt*

Before *Mempa,* the Court had ruled in Douglas v. California, 372 U.S. 353 (1963), that an indigent defendant has a right to appointed counsel for his first appeal of right from a criminal conviction. The Court relied, for the first and only time, on an equal protection rationale for requiring provision of counsel: because a person with means would retain counsel for an appeal of right, the denial of counsel to an indigent was discrimination that violated the Equal Protection Clause.

The problem with an equal protection rationale is that there would appear to be no limits to it; stated broadly, *Douglas* appeared to endorse a form of wealth equalization. See Harris, The Constitution and Truth Seeking: A New Theory on Expert Services for Indigent Defendants, 83 J.Crim.L. and Crim. 469 (1992) ("While the equality principle surely represents an earnest and well-intentioned effort to deal with the effect of poverty on criminal defendants, it is, if nothing else, too open-ended.").

Over time, the Court switched from an equal protection rationale to a due process rationale in assessing whether indigents had a right to appointed counsel in the appeal process. Under this approach, the state has an obligation to appoint counsel for an indigent whenever counsel would be necessary for adequate access to court relief. Thus, in Ross v. Moffitt, 417 U.S. 600 (1974), the Court refused to extend the *Douglas* reasoning to require counsel for discretionary appeals. Ross received counsel for his first appeal to the state's intermediate appellate court. But he was denied counsel for his subsequent appeal to the state supreme court. Justice Rehnquist, writing for the court, declared that the Fourteenth Amendment "does not require absolute equality or precisely equal advantages, nor does it require the State to equalize economic conditions." Applying the due process test of *adequate access*, Justice Rehnquist found that counsel was not reasonably necessary for discretionary appeals:

[P]rior to his seeking discretionary review in the State Supreme Court, [respondent's] claims had once been presented by a lawyer and passed upon by an appellate court. Douglas v. California. We do not believe it can be said, therefore, that a defendant in respondent's circumstances is denied meaningful access to the North Carolina Supreme Court simply because the State does not appoint counsel to aid him in seeking review in that court. At that stage he will have, at the very least, a brief on his behalf in the Court of Appeals setting forth his claims of error, and in many cases an opinion by the Court of Appeals disposing of his case. These materials, supplemented by whatever submission respondent may make *pro se,* would appear to provide the Supreme Court of North Carolina with an adequate basis on which to base its decision to grant or deny review. * * *

This is not to say, of course, that a skilled lawyer * * * would not prove helpful to any litigant able to employ him. * * * [But] the fact that a particular service might be of benefit to an indigent defendant does not mean that the service is constitutionally required. The duty of the State under our cases is not to duplicate the legal arsenal that may be privately retained by a criminal defendant in a continuing effort to reverse his conviction, but only to assure the indigent defendant an adequate opportunity to present his claims fairly in the context of the State's appellate process.

### Applying Ross to Other Post-Trial Stages

Reasoning from Ross v. Moffitt, the Court held, in Wainwright v. Torna, 455 U.S. 586 (1982) (per curiam), that a defendant could not challenge his retained lawyer's failure to file a timely petition for discretionary review in the state supreme court. Torna argued that counsel had been ineffective. But under *Ross,* Torna had no right to counsel in his appeal to the state supreme court; so there could be no claim of ineffective counsel. Justice Marshall, dissenting, argued that the defendant was denied due process.

Chief Justice Rehnquist wrote for the Court in Pennsylvania v. Finley, 481 U.S. 551 (1987), as it relied on Ross v. Moffitt to hold that a defendant has no right to counsel in postconviction (habeas corpus) proceedings. Because such right is lacking, the Court held that a lawyer, who is appointed to represent a defendant in such a proceeding and who finds the defendant's claims to be frivolous, need not file a brief referring to anything in the record that would support the defendant's claims. Such a brief (or a similar showing by counsel) is required on direct appeal as of right under the Supreme Court's decision in Anders v. California, 386 U.S. 738 (1967), but the requirement is derived from the right to counsel itself. When the right is nonexistent, there is no requirement of an *Anders* brief or any other comparable effort by counsel. The Chief Justice also rejected due process and equal protection arguments made in support of a briefing requirement.

In Murray v. Giarratano, 492 U.S. 1 (1989), the Court relied on *Ross* and *Finley* to hold that the state was not required to provide counsel for death-row inmates pursuing post conviction habeas corpus remedies. The plurality opinion, written by Chief Justice Rehnquist, "declined to read either the Eighth Amendment or the Due Process Clause to require yet another distinction between the rights of capital case defendants and those in noncapital cases." The Chief Justice noted, however, that many states "automatically provide counsel to death-row inmates in state habeas corpus proceedings, as a matter of state law." Justice Kennedy concurred in the judgment "on the facts and record of this case" noting that "no prisoner on death row in Virginia has been unable to obtain counsel to represent him in postconviction proceedings." Justice Stevens, joined by Justices Blackmun, Marshall, and Brennan, dissented. He noted that under Virginia law, some claims that would ordinarily be brought on direct review are deferred until habeas corpus proceedings, such as claims concerning ineffective assistance of counsel. He concluded that review of those claims in a habeas proceeding is tantamount to a first appeal of right, as to which the defendant does have a right to counsel under *Douglas*. Justice Stevens also argued that capital litigation is more complex and subject to a greater time pressure than the postconviction proceedings considered in *Finley*.[5]

In Halbert v. Michigan, 545 U.S. 605 (2005), the Court held that an indigent defendant had a constitutional right to the assistance of counsel in a first appeal of a conviction entered after a guilty plea. The Court likened that appeal to a first appeal of right from a conviction after trial, as to which the right to counsel is guaranteed under *Douglas*.

### Parole and Probation Revocation Proceedings: *Gagnon v. Scarpelli*

Once the defendant has been properly convicted and sentenced, some constitutional protections diminish or disappear. A defendant has no absolute right to counsel at parole or probation revocation proceedings, for example. In Gagnon v. Scarpelli, 411 U.S. 778 (1973), the Court adopted a case-by-case approach to the appointment of counsel at these revocation hearings. Relying on Morrissey v. Brewer, 408 U.S. 471 (1972), which held that due process protections apply to parole revocation proceedings (in other words, that they have to be fundamentally fair

---

[5]   21 U.S C. § 848(q)(4)(B) entitles capital defendants to qualified legal representation in any "post conviction proceeding" brought under 28 U.S.C. § 2254 or § 2255, sections of the federal habeas corpus statute.

because liberty interests are threatened), the *Gagnon* Court first determined that due process also applied to probation revocation hearings. However, the Court rejected the contention that states are under a constitutional duty to provide counsel for indigents in all probation and parole revocation cases. Acknowledging that its case-by-case approach to counsel is similar to the fundamental fairness approach of *Betts,* which was rejected in *Gideon,* the Court distinguished criminal trials from probation or parole revocation hearings, reasoning as follows:

> In a criminal trial, the State is represented by a prosecutor; formal rules of evidence are in force; a defendant enjoys a number of procedural rights which may be lost if not timely raised; and, in a jury trial, a defendant must make a presentation understandable to untrained jurors. In short, a criminal trial under our system is an adversary proceeding with its own unique characteristics. In a revocation hearing, on the other hand, the State is represented, not by a prosecutor, but by a parole officer with a different orientation; formal procedures and rules of evidence are not employed; and the members of the hearing body are familiar with the problems and practice of probation or parole. The need for counsel at revocation hearings derives, not from the invariable attributes of those hearings, but rather from the peculiarities of particular cases.

The Court in *Gagnon* articulated the relevant considerations:

> * * * Presumptively, it may be said that counsel should be provided in cases where, after being informed of his right to request counsel, the probationer or parolee makes such a request, based on a timely and colorable claim (i) that he has not committed the alleged violation of the conditions upon which he is at liberty; or (ii) that, even if the violation is a matter of public record or is uncontested, there are substantial reasons which justified or mitigated the violation and make revocation inappropriate, and that the reasons are complex or otherwise difficult to develop or present. In passing on a request for the appointment of counsel, the responsible agency also should consider, especially in doubtful cases, whether the probationer appears to be capable of speaking effectively for himself.

### Juvenile Proceedings: In re Gault

When guilt is adjudicated at a particular stage, the Court has shown a special sensitivity to the need for counsel. This helps to explain In re Gault, 387 U.S. 1 (1967), which involved a fifteen-year-old who was confined to a State Industrial School until he reached majority. Before being committed as a juvenile delinquent, he was given a hearing without counsel. In holding that due process required that he be appointed counsel, the Court focused on the juvenile's need for assistance of counsel to cope with the problems of law. Underlying the majority's opinion is the concern that the proceeding, though ostensibly civil in nature, involved the potential for incarceration that was as real as a similar threat in a criminal case.[6]

## C.  THE RIGHT EXTENDED TO EXPERTS

Using the principle of adequate access, the Court in Ake v. Oklahoma, 470 U.S. 68 (1985), held that an indigent defendant may in some cases be entitled to appointed expert assistance in addition to appointed counsel. Ake was arrested and charged with murdering a couple and wounding their two children. He was hospitalized after initially being found incompetent to stand trial. Subsequently, he responded sufficiently well to medication that he was declared fit to stand trial. At the guilt stage of the capital proceeding, he raised an insanity defense. Defense counsel called and questioned each psychiatrist who had examined Ake while he was hospitalized. But each doctor indicated on cross-examination that he had not diagnosed Ake's mental state at the time of the offense. The jury convicted. During the sentencing stage no new evidence was presented.

Justice Marshall's opinion for the Court reasoned that Ake should have had a psychiatrist appointed to assist his defense at both stages. The Court borrowed a procedural due process test it uses in civil cases to balance the defendant's need for help against the burden on the state of providing help. It found a strong "private interest" in life and liberty and the importance of avoiding an unjust conviction; no governmental interest in prevailing at trial if the result "is to cast a pall on the accuracy of the verdict obtained"; and a great value in providing expert assistance to a defendant when his sanity at the time of the offense is to be a significant factor at trial and when the government presents psychiatric evidence concerning future dangerousness in a capital sentencing proceeding. Thus, it held that Ake had been denied due process when he was not afforded access to a competent psychiatrist who might have conducted an appropriate examination and assisted in the evaluation, preparation, and presentation of the defense.

An indigent defendant's right to an appointed expert under *Ake* is not automatic. It is only triggered when the defendant will be deprived of a fair opportunity to present his defense without the expert assistance. For example, in Caldwell v. Mississippi, 472 U.S. 320 (1985), the defendant sought the appointment of several experts, including a ballistics expert.

---

[6]   In contrast, in Middendorf v. Henry, 425 U.S. 25 (1976), the Court refused to hold, on the basis of *Argersinger,* that a summary court-martial is a criminal prosecution because it results in a loss of liberty. The peculiarities of the military setting and its procedures led the Court to distinguish the summary court-martial from the traditional criminal trial. The Court was concerned that counsel would alter the nature of the proceeding, which is informal and flexible.

As support for his request, he stated only that the expert "would be of great necessarius [sic] witness." The trial court denied the request. The Supreme Court affirmed and stated that Caldwell's "undeveloped assertions" were not sufficient to require appointment of an expert. See also Bowden v. Kemp, 767 F.2d 761 (11th Cir.1985) (appointment of psychiatrist not required where no showing was made that sanity would be a real issue at trial).

Generally speaking the courts have read *Ake* narrowly, and have refused to require appointment of an expert unless it is absolutely essential to the defense. See Harris, *Ake* Revisited: Expert Psychiatric Witnesses Remain Beyond Reach for the Indigent, 68 No.Car.L.Rev. 763 (1990). For a discussion of when and whether *Ake* mandates the appointment of a DNA expert in cases where DNA evidence is proffered, see Developments in the Law—Confronting the New Challenges of Scientific Evidence, 108 Harv.L.Rev. 1481, 1559 (1995).

Professor Giannelli contends that the limited right to expert assistance provided by *Ake* must be expanded in light of two important developments: 1) the government's substantially increased use of expert testimony, most prominently DNA identification; and 2) the Supreme Court's opinion in *Daubert*, requiring district courts to act as gatekeepers in excluding unreliable expert testimony—including non-scientific expert testimony. See Giannelli, Ake v. Oklahoma: The Right to Expert Assistance in a Post-Daubert, Post-DNA World, 89 Cornell L. Rev. 1305 (2004). He concludes as follows:

> In 1985, the *Ake* Court could not have anticipated how the advent of DNA evidence would revolutionize forensic science or how [*Daubert*] would alter the judicial approach to scientific evidence. It could not have foreseen the scientific fraud cases or the expanded use of social science and modus operandi experts. All of these developments have increased the need for defense experts.

> While *Ake* settled the core issue by recognizing a right to expert assistance, significant issues were left unresolved. *Ake's* rationale extends to nonpsychiatric experts, to noncapital trials, and to other proceedings such as juvenile transfer hearings and sex offender commitments. Developing a useful standard for the appointment decision remains critical; courts have often applied a far too demanding standard. Finally, the role of the expert should be viewed as grounded in the right to counsel—i.e., a *defense* rather than neutral expert should be provided.

## D.  CIVIL CONTEMPT PROCEEDINGS

The Sixth Amendment right to counsel is limited by its terms to criminal prosecutions. In Turner v. Rogers, 131 S. Ct. 2507 (2011), Justice

Breyer's opinion for the Court examined how South Carolina's Family Court enforces its child support orders by threatening with incarceration for civil contempt those who are (1) subject to a child support order, (2) able to comply with that order, but (3) fail to do so. The Court held that "where as here the custodial parent (entitled to receive the support) is unrepresented by counsel, the State need not provide counsel to the noncustodial parent (required to provide the support)," but added "that the State must nonetheless have in place alternative procedures that assure a fundamentally fair determination of the critical incarceration-related question, whether the supporting parent is able to comply with the support order."

Justice Breyer relied upon factors set out in Mathews v. Eldridge, 424 U.S. 319, 335 (1976) (considering fairness of an administrative proceeding) in determining the Due Process requirements in a civil contempt proceeding. He reasoned that the risk of incarceration argued for a right to counsel but countervailing considerations of fairness to an unrepresented parent and delay argued against and concluded that alternative procedures could provide a parent with a fair hearing.

Justice Breyer identified the following safeguards that would increase the fairness and accuracy of proceedings: "(1) notice to the defendant that his "ability to pay" is a critical issue in the contempt proceeding; (2) the use of a form (or the equivalent) to elicit relevant financial information; (3) an opportunity at the hearing for the defendant to respond to statements and questions about his financial status, (e.g., those triggered by his responses on the form); and (4) an express finding by the court that the defendant has the ability to pay."

Justice Breyer chose not to address civil contempt proceedings where the underlying child support payment is owed to the State—for example, to recover welfare funds paid to the parent with custody. He observed that such proceedings more closely resemble debt-collection proceedings in which the government is likely to have counsel or some other competent representative.

Justice Thomas, joined by Justice Scalia, and in pertinent part by Chief Justice Roberts and Justice Alito, dissented. He agreed that there was no right to counsel for all indigent defendant facing incarceration in civil contempt proceedings but would not have addressed whether Due Process required safeguards other than counsel.

## V. THE PROMISE OF *GIDEON*

In Gideon's Broken Promise: America's Continuing Quest for Equal Justice, A Report on the American Bar Association's Hearings on the Right to Counsel in Criminal Proceedings (December 2004), an ABA

Committee reported on the results of hearings that it held in 2003 throughout the United States.

Part V of the Report outlined the principal findings of the Committee:

- Forty years after *Gideon v. Wainwright*, indigent defense in the United States remains in a state of crisis, resulting in a system that lacks fundamental fairness and places poor persons at constant risk of wrongful conviction.

- Funding for indigent defense services is shamefully inadequate.

- Lawyers who provide representation in indigent defense systems sometimes violate their professional duties by failing to furnish competent representation.

- Lawyers are not provided in numerous proceedings in which a right to counsel exists in accordance with the Constitution and/or state law. Too often, prosecutors seek to obtain waivers of counsel and guilty pleas from unrepresented accused persons, while judges accept and sometimes even encourage waivers of counsel that are not knowing, voluntary, intelligent, and on the record.

- Judges and elected officials often exercise undue influence over indigent defense attorneys, threatening the professional independence of the defense function.

- Indigent defense systems frequently lack basic oversight and accountability, impairing the provision of uniform, quality services.

- Efforts to reform indigent defense systems have been most successful when they involve multi-faceted approaches and representatives from a broad spectrum of interests.

- The organized bar too often has failed to provide the requisite leadership in the indigent defense area.

- Model approaches to providing quality indigent defense services exist in this country, but these models often are not adequately funded and cannot be replicated elsewhere absent sufficient financial support.

Part VI of the Report sets forth seven recommendations to respond to the principal findings.

- State governments should provide increased funding for the delivery of indigent defense services in criminal and juvenile delinquency proceedings at a level that ensures the provision of uniform, quality legal representation. The funding for indigent defense should be in parity with funding for the prosecution function, assuming that prosecutors are funded and supported adequately in all respects.

- The federal government should provide substantial financial support for the provision of indigent defense services in state criminal and juvenile delinquency proceedings.

- State governments should establish oversight organizations that ensure the delivery of independent, uniform, quality indigent defense representation in all criminal and juvenile delinquency proceedings.

- Attorneys and defense programs should refuse to continue indigent defense representation, or to accept new cases for representation, when, in the exercise of their best professional judgment, workloads are so excessive that representation will interfere with the rendering of quality legal representation or lead to the breach of constitutional or professional obligations.

- Judges should fully respect the independence of defense lawyers who represent the indigent, but judges should also be willing to report to appropriate authorities defense lawyers who violate ethical duties to their clients. Judges also should report prosecutors who seek to obtain waivers of counsel and guilty pleas from unrepresented accused persons, or who otherwise give legal advice to such persons, other than the advice to secure counsel. Judges should never attempt to encourage persons to waive their right to counsel, and no waiver should ever be accepted unless it is knowing, voluntary, intelligent, and on the record.

- State and local bar associations should be actively involved in evaluating and monitoring criminal and juvenile delinquency proceedings to ensure that defense counsel is provided in all cases to which the right to counsel attaches and that independent and quality representation is furnished.

- In addition to state and local bar associations, many other organizations and individuals should become involved in efforts to reform indigent defense systems.

Anthony Lewis, former New York Times columnist and author of Gideon's Trumpet, described the importance of the Report in his Foreword to it:

> In recent years we have all read accounts of criminal proceedings that showed how far we were from realizing the promise of the *Gideon* case. There was the Texas defendant whose lawyer slept through parts of his trial—a trial for his life. A number of convicts on death row, awaiting execution, were belatedly found to be innocent;

they had been convicted with lawyers who lacked the skill, determination or resources to defend them adequately.

We knew the stories, the anecdotal evidence. Now we have a systematic exploration of the problem, thanks to the American Bar Association's Standing Committee on Legal Aid and Indigent Defendants. Its report, "*Gideon's* Broken Promise," is a challenge to the country: to legislators, state and federal; to judges; and to lawyers. It asks all of us to think of our commitment to the very idea of law.

The United States Supreme Court can recognize a right to counsel and make it binding on both the federal government and the states. But, funding that right and making it a reality inevitably depends on legislatures. Spending on indigent defense is rarely popular. In difficult economic times, spending on all aspects of criminal justice may be strained. The challenge of *Gideon* is to make what the Supreme Court has promised a reality.

# CHAPTER 6

# THE SCREENING AND CHARGING PROCESS

■ ■ ■

## I.   INTRODUCTION

Once the police have made an arrest, the suspect's fate lies mainly in the hands of the prosecutor. The prosecutor has very broad discretion to decide whether to file a formal charge against the suspect, and if so, what crime to charge. As a practical matter, this is so even if the charge actually is made by a grand jury or is screened by a magistrate. The prosecutor's discretion continues even after the charging decision has been made, because a prosecutor usually can obtain a dismissal of a criminal case prior to trial or the entry of a guilty plea.

A decision to charge a defendant with criminal activity puts into motion several formal and informal procedures. These will be considered in this Chapter. Two of the most important are the preliminary hearing and the grand jury investigation. These procedures and their relationship to the prosecutor's role in the screening of cases and the charging process receive most of the attention in the material that follows.

## II.   CHOICES AND THE CHARGING PROCESS

### A.   CONTROLLED AND UNCONTROLLED CHOICES

Choices must be made at all levels of our criminal justice system. The police must decide whether to arrest or to investigate. Prosecutors must decide whether to initiate cases, what charges to file, and whether to plea bargain. Magistrates issuing search and arrest warrants, or sitting in preliminary hearings, must decide whether probable cause exists or whether a suspect should be released on bail or pursuant to other conditions of pre-trial release. Grand juries must decide whether to indict, and prosecutors must decide whether to take cases to grand juries or to bring charges when grand jury indictments are not required. Trial judges must decide whether there is enough evidence for cases to go to petit juries, and petit juries must decide whether to convict or acquit. Judges or juries must determine the sentences to be imposed on convicted offenders. Correctional authorities must decide how to treat incarcerated offenders, and parole or pardon authorities must determine whether to release offenders before their formal sentences have been served.

Some of these choices are controlled by standards—e.g., whether probable cause exists, whether there is enough evidence to go to a jury, and how convinced the jury must be before it convicts—and the task of government officials or jurors is to apply the standards to particular facts. Other choices—sentencing is an example—might be controlled by minimum and maximum provisions but provide the decisionmaker some latitude in choosing where to settle within the permissible range. Still other choices are essentially discretionary. The screening and charging process involves many uncontrolled choices, and these are a cause of concern. As you proceed in this chapter, keep in mind what choices are possible and what controls, if any, are placed upon them by the agency making the choice, or by some external authority.

## B. LESS THAN FULL ENFORCEMENT OF THE LAW

One of the realities of law enforcement is that not all crimes are investigated, not all criminals are prosecuted, and not all laws are enforced. Nowhere in the United States is there a full enforcement policy—i.e., one that seeks to impose a sanction on every criminal act that occurs.

There is no such thing as full enforcement because it would be too costly. We are not willing to pay for the police, the prosecutors, the public defenders, the judges, the courtrooms, and the penal institutions that would be required to punish all criminal acts that occur. But apart from economics, there are reasons why choices are made in the processing of cases. The notion of individualized justice runs deep in this country. Actions that technically fall under the same statutory proscription may not be equally reprehensible.

Moreover, legislative "overcriminalization" has resulted in criminal codes that, if they were fully enforced, might be intolerable. Laws are sometimes passed as "state-declared ideals," such as adultery statutes, which are "unenforced because we want to continue our conduct, and unrepealed because we want to preserve our morals."[1] Other laws, e.g., gambling laws, are drafted broadly for administrative convenience but are never intended to be fully enforced: the legislature never really wanted to prohibit private poker games among friends. Outdated laws, which would cause public outrage were they enforced, remain unrepealed, sometimes because legislators do not want to go on record as having repealed *any* criminal law for fear of being labelled as "soft on crime".[2]

---

[1]  LaFave, The Prosecutor's Discretion in the United States, 18 J.Am.Comp.L. 532, 533 (1970).

[2]  An example of this problem is mentioned in Misner, Recasting Prosecutorial Discretion, 86 J.Crim.L. & Crim. 717 (1996). When the Arizona legislature adopted its revised criminal code, a majority of legislators refused to go on record as voting for a repeal of any of the old sex offense statutes, even if they had become outmoded or superfluous. So that left two sets of sex offense

It seems, then, that legislatures pass and refuse to repeal statutes that invite choices by those who screen cases and make charging decisions. See Misner, Recasting Prosecutorial Discretion, 86 J.Crim.L. & Crim. 717 (1996) (arguing that legislatures, "by creating too many policy choices, have effectively abdicated policy-making to the prosecutor since it is the prosecutor, and not the legislature, that has the final decision in determining which public policy, if any, is breached by an individual's conduct."). See also Richman and Stuntz, Al Capone's Revenge: An Essay on the Political Economy of Pretextual Prosecution, 105 Colum. L.Rev. 583 (2005) (arguing that the "overexpansion of the federal criminal code" has invited "pretextual enforcement" whereby a prosecutor who suspects a person of one crime can "charge and convict him of a different crime, unrelated to and less severe than the first.").

Some other countries purport to operate on the principle that the police and prosecutor have no discretion to exercise at all. If the case is one in which there is sufficient evidence to prosecute, it must be prosecuted. Whether these systems operate in practice as they are designed to in theory is questionable. Two observers make the following comment:

> The principle of compulsory prosecution which formally permeates the German and Italian systems, and informally the French, demands the impossible: full enforcement of the law in a time of rising crime and fierce competition for resources. Inevitably, adjustments must be made in the way in which the principle is to be applied; where formal law or ideology does not permit these adjustments, informal processes are created that do.[3]

This observation serves as a reminder that it may be more difficult to make a mandatory system of prosecutions work in practice than it is to posit such a system in theory.

Judge Miner, in The Consequences of Federalizing Criminal Law, 4 Crim.Just. 16 (1989) argues that a prosecutor's decision not to prosecute someone who is guilty of a crime invades the province of the jury and creates a public perception of unfairness. Professor Green, in "Hare and Hounds": The Fugitive Defendant's Constitutional Right to be Pursued, 56 Brooklyn L.Rev. 439 (1990), disagrees with Judge Miner and argues that it makes sense that the prosecutor enjoys "virtually unfettered discretion in deciding how to allocate investigative and prosecutorial resources." Professor Green contends that the prosecutor is in the "best position" to decide how to use the finite resources allocated to prosecuting crime.

---

statutes, using different terminology and imposing different punishment—thus increasing prosecutorial discretion.

[3] Goldstein & Marcus, The Myth of Judicial Supervision in Three Inquisitorial Systems: France, Italy, and Germany, 87 Yale L.J. 240, 280 (1977).

## III.   SCREENING BY THE POLICE

## A.  THE NATURE OF POLICE CHOICES

Before reaching the question of what choices should be available to those responsible for charging suspects with criminal offenses, it is necessary to focus on the police. Generally, officials who have the ultimate responsibility for charging decisions do not themselves investigate criminal conduct—other than through grand jury investigations. Obviously, then, if the police do not turn information over to the charging officials, it is unlikely that those officials will have any real choice to make.

In Chapter 2, the restrictions on police investigations, arrests, and searches were examined. The assumption there was that the police wanted to proceed against citizens, and the question was what limits, if any, should be placed on police activity. Sometimes, though, the police decide they do not want to take action against individuals, even though such action might be permissible under the rules previously discussed. When the police decide not to act, the effect is usually to screen cases from the criminal justice process.

### *The Choice Not to Arrest*

The first level of screening occurs when the police decide whom to arrest. Although a decision to make an arrest must be reviewed by an impartial magistrate, either before or after the arrest is made, a decision *not to arrest* is essentially unreviewable.

The suggestion has been made that police cannot properly be given the choice whether or not to arrest, and that they must arrest when they have probable cause to do so.[4] In fact, police in all American jurisdictions make decisions not to arrest people whom they could arrest. Several explanations can be offered for this phenomenon.

Were the police to arrest every suspect who they reasonably believed committed a crime, an already overburdened judicial system would be further burdened. Thus, we tolerate choices by the police because we are not prepared to handle more cases. Actually, the police themselves are not prepared to handle more cases. If they spent more time in processing cases, they would have less time to spend on the street to deal with crimes that they view as more serious than the ones they now choose to ignore.

Also, police officers learn that courts and prosecutors will not proceed very far in processing certain kinds of cases. Rather than initiating a

---

[4]   Hall, Police and Law in a Democratic Society, 28 Ind.L.J. 133, 155 (1953).

process that they know will be shortlived, the police may decide not to make arrests for certain crimes and to devote their energies to other activities. For an interesting discussion of the interrelationship between the police investigatory function and the prosecutor's function, see Richman, Prosecutors and Their Agents: Agents and Their Prosecutors, 103 Colum.L.Rev. 749 (2003).

Police also might refrain from an arrest when they are engaged in a community caretaking function, in which case they need to maintain good relations with community elements who might resent the filing of criminal charges in some instances. The police officer may approach a disruptive incident "not in terms of enforcing the law but in terms of handling the situation."[5] Arrest is only one of several tools that the officer may use to maintain order and protect the public. The officer may rely on personal qualities and an aura of authority, rather than the arrest power, to maintain and restore order.

Police officers are also aware that complete enforcement of certain crimes by arrest would create a public backlash. If police officers arrested every driver who drove 56 miles per hour in a 55 mile per hour zone, it is clear that the police would hear about it. Upset drivers might create a risk of violence during the arrest for such a minimal offense. (Witness Walter White's reaction to simply being ticketed for a cracked windshield in "Breaking Bad"). Requiring police officers to arrest whenever they have probable cause of a violation of any of the thousands of offenses that legislatures have enacted would simply be unworkable.

That said, there is an undeniable problem in the police having virtually unfettered discretion in determining whom to arrest and whom not to arrest. Professor Davis, in Prosecution and Race: The Power and Privilege of Discretion, 67 Fordham L.Rev. 13 (1998), notes the racial impact that such discretion can have:

> Because police officers are not required to make an arrest when they observe conduct creating probable cause, their discretion may result in the failure to detain or arrest whites who commit acts for which their African American counterparts would often be detained or arrested.

As an illustration, Professor Davis notes an event in Prince George's County, Maryland, "where white officers observed three white adults smoking crack cocaine in a car with a baby and neither made arrest nor filed charges." If someone can prove that police arrest racial minorities but not white suspects for particular crimes, an equal protection violation may be established. But, as we shall see later in this Chapter, it is difficult to gather sufficient evidence to prove racial discrimination.

---

[5]   J. Wilson, Varieties of Police Behavior 33 (1968).

## B. SOME TYPICAL CASES

Consider the following situations that a police officer might expect to confront, and in which a choice to arrest or not will be made.

1. An officer responds to a call from a woman who says her husband is going to beat her. When the officer arrives, the woman has a broken nose and several facial bruises, but she refuses to sign a complaint. Should the officer arrest the husband anyway? Should he suggest that the couple see a marriage counselor? Should his decision be affected by whether the couple has children who witnessed the beating?

2. An officer watches an adult sell an ounce of marijuana to a juvenile. When he apprehends the seller, the seller offers to work as an informant in exchange for favorable treatment, but only if no arrest is made. What should the officer do? Does it make a difference that the sale was to a juvenile rather than to an adult?

3. Suppose two officers are operating a speed trap and a car whizzes by at 30 miles per hour over the speed limit. They usually make an arrest of anyone speeding more than 15 miles over the limit. Should they make an arrest if the driver is a parent rushing to the hospital to see an ill child? If the driver is an employee who is late to work and may be facing the loss of a job if tardy one more time? If the driver is from out of town and did not realize that he was speeding?

4. Officers enter a house without a warrant believing that they will find illegal narcotics. They find the drugs they were looking for but have grave reservations about whether they had exigent circumstances excusing the warrantless entry. Should the officers arrest the occupants and let the prosecution and the court figure it out? Or should they just seize and destroy the narcotics as an informal sanction? Does it matter if the officers believe that if they make an arrest, a motion to suppress will likely follow that will probably lead to a conclusion that the officers violated the Fourth Amendment and could be disciplined for the warrantless entry?

5. An officer stationed at a security checkpoint in front of a courthouse witnesses a purse-snatching. Should he chase after the perpetrator in order to make an arrest, or maintain the checkpoint and let the perpetrator escape?

Is police rulemaking a means by which an officer's discretion to arrest or not to arrest can be limited? Would rulemaking make decisions easier in the five examples set forth above? Ironically, if police departments contemplate adopting rules that would indicate circumstances in which an arrest could be, but probably ought not be, made, they may be criticized. There would be no deterrent effect to a law that the police have advertised will not be enforced. Yet, without rules, decisions are left to individual officers at the lowest enforcement level.

# IV. THE PROSECUTORIAL DECISION WHETHER TO CHARGE

## A. THE POWER OF THE PROSECUTOR

While discretion runs through the criminal justice system, it is the discretionary decisions made by the prosecutor that have the most impact. Professor Misner, in Recasting Prosecutorial Discretion, 86 J.Crim.L. & Crim. 717 (1996), notes the awesome authority granted to prosecutors—authority that has increased over time.

The prosecutor's authority is evident in bail hearings, grants of immunity, and in trial strategy. But in the areas of charging, bargaining, and sentencing, it has become clear that the prosecutor plays the pivotal role in the criminal justice process. Despite criticism, plea bargaining continues unabated. While a few courts have rather unsuccessfully attempted to formulate "a common law of prosecutorial discretion," the authority of the prosecutor continues to grow.

Three closely related trends have been at work to promote the authority of the prosecutor. First, current criminal codes contain so many overlapping provisions that the choice of how to characterize conduct as criminal has passed to the prosecutor. In many cases the legislature has effectively delegated its prerogative to define the nature and severity of criminal conduct to the prosecutor. Legislative mandates regarding sentencing maxima, sentencing minima, and sentencing guidelines are dependent upon the substantive charge chosen by the prosecutor. In addition, prosecutors have the untrammeled authority to select the number of separate criminal acts for which the defendant will be charged. The prosecutors also determine whether to seek sentencing enhancements.

Second, the increase in reported crime without a concomitant increase in resources dedicated to the prosecution and defense of criminal conduct has resulted in a criminal process highly dependent upon plea bargaining. There are very few restraints placed upon the prosecutor in the bargaining process.

Third, the development of sentencing guidelines and a growth of statutes with mandatory minimum sentences have increased the importance of the charging decision since the charging decision can affect the range of sentences available to the court. * * *

## B.  THE NATURE OF THE CHARGING DECISION

The prosecutor's decision whether to charge a suspect with a crime is of a different character than the officer's decision whether to arrest. While the officer usually must make an on-the-spot decision, the prosecutor has time, a fuller knowledge of the facts, and the opportunity to consult with colleagues. The consequences of a decision to charge are far greater than those of the decision to arrest. A decision to charge constitutes a finding that the suspect should bear the monetary and social costs of trial and, in some cases, that the suspect's freedom should either be conditioned on payment of bail or suspended as a means of preventive detention. That the defendant may reduce some of these costs by pleading guilty to a lesser charge only makes the prosecutor's decision more consequential.

Professor Davis, in Prosecution and Race: The Power and Privilege of Discretion, 67 Fordham L.Rev. 13 (1998), describes the importance of the prosecutor's decision to charge a person with a crime:

> The first and most important function exercised by a prosecutor is the charging decision. Although police officers decide whether to arrest a suspect, the prosecutor decides whether he should be formally charged with a crime and what the charge should be. This decision is entirely discretionary. Even if there is probable cause to believe the suspect has committed a crime, the prosecutor may decide to dismiss the case and release the suspect. She may also file a charge that is either more or less serious than that recommended by the police officer, as long as there is probable cause to believe the suspect committed the crime. Other than a constitutional challenge by a criminal defendant, there is very little process for review of these decisions.

> The charging decision is one of the most important decisions a prosecutor makes. In conjunction with the plea bargaining process, the charging decision almost predetermines the outcome of a criminal case, because the vast majority of criminal cases result in guilty pleas or guilty verdicts. The charge also often determines the sentence that the defendant will receive * * *.

At the outset, does it trouble you that the prosecutor's decision to charge, carrying the grave consequences that it does, is largely discretionary? If you think the prosecutor's unfettered discretion is a problem, what safeguards would you impose?

## C.  THE FACTORS THAT ARE CONSIDERED

The prosecutor must decide whether to charge and what crime to charge. The decision whether to charge depends on the prosecutor's belief that (1) the suspect is guilty, (2) the evidence is sufficient to secure conviction, and (3) it is in the community's best interest to prosecute the suspect. General criteria to be employed by the prosecutor are set forth in the ABA Standards for Criminal Justice: The Prosecution Function, approved by the ABA's House of Delegates in February, 1992:

### Standard 3–3.9 Discretion in the Charging Decision

(a) A prosecutor should not institute, or cause to be instituted, or permit the continued pendency of criminal charges when the prosecutor knows that the charges are not supported by probable cause. A prosecutor should not institute, cause to be instituted, or permit the continued pendency of criminal charges in the absence of sufficient admissible evidence to support a conviction.

(b) The prosecutor is not obliged to present all charges which the evidence might support. The prosecutor may in some circumstances and for good cause consistent with the public interest decline to prosecute, notwithstanding that sufficient evidence may exist which would support a conviction. Illustrative of the factors which the prosecutor may properly consider in exercising his or her discretion are:

(i) the prosecutor's reasonable doubt that the accused is in fact guilty;

(ii) the extent of the harm caused by the offense;

(iii) the disproportion of the authorized punishment in relation to the particular offense or the offender;

(iv) possible improper motives of a complainant;

(v) reluctance of the victim to testify;

(vi) cooperation of the accused in the apprehension or conviction of others; and

(vii) availability and likelihood of prosecution by another jurisdiction.

\* \* \*

(d) In making the decision to prosecute, the prosecutor should give no weight to the personal or political advantages or disadvantages which might be involved or to a desire to enhance his or her record of conviction.

(e) In cases which involve a serious threat to the community, the prosecutor should not be deterred from prosecution by the fact that in the jurisdiction juries have tended to acquit persons accused of the particular kind of criminal act in question.

(f) The prosecutor should not bring or seek charges greater in number or degree than can reasonably be supported with evidence at trial or than are necessary to fairly reflect the gravity of the offense.

---

Professor Fairfax discusses a number of nonevidentiary factors that the prosecutor may consider in a charging decision, including:

> whether the defendant is a recidivist or is likely to offend again, whether the prosecutor has a heavy caseload at the time, whether the type of case is career-advancing, whether the investigating law enforcement agency is pleasant to work with, whether the case has jury appeal, whether a matter is more appropriately prosecuted by a different sovereign or handled as a civil matter, and whether the criminal conduct is a priority area for the prosecutor's superiors.

Fairfax, Grand Jury Discretion and Constitutional Design, 93 Cornell L. Rev. 703, 735 (2008). See also Green and Zacharias, Prosecutorial Neutrality, 2004 Wis. L.Rev. 837 (discussing criteria for a charging decision and the difficulty of crafting clear standards given the need for prosecutorial discretion in charging).

## *Sample Cases*

Using the criteria from the standards set forth above, consider whether the prosecutor should have brought the following cases:

1.    Congressman Mel Reynolds, an African-American, was charged and convicted of statutory rape and obstruction of justice. The evidence showed that he had a long-term sexual relationship with a teenage girl, and that he tried to cover-up the relationship when an investigation began. The relationship was consensual and the girl was at best a reluctant witness against him. In such a case, should the prosecutor take into account (a) the fact that Reynolds is an elected official, and (b) the attempted cover-up? If so, how important are these factors?

2.    In the Southern District of New York, the U.S. Attorney promulgated a "Federal Tuesday" program, in which low-level drug dealers were arrested on the streets while making narcotics transactions. These low-level dealers were prosecuted under the federal narcotics laws, and given much harsher sentences than they would have received had they been prosecuted in the state system. Does deterrence justify prosecuting ordinary dealers caught on one week day in federal court while similarly situated dealers arrested every other day are prosecuted in state court?

3.    Leona Helmsley was charged and convicted of tax fraud. The government proved that she evaded taxes by charging renovations to her

home as business expenses. On balance, however, Ms. Helmsley paid millions of dollars a year in taxes—the amount of evasion was a rather small percentage of the amount she paid. Mrs. Helmsley was a well-known hotelier. Assuming that a prosecutor would not ordinarily bring a criminal prosecution for a relatively small amount of unjustified deductions, is a prosecution justifiable if it focuses public attention on tax evasion and the possible consequences?

4. Los Angeles police officers Stacy Koon and Lawrence Powell were convicted in federal court for violating the civil rights of Rodney King. The convictions arose out of the use of excessive force after the officers had lawfully pursued King in a high-speed chase and stopped and arrested him. The Rodney King beating was on videotape. A state prosecution had already been brought, resulting in acquittal on most of the counts and a hung jury on one count. The case was highly publicized and was widely watched both in Los Angeles and around the nation. Should a federal prosecutor consider filing federal charges if she believes that the acquittals were largely attributable to the fact that the entire jury was white while the victim in the case was black?

5. The accused snipers who tormented Maryland, Virginia and the District of Columbia, John Muhammad and Lee Malvo, were going to be tried in Maryland, where most of the sniper attacks occurred. But the Justice Department intervened to assure that the defendants would be prosecuted in Virginia. The apparent reason for this decision was that prosecutors could seek the death penalty for Malvo in Virginia but not in Maryland (because Malvo was a juvenile at the time of the crimes, and Maryland does not permit the use of the death penalty when the crime is committed by a juvenile). Should the Department of Justice be deciding whether Maryland or Virginia has the better criminal justice policy when it comes to juveniles and the death penalty?

6. Martha Stewart was charged and convicted of misleading authorities who were investigating whether she engaged in a stock transaction. There was no charge made in the case that the stock transaction was in fact illegal. Is it fair to charge and imprison a person for misleading a government investigation of a transaction that is not itself charged in the case? Is it relevant that Martha Stewart is a famous personality?

7. Arthur Anderson, the accounting firm, was indicted for destroying records that were pertinent to the SEC investigation of Enron. The indictment essentially resulted in the dissolution of the firm. The conviction, which was based on a single e-mail from a single lawyer concerning records destruction, was overturned by the Supreme Court, but by that time the firm was all but destroyed. Should a prosecutor

consider the effects of a conviction on a partnership or corporation in deciding whether to charge the entity along with or in lieu of individuals?

### Politics, and the Chance of a Favorable Outcome

Of course, an important factor in a prosecutor's decision to prosecute is whether the prosecutor thinks a case can be won. A prosecutor with a high conviction rate is not only more likely to be successful in a reelection bid (in jurisdictions where prosecutors are elected), but also will have enhanced credibility when she does file charges. Therefore, she is likely to want to carry all the way to trial only those cases that are supported by a great deal of evidence to which the judge and jury will be sympathetic.

That said, it is undeniably true that politics can often affect a charging decision. Attorney General Reno's decision to seek the death penalty in the prosecution of the bombing of the Federal Building in Oklahoma City is a prominent example. She announced that the death penalty would be sought even before the perpetrators were apprehended. And Attorney General Ashcroft ordered United States attorneys to seek the death penalty in certain cases even though the attorneys initially exercised discretion not to do so.

Problems can arise if charging decisions are dominated by politics and the goal of maintaining high conviction rates. Prosecutors could become less concerned about the danger of convicting innocent persons. Conviction rates could be reached by offering very favorable plea bargains to people against whom the evidence is quite weak and who might well be acquitted at trial. In short, it is not clear that a prosecutor's office should be judged on the basis of its rate of conviction. But the reality is that it probably will be.

## D. THE DECISION NOT TO PROSECUTE

A prosecutor's decision not to prosecute a suspect is generally protected from judicial review. This means that the effect of a prosecutor's decision not to charge a suspect is a final resolution of the case in favor of the suspect. Of course, the prosecutor may change her mind and decide to charge the suspect within the time prescribed by the applicable statute of limitations, but courts rarely attempt to compel the prosecutor to file charges.

Even when statutory language appears to make prosecution of all violations of a statute mandatory, courts have been extremely reluctant to *require* prosecution where the prosecutor has decided against it. See, e.g., Inmates of Attica v. Rockefeller, 477 F.2d 375 (2d Cir.1973) (statutory language that prosecutor is "required" to institute prosecutions "has never been thought to exclude the exercise of prosecutorial discretion").

The court in *Attica* relied on separation of powers principles and refused to order the prosecutor to instigate prosecutions against state officials.

### Refusing to Prosecute a Certain Type of Crime

In some situations, a prosecutor might decide that a certain type of crime will not be prosecuted. A prosecutor's decision not to prosecute a certain type of crime is often based on a judgment that the violation of law involved is simply not worth the resources that would have to be expended in a prosecution. Prosecutors might also be concerned about a public backlash in prosecuting certain crimes. Local and cultural conditions might be involved as well.

An example of the non-prosecution of a class of crime arose in Utah, as reported in an article in the National Law Journal, Aug. 10, 1998, p. A10:

> Facing criticism for suggesting that polygamy may fall under religious freedoms, Gov. Mike Leavitt turned to Utah's attorney general for advice on why the state fails to prosecute polygamists when the practice is widespread. * * * The Tapestry of Polygamy, a self-help group for former polygamist wives and children, held a news conference outside the governor's office July 27 and presented his chief of staff, Vicky Varela, a letter urging that the state constitutional ban on polygamy be enforced.

> \* \* \*

> Ms. Varela drew a distinction between prosecuting the act of polygamy itself and prosecuting crimes that may occur within plural marriages. "Polygamy is against the law in Utah," she said. "We do not know why prosecutors do not choose to prosecute it."

> There has not been a prosecution of anyone solely for practicing polygamy in Utah since 1952, when federal and state agents raided the border community of Short Creek * * *. The raid turned into a public-relations debacle as children were pulled from their parents' arms and husbands were jailed.

> Ms. Varela said the governor will ask Utah Attorney General Jan Graham for a "policy statement" on polygamy prosecutions. But Ms. Graham's chief deputy, Reed Richards, said the policy is simple: "Crimes are prosecuted when we know about them, and the vast majority of these relationships are consenting adults."

Does the explanation given by Chief Deputy Graham make any sense? If crimes are prosecuted when the prosecutor knows about them, and consent is no defense to polygamy, then why does consent justify non-prosecution?

### Overriding the Grand Jury's Decision to Indict

No federal prosecutor can lawfully sign an indictment not approved by the grand jury, but he or she may *decline* to sign off on charges that the grand jury wishes to file. See, e.g., United States v. Navarro-Vargas, 408 F.3d 1184 (9th Cir. 2005) ("The prosecutor has no obligation to prosecute the [grand jury's] presentment, to sign the return of an indictment, or even to prosecute an indictment properly returned.").

Several years ago, a dozen grand jurors in Colorado rebelled against a prosecutor's decision not to indict Rockwell International for polluting a site with nuclear waste. During its term, the grand jury heard from more than 100 witnesses and examined hundreds of thousands of documents. The evidence indicated that the cost of the clean-up at the site would be $2 billion. But the prosecutor pulled the plug on the grand jury by entering into a deal whereby Rockwell would pay an $18 million fine. The grand jurors made statements to the press that they wanted to indict Rockwell but were overruled by the prosecutor. They then wrote a report about their findings and sent it to a federal judge, requesting judicial intervention. The judge not only refused to intervene in the prosecutor's decision; he asked the U.S. Attorney General to determine whether criminal charges could be brought against the grand jurors for violation of grand jury secrecy. The foreman of the grand jury was quoted as saying: "The judge's instructions were very vivid and clear to us. He said that we were not to be a rubber stamp for the prosecutor. What we've done is in the best interest of the prosecutor and the nation." Do you agree? Subsequently the grand jurors brought a petition to release materials associated with the grand jury's investigation. See In re Special Grand Jury, 450 F.3d 1159 (10th Cir. 2006).

### Explaining the Decision Not to Prosecute

The public is rarely made aware of a prosecutor's decision not to bring charges. In highly publicized cases, however, prosecutors may have to worry about public opinion. Some prosecutors have found it necessary to explain their decisionmaking process when they decide not to charge in a high profile case.

For example, U.S. Attorney Otto Obermaier decided not to bring charges against Salomon Brothers, a Wall Street Brokerage house, in connection with Salomon's admission of submitting false bids in treasury securities auctions. He made a public statement explaining why he decided not to seek charges. Obermaier singled out four pertinent factors: (1) Salomon's extensive cooperation with the authorities; (2) Salomon's replacement of those senior management officials who had failed to promptly report the offenses to the authorities after first learning of it; (3) heavy fines and other punishments imposed as part of Salomon's civil settlement with the SEC, the Federal Reserve Bank, and the Treasury Department; and (4) the "negative effect on the company's innocent employees and shareholders" that would have resulted from criminal charges against the corporation. Obermaier, Drafting Companies to Fight Crime, New York Times, May 24, 1992, sec. 3, p.11, col.2.

Are these sufficient reasons to decline to prosecute? Should there be a general practice of public notice of a decision not to prosecute, just as there is public notice for a decision to prosecute? What good can come out of a prosecutor's disclosure of why she chose not to prosecute? Could a publicized decision not to prosecute become a source of abuse, by casting public suspicion upon the target?

## E. PROSECUTORIAL RULEMAKING

Just as there have been numerous calls for rulemaking by the police, there have been a number of suggestions that chief prosecutorial officers should formulate regulations to govern the conduct of their offices. See, e.g., ALI Model Code of Pre-Arraignment Procedure § 10.3 (calling for regulations); ABA Standards, The Prosecution Function § 3–3.4 (1992) (calling for policy guidelines to determine "whether criminal proceedings should be instituted").

Some guidelines have been drafted, but they leave much room for individualized charging judgment on the part of particular prosecutors. See, e.g., U.S. Dept. of Justice, Materials Relating to Prosecutorial Discretion. See also Baker, A View to the Future of Judicial Federalism: "Neither Out Far Nor In Deep," 45 Case W. Res. L. Rev. 705, 749 (1995) (discussing the process by which "the Department of Justice and the typical U.S. Attorney's Office have written prosecution guidelines, often labeled 'declination policies,' that describe principles for informed exercise of federal prosecutorial discretion."). The arguments for prosecutorial rulemaking are similar to those made in favor of police rulemaking, but they are even stronger, because policy-making executive officials are likely to be trusted with greater power to make enforcement decisions than are lower level police officers.

Arguments against prosecutorial rulemaking have been made, however. They are the following:

- the application of rules in particular cases would be challenged, thus raising the costs of the criminal process;

- rules would reduce the deterrent effect of the criminal law by announcing which laws would not be vigorously enforced;

- individual treatment would be sacrificed in order to have uniformity;

- problems in law enforcement change rapidly (e.g., post-September 11) and rulemaking would inhibit a rapid prosecutorial response to new problems; and

- adequate rules cannot be devised because discretion cannot be controlled by any clear criteria.[6]

Are these arguments persuasive? For an argument that internal standards are critical to assure the public integrity of a prosecutor's decisions, see Green and Zacharias, Prosecutorial Neutrality, 2004 Wis. L.Rev. 837.

## F. SELECTIVE ENFORCEMENT

Whether by rules or by ad hoc decisions, prosecutors operating in a world of partial enforcement must somehow choose whom to prosecute. The selection of a certain type of case or person for enforcement may raise questions of arbitrariness and even equal protection. Understandably, however, courts are reluctant to regulate the traditional discretion of the prosecutor to charge. As Judge Posner has stated:

> A judge in our system does not have the authority to tell prosecutors which crimes to prosecute or when to prosecute them. Prosecutorial discretion resides in the executive, not in the judicial, branch, and that discretion, though subject of course to judicial review, is not reviewable for a simple abuse of discretion.

United States v. Giannattasio, 979 F.2d 98 (7th Cir.1992).[7]

### 1. Charges on Collateral Matters

It should be no surprise that a disproportionate number of prosecutions are brought against career offenders, members of organized crime, and suspected terrorists. Often prosecutors hunt to bring a charge that will "stick," even if the crime charged might be considered collateral to the central criminal activity of the defendant. The classic example is the successful prosecution of Al Capone for tax violations. Another example is the prosecution of the Muslim student Awadallah in San

---

[6] See generally, Beck, The Administrative Law of Criminal Prosecution: The Development of Prosecutorial Policy, 27 Am.U.L.Rev. 310, 337–80 (1978). See also, Vorenberg, Decent Restraint of Prosecutorial Discretion, 94 Harv.L.Rev. 1521 (1981), which suggests appropriate ways of controlling discretion. Frase, The Decision to File Federal Criminal Charges: A Quantitative Study of Prosecutorial Discretion, 47 U.Chi.L.Rev. 246 (1980), focuses on one United States Attorney's office and documents the tremendous discretion afforded federal prosecutors and the factors they most often consider in exercising it.

[7] In Imbler v. Pachtman, 424 U.S. 409 (1976), the Court held that a prosecutor has absolute immunity from liability for all claims concerning the initiation of charges and the trying of the case. See also Buckley v. Fitzsimmons, 509 U.S. 259 (1993) (prosecutor entitled to absolute immunity for charging decisions, but receives only qualified immunity for statements to the media and for actions taken during the preliminary investigation of an uncharged crime).

Diego for lying to the grand jury about knowing some of the 9/11 terrorists (as opposed to taking part in the 9/11 conspiracy).

Should a prosecutor be able to tell law enforcement officials to "go after X who I believe is an organized crime official. Check his tax records, his business dealings, everything"? Professors Richman and Stuntz, in Al Capone's Revenge: An Essay on the Political Economy of Pretextual Prosecution, 105 Colum. L.Rev. 583 (2005), argue that pretextual decisions to charge create social costs:

> There is a strong social interest in non-pretextual prosecution, and that interest is much more important than the "fairness to defendants" argument that has preoccupied the literature on this subject. Criminal charges are not only a means of identifying and punishing criminal conduct. They are also a means by which prosecutors send signals to their superiors, including the voters to whom they are ultimately responsible. When a murderer is brought to justice for murder rather than for tax evasion, voters learn some important things about their community and about the justice system: that a given homicide has been committed in a particular way * * * ; that the crime has been solved; that the police and prosecution have done a good job of assembling evidence against the killer, and so forth. If there is a legislative body that oversees the relevant law enforcement agencies, those same signals are sent to the legislative overseers. When a prosecutor gets a conviction * * * for an unrelated lesser crime than the one that motivated the investigation, the signals are muddied. They may disappear altogether. * * *

> Another audience also gets a muddied signal: would-be criminals. Instead of sending the message that running illegal breweries and bribing local cops would lead to a term in a federal penitentiary, the Capone prosecution sent a much more complicated and much less helpful message: If you run a criminal enterprise, you should keep your name out of the newspapers and at least pretend to pay your taxes. * * * [T]he political economy of criminal law enforcement depends on a reasonably good match between the charges that motivate prosecution and the charges that appear on defendants' rap sheets. When crimes and charges do not coincide, no one can tell whether law enforcers are doing their jobs. The justice system loses the credibility it needs, and voters lose the trust they need to have in the justice system. Individual agents and prosecutors pay only a tiny fraction of that price, which is why they continue to follow the Capone strategy. The larger price is paid only over time— by crime victims, by law enforcement agencies, and (not least) by the voting public.

### 2.   Constitutional Limitations on the Charging Decision

The following case sets forth strict requirements for proving a constitutional claim of selective prosecution.

## UNITED STATES V. ARMSTRONG
Supreme Court of the United States, 1996.
517 U.S. 456.

### CHIEF JUSTICE REHNQUIST delivered the opinion of the Court.

In this case, we consider the showing necessary for a defendant to be entitled to discovery on a claim that the prosecuting attorney singled him out for prosecution on the basis of his race. We conclude that respondents failed to satisfy the threshold showing: They failed to show that the Government declined to prosecute similarly situated suspects of other races.

In April 1992, respondents were indicted in the United States District Court for the Central District of California on charges of conspiring to possess with intent to distribute more than 50 grams of cocaine base (crack) and conspiring to distribute the same, in violation of 21 U.S.C. §§ 841 and 846, and federal firearms offenses. * * * On seven separate occasions * * * informants had bought a total of 124.3 grams of crack from respondents and witnessed respondents carrying firearms during the sales. * * *

[R]espondents filed a motion for discovery or for dismissal of the indictment, alleging that they were selected for federal prosecution because they are black. In support of their motion, they offered only an affidavit [alleging] that, in every one of the 24 §§ 841 or 846 cases closed by the office during 1991, the defendant was black. Accompanying the affidavit was a "study" listing the 24 defendants, their race, whether they were prosecuted for dealing cocaine as well as crack, and the status of each case.

The Government opposed the discovery motion, arguing, among other things, that there was no evidence or allegation "that the Government has acted unfairly or has prosecuted non-black defendants or failed to prosecute them." The District Court granted the motion. It ordered the Government (1) to provide a list of all cases from the last three years in which the Government charged both cocaine and firearms offenses, (2) to identify the race of the defendants in those cases, (3) to identify what levels of law enforcement were involved in the investigations of those cases, and (4) to explain its criteria for deciding to prosecute those defendants for federal cocaine offenses.

The Government moved for reconsideration of the District Court's discovery order. With this motion it submitted affidavits and other evidence to explain why it had chosen to prosecute respondents and why respondents' study did not support the inference that the Government was singling out blacks for cocaine prosecution. The federal and local agents participating in the case alleged in affidavits that race played no role in their investigation. An Assistant United States Attorney explained in an affidavit that the decision to prosecute met the general criteria for prosecution, because

> "there was over 100 grams of cocaine base involved, over twice the threshold necessary for a ten year mandatory minimum sentence; there were multiple sales involving multiple defendants, thereby indicating a fairly substantial crack cocaine ring; ... there were multiple federal firearms violations intertwined with the narcotics trafficking; the overall evidence in the case was extremely strong, including audio and videotapes of defendants; ... and several of the defendants had criminal histories including narcotics and firearms violations."

The Government also submitted sections of a published 1989 Drug Enforcement Administration report which concluded that "large-scale, interstate trafficking networks controlled by Jamaicans, Haitians and Black street gangs dominate the manufacture and distribution of crack."

In response, one of respondents' attorneys submitted an affidavit alleging that an intake coordinator at a drug treatment center had told her that there are "an equal number of caucasian users and dealers to minority users and dealers." Respondents also submitted an affidavit from a criminal defense attorney alleging that in his experience many nonblacks are prosecuted in state court for crack offenses, and a newspaper article reporting that Federal "crack criminals ... are being punished far more severely than if they had been caught with powder cocaine, and almost every single one of them is black," Newton, Harsher Crack Sentences Criticized as Racial Inequity, Los Angeles Times, Nov. 23, 1992, p. 1.

The District Court denied the motion for reconsideration. When the Government indicated it would not comply with the court's discovery order, the court dismissed the case.

A divided three-judge panel of the Court of Appeals for the Ninth Circuit reversed, holding that, because of the proof requirements for a selective-prosecution claim, defendants must "provide a colorable basis for believing that 'others similarly situated have not been prosecuted'" to obtain discovery. (Quoting United States v. Wayte, 710 F.2d 1385, 1387 (C.A.9 1983), aff'd, 470 U.S. 598 (1985)). The Court of Appeals voted to rehear the case en banc, and the en banc panel affirmed the District Court's order of dismissal, holding that "a defendant is not required to demonstrate that the government has failed to prosecute others who are similarly situated." We granted certiorari to determine the appropriate standard for discovery for a selective-prosecution claim.

[The Court held that Federal Rule of Criminal Procedure 16 did not mandate disclosure of material supporting a selective prosecution claim. That Rule requires disclosure of documents "material to the preparation of the defendant's defense" and the Court construed that phrase to refer to a defense that was responsive to the government's case-in-chief (e.g., that the defendant is not guilty). A selective prosecution attack was not material to the "defense" in this sense. See the discussion of this aspect of the opinion in Chapter 8, infra.]

\* \* \*

A selective-prosecution claim is not a defense on the merits to the criminal charge itself, but an independent assertion that the prosecutor has brought the charge for reasons forbidden by the Constitution. Our cases delineating the necessary elements to prove a claim of selective prosecution have taken great pains to explain that the standard is a demanding one.\* \* \*

A selective-prosecution claim asks a court to exercise judicial power over a "special province" of the Executive. The Attorney General and United States Attorneys retain broad discretion to enforce the Nation's criminal laws. \* \* \* In the ordinary case, so long as the prosecutor has probable cause to believe that the accused committed an offense defined by statute, the decision whether or not to prosecute, and what charge to file or bring before a grand jury, generally rests entirely in his discretion.

Of course, a prosecutor's discretion is subject to constitutional constraints. One of these constraints, imposed by the equal protection component of the Due Process Clause of the Fifth Amendment, is that the decision whether to prosecute may not be based on "an unjustifiable standard such as race, religion, or other arbitrary classification," Oyler v. Boles, 368 U.S. 448, 456 (1962). A defendant may demonstrate that the administration of a criminal law is "directed so exclusively against a particular class of persons . . . with a mind so unequal and oppressive" that the system of prosecution amounts to "a practical denial" of equal protection of the law. Yick Wo v. Hopkins, 118 U.S. 356, 373 (1886).

In order to dispel the presumption that a prosecutor has not violated equal protection, a criminal defendant must present "clear evidence to the contrary." We explained in *Wayte* why courts are "properly hesitant to examine the decision whether to prosecute." Judicial deference to the decisions of these executive officers rests in part on an assessment of the relative competence of prosecutors and courts. "Such factors as the strength of the case, the prosecution's general deterrence value, the Government's enforcement priorities, and the case's relationship to the Government's overall enforcement plan are not readily susceptible to the kind of analysis the courts are competent to undertake." It also stems from a concern not to unnecessarily impair the performance of a core executive constitutional function. "Examining the basis of a prosecution delays the criminal proceeding, threatens to chill law enforcement by subjecting the prosecutor's motives and decisionmaking to outside inquiry, and may undermine prosecutorial effectiveness by revealing the Government's enforcement policy."

The requirements for a selective-prosecution claim draw on ordinary equal protection standards. The claimant must demonstrate that the federal prosecutorial policy had a discriminatory effect and that it was motivated by a discriminatory purpose. To establish a discriminatory effect in a race case, the claimant must show that similarly situated individuals of a different race were not prosecuted. * * *

The similarly situated requirement does not make a selective-prosecution claim impossible to prove. [In Yick Wo v. Hopkins], we invalidated an ordinance, * * * adopted by San Francisco, that prohibited the operation of laundries in wooden buildings. The plaintiff in error successfully demonstrated that the ordinance was applied against Chinese nationals but not against other laundry-shop operators. The authorities had denied the applications of 200 Chinese subjects for permits to operate shops in wooden buildings, but granted the applications of 80 individuals who were not Chinese subjects to operate laundries in wooden buildings "under similar conditions."

* * *

Having reviewed the requirements to prove a selective-prosecution claim, we turn to the showing necessary to obtain discovery in support of such a claim. If discovery is ordered, the Government must assemble from its own files documents which might corroborate or refute the defendant's claim. Discovery thus imposes many of the costs present when the Government must respond to a prima facie case of selective prosecution. It will divert prosecutors' resources and may disclose the Government's prosecutorial strategy. The justifications for a rigorous standard for the elements of a selective-prosecution claim thus require a correspondingly rigorous standard for discovery in aid of such a claim.

The parties, and the Courts of Appeals which have considered the requisite showing to establish entitlement to discovery, describe this showing with a variety of phrases, like "colorable basis," "substantial threshold showing," "substantial and concrete basis," or "reasonable likelihood". However, the many labels for this showing conceal the degree of consensus about the evidence necessary to meet it. The Courts of Appeals "require some evidence tending to show the existence of the essential elements of the defense," discriminatory effect and discriminatory intent. United States v. Berrios, 501 F.2d 1207, 1211 (C.A.2 1974).

In this case we consider what evidence constitutes "some evidence tending to show the existence" of the discriminatory effect element. The Court of Appeals held that a defendant may establish a colorable basis for discriminatory effect without evidence that the Government has failed to prosecute others who are similarly situated to the defendant. We think it was mistaken in this view. The vast majority of the Courts of Appeals require the defendant to produce some evidence that similarly situated defendants of other races could have been prosecuted, but were not, and this requirement is consistent with our equal protection case law. As the three-judge panel explained," selective prosecution implies that a selection has taken place."

The Court of Appeals reached its decision in part because it started "with the presumption that people of all races commit all types of crimes—not with the premise that any type of crime is the exclusive province of any particular racial or ethnic group." It cited no authority for this proposition, which seems contradicted by the most recent statistics of the United States Sentencing Commission. Those statistics show that: More than 90% of the persons sentenced in 1994 for crack cocaine trafficking were black; 93.4% of convicted LSD dealers were white.; and 91% of those convicted for pornography or prostitution were white (Table 13). Presumptions at war with presumably reliable statistics have no proper place in the analysis of this issue.

The Court of Appeals also expressed concern about the "evidentiary obstacles defendants face." But all of its sister Circuits that have confronted the issue have required that defendants produce some evidence of differential treatment of similarly situated members of other races or protected classes. In the present case, if the claim of selective prosecution were well founded, it should not have been an insuperable task to prove that persons of other races were being treated differently than respondents. For instance, respondents could have investigated whether similarly situated persons of other races were prosecuted by the State of California, were known to federal law enforcement officers, but were not prosecuted in federal court. We think the required threshold—a credible showing of different treatment of similarly situated persons— adequately balances the Government's interest in vigorous prosecution and the defendant's interest in avoiding selective prosecution.

In the case before us, respondents' "study" did not constitute "some evidence tending to show the existence of the essential elements of" a selective-prosecution claim. The study failed to identify individuals who were not black, could have been prosecuted for the offenses for which respondents were charged, but were not so prosecuted. This omission was not remedied by respondents' evidence in opposition to the Government's motion for reconsideration. The newspaper article, which discussed the discriminatory effect of federal drug sentencing laws, was not relevant to an allegation of discrimination in decisions to prosecute. Respondents' affidavits, which recounted one attorney's conversation with a drug treatment center employee and the experience of another attorney defending drug prosecutions in state court, recounted hearsay and reported personal conclusions based on anecdotal evidence. The judgment of the Court of Appeals is therefore reversed, and the case is remanded for proceedings consistent with this opinion.

[The concurring opinions of JUSTICES SOUTER, GINSBURG and BREYER are omitted.]

**JUSTICE STEVENS, dissenting.**

\* \* \*

[I]t is undisputed that the brunt of the elevated federal penalties [for crack cocaine] falls heavily on blacks. While 65% of the persons who have used crack are white, in 1993 they represented only 4% of the federal offenders convicted of trafficking in crack. Eighty-eight percent of such defendants were black.. \* \* \*

The extraordinary severity of the imposed penalties and the troubling racial patterns of enforcement give rise to a special concern about the fairness of charging practices for crack offenses. \* \* \* In my view, the District Judge, who has sat on both the federal and the state benches in Los Angeles, acted well within her discretion to call for the development of facts that would demonstrate what standards, if any, governed the choice of forum where similarly situated offenders are prosecuted.

### Critique of Armstrong

Professor Davis, in Prosecution and Race: The Power and Privilege of Discretion, 67 Fordham L.Rev. 13 (1998), provides the following critique on the intent-based test of selective prosecution set forth by the Court in *Armstrong*:

> \* \* \* Instead of focusing on the harm experienced by African Americans as a result of actions by state actors, the Court has focused on whether the act itself is inherently invidious and whether the actor intended to cause the harm. In addition, the Court has placed the burden of proving intent on the shoulders of the victim. \* \* \*
>
> The main problem with this intent-focused analysis is that it is backward-looking. Although perhaps adequate in combating

straightforward and explicit discrimination as it existed in the past, it is totally deficient as a remedy for the more complex and systemic discrimination that African Americans currently experience. When state actors openly expressed their racist views, it was easy to identify and label the invidious nature of their actions. But today, with some notable exceptions, most racist behavior is not openly expressed. More significantly, some racist behavior is committed unconsciously, and many who engage in this behavior are well-intentioned people who would be appalled by the notion that they would be seen as behaving in a racist or discriminatory manner.

Unconscious racism, although arguably less offensive than purposeful discrimination, is no less harmful. In fact, in many ways it is more perilous because it is often unrecognizable to the victim as well as the perpetrator. And the Court, by focusing on intent rather than harm, has refused to recognize, much less provide a remedy for, this most common and widespread form of racism. * * *

For another critique of the *Armstrong* standards, see McAdams, Race and Selective Prosecution: Discovering the Pitfalls of *Armstrong*, 73 Chicago-Kent L.Rev. 605 (1998).

### *Unprosecuted Similar Conduct*

In United States v. Parham, 16 F.3d 844 (8th Cir.1994), the defendants were African-Americans who were convicted of voting more than once in the same Arkansas election. The defendants, pursuing selective prosecution claims, proffered evidence of numerous voter irregularities attributable to whites that went unprosecuted. These included episodes where African-American disabled or elderly voters were refused assistance while whites were helped, and cases of intimidation of African-American voters by whites brandishing guns. While the court found that these acts by whites warranted prosecution, they were held irrelevant to the defendants' selective prosecution claims. This is because the acts by whites were

> not sufficiently similar to the acts of voter fraud for which Parham and Johnson were prosecuted to constitute a prima facie case of selective prosecution. Parham and Johnson were in effect charged with forging names on absentee ballots. They presented no evidence that other's acts of absentee ballot forgery or fraud were tolerated without prosecution. Where a defendant cannot show anyone in a similar situation who was not prosecuted, he has not met the threshold point of showing that there has been selectivity in prosecution.

Judge Heaney dissented in *Parham*, reasoning that the defendant need only establish that unprosecuted crimes are *similar*, not that they are identical.

### Example of a Case in Which Discovery Was Ordered on a Selective Prosecution Claim

United States v. Jones, 159 F.3d 969 (6th Cir.1998), is one of the rare cases in which discovery was ordered to permit investigation of a selective prosecution claim, after the defendant was convicted of drugs and weapons offenses. The shocking facts were related by the court as follows:

> Jones argues on appeal that he was prosecuted based on his race, citing to the Government's decision to prosecute him in federal court instead of state court and the egregious and unprofessional conduct of the arresting local law enforcement officers, Kerry Nelson and Terry Spence.
>
> The conduct of officers Nelson and Spence was undeniably shameful. Prior to the planned arrest of Jones and his wife, the two officers had t-shirts made with Jones's picture emblazoned on the front accompanied by the printed words, "See ya, wouldn't want to be ya" above the picture, and below, "going back to prison." On the back of the t-shirts appeared a picture of Jones's wife, a co-defendant, with the words, "wait on me, Slow, [Jones' nickname was "Slow Motion"] I am coming, too." The two officers were wearing the t-shirts when they arrested Jones in August of 1995. Over one year later, while on a Caribbean cruise, Officer Spence mailed a postcard purchased in Jamaica to Jones while he was in custody awaiting trial. Jones regards Spence's mailing of the postcard, that pictured a black woman with a basket of bananas on her head, as a racial insult. On the postcard, postmarked from Cozumel, Mexico on October 24, 1996, appeared the following handwritten message:
>
> > Slow Motion. What's up? Haven't talked to you since you were in court and lost all your motions. Sorry, but life goes on. Just wanted to drop you a line and let you know that Cozumel, Mexico is beautiful. I'm on vacation and I'll be back Monday for trial, and chances are good you're going to jail for a long time. See ya, Officer Spence.
>
> Spence testified that he sent the postcard to relieve "stress I was feeling while I was on the cruise." Regarding the t-shirts, Spence explained that "It was just—I took pride in arresting [Jones]." Nelson also testified that he wore the t-shirt to demonstrate "a great deal of pride in Mr. Jones's arrest."

In addition, there was testimony at the hearing with respect to Jones's claim that local law enforcement agents improperly referred his case for federal prosecution based on his race. [Federal prosecution subjected to the defendants to much harsher sentencing penalties]. The testimony showed that the Murfreesboro Police Department had referred fourteen defendants, including Jones and his Caucasian co-defendant, Donnie Billings, for federal prosecution in the preceding five years. Of those fourteen defendants, four were African-American, two were Columbian, two were Lebanese, one was Israeli and five were Caucasian. Of the cases referred for federal prosecution in the preceding five years, however, only Jones's and Billings's prosecutions involved crack cocaine. Further, Jones presented evidence of eight non-African-American defendants prosecuted for crack cocaine offenses who were not referred for federal prosecution.

The court found that Jones had established a prima facie case of discriminatory intent, which is the first part of the intent/impact test imposed by *Armstrong*.

The court found, however, that there was not enough evidence of discriminatory impact to require dismissal of the indictment. Yet there was enough to justify further discovery.

The second prong of a selective prosecution claim— discriminatory effect—creates a greater challenge for Jones. * * * The evidence that Jones has presented to this point does not establish that law enforcement failed to refer similarly situated non-African-Americans for federal prosecution. Accordingly, Jones thus far has not established a prima facie case of discriminatory effect.

In *Armstrong*, the Supreme Court stated that in order for a defendant to obtain discovery in a selective prosecution case, there must be a showing of "some evidence tending to show the existence of the essential elements of the defense, discriminatory effect and discriminatory intent." As we have stated, Jones has established a showing of discriminatory intent. With respect to discriminatory effect, we believe that Jones has set forth some evidence "tending to show the existence of discriminatory effect," despite the fact that Jones was unable to establish a prima facie case of discriminatory effect on the merits of his selective prosecution claim. Obviously, a defendant need not prove his case in order to justify discovery on an issue.

Jones has presented evidence that law enforcement referred only him and his co-defendant Billings for a federal prosecution that involved crack cocaine, and failed to refer for federal prosecution eight non-African-Americans who were arrested and prosecuted for crack cocaine. The harshness of the crack cocaine guidelines in federal court is certainly a factor that may have been considered in referring defendants for federal prosecution. The fact that law enforcement never considered foregoing the prosecution of Billings, Jones's white co-defendant, in federal court does not change our analysis. It would have been beyond foolish for law enforcement to have done such a thing, considering that Jones's and Billings's cases involved the same events.

Accordingly, Jones has set forth "some evidence" tending to show the existence of discriminatory effect that warrants discovery on his selective prosecution claim. * * * If Jones is able to obtain evidence that establishes a prima facie case of discriminatory effect, Jones may renew his motion to dismiss the indictment.

## 3. Choice of Forum

In the American system of dual sovereignty, the same criminal conduct is often prosecutable under either federal or state law. It is also possible for the choice of forum to be outcome-determinative. For example, in drug cases—as indicated in *Jones* above—the relevant sentencing laws generally provide for much harsher sentences than could be given for the same conduct in a state prosecution. Suppose that the defendant can show that a federal prosecution was brought in order to trigger the harsher federal sentences—but unlike in *Jones, supra,* there is no allegation that the decision was based on racial or other discriminatory grounds. Is the defendant entitled to relief?

A typical response to a challenge to the prosecutor's choice of forum is found in United States v. Jacobs, 4 F.3d 603 (8th Cir.1993), a case in which the defendant would have received probation had he been convicted on state charges, but instead received a five-year prison sentence after being convicted in federal court. As the court noted:

> Prosecutors have broad discretion in making prosecutive decisions. So long as the prosecutor has probable cause to believe that the accused committed an offense defined by statute, the decision whether or not to prosecute, and what charge to file, generally rests entirely in his discretion. In exercising this discretion, the prosecutor may take into account the penalties available upon conviction. The prosecutor may not, of course, base the decision to prosecute upon impermissible factors such as race, religion, or other arbitrary and unjustifiable classifications. Likewise the prosecutor may not file charges out of vindictiveness nor in retaliation for a defendant's exercise of legal rights.

The fact that the federal government prosecutes a federal crime in a federal court that could have been or has been prosecuted as a state crime in a state court does not itself violate due process. Choice of forum lies within the realm of prosecutorial discretion.

See also United States v. Dockery, 965 F.2d 1112 (D.C.Cir.1992) (it was permissible for the U.S. Attorney in the District of Columbia to terminate prosecutions in the D.C. Superior Court and reinstitute them in the U.S. District Court a block away to take advantage of the sterner penalties set by the federal sentencing law; defendant received a ten-year minimum sentence, which would have been 1–5 years in the Superior Court); United States v. Williams, 963 F.2d 1337 (10th Cir.1992) (defendant received 20 years under federal law, and would have received 5 years under state law: "prosecution in a federal rather than a state court does not violate due process despite the absence of guidelines for such referral"); United States v. Ucciferri, 960 F.2d 953 (11th Cir.1992) (it was irrelevant that a federal prosecution was motivated by a desire to avoid more rigorous state constitutional protections).

## 4.  Choice of Crime

What if two criminal statutes cover the same conduct—does the prosecutor have the discretion to charge under the statute resulting in the longer prison sentence? In United States v. Batchelder, 442 U.S. 114 (1979), Justice Marshall wrote for the Court as it held that a defendant who was convicted of receiving a firearm that had traveled in interstate commerce could be sentenced to five years' imprisonment, the maximum term under the statute, and that he was not entitled to be sentenced under another statute that punished felons for transporting firearms with a maximum penalty of two years. Justice Marshall reasoned that a wrongdoer has notice that more than one statute covers his conduct. Thus, the fact that conduct violates two statutes does not require a prosecution under the more lenient of them. The Court emphasized the deference due to the prosecutor in making a charging decision and reiterated that a defendant's sole complaint is against invidious discrimination.

Prosecutors may, however, be limited in their ability to charge a defendant in a certain way as punishment for a defendant's exercise of constitutional rights. The subject of vindictive prosecutions is considered in Chapter 12, infra.

# V.   THE GRAND JURY

The American criminal justice system, like the American political system, has checks and balances to prevent against too much centralized authority being placed in the hands of the executive. In some instances, depending on the jurisdiction and the seriousness of the crime, the grand jury operates as a check on the prosecutor's decision to charge. In other instances, the preliminary hearing serves this function. In some rare instances, both checks are available. Where a minor offense is charged, it is possible that no pretrial screening procedure will be utilized. This section will focus on the grand jury and how it operates.

## A.  BACKGROUND ON THE GRAND JURY

The Ninth Circuit, in United States v. Navarro-Vargas, 408 F.3d 1184 (9th Cir. 2005) provides a good summary of the history and purpose of the grand jury, and addresses critiques about its modern function. The court relies on an extensive list of sources, most of which are deleted from the entry below.

### *The Historical Role of the Grand Jury*

### *1.   The Early English Grand Jury: Quasi-Prosecutor*

The modern grand jury is a direct descendant of the English grand jury first employed more than 800 years ago. Its origins belie its modern role as intermediary between the people and their government. The earliest grand juries were the tool of the Crown. In 1164, anxious to consolidate power held by the church and feudal barons, King Henry II signed the Constitutions of Clarendon, which created a jury to charge all laity who were to be tried in ecclesiastical courts. Two years later he established the Assize of Clarendon, which was composed of twelve men who would "present" those suspected of crimes to the royal courts. These acts reasserted the King's power over his subjects and filled his coffers with the proceeds from chattels confiscated after conviction.

During its first hundred years, * * * the English grand jury was somewhat like a quasi-prosecutor for the King. Indeed, grand juries were expected to bring charges based on their own knowledge, as well as consider charges brought by prosecutors. * * *

The first real evidence of the grand jury acting as a shield to protect the accused was in 1681 when two London grand juries refused to indict the Earl of Shaftesbury and his follower Stephen Colledge, the political enemies of King Charles II. The King wanted them held over for public proceedings before the grand jury, but the grand jury insisted on conducting its inquiry in private. Given its powerful influence, the Crown expected a quick indictment pursuant to its charges. However, the grand jury returned the equivalent of a no-bill in the matter, defying the Crown's will both in holding private proceedings and in its ultimate decision not to indict. The Shaftesbury and Colledge cases established grand jury secrecy, which continues to be a crucial element in grand juries serving as an independent screen. * * *

### 2. The Colonial Grand Jury: Quasi-Legislative, Quasi-Administrative

American colonists adopted the grand jury as integral to the common law system. * * * In America, the institution gained broad powers to propose legislation and perform various administrative tasks. Grand juries "exercised broad, unorthodox powers," inspecting roads, jails, and other public buildings; monitoring public works expenditures, construction and maintenance; proposing new legislation; and criticizing poor administration. The colonial grand jury still performed a quasi-prosecutorial role by accusing individuals suspected of crimes, but colonial grand juries demonstrated greater independence than their English counterparts, due in part to the relatively weak position of colonial governments. With their expanding quasi-legislative and quasi-administrative roles, grand juries acquired greater popularity because they were regarded as more representative of the people. * * * [T]he American grand jury in effect enjoyed a roving commission to ferret out official malfeasance or self-dealing of any sort and bring it to the attention of the public at large * * *. Following the English traditions established in the Shaftesbury and Colledge cases, grand jury secrecy remained an important part of grand jury proceedings in the colonies. Grand jurors pledged to an oath of secrecy, and its violation was both a contempt and a crime.

While Colonial grand juries continued to serve as accusatory bodies, they occasionally refused to return indictments in high-profile cases. The most celebrated example in American history is that of John Peter Zenger, a newspaper publisher charged with libel after criticizing the Governor of New York. Based on the jury instructions, it seems clear that Zenger was guilty of the crime of libel. Nevertheless, three grand juries refused to indict not because of insufficient evidence but rather because the jurors were politically opposed to the prosecutions. As the Revolutionary War drew closer, the grand jury became popular at least as much from its success as a political weapon as from its role in the criminal justice system. * * * Grand jurors, selected from the public, frustrated prosecutors loyal to the king by refusing to indict those charged under unpopular laws imposed by the Crown, often on the urging of colonial judges. Grand jury presentments served an additional function during this time: they became excellent mediums of propaganda as grand juries issued stinging denunciations of Great Britain and stirring defenses of their rights as Englishmen. * * *

* * * In early debates over the ratification of the Constitution, before the Bill of Rights had been written, some feared that "there is no provision ... to prevent the attorney-general from filing

information against any person, whether he is indicted by the grand jury or not; in consequence of which the most innocent person in the commonwealth may be taken by virtue of a warrant issued in consequence of such information. . . ." Because of this fear, the Grand Jury Clause, located in the Fifth Amendment, was adopted with little debate or discussion.

### 3. The Post-Revolutionary and Nineteenth Century Grand Jury: Screening Function

As they had in colonial times, nineteenth century grand juries occasionally asserted their independence by refusing to indict under unpopular laws, even when the grand jury was instructed to indict if the facts satisfied the law. Prominently, grand juries in Kentucky and Mississippi refused to indict former Vice President Aaron Burr, although he was finally indicted in Virginia; refused to indict Americans who aided French privateers in violation of the Neutrality Proclamation of 1793; and resisted indicting those accused of violating the controversial Alien and Sedition Acts. Throughout the nineteenth century, courts continued to recognize the necessity of secrecy in grand jury proceedings. This secrecy allowed grand juries to independently determine whether to indict, despite a judge's instructions.

\* \* \*

The political potential in the screening function of the grand jury was \* \* \* manifest during the Civil War era. Prior to the war, Southern grand juries readily indicted those involved in crimes related to abolition of the slave trade, while Northern grand juries were slow to indict those charged with violations of the fugitive slave laws. Following the Civil War, Southern grand juries frustrated enforcement of Reconstruction-era laws by refusing to indict Ku Klux Klan members and others accused of committing crimes against newly-freed blacks. \* \* \*

### 4. The Modern Grand Jury

By the twentieth century, dramatic confrontations between prosecutors and jurors in grand jury proceedings had become rare. Currently, grand jurors no longer perform any other function but to investigate crimes and screen indictments, and they tend to indict in the overwhelming number of cases brought by prosecutors. Because of this, many criticize the modern grand jury as no more than a "rubber stamp" for the prosecutor. *See* Federal Justice Statistics Resource Center, Federal Justice Statistics Database, *at* http://fjsrc.urban.org (noting that federal grand juries returned only twenty-one no-bills in 2001). \* \* \* As the grand jury's tendency to indict has become more pronounced, some commentators claim that the modern grand jury has lost its independence. * * * Against this criticism, the Supreme Court has steadfastly insisted that the grand jury remains as a shield against unfounded prosecutions.

---

So as a historical matter, the grand jury served two major functions. On one hand, it was a "buffer" protecting citizens from unjust prosecution by the state. On the other hand, it served an enforcement function by investigating incidents or offenses that the grand jurors thought suspicious. These functions were considered so important that they are expressed in the Fifth Amendment, which states in relevant part:

> No person shall be held to answer for a capital, or otherwise infamous crime, unless on a presentment or indictment of a Grand Jury, except in cases arising in the land or naval forces, or in the Militia, when in actual service in time of War or public danger; * * *.

The Supreme Court has stated that the grand jury's dual historic functions "survive to this day. Its responsibilities continue to include both the determination whether there is probable cause to believe a crime has been committed and the protection of citizens against unfounded criminal prosecutions." United States v. Calandra, 414 U.S. 338 (1974).

Many observers, however, see the modern grand jury as performing only the first (prosecutorial) function and ignoring the second (protective) function. For example, Hafetz and Pellettieri conclude that

> whatever its historic antecedents, the grand jury has long ceased to function as an independent entity acting both as shield for the citizenry as well as sword for the prosecutor. * * * [T]he grand jury functions as an investigative tool of the prosecutor. Employing the power of compulsory process in a secret proceeding the prosecutor investigates and determines with virtually no check by the grand jury who gets indicted and for what.

Time to Reform the Grand Jury, The Champion, at 12 (Jan. 1999).

As you read the materials in this Chapter, consider whether the assessment of the grand jury as only a tool for the prosecutor is correct, and if so, whether reforms can be instituted to return the grand jury to its role as protector of citizens from unfounded prosecutions.

### *A Right Not Incorporated*

Unlike most other provisions of the Bill of Rights examined thus far, the right to a grand jury indictment does not extend to defendants accused of state crimes. In Hurtado v. California, 110 U.S. 516 (1884), the Supreme Court held that the right to a grand jury indictment is not incorporated in the Due Process Clause of the Fourteenth Amendment.

Today, slightly less than half the states require prosecution by indictment for serious crimes as a matter of state constitutional or statutory law. The majority of the states use the alternatives of preliminary hearing and the filing of an information, methods of charging discussed later in this Chapter.

### What Is an Infamous Crime?

The Fifth Amendment requires a grand jury indictment for the prosecution of an "infamous crime." Courts have held that a crime is "infamous" only if it can result in either hard labor or imprisonment in a penitentiary. Ex parte Wilson, 114 U.S. 417 (1885). Thus, the court in United States v. Armored Transport, Inc., 629 F.2d 1313 (9th Cir.1980), held that an indictment was not constitutionally required for a corporation to be convicted of an antitrust felony—a corporation is subject only to a fine and a fine is not an infamous punishment. See also United States v. Colt, 126 F.3d 981 (7th Cir.1997) (no right to grand jury indictment where statute authorized imprisonment in a federal prison camp, but not in a federal penitentiary: "The distinction between penitentiaries and other places of imprisonment survives in today's federal prison system. * * * Only eight of the Bureau of Prisons' institutions are designated as U.S. Penitentiaries, which feature the highest security and the closest control of prisoner actions.").

### How the Grand Jury Works

The court in In re Motions of Dow Jones & Co., 142 F.3d 496 (D.C.Cir.1998), provided this summary of the operation of the grand jury:

> Grand juries summon witnesses and documents with subpoenas. Witnesses, including custodians of documents, report on the scheduled date not to a courtroom, but to a hallway outside the room where the grand jury is sitting. The witness must enter the grand jury room alone, without his or her lawyer. No judge presides and none is present. See Beale et al., Grand Jury Law and Practice § 4.10, at 4–44 (2d ed.1997). Inside the grand jury room are sixteen to twenty-three grand jurors, one or more prosecuting attorneys, and a court reporter. 18 U.S.C. § 3321; Fed.R.Crim.P. 6. The witness is sworn, and questioning commences, all to the end of determining whether "there is adequate basis for bringing a criminal charge." United States v. Williams, 504 U.S. 36 (1992). Other than witnesses, each person present in the grand jury room or otherwise assisting the prosecutor is forbidden from disclosing matters occurring before the grand jury, Fed.R.Crim.P. 6.

The court explained judicial oversight of the grand jury in the following paragraph:

Although the grand jury normally operates, of course, in the courthouse and under judicial auspices, its institutional relationship with the Judicial Branch has traditionally been, so to speak, at arm's length. Still, at many points, from service of the subpoena through the completion of the witness's grand jury appearance, judicial proceedings relating to the grand jury may take place. The judge may be called upon to decide a witness's motion to postpone the date of testimony or to quash the subpoena. If a witness refuses to answer questions on the basis of a testimonial privilege, such as attorney-client or husband-wife, the grand jury may seek a court order compelling the witness to answer. This may be done forthwith, through an oral presentation to the court, or upon the filing of pleadings, followed by a hearing. A hearing will also be needed if a witness asserts his or her privilege against self-incrimination, and the prosecutor seeks an order from the court granting the witness immunity. See 18 U.S.C. § 6003(a).

## B.  THE CHARGE TO THE GRAND JURY

What follows are excerpts from the Model Grand Jury Charge approved by the Judicial Conference of the United States. It provides a useful introduction to the work of the grand jury and the expectations that the community has for this body. The charge is given by the judge who empanels and supervises the grand jury.

### MODEL GRAND JURY CHARGE

Ladies and Gentlemen:

1.    Now that you have been empaneled and sworn as a Grand Jury, it is the Court's responsibility to instruct you as to the law which should govern your actions and your deliberations as Grand Jurors.

2.    * * * The purpose of the Grand Jury is to determine whether there is sufficient evidence to justify a formal accusation against a person—that is, to determine if there is "probable cause" to believe the person committed a crime. If law enforcement officials were not required to submit to an impartial grand jury proof of guilt as to a proposed charge against a person suspected of having committed a crime, they would be free to arrest a suspect and bring that suspect to trial no matter how little evidence existed to support the charge.

3.    The Grand Jury is an independent body and does not belong to any branch of the government. As members of the Grand Jury, you, in a very real sense, stand between the government and the person being investigated by the government. A federal grand jury must never be made an instrument of private prejudice, vengeance, or malice. It is your duty to see to it that indictments are returned

only against those who you find probable cause to believe are guilty and to see to it that the innocent are not compelled to go to trial.

4.   A member of the Grand Jury who is related by blood or marriage to a person under investigation, or who knows that person well enough to have a biased state of mind as to that person, or is biased for any reason, should not participate in the investigation of that person or in the return of the indictment. This does not mean that if you have an opinion you should not participate in the investigation. However, it does mean that if you have a fixed opinion before you hear any evidence, either on a basis of friendship or ill will or some other similar motivation, you should not participate in that investigation and in voting on the indictment.

5.   Sixteen of the twenty-three members of the Grand Jury constitute a quorum and must be present for the transaction of any business. If fewer than this number are present, even for a moment, the proceedings of the Grand Jury must stop.

## Limitation on the Power of the Grand Jury

6.   Although as Grand Jurors you have extensive powers, they are limited in several important respects.

7.   You can only investigate conduct which violates federal criminal laws. Criminal activity which violates state law is outside your inquiry. Sometimes, though, the same conduct violates both federal and state law, and this you may properly consider.

8.   There is also a geographic limitation on the scope of your inquiries in the exercise of your power. You may inquire only to federal offenses committed in this district.

9.   You cannot judge the wisdom of the criminal laws enacted by Congress, that is, whether or not there should or should not be a federal law designating certain activity as criminal. That is to be determined by Congress and not by you.[8]

10. Furthermore, when deciding whether or not to indict, you should not consider punishment in the event of conviction.

## The Grand Jury Procedures

11. The cases which you will hear will come before you in various ways. Frequently, suspects are arrested during or shortly after the commission of an alleged crime, and they are taken before a Magistrate Judge, who then holds a preliminary hearing to determine whether there is probable cause to believe that the person

---

[8]   The court in United States v. Navarro-Vargas, 408 F.3d 1184 (9th Cir. 2005), rejected the defendants' claim that this charge unconstitutionally impinged upon the grand jury's independence. See the discussion on grand jury nullification later in this Chapter.

has committed a crime. If the Magistrate Judge finds such probable cause, he or she will direct that the person be held for the action of the Grand Jury so that you can independently consider whether there should be an indictment.

12. Other cases will be brought before you by a government attorney—the U.S. Attorney or an Assistant U.S. Attorney before an arrest but after an investigation has been conducted by a governmental agency such as the Federal Bureau of Investigation, the Treasury Department, the Drug Enforcement Administration, Postal Authorities, or other federal law enforcement officials.

13. Since the government attorney has the duty of prosecuting persons charged with the commission of federal crimes, the government attorney will present the matters which the government desires to have you consider. The government will point out to you the laws which it believes have been violated, and will subpoena for testimony before you such witnesses as the government attorney may consider important and necessary and also any other witnesses that you may request or direct be called before you.

14. If during the course of your hearings, a different crime other than the one you are investigating surfaces, you have the right to pursue this new crime. Although you can subpoena new witnesses and documents, you have no power to employ investigators or to expend federal funds for investigative purposes. If the government attorney refuses to assist you or if you believe he or she is not acting impartially, you may take it up with me or any Judge of this Court. You may use this power even over the active opposition of the government's attorneys, if you believe it is necessary to do so in the interest of justice.

## Evidence

15. The evidence you will consider will normally consist of oral testimony of witnesses and written documents. Each witness will appear before you separately. When the witness first appears before you, the Grand Jury foreperson will administer the witness an oath or affirmation, to testify truthfully. After this has been accomplished, the witness may be questioned. Ordinarily, the government attorney questions the witness first. Next, the foreperson may question the witness, and then any other members of the Grand Jury may ask questions. In the event a witness does not speak or understand the English language, an interpreter may be brought into the Grand Jury room to assist in the questioning.

16. Witnesses should be treated courteously and questions put to them in an orderly fashion. If you have any doubt whether it is

proper to ask a particular question, ask the government attorney for advice. If necessary, a ruling may be obtained from the court.

17.  You alone decide how many witnesses you want to hear. You can subpoena witnesses from anywhere in the country, directing the government attorney to issue necessary subpoenas. However, persons should not ordinarily be subjected to disruption of their daily lives, harassed, annoyed, or inconvenienced, nor should public funds be expended to bring in witnesses unless you believe they can provide meaningful evidence which will assist you in your investigation.

18.  Every witness has certain rights when appearing before a Grand Jury. Witnesses have the right to refuse to answer any question if the answer would tend to incriminate them and the right to know that anything they say may be used against them. The Grand Jury should hold no prejudice against a witness who exercises the right against compulsory self-incrimination, and this can play no part in the return of any indictment.

19.  Although witnesses are not permitted to have a lawyer present with them in the Grand Jury room, the law permits witnesses to confer with their lawyer outside of the Grand Jury room. Since an appearance before a Grand Jury may present complex legal problems requiring the assistance of a lawyer, you also can not hold it against a witness if a witness chooses to exercise this right and leaves the Grand Jury room to confer with an attorney.

20.  Ordinarily, neither the person being investigated by the government nor any witnesses on behalf of that person will testify before the Grand Jury. Upon his or her request, preferably in writing, you may afford that person an opportunity to appear before you. Because the appearance of the person being investigated before you may raise complicated legal problems, you should seek the government attorney's advice and, if necessary, the Court's ruling before his or her appearance is permitted. Before that person testifies, he or she must be advised of his or her rights and required to sign a formal waiver. You should be completely satisfied that the person being investigated understands what he or she is doing. * * *

21.  The determination of whether a witness is telling the truth is something that you must decide. * * * You may consider in that regard whether the witnesses are personally interested in the outcome of the investigation, whether their testimony has been corroborated or supported by other witnesses or circumstances, what opportunity they have had for observing or acquiring knowledge concerning the matters about which they testify, the reasonableness or probability of the testimony they relate to you, and their manner and demeanor in testifying before you.

22. Hearsay is testimony as to facts not known by the witness of the witness's own personal knowledge but which have been told or related to the witness by persons other than the person being investigated. Hearsay testimony, if deemed by you to be persuasive, may in itself provide a basis for returning an indictment. You must be satisfied only that there is evidence against the accused showing probable cause, even if such evidence is composed of hearsay testimony that might or might not be admissible in evidence at a trial.

23. Frequently, charges are made against more than one person. It will be your duty to examine the evidence as it relates to each person, and to make your finding as to each person. In other words, where charges are made against more than one person, you may indict all of the persons or only those persons who you believe properly deserve indictment.

**Deliberation and Vote**

24. After you have heard all the evidence you wish to hear in a particular matter, you will then proceed to deliberate as to whether the person being investigated should be indicted. No one other than your own members or an interpreter necessary to assist a juror who is hearing or speech impaired is to be present while you are deliberating or voting.

25. To return an indictment charging an individual with an offense, it is not necessary that you find that individual guilty beyond a reasonable doubt. You are not a trial jury and your task is not to decide the guilt or innocence of the person charged. Your task is to determine whether the government's evidence as presented to you is sufficient to cause you to conclude that there is probable cause to believe that the person being investigated committed the offense charged. To put it another way, you should vote to indict where the evidence presented to you is sufficiently strong to warrant a reasonable person's belief that the person being investigated is probably guilty of the offense charged.[9]

---

[9] In United States v. Navarro-Vargas, 408 F.3d 1184 (9th Cir. 2005), the defendants challenged this instruction because it told grand jurors that they "should" indict when they find probable cause, but it did not explain that grand jurors can refuse to indict even if they find probable cause. The court rejected the challenge, stating that the instructions as a whole "remind the grand jury of its independence from the federal government and leave room for it to refuse to indict." That is, the word "should" does not mean "must." On February 11, 2013, the American Bar Association adopted Resolution 104 J, which urges an amendment to paragraph 25 so that it would read as follows: "To return an indictment charging an individual with an offense, it is not necessary that you find that individual guilty beyond a reasonable doubt. You are not a trial jury and your task is not to decide the guilt or innocence of the person charged. Your task is to determine whether the government's evidence as presented to you is sufficient to cause you to conclude that there is probable cause to believe that the person being investigated committed the offense charged. To put it another way, you may vote to indict only where the evidence presented

26. Each juror has the right to express his or her view of the matter under consideration. Only after all Grand Jurors have been given full opportunity to be heard will a vote be taken. You may decide after deliberation among yourselves that further evidence should be considered before a vote is taken. In such case you may direct to subpoena the additional documents or witnesses you desire to consider.

27. When you have decided to vote, the foreperson shall designate a juror as secretary who will keep a record of the vote, which shall be filed with the Clerk of Court. The record does not include the names of the jurors but only the number of those voting for the indictment. Remember, at least sixteen jurors must be present at all times, and at least twelve members must vote in favor of an indictment before one may be returned.

28. If twelve or more members of the Grand Jury, after deliberation, believe that an indictment is warranted, then you will request the government attorney to prepare the formal written indictment if one has not already been prepared and presented to you. The indictment will set forth the date and place of the alleged offense, will assert the circumstances making the alleged conduct criminal, and will identify the criminal statute violated. The foreperson will sign the indictment as a true bill, in the space followed by the word "foreperson." It is the duty of the foreperson to sign every indictment, whether the foreperson voted for or against. If less than twelve members of the Grand Jury vote in favor of an indictment which has been submitted to you for your consideration, the foreperson will endorse the indictment "Not a True Bill" and return it to the Court and the Court will impound it.

29. Indictments which have been signed as a true bill will be presented to a Judge [or a Magistrate Judge] in open court by your foreperson at the conclusion of each deliberative session of the Grand Jury. In the absence of the foreperson, a deputy foreperson may act in place of the foreperson and perform all functions and duties of the foreperson.

---

to you is sufficiently strong to warrant a reasonable person's belief that the person being investigated is probably guilty of the offense charged." The same resolution urged a change in the language of paragraph 23 so that it would read as follows: "Frequently, charges are made against more than one person. It will be your duty to examine the evidence as it relates to each person, and to make your finding as to each person. In other words, where charges are made against more than one person, you may indict only those persons who you believe properly deserve indictment. You must remember to consider the charges against each person separately." The resolution also recommended deletion of paragraph 10.

## Independence of the Grand Jury

30. It is extremely important for you to realize that * * * the Grand Jury is independent of the United States Attorney and is not an arm or agent of the Federal Bureau of Investigation, the Drug Enforcement Administration, the Internal Revenue Service, or any governmental agency charged with prosecuting a crime. Simply put, as I have already told you, the Grand Jury is an independent body and does not belong to any branch of the government.

31. However, as a practical matter you must work closely with the government attorneys. They will provide you with important service in helping you to find your way when confronted with complex legal matters. It is entirely proper that you should receive this assistance. If past experience is any indication of what to expect in the future, then you can expect candor, honesty and good faith in matters presented by the government attorneys.[10] However, ultimately, you must depend on your own independent judgment, never becoming an arm of the United States Attorney's office. The government attorneys are prosecutors. You are not. If the facts suggest that you should not indict, then you should not do so, even in the face of the opposition or statements of the government attorney. You would violate your oath if you merely "rubber-stamped" indictments brought before you by the government representatives.

* * *

## The Obligation of Secrecy

33. Your proceedings are secret and must remain secret permanently unless and until the Court decrees otherwise. You cannot relate to your family, to the news or television reporters, or to anyone that which transpired in the Grand Jury room. There are several important reasons for this requirement. A premature disclosure of Grand Jury action may frustrate the ends of justice by giving an opportunity to the person being investigated to escape and become a fugitive or to destroy evidence. Also, if the testimony of a witness is disclosed, the witness may be subject to intimidation, retaliation, bodily injury, or other tampering before testifying at trial. Thirdly, the requirement of secrecy protects an innocent person who may have come under investigation but has been cleared by the actions of the Grand Jury. In the eyes of some, investigation by a Grand Jury alone carries with it a suggestion of guilt. Thus great

---

[10] In United States v. Navarro-Vargas, 408 F.3d 1184 (9th Cir. 2005), the defendants challenged this instruction because it amounted to a "vote of confidence" by the judge on the honesty of government attorneys and therefore undermined the independence of the grand jury. The court rejected the defendants' argument by looking to the instruction as a whole, reasoning that the passage would be problematic if it stated that the Grand Jury was an agent of the U.S. Attorney—but it did not.

injury can be done to a person's good name even though the person is not indicted. And fourth, the secrecy requirement helps to protect the members of the grand jury themselves from improper contacts by those under investigation. For all these reasons, therefore, the secrecy requirement is of the utmost importance and must be regarded by you as an absolute duty. If you violate your oath of secrecy, you may be subject to punishment.

34. To insure the secrecy of Grand Jury proceedings, the law provides that only authorized persons may be in the Grand Jury room while evidence is being presented. Only the members of the Grand Jury, the government attorney, the witness under examination, the court reporter, and an interpreter, if required, may be present.

* * *

## Conclusion

36. The importance of the service you will perform is demonstrated by the very comprehensive and important oath which you took a short while ago. It is an oath rooted in history and thousands of your forebears have taken similar oaths. Therefore, as good citizens, you should be proud to have been selected to assist in the administration of the American system of justice.

## C. THE PROCEDURES OF THE GRAND JURY

Rule 6 of the Federal Rules of Criminal Procedure illustrates typical procedures of the grand jury—providing for number of jurors (16 to 23), provisions on secrecy, and the process and requirements for handing down an indictment. State grand juries may have fewer members and operate somewhat differently. But, the limitations on who can be present in the grand jury room and other aspects of Rule 6 are common to most grand juries. See Fed.R.Crim.P. 6 in the Statutory Supplement.

### *Discriminatory Selection of Grand Jurors*

The Equal Protection Clause prohibits racial or ethnic discrimination in the selection of grand jurors. See Rose v. Mitchell, 443 U.S. 545 (1979) (racial discrimination in the selection of grand jurors is a valid ground for setting aside a criminal conviction, even where the defendant has been found guilty beyond a reasonable doubt by a properly constituted petit jury at a trial that was free from other constitutional error). In Castaneda v. Partida, 430 U.S. 482 (1977), the Court established that statistics could be used to make out a prima facie case of discrimination against Mexican-Americans, even where a majority of a county's population were Mexican-Americans. Challenges under the Fourteenth Amendment are like all of the challenges to government action on the basis of suspect classifications. See also Jefferson v. Morgan, 962 F.2d 1185 (6th Cir.1992) (statistical evidence, adjusted by standard deviation, shows systematic exclusion of African-Americans from grand jury; conviction reversed and indictment dismissed; error was not harmless simply because the defendant was convicted at trial).

### Discriminatory Selection of Grand Jury Forepersons

Chief Justice Burger wrote for the Court in Hobby v. United States, 468 U.S. 339 (1984), as it held that discrimination in the selection of grand jury forepersons and deputy forepersons in a federal district did not require reversal of a conviction. Chief Justice Burger condemned all discrimination in the selection of grand jurors, but found that the ministerial functions of the foreperson and the deputy added little to the role that any particular grand juror plays. Thus, as long as the grand jury itself was validly selected, discrimination in the selection of the two ministerial leaders did not prejudice the defendant.

### Secrecy of Grand Jury Proceedings

The Supreme Court has consistently recognized the importance of grand jury secrecy:

> First, if preindictment proceedings were made public, many prospective witnesses would be hesitant to come forward voluntarily, knowing that those against whom they testify would be aware of that testimony. Moreover, witnesses who appeared before the grand jury would be less likely to testify fully and frankly, as they would be open to retribution as well as to inducements. There also would be the risk that those about to be indicted would flee, or would try to influence individual grand jurors to vote against indictment. Finally, by preserving the secrecy of the proceedings, we assure that persons who are accused but exonerated by the grand jury will not be held up to public ridicule.

Douglas Oil Co. v. Petrol Stops N.W., 441 U.S. 211 (1979).

### Grand Jury Witnesses and Secrecy

Note that Federal Rule 6 does not require grand jury witnesses to maintain secrecy as to their own testimony. The argument has been made that a secrecy requirement for the witness's own testimony would be impractical. Do you agree with this? If witnesses are free to talk, how effective do you think the secrecy rule is likely to be?

## D.  THE RELATIONSHIP OF THE GRAND JURY TO THE PROSECUTOR AND TO THE COURT

The roles played by the prosecutor, the court, and the grand jury are not exactly the same in all jurisdictions. However, it is common for courts to view the prosecutor's relationship to the grand jury as subject to little, if any, judicial scrutiny. United States v. Chanen, 549 F.2d 1306 (9th Cir.1977), illustrates this. The government presented its case three times to a federal grand jury. The first time the government did not ask for an indictment, and no vote was taken before the grand jury was discharged. A second grand jury indictment was dismissed because no transcript was made, and the government failed to present the jury with the evidence presented to the first grand jury. On the third attempt, the government secured an indictment against defendants for statutory fraud. The government presented its evidence to the third grand jury by reading testimony from its first grand jury presentation. The district court quashed the indictment because the judge felt that where the first grand jury failed to indict on the basis of live testimony, a subsequent grand jury should hear live testimony as well. The court of appeals reversed. It held that the prosecutor's action was not "fundamentally unfair" and therefore did not constitute a basis for dismissal. It reasoned as follows:

> Respecting the work of the grand jury, both court and prosecutor play supportive and complementary roles. As a practical matter, the grand jury generally relies on the prosecutor to determine what witnesses to call. Also, in practice the prosecutor conducts the examination of the witnesses and otherwise determines what evidence to present before the grand jury. In addition, it is the prosecutor who normally prepares the indictment, although of course the grand jury must review the indictment and adopt it as its own. Some of these functions—such as initiating a criminal case by presenting evidence before the grand jury—qualifies as an executive function within the exclusive prerogative of the Attorney General.

> The court, on the other hand, exercises its power to summon witnesses to attend and to give testimony before the grand jury. Also, it is the court which must compel a witness to testify if, after appearing, he refuses to do so. In addition, the court exercises a form of authority over the grand jury when, for example, it dismisses an indictment for failure to charge all elements of the offense or to warn the defendant fairly of the charge against which he must defend. Likewise, the court exercises authority over the prosecutor when it dismisses an indictment because of prosecutorial misconduct. * * *

> Nevertheless, given the constitutionally-based independence of each of the three actors—court, prosecutor and grand jury—we believe a court may not exercise its "supervisory power" in a way

which encroaches on the prerogatives of the other two unless there is a clear basis in fact and law for doing so. If the district courts were not required to meet such a standard, their "supervisory power" could readily prove subversive of the doctrine of separation of powers.

Application of this standard to the present case requires reversal. The asserted legal basis for the district court's interference with a standard prosecutorial decision—what evidence to present to the grand jury and how to present it—is the need to preserve the integrity of the judicial process and to avoid any fundamental unfairness. But it is far from clear that the prosecutor's decision in this case regarding the presentation of evidence to the third grand jury implicates any of those interests.

See also United States v. Strouse, 286 F.3d 767 (5th Cir. 2002) (federal court does not have supervisory power to dismiss a grand jury indictment based on perjured testimony, unless it is shown that the prosecutor knew that the testimony was perjurious: "a rule allowing dismissal of an indictment without a showing of government misconduct would open the door to attacks on grand jury evidence for which there are large incentives including discovery by the accused").[11]

### *Role of the Prosecutor*

The role of the prosecutor may vary somewhat from place to place in grand jury proceedings, but generally she serves the following functions:

(a) She is the legal advisor to the grand jury. Many critics maintain that the grand jury should have separate counsel at its disposal to reduce the prosecutor's control over the grand jury. But traditionally the prosecutor is also the grand jury's counsel. See Mogul Bent on Grand Jury Reform, Nat.L.J. July 27, 1998, p. A10 (discussing an "Open Letter" sent to grand jurors suggesting that grand jurors should retain their own counsel, as "a simple way to the Grand Jury to reclaim its legal independence").

(b) She presents evidence to the grand jury. The grand jury can always hear any additional evidence that it requests, but as a practical matter grand juries usually rely on the prosecutor to explain criminal offenses and to present the evidence that the grand jury considers. The prosecutor can subpoena witnesses to attend grand jury hearings, and once the witnesses are present the grand jury will hear them.

---

[11] United States v. McKenzie, 678 F.2d 629 (5th Cir.1982), indicates that an indictment will be quashed because of prosecutorial misconduct before a grand jury "only when prosecutorial misconduct amounts to overbearing the will of the grand jury so that the indictment is, in effect, that of the prosecutor rather than the grand jury." The court indicated that a prosecutor could tell the grand jury that the evidence shows the defendant is guilty.

(c) The prosecutor may negate a grand jury's decision to return an indictment by refusing to sign the indictment, or by nolle prosequi, which dismisses the charges. And a grand jury decision not to indict can be circumvented if the prosecutor resubmits the case to another grand jury. In some jurisdictions such action requires court approval.

## E. THE GRAND JURY AS A PROTECTION AGAINST UNJUST PROSECUTION

The traditional view of the grand jury as a protection against unwarranted prosecution has been described by the Supreme Court as follows:

> Historically, this body has been regarded as a primary security to the innocent against hasty, malicious and oppressive persecution; it serves the invaluable function in our society of standing between the accuser and the accused, whether the latter be an individual, minority group, or other, to determine whether a charge is founded upon reason or was dictated by an intimidating power or by malice and personal ill will.

Wood v. Georgia, 370 U.S. 375, 390 (1962).

More recently this view has been challenged. Commentators and courts now see a grand jury indictment as little more than a rubber stamp for the prosecutor's decision to go forward. See Leipold, Why Grand Juries Do Not (And Cannot) Protect the Accused, 80 Cornell L.Rev.260 (1995) (noting that during 1984, federal grand juries returned 17,419 indictments and only sixty-eight no bills, a success rate of 99.6%). In Hawkins v. Superior Court, 22 Cal.3d 584, 150 Cal.Rptr. 435, 586 P.2d 916 (1978), the California Supreme Court expressed its somewhat cynical view of the modern grand jury:

> The prosecuting attorney is typically in complete control of the total process in the grand jury room: he calls the witnesses, interprets the evidence, states and applies the law, and advises the grand jury on whether a crime has been committed. The grand jury is independent only in the sense that it is not formally attached to the prosecutor's office; though legally free to vote as they please, grand jurors virtually always assent to the recommendations of the prosecuting attorney, a fact borne out by available statistical and survey data. * * * The contemporary grand jury investigates only those whom the prosecutor asks to be investigated, and by and large indicts those whom the prosecutor wants to be indicted. * * *

> The domination of grand jury proceedings by the prosecuting attorney no doubt derives at least in part from the grand jury's institutional schizophrenia: it is expected to serve two distinct and largely inconsistent functions—accuser and impartial factfinder. * * *

The high proportion of true bills (i.e., decisions to charge) compared to no bills is not surprising. The grand jury is a body that hears only one side of a case. And it reacts to that side. Moreover the relevant standard of proof for issuing an indictment is low.

The principal function of the grand jury today probably is not to refuse indictment, but rather to force the prosecution to gather and to offer evidence in some systematic way before a charge is brought. What often is overlooked in discussions of grand juries is the fact that when the evidence, once put together, turns out to be weak, prosecutors sometimes decide not to ask for indictments or to seek indictments on lesser offenses than they might have charged on their own.

## F.  THE EVIDENCE BEFORE THE GRAND JURY

One reason that the screening function of the grand jury does not work better than it otherwise could is that prosecutors are permitted to offer a good deal of evidence to grand juries that could not be offered at trials. The next case is an illustration.

### COSTELLO v. UNITED STATES
Supreme Court of the United States, 1956.
350 U.S. 359.

**MR. JUSTICE BLACK delivered the opinion of the Court.**

We granted certiorari in this case to consider a single question: "May a defendant be required to stand trial and a conviction be sustained where only hearsay evidence was presented to the grand jury which indicted him?"

Petitioner, Frank Costello, was indicted for wilfully attempting to evade payment of income taxes due the United States for the years 1947, 1948 and 1949. * * * Petitioner promptly filed a motion for inspection of the minutes of the grand jury and for a dismissal of the indictment. His motion was based on an affidavit stating that he was firmly convinced there could have been no legal or competent evidence before the grand jury which indicted him since he had reported all his income and paid all taxes due. The motion was denied. At the trial which followed the Government offered evidence designed to show increases in Costello's net worth in an attempt to prove that he had received more income during the years in question than he had reported. To establish its case the Government called and examined 144 witnesses and introduced 368 exhibits. * * * The prosecution concluded its case by calling three government agents. Their investigations had produced the evidence used against petitioner at the trial. They were allowed to summarize the vast amount of evidence already heard and to introduce computations showing, if correct, that petitioner and his wife had received far greater income than they had reported.

\* \* \*

Counsel for petitioner asked each government witness at the trial whether he had appeared before the grand jury which returned the indictment. This cross-examination developed the fact that the three investigating officers had been the only witnesses before the grand jury. After the Government concluded its case, petitioner again moved to dismiss the indictment on the ground that the only evidence before the grand jury was "hearsay," since the three officers had no firsthand knowledge of the transactions upon which their computations were based. Nevertheless the trial court again refused to dismiss the indictment, and petitioner was convicted. \* \* \*

\* \* \* [N]either the Fifth Amendment nor any other constitutional provision prescribes the kind of evidence upon which grand juries must act. \* \* \* There is every reason to believe that our constitutional grand jury was intended to operate substantially like its English progenitor. The basic purpose of the English grand jury was to provide a fair method for instituting criminal proceedings against persons believed to have committed crimes. Grand jurors were selected from the body of the people and their work was not hampered by rigid procedural or evidential rules. \* \* \*

\* \* \* If indictments were to be held open to challenge on the ground that there was inadequate or incompetent evidence before the grand jury, the resulting delay would be great indeed. The result of such a rule would be that before trial on the merits a defendant could always insist on a kind of preliminary trial to determine the competency and adequacy of the evidence before the grand jury. This is not required by the Fifth Amendment. An indictment returned by a legally constituted and unbiased grand jury, like an information drawn by the prosecutor, if valid on its face, is enough to call for trial of the charge on the merits. The Fifth Amendment requires nothing more.

\* \* \* In a trial on the merits, defendants are entitled to a strict observance of all the rules designed to bring about a fair verdict. Defendants are not entitled, however, to a rule which would result in interminable delay but add nothing to the assurance of a fair trial.

[MR. JUSTICE CLARK and MR. JUSTICE HARLAN took no part in the consideration or decision of this case.]

[The concurring opinion of JUSTICE BURTON is omitted.]

## *Analysis of Costello*

Aside from historical justifications, several arguments can be offered in support of *Costello*. First, inadmissible evidence often has probative value, and the grand jury's function is *investigative,* not adjudicative. Second, many evidentiary rules are designed to ensure fairness in an *adversary proceeding*, and the grand jury is not adversarial. See Federal Rule of Evidence 1101 (providing that the Rules of Evidence, except those related to privilege, are not applicable in grand jury proceedings). Evidence rules operate by way of objection; a prosecutor cannot be expected to object to her own evidence. Third, any misleading effect of inadmissible evidence will be remedied at trial. Fourth, grand jury proceedings would be greatly burdened if the rules of evidence were applicable to them. The court would have to review decisions as to the admissibility of evidence, because defense counsel would not be there to object. In order to make relevance and other rulings, supervising courts would have to ask grand juries why they wanted certain evidence, and this might infringe upon the independence of the grand jury.

Note that the fact situation of *Costello* was rather unique because defense counsel was able, by questioning witnesses at trial, to determine that hearsay statements were the only evidence presented to the grand jury. More commonly, the defendant will never know the degree to which hearsay and other inadmissible evidence is considered by the grand jury. Grand jury minutes are exempt from disclosure under Fed.R.Crim.P. 6. And the witnesses who render hearsay and other inadmissible testimony might not, for that very reason, testify at trial. As long as a defendant is convicted at trial on the basis of admissible evidence, he cannot complain that what occurred before the grand jury somehow affecte the trial. See United States v. Mechanik, 475 U.S. 66 (1986) (challenge to indictment based upon prosecutorial misconduct was rendered moot by conviction at a fairly conducted trial).

## *Use of Illegally Obtained Evidence*

In Chapter 2, we saw that illegally seized evidence can be used in the grand jury proceeding. United States v. Calandra, 414 U.S. 338 (1974). The Court in *Calandra* reasoned that applying the exclusionary rule "would unduly interfere with the effective and expeditious discharge of the grand jury's duties" and that sufficient deterrence of illegal police activity would flow from the fact that the tainted evidence could not be used at trial.

## *Exculpatory Evidence: United States v. Williams*

Does the prosecutor have an obligation to present all relevant evidence to the grand jury—including evidence that would exculpate the accused? Justice Scalia wrote for the Court in United States v. Williams, 504 U.S. 36 (1992), as it rejected a Tenth Circuit supervisory rule that required prosecutors to present "substantial exculpatory evidence" to the grand jury. He concluded that a rule requiring the prosecutor to present all substantially exculpatory evidence exceeded the courts' supervisory authority, because "the grand jury is an institution separate from the courts, over whose functioning the courts [do] not preside."

Justice Scalia stated that "any power federal courts may have to fashion, on their own initiative, rules of grand jury procedure is a very limited one, not remotely comparable to the power they maintain over their own proceedings." He asserted that the Tenth Circuit's rule was far from so limited, because it would result in the "judicial reshaping of the grand jury institution, substantially altering the traditional relationships between the prosecutor, the constituting court, and the grand jury itself." Justice Scalia reasoned that "requiring the prosecutor to present exculpatory as well as inculpatory evidence would alter the grand jury's historical role, transforming it from an accusatory to an adjudicatory body." He explained as follows:

> It is axiomatic that the grand jury sits not to determine guilt or innocence, but to assess whether there is adequate basis for bringing a criminal charge. That has always been so; and to make the assessment it has always been thought sufficient to hear only the prosecutor's side. * * *

> Imposing upon the prosecutor a legal obligation to present exculpatory evidence in his possession would be incompatible with this system. If a "balanced" assessment of the entire matter is the objective, surely the first thing to be done—rather than requiring the prosecutor to say what he knows in defense of the target of the investigation—is to entitle the target to tender his own defense. To require the former while denying (as we do) the latter would be quite absurd. It would also be quite pointless, since it would merely invite the target to circumnavigate the system by delivering his exculpatory evidence to the prosecutor, whereupon it would *have* to be passed on to the grand jury * * *

Justice Scalia observed that the grand jury itself might choose not to hear more evidence than that which suffices to support an indictment. That is, the grand jury is free on its own to refuse to consider evidence that exculpated the target. He reasoned that if "the grand jury has no obligation to consider all substantial exculpatory evidence, we do not understand how the prosecutor can be said to have a binding obligation to present it." The Court thus rejected "the attempt to convert a nonexistent duty of the grand jury itself into an obligation of the prosecutor."

Justice Stevens, joined by Justices Blackmun and O'Connor and in relevant part by Justice Thomas, dissented. Justice Stevens stated that he was "unwilling to hold that countless forms of prosecutorial misconduct must be tolerated—no matter how prejudicial they may be, or how seriously they may distort the legitimate function of the grand jury— simply because they are not proscribed by Rule 6 of the Federal Rules of Criminal Procedure or a statute that is applicable in grand jury proceedings."

As to the scope of the prosecutor's duty to disclose exculpatory evidence to the grand jury, the dissenters endorsed the position expressed in the Department of Justice's United States Attorneys' Manual, Title 9, ch. 7, par. 9–11.233,88: "When a prosecutor conducting a grand jury inquiry is personally aware of substantial evidence which directly negates the guilt of a subject of the investigation, the prosecutor must present or otherwise disclose such evidence to the grand jury before seeking an indictment against such a person."

## G.  THE GRAND JURY'S POWERS OF INVESTIGATION

The Supreme Court has emphasized that the role of the grand jury is to investigate any and all potential criminal conduct, and that the power to obtain information is broad. See, e.g., Branzburg v. Hayes, 408 U.S. 665 (1972) (grand jury has a right to disclosure of journalist's sources); United States v. Nixon, 418 U.S. 683 (1974) (communications protected by executive privilege must be disclosed to the grand jury). To understand how broadly the grand jury can sweep, it is helpful to think back to the search and seizure material in Chapter 2. You will recall that the government generally cannot search for evidence unless it has probable cause, and the government cannot arrest a person without probable cause. This is in sharp contrast with the standards used by a grand jury. The grand jury can call anyone to testify before it upon the hint of suspicion or on the basis of a prosecutor's speculation about possible criminal activity. People called before the grand jury can be directed to bring documents and other tangible objects with them. Although certain privileges (such as Fifth Amendment and attorney-client) can be raised before the grand jury, the burden is on the person called to raise them and sometimes to be willing to litigate in order to preserve them. Any aspect of a person's life that might shed light on some criminal activity by somebody is within the proper scope of a grand jury inquest. See, e.g., In re Grand Jury, 286 F.3d 153 (3d Cir. 2002) (grand jury has the power to demand the production of material even where it is covered by a protective order in a civil case).

## *Grand Jury Subpoena Power*

The scope of the subpoena power of a federal grand jury is nationwide, which means that the burden of traveling to testify can be considerable. The state grand jury has no such nationwide reach, but it too can impose travel burdens on witnesses. When it is recognized that often the prosecutor subpoenas witnesses without prior consultation with the grand jurors, it is apparent that a prosecutor can call witnesses who are considerably burdened by the duty of responding to a subpoena but who might end up having little to tell the grand jury.

For example, one of the cases consolidated for hearing in Branzburg v. Hayes, supra, involved Earl Caldwell, a New York Times reporter who covered the Black Panther Party. Caldwell claimed that his appearance before the grand jury would compromise his relationship with the Party. The Supreme Court held that this risk of harm gave him neither the right to refuse to appear before the grand jury nor the right to refuse to answer questions based on information related to him in confidence. Under the Court's opinion, even if the grand jury did not have any significant need for answers to questions, and even if, by answering, Caldwell's ability to function as a reporter covering the Party would be destroyed, the grand jury had a right to the information.

The breadth of grand jury power was evidenced once again in the grand jury investigation into charges of impropriety by then-President Clinton. The grand jury subpoenaed information from a bookstore concerning a purchase made by Monica Lewinsky. Despite the First Amendment ramifications, the subpoena was found valid. See Stout, Lewinsky's Bookstore Purchases Are Now Subject of a Subpoena, N.Y. Times, March 26, 1998, at A16 (quoting a legal director for the ACLU as stating that "people in this country ought to have the right to buy books without government scrutiny").

In Blair v. United States, 250 U.S. 273 (1919), the Supreme Court established the appropriate degree of deference to be accorded grand jury subpoenas by judicial officers:

> [T]he giving of testimony and the attendance upon court or grand jury in order to testify are public duties which every person within the jurisdiction of the Government is bound to perform upon being properly summoned, and for performance of which he is entitled to no further compensation than that which the statutes provide. The personal sacrifice involved is a part of the necessary contribution of the individual to the welfare of the public. The duty, so onerous at times, yet so necessary to the administration of justice * * * is subject to mitigation in exceptional circumstances; there is a constitutional exemption from being compelled in any criminal case to be a witness against oneself, entitling the witness to be excused from answering

anything that will tend to incriminate him; some confidential matters are shielded from considerations of policy, and perhaps in other cases for special reasons a witness may be excused from telling all that he knows.

But, aside from exceptions and qualifications—and none such is asserted in the present case—the witness is bound not only to attend but to tell what he knows in answer to questions framed for the purpose of bringing out the truth of the matter under inquiry.

\* \* \*

[The grand jury] is a grand inquest, a body with powers of investigation and inquisition, the scope of whose inquiries is not to be limited narrowly by questions of propriety or forecasts of the probable result of the investigation, or by doubts whether any particular individual will be found properly subject to an accusation of crime. As has been said before, the identity of the offender, and the precise nature of the offense, if there be one, normally are developed at the conclusion of the grand jury's labors, not at the beginning.

### Grand Jury Cattle Call: United States v. Dionisio

An objection to the breadth of a grand jury investigation, and correspondingly to the broad use of its subpoena power, is ordinarily dismissed out of hand. A case in point is United States v. Dionisio, 410 U.S. 1 (1973). The next excerpt contains the Court's description of the facts and the Court's deferential approach to grand jury subpoenas.

A special grand jury was convened in the Northern District of Illinois in February 1971, to investigate possible violations of federal criminal statutes relating to gambling. In the course of its investigation, the grand jury received in evidence certain voice recordings that had been obtained pursuant to court orders.

The grand jury subpoenaed approximately 20 persons, including the respondent Dionisio, seeking to obtain from them voice exemplars for comparison with the recorded conversations that had been received in evidence. Each witness was advised that he was a potential defendant in a criminal prosecution. Each was asked to examine a transcript of an intercepted conversation, and to go to a nearby office of the United States Attorney to read the transcript into a recording device. \* \* \* Dionisio and other witnesses refused to furnish the voice exemplars \* \* \*.

\* \* \*

The Court of Appeals found critical significance in the fact that the grand jury had summoned approximately 20 witnesses to furnish voice exemplars. We think that fact is basically irrelevant to the constitutional issues here. The grand jury may have been attempting to identify a number of voices on the tapes in evidence, or it might have summoned the 20 witnesses in an effort to identify one voice. But whatever the case, a grand jury's investigation is not fully carried out until every available clue has been run down and all witnesses examined in every proper way to find if a crime has been committed * * *. The grand jury may well find it desirable to call numerous witnesses in the course of an investigation. It does not follow that each witness may resist a subpoena on the ground that too many witnesses have been called.

In dissent, Justice Marshall argued that some protection against prosecutorial control of the grand jury is necessary. Justice Marshall urged that the government should have to make a showing of reasonableness before real evidence is gathered by the grand jury over the objection of a witness.

### *Subpoenaing Criminal Defense Attorneys*

Grand juries, guided by prosecutors, have sometimes sought to obtain information from criminal defense attorneys concerning monetary arrangements between the defense attorneys and their clients. Defense attorneys contend that fee-related information is protected by the attorney-client privilege, but this argument has been roundly rejected, because the fee itself is not a privileged communication. Nor is the Sixth Amendment right to counsel implicated when a grand jury subpoena is served, because the client has by definition not yet been formally charged with a crime. See Massiah v. United States, in Chapter 3.

Defense attorneys argue more broadly that serving a grand jury subpoena upon a defense attorney chills the attorney-client relationship, and might lead to disqualification because the attorney could be forced into being a witness against her own client. Yet this argument as well has generally fallen on deaf ears. Thus, in In re Grand Jury Proceeding (Schofield), 721 F.2d 1221 (9th Cir.1983), the court reversed an order requiring the government to make a preliminary showing of relevance before obtaining information concerning fees and expenses paid to a lawyer: "No preliminary affidavit, disclaiming ill intent, will be required of the government where a grand jury has subpoenaed testimony or material evidence in good faith." Accord, In re Grand Jury Subpoena Served Upon Doe, 781 F.2d 238 (2d Cir.1986) (en banc).

It should be noted, however, that ethical standards in some states prohibit the prosecutor from subpoenaing defense attorneys without prior court approval. These rules require the prosecutor to make a showing of relevance and a lack of other reasonable alternative sources for the fee-related information. See ABA Model Rules of Professional Conduct, Rule 3.8(f) (providing that a prosecutor shall not subpoena a lawyer in a grand jury or other criminal proceeding for information concerning a past or present client unless the evidence sought is essential, there is no feasible alternative to obtain the information, and the prosecutor "obtains prior judicial approval after an opportunity for an adversarial proceeding"). Most courts have held, however, that these ethical standards cannot be enforced in court because to do so would impair the subpoena power of grand juries. See, e.g., Stern v. United States Dist. Court for Dist. of Mass., 214 F.3d 4 (1st Cir. 2000) (invalidating Rule 3.8(f) because it "encroaches on grand jury prerogatives").

### *Minimal Limits on Grand Jury Subpoenas: United States v. R. Enterprises, Inc.*

The Court in United States v. Nixon, 418 U.S. 683 (1974), held that a *trial* subpoena must satisfy a three pronged test of relevancy, admissibility, and specificity. However, in United States v. R. Enterprises, Inc., 498 U.S. 292 (1991), the Court rejected the application of the *Nixon* standards to grand jury subpoenas. Justice O'Connor, writing for a unanimous Court on this point, stressed the distinction between a grand jury investigation and a trial proceeding. She stated that "the Government cannot be required to justify the issuance of a grand jury subpoena by presenting evidence sufficient to establish probable cause because the very purpose of requesting the information is to ascertain whether probable cause exists." The Court also noted that the multifactor *Nixon* test would produce unacceptable procedural delays that would frustrate the grand jury's investigation.

Justice O'Connor noted, however, that the grand jury's investigatory powers are "not unlimited." Under Federal Rule of Criminal Procedure 17(c), subpoenas may be quashed if compliance would be "unreasonable or oppressive." The Court held that a subpoena would be unreasonable under Rule 17(c) only if "there is no reasonable possibility that the category of materials the Government seeks will produce information relevant to the general subject of the grand jury's investigation." Justice O'Connor recognized that this standard would be extraordinarily difficult to meet in practice, especially given the difficult position of subpoena recipients, who may have no knowledge of the government's purpose in seeking production of the requested information. The Court suggested that an *in camera* proceeding should be employed in cases where the recipient of the subpoena is unaware of the nature of the investigation.

### *Warnings to Witnesses Testifying Before the Grand Jury*

Witnesses can be called to testify before the grand jury without being told why they are being called, what the purpose of the inquiry is, or whether they are suspected of criminal wrongdoing. Ignorance of the nature of the inquiry is compounded by the absence of counsel for the witness in the federal grand jury room (as well as in many states). Because grand jurors and prosecutors can ask leading questions, a witness who might be a target of the grand jury has good reason to fear that a slip of the tongue may come back to haunt her. Yet, the witness will have difficulty in answering carefully without knowledge of what the investigation is all about. Without a lawyer present to assist, vague or confusing questions may be asked, and a witness may later discover that what she said to the grand jury can be cast in a more negative light than she would have supposed while testifying.

In response to concerns about the possible unfair treatment of grand jury witnesses, the Department of Justice has added to the guidelines for United States Attorneys, found in the United States Attorney's Manual,[12] sections that require that a witness be advised of several things before testifying: of the general subject matter of the grand jury's inquiry (to the extent that an investigation would not be compromised); that the witness may refuse to answer questions that would tend to incriminate; that any answers may be used against the witness; and that the witness may step outside the grand jury room to consult with counsel. The guidelines provide that a target of an investigation may be subpoenaed, but known targets should be advised that they are targets and should be invited to testify voluntarily; if they refuse, a subpoena should be issued only after the grand jury and the responsible prosecutor have approved the subpoena. The prosecutor is encouraged to offer a target an opportunity to testify before the grand jury hands down an indictment.

It is notable, however, that there is no private right of action for violation of the DOJ guidelines on warnings. If they are ignored by the prosecutor, the most that will occur is a referral by the court to the Justice Department for internal (and confidential) discipline. See United States v. Gillespie, 974 F.2d 796 (7th Cir.1992) (asserting that judicial enforcement might deter the DOJ from adopting such rules in the first place). It should also be noted that a witness before the grand jury is not entitled to *Miranda* warnings, even if he is a target or subject of the investigation; such a witness is not in custody within the meaning of *Miranda*. See United States v. Mandujano, 425 U.S. 564 (1976).

---

[12] United States Department of Justice, United States Attorneys' Manual, Title 9, Ch.11, ¶ 9–11.50.

## Counsel in the Grand Jury Room

As discussed above, under Federal practice, a witness has no right to counsel while in the grand jury room. The Supreme Court reaffirmed the nonexistence of any right to counsel in Conn v. Gabbert, 526 U.S. 286 (1999). The plaintiff in *Conn* was a criminal defense attorney. He sued prosecutors and others for subjecting him to a search while his client was testifying before a grand jury. Before the Supreme Court, the attorney did not press a Fourth Amendment claim. Rather, he argued that the search "interfered with his client's right to have him outside the grand jury room and available to consult with her." Chief Justice Rehnquist, writing for the Court, analyzed this claim in the following passage:

> A grand jury witness has no constitutional right to have counsel present during the grand jury proceeding, United States v. Mandujano, 425 U.S. 564 (1976), and no decision of this Court has held that a grand jury witness has a right to have her attorney present outside the jury room. We need not decide today whether such a right exists, because Gabbert clearly had no standing to raise the alleged infringement of the rights of his client Tracy Baker.

Thus, the Court in *Conn* does not even concede that a grand jury witness has a right to have counsel *outside* the room, much less inside. In practice, counsel is permitted to park herself outside the grand jury room, and the witness can excuse himself for consultation.[13]

A number of states permit witnesses to be accompanied by counsel in the grand jury room. A subcommittee of the Judicial Conference Advisory Committee on Criminal Rules considered making such a change in federal procedure, and ultimately decided against it. The Report of the Subcommittee reasons that allowing counsel to be present before the grand jury would create the following problems:

1.   Loss of spontaneity of testimony.

2.   Transforming the grand jury investigation into an adversary proceeding.

3.   Loss of secrecy with resultant chilling effect on witness cooperation.

The Subcommittee also notes a "potential ancillary issue. Would an indigent witness summoned to the grand jury be entitled to the appointment of counsel at the obvious cost to the Treasury?"

---

[13] This limited opportunity to consult counsel probably reflects a practical consideration: if the witness refuses to answer, the grand jury would have to seek a contempt citation to make the witness answer; before going through that process, the grand jury may be better advised to let the witness discuss with counsel the question, because the witness may after consultation find that there is no Fifth Amendment or other privilege that is implicated.

To these concerns, the head of the Criminal Division of the Justice Department added another:

> [A]llowing defense counsel to accompany a witness before a grand jury would have adverse consequences for investigations of serious crimes by organizations, such as organized crime groups, corporations, or unions where typically a single lawyer represents all or several members of the organization. Currently, if a member of the organization wishes to cooperate with the grand jury secretly, the member may do so by appearing alone before the grand jury. But if the law allowed the member to bring the attorney, failure to do so would be a tip-off that the witness was likely cooperating, which would deter cooperation in many instances (or result in retaliation).

Letter from James K. Robinson to Subcommittee on Grand Jury Proceedings, Judicial Conference Advisory Committee on Criminal Rules, Dec. 22, 1998.

Despite these dire predictions, the evidence from the States that permit counsel in the grand jury room indicates that counsel's presence can have a positive rather than negative effect. For example, Colorado passed a law in the late 1970's permitting a witness's counsel to be present in the grand jury room. Jeffrey Bayles, a former Denver deputy district attorney, explains the salutary effect of the law as follows:

> Not only does the new law speed the process by eliminating the walk outside the room on every question, but it also reduces the number of questions requiring conferences between the witness and counsel. The educational process, which of necessity accompanies having counsel in the grand jury room, promotes a better understanding of the grand jury within the bar. The more the processes are known, the less is the aura of mystery surrounding the grand jury. * * * The demand for abolition of the grand jury will decrease in direct proportion to the number of counsel who attend grand jury sessions with their clients.

Bales, Grand Jury Reform: The Colorado Experience, A.B.A.J., May, 1981, at 568. See also Hixson, Bringing Down the Curtain on the Absurd Drama of Entrances and Exits—Witness Representation in the Grand Jury Room, 15 Am.Cr.L.Rev. 307 (1978) (given that the witness is allowed to go in and out of the room to get advice of counsel, it is more efficient to permit counsel to be present in the grand jury room.).

### Suggested Reforms of Grand Jury Procedures

Many commentators suggest that the abuses seen in grand jury practice can be eliminated by imposing reforms. The ABA Criminal

Justice Section Committee on the Grand Jury proposed the following reforms:

   1.   A witness before the grand jury shall have the right to be accompanied by counsel in his or her appearance before the grand jury. Such counsel shall be allowed to be present in the grand jury room only during the questioning of the witness and shall be allowed to advise the witness. Such counsel shall not be permitted to address the grand jurors or otherwise take part in proceedings before the grand jury.

   2.   No prosecutor shall knowingly fail to disclose to the grand jury evidence which will tend substantially to negate guilt.

   3.   The prosecutor shall not present to the grand jury evidence which he or she knows to be constitutionally inadmissible at trial.

   4.   A target of a grand jury investigation shall be given the right to testify before the grand jury. Prosecutors shall notify such targets of their opportunity to testify unless notification may result in flight, endanger other persons, or obstruct justice, or unless the prosecutor is unable to notify said persons with reasonable diligence. A target of the grand jury may also contact the foreperson in writing to offer information or evidence to the grand jury.

   5.   Witnesses should have the right to receive a transcript (at their own expense) of grand jury testimony.

   6.   The grand jury shall not name a person in an indictment as an unindicted coconspirator to a criminal conspiracy.[14]

The Criminal Justice Section report, proposing the above reforms, was issued in 1977. Congress held hearings on the proposals, but did not act on them. It is easy to see why no action was taken. The reforms would overrule Supreme Court doctrine, and would create a sea-change in the historically-ingrained federal grand jury practice. The reform proposals were staunchly opposed by the Justice Department. It is unlikely that the political climate will ever warm up enough for these or similar proposals to be enacted. See, e.g., Rovella, Grand Jury Battle Begins, Nat'l L.J., May 29, 2000, p. A4 (discussing attempt by Congressman Delahunt to revive the 1977 proposals under the new title "Federal Grand Jury Bill of Rights"; no legislation resulted).

---

[14]   See United States v. Briggs, 514 F.2d 794 (5th Cir.1975) ("the grand jury that returns an indictment naming a person as an unindicted coconspirator does not perform its shielding function but does exactly the reverse. If the charges are baseless, the named person should not be subjected to public branding, and if supported by probable cause, he should not be denied a forum.").

## *Grand Jury Nullification*

Professor Laurie Levinson suggests another reform for grand jury practice: that grand jurors be told that they have the right to nullify, i.e., that they do not have to return an indictment even when they find probable cause. She notes that the history of the grand jury is laced with important cases of nullification, such as the refusal to indict John Peter Zenger on charges of sedition (as discussed in the section on the history of the grand jury, supra). She argues that there are compelling modern justifications for the nullification power:

> Federal prosecutors are not directly accountable to the community in which they serve. Rather, their appointments are made in Washington, and line prosecutors are increasingly receiving direction from Department of Justice officials who set national policy. Whether it is the war on drugs, the war on white-collar crime, or the war on terrorism, the national agenda may not adequately consider the needs of a particular community. A grand jury can perform this role.

> \* \* \*

> The grand jury process, unlike trial jury deliberations, lends itself to a more thoughtful evaluation of community priorities and an evaluation of whether prosecutors are using the law for improper reasons, such as political grandstanding or witch-hunting of opponents.

> If grand juries have the discretion to reject charges that they think are improperly motivated or unwise, prosecutors will actually benefit in the long run because there will be greater moral authority behind the charges that grand jurors do bring.

Levinson, Grand Jury Nullification, Nat'l L. J. June 14, 2004 at 14.

Yet as shown earlier in this Chapter, the model charge given to federal grand jurors does not inform them that they have the right to decline to bring charges when the prosecutor establishes probable cause. The model charge says that when probable cause is established, the grand jury "should" return an indictment; and it further states that it is not for the grand jurors to second-guess the wisdom of laws passed by Congress. These charges have withstood attack. Thus, in United States v. Navarro-Vargas, 408 F.3d 1184 (9th Cir. 2005), the court noted that the grand jury has the *power*, as a matter of practice, to nullify a law because there is no means to review a grand jury's refusal to return an indictment. But according to the court, that does not mean that grand jurors have the *right* to nullify laws—or that they should in effect be invited to nullify by an instruction of informing them of their power to do so. The court stated: "we cannot say that the grand jury's power to judge the wisdom of the laws is so firmly established that the district court must either instruct the jury on its power to nullify the laws or remain silent."

Note that if the grand jury does nullify and refuses to return an indictment, all the prosecutor has to do is empanel another grand jury; it is not like petit jury nullification, which triggers double jeopardy protection. Given the fact that grand jury nullification can be so easily trumped, is there any reason to encourage it?

For a comprehensive discussion of grand jury nullification, see Fairfax, Grand Jury Discretion and Constitutional Design, 93 Cornell L. Rev. 703, 711–16 (2008).

## VI.   THE PRELIMINARY HEARING AND ITS RELATIONSHIP TO INDICTMENTS AND INFORMATIONS

Federal Rule of Criminal Procedure 5 provides that when an arrest is made, the arrested person must be taken without unnecessary delay before the nearest available federal magistrate. You will recall that Gerstein v. Pugh, 420 U.S. 103 (1975), and County of Riverside v. McLaughlin, 500 U.S. 44(1991), discussed in Chapter 2, requires that, if there has been no previous probable cause determination, one must be made promptly. Fed.R.Crim.P. 5 provides for such a determination when the person arrested is brought before the magistrate. The rule provides that a defendant is entitled to a preliminary examination for any crime except a petty offense. Fed.R.Crim.P. 5.1 governs preliminary examinations.

Note that an indictment cuts off the right to a preliminary hearing, because probable cause is held to be validly established by the indictment itself. It is common in some federal districts for prosecutors to avoid preliminary hearings by indicting as many defendants as possible.

Virtually every state that requires felony prosecutions to commence by indictment establishes some right to a preliminary examination. In most, the filing of the indictment cuts off the right to a preliminary hearing, just as does Federal Rule 5. About half the states do not require indictments in felony cases. In these states, prosecutors can begin felony cases by filing informations. A typical information procedure is to require a magistrate's determination of probable cause following a preliminary examination. In special cases prosecutors may utilize grand jury indictments, but usually they will file the information, since it is a less burdensome way of beginning a case.

Most states that permit the filing of an information in a felony case make a magistrate's decision to bind the defendant over for trial a prerequisite to the filing of the information. A few states do allow the prosecutor to file the information directly, however. The Supreme Court has upheld the direct filing of an information in Lem Woon v. Oregon, 229 U.S. 586 (1913), and Ocampo v. United States, 234 U.S. 91 (1914). Of course, after Gerstein v. Pugh, supra, a magistrate will have to make a probable cause determination, if the accused is deprived of freedom. But the *Gerstein* opinion indicates that the limited hearing it requires is to protect against erroneous detention; it is not a screening device to check the validity of the prosecutor's charges against a defendant.

## Procedural Requirements for a Preliminary Hearing

Most states have time limits in which the preliminary hearing must be held. But other aspects of the hearing are often not covered by any rule. Even the standard to be used by the magistrate who conducts the preliminary hearing often is unclear. It is apparent that different judges sitting in the same jurisdiction have different ideas about what screening function the hearing is to serve. Some judges believe that their function is to determine probable cause, with the evidence viewed in the light most favorable to the government, ignoring credibility questions. This is the standard set forth in the federal system. See Fed.R.Crim.P. 5.1. Others take the view that there must be enough evidence for a trier of fact to find guilt beyond a reasonable doubt. Some magistrates probably consider whether a defendant should be burdened by going to trial in some cases, even if there is enough evidence to warrant a bindover.

The standard that is chosen indicates how much screening a jurisdiction wants its magistrates to do. It probably is true that if a prosecutor presents all her evidence to the magistrate and the magistrate concludes that no reasonable jury could convict, it is silly to bind the defendant over for trial, even if technically there is probable cause. But it is burdensome to require the prosecutor to present all of her evidence to the magistrate as a prerequisite to bringing charges. The more thorough the screening at the preliminary hearing, the more it resembles a trial, and the more duplicative and costly it is.

Although some jurisdictions require magistrates to follow the usual rules of evidence at preliminary hearings, most others (including the federal system, see Fed. R. Evid. 1101) provide that trial evidence rules need not be followed—which means in most cases that hearsay evidence can be used, as it can be used before grand juries. Again, the approach to the question whether evidence rules should be followed at the preliminary hearing depends on the kind of hearing that is to be held. Obviously, the more closely the evidence rules resemble the rules that will be used at trial, the more screening the magistrate is able to do. But the more screening that is done, the more time-consuming and duplicative the procedure is likely to be.

Another obvious difference among jurisdictions is in their approach to the hearing as a discovery device. If the hearing is not intended to serve a discovery purpose—as under Fed.R.Crim.P. 5.1, which does not mention discovery as a proper subject for the hearing—then questions asked for discovery reasons are unlikely to be permitted over objection.[15] If, however, a jurisdiction recognizes a discovery purpose, the scope of questioning may be quite broad.

### Preclusive Effect of a Preliminary Determination

If the case is a felony case that will begin by a grand jury indictment, a decision by the magistrate at a preliminary hearing that there is no cause for bindover generally is not determinative for a grand jury. The grand jury still can indict, because it is an institution independent from the judiciary. See Fed.R.Crim.P. 5.1(f) ("A discharge does not preclude the government from later prosecuting the defendant for the same offense."). Likewise, a decision by the magistrate that bindover should be limited to designated offenses does not limit the grand jury in most jurisdictions. The grand jury can charge any offense for which it finds probable cause.

If the prosecution can begin by information, generally the prosecutor is limited by the bindover in the charges that can be brought. In some states only those charges designated by the magistrate can be brought. In other states the offense for which the defendant is bound over or others supported by the evidence at the preliminary hearing may be charged. Still others use a transactional test, which allows all crimes related to the same transactions and facts adduced at the examination to be charged. Under all these approaches, the defendant can challenge the information in the trial court, although it is likely that the trial court will defer to the preliminary hearing judge (and the absence of a formal record may make a challenge especially difficult). If the prosecutor is not satisfied with the bindover decision, she may drop the prosecution, file a new information, and hope for a better bindover ruling from another magistrate. Generally, the refusal to bind the defendant over is not appealable, although sometimes mandamus may be possible. If the prosecutor cannot get a favorable bindover decision, she might decide to present the case, even if it is a misdemeanor, to the grand jury, or decide to file charges directly against the defendant, if that is possible.

## VII.   NOTICE OF CHARGES, CONSTRUCTIVE AMENDMENT, AND VARIANCE

In Stirone v. United States, 361 U.S. 212 (1960), the Supreme Court reversed a conviction for violation of the Hobbs Act (interfering with

---

[15] The preliminary hearing may be used as a device to preserve testimony, and to precipitate bargaining that will lead to a guilty plea.

interstate commerce) because the government's proof of the defendants' effect on interstate commerce involved shipments of steel from inside Pennsylvania to points outside the state, whereas the indictment charged that the effect was on shipments from outside the state into Pennsylvania. The Court said that it could not permit a defendant to be tried on charges not made in the indictment, because to do so would undermine the defendant's constitutional right to an indictment by grand jury, and also would deny the defendant his constitutional right to be notified of the charges against him.

An indictment, to be sufficient under the Grand Jury Clause, must sufficiently state all elements of the crime. See, e.g., United States v. Villarreal, 707 F.3d 942 (8th Cir. 2013) ("An indictment is fatally insufficient when an essential element of the crime is omitted.").

United States v. Pickett, 353 F.3d 62 (D.C. Cir. 2004), is a case involving a defective indictment. Pickett was a security guard in the Capitol building who was indicted for lying to a government official. The prosecution involved the scare that arose when several Senators received anthrax in the mail. The defendant, as part of a "bad joke," placed a white substance on a table in the Capitol, and then lied about doing it. But the statute (18 U.S.C.§ 1001) requires that the lie to the government official must be made during an "investigation or review." That element was not charged in the indictment. The court dismissed the indictment, noting that on the plain language of the statute, the conduct charged against Pickett, making false statements, "does not constitute an offense" unless it occurs during the course of and investigation or review. The court concluded that "it is a fundamental protection, which an indictment is intended to guarantee, that the indictment contain the elements of the offense intended to be charged and sufficiently apprise the defendant of what he must be prepared to meet."

In contrast, the Court in United States v. Miller, 471 U.S. 130 (1985), held that the Fifth Amendment's protection of indictment by grand jury is not violated "when a defendant is tried under an indictment that alleges a certain fraudulent scheme but is convicted based on trial proof that supports only a significantly narrower and more limited, though included, fraudulent scheme." The government had charged Miller with fraudulent acts in consenting to a burglary of his business and lying to the insurer about the value of his loss. The proof focused only on the value of the loss and Miller's lying about it. Justice Marshall wrote that "[a]s long as the crime and the elements of the offense that sustain the conviction are fully and clearly set out in the indictment, the right to a grand jury is not normally violated by the fact that the indictment alleges more crimes or other means of submitting the same crime." He distinguished *Stirone* on the ground that the offense proved at Stirone's trial was *not* fully charged in the indictment.

## Constructive Amendments and Variance
## from Indictment at Trial

Besides an indictment that simply does not state all the elements of a crime, a situation might arise in which the indictment pleads elements that are different from the proof presented by the prosecution at trial. Courts have found two types of claims that arise when a grand jury indictment is allegedly altered during the trial. One claim is that the indictment was *constructively amended*; the other claim is that there has been a *variance* between the indictment and the proof elicited at trial. The court in Martin v. Kassulke, 970 F.2d 1539 (6th Cir.1992), discussed the difference between these two claims:

> An amendment of the indictment occurs when the charging terms of the indictment are altered, either literally or in effect, by prosecutor or court after the grand jury has last passed upon them. A variance occurs when the charging terms of an indictment are left unaltered, but the evidence offered at trial proves facts materially different from those alleged in the indictment. An amendment is per se prejudicial, as it directly infringes the defendant's right to know of the charges against him by effectively allowing the jury to convict the defendant of a different crime than that for which he was charged. * * *
>
> A variance, on the other hand, is not reversible error unless the accused has proved a prejudicial effect upon his defense, because it merely permits the prosecution to prove facts to establish the criminal charge materially different from the facts contained in the charging instrument. Although it is generally subject to the harmless error test, a variance infringes upon the apprisal function of the sixth amendment which requires that in all criminal prosecutions, the accused shall enjoy the right to be informed of the nature and cause of the accusation. If a variance infringes too strongly upon a defendant's sixth amendment rights, it is considered a constructive amendment, which is a variance that is accorded the per se prejudicial treatment of an amendment. * * * A constructive amendment occurs when the terms of an indictment are in effect altered by the presentation of evidence and jury instructions which so modify essential elements of the offense charged that there is a substantial likelihood that the defendant may have been convicted of an offense other than that charged in the indictment.

* * *

A variance is not material, or does not rise to the level of a constructive amendment, unless the variance misleads the accused in making her defense or exposes her to the danger of double jeopardy.

In *Martin*, the defendant was charged with rape by engaging in sexual intercourse "by forcible compulsion." The evidence showed, and the prosecutor argued, that the rape occurred while the victim was "physically helpless"—i.e., while unconscious. The pertinent rape statute criminalized sexual intercourse either by forcible compulsion or when the victim was physically helpless. The *Martin* court found that the difference between the proof at trial and the charging instrument constituted a variance, but did not rise to the level of a constructive amendment of the indictment. Under the statute, rape was a single crime, which could be committed by two alternative methods. The defendant was not prejudiced by the prosecution's proof of a method other than that charged, because his defense was that the victim was a willing participant in *whatever* sex occurred. This defense "clearly negates any possibility that the victim was physically helpless and that her helplessness meant that he was not guilty of the crime with which he was charged." See also United States v. Moore, 198 F.3d 793 (10th Cir. 1999) (defendant was not prejudiced by a variance where he was charged with carjacking, and the victim named in the indictment was Brent Beyers, whereas the government proved that the car was owned by his wife, Anne Byers).

A case that can be compared usefully with *Martin* is United States v. Lawton, 995 F.2d 290 (D.C.Cir.1993). Lawton was an official of a local union. He was charged with embezzling money from the Local. His defense was that he had an oral arrangement with the Local to write checks to himself to pay his salary. The federal labor embezzlement statute makes criminal only the embezzlement of the funds of a labor organization of which the defendant "is an officer, or by which he is employed, directly or indirectly." The trial court instructed the jury, however, that it could convict Lawton if it found that he embezzled the Local's funds, *or* the District Labor Council's funds, *or* the International Union's funds. It was clear that Lawton was neither an officer nor an employee of these latter two groups. The court found that the trial judge's charge constituted a constructive amendment of the indictment, which was per se reversible error:

> Under the Fifth Amendment, the infamous crimes on which a defendant must stand trial are limited by the charges contained in the grand jury's indictment. The district court's embezzlement instructions, however, allowed the petit jury to convict Lawton of additional charges. The trial court's instructions thus violated the Grand Jury Clause just as surely as if the court had written additional charges onto the grand jury's "true bill." Still worse, the instructions allowed the jury to convict on the basis of conduct that, on the face of the evidence, did not amount to a violation of [the labor embezzlement statute].

See also Lucas v. O'Dea, 169 F.3d 1028 (6th Cir.1999) (where the defendant was charged in the indictment with murder by shooting the victim with a pistol, it was a fatal variance for the jury to be instructed that the defendant could be convicted if his coconspirator fired the shot: the defendant was clearly prejudiced because his defense to the murder charge was that he was not the shooter: "Because it exposed Lucas to charges for which he had no notice and thus no opportunity to plan a defense, the variance from the indictment to the jury instruction constituted a constructive amendment that violated his Fifth Amendment rights."); Geboy v. Brigano, 489 F.3d 752 (6th Cir. 2007) (defendant was not prejudiced by variance between the indictment and the evidence as to the location of charged crimes).

### *Inspecific Charges*

The concern of *Stirone* and its progeny is that an amendment or variance at trial will deprive the defendant of sufficient notice and so impair his ability to prepare a defense. But a notice problem can also arise when the indictment, though stating the elements of the crime, provides factual assertions so general that it is difficult or impossible to prepare a defense.[16] One remedy for inspecific factual assertions is provided by Fed.R.Crim.P. 7(f), which permits the court to direct the filing of a bill of particulars. The court in United States v. Salisbury, 983 F.2d 1369 (6th Cir.1993), described the function of a bill of particulars:

> A bill of particulars is meant to be used as a tool to minimize surprise and assist defendant in obtaining the information needed to prepare a defense and to preclude a second prosecution for the same crimes. * * * The decision to order a bill of particulars is within the sound discretion of the court. * * * A court does not abuse its discretion in light of a detailed indictment.

If the defendant moves for a bill of particulars and that motion is denied, the defendant is not entitled to relief on appeal unless he can show that he was "actually surprised at trial and suffered prejudice from the denial." United States v. Livingstone, 576 F.3d 881 (8th Cir. 2009) (no error in denying motion for bill of particulars where the defendant's strategy was to attack the credibility of government witnesses, and he could not show how a bill of particulars could have affected his defense).

Whether or not supplemented by a bill of particulars, it is at least possible for an indictment to be so vague as to provide constitutionally inadequate notice. The test for constitutional sufficiency was stated by Judge Easterbrook in Fawcett v. Bablitch, 962 F.2d 617 (7th Cir.1992):

---

[16] Fed.R.Crim.P. 7(c)(1) requires the indictment to set out the essential facts constituting the offense charged, in order to inform the defendant of the offense against which he must defend.

"[A] charge is sufficiently specific when it contains the elements of the crime, permits the accused to plead and prepare a defense, and allows the disposition to be used as a bar in a subsequent prosecution." The *Fawcett* court rejected the argument that an indictment is constitutionally defective whenever the prosecution could have provided more specific information in the indictment. It declared that "the prosecutor's ability to do better does not vitiate the conviction."

In *Fawcett*, the defendant was charged with two events of unlawful sexual contact with a minor "during the six months preceding December 1985." Fawcett argued that the time period was impermissibly broad, because it was impossible for him to provide an alibi for the entire six month period. The court rejected this contention, finding that sufficient notice had been given, and noting that Fawcett was free to attack the complainant's veracity and to deny participation. Do you agree that sufficient notice was given? Would the indictment have been sufficient if it charged one act of sexual misconduct within a ten-year period? Compare United States v. Salisbury, 983 F.2d 1369 (6th Cir.1993) (indictment insufficiently specific where it charges the defendant with "voting more than once," and that term is not defined in the criminal statute).

### The Elements of the Crime: Apprendi v. New Jersey

Under *Stirone* an indictment that does not set forth all of the elements of the crime charged is constitutionally deficient. Sometimes however it is difficult to determine just what *is* an element of the crime— as distinct from a sentencing factor that can be left for the judge. This issue is discussed in detail in Chapters 10 and 11. At this juncture, it is sufficient to note that in Apprendi v. New Jersey, 530 U.S. 466 (2000), the Court held that a factual determination authorizing an increase in sentencing beyond a statutory maximum is an element of the crime, and therefore is a question for the jury that must be proved beyond a reasonable doubt—and it must accordingly be set forth in the charging instrument. So for example, if the legislature has authorized a sentencing enhancement, beyond the statutory maximum sentence, for possession of a certain amount of drugs, the jury must determine the amount that the defendant possessed, and that amount must be set forth in the indictment. The opinion in *Apprendi* is set forth in Chapter 10. In states where no indictment is required, it should be sufficient for any charging instrument to allege all of the essential elements of an offense.